I0797087

THE BAKER ILLUSTRATED BIBLE BACKGROUND COMMENTARY

THE BAKER ILLUSTRATED BIBLE BACKGROUND COMMENTARY

Edited by

J. Scott Duvall and J. Daniel Hays

BakerBooks
a division of Baker Publishing Group
Grand Rapids, Michigan

Published by Baker Books
a division of Baker Publishing Group
PO Box 6287, Grand Rapids, MI 49516-6287
www.bakerbooks.com

Printed in China

Library of Congress Cataloging-in-Publication Data

Names: Hays, J. Daniel, 1953– editor. | Duvall, J. Scott, editor.
Title: The Baker illustrated Bible background commentary / edited by J. Scott Duvall and J. Daniel Hays.
Description: Grand Rapids, Michigan : Baker Books, a division of Baker Publishing Group, [2020] | Includes bibliographical references.
Identifiers: LCCN 2019035113 | ISBN 9780801018374 (cloth)
Subjects: LCSH: Bible—Commentaries.
Classification: LCC BS491.3 .B345 2020 | DDC 220.7—dc23
LC record available at https://lccn.loc.gov/2019035113

24 25 26 7 6 5 4 3 2

We dedicate this book to our wives, Judy Duvall and Donna Hays,
for their never-ending love and support.

Contents

Commentary

Acknowledgments

We wish to express our appreciation to the great editorial team at Baker for their outstanding work on this volume. Likewise we thank the fifty-five scholars who took time out of their busy schedules to write the articles for this project. A special thanks goes to Russell Meek for helping locate and acquire many of the beautiful and helpful pictures that illustrate this volume. Finally, we want to recognize and thank our undergraduate student worker, Caroline (Poole) Winkler, for her invaluable assistance in editing this book.

Contributors

George Athas. University of Sydney (BA); Moore Theological College (DipMin, BD); University of Sydney (PhD); Director of Postgraduate Studies and Senior Lecturer in Old Testament, Moore Theological College, Sydney. George has written/coedited five books, including *The Tel Dan Inscription: A Reappraisal and a New Interpretation*; *Biblia Hebraica Stuttgartensia: A Reader's Edition*; *Elementary Biblical Hebrew: An Introductory Grammar*; and *Deuteronomy* (Reading the Bible Today). **(Haggai; Zechariah)**

Alan S. Bandy. Clear Creek Baptist Bible College (BA); Mid-America Baptist Theological Seminary (MDiv); Southeastern Baptist Theological Seminary (PhD); Rowena R. Strickland Associate Professor of New Testament and Greek, Oklahoma Baptist University. Alan has written several books, including *The Prophetic Lawsuit in the Book of Revelation* (NTM) and *Understanding Prophecy: A Biblical-Theological Approach*. Alan has also led several study trips to Turkey, Greece, and Italy. **(The City of Ancient Rome; Jewish Marriage Customs; Roman Citizenship; The Roman Military)**

Marcella Barbosa. Lycoming College (BA); Southwestern Baptist Theological Seminary (MA). Marcella serves as Collections Manager and Educational Coordinator for the Tandy Archaeological Museum, Fort Worth. She has participated in archaeological excavations at Sanisera (Roman City and Necropolis Dig, Menorca, Spain) and has been square supervisor for a number of years at the Tel Gezer Excavation Project. **(Women's Fashion in the Old Testament World)**

Mark J. Boda. Canadian Bible College (BTh); Westminster Theological Seminary (MDiv); University of Cambridge (PhD); Professor of Old Testament, McMaster Divinity College. Mark has written/coauthored/edited/coedited thirty books, including *The Book of Zechariah* (NICOT); *1–2 Chronicles* (CBC); *A Severe Mercy*; *The Prophets Speak on Forced Migration*; and *Haggai,*

Zechariah (NIVAC). He has led numerous student trips to Israel and Jordan. **(The Persians)**

James K. Bruckner. North Park College (BA); North Park Theological Seminary (MATS); Luther Northwestern Theological Seminary (MDiv); Luther Seminary (PhD); Paul W. Brandel Professor of Biblical Interpretation, North Park Theological Seminary. Jim has written/coedited several books, including *Exodus* (Understanding the Bible Commentary); *Living Faith: Reflections on Covenant Affirmations*; *Healthy Human Life: A Biblical Perspective*; *Jonah, Nahum, Habakkuk, Zephaniah* (NIVAC); and *Implied Law in the Abraham Narrative*. **(Habakkuk)**

M. Daniel Carroll R. (Rodas). Rice University (BA); Dallas Theological Seminary (ThM); University of Sheffield (PhD); Blanchard Professor of Old Testament, Wheaton College. Danny has authored/coauthored/coedited thirteen books, including *Family in the Bible: Exploring the Customs, Culture, and Context*; *Amos* (NICOT); *Amos—The Prophet and His Oracles: Research on the Book of Amos*; *Wrestling with the Violence of God: Soundings in the Old Testament Texts*; and *Christians at the Border: Immigration, the Church, and the Bible*. **(Amos; Obadiah; Jonah)**

Mark W. Chavalas. California State University, Northridge (BA); University of California, Los Angeles (MA, PhD); Professor of History, University of Wisconsin, La Crosse. Mark has authored/coauthored/coedited numerous books, including *New Horizons in the Study of Ancient Syria*; *Emar: The History, Religion, and Culture of a Syrian Town in the Late Bronze Age*; *Women in the Ancient Near East*; *Mesopotamia and the Bible*; *The IVP Bible Background Commentary*; and *The Ancient Near East: Historical Sources in Translation*. He has worked as the field director, field supervisor, or field epigraphist at a number of archaeological sites, including Tel Ashara/Terqa, Tel Qraya, and Tel Mozan/Urkesh. **(Women in the Old Testament World; Joel)**

Robert B. Chisholm Jr. Syracuse University (BA); Grace Theological Seminary (MDiv, ThM); Dallas Theological Seminary (PhD); Chair and Senior Professor of Old Testament Studies, Dallas Theological Seminary. Bob has authored numerous books, including *1 & 2 Samuel* (TTCS); *A Commentary on Judges and Ruth* (KEL); *Interpreting the Historical Books: An Exegetical Handbook* (HOTE); *Handbook on the Prophets*; and *Interpreting the Minor Prophets*. **(1–2 Samuel)**

Roy E. Ciampa. Gordon College (BA); Denver Seminary (MDiv); University of Aberdeen (PhD); S. Louis and Ann W. Armstrong Professor of Religion and Chair of the Department of Religion, Samford University. Roy has written two books: *The Presence and Function of Scripture in Galatians*

1 and 2 (WUNT) and *The First Letter to the Corinthians* (PNTC), coauthored with Brian S. Rosner. **(The Jewish Rite of Circumcision; Galatians)**

R. Dennis Cole. University of Florida (BA); Western Conservative Baptist Seminary (MDiv, ThM); New Orleans Baptist Theological Seminary (PhD); Professor of Old Testament Hebrew and Archaeology and Mcfarland Chair of Archaeology, New Orleans Baptist Theological Seminary. Dennis has written *Numbers* (NAC) and "Numbers" (*ZIBBCOT*). He has participated in archaeological excavations at Beersheba, Tel Batash-Timnah, Tel Qasile, Tel Beth Shean, Tel Rehob, and Tel Gezer. **(Leviticus)**

Bernie A. Cueto. Florida International University (BA); Dallas Theological Seminary (ThM, PhD); Campus Pastor and Associate Professor of Biblical and Theological Studies, Palm Beach Atlantic University. **(Athletics in the New Testament World; Demonization and Exorcism in the Greco-Roman World)**

J. Andrew Dearman. University of North Carolina (BA); Princeton Theological Seminary (MDiv); Emory University (PhD); Professor of Old Testament, Fuller Theological Seminary. Andy has written numerous books, including *Hosea* (NICOT); *Jeremiah and Lamentations* (NIVAC); *Studies in the Mesha Inscription and Moab*; *Religion and Culture in Ancient Israel*; and *Property Rights in the Eighth-Century Prophets: The Conflict and Its Background.* He has served as field supervisor, staff member, or survey director at Khirbet Iskander, Khirbet al Mudaynah, and for the Central Moab Survey and Northern Moab Survey. **(Ruth; Hosea)**

Stephen G. Dempster. University of Western Ontario (BA); Westminster Theological Seminary (MAR); University of Toronto (MA, PhD); Professor of Religious Studies, Crandall University. Stephen has written several books, including *Dominion and Dynasty: A Biblical Theology of the Hebrew Bible* and *Micah: A Commentary* (THOTC). **(Micah)**

Jason S. DeRouchie. Taylor University (BA); Gordon-Conwell Theological Seminary (MDiv); Southern Baptist Theological Seminary (PhD); Research Professor of Old Testament and Biblical Theology, Midwestern Baptist Theological Seminary. Jason has authored/coauthored/edited numerous books and articles, including *A Modern Grammar for Biblical Hebrew*; *What the Old Testament Authors Really Cared About*; "Zephaniah" (ESVEC); and *Zephaniah* (ZECOT). **(Zephaniah)**

Joseph R. Dodson. Ouachita Baptist University (BA); Southwestern Baptist Theological Seminary (MDiv); University of Aberdeen (PhD); Associate Professor of New Testament, Denver Seminary. Joey has authored/edited/

coedited numerous books, including *The "Powers" of Personification; Paul and the Second Century; Paul and the Greco-Roman Philosophical Tradition*; and *Paul and Seneca in Dialogue.* **(Crucifixion; 1–2 Thessalonians)**

J. Scott Duvall. Ouachita Baptist University (BA); Southwestern Baptist Theological Seminary (MDiv, PhD); Chair of Biblical Studies and Fuller Professor of New Testament, Ouachita Baptist University. Scott is author/coauthor of over a dozen books, including *Revelation* (TTCS); *The Heart of Revelation; The Baker Illustrated Bible Handbook; Grasping God's Word; Living God's Word; Experiencing God's Story of Life and Hope*; and *Biblical Greek Exegesis.* He has led numerous study trips to Turkey and Israel. **(The New Testament, general editor)**

James R. Edwards. Whitworth University (BA); Princeton Theological Seminary (MDiv); New Testament Studies, University of Zurich, Switzerland; Fuller Theological Seminary (PhD); Bruner-Welch Professor of Theology Emeritus, Whitworth University. James has written twelve books, including *The Gospel According to Mark* (PNTC); *Is Jesus the Only Savior?*; *The Hebrew Gospel and the Development of the Synoptic Tradition*; and *The Gospel According to Luke* (PNTC). James has also led numerous study tours to Israel and Turkey, and has published several articles on Greek epigraphy in Turkey. **(Mark)**

Craig A. Evans. Claremont McKenna College (BA); Western Seminary (MDiv); Claremont Graduate University (MA); Claremont Graduate University (PhD); Károli Gáspár Református University, Budapest (DHabil); John Bisagno Distinguished Professor of Christian Origins, Houston Baptist University. Craig has written eighty books, including *Jesus and the Remains of His Day; God Speaks: What He Says, What He Means; Matthew* (NCamBC); *Jesus and His World*; and *Ancient Texts for New Testament Studies.* He has participated in archaeological digs at Mount Zion (Jerusalem) and Kourion (Cyprus) and has led several study trips to Israel. He also serves as a consultant for the Museum of the Bible. **(Luke)**

Constance E. Clark Gane. Pacific Union College (BS); University of California, Berkeley (MA, PhD); Associate Professor of Archaeology and Old Testament, Curator of the Horn Archaeological Museum, and Associate Director of the Institute of Archaeology, Seventh-day Adventist Theological Seminary, Andrews University. Connie has written *Composite Beings in Neo-Babylonian Art* and *Esther* (SDAIBC). She has participated in archaeological excavations at Tel Dor, Tel Dan, and Nineveh (Iraq). She has worked as field archaeologist at Tel Gezer, San Miceli (Sicily), and Kurion (Cyprus), and as field supervisor or codirector at Tall Jalul (Jordan), Madaba Plains Project. She has led study tours to Egypt, Israel, and Jordan. **(Esther)**

Roy E. Gane. Pacific Union College (BA, BMus); University of California, Berkeley (MA, PhD); Professor of Hebrew Bible and Ancient Near Eastern Languages, Seventh-day Adventist Theological Seminary, Andrews University. Roy has written/coedited nine books, including *Leviticus, Numbers* (NIVAC); *Cult and Character: Purification Offerings, Day of Atonement, and Theodicy*; *In the Shadow of Shekinah: God's Journey with Us*; and *Ritual Dynamic Structure.* He has worked as Akkadian epigrapher and area supervisor for archaeological work at Nineveh (Iraq) and as square supervisor and Northwest Semitic epigrapher for excavations at Tall Jalul (Jordan), as part of the Madaba Plains Project. **(Numbers)**

Gregory Goswell. University of Sydney (BSc[Med]); University of London (BD); Australian College of Theology (MTh); University of Sydney (PhD); Academic Dean and Lecturer in Old Testament, Christ College, Sydney. Greg has written *Ezra-Nehemiah* (EPSC) and coauthored *Unceasing Kindness: A Biblical Theology of Ruth* (NSBT). **(Ezra–Nehemiah)**

Michael A. Grisanti. Pillsbury Baptist Bible College (BA); Central Baptist Theological Seminary (MDiv, ThM); Dallas Theological Seminary (PhD); Professor of Old Testament, Chair of the Old Testament Department, Director of the TMS Israel Study Trip, and Distinguished Research Professor of Old Testament, The Master's Seminary. Michael has authored/coauthored numerous articles and books, including "Deuteronomy" (*EBC*); *The World and the Word: An Introduction to the Old Testament*; and *Giving the Sense: Understanding and Using Old Testament Historical Texts.* He has led numerous trips to the Holy Lands. **(Deuteronomy)**

George H. Guthrie. Union University (BA); Southwestern Baptist Theological Seminary (MDiv); Trinity Evangelical Divinity School (ThM); Southwestern Baptist Theological Seminary (PhD); Professor of New Testament, Regent College. George has written numerous books, including *Hebrews* (NIVAC); *2 Corinthians* (BECNT); "Hebrews" (*CNTUOT*); and "Hebrews" (*ZIBBCNT*). George has taught courses to graduate students or Israeli pastors on four occasions in Israel. **(2 Corinthians)**

H. H. Hardy II. University of Oklahoma (BA); Southern Baptist Theological Seminary (MDiv); University of Chicago (MA, PhD); Assistant Professor of Old Testament and Semitic Languages, Southeastern Baptist Theological Seminary. Chip has contributed to *Semitic Inscriptions: Analyzed Texts and English Translations; Complete Biblical Hebrew and Aramaic Glossary; Studies in Semitic Language Contact*; and *Linguistic Methods in Biblical*

Hebrew. He has participated in the excavations at Zincirli, Turkey. **(Daily Life in Ancient Israel)**

Dana M. Harris. Stanford University (BA); Trinity Evangelical Divinity School (MA, PhD); Associate Professor of New Testament, Trinity Evangelical Divinity School. Dana has written numerous articles and books, including *The Eternal Inheritance in Hebrews: The Appropriation of the Old Testament Inheritance Theme by the Author of Hebrews*; *Hebrews* (EGGNT); *Revelation* (KEL); and *Introduction to the Book of Revelation*. She has participated in archaeological excavations at Qeiyafa and Abel Beth Maacah, and led student study trips to Turkey and Israel. **(Hospitality in the New Testament World; Magic in the New Testament World; Messianic Expectations in Jesus's Day; New Testament Household Codes; The Sea of Galilee and Fishing in the First Century; Slavery in the New Testament World; Hebrews)**

John E. Hartley. Greenville College (BA); Asbury Theological Seminary (BD); Brandeis University (MA, PhD); Professor Emeritus, Azusa Pacific Seminary. John has authored/edited/coedited numerous articles and books, including *The Book of Job* (NICOT); "From Lament to Oath: A Study of Progression in the Speeches of Job," in *The Book of Job* (BETL); *The Book of Leviticus* (WBC); *Genesis* (UBCS); *The Semantics of Ancient Hebrew Colour Lexemes*; and *Proverbs* (NBBC). **(Job)**

J. Daniel Hays. New Mexico State University (BS); Dallas Theological Seminary (ThM); Southwestern Baptist Theological Seminary (PhD); Dean and Professor of Biblical Studies, Ouachita Baptist University. Danny is the author/coauthor of over a dozen books, including *The Message of the Prophets*; *From Every People and Nation*; *Jeremiah, Lamentations* (TTCS); *The Temple and the Tabernacle*; and *Grasping God's Word*. He has led numerous study trips to the Holy Lands. **(The Old Testament, general editor; The Cushites; Musical Instruments in Israel and the Ancient Near East)**

Larry R. Helyer. Biola University (BA); Western Seminary (MDiv); Fuller Theological Seminary (PhD); Emeritus Professor of Biblical Studies, Taylor University. Larry has written numerous books, including *Exploring Jewish Literature of the Second Temple Period*; *Yesterday, Today, and Forever: The Continuing Relevance of the Old Testament*; *The Witness of Jesus, Paul, and John: An Exploration in Biblical Theology*; *The Life and Witness of Peter*; and *Mountaintop Theology: Panoramic Perspectives of Redemptive History*. He has led numerous trips to the Holy Lands. **(Intertestamental History)**

Gordon H. Johnston. University of Nebraska (BA); Dallas Theological Seminary (ThM, ThD); Professor of Old Testament Studies, Dallas Theological Seminary. Gordon has published over fifty articles and essays. He coauthored *Jesus the Messiah: Tracing the Promises, Expectations, and Coming of Israel's Kingdom*, and is writing commentaries on Song of Songs and Ecclesiastes. He has participated in several archaeological excavations in Israel as a square supervisor (Tel Malhata, Khirbet Makater) and has led numerous study trips to the Holy Lands. **(Song of Solomon; Nahum)**

Christine Brown Jones. Ouachita Baptist University (BA); George W. Truett Theological Seminary (MDiv); Baylor University (PhD); Associate Professor of Religion, Carson-Newman University. **(Psalms)**

Mariam Kamell-Kovalishyn. Davidson College (BA); Denver Seminary (MA); University of St. Andrews (PhD); Assistant Professor of New Testament, Regent College. Mariam has coauthored *James* (ZECNT). She lived in Greece for six months, studying Classical Greek art and architecture, when she also spent time on sites in Athens, Corinth, and Rome. She also co-led a study trip to Greece and Turkey. **(The City of Corinth; Roman Rule of Judea; Traditional Greek and Roman Gods; James)**

Andreas J. Köstenberger. Vienna University of Economics (Mag. rer. soc. oec.); Columbia International University (MDiv); Vienna University of Economics (Dr. rer. soc. oec.); Trinity International University (PhD); Research Professor of New Testament and Biblical Theology and Director of the Center for Biblical Studies at Midwestern Baptist Theological Seminary. Andreas is the author or editor of more than fifty books, including *John* (BECNT); *A Theology of John's Gospel and Letters* (BTNT); *Encountering John*; *The Missions of Jesus and the Disciples in the Fourth Gospel*; and "John" (*CNTUOT*). **(The Family of Jesus; Jewish Festivals; Pharisees and Sadducees; Pontius Pilate; The Sabbath; Samaritans; John)**

Kelly D. Liebengood. San José State University (BS); University of Kansas (MA); Midwestern Baptist Theological Seminary (MDiv); University of St. Andrews (PhD); Associate Professor of Biblical Studies and Theology, Dean of the School of Theology and Vocation, and Director of the Honors College, LeTourneau University. Kelly has written or coedited several books, including *The Eschatology of 1 Peter: Considering the Influence of Zechariah 9–14* (SNTSMS) and *Engaging Economics: New Testament Scenarios and Early Christian Reception*. Kelly also regularly teaches a class in Israel, Greece, and Turkey that explores the physical setting of the Bible. **(1–2 Peter, Jude)**

Tremper Longman III. Ohio Wesleyan University (BA); Westminster Theological Seminary (MDiv); Yale University (PhD); Distinguished Scholar of Biblical Studies, Westmont College. Tremper is the author/coauthor of over thirty books, including *Genesis* (Story of God Commentary); *How to Read Genesis*; *Psalms* (TOTC); *Ecclesiastes* (NICOT); *Daniel* (NIVAC); *A*

Biblical History of Israel; and *The Fear of the Lord Is Wisdom: A Theological Introduction to Wisdom in Israel.* **(Genesis)**

Safwat Marzouk. Evangelical Theological Seminary in Cairo (MTh, MATS); Union Theological Seminary (STM); Princeton Theological Seminary (PhD); Associate Professor of Hebrew Bible/Old Testament, Anabaptist Mennonite Biblical Seminary. Safwat has written *Egypt as a Monster in the Book of Ezekiel,* and he leads study trips to Egypt. **(The Egyptians)**

Josiah McDermott was born to Taiwanese-Canadian parents and grew up in East Asia. He holds a BComm in Finance from the University of British Columbia and a MA in Biblical Studies from Regent College. He currently lives with his wife and son in Vancouver, British Columbia. **(The City of Corinth; Roman Rule of Judea; Traditional Greek and Roman Gods; James)**

Catherine L. McDowell. University of North Carolina, Chapel Hill (BA); Gordon-Conwell Theological Seminary (MA); Harvard University (MA, PhD); Associate Professor of Old Testament, Gordon-Conwell Theological Seminary. Catherine has written *The Image of God in the Garden of Eden: The Creation of Humankind in Genesis 2:5–3:24 in Light of* mīs pî pīt pî *and* wpt-r *Rituals of Mesopotamia and Ancient Egypt.* She has worked as volunteer, staff member, object and material culture registrar, or square supervisor at a number of archaeological sites and projects, including Ashkelon, Tel Miqne-Ekron, Tel Beth Shean, Caesarea Maritima, and the Deep Sea Archaeology Project. She has been the curator for the Cooley Collection of the Robert C. Cooley Center for the Study of Early Christianity (Charlotte, NC), and she was a research fellow at the W. F. Albright Institute of Archaeological Research (Jerusalem), where she did research on material from Tel Dothan. **(The Canaanites and Canaanite Religion; The Philistines; 1–2 Kings)**

Samuel A. Meier. University of California, Los Angeles (BA); Dallas Theological Seminary (ThM); Harvard University (PhD); Professor at the Melton Center for Jewish Studies, Ohio State University. Sam has written several books, including *The Messenger in the Ancient Semitic World*; *Speaking of Speaking: Marking Direct Discourse in Biblical Hebrew*; and *Themes and Transformations in Old Testament Prophecy.* **(Prophets in the Old Testament World; 1–2 Chronicles)**

Eric Alan Mitchell. Baylor University (BBA); Mid-America Baptist Theological Seminary (MDiv); Southern Baptist Theological Seminary (PhD); Associate Professor of Old Testament and Archaeology, Southwestern Baptist Theological Seminary. Eric has authored/coauthored/coedited numerous books, including *The Holman Illustrated Bible Dictionary*; *Old Testament Survey*; *A Literary Examination of the Function of Satire in the* Mišpaṭ Hammeleḵ *of*

1 Samuel 8; and *Old Testament Survey: A Student's Guide*. He has participated in archaeological excavations at Tel Hazor and Tel Megiddo and since 2007 has been the project codirector and principal investigator of the Tel Gezer Regional Survey Project. He has been an Associate Fellow at the W. F. Albright Institute of Archaeological Research in Jerusalem and has led more than twenty study tours to Israel, Jordan, Egypt, Turkey, and Cyprus. **(Exodus)**

William B. Nelson. Westmont College (BA); Jerusalem University College (MA); Princeton Theological Seminary (MDiv); Harvard University (MA, PhD); Professor of Old Testament, Westmont College. Bill has written *Daniel* (UBCS). **(Daniel; Malachi)**

Douglas J. E. Nykolaishen. University of Saskatchewan (BA); Trinity Evangelical Divinity School (MDiv, MA); University of Edinburgh (PhD); Associate Professor of Biblical Studies, Ouachita Baptist University. Doug has coauthored *Ezra-Nehemiah and Esther* (TTCS). **(The Babylonians)**

Osvaldo Padilla. Moody Bible Institute (BA); Trinity Evangelical Divinity School (MA); University of Aberdeen (PhD); Associate Professor of Divinity, Beeson Divinity School. Osvaldo has written two books, *The Speeches of Outsiders in Acts: Poetics, Theology, and Historiography* and *The Acts of the Apostles: Interpretation, History, and Theology*. **(Ephesians; Philippians; Colossians; Philemon)**

C. Marvin Pate. Moody Bible Institute (Diploma); University of Illinois (BA); Wheaton Graduate School (MA); Marquette University (PhD); Professor of Christian Theology, Ouachita Baptist University. Marvin has written or coauthored over fifteen books, including *Romans* (TTCS); *The Writings of John*; *Interpreting Revelation*; *Deliverance Now and Not Yet: The New Testament and the Great Tribulation*; and *Apostle of the Last Days*. **(Romans)**

Rodney Reeves. Southwest Baptist University (BA); Southwestern Baptist Theological Seminary (MDiv, PhD); Dean and Redford Professor of Biblical Studies in the Courts Redford College of Theology and Ministry, Southwest Baptist University. Rodney has authored or coauthored six books, including *Matthew* (SGBC); *Rediscovering Paul: An Introduction to His World, Letters, and Theology*; *Rediscovering Jesus: An Introduction to Biblical, Religious, and Cultural Perspectives on Christ*; *Spirituality according to Paul: Imitating the Apostle of Christ*; and *A Genuine Faith: How to Follow Jesus Today*. **(Baptism in the New Testament World; Honor and Shame in the New Testament World; The Sanhedrin; Scribes and Teachers of the Law; Matthew)**

E. Randolph Richards. Texas Wesleyan College (BS); Southwestern Baptist Theological Seminary (MDiv, PhD); Provost and Chief Academic Officer,

Palm Beach Atlantic University. Randy has written numerous books, including *A Little Book for New Biblical Scholars*; *Paul Behaving Badly*; *Misreading Scripture with Western Eyes*; *Rediscovering Paul*; and *Paul and First-Century Letter Writing*. Randy has led numerous student study trips to Israel, Turkey, and Greece and worked with the Scholars Initiative of the Museum of the Bible. **(Ancient Letter Writing; Banquets and Meals in the Greco-Roman World; Money in the New Testament World; Shipping Practices in the First Century)**

Mark F. Rooker. Rice University (BA); Dallas Theological Seminary (ThM); Brandeis University (MA, PhD); Senior Professor of Old Testament and Hebrew, Southeastern Baptist Theological Seminary. Mark has authored/coauthored numerous books, including *Leviticus* (NAC); *Ezekiel* (HOTC); *Biblical Hebrew in Translation: The Language of the Book of Ezekiel*; and *The Ten Commandments: Ethics for the Twenty-First Century*. Twice he has been a visiting student at Hebrew University in Jerusalem. **(Ezekiel)**

Richard L. Schultz. Michigan State University (BA); Trinity Evangelical Divinity School (MDiv); Yale University (MA, PhD); Blanchard Professor of Old Testament, Wheaton College. Richard has authored/coauthored several books, including *Search for Quotation: Verbal Parallels in the Prophets*; *Bind Up the Testimony: Explorations in the Genesis of the Book of Isaiah*; and *Out of Context: How to Avoid Misinterpreting the Bible*. **(Proverbs; Ecclesiastes)**

Boyd Seevers. Wheaton College (BA); Dallas Theological Seminary (ThM); Trinity Evangelical Divinity School (PhD); Professor of Old Testament Studies, University of Northwestern. Boyd has written several books, including *Warfare in the Old Testament: The Organization, Weapons, and Tactics of Ancient Near Eastern Armies*; *Hidden in Plain Sight: Finding Wisdom and Meaning in the Parts of the Bible That Most People Skip*; and *The Quick-Start Guide to the Bible*. Over the last thirty years he has worked at numerous archaeological sites (Khirbet el-Maqatir, Shiloh, Bethsaida, Tiberias, Har Tuv) as volunteer, group leader, square supervisor, or supervisor of archaeological excavation. **(Warfare in the Old Testament; Joshua; Judges)**

Gary V. Smith. Wheaton College (BA); Trinity Evangelical Divinity School (MA); Dropsie College for Hebrew and Cognate Learning (PhD); Professor of Christian Studies (retired), Union University. Gary has authored/coauthored thirteen books, including *Isaiah* (NAC); *Hosea, Amos, Micah* (NIVAC); *The Prophets as Preachers: An Introduction to the Hebrew Prophets*; *Ezra, Nehemiah, Esther* (CBC); and *Old Testament Survey: Broadening Your Biblical Horizons*. He has led several tours to the Holy Lands. **(The Assyrians; Isaiah)**

Mark L. Strauss. Westmont College (BA); Talbot School of Theology (MDiv; ThM); University of Aberdeen (PhD); University Professor of New Testament, Bethel Seminary, San Diego. Mark is the author/coauthor of fifteen books and editor/coeditor of forty. Books include commentaries on the Gospels of Mark (ZECNT; *EBC*) and Luke (*ZIBBCNT*); *How to Read the Bible in Changing Times*; *Four Portraits, One Jesus*; and *The Davidic Messiah in Luke-Acts*. He is also Vice-Chair of the Committee on Bible Translation for the NIV. **(Jerusalem in the Time of Jesus; The Jerusalem Temple; The Jewish Synagogue; Acts)**

Mark E. Taylor. Mississippi State University (BBA); Mid-America Baptist Theological Seminary (MDiv); Southwestern Baptist Theological Seminary (PhD); Professor of New Testament and Associate Dean of Masters Programs, Southwestern Baptist Theological Seminary. Mark has written two books, *A Text-Linguistic Investigation into the Discourse Structure of James* and *1 Corinthians* (NAC). **(1 Corinthians)**

David L. Turner. Cedarville University (BA); Grace Theological Seminary (MDiv, ThM); Hebrew Union College-Jewish Institute of Religion (MPhil); Grace Theological Seminary (ThD); Hebrew Union College-Jewish Institute of Religion (PhD); Emeritus Professor of New Testament, Grand Rapids Theological Seminary. David has written numerous books, including *Matthew* (BECNT); *Matthew* (CBC); *Israel's Last Prophet: Jesus and the Jewish Leaders in Matthew 23*; and *The Gospels and Acts* (KHNTE). David also studied at Jerusalem University College and has twice taught study groups in Israel. **(1–3 John)**

Ray Van Neste. Union University (BA); Trinity Evangelical Divinity School (MA); University of Aberdeen (PhD); Professor of Biblical Studies and Director of the Ryan Center for Biblical Studies, Union University. Ray has written or contributed to eight books, including *Cohesion and Structure in the Pastoral Epistles* (JSNTSup). **(1–2 Timothy, Titus)**

Mark Wilson. Trinity Bible College (BA); Regent University (MA); University of South Africa (D.Litt. et Phil.); Associate Professor Extraordinary of New Testament, Stellenbosch University. Mark is the author or editor of fifteen books, including *The Victor Sayings in the Book of Revelation*; *Charts on the Book of Revelation: Literary, Historical, and Theological Perspectives*; *Revelation: Illustrated Bible Backgrounds Commentary*; *Victory through the Lamb: A Guide to Revelation in Plain Language*; and *Biblical Turkey: A Guide to the Jewish and Christian Sites of Asia Minor*. He served as a cofacilitator for the synagogue excavation at Priene, Turkey. He is the English editor for the archaeological publications of the Mediterranean Civilizations Research

Center (AKMED) in Antalya, Turkey. He has led numerous study trips to Turkey, Greece, Cyprus, Malta, Italy, Macedonia, and Albania. **(The City of Ephesus; Roman Roads and Travel; Revelation)**

Gary E. Yates. Washington Bible College (BA); Dallas Theological Seminary (ThM, PhD); Professor of Old Testament Studies, Liberty University School of Divinity. Gary has authored/coauthored/coedited several books, including *The Message of the Twelve: Hearing the Voice of the Minor Prophets* and *The Essence of the Old Testament: A Survey*. **(Jeremiah; Lamentations)**

Introduction

J. Scott Duvall and J. Daniel Hays

Welcome to *The Baker Illustrated Bible Background Commentary* and the world of biblical backgrounds! We pray that this book will help you in your study of Scripture and enrich your understanding of it. This is a very different kind of commentary. Usually, commentaries on the Bible seek to explain the theological meaning of the text and perhaps how it applies to you. That is a very important task, and we encourage you to continue to use regular commentaries, along with your personal study of God's Word. But often, since we are so far removed from the biblical world by time and culture, our lack of insight into those cultural and historical contexts can limit our understanding. The mission of this book is to provide cultural and historical background information about the biblical text that will give you a better appreciation for and understanding of the text.

Thus in this book we are not trying to explain the theological meaning of the Bible to you, but rather we are providing relevant background information that you can combine with your own personal study and input from other regular commentaries to arrive at the correct interpretation and application of biblical passages. Furthermore, we believe that helpful and relevant background material often helps make the biblical texts more "colorful"; that is, it brings them alive and helps us to relate to them. We want to enter the world of the biblical characters, and we ask, "What were things like back then?" This book tries to help you envision and connect to biblical times.

The amount of historical and cultural background material for each chapter of the Bible is overwhelming, and it is impossible for us in one volume to provide all of the available material on every passage. What we have done in this volume is select outstanding biblical scholars to write the articles on each book of the Bible. Within the page limits of this one volume we asked these biblical scholars to include the material that they thought was most relevant, helpful, and/or interesting. So for each book of the Bible we are not presenting a comprehensive discussion of background material, but rather we are offering information that we (the authors of the articles) think is the most illuminating.

Also, because it is true that a picture is worth a thousand words, we have included hundreds of pictures and other illustrative material that will help you envision and understand the biblical world. We think that the pictures are just as important as the written commentary.

This background commentary is written for people in the church, and it is not directed at scholars. Nonetheless, it is written by outstanding biblical scholars who understand and can access the academic world in which much of this material lies. Yet we have tried to minimize the technical language normally used by scholars and to be as clear and understandable as possible. Likewise, we have tried to minimize extensive documentation, and we have placed that kind of material as endnotes in the back of the book.

Differences between the Testaments. It is important to note that historical context and cultural-religious practices change over time. The Bible spans nearly two thousand years of history. Culturally, historically, and technologically, things change. There is no monolithic unchanging or common "biblical world." The cultural, historical, and technological world of King David (ca. 1000 BC), for example, is extremely different from that of the apostle Paul (ca. AD 50). Also, in our study of the OT we will be looking at the religious practices of the ancient Egyptians, Canaanites, and Mesopotamians, while in the NT we will be looking at Greco-Roman or Jewish religious backgrounds or practices. Clearly, historical and cultural information from 700 BC can be misleading or irrelevant for understanding the NT in the first century AD (and vice versa). For this reason, the kinds of biblical background material that we discuss in the OT and in the NT are usually quite different, and there is little cross-referencing between the two.

Cross-Referencing. Because we have so much helpful and relevant material to present in one volume, we have tried to minimize repeated discussions on the same topic. Thus, for example, since the Babylonians appear numerous times throughout the OT, we have decided to present one main article, "The Babylonians," in the OT section and then to cross-reference this article whenever we need a discussion on the Babylonians. A list of these special articles for both the OT and the NT are provided in the table of contents. Also, sometimes within the discussion on a specific background issue from a biblical text we have a good, thorough discussion that is also relevant for the same issue in other texts. Rather than repeat that same discussion, we will cross-reference it. For example, if there is a good discussion on a relevant topic in 2 Kings 17:16, we will cross-reference it in this form: See comments on 2 Kings 17:16. Often, however, we will just want to refer to the Bible and point you to other Bible passages rather than to our discussion. In those instances we will simply provide Bible citations (e.g., 1 Cor. 16:19).

Old Testament Quotations in the New Testament. The Christian Standard Bible, which this commentary follows, puts NT quotations of the OT in boldface type. Because this book uses boldface type for Christian Standard Bible verses in the commentary sections, we have put such quotations in italics as well as boldface.

Abbreviations. A list of abbreviations for the dictionaries, journals, and ancient sources used in the endnotes is presented at the end of the book with the endnotes. Here, however, we list the abbreviations used throughout the articles within this book.

Aram.	Aramaic
ca.	in regard to historical time eras, this means "about"
cf.	compare
chap(s.)	chapter(s)
e.g.	for example
esp.	especially
ET	English translation
et al.	and others
Gk.	Greek
Heb.	Hebrew
Lat.	Latin
LXX	Septuagint
no(s).	number(s)
NT	New Testament
OT	Old Testament
s.v.	under the word
v(v).	verse(s)

THE OLD TESTAMENT

Introduction to the Old Testament

J. Daniel Hays

The Historical and Geographical Setting. As we mentioned in the introduction, it is important to remember that the events and the writing of the NT and the OT take place in very different time settings and with very different cultural background settings. The OT was written over the span of nearly one thousand years, running roughly from the mid-second millennium BC to the mid-first millennium BC. This time period, and the tumultuous changes that took place throughout the biblical world during this time, form the primary historical and cultural context in which to explore the background for the OT.

Throughout this book we will use the term "ancient Near East." Geographically, this term refers primarily to the region in the Middle East that today comprises the countries of Egypt, Sudan, Israel, Palestinian Territories, Jordan, Lebanon, Syria, Iran, Iraq, and Turkey. Chronologically, the phrase "ancient Near East" starts approximately with the rise of civilizations in Sumer (in Mesopotamia) and in Egypt around 3300 BC and continues until Alexander the Great (ca. 330 BC), who conquered most of this area and spread Greek culture throughout the region.

The story of the OT moves across much of this region and time. In Gen. 11:27–32, as Abraham and his family are first introduced, they are living in Mesopotamia (now modern Iraq and Syria). God calls him from there and leads him into the land of Canaan, where he and his family interact with the inhabitants of that region. At the end of Genesis, Abraham's descendants have moved to Egypt, where they reside for four hundred years, no doubt picking up some strong Egyptian cultural influence. In Exodus God delivers Abraham's descendants, now called the "sons of Israel" (i.e., the Israelites), from Egypt and leads them back into Canaan, where for the next thousand years or so they will interact militarily and culturally with both the inhabitants of their land (the Canaanites and a number of other closely related peoples) and their close neighbors (Philistines, Edomites, Moabites, Ammonites, Arameans). In the late eighth century BC (i.e., the 700s BC) the Assyrians (from Mesopotamia, in the area that is now modern Iraq) conquer most of the region and establish the Assyrian Empire (see the article "The Assyrians"). Next, in the late seventh century BC, the Babylonians (also from Mesopotamia) defeat the Assyrians and replace them as the primary power and ruler over most of the ancient Near East. It is the Babylonians who conquer and destroy Jerusalem (586 BC), exiling much of the Judean population to Babylon (see the article "The Babylonians"). In 539 BC the Babylonians will then be defeated and replaced by the Persians (from what is now Iran), who likewise will establish an empire that encompasses most of the ancient Near East, including Judah, the homeland of the Jews, as well as all the regions to which Jews had been exiled (see the article "The Persians"). The Persian Empire lasts until Alexander the Great overruns it in 331 BC.

The Bible Background Material to Be Discussed. Examining the history and the culture of this very complex ancient Near East will help us in our understanding and appreciating the OT. In the OT articles we will be presenting helpful background information and visual illustrations that fall into the following categories:

1. **Historical people and geopolitical events.** We will identify many of the foreign nations and their kings (and generals, etc.) that the Israelites will encounter as well as the interactions that the Israelites have with these nations. When it is available, we will share relevant information from written historical annals or records that these foreign kings made, which presents their side of the story (often quite propagandistic!). There will be huge geopolitical events taking place in the ancient Near East in which Israel may not be one of the main players but the results of which impact them profoundly (e.g., the conflict between Babylonia and the Assyria/Egypt alliance in 612–605 BC). Thus we will try to explain these "big picture" events and movements occurring in the world around Israel and the way in which these events affect Israel.

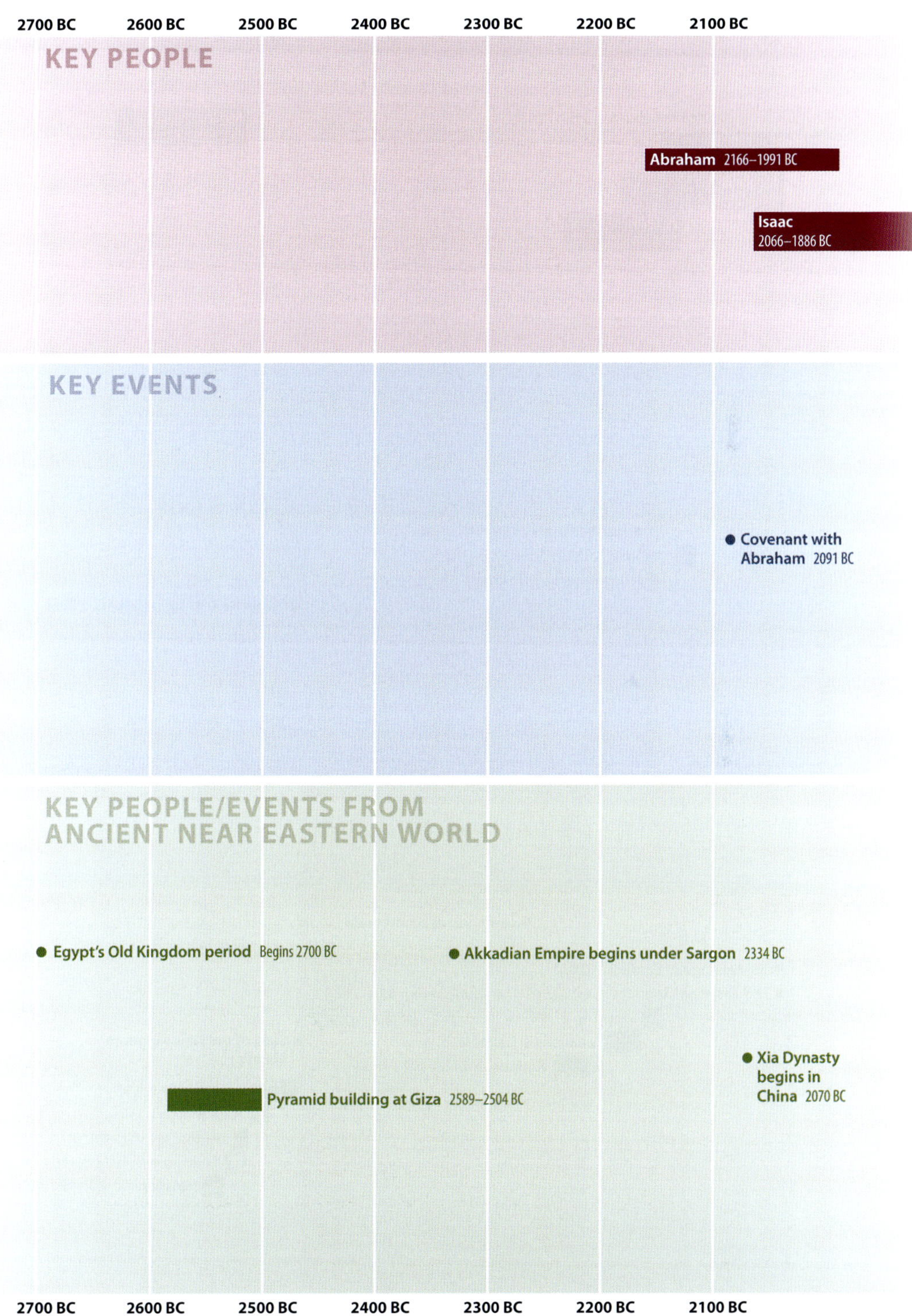
2700 BC
2600 BC
2500 BC
2400 BC
2300 BC
2200 BC
2100 BC
KEY PEOPLE
Abraham 2166–1991 BC
Isaac 2066–1886 BC
KEY EVENTS
Covenant with Abraham 2091 BC
KEY PEOPLE/EVENTS FROM ANCIENT NEAR EASTERN WORLD
Egypt's Old Kingdom period Begins 2700 BC
Akkadian Empire begins under Sargon 2334 BC
Xia Dynasty begins in China 2070 BC
Pyramid building at Giza 2589–2504 BC
2700 BC
2600 BC
2500 BC
2400 BC
2300 BC
2200 BC
2100 BC

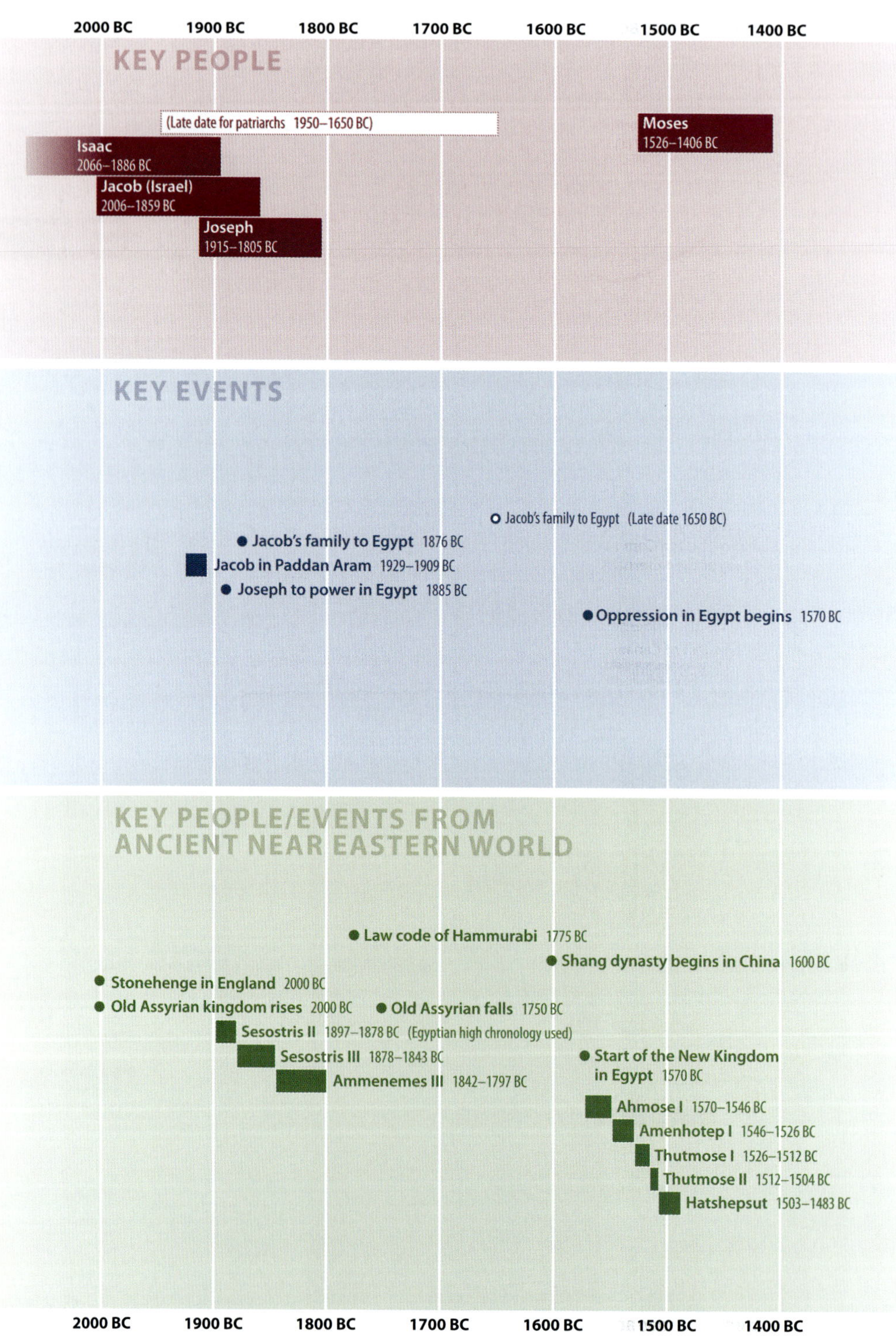
2000 BC
1900 BC
1800 BC
1700 BC
1600 BC
1500 BC
1400 BC
KEY PEOPLE
(Late date for patriarchs 1950–1650 BC)
Moses 1526–1406 BC
Isaac 2066–1886 BC
Jacob (Israel) 2006–1859 BC
Joseph 1915–1805 BC
KEY EVENTS
Jacob's family to Egypt (Late date 1650 BC)
Jacob's family to Egypt 1876 BC
Jacob in Paddan Aram 1929–1909 BC
Joseph to power in Egypt 1885 BC
Oppression in Egypt begins 1570 BC
KEY PEOPLE/EVENTS FROM ANCIENT NEAR EASTERN WORLD
Law code of Hammurabi 1775 BC
Shang dynasty begins in China 1600 BC
Stonehenge in England 2000 BC
Old Assyrian kingdom rises 2000 BC
Old Assyrian falls 1750 BC
Sesostris II 1897–1878 BC (Egyptian high chronology used)
Sesostris III 1878–1843 BC
Ammenemes III 1842–1797 BC
Start of the New Kingdom in Egypt 1570 BC
Ahmose I 1570–1546 BC
Amenhotep I 1546–1526 BC
Thutmose I 1526–1512 BC
Thutmose II 1512–1504 BC
Hatshepsut 1503–1483 BC
2000 BC
1900 BC
1800 BC
1700 BC
1600 BC
1500 BC
1400 BC

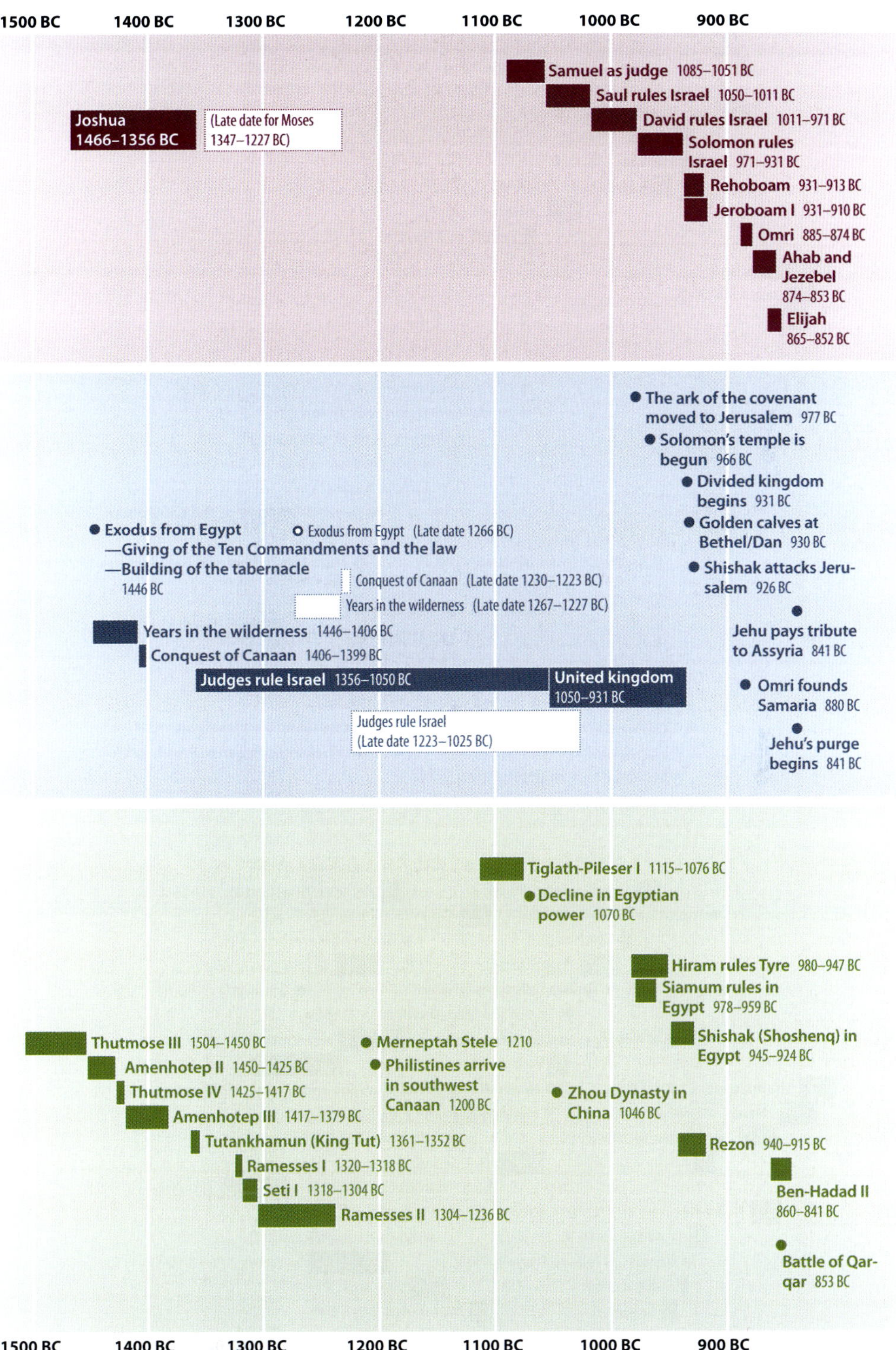

1500 BC
1400 BC
1300 BC
1200 BC
1100 BC
1000 BC
900 BC
Samuel as judge 1085–1051 BC
Saul rules Israel 1050–1011 BC
Joshua 1466–1356 BC
(Late date for Moses 1347–1227 BC)
David rules Israel 1011–971 BC
Solomon rules Israel 971–931 BC
Rehoboam 931–913 BC
Jeroboam I 931–910 BC
Omri 885–874 BC
Ahab and Jezebel 874–853 BC
Elijah 865–852 BC
The ark of the covenant moved to Jerusalem 977 BC
Solomon's temple is begun 966 BC
Divided kingdom begins 931 BC
Golden calves at Bethel/Dan 930 BC
Exodus from Egypt —Giving of the Ten Commandments and the law —Building of the tabernacle 1446 BC
Exodus from Egypt (Late date 1266 BC)
Shishak attacks Jerusalem 926 BC
Conquest of Canaan (Late date 1230–1223 BC)
Years in the wilderness (Late date 1267–1227 BC)
Years in the wilderness 1446–1406 BC
Jehu pays tribute to Assyria 841 BC
Conquest of Canaan 1406–1399 BC
Judges rule Israel 1356–1050 BC
United kingdom 1050–931 BC
Omri founds Samaria 880 BC
Judges rule Israel (Late date 1223–1025 BC)
Jehu's purge begins 841 BC
Tiglath-Pileser I 1115–1076 BC
Decline in Egyptian power 1070 BC
Hiram rules Tyre 980–947 BC
Siamum rules in Egypt 978–959 BC
Thutmose III 1504–1450 BC
Merneptah Stele 1210
Shishak (Shoshenq) in Egypt 945–924 BC
Amenhotep II 1450–1425 BC
Philistines arrive in southwest Canaan 1200 BC
Thutmose IV 1425–1417 BC
Zhou Dynasty in China 1046 BC
Amenhotep III 1417–1379 BC
Tutankhamun (King Tut) 1361–1352 BC
Rezon 940–915 BC
Ramesses I 1320–1318 BC
Seti I 1318–1304 BC
Ben-Hadad II 860–841 BC
Ramesses II 1304–1236 BC
Battle of Qarqar 853 BC
1500 BC
1400 BC
1300 BC
1200 BC
1100 BC
1000 BC
900 BC

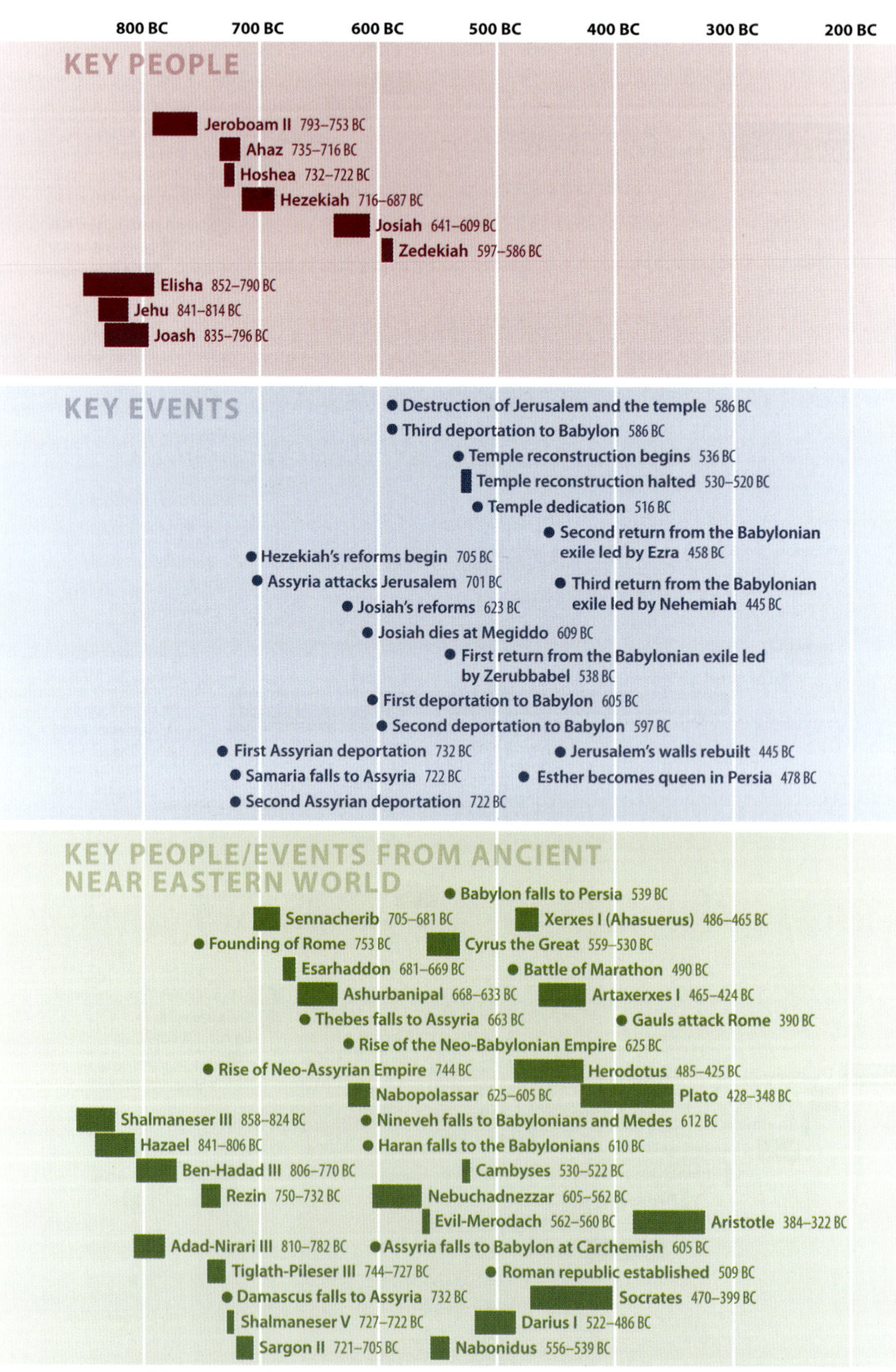

800 BC
700 BC
600 BC
500 BC
400 BC
300 BC
200 BC
KEY PEOPLE
Jeroboam II 793–753 BC
Ahaz 735–716 BC
Hoshea 732–722 BC
Hezekiah 716–687 BC
Josiah 641–609 BC
Zedekiah 597–586 BC
Elisha 852–790 BC
Jehu 841–814 BC
Joash 835–796 BC
KEY EVENTS
Destruction of Jerusalem and the temple 586 BC
Third deportation to Babylon 586 BC
Temple reconstruction begins 536 BC
Temple reconstruction halted 530–520 BC
Temple dedication 516 BC
Second return from the Babylonian exile led by Ezra 458 BC
Hezekiah's reforms begin 705 BC
Assyria attacks Jerusalem 701 BC
Third return from the Babylonian exile led by Nehemiah 445 BC
Josiah's reforms 623 BC
Josiah dies at Megiddo 609 BC
First return from the Babylonian exile led by Zerubbabel 538 BC
First deportation to Babylon 605 BC
Second deportation to Babylon 597 BC
First Assyrian deportation 732 BC
Jerusalem's walls rebuilt 445 BC
Samaria falls to Assyria 722 BC
Esther becomes queen in Persia 478 BC
Second Assyrian deportation 722 BC
KEY PEOPLE/EVENTS FROM ANCIENT NEAR EASTERN WORLD
Babylon falls to Persia 539 BC
Sennacherib 705–681 BC
Xerxes I (Ahasuerus) 486–465 BC
Founding of Rome 753 BC
Cyrus the Great 559–530 BC
Esarhaddon 681–669 BC
Battle of Marathon 490 BC
Ashurbanipal 668–633 BC
Artaxerxes I 465–424 BC
Thebes falls to Assyria 663 BC
Gauls attack Rome 390 BC
Rise of the Neo-Babylonian Empire 625 BC
Rise of Neo-Assyrian Empire 744 BC
Herodotus 485–425 BC
Nabopolassar 625–605 BC
Plato 428–348 BC
Shalmaneser III 858–824 BC
Nineveh falls to Babylonians and Medes 612 BC
Hazael 841–806 BC
Haran falls to the Babylonians 610 BC
Ben-Hadad III 806–770 BC
Cambyses 530–522 BC
Rezin 750–732 BC
Nebuchadnezzar 605–562 BC
Evil-Merodach 562–560 BC
Aristotle 384–322 BC
Adad-Nirari III 810–782 BC
Assyria falls to Babylon at Carchemish 605 BC
Tiglath-Pileser III 744–727 BC
Roman republic established 509 BC
Damascus falls to Assyria 732 BC
Socrates 470–399 BC
Shalmaneser V 727–722 BC
Darius I 522–486 BC
Sargon II 721–705 BC
Nabonidus 556–539 BC
800 BC
700 BC
600 BC
500 BC
400 BC
300 BC
200 BC

2. **Religious background material.** Between significant archaeological remains and the discovery of thousands of ancient literary documents we have quite an extensive knowledge of many religious beliefs and practices of people throughout much of the ancient Near East. In the OT the Israelites are frequently struggling against the strong influence of pagan religions and the associated religious practices and mindset of their neighbors. Throughout the OT articles we will try to explain these influences. Also, we certainly affirm that the God of Abraham, Isaac, Jacob, and Moses is the one, true God and the creator of the universe. In this sense he is completely unique. But God communicates and reveals himself to his people in the OT within the context of their world—that is, the world of the ancient Near East. Thus while there are critical differences between the religious beliefs and practices of Israel and their pagan neighbors (and we will point those out), there are also lots of similarities in practices as well, especially in the basic conceptual world. Several representative examples of this include the following: (1) the basic architectural layout of the temple that Solomon builds in Jerusalem is similar to the layout found in the pagan temples of Israel's neighbors in the region; (2) hundreds of depictions of lower-level divine beings have been discovered that are composite in nature, with wings and human, bull, or lion bodies and heads, which are very similar to the cherubim described in the OT; and (3) numerous altars and incense burners similar to those used in Israel have been discovered in archaeological excavations. This wealth of information from the nations around Israel can often help us better understand the religious practices and beliefs of Israel, both through comparison and through contrast.

The Ain Dara temple, near Aleppo, Syria, had the same basic layout as the temple of Solomon in Jerusalem. Shown here are the ruins of the entrance, guided by a cherubim-like creature with the head of a man, the body of a lion, and the wings of a bird.

3. **Daily life and technological developments.** Although no doubt there were regional variations and differences, especially across time, in general there was a great deal of commonality throughout the ancient Near East during the OT period in regard to farming, livestock, food preparation, commerce, manufacturing (pottery, glassblowing, metallurgy, etc.), travel, building construction, shipping, methods and

equipment of warfare, and writing, among others. Thus the knowledge that we have of these activities and practices from the ancient Near East can shed light on the day-to-day lives of those in ancient Israel.

4. **Literature.** As discussed below, thousands and thousands of literary documents from the ancient Near East have been discovered and translated. In many places of the OT there are literary similarities between sections of the OT and literary documents from the ancient Near East. For example, the structure and format of the book of Deuteronomy (the great law code given by God to Israel) is very similar to the structure seen in several ancient Hittite treaties. Thus it appears that when God entered into his great covenant relationship with Israel and defined it in writing through the book of Deuteronomy, he employed a style of literature that the people of the ancient world (educated people like Moses, especially) would recognize as a legal treaty style of writing. Likewise, some of the laws in the Pentateuch are similar to laws that show up in ancient law codes, such as that of the Babylonian king Hammurabi. From ancient Egypt there are written compositions of wisdom literature that have strong similarities to parts of Proverbs. There are also several ancient literary compositions from Israel's neighbors, apparently well known throughout the region, which describe how the world was created by the pagan gods. The story in Gen. 1–2 explicitly refutes much that is in these pagan accounts, but nonetheless it apparently is well aware of them and follows the general genre (or literary style) of these other stories as it interacts with them. Thus from a literature point of view, it is helpful to explore other literary works that bear similarities in style or content to the biblical text, even if the overall orientation (the Lord created the world and is one God) is different.

The Sources. Over the last 150 years extensive archaeological excavations have been undertaken throughout many regions of the ancient Near

Ancient clay tablet with cuneiform writing, containing the story of Gilgamesh.

East. Thus there is a wealth of archaeological data available from the larger region and from the same basic time period as the OT. Particularly helpful are the hundreds of thousands of literary documents (monument inscriptions, papyri documents, tomb inscriptions, and entire libraries full of thousands of clay tablets, etc.) that have been discovered, many of which have been translated into English. Just as one example, in the ancient city of Mari, located in northern Syria near the Euphrates River, over 25,000 clay tablets were discovered, most from 1800 to 1750 BC (near the time of Abraham). These tablets are written in the cuneiform style of writing in the Akkadian language. Within this rich literary collection are administrative texts dealing with food rations and distribution, expense reports, texts relating to the royal harem, palace administration texts, provincial administration texts, treaties, poems and other literary compositions, expense texts regarding the royal temples, ritual "omen" texts, and over three thousand letters. Here we have a tremendous amount of information relating to how people in this ancient city lived and believed during the patriarchal period of the OT. There are likewise large archives of texts from other ancient Near Eastern locations, the most famous including several sites in the region of Sumer; the cities of Ebla, Ugarit, and Nuzi; several sites in the Hittite Empire (in modern Turkey/Syria); the island of Elephantine (in Egypt); the region of Amarna (in Egypt); numerous other cities in Egypt; and others. Thus throughout the OT articles we will be referring to these "ancient documents," "archives," or "royal annals" from the ancient Near East that enlighten our understanding of the religion, culture, and history of the OT period. Many of the most relevant documents have been translated into English and published in several helpful and accessible volumes, such as *The Context of Scripture*, 3 vols. (Brill, 2000–2003); *Ancient Near Eastern Texts Relating to the Old Testament* (Princeton University Press, 1969); and *Ancient Egyptian Literature*, 3 vols., 2nd ed. (University of California Press, 2006).

How Do We Know What Year It Was? Throughout the OT articles we will frequently be providing historical dates for people and events. But how do scholars know what year it was for these kings and battles? One of the documents discovered from ancient Assyria is called the Assyrian King List. This document lists out the Assyrian kings in order. Also in this list the Assyrians assign a personal name, called an eponym, to each consecutive year. Thus each year of Assyrian history in the king list is identified by one of these eponyms. These eponyms can thus be used within the king list to establish a fairly tight internal chronology—that is, the time period of each king's rule and the time period from one king to another. One of the entries in this list notes that during one particular eponym year during the reign of Assyrian king Ashur-dan III a solar eclipse occurred. Astronomers today can identify the exact date for that eclipse (June 15, 763 BC). By using this exact date and the tight internal chronology of the Assyrian King List, scholars can date most of Assyrian history (reigns of kings, campaigns, sieges of foreign cities, etc.) with precision. The Babylonians likewise have king lists that interconnect with the Assyrian King List, and Persian history can also be connected and thus dated precisely. At numerous places in the Bible, especially in 1–2 Kings, Assyrian history (kings, invasions, battles, etc.) intersects with Israelite history, and thus scholars can date those events with some confidence. Then within 1–2 Kings, 1–2 Chronicles, and 1–2 Samuel the chronology for the reigns of Israelite and Judahite kings and the dates for key events can be worked out internally. Postexilic books like Ezra and Nehemiah, as well as Haggai and Zechariah, provide tight chronology connections to the reigns of Persian kings, and thus can also be dated quite accurately.

General Background Articles

The Assyrians

Gary V. Smith

Geography. The central territory of the nation of Assyria coincided with the northern part of modern Iraq. Assyria was located north of Babylon, east of Syria, south of the Urartu Mountains, and west of Medo-Persia. The Euphrates River meandered through the southern and western side of the country, while the Tigris River watered the eastern part. During the eighth to seventh centuries BC, Assyria became one of the most powerful and expansionistic nations in the ancient Near East. At the height of its power, the Neo-Assyrian Empire included Babylonia, Syria, Palestine, parts of Asia Minor, Elam, and Egypt.

Early History. Genesis 10:22 identifies the original people in this area as descendants of Asshur, the second son of Shem. Archaeological evidence indicates that people lived in this area as early as around 5000 BC. Some southern Babylonian kings (Sargon of Akkad, reigned approx. 2340–2284 BC) constructed buildings in this territory before it became an independent nation, but the first organized attempts to establish political control of the whole area appear to have been made by Shamshi-adad I (1813–1781 BC),[1] not long after Abram passed through this area on his way to Haran (Gen. 11:31). Shortly after this, invasions by the Hittites, the Hurrians, and the Kassites resulted in a time of chaos that lasted for nearly four hundred years.

Middle Assyrian Period (1364–934 BC). Assyria became a political state under the leadership of Ashur-uballit I (1364–1329 BC) and his son Shalmaneser I. They defeated the Hittites, the Arameans, the Hurrians, and the Babylonians, and thus were able to expand the nation's power and influence considerably. Following a period of decline (about one hundred years)

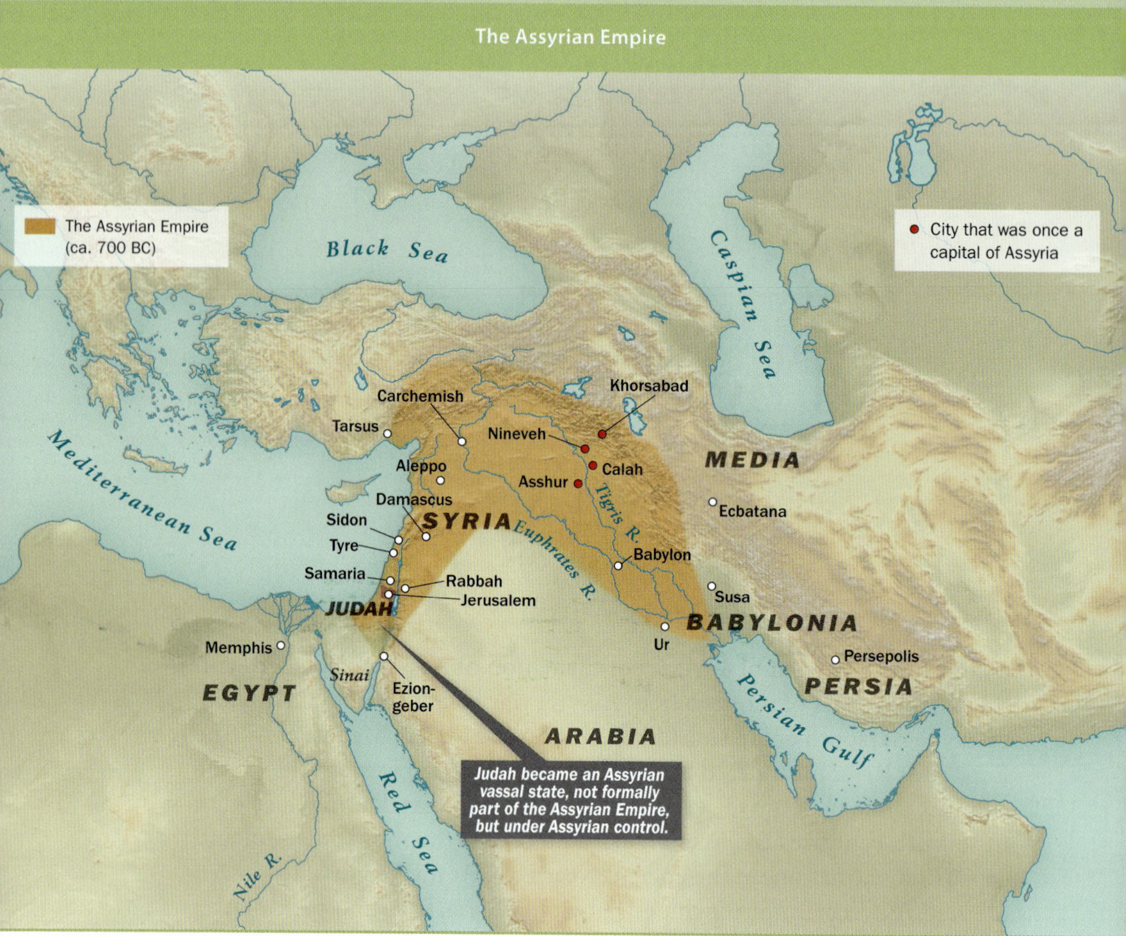

there was a revival of Assyrian power, mainly due to the efforts of the strong Assyrian king Tiglath-pileser I (1115–1077 BC), who gained control of Babylon for a short time and also conquered forty-two other city-states (even Byblos, Tyre, and Sidon on the Mediterranean Sea).[2] After Tiglath-pileser's death the Assyrians were unable to maintain control over the large area they had conquered, and they were further weakened by an invasion of Arameans from Syria. This period of Assyrian weakness coincided with the northward expansion of Israel under the reigns of David and Solomon.

Neo-Assyrian Period (934–612 BC). A new era of power began with the rise of the Assyrian king Ashur-dan II (934–912 BC) and his descendants. They were strong military leaders who won several military campaigns and were able to complete numerous building projects in Assyria (e.g., the building of a citadel, palace, and temples at the city of Calah). One example of this military expansion was the war that Shalmaneser III (859–824 BC) fought against Damascus and other entities in the west.[3] In order to stop this Assyrian aggression, King Hadadezer of Damascus and King Irhuleni of Hamath put together a coalition of twelve nations (including King Ahab of Israel, who provided a significant number of troops and chariots), and they fought the Assyrians in a major battle at Qarqar in 853 BC. In their written royal annals the Assyrians claim a victory, but this is far from clear. Yet not too long afterward (in 841 BC) Tyre, Sidon, and Israel (under King Jehu)[4] were forced to submit to the Assyrians and to pay tribute to them. After this, however, internal conflicts led to the decline of Assyrian power. It was during this time of Assyrian weakness that the prophet Jonah came to the Assyrian capital city of Nineveh warning them of judgment. Continued Assyrian weakness during the reign of Ashur-dan III (772–755 BC) enabled the Israelite king Jeroboam II to expand his influence into the region (2 Kings 14:24–26; Amos 1) and to make Israel a powerful and wealthy nation (Amos 3:15; 6:4–6, 8).

The rise of the Assyrian king Tiglath-pileser III (745–727 BC) brought major changes in Assyrian power. In the first few years of his reign he subdued several nations that had rebelled against him, including a coalition between Rezin, king of Aram (Syria), and Pekah, king of Israel. These two kings wanted Ahaz, king of Judah, to join their coalition against Assyria, but Ahaz refused. Consequently, in 734 BC the Aramean (Syrian) and Israelite armies attacked Judah to force it to cooperate, a time of crisis in Judah that provides the background for Isa. 7–8. In desperation, Ahaz sent messengers and gold to the Assyrian king Tiglath-pileser III, pleading for his help (2 Kings 16:7; 2 Chron. 28:16). In response to this request Tiglath-pileser III defeated both the Syrian forces and the Israelite forces (2 Kings 16:9). However, then he also made Ahaz his vassal servant (2 Chron. 28:20). Later Tiglath-pileser III defeated the Babylonians and was installed as the king of Babylon.

A few years later the Assyrian king Shalmaneser V (726–722 BC) determined that King Hoshea of Israel was withholding tribute and was also conspiring with the Egyptians, so he invaded Israel and attacked the Israelite capital city of Samaria (2 Kings 17:1–5). Shalmaneser V died at this time, but the next Assyrian king, Sargon II (722–705 BC),

The Assyrian King Tiglath-pileser III (reigned 745-727 BC).

A wall relief from the palace of the Assyrian king Sennacherib (reigned 705–681 BC) depicting Judahite prisoners from the captured city of Lachish being tortured.

finished the conquest of Israel, and in 722 BC he exiled many of the people (in the Assyrian royal annals Sargon claims that he exiled 27,900 people)[5] into various parts of the Assyrian Empire (2 Kings 17:6). He also resettled many foreigners into the land of Israel (2 Kings 17:24). In 715–711 BC Sargon attacked the Philistine cities of Gath and Ashdod for conspiring with Egypt (see Isa. 20), and this campaign may be reflected in Micah's lament in Mic. 1:8–16.

Sennacherib (705–681 BC), the next Assyrian king, faced rebellions by Merodach-baladan in Babylon and by Hezekiah in Judah (2 Kings 18:7–9, 13; Isa. 39:1–8). Sennacherib first moved to restore order in Babylon (702 BC) and then turned to deal with Hezekiah in Judah (701 BC) (Isa. 36–37). In his annals Sennacherib claims that he defeated the Egyptians' ally Judah at Eltekeh (cf. 2 Kings 18:9) and then destroyed forty-six walled cities in Judah, including the city of Lachish (2 Kings 18:14, 17).[6] Hezekiah quickly paid his back taxes (2 Kings 18:14–16), but this did not stop a large Assyrian army from coming to attack Jerusalem. At that time Hezekiah prayed for God's deliverance (2 Kings 19:14–19), and God sent an angel to kill 185,000 Assyrian soldiers (Isa. 37:36). The surviving Assyrian soldiers fled homeward (2 Kings 19:36). Because of another rebellion in the city of Babylon, Sennacherib leveled that city in 689 BC, perhaps fulfilling the prophecy of Isa. 46–47. A few years later (681 BC) Sennacherib was killed by his own sons while he was worshiping in a temple in Nineveh, just as Isaiah had prophesied (Isa. 37:38).

The next Assyrian king, Esar-haddon (681–669 BC), continued to require tribute from his many vassals throughout the region. Manasseh, king of Judah, paid tribute to Esar-haddon, but apparently Manasseh was also involved in some rebellious conspiracies against Assyria. Consequently, the Assyrians put Manasseh in prison in Babylon (2 Chron. 33:11).[7] Manasseh repented of his sins, and God graciously restored him to his throne in Jerusalem (2 Chron. 33:12–13). Shortly before King Esar-haddon died, he appointed one of his sons (Ashurbanipal) to rule Assyria and his other son (Shamesh-shum-ukin) to rule over Babylon. This resulted in civil war between the brothers and set the stage for the fall of Nineveh, as prophesied by the prophet Nahum (around 630 BC). At the beginning of King Josiah's reign in Judah (640–609 BC), Judah was still under the control of the Assyrians, but with the death of Ashurbanipal (627 BC), Josiah was able to declare his independence from Assyrian rule and to carry out needed religious reforms (2 Chron. 34:1–8; Zeph. 1:4). Meanwhile, in Babylon, Nebopolasser (626–605 BC) was rising to power, and with the help of the Medes he defeated Assyria in 612 BC. The final outpost of Assyrian resistance was eventually eliminated by the Babylonians in 605 BC (see the article "The Babylonians").

Culture and Religion. The people in Mesopotamia believed that kingship was lowered from heaven by the gods, and that the king (often called a priest) was chosen by the gods. Nevertheless, they knew that the real ruler who controlled the world was their god. Beneath the king were high military officials, the king's advisors, and then provincial governors. The duty of the government was to provide security, to maintain the state's religions and associated temples, and to establish just order and economic prosperity for its citizens. Both biblical accounts and Assyrian royal annals testify that Assyria was involved in militaristic expansionistic activities almost continuously. Indeed, Assyrian literature and inscriptions boast of their victories and the plunder they took. They required heavy taxation and tribute from the vassal states they had conquered, using it to fund the building projects of their kings.

A wide range of Assyrian religion and culture is revealed through their art on cylinder seals, figurines, plaques, toy-like models, pottery, and mural carvings. Their culture was also rich in literature. King Ashurbanipal established a large library of cuneiform texts in Nineveh containing hymns, laws, treaties, omens, divination interpretations, letters, myths, prayers, king lists, and historical annals.

The religion of the Assyrians was polytheistic, with the gods organized in a hierarchical order. The highest god was Ashur, but also frequently worshiped were the gods Ishtar, Ninurta, Shamesh, Adad, Dagan, Nergal, and Sin, along with some Babylonian gods, plus hundreds of minor gods. The Assyrians believed that divine powers controlled the growth and fertility of plants and animals, produced rain from the clouds, determined the outcome of wars, and communicated the

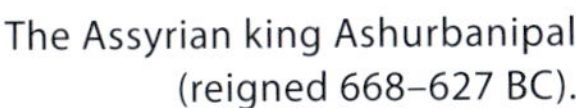

The Assyrian king Ashurbanipal (reigned 668–627 BC).

future to humankind through the movement of the moon and stars (astrology). Since the gods controlled everything, it was essential for everyone to be aware of the will of the gods and to take care not to offend them. Divination was practiced to determine the will of the gods through the examination of the entrails of animals, the movement of oil on water, and the interpretation of dreams. Fear of the future resulted in the widespread use of witchcraft and magic to influence the behavior of the gods. Assyrian religious literature included myths, hymns, prophecies, prayers, and laments to various gods.

The Babylonians

Douglas J. E. Nykolaishen

Introduction. For two main reasons, the Babylonians are among the most important groups for gaining an understanding of the background of the OT. The first is that fifteen of the thirty-nine books in the OT canon contain direct references to Babylon (287 total references to Babylon or Babylonians; 82 references to Chaldeans, on which see below). The second, and more subtle reason, although possibly more important, is that Babylonian culture and religion had an extensive influence on the thought world of the OT. How greatly ancient Near Eastern society was shaped by Babylonian ideas is exemplified in the fact that although the Assyrians dominated Babylon politically and militarily for much of the period from 729 to 626 BC, the Assyrians were much more influenced by Babylonian culture, rather than the other way around. Often the writers of Scripture, especially the prophets, are attempting to revise or refute the "worldview" of the ancient Near East, a way of thinking that was heavily influenced by the Babylonians.

The Neo-Babylonian Empire. The name Babylon is used in the Bible to refer to a city, a region, and an empire. The city was located on the Euphrates River, about fifty miles south of modern Baghdad, and was the capital of the empire that flourished in the seventh and sixth centuries BC. Although there were earlier prominent empires associated with Babylon, this one, usually known as the Neo-Babylonian Empire, is the focus for most of this article. The geographic region of Babylon (also called Babylonia) included several cities along the Euphrates and the plain between the Euphrates and Tigris Rivers, from the Persian Gulf as far north as the cities of Mari and Ashur.

The Babylonian Empire

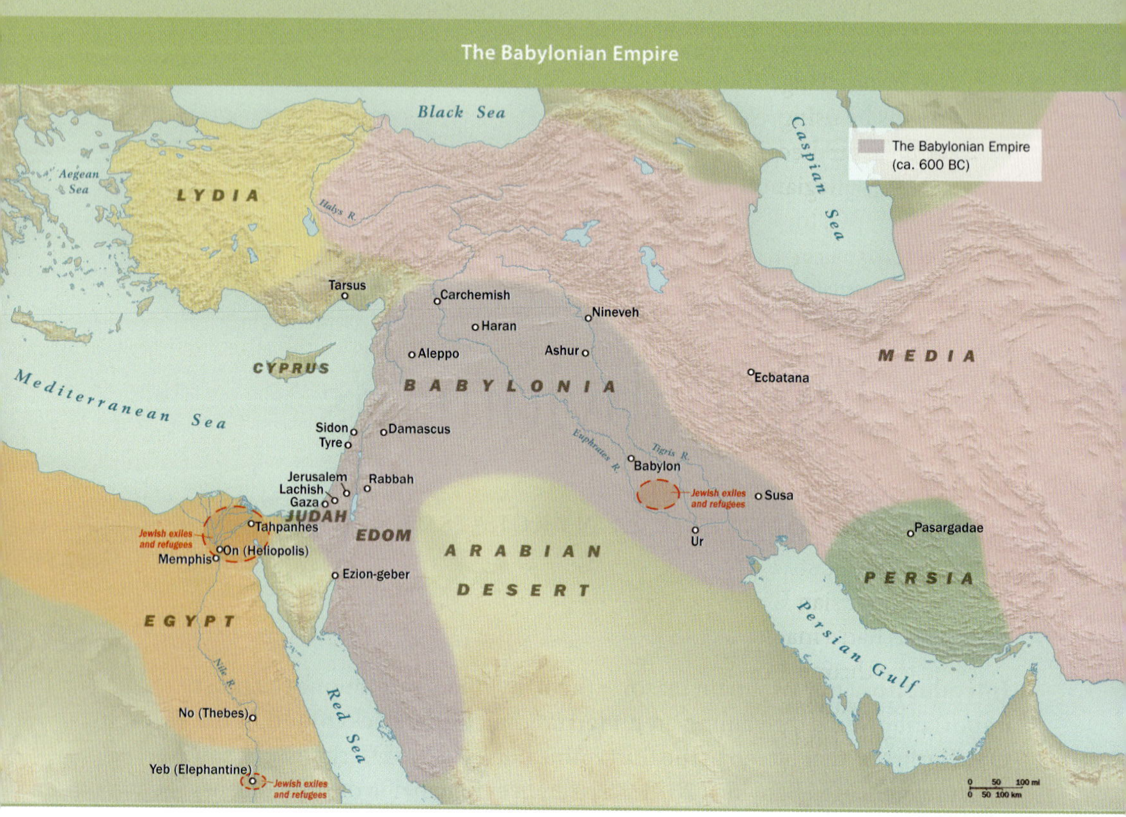

Typically, the Babylonians were an ardently independent people throughout their history. This resulted in centuries of struggle with the Assyrians, who frequently sought to control Babylonian territory. The Neo-Assyrian Empire did manage to dominate Babylon for much of the ninth through seventh centuries BC, but in 626 BC the Babylonian king Nabopolassar took control of Babylon. Allied with the Medes, his army then managed to conquer the Assyrian capital of Nineveh in 612 BC. With the Assyrian Empire virtually destroyed, Nabopolassar placed the crown prince, Nebuchadnezzar, in command of the army and sent him to take control of Syria-Palestine. The Egyptians tried to support what remained of the Assyrian army, but in 605 BC the Babylonians defeated them at the battle of Carchemish (Jer. 46:2), and the Babylonians subsequently became heirs of most of the lands that Assyria had controlled. As a result, the kingdom of Judah became subject to Babylon as well.

Prior to taking control of Babylon, Nabopolassar was the governor of Chaldea, a district in southern Babylonia. After he led the Babylonian army to supremacy over much of the ancient Near East, Chaldea became an alternative name for Babylonia. Something similar also happened earlier, when the Chaldean king Merodach-baladan ruled Babylon for fourteen years in the eighth century BC. At that time also the names Chaldea and Babylon were used interchangeably (e.g., Isa. 13:19; 47:1; some English translations obscure this by using "Babylon" where the Hebrew text has "Chaldea").

Nabopolassar died in 604 BC, and Nebuchadnezzar became king. When Judah gave its allegiance to the Egyptians, Nebuchadnezzar captured Jerusalem in 597 BC, took valuables from the temple and the royal palace, and returned to Babylon with King Jehoiachin of Judah and thousands of people, including many officials, captive (2 Kings 24:10–17). Later, under King Zedekiah, Judah rebelled again, and Nebuchadnezzar marched south and laid siege to Jerusalem. In 586 BC Jerusalem fell, and this time the city and temple were destroyed, the rest of the valuables taken from the temple, and many more captives taken to Babylon (2 Kings 25:1–12).

The grandeur of the Neo-Babylonian Empire did not last. Nebuchadnezzar died in 562 BC, and the next three kings reigned for a total of six years. Maintenance of this magnificent kingdom required very high taxes, and famine and domestic strife eventually appeared. While Babylon was becoming weaker, the Persian Empire to the east was becoming stronger. In 556 BC Nabonidus had a major role in murdering Nebuchadnezzar's grandson and usurped the throne. His mother was a devoted worshiper of the moon god Sin, and Nabonidus also seems to have given priority to this deity. For most of a ten-year period beginning around 553 BC, he lived in Teima, a desert oasis in Arabia, possibly to avoid clashing with the influential Marduk priests in Babylon, while his son Belshazzar acted as regent. Consequently, he was absent from the Akitu festival throughout this time, which made him very unpopular with the Babylonian people. Nabonidus did return to Babylon shortly before it was attacked by Cyrus the Great of Persia in 539 BC, but the Persians captured the city, and therefore the empire. The region of Babylon became a province in the Persian Empire.

The City of Babylon. King Nebuchadnezzar used the resources from his subjugated lands to decorate his capital city with impressive architecture. In fact, although Babylonian records document many of Nebuchadnezzar's military endeavors, he is best known in the annals for his expansion and restoration of Babylon, which became the largest of any city known in ancient times.

The spectacular Ishtar Gate from the ancient city of Babylon has been excavated, transported, and reconstructed in the Pergamon Museum in Berlin, Germany.

Two massive walls encircled the city, one more than twelve feet thick and the other more than twenty. There was also a moat outside the outer wall that was two hundred feet wide in places. Eight gates led into the city, and the most spectacular was the Ishtar Gate. It had a forty-foot-high double gateway covered with brightly colored enameled brick reliefs of dragons and bulls. The wide, impressive road running through the gate led to *Esagila*, the temple of Marduk, lavishly decorated with gold, and the nearby seven-terraced ziggurat (named *Etemenanki* in Akkadian, the Babylonian language, meaning "house of the foundation of heaven and earth"), which may have been three hundred feet tall.

Given the remarkable, even extravagant, appearance of Babylon, it is not surprising that Nebuchadnezzar boasted, "Is this not Babylon the Great that I have built to be a royal residence by my vast power and for my majestic glory?" (Dan. 4:30). To those from outside, such as the Judean exiles, the evident luxury and cosmopolitan atmosphere, combined with pervasive idolatry, made the city seem both sophisticated and immoral.

Religion. Marduk was the patron god of the city of Babylon and of the royal family and was worshiped by Babylonians as the king of the gods. He was said to be the son of Ea, the god of the sweet water under the earth, as well as the god of wisdom and magic. The Babylonian pantheon contained hundreds of gods, most of them related to natural phenomena. These deities were sexual beings who married and raised families, but were limited in power and could even experience injury. Many deities had a temple in the city that was considered to be their home. The city of Babylon itself contained at least fifty temples.

In the Babylonian creation epic (known as the Enuma Elish), Marduk defeated Tiamat, the goddess of chaos, in a cosmic struggle. Because of this, the other gods established his temple at Babylon and gave him the scepter of authority and the tablets of destiny. Using the blood of another god who had been killed, Ea and Marduk created human beings and also showed them how to use divination to discover the will of the gods. The last part of the epic lists fifty names of Marduk. One of these, Bel (similar to Canaanite Baal), meaning "lord," became a popular alternative designation that is seen, for example, in the apocryphal text Bel and the Dragon. His son Nabu (also known as Nebo) was the god of writing and science.

At the beginning of every new year the Babylonians observed a festival called Akitu, which celebrated Marduk's rise to the head of the pantheon and his enthronement in his temple in the city of Babylon. During the twelve-day festival the statues of other gods were brought from the cities where they were normally kept to visit Marduk in Babylon, and the Enuma Elish was recited. The priest stripped the king of his symbols of authority and struck him. The king then bowed before Marduk and asked for forgiveness and pledged to uphold his sacred duties. Finally, he would "take the hand of Bel" in a procession that led out of the city. All of this was to reaffirm the king's loyalty to Marduk and to guarantee fertility in the land.

The Babylonians believed that the main function of human beings was to serve the gods. This included clothing the statues of the gods and bringing them food each day in their temples. Although ordinary people brought items to the temple, they did not have direct access to the gods, and it was the priests and other ritual specialists who performed the formalities. Personnel at the temple also included musicians, singers, prophets, diviners, and prostitutes. Texts from this period have been discovered that document incantations believed to ward off evil spirits or demons. Divination involved the interpretation of dreams and also the observation of specific natural phenomena and the entrails of sacrificial animals.

Literature and Culture. The Neo-Babylonian Empire inherited and developed many prominent cultural features from the earlier periods of Babylonian history. One of the most influential throughout the ancient Near East was cuneiform writing. In this system, one sign represented one syllable rather than one sound as in the modern Roman alphabet. Speakers of several ancient Near Eastern languages adapted cuneiform in order to write their documents.

Not surprisingly, then, the early Babylonians were among the first to produce a large body of literature of various kinds. Law was also an important institution throughout their history, and several Babylonian law collections have been discovered, including the famous Code of Hammurabi, dating from 1754 BC. Its 282 paragraphs reflect existing standards at the time, rather than introducing new legislation, and display a concern for justice and human welfare. They touch on property, theft, marriage, divorce, adoption, inheritance, commerce, agriculture, judicial procedures, and punishment for crimes.

The Neo-Babylonians also extended the scientific traditions that they inherited. Many cuneiform lists of plants, animals, and minerals have been found, as well as remarkably accurate reports of astronomical observations. These were combined with their

A Babylonian stela with King Nabonidus and astrological religious symbols (the star of Ishtar-Venus, the winged disc of the sun god Shamash, and the crescent of the moon god Sin).

belief in omens to produce what we today would call astrology. There are also mathematical texts describing multiplication, division, determination of square and cube roots, exponential functions, algebra, and geometry. Babylonian scholars used a base-ten number system, as is common today, but also a base-sixty system, which survives in our sixty-minute hour and 360-degree circle.

In addition to the Enuma Elish, the Babylonians produced many other religious poems, prayers, and hymns, as well as epics, proverbs, and various kinds of wisdom literature. In "The Poem of the Righteous Sufferer," for example, the protagonist is opposed by the king, taken advantage of by others, stricken with diseases, spurned as a social outcast, and abandoned by the gods. He cannot understand why these things have happened, since he has been faithful in carrying out the prescribed rituals. He eventually discovers that Marduk himself is responsible for his plight, although he does not learn why. Ultimately, he has a series of dreams and finds that the wrath of Marduk has been satisfied, and his condition begins to improve. He ends the poem by calling on all people to praise Marduk.

The Canaanites and Canaanite Religion

Catherine L. McDowell

Etymology. The origin of the terms "Canaan" and "Canaanite" is unknown. The terms may be associated with Akkadian and Ugaritic words that designate a bluish-purple color, or with a Hurrian word that refers to blue cloth. Later Canaanites, known as Phoenicians, were famous for their expensive textiles and garments dyed various shades of blue, red, and purple with the natural dye extracted from the murex shell native to Phoenicia. This view, however, has been largely discredited in recent years. The terms instead probably derive from the West Semitic root *kn'*, which means "to bend, to humble, to subdue, to sink, to be low."[1] Whatever the origin, the term "Canaanites" designated the inhabitants of the land of Canaan from at least the eighteenth to the thirteenth centuries BC.

Extrabiblical Sources for the Canaanites. The oldest uncontested reference to the Canaanites appears in a letter from the city of Mari (eighteenth century BC) that mentions "Canaanites" together with "thieves" who were living in the Mesopotamian city of Rahisum.[2] The actual phrase "land of Canaan" appears in a fifteenth-century-BC (or late thirteenth-century-BC) inscription on a statue of Idrimi, king of Alalakh, from the city of Ammia (near Tripoli in southern Lebanon), said to be in "the land of Canaan."[3] The city of Ugarit, north of Ammia, however, apparently lay outside Canaan, as indicated by a Ugaritic legal text that distinguishes between "the sons [citizens] of Ugarit" and "the sons [citizens] of Canaan."[4] Furthermore, a Ugaritic administrative text includes "Ya'ilu, a Canaanite" in a list of *foreign* merchants.[5] These texts indicate that at Ugarit, and perhaps more broadly, the term "Canaanite" referred to indigenous or assimilated inhabitants of the geopolitical entity known in antiquity as "Canaan/the land of Canaan" rather than to a person of a particular ethnic origin.[6]

Several hundred clay tablets like this one were discovered in Amarna, Egypt. Most of them contain correspondence between Canaanite rulers in Canaanite cities and their Egyptian overlords, Pharaoh Amenophis III (1386–1349 BC) and Pharaoh Akhenaten (1350–1334 BC).

"Canaan" and "Canaanite" are also attested in Egyptian sources. In a victory stela (stone monument) discovered at Memphis, Amenhotep III boasts that he captured "640 Canaanites" during his first campaign in the late fifteenth century BC.[7] Two centuries later Pharaoh Merneptah claims on a victory stela that he conquered territory in Syria-Palestine that included Canaan. In addition to these inscriptions, several hundred letters on clay tablets, most of which were written by rulers of Canaanite cities to their Egyptian overlords, Pharaoh Amenophis III (1386–1349 BC) and Pharaoh Akhenaten (Amenophis IV, 1350–1334 BC), were discovered in Amarna, Egypt. These tablets depict Canaan in the fourteenth century BC as a conglomeration of independent city-states under Egyptian control whose kings often were at odds with one another. Their letters record complaints and accusations against neighboring kings as well as requests for military support against their local enemies.[8]

Canaanites in the Old Testament. The Canaanites are best known from the OT books of Genesis, Exodus, Numbers, Deuteronomy, Joshua, and Judges. They are described as one of several groups living in the land of Canaan, the borders of which extended from modern Lebanon south along the Mediterranean coast to Gaza, west to the Jordan River and north into southern Syria (cf. Gen. 10:19; Num. 34:1–12; Josh. 15:2–4; Ezek. 47:15–19). The books of Numbers, Deuteronomy, and Joshua locate the Canaanites specifically along the coastal plain (Num. 13:29; Deut. 1:7; Josh. 5:1), in the valleys (Num. 14:25), in the hill country (Num. 14:45), and in parts of the Negev (the southern arid region) (Num. 21:1; 33:40). Under Joshua, the Israelites largely defeat the Canaanites and conquer much of their territory, but they fail to completely drive out all the Canaanites from the land as God had commanded. Some of the remaining Canaanites are subjected to forced labor (Josh. 16:10; 17:13; Judg. 1:28, 30, 33). Many Canaanites persist in pockets scattered throughout Israel (Judg. 1:27–33). According to Judg. 3:1–4, God used the Canaanites, as well as other native and assimilated groups living in the land, to test Israel's fidelity as specified in the Mosaic covenant.

Canaanite Religion. Among the thousands of tablets discovered at the ancient city of Ugarit (modern Ras Shamra on the Syrian coast) from the period about 1450–1200 BC, the mythological texts rank as the most important textual sources for the study of Canaanite religion. Although Ugarit is located just beyond the northern border of Canaan proper, it lies within the same historic stream and within geographic, chronological, and cultural proximity to Canaan. Its mythological texts, therefore, provide a reliable source of information on the Canaanite pantheon of gods, although some regional differences may have existed.[9]

One of the clay tablets discovered at Ras Shamra (Ugarit).

The chief god of the pantheon was El ("god"), a wise elderly male deity who presided over the divine assembly. He was the creator of earth and the progenitor of the other gods ("the sons of El") and humanity. He was known as "King," "Bull," "Beneficent El, the Benign," and "Father of Years." His consort and cocreator of the gods, Athirat, was named "lady of the Sea." She often was depicted as a life-giving tree surrounded by animals eating from her branches. In the OT she is known by the name Asherah, and her symbol, the *asherah*, probably was a stylized tree.

Three other gods figured prominently in Canaanite religion: Baal ("lord"), whose domain is the sky; Yam ("sea"), lord of the sea; and Mot ("death"), the god of the underworld. These three battled one another for supremacy over the gods, humanity, and the earth. Of the three, Baal predominated. He was god of the storm, and the one who controlled the rain and, hence, fertility. He is depicted in statuary and in carved relief in a striding position, bearing a mace or a thunderbolt in his raised hand. His epithets include "Prince Baal of the Earth," "Mighty Baal," "Mightiest of Warriors," "Rider of the Clouds," and "Most High."

Baal had two female consorts. Astarte, the biblical Ashtoreth, played a lesser role. His primary female companion is the hot-tempered, vengeful, and bloodthirsty warrior goddess Anat, described in the Ugaritic literature as affixing decapitated heads and severed hands of her enemies to her body and wading knee-deep in their blood and neck-deep in their gore. In her zeal for her beloved Baal and by means of vicious threats against El,

The Canaanite storm god Baal brandishing a club and unleashing a storm. Also known as the god of fertility, with his other hand he thrusts a spear into the ground sprouting vegetation.

An aerial view of the ancient city of Megiddo.

Anat secures El's permission for Baal to build a palace after his victory over Yam. Once the palace is complete, however, Baal is killed by Mot. Grieved and angry, Anat seeks revenge against Mot, utterly destroying him. Baal is then resurrected and reinstated to the throne. Mot miraculously reappears, however, and engages Baal once again in fierce combat. El comes to Baal's aid, and the story concludes with Baal's victory over Mot.

In addition to the rich cache of mythological texts, the remains of Baal's temple at Ugarit were also discovered.[10] The temple was built on the acropolis, at the highest point in the city. A set of stairs led up to a square-shaped antechamber that opened into a large, rectangular room (likely the cella, or sanctuary). On the east side of the second room was a monumental stone staircase, indicating that this section of the temple had multiple stories that stood an estimated fifty to sixty-five feet tall. Other finds included an open-air stone altar, seventeen stone ship anchors that had been incorporated into the building or left as offerings to Baal by devoted sailors, and a large stone stela depicting Baal in a striding position, with mace and lightning bolt in hand. Given the temple's location on the acropolis and the height of the temple's tower, it may have functioned as a beacon to guide sailors into port. If so, the anchors may have been offerings of gratitude for a safe journey or in petitionary prayer for safety on the sea.

Several other Canaanite temples from this time period have been excavated in Canaan proper. These buildings exhibit a wide variety in plan and in size. The largest are the monumental temples, such as those discovered at Hazor and Megiddo. The Hazor temple was built sometime between 2000 and 1550 BC, and it continued in use until about 1200 BC. This large, rectangular building was divided on the interior into three rectangular areas: an entryway, a middle room, and a back room with a niche for an image of the god or goddess. This particular style apparently had its origins in Syria, with the closest parallels found in the roughly contemporary temple in Alalakh.

The monumental temple at Megiddo was also rectangular in shape but consisted only of two rooms: a columned entryway and a large inner room with a niche for the image of the god or goddess in the rear wall. It resembled the fortress-style temple known from Shechem. The Canaanite temple discovered at the city of Lachish consisted of a smaller, rectangular room with an entry point on the north wall, and a second, larger room containing several benches, four column bases, and a raised platform or dais for the image/idol of the deity.[11]

The prominence of Canaanite religion in the life of Canaan's inhabitants extended into the Iron Age (ca. 1200–586 BC) and, through the descendants of the Canaanites known as the Phoenicians, had a significant and devastating impact on ancient Israel, as the OT prophets and the books of 1–2 Kings make clear. For example, in the 1970s archaeologists discovered a shrine, dating from the ninth century to eighth century BC, at Kuntillet Ajrud, located on an ancient trade route about thirty miles south of Kadesh Barnea in the northern Sinai desert.[12] Several large store jars found in the shrine were decorated in red ink with a variety of rather crudely drawn religious images, including a stylized tree of life, a group of human worshipers, and what appear to be the Egyptian gods Bes and Bastette. An inscription written above the latter, but apparently unrelated to it, reads, "I have blessed you by Yahweh of Samaria and his A/asherah." "Yahweh" is the specific name of the God of Israel in the OT, usually translated in English Bibles as "Lord." Another blessing or prayer, this time to "Yahweh of Teman and his A/asherah," was discovered on one of the shrine's plastered walls. A similar and contemporary inscription was discovered near Jerusalem.[13] It reads, "Blessed by Uriyahu by Yahweh and by his A/asherah; from his enemies he saved him!" These inscriptions with the reference to "his A/asherah" may refer to the Canaanite goddess, but it would be unusual for the goddess's name to appear with the possessive pronoun "his." It is more likely that this term refers to Asherah's cult symbol, a wooden pole (the *asherah*). Whichever is intended, these inscriptions provide an extrabiblical witness to the widespread influence of Canaanite (and Phoenician) religion on ancient Israel, just as reported in the OT.

The Cushites

J. Daniel Hays

Introduction. Cush was an African kingdom located along the Nile River to the south of Egypt in the region that is now part of the country of Sudan. The Hebrew words "Cush" or "Cushite" occur over fifty times in the OT. Since the Greeks used the term "Ethiopia" in a generic sense to refer to everything south of Egypt, including Cush, and some historians occasionally refer to the Cushite kingdom as Nubia, English Bible translations occasionally translate the Hebrew word "Cush" as "Ethiopia" or "Nubia." Likewise, the NT character referred to as the "Ethiopian eunuch" (Acts 8:27) is not from the region now occupied by modern Ethiopia, but rather from this same kingdom on the Nile, south of Egypt, called Cush throughout the OT and in much of the literature of the ancient Near East.

History. Cush was an identifiable entity on the Nile River south of Egypt as early as 2500 BC. Cush quickly became a very important region because it contained some of the most productive gold mines in the ancient Near East. During the ninth and tenth dynasties of Egypt (2160–2040 BC), the Egyptians conducted numerous military campaigns into Cush in an attempt to capture control of the

Cushites bringing tribute, including gold, to the Egyptian pharaoh.

gold mines. By around 1800 BC Cush was nominally under Egyptian control. During the eighteenth, nineteenth, and twentieth dynasties of Egypt (1570–1090 BC), however, Cush was firmly under Egyptian control and was practically part of Egypt. Trade flourished between the two regions. Numerous Cushites are depicted in the artwork of Egypt from this period, shown as servants, workers, soldiers, and police, including the pharaoh's elite bodyguards. Others, however, were wealthy and of high social standing, embracing Egyptian culture and religion.[1]

Egypt, however, then came under the rule of several Libyan-related dynasties and declined in power. As the power of Egypt waned, the power of Cush grew. In 720 BC the Cushite king Piye conquered Egypt, and by 715 BC there was a Cushite dynasty (the Twenty-Fifth) well established in Egypt.[2] The Cushites ruled Egypt from 715 to 663 BC, and they were continually involved in the affairs of Judah and its neighbors.[3] During this time there was a marked increase in commercial and political relations between Judah and Cushite-ruled Egypt.[4] According to Assyrian inscriptions, King Hezekiah of Judah sent Sennacherib a wide variety of valuable tribute, including several items of probable African origin: elephant hides, ivory, ivory-inlaid furniture, and ebony.[5] Syrian elephants were extinct by this time, and thus the ivory mentioned in these inscriptions almost certainly came from Cush.[6] There would have been numerous Cushite soldiers, diplomats, and merchants in Judah at this time, as well as Judahite merchants and diplomats in Cushite-ruled Egypt.

Initially, the Cushites also established cooperative military/economic relations with the Assyrians, a relationship that probably began even before Piye conquered Egypt. Some Assyrian cuneiform texts from this time, labeled "Horse Lists," refer to the Assyrian chariot horses as *kusaya* ("from Cush"). Stephanie Dalley writes, "From this evidence there is a strong possibility that many of the chariotry horses used in the Levant during the 9th and 8th centuries were imported from Nubia [Cush] via Egypt."[7] The Assyrians never controlled Cush directly, so they depended on trade to acquire the specialized Cushite horses. War technology was changing, and

In the early stages of Cushite history the Egyptians controlled Cush. Depicted on this painted chest is the Egyptian king Tutankhamun (reigned 1332–1323 BC) defeating the Cushites. This painting provides us with a representation of how the Egyptians depicted Cushite soldiers at this time.

horses were a critical component. Indeed, Tiglath-pileser III opened a trade station in Egypt, evidently for the primary purpose of acquiring Cushite horses for his chariots.

In the Wine Lists of Tiglath-pileser III, individual Cushites are also mentioned by the name *Kusaya* ("the Cushite"). In one text the man *Kusaya* delivered twenty bales of straw and fifteen homers of barley, presumably for horses. Dalley connects the reference to the Cushite horses in the Horse Lists with the Cushite administrators in the Wine Lists, and she concludes that some of the Cushites in the Wine Lists of Tiglath-pileser III were employed as equestrian experts in the Assyrian army. This practice, Dalley suggests, continued down into the reign of Ashurbanipal.[8] This is further evidence that Cush had commercial and military relationships with nations throughout the ancient Near East, and probably sent numerous envoys back and forth to these nations. Cush was not an isolated backwater entity during the eighth and seventh centuries BC, but rather was a major geopolitical and economic world player.

Although the Cushites probably had warm relations with the Assyrians during the reigns of Tiglath-pileser III (745–727 BC) and Shalmaneser V (726–722 BC), during the reign of Sargon II (721–705 BC) the Cushites, who by then had total control of Egypt, began to fight directly against Assyria, which had by now conquered and depopulated the northern kingdom of Israel (722 BC). Thus the Cushites began to form alliances with the enemies of Assyria in this region. One of the main allies of the Cushites was Judah.

Assyrian art of this time period implies that Cushites were actively serving alongside the Judahites and their neighbors as they tried to stop the Assyrian juggernaut from moving southward. Reliefs on the walls of Sargon's palace at Khorsabad depict foreign foot soldiers, including what appears to be a Cushite soldier, fighting against the Assyrian army during Sargon's campaign against Palestine in 720 BC.[9] This conclusion correlates well with Isa. 20.

The Assyrian king Sargon dies in 705 BC, and Sennacherib (704–681 BC) becomes the new Assyrian king. Soon the Cushites are at open war with the Assyrians. The death of Sargon encourages plots and intrigues among the Assyrian vassal states, especially in the southern region of Palestine. Meanwhile, a new Cushite king, Shebitku, becomes pharaoh. Sennacherib is trying to consolidate Assyrian control of Palestine while the smaller rulers of these various Palestine states are plotting to overthrow Assyrian rule. One of the central players in this coalition is Hezekiah of Judah (2 Kings 18–20; Isa. 36–39). Hezekiah and his coalition apparently join forces with the Cushite pharaoh Shebitku in an attempt to throw off Assyrian control.[10]

In 701 BC Sennacherib sends an army to invade Phoenicia, Philistia, and Judah. In response, Shebitku sends an army under the command of his brother Tirhakah (Taharqa in Egyptian/Cushite sources), who will become pharaoh after Shebitku in 690 BC (although there is quite a bit of debate over exactly who leads this expedition).[11] The Cushite-Egyptian force, along with the various allies of the coalition, first engages the Assyrians at Eltekeh (in Palestine), where they are defeated but not destroyed.[12] They retreat while the Assyrians attack the Judahite fortress of Lachish (2 Kings 18:13–16).[13]

Assyrian reliefs portraying Sennacherib's siege of Lachish (701 BC) depict captured enemy soldiers who appear to be Cushites.[14] This suggests that, besides challenging Sennacherib in open battle, the Cushites had also lent their support to defending the Judahite fortresses. The strong implication of this observation is that black Cushite troops and Judahites were fighting side by side in an attempt to defend the town of Lachish.

After Lachish falls, Hezekiah pays tribute to the Assyrians, but they advance on Jerusalem anyway. The Assyrian commander delivers a speech to the defenders of Jerusalem (2 Kings 18:19–25; Isa. 36:4–10), mocking their reliance both on the pharaoh of Egypt (i.e., the Cushite king Shebitku) and on their god. However, in the meantime, Tirhakah the Cushite regroups and advances again against the Assyrians (Isa. 37:9). They withdraw from the siege of Jerusalem to deal with Tirhakah. Sennacherib defeats Tirhakah, who then retreats back into Egypt.[15]

Sennacherib's annals do not mention Tirhakah by name, as later Assyrian annals do, but they do mention this event. According to Sennacherib's account, Hezekiah appeals to Egypt and Cush (both under Cushite rule) for help against the Assyrian siege, and the Cushite king responds with an army. Sennacherib apparently turns from his siege of Jerusalem to defeat this

Cushite soldiers in the Egyptian army.

Egyptian/Cushite relief expedition, and then he returns to his siege, which proves unsuccessful (2 Kings 19:14–37). Likewise, it is interesting to note that the Assyrians do not venture down to tangle with the Cushites for another twenty-six years.

After Sennacherib's withdrawal Tirhakah and the Cushites continue to stay involved in Palestine, particularly along the coastal areas (Phoenicia) that controlled the trade roads.[16] The next Assyrian king, Esar-haddon, attacks Tirhakah in 674 BC, but he is defeated and retreats back to Assyria. However, ultimately Assyrian power proved to be too much for the Cushites. Esar-haddon returns in 671 BC and drives Tirhakah completely out of Palestine and Egypt. The Cushites withdraw up the Nile River to Cush, behind the natural protection of the Nile's cataracts. For the next eight years the Cushites play a dangerous game of cat and mouse with the Assyrians. When the Assyrian army moves into Egypt, the Cushites retreat to the safety of Cush. When the Assyrian army leaves, the Cushites sweep back down the Nile Valley, destroy the small Assyrian contingents left behind along with any puppet government structures, and reestablish control over Egypt. When the Assyrian army returns to put down the rebellion, the Cushites flee again up the river to Cush. Finally, in 664 BC the Assyrian king Ashurbanipal, after driving the Cushites out of Egypt once again, destroys the temple city of Thebes, the base of Cushite power in Egypt.[17] The Cushites never again control Egypt or engage in empire building, although they do continue to carry out trade and commerce with both Egypt and other nations of the ancient Near East.

Daily Life in Ancient Israel

H. H. Hardy II

Introduction. Day-to-day life in ancient Israel centered on activities providing sustenance and security. The fundamental social institution was the family unit, which furnished food and shelter. All other communal endeavors served the needs of both individual families and broader society.

Family Life. Israel was patriarchal and tribal (Judg. 21:24). Family descent was based on the father's lineage (patrilineal). Land was inherited within the paternal clan (patrimony). The basic family unit was designated as a "father's family" (literally, "father's house"; Num. 1:2) or simply a "family" (literally, "house"; NRSV: "household"; Josh. 7:18). This structure included three or four generations, usually led by a grandfather with several sons, living in close proximity or even the same house. Two foundational kinship relations defined the household: sibling and parent-child relationships. The household also provided a pattern for the clan, tribe, and nation; at each of these levels the social organization was analogous to the family unit.[1] A grandparent, stepparent, or elder could be called mother or father; a child's spouse, grandchild, or youth was called a daughter or son; and a cousin or fellow Israelite was a sister or brother.

The household also included individuals not blood-related. These included slaves and hired workers. The reciprocal terms "master" and "mistress" were extended to other relationships: wife to husband (1 Kings 1:17), daughter to father (Gen. 31:35), brother to brother (Gen. 32:5), wife to stranger (Judg. 4:18), king to prophet (2 Kings 8:12), and household to wife (1 Kings 17:17). Familial status and protection were to be extended to hired workers (Deut. 24:14) and refugees (Lev. 25:35).

Responsibility and power within these relationships were interwoven into the cultural tapestry. An individual had purpose in the family unit (Ruth 1:11–13, 20–21). Social conventions such as the dowry (1 Kings 9:16) and the divorce decree (Deut. 24:1–4) protected vulnerable individuals from losing their status. Patrilineal inheritance (Num. 36:1–9; Prov. 19:14) ensured a balance of resources (Gen. 31:14; 1 Kings 21:3–4) needed for provisions and security (Lev. 25:23–34). This was transmuted only in exceptional circumstances in the absence of a male heir (Num. 27:1–11; Josh. 17:3–6) or because of vast wealth (Job 42:15).

Customs such as marriage, adoption, slavery, and tenancy provided kinship between individuals outside of bloodlines. A wife would become like a sister to her husband (Song 4:9–10, 12; see also Gen. 20:12) and a daughter to her in-laws (Judg. 12:9; Ruth 1:11, 13). Adoption extended the parent-child relationship (Ruth 1:16–17; Ps. 2:7). Both required an agreement, or covenant, to produce the kinship relation.[2] In such covenants an individual's household transferred from one to another (Gen. 2:24), but a blood relative could not be demoted, as, for example, to a slave (Exod. 21:16; Deut. 24:7).

Provisioning Life. Most ancient Israelites spent their days provisioning their household through tending livestock (pastoralism) and farming small plots of land (agriculture). Although specialization within one of these livelihoods (Gen. 4:2) or outside of these occupations existed (cooks and bakers, 1 Sam. 8:13; merchants and traders, 1 Kings 10:15; metalsmiths, Judg. 17:4; musicians, 1 Kings 10:12; scribe-treasurer, 2 Sam. 8:17), a household's activities characteristically revolved around the flock and the field.

As in ancient Israel, shepherds and sheep can be seen throughout the Middle East today.

Egyptian cattle and herder, from an Egyptian tomb-chapel painting (1350 BC). This gives us a good idea of what kind of cattle were in Egypt during Old Testament times.

The manner in which Israel raised livestock varies throughout OT history. Early in Israel's history, the patriarchs (such as Abraham, Isaac, and Jacob) followed nomadic sheepherding characterized by itinerant migrations. After the settlement of the Israelite tribes in the land (i.e., the time of Joshua), animal husbandry became largely village-based.[3] Both women (Gen. 29:9; Exod. 2:16–17) and men (Gen. 46:31–34) participated in shepherding. The shepherd led small animals, normally sheep and goats (Judg. 5:16; 1 Sam. 16:11; Isa. 40:11), and cared for the larger animals, such as cattle (Isa. 7:25). Horses were rare.[4] Herding duties included providing grazing in pasturage or folds (1 Chron. 4:39–40; 2 Chron. 32:28), supplying feed and water (Exod. 2:17; 1 Sam. 17:15), counting sheep (Jer. 33:13), searching for lost animals (Ezek. 34:12), protecting against predators (1 Sam. 17:34; Amos 3:12), breeding (Gen. 30:25–43; 2 Kings 3:4; Amos 1:1), caring for young (Prov. 27:23; Isa. 40:11), shearing (Deut. 18:4; 1 Sam. 25:2; 2 Sam. 13:23), selecting sacrifices (Lev. 27:32), slaughtering (Isa. 53:7), and securing water rights (Gen. 26:18–22; 29:7). The typical equipment of a shepherd included a satchel or bag (1 Sam. 17:40), a staff (1 Sam. 17:40–43; Mic. 7:14), and a tent (Song 1:8; Isa. 38:12). In addition to wool, skins, and manure for fuel and fertilizer, flocks provided various kinds of food (dairy products and meat).

Land cultivation, however, became the primary means of producing food. As with all creation (Deut. 10:14), the land was God's (Lev. 25:23). It was effectively leased to be managed by individual families and passed down generationally (Deut. 21:16). If poor management occurred, land could be leased to another for a period of, at most, fifty years (Lev. 27:24). Afterward it was returned to the original tenants (Lev. 25:8–55). The hill country was farmed by first clearing stones (Isa. 5:2) and trees (Josh. 17:18) and then terracing (2 Chron. 26:10; Isa. 5:2–5). Watering was accomplished through rainfall (Deut. 11:14; Jer. 5:24), cisterns (Jer. 2:13), and irrigation systems (Ps. 1:3). Locusts were feared pests (Amos 7:1; Joel 1:4). Farming implements—for example, yokes (1 Sam. 6:7) and yoke-harnessing (Jer. 27:2) for oxen and donkeys (Deut. 22:10; 1 Kings 19:19), threshing and harrowing utensils (Isa. 28:24; Hosea 10:11), cattle goads (1 Sam. 13:21), hoes (Isa. 7:25), plowshares, mattocks, axes, and sickles (1 Sam. 13:20)—were made from wood and sometimes reinforced with bronze or iron, although all metals were expensive.

Crops were grown in fields, gardens, and orchards according to an annual cycle. Grains included wheat, barley, millet, and spelt (2 Sam. 17:28; Ezek. 4:9). The growing season began in October-November with plowing and seeding after the rainy season (Song 2:11; Isa. 45:8). Barley was ingathered in early spring (Passover; Exod. 12), and wheat between April and May (Festival of Weeks; Exod. 34:22). In small gardens planted in late December to February, legumes such as lentils, chickpeas, peas, and broad beans (2 Sam. 23:11) were raised along with various other edible plants, including sesame, flax, dill, cumin, and coriander (Isa. 28:25). Trees bore olives, figs, pomegranates, dates, carobs, mulberries from sycamores, pistachios, almonds, and walnuts (Deut. 8:8; Eccles. 2:5; Song 6:11; Amos 4:9).[5] Grape vineyards were also common. Grapes were collected in June-July. Summer fruit was picked in late July into August (Mic. 7:1). Olive trees were beaten (Isa. 24:13) and their fruit gathered at the end of September (Festival of Tabernacles; Lev. 23:33–43).

Food storage was essential for sustaining life (Prov. 21:20), particularly in seasons without produce (Gen. 41:47–49). The harvest included processing and storage in jars (Jer. 40:10). Grain required gathering (Mic. 4:12) into heaps (Jer. 50:26), threshing (Lev. 26:5; Ruth 3:2), winnowing (Isa. 30:24, 28), milling (Eccles. 12:3–4; Isa. 47:2; Jer. 25:10; Lam. 5:13), and storing (Jer. 41:8). Grapes were pressed or threshed (Amos 9:13); the wine was collected in vats (Isa. 5:2; Joel 2:24) or skins (Josh. 9:4, 13). At ingathering, the tithe was to be collected by apportioning the produce (Deut. 14:22–29; Neh. 12:44; 13:15).

Food preparation entailed making various breads (Exod. 29:2; Num. 6:15; 1 Chron. 16:3) from milled flour and oil (Num. 11:7–8) and sometimes honey (Ezek. 16:19) on griddles (Lev. 6:21) or in ovens (Lev. 26:26).[6] Meat from wild and domestic animals (except the meat from those animals declared to be unclean; Deut. 14:1–21) was consumed mostly during religious and civil celebrations (1 Kings 4:22–23). Dairy products were milk and curds (Gen. 18:8), cheese (1 Sam. 17:18), yogurt, and butter. Sweeteners and syrups were made from honeycombs (Ps. 19:10) and sweet fruits such as dates (2 Kings 18:32).

Products for day-to-day living were either made in the household or obtained through trade at the market. This would include clothing (Exod. 25:3–5), cosmetics (Esther 2:12), perfumes (Exod. 30:22–32; 37:29), metal farming implements (Deut. 8:9), medicine (Isa. 1:6), cleansing agents

(Deut. 33:24), and pottery (Jer. 19:11).

Artist's conception of an Israelite four-room house.

The work cycle included regular cessation of labor on the Sabbath (Lev. 23:3). The six-plus-one rotation of work and rest was intended to be applied to days and years extending to masters, slaves, hired workers, refugees, and even beasts of burden (Exod. 20:9–10). This occasioned time for rest and assembly (Lev. 23:3).

Protecting Life. Urban life provided a concentrated populace for protection and sustenance. Cities were formed of houses connected by streets (Isa. 15:3) within defensive walls (Deut. 3:5). The traditional four-room house normally was constructed of mud brick on stone foundations, large enough to house a family and animals (Judg. 19:21). In this typical four-room house would be a first-floor main hall or courtyard, surrounded on three sides by other rooms for storage and living space.[7] Sometimes a second floor provided an open area for family activities and lodging (1 Kings 17:19; 2 Kings 4:10). Likewise, most houses had an accessible flat roof, providing a cool place for sleeping (1 Sam. 9:25).

Cities and surrounding settlements ("daughters" [Isa. 16:2]) were strategic, economic, religious, and political centers. They served to defend against wild animals (Ps. 22:21), marauders (Hosea 6:9), and the elements (Isa. 32:2). Public endeavors took place in the open squares, religious sites, and city gates.[8] Governmental structures (1 Chron. 27:25–34), taxation (2 Kings 23:35), and storehouses (2 Kings 20:13) were organized in these population centers.

Other pursuits supported life and served the needs of society. Religious practices involved various sacrifices (firstfruits, Num. 18:12; offerings, 2 Chron. 31:5), tithes (Neh. 10:37–39; 13:5, 12), festivals at places of worship (Exod. 23:14–16), circumcision (Lev. 12), and burial rites (Gen. 23:1–9). Trade (1 Kings 5:11; Prov. 31:31) and the production of goods (2 Chron. 2:7–10) were conducted. In the city gates elders arbitrated legal disputes and carried out punishment (Deut. 21:18–20). Protection from foreign armies required military personnel and action, included oiling shields (2 Sam. 1:21; Isa. 21:5), siege preparations (2 Chron. 11:11), and gathering supplies (1 Chron. 12:38–40). Travel between towns normally was on foot or by donkey (Judg. 19:3).

The Egyptians

Safwat Marzouk

Ancient Egypt. Ancient Egyptian history usually is divided into times of stability and other times of instability: Old Kingdom (2686–2125 BC), First Intermediate Period (2160–2055 BC), Middle Kingdom (2055–1650 BC), Second Intermediate Period (1650–1550 BC), New Kingdom (1550–1069 BC), Third Intermediate Period (1069–664 BC), and the Late Period (664–332 BC). The name Egypt comes from the Greek *Aigyptos*, which is an appropriation of an ancient Egyptian phrase that was used to refer to the land of Egypt as *hwt-ka-ptah* ("the house of the ka [life force] of Ptah"). Ancient Egyptians called their country *kemet* ("black land") in reference to the fertile land of the Nile Valley, and they used the term *dešret* ("red land") in reference to the desert that surrounds the valley, which constitutes the majority of the land. Contemporary Egyptians use the name *Miṣr* to refer to their country, which relates to the Hebrew word *Mitsrayim*.

Egyptian Religion. Ancient Egyptian religion lasted more than three thousand years, from the predynastic

The cobra symbolized Lower Egypt. The Egyptian pharaohs often placed images of cobras on their crowns, signifying their rule over Lower Egypt.

Painted on the walls of an Egyptian tomb are these scenes of the afterlife in Egyptian religion. The deceased is depicted as participating in agriculture and in worshiping the gods.

period to the Greco-Roman era. Despite the many changes that occurred in the expression of the ancient Egyptian religious beliefs, some of the fundamental beliefs continued over this long period of time. "Those included the emphasis on the need for continued maintenance of order over chaos—a balance known as *ma'at,* the belief in the numinous nature of the world, and the hope of living for eternity in the afterlife."[1] The ancient Egyptians' belief in life after death permeated the various aspects of their life. This central belief was inspired by the well-known myth of the death of Osiris at the hand of his brother Seth and his mummification and resurrection with the help of his wife, Isis. Essentially, for ancient Egyptians, death was not the end of life; rather, it was an interruption to life. Taking care of the body of the deceased through mummification as well as equipping the tombs with the food, drink, figurines, pottery, and other necessities needed by the deceased testifies to the belief that life continued beyond death. More importantly, the tombs contained texts and paintings that aimed at helping the deceased in their journey in the underworld. The Pyramid Texts from the Old Kingdom provided instructions to the king on how to safely ascend to heaven, the Coffin Texts of the Middle Kingdom provided abbreviated spells to help the deceased navigate their way through the sky and the underworld, and the New Kingdom funerary texts, such as the Amduat (the Netherworld) and the Book of Gates, focused on the twelve-hour journey of the sun god Re through the underworld. This journey happened every night between sunset and sunrise. Accompanied by other gods and the deceased king, Re would encounter the monster Apophis, who would try to throw the world into chaos by obstructing the rise of the sun. The rejuvenation of the sun on the eastern horizon every day meant that Re reunited with Osiris, the god of the dead, and defeated the monster of chaos, guaranteeing the order of creation and the stability of the society.[2]

In his analyses of the ancient Egyptian religion, Jan Assmann highlights two concepts. The starting point to his analyses is the following text: "Ra has placed the king in the land of the living, forever and ever, judging humankind and satisfying the gods, realizing Maat and destroying Isfet, He [the king] gives offerings to the gods and mortuary offerings to the deceased."

An ancient Egyptian temple at Thebes (Luxor).

Although the text focuses on the role of the king, the passage underlines two essential facets of the Egyptian religion: "(1) ethics and the dispensing of justice (the creation of solidarity and abundance in the social sphere through dispensing justice, care, and provisions), and (2) pacifying the gods and maintaining adequate contact with them, as well as provisioning the dead."[3] Connecting with the gods through offerings, therefore, is not separated from making justice in the human realm. The latter aspect of ancient Egyptian religion was expressed in a positive way, "realizing *ma'at*," which refers to a just distribution of the blessings that the gods have bestowed upon the people. This ordered and just view toward the world was constantly under the threat of Isfet ("lack"). "Sickness, death, scarcity, injustice, falsehood, theft, violence, war, enmity—all these are manifestation of lack in a world that has fallen into disorder through loss of its original plenitude of meaning."[4] Ancient Egyptians had an unshaken belief in the presence of the divine in all aspects of the cycle of life, which led them to consider all of life's activities to be numinous. Thus ancient Egyptian religion created multiple layers for human-divine interaction. Although access to the inner rooms of the temples was restricted to high priests, there were festivals that enabled the people to get a glimpse of the deities and to take part in communal religious rituals. In addition, ancient Egyptians used "local chapels" in order to offer their prayers to the gods.[5]

Egypt in the Bible. The Hebrew word *Mitsrayim* ("Egypt, Egyptians") appears well over six hundred times in the Hebrew Bible. It first appears as part of the table of the nations in Gen. 10, where the Egyptians are considered part of the children of Ham, Noah's second son (vv. 6, 13). Egypt plays a central role in the Bible and figures prominently in the ancestral narratives, the exodus narrative, and the prophetic oracles that condemn political alliances between Israel/Judah and Egypt. The way the Bible speaks about Egypt escapes any easy classification, because sometimes Egypt is seen as a threat to the well-being of the Israelites, while at other times Egypt is seen as a place of refuge for the Israelites during periods of famine and war.

One of the most lasting images of Egypt in the Bible is that of Egypt as a house of slavery. Thirteen times the Hebrew Bible puts the phrase "house of slavery" in apposition with the word "Egypt" (e.g., Exod. 13:3, 14; Deut.

5:6; Josh. 24:17; Mic. 6:4). A cornerstone in the collective memory of the Israelites is the story of the divine miraculous deliverance of their ancestors from Egyptian slavery. The deliverance of the Israelites from their Egyptian slavery was seen as an essential part of the fulfillment of the divine promises to the ancestors (Exod. 2:24–25): it was the basis on which the God of Israel established his covenant with them in the wilderness (Exod. 20:1–2); it was the theological basis for their ethics of compassion toward the oppressed and the marginalized (e.g., Deut. 24:10–22); and it was the explanation for the divine judgment (Amos 3:1–2) and the foundation for the hope in a new future, expressed as a new exodus (Isa. 51:9–16; Jer. 31:31–34; Ezek. 20). In other words, Egypt and the exodus from Egypt play a central role in forming Israel's identity and its relationship with God.

Although the prevalent image of Egypt in the Hebrew Bible is that of a house of slavery, this image is destabilized when we consider the reversal that takes place in the story of Hagar, the Egyptian maidservant, who was oppressed by Sarah, the matriarch of the Israelites. The Hebrew Bible uses the same verb to describe the oppression that Hagar the Egyptian and the Israelites have endured (*ʿnh* in Gen. 16:6; Deut. 26:6), and the same verbs to describe their "exodus" or "flight" (*brh* in Gen. 16:6; Exod. 14:5; *grsh* in Gen. 21:10; Exod. 10:11; 11:1; 12:39). Furthermore, as the Israelites wandered in the wilderness, so did Hagar the Egyptian (*tʿh* in Gen. 21:14; Ps. 95:10; 107:4), and in both cases God benevolently provided water for the thirsting Israelites and for Hagar. By preserving the Hagar-Ishmael stories, the Hebrew Bible underscores God's providence for the Egyptians and the Israelites.

The Bible also describes Egypt as a place of refuge for those who were escaping famine and violence. Abraham and Sarah descend to Egypt during a time of famine (Gen. 12), and Jacob and his family go down to Egypt to reunite with Joseph, escaping a severe famine in Canaan (Gen. 42–50). In 1 Kings 11:14–12:24 two figures, Hadad and Jeroboam, take refuge in Egypt to flee from imminent life-threatening danger. Hadad of Edom manages to escape the massacre that Joab, the commander of David's army, conducts against the Edomite males (1 Kings 11:14–22). Jeroboam flees to Egypt, running from Solomon, who seeks his life because Jeroboam had been promised a kingdom. Jeremiah 36–45, which tells the story of the fall of Jerusalem to the Babylonians and the flight of some Judeans to Egypt, castigates the Judeans who take refuge in Egypt, highlights that Israel's story "ends where it originated: in Egypt," and finally points out that "Jeremiah's personal history ends in the land where Moses started."[6] These incidents of seeking refuge in Egypt become more significant when one considers the other times in which God commands individuals and the people of Israel not to seek help from Egypt (Gen. 26:1–3; Deut. 17:16). In the Gospel of

Matthew Egypt functions as a place of refuge for Jesus and the holy family, who escape the violence of King Herod. In this story we find a reversal of the exodus narrative, where Egypt is not a threat to the life of the hero of the story, but rather a place of protection.

The interaction between Egypt and Israel/Judah during the monarchy is reflected in the Deuteronomistic History and in the prophetic literature with a special focus on castigating political alliances between Egypt and Israel/Judah. The political treaties between Egypt and Israel started during the early reign of Solomon, who married the pharaoh's daughter and whose dowry was the city of Gezer (1 Kings 9:16). Shoshenq I (945–924 BC) led a campaign against Philistia, Israel, and Judah that resulted in the imposition of a heavy tribute on Jerusalem (1 Kings 14:25–26). During the Neo-Assyrian imperial control of the Levant, Egypt's relation with Israel and Judah varied. For example, Hoshea, king of Israel, sought an alliance with So, king of Egypt (726 BC) (2 Kings 17:4), and Hezekiah, king of Judah, sought an Egyptian military support against the Assyrians in 701 BC (see the article "The Cushites"). Pharaoh Neco attempted to assist the Assyrians against the Babylonians, and on his way to the battle of Carchemish, a battle that the Egyptian-Assyrian coalition lost to the Babylonians, he was obstructed by King Josiah of Judah, who died as a result of his battle against Neco at Megiddo (609 BC) (2 Kings 23:29). During the last decade of the kingdom of Judah, Egyptian pharaohs Psammetichus II (595–589 BC) and Apries (589–570 BC) failed to assist king Zedekiah in his rebellion against the Babylonians, which resulted in the catastrophic exile of the Judeans to Babylon and the destruction of Jerusalem and its temple in 586 BC.

The books of the prophets Hosea (8–11), Isaiah (19–20; 29–30), Jeremiah (46), and Ezekiel (29–32) considered Israel's/Judah's political alliance with Egypt as not only a political rebellion against the Assyrians or the Babylonians but also a rebellion against the God of Israel.[7] The prophetic criticism of Judah's trust in Egypt focused on two themes: deconstructing the political propaganda of the pharaoh, and showing the shallowness of Egypt's economic power should the waters of the Nile dry up (Isa. 19:1–15; Ezek. 29:1–16). Even though these oracles were written for a Judean audience, it is clear that the audience was familiar with the Egyptian worldview, in which the pharaoh's status as a representative of the deity was closely tied to the political order and the economic prosperity that relied on the stability of the cycle of the flooding Nile.[8] Despite the negative attitude of the Israelite prophets toward Egypt, there is a stark exception in Isa. 19:18–25, where the prophet paints a utopian picture in which the history of enmity between the Israelites, the Assyrians, and the Egyptians is replaced by a divine blessing to these neighboring countries. The phrase "blessed be my people Egypt" and the prophecy of building a temple for the Lord in the middle of Egypt have played a central role in the identity formation of the Christian Egyptian community in the face of its continuous political marginalization.

The relationship between Egypt and Israel extends beyond the political realm into the cultural and religious spheres. Scholars have noted the many similarities shared by Ps. 104 and the Great Hymn to the Aten. Both the psalm and the hymn speak of the natural order in similar patterns (Ps. 104:20), human activities (Ps. 104:23), and the dependence of the natural world on the providence of the deity (Ps. 104:27–29). These similarities do not necessarily indicate dependency, but rather reflect a shared worldview and theological perspectives used by each textual tradition to praise its deity. The case of dependency, however, has been argued by many scholars with regard to the sayings of the sage that are recorded in Prov. 22:17–23:11, which seems to be an appropriation of the teachings of the Egyptian sage Amenemope. Both traditions of wisdom mention in the introduction that the sayings are thirty in number (Prov. 22:20; Amenemope 30.1); Prov. 22:18 employs a unique Egyptian idiom for remembering the instructions: "Keep [my words] in the casket of your belly" (Amenemope 1.13); both traditions exhort the listener not to rob the lowly or oppress the poor (Prov. 22:22; Amenemope 2.4–5); both sets of teachings liken wealth that was gained in a crooked way to a bird that flies away. The author of Prov. 22–23 used the wisdom of Amenemope and thus reflects the international character of wisdom literature, but at the same time the author appropriated these teachings for his own sake and has given them an Israelite color of personal piety when he says, "so that your confidence may be in the LORD" (Prov. 22:19).[9]

Musical Instruments in Israel and the Ancient Near East

J. Daniel Hays

Introduction. Music played on instruments, along with singing and dancing, was an integral part of daily life and culture throughout the history of Israel as well as throughout the ancient Near East. Evidence of instruments and musicians appears frequently in the archaeological records and literature of the ancient Near East from as early as 3000 BC. Likewise, very early in the Bible the origins of three major occupations are singled out: herding, metallurgy, and music (Gen. 4:20–22).[1]

In Israel, as throughout the ancient Near East, musical instruments were associated with religious ceremonies (both temple worship and large communal festivals), royal court functions (including banquets, feasts, and personal entertainment for the king), military activities (communication among troops, celebration of victories), prophetic activity, and personal use.

Musical instruments are mentioned frequently throughout the book of Psalms, underscoring the

An ancient Sumerian boat-shaped harp that has been refurbished and restrung.

important role that music played in the worship of Israel. Interestingly, however, although references to musical instruments (along with singers) are closely associated with temple worship both in Israel and throughout the ancient Near East, there is no mention of performed music in the instructions and guidelines that God gave to Moses in the books of Exodus and Numbers in regard to the tabernacle. There were trumpets that the priests used for announcements and signaling (see comments on Num. 10:2) and that were blown at the time of offerings, sacrifices, and festivals (Num. 10:10), but this seems to be more of a trumpet "blast" than a musical performance (cf. Num. 10:9). It will be King David who later introduces music, along with instruments and singers, on a large scale into the mainstream of Israel's worship (see comments on 1 Chron. 6:31).

Terminology. In the archaeological remains of the ancient Near East there is a wealth of information regarding what ancient musical instruments looked like. This evidence includes rough drawings/sketches on walls, clay and metal figurines of musicians, impressions from personal seals, decorative depictions on utensils such as pots and incense burners, carvings on stone wall panels that lined the palaces of Mesopotamian kings, exquisitely detailed paintings on the walls of Egyptian tombs, and the remains of the actual instruments themselves. The challenge is in determining which of these instruments are being referenced by the many different Hebrew words used in the OT in regard to musical instruments. The OT has twenty-two different terms for musical instruments.[2] Major biblical passages that mention two or more musical instruments include Gen. 4:21; 1 Sam. 10:5; 18:6; 2 Sam. 6:5; 1 Kings 10:12; 1 Chron. 13:8; 15:16, 28; 16:5, 42; 25:1, 6; 2 Chron. 5:12–13; 9:11; 15:14; 20:28; 29:25, 27; Neh. 12:27; Job 21:12; Ps. 33:2; 57:8; 71:22; 81:2; 92:3; 108:2; 149:3; 150:3–5; Isa. 5:12; 30:32; Dan. 3:5–15. Most of the terms used in these passages can be identified with some confidence, but exact identification of every term is difficult, and scholars disagree on some of the identifications. Also, some of the terms occurring in lists of instruments may refer to larger groupings of instruments (e.g., "strings" in Ps. 150:4; "every kind of music" in Dan. 3:5). Basically, however, the musical instruments used in the ancient Near East and in Israel fall into three major categories: strings, wind, percussion.

Stringed Instruments. There were two very popular stringed instruments used in ancient Israel, the *nebel* (usually translated as "harp") and the *kinnor* (usually translated as "lyre"). In the OT the term *nebel* occurs twenty-seven times and the term *kinnor* forty-two times, and often they occur together (e.g., Ps. 108:2). These were similar instruments, distinguished primarily by number of strings and size. Both had a rectangular wooden soundbox and some kind of frame to hold the strings. The *kinnor,* however, was

This painting from a fifteenth-century-BC Egyptian wall tomb presents a good depiction of what several instruments used in Israel probably looked like. From right to left, the instruments depicted are the harp (*nebel*), the lute, and the flute or double pipe (*halil*).

smaller in size and typically had four to eight strings. The strings were played with a "plectrum" (a hard, hand-held object similar to a guitar pick).[3] In most depictions this instrument looks to be around twelve to fifteen inches high. It was easily carried and allowed the player to walk, dance, and/or sing during the performance, although depictions show the players in several different positions—sitting, standing, and walking. The *nebel* was larger, typically having ten to twelve strings, and the strings were strummed or plucked with the fingers. In depictions of this instrument throughout the ancient Near East, the size varies dramatically (from about twenty-four inches high to over five feet high).[4] Although larger than the lyre, some harps were still small enough to be carried as they were being played. Others, however, rested on the ground while being played. There are numerous depictions in the archaeological remains from the ancient Near East that show small groups of musicians (like a "combo" or "band"), some playing harps and some playing lyres, indicating that these two instruments often were used together.

In several regions of the ancient Near East depictions of lutes have been found. A lute was a guitar-like instrument, with a rectangular soundbox and a long, thin, single arm to which strings were attached. One apparent reference to this type of instrument in the OT is in Dan. 3:5–15, although this scene takes place in Babylon and not in Israel. The Hebrew term used here is actually a Greek "loanword" derived from the Greek word for that instrument. In Dan. 3:5–15 it often is translated as "zither" (see comments on Dan. 3:5). Another possible reference to a lute, though using a different term, is in 1 Sam. 18:6. The name of the instrument in that text is related to the number three, perhaps suggesting three strings, but this is far from clear, and translations for this term vary widely (CSB: "three-stringed instruments"; NIV: "lyres"; NASB, NRSV, ESV: "musical instruments"; NLT: "cymbals").

Wind Instruments. The most commonly mentioned wind instrument in the OT is the *shophar* ("ram's horn"), occurring seventy-two times. However, since the ram's horn only had one loud tone (or "blast"), it is questionable whether it should be considered a musical instrument, and the common translation as "trumpet" is a little misleading. Nonetheless, the *shophar* was used frequently in worship/religious services, in royal ceremonies and proclamations, and in military operations. Another term, *yobel,* seems to be used synonymously with *shophar* (Josh. 6:4–8). A more trumpet-like instrument is the *hatsotserah* (Num. 10:1–10) (see comments on Num. 10:2). This term occurs twenty-nine times in the OT and refers to a long, tubed, metal instrument with a flared end. The trumpets for the priests in Num. 10:2 were hammered out of silver. Yet even these "trumpets" did not have valves like a modern trumpet, and so were more like today's bugles.[5]

The Hebrew word *halil,* occurring six times, refers to a double-pipe instrument made of two thin tubes of reed, metal, or ivory. Sometimes translated as "flute" or "pipe," it is perhaps best rendered as "double pipe" (1 Sam. 10:5; 1 Kings 1:40; Isa. 5:12; 30:29; Jer. 48:36). Another term, *ugab,* occurring only four times, may also refer to some kind of flute or pipe instrument (Gen. 4:21; Job 21:12; 30:31; Ps. 150:4), perhaps the single-tubed flute in contrast to the double flute (*halil*). However, some argue that this term refers to a stringed instrument or perhaps a collective term for wind instruments in general (Ps. 150:4).[6]

Percussion Instruments. The Hebrew word *top* occurs seventeen times and seems to refer to a range of small hand-held drums or tambourines. Although usually translated as "tambourine" or as "timbrel," what the archaeological evidence from the ancient Near East depicts seems to be more of a small, thin drum, about the same size as a tambourine, but without any jingling circlets of metal.[7]

Numerous bronze cymbals have been discovered throughout the ancient Near East and are mentioned in Ps. 150:5 and 2 Sam. 6:5 (*tseltselim*). They usually come in two sizes, the smaller version being about three inches in diameter and the larger version being about six inches in diameter.[8] Typically, these cymbals had small wires in the center that attached to the musician's fingers. There are also possible references in the OT to some type of "wooden clappers" and/or "rattles" (*menaanim*), perhaps better rendered as "sistrums" (2 Sam. 6:5). Likewise, "bells" (*paamonim*) are mentioned in association with the priests serving in the tabernacle, but the relationship between these bells and "music" is unclear (Exod. 28:33–35; 39:25–26).[9] Although large drums do appear in the ancient Near East, they are not mentioned in the OT.

Examples of ancient Egyptian double-pipe and single-tubed flutes.

The Persians

Mark J. Boda

Introduction. Located largely in the region that is now known as Iran, in the late sixth century BC the Persians became one of the most powerful nations in the ancient Near East. They dominated much of the ancient Near East until the late fourth century BC, with an empire that at its peak stretched from Asia Minor (modern Turkey) in the west to India in the east, and from the Black Sea and Caspian Sea in the north to Egypt and Cush in the south.

Cyrus. The Persian (Achaemenid) Empire traces its roots to a group of small tribes on the northern side of the Persian Gulf. It was Cyrus, king of Anshan, who led the Persians onto the world stage. His mother was a Median princess, her father the final Median king, Astyages, who ruled from his mountain fortress of Ecbatana. Astyages's grandson Cyrus revolted against his grandfather in 553 BC, defeating the Medes near the city of Pasargadae, the site on which Cyrus would build his capital and where he would be buried. By defeating Astyages, Cyrus assumed control of a small empire, but he soon expanded it in 547–546 BC by crossing the Halys River and conquering King Croesus's Lydian kingdom. Afterward Cyrus marched east, extending his holdings northeast to the Jaxartes (Syrdar'ya) River.

Cyrus's success in the territory surrounding the Babylonian Empire and especially his defeat of the Babylonian ally Croesus raised concern within the deeply conflicted Babylonian Empire of Nabonidus and his son Belshazzar.

The tomb of King Cyrus of Persia.

The Persian Empire

Originally, Nabonidus had been comforted by the rise of Cyrus against Astyages, thinking that this signaled weakness within his main nemesis (the Medes), but Cyrus's aggressive movements in the years that followed his conquest of Media prompted Nabonidus's return to the capital of Babylon, which he had abandoned for nearly a decade to invest his energies in the building of a temple at Teima in Arabia. Nabonidus was not well liked at the center of the empire, especially among the priests who were offended by his lack of attendance at the annual New Year festival and his offense to various cults in the southern Mesopotamian region whose gods he had transported to Babylon. In 539 BC Cyrus crossed the Zagros Mountains, forded the Tigris River, and conquered the city of Babylon. Cyrus appears to have been welcomed as liberator of Babylon as he incorporated the now much smaller Babylonian kingdom into his massive empire. Cyrus's policy was to win the population over through liberal religious policies linked to the return of temple paraphernalia and people to their homeland, as well as through minimal shifts in political and administrative bureaucracy. The Cyrus Cylinder, on which Cyrus grants permission for the return of divine images and the rebuilding of their shrines, showcases one of his key religious policies.[1] With the western side of his empire under control, Cyrus shifted his attention to the east, where on a military expedition in 530 BC he was killed.

Cyrus's reign had considerable impact on the Jewish community. Not only was his appearance promised in the book of Isaiah (44:28; 45:1, 13) but also his religious policies benefited the Jewish community, as evidenced in Ezra 1:1–4 (cf. 2 Chron. 36:22–23) and 6:1–5. Looted temple utensils and exiled Jewish people were allowed to return home early in Cyrus's reign (Ezra 1:9–11; 5:13–14), and an initial attempt at rebuilding the temple in Jerusalem was allowed (Ezra 5:15–16). The Jewish community was led during this period by a governor, Sheshbazzar (Ezra 1:8; 5:14). The TAYN archives, a collection of nearly one hundred texts from Jewish settlements in Mesopotamia, highlight the role of the Jewish community in financial and legal affairs (the texts reflect a number of financial transactions) at the center of the empire.[2]

Cambyses. Cyrus's son Cambyses (530–522 BC) assumed the rule of the empire from his father without any disruption, and this enabled Cambyses to fulfill one of Cyrus's dreams for the southwestern side of the empire: the conquest of Egypt, accomplished with the naval assistance of the Greeks and Phoenicians. In 525 BC Cambyses was crowned pharaoh of Egypt, advised by his Egyptian vizier Uzahor-Resenet. With Cambyses in Egypt and far from home at the western frontier of his massive empire, a challenger arose back at the center of the empire in March of 522 BC. A certain magus (combination of astrologer, intellectual, and magician), Bardiya by name, claimed to be Cambyses's brother Smerdis, whom Cambyses had quietly eliminated prior to marching to Egypt. The core of the empire supported Bardiya, most likely due to his easing of taxation. Cambyses responded to this challenge by marching toward Persia with his army, but he wounded himself with his knife en route and died in Syria.

Darius. It would be Darius (522–486 BC), one of Cambyses's generals, who would assume control of the Persian army and ultimately defeat the usurper Bardiya in September of 522 BC. Rebellions continued for the next four years (522–518 BC), recorded in detail on the Behistun inscription,[3] but once the situation was stabilized, Darius would lay the foundation for an empire that would last under his dynastic line for nearly two centuries. Darius extended the Persian Empire eastward to the Indus Valley in India, and thus for the first time in history the Nile, the Tigris-Euphrates, and the Indus river valleys were under a single political jurisdiction. An empire of this size demanded effective administrative reforms, and Darius set to work carefully delineating political regions as satrapies, subsatrapies, provinces, and subprovinces, administered by imperial officials as well as by native dynasties. Darius administered his empire through these satrapal administrative bureaucracies, but he also maintained control through direct reporting through the military command as well as through royal officials (eyes and ears of the king) who served throughout the empire, providing "intelligence" information for the emperor regarding who was loyal and who was not. While the capitals of the former kingdoms that were incorporated into the Persian Empire continued to function as key centers of administration (the city of Babylon from the Babylonian Empire, the city of Susa from the Elamite Empire, and the city of Ecbatana from the Median Empire), Darius also expended much energy in building a new showcase capital that was Persian in origin, the city that the Greeks called Persepolis ("Persian City"). Cyrus's earlier capital, Pasargadae, lacked adequate water resources and probably was too closely linked with Cyrus's exploits, besides being too distant from the Persian heartland. So Darius built a grand city fifty miles to the west of Pasagardae, a city without walls, testimony to the greatness of the Persian accomplishments as well as their confidence in the "peaceful" conditions they had created. Darius also expanded the royal road network throughout the empire, as well as maritime routes, and in particular a canal connecting the Red Sea with the Nile Delta. However, it was Darius's desire to extend his empire to the northwest, across the Hellespont (i.e., the Dardanelles Strait between Asia Minor and Europe) into Europe, that spoiled the final decades of his rule. His defeat by the Greeks at Marathon (490 BC) typifies his setbacks during this final phase and may have prompted a rebellion in the southwest (Egypt) in 486 BC, shortly after which Darius died.

Darius also made a significant impact on the Jewish community. During his reign Jews continued to return to their homeland in the province of Yehud (former Judah), building an altar, reinstating sacrifices and feasts, and reconstructing the temple, all by 516 BC (Ezra 2–6). The books of

The palace of King Darius at Persepolis.

From the palace of the Persian king Darius I in Susa, these double-bull capitals sat atop stone columns and supported the ceiling beams.

Haggai and Zechariah (cf. Ezra 5:1–2) are both dated to the initial phase of Darius's reign and reveal the reemergence of the preexilic leadership families, with the royal Zerubbabel (a Davidic descendant; Hag. 1:1, 14; Zech. 4:6–10) and the priestly Joshua (a descendant of David's priest Zadok; Hag. 1:1, 14; Zech. 3; 6:9–15) supervising rebuilding efforts (Ezra 3). Darius's punishment of Babylon at the outset of his reign is key to the vision of restoration in the book of Zechariah, placing Darius on the same level as Cyrus as the one who brought an end to the seventy-year Babylonian abuse of the Jewish community. Again the TAYN archives highlight the continuing role of the Jewish community in economic affairs at the center of the empire, even as some Jews returned to the land.[4] Official seals of Zerubbabel's daughter Shelomith and her husband, the governor Elnathan, discovered by archaeologists, attest to the final connections between the Davidic line and rule in the former kingdom of Judah.[5] Yeho'ezer, another governor of the Persian province of Yehud, is also attested on a jar impression, most likely during the period of Darius.

Xerxes. Darius's son Xerxes (486–465 BC) assumed control of the Persian throne and quickly stabilized the empire, quashing the rebellion in Egypt as well as others in Babylon. This positive start, however, did not lead to any more success against the Greeks than that of his father, since even after his great "defeat" of the Spartans at Thermopylae and his "sack" of an empty Athens (480 BC), his mighty army was defeated at Salamis, Plataea, and Mycale. In spite of this, Xerxes continued the development of Persepolis as the showcase capital of the Persian Empire. One key political reform during this time was the division of the former Babylonian satrapy Beyond the River into two separate regions. In 465 BC Xerxes was assassinated in his sleep by two close aides.

The influence of Xerxes on the Jewish community can be discerned in the discovery of a series of fortresses in and around the province of Yehud, evidence of Persian efforts to solidify their holdings of the western portion of the empire, especially in light of the Egyptian revolts. Reference to a letter of opposition against the Jews' rebuilding efforts is found in Ezra 4:6. The book of Esther is set within the court of Xerxes, and the book of Malachi possibly emerges during his reign. A jar impression with the name of a Yehud governor, Ahazai, is linked most likely to the reign of Xerxes.

Artaxerxes I. With the murder of his father and his older brother (the crown prince), Artaxerxes I (465–424 BC) assumed the throne of Persia. The Greeks called him Longimanus ("long-armed"), understood either literally because he had one arm longer than the other (Plutarch) or symbolically because of his far-reaching power (Pollux). Artaxerxes faced several early revolts in Bactria (central Asia) as well as in Egypt (460–454 BC), the latter prompted by Greek intervention. But he was able to quell these rebellions, especially with the help of his brother-in-law Megabyzus. This same brother-in-law, however, would later rebel against Artaxerxes, with peace between the two being secured only by the intervention of Artaxerxes's mother and his sister (the wife of Megabyzus). After Greek attacks on Cyprus in 450 BC Artaxerxes agreed to the Peace of Callias, a deal struck between Athens, Argos, and Persia that ensured Persian control of Egypt, Cyprus, and the coastal cities of Anatolia (modern Turkey). Artaxerxes's great building achievement was the throne hall of one hundred columns at Persepolis. He died of natural causes in 424 BC.

The vast majority of documents from the Murashu archives are from the reign of Artaxerxes I, some of which highlight the role of Jews within the economy.[6] While the letters recorded in Ezra 4:7 and 4:8–23 present a fairly negative influence linked to Artaxerxes I, elsewhere in the OT Artaxerxes is presented more positively, as shown clearly in Ezra 7–10 and Nehemiah 1–13 (Ezra 7:7–8; Neh. 2:1; 5:14; 13:6), where he commissions Ezra and

Persian archers from the palace of Darius I.

Nehemiah for leadership within the province of Yehud (Ezra 6:14). Nehemiah is twice identified as a governor of the province of Yehud (Neh. 5:14; 12:26). Ezra is given a more limited commission to promote the law (Ezra 7:11–26).

Xerxes II and Darius II. Artaxerxes I was succeeded by his son Xerxes II (424–423 BC), who lasted on the throne for only forty-five days. His assassination was followed by an intense civil war from which emerged his victorious brother Darius II (423–404 BC). As Sparta and Athens vied for control of their own region, Darius II entered into a relationship with the Spartans, who ultimately emerged victorious.

Significant documents from a Jewish military colony in southern Egypt on the island of Elephantine (in the Nile River) reveal life for Jews outside the homeland and their orientation toward the community in Jerusalem.[7] The Passover Letter (419 BC) showcases the desire of the community to properly keep the Jewish feasts, and the Petition to Bagoas, the governor of Yehud (407 BC), appeals for assistance in building a Jewish temple in Elephantine, mentioning Sanballat I, the governor of the province of Samaria and the nemesis of Nehemiah (see comments on Neh. 2:10). These two documents highlight the connection between Jewish exilic communities and the homeland.

The Final Years of the Persian Empire. The final seventy-five years of Persian (Achaemenid) hegemony of the ancient world are not explicitly evidenced in the OT, although the book of Chronicles most likely is finalized during this period, as seen in the genealogies of the Davidic house in 1 Chron. 3.

Rebellion in the western part of the empire typified the reign of Artaxerxes II (404–359 BC), son of Darius II. Egypt's rebellion at the outset of his reign was a considerable concern (404–400 BC), but even more troubling was the challenge of Artaxerxes's brother Cyrus, backed up by ten thousand Greek mercenaries in 401 BC. Both of these rebellions were quelled by Artaxerxes II. The first quarter of the fourth century BC entailed considerable peace negotiations between Sparta, Athens, Corinth, Argos, and Persia, with Egypt being a constant source of rebellion as it allied at times with Sparta. The King's Peace of 386 BC between Sparta and Persia ensured Persian dominance of Asia Minor and allowed Artaxerxes II to focus attention on Egypt. But rebellions continued to plague Artaxerxes II in his final years, mostly coming from satraps in Asia Minor. Conditions were not much better under Artaxerxes II's son Artaxerxes III (359–338 BC), who also faced rebellions in the northwest and southwest. The revolts by Tachos and then the Egyptian Nectanebo II in 360–359 BC were highly problematic for the Persian king. Artaxerxes III failed to retake Egypt in 354 and 351 BC, which bolstered the confidence of the Phoenician cities, and Tennes, king of Sidon, rebelled with the support of Nectanebo II in 345/44 BC. This Phoenician rebellion was put down by Artaxerxes's faithful satraps (regional governors), and finally the Egyptian king Nectanebo II was defeated by Artaxerxes himself in 342 BC. With Egypt under his control, Artaxerxes focused his attention on Macedonia, with the primary mission to curb the ambition of its king, Philip. Philip would outlast Artaxerxes III, who died in 338 BC, possibly in a palace coup (according to Greek sources), although this is not certain (according to a Babylonian source). His son Artaxerxes IV (338–336 BC) would last only two years, dying in the same year as Philip of Macedonia. Thus Artaxerxes IV's cousin Darius III (336–330 BC) would ascend the throne of Persia in the same year as Alexander of Macedonia, the one called "the Great," who would be responsible for the ultimate demise of the Persian royal house and the empire that had lasted for over two centuries.

The Philistines

Catherine L. McDowell

One of the earliest extrabiblical records of the Philistines is preserved in an inscription on the northern wall of Pharaoh Ramesses III's mortuary temple at Medinet Habu in Thebes, Egypt. The text describes Ramesses III's fierce battles in about 1190 BC against the so-called Sea Peoples. This confederation of groups, including the Sherden, the Tjekker, the Denyen, the Weshesh, and the Philistines, apparently sailed from the Aegean islands (possibly Caphtor/Crete, which both Amos 9:7 and Jer. 47:4 identify as the Philistine homeland) to the shores of Egypt and the Levant (the eastern Mediterranean area) in search of a new home. The battles took place on land and at sea, and both are vividly depicted in the accompanying reliefs carved on the temple wall. The land war, apparently fought north of Egypt on the Phoenician coast, depicts a chaotic mass of Egyptian soldiers and Sea Peoples in hand-to-hand combat. Several young women or girls in an ox-drawn cart lift their hands in a gesture of submission before the Egyptian soldiers while dead bodies lie prostrate around them. The naval battle, fought at the mouth of the Nile, depicts Egyptian soldiers engaged with bows and arrows, lances, clubs, and rectangular shields, while the Sea Peoples fight with spears, swords, and rounded shields. The Philistines, along with some of the other Sea Peoples, are distinguished from the Egyptians by their feathered helmets, short skirts with tassels, and ribbed breastplates.[1] Ramesses decisively defeated the invading migrants, boasting, "Those who came forward together on the sea, the full flame was in front of them at the river-mouths, while a stockade of lances surrounded them on the shore. They were dragged in, enclosed, and prostrated on the beach, killed, and made into heaps from tail to head. Their ships and their goods were as if fallen into the water."[2] Captives, many of whom are depicted in the Medinet Habu reliefs with arms shackled, were either conscripted into the Egyptian military or given permission to settle in areas of Canaan where the Egyptians maintained a strong military presence. This included the southern Canaanite coast (roughly what is known today as the Gaza Strip plus about twelve miles to the north), where the Philistines displaced the indigenous Canaanite population and established themselves as a rival power. By 1175/1150 BC the Philistines had gained their independence from a weakened Egypt and had founded the five major cities known as the Philistine Pentapolis: Ashdod, Ashkelon, Ekron (Tel Miqne), Gaza, and Gath, each with its own ruler.

At the mortuary temple of the Egyptian pharaoh Ramesses III are depictions of his victory over the Sea Peoples (Philistines). Pictured here are several captured Philistine soldiers, identifiable especially by their feathered helmets.

During the next one hundred years (ca. 1150–1050 BC) the Philistines expanded north as far as Tell Qasile (Tel Aviv), south to Raphia along the coast toward Egypt, southeast toward the Negev (the arid region south of Judah), east to Megiddo and Beth-shan and into the Judean foothills (Shephelah). Their eastward expansion brought them into direct contact with Israel, whom they apparently dominated by about 1050/1000 BC (Judg. 14:4; 15:11). The frequent and fierce battles between Israel and the Philistines are recorded in Judges and 1 Samuel, and include the famous stories of Samson (Judg. 13–16), the capture of the ark of the covenant (1 Sam. 4–6), and the battle between David and Goliath (1 Sam. 17). Although Saul (1 Sam. 13–31) had initial military success against the Philistines, they managed to establish garrisons in the hill country and were fighting Israel near Jerusalem. Only in about 975 BC, when David became king, were the Philistines finally driven back to their initial area of settlement along the Canaanite coast. From there the Philistines engaged in periodic skirmishes with Israel and Judah for control of the hill country (1 Kings 15:27; 16:15; 2 Chron. 17:11; 21:16–17; 26:6; 28:18; Amos 1:6–8) until the late eighth century BC, when the Assyrian King Tiglath-pileser III (745–727 BC) and his successors Shalmaneser V (727–722 BC) and Sargon II (722–705 BC) gained control of Syria and Palestine, including Philistia, and subjugated its inhabitants (see the article "The Assyrians"). Among the many cities taken were Ekron, Gaza, Gath, and Ashdod. The siege of Ekron (712 BC) is depicted in the reliefs from Sargon's palace at Khorsabad.

The Philistines remained Assyrian vassals under Sennacherib and his successors. Esar-haddon required the Philistines to supply corvée labor for building projects in Nineveh. Ashurbanipal conscripted the Philistines for military service in his war against Egypt. Ashurbanipal was victorious, but about a decade later Egypt gained its independence from an overextended and weakened Assyrian Empire and took control of Philistia once again. Egyptian presence is particularly well attested at Ashkelon, where excavators discovered vessels made of Nile clay, an Egyptian jewelry box, twenty-six Egyptian bronze statuettes, a cache of bronze bottles decorated with Egyptian motifs, and over a dozen other Egyptian artifacts made of bronze.[3] Egyptian dominance over Philistia, however, was short-lived. In 605 BC the powerful Babylonian army defeated Egypt at Carchemish in western Syria (cf. Jer. 25:8–11; 46:2–8, 22–26) and then moved south. Ekron, located on the inner coastal plain, and Ashkelon, an international and cosmopolitan seaport, were conquered in 604 BC, and their destruction is well attested in the archaeological record at both sites.[4] The Babylonian Chronicle reports, "(Nebuchadrezzar) marched to the city of Ashkelon and captured it in the month of Kislev (November/December). He captured its king and plundered it and carried off [spoil from it . . .]. He turned the city into a tell and heaps of ruins"[5] (cf. Jer. 47:1–7; Ezek. 25:15; Zeph. 2:5). This fulfilled the words of the prophet Amos: "'I will cut off the ruler from Ashdod, and the one who wields the scepter from Ashkelon. I will also turn my hand against Ekron, and the remainder of the Philistines will perish.' The Lord God has spoken" (Amos 1:8).

Babylonian records from the early sixth century BC preserve the last few historical references to the Philistines. The names of the sons of Aga, the last king of Ashkelon, along with several names of deported sailors, officials, and musicians from Ashkelon, appear in a Babylonian rations list dated to about 592 BC.[6] The kings of Gaza and Ashdod are mentioned in a Babylonian court document from about 570 BC for their participation in the dedication of Nebuchadnezzar's new palace. Finally, a list from the Murashu Archives (mid-late fifth century BC) at the city of Nippur preserves the names of settlements, including Ashkelon and Gaza,[7] suggesting that the descendants of exiled Philistines had established their own communities in the region of Nippur and named them after their original pentapolis cities back in Philistia. These references to Ashkelon and Gaza provide the final glimpse of the Philistines, who then disappear from the historical record, leaving only their name (Palestine) on the region where they once lived.

Prophets in the Old Testament World

Samuel A. Meier

The belief in the ancient Near East was that certain individuals might have regular, but not necessarily predictable, access to information from the gods that was not available to most humans. These "prophets" attained this information through a personal encounter with gods and consequently were able to communicate their extraordinary realities to their peers as messages from gods. Unlike individuals who tried to gain access to such information through technical means (e.g., inspecting animal entrails, interpreting omens, astrology, consulting the dead; cf. Deut. 18:10–12), a prophet claimed to engage in a personal encounter with a god, often by means of a verbal or visual communication, or by the god taking over the personality of the prophet.

A variety of terms could be used to designate such individuals, both in the OT and in the ancient world. Just as in Hebrew where the terms *hozeh* and *roeh* both identify someone who could see ("seer"), pointing toward more visionary dimensions of insight, so this same term, "seer" (*hozeh*), is attested outside the Bible in Aramean and Transjordanian texts from the first millennium BC (Zakkur Stela; Deir Alla). The Hebrew word *nabi* ("prophet"), of uncertain derivation and the general term in the OT identifying one called by God to convey special messages to humans, is attested also in texts from northern Mesopotamia in the second millennium BC.

Terminology that is not found in the Bible to identify prophets includes the Akkadian term *muḫḫû* ("ecstatic"), which identified someone associated with frenzied or bizarre behavior, perhaps spontaneous, while the *āpilu* ("one who answers") may have been one who conveyed responses from the gods to specific human inquiries in a more deliberate fashion. It is possible that the latter two were distinguished by their place of activity, with the former being more mobile and not confined to a specific holy place. In first-millennium-BC Assyria, the *raggimu* ("one who proclaims") is the term most often used for prophets. Both male and female prophets appear in the Bible and elsewhere in the ancient Near East.

Prophetic activity is particularly well documented in two clusters of documents in northern Mesopotamia. Scores of texts from the palace of eighteenth-century-BC Mari, a city-kingdom on the Euphrates River, preserve encounters with prophets whose messages pertained to the king and the well-being of the kingdom. A thousand years later, much evidence about prophets surfaces again during the reigns of Esar-haddon and Ashurbanipal, two seventh-century-BC Assyrian kings who exhibited an intense interest in determining the will of the gods.

Prophetic oracles, particularly associated with the goddess Ishtar, who was venerated in the city of Arbel, were collected and archived by the Assyrian palace. Prophetic oracles in the kingdom of Mari were characteristically recorded in letters destined for the king. Any prophetic activity outside of royal concerns is thus not available to us. In all these cases prophetic oracles were oral in origin, sometimes even clearly dramatized by prophets with actions that reinforced the message, relayed by humans speaking as if they were the god in question. Oracles could be short (a sentence or two) or long (several paragraphs). The messages could be imperious and coercive, allowing no compromise and threatening dire consequences for the king's failure to obey. Messages could also be encouraging, even affectionate, for the king who was heeding the god's will.

In Mesopotamian texts, particularly in the second millennium BC, a clear suspicion of prophets also surfaces in the sources. Some form of authentication for their oracles is characteristically required, and a greater trust was placed in interpreting the entrails of animals. For this reason, specific names of prophets are regularly associated with specific oracles in order to track their reliability.

On this stela a king named Zakkur describes how his god Ba'al-shamayn spoke to him through seers and diviners, giving him assurance of the god's help and thus upcoming victory.

Warfare in the Old Testament

BOYD SEEVERS

Introduction. Wars, battles, and military imagery appear throughout the OT, in its history, prophecy, poetry, and even laws. For some readers, all this bloodshed raises ethical questions: Why so much fighting? How could a good God command such violence, even genocide? Others ask more practical questions: How did the ancients actually fight? What weapons and tactics did they use?

Why So Much Fighting? The OT includes so many references to warfare because the ancient Israelites fought often, just like other contemporary peoples in the ancient Near East. Good land and other resources were quite limited, so nations often fought to defend their interests, take what they needed, or take what they wanted. Throughout the ancient Near East during the OT era, peoples and nations fought one another a great deal.

The Bible also shows that the God of Israel was heavily involved in his people's wars, just like the supposed gods of nearby peoples were thought to be involved in theirs. Ancient texts from many nations include statements of how their gods commanded, accompanied, and fought for their national armies. Ancient carved reliefs often show symbols of those gods hovering over their king and their armies. All the nations assumed that their gods helped them with their fighting, and Israel was no exception.

Why the Apparent Atrocities? Although the Israelites' military activities can seem harsh to the modern reader, they were typical for the time. For example, just as the Israelite army killed thousands of Canaanites in Jericho and Ai because God commanded it (Josh. 6–8), so the king of Moab killed thousands of Israelites in two cities because his god, Kemosh, commanded it. The modern reader should also remember that God sometimes used Israel's military as his instrument of rather harsh judgment, just as God would later use the Assyrian and Babylonian armies in harsh judgment of the idolatrous Israelites.

How Did the Israelites Carry Out Warfare? Israel's military changed significantly over the many centuries of OT history. From Israel's time in the wilderness through the period of the judges, its military apparently was organized by clans and tribes, with leaders of those groups (1 Chron. 27:1, 16–22) answering to an overall commander such as Joshua or one of the judges. The soldiers probably had just simple weapons and little or no formal training. The troops would have served like a militia, called up during emergencies and then released to return home when the fighting ended (Judg. 7:7–8). Such weaknesses in this type of system contributed to the nation's desire for a king with a standing army (1 Sam. 8:19–20).

Israel's military experienced tremendous change and expansion during the monarchy. Saul, the first king, formed the nucleus of a standing army (1 Sam. 14:50, 52). When David and Solomon elevated the nation to regional dominance, the military expanded to support the nation's growth (1 Chron. 27:1–24), requiring a large portion of the nation's resources to support it (1 Kings 4:7–19).

During this period Israel also developed a substantial chariot force to supplement its infantry (2 Sam. 8:4; 1 Kings 10:26). When earlier Israel

This Assyrian wall panel depicts Assyrian soldiers at the siege of Lachish, a city in Judah. Note the rows of archers with bows and then the rows of soldiers with slings.

had been a weak nation confined to the hill country, it would have lacked both the need and ability to acquire and use chariots. Chariots were the most powerful military weapons of the time, but they were expensive to build and maintain and were far more effective in lower, flat, open regions. David and Solomon started Israel's use of chariotry, a practice that continued throughout the divided kingdom as well.

Israel's forces were led by a corps of officers and by their God. The king or a designated general served as the overall leader, often physically leading the troops in battle (1 Sam. 31:1–7; 2 Sam. 20:23; 21:15–17). Lesser officers commanded smaller units whose number and size often are unclear and may have changed fairly often. In those time periods when Israel was obedient and faithful, Israel's God led their army, sometimes giving specific directions as well as victories. Unlike the armies of its enemies, Israel's army did not possess a visible symbol of its God, such as an idol for the priests to carry in front of the army, except when the ark of the covenant served that purpose (Josh. 6:6–7).

What Weapons Did the Israelites Use? Like its neighbors, Israel's troops used different offensive weapons for close-, medium-, or long-range fighting. Much fighting took place hand-to-hand, so soldiers typically carried close-range swords or spears in one hand and shields in the other. Some soldiers used medium-range javelins, which could be thrown a moderate distance. The sling and bow were effective long-range weapons that could fire numerous rounds with great accuracy. Slings were cheap, easy to make, and surprisingly effective, as David's victory over Goliath demonstrated. Bows could be relatively cheap and simple if fashioned from single pieces of wood, while more expensive, yet more powerful, compound bows were made by gluing together multiple pieces of wood and animal horn.

Soldiers attacked using such weapons, and they defended themselves with

Chariots were the most powerful weapon of the time, but were expensive to build and maintain and were restricted to relatively flat ground.

This Assyrian wall panel depicts the siege of Lachish, a city in Judah. Note the siege ramps and the battering ram siege machine.

shields of different sizes, plus body armor if possible. Soldiers in poor armies might have simple leather garments or no armor at all. If the nation had the money and skill, it fashioned armor from metal scales or larger plates, especially for the highest officers and the charioteers (1 Sam. 17:38; 1 Kings 22:34; 2 Chron. 26:14).

What Tactics Did the Israelites Use? Armies such as Israel's used different tactics depending on their resources, their opponent, and the current circumstances and terrain. Outmatched armies, such as in early Israel, often used guerilla tactics. They practiced stealth, moving troops and launching attacks at night (Josh. 8:3; 10:9; Judg. 7:19) or from ambush (Josh. 8:4–23). Large, capable armies such as Israel under David (2 Sam. 10:7–14; 1 Chron. 19:17) were more likely to arrange their soldiers in battle lines and face opponents out in the open.

To protect their cities from invaders, Israel and other nations often built high, thick walls out of stone and/or mud-brick, with strong wooden gates that could be closed when attack was imminent. Attackers could try to penetrate the walls with battering rams, climb over the walls using ladders, tunnel under the walls, or talk their way in by threat or subversion (Judg. 1:22–25). Alternately, attackers could ring the city with troops and siege works such as fences and watchtowers in preparation for direct attack (2 Sam. 11:1, 14–25; 12:26–31; 20:15–22) or to starve the inhabitants into surrender (2 Kings 6:24–30).

Conclusion. The OT is full of warfare because it accurately describes a violent era. Israel's military organization, weapons, and tactics were largely like those of the other nations of the time. Earlier, less-capable Israel used poorly trained and poorly armed troops organized along family lines, and only during emergency. More mature, wealthier Israel had a much larger, better trained, and better equipped army of infantry and chariots, using weapons and tactics common to the time. The Bible notes that Israel's God often was involved in the nation's military activity, giving direction and victory as he knew best, based largely on the obedience and covenantal loyalty of his people.

Women in the Old Testament World

Mark W. Chavalas

Background from Mesopotamian Sources. In order to understand the nature and status of women in the OT, one needs to become acquainted with the world of the ancient Near East, especially Mesopotamia. Beginning in the mid-nineteenth century, thousands of cuneiform (the writing style of Mesopotamia) texts have been discovered and translated, opening up an opportunity for the scholarly world to study Mesopotamian women from Mesopotamian sources (rather than rely on the opinions of an outsider, such as the Greek historian Herodotus). This has also provided a context for understanding women in the OT, as it is clear that the biblical writers claimed Mesopotamian origins for their ancestors. Moreover, the nature of the cuneiform texts provides an excellent resource for understanding women in the ancient world. The documents, written over a three-thousand-year period (ca. 3100 BC to ca. AD 100), are written mostly in Sumerian (the world's first known written language; it is unrelated to any other known language) and Akkadian (a linguistic relative to Biblical Hebrew). They are primarily administrative in nature (receipts, contracts, legal statements, economic transactions) and thus refer to both male and female subjects. Furthermore, there are a number of law codes that often refer to topics concerning women (e.g., marriage, divorce, and abduction), as well as some personal letters that reveal much about women.

Women in Ancient Law Codes. Archaeologists have uncovered only a small sampling of law codes from excavations.[1] They include two Sumerian codes, the Ur-Namma Code (from Ur, ca. 2100 BC) and the Lipit-Ishtar Code (from Isin, ca. 1930 BC), and four Akkadian codes: Dadusha of Eshnunna (ca. 1770 BC), Hammurabi of Babylon (ca. 1750 BC), Middle Assyrian laws (ca. 1100 BC), and Neo-Babylonian laws (ca. 700 BC). In fact, the Hittite Codes (ca. 1400–1200 BC) and even the Mosaic laws (Exodus through Deuteronomy) appear to come from the same legal and social environment. However, these ancient Near Eastern laws are not to be taken at face value. They are literary creations that perhaps describe elite ideals concerning legal situations. Interestingly, the verdicts in the codes are never cited in the numerous legal decisions from Mesopotamia, which causes one to wonder about their purpose.

Though some are heavily fragmented, most law codes appear to consist of three major parts: a prologue and an epilogue, both of which articulate the royal attributes and deeds of the monarch, and a collection of case-law provisions that contain "if-then" clauses, dealing with a variety of criminal (e.g., murder, robbery, assault, bodily injury) and civil issues (e.g., inheritance, adoption, marriage, real estate, rental). Though not the same in all cases, the law codes appear to differentiate between the upper class, an amorphous middle class (probably semi-independent peasants and laborers who were in some way dependent upon the king), and slaves.

The law codes involve women of all classes; there are laws concerning priestesses, workers, and slaves. It appears that many free women often were employed, but they probably were not fulfilling any vocational destiny. A woman who worked outside of the domestic environment either did not have a male guardian to protect her interests or had a male guardian who could not support her economically.

There are a number of interesting laws regarding female priests. The Code of Hammurabi law 110 makes it clear that certain celibate priestesses were forbidden to enter taverns, under penalty of death by burning. Perhaps this is because inns and taverns were places of male relaxation, and the priestesses were not to be defiled. One

A tablet containing the Sumerian Ur-Nammu law code (2111–2095 BC).

type of Mesopotamian priestess was called *naditum*. The *naditum* priestess was a celibate who apparently was chosen by divine lottery from among upper-class families. In some towns they were allowed to be married, but still they remained celibate. Married *naditum* priestesses were required to furnish their husbands with children (presumably through adoption). Unmarried *naditum* priestesses received an inheritance from their families, which they used for daily needs. However, one *naditum*, Erishti-Aya, the cloistered daughter of King Zimri Lim of Mari (ca. 1770 BC), complained in hyperbolic terms to her parents about their lack of support for her.[2]

Marriage and Divorce in Ancient Law Codes. Marriage was a contractual agreement between families. The process could be lengthy, and the giving of gifts and the negotiations could go on for years. The arrangement was completed when the future husband came to take his wife-to-be to the wedding chamber, similar to Jacob asking to take Rachel (Gen. 29:21). Until then, the maiden was considered a virgin bride (i.e., betrothed, similar to the story of Mary in Matt. 1). If a man took a wife without a contract, the woman was not legally his wife, and thus legally vulnerable. If a woman was accused by her husband of adultery, she had to take a divine oath of innocence (similar to the law in Num. 5). If, however, someone else accused her of adultery, she had to endure the divine River Ordeal, a type of divine water trial that apparently was imposed somewhat differently across the region.

Divorce was not uncommon, although women appear to have been protected economically. The husband was required to give back the monetary equivalent of double her bride wealth. If a woman for whatever reason refused to accompany her husband to the wedding chamber, the neighborhood made the determination as to whether she was "in good standing." If so, she was allowed to leave the house with her bride wealth; if not, she was put to death. If the woman was incapable of fulfilling her marital duties (e.g., because of illness), the husband could not divorce her. He often married a second wife, who was contracted to take care of the first one. Although women could divorce their husbands, there was a heavy cost. If there were children, they usually stayed in the husband's family, since women left their family of origin to enter their husband's family.

The legal codes generally describe passive women (i.e., women who are subject to laws and are not legally proactive). However, the

A statue of an Egyptian high-ranking official, Meryre, with his wife, Inyuia, seated beside him.

lawgivers conceived of women who "took out a contract" on their husbands. Interestingly, in one murder trial a woman was declared innocent because the judges found it hard to believe that a woman would actively participate in her husband's demise.[3]

From the myriad of administrative documents from Mesopotamia, one can surmise that women had a relative degree of economic freedom. Many contracts depict women as buying and selling property, arranging marriages, claiming inheritances, and engaging in lawsuits.

Women, Literacy, and Business in the Old Testament World. In some ways, the collection of ancient personal letters from Mesopotamia is the most authentic depiction of the nature and status of women in the ancient Near East. Some women in the Assyrian city of Ashur during the period of the Assyrian merchant letters (ca. 2000–1750 BC) were able to compose their own letters to their husbands. In fact, it is possible that a good percentage of the women were at least partially literate. Assyrian merchants traveled frequently from Ashur to Kanesh, a trade colony in central Anatolia (modern Turkey). In Kanesh over twenty-five thousand texts have been found that document this trade activity. Most of these women stayed home and were the functional heads of their households, representing their husbands in commercial transactions, trade, and performing domestic tasks, such as the weaving of textiles.[4] In fact, the money they received for the textiles was used to supply the family with daily needs. Some of them even complained bitterly to their distant husbands about the lack of monetary support they were receiving.

One of the most powerful people in Egypt was a priestess in Thebes with the title "God's Wife of Amun." One of the women who held this title is depicted in this relief.

Examples concerning royal women abound from the ancient Syrian city of Mari, located along the Euphrates River (ca. 1770 BC). Of the thousands of letters found there, over three hundred were composed either by or to women. The monarch Zimri-Lim received numerous letters from his wife, Shibtu, who clearly ran the royal palace while her husband was away. Of special interest was her inclination to pray for her husband's welfare and warn him of bad omens or prophecies that concerned the crown. She even commented on international relations; ironically, she reported to her husband about the evil designs of Hammurabi of Babylon, who eventually destroyed the Mari kingdom.[5] Zimri-Lim also received letters from his sister and his many daughters. In fact, he sent two of his daughters, Kiru and Shimatum, to marry the same ally. Kiru remained faithful to her father, but she bitterly complained that her new husband hated her, and so she wanted to return home. Shimatum evidently became estranged from her sister.

Many of the nearly three hundred letters from Tell al Rimah (most likely ancient Qattara) in northern Iraq (ca. 1750 BC) were connected to the queen, Iltani, who appears to have run her palatial estate similarly to Shibtu at Mari. However, her husband, Aqba-hammu, clearly had trouble controlling his anger, as he threatened to cut up his wife into twelve pieces! In addition, the queen received numerous requests from individuals hoping to take advantage of her high position. One individual had known Iltani when she lived in Eshnunna and hoped to capitalize on their previous relationship.[6]

Conclusions. Although few generalizations concerning women can be made from studying the myriad of texts from the ancient Near East, the wealth of information in these documents does provide a helpful context in which to study the women of the OT. For example, the many laws concerning women in Exodus, Leviticus, Numbers, and Deuteronomy are now better understood in the wider context of the ancient Near Eastern legal environment. Just as important, the manner in which women are depicted in narrative texts (especially in Genesis) reflects a sociocultural environment and customs that are generally consistent with what is found in Old Babylonian contracts and in texts from Nuzi in northern Iraq (ca. 1600–1350 BC), especially those concerning adoption and inheritance.[7]

Women's Fashion in the Old Testament World

Marcella Barbosa

Introduction. Women's fashion in the OT world included many of the same things that today's fashion does—clothing, hairstyles, shoes, jewelry, makeup, and perfume. Just like today, fashion in the ancient Near Eastern world evolved over time and likewise varied according to region and according to the message that the wearer was hoping to convey. At times that message concerned a specific event or special purpose, such as a wedding celebration or a time of mourning. Clothing, whether worn for a special occasion or not, did always convey a message, sometimes consciously and sometimes subconsciously, especially regarding social status, as there was clothing specific to gender, age, marital status, wealth, rank, modesty, place of origin, or occupation.[1] Unfortunately, we do not have enough information about women's fashion of the OT world to get the entire picture, mostly due to the entirely expected reason that not everything will survive that length of time. Our lack of information is due to the perishable nature of clothing and associated items in conjunction with the fact that many of the lands that produce the settings for the Bible do not have environments conducive to preserving such perishable material. Even so, there are a few areas that have the right conditions, and these have produced a few rare examples of clothing or at least fragments of it. More endurable objects like jewelry and containers for makeup and perfume are much more likely to be preserved over time, and indeed many have been found at biblical sites. Finally, to enhance our understanding of women's fashion of this time, we have numerous references in texts, along with depictions from the art of the time. The two main artistic sources for the fashion of Canaanite, Israelite, and Judean women are the painting at the Beni Hasan tomb in Egypt dating to the time of the patriarchs (nineteenth century BC)[2] and the Assyrian relief of Sennacherib's siege of Lachish, which dates to the time of the divided kingdom (701 BC).[3]

Assyrian wall panel depicting the fall of the Judahite city of Lachish. These two Judean women are being led off into captivity. They wear unadorned, simple garments that are cloak-like and ankle-length with short sleeves.

Women's Clothing. The main garment worn by women of the ancient Near East was formed from a single large, rectangular piece of cloth wrapped around the body so that it was ankle-length, leaving the right arm and shoulder bare.[4] This style of clothing can be seen in the Beni Hasan painting, which also indicates that these garments perhaps could be made of brightly colored, patterned material. It also allowed for warmth or coolness in an environment that could vary greatly in temperature.[5] Later, in the Lachish relief, the women are dressed in unadorned, simple garments that were cloak-like and ankle-length with short sleeves; they also wore mantles that could cover their heads.[6] In biblical texts the women's main garment is called a *ketonet*.[7] This term often is translated as "robe," and it could be used of a man's garment (Gen. 37:31; Exod. 28:39) or a woman's garment (2 Sam. 13:18; Song 5:3). For most Israelites and Judeans, their clothing was likely to be made of wool, since it was readily available in that region. In other areas, such as Egypt, linen was often used for clothing.[8]

The style of clothing definitely differed in other lands, though perhaps only minutely, and sometimes the wealthy Israelites and Judeans adopted the style of these neighboring cultures.[9] In Syria, to the north, the basic garment was similar, in that it was wrapped, draped over one shoulder, left the arms bare, and was of a variety of bright patterns, but it hung to about mid-calf.[10] The style was also similar in Mesopotamia, with simple linen garments that wrapped around the body from shoulder to ankle and left the right arm and shoulder bare, though sometimes women also wore tufted skirts and cloaks.[11] In Egypt, however, women wore garments that were of plain white linen, tubular and ankle-length, starting above or below the breasts, and sometimes supported by shoulder straps.[12] Upscale versions worn by the wealthy could be pleated.[13] Egyptian women might also wear elaborate beaded net dresses over these linen garments.[14]

This ancient Egyptian painting depicts foreign women, similar to Israelites. Note the ankle-length wrap, the bright colored pattern, the exposed shoulder, and the shoes. This may be one of our bes portrayals of what Israelite women looked like in th Old Testament.

Headdresses and Hairstyles. It was a common style of both men and women to wear a headband that held the hair in place. However, hairpins have also been discovered.[15] Other styles include a turban-like headpiece[16] and headdresses of bright colors or patterns that could also be used to support the carrying of an object.[17] Veils seemed to be used only to celebrate special occasions like weddings (Gen. 24:65), or to identify the social status of either an elite lady or even a prostitute (Gen. 38).[18] In the Megiddo ivories, beautifully carved pieces dating to before 1200 BC, women are depicted wearing stiff caps with fabric that hangs behind the head like a short veil in the back.[19] As for hair, while the information is limited, it does appear that long hair was the preferred style. It was a mark of beauty for both men and women.[20] At the site of Lachish archaeologists uncovered what amazingly looks to be a curling iron that dates to about 1400 BC.[21]

In Egypt there are multiple artistic depictions of the Egyptians' elaborate hairstyles, wigs, and headdresses. Likewise, examples of each have been found in Egyptian tombs.[22] In Mesopotamia there are a few examples in art pieces (such as statues) portraying the large headdresses that women wore.[23] But perhaps the most fantastic example is that of the burial of Queen Shub-ad of Ur, where the actual headdresses themselves were found.[24] The queen wore an elaborate headdress over a bouffant wig, while her ladies-in-waiting, who were killed and buried with her, each had her own ornate headdress of silver and gold.[25]

Footwear. Once again, not much remains of women's footwear, and most of our information comes from textual and artistic sources. Early footwear seemed to cover the entire foot, coming up over the ankle, with a white border at the top, as seen in the Beni Hasan painting.[26] Later, it appears that it was more common among the Israelites and Judeans, as well as other contemporary peoples, to wear sandals made of leather.[27] The poor were more likely to go barefoot all the time, while everyone probably went barefoot when indoors.[28]

Cosmetics and Perfumes. Cosmetics and perfumes are likewise not often preserved over time. However, many of the containers that held them have been found, sometimes containing detectable traces of the cosmetics or perfumes that they held. Makeup applicators have also been found. Yet once again we rely primarily on texts and art to provide a picture of the type of makeup and perfumes that were used and particularly how they were applied. Ironically, nearly nothing is known about the application of makeup among Israelite and Judean women, but we do know that makeup certainly was used, because containers and applicators have been found at various sites.[29] Makeup served the dual purpose of beautification and personal cleanliness. It also appears to have been used in cultic (i.e., religious) contexts where it was applied to statues of gods and their attendants.[30]

Some of the cosmetic objects that have been preserved and found within biblical lands are containers, applicators, spatulas, kohl sticks, unguent spoons, tweezers, mirrors, cosmetic burners, combs, and cosmetic palettes.[31] These items were made of various materials such as wood, bone, or metal.[32] While not much is known about the use of makeup in Israel, one cosmetic that was known to be in use was eye makeup. Not only have containers and applicators been discovered but also there are a number of references to eye makeup in the Bible (2 Kings 9:30; Jer. 4:30; Ezek. 23:40), though these examples have bad connotations.[33] Kohl or manganese was used to outline the eyes, and color for the eyelids was produced by mixing dry powders of different minerals and materials with water or gum.[34]

Even though the use of makeup seemed to be widespread in Egypt, the Egyptian aristocracy had a particularly high concern for personal hygiene, as well as for aesthetics. Thus Egypt provides much of the information available on cosmetics.[35] Egyptian men and women both used cosmetics. Some of the essential items were skin-softening ointments, which helped with skin that dried out due to dust or heat or washing, and eye paint, which prevented eye infections, killed parasites (due to the materials being used), and enhanced the beauty of the eyes.[36] Egyptian women preferred to paint their upper eyelids black and the lower ones green, while Mesopotamian

Canaanite mirrors, combs, perfume containers, and kohl eye-makeup containers.

women favored reds and yellows for their eyelids.[37] Also, red ocher was used to color their lips.[38]

Perfumes, as well as other ointments and creams, served multiple purposes as well—for protecting the skin, for healing, for masking odors, and even as a sacred symbol.[39] Perfumes were produced from different plants, and the OT mentions several different kinds of perfumes and ointments: aloe, balm, cinnamon, frankincense, and myrrh.[40]

Jewelry and Ornaments. Both men and women wore jewelry, and the jewelry served multiple functions. It could be used as adornment, as currency, as a symbol of status, or for religious purposes.[41] While not exactly a common find, jewelry is still something that is found at many tombs and biblical sites. This jewelry usually is split into two categories. Group one includes jewelry that is expertly made, crafted from precious metals like gold and silver, and generally found in hidden hoards, treasuries, or in the tombs of the wealthy. Group two is found in more common, everyday locations and consists of jewelry made of more common materials like bronze and iron. It is attributed to the average person.[42]

Some of the most common types of jewelry worn by women are rings, nose rings, bracelets, jewels, and necklaces.[43] Of course, there were other pieces of jewelry besides these, and sometimes only fragments of jewelry remain for excavators to find. For instance, beads, which can be made from many different materials, are the most common jewelry found, though they are rarely found in their original setting.[44] Other types of jewelry include armlets, anklets, pendants, earrings, amulets, and signet rings.[45] Amulets were worn for religious purposes, either for divine protection or gifted benevolence.[46] Signet rings were symbols of status, as they were used to authenticate and to seal documents. These rarely belonged to women, though there are a few examples, including a recent find from excavations in Jerusalem of a signet ring belonging to Elihana, the daughter of Gael (dating to about the seventh century BC).[47] Finally, other ornaments include hairpins and different types of clasps that helped keep clothing in place.[48]

Canaanite jewelry.

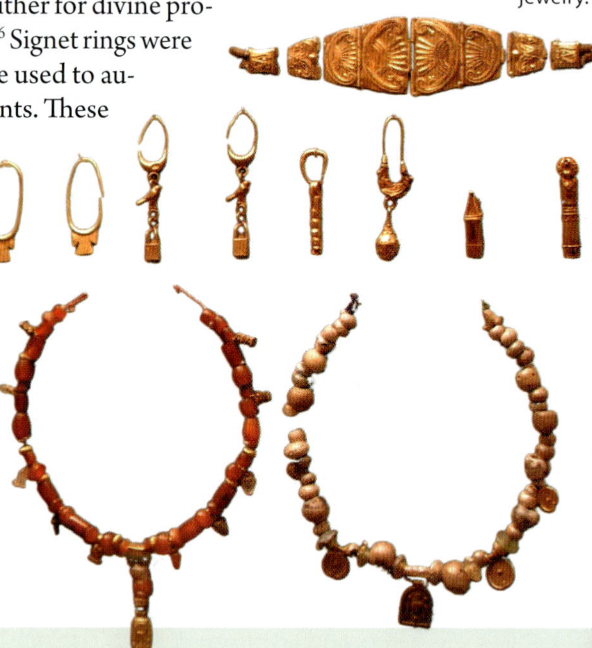

Commentary

Genesis

- Exodus
- Leviticus
- Numbers
- Deuteronomy
- Joshua
- Judges
- Ruth
- 1 Samuel
- 2 Samuel
- 1 Kings
- 2 Kings
- 1 Chronicles
- 2 Chronicles
- Ezra
- Nehemiah
- Esther
- Job
- Psalms
- Proverbs
- Ecclesiastes
- Song of Songs
- Isaiah
- Jeremiah
- Lamentations
- Ezekiel
- Daniel
- Hosea
- Joel
- Amos
- Obadiah
- Jonah
- Micah
- Nahum
- Habakkuk
- Zephaniah
- Haggai
- Zechariah
- Malachi

Genesis

Tremper Longman III

Introduction. Genesis means "Beginnings," a name well suited to the contents of the book. In this first part of the five-part Torah (Pentateuch) we read about the beginning of the cosmos, the beginning of humanity, the beginning of sin and death, and the beginning of redemption.

The book of Genesis has three major parts. The book opens with what often is called the primeval history (Gen. 1–11). These chapters tell the story of the far distant past, beginning with creation (Gen. 1–2) and followed by human rebellion against God (Gen. 3). The rest of the section (Gen. 4–11) recounts other episodes (Cain and Abel, the flood, and the tower of Babel) of human sin. Though God judges sinful humanity, he also extends to them grace and passionately pursues reconciliation. Genealogies connect these stories with one another.

By the end of Gen. 11 there is still no apparent resolution between God and his sinful human creatures. God thus calls Abraham to leave his homeland and go to a new place to start a new people. He promises to make Abraham's descendants a "great nation" and to bless them. In addition, he promises that, through them, he will bring blessing to the nations (12:1–3). Thus begins the second part of the book (Gen. 12–36), commonly referred to as the patriarchal narratives because it follows the story of the three "fathers" of Israel: Abraham, his son Isaac, and Isaac's son Jacob.

A tablet containing a portion of the Enuma Elish, the Babylonian epic of creation.

The final part of Genesis (Gen. 37–50) tells the story of the twelve sons of Jacob, particularly Joseph. The story of Joseph provides a bridge to the book of Exodus by telling the reader how the family called by God to special service ended up in Egypt. The story of Joseph shows how God guided this family through his providence, even using evil people for redemptive purposes (50:19–20).

The book of Genesis does not name an author, but later biblical texts and tradition associate the book with the towering figure of Moses (Josh. 1:7, 8; 2 Chron. 25:4; Ezra 6:18; Neh. 13:1; Matt. 19:7; 22:24; Mark 7:10; 12:26; John 1:17; 5:46; 7:23). Moses, who lived in the second half of the second millennium BC, was the leader of the Israelites at the time of the exodus and the journey through the wilderness toward the promised land. While never specifically named as the author of the book, he is described as writing things down during his lifetime (see Exod. 24:4; 34:27; Num. 33:2; Deut. 31:22). Of course, the events of Genesis took place long before he was alive, but there are indications that he used sources to write the book that were passed down to him (see comments on Gen. 2:4). That said, there are also a number of passages in the Torah that refer to places by names that those places did not acquire until after the death of Moses or to events that happened after the death of Moses (e.g., Gen. 11:28; 14:14; Deut. 34). These so-called post-Mosaica imply that later anonymous editors were involved in the final composition of the Torah as we know it.

The First Creation Account (1:1–2:3)

God created (1:1). Thus begins the first of two accounts of creation at the beginning of the first book of the Bible. It is likely that not only the author but also the original readers of Genesis were well aware of other ancient Near Eastern literary compositions that purported to describe the origin of the cosmos and humanity. These were rival claims that stated that other gods, rather than the God of the Hebrews, created everything. One of the purposes of Genesis is to counter these rival claims. Three of these stories have particular relevance to the biblical creation account.

First is the Enuma Elish, a Babylonian creation account that described creation as the result of a conflict among the gods.[1] Tiamat and Apsu were gods representing the waters and were just there at the beginning. Their intermingling waters led to the birth of the younger gods, who disturbed their tranquil existence. Apsu determined to kill his divine offspring, but Ea, the god of wisdom, learned of his intentions and killed him first. At this point, Tiamat became enraged and took up Apsu's purpose, gaining the support of Qingu and his demonic horde. Ea, knowing he was no match for the powerful Tiamat, enlisted his son Marduk, who agreed to battle Tiamat on condition that if victorious he would become king of the pantheon of gods. After an intense battle Marduk did defeat Tiamat, and from her body he created the cosmos. He placed her upper half above and with it created the sky. He put the gods there as the celestial bodies: the sun, moon, and stars. With her lower half he created the earth by pushing back the waters to create land. At this point, he executed the demon god Qingu and, mixing his blood with the clay of the earth, created human beings.

The second story is the Atrahasis Epic, also a Babylonian story, which combines an account of creation followed by a description of a flood (see comments on Gen. 6:7).[2] The focus of interest is on the creation of humans, who were created to replace the lesser gods, who up to that point had been commissioned to dig the irrigation ditches. The more powerful gods created humans from the clay of the earth, the blood of a minor god, and the spit of the gods. They were created in order to do the menial tasks that the lesser gods refused to do.

Third, in 1929 a number of cuneiform texts written in a language now called Ugaritic were discovered in northern Syria, including texts describing what looks like a creation story very similar to the Enuma Elish.[3] The Ugaritic people were more closely related by geography and language to the ancient Hebrews and may represent Canaanite culture. Like the Enuma Elish, the focus of the story is on a conflict between the creator god, in this case Baal, and the god of the waters, Yam. Baal is able to defeat Yam, and most scholars believe that the now broken part of the tablet that follows the account of this struggle was a creation text similar to the story found in the Enuma Elish.

Then God said (1:3). The biblical account of creation often is contrasted with ancient Near Eastern creation texts, since it pictures God creating the world by the power of his speech. This statement is generally true, but we should note that there was a myth from Egypt that described creation as the result of the speech of the god Ptah. This account, known as the Shabaka Stone, is on a black granite slab dating to the eighth century BC, but the story itself goes back to the Old Kingdom period of Egypt (ca. 2700–2200 BC) and describes Ptah bringing creation into being by speech.

Expanse (1:6). On the second day of creation God separates the waters by an "expanse" (*raqia*). The expanse is called the "sky"; thus the waters above the expanse are the source of rain. On day four God places the sun, moon, and stars in the expanse (1:14–19), and on the fifth day he makes the birds that fly across the expanse (1:20).

The Hebrew noun *raqia* derives from a verb that refers to hammering metal into sheets; thus most scholars believe that the ancient Hebrews thought that there was a hard dome above the earth in which the planets were set and from which the rain came. Genesis does not give us a scientific explanation of cosmology, but rather one that would have been familiar to its ancient audience.

Kinds (1:11, 12, 21, 24, 25). While the language of different kinds of creatures reminds one of the modern technical term "species," it is important to read the text in light of ancient thought, not modern science. The biblical term "kind" (*min*) is based on similar visual characteristics and is used for broad categories like birds and fish.

Let there be lights . . . they will serve as signs for seasons (1:14). In the Babylonian creation stories the sun, the moon, and the stars were gods and goddesses. In stark contrast, in the biblical account God *creates* these celestial bodies on the fourth day. They are not deities, but rather are part of the creation.

Let us (1:26). God announces his intention to create humans by stating, "Let us make man in our image." Some Christian readers suggest that "our image" is a reference to the different persons of the Trinity—Father, Son, Holy Spirit. Yet since God chose to wait until the NT time period to reveal his trinitarian nature, that would make little sense to the original author or reader. Reading this passage in its ancient Near Eastern context leads us to conclude that the reference here is to the divine council. In ancient Israel God was the divine king, and he was attended by other heavenly beings who elsewhere are called angels. Thus God here announces to his angelic servants his intention to create human beings.

Image of God (1:26–27). Through the creation story the author highlights the exalted status of human beings among God's creatures. The exact meaning of "the image of God" is uncertain, but reading the text in its ancient Near Eastern context leads us to understand the idea as similar to the way images (statues) of kings project and represent the kings' power and authority throughout their kingdoms. Support for this understanding can be seen in a ninth-century-BC Aramaic-Akkadian inscription recently discovered in Syria. Here a statue is said to be the "likeness" and "image" of the reigning king.[4] Humans are God's representatives in creation, taking on a royal status where they are to "rule the fish of the sea, the birds of the sky, and every creature that crawls on the earth" (1:28).

God blessed the seventh day and declared it holy (2:3). Nowhere else in the ancient Near East is time calculated based on a seven-day cycle with a rest day on the seventh. However, the idea of deity resting after creation is found in the Egyptian creation account on the Shabaka Stone (see comments on Gen. 1:3). God's resting shows that the work of creation is completed and now God stays involved in sustaining and maintaining his work.

The Second Creation Account (2:4–25)

These are the records of (2:4). The formula statement "these are the records of," or similarly "these are the family records of," appears eleven times in the book of Genesis (2:4; 5:1; 6:9; 10:1; 11:10, 27; 25:12, 19; 36:1, 9; 37:2) and usually is followed by a personal name, though here in its first occurrence the "records" are those of "the heavens and the earth." In all but its first appearance here, it is clear that the formula introduces the material that follows it. The "family records of person X" is really the story of that person's children. Thus the "family records of Terah" (11:27), for example, is an account of Terah's offspring, in particular Abraham (11:26–25:11). Not only do these "family records" provide a structure of the book of Genesis but also they evidence the use of earlier oral and/or written sources in the writing of the book (see comments on Gen. 5:1).

Formed the man out of the dust from the ground and breathed the breath of life into his nostrils (2:7). Genesis describes the creation of man from the dust of the ground, representing his creaturely status, and the breath of God, indicating his special relationship with the Creator. Mesopotamian accounts speak of the creator god making humans from an earthly component (clay) and a divine element (the blood of a demon god [in the Enuma Elish] or the blood of a lesser god and the spit of the gods [in the Atrahasis Epic]). The similarities and differences are striking. The picture of the creation of man from the breath of God indicates humanity's dignified status and primal innocence in comparison to the demeaning picture given in Mesopotamian tradition.

Tree of life (2:9). Trees often were symbolic of life and fertility. Since Adam and Eve are allowed to eat from every tree in the garden except for the tree of the knowledge of good and evil, it is likely that they ate from the tree of life as well (see comments on Gen. 3:22). In the Babylonian Adapa legend, Adapa is offered "food" and the "water of life," but on the advice of Ea, the god of wisdom, he refuses, thus forfeiting the possibility of eternal life.[5]

Eden . . . Pishon . . . Havilah . . . Gihon . . . Cush . . . Tigris . . . Assyria . . . Euphrates (2:10–14). Eden is the name of the land in which God places the garden where Adam and Eve live. The name Eden means "abundance" or "luxury." A river, which divides into four headwaters, provides water for the garden. Two of these rivers were well known, the Tigris and the Euphrates, and they flowed across the Mesopotamian alluvial plain (today in Iraq). The other references are puzzling. The Gihon was a small watercourse in the vicinity of Jerusalem, and the Pishon, otherwise unknown, is mentioned only here in this passage. Assyria (Heb. *ashur*; cf. NIV) is known in later times as a region in northern Mesopotamia. Throughout the rest of the

OT, Cush normally refers to the region south of Egypt (see the article "The Cushites"), but here it seems to suggest a place in Mesopotamia. Havilah's location is unknown.

To work it and watch over it (2:15). God creates humans in order to work in the garden. Contrast this to the Atrahasis Epic (see comments on Gen. 1:1), where humans were created to carry out menial work in the irrigation ditches. The Bible presents a more dignified picture of humans created in the image of God to take care of the garden as opposed to being created from the blood of a demon god and the spit of the gods to do the menial task of digging the irrigation ditches that the lesser gods refused to dig.

A helper corresponding to him (2:18). The Hebrew word translated as "helper" (*ezer*) does not denote subordination. It is used elsewhere of God, who is Israel's helper (Deut. 33:29; Ps. 33:20; 89:18). Perhaps "ally" is a better translation in this context, as both Adam and Eve worked together in the garden to tend it and guard it.

The man (2:20). The Hebrew word *adam* means "human" or "man" in the generic sense. Indeed, it is not clearly used as a personal name until 4:25. The word is also related to the word for "ground" (*adamah*), perhaps highlighting humanity's status as creature in contrast to the Creator.

God made . . . a woman (2:22). No other ancient Near Eastern creation story contains an independent account of the creation of a woman. Throughout the biblical creation accounts women as well as men are presented as the apex of God's creation.

Rebellion and Punishment (3:1–24)

The serpent (3:1). The serpent appears from nowhere and works against the purposes of God by tempting Adam and Eve to eat from the forbidden tree. Ancient Near Eastern readers would have recognized immediately that a walking serpent represented evil, since serpents, particularly walking serpents, regularly played negative roles in ancient Mesopotamian and Egyptian stories. In the Gilgamesh Epic a serpent steals the "plant of life," denying Gilgamesh the possibility of life. In the Enuma Elish (see comments on Gen. 1:1) Tiamat is pictured as a walking serpent.

He will strike your head (3:15). This reflects an ancient Near Eastern image of complete dominance and victory.

The man named his wife Eve (3:20). Eve's name is related to the Hebrew verb "to live," thus the explanation of her name is "the mother of all the living" or "kin-maker."

Take from the tree of life . . . and live forever (3:22). The tree of life (see comments on Gen. 2:9) does not produce magical fruit that if eaten one time renders someone permanently eternal. Adam and Eve have been eating from this fruit, and now their ejection from the garden will distance them from it, symbolizing the entrance of aging and death into the human condition.

Cherubim (3:24). Cherubim are powerful angelic creatures (Ezek. 1:4–21; 10:1–22) who serve as protectors of God's holiness, as indicated by their placement near the presence of God in the tabernacle (Exod. 26:1, 31) and in the temple (1 Kings 6:23–29; 7:29, 36; 8:6–7; 2 Chron. 3:14) (see comments on 1 Kings 6:23–28; Ezek. 10:1).

Winged, composite, cherubim-like creatures such as the one depicted on this ivory carving were common in the art and religion of the ancient Near East.

Cain and Abel (4:1–16)

Abel became a shepherd of flocks, but Cain worked the ground (4:2). Shepherding and farming are the first two occupations mentioned in the Bible, and since they compete for the same land, throughout history there has frequently been tension between the two. Indeed, in the Sumerian composition Dumuzid and Enkimdu they are presented as competing entities, as a shepherd and a farmer try to win the same woman.[6]

Land of Nod (4:16). Though we do not know the location of Nod, it is significant that it comes from a Hebrew verb meaning "to wander."

The Cainite Genealogy (4:17–26)

Gave birth to Enoch (4:17). Here begins the first extended genealogy in Genesis. Ancient peoples constructed and used genealogies differently than people do today. Studying biblical genealogies in the light of ancient Near Eastern genealogies shows that although they are not completely disconnected from actual history, they are constructed primarily for theological purposes. For instance, here the author wants to point out that civilization (making of cities, technology, music) has a suspect origin in the line of Cain. If

The Sumerian King List.

we compare genealogies that cover the same time period in the Bible, we see that they are fluid and can skip entire generations.

Cain . . . named the city Enoch after his son (4:17). The first cities in the ancient Near East emerge in the middle of the fourth millennium BC, long after the appearance of the first human beings. According to the Sumerian King List,[7] the first city was Eridu, a name tantalizingly similar to Cain's grandson Irad (4:18).

Lamech took two wives (4:19). Although polygamy was known throughout the ancient Near East and also in later Israel (Exod. 21:7–11), God's ideal established in Eden was monogamy (Gen. 2:20–25).

The father of all who play the lyre and the flute (4:21). The first nonbiblical evidence we have of musical instruments comes from the fourth and third millennia BC. Mesopotamian texts speak of instruments as coming from the divine realm, but here music is explained as a human development (see the article "Musical Instruments in Israel and the Ancient Near East").

The Sethite Genealogy (5:1–32)

This is the document containing the family records (5:1). Here note that the "family records" came to the author in a written form (see comments on Gen. 2:4).

In the likeness of God (5:1). See comments on Gen. 1:26–27.

He fathered a son (5:3). After the genealogy of Cain, we now have a genealogy of the third son of Adam and Eve, named Seth (4:25). (For genealogies in general, see comments on Gen. 4:17.) This genealogy has similarities with the Sumerian King List, which lists kings both before and after the flood as well as their immensely long reigns (King Alagar lives thirty-six thousand years!), making Methuselah's life of 969 years seem small. The diminishing life spans as we move from Seth to Noah intend to show the effects of sin on humanity.

The Sons of God and the Daughters of Mankind (6:1–4)

The sons of God . . . the daughters of mankind (6:2). This strange (at least to modern readers) story has challenged commentators for centuries. However, the OT "sons of God" is a phrase that points to angels (Ps. 29:1; 89:5–7). Likewise, both early Jewish interpretation (*1 Enoch* 6–36) and early Christian interpretation (2 Pet. 2:4; Jude 6) appear to have understood this passage as referring to angels cohabiting with human women. The story is an example of the type of horrible sin that led to the judgment of the coming flood.

Nephilim (6:4). The offspring of the union between the sons of God and the daughters of humans are called Nephilim. The name means "fallen ones," but we do not know the entire significance of the name. That they were "heroes of old" may signify that they inspired stories like the Gilgamesh Epic. Nephilim is the name of a warlike tribe later encountered by the Israelites in Canaan (Num. 13:33). Those Nephilim, however, were not the descendants of the Nephilim of Genesis, and probably were given the name because they were fearsome warriors.

The Flood (6:5–9:17)

Human wickedness (6:5). In the stories of Atrahasis and Gilgamesh (see comments on Gen. 6:7) the chief god decides to destroy humanity because they make too much noise. In the Bible, however, God's decision is based on humanity's moral failure.

I will wipe mankind . . . off the face of the earth (6:7). God will bring his judgment on humanity in the form of a devastating flood. Sumerian and Akkadian literature abounds with references to a flood that annihilates humanity except for a few survivors. In Sumerian literature the flood is mentioned in the Sumerian King List (see comments on Gen. 5:3) as well as the Eridu Genesis (ca. 1600 BC). Enki, the god of wisdom, tells a man named Ziusudra to build an ark before the flood. He survives and offers a sacrifice afterward. In Akkadian literature the Atrahasis Epic, whose title comes from the name of the flood hero, after describing the creation (see comments on Gen. 1:1), narrates the flood sent by the god Enlil, who is disturbed by the noise that humans were making. Enki informs his devotee Atrahasis of the coming flood, and he builds an ark and survives the flood.

The most detailed flood story is found at the conclusion of the Gilgamesh Epic. In his search for long life, Gilgamesh goes to Utnapishtim to find out why he was the only human to be given eternal life. Utnapishtim replies by telling Gilgamesh the story of the flood, whose details often are very similar

Mount Ararat, the area where Noah's ark came to rest (Gen. 8:4).

to the biblical flood story. The similarities and differences will be cited in the notes that follow.

An ark (6:14). Noah, his family, and the animals survive the flood by riding it out in a large boat known as an ark. The flood stories of Mesopotamia (see comments on Gen. 6:7) also feature arks on which the hero, animals, and various others survive the devastating flood. The biblical ark is a huge (450 feet long, 75 feet wide, 45 feet high) wooden ship by ancient and even modern standards, but it is boatlike in its dimensions. Most scholars understand the description of the ark in the Gilgamesh Epic as a cube (which would not be seaworthy), although some today would interpret the measurements as picturing a rounded boat like a coracle.[8]

I will establish my covenant with you (6:18). For the first time, the Bible speaks of a covenant, in this case a covenant between God and Noah. Studies in the mid-twentieth century demonstrated that the biblical covenant is similar to ancient Near Eastern treaties between a great king and a vassal king. We have two collections of such treaties from the Hittites (mid-second millennium BC) and the Assyrians (seventh century BC).

On the mountains of Ararat (8:4). Mount Ararat (known today as Agri Dagh), located at the border of Turkey and Iran near Lake Van in Kurdistan, is seventeen thousand feet high and is the tallest mountain in the region. In the Gilgamesh Epic the ark also ends its journey lodged on a high mountain, Mount Nisir.

Raven . . . dove . . . dove (8:6–12). In order to check how far the waters had receded, Noah sent out a series of three birds. In what is perhaps the most striking similarity with the Gilgamesh Epic, Utnapishtim tells Gilgamesh how he sent out birds for the same purpose, except that he did so in reverse order (dove, dove, raven).

Built an altar . . . and offered burnt offerings (8:20). Altars, places of sacrifice, have been found throughout the ancient Near East. Interestingly, Utnapishtim's first act after disembarking was to offer sacrifices. Since in ancient Mesopotamia the gods were dependent on the sacrifices of their adherents for food, the story presents an uncomplimentary portrayal of the gods as they gathered "like flies" around Utnapishtim's offering.

God made humans in his image (9:6). See comments on Gen. 1:26–27.

I am establishing my covenant with you (9:9). See comments on Gen. 6:18.

The Drunkenness of Noah (9:18–28)

Saw his father naked (9:22–23). The culprit of this story is Ham, Noah's son, who sees his father in a helpless state and yet does nothing to help him.

Ancient Egyptians picking grapes and making wine (from the tomb of Nakht).

Shem and Japheth, on the other hand, act as good sons toward their father. The Ugaritic Aqhat text alerts the modern reader to the ancient context by describing the ideal son as one who takes "his (father's) hand when (he is) drunk, to bear him up [when] (he is) full of wine."[9]

From the Sons of Noah to Abram (10:1–11:26)

These are the family records (10:1). See comments on Gen. 2:4.

They also had sons (10:1). See comments on Gen. 4:17.

Each with its own language (10:5). This genealogy reads like an ancient political and linguistic map. Genealogies in the ancient Near East sometimes used the language of kinship to reflect political and, in this case, linguistic relationships. The relationship between languages as expressed in Gen. 10 does not reflect modern understanding, but rather is based on phenomenological connections. An explanation of the variation of languages among humans comes after this map that presumes multiple languages in the episode of the tower of Babel (11:1–9).

Nimrod (10:8). Nimrod, whose name may be connected to the Hebrew word for "rebellion," is associated first with southern Mesopotamian cities (Babylon, Uruk, Akkad, and Kalneh) and is said to have established northern Mesopotamian cities (Nineveh, Rehoboth Ir, Calah, and Resen). There have been attempts to identify Nimrod with specific Mesopotamian rulers (Sargon the Great, Shulgi, or Hammurabi), but it is more likely that he is a type that represents several such rulers rather than a specific individual.

Shinar (10:10). Another name for Mesopotamia, the region between the Tigris and the Euphrates in the location now occupied by Iraq.

By their clans, according to their languages (10:20, 31). See comments on Gen. 10:5.

The same language and vocabulary (11:1). The story looks back to a time before the situation described in Gen. 10, since the earlier chapter names many different languages. Human rebellion will lead to difficulty in

A partially reconstructed ziggurat at Ur.

human communication. While some scholars point to the Sumerian myth of Enmerkar and the Lord of Aratta as comparable with its description of a time when there was "but a single tongue," it is not certain whether this myth describes the distant past or the future.

Shinar (11:2). See comments on Gen. 10:10.

Brick for stone and asphalt for mortar (11:3). Mud-brick with asphaltic tar, rather than stone and mortar, were the regular building materials of ancient Mesopotamia.

A city and a tower with its top in the sky (11:4). God had scattered rebellious humans not only as punishment but also for their own good. When wicked people gather together, their wickedness only increases. The description of this tower suggests that they were building a ziggurat, a stepped pyramid. Ziggurats were built in cities and were thought to connect heaven and earth. Indeed, the ziggurat built in the city of Babylon, perhaps the one in mind in this story, had the name *E-temen-an-ki*, meaning the "house of the foundation of heaven and earth." Building such a structure would have been seen as an attack on heaven itself.

Therefore it is called Babylon (11:9). The narrator derives a negative etymology for the city of Babylon. In Akkadian, the language of the Babylonians, the name means "gate of the gods" (*bab ili*), but here the name is connected to the Hebrew verb *balal*, which means "to confuse."

These are the family records (11:10). See comments on Gen. 2:4.

He fathered (11:10–26). See comments on Gen. 4:17.

God's Promises to Abraham (11:27–12:9)

These are the family records (11:27). See comments on Gen. 2:4.

Ur of the Chaldeans (11:28). Ur was an ancient city dating back to the early fourth millennium BC, located in southern Mesopotamia near the place where the Euphrates River flows into the Persian Gulf. The time of Abraham cannot be precisely dated, but likely is in the first quarter of the second millennium BC. The reference to the Chaldeans clarifies for a later audience that the reference is to the Ur in Mesopotamia and not another Ur somewhere else. Since the Chaldeans were an Aramaic-speaking tribe that occupied southern Mesopotamia centuries after Abraham and even

after Moses, this reference is often seen as a later addition (a so-called post-Mosaica), updating the name of the region for later audiences.

Sarai was unable to conceive (11:30). To be without child in the ancient Near East was devastating because a couple would have no one to care for them in their old age. The childlessness of Abraham and Sarah will be a particularly difficult issue for them, especially in light of the divine promises in 12:1–3.

Terah . . . died in Haran (11:32). Haran was located in what is today southeastern Turkey near Syria, about sixty miles north of where the Euphrates River and Balikh River meet. It was known as a center for the worship of the moon, which is significant because Terah's name means "moon," and he was known as a pagan (Josh. 24:2).

The oak of Moreh (12:6). Moreh was near the well-known city of Shechem in the hill country about forty miles north of Jerusalem. Tell Balata between Mount Ebal and Mount Gerizim has been identified as the ruins of the ancient city of Shechem. The mention of the tree is probably not an accidental feature of the narrative. The association of a tree with the place where God makes his presence known to his human creatures likely intends to remind people of the garden of Eden.

Altar (12:7–8). See comments on Gen. 8:20.

With Bethel on the west and Ai on the east (12:8). Bethel was also in the central hill country south of Shechem (about ten miles north of Jerusalem). Bethel (modern Beitin) was strategically situated at the juncture of the main north-south road as well as an important road that ran west from Jericho. Ai (Et-Tell) was located east of Bethel a few miles away.

Journeyed by stages to the Negev (12:9). The Negev was a region south of Judah that stretched to the Gulf of Aqaba. Its name means "the south," and it was a very dry area.

Famine in the Land (12:10–20)

Abram went down to Egypt (12:10). As we learn later from the Joseph story (Gen. 37–50), as well as from ancient documents such as the Egyptian Papyrus Anastasi VI and ancient paintings on Egyptian tombs, it was not unusual for Semitic people like Abraham to seek refuge in Egypt during times of crisis such as a famine.

Abraham and Lot Part Ways (13:1–18)

To the Negev (13:1). See comments on Gen. 12:9.

Between Bethel and Ai (13:3). See comments on Gen. 12:8.

The entire plain of the Jordan as far as Zoar was well watered (13:10). Lot sets his eyes on the luxurious region around the Jordan River with special focus on the region around the Dead Sea. The description of the region

The Dead Sea.

as being like the Lord's garden (see comments on Gen. 2:10–14) and like Egypt (with the Nile and extensive irrigation) provides quite a contrast with the area after God's judgment (Gen. 18–19). Sodom and Gomorrah and the lesser-known site of Zoar were in this region, though today we do not know their precise location.

The oaks of Mamre at Hebron (13:18). Mamre is the name of a location near the important town of Hebron, which was eighteen miles south (and a little east) of Jerusalem in the central hill country (identified with Tell Hebron [Jebel er-Rumeidah]) (see comments on Gen. 12:6).

The Four Kings of the East (14:1–24)

King Amraphel of Shinar, King Arioch of Ellasar, King Chedorlaomer of Elam, and King Tidal of Goiim (14:1). Four kings come from the east in order to plunder Canaan. Their identity is difficult to pin down precisely, but some things are certain. Shinar is Mesopotamia, specifically Babylon (see comments on Gen. 10:8). Elam is the name of an ancient nation-state that was located in what is today southwestern Iran, and *goyim* (Goiim) is a Hebrew term that means "nations," often used for non-Semites (here perhaps the Hittites or the Umman-manda). Chedorlaomer is an authentic-sounding Elamite royal name. Ellasar is the most difficult place to identify, but may be a reference to the city-state Larsa in southern Mesopotamia. In spite of great effort the identity of these specific kings has not been determined, although such a coalition was most likely to have occurred before the Old Babylonian period (so before the eighteenth century BC), which was around the time the Bible places Abraham.

King Bera of Sodom . . . King Shemeber of Zeboiim, as well as the king of Bela (14:2). For Sodom and Gomorrah, see comments on Gen. 13:10. The other sites and kings are not known outside of this story.

The Rephaim . . . the Zuzim . . . the Emim . . . the Horites . . . the Amalekites . . . the Amorites (14:5–7). The invading kings defeat a number of tribes listed with their locations. The Rephaim, located in a city in Gilead (Ashteroth Karnaim), are also known as Anakim, a giant tribe (Num. 13:33; Deut. 2:11; 3:11; Josh. 12:4). The Zuzim, or Zamzummim (Deut. 2:20), and Emim (Deut. 2:10–11) were also known for their height. The former lived in Ham (sometimes a reference to Egypt, but here an unknown location in Canaan), and the latter in Shaveh ("plain of") Kiriathaim, located on the east side of the Jordan River. The Horites (also known as Hurrians) lived in the hill country of Seir (south of the Dead Sea) to El Paran (probably Elath on the northern shore of the Red/Reed Sea). En Mishpat was an early name of Kadesh, short for Kadesh Barnea, a location in the northern

An ancient mud-brick gate at Dan (Laish) that dates back near to the time of Abraham.

Sinai Peninsula. The Amalekites were fearsome warriors who lived in the Negev (see comments on Gen. 12:9). Amorite is often used as another term for Canaanite.

The Siddim Valley (14:8). This area, the northern shore of the Dead Sea (cf. 14:3), was about an eighteen-mile walk east of Jerusalem.

The oaks belonging to Mamre (14:13). See comments on Gen. 13:18.

As far as Dan (14:14). Dan refers to a town to the far north of future Israel. Since the town did not receive this name until the period of the Judges (Judg. 18), referring to the city this way shows clear signs of updating after the death of Moses. The ancient city was called Laish.

As far as Hobah to the north of Damascus (14:15). Damascus was a major ancient city (and is the modern capital) of Syria, located fifty miles from the Mediterranean, northeast of Mount Hermon, the northernmost point of the future land of Israel. Hobah is otherwise unknown.

The Shaveh Valley (that is, the King's Valley) (14:17). The reference to the King's Valley in 2 Sam. 18:18 suggests that this valley was south of Jerusalem.

Melchizedek, king of Salem (14:18). Surprisingly, Abraham recognizes that Melchizedek (whose name means "king of righteousness"), the Canaanite priest-king of Salem (the ancient name of Jerusalem), shares his belief in the same God.

Reaffirming the Promises (15:1–21)

The heir of my house Eliezer of Damascus (15:2). Tablets found at the city of Nuzi (in modern Iraq) explain the ancient custom in which a childless couple could adopt a household servant who would take care of them in their old age in return for inheriting their property. In this way, Abraham uses human conventions to manufacture an heir rather than waiting for God to act.

Ur of the Chaldeans (15:7). See comments on Gen. 11:28.

Bring me a three-year-old cow (15:9–21). In order to assure Abraham that he would fulfill his promise of descendants, God tells him to cut a number of animals into two parts and line them up. Then God, in the form of a "smoking firepot with a blazing torch" (15:17), passes through the divided parts. We learn about this ritual from texts found at ancient Alalakh, Mari, and Hatti. By passing through the parts, God is taking on a self-curse: "If I break my promise, may I become like these animals." In the ancient Near Eastern texts, two people who make an agreement pass through the parts assuring each other that they will not break their promise to each other on pain of death. Here it is only God who passes through the parts. Of course, God cannot die, but neither can he break his promises.

Made a covenant with Abram (15:18). See comments on Gen. 6:18. The heart of the content of the covenant here reaffirmed is found in 12:1–3, where God promises that Abram's descendants would be a great nation that God would bless and that through them God would bless the nations.

From the brook of Egypt to the great river, the Euphrates River (15:18). For the first time, the extent of the promised land is described. The Euphrates was the major river that flowed out of Armenia through Syria and then across Mesopotamia into the Persian Gulf. Certainly the northern reaches of the Euphrates were in mind here. The Wadi ("brook") of Egypt probably was in northeastern Sinai.

The land of the Kenites . . . Jebusites (15:19–21). The inhabitants of the promised land are listed as ten tribes, though we cannot be sure in every case precisely where they were located within Canaan.

Abraham Takes a Concubine (16:1–16)

Perhaps through her I can build a family (16:2). In the previous chapter Abram thought to manufacture an heir through adopting his household servant (see comments on Gen. 15:2). God had reassured him of his intention to provide an heir through natural means, but now Abram agrees to follow Sarai's instructions to produce an heir by utilizing yet another ancient Near Eastern custom: taking a secondary wife (a concubine). Marriage contracts from Nuzi and the Neo-Assyrian period contain provisions that the man will not take a secondary wife unless the first wife cannot produce children.

The way to Shur (16:7). This is the southernmost route to Egypt from Canaan. Shur is Hebrew for "wall" and may refer to a wall erected by the Egyptians or a wall-like limestone ridge near Gebel Halal and Gebel Maghara.

The well is called Beer-lahai-roi . . . between Kadesh and Bered (16:14). The well, whose name means "the well of the Living One who sees me," was located in the Negev, the arid area south of Judah (see comments on Gen. 14:5–7).

Reaffirming the Promises (17:1–27)

I will set up my covenant between me and you (17:2). See comments on Gen. 6:18; 15:18.

Abram . . . Abraham (17:5). Abram is Hebrew for "exalted father," while Abraham means "father of a multitude," appropriate for the one who will be "the father of many nations" (17:4).

Must be circumcised (17:10). There is evidence that circumcision was practiced by a number of nations (Jer. 9:25–26) and by the Syrians and the Egyptians even before the time of Abraham. Thus God does not introduce a new practice into the world, but he gives it a new significance. As a sign of the Abrahamic covenant, it serves as a reminder of God's promises and his people's obligations. Since the promises center on descendants, it is appropriate that the sign of this covenant is associated with the male reproductive organ.

Sarai . . . Sarah (17:15). Abraham's wife also has her name changed, but it is a subtle change. Both Sarai and Sarah mean "princess," but the former is how the word is pronounced in Mesopotamia and the latter how it is pronounced in the promised land. Perhaps the name change is related to the move from Mesopotamia to their new home in Canaan.

Sodom and Gomorrah (18:1–19:38)

The oaks of Mamre (18:1). See comments on Gen. 13:18.

Let a little water be brought (18:3–8). In the ancient Near East the quality of hospitality offered to a stranger indicated the quality of one's character. In this section Abraham displays impeccable hospitality toward his visitors, providing water so they could wash their feet (dusty from the trail) and providing a bounteous meal ("three measures" of grain would be thirty-six pounds!).

Sodom (18:16). See comments on Gen. 13:10.

Sodom's gateway (19:1). The gate of an ancient city was a public area where leaders met. Lot's presence at the gate may indicate that he is a leader in the city of Sodom.

Wash your feet (19:2). Lot too shows hospitality to strangers (see comments on Gen. 18:3–8). Though Abraham is portrayed as a more enthusiastic host, Lot's actions differentiate him from the other inhabitants of the city.

So we can have sex with them (19:5). Their desire for sex with the men does not necessarily mean that they are homosexual. In the ancient Near East the act of men forcing themselves on other men was thought to be a sign of power that shames those who are forcibly violated.

I'll bring them out to you (19:8). Lot's offer to give the men of Sodom his two daughters in place of the visiting strangers is a perversion of the ancient Near Eastern practice of hospitality. His suggestion shows that he has been changed in a negative way by living in such a corrupt town.

Zoar (19:22). We do not know the exact location of Zoar (see comments on Gen. 13:10), but the town's name is appropriately "Small."

Named him Moab . . . named him Ben-ammi. He is the father of the Ammonites (19:37–38). Ammon and Moab both later became enemies of Israel. Moab was directly east of Israel, on the eastern shores of the Dead Sea; Ammon was north of Moab, to the east of the Jordan River and extending to the desert on its eastern boundary. By highlighting the dubious origins of the men who founded those nations, the book of Genesis casts aspersions on those future enemies.

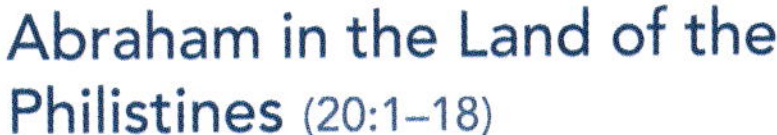

Abraham in the Land of the Philistines (20:1–18)

Negev . . . between Kadesh and Shur (20:1). See comments on Gen. 12:9; 14:5–7; 16:7.

Abimelech of Gerar (20:2). Gerar, a Philistine city (21:32, 34), was located between Beer-sheba, a city in the Negev, and Gaza, a city in southern Canaan on the Mediterranean coast. The origin of the Philistines, especially these early examples in biblical history, is difficult to ascertain, but it is thought that they originated in the area of the Aegean Sea (see the article "The Philistines"). The name Abimelech ("my father is king") may be a throne name (see comments on Gen. 26:1).

Enormous guilt (20:9). The term "enormous guilt" may be specific to the crime of adultery. An Ugaritic text accuses the wife of King Ammishtamru of committing the "great sin" of adultery. This language is also found in Egyptian marriage contracts.

One thousand pieces of silver (20:16). This amounted to twenty-five pounds of silver.

The Promised Birth (21:1–7)

Abraham circumcised him (21:4). See comments on Gen. 17:10.

This ancient well stands next to the archaeological site of Beer-sheba, which was named for the oath that Abraham made there (Gen. 21:31).

Hagar Sent Away (21:8–21)

Abraham held a great feast on the day Isaac was weaned (21:8). This probably occurs around Isaac's third year. Due to the high infant mortality rate, his reaching this age is a cause for celebration.

Abraham . . . sent her and the boy away (21:14). The Hebrew word used here (*shalah*) implies that this was a divorce (cf. Deut. 22:19, 29; 24:1, 3; Jer. 3:1; Mal. 2:16).

The Wilderness of Beer-sheba (21:14). The city of Beer-sheba was in the far south of Canaan, surrounded by areas that experienced little rainfall.

The Wilderness of Paran (21:21). The Desert of Paran was in the Negev to the south of Beer-sheba, not too far north of the Sinai Peninsula, thus on the way to Egypt.

Abraham and Abimelech (21:22–33)

Swear to me by God here and now (21:23). Abimelech, the king of the Philistine city of Gerar (see comments on Gen. 20:2), asks Abraham to enter into a formal treaty with him. There are about forty treaties preserved from the ancient Near East. Most of these are Hittite treaties (written in Akkadian) from the mid-second millennium BC, while some are from the Neo-Assyrian period (also written in Akkadian) from the seventh century BC. These are political arrangements between two nations in which the two parties agreed to certain regulations between them.

Because of the well (21:25). Water was a scarce commodity in most of the ancient Near East. The negotiations between Abimelech and Abraham here have analogies in the discussion over water rights that occurs in the correspondence between King Rim-Sin of Larsa and the king of a city named Eshnunna from the Old Babylonian period in the eighteenth century BC.

As my witness (21:30). As a legal agreement, a treaty (see comments on Gen. 21:23) required witnesses to serve as third-party reminders of the arrangement.

That place was called Beer-sheba (21:31). The name Beer-sheba (see comments on Gen. 21:14) is explained as a Hebrew phrase that means "well of the oath," though it can also mean "well of seven" or "seven wells."

A tamarisk tree . . . and there he called on the name of the LORD (21:33). See comments on Gen. 2:9; 12:6; 13:18.

The Binding of Isaac (22:1–19)

The land of Moriah (22:2). Moriah is mentioned only here and in 2 Chron. 3:1, where it is named as the site of Solomon's temple. Thus the location was near or in Jerusalem, and it may have been another name for Zion or perhaps the name of the mountain range on which Zion was a peak.

Offer him there as a burnt offering (22:2). On child sacrifice, see comments on 2 Kings 3:27.

Abraham built the altar (22:9). See comments on Gen. 8:20.

Beer-sheba (22:19). See comments on Gen. 21:14.

The Death and Burial of Sarah (22:20–23:20)

Milcah also has borne sons (22:20). This genealogy (see comments on Gen. 4:17) presents Abraham's eastern relatives who live in Paddan-aram, or northwest Mesopotamia (see comments on Gen. 25:20), as a way of introducing Rebekah, who will marry Isaac.

Kemuel the father of Aram (22:21). Kemuel, elsewhere called Bethuel the Aramean (25:20; 28:5), is called the father of Aram, a group of Semitic tribes located in northwest Mesopotamia and into Syria that will have frequent interaction with later Israel.

His concubine (22:24). See comments on Gen. 16:2.

Kiriath-arba (that is, Hebron) (23:2). Hebron was the later name of this city, located in the Judean highlands about eighteen miles south-southwest of Jerusalem.

The arid area known as the Negev, south of Beer-sheba.

The Hethites (23:3). The Hethites were an indigenous Canaanite tribal group (15:18–21; Exod. 3:8) whom God would later drive out of the land (Exod. 23:28). Israel was to totally destroy them (Deut. 7:1–2; 20:17). They are not to be confused with the Hittites, the better-known Indo-European inhabitants of Anatolia, well to the north, from 1800 to 1200 BC.

The cave of Machpelah (23:9). Caves often were used as burial sites. This cave was located near Mamre, which is near Hebron (13:18; 23:19). Caves were used not just for individual burials but also for family burials over the generations (49:31).

I give you the field (23:11). Ephron the Hethite and Abraham barter for the burial site in a manner typical of ancient Near Eastern practices. Abraham would have been expected to counteroffer with a price. In any case, it was important that he clearly own this land, which is the first piece of the promised land that comes into his actual possession.

Four hundred standard shekels (23:16). While we cannot be certain about the exact value at this time, four hundred shekels would be equivalent to over seven pounds of silver. Ephron cites this figure earlier as the amount the land was worth (23:15).

Marriage Negotiations (24:1–67)

Aram-naharaim . . . Nahor's town (24:10). Aram-naharaim referred to northwest Mesopotamia, the transitional area between Mesopotamia proper and Syria. Nahor was a city named after Abraham's brother (11:27).

Beside a well outside the town (24:11). The well was a shared water source and a public place in a community like this one. It is interesting that there are a number of occasions where marriages begin with meetings at a public well (29:1–14; Exod. 2:15–25). In this story Abraham's senior servant is a surrogate for Isaac.

Let the girl to whom I say (24:14). Abraham's servant sets up what might be called a "word oracle," a feature seen elsewhere in the Bible as well as in the literature of the ancient Near East. It is similar to posing a question and then casting lots (see comments on 1 Sam. 14:41–42). The servant is asking God to guide his decisions based on the response that he will receive from a young woman. The word oracle also serves as a gauge of her character.

A gold ring . . . two bracelets weighing ten shekels of gold (24:22). Marriages at this time in the ancient Near East involved an exchange of gifts between the two families involved.

Gold bracelets from ancient Egypt.

The nose ring, weighing about one-fifth of an ounce, and the two gold bracelets, weighing about four ounces, likely functioned as a down payment on the marriage price, the price that a groom would pay his future bride.

A place to spend the night (24:25). In the ancient Near East hospitality was essential and customary, and Rebekah shows herself to be an exemplary host to this out-of-town visitor.

He also gave precious gifts to her brother and her mother (24:53). See comments on Gen. 24:22.

Beer-lahai-roi, for he was living in the Negev (24:62). See comments on Gen. 16:14.

The Death of Abraham (25:1–11)

Another wife, whose name was Keturah (25:1). Abraham had another wife—actually a concubine (see comments on Gen. 16:2)—Keturah, to whom we are introduced at the end of the account of Abraham's life, though he must have been married to her for some time to produce so many children. These children are the ancestors of many future nations, thus showing that Abraham truly was "the father of many nations" (17:4).

Abraham gave everything he owned to Isaac (25:5). Isaac, as the first and only-born son to Abraham and his primary wife, Sarah, receives the inheritance from his father.

Gathered to his people (25:8). When Abraham dies, his body is placed in the cave where Sarah had been buried (25:9). Thus in a literal sense, as his bones are placed in the cave, he is gathered to his people.

The cave of Machpelah near Mamre (25:9). See comments on Gen. 23:9.

Beer-lahai-roi (25:11). See comments on Gen. 16:14.

The Account of Isaac's Family (25:12–18)

These are the family records of Abraham's son Ishmael (25:12). See comments on Gen. 2:4. Interestingly, a brief family record of the nonchosen son, Ishmael, is given before the longer family record of Isaac. The nonelect son is not ignored, but neither is he the one through whom the covenant promises will pass down through history.

From Havilah to Shur, which is opposite Egypt as you go toward Asshur (25:18). This was a large region, as would be appropriate for the nomadic Ishmaelite tribes. Havilah here may refer to the Arabian Peninsula, while Shur was connected to the Sinai Peninsula. Asshur was in northern Mesopotamia.

The Birth of Jacob and Esau (25:19–34)

These are the family records of Isaac son of Abraham (25:19). See comments on Gen. 2:4.

The Aramean from Paddan-aram (25:20). Like Aram-naharaim (24:10), Paddan-aram referred to northwest Mesopotamia, a transitional zone between Mesopotamia proper and Syria-Palestine. This was the ancestral homeland of Abraham's family, who came from Aramaic stock (22:21). The Arameans were closely related to the later Hebrew tribes.

They named him Esau . . . he was named Jacob (25:25–26). Esau means "hairy," and Jacob can mean both "he grasps the heel" and "he deceives," both of which are appropriate for his actions in the story.

He was also named Edom (25:30). Edom means "red," and Esau/Edom was the father of the Edomites, a later people who were often in conflict with Israel (Num. 20:14–21; 2 Sam. 8:14; 2 Kings 8:20). Edom was located to the southeast of the Dead Sea below Moab.

Sell me your birthright (25:31). Esau is born first and thus is due the largest share of his father's future inheritance. Jacob demands that Esau sell him his birthright for a bowl of stew. The fact that Esau is willing to do so shows that he lightly esteems his birthright. However, there is no reason to think that the sale would be considered binding in any formal, legal sense.

Famine in the Land—Again (26:1–35)

There was another famine in the land (26:1). See comments on Gen. 12:10.

Abimelech, king of the Philistines, at Gerar (26:1). See comments on Gen. 20:2. Since Abimelech ("my father is king") may be a throne name, this Abimelech may be a successor/son of the Abimelech from the time of Abraham (Gen. 20–21).

Brought guilt on us (26:10). See comments on Gen. 20:9.

The wells (26:15). See comments on Gen. 21:25.

Esek . . . Sitnah . . . Rehoboth (26:20–22). Water rights (see comments on Gen. 21:25) often were the occasion of arguments in areas that had little rainfall. Isaac's servants dig new wells. The Philistine herders fight over the rights of the first two wells, whose names mean "dispute" and "opposition." The third well must have provided enough water for everyone, so they name it "room."

Beer-sheba (26:23). See comments on Gen. 21:14.

Altar (26:25). See comments on Gen. 8:20.

Let us make a covenant with you (26:28). See comments on Gen. 21:23.

Prepared a banquet for them (26:30). The formation of a treaty between two political groups often was sealed by a shared feast. The act of eating a meal together recognized the formal relationship between the two groups.

Sheba (26:33). Sheba can mean "seven" or "oath." Either would be relevant to the context. The well also gave its name to the town of Beer-sheba, which can mean "the well of seven" or "the well of the oath."

Hethite (26:34). See comments on Gen. 23:3.

Jacob Deceives Isaac and Receives the Blessing (27:1–28:9)

I can bless you (27:4). Isaac, the patriarch of the family, now announces his intention to confer his blessing on Esau, the older son. It was typical in the ancient Near East that the oldest son received the lion's share of the inheritance. In this particular family, inheritance is bound up with the promises given to Abraham (12:1–3). The issue here is who will carry forward the promises of the covenant that includes land, many descendants, and blessing into the next generation. The blessing determines who would be the one to administrate the family's wealth in the next generation. It is also an announcement of one's future destiny. That Isaac is going to confer this blessing on Esau and not Jacob shows that Esau's earlier sale of his birthright has no legal standing with Isaac (see comments on Gen. 25:31).

Bless me too, my father! (27:34). The blessing is not magical, but has behind it the weight of patriarchal authority. Once announced, it could not be taken back or reversed.

He took my birthright (27:36). See comments on Gen. 25:31.

These Hethite girls (27:46). See comments on Gen. 23:3.

A Canaanite girl (28:1). Canaanite is a general term for the pre-Israelite inhabitants of the promised land.

Paddan-aram (28:2). See comments on Gen. 25:20.

The Aramean (28:5). See comments on Gen. 22:21.

A stepped pyramid from ancient Egypt.

A Stairway to Heaven (28:10–22)

Beer-sheba . . . Haran (28:10). See comments on Gen. 11:32; 21:14.

A stairway . . . with its top reaching the sky (28:12). Jacob sees a portal connecting earth and heaven with angels coming to earth to perform tasks for God and then returning to heaven. This is a stairway, not a ladder. The idea was similar to a Mesopotamian ziggurat, or stepped pyramid, which was thought to be the stairway used by the gods to descend to earth.

The house of God . . . the gate of heaven (28:17). The language again (see comments on Gen. 28:12) suggests that Jacob sees a portal between heaven and earth as a stairway between the two. "House of God" is language denoting a temple. Often temples were built at such holy places. A gate was an entrance to and from a place, and thus the phrase "gate of heaven" is appropriate for this location.

Jacob took the stone . . . and set it up as a marker. He poured oil on top of it (28:18). Such "standing stones" marked sacred places where God would make his presence known. Standing stones that have survived from antiquity may still be observed in Israel today. The pouring of oil on the stone was a form of consecration.

Bethel . . . Luz (28:19). Luz was the name of the town up to this moment, but due to Jacob's experience of God's presence, the town is renamed Bethel, "the house of God" (see comments on Gen. 28:17).

Jacob, His Wives, and Their Children (29:1–30:24)

The eastern country (29:1). This was another way to refer to Paddan-aram (25:20) or Aram-naharaim (24:10). Located in northwest Mesopotamia, this region was northeast from the promised land.

He looked and saw a well (29:2). See comments on Gen. 24:11.

We can't (29:8). The shepherds tell Jacob that they cannot roll away the stone from the well until all the flocks have gathered. Their unwillingness is likely the result of an agreement of the type that was common for water rights in the ancient Near Eastern world among different shepherds to assure equal distribution of water from the well. Jacob probably would not have been bound by such an agreement.

I'll work for you seven years (29:18). In the ancient Near East the groom and his family would pay the bride's family a sum as a bride-price. Jacob brought no wealth with him, so he works off his debt to Laban's family in this way.

This week of wedding celebration (29:27). Marriages were consummated on the first night, but the celebrations could last a week.

She named him (29:32). Naming had great significance in the ancient Near East and often had to do with the circumstances surrounding the birth, but also sometimes portended the future in some way. Beginning with Reuben, the significance of the names of the children born to Jacob, his wives, and his concubines is explained as the story unfolds in the following verses.

She was not bearing Jacob any children (30:1). Barrenness was not only disappointing but also threatening to the well-being of a woman. If she had no children, her husband might lose interest in her, and in any case she would have no one to protect and take care of her when she grew old.

Some mandrakes in the field (30:14). Mandrakes were thought to be an aphrodisiac that also helped women to conceive children. The word for "mandrake" in Hebrew also sounds similar to the word that refers to physical love or lover (see comments on Song 7:13).

A model of a liver, used for divination.

Jacob Returns to the Promised Land (30:25–31:55)

I have learned by divination (30:27). Divination refers to ritual actions by which human beings try to answer a question, find guidance, or determine the future. In the ancient Near East divination took many different forms, including astrology, dream interpretation, haruspicy (reading a sheep's liver), casting lots, and more. We do not know what type of divination Laban uses to learn about the blessing of Jacob's presence, but we do know that later OT texts strongly prohibit such practices (Deut. 18:9–13).

Jacob then took branches of fresh poplar, almond, and plane wood (30:37). It is not clear why two white lambs or goats would produce offspring with speckles, stripes, or dark color simply because they mated in front of Jacob's branches. There is no ancient Near Eastern background or any scientific reason for this outcome. The presumption is simply that God worked it out so that Jacob could finally get paid for his work for Laban.

The God of Bethel, where you poured oil on the stone marker (31:13). See comments on Gen. 28:18.

Her father's household idols (31:19). These household gods (*teraphim*) likely were figurines representing Laban's departed ancestors. They would be venerated as part of ancestor worship. Based on some texts from the ancient site of Nuzi, it can be inferred that the possession of household gods may also be connected to inheritance rights,

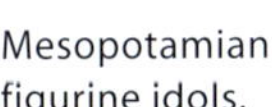

Mesopotamian figurine idols.

The Jabbok River. Jacob wrestled with an angel of God near this river (Gen. 32:22–37).

since typically they were passed down to the main heir.

Let's make a covenant (31:44). Jacob and Laban then establish a covenant (i.e., a treaty) between them (see comments on Gen. 6:18; 21:23). Jacob is the patriarch of the later Israelites and Laban of the Arameans.

Jacob picked out a stone and set it up as a marker (31:45–47). Jacob sets up a pillar and then tells his relatives to pile up a heap of stones (on such pillars or standing stones, see comments on Gen. 28:18). The names given to the heap (Jegar Sahadutha and Galeed) both mean "witness heap." Treaties needed witnesses to affirm that a formal, legal agreement had been established. The witnesses would then also serve as accusers if one of the parties broke the agreement. The pillar/standing stones functioned like such a witness.

A meal (31:54). See comments on Gen. 26:30.

Jacob Threatened by God and Humans (32:1–33:20)

Mahanaim (32:2). Mahanaim means "two camps," and in 32:2 presumably the two camps are that of Jacob's family's and the "camp of God," though in 32:10 Jacob will refer to his own group as "two camps." Later Mahanaim referred to a Levitical city located on the border of Gad and Manasseh (Josh. 13:26, 30; 21:38), and it played an important role in later Israelite history (2 Sam. 2:8, 12, 29; 17:24, 27; 19:32).

Seir, the territory of Edom (32:3). Edom was another name for Esau and referred to the region southeast of the Dead Sea just south of Moab (25:30). Seir means "hairy," a term also associated with Esau (25:25). Here Seir may be another name for Edom, or it could refer to a place within Edom.

The ford of Jabbok (32:22). Jabbok was a river that flowed into the Jordan River from the east about twenty miles north of the Dead Sea. In Hebrew the river's name was *yabboq*, perhaps a wordplay with Jacob's name (*yaaqob*) and the verb "wrestled" (*yeabeq*).

Peniel (32:30). Due to his encounter with God, Jacob names the place Peniel, meaning "the face of God." Peniel was located on the Jabbok River (32:22).

The thigh muscle that is at the hip socket (32:32). The custom of not eating the tendon of the socket of the hip is not mentioned elsewhere in

Scripture, but the explanation for it is provided: God had touched Jacob's hip and thus rendered that joint sacred.

Bowed to the ground seven times (33:3). Seven was a number of completion or totality, and to bow seven times would be to show utter respect and subordination. An interesting parallel to Jacob's action can be seen in the opening phrases of the letters that the subordinate leaders of various Canaanite cities sent to the Egyptian pharaoh during the Amarna period, which state, "At the feet of the king, my lord, and my Sun-god, seven times and seven times I fall."[10]

He accepted (33:11). At first Esau refuses Jacob's offer of a gift, but later he accepts it. Such give-and-take was typical of ancient, as well as modern, Near Eastern bartering. It is likely that Jacob and Esau both knew that Esau would eventually accept this gift (see comments on Gen. 23:11).

Seir (33:16). See comments on Gen. 32:3.

Succoth (33:17). Rather than going to Seir as he told Esau, Jacob sets up a camp at Succoth, located near where the Jabbok and Jordan came together (see comments on Gen. 32:22). The name Succoth means "shelters," after the shelters Jacob constructed for his family and their animals. Succoth is mentioned later in Scripture (Josh. 13:27; Judg. 8:5–9, 13–17).

Paddan-aram . . . Shechem (33:18). Jacob settles outside the city because he is a shepherd and needs rooms for his flocks. Shechem, a well-known and bustling city in the time of the patriarchs, has been identified with Tell Balata, and was located in a valley between Mount Gerizim and Mount Ebal, on the central hill road a little over sixty miles north of Jerusalem.

A hundred pieces of silver (33:19). Jacob bought land from the local inhabitants, the second parcel of real estate purchased by Abraham and his descendants (23:16), for one hundred *qesitah*. Since we do not know the exact value of a *qesitah*, many English translations translate it vaguely as "pieces" of silver.

Jacob in Shechem (34:1–31)

The young women of the area (34:1). The women of the land are Canaanites who live in the city of Shechem (see comments on Gen. 33:18), in whose outskirts Jacob and his family settled.

The Hivite (34:2). The Hivites were the descendants of Ham through Canaan (10:17). Beyond the fact that they were counted among the pre-Israelite inhabitants of the promised land, little is known about them. God did not want his people to have intimate relationships with the people of the land, but rather to stay separate from them.

An outrage (34:7). Whether consensual or, as is likely in this case, forced, sexual relations outside of marriage were a great affront not only to the woman, who would then be less likely to be married, but also against the family. Levi and Simeon are Dinah's full brothers having the same mother (Leah). In the ancient Near East brothers participated in the marriage negotiations of their sister.

A high compensation and gift (34:12). Marriages required economic transactions between families. Here the groom's father offers a large payment to both the bride and the bride's family.

An uncircumcised man (34:14). See comments on Gen. 17:10.

The gate of their city (34:20). See comments on Gen. 19:1. Archaeologists have discovered a gate at Shechem that dates to the Middle Bronze Age (2200–1550 BC), the time of the patriarchs.

The Canaanites and the Perizzites (34:30). These were some of the pre-Israelite inhabitants of the promised land. Canaanite was often used as a general term for the people of the land, while Perizzite was a subset, probably a tribe that lived in the vicinity of Shechem. They are in the northern coalition of Canaanites who fight Joshua at the time of the conquest (Josh. 11:3).

Jacob Returns to Bethel (35:1–15)

Get rid of the foreign gods (35:2). Foreign gods probably refer to personal idols that various members of Jacob's entourage kept with them. While we might rightly think that these foreign gods were mostly kept by foreign individuals who had been added to the family, we have already read that Rachel had stolen Laban's household idols (31:32), though these probably are images of departed ancestors. The presence of these idols, however, has ritually defiled the family of God, who now need to purify themselves after the idols are removed from their camp. They also need to change their clothes, a ritual that symbolizes the transition into the realm of the holy since they are coming into the presence of God in Bethel.

And their earrings (35:4). That these earrings must be buried along with the foreign gods indicates that they have some kind of religious significance, though the precise nature of this is unclear. It is possible that these earrings belonged to the idols or perhaps had depictions on them representing foreign deities.

The oak near Shechem (35:4). This is perhaps the same tree mentioned in 12:6 (see comments on Gen. 12:6). If so, the tree was

A household idol (*teraphim*) such as Rachel stole from her father, Laban.

associated with the presence of God, and the burial there may be seen as a way of turning over these blasphemous idols to God.

Standing stones at the ancient city of Gezer.

Luz (that is, Bethel) (35:6). See comments on Gen. 28:19.

El-bethel (35:7). The altar's name means "The God of Bethel."

Named it Allon-bacuth (35:8). The name of the oak marking the burial spot means "Oak of Weeping."

Paddan-aram (35:9). See comments on Gen. 25:20.

Jacob set up a marker . . . a stone marker (35:14). Jacob now erects a second "standing stone" at Bethel (see comments on Gen. 28:18). Standing stones sometimes represented deities, but often, as here, they were memorial stones that simply commemorated an event, here the encounter with God, who reaffirmed the covenant promises to Jacob. Jacob pours oil to consecrate the stone and offers a drink offering. For the latter, the worshiper normally would pour a liquid, usually wine or some other alcoholic drink (Num. 28:7), as an offering.

The Death of Rachel (35:16–29)

Bethel . . . Ephrath (35:16). Jacob and his family travel from Bethel (see comments on Gen. 12:8) heading toward Mamre near Hebron (35:27). As they approach Ephrath (a town associated with Bethlehem [Mic. 5:2], four miles south of Jerusalem), Rachel dies while giving birth to Benjamin.

Ben-oni . . . Benjamin (35:18). Rachel names her baby "son of my affliction," but Jacob calls him "son of my right hand," the right hand being a place of honor and power.

Set up a marker (35:20). See comments on Gen. 35:14.

Tower of Eder (35:21). This site, whose name means "watchtower of the flock," was associated with the "stronghold of Daughter Zion" in Mic. 4:8 and thus was likely near Jerusalem.

His father's concubine (35:22). A concubine was a secondary wife (see comments on Gen. 16:2).

Paddan-aram (35:26). Northwest Mesopotamia (see comments on Gen. 25:20).

Mamre in Kiriath-arba (that is, Hebron) (35:27). See comments on Gen. 13:18. Kiriath-arba, meaning "the city of Arba" (a man described in Josh. 14:15 as the greatest of the Anakim, the original inhabitants), was its ancient name.

From an Assyrian wall panel, a scene of Assyrian soldiers fighting against camel-mounted Arabs.

The Account of Esau's Family (36:1–37:1)

These are the family records (36:1). See comments on Gen. 2:4; 5:1. Like Ishmael, Esau, though not the chosen son, has his own "family records" before the "family records" of his brother Jacob (see comments on Gen. 25:12).

Edom (36:1). See comments on Gen. 25:30.

Hethite . . . Hivite (36:2). The Hethites (see comments on Gen. 23:3) and the Hivites (see comments on Gen. 34:2) were tribal elements from among the pre-Israelite inhabitants of the promised land.

The mountains of Seir (36:8). See comments on Gen. 32:3.

Joseph Sold into Slavery (37:2–36)

These are the family records (37:2). This is the final "family records" of the book of Genesis (see comments on Gen. 2:4; 5:1).

A robe of many colors (37:3). It is not known what made this robe special, but the gift of distinctive clothing is a sign that Joseph is his father's favorite son.

Joseph had a dream (37:5). In the ancient Near East dreams often were viewed as symbolic and were considered to have come from the divine realm, thus often informing the dreamer about the future. In ancient Egypt and Mesopotamia dreams were interpreted by specialists who utilized commentaries on the significance of different elements in dreams. Here Joseph shows himself to be an expert dream interpreter.

At Shechem (37:13). See comments on Gen. 12:6. The brothers have traveled about eighty miles on the central hill route passing Jerusalem on the way.

Hebron Valley (37:14). See comments on Gen. 23:2; 35:27.

Dothan (37:17). A town another thirteen miles to the west of Shechem at the southern end of the Carmel Mountain range.

One of the pits (37:20). A cistern was a pit dug into the ground to catch rainwater runoff in order to provide water for people and animals.

Ishmaelites coming from Gilead (37:25). Dothan was on a busy international highway that ran along the coast that connected Egypt with Syria-Palestine and beyond. The Ishmaelites were a nomadic people who had descended from Ishmael, Isaac's half-brother (25:12–16; Judg. 8:24; Ps. 83:6).

Their camels (37:25). Camels were well suited for this type of international trade. At one time, due to lack of early evidence, it was thought that camels were not domesticated until the twelfth century BC, long after the time of Joseph and the other patriarchs. Now, however, though it is not beyond controversy due to the lack of clear extrabiblical evidence, "it may be the case that domesticated camels were in use . . . sometime in the mid-second millennium BC among pastoral people with whom the Israelites had some acquaintance."[11]

Midianite traders (37:28). Here the Ishmaelites are called Midianites. The Midianites were another people also descended from Abraham, but through his concubine (see comments on Gen. 16:2) Keturah (25:1–2). It could be that Ishmaelite is here used as a general term for nomad, while Midianite is a more specific term (Judg. 8:22–24). Or perhaps they looked like Ishmaelites when they were far away but then close up it becomes clear that they are Midianites.[12]

Twenty pieces of silver (37:28). Slave prices changed throughout the OT time period. According to extrabiblical sources, the going rate for a male adult slave in the first half of the second millennium was twenty shekels, thus supporting the idea that the Joseph story well reflects that time period.[13]

Judah and Tamar (38:1–30)

An Adullamite named Hirah (38:1). Adullam was a Canaanite town about ten miles northwest of Hebron and about fifteen miles southwest of Jerusalem. Nothing further is known about Hirah except that he was a Canaanite and a friend of Judah.

Perform your duty as her brother-in-law (38:8). Later, the Mosaic law prescribes that it is the duty of a man to marry the childless wife of his deceased brother so that she might have a son to take care of her and continue the family line (Deut. 25:5–6). This later law apparently institutionalizes an earlier custom that also shows up in other ancient Near Eastern sources, including Assyrian and Hittite laws.[14]

Timnah (38:12). This town was not the same as the more well-known Timnah featured in the Samson story (Judg. 14); it was located to the southeast of Hebron.

Veiled her face (38:14). In and of itself, a veil did not designate a woman as a prostitute. The woman in Song of Songs, for example, is depicted as wearing a veil (4:1, 3; 6:7). However, it appears that prostitutes did wear

veils, and the Genesis narrator tells us that Judah thinks she is a prostitute because "she had covered her face" (38:15).

Your signet ring, your cord, and the staff in your hand (38:18). These were items that would serve as identity markers. A signet ring had distinctive features that when pressed into soft clay marked an item as property of the owner of the signet ring, who would wear the ring on a cord around his neck. The staff was a walking stick that also had markings that would reveal a person's identity.

Cult prostitute (38:21). The word for "prostitute" here is different from the general term used earlier in the chapter and comes from a verb that means "to be holy" or "consecrated." It is not clear whether Judah really thinks that she is a prostitute connected to a holy place or whether his friend is trying to make the situation look better than simply sleeping with a woman for sex. Such women are mentioned in Ugaritic texts, but their exact function is unclear.

Joseph in Potiphar's House (39:1–23)

The captain of the guards (39:1). The Hebrew words used for Potiphar's office are literally "captain of the butchers" or "captain of the executioners," indicating that Potiphar holds an office that utilizes violence. The fact that Joseph is not executed for the charge that he raped Potiphar's wife thus suggests that Potiphar probably does not believe his wife's accusation.

Joseph Meets the Pharaoh (40:1–41:57)

The Nile River.

Cupbearer and baker (40:1). These were more than menial servants in the palace. They may have delivered the food and drink to the king, but poisoning was such an ever-present danger that only trusted advisors held such posts.

In the house of the captain of the guards (40:3). The prison in which Joseph is incarcerated is the same as the house of Potiphar, who is the captain of the guard (see comments on Gen. 39:1). This too is an indication that Potiphar is aware that his wife's accusation is not true.

Had a dream (40:5). See comments on Gen. 37:5.

Don't interpretations belong to God? (40:8). Egyptians believed that dreams could carry a message from the gods. Typically, these dream messages were determined by researching the content of the dreams in written commentaries, the Dream Books. Joseph, on the other hand, believed that God would give him the interpretation of dreams without the need to consult the commentaries (see comments on Gen. 37:5).

Pharaoh's birthday (40:20). Egyptian evidence for the celebration of the pharaoh's birthday does not exist for this early in history; thus some believe that this day celebrates not his birthday, but rather the day the pharaoh ascended the throne, a celebration for which there is evidence.[15]

Pharaoh had a dream . . . beside the Nile (41:1). See comments on Gen. 37:5; 40:8. The Nile was the major river that ran through the heart of Egypt. Every year the Nile would flood, depositing rich and fertile soil that was essential to farming and thus to the prosperity of Egypt.

All the magicians of Egypt and all its wise men (41:8). The Hebrew word for "magician" derives from an Egyptian title that means "chief lector priest," and most probably referred to priests connected to the House of Life, the place where ritual texts, like the dream commentaries, were studied.[16]

Seven years of famine (41:27). A seven-year famine during the reign of Pharaoh Djoser (twenty-seventh century BC, though the text is from the third to first centuries BC) is mentioned in an Egyptian text known as the Famine Stela of Sehel Island. While this famine is not the one mentioned in the Joseph story, it indicates that "seven" might be symbolic for a long time and that such long famines were not unprecedented in Egypt.

Signet ring . . . fine linen garments . . . gold chain (41:42). Egyptian evidence indicates that such a ceremony that includes these gifts could be either a reward for Joseph's dream interpretation or a commissioning for his new status as second only to the pharaoh.[17] Due to a lack of surviving documentation from this time period, there is no direct Egyptian evidence of Joseph's high position. However, we do know that there were other non-Egyptian and even Semitic people who at various times in Egyptian history rose to similar high positions. A Syrian named Bay, for example, was the second most important person during the reign of Seti II in 1194 BC.[18]

Asenath daughter of Potiphera, priest at On (41:50). On was an important city also known as Heliopolis, seven miles northeast of Cairo. The names of Joseph's wife and her father are clearly Egyptian and in a form that was appropriate to the first quarter of the second millennium BC, the time setting for the Joseph story.[19]

Joseph's Brothers' First Trip (42:1–38)

You are spies (42:9). In general the Egyptians distrusted Semitic people like the family of Jacob (see comments on Gen. 43:32). Thus it would not

The Famine Stela on Sehel Island.

be unusual for them to suspect traveling Semites of planning a raid on the stored grain. This fear gave Joseph's accusation some substance, though of course Joseph knew that they were not spies.

Joseph's Brothers' Second Trip (43:1–44:34)

Egyptians could not eat with Hebrews (43:32). The Egyptians generally seemed to detest "the Asiatics," the term they used for the various Semitic groups (including the Hebrews) that lived to the east and northeast of them. This was related to the fact that the Egyptians had an advanced and wealthy urban society, while the Semites typically lived as nomads. This attitude is well illustrated by the Egyptian wisdom book known as the Instruction of Merikare, a Middle Kingdom (ca. 2133–1786 BC) document in which the main speaker warns the reader to beware "the hated Asiatic."[20]

The cup that my master . . . uses for divination (44:5). There were various ways that a cup could be used for the purposes of divination in an ancient Near Eastern context. In Mesopotamia diviners poured oil in water and then watched the shapes that were formed by the oil. Such practices are condemned in Deut. 18:9–13, since divination does not leave room for God to decide not to answer the diviner's question. It is not clear why Joseph is in possession of a diviner's cup, but it is interesting that he uses it to test his brothers' character.

Family Reconciliation (45:1–47:31)

Father to Pharaoh (45:8). In both Egyptian and later Israelite literature (Proverbs) fathers were those who gave advice to their sons, and thus Joseph tells his brothers that he has been an advisor to the pharaoh.

Land of Goshen (45:10). A location in the eastern part of the Nile Delta, in northern Egypt.

Beer-sheba (46:1). See comments on Gen. 21:14.

Paddan-aram (46:15). See comments on Gen. 25:20.

All shepherds are detestable to Egyptians (46:34). See comments on Gen. 43:32.

The land of Rameses (47:11). This probably was a (post-Mosaic) name for Goshen (45:10). It is a name of the city that will later be built by Israelite slaves during the time of Moses (Exod. 1:11) and the place from which the Israelites depart from Egypt at the time of the exodus (Exod. 12:37).

Looking to the Future (48:1–49:28)

Luz (48:3). Another name for Bethel (see comments on Gen. 28:19).

Paddan (48:7). Northwest Mesopotamia (see comments on Gen. 25:20).

Ephrath . . . Bethlehem (48:7). See comments on Gen. 35:16.

With his right hand Ephraim (48:13). In this context, the laying on of hands signifies commission to a status. Jacob raises these two boys, his grandsons, to the status of sons with all that entails in terms of inheritance. The right hand is the hand of power and prestige, probably because most people are right-handed. Typically, the older received preferential position, but here the younger is chosen contrary to expectations.

The scepter will not depart from Judah (49:10). The scepter was an ornamental mace and was a symbol of kingship in the ancient Near East. Jacob thus anticipates the rise of kingship in the tribe of Judah, an expectation that is realized when David becomes the second king of Israel and God grants him a dynasty (2 Sam. 7).

The Deaths of Jacob and Joseph (49:29–50:26)

The cave in the field of Machpelah near Mamre (49:30). See comments on Gen. 23:9.

Gathered to my people (49:29). See comments on Gen. 25:8.

Statuette of a funeral bier for the Egyptian prince Thutmose (ca. 1360 BC).

To embalm his father (50:2). Embalming and mummification were well-known burial practices in Egypt. Body organs were removed and stored in jars. Natron was used to dry out the body, which was then washed and anointed with various oils and resins. The embalmers then wrapped the body in linen. This procedure preserved the body. Embalming in Egypt was connected to the distinctive Egyptian beliefs about the afterlife, which there is no evidence that Joseph shared. The purpose of embalming here might be simply to preserve the body for transport to the promised land for burial.

Abel-mizraim (50:11). The name means "Mourning of Egypt."

They embalmed him and placed him in a coffin (50:26). See comments on Gen. 50:2.

Exodus

Eric Alan Mitchell

Introduction. Although the opening verses of Exodus do not address the issue of authorship, there are numerous references throughout the book that allude to Moses's involvement in writing Exodus. For example, 24:4 states, "Moses wrote down all the words of the Lord" (i.e., the covenant laws up through 23:30). Twice in other texts Moses is commanded by God to "write" something down (17:14, God's curse against Amalek; 34:27, all the covenant laws of Exodus). Thus later biblical texts and tradition attribute the book of Exodus to Moses (see the introduction in the commentary on Genesis). Likewise, keep in mind that there are several references to the fact that God himself "wrote" the Ten Commandments (first set of tablets: 31:18; 32:16; second set of tablets: 34:1, 28).

The major themes in Exodus are deliverance from bondage, redemption from judgment, and God's revelation of himself as the covenant God of Israel (both as a continuation of the covenant that he made with Abraham and in regard to the new national covenant that he is making with Israel).

An Outline of Exodus

1:1–2:25	God raises a deliverer
3:1–4:31	God calls Moses to deliver Israel
5:1–7:7	God reassures Moses about his calling; God's plan that Israel and Egypt will know him
7:8–11:10	God smites Egypt with miraculous judgments
12:1–13:16	God passes over Israel and redeems them from judgment

The Beni Hasan painting from Upper Egypt showing Semite families entering Egypt.

13:17–15:21	God leads Israel out of Egypt through the sea
15:22–18:27	God provides for and protects Moses/Israel despite their grumbling
19:1–31:18	God makes his covenant with Israel at Mount Sinai
32:1–34:35	Israel breaks the covenant; God restates his willingness to abide with Israel
35:1–39:43	Israel builds the tabernacle according to God's specifications
40:1–38	Moses sets up the tabernacle; God's glory abides in the midst of Israel

The book of Exodus opens with the descendants of Abraham residing in Egypt. They have left Canaan, the land of promise, and migrated into Egypt in the hopes of surviving a famine. During this time period it was common for traders and immigrants to seek to enter Egypt, especially in times of drought. Egypt had a constant supply of water and well-fertilized land due to the annual flooding of the Nile. In fact, at times the pharaohs maintained a string of fortresses along their eastern border and on the roadway toward Canaan along the Mediterranean coast in order to limit immigration. No doubt there were also other groups of people who had migrated down into Egypt. The Beni Hasan painting from Upper Egypt depicts a family of Semites (similar to the Hebrews) entering Egypt with wives, children, and livestock, all dressed in the multicolored style of clothing apparently similar to that mentioned in the account of Joseph's coat (Gen. 37:3).

Although Egypt had plenty of water, there were numerous challenges for the immigrants. The Egyptian culture and religion differed greatly from their own. Within Egyptian society the "sons of Israel" were outsiders and were considered to be part of a lower caste, especially due to their unshaven faces and work with animals (Gen. 41:14; 43:32; 46:33–34) (see comments on Gen. 43:32).

Egyptian inscription depicting an Egyptian woman giving birth on a "birthing stone."

Israel in Slavery (Chap. 1)

These are the names (1:1). This first phrase reflects the name of the book in Hebrew (*Shemot*) as well as the connection and continuation of the story of the sons of Israel found in Genesis (see the introduction in the commentary on Genesis).

A new king, who did not know about Joseph, came to power in Egypt (1:8–11). The name of this pharaoh is not mentioned in Exodus. There are two competing dates for the exodus event (referred to as the early date and the late date), and the identification of which pharaohs are in the story is determined by which date is used. For the early date (ca. 1446 BC), this new pharaoh who would oppress and enslave Israel may have been either from the Semitic Hyksos dynasty (which entered northern Egypt around 1650 BC and ruled there for over a century) or from the later Eighteenth Egyptian dynasty who drove the Hyksos out of Egypt. Pharaoh Ahmose I established the Eighteenth Dynasty when he expelled the Hyksos in about 1550 BC. So Ahmose I may have expelled the Semitic Hyksos dynasty and then enslaved all the Hebrews (likewise a Semitic people group) in the land of Goshen. For the later date of the Exodus (ca. 1250 BC), the pharaoh of the oppression could be any pharaoh from Pharaoh Ay (ca. 1330 BC)[1] to Pharaoh Ramesses II (ca. 1290 BC).

Pithom and Rameses (1:11). The names and locations of these two cities are not clear and are part of the debate about the date of the exodus. The city of Pithom (probably a Hebrew rendering of Egyptian "Temple of Atum") has been connected with two sites; the earliest is Tell Retabeh (ca. 1300–700 BC), a city later moved to another site, Tell el-Maskhuta (ca. 700 BC–AD 400).[2] The city of Rameses (Pi-Rameses) has been identified with the site of Qantir (which was in use from 1270 to 1120 BC, before the nearby branch of the Nile River silted in).[3] If Qantir is the city of Rameses, then the early date for the exodus is unlikely. While the Nineteenth Dynasty had a royal complex at the site of Qantir/Pi-Rameses, the Eighteenth Dynasty (early date) reveals only a fort/military compound there and overall has no site called (Pi-)Rameses.[4] Pharaoh Ramesses II did build a store-city (perhaps a regional capital) with this name (*Pi-Ramesse A-nakhtu*, "Domain of Ramesses II, Great in Victory"), which was in use from 1270 to 1130 BC.[5] Establishing whether these cities had an Israelite presence is difficult; ethnicity is hard to determine with great accuracy when there is only archaeological data from things like pottery. The Israelites were likely utilizing Egyptian material culture (pottery, house construction, etc.) in their daily lives, and thus the archaeological record that they left would be difficult to distinguish from that of the Egyptians.

The use of the name Rameses, however, could be an editorial update to explain the later name of the town that the Israelites had built, or perhaps the eventual name of the construction at the site of Tell el-Daba/Qantir (which began under Pharaoh Horemheb [1323–1295 BC] and continued under Pharaoh Seti I [1294–1279 BC]).[6] It is also possible that the name Rameses was not tied to a ruling pharaoh.

Moses's Early Life (Chap. 2)

A papyrus basket . . . coated it with asphalt and pitch (2:3). God orchestrates the events of Moses's birth into a hero birth story not unfamiliar to people in the ancient Near East. Moses is not the only child in ancient literature to be set out on a river in a pitch-covered basket. For example, one such story in ancient literature is "The Birth Legend of Sargon of Akkad." Written in about 700 BC, during the reign of King Sargon II, the story recounts the birth of the king's namesake, an earlier King Sargon (ca. 2300 BC). The Sargon legend follows the ancient "birth of a hero" account pattern where the child/hero is abandoned or exposed in a basket at birth (at times on water) and fortuitously is rescued from harm to go on to great accomplishments.[7] "The Birth Legend of Sargon of Akkad" reads,

> She placed me in a reed basket, she sealed my hatch with pitch.
> She left me to the river, whence I could not come up.[8]

She named him Moses (2:10). The pharaoh's daughter gives the baby an Egyptian name. The name Moses means "drawn from" or "birthed from." It is partially the same name as occurs in pharaohs named Ramesses. The Egyptian name Ramesses was actually spoken *meses-ra*, meaning "born from (the sun-god) Ra." However, the Egyptians always wrote the "god" element first. So when written, it becomes Ra-meses. It is possible that the pharaoh's daughter originally named him Moses-Hapi (after the Egyptian idol god of the annual Nile floods), or she could have used one of the many other god-names connected with the Nile. If that is the case, then Moses apparently later dropped the name of the other god, for obvious theological reasons.

A papyrus basket from ancient Egypt, similar to the basket used by Moses's mother.

Moses fled . . . and went to live in the land of Midian (2:15). The Midianites were a people group related to Israel, descended from Abraham and his second wife, Keturah (Gen. 25:4). Midian was located in what are now southern Jordan and the northwestern Arabian Peninsula.

Moses Meets God (Chap. 3)

The mountain of God (3:1). Moses is pasturing the flock of Jethro, his father-in-law, on the back or far side of Sinai. From a perspective in Midian, this would be the opposite side of the Sinai Peninsula from Midian (i.e., southern or western Sinai). However, if Moses is writing from the perspective of standing in Egypt, then this would be to the east or to the south of Sinai. When Moses first speaks of going to Egypt, probably relating the account of his "burning bush" experience, it is to Jethro in Midian (4:18). However, the far side of Sinai may reflect when Moses relates the account to Aaron in the wilderness and speaks to his (and Israel's) Egyptian perspective (4:28–31). Shepherds normally wintered their flocks near home, then stayed close to their home base in the spring, when forage was nearby. Later in the summer they traveled farther afield to find forage for their flocks. When Jethro later visits Moses at Mount Sinai/Horeb (chap. 18), he leaves from there to go to his own land, so Sinai is not located in the land of Midian (as some have recently conjectured). The Sinai Wilderness was more of a mountainous desert region than a forested wilderness region. Even though it was a dry desert area, it still would have been possible to pasture a flock in the mountainous higher elevations of Horeb. This would be the reason why Moses led Jethro's flock there.

The Sinai region.

A land flowing with milk and honey (3:8, 17). God had promised Abram that his descendants would return triumphantly to the promised land (Gen. 15:14). In the beginning of Exodus the people of Israel are mainly situated in the land of Goshen, located in the northeastern Nile Delta of Egypt. Goshen was a good land for growing crops and for herding animals, but the people would be hemmed in by the tributaries of the Nile and unable to expand or to spread out. So when God speaks of the land to which he will take them, he describes it as a good and spacious land. It is a land with grass for sheep and cattle (i.e., milk), and a land full of the greenery of productive crops (thus the honey from bees). While the land of promise had regions that were arid, there were also regions that were very productive in ancient times. Honey that is easily available on the ground is later mentioned in the accounts of Samson (Judg. 14:8) and Jonathan (1 Sam. 14:26). There is also archaeological evidence from around 850 BC for industrial beekeeping at Tel Rehov, a densely settled city in the northern Jordan Valley. It is also possible that the honey mentioned here in Exod. 3 refers to a product made from the fruit of date palm trees. If this is the case, then the reference to a land flowing with milk and honey is declaring that the produce of animals (milk) and plants (date honey) in the land will be bountiful and will satisfy the Israelites.

Moses Convinced to Go Back to Egypt (Chap. 4)

The staff . . . became a snake (4:3). Moses is given three signs to convince the people that he speaks for the Lord. In the first, his staff turns into a serpent. For the Israelites, a snake/serpent reference brought connotations of the animal in the garden of Eden that deceived Eve. Moses's control of the serpent may have revealed to the Israelites an image of Eve's seed returning to take dominion over the serpent and creation—something only God could make happen. On the other side, snakes played an important symbolic role in Egypt. The Egyptians had a gigantic serpent idol god, Apophis, who was the master of chaos and enemy to the sun god Ra, the patron deity of most pharaohs. In Egyptian understanding, this giant snake Apophis tried to swallow the sun every day.

The Egyptian pharaohs were often portrayed holding a flail and a shepherd's crook, as seen in this *shabti* (funerary figurine) of King Tutankhamun.

So the Egyptians worshiped Ra and set spells against Apophis. For Moses to control this god or his image (serpent staff) was to establish that God and his spokesman Moses were more powerful than the god Apophis and thus posed a very serious threat to the pharaoh. Also, Moses's staff is probably a shepherd's crook. The pharaohs of Egypt carried scepters in the shape of a small shepherd's crook as an image of their rule. When Moses's staff swallows all the other staffs of the pharaoh's magicians, it demonstrates that the God of Moses rules over all, including Egypt.

Collection of ancient Egyptian staffs.

His hand was diseased (4:6). The second sign is similar to the first, showing God as having control over the physical realm of disease. The Hebrew term often translated as "leprosy" (*tsara*) refers to a range of unsightly skin diseases for which no cure was known.

The water you take from the Nile will become blood (4:9). This sign would reveal God's power over the life source of Egypt and at the same time show God's power over Hapi, the Egyptian god of the Nile, as well as over several minor gods represented by animals within the Nile (crocodiles, hippopotamuses, frogs, etc.). This sign/plague also recalls the earlier Egyptian bloodshed against Israel when the pharaoh ordered that all Hebrew baby boys be thrown into the Nile River (1:22).

A bridegroom of blood (4:25). Moses is on his way to Egypt. Although commissioned to deliver Israel, he had never circumcised his son Gershom according to the conditions of God's covenant with Abraham (Gen. 17:10). The reason for this laxity is unknown, but Moses would seem to be the guilty one responsible. Perhaps Moses had given in to Zipporah's reluctance when the time came (on the eighth day after birth) to circumcise Gershom. Thus now perhaps it is Zipporah who acquiesces and (to save Moses from God's wrath) reluctantly circumcises her son, making him (and indicating that she also is) connected to the covenant people of God (see comments on Gen. 17:10). Although not required, circumcision was practiced among the Egyptians, especially among the upper classes. In later times in Egypt it was restricted to the priestly class.

The Egyptian god Amun-Re (left). The Egyptian goddess Ma'at (right).

Israel Oppressed (Chap. 5)

Pharaoh responded, "Who is the Lord? . . . I don't know the Lord, and besides, I will not let Israel go" (5:2). The

Scene of slaves making mud-bricks in Egypt, from a wall painting in the tomb of Rekhmire, the vizier under Thutmose III (1479–1425 BC).

Egyptians had over two thousand gods, each with its own sphere of influence or power. There were creator gods (Ptah, Ra/Re), gods for the physical features of the cosmos (Amun-Re, the sun god; Nut, the sky goddess; Khonsu, the moon god), gods for physical features of the land (Hapi, the Nile River god), gods exhibited as animals (Bastet [cat], who supported Amun-Re; Hathor, the cow goddess), gods over childbirth (Bes), and a god of death, disorder, storms, and violence (Seth). The pharaoh was seen as a manifestation both of the god Horus (who smites death/disorder/enemies) and of Amun-re the sun god (father of Ma'at). Ma'at, as the goddess of divine order and justice, kept societal order (called *ma'at*). To please her, one kept one's place in that order. To have success in life and in the afterlife, one needed to keep the gods pleased through sacrifice, worship, right actions, and proper funerary preparation. The pharaoh was charged with upholding *ma'at* (divine order) and destroying Isfet (the god of chaos). When Pharaoh says that he does not "know" the Lord, he may mean that he does not recognize him as having any power or influence over him because the Lord is not an Egyptian god. In response, God states in 7:3–5 that he will bring upon Egypt many signs and wonders, and then they will "know" that he is the Lord. As the Lord does so, he reveals himself to be the ruler of the divine/creative order. He also reveals the pharaoh to be impotent and unable to keep *ma'at* (order), since in the Egyptian worldview the plagues would be Isfet (chaos) personified.

Don't continue to supply the people with straw for making bricks (5:7). Mud-brick was a common building material in Egypt. While certain structures (temples, palaces, pyramids, etc.) were built of stone, such stone blocks had to be quarried and then moved great distances, usually at great cost. Thus most structures were built of less-expensive and readily available mud-brick. Similar to modern adobe, mud-brick in the ancient world was made by mixing water, clay, sand, and straw (as a binding agent). The mixing process was very labor-intensive, carried out in a shallow pit by stamping and mixing the ingredients with the feet. The mixture was then pressed into wooden forms and left in the sun to dry for days. When stacked together with a mud-based mortar, these mud-bricks made for a solid and well-insulated structure. When regularly plastered on the exterior, structures made of mud-brick could last quite a long time. When the Israelites are ordered to scavenge their own straw, this is a severe hardship on them, increasing their workload and taxing their productivity.

Covenant Fulfillment (Chap. 6)

Because of a strong hand (6:1). The "strong hand" or "mighty hand" of God (cf. 13:3, 9, 14, 16) often is juxtaposed with the phrase "outstretched arm" (e.g., Deut. 4:34). The classic pose in Egyptian paintings and statuary for every pharaoh from the first, Narmer (ca. 3000 BC), down to Ramesses III (ca. 1153 BC) was one of a bigger-than-life pharaoh standing over his small enemies ready to strike them dead. Often in these images the pharaoh grasps his enemies by the hair in his left hand, with his right hand raised and stretched out overhead holding a mace/club ready to smite them on the forehead. The foreigners in this classic iconography were viewed by Egyptians as agents of Isfet/chaos whom the pharaoh subdues to fulfill *ma'at* (order). This image of the pharaoh may reflect the Egyptian belief in the mythological battle between Horus and Seth for the throne of Egypt. In the image of Pharaoh Narmer he decapitates ten enemies. Much later, in an image in the temple at Edfu (ca. 110 BC) the god Horus harpoons the god Seth ten times.

A pharaoh with "outstretched arm" ready to strike a multiethnic collection of his enemies.

Here in Exodus the Lord, the God of Israel, takes up a similar image for himself, polemically countering the Egyptian belief, and essentially claiming that he alone is the one who orders the universe (not the goddess Ma'at). Furthermore, he alone is the all-powerful ruler capable of delivering his people (not the pharaoh). Likewise, the implication from this imagery is that he is about to strike Egypt ten times, and, indeed, this transpires in the ten plagues. This iconographic religious imagery intermixed throughout the exodus story would have been well understood by both Israelites and Egyptians.

I am such a poor speaker (6:12). Literally, Moses says here that he is a man of "uncircumcised lips." This statement may reflect not that Moses stutters, but that he is reticent to speak in the pharaoh's presence. No doubt Moses in his youth once spoke Egyptian fluently in the pharaonic court (2:9–10; Acts 7:20–22). Yet now, decades later, perhaps he feels inadequate. Eloquence of speech was highly valued by the Egyptians. It was one of the hallmarks of Egyptian wisdom and rhetoric. A person who could be self-composed and speak eloquently was considered truthful and could prevail before the pharaoh's court. This is seen in Egyptian literature, particularly in the story titled "The Tale of the Eloquent Peasant." In this story a peasant who is oppressed by a wealthy man so enthralls the pharaoh by his eloquence that his imprisonment is extended just so the pharaoh can listen to him every day. Ultimately, this eloquent peasant wins his case.

Staff to Snake, Water to Blood (Chap. 7)

The waters of Egypt . . . will become blood (7:19). Most of the plagues sent upon the Egyptians are indeterminate in length, though the first, ninth, and tenth plagues last seven days, three days, and one day, respectively. It probably is safe to assume that most of the plagues lasted several days. It is also not known how much time takes place between most of the plagues (with the exception of the seven days mentioned in 7:25 between the first and second plagues). There is a reasonable end date (Passover), plus a few key markers in between (the plagues of hail and locusts). The plagues likely begin in August/September, at the height of the Nile annual flooding, and stretch across six months, ending with the tenth plague (death of the firstborn) in March/April.[9]

In the Egyptian worldview the flooding of the Nile River was connected to the resurrection of the god Osiris, who brought rebirth, renewal, and fertility. Thus the water of the Nile turning into blood might have been viewed by the Egyptians as indicating Osiris's death.[10] Furthermore, also in Egyptian mythology the Nile ran with human blood when the goddess Sekhmet was created by Re to kill humankind. However, Re had a change of heart and, by pouring out red-colored beer on the ground, tricked Sekhmet into thinking that all humankind had been killed. To the Egyptians the first plague could have been taken as a portent of the judgment of Re and Sekhmet upon them. Perhaps the pharaoh's magicians used this same trick of barley beer colored with red ochre to mimic the Nile water turning to blood.[11] The blood may also recall the blood of the Hebrew children thrown into the Nile by the pharaoh of the oppression (1:22). While some would like to attribute the first nine plagues solely to natural causes, the immediacy and the pervasive extent of the water turning to blood stress this as a supernatural event.

Frogs, Gnats, and Flies (Chap. 8)

Plague all your territory with frogs. . . . gnats. . . . flies (8:1–32). As God smites Egypt with the plagues, he begins with attacking the life-giving waters of the Nile River, demonstrating his control over both the waters and the creatures within the Nile. The fouled water certainly upset the *ma'at*/order within the land, sending the birds and wildlife out from their normal abodes in search of water. Next, God judges Egypt with gnats (stinging insects, perhaps mosquitos), flying insects that move in the space above the Nile waters. Moses then meets the pharaoh again by the Nile, and God judges Egypt by sending flies, whose area of movement is the space above the ground but stretching all across Egypt. In Egyptian mythology the god Uatchit, represented by a fly, protected against misfortune and disease, but in this instance it could do neither. In each case the miraculous timing of the starting and stopping of the plague, the spectacular overabundance (evidencing both the imbalance of nature and, to Egyptians, their gods' impotence), and the expanding realm of influence of each plague increasingly show that the Lord has power over creation, the space and powers attributed to the Egyptians' gods, and the space and powers attributed to the pharaoh and his servants.

What we will sacrifice . . . is detestable to the Egyptians (8:26). Because they worked as shepherds, the Israelites in general were detestable to the Egyptians (see comments on Gen. 43:32). However, the Egyptians also sacrificed animals to their gods (mainly goats, bulls, antelopes, and geese, though cats, birds, and crocodiles apparently were also used). Millions of these animals in mummified form have been found in Egypt. They probably would have been purchased and then donated as a sacrifice. The Greek historian Herodotus indicates that the Egyptians in general sacrificed in a manner similar to Israel. While they would sacrifice bulls, the regulations were tight, and if one sacrificed a bull that an Egyptian priest had not properly marked, the penalty was death. The Egyptians did not sacrifice cows (females) because they were sacred to Isis.[12] The Israelites, however, sacrificed both bulls and cows, thus perhaps offending the Egyptians.

Another interesting aspect is that Moses and Israel, foreigners in Egypt, were asking to go into the desert (or wilderness) to sacrifice. The desert/wilderness was considered by the Egyptians to be the abode of the Egyptian god Seth, the god of the desert, foreigners, and usurpers, as well as the god of chaos and confusion. Thus Seth was somewhat of a hostile god to the Egyptians. They probably would have viewed sacrificing to a god in the desert as sacrificing to Seth, their "enemy" god.

Plagues on Beast, Man, Crops (Chap. 9)

The LORD's hand will bring a severe plague against your livestock (9:3). The plague on livestock creates both an economic burden to Egypt and a boon to Israel (instantly inflating the value of their herds). Some of the cattle of Egypt were in the delta region near the Hebrew cattle, yet the Hebrew cattle did not get sick and die as the Egyptian cattle did. This may be why the pharaoh "investigated" the matter to see if it were so. This plague also judges the idol gods of the Egyptians who were represented in animal or a combined human-animal form. When the time of plowing came (October/November), the shortage of oxen to plow the fields for the next crop would be disastrous. Many animals—such as rams, cats, dogs, horses, cows, and bulls—were sacred to the Egyptians. One of the most important animals that would have been affected by this plague was the Egyptian Apis bull, viewed as the god Apis incarnate. The Apis was a bull specially selected by its markings, and it was worshiped as a representative of the pharaoh's power and the fertility of the land. This plague would have killed the Apis bull not by natural causes—as happened occasionally—but rather by God's command, resulting in a great time of mourning in Egypt and a necessary search for a new Apis bull. Since all the cattle of the Egyptians would be dead, however, they would have had to seek a replacement from outside Egypt, ironically perhaps from the cattle of the Hebrews.

It will become fine dust . . . festering boils on people and animals (9:9). This plague attacks the gods of Egypt who held power over humankind, health, and healing. Once again, worship at all the temples of Egypt would be disrupted. Note that each of the earlier plagues (water changing to blood, dead frogs, bites from gnats/mosquitos, dead livestock) tended to bring blood or dead animals into the Egyptian temple precincts, resulting in defilement of the temple and thus a stoppage in worship. Now with skin infection/boils on everyone, including the priests, their temple worship would once again be seriously disrupted. The Egyptian priests, who normally shaved their entire bodies, were extremely concerned with maintaining purity of their physical bodies. The presence of boils would disqualify a priest from service. These same types of boils are later promised to come upon the Hebrews if they do not keep their covenant with God (Deut. 28:27).

The worst hail (9:18). This plague belittles the Egyptian gods who supposedly ruled over the sky, soil, crops, and fertility. The Egyptians had three

The Israelites Leave Egypt

seasons: rain/flood, planting/growing, and harvest. They grew a wide variety of crops (cf. Num. 11:5), including grains (wheat, spelt, barley), vegetables (leeks/onions, cucumbers, garlic, lettuce/cabbages, beans/lentils, radishes/turnips), fruits (figs, grapes, melons), flax (for making linen clothing and rope), and papyrus (for writing texts and for utilitarian items). The rain/flood season was from June to September, the planting/growth season from October to February, and the harvesting season from March to May. The hail plague came in the middle of the growing season after the flax and barley were in bloom but before the wheat and spelt had ripened. This likely was in February.

Locusts and Darkness (Chap. 10)

Tomorrow I will bring locusts (10:4). The locust plague reveals that those Egyptian gods who were connected to the sky, to plants, to the harvest, and to general protection of the people are impotent before the Lord. While moving in large swarms is not the normal behavior of locusts, they are known to swarm occasionally after long periods of drought followed by rain-fed new vegetation growth. However, it takes the right environment as well as several generations of increasing numbers in close contact with increasingly larger swarms to build their numbers up into the proportions of a plague. Passively directed by prevailing wind patterns, the swarms fly until temperatures cool. Then they rest, eat, and move on. In this manner they could devour almost all vegetation in their path. A swarm of the desert locust variety can cover nearly 500 square miles—containing up to 200 million locusts per square mile—and can eat over 400 million pounds of plants per day.[13] The swarm described in 10:1–20 is supernaturally timed, directed, and sized, and the scale of the swarm is devastating for Egypt.

There will be darkness over the land of Egypt (10:21). By the mid-third millennium BC, the creator god Amun had been combined with the sun god Ra/Re to become Amun-Re, the chief of the Egyptian pantheon (in one inscription he is described as "king of the gods"). The pharaoh was viewed as the son of Amun-Re and served as his representative on earth. Amun-Re was the state god during the New Kingdom period and so was worshiped by every pharaoh during the Eighteenth and Nineteenth Dynasties of Egypt (covering the entire range of possible dates for the exodus events). During the day Amun-Re traveled in his boat (called a bark) across the sky. During the night he traveled in a boat through the netherworld. In order to rise again, Amun-Re had to defeat his evil enemy the snake god Apophis with the help of another god, Seth. The pharaoh would perform rituals to aid him in this fight. The plague of darkness, therefore, was a direct attack on the power of Amun-Re, demonstrating that both Amun-Re and the pharaoh were powerless before the Lord, the all-powerful God of Israel. To the Egyptians, the darkness during the daytime meant that Amun-Re had lost or was losing his fight, and that the pharaoh obviously could not help him, thus also failing to uphold order in the world (*ma'at*). To make things even worse for the Egyptians, while the darkness covered all Egypt for three days, the sun continued to shine on the Israelites. In the understanding of the Egyptians, this would imply that the sun (or the chief god Amun-Re) was merely a servant of the Lord, the God of the Israelites, shining where and when he willed it. In regard to human power, this would also elevate Moses, the Lord's representative, above the pharaoh in the eyes of the Egyptians. Furthermore, the three final plagues each contain a reference to darkness or night (10:5, 15; 10:22–23; 11:4; 12:12, 29, 31), implying perhaps that this attack on Amun-Re extended across these three final plagues.[14]

God's Wonders Multiplied (Chap. 11)

About midnight . . . every firstborn male in the land of Egypt will die (11:4–5). Throughout most of the ancient Near East, upon the death of his father, the firstborn son would receive a double portion of his father's estate and become the authority and the spiritual leader over the

This wooden chariot was a gift from Pharaoh Amenhotep III.

remaining family members. Thus the firstborn son had a special status. Back in 1:15–22 the pharaoh had killed many sons of Israel. Thus God's actions now in striking dead all the firstborn of Egypt, even the firstborn son of the pharaoh himself, is a fitting "poetic justice." The Egyptian god who provided protection during the night was the moon god Khonsu (also known as Khons). He was also the patron deity of the firstborn son of the pharaoh. The height of Khonsu's power was on the night of the full moon. The Passover was to take place on the fourteenth day of a lunar month—the night of the full moon (12:6). So at the height of Khonsu's power—the god charged with protecting Egyptians during the night, especially the firstborn of the pharaoh—the God of Israel comes and strikes dead all the firstborn in Egypt.

Egypt Judged (Chap. 12)

I will . . . strike every firstborn male . . . I will execute judgments against all the gods of Egypt (12:12). Egypt lay devastated. Economically, the disruption and the loss were catastrophic—food was scarce, animals were gone (even wild animals would have had to flee in search of food). The temples of Egypt were without offerings, and the court of the pharaoh was lacking taxes and income. Each one of the plagues brought additional disorder, pestilence, suffering, and death, all of which disrupted and/or destroyed *ma'at* (order and balance in the world), something that lay at the very center of Egyptian worldview and mythology. Such disorder was an affront

From the Egyptian "Book of the Dead," a scene depicting the "judgment of the dead" ceremony. Note the feather of Ma'at on one side of the scale and the heart of the deceased on the other. Anubis, god of the dead, operates the scales while the crocodile-headed Ammit, god of the underworld, looks on expectantly and the god Thoth writes down the results. The god Osiris is seated to the right.

Jebel Musa, a Probable Location of Mount Sinai

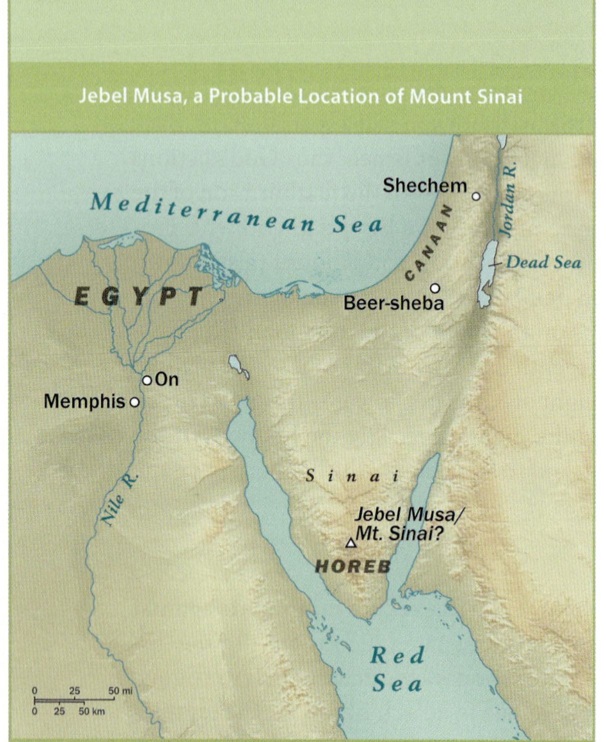

to the Egyptian goddess Ma'at (daughter of Re and goddess of order) and to the pharaoh, who was to keep order. Ma'at was often represented as a seated woman with a feather on her head. The Egyptian "Book of the Dead" describes a "judgment of the dead" ceremony taking place on the night in which a person passed into the afterlife. In this ceremony the deceased's heart was weighed in the balance of the goddess Ma'at—balanced against her feather on the other side of the scale. If the heart was out of order, not in balance with *ma'at*, it would be devoured by the god Ammit (a crocodile-headed lion/hippo griffin). Through the plagues that the Lord brings on the Egyptians he destroys any notion of order or balance (*ma'at*) that they have left in their world. Then in the final plague, at the Lord's command all firstborn are stricken dead all across Egypt. This takes place "about midnight" (11:4), suggesting a possible allusion to the Egyptian "judgment of the dead" ceremony. There is no *ma'at* left in Egypt, only terrible judgment. The Egyptians probably would perceive this as a direct judgment on them, their pharaoh, and their gods, as the Lord himself declares in 12:12.

Commemorate the Passover (Chap. 13)

So he led the people (13:18). Israel left Egypt heading toward Mount Sinai (3:12) on a route southeast through the Wadi Tumilat passing Succoth (a chariot city of the pharaoh). They moved toward the wilderness of Shur, located in northern central Sinai (15:22; 1 Sam. 15:7).[15]

Crossing the Sea (Chap. 14)

Pi-hahiroth, in front of Baal-zephon (14:9). The location of the crossing of the sea traditionally has been placed at the Bitter Lakes or farther south on the coast of the Gulf of Suez. The Israelites were leaving Egypt by a southeasterly route when God had Moses tell them to "turn back" (i.e., to the north). Doing so could have "boxed in" (14:3) Israel in the northeast Nile Delta region with a canal and Egyptian fortresses stretching into the coastal desert to their east. Others propose that this crossing took place at the northern end of the el-Ballah lake system and near the southern tip of a nearby ancient lagoon (i.e., the proposed location of the frontier fortress of Migdol).[16] This does not mean that it was God's intent to lead Israel to Canaan by the coastal route ("the road through the Philistine country"), but that he was intent on displaying his power over the pharaoh (13:17; 14:4). The account notes that the crossing took place at Migdol (a place name meaning "tower"),[17] that it was also near Pi-hahiroth ("mouth of the canal" or "the canal[s]"; there was a frontier canal that connected lakes in the northeast),[18] and that it faced Baal-zephon ("Lord of the North," referring to an idol god who protected mariners at sea).[19] The name Baal is mentioned in an Egyptian text referring to a body of water in this region, and it is near an ancient coastal lagoon for the Mediterranean Sea.[20] This frontier canal "ran north from Lake Timsah to Lake el-Ballah, and then proceeded in a northeasterly direction from the north side of that lake to the Mediterranean coast, just west of Tell Farama."[21] The term in the Bible for the body of water crossed is "Yam Suph"—literally, "Reed Sea" (note that Lake el-Ballah had many reeds and rushes). In Egyptian mythology the term Yam Suph stood for a location where the deceased "would pass through the lake or marsh and be purified in its waters before ascending to new life" in the spiritual realm.[22]

God miraculously leads the Israelites through the sea and destroys the Egyptian army led by the pharaoh just after he defeats the gods of Egypt, destroys Egypt's firstborn, and plunders its people. God carries out this final judgment in the sea, in front of the temple to Baal-zephon (who, in Egyptian mythology, perhaps should have protected the Egyptians in the midst of the sea). Likewise, the imagery of God leading Israel through purifying waters would not have been lost on the Israelites and those who traveled with them.

The Bitter Waters (Chap. 15)

They could not drink the water at Marah because it was bitter (15:23–25). The Sinai is mostly an empty, arid desert that receives very little rainfall. Water is rare and found only at a few oasis locations. Finding a well with undrinkable water could have been tragic. The piece of wood that Moses throws into the water to purify it may have been from the *Moringa oleifera* (horseradish tree), a tree native to India but also grown in North Africa. In some cases the ground-up seeds of this tree can have a purifying effect on water. Trees of any kind, however, are rare in central Sinai. So even given the possibility of a natural remedy, both the timing and the large scale of this purification process reveal God's power, provision, and healing care for Israel.

Manna and Quail (Chap. 16)

At evening quail came and covered the camp (16:13). Millions of quail annually migrate northward from Africa to Europe in the spring and back south in the fall. The quail generally fly in the evening and drop to the ground exhausted in the mornings to rest, though northbound migrations may reverse this and rest in the evening. Some of the eastern migrations do pass through Sinai on their journey north. Yet the timing of the quails' arrival and the fact that they arrive in numbers large enough to feed all the Israelites are miraculous.

The Amalekites (Chap. 17)

Amalek (17:8). Amalek, son of Eliphaz, was the grandson of Esau and a chief of his own tribe (Gen. 36:12, 16). The Amalekites lived in northern Sinai and in the Negev, the arid area south of Judah.

Jethro and Judges (Chap. 18)

Moses's father-in-law Jethro (18:1–12). After Sarah died, Abraham took a concubine-wife, Keturah. She bore Abraham six sons, the fourth of which was Midian (Gen. 25:1–6). This tribe settled in the northwestern Arabian Peninsula. Midian had a friendly relationship with both Amalek (to their west) and Moab (to their north) and oppressed Israel at times (Num. 22:7; Judg. 6–8). After killing the Egyptian, Moses flees to Midian and marries Zipporah, daughter of Reuel. Reuel, though living among—and a priest of—Midian, was a Kenite (Exod. 2:16; Judg. 1:16). The Kenites were a tribe of metalsmiths who later lived among and were loyal allies to Israel (1 Sam. 15:6). Reuel is identified as Zipporah's father (Exod. 2:18). Thus he would become Moses's "father-in-law" after the marriage. Later Hobab, son of Reuel, is also called Moses's "father-in-law" (Num. 10:29; Judg. 1:16; 4:11). The term translated as "father-in-law" (*hatan*), however, probably is more of a generic term that means just "in-law," a close relative by marriage (i.e., Zipporah's father, uncle, brother, or close blood relation). So Reuel could be Moses's father-in-law and Hobab his brother-in-law. Jethro could be another name used by Reuel. However, Jethro could also be a separate person. Jethro, also called "in-law," could be the priestly Midianite tribal leader into whose family Reuel (the Kenite) married. In this instance, Jethro—as "in-law," perhaps after Reuel's death—brings Zipporah and sons to Moses (along with Hobab, son/grandson of Reuel) at Sinai (Exod. 18). In either case, Jethro (or Jethro/Reuel) comes to faith in the Lord (Exod. 18:11) and makes a covenant of peace with Israel's leaders by sharing a meal with them. Then he leaves Sinai and goes home (Exod. 18:27), while Hobab, son/grandson of Reuel, joins Israel and dwells with them (Num. 10:29; Judg. 4:11).

Sinai (Chap. 19)

Came to the Sinai Wilderness . . . camped there in front of the mountain (19:1–2). Sacred mountains were well known in most cultures of the ancient Near East; the gods were thought to live on them. Within the Pentateuch there are two different names associated with this mountain (Horeb and Sinai). Horeb is called the "mountain of God" in 3:1. Yet the meaning of the term "Horeb" is "desert," suggesting a more regional nuance of the term. The word "Sinai" is also used as a regional term (e.g., "wilderness/desert of Sinai") three times in Exodus, ten times in Numbers, and once in Leviticus. Yet "Sinai" is also used ten times in Exodus to refer specifically to Mount Sinai, the mountain where Moses meets God. Likewise, while "Horeb" is used for this mountain in 3:1 and 33:6, as well as nine times in Deuteronomy, in Exod. 17:1–7 Horeb seems to be referring to a region broader than just Mount Sinai itself. The relationship between the two terms can best be understood by viewing Sinai as the proper name for the specific mountain, while Horeb is the region in which the mountain lies. The Wilderness of Sinai would be the region immediately around the mountain.[23]

The central plateau of what is now called the Sinai Peninsula covers a desolate 13,200 square miles of chalky plateaus, limestone escarpments, and granite mountains, with wide valleys between.[24] It is not known for certain which of the many mountains in this region was the biblical Mount Sinai, and several different mountains have been suggested as possibilities. Note that the Israelites take six weeks to travel from Egypt to Mount Sinai. The six weeks following Passover (approximately mid-April to June 1) are the best time of year to travel in this region; it is a cool 46–57 degrees in the evenings and a tolerable 73–84 degrees during the day. Yet even then, traveling under the hot sun with children, elderly people, and animals, the Israelites probably did not cover more than about fifteen miles per day and perhaps less. Even this slow pace, however, would allow enough time for

Israel to reach most of the mountains that have been proposed, including the traditional southernmost site of Jebel Musa (165–220 miles).[25]

The Law (Chaps. 20–22)

The Covenant (20:1–26). In the ancient Near East a conquering overlord or king would make (or impose) a treaty/covenant upon a lesser king/people for mutual support and benefit. The powerful king (often called suzerain) imposed his stipulations, and the lesser king and his people voluntarily agreed to them and became his vassals. In the mid-to-late second millennium BC international suzerainty treaty/covenants had a literary form containing certain elements. In this time frame the form found in Exodus and in Deuteronomy most closely resembles the Hittite treaty structure unique to the period of 1400–1200 BC.[26] The elements of a Hittite treaty are (1) preamble, (2) historical prologue, (3) covenant stipulations, (4) covenant blessings or curses, and (5) witnesses. The structure of the book of Deuteronomy is very similar to this Hittite treaty form (see comments on Deut. 4:2). These covenant elements of God as suzerain and Israel as his vassal are also present in Exodus, but the elements are presented in a slightly different order.[27]

These are the ordinances that you are to set before them (21:1). There are several ancient Near Eastern law codes with laws similar to those in Exodus: Shulgi/Ur-Nammu (2100 BC), Lipit-Ishtar (1900 BC), and the more famous Code of Hammurabi (1700 BC). Most of these law codes are descriptive civil or criminal case law ("If a man does X, then Y should be the result/punishment") rather than prescriptive absolute statements that limit behavior ("Thou shalt not X"). So the ancient Near Eastern laws were more about the king's role of keeping order after the fact than about a systematic legislation governing rules of behavior.[28] In Egypt criminal and civil law was adjudicated by regional governors, officials of the pharaoh, and ultimately the pharaoh himself. No law code of the Egyptians remains, but there is evidence of harsh punishment for certain crimes such as tomb robbing, and there is evidence that the legal system was rather arbitrary. The Egyptian "Tale of the Eloquent Peasant," for example, reveals how the rich oppressed the poor, and how while justice might come, it was arbitrary, capricious, and dependent upon how well a complainant could present a case.[29] While the legal forms are similar, the biblical law differs from other law codes in the ancient Near East in focus. Biblical laws highlight the relationship Israel has with the Lord; indeed, their covenant relationship with him was the basis for the law. The Ten Commandments, as the core of covenantal requirement, are absolute statements of prescribed behavior that include religious, moral, civil, and criminal elements.[30]

Festivals (Chap. 23)

You must not boil a young goat in its mother's milk (23:19). The context here is one of bringing sacrifices to the annual festivals. Lambs usually are weaned from sixty to ninety days of age, though it can take place as early as fourteen days and as late as six months. "One-year-old lamb(s)" are mentioned 268 times as required sacrifices in the OT. So a lamb that is too young (under a year), and needing its mothers' milk, is too young to sacrifice. The proscription is stated again in 34:26 in a context of prohibition against putting together that which is holy and that which is common or impure. The proscription is stated also in Deut. 14:21 in the context of a prohibition against eating animals that have died on their own (implying that they are unclean). Ultimately, the issue may be to avoid the conjoining of the opposites of life and death—that is, a slaughtered or sacrificed lamb being cooked in the life-supporting milk of its mother (see comments on Deut. 14:21).

Confirming the Covenant (Chap. 24)

An altar and twelve pillars . . . they ate and drank (24:1–11). In the ancient Near East sometimes stones would be set up within a temple context (as at Arad) to represent a god, but they could also be set up to represent ancestors or, as here, witnesses to a covenant or treaty. After reading the covenant laws to Israel (20:1–23:33), the people agreed to be bound by the covenant. Then Moses sprinkled the blood of the sacrifice upon them and upon the altar. This sprinkling bound the people by the sacrificial blood to God (represented by the altar on which the covenant sacrifice took place). Moses and the leading elders of Israel went up the side of Mount Sinai and ate a covenantal fellowship meal, with God actually standing next to them and so participating in the meal.

The Tabernacle (Chaps. 25–27)

They are to make an ark of acacia wood . . . overlay it with pure gold (25:10–22). The ark of the testimony (or ark of the covenant) consisted of a wood box (45 inches long by 27 inches wide by 27 inches high) and long poles for carrying—all overlaid with gold, as well as a solid-gold lid that had two cherubs on top facing each other and bowing with outspread wings covering their faces. The lid was called the atonement cover (or mercy seat), and it was there that God's presence appeared in a cloud between the wings of the cherubs (Lev. 16:2). It was from here that God spoke to Moses (Num. 7:89). The ark was called God's footstool by David (1 Chron. 28:2). The prophet

Isaiah quotes the Lord, "Heaven is my throne, and earth is my footstool" (Isa. 66:1); the ark may be similar to Isaiah's imagery, with God's presence above the lid of the ark revealing heaven and the box below denoting the earth. The two tablets with the Ten Commandments were kept inside the ark along with a jar of manna and Aaron's rod that budded. On the Day of Atonement the high priest came into the holy of holies and sprinkled the blood of the sacrifice upon the atonement cover (Lev. 16:14–15). So the sacrificial blood came between the covenant law (Ten Commandments) and the presence of God above—literally covering the law. In the mindset of the Israelites the ark may have been similar to the Egyptian sacred bark. In Egypt the gods often rode in the bark, a sacred boat carried by priests on poles.[31] However, whereas the bark carried an idol image, the ark of the testimony was aniconic (without an image); God was actually there, and no image was necessary. A depiction of Pharaoh Ramesses II's tent shows his cartouche (inscribed name) within his tent in the midst of his camp, and the cartouche is flanked by two winged creatures, which is similar to the image of the mercy seat described on the ark.[32]

Put the tablets of the testimony that I will give you into the ark (25:16). The Ten Commandments were not spread out over two tablets. There were two copies of the Ten Commandments, each one containing all ten (also called "the testimony" [25:21]). In the ancient Near East if two kings/nobles made a covenant, one copy of that covenant would be placed in the temple (between the feet) of the idol god of one party, and one copy would be placed in the temple (between the feet) of the idol god of the other party. In the instance of the Israelites, the tabernacle and the ark as God's footstool (1 Chron. 28:2) belonged to God as suzerain and to Israel as vassal. So both copies of the Ten Commandments are placed in the same place—the ark of the testimony/covenant.[33]

Construct a table of acacia wood (25:23). The table of showbread was overlaid with gold, with an edge molding to keep its plates, pitchers, dishes, and bowls on the table as it was carried from place to place. The twelve loaves of the bread of presence, representing the twelve tribes, were literally "bread of the face" or "bread in the presence of" the Lord and before him continually. The bread of presence was holy and was replaced each Sabbath. Unlike the food offerings made to ancient Near Eastern temple idols of Israel's neighbors, the bread of presence was not to feed God. However, in a manner similar to ancient Near Eastern temples, the removed bread was eaten by the high priest and his sons (Lev. 24:7–9).

Make a lampstand (25:31). The lampstand (or menorah) was an elaborate candle stand with seven oil lamps to provide light in the holy place. The description of the lampstand suggests that it resembled a stylized almond tree, thus probably representing the tree of life in the garden of Eden, the burning bush that Moses encountered, or both.

Construct the altar . . . make horns for it on its four corners . . . overlay it with bronze (27:1–2). The nature of the horns for the altar was not well understood until archaeologists uncovered a horned altar of stone at the ancient city of Beer-sheba. That altar has four horn-like appendages projecting upward from its corners that apparently served to keep the wood and the sacrifice in place on the altar. The bronze altar for the tabernacle also had a grate through which the ashes from the fire/sacrifice would fall. These ashes were removed periodically (Lev. 6:10), but this imagery of the used-up sacrifice being under the altar may be the imagery later used in the NT book of Revelation, where the souls of those who were slain for their faith were under the altar in heaven before God (Rev. 6:9).

Priestly Garments and Consecration (Chaps. 28–29)

Make holy garments (28:2). Throughout the ancient Near East sacred garments typically were used by priests and temple workers in their daily service.[34] In Egypt priests were required to have clean/pure bodies and garments.[35] When the pharaoh participated in temple ceremonies, there was a robing ceremony that included a ritual cleansing that involved the use of incense.[36] In Mesopotamia there is an account of the king of Babylon giving a year's worth of clothing (ten different types of garments) made of fine linen and wool—including garments colored red and purple—to a temple high priest at the city of Sippar in order to support him in his work (ca. 839 BC).[37] The priestly garments set apart the high priest as holy before God. Elements of the priestly clothing were symbolic (i.e., bearing the names of the tribes on his shoulder and chest). The Urim (lights) and Thummim (perfections) were kept in the breastpiece of decision (ephod) for the priest to use to inquire of the Lord (Num. 27:21), likely by casting lots (cf. 1 Sam. 14:41). It may be that these had one side light and one side dark (in this manner, two lights could be a yes, and two darks a no, with a mixed set being a nonanswer [cf. 1 Sam. 28:6]). Casting lots was often done to determine the guilty party in a situation (1 Sam. 14:41; cf. Josh. 7:14), so perhaps two

A reconstructed horned altar at Beersheba.

Urim selected the guilty person (since the term *urim* may be based upon a root word meaning "curse"). If so, the two terms may be "curses" and "innocents." In other instances these were used to get a "yes" or a "no" answer from God, and then the priest might add a further word from the Lord (1 Sam. 23:9–12) (see comments on 1 Sam. 14:41–42).

Oil and Incense (Chap. 30)

Make an altar for the burning of incense; make it of acacia wood (30:1–10, 34–38). Incense was widely used in temples across the ancient Near East as an offering to the gods. Typically it was offered in censers held by worshipers, placed upon altars along with animal sacrifices and grain offerings, or, as in this instance, upon a separate altar used solely for the purpose of incense. Incense allowed for use in the tabernacle was made from clear resin taken from unripe almonds, ground spiral seashells, aromatic gum resin (from a plant in the parsley family and used in Egypt for incense), frankincense, and other spices (30:34–38). When burned, it gave off a pleasant-smelling perfume as well as smoke. Each day (morning and twilight) the high priest (and no one else) was to place incense upon this altar within the holy place, right before the veil that covered the entrance to the holy of holies (30:1–10). The psalmist compares his prayers to this burning incense, so the incense may figuratively represent the prayers of the people rising to God as a pleasing aroma (Ps. 141:1–2; see also Luke 1:10; Rev. 5:8; 8:3–4). On the Day of Atonement, however, as he entered the holy of holies, the high priest was to offer two handfuls of finely ground incense using a censer full of coals from the altar. The smoke from the incense would thus keep him from "seeing God" seated above the ark and protect him from being killed (Lev. 16:12–13). Aaron's sons Nadab and Abihu were killed when they offered incense in a manner contrary to God's command, thus showing disrespect for God (Lev. 10:1–2).

Prepare from these a holy anointing oil (30:25). This anointing oil was used to sanctify, or set apart as holy, the tabernacle and all of its articles of service and its furnishings (tent, ark, altars, utensils, laver, etc.). Made from myrrh, cinnamon, spice-reed, clove of cinnamon, and olive oil, it was to be sprinkled even upon Aaron and his sons, consecrating them as priests. The dry spices were boiled, distilled, and infused into the olive oil in the manner of a perfumer (30:25). Anyone who copied its formula and made it for common use was to be excommunicated from the people of Israel. The Hebrew verb for "anoint" (*mashah*) can be used for common things (Isa. 21:5; Jer. 22:14; Amos 6:6) or for higher purposes (as here, anointing religious objects and priests; or as in 1 Kings 19:16, prophets and kings).

As kings, both Saul and David were called "the Lord's *anointed*" (*mashiah*, 1 Sam. 26:11; 2 Sam. 19:21). This is the term transliterated as "Messiah" in the OT (cf. Dan. 9:25–26); in the NT the equivalent Greek term (*christos*) is transliterated as "Christ" (Matt. 1:1; cf. Isa. 61:1, quoted by Jesus in Luke 4:18; and Acts 10:38).

The Sign of the Covenant (Chap. 31)

You must observe my Sabbaths (31:13). The origins of the Sabbath (a word that means "to cease, rest") are found in Gen. 2:2–3 (God rests, blesses, makes it holy), Exod. 20:8–11 (keep the Sabbath because God rested on the seventh day, blessed it, and made it holy), and Deut. 5:12–15 (keep the Sabbath, remembering God's deliverance of Israel from Egypt). This appears to reflect a movement of focus in covenant observance from God's creation to God's deliverance.

The Golden Calf (Chap. 32)

Made it into an image of a calf (32:4). In the Canaanite pantheon of gods both the father god El and frequently the fertility/storm god Baal/Haddad are represented as standing upon the back of a bull. Thus Aaron's handiwork could be intended as a throne for the Lord, who would be present above the bull. However, by the time the image was complete, the people say, "Israel, these are your gods," thus breaking the second commandment before the law was even delivered by Moses. For several centuries Israel had been steeped in the Egyptian culture of idolatry and deified idols/icons. Thus the bull image may have been influenced by the worship of the Apis bull, which was of great importance in Egypt. However, this "young bull" figurine that Aaron shaped from the golden earrings of the people most likely was intended to be an image of the Lord, since they made a feast to the Lord (32:5–6). Much later, in the period of the divided kingdom, Jeroboam I, king of the northern Israelite tribes (ca. 930 BC), likely looked back to this event when he set up two golden calf-idols, thus leading Israel, yet again, into idolatry.

Erase me from the book you have written (32:32). The term translated as "book" is no doubt referring to a rolled scroll (books with leaf pages, or codices as they are called by scholars, do not come into common usage until fifteen hundred years or so after the exodus). Leather scrolls or parchments were written on in ancient times with ink made from a mixture of soot, water, and gum arabic. In order to reuse a leather scroll, a scribe had to scrape off the writing and then sand the surface to remove the ink that had penetrated the hide. Sometimes a reused scroll's original writing can still be seen in part on the scroll. A scroll like this is called a palimpsest, but in the imagery used here, the "wiping out" of a name from God's scroll is permanent and complete. This same term is applied to judgment on the Amalekites in 17:14 for their attack upon Israel. Forty years later at the end of the wanderings, God states that if anyone commits idolatry and serves other gods, he will curse them and "blot out" their name from under heaven (Deut. 29:20). The conceptual setting for a "book of life" comes from the practice of creating a list of names in a town or city of the clans, families, and individuals living there.[38] The psalmist speaks of a "book of life" in whose names the righteous are listed but from which his wicked adversaries might be blotted out (Ps. 69:28; see also Dan. 12:1; Mal. 3:16; Phil. 4:3; Rev. 13:8; 17:8; 20:15).

Moses Brings the Covenant (Chaps. 34–39)

Come up Mount Sinai . . . no one may go up with you (34:2–3). Sacred space was well understood among the people of the ancient Near East. Temples were considered to be ideal representations of the sacred spaces where the gods lived upon their holy mountains. God warns Moses again about the prohibition against Israel approaching the holy mountain. Yet Moses is called to the summit, where God will again write the Ten Commandments on two new stone tablets (34:1). Often when God reveals his presence, the place is considered holy, with special stipulations added regarding how to approach him (the garden of Eden, "you shall not eat from the tree" [Gen. 2:17]; the burning bush, "remove your sandals" [Exod. 3:5]; the guarding of the tabernacle [Num. 1:53]; the angelic commander, "take off your sandals" [Josh. 5:15]). Upon reaching the summit, Moses falls prostrate in the cleft of the rock before God as he passes by, declaring his name to Moses (34:5–8; cf. 33:19–22). In Moses's song after crossing the sea, he states, "You will bring them in and plant them on the mountain of your possession; Lord, you have prepared the place for your dwelling; Lord, your hands have established the sanctuary" (15:17). While Israel is reticent, fearful, and restrained from approaching God now, their destiny is to dwell upon God's mountain with him.

Chop down their Asherah poles (34:13). See comments on 1 Kings 15:13.

Make everything that the Lord has commanded (35:10). Much of the material in chapters 35–39 is similar to that presented in chapters 25–29 regarding the construction of the tabernacle and associated utensils. Some scholars have argued that the repetition of the content in these two sections stems from the use of multiple sources in the composition that were edited together. However, the two sections are part of the same story. The difference in the two sections is that in chapters 25–29 God instructs Moses and the Israelites in how to construct the tabernacle and associated utensils, and in chapters 35–39 Israel obediently carries out the actual construction. Also, note that in the mid to late second millennium BC it is common in ancient Near Eastern texts to find repeated texts/topics, commands, or accounts varying in this manner, with different sections focusing in on different specific aspects. So this repetition reinforces the message—the sovereignty of God—and the obedience of Moses and the people in stressing that his word was carried out exactly as God directed Moses.

The Glory of the Lord Fills the Tabernacle

(Chap. 40)

The glory of the Lord filled the tabernacle (40:34). God had said, "They are to make a sanctuary for me so that I may dwell among them" (25:8). The imagery of a special tent inhabited by a god was an image with which both the Egyptians and the Israelites would be familiar. The pharaoh, considered by the Egyptians to be a divine king, occasionally went forth on campaigns against neighboring countries and peoples (e.g., Libya, Cush, Canaan, the Hittites, Assyria). In the Egyptian wall relief from one of these campaigns (the battle of Kadesh) the pharaoh is depicted in the midst of his army, camped in a tent with a layout very similar to that of the tabernacle (a rectangular courtyard oriented east-west with the entrance on the east, a reception tent/holy place, a square throne tent/holy of holies).[39]

This stela contains the law code of the Babylonian king Hammurabi (1792–1750 BC) and addresses a wide range of civil laws (agricultural, domestic, commercial, etc.).

Leviticus

R. Dennis Cole

Introduction. The book of Leviticus stands at the center of the Pentateuch with its key theme of "holiness" as that which is both a central attribute of God and an essential need for the people of God. The Israelite people were to be a holy people living a distinctive holy life before a holy God. The title of the book of Leviticus is derived from the Latin, reflecting the function of the Levite tribe and the Aaronic priesthood. Leviticus contains divine instructions for the collective and individual people of Israel, setting forth the parameters for maintaining a holy relationship to God through a variety of sacrifices, laws, and celebrations.

The ancient Near East abounds with literary and archaeological evidence of cultic (i.e., religious) practices involving ritual sacrifices, priestly personnel, prayers and hymnic recitations, and laws. From the earliest civilizations of the ancient Near East and the Mediterranean world, sacrificial acts of ritual slaughtering of animals, the rendering of liquid libations of oil, water, and wine, the presentations of grain products, and the utilization of incense were means by which people attempted to interact with their deities. Many of these practices find close parallels with the biblical instructions, reflecting a vibrant international world of socioreligious interaction and a common desire to engage the divine through ritual processes.

Among the most well-known texts are the Hittite "Instructions to Priests and Temple Officials," the Laws of Eshnunna, Ur-Nammu, and Lipit-Ishtar, the Code of Hammurabi, and later Assyrian and Babylonian law codes that date from between 2500 and 500 BC, the time frame of the OT. These texts from Mesopotamia, Egypt, Syria, and Anatolia (Turkey) reflect a background

A stone wall relief that depicts Ashurbanipal pouring out a libation offering at an offering table.

of magic, divination, and sorcery by which the divine and demonic forces could be engaged to bring about positive or negative results, blessing or cursing to individuals, families, or nations.

The historical setting of Leviticus within the structure of the Pentateuch is the year or so following Israel's exodus from Egypt. The biblical time frame is the second half of the second millennium BC (1500–1200 BC) (see comments on Exod. 1:8–11; 1:11), during the era of the empires of the Egyptians and the Hittites, the seafaring people of Ugarit, and the world of the Canaanites, Amorites, Aramaeans, and others. The instructions of Leviticus will be compared to similar instructions of those people groups of the second millennium.

Geographically, the Israelites are camped at Mount Sinai (Lev. 25:1; 26:46; 27:34) in the region of the Sinai Wilderness, generally located in the southern half of what is known today as the Sinai Peninsula.

Ritual Sacrifices (1:1–3:17)

The Lord summoned Moses and spoke to him (1:1). The divine speech formula occurs more than twenty times in Leviticus. Divine speech formulas in various literary contexts of the ancient Near East set forth the concept that the order of civilization was instructed and ordained by deity. The texts reflected a symbiotic relationship between humans and the divine whereby deity can be invoked, provided for, placated, or manipulated into bringing desired results. The stela of the Code of Hammurabi, for example, reflects the wise sun god Shamash giving the law to the king of Babylon.

Offering from the herd or the flock (1:2). Evidence of the ritual slaughtering of animals in the socioreligious context of the ancient Near East has been dated at least as far back as 8000 BC, and this practice continued into the NT era of Greece and Rome. The purpose of these offerings was viewed variously as a means of providing for the needs of deity, placating deity's displeasure with people, and bringing desired results for human benefit. The Israelite sacrifices are restricted to "the herd or the flock" and designated as "clean" animals. Other civilizations sacrificed wild animals, as well as donkeys, pigs, and other animals that were disallowed in Israelite practice.

Burnt offering (1:3–17). The burnt offering was one of the most common sacrifices among the Israelites and neighboring peoples. In Ugarit (an ancient city in Syria) there was a "whole offering" that was similar in kind and function. The "burnt offering" first occurs in Gen. 8:20 when Noah honored God by offering clean animals after deliverance from the judgment of the flood (see comments on Gen. 8:20).

Unblemished male (1:3). Other animal offerings, such as the peace offering (3:1), could come from the female population. Israelite religious instructions emphasized the high quality of all offerings—only the best could be presented to God.

Lay his hand on the head of the burnt offering (1:4). A practice known among Hittite rituals, the laying on of the hand was an identification ritual that conferred the personal identity of the offerer upon the sacrificial victim. The effect was a substitutionary ritual whereby the sacrifice of the life of the animal was equivalent to the submission of the life of the offerer.

Accepted on his behalf to make atonement (1:4). The two concepts "acceptability" and "atonement" denote the human-divine reconciliation process by which God is pleased as the impurity is removed. The parallel term in Akkadian, the language of the Assyrians (see the article "The Assyrians"), denotes a removal of evil or impurity, and ritual cleansing is effected (cf. 16:19, 30; Num. 8:21).

Aaron's sons the priests (1:5–9). Priestly oversight of ritual activity is well documented among most ancient Near Eastern cultures of the OT era. Priests carried several responsibilities of maintaining separation between the sacred and the profane, between impure humanity and the sacred divine, carrying out ritual acts properly, and mediating divine response via divination, incantation, and other means.

Present the blood and splatter it on all sides of the altar (1:5, 11, 15). The use of blood for ritual purification was practiced by the Israelites and the Hittites, though unknown in Ugarit and Mesopotamia. However, the special significance of blood as the source of life, with highly restrictive practices ensuring its proper collection and distribution, was unique to ancient Israel. Though the Hittites believed that blood carried life (or conversely death) and strength, in their blood sacrifices of the *zurki* ritual, "no special precautions against defilement or contamination are called for in the handling of blood in sacrifice, and . . . its consumption by humans is never enjoined or even restricted."[1]

A fire offering of a pleasing aroma (1:9, 13, 17). See comments on Lev. 3:11, 16.

Grain offering (2:1–16). The finest flour combined with oil and incense was offered alone or in combination with animal and/or libation offerings. Typically, the oil was olive oil extracted through the chopping and crushing of olives in a press. Examples of these presses abound in excavations throughout the ancient Near East. Hittite grain offerings were part of their seasonal festivals as recorded in "Instructions to Priests and Temple Officials," which reads, "He must celebrate with festival cattle, sheep, bread, and beer. He may not omit (even) the thin loaf. Whoever neglects it . . . let it be a great sin to that one."[2]

Memorial portion (2:2). The memorial portion was offered to God, and the remainder eaten by the priests. There is a Hittite text that mentions the provision of certain bread portions for the priestly families, though the beer and the wine were not to be taken outside the temple. The inventory of a festival for the storm god of the city of Wattarwa included a bull, sheep, two kinds of flour, and two grades of beer.

Baked in an oven . . . unleavened (2:4). The oven was made from hand-shaped clay and formed into a dome-like shape. Each family probably owned one. The restriction against leavening in the grain offering may have derived from the connotation that leaven symbolized fermentation, deterioration, and death, and hence was taboo on the altar of blessings and life.[3]

You are not to burn any yeast or honey (2:11). Though some offerings could include leavening, honey, wine, or beer, they were not to be burned on the altar as an offering of savory aroma to God. As mentioned above, leavening carried a connotation of death and impurity and thus was not to be rendered by smoke into the realm of the holy, life-giving God. Honey was derived from dates, which were susceptible to fermentation.

Salt of the covenant with your God (2:13). Peoples from the ancient Near East (as well as Greece) shared salt as they entered into treaties and alliances. Salt, once a medium of exchange, denoted preservation, mutual support, and enhancement of relationships. Note that loyalty to the Persian king Artaxerxes is symbolized through the phrase "we eat the salt of the palace" (usually translated as something related to an oath of loyalty) (see comments on Ezra 4:14). Salt as a preservative inhibited fermentation and deterioration.

Fellowship sacrifice (3:1). The fellowship (or peace) sacrifice was a male or female animal from the cattle, sheep,

Grain offerings or incense were most likely burned on an offering stand such as this one, discovered at the ancient city of Megiddo.

or goats category. This offering of well-being was also practiced regularly in the city of Ugarit (in Syria), where the king offered in sequence a burnt offering and a peace offering on the roof of the Baal temple.

Fire offering . . . fat . . . kidneys (3:3–4, 9–10, 14–15). These portions were always dedicated to the Lord, whereas others could be consumed by the offerer and the priests (5:11–36). All portions of fat under the skin and around and between the internal organs were considered the choicest portions to be rendered by fire on an altar unto God.

Burn the food on the altar, as a fire offering (3:11, 16). Most ancient Near Eastern cultures considered their deities as needing sustenance like humans, and they envisioned sacrifice as a means of feeding them. In Hittite rituals, feeding the gods involved "divine" portions of the heart and liver. Food for the deities could be supplemented with baked goods, sweets, and beverages. A text from the city of Ugarit (in Syria) described the god 'Ilu (El) throwing a banquet for the gods by slaughtering animals and inviting them to eat meat and drink new wine to drunkenness. Israelite religion did not consider God as needing sustenance, though the "food" offering was prepared in the same manner as for human consumption, but via the savory smoke the offering entered into the symbolic nostrils of God.

Sin Offerings (4:1–6:7)

Someone sins unintentionally (4:2, 22, 27). Unwittingly or ignorantly violating the will of the gods is reflected in the Egyptian prayer for forgiveness to Re-Harakhti: "Visit not my many offenses upon me, I am one ignorant of himself; I am a mindless man who all day follows his mouth like an ox after grass."[4] Similarly, the Babylonian "Poem of the Righteous Sufferer" reflects, "I wish I knew the things which were pleasing to the gods! What seems good to one's self could be an offense to one's god! Who could learn the reasoning of the gods in heaven?"[5]

Sprinkle . . . seven times (4:5–7). The sevenfold sprinkling reflects the concept of wholeness or completeness similar to the Day of Atonement, moving outward in a three-step process from a position in front of the veil, then to the incense altar, and finally the remainder is poured out in front of the altar just inside the entrance (cf. chap. 17). Sevenfold recitations over sacrificial acts to invoke deity are known from other locations such as the city of Ugarit (in Syria).

Horns of the altar of fragrant incense (4:7, 18). See comments on Exod. 27:1–2; 30:1–10, 34–38. Incense altars have been discovered in excavations throughout the ancient Near East. Often made from stone, bronze, or other materials, these altars were relatively small structures. The excavations at Ekron (a Philistine city) yielded numerous small stone horned altars.

A horned altar from the ancient city of Megiddo.

Outside the camp (4:12, 21). The removal of sources of impurity such as sacrificial remnants to a location outside the holy assembly occurs frequently in Israelite as well as in ancient Near Eastern law. The Hittites disposed of ritual remnants on burning trash heaps outside the city.

He will be forgiven (4:26, 31, 35). The concept of forgiveness (*nislach*) finds a parallel in a Ugaritic text listing sacrifices in the context of a person seeking forgiveness (*slch nepesh*).

Guilt offering (5:14–6:7). The Hebrew guilt offering (*asham*) finds its semantic equivalent in the *atam* of Ugarit (an ancient city in Syria). This "reparation offering" remedied a variety of offenses against both God and people. Punishment of guilt was one of the most common forms of ancient Near Eastern case law. One such case is the neglect of providing testimony as a witness in a legal matter after being confronted publicly. In the Code of Hammurabi (an ancient Babylonian king), as in Israelite law, an observer of a crime was required to step forward and testify.

Two turtledoves (5:7). A variety of birds are mentioned among the offerings at the temple of Baal Saphon, including a group of sacrifices that could be offered by a poor person, as here in 5:7.

Holy things (5:14). Restitution for sacrilege against the sanctuary or its holy things finds parallel among the Hittites, who in one particular situation feared that a plague had come because of their failure to carry out the proper rituals.

Adding a fifth of its value to it (5:16). The animal offering could be converted into currency, with a one-fifth "penalty." A parallel from the ancient Mesopotamian city of Nuzi specifies certain animals for restoration in which fixed fines of currency could substitute for the animal.

Deceiving his neighbor (6:2). Fraud, extortion, and breaking an oath against another person in property and financial matters were a sacrilege against God. Atonement reparation required restitution of adding a one-fifth penalty to the offended party, plus an animal sacrifice of an unblemished ram. The Egyptian "Instruction of Amenemope" (chaps. 5–7) contains numerous warnings against greed and defrauding of others, including the sanctuary. Many warnings apply to the abuse and oppression of the poor and the weak, warning that the offender may reap the judgment of the gods.

The law code of the ancient Babylonian king Hammurabi carried severe punishments for cases of theft and fraud, often death.

Priestly Roles and Provisions in Offerings (6:8–7:38)

The fire of the altar is kept burning (6:9). The perpetual fire in the tabernacle is unlike Hittite priestly regulations, which required that sacrificial fires be extinguished overnight lest they cause the temple to catch fire.

Aaron's descendants may eat it (6:18, 26; 7:6). Provision for the priesthood through the consumption of portions of sacrificial offerings was common among ancient Near Eastern rituals. In the Zukru festival at Emar (an ancient city in Syria) the divination priest was provided with portions of animal sacrifices, including the right breast, the hide, and the head. In Assyrian texts the right thigh and other cuts were provided for the various attendant priests.

Priesthood (8:1–10:20)

Consecrate them (8:1–36). The Babylonian Akitu festival of the New Year and the Emar (a city in ancient Syria) "Installation of the High Priestess of the Storm God" provide ancient Near Eastern parallels to the ritual installation of priestly personnel.

Take Aaron . . . anointing oil (8:2). On the first day of the seven-day dedication at Emar (an ancient city in Syria), fragrant oil from the palace and Ninkur's temple was placed on the high priestess's head, and numerous sacrifices followed. Among the Egyptians and the Hittites oil anointing was viewed as a means of protecting one from the gods of the underworld. In Israel the anointing oil also consecrated the tabernacle and its installations, a practice paralleled in ancient Near Eastern cultures.

Urim and Thummim (8:8). See comments on Exod. 28:2; 1 Sam. 14:41–42; 23:6. A parallel practice in Assyria for ritual divination utilized black and white stones with incantations evoking the sun god Shamash. Casting of lots was also used in the choosing of a new high priestess at Emar (an ancient city in Syria).

Right earlobe . . . thumb of his right hand . . . big toe of his right foot (8:23). The threefold blood-smearing purification ritual echoes a further fulfillment of the ordination of the priesthood: the totality of the officiant had been sanctified and cleansed. Ritual daubing is widely attested in the literature of the ancient Near East. Usually accompanied by incantations, the smearing of a variety of liquids and potions was a means to purify persons, deities, objects, and buildings.

Aaron, his sons . . . approach the altar and sacrifice (9:1–24). Following the seven-day consecration and ordination of the priesthood, the prescribed ritual offerings were inaugurated. The sequence of the offerings followed the standard ritual sequence of sin offering (9:2, 8, 15), burnt offering (9:2, 12, 16), and then the peace (fellowship) offering (9:18). The lifting of the hands (9:22) was a common gesture in invoking the blessing of deity, a symbol of humility as when King Kirta (a mythological Canaanite hero) "washed and rouged himself," sacrificed a kid goat and a bird, then lifted his hands heavenward to invoke 'Ilu (El) to have Ba'lu (Baal) to descend and provide for the people in preparation for defending the city. More so than the occasional ancient Near Eastern reference to water lustration, ceremonial washing was an essential part of numerous ritual texts in the Bible.

Firepan . . . unauthorized fire (10:1–4). Firepans of gold were used with the golden lampstand (Exod. 25:38), and bronze with the bronze altar (Exod. 27:3). Several aspects indicate the improper nature of the ritual act performed by Nadab and Abihu: each priest took his own firepan, they both burned a "strange" fire, the act was not commanded by God, and they did not honor God as holy. Strict rules for cultic practice are evidenced in Mesopotamia, Anatolia, and Egypt. The worship of Amon-Re at Karnak entailed a precise ritual sequence for incense offerings. Special incantations preceded each stage of the process, several times concluding with a proclamation of purity.

Do not let your hair hang loose and do not tear your clothes (10:6). The consecrated priests were not to engage in mourning rituals for the dead, such as exposing the head via removal of the turban or showing remorse by the rending of garments. These and other aspects of priestly mourning are reflected in the dual texts of Mesopotamia, "The Descent of Inanna" and "The Descent of Ishtar to the Underworld."

You . . . are not to drink wine or beer when you enter the tent (10:9). In the Hittite document "Instructions to Priests and Temple Officials" the Hittite priests were permitted to drink alcohol, but they were warned against careless behavior that might come from their drinking, which could result in a serious beating. Israelite priests were restricted from any consumption of fermented beverages while performing sacred service in the tabernacle, and the punishment for violating this was death.

Purity Laws and Purifications (11:1–15:33)

You may eat . . . do not not eat (11:1–47). The strict delineation of clean versus unclean animals for consumption in Israel is unparalleled in the literature of the ancient Near East. Most cultures limited some animals (such as cattle, donkeys, wild animals, birds) from consumption or use in their sacrificial systems, but none compared to the extensive details of Israelite law. The Egyptians would not consume cows because the cow was a symbol associated with either the cow goddess Hathor or the related cow goddess Bat. Followers of the Egyptian god Horus considered the pig an abomination to the gods based on a mythological conflict between Horus and Seth (the god of chaos, who in this incident took the form of a pig) in which Horus lost an eye.[6] The diet of the Hittites included pigs, wild boars, wild animals, fish, sharks, badgers, weasels, and bears, among others. Later in history, among the Greeks and the Romans, pigs were acceptable for sacrifice.

Winged insects (11:20–23). Certain winged insects, such as locusts and crickets, were consumable both in Israel and in other regions of the ancient Near East, as evidenced by dietary texts of Mesopotamia.

When a woman . . . gives birth . . . she will be unclean (12:1). Across the ancient Near East genital discharges from males or females were considered religious contaminants, rendering one impure for specified periods of time. Among the Hittites a purification ritual was required for women after they gave birth. Likewise, if a birthing stool broke during childbirth, it was considered unclean, and a blood purification ritual was enacted. Menstrual uncleanness derived from blood was also a common impurity among ancient Near Eastern cultures. Fear was widespread in the ancient Near East that menstrual blood was the source of demonic forces. In Israel the impurity period for the new mother lasted forty days for the birth of a son and eighty days for the birth of a daughter (12:2–5). Similarly, Persian and Greek women were restricted from sacred areas for forty days after giving birth. Likewise, among the Hittites the impurity period for a male child was three months, and for a female child four months.

Make atonement on her behalf (12:7). Atonement here is for ritual impurity, not moral or ethical sin.

Infection of leprosy (13:2). The disease popularly known as leprosy is more technically known in the medical world today as Hansen's disease. It is unlikely that the disease described in Lev. 13 is specifically Hansen's disease because the description of the symptoms in that chapter does not match the known effects of Hansen's disease. Instead, Lev. 13 probably is referring to a wide variety of skin diseases, ranging from psoriasis and eczema to favid or sebhorrea, or even boils and abscesses. In Mesopotamia a variety of omens were used to address the problem of physical diseases and skin problems, such as a mole that turns white. Such infections were considered punishment from the gods.

He must live alone in a place outside the camp (13:46). Many ancient Near Eastern cultures carried restrictions against unclean persons whom they believed had been stricken by the gods with disease. Likewise, priests who

While some uncertainty exists, this probably is the plant referred to as "hyssop" in the Old Testament.

became unclean (for a variety of reasons) often were required to undergo purification rituals before entering into temple areas. For example, the Mesopotamian priests rendered unclean through their purification of the sanctuaries of the Mesopotamian gods Nabu, Bel, or Beltiya could not enter the sanctuary again until purified. Yet in general Israelite priestly practice was much more restrictive with regard to numerous impurities.

Two live clean birds (14:4). After the diseased person was healed, two "clean" birds, plus cedar, some scarlet yarn, a hyssop plant, and water, were used to perform a ritual purification, after which bathing and shaving enabled one to return to the camp as clean (14:1–9). The use of birds in the removal of impurity is evidenced in Hittite and Mesopotamian ritual texts as well, though the Hittite ritual involved a hawk and an eagle, birds that were considered unclean in Israel.

Fresh water (14:5–6, 50–52). This Hebrew phrase literally means "living water" and refers to water that was moving, such as in a stream or a river. Mesopotamian rituals utilized water from the Tigris and/or the Euphrates Rivers for cleansing for the annual New Year festival.

A mildew contamination in a house (14:34–53). The same term is used here in reference to household fungus, mold, or mildew, as is used throughout Lev. 13–14 in reference to "skin disease," further underscoring the conceptual difference between the modern world and the ancient world in regard to diseases and terminology. The ritual cleansing process is much the same for the person as for the house. In Mesopotamian omen texts the appearance of black fungus or mold could portend successful business, but red and green mold could portend evil or death (cf. 14:37).

During the Second Temple period bathing for ritual purity (as prescribed in Lev. 15) often occurred in a mikvah, a ritual bath. The mikvah shown here was excavated near the southern wall of the Temple Mount in Jerusalem.

When any man has a discharge (15:2). See comments on 12:1. Hittite priests were prohibited from engaging in sexual intercourse during their temple service. If they did, and did not purify themselves properly, it was a capital offense.

An emission of semen (15:16). Seminal fluids were considered a minor impurity, requiring bathing and an unclean status until evening, the beginning of the next day. In Mesopotamian omen texts a nocturnal emission was considered a sign of prosperity.

Atonement and Blood, Life and Death (16:1–17:16)

Atonement will be made for you on this day (16:1–34). The Day of Atonement was an annual culmination of the Israelite sacrificial and purification system. On this day the sanctuary was cleansed of the brazen sins of the Israelites. In Babylon rites of penitence marked the springtime New Year festival on days two through five of the month of Nisan (springtime). The priest bathed, put on special garments, entered the temple with a censer of aromatics, and cleansed the sanctuary with water from the Tigris and Euphrates Rivers. Purgation was accomplished with the body of a decapitated ram, after which the ram was thrown into the river flowing outward from the city. The same was done with the ram's head, after which the priest and the slaughterer were required to go out of the city into the open country and remain there for a week. The king/priest would then be subject to a ritual of confession and penitence.

Behind the curtain (16:2). The Hebrew word *paroket* refers to the inner curtain that separated the most holy sacred space from the central hall. The Akkadian word *parakku* was related and denoted the sacred space surrounding the statue of a god or the pedestal on which the statue sat.

The goat . . . sending it into the wilderness . . . will carry all their iniquities (16:10, 22). The "scapegoat," which symbolically carried away the sins and iniquities of the Israelites, finds a parallel in several ancient Near Eastern texts. The Hittite rituals of Huwarlu and Ambazzi utilized a dog and a mouse, respectively, to carry away evil from the royal court or city.

Atonement for the most holy place (16:16). Even the most sacred space, which held the ark of the covenant as the center of the divine presence, apparently would become contaminated by its residing in the midst of an unholy community (16:16). The concept of moving inward for purification and then outward to reflect expiation is paralleled in Mesopotamian and Hittite temple purification rituals. In those ritual texts temples and their implements were smeared with liquids or wiped clean using a variety of materials such as oil, bread loaves, or even the carcass of a ram or sheep. In the Hittite Ulippi ritual, for example, a new temple was purified by the smearing of blood on the statue of the deity, as well as on the walls and the temple service implements.

Practice self-denial and do no work (16:29). Individual participation on the Day of Atonement required cessation from work, self-denial, humility of soul, and later fasting. Similarly, in the "Adad-Guppi Autobiography" the mother of the Babylonian king Nabonidus demonstrated her humble devotion to several deities who were believed to have brought judgment on Babylon by denying herself the pleasures of fine clothing, silver and gold, perfumes, and oils, and instead dressing in torn sackcloth.

No longer offer their sacrifices to the goat-demons (17:7). This text implies that there existed a cult for the worship of goat-demons. Numerous Hittite and Mesopotamian elimination rituals were intended to drive out demonic forces from human habitations, from households to cities and royal palaces, forces that were believed to cause plagues, infertility, and a variety of diseases.

Aliens who reside among them (17:8). Unlike other ancient Near Eastern cultures that had laws in which the adjudication of law was differentiated according to one's status in society, Israelite law was explicit that one law code existed for both Israelites and resident aliens (Exod. 12:48–49; Lev. 16:29; 17:8–16; Num. 9:14; 15:14–16). The Code of Hammurabi, for example, provides numerous examples of how Babylonian law differentiated between the wealthy and the poor.

None of you . . . may eat blood (17:12). See comments on Deut. 12:16, 20. Both in Israel and in the ancient Near East blood was thought to carry both pure and impure properties. In Israel blood was a symbol of both life and death. Blood purification rites were practiced among the Hittites and other ancient Near Eastern cultures, but Israel's religious intensity, level of restrictions, and detailed delineations regarding the collection and utilization of blood were unsurpassed. The core concept for ancient Israel was that blood as a symbol of life was always to be rendered back to God, the source of life. Consumption of blood was thus prohibited for the Israelites. In contrast, in an Egyptian coffin text blood consumption was one of the secrets to longevity in the afterlife.

Purity Laws (18:1–30)

Do not follow the practices of the land of Egypt (18:3). The following passage (18:6–30) implies that the practices of Egypt being referred to here were sexual in nature, and in particular were related to sexual impropriety within the family. Incest was common in ancient Egypt within the royal families of the pharaohs, for the Egyptian pharaohs often married their sisters. Recent DNA tests conducted by the University of Zurich have shown incestual relationships among pharaohs such as Tutankhamun, whose parents were brother and sister.

You are not to come near any close relative for sexual intercourse (18:6–23). Hittite law prohibited a man from having sexual relations with his daughter or son, sister or cousin. Among the omen texts of Mesopotamia are a variety of portended results from men having intercourse with their niece, grandniece, or other relative, or even homosexual acts with other men.

You are not to sacrifice any of your children in the fire to Molech (18:21). On child sacrifice, see comments on 2 Kings 3:27. Molech (also known as Milcom, Malkam, Moloch) was a deity worshiped by the Ammonites and the Phoenicians (see comments on 1 Kings 11:5).

You are not to sleep with a man as with a woman (18:22). Male homosexual activity was taboo in ancient Israel, punishable by death (20:13). However, in some other ancient Near Eastern cultures the practice was acceptable.

You are not to have sexual intercourse with any animal (18:23). Bestiality was strictly forbidden in Israel. Restrictions varied among other ancient Near Eastern cultures. In many mythological texts gods and goddesses take the form of bulls, cows, donkeys, or other animals in order to copulate, thereby bringing fertility. In Hittite law, however, bestiality with certain animals was potentially punishable by death, unless the king granted mercy.

Idolatry and Other Delimitations (19:1–37)

Be holy because I, the Lord your God, am holy (19:2). In the Mesopotamian hymn to the goddess Nanshe, the priests were expected to live up to the ethical standards of purity and faithfulness of the goddess. In contrast, in Lev. 19:2 the entire Israelite community is called to holy living.

Do not turn to idols or make cast images of gods (19:4). The worship of gods and goddesses utilizing anthropomorphic and zoomorphic images was normative for all nations throughout the ancient Near East except Israel (Exod. 20:3–4).

Do not oppress your neighbor or rob him (19:13–18). All forms of injustice, oppression, and abuse of others were condemned in Israelite law. Likewise, the law codes of other ancient Near Eastern nations centered on the theme of establishing justice in the land. One of the concluding statements of the Babylonian king Hammurabi's law code states, "I am Hammurabi, king of justice, to whom the god Shamash has granted the truth."

If a man has sexual intercourse with a woman who is a slave (19:20). Hittite and Mesopotamian laws also address the matter of sexual relations between a man and a slave, providing a variety of responses of payments or penalties, depending on the ownership of the slave and the societal status of those involved.

Terracotta plaque figurine from Sumer, late third millennium BC. It depicts Nanshe, the Sumerian goddess of fish, water birds, and social justice, responsible for the accuracy of weights and measures. She is portrayed here with two pelicans.

You are not to practice divination or witchcraft . . . mediums . . . spiritists (19:26, 31). See comments on Deut. 18:10–11. Prohibited in Israel but common in the literature of the ancient Near East are varieties of sorcery, divination, witchcraft, and the use of mediums in invoking deity to bring blessings and curses upon others. The use of apotropaic magic (symbolic forms to ward off evil), extispicy (reading patterns in the internal organs of animals), necromancy (consulting the dead; see comments on 1 Sam. 28:3, 9), and other special sacrificial rituals, accompanied by incantations and oath formulas, was common throughout Sumer, Babylonia, Assyria, Hatti, Egypt, and Ugarit.

You are not to make gashes on your bodies for the dead (19:28). Like the prophets of Baal who attempted to arouse their god to respond (see comments on 1 Kings 18:28), texts from Ugarit (an ancient city in Syria) described the ritual of the god El in preparation to rescue Baal from the underworld. He descends from his throne, heaps dust upon his head, clothes himself in garments of mourning, and cuts his body and face with stone implements and a razor.

You are to have honest balances, honest weights (19:35–36). Economic justice is delineated in several genres of ancient Near Eastern texts, both in law codes such as Hammurabi's (the ancient Babylonian king), and in Egyptian wisdom literature such as in the teaching of Amenemope, as well as in confessions in the Egyptian "Book of the Dead."

Priesthood (21:1–22:32)

A priest is not to make himself ceremonially unclean for a dead person (21:1–24). Priests of other nations likewise were commanded to maintain ritual purity in order to carry out their prescribed duties. In the ancient Near East impurities due to proximity to death, marriage adulteration, physical deformity, or moral failure were all matters by which priests could be disqualified from performing their ritual duties.

If any man . . . is in a state of uncleanness yet approaches the holy offerings (22:3). Any form of physical or ritual impurity rendered an Israelite priest unfit for sacred service. Likewise, disabled Hittites were restricted from temple service. In the Egyptian "Book of the Dead" a petitioner, after listing scores of ways in which he has not offended Osiris, declares, "I am pure, I am pure, I am pure, I am pure! My purity is the purity of that great phoenix in Herakleopolis."

Holy Days and Redemption (23:1–24:21)

These are my appointed times (23:1–44). Israel's annual ritual calendar was built on the agricultural cycle reflecting God's beneficent provision for the needs of his people, and the redemptive cycle of God's handiwork and revelatory work in history. Leviticus 23 focuses on the natural creation aspect, from resting on the Sabbath to harvesting of grain in the springtime.

These are the Lord's appointed times, the sacred assemblies (23:4, 37). Daily, monthly, and annual rites among ancient Near Eastern cultures were marked by special sacrifices, prayers, festival meals, and other practices. Priests of Ugarit, for example, offered burnt offerings, peace offerings, and other offerings according to appointed daily, monthly (lunar), and annual times. The Zukru festival at Emar (a city in Syria) has some parallels with the

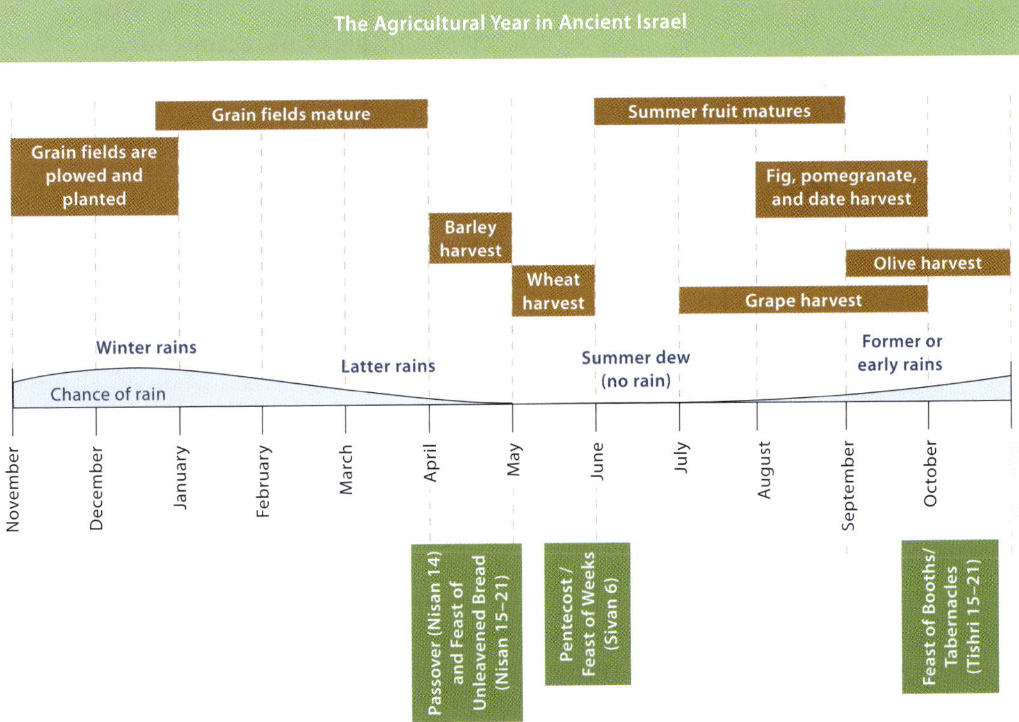

agricultural background of the Israelite Passover. The festival was celebrated every seventh year (sabbatical) with sacrifices of lambs, breads, oil, and wine for the seventy gods of Emar, such as Dagan and Ninurta.

In the seventh month . . . first day . . . trumpet blasts (23:24). Later Israelites may have adopted this as Rosh Hashanah to distinguish it from the Babylonian springtime Akitu festival of New Year, a twelve-day celebration of the reenthronement of the king of Babylon and the life-death-rebirth cycle of the patron god Marduk.

Festival of Shelters to the Lord (23:33–36, 39–43). The booth/shelter was to be constructed as a temporary shelter for a week each year to commemorate God's provision of the people's needs during their wilderness experience after the exodus. Branches from several leafy trees—palms, willows, citron, myrtle, and/or others—formed the canopy over the hut (23:40).

Bake it into twelve loaves . . . Aaron and his sons, who are to eat it (24:5–9). In most regions of the ancient Near East gifts of baked loaves of bread, or even unbaked dough, were common in providing for the needs of the gods. Here the twelve loaves reflecting the nation of twelve tribes were offered to celebrate God's faithful provision for his people and then were consumed by the priests.

Cursed and blasphemed the Name (24:11). Blasphemy against the name of God was punishable by death, as was the case in several ancient Near Eastern cultures where speaking evil or pronouncing a curse against a deity, a temple, or even a king could result in severe punishment, even death. Assyrian texts describe how blasphemers could have their tongues cut out or their flesh flayed.

Life for life . . . eye for eye, tooth for tooth (24:17–21). See comments on Deut. 19:21. Talionic justice was a common form of ancient Near Eastern law, where penalty or adjudication was compensatory with the crime. Many of the laws of the Babylonian king Hammurabi's code contain such penalties, and thefts of temple sacrifices and treasures were to be recompensed up to tenfold.

Sabbatical Year and Jubilee; Redemption Laws for Land and People (25:1–26:46)

You are to consecrate the fiftieth year . . . it will be your Jubilee (25:8–35). The land belonged to God, and

the Israelites were mere tenants sharing in the communal ownership of their tribal and clan territories. Land could be traded or sold, but only temporarily. In the Jubilee Year (the fiftieth year) ownership of property was to revert to its original household. Similarly, property documents and law codes of Ugarit (a city in Syria), Anatolia (Turkey), and Mesopotamia contained provisions for the potential return of land to its original owners. The law code of the Babylonian king Hammurabi provided for the redemption of land in a variety of cases, such as military service or state business.

Do not profit or take interest from him (25:36). In an Aramaic document from Elephantine, a Jewish colony on the Nile River, interest on a small loan of four shekels of silver to a woman was placed at 5 percent monthly, and if unpaid the interest accumulated. Security could be claimed against the woman or her family in terms of their property. Annual interest rates in Mesopotamia often fell in the range of 20–33 percent.

Do not make idols (26:1). Distinct from the peoples and nations of the ancient Near East, Israel was prohibited from making any kind of iconic image

The island of Elephantine, on the Nile River.

of deity for worship (Exod. 20:3–4). Memorial stones could be erected, such as those placed by Jacob at Bethel (Gen. 28:18–22) and at Galeed/Mizpah (Gen. 31:45–49), as reminders of relationships with God and with people, but not for worship (see comments on Josh. 4:7).

If you follow my statutes . . . but if you do not obey me (26:3, 14). Covenant blessings for faithful obedience and curses for rebellious disobedience were an essential part of making treaties and covenants in the ancient Near East. Examples from Sumerian, Babylonian, Assyrian, Hittite, and Egyptian literature from 2000 to 586 BC are plentiful.

I will give you rain at the right time (26:4). Blessings for covenant obedience included abundant rainfall in a region where rain falls only about half of the year. Since rain was so critical in the ancient Near East, numerous gods were associated with storms and rainfall. The Baal Cycle from Ugarit presents their god as the provider of rains. The challenge of Elijah versus the prophets of Baal and Asherah on Mount Carmel centered on which god truly supplied the rain (see comments on 1 Kings 17:1).

I will turn against you (26:17–20). In contrast to the priestly blessing in Num. 6:24–26, in which God's shining face brings grace, peace, and blessings toward the faithful, those who rebel against his covenant will see defeat, destruction, disease, and drought. Such depiction of the wrath of the gods due to people's unfaithfulness is seen in numerous ancient Near Eastern omen and divination texts, prayers, and hymns.

I will make your sky like iron and your land like bronze (26:19). This metaphor occurs in the "Succession Treaty of Esar-haddon," in which the gods are called upon to curse the rebellious party with ground like iron that would not sprout and with brazen heavens that would not bring rain.

You will eat the flesh of your sons . . . of your daughters (26:29). In the succession/vassal treaties of the Assyrian king Esar-haddon cannibalism was one of the potential results from failure to keep the covenant stipulations.

Vows and Valuations (27:1–34)

When someone makes a special vow to the LORD that involves the assessment of people (27:2). Vows in the ancient Near East concerning slaves, indentured servants, or household personnel were not uncommon. In Egypt the "Lawsuit over a Syrian Slave" depicts a case in which a young woman was valued in terms of multiple garments of fine linen, copper and silver articles, and other valuables. Vows were made at the conclusion of the lawsuit.

Every tenth . . . is holy to the Lord (27:30, 32). The practice of tithing is known in temple and royal texts from Ugarit (an ancient city in Syria) and Mesopotamia. Numerous gods were rendered tithes in the contexts of temple gifts, including a range of items such as garments, grains, silver, and dates.

Numbers

Roy E. Gane

Introduction. As the book of Exodus ends, the Israelites are still at Mount Sinai, having entered into covenant relationship with God and having constructed the tabernacle as he instructed. At the end of Exodus God comes to dwell in the tabernacle. Leviticus establishes a God-centered holy community out of the Israelites, carefully explaining how they were to live with the holy, awesome God living right in their midst. Numbers picks up the story of the Lord's chosen Israelite people right after this, while they are still at Mount Sinai. The Hebrew name of the book translates as "In the Wilderness," taken from the opening words of the first verse. This aptly describes the setting of the events recounted here, which start at Sinai and continue during the Israelites' resumed journey to Canaan, followed by decades of wandering in the wilderness due to the Israelites' faithless rebellion against the Lord. The English title Numbers derives from the Latin title *Numeri*, which was based on the earlier Septuagint Greek title of the book, *Arithmoi*. This reflects the prominence of census reports in the book of Numbers. Indeed, the census of the (subsequently rebellious) adult generation that left Egypt in chapter 1 and the census of the next generation in chapter 26 provide the basic structural markers of the book, which can be divided into two parts: chapters 1–25 (the disobedient generation of the first census) and chapters 26–36 (the obedient generation of the second census).[1] The book of Numbers contains fascinating cultural, historical, and geographical elements and utilizes a greater variety of literary genres than any other book of the Bible.[2]

Military Census (1:1–46)

All the Israelites twenty years old or more, everyone who could serve in Israel's army (1:45–46). This military census ordered by God is in preparation for mobilizing the Israelites so that they could cooperate with the Lord in conquering the land of Canaan. Compare the directions for the beginning of a military campaign that the god 'Ilu gave to Kirta the king in a dream, as recounted in a Ugaritic epic (from Tell Ras Shamra in Syria): "A throng will be provisioned and march forth, a mighty throng will be provisioned, a throng will indeed go forth. Your army will be a numerous host, three hundred myriads, soldiers without number, archers without count."[3]

Exemption from Census and Introduction to Duties of the Levites (1:47–54)

But the Levites were not registered with them by their ancestral tribe (1:47). The Levites are not included in the military census because their permanent duty is to care for the sanctuary (i.e., the tabernacle) (1:50). Similarly, a number of Egyptian pharaohs granted exemption from forced labor to temple-related personnel as a gift to the gods so that the gods would not be deprived of their service.[4]

Any unauthorized person who comes near it is to be put to death . . . the Levites are to camp around the tabernacle (1:51–53). Throughout the ancient Near Eastern world sanctuaries/temples were treated as the palaces and residences of powerful deities, so access to sanctuaries and temples was limited and tightly controlled. Since God himself dwells and rules in the Israelite tabernacle, the situation is similar. Levitical guards are responsible for stopping (i.e., killing) any unauthorized person who tries to enter the tabernacle. If they failed to do this, divine wrath would break out against the Israelites (3:10, 38; 18:1–7). The life-and-death importance of guarding a divine residence also appears, for example, in the Hittite "Instructions to Priests and Temple Officials" (second millennium BC), which commands temple personnel as follows: "Guard the temples very carefully, and let there be no sleep for you. Further, let the watch be divided among you. In whose watch a sin occurs, he shall die. Let him not be pardoned."[5]

Military Camp (2:1–34)

The Israelites are to camp under their respective banners (2:2). The Israelite encampment is a mobile military camp on the way to conquer Canaan, as indicated by the fact that the census in Num. 1 counts Israelite males of fighting age. The war camp is configured in a hollow square, with four groups of three tribes each arranged on four sides around a rectangular courtyard containing the two-room (most holy place and holy place) tabernacle of the divine king and commander in the middle (cf. 23:21). This is strikingly similar to the war camp of the Egyptian pharaoh Ramesses II (1279–1213 BC) at the Battle of Qadesh (ca. 1275 BC) in Syria, as depicted in a diagram carved on the stone interior of a temple at Abu Simbel, in southern Egypt. In the diagram the two-room tent of the god-king is a mobile palace-shrine at the center of the rectangular camp (similar to the court of the Israelite tabernacle), surrounded and protected by army divisions on all four sides. The name of the pharaoh, framed by divine falcons facing each other (like the winged cherubim overshadowing the cover of the ark, where Israel's

God was enthroned [Exod. 25:10–22; 1 Sam. 4:4; 2 Sam. 6:2]), is placed in the smaller room that is equivalent to the most holy place in the Israelite tabernacle (cf. Exod. 26:34).[6] But the Egyptian pharaoh was human, far inferior to the monarch at the center of the Israelite camp—God himself.

Sanctuary Personnel (3:1–4:49)

Take down the screening curtain . . . and insert its poles (4:5–6). When the tabernacle was to be moved (see comments on Num. 4:31), the priests were to prepare the most holy items so that the Levites could transport them (4:15). They were to carry the ark at a distance from themselves on two poles over their shoulders (7:9). The poles passed through two rings on each side of the sacred chest. A box with such rings and poles was found in the famous tomb of the young pharaoh Tutankhamun (fourteenth century BC).[7] This means of transport was safer for valuable items than a cart (cf. 2 Sam. 6:3–7).

The supports of the tabernacle, with its crossbars, pillars, and bases (4:31). The small Israelite tabernacle was a mobile shrine. It consisted of a rigid framework formed by upright, gold-covered wooden boards, set on bases, that were held in place by gold-covered horizontal crossbars passing through rings on the planks (Exod. 26:15–29). Over this framework several layers of curtains were draped (Exod. 26:1–14). All of these components were disassembled and transported by the Levites when the Israelite camp moved. Archaeologists have discovered framework portions of similar structures in Egypt that date to the third millennium BC, more than a thousand years before the Israelites built the Lord's tabernacle, confirming that such technology was available to them. Parts of poles were found in a tomb at Saqqara (ca. 2900 BC) and in the storerooms of the Step Pyramid (ca. 2700 BC). Better preserved are the disassembled parts of a tabernacle structure that had enclosed the bedroom suite of Queen Hetepheres, which were discovered in her tomb at Giza (ca. 2600 BC). Nearby were found the remains of a religious tabernacle. Several Egyptian tomb chapels dating to the mid-third millennium BC contain pictures of curtained pavilions held up by vertical poles

A replica of the tabernacle. Note the altar in the foreground.

connected by horizontal rods. Also, some texts from Mari in Syria that date to about the eighteenth century BC speak of large public tents held up by wooden frames on bases. One of these texts mentions that forty-three men were needed to transport the parts of such a structure.[8]

Community Purity, Holiness, and Blessing (5:1–6:27)

Send away anyone from the camp who is afflicted with a skin disease . . . or anyone who is defiled (5:2). A person who has a serious physical ritual impurity (Lev. 12–15; Num. 19) is to stay outside the war camp to keep from defiling the holiness of the camp in which God dwells among his people (Lev. 15:31; Num. 5:3). Other ancient Near Eastern peoples likewise were concerned to remove impurities from their dwelling places. Both in Mesopotamia and among the Hittites a wide variety of ritual methods were used to expel impurities, which they viewed as originating from and belonging to the underworld.[9] For the Mesopotamians, impurities were harmful evils caused by demons, but for the Hittites, they were generally nondemonic evils.[10] According to the Bible, however, impurities that affected the Israelites were neither demonic nor from the underworld,[11] but rather were caused by the people themselves and represented the birth-to-death cycle of mortality resulting from sin (Gen. 3; Rom. 6:23). This is why such impurities could not be associated with the presence of the pure, immortal, holy God.[12]

If a feeling of jealousy comes over the husband (5:14). Suspicion of marital infidelity is an old problem. A Mesopotamian composition from about 1900–1800 BC (with an earlier version dating to 2600–2500 BC) presents wise teachings, like proverbs, as if they were addressed by the pre-flood ruler Shuruppak to his son Ziusudra, the hero of their flood story (like Noah). Two timeless warnings from Shuruppak on this topic are included: "Do not laugh with a girl who is married; the slander is strong. My son, do not sit (alone) in a chamber with a woman who is married."[13]

The priest will require the woman to take an oath (5:19). Similarly, in the Code of Hammurabi (king of Babylonia) is a law that calls for a wife to swear an oath in order to address her husband's unproven suspicion that she has committed adultery. It reads, "If her husband accuses his own wife (of adultery), although she has not been seized lying with another male, she shall swear (to her innocence by) an oath by the god, and return to her house."[14] As in the biblical procedure, the oath turned the case over to the all-knowing deity, who could hold the woman accountable if she were lying. However, whereas the Babylonian wife was to simply swear her innocence (cf. Exod. 22:11), the Israelite oath is a conditional self-curse to the effect that if the woman is innocent, she will suffer no harm, but if she is guilty, she will experience serious gynecological damage (5:19–22).

He will require the woman to drink the bitter water that brings a curse (5:24). This symbolically takes the effect of the conditional self-curse into her body, with God controlling the outcome according to his knowledge. There is no inherent physical danger in drinking the liquid, so an innocent woman is safe. Contrast that with the Babylonian river ordeal described in the Code of Hammurabi (law 132),[15] in which the accused woman was required to go into a river for judgment (the river being regarded as divine). If the woman survived, she was viewed as having been judged innocent, but if she drowned, she was considered guilty.

A man or woman makes a special vow, a Nazirite vow, to consecrate himself to the Lord (6:2). Egyptian temple religion mostly consisted of performances by a few elite people.[16] By contrast, ordinary Israelite men and women are welcome to bring their offerings to the sanctuary (Lev. 1–7), although they are still not permitted to officiate as priests and do not have access to the inside of the tabernacle (Num. 3:10, 38; 18:7). Common Israelites were also welcome to participate in a high degree of holiness by taking the Nazirite vow, which temporarily bound them to some lifestyle restrictions similar to those observed by priests, including avoidance of corpse contamination (Num. 6:6–7; cf. Lev. 21:1–4, 11) and alcoholic beverages (Num. 6:3; cf. Lev. 10:9).

The Lord bless you and protect you; may the Lord make his face shine on you (6:22–27). The Israelites cherished this profoundly beautiful blessing of the people by the priests, as shown by the discovery in 1979 of two tiny silver scrolls (about three inches and two inches long, respectively) on which are inscribed two versions of this blessing, along with some other expressions found in other biblical verses. The scrolls, designed to be used as amulets, were found in a burial chamber at Ketef Hinnom, just outside ancient Jerusalem. They date to the late seventh or early sixth century BC and thus are among the oldest known written texts that we have of any biblical passage.[17] Elsewhere, some inscriptions from Mesopotamia and Kuntillet Ajrud in the upper Sinai Peninsula contain wording that resembles parts of this priestly blessing.[18]

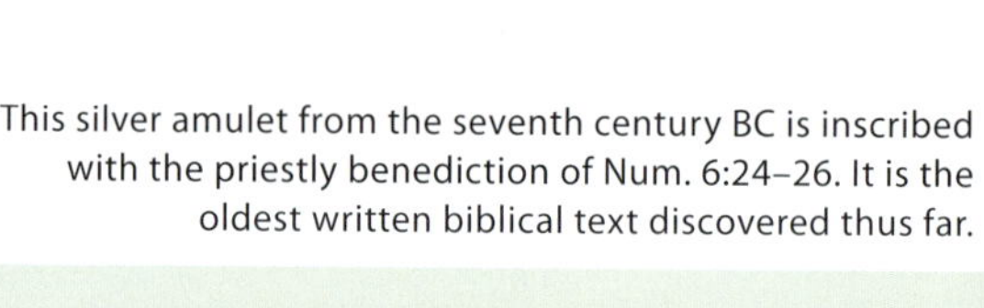

This silver amulet from the seventh century BC is inscribed with the priestly benediction of Num. 6:24–26. It is the oldest written biblical text discovered thus far.

Sanctuary Supplies and Service (7:1–8:26)

The leaders of Israel . . . brought as their offering before the LORD six covered carts and twelve oxen (7:1–11). When the construction of the tabernacle is complete and after Moses consecrates it along with all of its furnishings, then the Israelite tribal leaders bring gifts to the Lord. For transporting the tabernacle, they bring carts and oxen. For service at the altar, they also bring silver and golden vessels, food items, incense, and sacrificial animals (7:10–88). Similarly, Gudea, ruler of the Mesopotamian city of Lagash (ca. 2100 BC), gave gifts to the god Ningirsu and his wife Baba when they were installed in a new temple that Gudea had built for them. The gifts included a war chariot with its weapons, along with utensils and furniture for eating and sleeping.[19]

Sprinkle them with the purification water. Have them shave their entire bodies and wash their clothes (8:7). Before the Levites could assist the priests at the holy sanctuary, they had to be ritually purified. The "purification water" is to purify them from corpse contamination (cf. 19:9, 11–20). Regarding the requirement to shave as part of a consecration process, an ancient document in Akkadian from the city of Emar (in modern Syria) provides an extensive description of the long nine-day consecration process involved in the installation of a new high priestess, including shaving her at the entrance to the temple on the second day.[20]

Resuming the Journey (9:1–10:36)

Make two trumpets of hammered silver (10:2). Two such signal trumpets, with long, narrow tubes and flared at the end, were found in the Egyptian tomb of Tutankhamun. One was made of silver and the other of copper or bronze overlaid with gold. In Num. 10 the trumpets are to be blown in various ways to send messages throughout the entire camp of people, signaling the time for assembly, the gathering of leaders, the start of the day's journey, and so on. Trumpets like these, which produced loud, piercing blasts, were used similarly in Egypt to assemble people, call them to battle, or to celebrate religious festivals.[21]

Troubles in the Wilderness (11:1–12:16)

A wind sent by the LORD came up and blew quail in from the sea (11:31). See comments on Exod. 16:13. From antiquity until recent times millions of quail migrate every spring across the Sinai Peninsula from Africa to Europe and Asia.[22]

In this Egyptian tomb wall painting, Cushites (also called Nubians) are bringing tribute to the pharaoh. This painting provides a very detailed depiction of the Cushites.

Miriam and Aaron criticized Moses because of the Cushite woman he married (12:1). Cush (referred to by historians as Nubia and by the ancient Greeks as Ethiopia) was a kingdom along the Nile River in southern Egypt and northern Sudan that was inhabited by dark-skinned people (see the article "The Cushites"). Moses's wife, Zipporah, was from Midian (Exod. 2:15–21), so the Cushite wife in 12:1 may be another woman whom he married after Zipporah died. Interestingly, the Jewish historian Josephus, writing much later (in the latter part of the first century AD), also portrays Moses as marrying a Cushite (Josephus writes in Greek; thus he uses the Greek term "Ethiopian" for the inhabitants of ancient Cush). Josephus usually follows the OT story fairly carefully, but in this instance his account is quite different. He depicts Moses as a young man leading an army of Egyptians and Hebrews against Cush. During the siege of the Cushite capital city, Tharbis, the daughter of the Cushite king, sees Moses, falls in love, and proposes marriage, which he accepts, sealing the peace between Egypt and Cush.[23] While this account probably is more legend than history, and many of the historical details of Josephus's account are doubtful, the fact that he depicts Moses as marrying an African woman from Cush/Ethiopia correlates well with this account in Numbers.

Rebellion at Kadesh (13:1–14:45)

I [the Lord] will strike them with a plague . . . Moses replied to the Lord (14:12–13). There are examples of people in the ancient Near East attempting to placate their gods, who, they believed, caused plagues. For instance, there was a terrible plague during the reign of the Hittite king Muršili II that lasted for years and caused the death of many of his people. He (or his scribes) composed several prayers to try to persuade the gods to end the epidemic. In these prayers he confessed guilt, referred to restitution, and pointed out that more deaths would only reduce service to the gods: "These few bakers of offering bread and libation bearers who [are still here]—if they perish, no one will any longer give you offering bread or libation."[24] When Moses intercedes for the rebellious Israelites, however, he appeals to the preservation of the Lord's reputation and to the Lord's merciful character (14:13–19; cf. Exod. 34:6–7).

Loyalty versus Disloyalty (15:1–41)

A grain offering . . . a drink offering (15:4–5). Conceptually, grain and drink offerings that accompany animal sacrifices make the "meals" complete for God. Compare the meal of hospitality that Abraham offered to three heavenly visitors, including the Lord, which included a calf, cakes of fine flour, and curds and milk (Gen. 18:6–8). Other ancient Near Eastern peoples also gave meals to their deities that included meat, grain products, and drink. For example, on the fifth day of the Babylonian New Year festival of spring the high priest was to serve the regular afternoon meal to Bēl (Marduk), the city god of Babylon:

> [. . . hours . . .] the day, the high priest [enters into the presence of B]ēl, and . . . He [performs the ceremony of] the golden table: He places roasted meats upon it, he places . . . [upon i]t, he places the twelve usual (loaves) upon it, he fills a [gold]en . . . with salt and places it upon it, he fills a [gold]en . . . with honey and places it upon it, he places . . . upon it, four golden containers . . . he places [up]on the table, a golden censer . . . he places [in] front of the table, aromatic material and an aromatic substance of the juniper tree [he mixes on top (of the censer)], he pours out a libation of wine.[25]

This plaque, depicting a *mushhushshu* dragon, the sacred animal of Marduk, the principal Babylonian god, probably was used as a protective amulet.

If one person sins unintentionally . . . he will be forgiven (15:27–28). The Lord communicated his will to the Israelites in the form of commandments, and if they inadvertently violated them, he provided sacrificial remedies through which they could receive forgiveness when they realized their mistakes (compare Lev. 4). This removed the stress, fear, and uncertainty experienced by other ancient Near Eastern peoples, whose lives were complicated by the need to figure out unclear and sometimes temperamental desires of multiple gods.[26] An eloquent Babylonian prayer to the god Marduk, which also appeals to other deities, reflects this sense of uncertainty:

> I am left anxious by speech unheeded,
> My hopes are deceived by outcry unanswered,

Such as has sapped my courage,
And hunched me over like an aged man.
O great lord Marduk, merciful lord!
Men, by whatever name,
What can they understand by their own efforts?
Who has not been negligent, which one has committed no sin?
Who can understand a god's behavior? . . .
I am surely responsible for some neglect of you,
I have surely trespassed the limits set by the god.[27]

Rebellion of Korah and Aftermath (16:1–17:11)

The earth opened its mouth and swallowed them . . . they went down alive into Sheol (16:32–33). See comments on Ps. 6:5. Compare this with Isa. 5:14, where the realm of the dead (Hebrew *Sheol*; i.e., the grave, viewed as an underworld) is personified as a monster that opens its jaws to swallow the wicked. In the Ugaritic myth of the god Ba'lu (Baal), the god Môtu (Death), who has crushing jaws and a huge throat, swallows Ba'lu.[28]

Aaron's staff . . . formed buds, blossomed, and produced almonds (17:8). Recall that the cups on the lampstand in the tabernacle were "shaped like almond flowers with buds and blossoms" (Exod. 25:33–34). The Hebrew word for "almond" is derived from a Hebrew root that refers to watchfulness (cf. Jer. 1:11–12), because almond trees blossom in the spring before other trees. The sanctuary lamps were to burn all night (Exod. 27:20–21), showing that the Lord was always awake and watchful (Ps. 121:4). So the almond blossoms on Aaron's staff imply that God was watching out against opposition toward the priest (Aaron) whom he had chosen (Num. 17:5, 10).

A flowering almond tree.

Staffs and rods were used as walking sticks and as symbols of authority.

Danger Borne by Priests and Levites and Their Remuneration (17:12–18:32)

All the holy offerings of the Israelites, I have given them to you and your sons as a portion (18:8). Just as the servants of a human king receive support from him that includes eating from his food, so the Lord provides for his priests and Levites by allocating to them portions of the sacred offerings and gifts that the Israelites brought to him. These perquisites also compensated for the sensitive and potentially dangerous nature of service in close proximity to the awesome deity. Priests in other ancient Near Eastern religious systems likewise received remuneration for their high responsibilities. For example, the Hittite document "Instructions to Priests and Temple Officials" required priests first to serve the god his food and drink, but afterward, when he had finished eating in some sense, they could consume what remained.[29] A text from Emar (in modern Syria) from the second millennium BC lists a number of items included in the yearly salary of the high priestess of the storm god.[30]

Purification from Corpse Impurity (19:1–22)

The person who touches any human corpse will be unclean for seven days (19:11). In Israel dead bodies and graves are impure (19:14–16), so people who are defiled by coming into contact with them are required to undergo purification so that they will not pollute the Lord's holy sanctuary, even from a distance (19:12–13, 17–20). Tombs discovered in the vicinity of Jerusalem dating from the period of the Israelite monarchy are located outside the inhabited area of the city in order to avoid making the people impure. As Jerusalem expanded, some tombs were emptied so that the corpses in them would no longer be inside the city.[31] The Israelite view of death was that it was an evil intruder not part of the divine plan (see Gen. 1–3). Thus it is something that is impure and conflicts with holiness. This is in strong contrast to the perspective of death in Egypt, where death was regarded as sacred and the beginning of the next life. In Egypt tombs were treated as temples.

Failures and Victories (20:1–21:35)

Struck the rock twice with his staff, so that abundant water gushed out (20:11). Aquifers are known to exist under the surface of the sedimentary rock layers in some parts of the Sinai Peninsula. However, even if a physical blow could dislodge the natural plug to such a water source, normally there would hardly be enough water to supply the entire Israelite community.[32]

Edom (20:14). See comments on Ezek. 25:12; Obad. 1. Edom was the kingdom to the southeast of Israel, across the Dead Sea.

A bronze serpent found in Timna, Israel, perhaps similar to the bronze snake made by Moses (Num. 21:8–9).

The King's Highway (20:17). This international route, mainly used for trade, linked Damascus in the north (in Syria) to Elath, on the north coast of the Gulf of Aqaba, from where other routes connected to Egypt and Arabia. The fact that the King's Highway ran through the Transjordan (east of the Jordan River) increased the political importance of this area.[33]

Whenever someone was bitten, and he looked at the bronze snake, he recovered (21:9). A five-inch-long copper snake has been found at the remains of a shrine (Midianite occupation; period of the judges) at Timna, a copper-mining site near the Red Sea. Ancient Egyptians used images of snakes as sympathetic magic to prevent snakebites and to provide healing from them. Healing by looking at the bronze snake made by Moses was not due to power inherent in the image, however, but rather to empowerment from the Lord.[34]

The King's Highway (21:22). See comments on Num. 20:17.

Israel took all the cities and lived in all these Amorite cities (21:25). Such a report of military victory, in this case over the country of King Sihon (21:21–24), was common in the ancient Near East, especially in annals of kings. For example, part of the record of a military campaign by the Assyrian king Shalmaneser III, inscribed on a large stone monument at Kurkh from about 853–852 BC, reads, "I approached the cities of Irḫulēni, the Hamathite. I captured Adennu, Pargâ, (and) Arganâ, his royal cities."[35]

Balaam's Attempts to Curse Israel (22:1–24:25)

The plains of Moab (22:1). See comments on Deut. 34:8.

Please come and put a curse on these people for me because they are more powerful than I am (22:6). Such a curse is a kind of weapon that calls on a superhuman being to inflict harm, especially when human power is inadequate. Some ancient Near Eastern inscriptions on statues of rulers called on gods to curse anyone who disturbed them.[36] A curse could also appeal for one or more gods to strike a larger entity, as in a curse on the Mesopotamian city of Uruk, part of a Sumerian hymn to the goddess Inanna.[37]

God came to Balaam at night and said to him (22:20). Interestingly, Balaam, son of Beor, appears in some nonbiblical inscriptions. At Deir Alla, about five miles east of the Jordan River, archaeologists discovered ink writing on fragments of plaster, dated to about 800 BC, that had fallen from the inner walls of a building on which inscriptions had been displayed. The texts are written in a dialect probably related to Hebrew. They portray Balaam, son of Beor, as a diviner and seer/prophet of the gods, who communicated with him in a night vision, bringing a message of doom from the high god El. The vision showed Balaam that a council of gods, in rebellion against El, had commanded the goddess Shagar-and-Ishtar to sew up the heavens, thereby producing darkness. Balaam interpreted the mythological vision as an omen of disaster in the land, and he successfully averted the catastrophe by using magic to free the goddess from the decree of the divine council. Although the Deir Alla writings may have been written by Israelites, they reflect a pagan worldview that includes polytheism and acceptance of divination, magic, and apparently also exorcism.[38]

Then the Lord opened the donkey's mouth (22:28). Balaam's donkey saves him from being killed by the angel of the Lord (22:33). In "The Story of Two Brothers," an Egyptian folk tale dated about 1225 BC, talking cows save the life of a man whose older brother was about to kill him because the wife of the latter falsely accused the former of proposing adultery with her.[39]

Apostasy with Baal of Peor (25:1–18)

Baal of Peor (25:3). The Israelites are camping below Mount Peor (23:28) near Beth-peor (Deut. 3:29), and they begin worshiping Baal, the local god of Peor. Other places similarly associated with Baal are Baal-meon (Num. 32:38) and Baal-zephon (Num. 33:7). Baal, whose name means "lord/owner," was the Canaanite god of fertility who became prominent in the second half of the second millennium BC (see the article "The Canaanites and Canaanite Religion"). Baal of Peor likely represented a netherworld aspect of Baal, as indicated by two factors. First, the name Peor is from the same Hebrew root as the verb in Isa. 5:14 that refers to Sheol (the grave/netherworld) as "opening wide" its mouth. Second, in Ps. 106:28 those who yoked themselves to Baal of Peor ate "sacrifices of the dead." Likewise, in the Ugaritic myth of Ba'lu (Baal), this god suffered temporary defeat, was swallowed by Môtu, the god of death (see comments on Num. 16:32–33), and went down into the netherworld to dwell among the dead. This mythological event was thought to coincide with the waning of natural fertility in autumn and winter. It appears that sexual rites practiced in the cult of Baal of Peor were intended to help Baal's revival of fertility.[40]

Transfers to the Next Generation (26:1–27:23)

When a man dies without having a son, transfer his inheritance to his daughter (27:8). Similar laws and stipulations have been discovered throughout the ancient Near East. For example, documents from the Mesopotamian city of Nuzi show that a man who had no sons could designate his daughter as the sole heir to his estate. If he died without having made such an arrangement, however, his property went to his male relatives, in which case his unmarried daughter was left without a dowry.[41] According to an inscription from the Mesopotamian city of Lagash (ca. 2100 BC), Gudea, the ruler of the city, sought to provide justice in such a situation: "In the house that had no male heir, he installed its daughter as the heir."[42] The laws of the Mesopotamian king Lipit-Ishtar (ruled 1934–1924 BC) include a similar provision: "If a man dies without male offspring, an unmarried daughter shall be his heir."[43]

Calendar of Communal Sacrifices (28:1–29:40)

Each day present two unblemished year-old male lambs as a regular burnt offering (28:3). As creator-provider (Ps. 145:15–16), the God of Israel does not need daily food as sustenance or any other form of care (Ps. 50:12–13).[44] In contrast, elsewhere in the ancient Near East priests regularly carried out the daily care and feeding of their gods, which were represented by their idols. Generally, the idols received food and drink, which could be served with incense, every morning and afternoon/evening (see comments on Num. 15:4–5). An elaborate regular morning liturgy in an Egyptian temple was to include "spells of prostration, praise and offerings, after which the cult statue is removed, salved, clothed, adorned,

Statue of Gudea, ruler of the Mesopotamian city of Lagash (ca. 2100 BC).

and provided with unguent and eyepaint . . . fresh sand is strewn on the chapel floor, and the god is purified by water and natron."[45] Thus ancient Near Eastern gods were treated like human monarchs in a number of ways. Furthermore, in contrast to the God of Israel, they were believed to actually need human food. For instance, in the old Babylonian epic Atrahasis, a great flood wiped out the human population. With nobody to provide for them, the gods suffered hunger and thirst until Atrahasis offered a sacrifice after the flood. When the gods smelled the sacrifice, they crowded around like flies to consume it.[46]

On the fifteenth day of this month there will be a festival (28:17). Ancient Near Eastern peoples celebrated many religious festivals to various gods at certain times during the year.[47] Some of these festivals were exceedingly elaborate. For example, the Babylonian New Year festival of spring lasted eleven or twelve days, included grand processions of idols witnessed by the entire populace, and involved the direct participation of the king.[48] One of the Hittite festivals, apparently a religious tour by the king (and often the queen), lasted thirty-eight days each spring and contained several shorter festivals embedded in it.[49] By comparison, the Israelite festivals are fairly simple (cf. Lev. 23).

Instructions concerning Vows (30:1–16)

When a woman in her father's house during her youth makes a vow to the Lord (30:3). Many ancient Near Eastern people made vows to divine beings and took them very seriously, so that they would not offend their deities. Women as well as men could make vows (see comments on Num. 6:2). For example, in a Hittite record of vows made by the royal family the queen made the following vow: "If you, O goddess, my lady, will preserve the life of His Majesty, i.e., you will not allow him to come to harm, I will make for Ḫebat a gold statuette."[50] In this Hittite example the vow promises to give something of value to the deity, which would be no problem for a queen. Numbers 30 deals with the situation that a common Israelite woman would face if she made a binding promissory vow to give an animal as a sacrifice to the Lord without getting prior approval from her father or husband (who managed the family property).

Punishment of the Midianites (31:1–54)

Brought the prisoners, animals, and spoils of war to Moses (31:12). This was standard procedure for the aftermath of a military victory in the ancient Near East. Compare a text found on a statue of King Idrimi of the Mesopotamian city of Alalaḫ (probably ca. 1500 BC): "I took them as captives; I took their goods, their possessions and their valuables and divided (them) among my auxiliaries. I took my brothers and my comrades together with them and returned to Mukiš. I entered my city Alalaḫ with captives."[51]

Journey Completed and Land to Inherit (32:1–34:29)

These were the stages of the Israelites' journey when they went out of the land of Egypt (33:1). Carved on walls of the temple of Karnak in Egypt, the record of an Asiatic campaign of Thutmose III (ca. 1490–1436 BC) similarly lists stages in an itinerary, in this case of the pharaoh and his conquering army.[52]

When you enter the land of Canaan, it will be allotted to you as an inheritance with these borders (34:2). These boundaries delineate the territory of Canaan, an area previously dominated by Egypt, as shown by a number of Egyptian texts.[53] In this description (34:12) Canaan does not include the Transjordanian territories (i.e., the region east of the Jordan) that the Israelites conquered, and in which the tribes of Reuben, Gad, and half of the tribe of Manasseh settled (Num. 32).

Levite Towns and Asylum for Unintentional Manslayers (35:1–34)

Designate . . . cities of refuge for you, so that a person who kills someone unintentionally may flee there (35:11). Intentional murder necessarily incurs capital punishment (35:31), but a person who commits accidental manslaughter is to be given protection from the death penalty, especially from that administered by a relative of the slain person. There is no direct evidence for cities of refuge like this in other ancient Near Eastern societies, but lesser penalties for accidental manslaughter do appear in Hittite laws.[54]

Bloodshed defiles the land (35:33). A prayer of the Hittite king Muršili II acknowledged that the murder of Tudḫaliya during his father's reign affected the whole land of the Hittites, causing it to suffer a devastating plague (see comments on Num. 14:12–13).[55]

Keeping Land in the Extended Family (36:1–13)

They may marry anyone they like provided they marry within a clan of their ancestral tribe (36:6). This solves a potential problem resulting from inheritance of real estate by daughters (27:8). Inheritance by a woman would be treated as a dowry, which she would take into the estate of her husband. Marriage to a relative would ensure that the property remains within the extended family.[56]

Deuteronomy

Michael A. Grisanti

Introduction. If we accept Moses as the author of Deuteronomy and embrace an early date for the exodus from Egypt (1446 BC), Moses would have completed the book of Deuteronomy (in near final form) in 1407/1406 BC, just prior to Israel's crossing the Jordan River. Among other things, this book sets the stage for the initial fulfillment of the Lord's promise to make Israel into a nation and provide for them a land. Deuteronomy contains Moses's exhortation to a relatively new generation of Israelites just before they possess that land of promise, reminding them of God's demand for their undiluted loyalty and heartfelt obedience to his covenant demands.

In Deuteronomy Moses presents an overview of the Lord's dealings with his chosen people from his encounter with them at Mount Sinai until their encampment on the plains of Moab (chaps. 1–3), demonstrating that the Lord is their provider, protector, and redeemer. Consequently, God's people must not worship any other gods or attempt to make an image of their incomparable God (chap. 4). Moses reminds his people of the Lord's expectations of them in chapters 5–26. Moses presents those demands in two sections: the Lord's broad expectation of absolute allegiance (chaps. 5–11) and the Lord's specific legislative demands (chaps. 12–26). These expectations reach a crescendo at the end of chapter 26, where Moses reminds Israel of their divine calling: to represent the Lord's character before the surrounding pagan nations (26:16–19). The Lord promises to bless the Israelites if they obey him and to curse them if they rebel against him (27:1–29:1). The nation must renew their wholehearted commitment to their covenant relationship with the Lord (29:2–30:20). A casual, ritualistic attempt to conform to God's demands was incompatible with a genuine relationship with the Lord. Moses ends the book by dealing with issues related to the transfer of national leadership to Joshua as well as giving final challenges to the nation (chaps. 31–34).

General Introduction (Preamble) (1:1–5)

Across the Jordan in the wilderness (1:1). The events of Deuteronomy take place during Israel's travels on the east side of the Jordan Valley.

King Sihon . . . King Og (1:4). Both of these kings were Amorites. Sihon ruled the area between Ammon and Moab. Og ruled over the northern part of the Transjordan (in the vicinity of the modern Golan Heights). They were the first "Canaanites" conquered as part of God delivering the land of promise into Israel's hands.

Amorites (1:4). The Amorites migrated from Syria into Canaan around 2500 BC. It appears that the Amorites displaced the Canaanites in the hill country region (Num. 13:29; Josh. 10:6) and even drove out the Moabites from some of their territory (Num. 21:26).

The Lord's Past Dealings with Israel (from Horeb to the Jordan River) (1:6–3:29)

The descendants of the Anakim (1:28). Among the fearsome defenders of the land of Canaan were the Anakim, described as both strong and tall (cf. Num. 13:28, 33; Deut. 1:28; 2:10–11, 21; 9:2). They descended from a certain Anak, whose own ancestor Arba founded the city of Kiriath-arba—that is, Hebron (Josh. 21:11). Although the Anakim are associated with the Nephilim (the offspring of the union of the sons of God and daughters of men in Gen. 6 [cf. Num. 13:33]), all of those Nephilim (and their genetic code) would have perished in the Noahic flood (Gen. 6–9).[1] Most likely this association of the Anakim with the Nephilim would have served to instill fear in the hearts of any people who intended to come against them in battle. Eventually, the Israelites drove all the Anakim out of the land of promise, and the survivors settled in Philistia (Gaza, Gath, and Ashdod [Josh. 11:22]). This suggests that Goliath, who was from Gath, was an Anakite (1 Sam. 17:4; cf. 2 Sam. 21:16–22; 1 Chron. 20:4–8).

Caphtorim (2:23). Although scholars debate the exact origin of the Philistines, it appears that Caphtor, an island or coastland in the area of the Aegean Sea, was the point of origin for the Philistines (Gen. 10:14; 1 Chron. 1:12; Amos 9:7; Jer. 47:4; cf. Zeph. 2:5) (see the article "The Philistines").[2]

Only King Og of Bashan was left of the remnant of the Rephaim (3:11). The term "Rephaim" can refer to a people group that Deuteronomy connects to the Emim (2:10–11). The Rephaim were tall like the Anakim (2:20–21; cf. Num. 13:33). Og was the last survivor of the Rephaim. He must have been a very tall man, as 3:11 states that his bed (or sarcophagus) was thirteen feet long and six feet wide. Contrast this with the average height of Israelite men (and others in the ancient Near East) at this time, which was only around five feet six inches.

Vassal treaty between the Hittite king Mursili II and Talmi-sharruma of Aleppo (ca. 1300 BC), written in cuneiform.

Moses Exhorts God's People to Obey God's Law (4:1–40)

You must not add anything to what I command you (4:2). This expression fits the covenant context suggested by the treaty structure of Deuteronomy. In suzerain-vassal treaties of the ancient Near East, which are the model followed by the bulk of Deuteronomy, only the sovereign sets the terms of the covenant. The vassal could not tamper with or adjust those demands. This "nontampering" clause is found in various ancient Near Eastern treaties with that same significance.[3]

Baal of Peor (4:3). See comments on Num. 25:3. Deuteronomy 3:29 refers to the place Beth-peor, likely pointing to the place near Pisgah where Balaam attempted to curse the nation Israel (Num. 23:28). Deuteronomy 4:3 highlights the fact that the Moabites also worshiped Baal there by the name "Baal [of] Peor."

Two stone tablets (4:13). See comments on Exod 25:16. These two tablets were likely two copies of the Ten Commandments. It was common in ancient Near Eastern treaties for the suzerain and the vassal each to receive a copy of the covenantal agreement, which they deposited in their temples.[4] Both copies of the Ten Commandments were deposited in the ark of the covenant, housed in the most holy place (Exod. 25:16, 21; 40:20; Deut. 10:2).

The sun, moon, and stars . . . do not . . . bow in worship (4:19). See comments on Deut. 17:3.

Iron furnace (4:20). This type of furnace was not used as a source for household heat, but rather for the refinement of precious metals by liquefying those metals and burning away their impurities.

I call heaven and earth as witnesses against you (4:26). Since court proceedings required the testimony of witnesses, the Lord summons heaven and earth to testify to his faithfulness, Israel's disobedience, and the threat of judgment. These "witnesses" offered enduring, unchanging testimony, unlike humankind's penchant for rebellion (Deut. 30:19; 31:28; Isa. 1:2; 3:13; Jer. 2:9).

The Ten Commandments (5:1–6:3)

The Lord our God made a covenant with us at Horeb (5:2). The idea of a god making a covenant with his subjects is generally unheard of in the ancient Near Eastern world. The "gods" of the other nations expected their subjects to meet their needs. In the Bible the one and only true God enters into a covenant relationship with his subjects.

And he said (5:5). Unlike throughout the ancient Near Eastern world, where it is the king who creates law codes to establish justice in his kingdom in an attempt to satisfy his gods, with Israel it is the Lord who establishes the covenant requirements for his chosen people.

This scene from the Egyptian "Book of the Dead" depicts a number of the many gods worshiped in Egypt.

Do not have other gods besides me (5:7). God's demand for Israel to worship him exclusively stands in direct contrast to the practice of polytheism among the nations that surrounded Israel. Throughout the ancient Near East people worshiped many gods, attempting to make the gods happy and thus to avoid their wrath. Yet those gods never demanded exclusive worship. The LORD's demand for Israel's total loyalty is quite distinct from that mindset, as is his jealousy for Israel's affections.

I, the LORD your God, am a jealous God (5:9). As a jealous God, the Lord demanded an exclusive relationship with his covenantal people. Not only was this kind of exclusivity unheard of in other ancient Near East religious systems but also it must not be compared with the petty jealousy and anger that often characterize human relationships. God has the right to a monopoly on the loyalty of his followers, and he will act to protect that special relationship (as in a husband-wife relationship).

Be careful to remember the Sabbath day (5:12). God demanded that Israel celebrate his great accomplishments in creation as well as his redemption of Israel from Egypt by setting aside one day each week to worship him and to place focused attention on his character and activity on their behalf. Nothing like this was practiced by other ancient Near Eastern religions.

Do not commit adultery (5:18). Although adultery was a serious offense throughout the ancient Near East, the Mosaic law regards it as the height of treachery. Just as the Lord demands absolute loyalty from his subjects, so also he requires that husbands and wives maintain absolute loyalty toward each other. Adultery represented an offense against both the spouse and the Lord.

Moses Exhorts Israel to Tangibly Manifest Their Love for the Lord (6:4–25)

A land flowing with milk and honey (6:3). See comments on Exod. 3:8, 17. This expression occurs eighteen times in the OT, including five times in Deuteronomy (6:3; 11:9; 26:9, 15; 27:3). It depicts the land of Canaan as one of abundance and fertility. In addition to signifying potential and comparative agricultural abundance, this expression probably also serves as a polemical critique of what Baal (the god of fertility, who died and came back to life each year) attempted to do. In absolute contrast, the Lord, the living God, will do much more than what Baal tried to do but could not.

The LORD is one (6:4). Although many English translations render this expression with the idea of "one," the Hebrew term signifies the concept of "alone" or "only" in several other passages (Josh. 22:20; 1 Chron. 29:1; Zech. 14:9). The contextual emphasis that the Lord is the only God for Israel as well as the incomparable God provides compelling evidence that the phrase would be better translated as "the Lord alone," as in the NRSV and the footnote of the CSB. Unlike most ancient Near Eastern religions, in which the subjects worshiped numerous gods responsible for various areas of their existence, the Lord was Israel's only God and the God who demanded their exclusive allegiance ("alone").

For the Lord your God . . . is a jealous God (6:15). See comments on Deut. 5:9.

The Blessings and Requirements Occasioned by the Lord's Choice of Israel (7:1–26)

Tear down their altars (7:5). In the religious realm the Israelites must destroy any item involved in Canaanite worship: altars, sacred stones, Asherah poles, and idols (see the article "The Canaanites and Canaanite Religion"). Failure to do this would provide a temptation for the Israelites to depart from total allegiance to the Lord, as actually happened later in the period of judges (Judg. 2:3; 3:6–7; 8:34).

Cut down their Asherah poles (7:5). See comments on 1 Kings 15:13.

The Need for Israel to Depend Totally on the Lord (8:1–20)

A land of olive oil and honey (8:8). See comments on Exod. 3:8, 17; Zech. 4:3.

Moses Warns Israel against Self-Righteousness and Rebellion (9:1–10:11)

The Anakim (9:2). See comments on Deut. 1:28.

Shattering them before your eyes (9:17). Moses intentionally threw the two stone tablets to the ground, causing them to shatter, as a symbol or emblem of the broken covenant. Breaking a tablet in ancient Near Eastern legal and covenantal traditions signified the cancellation of the validity of a document.[5]

Two stone tablets (10:1). See comments on Deut. 4:13.

The Lord Deserves and Demands Israel's Undivided Loyalty (10:12–11:32)

Circumcise your hearts (10:16). Circumcision was practiced by numerous peoples in the ancient Near East. The Israelite practice of circumcision differed from the Egyptian practice in at least two ways. The Egyptians did not circumcise infants but circumcised a male before adulthood or marriage. Also, they only slit the foreskin to let it hang free rather than removing it.[6]

Taking no bribe (10:17). See comments on Deut. 16:19.

A land flowing with milk and honey (11:9). See comments on Exod. 3:8, 17; Deut. 6:3.

From the wilderness . . . to the Mediterranean Sea (11:24). Moses gives the boundaries of the promised land in general directional terms: the desert (wilderness) to the south, Lebanon to the north, the Euphrates River to the east, and the Mediterranean Sea to the west (cf. Gen. 15:18–20; Exod. 23:31).

Mount Gerizim . . . Mount Ebal (11:29). Mount Ebal (3,080 feet high, north of Shechem) and Mount Gerizim (2,849 feet high, south of Shechem) are situated just off the main north-south road as well as above the valley between, through which a main route heading to the coast passes. The curses and blessings of the covenant were recited antiphonally by the participants, positioned in the narrowest part of the valley, opposite each other (cf. 27:13–26; cf. Josh. 8:30–35). Archaeologists have found a structure on Mount Ebal that may be an altar, but its exact date and function are debated.[7] The city of Shechem, rich in patriarchal history (Gen. 12:6–7; 33:19–20; cf. John 4:5–6; Acts 7:16), sits at the base of the two mountains mentioned.

God Demands That Israel Be Totally Distinct in Their Object, Place, and Manner of Worship (12:1–13:18)

These statutes and ordinances (12:1). Many scholars have pointed out various similarities between the Mosaic law (case law) and ancient Near Eastern law codes, in particular the Code of Hammurabi (from Babylonia). On the one hand, the genre of law that occurs in the Pentateuch and ancient Near Eastern law codes (case law: "If this happens, do this") is quite similar. Beyond that, the kinds of life issues addressed in the Mosaic law and these ancient Near Eastern law codes are quite similar as well. On the other hand, there are significant differences between these two categories of law codes. Unlike the ancient Near Eastern law codes, the Mosaic law almost never describes the law to be followed in accordance with any "social ladder." Under the Mosaic law, the laws and associated penalties are generally the same for the top as for the bottom of society. In addition, in the Mosaic law God is pursuing a relationship with his chosen people, and their obedience is presented as an essential part of that relationship. The concept

Figurine of El, head of the Canaanite gods, which the Israelites were warned not to worship (Deut. 11:16).

of ancient Near Eastern gods having a relationship with their subjects is absent from ancient Near Eastern law codes. Finally, God is the author of the laws in the OT, whereas elsewhere throughout the ancient Near East it is the king who authors the laws in his law code.

On the high mountains, on the hills, and under every green tree (12:2). Throughout the ancient Near East the mountains and hills were recognized as prime spots for worship and other religious rituals.[8] Numerous OT passages describe or condemn false worship that took place on high hills (e.g., Deut. 12:2; 1 Kings 14:23; 2 Kings 16:4; 17:10; Isa. 65:7; Jer. 2:20; 17:2).

Tear down their altars . . . burn their Asherah poles (12:3). See comments on Deut. 7:5; 1 Kings 15:13.

Wipe out their names from every place (12:3). As with the Lord (see comments on Deut. 12:5), a person's name points to the sum total of their identity and character. In Egypt names were used in execration texts where the names of certain rulers or cities were written on clay objects and then smashed, highlighting Egypt's hope to remove them from existence.[9] God required Israel to remove the Canaanites from existence in the land of promise (for the concept of wiping/blotting out a name, cf. Deut. 7:24; 9:14; 29:20).

Don't worship the Lord your God this way (12:4). The Lord called the Israelites to worship him as their one and only God, the incomparable great God of the universe. Their worship of him was to arise out of genuine gratitude for what he had done for them and in light of the relationship that he expected them to have with him. In clear contrast to that mindset, Canaanite worship of the god Baal involved fertility worship. Having sexual relations with a temple prostitute at the temple of Baal was meant to provoke Baal into giving fertility to their family, crops, and herds and flocks, a form of sympathetic magic. The Lord presents himself instead as the suzerain of Israel, not as a god for Israel to manipulate for their own purposes.

To the place the Lord your God chooses . . . to put his name for his dwelling (12:5). First, the "place" referred to here stands in clear contrast to the many places where the Canaanites worshiped their gods (12:2–4). Second, the names of pagan gods were attached to the places where they appeared or were connected to a given location, especially a cultic location or shrine. In a similar way, God instructed Israel that he would put his name at those places where he chooses to be recognized and worshiped. The name of a deity in the Bible and generally throughout the ancient Near East defined in an

Egyptian execration texts/fragments.

essential way the character, nature, and function of that deity. Hence, when a god's name was "placed" somewhere (e.g., Baal [of/at] Peor), the god allegedly was there.

You must not eat the blood . . . the blood is life (12:16, 20). Although various non-Israelite ancient Near Eastern texts employ "blood" and "life" as word pairs (showing an awareness of the connection between the two terms), many texts refer to the drinking of blood as part of a god's or a king's victory over his enemies. The stress on blood as signifying life and the central role of blood in Israel's sacrificial system are unparalleled in the ancient Near Eastern world.

They even burn their sons and daughters in the fire to their gods (12:31). See comments on 2 Kings 3:27. Archaeological evidence and several ancient Near Eastern literary texts give evidence of human sacrifice as well as child sacrifice in various parts of the ancient Near East.[10]

If a prophet or someone who has dreams arises among you (13:1). Although the Lord occasionally made use of dreams to communicate his will (Gen. 28:12; 37:5–11; Dan. 2; 4), references to dreams as a means of communication from the gods occur frequently in the ancient Near East.[11] The point that Moses makes is that anyone who calls upon the Israelites to worship other gods, even a person who dreams something that comes true, must be put to death.

Completely destroy everyone (13:15). The threat to turn a town into a ruin was a common curse found in ancient Near Eastern treaties.[12]

Daily Implications of Bearing the Lord's Name (14:1–21)

Do not cut yourselves . . . on behalf of the dead (14:1). See comments on 1 Kings 18:28. Moses prohibits the Israelites from imitating pagan practices associated with mourning the dead (cf. Lev. 21:5; Jer. 16:5). In a text from Ugarit (an ancient city in Syria) the god El lacerates himself with a stone, cutting off his hair while mourning Baal's death. According to various other Ugaritic texts, professional mourners cut their skin or lacerated themselves on behalf of a dying righteous person.[13]

His own possession (14:2). A related form of the same Hebrew noun that is used here occurs in various ancient Near Eastern texts to refer to "accumulated assets." Yet it can also be used to describe people as well. A king, for example, identified himself as the "treasured possession of the god Hadad." In another text this term is used to signify the favored status of the king of Ugarit to his Hittite overlord.[14]

You must not eat any detestable thing (14:3). Although various Mesopotamian texts indicate that certain foods may have been prohibited for short periods, there is no indication of any overriding system of clean/unclean food in Mesopotamian religion like what the Lord demanded of Israel.[15]

Do not boil a young goat in its mother's milk (14:21). See comments on Exod. 23:19. Scholars are uncertain about the reason for this prohibition (cf. Exod. 23:19; 34:26). Some scholars in the past viewed this law as referring to a pagan religious practice that the Lord outlawed, but that interpretation has been abandoned by many scholars in recent years. Among the various suggestions that have been offered, the most plausible option seems to be that the Israelites are told that they must not use what gives life to take away life.[16]

Tribute for the Lord, the Covenant Lord (14:22–16:17)

Each year you are to set aside a tenth (14:22). Kingdoms in the ancient Near East had various systems of taxation to provide for the needs of their bureaucracies and religious institutions. They also received tribute from subject nations. In most of these cases, however, the tithe/tax and tribute were submitted to the government and were totally unrelated to any relationship with their gods. Thus the OT tithing system was quite distinct from the taxation system of the surrounding nations in that it went directly to support the needs of the worship system and its attendants (priests and Levites), and was anchored in Israel's relationship with their suzerain, the Lord.

At the end of every seven years you must cancel debts (15:1). The nations and peoples in the ancient Near East regularly made use of loans and debt. Although there may have been periodic decrees that required the remission of debt for a year, in general across the ancient Near East there was no systemic or regular practice of canceling debts. Thus the cyclical debt cancellation in Israel and its connection to the Sabbatical Year was unique in the ancient Near East.

Do not be hardhearted or tightfisted toward your poor brother (15:7). Various hymns in the literature of the ancient Near East refer to a goddess who cares for the widow and the poor. Likewise, the prologues and epilogues of ancient law codes from Mesopotamia often manifest concern for the poor.[17] In contrast to these ancient law codes, however, which contained lofty statements about this issue in their prologues and epilogues, the Mosaic law contains clear legislation that required God's people to care for the needy (cf. Exod. 23:6, 11; Deut. 15:9, 11; 24:14). This requirement upon the Israelites is an aspect of their covenant loyalty and is modeled after the way that God defends the cause of the fatherless, the widow, and the resident foreigner (Deut. 10:18).

If your fellow Hebrew, a man or woman, is sold to you (15:12). In Israel and in the surrounding nations of the ancient Near East slavery or servitude often was the result of a family's economic calamity. While law 117 of the Code of Hammurabi (from Babylonia) limited the term of servitude for the repayment of debt to three years,[18] the Mosaic law provided a six-year term for debt repayment by an Israelite (cf. Exod. 21:2–6; Lev. 25:39–46). The law allowed Israelites to have slaves for life if they were from a conquered people (Num. 31:7–12; Deut. 21:10–14). Unfortunately, it appears that Israel did not always submit to the requirement to release slaves after they had completed their required time (Jer. 34:8–16).

But you must not eat its blood (15:23). See comments on Deut. 12:16, 20.

Abib (16:1). The month of Abib (March-April) was considered the first month of the Israelite religious calendar. The Passover and the Festival of Unleavened Bread and the exodus from Egypt took place in this month (Exod. 12:2; 13:4; 23:15). Later in history, during the exilic and postexilic periods, the Babylonian word for this month, Nisan, replaced the earlier Hebrew term Abib (Neh. 2:1; Esther 3:7).

Kingdom Officials (16:18–18:22)

Do not deny justice or show partiality to anyone (16:19). Through various law codes the kings in the ancient Near East often declared their mission to establish justice and to liberate the oppressed. Occasionally they put in place various social reforms to seek to provide justice for the weak in society. However, this justice was elusive and almost inaccessible to the lower classes. In direct contrast to the Mosaic law, many of the laws in the Code of Hammurabi (from Babylonia) had diminished penalties for crimes committed against poor people or slaves.[19]

Do not accept a bribe (16:19). The OT consistently prohibits taking bribes because it corrupts justice (Exod. 23:8). Law 6 of the Code of Hammurabi (from Babylonia) may refer to a bribe when it indicts a judge who renders a judicial decision and then abruptly changes it for no apparent cause.[20] Besides that example, there are no clear examples where bribery is condemned in the ancient Near East.

Do not set up an Asherah (16:21). See comments on 1 Kings 15:13.

Bowing in worship to the sun, moon, or all the stars in the sky (17:3). See comments on 2 Kings 17:16. The worship of the celestial bodies (sun, moon, planets, stars) was common

This boundary marker of King Meli-Shipak shows the symbols of three astral deities worshiped in Mesopotamia.

throughout the ancient Near East. In Mesopotamia, Shamash was a sun god and Sin a moon god (Thoth in Egypt and Yarah in Canaan). In contrast, besides condemning the worship of any God except the Lord (Deut. 5:7; cf. Josh. 23:16), the Lord explicitly prohibited Israel from making an image of him comparable to any celestial body (Deut. 4:19).

To your city gates (17:5). Throughout the history of Israel, as in the ancient Near East, city gates were important places for commerce and defense, as well as for adjudicating disputes between people (Deut. 21:19; Ruth 4:1–12; Amos 5:15). In the ancient Near East town leaders often handled disputes in the gate area, so the gates carried a judicial connotation.[21]

On the testimony of two or three witnesses (17:6). Witnesses served as a critical part of the judicial process in Israel (Exod. 20:16; Num. 35:30; Deut. 19:16–19; Jer. 32:44) and throughout the ancient Near East. Certain Middle Assyrian laws required a minimum of two witnesses, while others needed five or six.[22]

The king the Lord your God chooses (17:15). The Sumerian King List begins with the statement "When the kingship was lowered from heaven." Likewise, in the prologue of his law code Hammurabi (1792–1750 BC) refers to the gods Anum and Enlil as choosing him to rule over the people. Unlike the kings of Mesopotamia, the Egyptian pharaohs (in the Old Kingdom in particular) were considered to be gods themselves.[23] In the OT, however, while the Israelite king is to be chosen by the Lord and held accountable to the Lord's explicit instructions in the Mosaic law, he is not given divine status.

Must not acquire many horses . . . many wives . . . large amounts of silver and gold (17:16–17). Throughout the ancient Near East horse-mounted soldiers (cavalry) and chariots found wide usage in the first millennium BC, and were the backbone of most powerful armies in the region. Likewise, kings often entered into marriage with princesses of other nations specifically to establish treaties with those nations. Of course, the accumulation of great wealth dominated the ruling class of every nation around Israel.

The Levitical priests (18:1). See comments on Lev. 1:5–9. In contrast to Israel, in Egypt and among the Hittites the king was the high priest and often exercised priestly functions. Various ancient Near Eastern nations also had priestesses and referred to some of those priestesses as a mother, priestess, or wife or concubine of the god. In some of the nations the king and queen ate from the sacrifices offered to their gods.[24]

No one among you is to sacrifice his son or daughter (18:10). See comments on 2 Kings 3:27.

Practice divination . . . practice sorcery . . . inquire of the dead (18:10–11). See comments on Lev. 19:26, 31; 2 Kings 16:14; 17:17. There was a wide range of divination practices in the ancient Near East used to determine the will of the gods and to predict the future. These included the examination of the entrails of sacrificial animals (extispicy), the analysis of omens of various types, the reading of the future in natural and unnatural phenomena (see Gen. 44:5), and the interpretation of dreams (specific Babylonian texts contain lists of dreams and what they portend—accidents, deaths, military defeats or victories; see Dan. 2:9).[25]

The Lord your God will raise up for you a prophet (18:15). Individuals in prophet-like roles were common throughout the ancient Near East, especially in royal courts. Texts from Mesopotamia, Syria, and Anatolia (modern Turkey) contain a large number of prophetic utterances from different periods of ancient Near Eastern history. Many of these utterances involved men or women who claimed to have received a message from a god, often through dreams or omens.[26]

When . . . the message does not come true (18:22). The broad principle of testing the truthfulness of a prediction was recognized at Mari (a city in ancient Syria where over twenty thousand ancient literary texts were discovered), where a prophecy was tested by getting another opinion. Often royal written records were kept in order to check on a prediction's fulfillment or nonfulfillment.[27]

Laws Delineating the True Administration of Justice (19:1–22:8)

Do not move your neighbor's boundary marker (19:14). In the ancient world landowners often marked out their property with boundary stones. Removing these stones was regarded as a serious form of theft. Every major region of the ancient Near East had laws outlawing the relocation of someone else's boundary stones.

The testimony of two or three witnesses (19:15). See comments on Deut. 17:6.

If a malicious witness testifies (19:16). Various ancient Near Eastern law codes address the issue of false witnesses and demand a punishment for it—either a fine, the death of the false witness, or, as Deuteronomy demands here, that the false witness receive the same penalty that the accused person would have received if found guilty (19:19).

Eye for eye, tooth for tooth (19:21). The legal principle of *lex talionis* or "law of retaliation" occurs in the Mosaic law (cf.

Ancient Babylonian boundary stone (*kudurru*) recording a gift of land with its boundaries carefully defined.

Exod. 21:23–25; Lev. 24:19–20) as well as in various law codes of the ancient Near East. In general, this principle dictates that the guilty party receive the exact equivalent injury that he or she inflicted on the victim. Among non-Israelite nations in the ancient Near East, however, the penalty also varied depending on the social status of the injured party and the accused. Thus in those regions *lex talionis* would be precisely applied only if the accused and injured parties had the same social standing. If the injured party was from a lower class, however, a less demanding punishment would be required for the guilty person. By contrast, under the Mosaic law a person's social standing had nothing to do with the kind of penalty applied, although it did allow for some kind of compensation in certain cases.

You may take . . . all its spoil—as plunder (20:14). The practice of looting and burning conquered cities was common throughout the ancient Near East. Generally, however, the looting was selective; not every item was taken, nor every person killed, nor everything of value destroyed. Tribute often was imposed on conquered peoples.[28]

You must completely destroy them (20:17). Only rarely did kings in the ancient Near East totally destroy a conquered city. The Assyrians, however, were well-known for causing more destruction than normal to a defeated city.

Do not destroy its trees by putting an ax to them (20:19). In contrast to this command to the Israelites, generally the Egyptians and the Assyrians would cut down all the fruit trees after they conquered an area.[29]

If a man has two wives (21:15). Polygamy was very common in the ancient Near East. Most of the law codes in the ancient Near East clearly delineated the inheritance share for the first wife as well as later wives. Polygamy was allowed briefly in Israel, but the practice represented a departure from God's ideal (Gen. 2:22–25) and was never encouraged. In general, the details of ancient Near Eastern inheritance practices are quite varied, though a common feature was that the first wife and the firstborn son received a larger share than the others.[30]

If a man has a stubborn and rebellious son . . . all the men of his city will stone him to death (21:18, 21). In the ancient Near East the phenomenon of rebellious children was basically a societal issue, but still it was considered a grave offense. Penalties delineated in various ancient Near Eastern law codes for delinquent children involved enslavement, mutilation, or disinheritance.[31]

You are not to leave his corpse on the tree overnight (21:23). This verse is not describing the means of execution (by hanging), but rather the exhibition of a dead criminal's body hanging from a tree in order to bring shame to the criminal (cf. Josh. 8:29; 10:26–27; 1 Sam. 31:11–13; 2 Sam. 4:12). The public exposure of the bodies of executed criminals, which enabled various birds and animals to eat their bodies, was also common in the ancient Near

East. Sennacherib, king of Nineveh (704–681 BC), displayed images of impaled Israelites on the reliefs of several walls in his palace celebrating his victory over the Israelite city of Lachish.[32]

A woman is not to wear male clothing, and a man is not to put on a woman's garment (22:5). Although the meaning of this passage is not altogether clear, it seems to refer to transvestism. Throughout the ancient Near East transvestism appears to be strictly prohibited, except when used as a punishment. The Hittites, for example, made conquered soldiers wear feminine scarves to shame them. Some scholars have argued that transvestism was also part of pagan worship.[33]

Various Laws of Distinctiveness/Purity (22:9–23:18)

With another man's wife (22:22). See comments on Deut. 5:18.

And sleeps with her (22:23). Deuteronomy 22:23–29 presents four scenarios involving premarital sex: (1) consensual sex between a man and engaged woman; (2) a man who rapes an engaged woman in the city; (3) a man who rapes an engaged woman in the country; and (4) a man who rapes an unattached woman in the country. The law codes of non-Israelite nations in the ancient Near East likewise view several of these actions as punishable, but vary in their punishment from that prescribed here. These ancient law codes are fairly unanimous that the man in scenario 3 would be executed.[34] The penalty in those law codes for the man and woman in scenario 2 is quite varied.[35] Scenarios 1 and 4 are not clearly addressed in ancient Near Eastern law codes. These differences suggest that the Bible placed more value on sexual intimacy as appropriate only for marriage than did the surrounding nations, and likewise was concerned with guarding the welfare of the unengaged woman (and any children that might be conceived through rape).

Give the young woman's father fifty silver shekels (22:29). This would be the "bride-price" mentioned in three other OT passages (Gen. 34:12; Exod. 22:16; 1 Sam. 18:25). The practice of the groom's family providing a bride-price for the bride's family was common throughout the ancient Near East. The amount of the bride-price likely varied over time and in light of different family circumstances.

Do not return a slave to his master when he has escaped (23:15). In strong contrast to this biblical law, in most law codes of the ancient Near East harboring an escaped slave was a serious crime. In fact, certain treaties included clauses that required extradition of escaped slaves to their rightful owners.

No Israelite woman is to be a cult prostitute (23:17–18). Prostitution in general was legally and socially permitted throughout the ancient Near

East.[36] What is not as clear is the extent to which prostitution was connected to pagan worship centers (i.e., cult prostitution) and served as part of fertility worship practices. Although recently some scholars have questioned whether cult prostitution was widespread in the ancient Near East, texts like Deut. 23:17–18, along with Gen. 38, appear to suggest that some version of religious prostitution existed in Israel at times and probably was related to pagan fertility religious practice.

Laws of Interpersonal Relationships (23:19–25:19)

Do not charge your brother interest (23:19). Charging high interest occurred regularly and widely in the ancient Near East. Israelites, however, were allowed to charge interest to foreigners (23:20), but not to fellow Israelites.

He may write her a divorce certificate (24:1). Throughout the ancient Near East, outside of Israel, a husband could divorce his wife for a wide number of reasons (often to the wife's detriment). Once children were born, divorce was more complicated but still possible. A wife could not divorce her husband.[37]

Do not take a pair of grindstones . . . as security for a debt (24:6). Although an Israelite lender could not charge a fellow Israelite interest, the person borrowing money could offer some form of collateral to express a commitment to repay the debt. This passage prohibits an Israelite from taking a person's millstone as collateral, because that would prevent its owner from caring for important daily needs, like the provision of food for the family. A millstone involved two stones, often made of a hard stone like basalt. Grain or corn was placed between the two stones. The pressure applied by the upper stone crushed the grain or corn into flour or meal. Each family would own a small millstone for the daily grinding of wheat into flour for that day's meals.

Children are not to be put to death for their fathers (24:16). In the ancient Near Eastern world some law codes prevented those who did not commit the crime from being punished along with the guilty party.[38] However, others required family members of the guilty party to be punished along with the guilty party.[39]

Do not deny justice to a resident alien or fatherless child, and do not take a widow's garment as security (24:17). The care for widows and orphans receives attention in many ancient Near Eastern law codes. This literature often presents the gods as interested in guarding the interests of these needy people.[40]

Her brother-in-law is to take her as his wife (25:5). When a married man died before he had an heir, one of his brothers was responsible to take his widow as his wife and have a child by her who would serve as the deceased brother's heir, a practice known as levirate marriage (see Gen. 38:6–10, 26; cf. Ruth 2:8; 3:12; 4:6). Among other things, this would keep the land allotted by the Lord in the family. Some version of this practice existed in different parts of the ancient Near East. Although the motive or rationale behind the ancient Near Eastern practice varied, a general concern was to maintain a family's seed and inheritance. The idea of land allotted by their god was never addressed in non-Israelite ancient Near Eastern laws.[41]

Ceremonial Fulfillment of the Law (26:1–15)

A wandering Aramean (26:5). Aram was a region to the north of Israel, corresponding to that occupied by biblical Syria at the height of its power. Both Isaac and Jacob married women from Abraham's family who lived in that region. Since Jacob himself left Canaan and lived in that region for twenty years, this expression describes him (Gen. 28:5).

A land flowing with milk and honey (26:9). See comments on Exod. 3:8, 17; Deut. 6:3.

The tenth of your produce . . . fatherless children and widows (26:12). See comments on Deut. 14:22. Although taxes were used to support temples and priests in the ancient Near East, there is no evidence of a tithe used to assist the disadvantaged of society.

I have not . . . offered any of it for the dead (26:14). These words refer to the anticipated confession of a godly Israelite widow, orphan, or resident foreigner (26:12–13) who did not eat anything provided to them as part of this tithe while participating in a pagan fertility or mourning ritual.

Mutual Commitments of Covenant Renewal (26:16–19)

His own possession (26:18). See comments on Deut. 14:2.

Covenant Blessings and Curses (27:1–29:1)

Set up large stones and cover them with plaster (27:2). Since inscribing texts into stone was very difficult, an alternative method for writing on stone monuments was to coat the stone surface with plaster and then write in the soft plaster. Several examples of this method have been discovered in the Palestine region, including the inscriptions at Deir Alla and Kuntillet Ajrud.[42]

A land flowing with milk and honey (27:3). See comments on Exod. 3:8, 17; Deut. 6:3.

Mount Ebal (27:4). See comments on Deut. 11:29.

To bless the people . . . to deliver the curse (27:12–13). The offensive conduct condemned in 27:15–26 as well as the blessings and curses presented in chapter 28 broadly resonate with the blessings and curses found in many ancient Near Eastern treaties. Some of these points of similarity involve various categories of disease, drought and famine, sale of family members into slavery, defeat, and cannibalism.[43] One of the key differences is the threat of eviction from the land of promise in the Mosaic covenant curses.

The LORD will establish you as his holy people . . . all the peoples of the earth will see (28:9–10). Although typically ancient Near Eastern treaties promised blessing for obedience, and even blessings that would be delivered by their gods, the concept that the Lord desires to exalt his chosen people over the other nations in order to bring glory to himself is found only in the OT.

The sky above you will be bronze, and the earth beneath you iron (28:23). At least two ancient Near Eastern treaties threaten bronze skies and iron-hard land to a nation that violates the covenant, specifying the absence of rain and dew as well as the dryness of the ground (see comments on Lev. 26:19).[44]

The Grounds and Need for Covenant Renewal (29:2–30:20)

Sodom and Gomorrah (29:23). See comments on Deut. 32:32.

Circumcise your heart (30:6). See comments on Deut. 10:16.

This command that I give you today is certainly not too difficult (30:11). In the Gilgamesh Epic, after the death of his friend, Gilgamesh sets out on a voyage to discover the secret of life, something unattainable.[45] In Babylonian wisdom literature a person experiencing suffering or pursuing wisdom might confess to being unable to grasp any of the gods' purposes.[46] In direct contrast to that impossibility of understanding any of the deity's intentions, Moses affirms that his God has clearly revealed his intentions to his covenant people.

I call heaven and earth as witnesses (30:19). See comments on Deut. 4:26.

The Continuity of the Covenant from Moses to Joshua (31:1–34:12)

Sihon and Og . . . the Amorites (31:4). See comments on Deut. 1:4.

You are about to rest with your fathers (31:16). The expression "rest with your fathers" was a common OT idiom of dying (based on a verb meaning "to lie down in sleep") (Gen. 47:30; 1 Kings 1:21; 2:10; 11:21, 43; 14:20). It probably is to be connected to the burial practice in the OT of burying people in the family tomb and later having their bones put in a bone repository with the bones of their ancestors.

A view from the top of Mount Nebo, looking across the Dead Sea to the land of Israel.

A land flowing with milk and honey (31:20). See comments on Exod. 3:8, 17; Deut. 6:3.

Heavens . . . earth (32:1). See comments on Deut. 4:26.

Rams from Bashan (32:14). See comments on Amos 4:1. The region of Bashan, a fertile area east of the Jordan River, was renowned for its impressive oak forests (Isa. 2:13; Ezek. 27:6), abundant grazing lands (Jer. 50:19), and especially its well-fed cattle (Ps. 22:12; Ezek. 39:18).[47]

From the vine of Sodom and from the fields of Gomorrah (32:32). Sodom and Gomorrah are mentioned metaphorically to exemplify the soil of perversion that produces the fruit that Moses condemns here (cf. Gen. 18:20; 19:4–28), and perhaps to warn of judgment such as that which fell on those cities (see comments on Zeph. 2:9).

Go up Mount Nebo in the Abarim range in the land of Moab (32:49). The Abarim mountain range sits northeast of the Dead Sea, near the plains of Moab. Mount Nebo, from which the Lord allowed Moses to view the land of promise, is part of this range (Num. 27:12; 33:47–48; Deut. 34:1; Jer. 22:20).[48]

The Lord came from Sinai . . . from Seir . . . from Mount Paran (33:2). These are mountains and regions in the wilderness area where Israel spent almost forty years on their journey to the land of promise, areas where God revealed himself as the one who cared for his people (Judg. 5:4–5; Ps. 68:7–8; Hab. 3:3–4).

Thummim and Urim (33:8). See comments on Exod. 28:2.

Out of Bashan (33:22). See comments on Deut. 32:14.

To Mount Nebo, to the top of Pisgah (34:1). See comments on Deut. 32:49.

Facing Beth-peor (34:6). See comments on Deut. 4:3.

Plains of Moab (34:8). This refers to the broad plain immediately north of the Dead Sea, at the base of Mount Nebo, and east of the Jordan River, just opposite the "plains of Jericho" (Josh. 4:13). Its location served as the jumping-off point for Israel's conquest of Canaan (cf. Num. 22:1; 26:3, 63; 31:12; 33:48–50; 35:1; 36:13; Josh. 13:32).

Joshua

Boyd Seevers

Introduction. The book of Joshua is named after the man who led Israel to conquer Canaan. In fact, some of the book appears to have been written by Joshua himself (24:26). Joshua had been an aide to Moses (1:1; Exod. 24:13–14), had led Israel into battle (Exod. 17:8–13), and was one of the two faithful spies who had scouted out Canaan (Num. 13–14). Following Moses's death, Joshua is handed the responsibility of leading Israel to conquer and take possession of the land promised to them in the time of Abraham (Gen. 12:7) centuries earlier.

The account in Joshua begins forty years after the exodus from Egypt, which apparently occurred either in 1446 BC or around 1260 BC (see comments on Exod. 1:8–11; 1:11). Regardless of the exact date, much of central Canaan was vulnerable to conquest. Many of the region's earlier powerful cities had been abandoned or had become greatly weakened, and Egypt no longer kept the region under tight control. The central hill country was sparsely populated, with most of the population located in a few cities governed by leaders called "kings" who also controlled smaller, nearby villages. Defeating the relatively small armies of these Canaanite city-states would allow the invading Israelites to settle into the land and set up small agricultural villages in the hills.

The book of Joshua describes how God leads Joshua to use a classic strategy of divide-and-conquer to subdue central Canaan. Following the miraculous crossing of the flooded Jordan River (1:1–5:15), the Israelites cut through Canaan from east to west with victories at Jericho in the Jordan Valley, at Ai and Gibeon up in the central hills, and then down into the western lowlands

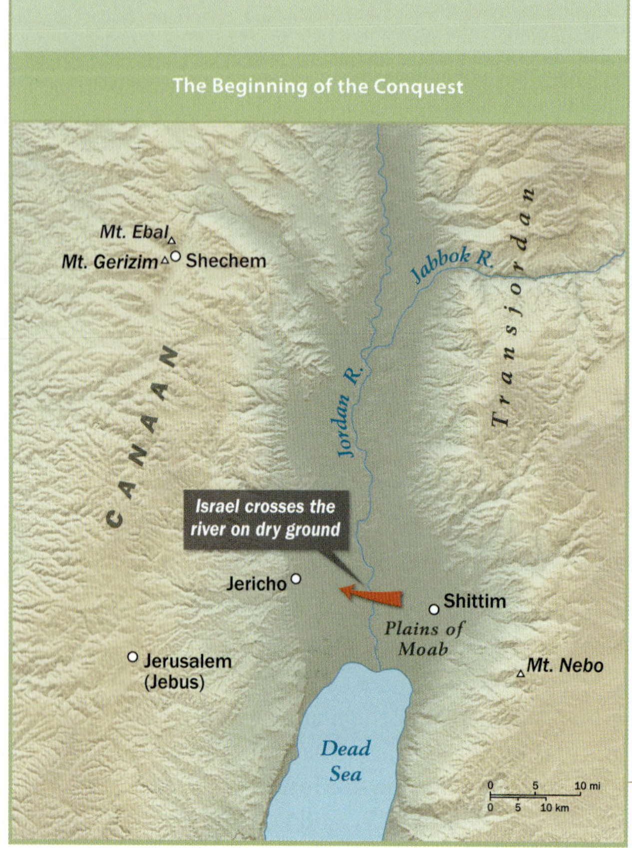

(6:1–10:27). They then sweep through the southern part of Canaan (10:28–43) and then through the north (11:1–15), defeating the armies of major cities in those regions. After summarizing the conquest (11:16–12:24), the remainder of the book describes the division of the land among the Israelite tribes (13:1–21:45) and the final events that closed out this generally positive and successful period of conquest (22:1–24:33).

Preparations for Conquest (1:1–5:15)

Moses my servant is dead (1:2). In 1:1–9 God commissions Joshua to assume leadership of Israel after the death of Moses—Israel's leader, judge, general, and prophet for the past forty years. Transition of leadership often was difficult in the ancient Near East, where power tended to be concentrated at the top and remain within families. Many ancient Near Eastern military campaign accounts commenced with the king receiving encouragement and assurances of victory from his gods. For example, in 1392 BC in Egypt, Pharaoh Thutmose IV prepared to campaign in Nubia by consulting the god Amun in Thebes, who offered him encouragement.

To the land I am giving the Israelites (1:2). God is giving the land of Canaan to Israel, fulfilling a promise dating back to Abraham (Gen. 12:7). Grants of land from greater to lesser parties appear frequently in the ancient Near East. For example, a land grant from eighteenth-century-BC Alalakh (a city-state along the modern Syrian-Turkish border) described the gift of the site by a powerful king to the man who would begin a dynasty there. This land grant document included two sections, one recounting the history that led to the grant (cf. Josh. 1–11), and the other containing a town list (cf. Josh. 12). This land grant portrayed the greater king as the main character (like God in the book of Joshua), who promised the land to the faithful recipient who had participated in its conquest (like Israel in the book of Joshua).

Be strong and very courageous to observe carefully the whole instruction my servant Moses commanded you (1:7). As new Egyptian pharaohs demanded obedience from subject kings by having them swear an oath of loyalty, so God challenges Joshua to remain faithful, and the rest of the Israelites pledge their obedience.

Joshua . . . secretly sent two men as spies (2:1). See comments on Josh. 9:4. Texts from Mari, a city in Syria, indicate that the use of spies was known from as early as the eighteenth century BC.

The king of Jericho sent word to Rahab and said, "Bring out the men who came to you . . . for they came to investigate" (2:3). There is evidence that in some areas of the ancient Near East rulers required tavern keepers to pass along information about suspicious individuals. For example, law 109 in the Code of Hammurabi (an ancient Babylonian king) states, "If conspirators meet in the house of a woman wine-seller, and these conspirators are not captured and delivered to the court, the wine-seller shall be put to death."[1]

I don't know where they were going (2:5). To save the spies—and probably herself as well—Rahab lies about their whereabouts. For people in the ancient Near East, telling the truth in general probably was less important than it is in modern Western cultures. Note how even godly biblical characters such as Abraham (Gen. 12:11–13; 20:2) and David (1 Sam. 27:10–12) lied. God seems to overlook Rahab's lying to honor her belief and her faithfulness to the Israelites.

But she had taken them up to the roof (2:6). Homes built into a city's wall were not uncommon for this period. Sometimes homes were built in a continuous ring around a settlement so that their adjoining back walls served as the city wall; other times city walls were built with hollow chambers called "casemates" that homeowners could use as living space. Whatever the style of Jericho at that time, homes in this region typically were built with flat roofs that could be used for additional activities such as drying agricultural produce like flax.

Go to the hill country so that the men pursuing you won't find you (2:16). Jericho was located approximately one-half mile east of the cliffs of the Rift Valley, where the many caves would offer excellent cover for the spies, especially when their pursuers were searching further east, toward the Jordan River.

Acacia Grove . . . Jordan . . . Gilgal (3:1; 4:19). To cross the Jordan and reach the site of their new base camp in Canaan, the Israelites would have marched about eight miles from Acacia Grove (translated as "Shittim" in some English versions) to the Jordan River, and then another six miles to their next camp at Gilgal near Jericho.

He said to the priests, "Carry the ark of the covenant and go on ahead of the people" (3:6). As ancient kings had bodyguards who accompanied them on the march, so the gold-covered box symbolizing Israel's God is accompanied by priests. The Hittite document "Instruction for the Royal Bodyguard" even specified the distance that the king's guards had to keep from their sovereign (cf. with 3:4).

The water flowing downstream stood still, rising up in a mass . . . as far as Adam, a city next to Zarethan (3:16). At flood stage during the spring the Jordan could measure 10–12 feet deep and 140 feet across. Sixteen miles upstream from Jericho at Adam, the Jordan runs below a bluff on its east bank. Periodically the bank collapses and stops the flow of water for a short time until the water cuts back through the blockage. This occurred in AD 1160, 1267 (for 16 hours), 1546, 1834, 1906, and most recently in 1927 during an earthquake (for 21 hours). Such a collapse, although this time orchestrated by God's intervention, likely caused the stoppage described in Josh. 3. Ancient Near Eastern armies often began campaigns in the spring (2 Sam. 11:1) when rivers were flooding, so they faced this same problem of crossing flooded rivers. Sargon II of Assyria boasted that his army crossed the Tigris and Euphrates Rivers "at the highest flood, the high water of the spring of the year."[2]

These stones will always be a memorial (4:7). Since large stones are readily available throughout most of Israel, people there often have used them as commemorative markers to signify boundaries (Prov. 22:28), places of worship (Gen. 28:18–22; cf. Exod. 24:4), or momentous events, as here. Kings in the ancient Near East were known to erect memorial stones, often carved with images and inscriptions, to mark the border of a conquered territory. Thutmose II of Egypt, for example, erected such a stone next to the stone of his grandfather on the east side of the Euphrates River, as well as two on the west side and one at Niy in northern Syria. Similarly, the stone monument here in 4:1–24 may represent (the beginning of) God's conquest of Canaan.

The LORD your God dried up the water of the Jordan (4:23). In Egypt and Mesopotamia rivers were considered as either gods or under the control of the gods. When Israel's God manipulates the Jordan River for his people (as he had the Red Sea), he is demonstrating his sovereignty in a way that even the locals probably understood and feared.

Flint knives (5:2). Flint is a hard stone (cf. Ezek. 3:9) that people have shaped into blades and other tools for thousands of years. It can be found easily in the region of Jericho and makes an excellent cutting tool like that needed for circumcision (Exod. 4:25).

A land flowing with milk and honey (5:6). See comments on Exod. 3:8, 17; Deut. 6:3. Similarly, an Egyptian official named Sinuhe from about the time of Abraham described Canaan as "a good land . . . abundant was its honey . . . and milk dishes of all kinds."[3]

They stayed where they were in the camp until they recovered (5:8). Had the Israelites been circumcised in their camp back across the Jordan, they could have healed in relative safety. Here at Gilgal they are perhaps only a mile from the enemy at Jericho and highly vulnerable (cf. Gen. 34:24–29).

From the produce of the land (5:11). God stops the miraculous supply of manna, forcing the Israelite invaders to forage for food. Ancient military invaders typically did the same. Egyptian records indicate that when Pharaoh Thutmose III invaded Canaan in the fifteenth century BC, his troops harvested 207,300 sacks of wheat from the fields near Megiddo.

The commander of the LORD's army (5:15). As God had appeared to Jacob at the edge of Canaan (Gen. 32:22–30) and to Moses at the burning bush (Exod. 3:5–6), so he appears to Joshua at Jericho. On the eve of the first battle in Canaan, God assures Joshua of his presence and that Joshua's mission will succeed.

Conquest of Canaan (6:1–12:24)

The Israelites begin their conquest of the promised land by attacking central Canaan from the east (6:1–10:27). Their early victories cut across Canaan from east to west with the battles at Jericho, Ai, and Gibeon (and the series of battles associated with defending Gibeon).

Jericho Falls (6:1–27)

March around the city . . . for six days (6:3). Tactics used in a number of ancient battles are known, but none resemble God's strategy for Israel at Jericho. Parading in front of the enemy repeatedly calls for obedience but makes little strategic sense, as it removes all element of surprise.

Have seven priests carry seven ram's-horn trumpets in front of the ark (6:4). See comments on Josh. 3:6.

Then the city wall will collapse (6:5). The inconclusive archaeological remains at Jericho have generated great debate, with some researchers even arguing that the site had no meaningful city to conquer at the time of Joshua.

An ancient flint knife.

Aerial view of the excavations of ancient Jericho.

The city fortifications might have been as simple as a ring settlement (see comments on Josh. 2:6), or the city could still have been using walls built much earlier. Ancient Jericho had an inner wall dating to before 2200 BC and an outer wall dating to about 1550 BC. Both could have been in use until the time of Joshua.

They marched around the city seven times (6:15). This author's personal march around the rather small site of Jericho took about fifteen minutes. If the ancient Israelite troops circled Jericho at least a bowshot (up to two hundred yards) away from the walls, a circuit might take approximately forty-five minutes. Thus seven circuits on the seventh day would take several hours, suggesting that the Israelites marched from daybreak until midday in a warm climate, tiring themselves while the defenders rested—an additional act of obedience to God that made little sense militarily.

The troops gave a great shout, and the wall collapsed (6:20). God orchestrated the collapse of Jericho's walls, perhaps using an earthquake. The city is located along a major geological fault and has experienced many earthquakes throughout history, including one of magnitude 5.3 in February 2004 and another of 4.5 in November 2007.

They completely destroyed everything in the city (6:21). The Israelites killed the inhabitants of Jericho and destroyed the plunder from the city (except the metal goods) as God had commanded (cf. Deut. 20:16–18). This practice was common throughout the ancient Near East and was a common way for armies to give to their god a portion of what he had given them through military victory. Similarly, in the ninth century BC a Moabite king killed all seven thousand Israelites in a conquered city that he had dedicated to his god Chemosh.

The man who undertakes the rebuilding of this city, Jericho, is cursed before the Lord (6:26). To preserve the ruined city of Jericho as a gift to God, Joshua curses any potential rebuilder of the site (cf. 1 Kings 16:34). Cursing and/or sowing salt on a captured and destroyed city were not unusual practices in the ancient world. The Israelites salted Shechem (Judg. 9:45), and in 146 BC Rome allegedly salted Carthage after destroying that city. Given Jericho's good water source, as well as its key location guarding access to central Canaan, forsaking the site of Jericho would have been a great sacrifice for Israel as it settled Canaan.

Failure at Ai (7:1–26)

The things set apart for destruction (7:1). See comments on Josh. 6:21.

The men went up and scouted Ai (7:2). The comments of Joshua ("go up") and the spies ("don't wear out all our people") hint at the challenging climb from Gilgal, located down in the Jordan Valley, up to Ai in the central hill country, an ascent of thirty-five hundred feet over twelve miles.

The quarries . . . the descent (7:5). The valley that leads east from Ai toward Jericho has some unusual deep fissures approximately three miles east of Ai as the land slopes down toward the Jordan Valley and Jericho.

They have taken some of what was set apart . . . this is why the Israelites cannot stand against their enemies (7:11–12). Since ancient Near Eastern people assumed that their gods commanded and aided them in the conquest of their enemies, defeat on the battlefield generally was interpreted as divine anger for some violation that they needed to correct. For example, the ancient Hittites placated their offended god and purified their troops using a ritual ceremony called "The Far Side of the River." On the opposite bank of a nearby river the army would construct a gate of hawthorn. On each side of the gate were hung the severed halves of a goat, a puppy, a piglet, and a sacrificed prisoner, with fire on each side as well. As the troops passed through the gate and reached the river, they were splashed with water from the river to complete the cleansing.

Mesopotamian clay cuneiform tablet with astrological omens.

The one who is caught with the things set apart must be burned (7:15). An Old Babylonian liver omen tablet commanded that a high priestess who repeatedly stole offerings consecrated to the gods be seized and burned. Another Mesopotamian text likewise specified that those guilty of such an offense should be seized and put to death. Stealing devoted items meant that the person had stolen from the god, which was a grave offense.

Achan . . . was selected (7:18). Joshua probably is casting lots to determine the guilty party. Lots were objects of unknown form made of stone or wood that were shaken and tossed onto a surface to reveal a pattern (much like modern dice) that was understood to indicate a god's choice. Many peoples throughout the ancient Near East practiced the casting of lots. Through lots God could designate a guilty party, such as when Jonathan ate and broke Saul's oath (1 Sam. 14:41–42) or when Jonah disobeyed and the pagan sailors' lots pointed to him (Jon. 1:7).

Give glory to the Lord . . . and make a confession to him (7:19). Joshua put Achan under oath before God to force him to confess what he had done. Oaths were common throughout the ancient world and typically were made in the name of the speaker's god to prompt a confession or to support the truth of a statement.

A beautiful cloak from Babylon (7:21). Babylonians exported garments north to Assyria and west to Syria and Asia Minor from the eighteenth century BC onward. Babylonian merchants were traveling to Egypt as early as the fourteenth century BC, so a valuable Babylonian robe could well have ended up in Canaan at Jericho.

Joshua . . . took Achan . . . his sons and daughters, his ox . . . his tent, and all that he had (7:24–25). Contrary to modern Western individualistic thinking and legal practice, ancient Near Eastern people thought and acted primarily as families and/or tribes. They often lived and made decisions together and subsequently benefited or suffered together the results of what the group or even one member had done. Just as Achan's family dies with him, so do the families of the guilty Israelites in Num. 16:25–33 and the guilty Babylonians in Dan. 6:24.

Raised over him a large pile of rocks (7:26). Cairns or piles of stones over burial sites have long been used in the Middle East. Used normally to cover kings and other dignitaries, the stones protected the corpse and served as a visible reminder of the deceased. Large burial mounds west of Jerusalem may still mark the graves of Judah's kings. Stones over Achan's grave remind the Israelites of the consequences of disobedience, just as the pile of stones from the Jordan (see comments on Josh. 4:7) commemorated the fruit of obedience.

Victory at Ai (8:1–29)

The Treaty of Kadesh, resulting from the defeat of the Egyptian army by the Hittite chariots.

You may plunder its spoil and livestock for yourselves (8:2). God forbade Israel to take any plunder from Jericho, but now he permits the Israelites to take plunder from Ai, a typical reward for ancient soldiers and armies. Soldiers in the ancient Near East were motivated to fight partly by the prospect of acquiring possessions (Deut. 20:14; 2 Kings 3:23: "To the spoil!"), and kings sought to enrich their nations by acquiring great quantities of goods. The list of war plunder taken by Thutmose III following Egypt's victory over a Canaanite coalition at Megiddo in the fifteenth century BC includes 3,400 prisoners, 83 hands (severed from the bodies of enemy soldiers), 2,238 horses, 892 chariots including one decorated with gold, 22 coats of mail, 502 bows, 1,929 cows, 2,000 goats, and 20,500 sheep.

Set an ambush behind the city (8:2). Although it still comes from God and still requires obedience, Israel's military strategy shifts from the highly unusual parade with trumpet blasts at Jericho to a much more logical tactic using ambush at Ai. Many ancient armies, including those of Egypt, Assyria, and Israel (Judg. 9:43–45; 20:29–45), used ambushes. Likewise, when the Egyptians and Hittites fought at Kadesh in 1274 BC, the Hittites used the ambush tactic with great success. Aided by phony spies and misinformation (see comments on Josh. 2:1), the Hittite chariots ambushed and almost wiped out one of four Egyptian divisions (five thousand troops) arriving for battle, nearly sealing a decisive victory.

Joshua selected thirty thousand of his best soldiers (8:3). The numbers of Israelite troops given in the Bible often appear quite large, including those in this passage. Yet note that the same Hebrew word translated here as "thousand" can also mean "clan," "unit," or, with minor modification, even "champion." Perhaps the author of Joshua meant thirty *units* of soldiers mustered from clans or even perhaps, although less likely, thirty *elite troops*.

Lie in ambush behind the city (8:4). A large valley lies between Bethel and Ai in which a sizable number of troops could easily hide from Ai's defenders. This author's personal experiment showed that a five-minute run would bring troops from the lip of the valley to the gate of Ai (assuming the more recently posited location of Ai at Khirbet el-Maqatir).

Arriving opposite Ai, and camped north of it (8:11). When the smaller Israelite force first approaches and attacks Ai (7:4–5), the soldiers probably ascend the ridge that approaches Ai directly from the east before being beaten back. When Joshua brings the entire army, they camp north of Ai. This suggests that they climb the next ridge to the north, leaving a deep valley between them and Ai for protection. When the two opposing forces engage the following day, the Israelites again fall back to the east, pulling Ai's defenders away from the city and the troops waiting in ambush to the west.

Javelin (8:18, 26). The word translated as "javelin" might better be translated as "sword" or "scimitar" and understood as a curved sickle sword common to the time. Either way, Joshua holds up a weapon as a visible signal to his troops, similar to how Moses had used his staff during a battle in the wilderness (Exod. 17:8–13).

Joshua burned Ai (8:28). Ancient armies often burned conquered cities, particularly those they wished to punish. Somewhat curiously, the book of Joshua records that the Israelites burned only the cities of Jericho, Ai, and Hazor, perhaps because the Israelites wished to inhabit most of the cities following the conquest (cf. Deut. 6:10–12).

He hung the body of the king of Ai on a tree (8:29). Sometimes translated as "hung on a tree," the phrase probably is better understood as "impaled on a pole" or some other wooden item, since impalement was practiced throughout much of the ancient Near East, including Egypt, Old Babylon, Assyria, and Persia. Law 153 in the Code of Hammurabi (an ancient Babylonian king) reads, "If a woman has procured the death of her husband on account of another man, they shall impale that woman."[4] An Assyrian relief depicting the conquest of the city of Lachish in Judah shows three Judeans impaled and set up in front of that city.

A large pile of rocks (8:29). See comments on Josh. 4:7; 7:26.

Covenant Renewal at Mount Ebal (8:30–35)

At that time Joshua built an altar on Mount Ebal to the Lord (8:30). Archaeologists have discovered a structure on Mount Ebal from the period of the Israelite settlement that some identify as a sacrificial altar. Although others dispute this interpretation, the structure was made of uncut stones (see 8:31; cf. Deut. 27:5–7), it faced an open area where a crowd could gather, and it was found along with many butchered and burned bones of animals suitable for sacrifice (cattle, sheep, goats, and deer, but no pigs, dogs, or donkeys), all of which suggest it could have been a sacrificial altar.

There on the stones, Joshua copied the law of Moses (8:32). Joshua fulfills God's earlier command (Deut. 27:4–8) to write God's law on stones.

Writing on plaster-coated stones is also known from sites in the wilderness of Sinai and in the Jordan Valley, where an inscription from the ninth to eighth centuries BC recounts visions of Balaam the seer, apparently the same one who appears in Num. 22–24.

All Israel . . . stood on either side of the ark of the Lord's covenant (8:33). In obedience to God's earlier command (Deut. 27), the Israelites perform a formal ceremony with God that appears to reflect a divine land grant ceremony. Known from Babylonian, Syrian, and Assyrian texts, such a ceremony produced a legal document (cf. 8:32) recording the transfer of property in the presence of witnesses (cf. 8:32–33) under the protection of the local gods, who would curse violators of the agreement (cf. 8:34).

Half of them were in front of Mount Gerizim and half in front of Mount Ebal (8:33). These two mountains frame the site of biblical Shechem and form a natural amphitheater well suited for such a public ceremony.

Gibeonite Treaty and Victory (9:1–10:27)

Hethites . . . Jebusites (9:1). This is a general list of the various people groups inhabiting Canaan at this time, sometimes collectively referred to generically as "Canaanites" (cf. 3:10; Deut. 7:1).

When all the kings heard about Jericho and Ai . . . they formed a unified alliance (9:1–2). Most of the kings mentioned in Joshua ruled not vast kingdoms but rather city-states, which included the primary cities and the nearby lands and villages connected to those cities politically and economically. During that period Canaan had numerous city-states with kings (who perhaps were more similar to mayors than kings in the modern sense of the words). In the Amarna letters (fourteenth century BC) Canaanite kings corresponded with the pharaoh of Egypt (their overlord) about various governmental matters, including groups of displaced people (much like the Israelites in Joshua) who sought to raid or seize control of Canaanite towns, sometimes killing the kings or burning their towns. The kings feared other cities joining with the marauders (as Gibeon did with Israel in Josh. 9), or they sometimes banded together against a common enemy (as in Josh. 10–11).

Gibeon (9:3). This important, prosperous Canaanite city was located a few miles north of Jerusalem in the central highlands. Gibeon lay at a key junction of north-south and east-west roads (see comments on Josh. 10:2).

They acted deceptively (9:4). Deception and misinformation have been important elements of warfare throughout history, including in the ancient Near East (see comments on Josh. 2:1). For example, before the Hittites engaged the Egyptians at Kadesh in Syria in 1274 BC, the Hittite king sent out two decoy scouts to be caught and give false information to the Egyptians about the location of the Hittite army. The ruse worked, luring the Egyptians into advancing too quickly on Kadesh and nearly suffering a disastrous defeat. Fearing destruction and death, the people of Gibeon also use deception to help secure a treaty that will save their lives.

They went to Joshua in the camp at Gilgal (9:6). The Israelites maintain their base camp at Gilgal near Jericho, so the Gibeonites must travel only about seventeen miles to reach them, and not, as they claimed, from "a distant land."

Hivites (9:7). See comments on Gen. 34:2; Josh. 9:17.

Joshua established peace with them and made a treaty (9:15). The Gibeonites ask that the Israelites make a treaty with them, likely a suzerain-vassal treaty common in the second millennium BC. In such treaties the suzerain claimed lordship and demanded loyal service by the vassal, who would expect protection by the suzerain in return. For example, a contemporary Hittite king named Murshili made suzerain-vassal treaties with a king named Manapa-Datta, ruler of the Seha River region, as well as with the Azzi people, in western Asia Minor. Manapa-Datta grew afraid when Murshili approached with his army, so he sent nonthreatening emissaries, including old men and women, to meet Murshili. As Manapa-Datta had hoped, Murshili refrained from attack and agreed to a treaty that subjected Manapa-Datta's people to servitude. In a similar event Murshili had been fighting successfully against the Azzi people, who were governed by elders rather than a king (cf. the elders in Gibeon in 9:11). An Azzi delegation presented itself to Murshili, bowed, and requested a treaty of peace in which they would serve the Hittites. Murshili wrote, "Then I . . . did not destroy them. I took them into servitude; and I made them slaves."[5]

Gibeon, Chephirah, Beeroth, and Kiriath-jearim (9:17). These four cities in the central and western hill country all lay within five and a half miles of Gibeon. All were inhabited by the same people group, the Hivites, who apparently had originated in Asia Minor and were one of many groups inhabiting Canaan at the time (see comments on Josh. 9:1).

The Israelites did not attack them, because the leaders of the community had sworn an oath (9:18). In the ancient world the two parties of a treaty customarily swore oaths by their respective gods, assuming that the gods would watch and hold them accountable. In one of his treaties the Babylonian king Hammurabi challenged his covenantal partner: "Swear by Shamash (god) of heaven! Swear by Addu of heaven! These are the gods that Hammurabi, son of Sin-muballiṭ, king of Babylon, invoked."[6] Even though their treaty with the Gibeonites had been based on deception, the Israelite leaders had sworn an oath in the name of the Lord. Thus they are bound to honor the treaty, since breaking it would mean risking God's wrath (9:20; Exod. 20:7).

Woodcutters and water carriers (9:21). The Israelites subject the Gibeonites to forced labor. This was a widely practiced custom in the ancient Near East in which a superior power forced people to serve with unpaid labor. The Israelites had been subjected to forced labor during their time in Egypt (Exod. 1:11), and they impose forced labor on the Gibeonites as well as on other Canaanites after the conquest (Judg. 1:28). During the time of the monarchy Israelite kings used forced labor to carry out major building projects like the temple (1 Kings 4:6; 5:13–18).

For the house of my God (9:23). Ancient places of worship often required large quantities of wood for burning incense and sacrifices as well as plentiful water to cleanse the site. Note Solomon's extensive sacrifices when worshiping at Gibeon (1 Kings 3:4).

Like one of the royal cities (10:2). A royal city was the center of a city-state and ruled by a king (see comments on Josh. 9:1–2). Although Gibeon was ruled by elders (9:11) rather than a king, the city's importance rivaled that of the royal cities (see comments on Josh. 9:3).

The five Amorite kings—the kings of Jerusalem, Hebron, Jarmuth, Lachish, and Eglon (10:5). The king of Jerusalem led a coalition of five cities in the central and southern hill country and in the foothills to the west. The inhabitants of these cities are Amorites, much like the Hivites inhabiting Gibeon and neighboring cities (see comments on Josh. 9:17). The Amorites had been a significant people in many parts of the ancient Near East for centuries, and the southern hill country of Canaan was one place they had settled (see comments on Deut. 1:4). The five Amorite cities in Josh. 10 join forces for military action against Gibeon for defecting to the side of the invading Israelites. This parallels how the kings of Canaanite city-states also attacked cities that sided with attackers, as reflected in the Amarna letters (see comments on Josh. 9:1–2).

Don't give up on your servants (10:6). The Gibeonites naturally appeal to the Israelites, who were obligated to aid their Gibeonite partners by treaty (see comments on Josh. 9:15).

After marching all night (10:9). Although battles in the ancient Near East typically were fought during the day, maneuvers and even attacks at night were not uncommon. The Hittite king Murshili II recorded a number of overnight marches and attacks. In a letter from Ugarit in northern Syria at about the same time, a general wrote, "My men were attacked (repeatedly) in the middle of the night, and a battle was fought."[7]

Before attacking Gibeon, Joshua and the Israelites would have marched through the night, which meant ascending some thirty-one hundred feet over a distance of about seventeen miles. Appearing suddenly at dawn, they caught the Amorite soldiers unprepared for battle. Although the Israelites had lost the night's sleep and were tired from the march and the climb, the successful approach gave them a clear tactical advantage.

Beth-horon . . . Azekah and Makkedah (10:10). The primary road heading west out of the central hill country down toward the Mediterranean Sea descended from Gibeon to the city of Beth-horon. From there another road ran southwest through the western foothills to the city of Azekah. The city of Makkedah lay farther south in the same general line.

The LORD threw large hailstones on them (10:11). People in the ancient Near East would have understood such a storm during a battle as being orchestrated by a god fighting for his people. The eighth-century-BC Assyrian king Sargon gave a similar description of one of his battles: "The rest of the people, who had fled to save their lives, whom [the enemy king] had abandoned that the glorious might of Assur [the Assyrian god], my lord, might be magnified . . . and with the flood cloud and hailstones, he totally annihilated the remainder."[8]

Sun . . . over Gibeon . . . moon, over . . . Aijalon (10:12). To modern readers, 10:12–14 reads as though God lengthens the day to give Israel extra time to win a decisive battle. While God undoubtedly could do this, ancient literature may suggest a different meaning. Many ancient peoples often understood celestial events as divine omens. When the sun appeared on the eastern horizon (over Gibeon) at the same time as the moon on the western horizon (over the Aijalon Valley, west of Beth-horon), followers of such omens would have thought of this as a divine sign for either good or bad, depending on which day it occurred. Although Joshua need not have believed in omens, he may have been asking God to arrange the celestial bodies in a way and at a time that would dishearten his Canaanite enemies. One ancient Near Eastern omen reads, "When the moon and sun are seen with each other on the fifteenth day (of the lunar month) a powerful enemy will raise his weapons against the land. The enemy will destroy the gate of my city."[9]

Book of Jashar (10:13). This apparently was a collection of national poems from Israel's early history (also mentioned in 2 Sam. 1:18), no longer available to us.

Almost a full day (10:13). Victorious ancient Near Eastern kings sometimes used hyperbole to describe great military feats as being accomplished in one day, even though the events could not have occurred within a twenty-four-hour period. For example, the Assyrian king Tiglath-pileser I claimed to have won numerous victories over a distance of about 250 miles "in a single day."[10] A governor of Susa in Elam boasted of conquering seventy towns "in one day."[11] If God did not literally lengthen the day (see comments on Josh. 10:12), this section of Joshua may also be using hyperbole to describe a great victory accomplished with God's help.

Put your feet on the necks of these kings (10:24). Victorious kings in the ancient Near East sometimes killed enemy rulers in ceremonial fashion to demonstrate superiority and to inspire their own troops. They might also literally put their feet on their opponents' necks, as here, or describe such subjection as using enemies as a footstool (see Ps. 110:1).

He hung their bodies on five trees (10:26). See comments on Josh. 8:29.

Conquest of Southern Canaan (10:28–43)

The long, detailed stories that describe Israel's successful entrance into Canaan (1:1–5:15) and central campaign (6:1–10:27) now give way to dramatically briefer summaries of the campaigns in southern (10:28–43) and northern (11:1–15) Canaan. This style of reporting military results, moving from detailed accounts to general reports, finds a clear parallel in the Egyptian records of the military exploits of Thutmose III in the fifteenth century BC. Thutmose III carried out seventeen campaigns over twenty years and conquered territory from the Euphrates River in the north to Cush in the south, as inscribed on the temple of Amun at Karnak. These records begin with a highly detailed account of the first campaign, including the decisive victory at Megiddo (see comments on Josh. 5:11; 8:2). The subsequent sixteen campaigns are covered in terse, stylized summaries with repetitive, stereotypical language. Similarly, the annals of Hittite king Murshili II in the fourteenth century BC begin with a long preface describing the hostility of neighboring rulers before giving rather brief formulaic accounts of his military campaigns.

Completely destroyed (10:28). See comments on Josh. 6:21.

Makkedah . . . Debir (10:28–39). The Israelites attack and conquer six additional cities in southern Canaan. They continue the success of the central campaign by attacking cities in the southern hill country and western foothills, which eliminates the locals' military ability to resist Israelite settlement in the region.

They laid siege to it and attacked it (10:31). The Israelites arrange troops to attack a settled site, perhaps one with city walls. Most Canaanite cities were rather weakly fortified at this

From the Egyptian temple at Karnak, a stone carving of Thutmose III smiting his enemies.

time, as some likely had centuries-old walls and others had no effective fortifications at all (see the introduction in the commentary on Joshua).

Hebron . . . its villages (10:36–37). See comments on Josh. 9:1–2.

Joshua conquered the whole region . . . completely destroyed every living being (10:40). The Israelites conquer the southern hill country with its western approaches, and the narrative describes that success apparently using the hyperbolic language common to the time. Pharaoh Merneptah reported around 1209 BC that "Israel is wasted, its seed (progeny) is not."[12] Similarly, King Mesha of Moab wrote around 830 BC that "Israel has gone to ruin, yes, it has gone to ruin forever."[13] Both kings obviously used hyperbole to describe victories over Israel.

Conquest of Northern Canaan (11:1–12:24)

King Jabin of Hazor . . . sent a message (11:1). Much like the king of Jerusalem had done (see comments on Josh. 9:1–2; 10:5), the king of Hazor summoned allies from various sites in northern Canaan to fight the Israelites (see comments on Josh. 11:10).

Hamstring their horses and burn their chariots (11:6). Cutting a hamstring tendon rendered a horse unable to gallop and thus of no military value. God did not want the Israelites to rely on their military abilities (Deut. 17:16), so they needed to forgo the chance to acquire horses and chariots—the most valuable military resources of the time.

Hazor . . . the leader (11:10). Hazor was the largest city (175 acres) in northern Canaan. Texts from second-millennium-BC Hazor, eighteenth-century-BC Mari in northern Syria, and fourteenth-century-BC Amarna in Egypt attest to Hazor's international importance. Hazor was destroyed in a massive fire in the thirteenth century BC, which is attributed by many to the events recorded in Josh. 11.

Wall carving of Ramesses II in an Egyptian war chariot fighting the Hittites.

Israel did not burn any of the cities . . . except Hazor (11:13). The book records that the Israelites burned only Hazor in the north and only Jericho and Ai in central Canaan, usually taking plunder but leaving the majority of conquered cities intact. The Israelites apparently sought to kill off the Canaanite leaders and reduce or eliminate Canaanite manpower so that Israel could later inhabit the cities (cf. Deut. 6:10–12) or settle in new villages in those regions. Similarly, Egyptian records indicate that following their successful campaigns the Egyptians preferred to avoid burning conquered cities in order to make them profitable sources of ongoing tax revenue.

So Joshua took all this land (11:16). The book of Joshua emphasizes Israel's success and obedience (11:12, 15) during the conquest but also acknowledges that the conquest was incomplete (13:1–5). Such dissimilar statements may appear inconsistent to the modern reader but were not uncommon for the time (see comments on Josh. 10:40).

The Anakim (11:21). These large, mighty warriors had earlier caused Israel to fear invading Canaan (Num. 13:33). Egyptian texts of the second millennium BC mention rulers called Anakim as well as other Canaanites who were extremely tall.

The Israelites struck down the following kings of the land (12:1). Joshua 12 summarizes Israel's victories both east (vv. 1–6) and west (vv. 7–24) of the Jordan River. The latter is a verbal equivalent to Egyptian semipictorial summaries of military campaigns inscribed on temples in the fifteenth, twelfth, and tenth centuries BC. These Egyptian accounts consist primarily of vertical ovals representing conquered fortified sites with the site's name inside the oval. A man's head is shown above the oval, and his features are typical of people from that region.

Division of Canaan (13:1–21:45)

A great deal of land remains to be possessed (13:1). See comments on Josh. 10:40; 11:16.

Distribute the land as an inheritance for Israel (13:6). The Israelites divide the land of Canaan according to tribes: first to the two and one-half tribes that settled east of the Jordan (13:8–33), then to the largest tribes west of the Jordan (14:1–17:18), and finally to the remaining seven smaller tribes also west of the Jordan (18:1–19:51). Land was allocated by lot (see comments on Josh. 7:18). The allotments typically begin with some introduction, are followed by boundary sequences and/or groups of towns within the region, and end with final remarks. Similar boundary descriptions and/or lists of towns are known as early as 2100 BC and were especially common during 1400–1200 BC, coming from Ur, Asia Minor, and Syria.

The Israelite tribal allocations are somewhat presumptive since they include land that Israel has not yet taken. In addition, special allotments are given to Caleb (14:6–14; 15:13–19) and Joshua (19:49–50), the faithful scouts from Israel's spying mission from Kadesh Barnea (Num. 13–14).

I was forty years old when Moses the LORD's servant sent me . . . here I am today, eighty-five years old (14:7, 10). Caleb's references to his ages at Kadesh Barnea and now at the land's division suggest that the conquest took approximately seven years (85 – 40 [age at Kadesh Barnea] – 38 [years from Kadesh Barnea until the beginning of the conquest = 7]).

Iron chariots (17:16). The military superiority of the Canaanites living on the coastal plain was exemplified by their chariotry. During this era chariots typically were made almost entirely of wood and leather with some metal fittings. The reference to iron could be to fittings such as pins holding the wheels to the axle or else to thin metal plates used as decorations. When Thutmose III led Egypt to victory at Megiddo (see comments on Josh. 5:11; 8:2), he rode in a chariot decorated with electrum (an alloy of gold and silver) and captured an enemy chariot decorated with gold. When iron first came into use it was rare, valuable, and sometimes used for jewelry and decoration. Alternately, the term "iron" could be a figure of speech meaning "strong" (cf. Jer. 1:18).

It is a forest; clear it (17:18). When the Israelites settle the central hills of Canaan, much of that region has not been cultivated for centuries. They would need to once again clear the native growth in order to use the land for agriculture.

Distributed to the Israelite tribes by lot (19:51). See comments on Josh. 7:18.

Cities of refuge (20:1). The Israelites practiced a system of familial and tribal justice common to the region in which close relatives avenged wrongs done to a person or family. To regulate this cultural practice, God designated six cities to which a person who had killed someone could flee and be tried for murder.

The Israelites, by the LORD's command, gave the Levites these cities (21:3). In fulfillment of Num. 35:1–8 God provides for the Levites, who did not receive a tribal allotment. Ancient Near Eastern priests often received lands as part of their support. All Egyptian temples had endowed lands for such use. At the time of Ramesses III the temple of Amun in Thebes owned fifty-six towns in Egypt.

Close of Conquest (22:1–24:33)

Return to your homes with great wealth (22:8). See comments on Josh. 8:2.

Joshua was old, advanced in age. So Joshua summoned all Israel (23:1–2). The book's concluding chapters include sections that resemble parts of ancient Near Eastern treaties, particularly those from the fourteenth and thirteenth centuries BC. Joshua's review of Israel's successes in the promised land (23:3–14) resembles covenantal blessings, and the warning in 23:15–16 bears similarities to covenantal curses. The introduction (24:2a), historical review (24:2b–13), stipulations (24:14–21), witnesses (24:22, 27), and curse (24:19–20) are very much like those used in contemporary suzerain-vassal treaties (see comments on Josh. 9:15).

Joshua . . . died at the age of 110 (24:29). Like Joseph before him (Gen. 50:22), Joshua lived to the age of 110, which was considered by the Egyptians to be the ideal length of life. One Egyptian prayer reads, "May I reach 110 years on earth such as every righteous man."[14]

Judges

Boyd Seevers

Introduction. The book of Judges is named for the men (and woman) who led Israel following the death of Joshua until the beginning of Israel's monarchy. They were not so much judicial figures deciding legal matters as they were military leaders who delivered the Israelites from neighboring peoples who raided and plundered them. Although most of the judges were flawed in character, God still used them for his purposes. The book of Judges includes twelve judges (six major and six minor), the same number as the Israelite tribes, perhaps to represent a full history.

Throughout the several centuries covered by the book the entire region that encompassed Israel and its neighbors was experiencing significant, and often chaotic, geopolitical changes. Egypt, which had ruled Canaan for centuries, was weakening and was losing its grip on the region. Other formerly strong nations in the wider region were likewise weakening or disappearing altogether. Significant migrations of entire people groups were taking place in the ancient Near East, and these new arrivals were fighting with the established peoples as well as one another for new territory and new homelands into which to settle. The Israelites and the Philistines were part of these massive relocations.

Along with recording Israel's history during this chaotic period, the book of Judges also stresses the nation's repeated unfaithfulness toward God. The story of Israel's unfaithfulness follows a repeated cycle: disobedience, oppression, repentance, and deliverance. Judges also emphasizes the need for a monarchy. Note the phrase that is repeated at the end of the book: "In those days there was no king in Israel; everyone did what seemed right to them" (17:6; 21:25

[see also 18:1; 19:1]). The book of Judges also implies a preference for the kings that would descend from Israel's second king, David. The positive portrayal of Judah (1:1–20; 3:7–11; 20:18) and the negative picture of Benjamin (1:21; 19:1–21:24), especially Gibeah in Benjamin (19:14–20:48), suggest that Judges was written around the time of David to support his line from Judah, rather than the line of Saul from Gibeah in Benjamin.

Joshua's victories, described in the book of Joshua, had eliminated the military ability of the inhabitants in central Canaan to prevent the Israelites from settling there. However, many people groups remained in various parts of the land, so the Israelites had to continue fighting to drive out the rest of these people. The opening section of the book of Judges (1:1–3:6) shows the Israelites' failures with these efforts.

Military Failures (1:1–2:9)

After the death of Joshua (1:1). Judges begins around 1400 or 1210 BC, depending on the date of the exodus (see comments on Exod. 1:8–11; 1:11) and concludes before the birth of Samuel (ca. 1050 BC). During this time period Israel has no clear strong, central leader like Moses and Joshua had been in the past, or like Samuel and the kings of the monarchy would be in the future. The lack of effective leadership and the general geopolitical chaos of the time combine to produce a generally dark period in the nation's history.

Such an era of weakness between periods of strength has parallels in other ancient Near Eastern kingdoms. Egypt experienced weakness and division between its Old and Middle Kingdoms and between the Middle and New Kingdoms. Likewise, in Mesopotamia the Old Babylonian Empire had an intermediate period during the early second millennium. King lists from both regions include kings who ruled in different locales at the same time. These overlapping reigns are listed in succession, much as Judges seems to describe sequential judges whose careers must have overlapped in different parts of Israel.

The Israelites inquired of the Lord (1:1). Ancient armies typically sought direction from their god(s) before campaigns or battles (cf. 1 Sam. 30:8). For example, in 1392 BC Pharaoh Thutmose IV prepared to campaign in Cush (Nubia) by consulting the Egyptian god Amun, who, according to Egyptian accounts, responded with assurances of success.

The first to fight (1:1). The Hebrew word translated as "fight" means literally "to go up." Since cities and fortresses typically were built atop hills, the phrase "go up" in this context means "attack" or "fight."

Judah (1:2). See the introduction in the commentary on Judges. Judah is the first tribe to continue Israel's conquest, and is generally successful.

I have handed the land over to him (1:2). Israel's God was the true owner of Canaan and gave it to the nation he chose. Likewise, other nations thought that their gods gave them land through victory. In 539 BC the Persian king Cyrus stated that Marduk, patron god of Babylon, "ordered (Cyrus) to march to (Marduk's) city Babylon . . . (and) . . . went at his side" until Cyrus "enter(ed) his city (in victory)."[1]

Judah . . . Simeon (1:3). The small tribe of Simeon inherited land within Judah's large allotment, so the two tribes have common interest and team up together.

The Canaanites (1:3). See the article "The Canaanites and Canaanite Religion."

They struck down ten thousand men (1:4). The numbers of troops given in the Bible often appear quite large, as here. The Hebrew word translated as "thousand" (*eleph*) can also mean "unit," "clan," or "family" (cf. 6:15: "my family [*eleph*] is the weakest"), possibly signifying the unit of soldiers mustered from a clan or family. Perhaps this passage means ten *units* of soldiers (like modern military terms such as "platoon," "company," "battalion"). Archaeological evidence also supports the smaller numbers that would come from translating this word as "units" rather than "thousand." Although not entirely precise, archaeological surveys estimate that the population of Israel was probably only about 21,000 at the time of Judges and only about 51,000 by the time of David.

They . . . cut off his thumbs and big toes (1:6). Ancient soldiers often severed body parts from a defeated enemy, sometimes as proof of kill (Judg. 7:25; 8:6; 1 Sam. 18:25–27). Other times, as here, victors disfigured the vanquished to disable and humiliate them (1 Sam. 11:2).

Seventy kings (1:7). Seven and ten were considered full numbers in the ancient Near East, and their multiples signified *very* full numbers.

God has repaid me (1:7). Ancient peoples assumed that gods observed human actions and intervened to administer justice. This king interprets his demise as divine punishment.

I will give my daughter Achsah to him as a wife (1:12). Marriages often were arranged to bring honor to one's family. Marrying into the family of a king (1 Sam. 18:17–27) or of an important person, as here, brought honor.

City of Palms (1:16). This is a reference to Jericho (cf. Deut. 34:3) in the Jordan Valley, famous for large plantations of date palms.

Completely destroyed the town (1:17). Victorious ancient Near Eastern armies sometimes totally destroyed a site and killed all of its inhabitants to give the site to their god(s). Israel did this at Jericho (Josh. 6). King Mesha (ninth century BC) of Moab did the same to an Israelite city, declaring, "I killed [its] whole population, seven thousand male citizens and aliens, and female citizens and aliens . . . for I had put it to the ban for Ashtar-Kemosh."[2]

Gaza . . . Ashkelon . . . Ekron (1:18). As with Jebus (see comments on Judg. 1:21), the conquests of these major coastal cities apparently were short-lived (cf. 1:19). The Philistines would later conquer them and use them as strongholds (see the article "The Philistines").

Judah . . . could not drive out the people who were living in the valley (1:19). Even Judah could not drive the Canaanites from the cities on the coastal plain. Most tribes experienced similar results, settling in the sparsely populated central hills but not the coastal plain or the major valleys. Modern archaeological results support this picture. Major lowland cities continue to reflect their Canaanite culture even after the Israelites arrive, while the highlands appear to undergo a change, becoming populated with hundreds of small rural settlements whose culture is noticeably different from that of the Canaanites. The simple homes in the highlands often reflect a four-room style, which becomes typical for Israelite homes. Groups of homes often are arranged in a circular pattern for defense with a central courtyard for animals.

Iron chariots (1:19). See comments on Josh. 17:16.

Jebusites . . . in Jerusalem (1:21). After the Judeans capture this city, the Jebusites apparently later recapture it.

House of Joseph (1:22). The patriarch Joseph had two sons, Ephraim and Manasseh (Gen. 41:50–52), so these two tribes are the "tribes of Joseph" who inherit the hill country north of Jerusalem.

Spies (1:23–24). See comments on Josh. 2:1.

Show us how to get into town (1:24). Perhaps they are asking about where the defenses are the weakest, or perhaps how to sneak in through the water system (cf. 2 Sam. 5:8).

They put the town to the sword (1:25). Swords were one of the most common weapons (see comments on Josh. 8:18, 26). The word is used here as a figure of speech for military action.

Land of the Hittites (1:26). The Hittite Empire had dominated most of Asia Minor in the mid-fourteenth century BC. By the time of Judges it had disintegrated, but remnants of the Hittite people continued in city-states as far south as northern Canaan.

Manasseh failed to take possession (1:27). See comments on Judg. 1:19.

The Canaanites (1:27). See the article "The Canaanites and Canaanite Religion."

When Israel became stronger (1:28). This is a reference to the future, during the time of David and Solomon (1 Kings 9:20–21).

Forced labor (1:28). See comments on Josh. 9:21.

Canaanites . . . among them (1:30). Zebulun's allotment included the highly desirable Jezreel Valley, but the tribe failed to drive out or subjugate the Canaanites until the time of David (see comments on Judg. 1:28).

The Asherites lived among the Canaanites (1:32). The Canaanite cities along the Mediterranean coast engaged in fishing and maritime commerce, so they needed nearby farmers to supply them with food. In the Amarna letters from Byblos, a major port farther north, the king repeatedly frets about whether his farmers will remain loyal. Perhaps the Asherites were similar, welcomed by the Canaanites to settle inland parts of their region to provide the Canaanite seafarers agricultural support (see comments on Josh. 9:1–2).

One of the Amarna tablets.

The angel of the Lord (2:1). This is a reference to God himself, an angel, or perhaps even a human messenger like a prophet. Contrast the "angel of the Lord" and his message here with "the commander of the Lord's army" and his message back in Josh. 5:13–15.

Tear down their altars (2:2). Altars in the ancient Near East often were made of stone or clay in a wide range of sizes. Incense, animal sacrifices, or foodstuffs were burned on them as offerings. Victorious armies often broke the altars and other religious symbols of a vanquished enemy to show dominance. Here the Israelite failure to destroy the Canaanite altars demonstrated disobedience (Deut. 12:3) and left religious snares for future generations.

Servant of the Lord (2:8). The word translated as "servant" could refer to either a high or a lowly position, depending on whom a person served. A "servant of the king" could be a high governmental minister. Numerous official seals or impressions of seals have been discovered that apparently belonged to high-ranking officials with the title "servant of king *so-and-so*," depending on which king they served.

The age of 110 (2:8). See comments on Josh. 24:29.

Religious Failure (2:10–3:6)

Gathered to their ancestors (2:10). In the ancient Near East deceased people often were buried in caves that served as family tombs (see comments on Gen. 25:8). As years passed, sometimes bones of the deceased were gathered and set aside to make room for the more recently deceased.

The Israelites did what was evil . . . the Lord raised up judges (2:11–19). The pattern of disobedience, oppression, repentance, and deliverance will repeat numerous times in Judges. The Israelites disobey God; God brings an enemy to plunder Israel; Israel repents and cries for release; God delivers Israel through a judge. After the judge dies, Israel again disobeys, and the cycle repeats. The concept of an offended god punishing disobedient followers until they repent was not uncommon in the region. In the thirteenth to twelfth centuries BC workers who cut royal tombs in Egypt's Valley of the Kings left inscriptions addressed to their gods. One worker wrote that his son had, "because of his wrongdoing" in the sight of Amun, been punished and was "ill and close to death. (After) supplications (to Amun), he delivered (the son)."[3]

Baals (2:11). *Ba'al* (usually transliterated as "Baal") means "lord" or "master," but it is also often used as a proper name for the chief Canaanite god of storms and war (see the article "The Canaanites and Canaanite Religion"). Many other peoples besides the Canaanites also worshiped Baal, including the Babylonians, who knew him as Bel (variant of *ba'al*) or Marduk. As the storm god, Baal gave rain that made the land fertile, important to agricultural people like the Israelites. The plural "Baals" refers to various local manifestations of the same god (2:12).

Ashtoreths (2:13). This is another plural for a popular ancient Near Eastern goddess, also known as Astarte in Ugarit, Ashtar in Ebla, and Ishtar in Mesopotamia. She was the goddess of fertility, love, and war, and the consort of Baal (see the article "The Canaanites and Canaanite Religion").

Marauders (2:14). These were neighboring enemy peoples who attacked the weaker Israelites to take their agricultural produce or other goods.

The Lord was against them (2:15). All ancient Near Eastern peoples believed that battles were determined by the gods. If the Lord was angry, Israel's defeat was certain. The Moabite king Mesha understood his nation's misfortune in the same way, declaring, "Omri was the king of Israel, and he oppressed Moab for many days, for Kemosh [the Moabite god] was angry with his land."[4]

Judges (2:16). On the meaning of "judges," see the introduction in the commentary on Judges. None of the judges discussed here are known from sources outside the Bible, but their style of leadership fits the general picture of this time period, when charismatic strongmen could establish small "kingdoms" for themselves and their people. For example, in the Amarna letters (see comments on Josh. 9:1–2) numerous Canaanite kings complain about the aggressive moves of an individual named Labayu, the "ruler" of Shechem. The Amarna letters also reflect the success of Abdi-ashirta and his son (cf. Gideon and his son Abimelech), who created a small kingdom in the mountains of northern Lebanon.

Prostituted themselves with other gods, bowing down to them (2:17). Idolatry was the Israelites' greatest temptation and downfall from the time of the judges until their exile in the sixth century BC.

Five rulers of the Philistines (3:3). The Philistines were one of several tribes of the so-called Sea Peoples from Crete and the Aegean Sea region who migrated around the eastern Mediterranean and settled along the coast of Canaan (see the article "The Philistines"). They occupied five major cities on the coastal plain of Canaan (Ashdod, Ashkelon, Ekron, Gaza, and Gath), each with its own ruler. They remained Israel's greatest military threat until the time of David.

Sidonians (3:3). Derived from the city of Sidon, this is a general term for Phoenician peoples inhabiting the coast north of Israel.

Hivites (3:3). This people group from Asia Minor settled north of Israel (see comments on Gen. 34:2; Josh. 9:17).

Canaanites . . . Jebusites (3:5). This verse lists various people groups inhabiting Canaan, sometimes collectively called Canaanites (see comments on Josh. 9:1; see the article "The Canaanites and Canaanite Religion").

Took their daughters as wives . . . and worshiped their gods (3:6). God forbade the Israelites to marry foreign peoples (Exod. 34:16) because intermarriage to them naturally led to the worship of foreign gods.

Othniel of Judah—Major Judge #1 (3:7–11)

Asherahs (3:7). A different goddess than Ashtoreth (mentioned in 2:13), Asherah was another fertility goddess worshiped widely in the region, often represented by a wooden pole or tree (Deut. 7:5; Judg. 6:25–30). Asherah was the consort of El, Baal's father, and mother of seventy gods (see comments on 1 Kings 15:13; see the article "The Canaanites and Canaanite Religion").

The Lord raised up Othniel (3:9). As the narrator in 1:1–11 dealt with the tribe of Judah first and in a positive manner, so here as the story of the judges begins, the writer deals first with Othniel (from the tribe of Judah) and in a positive manner.

King Cushan-rishathaim of Aram-naharaim (3:10). Cushan established a kingdom in the heartland of Aram (modern Syria). He extended his control southward until repulsed by Othniel.

Ehud of Benjamin—Major Judge #2 (3:12–30)

Moab (3:12). Moab was one of the bordering nations to the east of Israel. Although related (see comments on Gen. 19:37–38), the Israelites and Moabites traditionally were enemies, with one frequently oppressing the other. The Moabites worshiped Chemosh and Astarte (see comments on Judg. 2:13; 2 Kings 1:1).

Ammonites (3:13). Like the Moabites, the Ammonites bordered Israel to the east and were related to the Israelites (see comments on Gen. 19:37–38). The Ammonites inhabited a region north of Moab.

Amalekites (3:13). This was a nomadic tribe that often fought Israel (Exod. 17:8–16; 1 Sam. 30:13–20).

Eglon convinced the Ammonites and the Amalekites to join forces with him (3:13). These peoples from the drier Transjordan region (i.e., east of the Jordan River) form a coalition to attack and subject Israel, probably for the primary purpose of obtaining food.

City of Palms (3:13). This refers to the city of Jericho (see comments on Judg. 1:16), located near the major ford across the Jordan River. Eglon sets up his command post west of the Jordan at Jericho, a major site for east-west traffic between the regions east of the Jordan River and Israel. Recently at Jericho archaeologists have discovered an isolated building reflecting wealth and administrative activities that may have served as Eglon's palace.

The Israelites served King Eglon (3:14). Victorious kings often subjected conquered peoples to treaties that required them to deliver goods annually. Such tribute often consisted of precious metals or agricultural products (2 Kings 3:4).

He [the Lord] raised up Ehud . . . a left-handed Benjaminite (3:15). The term "left-handed" plays on the tribal name "Benjamin," which means literally "son of the right hand." Ehud's left-handedness facilitates hiding a dagger on his right thigh (3:21), opposite the normal side to strap a weapon.

Double-edged sword eighteen inches long (3:16). This short, straight, double-edged sword was unusual for the time.

Carved images (3:19). Victorious kings often erected stones engraved with text and images on the borders of their conquests or where they had won a decisive battle (see comments on Josh. 4:7). Perhaps Eglon had defeated Israel near Gilgal.

Upstairs room (3:20). Extra rooms sometimes were constructed on roofs of buildings (see comments on 1 Kings 17:19).

So they took the key and opened the doors (3:25). Ancient tumbler locks were constructed on the inside of a door (or pair of doors) with a hole for someone to reach through to unlock it from the outside. Such doors were locked by sliding

A ram's horn (*shofar*).

a bolt into place, again on the inside, if necessary by reaching through the hole. The lock was opened only by using a large key, again, from either the inside or by reaching through the hole.

Ram's horn (3:27). These horns were made from an animal's horn (often a ram) and were used for various types of signaling (Josh. 6:4–20).

Fords of the Jordan (3:28). A tributary flowing into the Jordan River near Jericho deposited enough sediment to create a natural ford typically only three to four feet deep (when not in flood stage) where people could wade across. Having command of the ford meant cutting off the Moabites' escape.

Ten thousand (3:29). See comments on Judg. 1:4.

Not one of them escaped (3:29). Ancient near Eastern literary works often used hyperbolic language to describe victories. See comments on Josh. 10:40.

Shamgar Son of Anath—Minor Judge #1 (3:31)

Shamgar son of Anath became judge (3:31). Shamgar's non-Hebrew name suggests that he is a foreigner, as does his lineage as "son of Anath." Anath was a goddess of war and a consort of Baal worshiped in Canaan, Egypt, and Syria (see the article "The Canaanites and Canaanite Religion"). In the twelfth century BC Egypt fought a unit of soldiers called "the troop of Anath," named after its patron goddess. Perhaps Shamgar is from this group. He may have joined the Israelites or simply helped them by defeating a common foe: the Philistines.

Cattle prod (3:31). A cattle prod (oxgoad) was a long, pointed stick, often with a sharp metal tip (1 Sam. 13:21), used by farmers to prod oxen to keep moving when plowing. These cattle prods (and other farm implements) could also be used as weapons in times of war.

Deborah—Major Judge #3 (4:1–5:31)

King Jabin . . . in Hazor (4:2). This is a different (and later) King Jabin than the one mentioned in Josh. 11:1–11. Names of former rulers often were taken by later rulers. For example, there were eleven different pharaohs named Ramesses. Apparently, the Canaanites had reestablished themselves at Hazor after Joshua had defeated them back in Josh. 11.

Harosheth of the Nations (4:2). This apparently is a reference to the plain east of Megiddo where armies often assembled.

Nine hundred iron chariots (4:3). In the fifteenth century BC, Pharaoh Thutmose III captured 924 chariots from a coalition of kings at Megiddo (see comments on Josh. 17:16).

Take with you ten thousand men (4:6). See comments on Judg. 1:4.

Mount Tabor.

Deploy the troops on Mount Tabor, and take . . . men from the Naphtalites and Zebulunites (4:6). The allotments of these two tribes included part of the Jezreel Valley, where the battle would take place. Mount Tabor was in the northeast corner of the valley next to the major north-south road that ran through the country between the Canaanite strongholds of Megiddo to the south and Hazor farther north.

Wadi Kishon (4:7). This small river drained the Jezreel Valley but often flooded, making travel difficult.

You will receive no honor . . . because the LORD will sell Sisera to a woman (4:9). Ancient Near Eastern societies were male-dominated, and honor, especially from victory in battle, was supremely important.

Kenites (4:11). This was a tribe of nomads related to Moses (Judg. 1:16).

Zaanannim, which was near Kedesh (4:11). These two sites were about nine miles east of Mount Tabor, south of the Sea of Galilee.

The LORD threw Sisera, all his charioteers . . . into a panic (4:15). Canaanite chariots advanced across the flat Jezreel Valley while the Israelite foot soldiers descended the slopes of Mount Tabor. The seemingly outmatched Israelites, however, rout the Canaanites and pursue them back across the valley to their camp. The key to the Israelite victory is explained in chapter 5.

Fell by the sword (4:16). See comments on Judg. 1:25.

Not a single man was left (4:16). See comments on Judg. 3:29.

A tent peg . . . a hammer (4:21). These were common items for tent-dwelling nomads (4:11).

She hammered the peg into his temple . . . and he died (4:21). Jael is lauded for taking the life of the enemy commander. To do so, she must defy her family's alliance (4:17), betray her assurance to Jabin (4:18), and violate the strong tradition in place that required hosts to protect their guests at all costs (cf. Gen. 19:8). Jabin then suffers the humiliation of dying at the hand of a woman (see comments on Judg. 4:9).

Deborah and Barak . . . sang (5:1). The narrative in chapter 4 is amplified by the song in chapter 5, much like the narrative in Exod. 14 is amplified by the song in Exod. 15. Triumphal hymns from this era are known from Egypt and Assyria.

Seir . . . Sinai (5:4–5). The Lord is pictured as a warrior coming from the heights of Seir/Edom and Sinai to fight for Israel.

The clouds poured water (5:4). Apparently a sudden rainstorm turned the eastern Jezreel Valley into a flooded, muddy pit. The chariots sank into the mud, giving the Israelite foot soldiers the clear advantage.

Shamgar (5:6). Like Jael, Shamgar was a foreigner who won a great victory for Israel (see comments on Judg. 3:31).

The main roads were deserted (5:6). Foreign oppression meant that the Israelites were unable to travel safely on the main roads and had to resort to the safer but more difficult side paths.

White donkeys . . . saddle blankets (5:10). Light-colored donkeys and ornamented saddle blankets were symbols of prestige for wealthy Canaanites.

Kishon (5:21). This is one of the rivers in the Jezreel Valley that flooded (see comments on Judg. 5:4).

Sisera's mother (5:28–30). Jael's victory is contrasted with the futile longing of Sisera's mother. She hopes that her son's delay is caused by time taken for the division of spoils (women, garments) that often followed military victories, but such is not the case this time.

Gideon—Major Judge #4 (6:1–9:57)

Midian (6:1). See comments on Exod. 2:15. The Midianites had already been defeated once by Moses (Num. 31).

As far as Gaza (6:4). Since invaders from the eastern desert could plunder as far as Gaza on the Mediterranean coast, the settled Israelites were in dire straits.

A great swarm of locusts (6:5). See comments on Exod. 10:4; Joel 1:4. Damage by the marauders is compared to that of plagues of locusts that periodically swept into Israel from northern Africa.

Modern-day farmer threshing wheat.

Camels (6:5). Camels were well suited to nomadic life on the eastern desert, providing milk, meat, and transportation, and were even used for warfare.

Amorites (6:10). See comments on Josh. 10:5.

Oak that was in Ophrah (6:11). This was a landmark at a town apparently in the east-central Jezreel Valley.

Abiezrite (6:11). This name indicates a member of a clan in Manasseh that descended from an ancestor named Abiezer (cf. 6:34).

Threshing wheat (6:11). Threshing is the process of separating kernels of wheat from their hulls and stalks, normally done on a large threshing floor in an exposed area where the wind could help separate the grain from the chaff.

Winepress (6:11). A winepress was a basin-like facility for pressing the juice out of grapes, often accomplished through trampling directly on the grapes with one's feet. Winepresses were sometimes chiseled from bedrock. A winepress usually was smaller and more protected than a threshing floor, reflecting Gideon's need to hide from the marauders.

You will strike Midian down as if it were one man (6:16). See comments on Judg. 1:4.

Goat . . . half bushel of flour (6:19). Gideon prepares an entire goat plus bread made from half a bushel of flour (an "ephah," around six gallons), perhaps reflecting his family's wealth.

Tear down the altar of Baal . . . and cut down the Asherah pole (6:25). See comments on Judg. 2:11; 3:7; 1 Kings 15:13; see the article "The Canaanites and Canaanite Religion." That the father of the chosen deliverer would have such pagan symbols reflects the deep-seated idolatry of the time.

If he is a god, let him plead his own case (6:31). People in the ancient Near East assumed that gods would enter statues or other symbols made to represent them, so attacking a god's symbol should naturally elicit their response. Gideon's father probably reflects such thinking, but he speaks in a way that also protects his son from the villagers.

The Spirit . . . enveloped (6:34). God's Spirit took possession of (literally, "clothed") Gideon to empower him. One Babylonian text states that a certain demon "has put on my body as if it were a garment."[5]

Ram's horn (6:34). See comments on Judg. 3:27.

Manasseh . . . Naphtali (6:35). Gideon calls his own tribe as well as other nearby tribes to fight the invaders.

Fleece . . . dew (6:36–40). Twice Gideon requests reassurance of future success, much like how diviners in other cultures sought confirmation by some divine sign. Gideon uses a fleece—the wool shorn from a sheep—and dew, common to the region. In the Jezreel Valley moisture blowing in from the nearby Mediterranean Sea creates abundant dew most mornings.

Spring of Harod (7:1). This copious spring is located at the base of Mount Gilboa in the southeast corner of the Jezreel Valley.

Twenty-two thousand (7:3). See comments on Judg. 1:4.

The camp of Midian was below (7:8). The Israelites are camped on Mount Gilboa, an arm of the central hills that extends into the Jezreel Valley. The Midianites are camped at the base of Mount Moreh, which lay across a narrow neck of the Jezreel.

Swarm of locusts (7:12). See comments on Exod. 10:4; Judg. 6:5; Joel 1:4.

A man was telling his friend about a dream (7:13). In the ancient Near East people understood dreams to be messages from the gods with either unambiguous information or symbols that needed interpretation. Egyptians and Babylonians used dream books with lists of symbols to help with the interpretation. Here, one Midianite soldier dreams, and his tentmate interprets correctly, giving Gideon a third confirmation of success.

Empty pitcher . . . with a torch inside (7:16). The torches probably are constructed of combustible pieces of wood or cloths soaked in oil and tied around sticks. A medium-sized pottery jar would conceal most of the light and restrict the airflow to the flame, dampening it. Once the jar is broken, additional oxygen would make the torch flare up.

Abel-meholah (7:22). This site is about twenty miles southeast of the battle and the location of a ford across the Jordan.

Ephraim (7:24). This large, important Israelite tribe resides south of the site of the battle but close to the route taken by the fleeing Midianites.

They took control of the watercourses (7:24). The Israelites rush to cut off the Midianites as they flee southeast toward one of the fords across the Jordan River (cf. 3:28).

Brought the heads of Oreb and Zeeb to Gideon (7:25). See comments on Judg. 1:6.

Men of Ephraim (8:1). This Israelite tribe, closely related to Manasseh in the "house of Joseph" (1:22), is upset that it was not called to help in the battle.

The gleaning . . . the grape harvest (8:2). Gleanings were the remainders of a crop, such as grapes, that the harvesters left (Deut. 24:21). Gideon placates the offended Ephraimites by stressing their greatness.

Succoth (8:5). This city is just east of the Jordan and more than thirty miles from the battlefield. After attacking in the middle of the night and traveling more than thirty miles, the men would have been exhausted.

Penuel (8:8). This is an Israelite city in the Transjordan region (i.e., east of the Jordan River), five miles east of Succoth.

Karkor (8:10). See comments on Judg. 8:11.

One hundred twenty thousand armed men (8:10). See comments on Judg. 1:4.

The caravan route (8:11). Gideon attacks the Midianites at Karkor, 120 miles southeast of Peniel, along the caravan route into the Arabian Desert.

The youth wrote down for him the names (8:14). The fact that this young man could write provides an indication of at least limited literacy during this time.

Seventy-seven (8:14). See comments on Judg. 1:7.

Took the crescent ornaments that were on the necks of their camels (8:21). Victors commonly took trophies from their conquests (1 Sam. 17:54), which sometimes represented the enemies' defeated gods. These ornaments from the camels likely were crescent-shaped, representing the moon god worshiped in Arabia.

I will not rule over you (8:23). Gideon seemingly rejects the offer but then certainly acts like a king—taking a major share of plunder (8:24–26), making a worship center (8:27), and taking a harem (8:30–31).

Ephod (8:27). This was a garment or breastplate for a priest or idol (Exod. 28:6–14; Judg. 17:5), here perhaps used for an idol and its adornment.

Seventy sons (8:30). This number of sons perhaps represents a full royal household (see comments on Judg. 1:7).

His concubine (8:31). A concubine was a secondary wife taken for sexual pleasure or to produce offspring, or both. Gideon marries into an important family in Shechem, perhaps to expand his power to that city.

Made Baal-berith their god (8:33). The name of this god means "Baal/ Lord of the Covenant," a clear sign of serious idolatry (see comments on Judg. 2:11).

Abimelech . . . went to Shechem and spoke to his uncles (9:1). Abimelech uses diplomacy and violence to take control of his mother's city. He hires scoundrels (9:4), much like Labayu of Shechem had utilized the Apiru earlier, as recorded in the Amarna letters (see comments on Josh. 9:1–2; Judg. 2:16).

Killed his seventy brothers (9:5). Usurpers sometimes wiped out entire royal lines to take power (2 Kings 11:1–3; 10:1–11 [also seventy]). An eighth-century-BC text from Asia Minor describes a usurper who "killed his father . . . and killed seventy brothers of his father."[6]

Mount Gerizim (9:7). This is a high hill flanking Shechem on the south, an excellent point from which to speak to Shechemites (see comments on Josh. 8:33).

Olive tree . . . fig tree . . . grapevine . . . bramble (9:8–15). Jotham's parable uses a succession of common plants presented in order of the most to the least valuable, comparing Abimelech to the nearly worthless thornbush.

Killed his seventy sons (9:18). By accepting Abimelech as king, the Shechemites participate in his brutal power grab.

Escaping to Beer (9:21). The Hebrew word "Beer" means "well," perhaps referring to a place name or some well where Jotham hid.

Gaal son of Ebed (9:26). This otherwise unknown person leads a rebellion that results in Abimelech warring against Shechem (9:45).

He tore down the city and sowed it with salt (9:45). See comments on Josh. 6:26.

Tower of Shechem (9:46). In Shechem archaeologists have uncovered the base of a tower with walls almost thirteen feet thick.

Thebez (9:50). This unknown city apparently was near Shechem, which also had a tower.

Upper portion of a millstone (9:53). This was a loaf-shaped stone that was rubbed on a lower, saddle-shaped stone to grind grain.

They'll say about me, "A woman killed him" (9:54). See comments on Judg. 4:9; 4:21.

Tola of Issachar—Minor Judge #2 (10:1–2)

Shamir (10:1). The location of this town is unknown.

Jair of Gilead—Minor Judge #3 (10:3–5)

Gilead (10:4). Gilead is the area east of the Jordan River, between the Yarmuk River and the Dead Sea, which had been largely allocated to the tribe of Gad.

He had thirty sons who rode on thirty donkeys (10:4). Jair apparently had a harem and, through his numerous sons, controlled a region in Gilead. The note that all of his sons rode donkeys is a reflection of Jair's wealth.

Jephthah of Gilead—Major Judge #5 (10:6–12:7)

They worshiped the Baals and the Ashtoreths . . . and the gods of the Ammonites and the Philistines (10:6). See comments on Judg. 2:11; 2:13; see the articles "The Canaanites and Canaanite Religion"; "The Philistines." The text lists seven groups of gods, implying a stress on the fullness or completeness of Israel's idolatry.

The Philistines and the Ammonites (10:7). The Philistines were the enemy to the west of the Israelites, and the Ammonites were the enemy to the east of the Israelites.

The Egyptians . . . and the Maonites oppressed you (10:11–12). Seven enemies of Israel are cited, suggesting a fullness or completion of enemies (cf. 10:6).

Mizpah (10:17). This Hebrew word means "watchtower." This is not the Mizpah in central Israel (1 Kings 15:22), but rather is an unknown site in Gilead.

Gilead (10:18). See comments on Judg. 10:4.

Prostitute (11:1). Ancient Near Eastern women could be driven into prostitution if they had no other means of support (Amos 7:17).

Inheritance (11:2). Children of prostitutes or secondary wives often were denied inheritance and social acceptance (Gen. 21:9–10).

Tob (11:3). This region, home to the "worthless men" who joined up with Jephthah, was north of Gilead.

Jephthah repeated all his terms in the presence of the Lord (11:11). Apparently, Jephthah swore an oath before God (see comments on Judg. 11:30).

Jephthah sent messengers (11:12). Jephthah addressed the Ammonites using formal diplomacy, negotiating through messengers.

They seized my land . . . we can have whatever the Lord our God conquers for us (11:13–27). The Ammonites' king claims that the region east of the Jordan River is theirs by historic right, but Israel claims it by divine grant.

You can have whatever your god Chemosh conquers (11:24). The Ammonites worshiped Milcom (1 Kings 11:5); the Moabites worshiped Chemosh (Num. 21:29). Perhaps Jephthah errs, perhaps he is mocking the Ammonites, or perhaps the worship of the related and neighboring Ammonites and Moabites overlapped.

Jephthah made this vow (11:30). Used widely in the ancient world, a vow was a formal, binding promise made by a person to give something to the deity in return for being aided as the person requested.

Whoever comes out the doors . . . I will offer that person as a burnt offering (11:31). Israelites often had homes where animals lived as well (1 Sam. 28:24), so Jephthah may have expected an animal.

Tambourines (11:34). These are small, flat, hand drums that may have had bells or metal pieces around the outside, frequently used with dancing at festivals (see the article "Musical Instruments in Israel and the Ancient Near East").

I have given my word to the Lord and cannot take it back (11:35). Many in the ancient Near East would think that even foolish vows needed to be fulfilled lest the deity be angered (cf. 1 Sam. 14:39, 44).

An ancient sculpture of a Phoenician woman with a tambourine.

Greek histories include stories of children killed in fulfillment of vows, and the Phoenician/Canaanite colony of Carthage in North Africa had a cemetery with perhaps twenty thousand infants sacrificed to Baal and his consort Tanit-Ashtart in fulfillment of parental vows.

Fords (12:5). See comments on Judg. 3:28; 7:24.

Shibboleth (12:6). This word means a "head of grain" (Gen. 41:5), but it was pronounced with "s" rather than "sh" by the Ephraimites.

Forty-two thousand (12:6). See comments on Judg. 1:4.

Ibzan of Bethlehem and Elon of Zebulun—Minor Judges #4 and #5 (12:8–12)

Bethlehem (12:8). This is probably the Bethlehem in Galilee (Josh. 19:15), not the one in Judah.

He had thirty sons (12:9). See comments on Judg. 10:4.

Abdon of Pirathon—Minor Judge #6 (12:13–15)

Forty sons . . . seventy donkeys (12:14). See comments on Judg. 10:4.

In the hill country of the Amalekites (12:15). Referring to this region as "of the Amalekites" implies that the nomadic Amalekites have recaptured this area and now control it.

Samson of Dan—Major Judge #6 (13:1–16:31)

Philistines (13:1). See comments on Judg. 3:3; see the article "The Philistines."

Zorah (13:2). This town was near Beth-shemesh in Dan, not far from the border with Philistia.

Angel of the Lord (13:3). See comments on Judg. 2:1.

Unable to conceive (13:3). Ancient people assumed that a barren woman was cursed by God (Deut. 28:18), but a formerly barren woman who gave birth (Gen. 21:2–7) was obviously blessed.

A Nazirite (13:5). The Nazirite vow is described in Num. 6:1–8 (see comments on Num. 6:2).

A decorated Philistine jug, probably used for serving beer.

Camp of Dan (13:25). Perhaps this phrase refers to a place where the tribe of Dan had camped at some point when they first settled into Canaan.

Timnah (14:1). Timnah is a Philistine town about four and a half miles west of Zorah. Archaeological excavations revealed a well-planned settlement with mud-brick homes and typical Philistine pottery.

Get her for me as a wife (14:2). Samson disregards clear divine commands (Deut. 7:3), parental desires, and cultural norms in demanding a Philistine wife.

The uncircumcised Philistines (14:3). The Egyptians, Hebrews, and most other ancient Near Eastern peoples practiced circumcision, but not these immigrants from the Aegean (see comments on Judg. 3:3). The term "uncircumcised" is used here as a religious and social slur.

A young lion came roaring at him (14:5). Asiatic lions were not uncommon in Israel (1 Sam. 17:36–37; 1 Kings 13:24) and throughout the region at the time.

There was a swarm of bees with honey (14:8). Honey was a desirable treat occasionally found in the wild (1 Sam. 14:26–29).

He had scooped the honey from the lion's carcass (14:9). Samson seriously violates the Nazirite vow to avoid corpses (Num. 6:1–8).

Thirty linen garments (14:12). Since many people in the ancient world had only one set of clothes, another set was valuable. Clothes were common war plunder (5:30; Josh. 7:21), and linen was expensive.

Ashkelon (14:19). This is a major Philistine city twenty-three miles southwest of Timnah.

Samson . . . visited his wife (15:1). In the ancient Near East a groom and bride could separate after the wedding for as long as several months while the groom finished preparing their home. During the separation he, often bringing gifts (i.e., young goat), could return for conjugal visits.

He burned . . . the standing grain . . . vineyards . . . olive groves (15:5). Grains, along with grapes and olives, formed the heart of the Mediterranean ancient Near Eastern diet (cf. Deut. 11:14).

The Philistines went to her and her father and burned them to death (15:6). Execution by burning was not uncommon in the ancient Near East. In Dan. 3 death by fire is the punishment for an act of disloyalty. Law 110 of the Code of Hammurabi prescribes the same punishment for a priestess who enters a tavern.

The Philistines rule us (15:11). This is an indication of the Philistine dominance at the time (see comments on Judg. 3:3; see the article "The Philistines").

They tied him up with two new ropes (15:13). These ropes were made of flax (15:14), among the strongest of natural fibers. "New" indicates that these ropes were made from the current year's crop and thus exceptionally strong.

Lehi (15:14). This is the Hebrew word for "jawbone," named for the battle that takes place here.

He . . . killed a thousand men (15:15). See comments on Judg. 1:4.

That is why he named it En-hakkore (15:19). The land of Israel includes numerous springs where a stratum of water-bearing rock intersects ground level. The Hebrew *En-hakkore* means "spring of the one who calls."

Gaza (16:1). Gaza was one of the Philistines' five major cities (see the article "The Philistines").

Doors of the city gate . . . gateposts . . . bar (16:3). The gates of fortified cities consisted of a pair of heavy wooden doors attached to pivoting gateposts. They were sealed shut by a horizontal beam set in brackets on the inside. Excavations of the gate at Ashdod from this same era indicate that the pair of doors would have been thirteen and a half feet wide.

To the top of the mountain overlooking Hebron (16:3). This is not near Hebron, which is thirty-eight miles to the east, but rather the top of the hill near Gaza in the direction of Hebron.

Who lived in the Sorek Valley (16:4). The Valley of Sorek is where the cities of Timnah, Zorah, and Beth-shemesh were located (see comments on Judg. 13:2; 14:1).

Each of us will then give you 1,100 pieces of silver (16:5). This represents more than three times the weight of the gold collected by Gideon in 8:26. Eleven hundred shekels weighed about 28 pounds, so the total from five kings would be about 140 pounds, a small fortune to be exchanged for the information to neutralize a major threat.

Seven fresh bowstrings (16:7). The Hebrew word translated as "bowstrings" is used not only for bowstrings (Ps. 11:2) but also for animal tendons and tent cords (Job 4:21). "Seven" (see comments on Judg. 1:7) connotes a full number, perhaps even considered magical.

New ropes (16:11). See comments on Judg. 15:13.

Reconstructed vertical loom.

The fabric on the loom (16:13). A loom was used to weave cloth, most commonly wool. Nearly every home contained a loom.

My hair has never been cut (16:17). Samson's lengthy hair is the result of his Nazirite vow (13:5; cf. Num. 6:5) and connected to God's gift of supernatural strength.

The Philistines . . . gouged out his eyes . . . forced [him] to grind grain (16:21). Such a fate was not uncommon for war captives.

A great sacrifice to their god Dagon (16:23). Dagon was an ancient Near Eastern god associated with grain, war, and rain who was worshiped by the Philistines (see the article "The Philistines").

Two middle pillars supporting the temple (16:29). A temple excavated at a northern Philistine city (ancient name unknown) had two central columns supporting the roof.

Israel Becomes like the Canaanites (17:1–18:31)

A man from the hill country of Ephraim named Micah . . . the Danite tribe was looking for territory to occupy (17:1–18:31). Two stories that apparently had occurred earlier (see comments on Judg. 18:30; 20:28) are placed at the end of Judges for rhetorical purposes, emphasizing the utter chaos of the time.

The 1,100 pieces of silver (17:2). See comments on Judg. 16:5.

My son, may you be blessed by the Lord (17:2). Ancient peoples assumed that the gods would enforce uttered curses, so this mother blesses her son to counteract her earlier curse.

I personally consecrate the silver (17:3). This indicates that Micah's mother is formally presenting this silver as a divine offering.

A carved image and a silver idol (17:3). Small statues often were made from wood or bronze and then covered with silver or gold.

Micah had a shrine (17:5). This shrine is perhaps a small building or section of the house that held the divine object(s).

Ephod (17:5). See comments on Exod. 28:2; Judg. 8:27. This priestly garment apparently was closely associated with the household idols (18:14, 17–20).

Installed one of his sons to be his priest . . . stay with me and be my father and priest (17:5–13). Micah first uses one of his sons and then a Levite as his family priest, likely seeking divine aid in childbearing, fertility of crops and flocks, and safety.

Four ounces of silver a year (17:10). This was the common wage for a laborer.

Five brave men from all their clans . . . scout out the land (18:2). There are strong and ironic parallels here with the twelve spies who had represented all the tribes in spying out the land in Num. 13.

Laish (18:7). This city is a fertile site in far northern Israel, too far away (twenty-five miles) for allies at the city of Sidon to give aid.

Six hundred Danites (18:11). This is a typical size for a fighting force (cf. 1 Sam. 13:15; 27:2).

Camp of Dan (18:12). This site is farther northeast than the one mentioned in 13:25.

Better for you . . . to be a priest for a tribe (18:19–20). Religious apostasy, misuse of force, and personal opportunism combine to supply the Danites with a priest and religious center.

The men who were in the houses near it (18:22–23). These are perhaps formal allies (cf. Gen. 14:13–14) or helpful neighbors willing to assist in battle.

They killed them with their swords and burned the city (18:27). Archaeological excavations have revealed the ruins of a prosperous Canaanite city on this site that was destroyed in about 1200 BC. The prosperous city

Excavations of the gate to the ancient city of Dan.

was replaced by a poor encampment with storage pits and simple pottery, apparently matching this story.

They rebuilt the city and lived in it (18:28). The poor encampment first built by the Danites was replaced by a proper town with a developing culture.

Jonathan son of Gershom, son of Moses (18:30). If Moses died at age 120 just before the conquest (Deut. 34:7), his grandson would have been an adult early in the time of Judges (see comments on Judg. 17:1–18:31).

Until the time of the exile from the land (18:30). This is a reference either to when the Philistines captured the ark (mid-eleventh century BC; 1 Sam. 4–6) or to when the Assyrians conquered and exiled the Danites (734 BC; 2 Kings 15:29).

Military Chaos—Civil War (19:1–21:25)

Concubine (19:1). See comments on Judg. 8:31.

He stayed with him for three days (19:4). This would be the classic length of hospitality.

Spend the night (19:9). The host attempts to convince the guest to stay extra time, probably to delay his daughter's departure (cf. Gen. 24:55).

Jebus . . . Gibeah . . . Ramah (19:10–13). From Bethlehem (19:2) to Jebus (Jerusalem) was about six miles; on to Gibeah and Ramah was another three to five miles.

Sat down in the city square (19:15). Since many cities did not have inns, travelers could go to a town's public area and expect a local to invite them in (cf. Gen. 19:1–3).

So we can have sex with him (19:22). The men of Gibeah are very poor hosts, just as evil as the Sodomites (see comments on Gen. 19:5).

Mizpah (20:1). This was a central location where Samuel would also gather the nation (1 Sam. 7:5–6).

All could sling a stone at a hair and not miss (20:16). This is a hyperbolic description of their great accuracy. On the use of slings in the ancient Near East, see comments on 1 Sam. 17:49.

Judah will be first (20:18). See the introduction in the commentary on Judges; see comments on Judg. 1:2. Judah goes first again, but this time Judah is attacking an Israelite tribe and not the Canaanites.

Phinehas son of Eleazar, son of Aaron (20:28). Phinehas was the great-nephew of Moses (Num. 25:7–11) and is a major character in the book of Numbers, implying that this story took place early in the time of the judges (see comments on Judg. 17:1–18:31; 18:30).

The Benjaminites . . . were drawn away from the city (20:31–48). What Joshua did to the Canaanites at Ai (Josh. 8), Israel now does to the Benjaminites, one of Israel's own tribes.

The men of Israel had sworn an oath (21:1). See comments on Judg. 11:11; 11:35.

There must be heirs for the survivors of Benjamin (21:17). The end of a family line was a terrible curse for people in the ancient Near East.

Ruth

J. Andrew Dearman

Introduction. The book of Ruth is a short story that provides fascinating information regarding the tribe of Judah during the time between the ancestor Judah and King David. Ruth, a Moabite woman, twice marries into a family from Bethlehem in Judah, accepting the faith and customs of Israel, and then she becomes the great-grandmother of David, Israel's greatest king. Ruth and her husband Boaz lived during the period of the judges (1:1), and their story functions like a bridge between that period and the rise of the Israelite monarchy in 1–2 Samuel. Ruth and Boaz worked out a commitment to each other and to the continuation of the family line by following the customs of marriage and inheritance of their day.

Introduction (1:1–5)

Moab (1:1). Moab was a region and country east of the Dead Sea. Some of the people living there were related to the Judahites through an ancestral connection with Lot (see comments on Gen. 19:37–38). Solomon married a Moabite princess and established a temple for the chief Moabite deity near the temple in Jerusalem (1 Kings 11:7). Because of bad blood between Israel and Moab, no Moabite was allowed into the sacred assembly of Israel (Deut. 23:3–8).

Bethlehem (1:1). Bethlehem was a town of modest size, although it possessed a wall and a gate (4:1). It became well known as the home of David, the future king over Israel (Luke 2:11).

Ruth and Naomi Travel from Moab

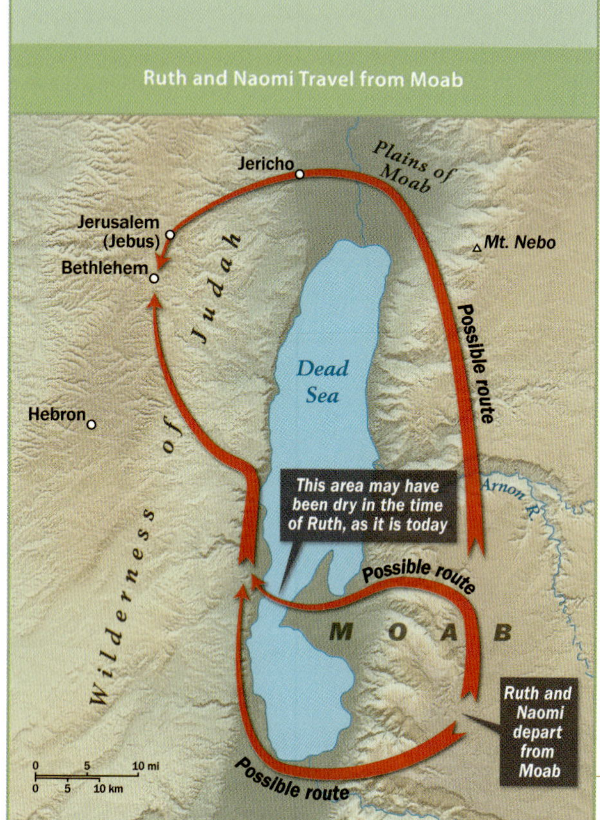

Ephrathites (1:2). Both Elimelech and Jesse, David's father, are described as Ephrathites from Bethlehem (1 Sam. 17:12). Ephrathah is an old clan name associated with the area (Mic. 5:2). It is assumed by the narrator that because of the famine Elimelech had exhausted his resources before leaving Bethlehem and that someone else had use of his property. This matter comes into play later in the story during the gate negotiations for Elimelech's property (4:1–12).

On the Road to Bethlehem (1:6–18)

The road leading back to the land of Judah (1:7). The route to Bethlehem taken by Ruth and Naomi is not specified, but most likely it was around the northern end of the Dead Sea.

Each of you go back (1:8). There were no customs of the region that bound a widow to her mother-in-law when her father-in-law was deceased. That Orpah remained in Moab when Naomi left is understandable.

Wherever you go, I will go (1:16–17). Ruth's vow to stay with Naomi is a free choice and it has an oath of judgment in it ("may the Lord punish me, and do so severely") if anything separates her from Naomi, even death. She commits herself to burial with Naomi as part of the family of Elimelech. Family burial plots kept the family together in life and death (cf. Gen. 49:29–32). Her later request that Boaz take her in marriage (3:9) is also rooted in her commitment to the continuation of Elimelech's and Mahlon's family.

Bitterness at Harvest Time (1:19–22)

Mara (1:20). Mara means "bitter" and is a wordplay on Naomi's name, which means "pleasant." Wordplays were an important cultural practice in the ancient world, and names could be vehicles for expressing a person's identity.

Barley harvest (1:22). The barley harvest would have begun at the end of March or early April. Barley and wheat were sown after the fall rains commenced in October, with the wheat harvest happening in May. Line 5 of the famous Gezer Calendar, dating to around 925 BC, refers to a period of barley harvest, using a phrase similar to that in 1:22. The events of 2:1–4:12 are set during the harvest and subsequent processing of these two cereals (cf. 2:23).

Reaping in Order to Eat (2:1–7)

Let me gather fallen grain (2:7). Ruth apparently did not know the family connection to Boaz when she asked the foreman of reapers in a field if she might come behind them and glean for leftover barley stalks. Boaz's reapers would have worked in teams and been paid a set wage, possibly from the produce of the field itself. First the stalks of grain would have been cut with a sickle and bound in sheaves. A poor person like Ruth would look for the opportunity to collect leftover stalks (cf. Lev. 19:9–10; 23:22; Deut. 24:19). The collected sheaves in a field would then be taken to a threshing floor, where the process of separating and securing the grain seed would take place.

Boaz Helps Ruth (2:8–16)

Haven't I ordered the young men not to touch you? (2:9). Ruth was in a precarious position when gleaning. As a single female and a foreigner, she lacked the protection of an extended family, and there was no such thing as a police force for public order. Boaz tells the male reapers not to lay a hand on her, implicitly extending his protection to her.

Have some bread and dip it in the vinegar sauce (2:14). Boaz also offers Ruth the food and drink that he provided for the reapers who worked for him. It included bread (probably roasted grain) and vinegar sauce. The grain perhaps was beaten from some stalks and roasted on the spot.

Scene from an Egyptian tomb painting, depicting the afterlife. Here a man cuts wheat while his wife gathers the bundles.

Threshing and Conversation (2:17–23)

Twenty-six quarts of barley (2:17). Ruth's long workday did not end with the gleaning of barley stalks. She also threshed or beat the heads of grain with a stick, separating the seed from the chaff that covered them, and collected nearly an ephah of barley to take back to Naomi. This would be nearly five gallons of grain, a large amount for a day of gleaning.

Family redeemers (2:20). The term translated as "family redeemer" refers to a male relative who could act on behalf of other family members when they were in various kinds of distress. Such a person could pay the debt on family property used as collateral or purchase it outright from family members, thereby assisting relatives in need (cf. Jer. 32:6–15). Inherited family property was not to be sold outside the clan, because, like family members, it helped to define the clan. Naomi knows that Boaz is kin to Elimelech, making him a potential family redeemer for her and Ruth.

Naomi Advises Ruth to Go to the Threshing Floor (3:1–5)

The threshing floor (3:2). Threshing floors could be communal open spaces or privately owned. The hooves of animals and often a sled pulled by them

The region near Bethlehem.

first cracked the heads of grain to help free the seed from the covering chaff. When the wind came up, wooden forks were used to toss the crushed stalks into the air, where the heavier heads of grain would fall to the ground and the lighter chaff would be driven downwind. Eventually the grain would then be run through a sieve, either at the threshing floor or in the homes of those who collected it. Work at the threshing floor would be intensive, as Boaz and his workers processed the barley sheaves in order to collect the grain. That he would sleep there at night may have been for the sake of convenience, but it also provided a measure of security against thieves. Naomi's instructions to Ruth were intended to give Boaz opportunity to serve as a "family redeemer" (2:20) for her daughter-in-law. He was not legally obligated to do so.

Commitments (3:6–13)

Take me under your wing (3:9). The Hebrew word translated as "wing" is the same word used for the edge of a garment, so this phrase can also be translated as "spread the edge/corner of your garment over me." Spreading his garment over her means that Boaz would take Ruth in marriage (cf. Ezek. 16:8) and thereby serve as family redeemer for her, Naomi, and the property of her deceased husband.

A redeemer closer than I am (3:12). While praising her family commitment, Boaz indicates that there is someone related to Elimelech more closely than he, someone who would have the first option of acting on behalf of the larger family. Readers are never told precisely how Boaz and the unnamed kinsman were related to Elimelech.

Anticipation (3:14–18)

He won't rest unless he resolves this today (3:18). Ruth and Naomi would be observers until Boaz sorted out matters of law and custom. As a male relative of Elimelech, Boaz could initiate action on certain family matters, but only in accordance with the customs of the community regarding marriage and inheritance. The connection between these customs may be difficult for modern Western readers to grasp. Note how a man's "house" (= family) is succinctly defined as both people and possessions in Exod. 20:17.

Buying and Building (4:1–12)

Gate (4:1). The gate of a city was the best place to meet inhabitants, since everyone who entered or left the city had to pass through it. Boaz is there early to catch the nearer kinsman coming out of the town for daily activities. Gates were also often the location of judicial hearings and legal decisions (see comments on Gen. 19:1; Deut. 17:5).

You are witnesses today (4:9–10). Since few could read or write, the testimony of the witnesses would be crucial if a dispute over this transaction later emerged.

I am buying from Naomi everything . . . also acquired Ruth the Moabitess, Mahlon's widow (4:9–10). In modern terms, the property that belonged to Elimelech would have a lien against it, almost certainly for support that he had received from a creditor before leaving for Moab. As family property, it can be sold in perpetuity only within the clan. The option to acquire the property from Naomi would appeal to the unnamed kinsman, who had the first right of acquisition among relatives, since Naomi had neither money nor male heir. Ruth is a complicating factor, however, since she is Mahlon's widow and still of childbearing age. Were she to marry Boaz or the unnamed kinsman and bear a child, then the child would be Elimelech's heir. This apparently is behind the phrase "to perpetuate the [deceased] man's name on his property" (4:5). The law in Deut. 25:5–10 envisions a similar situation where a man marries the childless widow of his dead brother with the goal of producing an heir for the deceased. This expansive understanding of what constitutes a family is seen also in the blessing extended by the people to Ruth that she bear children who would build up the family of Israel (4:11).

Ruth and Naomi Have a Son (4:13–17)

They named him Obed (4:17). The family of Elimelech and Mahlon continues through the son born to Boaz and Ruth. In that sense, Obed is both a family redeemer for and a son of Naomi (4:17). Moreover, the property acquired by Boaz when he married Ruth would belong to Obed.

Genealogy for David (4:18–22)

The family records of Perez (4:18–22). The genealogy connects Boaz with his ancestor Judah (through Perez his son; cf. 4:12 and Gen. 38:24–30) and with his great-grandson David. Not every person in this line is named, so that Boaz can be the seventh and David the tenth person listed. In the ancient Near East genealogies functioned as social maps and as memory hooks for important historical accounts. As such, they are common in the OT. Forty-two generations of this same family are preserved in the NT (Matt. 1:2–17).

1–2 Samuel

Robert B. Chisholm Jr.

Introduction. The books of 1 and 2 Samuel are central to the Bible's account of Israel's history. They cover a period of roughly 140 years (1110–970 BC), beginning with the birth of the great prophet Samuel in the latter part of Eli's career (the precise date is uncertain) and concluding just prior to David's death (recorded in 1 Kings 1–2).

The major events in 1–2 Samuel may be dated as follows:

1130–1090 BC	Eli's leadership (1 Sam. 4:18)
1090	The Philistines capture the ark of the covenant (1 Sam. 4:11; 6:1)
1090	The ark arrives in Kiriath-jearim (1 Sam. 7:2)
1070	Samuel's victory over the Philistines (1 Sam. 7:2–12)
1070–1050	Israel enjoys relief from Philistine oppression (1 Sam. 7:13–14)
1050	Samuel anoints Saul as king (1 Sam. 9–12)
1050–1010	Saul's reign
1010–1003	David's reign over Judah
1003–970	David's reign over Israel and Judah

This period was particularly significant in Israel's history. Since the time of the exodus (1446 BC) and conquest (1406–1399 BC), judges had led Israel. But finally the people demanded to have a king like the rest of the nations—a military leader with a standing army who would provide them with security. The Lord, of course, was fully capable of protecting his people,

Major Locations of Events in 1–2 Samuel

with or without a king. Despite being offended by the people's request, which was a rejection of his authority, the Lord gave them a king, though he made it clear that the king would be a vice-regent under his rule.

The books of Samuel focus on three major characters: Samuel, Saul, and David. Their careers overlap: Samuel (1 Sam. 1–16), Saul (1 Sam. 9–31), and David (1 Sam. 16–2 Sam. 24). David, however, is the central character of the story. As the Lord's chosen prophet, Samuel anointed both Saul and David. The prophet made it clear that the Lord had rejected Saul and had chosen David as his replacement. The author of 1–2 Samuel demonstrates David's superiority to Saul. Though David is flawed and tragically fails in many ways, in the end the Lord preserves his rule, in contrast to Saul, whom the Lord rejects and abandons.

1 Samuel

Elkanah . . . had two wives (1:1–2). Except for persons of royalty, monogamy was the norm in ancient Israel. In fact, Elkanah is the only example in Samuel-Kings of a common (nonroyal) person who had two wives.[1] His motivation for doing so probably was Hannah's barren condition. It was important for a man to have offspring, so a husband apparently could take a second wife or concubine when his first wife did not produce a child. This practice is attested earlier in the patriarchal accounts, though in these cases the secondary wife is viewed as a surrogate for the primary wife (Gen. 16:1–2; 30:1–3, 9).

Making a vow, she pleaded, "Lord of Armies, if . . ." (1:11). It was common in the ancient Near East and in ancient Israel for worshipers, when seeking help from a deity in the midst of a crisis, to promise something of value in return. For example, in a prayer from the ancient city of Ugarit worshipers promise the deity Baal a whole list of gifts if only he will drive an enemy army away from the city.[2] In Num. 21:2 the Israelites promise to devote defeated cities to the Lord if he gives them victory in battle. Several psalms speak of paying vows made to the Lord.[3] While this may seem like bargaining with God, it was an accepted way of praying in this culture and, from the worshiper's perspective, an expression of gratitude.

His hair will never be cut (1:11). Though the word "Nazirite" does not occur in verse 11, Hannah's vow that her son's hair would not be cut throughout his life suggests that Samuel was indeed a Nazirite (cf. Num. 6:5; Judg. 13:5). Nazirite vows typically were voluntary and made for a limited period of time, but Samuel's mother dedicated him to the Lord as a lifelong Nazirite.

My horn is lifted up by the LORD (2:1). Hannah, who had prevailed in her struggle with Peninnah, spoke of herself as a bull or ox with a powerful horn (cf. Deut. 33:17; 1 Kings 22:11; Ps. 92:10). Elsewhere "exalt the horn" is used of a military victory (Ps. 89:17, 24; 92:10; Lam. 2:17). In the ancient Near East powerful warrior-kings sometimes compared themselves to a goring bull that uses its horns to defeat its enemies. For example, Ramesses III called himself "a bull . . . relying upon his horns."[4] Hammurabi referred to himself as a "fierce, wild bull, who gores the enemies."[5]

There is no one holy like the LORD (2:2). In her thanksgiving song Hannah declares that the Lord is incomparable. When viewed in its historical setting, this declaration attests to Hannah's strong faith. Many in Israel are worshiping the Canaanite fertility god Baal in hopes that he would give them children (see comments on Judg. 2:11; 1 Sam. 7:4; see the article "The Canaanites and Canaanite Religion"). But Hannah looks to the Lord to provide her with a child. When he answers her prayer, she affirms that there is no one holy like the Lord. In the Ugaritic myths Baal has a prominent position among the assembly of the gods, who are called "sons of the Holy One" (a reference to the god El, who was viewed as the father of the gods). The goddess Anat affirms, "Baal is our king, our judge, over whom there is none."[6] Contrary to Anat's claim that Baal was incomparable, Hannah declares that the Lord alone is deserving of such praise.

The LORD brings death and gives life (2:6). In the Ugaritic myths Baal struggles with Mot, the god of death, and is even defeated and forced to descend temporarily into the underworld land of the dead. Hannah asserts that the Lord, in contrast to Baal, is absolutely sovereign over life and death (see the article "The Canaanites and Canaanite Religion").

He will thunder in the heavens against them (2:10). The fertility deity Baal was also the god of the storm. His worshipers trusted him to provide the rain needed for crops to grow. When they heard thunder, they thought it was the voice of Baal. As the god of the storm, Baal could sound his battle cry (thunder) and attack his enemies with lightning. Yet Hannah knew that the Lord, not Baal, controlled the storm. He thunders against his enemies. Hannah even applied one of Baal's titles ("Most High")[7] to the Lord, as if to emphasize his superiority over the Canaanite deity. Not too long after this, the Lord demonstrates

Statue of the Canaanite god El.

the truth of Hannah's words when he defeats the Philistine army by thundering against them (7:10).

Eli's sons were wicked men (2:12). Eli's sons, Hophni and Phinehas, violate the Lord's prescribed rules for sacrifices in two ways: (1) according to the law (Lev. 7:33–34; 10:14–15; Deut. 18:3), priests were to receive specified portions of the sacrificial animal, but Eli's sons would stick a three-pronged fork into the cooking pot while the meat was boiling and take whatever came out, undoubtedly a sizable amount;[8] (2) the law also specified that the fat of the sacrificial animal must be presented to the Lord and burned first (Lev. 3:16; 7:31), but Eli's sons would demand a portion of the meat before offering the fat.

Ancient oil lamp.

The lamp of God (3:3). According to Exod. 27:20, lamps were burned in the tabernacle during the night. These were small clay lamps filled with oil.

Philistines (4:1). See the article "The Philistines."

Ark of the Lord's covenant (4:3). See comments on Exod. 25:10–22.

A god has entered their camp (4:7). When the Philistines learn that the ark has entered the Israelite camp, they are afraid and declare, "A god [or perhaps "God"] has entered their camp." But then they speak of multiple gods (4:8: "these magnificent gods"). In ancient Near Eastern literature a primary god may come to execute judgment and/or engage in battle, but other gods sometimes would accompany this god. In the Gilgamesh Epic of the flood, Adad is the primary judge, but he is accompanied by other divine figures.[9] In his poetic account of his battle with the Hittites at Kadesh, Ramesses II attributes his success to Amun, but he also praises the goddess Sakhmet for her intervention.[10] In Assyrian annals kings sometimes praise more than one deity for help in battle. Similarly, in Judg. 5 the Lord comes in the storm with the stars (i.e., his angelic army) to fight for Israel against the enemy (vv. 3–4, 20). So the Philistines recognize that Israel's God was leading Israel's army into battle, but at the same time, being polytheistic, they assume that other gods are involved as well.

Thirty thousand of the Israelite foot soldiers (4:10). See comments on Josh. 8:3; Judg. 1:4.

Dagon (5:2–5). Dagon is described as if personally present in his temple. As verse 4 indicates, "Dagon" refers here to an image of the deity. Worshipers in the ancient Near East believed that a god was present in its image, which provided them with a tangible object of worship.[11] Dagon was the chief deity of the Philistines (see the article "The Philistines"). An older interpretation understood him as a fish god (Hebrew *dag* means "fish"), but it is more likely that he was a weather-fertility deity responsible for crops. Scholars debate whether he was fundamentally a storm god or a god of vegetation, but in either case he was associated with fertility. Hebrew *dagan* means "grain," as does Ugaritic *daganu*. In some accounts the storm god Baal is Dagon's son, suggesting the latter is a fertility deity.[12]

Dagon's head and both of his hands were broken off (5:4). The decapitation of Dagon would be viewed as a military defeat. Victorious warriors sometimes cut off the heads and hands of their defeated enemies (17:51; 31:9). In a Ugaritic myth the warrior goddess Anat ties the decapitated heads of her defeated foes into a necklace and attaches their disembodied hands to her belt.[13]

Tumors (5:6). The Hebrew word translated as "tumors" literally means "hills, mounds" and probably refers to swelling of some sort. One theory is that the Lord struck the Philistines with bubonic plague, a symptom of which is swollen lymph glands in the armpit and groin. In response to this affliction the Philistines made golden rats (or mice) and tumors as a guilt offering to the Lord (6:4). Rats are carriers of bubonic plague, a fact that was recognized in the ancient world. Another theory is that the swelling refers to anal ulcers or hemorrhoids brought on by dysentery.

Diviners (6:2). In the ancient Near East divination was a widely used means of discovering the will of the gods (see comments on Deut. 18:10–11). According to John Walton, there were two primary types of divination in the ancient world: (1) "inspired divination," which took the form of prophecy and dreams, was "initiated in the divine realm" and used "a human intermediary"; (2) "deductive divination" also originated with the gods, "but its revelation" was "communicated through events and phenomena that can be observed."[14] The OT law prohibited this type of divination (Deut. 18:10).[15] Deductive divination involved the interpretation of omens, which could be active (provoked) or passive (unprovoked). Active omens included examining the internal organs of animals and casting lots, as well as other methods. Passive omens came in celestial, terrestrial, and physiognomic forms.[16]

Magic also played an important role in ancient Near Eastern religion. Walton explains its relationship to divination: "While divination is concerned with gaining knowledge, magic involves exercising power." Magic involved the use of incantations and rituals designed "to manipulate cosmic forces in pursuit of self-interest" and to ward off the danger associated with bad omens.[17]

The Philistine priests and diviners used both divination and magic. Their suggestion regard-

The seated Philistine goddess Ashdoda (in the shape of a chair).

ing the two cows and the cart is an "ad hoc" form of divination designed to determine if Israel's God really is the source of the calamity they have suffered.[18] The reparation offering, in the form of golden tumors and rats, is a type of sympathetic magic designed to draw off the plague and to appease Israel's God (cf. Num. 21:8–9).[19]

Baals and the Ashtoreths (7:4). See the article "The Canaanites and Canaanite Religion." The plural forms here probably refer to idols present in various local shrines dedicated to the Canaanite deities Baal and Astarte, respectively.[20] The form "Ashtoreth" is a deliberate distortion of Astarte's name that vocalizes the last two syllables of the name to reflect the Hebrew word for "shame" (*bosheth*).[21] Astarte is one of Baal's female consorts in the myths from Ugarit.

The Lord thundered (7:10). See comments on 1 Sam. 2:10. It is no coincidence that the Lord revealed his powerful presence in this way. The people had just rejected Baal, the Canaanite god of the storm (7:4). So it was appropriate that the Lord came in the storm to do battle with his enemies, proving to Israel that he, not Baal, controls the rain and, with it, the power to grant fertility.[22] In the Lord's self-revelation as warrior the thunder was his battle cry. The sheer power of his thunderous voice terrified the Philistine army and sent them into a panic. The image of an enemy fleeing at the sound of the great king's battle cry is a military motif in ancient Near Eastern texts. For example, Amun-Re, in recalling how he had granted Thutmose III victories, states, "Hearing your battle cry they [the enemy] hid in holes."[23] In Ugaritic mythology when "Baal thunders in the clouds . . . The enemies of Baal take to the woods."[24]

A king to judge us the same as all the other nations have (8:5). Israel wants a king like all the nations have (8:4–5, 19). Ancient Near Eastern kings were responsible for ensuring social justice and national security. This sounded good in theory, but in reality royal bureaucracies often were oppressive because kings needed a standing army that must be armed and fed. Evidence from the second millennium BC from Syria-Palestine, particularly the sites of Alalakh, Mari, and Ugarit, supports Samuel's description of what this kind of king would do.[25] The typical king accumulated chariot warriors, craftsmen, and a palace support staff. He conscripted men for military and agricultural service, confiscated land and produce, and taxed crops and livestock.

Saul, an impressive young man . . . a head taller than anyone else (9:2). Reflecting the people's perspective and values, the text focuses on Saul's physical attributes, especially his height (cf. 10:23–24). Physical attributes were prominent in the ancient Near Eastern ideal of kingship.[26] One of the most vivid examples of this is Amenhotep II, who, according to an Egyptian

The mummy of Amenhotep II.

inscription, was "a beautiful youth who was well developed" and was "strong of arms."[27] Skilled in horsemanship, rowing, and archery, he could outrow all others, and he allegedly shot an arrow through a thick copper shield.[28] Miriam Lichtheim points out that "his mummy is that of an exceptionally tall and strongly built man."[29]

Harps, tambourines, flutes, and lyres (10:5). See the article "Musical Instruments in Israel and the Ancient Near East."

You will prophesy with them (10:6). Samuel gives Saul a threefold sign to verify that the Lord has chosen him to be Israel's king. The first two signs demonstrate God's providential presence (10:2–4); the third shows that God intends to empower Saul by his divine Spirit for the task at hand (10:5–6). In accordance with the third sign, Saul meets a group of prophets who are playing music and prophesying. The Spirit comes upon him, and he too begins prophesying, as if changed into a different person (10:9–11). Apparently prophets sometimes used music to induce a trance-like state, in which they would receive prophetic revelation (cf. 2 Kings 3:15–16). Sometimes the Spirit exhibited his presence by inducing the prophet to engage in ecstatic behavior. Later, Saul is overpowered by God's Spirit a second time, prompting him to engage in prophetic behavior (19:23–24). On this occasion he removed his clothing and lay naked on the ground for an entire day. Such ecstatic behavior is not limited to the Bible. In Mesopotamia there was a certain class of prophets who exhibited trance-like behavior when prophesying.[30] Such behavior is also attested at the Phoenician town of Byblos. In an Egyptian report dating to 1100 BC, Wen-Amun, a messenger sent from the pharaoh, tells how a god "took hold of a young man" and "put him in a trance." The young man then delivered a prophetic message from the deity.[31]

Ammonite (11:1). See comments on Gen. 19:37–38.

Gouge out everyone's right eye (11:2). Mutilating defeated enemies was commonplace in the ancient Near East and is vividly portrayed in Assyrian art.[32] There are instances in the OT of a victor blinding a defeated enemy. The Philistines gouged out Samson's eyes (Judg. 16:21), and the Babylonians blinded Zedekiah following the conquest of Jerusalem (2 Kings 25:7). Here, Nahash was willing to spare the lives of the men of Jabesh-gilead, but only if they agreed to let him remove their right eyes. In addition to humiliating them, this would make them incapable of fighting effectively in battle, but would still allow them to be able to grow and harvest crops as tribute to Nahash.[33]

I will call on the LORD, and he will send thunder and rain (12:17). Wheat was sown in November to December and harvested in May, after the rainy season, which ran from October to March.[34] Heavy rain at the time of wheat harvest would have been rare (Prov. 26:1) and consequently serves as a vivid sign of the Lord's displeasure. Samuel's reference to the exodus (12:6–8) would have prompted the people to remember the Egyptian plagues, the seventh of which was hail, accompanied by thunder and rain (the Hebrew terms used in Exod. 9:23, 33, occur together elsewhere only in 1 Sam. 12:18). The hail destroyed the Egyptians' barley and flax (Exod. 9:23–26, 31). So in Israel's case the thunder and rain are ominous, but Samuel does not call for hail. The Lord spares the crops, but the sign makes it clear that Israel must recommit to serving the Lord.

Three thousand chariots (13:5). According to the Hebrew text, the Philistines have 30,000 chariots. The number is either exaggerated for emphasis or the result of textual corruption. Some ancient witnesses read 3,000 (the reading followed by CSB and NIV). This figure, though still high, makes better sense in light of the reference to 6,000 charioteers (or perhaps chariot horses) that immediately follows. Other references to imposing chariot forces in the OT give figures of 900 (Judg. 4:3) and 1,400 (1 Kings 10:26). At the Red Sea the pharaoh had 600 select chariots, in addition to others (Exod. 14:7). These numbers are in line with those found in ancient Near Eastern texts. For example, Thutmose III says that he captured 924 chariots at the battle of Megiddo, and Shalmaneser III reports that the western coalition he faced had over 4,000 chariots, with Ahab of Israel contributing 2,000 of these.[35]

The LORD has found a man after his own heart (13:14). Appealing to ancient Near Eastern texts, some support Kyle McCarter's argument that this passage refers to "a man of God's own choosing." McCarter states that the expression "has nothing to do with any great fondness of Yahweh's [the LORD's] for David or any special quality of David."[36] But this is an incorrect conclusion. Surely the Lord would not just randomly choose someone. He would choose someone who was like-minded. Indeed, the use of the expression in 14:7 favors this: Jonathan's armor-bearer assures him, "I am with you, according to your heart" (that is, like-minded).[37] The Babylonian parallel cited by Philips Long, where Nebuchadnezzar appoints a "king according to his heart" (i.e., according to his choosing) over defeated Jerusalem, may be interpreted along similar lines.[38] The king (governor) chosen would be one who supported Nebuchadnezzar, in contrast to the deposed king of Judah.

No blacksmith could be found . . . because the Philistines (13:19–22). Prior to 1000 BC bronze was used more commonly than iron to make weapons and tools. Ancient furnaces were not capable of melting pure iron. Iron implements had to be heated and then hammered. This wrought iron, though softer than bronze, could hold an edge and a point, so it was used to make tools, plow tips, and swords. A shortage of copper and tin (used to make bronze) and the greater fuel efficiency of iron manufacturing (it required far less wood) led to a preference for iron.[39] As early as the time of Samuel and Saul (ca. 1050 BC) the Philistines had a monopoly on iron manufacturing. They do not allow Israel to have iron weapons and charge them for sharpening farm tools.

Two-thirds of a shekel (13:21). The Philistines charge two-thirds of a shekel to sharpen plow points and other cutting tools. The Hebrew word used for "two-thirds of a shekel" appears only here in the OT, but archaeologists have discovered stone weights inscribed with this word. Their average weight is 0.268 of an ounce.[40]

Urim . . . Thummim (14:41–42). See comments on Exod. 28:2. The Septuagint (an ancient Greek translation of the OT) preserves the original text in 14:41, which is reflected in most modern English translations (e.g., CSB, NIV, ESV). The CSB translation reads, "So Saul said to the Lord, 'God of Israel, why have you not answered your servant today? If the unrighteousness is in me or my son Jonathan, Lord God of Israel, give Urim; but if the fault is in your people Israel, give Thummim.' Jonathan and Saul were selected, and the troops were cleared of the charge."

The Urim (symbolizing condemnation) and Thummim (symbolizing innocence and acquittal) may have been marked lots, or objects, one probably having an inscribed *aleph* (the first letter of the name Urim in Hebrew and of the Hebrew alphabet), the other an inscribed *taw* (the first letter of the name Thummim in Hebrew and the last letter of the Hebrew alphabet).[41] One would phrase a question and then the Urim/Thummim would provide a "yes" or a "no" answer. Or, as in this instance, the Urim could designate one party, the Thummim the other.

The "pim" weight (two-thirds of a shekel).

Attack the Amalekites and completely destroy everything (15:3). See comments on Gen. 14:5–7; Exod. 17:8; 1 Sam. 30:17. The Lord intends to punish the Amalekites for "what the Amalekites did to the Israelites when they opposed them along the way as they were coming out of Egypt" (15:2; cf. Exod. 17:8–16). On that occasion Moses announced that the Lord would "be at war with Amalek from generation to generation" (Exod. 17:16). Moses later commanded Israel to "blot out the memory of Amalek under heaven," and he urged them, "Do not forget" (Deut. 25:19).[42]

The Hebrew verb translated as "totally destroy" (*haram*) in 15:3 indicates that this is a case of the "ban" (*herem*, the noun form). Earlier the Canaanites had been put under the ban (Deut. 7:1–6) and were to be "devoted" to the Lord for destruction (Josh. 6:17, 21), perhaps as an offering of gratitude for the Lord's help (Num. 21:2–3). This concept of the ban was not unique to Israel. It is also attested in the Moabite Stone (Mesha Stela), where King Mesha of Moab boasts that he devoted to his god seven thousand Israelite captives. He states that he had put them "to the ban for Ashtar Kemosh," his god.[43]

Kenites (15:6). See comments on Judg. 4:11.

Idolatry (15:23). See comments on 1 Sam. 19:13.

Saul will hear about it and kill me (16:2). When commissioned to go to Bethlehem to anoint a new king, Samuel expresses his concern that Saul would hear about it and kill him. Samuel lives in Ramah, located about ten miles north of Bethlehem. His journey would take him right through Saul's hometown of Gibeah (15:34) and likely prompt questions from the king.

The Lord sees the heart (16:7). Modern readers tend to associate the heart with the emotions, but the ancient Hebrews understood the heart as the seat of will, conscience, and motives, as well as the emotions.[44] The heart was viewed similarly in ancient Mesopotamia and Egypt.[45]

The lyre (16:16, 18, 23). See the article "Musical Instruments in Israel and the Ancient Near East."

A valiant man, a warrior (16:18). This may seem puzzling at first, for David is depicted in the previous scene as a youthful shepherd (16:11). However, David is old enough to kill wild animals (17:36). Shepherds had to be brave, adept fighters who could protect their flocks from predators and robbers. Ancient Near Eastern art depicts a shepherd carrying a club and portrays individual men protecting

Lyres were small, handheld stringed instruments. Shown here are prisoners playing lyres (from the palace of the Assyrian king Sennacherib).

a deer from a lion by using a curved sword.[46] David has proved himself in this regard (17:34–36). He is especially accomplished with the sling, a particularly deadly weapon (see comments on 1 Sam. 17:49). It is not clear whether David has actually participated in a battle yet, but Saul's servant can be excused if he engages in a bit of hyperbole. Knowing of David's exploits as a shepherd, he realizes that David certainly had the ability of a warrior, even if he lacks actual battle experience.

He was nine feet, nine inches tall (17:4). According to the Hebrew text, Goliath's height is 6 cubits (a cubit is the length of a forearm, approximately 18 inches) and a span (the distance from the tip of the thumb to the tip of the little finger when the hand is opened, approximately 9 inches). So Goliath's height would be approximately 6 × 18 inches + 9 inches = 117 inches, or 9 feet 9 inches. However, some early Greek manuscripts (the Septuagint), Josephus (a first-century Jewish historian), and the Qumran scroll from cave 4 (i.e., the Dead Sea Scrolls) all read "four cubits and a span," which would be 6 feet 9 inches. If these earlier textual witnesses preserve the correct reading, then the Hebrew text either reflects a later tradition that exaggerated Goliath's height or preserves an accidental textual error, perhaps influenced by the reading "six hundred" in 17:7. In Hebrew "six cubits" and "six hundred" are very similar. If the Hebrew text preserves the original reading, then the reading "four cubits" may be an attempt to tone down the story and give it more credibility.[47]

Choose one of your men and have him come down against me (17:8). Goliath challenges Israel to an ordeal of divine judgment through single combat.[48] There are other examples of single combat in ancient Near Eastern literature. A text from Middle Kingdom Egypt (ca. 1800 BC) tells how the hero Sinuhe engaged in single combat with a "hero of Retenu," who fought on behalf of his tribe. He attacked Sinuhe with battle-ax and bow, but Sinuhe brought him down with an arrow and then finished the job with his enemy's own ax.[49] In similar fashion David brings the Philistine champion down with a sling stone and then chops off his head with Goliath's own sword (17:49–51). The Hittite king Hattusilis (ca. 1250 BC) defeated the commander of an enemy army and then routed the enemy army, despite being vastly outnumbered. Following the victory, he dedicated his enemy's weapon to his goddess.[50] When Goliath falls, the Israelites rout the Philistine army (17:51–53) and David eventually dedicates his enemy's sword to the Lord, for it appears later in the sanctuary at Nob (21:8–9).

Put his hand in the bag, took out a stone (17:49). It appears that Goliath expected to fight at close quarters: (1) Saul attempts to outfit David with his armor and sword, as if assuming that there would be a hand-to-hand conflict; (2) David's reference to fighting wild animals at close range suggests that he would fight Goliath the same way; (3) Goliath's movements (17:41) and challenge "come to me" (17:44) indicate that he was expecting a close-range conflict. But David does the unconventional. He fights from a distance and uses a sling to bring Goliath down. Sling stones used in an ancient battle at Lachish (a city of Judah south of Jerusalem) are smooth and round, and made of flint; each is two to three inches in diameter and weighs approximately nine ounces. Philip King and Lawrence Stager estimate that one could propel a sling stone at a speed of 100–150 miles per hour.[51] David picks his ammunition from the stones in the stream, but probably he chooses stones that approximated the standard size used in battles. In the hands of a well-trained warrior the sling could be deadly accurate (Judg. 20:16) (see comments on 2 Kings 3:25).

Jonathan . . . and all Israel and Judah loved David (18:1, 16). Verse 1 states that Jonathan "loved" David as much as he did his own life. Here the word "loved" expresses not so much an emotional feeling, but rather devotion and allegiance (cf. 20:16–17). Likewise, the whole nation, Israel and Judah, "loved" David (18:16), in the sense that they were loyal to him. In the Amarna letters (fourteenth century BC) cities are said to "love" a leader; the term refers to loyalty. For example, in one letter the king of Byblos, writing to the pharaoh in Egypt, says, "Behold the city! Half of it loves the sons of Abdi-ashirta [a rebel] and half of it loves my Lord [Pharaoh]."[52]

Dancing with tambourines . . . three-stringed instruments (18:6). See the article "Musical Instruments in Israel and the Ancient Near East."

Saul was holding a spear, and he threw it (18:10–11). There are examples in the ancient Near East where ecstatic prophets sometimes engaged in violence in conjunction with their prophetic activity. In a text from Ugarit a man complains, "My brothers bathe in their own blood like ecstatics" (cf. 1 Kings 18:28–29).[53] According to the Mesopotamian creation myth Enuma Elish, the

Assyrian soldiers with slings.

goddess Tiamat was "beside herself" like an ecstatic and "turned into a maniac."[54] Saul's prophesying would have been a sign to those around him that the evil spirit was once more tormenting him.

Bride-price (18:25). A bride-price was an amount of money paid by the bridegroom to the bride's father as compensation for the loss of his daughter.[55] Sometimes the bride-price could take a different form, as when Laban accepted Jacob's labor in exchange for his daughters (Gen. 29:15–30) or when Caleb accepted Othniel's capture of a city in exchange for his daughter Achsah (Judg. 1:12). Saul's demand of one hundred Philistine foreskins is motivated by his desire to put David in harm's way so he would be killed. It was more common for warriors to cut off the heads and hands of defeated enemies, but an Egyptian inscription from Pharaoh Merneptah tells how his army cut off the uncircumcised phalli of his Libyan victims.[56]

The lyre (19:9). See the article "Musical Instruments in Israel and the Ancient Near East."

Then Michal took the household idol (19:13). The fact that an idol is in Michal's home, or at least readily accessible to her, is alarming. In the Hebrew text this "idol" is called a *teraphim*. This type of idol is mentioned in a few other passages: (1) Rachel stole Laban's *teraphim* when she left with Jacob (Gen. 31:19, 34–35); (2) Micah owned *teraphim* and used them in his own private shrine, and the Danites stole them (Judg. 17:5; 18:14, 17–18, 20); (3) Samuel told Saul that disobedience to God is as bad in God's sight as worshiping *teraphim* (1 Sam. 15:23); (4) Josiah banned *teraphim* and idols from the land, as required by the law (2 Kings 23:24); (5) the king of Babylon used *teraphim* for divination prior to a battle (Ezek. 21:21); (6) Hosea warned Israel that the Lord would remove *teraphim* from the land as part of his judgment (Hosea 3:4); (7) Zechariah stated that *teraphim*, like diviners, misguide those who consult them (Zech. 10:2).[57] *Teraphim* may have been household idols (Gen. 31:19; 1 Sam. 19:13, 16) used for divination (Ezek. 21:21). Patrick Miller suggests that the *teraphim* were "ancestor figurines" used by those wishing to communicate with the dead (see comments on Gen. 31:19).[58] In any case, the Lord prohibited their use (1 Sam. 15:23; 2 Kings 23:24).

Saul then removed his clothes and also prophesied (19:24). See comments on 1 Sam. 10:6.

Then he and Jonathan kissed each other and wept (20:41). Kissing between members of the same gender could signify a variety of things. A kiss could be an expression of respect and affection, as when a son kisses his father (Gen. 27:26–27; 50:1), a grandson kisses his grandfather (Gen. 48:10), or a son-in-law kisses his father-in-law (Exod. 18:7). It could also express joy, as when relatives or brothers meet, especially after a long separation (Gen. 29:13; 33:4; 45:15; Exod. 4:27). A kiss was also an appropriate expression of affection when people were parting (Ruth 1:9, 14). A kiss sometimes was a sign of honor, as when Samuel kissed the newly anointed king, Saul (1 Sam. 10:1), or a token of acceptance, as when David kissed Absalom (2 Sam. 14:33). In the case of David and Jonathan, their farewell kiss (cf. Ruth 1:9, 14) is a token of their mutual affection, as well as their binding commitment to each other (1 Sam. 20:42).

Every man who was desperate, in debt, or discontented rallied around him (22:2). Groups of mercenaries like this appear elsewhere in Israel's history (Judg. 9:4; 11:3–11; 1 Kings 11:23–25). These groups are similar to the *Habiru*, mercenaries mentioned in the Amarna letters who disturbed Canaan in the early fourteenth century BC. The *Habiru* were organized in small groups, probably consisting of fifty to one hundred, though one Amarna letter does mention a group of four hundred.[59]

The *Habiru* are mentioned in the ancient Amarna tablets, one of which is shown here.

The story of David's exile rings true in its ancient Near Eastern context. A similar story is found in an inscription from Alalakh dating to around 1500 BC. Idrimi eventually became king of Alalakh, but before that happened he had to flee his ancestral home in Aleppo because of an "act of hostility" that threatened his life. He eventually migrated to the land of Canaan, where he lived among *Habiru* warriors for seven years.[60]

He killed eighty-five men who wore linen ephods (22:18). There is evidence from Hittite texts that priests were bound by oaths of loyalty to their king. Violation of such an oath was severely punished. The guilty party would be punished along with his entire family. Saul apparently views his relationship to the priests of Nob in this way.[61] This explains the swift "justice" that he unleashes against all the priests of Nob. However, Saul's servants are not convinced of the justice of the king's decision and refuse to carry out the execution, probably because Ahimelech's defense, in which he assures the king of his loyalty, is convincing. Furthermore, these are the Lord's priests, as Saul acknowledges (22:17) and is emphasized by the narrator through repetition (22:17, 21). In the Hittite material, loyalty to the god is expressed through his representative, the king. But in Saul's case, the Lord has rejected Saul as king in favor of David, so the Lord would not have considered *his* priests bound to Saul.[62]

An ephod (23:6). David inquires of the Lord while in Keilah by consulting an ephod in the possession of Abiathar the priest (cf. 23:9–12). In Exod. 28:4–6 and several other texts an ephod appears to be a priestly or cultic garment. In some cases, as here, an ephod was used to obtain a divine oracle (see also 1 Sam. 30:7–8). McCarter theorizes that the ephod had a pouch containing the Urim and Thummim (see comments on 1 Sam. 14:41–42; Exod. 28:2).[63]

My father (24:11). Saul is David's father-in-law, but his use of "my father" here may indicate more than this literal sense. David may be addressing Saul as his benefactor and protector (see the use of the term "father" in Job 29:16; 31:18; Isa. 9:6; 22:21) to remind him of his dependence on him. In their role as protectors of their people, rulers sometimes viewed themselves as being a father or mother. In a ninth-century-BC Phoenician inscription the ruler Kulamuwa says, "I was to some a father; and to some a mother; and to some I was a brother."[64] Likewise, in a Phoenician inscription dating from around 700 BC the ruler Azitawada says that his god Baal "made me a father and a mother to the Danunians."[65]

A dead dog (24:14). In ancient Israel dogs were not friendly family pets, but rather scavengers that traveled in packs (see 1 Kings 22:38; 2 Kings 9:35–36).[66] The dog is used as a derogatory metaphor in texts from throughout the ancient Near Eastern world, including Mari, Amarna, Assyria, and Lachish.[67]

Three thousand sheep and one thousand goats (25:2). Sheep and goats were the most important domestic animals raised in ancient Israel. Though often sheep are associated with animal sacrifices, they were raised mainly for their wool. Sheep shearing, which took place in the spring, was a festive event. Goats were raised for their milk and also for their hides, which were used to make clothing and tents.[68]

Raisins . . . figs (25:18). Raisins and figs are particularly nutritious and good sources of energy. In 30:12 a famished Egyptian who has had nothing to eat or drink for three days is revived when given water, part of a fig cake, and two clusters of raisins.[69] Figs and raisins would have been especially valuable to David and his men, who spent a great deal of the time traveling.

Go and worship other gods (26:19). These men were basically telling David to go to a foreign country and worship other gods, which was strictly forbidden (Deut. 11:16; 13:6–18; 17:2–7; Josh. 23:16). The underlying assumption in their attitude was that gods had jurisdiction over specific geographical areas, a viewpoint that characterized the ancient Near Eastern world. The Lord, the God of Israel, ruled in Israel and Judah, but Chemosh was the patron deity of Moab, Dagon ruled in Philistine territory, and so forth. David, of course, always maintains his loyalty to Yahweh wherever he goes, but, when exiled, he is unable to participate in the formal worship of Israel's God.[70]

Mediums and spiritists (28:3, 9). The Mosaic law prohibited necromancy (Deut. 18:9–13), which involved conjuring up the spirits of the dead in order to learn about the future. To his credit, Saul had attempted to remove the necromancers (called here mediums and spiritists) from the land. The first term used for the necromancers in 28:3 (*obot*, "mediums"), when used in a singular form, refers to a pit used by a medium to conjure up the spirits of the dead.[71] Saul asks his servants to find "an owner of an *ob*" (28:7, literal translation); he told the medium, "conjure for me by (using) an *ob*" (28:8, literal translation), and Samuel is described as ascending from the ground (28:13; cf. 28:8, 14–15). By extension, the word can refer to the spirit that is conjured up by use of the pit (cf. Lev. 20:27, which reads literally, "a man or woman who has within them an *ob*," and Isa. 29:4, which reads literally, "and your voice will be like an *ob* from the ground"). However, in several other texts the term refers to the medium, especially when it is plural and paired with "spiritists," as here in 28:3 (see also 28:9). As with the case of the medium of Endor, these mediums attempted to conjure up the spirits of the dead, which would speak in a low voice from the pit (Isa. 29:4), perhaps even through the vocal apparatus of the conjurer (Lev. 20:27 may imply this).

The second term used for the necromancers in 28:3 (*yiddeonim*, "spiritists") literally means "knowing one(s)." This may mean that the one so designated had knowledge of how to conjure up the dead or, having contacted a spirit, possessed knowledge of the future. In Isa. 8:19 these mediums/spiritists are described as whispering and muttering, sounds that are associated elsewhere with the chirping and cooing of birds (Isa. 10:14; 38:14; 59:11). The muttering of incantations, used to conjure up the dead, probably is in view here.

The Lord did not answer him in dreams or by the Urim or by the prophets (28:6). As noted above (see comments on 1 Sam. 14:41–42), the Urim, along with the Thummim, may have been marked lots, or objects, one probably having an inscribed *aleph* (the first letter of the name Urim and of the Hebrew alphabet), the other an inscribed *taw* (the first letter of the name Thummim and the last letter of the Hebrew alphabet).[72] An inquirer would phrase a question, and then the Urim/Thummim would provide a "yes" or a "no" answer. Since this device would give a straightforward answer, it is puzzling why Saul received none. However, a similar ritual attested in ancient Assyria suggests that one had to receive the same answer multiple times in succession for it to be legitimate. The Assyrian ritual involved drawing out stones from a bag—a white stone meant "yes," while a black stone meant "no." Kenton Sparks writes, "For the portent to be valid, the procedure had to be repeated three times with the same result; mixed results indicated no answer from the gods."[73] Apparently, Saul could never get the Urim to yield a consistent message.

Why have you disturbed me? (28:15). Samuel's response suggests that he has been resting or sleeping. This same Hebrew verb for "disturb" (*ragaz*) appears in Isa. 14:9, where the arrival of the dethroned king of Babylon "stirs up" Sheol, the land of the dead. The spirits of the deceased kings who already sleep there then rise from their thrones and taunt the newly arrived Babylonian ruler. The word also appears in a fifth-century-BC Phoenician tomb inscription warning the reader not to "disturb" the one lying in the coffin (Tabnit, a former king of the city of Sidon).[74] Isaiah 14:9 depicts the land of the dead as a place where departed spirits are inactive, mirroring the corpse in the grave. Yet they also occupy positions that reflect their status in life. This is consistent with Samuel's response to Saul. He complains of being disturbed, yet still he wears his prophetic robe (28:14). Of course, Jesus later clarifies the nature of the afterlife (see Luke 16:22–26). The description of the afterlife in Isa. 14:9 and Samuel's response to Saul are accommodated to the understanding of ancient Israel, awaiting clarification in the progress of revelation.

Got on camels and fled (30:17). Assyrian art depicts Arabian soldiers fleeing on camelback from Assyrian warriors. One rider controls the camel with a staff, while a second rider shoots arrows at their pursuers. Two types of camels are known in the ancient Near Eastern world: the one-humped dromedary or Arabian camel, and the two-humped Bactrian variety. It is not certain which type is in view in any given OT reference. It is not surprising that the Amalekites used camels (cf. Judg. 6:3–5; 7:12; 1 Sam. 15:3), for they lived in the dry region south of Israel. Camels would have been ideal for transportation in such an area, for they can drink up to twenty-eight gallons of water and are capable of traveling approximately sixty to seventy-five miles in a day.[75]

Draw your sword and run me through (31:4). In the ancient Near East captured kings often were treated with great cruelty (cf. Judg. 1:6–7; 2 Kings 25:7). Assyrian art depicts this vividly, where captured kings are sometimes impaled on stakes. Here, the Philistines' treatment of Saul's corpse (31:9–10) shows that his fears of being tortured are well founded.

They cut off Saul's head (31:9). It was common for victorious warriors to cut off the heads of their defeated enemies. There is abundant evidence for this practice in ancient Near Eastern literature and art, as well as in the Bible. In a Ugaritic myth the warrior goddess Anat ties the decapitated heads of her defeated foes into a necklace.[76] An Assyrian sculpture shows King Ashurbanipal dining on his couch as the head of a defeated Elamite king hangs on a nearby tree.[77] David cut off Goliath's head and kept it as a trophy

The Assyrian king Ashurbanipal sits in the garden with the queen while the head of his enemy hangs in one of the nearby trees.

(1 Sam. 17:51, 54). The residents of the besieged town of Abel threw the head of the rebel Sheba over the wall to Joab (2 Sam. 20:21–22). When Jehu overthrew Ahab, he demanded that the residents of Samaria send him the heads of the king's sons, which he then stacked in two piles (2 Kings 10:6–8).

They . . . hung his body on the wall of Beth-shan (31:10). An Egyptian text describing the exploits of Amenhotep II (1450–1425 BC) tells how he hung the bodies of his enemies on a wall as tangible proof of his victory.[78]

Retrieved the body . . . burned the bodies . . . buried them (31:12–13). Cremation was not common in ancient Israel, though burning is mentioned as a form of execution (Lev. 20:14; 21:9; Josh. 7:25). In the case of Saul and his sons, the decaying flesh was burned and the bones then buried. This probably was an effort to purify the bodies because they had been so badly desecrated.[79]

2 Samuel

The daughters of the Philistines will rejoice (1:20). There are several instances in the Bible of young women celebrating the exploits of warriors (Judg. 10:34; 1 Sam. 18:6–7).

Mountains of Gilboa, let no dew or rain be on you (1:21). Since Gilboa was the site of Saul's violent death, David curses the mountains. In David's thinking, the land has been defiled by blood spilled there (cf. Isa. 24:4–11; 26:21). According to Num. 35:33–34, spilled blood defiles the ground. Similarly, in the Ugaritic story of Aqhat his unjust death at the hands of the goddess Anat prompts Aqhat's father to pronounce a curse. He "uttered

Mount Gilboa.

a spell upon clouds in the heat of the season, upon the rain that the clouds pour down on the summer fruits, upon the dew that falls on the grapes." This prompts Baal to withdraw fertility, so that there is "no dew, no showers, no upsurging (of water) from the deeps, no goodly voice of Ba'alu."[80]

The shield of Saul, no longer anointed with oil (1:21). Shields typically were made of wood covered with leather, which had to be treated with oil to keep it battle ready.[81] The reference to Saul's unoiled shield is a poetic way of saying that he was no longer fighting Israel's wars.

Your love for me was . . . wondrous (1:26). As noted earlier (see comments on 1 Sam. 18:1, 16), the love between David and Jonathan was mutual allegiance sealed by a covenant between them (cf. 1 Sam. 20:16–17).[82] When David says that Jonathan's love was greater than that of women, he does not suggest that it was sexual in nature. Rather, he is simply stating that Jonathan's love (loyalty) was stronger and more enduring than the love (in the romantic sense) he received from women.[83]

Let's have the young men get up and compete (2:14). Abner's description of this encounter suggests that this would be for entertainment. The verb translated as "compete" (NIV: "fight hand to hand") actually means "to make sport, entertain." Abner may have been speaking euphemistically, for this was deadly "entertainment" that precipitates a battle (2:17). It is likely this contest of champions is a variation on the practice of single combat (see comments on 1 Sam. 17:8). Perhaps this encounter between representatives of the warring armies was designed to decide a conflict without a bloody battle being fought. In this case, the outcome was a draw; all twenty-four combatants died.[84]

Abner hit him in the stomach with the butt of his spear (2:23). As archaeology attests, spears had a pointed metal covering on their butt end that gave the spear proper balance for throwing and also allowed it to be stuck in the ground. Asahel did not run into a blunt wooden spear butt, but rather into a pointed metal tip, which ran right through him from the sheer force of the momentum.[85]

Ahinoam . . . Abigail . . . Maacah (3:2–3). As was typical of kings in the ancient Near East, David begins building a harem. One of his wives is Maacah, the daughter of King Talmai of Geshur, located on the east side of the Jordan, north of the Sea of Galilee. David's rival for the throne of Israel, Saul's son Ishbosheth, claimed jurisdiction over Geshur (2:9). It is likely that David's marriage to Maacah is politically motivated, designed to further his royal interests in Geshur and to counter Ishbosheth's influence there. In the ancient Near East kings often arranged for such marriages with the daughters of neighboring kings in an effort to solidify alliances.[86]

Why did you sleep with my father's concubine? (3:7). At this early period in Israel's history a king's concubines were given to his successor (2 Sam. 12:8; 16:21–22; 1 Kings 2:13–25). So Ishbosheth is accusing Abner of plotting to overthrow him as king.

Give me back my wife, Michal (3:14). In the context of ancient Near Eastern law David was within his rights.[87] The Laws of Eshnunna allowed a man to reclaim his wife if he had left his country involuntarily as a captive.[88] Similarly, the Code of Hammurabi allowed a man, if leaving his country involuntarily, to reclaim his wife once he returned, even if she was remarried and had children by her second husband. However, if he voluntarily deserted his city, he could not reclaim his wife upon his return.[89] One could claim that David left voluntarily, but in actuality he was forced to do so by Saul.

For this reason, the law of remarriage in Deut. 24:1–4 does not apply in David's case. This law envisions a situation where a man divorces a woman who then marries a second husband. If the second husband then divorces her or dies, the first husband may not remarry the woman. The law does not apply in David's case because David apparently never agreed to a divorce from Michal; Saul simply took her from him while he was a fugitive and gave her to another man.[90]

A man who can only work a spindle (3:29). As is typical in ancient Near Eastern curses, David calls severe judgment down upon Joab for his crime of murder. The statement in 3:29 translated by the NIV as "who leans on a crutch" is better translated as "who can only work a spindle" (CSB; cf. ESV, NASB). The Hebrew word (*pelek*) refers to a spindle used in weaving (Prov. 31:19). The term is also used of a spindle in the related languages Phoenician

A woman of royalty with a spindle (from Susa).

and Ugaritic.[91] Apparently, since weaving typically was done by women, David is praying that at least some of Joab's descendants would be unfit for typically male work, whether due to disposition or a handicap.[92] Philips Long compares David's curse to a Hittite soldier's oath dating to the second millennium BC. If a soldier breaks his oath of loyalty to the king, the accompanying curse calls for his troops to become women whose weapons are replaced by "the distaff and spindle."[93]

Hung their bodies by the pool in Hebron (4:12). David ordered the assassins Rechab and Baanah to be executed and their hands and feet to be cut off. The Hebrew text reads at this point, "and they cut off their hands and their feet and they hung (them) near the pool in Hebron." There is no stated object for the verb "hung," so we are not certain if the hands/feet were displayed or the mutilated corpses. In either case, this public display lasted probably for just a few hours, as Deut. 21:22–23 prohibits the hanging of a corpse in public overnight.[94]

You will shepherd my people (5:2). Throughout the ancient Near Eastern world kings were viewed as divinely appointed shepherds of their people.[95] For example, a Sumerian text tells how the god Enlil chose Shulgi (2094–2047 BC) to be a shepherd-king: "Enlil chose Shulgi in (his) pure heart, he entrusted the people to him. The lead-rope and the staff he hung on his arm—he is (henceforth) the shepherd of all the lands."[96] According to a Babylonian text, the god Ea enabled King Ammiditana (1683–1647 BC) to shepherd his people. The king led them to "fine pastures and watering places" and made "them lie down in (safe) pastures."[97] The royal metaphor of a shepherd was an apt one, for a king, like a shepherd, was responsible for the safety and security of those entrusted to him.

Jebusites (5:6). See comments on Josh. 9:1; Judg. 1:21; see the article "Canaanites and Canaanite Religion." The Jebusites were one of the groups already inhabiting Canaan when the conquest began. They usually are included in the collective and more general term "Canaanites."

David inquired of the Lord (5:19, 23). Such oracles, delivered by a deity to a king, were common in the ancient Near East. For example, the goddess Ishtar assured the Assyrian king Esar-haddon, "Fear not, O King! Because I have spoken to you (in an oracle) I will not abandon you. Because I have encouraged you, I shall not let you come to shame. I will help you cross the river safely. . . . With my own hands, your foes I shall annihilate. . . . O Esarhaddon, in Arbela, I am your good shield."[98] King Zakkur of Hamath, when besieged by enemies, appealed to his god Ba'lshamayn, who replied, through "seers and diviners," "Do not be afraid! Since I have made [you king, I will stand] beside you. I will save you from all [these kings who] have besieged you." He reports that his god "answered" him.[99] The Egyptian king Ramesses III, following a victory, praised his god: "I have returned in valor, my arms (laden) with captives . . . through the decree which issued from thy mouth. That which thou hast promised has come to pass."[100]

The ruins of a city gate at Nineveh.

The Lord will have gone out ahead of you (5:24). The concept of a deity marching ahead of the appointed leader also appears in the Tel Dan Stela, where the author states that his god Hadad went before him into battle.[101]

They brought the ark of the Lord . . . David offered burnt offerings . . . a raisin cake to each one (6:16–19). This protocol is attested in Assyrian inscriptions. When Ashurnasirpal II (883–859 BC) dedicated his palace in his new capital city at Calah, he invited Ashur and the other gods to the city and offered abundant sacrifices to them. He also invited thousands of guests to a banquet. When Sargon II (721–705 BC) completed his royal city, he, like Ashurnasirpal before him, invited Ashur and the rest of Assyria's gods into the city, offered them sacrifices, and held a royal banquet. Sennacherib (740–681 BC) followed the same protocol when he dedicated Nineveh as his royal city, as did Esar-haddon (680–669 BC) when he restored the palace at Nineveh. Perhaps the most striking parallel to 2 Sam. 6 is the account of how Ashurbanipal (668–627 BC) brought Marduk, the patron deity of Babylon, back to his city after an eleven-year exile in Assyria. There was great rejoicing along the processional route, and sacrifices were offered at prescribed distances along the way.[102]

The Lord himself will make a house for you . . . Your house and kingdom will endure before me (7:11, 16). Some have compared God's covenantal promise to David with royal grants attested in the ancient Near East, especially in Hittite texts. In such grants a king bestowed on a subject a dynasty and/or land. Moshe Weinfeld proposed that the Davidic promise follows the pattern of the promissory grants, which, though typically conditional, could be unconditional in special cases.[103] Gary Knoppers, on the other hand, argues that the Davidic covenant differs from the grants in structure, form, and content.[104] While the grants are, for the most part, conditional, Knoppers does acknowledge that parallels exist between the formulation of the Davidic covenant in 2 Sam. 7 (and Ps. 89) and the Hittite treaty of Tudhaliya IV with Ulmi-Teshup. In both cases, a continuing dynasty is assured, even if a son is disobedient and must be severely disciplined.[105] Likewise, in Tudhaliya's treaty with Kurunta he assures Kurunta that "he will not throw out his son," even if the son sins and is subjected to severe discipline. The disobedient son will not lose his "house" (dynasty) or land; it must be given to his direct descendant.[106] It should be noted, however, that this treaty does make provision for the destruction of Kurunta and his posterity if he rebels against Tuhaliya or his descendants who succeed him on the throne.[107]

He hamstrung all the horses and kept a hundred chariots (8:4). Horse-drawn chariots were an essential part of Near Eastern armies and were greatly valued by kings. For example, in the Ugaritic Kirta Epic, King Pabil offers Kirta silver, gold, slaves, horses, *and* chariots if he will terminate his siege of Pabil's city. The OT frequently describes powerful armies, including those of Egypt, Assyria, and Babylon, as containing horses and chariots. The horse was a symbol of military might, and its very appearance and mannerisms struck fear into the heart of those being attacked (Jer. 8:16; Hab. 1:8). Because of its military importance, the horse was viewed as a guarantee of security (Isa. 30:16) and an object of trust (Ps. 20:7). In the Phoenician Karatepe inscription Azitawaddu boasts that he "acquired horse upon horse" with the aid of Baal and the gods.[108] However, the Lord wanted his people to trust in his ability to protect and deliver, not in horses and chariots. Moses urged Israel not to fear horses and chariots and assured them that the Lord would give them victory in battle (Deut. 20:1). The law of Moses explicitly prohibited Israel's king from accumulating horses and developing a chariot force (Deut. 17:16). David was faithful in this regard. Rather than keeping the horses of the defeated enemy and building a chariot force of his own, he disabled all but one hundred of them, which he may have used for non-military purposes.

Hanun . . . shaved off half their beards, cut their clothes (10:4). Hanun's treatment of David's servants is particularly humiliating in a culture where beards were a source of male identity and public nudity was

A wall relief from Assyria depicting a king in his chariot.

considered shameful (Isa. 20:4). But what made the action particularly insulting was that the messengers represented the one who sent them and were to be treated with the same respect as their master. This is why the angel of the Lord at times speaks as God (Gen. 31:11–13; Judg. 2:1–3), and humans who encounter the angel sometimes react as if they have seen God himself (Gen. 16:13; Judg. 6:22; 13:22). In the Ugaritic Baal myth the god Yam's messengers enter the divine assembly, refuse to bow before El, and report their lord's words. The god El addresses them as Yam and speaks to them as if he is talking directly to Yam.[109] When Hanun humiliates David's messengers, he insults David himself and the nation he rules. This explains why David regards the insult as an act of aggression and responds militarily.

A clay figurine of a bathing woman.

David . . . strolled around on the roof (11:2). The roof of David's palace, like the roof of the typical Israelite house, was flat, allowing one to walk around upon it. During warm weather, people sometimes slept on the roof.[110]

He saw a woman bathing (11:2). Bathsheba may have been sitting in a tub. A clay figurine found at Achzib dating to the eighth or seventh century BC shows a woman bathing herself as she sits in an oval tub.[111] Bathsheba probably is purifying herself of her menstrual uncleanness. According to Lev. 15:19–24, a menstruating woman was ritually unclean for seven days. It probably is right after this that David has relations with her.

When the time of mourning ended (11:27). The period of mourning probably was seven days in length (Gen. 50:10; 1 Sam. 31:13 = 1 Chron. 10:12).[112]

He must pay four lambs for that lamb (12:6). Exodus 22:1 provides the legal background for David's decision: "Whoever steals an ox or a sheep and slaughters it or sells it must pay back five head of cattle for the ox and four sheep for the sheep" (NIV). The fulfillment of David's self-proclaimed punishment comes in the following chapters, as he loses four sons: the anonymous child to whom Bathsheba gives birth, Amnon, Absalom, and Adonijah.

I gave . . . your master's wives into your arms (12:8). It was customary in the ancient Near East for a king to inherit his predecessor's harem.[113] Speaking within the framework of the cultural context of the time, the Lord is not endorsing polygamy, but is simply reminding David of all that he has given him.

I'll go to him, but he will never return to me (12:23). David's statement reflects the typical view of the afterlife in this culture at this time. David understood that no one returns from the land of the dead. Passage between the realms of the living and the dead is strictly one way. In ancient Mesopotamian texts the subterranean world of the dead is called "the land of no return." Seven gates close behind the one who enters this land, preventing a return to the land of the living.[114]

Rabbah of the Ammonites (12:26). This site is located in the modern city of Amman, the capital of Jordan. On the Ammonites, see comments on Gen. 19:37–38.

Joab . . . captured the royal fortress (12:26). Cities sometimes had a royal fortress that was heavily fortified and situated on steep terrain above the city proper. In this case, Joab took the fortress, but he left the rest of the city for David to conquer (12:28).[115]

Otherwise I will be the one to capture the city, and it will be named after me (12:28). Conquerors sometimes renamed a city, indicating that it now belonged to them (Num. 32:42). Joab may have this in mind here, or he may be speaking of some kind of ceremony in which the conqueror's name is invoked over the defeated city to indicate that he now officially possesses it.[116] The Hebrew text reads literally here, "Otherwise I will take the city and my name will be called over it." In either case, Joab was concerned that he, the general of the army, would be viewed as the city's conqueror, instead of King David.

Please, speak to the king, for he won't keep me from you (13:13). Tamar's proposal is difficult to harmonize with the Mosaic law, which prohibited a man from having sexual relations with his sister or half-sister. Violation of this law was a serious, perhaps even capital, offense (Lev. 18:9, 11; 20:17; Deut. 27:22; cf. Ezek. 22:11). It is possible that this law was not being followed at this time.

Sending me away is much worse (13:16). Tamar's request appears to reflect Deut. 22:28–29, which says that the rape of a virgin, while not a capital crime, requires the guilty party to pay a fine and to marry the victim. This law seems odd and even cruel to modern readers. While not reflecting God's perfect moral standard, it did provide some protection for the woman in this male-dominated society with its taboos. After being raped, a woman would be viewed as damaged goods and would be unable to find a husband. This law made sure that a woman in such circumstances at least was protected economically. Knowing this, Tamar realizes that marriage to Amnon would be her only chance to salvage her future. Of course, her proposal seems to assume that such a marriage would not violate the prohibitions against having sexual relations with one's sister (see comments on 2 Sam. 13:13).

Tamar put ashes on her head and tore the long-sleeved garment she was wearing (13:19). Tamar in her despair places ashes on her head, tears the long robe symbolizing her virginity (13:18), and puts her hand (the

Hebrew text has the singular "hand" in 13:19) on her head as she walks along wailing. Putting ashes on one's head and tearing one's garment were typical mourning rites (1 Sam. 4:12; 2 Sam. 1:11), and the torn garment additionally symbolized the violation of her virginity. Putting one's hand on one's head while walking along also symbolized the pain of grief. In the Egyptian story "The Two Brothers," dating to around 1225 BC, the older brother grieves his separation from his younger brother by smearing himself with dirt and putting his hand on his head as he returns to his home.[117]

The king is able to discern the good and the bad like the angel of God (14:17). The woman of Tekoa compares David to an angel who possesses wisdom and can discern between right and wrong. This is a quality possessed inherently by God as creator that he has granted to his angelic entourage (cf. Gen. 3:5, 22). In Prov. 30:2–4 Agur admits he is a mere human being and does not possess the supernatural wisdom that characterizes "the holy ones" (the form is plural in Hebrew) who surround God's heavenly throne (cf. Job 15:15; Ps. 89:5–7; Dan. 8:13; Zech. 14:5). Similarly, in the ancient Mesopotamian Gilgamesh Epic the Tarzan-like Enkidu's newly acquired wisdom makes him divine in the eyes of others. The woman responsible for helping him achieve this status says to him, "Thou art wise, Enkidu, art become like a god!"[118]

If only someone would appoint me judge in the land (15:4). Absalom presents himself to the people as a champion of justice, in contrast, he stresses, to his father's failed administration. In the ancient Near Eastern world one of a king's primary responsibilities was to promote and execute justice in his realm.[119] If a king failed to do so, he was considered unfit to rule. A good illustration of this can be seen in the Ugaritic Kirta Epic, which tells how King Kirta's son accuses his ill father of neglecting justice and declares his intention to take the throne: "You let your hands fall slack; you do not judge the widow's case, you do not make a decision regarding the oppressed and you do not cast out those who prey upon the poor. Before you, you do not feed the orphan, behind your back the widow. . . . So descend from your kingship, I will reign."[120]

Shimei . . . yelling curses as he approached (16:5–13). This does not refer to shouting obscenities or using profane language, as in modern English. A "curse" was a formal appeal to God to bring judgment down upon the one being cursed, whose guilt was assumed. For example, in 2 Kings 2:24 Elisha "cursed" "in the name of the Lord" the boys who were insulting him, and two bears immediately appeared and mauled them. Shimei is convinced that David is guilty of murdering members of Saul's royal household, so he calls upon God to judge David.

David's friend Hushai (16:16). Although some translations refer to Hushai as "David's friend," the expression is not referring simply to friendship as people think of it today. The expression used here probably is an official title for the king's "confidant" or "privy counselor." A similar title appears in Egyptian texts, and such an official is in view in 1 Kings 4:5, where the priest Zabud, the king's close advisor, is called "friend of the king."[121]

Absalom . . . slept with his father's concubines in the sight of all Israel (16:21–22). To show that he is the new king, Absalom takes David's concubines as his own and sleeps with them. This practice is attested elsewhere in the ancient Near East. For example, the Assyrian king Sennacherib (704–681 BC) took the concubines (literally, "women of the palace") of both Hezekiah, king of Judah, and Merodach-baladan, a Babylonian ruler, as spoils of war.[122]

All Israel will bring ropes to that city, and we will drag its stones (17:13). The reference to ropes may allude to using "grappling hooks attached to ropes" to tear down the city walls.[123] It was common practice to level a city and reduce it to rubble after a battle, especially if the city was viewed as rebellious (cf. Judg. 9:45; 20:48; 1 Kings 20:10; 2 Kings 3:25; 8:12; 25:10).[124]

The mule under him kept going, so he was suspended in midair (18:9). As Absalom is fleeing from David's men, his head gets caught in a tree. Tradition says his hair became entangled in the branches. Absalom's mule runs out from beneath him, leaving him dangling in midair. The mule is a royal mount (13:29), so this incident has symbolic significance. Just as Absalom loses his mule, so he is about to lose the throne he has stolen from his father.[125]

Raised up a huge mound of stones over him (18:17). This may have been a form of burial for accursed enemies. Both Achan and the king of Ai were buried in this fashion (Josh. 7:26; 8:29). These are the only other instances of this form of burial in the OT. A similar incident is described in Josh. 10:27, where Joshua buried five enemy kings in a cave and then covered its mouth with large stones.[126]

By . . . hating those who love you (19:6). Joab uses "love" and "hate" in their covenantal sense of loyalty/disloyalty. David's response suggests that he is more loyal to the disloyal Absalom than he is to his faithful soldiers. A good illustration of the use of love/hate terminology in this sense can be seen in the Amarna letters, where Abdi-Heba of Jerusalem asks the pharaoh's commissioner, "Why do you love the Apiru but hate the mayors?"[127]

Forced labor (20:24). Throughout the ancient Near Eastern world kings used forced-labor crews for building projects. Typically these crews comprised prisoners of war and criminals. The precise makeup of David's forced-labor crews is not specified, but later his son Solomon utilized the offspring of Canaanites whom Israel had not exterminated (1 Kings 9:20–21). According to 1 Kings 9:22, he did not assign Israelites to these work crews, yet 1 Kings 5:13–18 indicates that Israelites were used as stonecutters for special assignments.[128]

There was a famine for three successive years (21:1). The Gibeonite treaty, which Saul violated, was protected by an oath and its accompanying "curses" (see comments on Josh. 9:18; 9:21). Saul's crime brought famine upon the land, which was a typical curse in west Semitic treaties.[129] There is a parallel to this famine in Hittite literature from the fourteenth century BC.[130] The Hittites experienced a plague for several years. When the king inquired of the storm god, he was informed that his father had violated a peace treaty with the Egyptians. The Hittite king confessed this sin to his god, presented sacrifices, and offered to make compensation for the transgression.

Let seven of his male descendants be handed over to us so we may hang them (21:6–9). When David asks the Gibeonites how they might be appeased, they demand that seven of Saul's descendants be handed over. The Gibeonites execute them and then leave their corpses exposed. In violation of Israel's ancient treaty with the Gibeonites, Saul had tried to exterminate them. The continuation of their line was jeopardized, so much so that their standing in Israel was threatened. So from the Gibeonites' perspective, it was only fair that the punishment would in turn diminish Saul's line.[131] This might seem to violate Deut. 24:16, which states that children must not be punished for the sins of their parents. Yet the Lord warned his enemies that their sin would have negative consequences in their families throughout their lifetime (Exod. 20:5; 34:7; Num. 14:18).

There are several incidents in which God's punishment included the sinner's children. For example, the earth swallowed up the children of Dathan and Abiram when God judged their rebellious parents (Num. 16:27, 32). Achan's children were executed along with their disobedient father (Josh. 7:24–26). In accordance with David's self-imposed punishment, the Lord took the lives of four of his children because of his sin against Uriah (2 Sam. 12:5–6, 10; cf. 12:14–15; 13:28–29; 18:15; 1 Kings 2:25). In each case the sinner blatantly rebelled against God. The same is true in 2 Sam. 21, for the Lord was the guarantor of the treaty with the Gibeonites. When Saul sinned against the Gibeonites, he rebelled against God. Apparently in these cases where blatant rebellion against God was involved, the Lord, as the source of all life and the one who grants children as a blessing, was justified in punishing the sinner's children and removing his blessing.

There is a precedent for this in Hittite laws pertaining to sacrilege. Jacob Milgrom explains that in the Hittite laws, which deal with the "misappropriation of sanctums," there are three forms of punishment: (1) "death by the gods (collective—the family)," (2) "death by humans (collective)," and (3) "death by humans (criminal only)."[132] He explains, "If the Hittite gods are doing the punishing, then not only the offender but also his or her household are killed." In contrast, if "the juridical authorities convict the offender, they will execute the criminal alone and will not include his family." However, there is an exception to the latter: "the authorities may execute an offender together with his family, but only if the culprit has been *convicted* by the gods (by ordeal or by oracle)."[133] Saul's crime fits under Milgrom's second category, for God convicted Saul through an oracle given to David (2 Sam. 21:1). Under Milgrom's categories, the judgment upon Dathan and Abiram, as well as the punishment of David, would fall under category 1, and the punishment of Achan and Saul under category 2 (note the lot casting in Achan's case [Josh. 7:16–18] and the oracle in Saul's case [2 Sam. 21:1], not to mention the famine!). Milgrom states that "Israelite law operates with two postulates: (1) sins against God are not punishable by human beings; and (2) collective punishment is a divine right that may not be usurped by humans."[134]

He bent the heavens and came down, total darkness beneath his feet . . . blazing coals were ignited (22:10, 13). The description of the Lord thundering in the storm clouds and hurling lightning bolts (22:8–16) has numerous parallels in ancient Near Eastern literature. Such imagery is used of storm deities and also appears in royal annals where warrior-kings use such language to depict their prowess and exploits in battle.[135] The Ugaritic myths depict the Canaanite storm god Baal shaking the earth with his thunder. He is called "rider of the clouds" and hurls lightning bolts at his enemies.[136]

He rode on a cherub and flew (22:11). The image of the Lord mounting cherubim (in this case, one cherub) and soaring on the wings of the wind may seem bizarre to us, but it is similar to the way storm deities were depicted in the culture. Elsewhere in the Bible cherubim are described as winged creatures possessing both human and animal characteristics (Exod. 25:20; 37:9; 1 Kings 6:24–27; Ezek. 10:8, 19). Here in 22:11 the poetic parallelism suggests that the cherub is a personification of the wind, which carries the Lord along like a chariot (Ps. 104:3). There are numerous cases in ancient Near Eastern literature and art of deities riding both beasts and the wind. For example, the Sumerian god Ishkur rides the

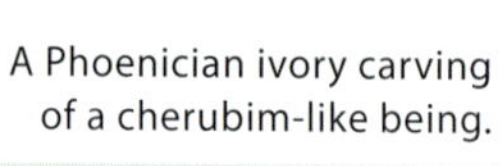

A Phoenician ivory carving of a cherubim-like being.

storm and a great lion, and he harnesses the seven winds as though they were a team of animals.[137] In the Atrahasis Epic, the Babylonian story of the flood, the storm god mounts a chariot that is pulled by the four winds.[138]

The LORD rewarded me according to my righteousness (22:21–25). In these verses David affirms his loyalty to the Lord as the basis for his deliverance. This notion that deities reward faithful servants is attested throughout ancient Near Eastern literature. For example, in Sargon II's letter to Ashur he asserts that he is loyal to the gods. He "carefully observes the law of Shamash" (the sun god who promotes justice) and waits "reverently upon the word of the great gods, never violating their ordinances." His commitment to justice prompts the gods to support him.[139]

With you I can attack a barricade . . . I pursue my enemies and destroy them (22:30–46). David tells how the Lord trained him for battle, assured him of victory, and enabled him to cut down his enemies on the battlefield. This report of the king's divinely aided victory in battle has numerous parallels in ancient Near Eastern texts from a variety of chronological periods and geographical locations. These include the Sumerian ruler Shulgi (2094–2047 BC), the Egyptian pharaoh Ramesses II (1290–1224 BC), the Assyrian king Ashur-nasir-apli II (883–859 BC), the Moabite king Mesha (830 BC), and the Assyrian ruler Sargon (721–705 BC).[140]

With my God I can leap over a wall (22:30). The Hebrew verb used here means "to leap, spring." To emphasize God's enablement, David describes himself leaping over the wall of the enemy's city. Similar hyperbolic descriptions appear in the Assyrian annals of Ashurnasirpal II and of Sargon.[141] Ashurnasirpal claimed that his warriors "flew" like a bird against a mighty citadel that "had the form of a mountain peak" and "hovered like a cloud in the sky." Sargon reported that his army jumped across the Lower Zab River as if it were a mere "ditch."

He trains my hands for war (22:35). David is emphasizing that the Lord is responsible for his success. Two Egyptian reliefs illustrate this nicely.[142] In one the god Seth stands behind young Thutmose III with his hands on his shoulder and arm as he teaches the king how to shoot a bow. The second shows the god Month helping Thutmose IV shoot his bow from his chariot.

You have given me the shield of your salvation (22:36). The image of the king receiving a weapon from his God is a common one in the ancient Near East, used to emphasize the deity's role in the king's victory.[143] In a relief from Medinet Habu, Ramesses III receives a sickle-sword from the god Amun. In the accompanying inscription Amun says to the king, "Take to thee the sword, my son, my beloved, that thou mayest smite the heads of the rebellious countries."[144] In another inscription Amun tells Ramesses III, "I give thee my sword as shield for thy breast, while I remain the (magical) protection of (thy) body in every fray."[145] Assyrian kings receive bows and javelins from their gods prior to battle. Sennacherib describes his battle preparations as follows: "The mighty bow which Assur had given me, I seized in my hands; the javelin, piercing to the life, I grasped." In another text he recalls, "Assur and Ishtar have given me an invincible weapon and have opened my hand for the destruction of the enemies of Assyria." Esar-haddon states, "Ishtar, queen of battle and warfare, a mighty bow, a monstrous javelin, she gave me as a gift."[146]

My enemies . . . fall beneath my feet (22:38–39). David's defeated foes grovel at his feet as they recognize his sovereignty. Parallels abound in ancient Near Eastern battle accounts. For example, the Egyptian god Amun tells Thutmose III, "I cause thy foes to fall beneath thy sandals."[147] It is said of Ramesses III, "As for the rebels who know not Egypt forever, they hear of his strength, coming with praise, trembling in their limbs at the (mere) mention of him, saluting with their hearts for terror of him." The Assyrian king Sargon, after a victorious campaign, boasts that subdued princes were overcome by his "awe-inspiring splendor," fell before him, "begged" him to "spare their lives," and kissed his feet.[148]

Like the morning light when the sun rises (23:4). David quotes the Lord as saying that a righteous ruler who fears God is "like the light of the morning at sunrise." Light may signify divine deliverance and renewed blessing (Isa. 9:2) associated with God's presence (Isa. 60:1–3). The comparison of a righteous king to the light of the sun brings to mind Ps. 84:11, where the Lord, in his role as a just king who protects his people, is called "sun and shield." The comparison of a king to the sun is common in ancient Near Eastern literature, where examples abound from the city of Ugarit (in letters to the Hittite overlord) and Amarna (in letters to the pharaoh). The Assyrian kings Shalmaneser III, Ashurnasirpal II, and Esar-haddon use the epithet "sun" of themselves.[149]

David's warriors (23:8). The mighty warriors listed here may have served as David's royal bodyguard. The list includes some foreigners, such as Zelek the Ammonite and Uriah the Hethite (23:37, 39). Foreign mercenaries were common in armies of the time. During the time David was running from Saul, he himself, along with his men, served as mercenaries to the Philistine king Achish (1 Sam. 27). Later, when he had become king, David hired mercenaries from the Kerethites, Pelethites, and Philistines (2 Sam. 8:18; 15:18).[150]

Benaiah . . . killed a lion (23:20). Ancient Near Eastern literature and art depict mighty warrior-kings hunting down lions to demonstrate their prowess.[151] Since shepherds sometimes had to protect their flocks from lions and other predators (cf. 1 Sam. 17:34–35), such a demonstration perhaps symbolized their ability to shepherd the people placed under their care.

Go, count the people (24:1). There is ample evidence for the taking of censuses in the ancient Near Eastern world. Typically a census was taken for levying taxes, organizing a state labor force, or assessing a state's military strength.[152] David's census was motivated by military concerns (24:2). It is not entirely clear why this census was wrong. Perhaps it reflected lack of faith (note Joab's objection in 24:3) or was not conducted according to regulations governing ritual purity (Exod. 30:11–16).[153]

1–2 Kings

CATHERINE L. McDOWELL

Introduction. Most scholars concur that the books of 1–2 Kings, which cover the period from the end of David's reign (ca. 970 BC) to the destruction of the Solomonic temple in 586 BC, were largely written and compiled during the Babylonian exile in the sixth century BC by an anonymous Judean or group of Judeans, for the purpose of providing a historical-theological explanation of Israel's demise. Earlier partial editions may well have existed in the preexilic period, but given that the concluding events reported in 2 Kings 25:27–30 occurred in 562/561 BC, the final form must postdate this event. The author(s) apparently had access to many historical sources, including the book of the annals of Solomon (1 Kings 11:41), the annals of the kings of Israel (1 Kings 14:19), the annals of the kings of Judah (1 Kings 14:29), and perhaps some of the preexilic prophetic books and other official records. The author(s) also had a strong acquaintance with Deuteronomy, as indicated not only by the use of Deuteronomic language (e.g., Deut. 4:29; 6:2; 8:6; 11:1) but also by the emphasis on the Mosaic covenant and the evaluation of Israel's kings in light of its stipulations.

1 Kings

The Contradiction of Solomon: Splendor and Apostasy (1 Kings 1–11)

King David was old (1:1). According to the figures in 2 Samuel 5:4 and 1 Kings 2:11, David would have been about seventy years old at this point, which was well beyond the average male lifespan in the first millennium BC.

He prepared chariots, cavalry, and fifty men to run ahead of him (1:5). Chariots were used throughout the ancient Near East for ceremonial parades, travel, hunting, and battle. A typical Egyptian chariot consisted of a lightweight, wooden and leather carriage that held the driver and an archer or a javelin thrower. Hittite chariots were larger, supporting a driver, a javelin thrower, and a shield bearer. The runners were a group of young men who ran before the king's chariot as escorts in parades and royal ceremonies.

Rests with his fathers (1:21). The Hebrew expression can be translated literally as "to lie down with one's fathers/ancestors." An Israelite family tomb from the seventh century BC discovered at Ketef Hinnom, just south of the Temple Mount in Jerusalem, illustrates this concept. The tomb contained several burial chambers, each of which was large enough to hold multiple bodies. This allowed for family members literally to "lie down" or be "laid to rest" with their ancestors.

Have my son Solomon ride on my own mule (1:33). In the ancient Near East mules were considered fitting transport for royalty (cf. 2 Sam. 13:29; 18:9; Zech. 9:9; Matt. 21:1–11). This is stated explicitly in a letter written to King Zimri-Lim (eighteenth century BC) of Mari in western Syria: "[If] you are the king of the Ḫaneans, you are, moreover, a 'king of the Akkadians.' [My lord] should not ride horses [i.e., in tribal fashion]. May my lord drive in a wagon and mules [i.e., in a "civilized" manner], and may he [thus] honor his royalty."[1]

The Cherethites . . . the Pelethites (1:38). Foreign soldiers frequently served in the armies of the ancient Near East. The Cherethites and the Pelethites probably were mercenaries from Crete and Philistia, as their names imply.

The main gate to Megiddo.

The ruins of a large building at Megiddo, possibly Solomon's stables.

Took the horn of oil . . . and anointed Solomon (1:39). In ancient Israel anointing with oil was part of the enthronement ceremony for the king (cf. 1 Sam. 10:1; 16:3; 2 Kings 9:6; 2 Kings 11:12). This apparently was practiced among the Hittites as well. Hattusili III, in a letter to the king of Assyria, complains that the king has neglected to send him the oil of kingship needed for his coronation. There is no decisive evidence from Egypt that pharaohs were anointed with oil at their accession. However, one of the Amarna letters (fourteenth century BC) refers to the installation of the Egyptian vassal Taku with oil: "When Manahpiya, the king of Egypt, your ancestor made [T]a[ku], my ancestor, a king in Nuhasse, he put oil on his head and [s]poke as follows: 'whom the king of Egypt has made a king, [and on whose head] he has put [oil], [no] one [shall . . .].'"[2]

David rested with his fathers (2:10). See comments on 1 Kings 1:21.

Solomon made an alliance with Pharaoh king of Egypt by marrying Pharaoh's daughter (3:1). Marriage among royal families was a common means of establishing political alliances, formalizing treaties, and securing the loyalty of one's vassals. The practice is well attested among the diplomatic correspondence of the Mari archives in Syria and the Egyptian Amarna letters. By marrying his daughter to Solomon, the pharaoh, likely Siamun (979–960 BC), secured a formidable ally on his northern border.

City of David (3:1). David conquered the Jebusite city known as the fortress of Zion (2 Sam. 5:7) and claimed it for himself. This area, known from then on as "the city of David," was located on a small spur of land situated between the Tyropoeon and Kidron Valleys in Jerusalem, just southeast of what would later become the Temple Mount.

The high places (3:2–3). The remains of what may have been an early Israelite high place (late thirteenth century to early twelfth century BC) were discovered in 1980 on Mount Ebal. Excavations revealed a large, rectangular structure (24 feet long by 29 feet wide by 9 feet high) made of unhewn stones and filled with dirt, ashes, and the bones of sacrificed animals.

In charge of forced labor (4:6). See comments on 2 Chron. 2:2. Solomon made extensive use of forced labor for the construction of his royal palace, the city wall surrounding Jerusalem, and his many building projects at Hazor, Megiddo, and Gezer (cf. 9:15). A reference to the use of forced labor in

Jerusalem during the Iron II period was discovered on a green quartz scaraboid seal dating to the seventh century BC. The inscription reads, "Belonging to Pela'yahu, who is over [in charge of] the forced labor."[3]

Stalls of horses for his chariots (4:26). Large, tripartite, pillared buildings from the period of the monarchy have been discovered at the cities of Megiddo, Hazor, and Beth-shemesh. Each unit consists of a central hall with aisles on either side, divided from the hall by rows of pillars. These buildings may have been horse stables, although some argue that they were storerooms.

All the wisdom of Egypt (4:30). Egypt was well known in antiquity for its wisdom literature, which addressed issues of justice, giving false testimony, avoiding evil, coveting, forgiving debts, parenting, humility, morality, and friendship. Given God's common grace and the universality of human experience, it comes as no surprise that some Egyptian and biblical proverbs are strikingly similar. Biblical wisdom is distinct, however, in claiming that the source of all wisdom is the Lord, the God of Israel (see the introduction in the commentary on Proverbs).

King Hiram of Tyre (5:1). The ancient city of Tyre was on a small island located just off the southern Phoenician coast of Lebanon. During Hiram's lengthy reign (969–936 BC or 980–950 BC) Phoenicia gained tremendous wealth through international sea trade, as exemplified in the gilded and emerald-studded columns at the entrance to the Melqart temple. The famous temple is described by Herodotus (*Histories* 2.44) and depicted in an Assyrian relief from Khorsabad dating from the late eighth or early seventh century BC.

The Lord put his enemies under his feet (5:3). This expression refers to the defeat and subjugation of one's enemies (cf. Mal. 4:3). The Behistun monument in Persia depicts such an action. On this monument King Darius I of Persia (522–486 BC) stands with his left foot firmly on the chest of his defeated enemy.

The Behistun monument in Persia. Note that King Darius I (third from left) stands with his foot on the chest of his enemy.

Your son . . . will build the temple (5:5) Although nothing of the Solomonic temple has survived, the archaeological remains of a Neo-Hittite temple in Ain Dara, Syria, in use from about 1300 to 740 BC, provide an excellent par-

Ruins of the Ain Dara temple (in Syria).

allel to the description of the Solomonic temple in 1 Kings 6–7 and 2 Chron. 2–4. Although larger than the temple Solomon would build, the Ain Dara temple had a similar three-part floor plan, including an entryway with two columns, a main hall, and a smaller room (holy of holies) at the rear of the building. Like the Solomonic temple, the Hittite temple was surrounded on three sides by multistoried rooms for storage, and its walls were decorated with lions, winged sphinxes (similar to the biblical cherubim), floral imagery, and geometric patterns (cf. 1 Kings 6:29, 32, 35). These parallels should not be surprising. Rather, they attest to a common ancient Near Eastern architectural and iconographic tradition that God used to reveal himself.

Cedars from Lebanon . . . not a man among us knows how to cut timber like the Sidonians . . . I will make them into rafts to go by sea (5:6–9). The word "Sidonian," derived from the name of the city of Sidon on the Phoenician coast (south of the modern city of Beirut), is a general term for "Phoenician." A relief from the Assyrian king Sargon II's palace at Dur-Sharruken (modern Khorsabad) depicts ten Phoenician ships, identified by their horse-headed prows and fish tails, transporting cedar logs.

Cherubim (6:23–28). The Lord's divine attendants referred to as "cherubim" are described as creatures with animal and human features, much like those supernatural beings depicted in numerous ivory carvings found at Fort Shalmaneser in Nimrud (ancient Kalhu), as well as the two Neo-Hittite creatures flanking the entrance to the Ain Dara temple (ca. 1300–740 BC) in northern Syria. The similarities demonstrate that the composite nature of the heavenly creatures identified in the Bible as cherubim was familiar to non-Israelites.

Palm trees . . . flower blossoms (6:29, 31, 35). Floral imagery was common in the sacred art and architecture throughout the ancient Near East because it represented the abundance and fertility associated with the presence of the gods. In a relief from Nineveh the Assyrian king Ashurbanipal (668–627 BC) is shown worshiping in a small temple or shrine. There is an altar situated outside the temple on the path leading up to the shrine. The sacred building is surrounded on all sides by a beautiful garden boasting a variety of trees, shrubs, and orchards, through which irrigation canals flow.

The cast metal basin (7:23). This large tank of cast bronze may have represented the forces of watery chaos alluded to throughout Scripture (Job 26:12; Ps. 29:3; 93:3–4; 107:25, 29; Isa. 51:9–10; Zech. 10:11) and personified by Egypt in the Song of the Sea (Exod. 15). Similar basins known as *apsu/abzu* tanks were set up in the courtyards of Babylonian and Assyrian temples. They symbolized the freshwater ocean thought to be located beneath the earth in the *absu,* or "watery deep." An example from the early seventh century BC was discovered in the temple of the god Ashur in the Assyrian city of Assur. Its elaborate carvings depict priests in their traditional fish-shaped cloaks performing various rituals.

Ten bronze water carts (7:27–39). A well-preserved wheeled bronze stand from the late thirteenth to twelfth century BC was discovered in Cyprus. Its construction and its decoration are strikingly similar to the description in 7:28–36.

The ark of the Lord's covenant (8:1). The ark is identified elsewhere in Scripture as king Yahweh's (the Lord's) royal footstool (Exod. 25:22; 1 Chron. 28:2; Ps. 99:5; 132:7; Lam. 2:1), above which God sat, flanked by cherubim, on his royal throne. Similar royal iconography is preserved on a tenth-century-BC sarcophagus from Byblos. On that sarcophagus the Phoenician king, Ahiram, is shown enthroned between two winged sphinxes while he rests his feet on a small box-shaped footstool. These parallels demonstrate that God contextualized his self-revelation. That is, he revealed himself as sovereign king in culturally intelligible ways.

The Phoenician king Ahiram seated on his throne between two winged cherubim-like sphinxes, with his feet on a footstool.

The wings of the cherubim (8:6–7). See comments on 1 Kings 6:23–28.

The supporting terraces (9:15). The term translated as "terraces" (*millo* [cf. NRSV, NASB]) is derived from a Hebrew verb meaning "to fill, fill up," and it occurs here and in 1 Kings 9:15, 24; 11:27; 1 Chron. 11:8; 2 Chron. 32:5. Some archaeologists have identified these terraces with a multistory stepped structure located on the eastern slope of the city of David. Excavations have confirmed that this stone structure predates the eighth-century-BC houses built on top of it.

Hazor, Megiddo, and Gezer (9:15). Excavations at these three sites have revealed similar fortification systems dating to Solomon's reign. At each site archaeologists discovered a six-chambered gate flanked by large stone towers and connected to a casemate wall (a wide wall constructed of two smaller parallel walls of stacked stone blocks, with the space between them filled with stone and dirt rubble).

Ezion-geber (9:26). Ezion-geber probably is to be identified with Jazirat Faraun, a small island off the Gulf of Eilat/Aqaba.

The queen of Sheba (10:1). See comments on 2 Chron. 9:1.

Lyres and harps (10:12). See the article "Musical Instruments in Israel and the Ancient Near East."

A large ivory throne . . . two lions standing beside the armrests (10:18–20). See comments on 1 Kings 8:1; 2 Chron. 9:17. This description of Solomon's throne recalls an earlier Canaanite throne depicted on an ivory plaque from Megiddo. It has a rounded back, armrests, and winged lions on either side of the throne, just as described here in 10:19. A strikingly similar throne is depicted on the sarcophagus of the Phoenician king Ahiram (tenth century BC).

Seven hundred wives . . . three hundred who were concubines (11:3). See comments on 1 Kings 3:1. Although the size of Solomon's harem shocks modern readers, it was not unusual at that time for a powerful monarch to have such a large harem. However, by intermarrying with foreigners and having so many wives, Solomon was in direct violation of the Mosaic law (Deut. 7:3–4; 17:17).

Ashtoreth, the goddess of the Sidonians (11:5). See the article "Canaanites and Canaanite Religion." Ashtoreth, also known as Astarte, was the Canaanite goddess of fertility and the wife of the god Baal. She is mentioned in the Ugaritic mythological texts and is likely represented on the so-called Astarte plaques as a nude female figure.

Milcom (11:5). This probably is the same god known elsewhere in the Bible as Molech, a god associated with the Ammonites here in 11:5, 7, 33. This god is mentioned in a ninth-century-BC building inscription or oracle discovered at Rabbath-Ammon (modern Amman, Jordan), capital of the ancient Ammonite kingdom. He may be the god to whom parents at Carthage (a Phoenician colony on the coast of North Africa) sacrificed their children, but the term *mlk* in those inscriptions may refer instead to a *mulk* sacrifice (an offering by fire), rather than to the god himself. Several eighth-century-BC sculptures of a crowned male figure were found in Amman and may be images of this god.

Solomon built a high place for Chemosh . . . and for Milcom (11:7). On "high places," see comments on 1 Kings 3:2–3. A high place from the Israelite period was found in the northern hills of Samaria. It consists of a large circle of stones measuring about sixty-five feet in diameter, a stone pavement with remains of several offerings, a possible sacred stone, and a small bronze bull. The bull may have represented either the Canaanite storm god Baal or the Lord, although the latter was prohibited by the Mosaic law (cf. Exod. 32:4, 8; 1 Kings 12:28). The shrines that Solomon built near Jerusalem for Chemosh and Molech (Milcom) were for his Moabite and Ammonite wives and their people.

Chemosh (11:7). Chemosh, the chief god of the Moabites, is mentioned eight times in the OT and over a dozen times in the Mesha Stela, a Moabite inscription from the late ninth century BC. According to that text, King Mesha of Moab received military directives from the god Chemosh, who delivered his people and restored their land. Mesha responded by building a high place for Chemosh in the city of Qarcho.

Milcom (11:7). See comments on 1 Kings 11:5.

Ashtoreth . . . Chemosh . . . and to Milcom (11:33). See comments on 1 Kings 11:5.

Fled to Egypt, to King Shishak (11:40). See comments on 2 Chron. 12:2. Shishak I, also known as Sheshonk, Sheshonq, and Shoshenq, ruled Egypt from 945 to 925 BC. His successful military campaigns into Palestine are commemorated in a twenty-six-foot-high triumphal relief engraved on the southern face of the Bubastite Portal, the gateway to the colonnaded first court of the grand temple of Amun at Karnak. Cities from the northern kingdom of Israel listed in this inscription include Ayalon, Gibeon, Beth-shean, Rehov, Shunem, Taanach, and Megiddo. Most of the Judahite city names are illegible. In addition, a stone fragment from a victory stela was found during the early excavations at Megiddo in Israel. This inscription states, "Bright is the form of (the sun-god) Re, Amun's beloved, Shishak."[4]

Reversing the Conquest and Dismantling the Empire
(1 Kings 12–16)

He set up one in Bethel, and put the other in Dan (12:29). During the excavations at Dan archaeologists discovered a sacred area that included a large, open-air platform, a sizable stone altar with the remains of staircases on either side, and a smaller, horned altar. A third altar accompanied by bronze incense shovels, ashes, and animal bones was also found in the complex. The structure is thought to be the Israelite sanctuary built by Jeroboam I that continued in use during the eighth century BC.

High places (12:31–32). See comments on 1 Kings 3:2–3; 11:7.

Shishak (14:25–26). See 1 Kings 11:40; 2 Chron. 12:2.

Asherah (15:13). The term *asherah* often refers to some kind of object, perhaps a wooden symbol or statue, that was constructed, set up, served, cut down, chopped, hewn, burned, crushed, beaten, or removed. Deuteronomy 16:21, in which Israel was prohibited from planting any type of tree as an *asherah*, indicates that the term could also refer to a living tree. Whether manufactured or natural, an *asherah* apparently was a Canaanite religious symbol representing the goddess Asherah and the forces of fertility and reproduction associated with her. Archaeological evidence for Asherah worship was discovered in the 1970s at Kuntillet Ajrud, a shrine dating from the ninth to eighth century BC located on an ancient trade route about thirty miles south of Kadesh Barnea in the northern Sinai. Several large store jars found in the shrine were decorated with a variety of crudely drawn religious imagery and the following inscription: "I have blessed you by Yahweh of Samaria and his A/asherah."[5] A similar blessing or prayer, to "Yahweh of Teman and his A/asherah," was discovered on one of the shrine's walls. These inscriptions may refer to the Canaanite goddess, but it would be unusual for the goddess's name to appear with the possessive pronoun "his." It is more likely that this term refers to Asherah's cult symbol, a wooden pole, which could be cut and burned, as Asa is said to have done with the image mentioned here in 15:13.

Queen mother (15:13). The office of queen mother is attested in Hittite texts and in the royal records of Ugarit (a city in Syria), Assyria, Babylon, and Persia. Some queen mothers held religious office, as in the case of the Hittite king Hattusili I. This has led some to wonder if Maacah's worship of Asherah in Judah was state-sanctioned. Whether or not she held a formal religious or political office (cf.

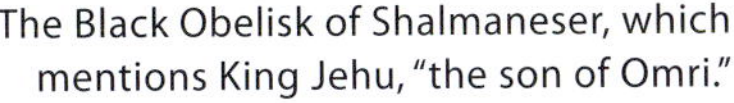

The Black Obelisk of Shalmaneser, which mentions King Jehu, "the son of Omri."

Jer. 13:18), queen mothers in Israel and Judah wielded significant power in matters of royal succession (1 Kings 1:11–31; 2 Kings 11).

The high places (15:14). See comments on 1 Kings 3:2–3; 11:7.

The dogs will eat . . . the birds will eat (16:4). See comments on 1 Kings 21:23–24.

Tirzah (16:6). King Jeroboam probably is to be credited with moving the capital of the northern kingdom of Israel from Shechem about three miles north to Tirzah (Tell el-Farah North), where it remained for about forty years until King Omri relocated it to Samaria (16:24).

Omri (16:16–28). Omri, king of Israel (ca. 884–874 BC), moved the capital from Tirzah to Samaria, where he and his son Ahab built their royal palace. Omri is mentioned in the Mesha Stela for his forty-year occupation of Moab and again on the Black Obelisk of Shalmaneser III (king of Assyria, 858–824 BC), which refers to the later Israelite king Jehu as "son [dynastic successor] of Omri."

Ahab son of Omri (16:29). Ahab, king of Israel (ca. 873–852 BC), expanded the acropolis in the city of Samaria by adding administrative buildings and extending the royal palace. He also rebuilt the cities of Megiddo and Hazor, expanding their administrative centers and defenses and constructing a water delivery system at Hazor.

Jezebel (16:31). An Egyptian-style seal inscribed with the name "Jezebel" (*yzbl*) was donated in the 1960s by a private collector to the Israel Department of Antiquities. Based on the form of its letters, scholars have dated it to the ninth century BC, when the Jezebel of 1–2 Kings lived as queen of Israel in Samaria.

He set up an altar for Baal in the temple of Baal . . . in Samaria (16:32). Although the Baal temple in Samaria has not been discovered, excavators did find the remains of an earlier Baal temple at the city of Ugarit, located on what is today the northern coast of Syria. A stairway led up to a large rectangular sanctuary. A monumental stone staircase on the east side indicated that this section of the temple originally had multiple stories and an estimated height of 52–65 feet. Excavators also found an open-air stone altar and a large stela on which Baal is shown striding forward with a lightning bolt in his hand.

Asherah (16:33). See comments on 1 Kings 15:13.

The seal of Queen Jezebel.

God Sends Prophets to Confront the Corrupt Monarchy

(1 Kings 17:1–2 Kings 8:15)

There will be no dew or rain . . . except by my command (17:1). In Canaanite religion it was believed that Baal, the god of the storm, controlled the rain. His absence brought drought, as noted in this lament from the Ugaritic "Tale of Aqhat": "Seven years shall Baal fail, eight the Rider of the Clouds. No dew, no rain, no welling up of the deep, no sweetness of Baal's voice."[6] For the Lord to withhold the dew and the rain, except by his word, was a direct challenge to the power and perhaps even to the existence of Baal.

The upstairs room (17:19). Typical houses of this period comprised a central courtyard surrounded by rooms on three sides. Cooking and other domestic activities took place on the dirt floor in the courtyard, while the side rooms functioned as stables for the family's animals. In two-storied houses the second floor was likely used for domestic activities and sleeping. An upper chamber would have been accessible by a ladder or by a set of exterior stairs, such as those discovered at an Iron Age house at Hazor.

Ahab (18:1). See comments on 1 Kings 16:29.

The Baals (18:18). See comments on 1 Kings 16:32; see the article "The Canaanites and Canaanite Religion." The plural "Baals" presumably refers to the many local manifestations of the Canaanite god Baal, who is identified in the texts from Ugarit (Ras Shamra) as the god of the rain, clouds, and the storm. According to the Baal myths from Ugarit, seasonal changes were the result of a recurring battle between Baal and Mot, the Canaanite god of death, who was associated with dry weather and sterility. A lack of rain signaled Mot's victory over Baal, but the rain's return signified Baal's resurgence.

Mount Carmel (18:19). This is located at the northwestern end of the Carmel mountain range, south of the modern-day Israeli city of Haifa. It is known in early Egyptian texts as "Holy Head" and is referred to by the

The Carmel mountain range.

Assyrian king Shalmaneser III (ninth century BC) as "Baal of the Headlands," suggesting that it may have had a long history as a holy mountain.

Prophets of Baal . . . prophets of Asherah (18:19). See comments on 1 Kings 15:13; 16:32; 18:18.

Maybe he's thinking it over; maybe he has wandered away; or maybe he's on the road (18:27). The gods of the ancient Near East were thought to share certain functions with humans, including eating, drinking, urinating, defecating, and sleeping. Thus the idea that Baal was busy or traveling would not have offended his devotees. The author's point, it seems, is that a true god transcends human limitations. The psalmist declares that the God of Israel neither slumbers nor sleeps (Ps. 121:4).

Cut themselves with knives and spears (18:28). In the ancient Near East self-mutilation was associated with mourning (Lev. 19:28; Deut. 14:1; Jer. 16:6; 41:5; 47:5), but it was also characteristic of certain prophetic behavior, as noted in an Akkadian wisdom text from the Old Babylonian or early Cassite period (ca. 1300 BC) found at Ugarit: "My brothers bathed in their own blood, like ecstatics."[7]

Mount Carmel (18:42). See comments on 1 Kings 18:19.

Chariot (18:44). See comments on 1 Kings 1:5.

Jezreel (18:45). See comments on 1 Kings 21:1.

Beer-sheba that belonged to Judah (19:3). Beer-sheba ("well of the oath" or "well of the seven") is located in the southern Judean desert about 120 miles from Mount Carmel, at a safe distance from Ahab and Jezebel.

A great and mighty wind . . . an earthquake . . . a fire (19:11–13). In the ancient Near East winds, storms, thunder, lightning, earthquakes, and fire often accompanied the presence of the gods, including the God of Israel (e.g., Exod. 19:16, 18; Judg. 5:4–5; Ps. 18:8–10; Hab. 3:3–6). In the Ugaritic texts Baal's arrival is described this way: "Seven lightning bolts he casts, eight magazines of thunder; He brandishes a spear of lightning. . . . He has thundered in the storm clouds, he has blazed his lightning to the earth . . . his holy voice shatters the earth . . . at his roar the mountains quake . . . the high places of the earth shake . . . the whole land shakes at his cry."[8] Note, however, that in this encounter with God in 1 Kings 19 the natural elements *precede* God's self-revelation, which itself is accompanied by a gentle whisper.

Hazael as king over Aram (19:15). Aram was the kingdom to the north of Israel in what is now modern Syria. Hazael became king of Aram in 842 BC after Ben-hadad II's assassination. His vassalage to the Assyrian king Shalmaneser III is mentioned in several royal Assyrian inscriptions, including the Black Obelisk and an inscription from Calah (modern Nimrud) in which Shalmaneser boasts,

> I fought with him and inflicted a defeat upon him, killing with the sword 16,000 of his experienced soldiers. I took away from him 1,121 chariots, 470 riding horses as well as his camp. He disappeared to save his life (but) I followed him and besieged him in Damascus, his royal residence. (There) I cut down his gardens (outside of the city, and departed). I marched as far as the mountains of Hauran, destroying, tearing down and burning innumerable towns, carrying booty away from them which was beyond counting. I (also) marched as far as the mountains of Ba'li-ra'si which is a promontory (lit: at the side of the sea) and erected there a stela with my image as king.[9]

Jehu son of Nimshi (19:16). See comments on 2 Kings 9:2.

Every knee that has not bowed to Baal and every mouth that has not kissed him (19:18). This universal act of submission is mentioned by Ashurbanipal, king of Assyria (668–633 BC), who says of his enemies, "They brought the booty safely to Nineveh, the town where I exercise my rule, and kissed my feet."[10] On the Black Obelisk of Shalmaneser III, king of Assyria (858–824 BC), Jehu, king of Israel, is shown on his knees bowing before his Assyrian suzerain. This is the only surviving image of an Israelite or Judean king.

King Ben-hadad of Aram (20:1). This probably is Ben-hadad II (860–841 BC), also known as Hadadezer, the son or successor of Ben-hadad (I) mentioned in 15:18.

Chariots (20:1). See comments on 1 Kings 1:5.

Sackcloth around our waists and ropes around our heads (20:31). Sackcloth was made of coarse animal hair and was irritating to the skin. It was worn to signify grief, repentance, submission, and/or surrender. In a relief from the mortuary temple of the Egyptian pharaoh Ramesses II (1279–1213 BC) at Abu Simbel, prisoners appear before the king on their knees with their arms tightly bound behind their backs. The rope tied around each neck functioned as a leash by which to lead and control the prisoners.

From the Egyptian mortuary temple of Abu Simbel, a scene depicting prisoners with ropes around their necks.

He is my brother (20:32). In the ancient Near East political agreements typically were expressed in kinship terms, even if the parties were not related by blood. Treaties among equals used the language of brotherhood, whereas treaties between a suzerain and a vassal employed a father-son metaphor. By referring to Ben-hadad as his brother, King Ahab honors Ben-hadad's royal status as king of Syria.

Jezreel (21:1). The city of Jezreel was located fifteen to twenty miles southeast of Mount Carmel at the eastern end of the Jezreel Valley. In the early mid-ninth century BC the city was fortified by King Omri and King Ahab with a wall, earthen rampart, a dry moat, and a gate. Royal ashlar masonry found near the gate may be the remains of Ahab and Jezebel's winter palace. The site probably was destroyed by Hazael, king of Aram, in the late ninth century BC.

A vegetable garden (21:2). The Hebrew phrase translated as "vegetable garden" may refer instead to a royal garden, similar to the Neo-Assyrian royal gardens mentioned in several ancient sources. These gardens included nonnative plants and trees from lands the king had visited or conquered. The Assyrian king Sennacherib boasted, "A great park, like unto Mount Amanus, wherein were set out all kinds of herbs and fruit trees; trees, such as grow on the mountains and in Chaldea, I planted by its (the palace's) side."[11] In an Assyrian relief from the north palace of king Ashurbanipal at Nineveh the royal couple enjoys a meal in the palace gardens.

Sealed them with his seal (21:8). See comments on 1 Kings 16:31. In the ancient Near East papyrus or leather documents typically were sealed with a small piece of moist clay. The sender's official seal was then impressed on the clay, leaving his or her unique signature. Seal impressions (bullae) of several biblical figures have been discovered, including a bulla of King Ahaz and six bullae from seals belonging to his son Hezekiah, king of Judah.

Dogs will eat Jezebel . . . anyone who belongs to Ahab . . . the birds will eat (21:23–24). In the ancient Near East to be denied a proper burial was a curse. Further, for one's corpse to be eaten by animals was both a curse and a sign of divine judgment (Deut. 28:26; cf. Gen. 40:19; Ezek. 39:17). When a rebellious Babylon fell to the Assyrian king Ashurbanipal, he reports that he destroyed the survivors in the following manner: "Their dismembered bodies I fed to the dogs, swine, wolves, and eagles, to the birds of heavens, and the fish of the deep."[12]

Ramoth-gilead (22:3). This city is located north of Amman, Jordan, in the territory that had belonged to the tribe of Gad. It had been seized by

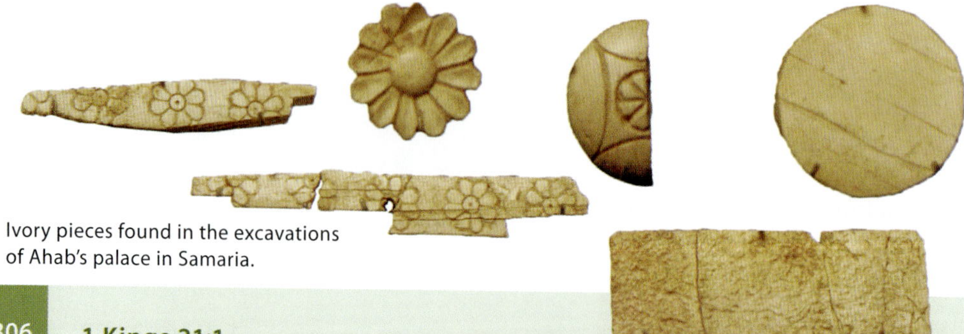

Ivory pieces found in the excavations of Ahab's palace in Samaria.

the Arameans in the mid-ninth century BC, but it was coveted by Israel and Judah because it provided access to lucrative east-west trade routes.

Please ask what the LORD's will is (22:5–8). In the ancient Near East kings regularly consulted the gods before entering into battle (cf. 2 Chron. 20:1–30; Isa. 7:4–9). A favorable reply, as determined by the priests, was thought to ensure victory. Hammurabi, king of Babylon, reports, "I now requested [an oracle about going to war with Larsa from the gods] Shamash and Marduk and they answered me with yes. I would not have risen to this offensive [against Larsa] without consulting a god [first]." He then commanded his troops, "Go [to Larsa], may the god go in front of you [into battle]!"[13]

Sitting on his own throne . . . at the entrance to the gate of Samaria (22:10). City gates and their adjoining plazas functioned as marketplaces, courtrooms (Deut. 22:15; Josh. 20:4; Ruth 4:1, 11), meeting halls (2 Chron. 32:6), news outlets (Ps. 69:12), and as places for prophetic consultation.

The ivory palace he built (22:39). Several hundred fragments from ivory panels and furniture inlay were found in the excavations of Ahab's palace at Samaria. Their subject matter and designs, which include the smiting pharaoh, Egyptian deities, winged sphinxes, and the palmette and lotus, demonstrate a strong Egyptian and Phoenician influence.

The high places (22:43). See comments on 1 Kings 3:2–3; 11:7.

The male cult prostitutes (22:46). The Hebrew term *qadesh*, here translated as "male cult prostitute," refers to a class of non-Levitical priests who apparently engaged in literal prostitution at various high places and temples. Although there is no conclusive evidence this is the case, it may be suggested by the fact that the feminine form of the word, *qedeshah*, appears in the OT as a synonym for *zonah* ("prostitute").

Ezion-geber (22:48). Ezion-geber may be identified with the small island off the coast in the Gulf of Eilat/Aqaba known today as Jazirat Faraun.

Baal (22:53). See comments on 1 Kings 16:32; 18:18; 18:19; see the article "The Canaanites and Canaanite Religion."

2 Kings

Moab rebelled against Israel (1:1). The Mesha Stela, also known as the Moabite Stone (ca. 850 BC), refers to this same rebellion but from the perspective of Mesha, the king of Moab. Mesha had been an Israelite vassal, forced to supply Ahab with agricultural produce and large quantities of sheep.

At Ahab's death he rebelled, gaining his freedom. In the Mesha inscription he credits his god, Chemosh, with the victory: "he saved me from all the kings and caused me to triumph over all my adversaries."[14]

Samaria (1:2). Samaria was the capital of the northern kingdom of Israel from the time of Omri (1 Kings 16:24) until the fall of the northern kingdom under Hoshea (2 Kings 17).

Baal-zebub (1:2). Literally "lord of the flies," this probably is an intentional corruption of "Baal-Zebul," which means "Baal the Exalted," "Baal the Prince," or "Lord of the Heavenly House" (cf. Beelzebul in Matt. 10:25; 12:24, 27; Mark 3:22; Luke 11:15, 18–19), intended to express the author's disdain for this so-called deity. There is no reference to "Baal of the flies" in the Ugaritic mythological texts, but the title "Baal-Zebul" ("Prince Baal") appears four times and is also used to describe several other deities at Ugarit (an ancient city in Syria).

Ekron (1:2). See the article "The Philistines." Ekron (Tel Miqne) was one of the Philistine Pentapolis cities, situated on the western edge of the coastal plain near the border with Judah. It was settled by the Philistines in the early twelfth century BC.

A hairy man with a leather belt around his waist (1:8). This may have been standard prophetic garb (cf. Zech. 13:4; Matt. 3:4). An Old Babylonian letter from the city of Mari reports the gift of a *laharum* garment to a prophetess in exchange for her prophecy. This is the only known occurrence of the term *laharum*, but if it is related to Akkadian *lahru* ("sheep"), as scholars suggest, it may denote a wooly, sheepskin garment.

From Gilgal . . . to Bethel (2:1–2). It was in Bethel, modern Beitin, ten miles north of Jerusalem, that Jeroboam established the southern Israelite sanctuary for worshiping one of the two golden calves (1 Kings 12:28–29). The site of ancient Gilgal has not yet been securely identified, but it might be modern Jiljulieh, about seven miles north of Bethel. It was in Gilgal that Saul was made king (1 Sam. 11:15), and it was in Gilgal that his kingship was later rejected. Later both Gilgal and Bethel were identified by Amos (4:4; 5:5) and Hosea (4:15; 9:15; 12:11) as illegitimate places of worship.

Jericho (2:4). Jericho is located in the Jordan Valley about ten miles northwest of the Dead

The Moabite Stone (Mesha Stela).

Sea. It was the first city the Israelites captured in their conquest of Canaan (Josh. 2:1).

Two shares (2:9). Elisha requests what an eldest son would expect of a father in ancient Israel: a double portion of the inheritance (Gen. 25:31–34; 27:1–46; 48:8–22; Deut. 21:15–17). In this case, however, the inheritance is not land but spiritual power. The inheritance of a double portion for the firstborn son is well attested in legal texts from Assyria, Nuzi, Mari, and Ugarit, even in the case of adoption. An adoption contract from Mari reads, "If Hillalum and Alitum should acquire (by adoption) many more sons, Iahatti-Il alone (is principal) heir. From the estate of Hillalum, his father, two (shares) he shall take. His younger brothers shall divide (the remainder of the inheritance) brother like brother (i.e., in equal shares)."[15]

A chariot of fire with horses of fire (2:11–12). In biblical tradition chariots and fire have close associations with God's self-manifestation. The storm cloud represents the divine chariot or throne (Ezek. 1; Hab. 3:8), and the fiery lightning bolts represent divine weapons (Ps. 18:14; Hab. 3:11). In the mythological texts from the city of Ugarit, it is Baal, the god of the storm, who rides in a chariot of clouds, armed with weapons of thunder and lightning. Given the prevalence of Baal worship in Israel during this period, God's manifestation as the fiery charioteer who arrives in a storm (whirlwind) is especially appropriate, as it challenges directly Baal's claim to be god of the storm.

Picked up the mantle that had fallen off Elijah (2:13). In a legal context, putting on a cloak was a symbolic act signifying inheritance, just as removing it signified disinheritance (cf. Gen. 37:23; Exod. 22:26; Ezek. 16:8–16). Here, Elisha's call to prophetic ministry, expressed symbolically when Elijah put his cloak around him (1 Kings 19:19), is reaffirmed. By taking Elijah's cloak, Elisha recognizes that he has indeed been granted the inheritance of the firstborn—that is, a double portion of Elijah's spirit. He is thus Elijah's legitimate successor, and he is acknowledged as such by the prophets of Jericho (2:15).

Mount Carmel (2:25). See comments on 1 Kings 18:19. Elisha returns to Samaria, the center of Baal worship in Israel, to continue his prophetic ministry.

Joram (3:1). Joram, the son of King Ahab, reigned from 849 to 843 BC. He is named in the Tel Dan Stela (late ninth century BC), a monument erected by Hazael, king of Aram-Damascus, to commemorate his defeat of Israel. The text reads, "[And I killed Jo]ram, son of A[hab,] king of Israel, and [I] killed [Ahazi]yahu, son of [Joram, kin]g of the House of David; and I set [their towns into ruins? . . . the ci]/ties of their land into de[solation? . . .] . . . other and to over[turn all their cities? . . . and Jehu] [ru]/led over Is[rael . . .]."[16] Second Kings 9 claims that Jehu (843–815 BC) killed Jehoram/Joram, but in the Tel Dan Stela, Hazael takes the credit. A previous

Kings of Israel and Judah

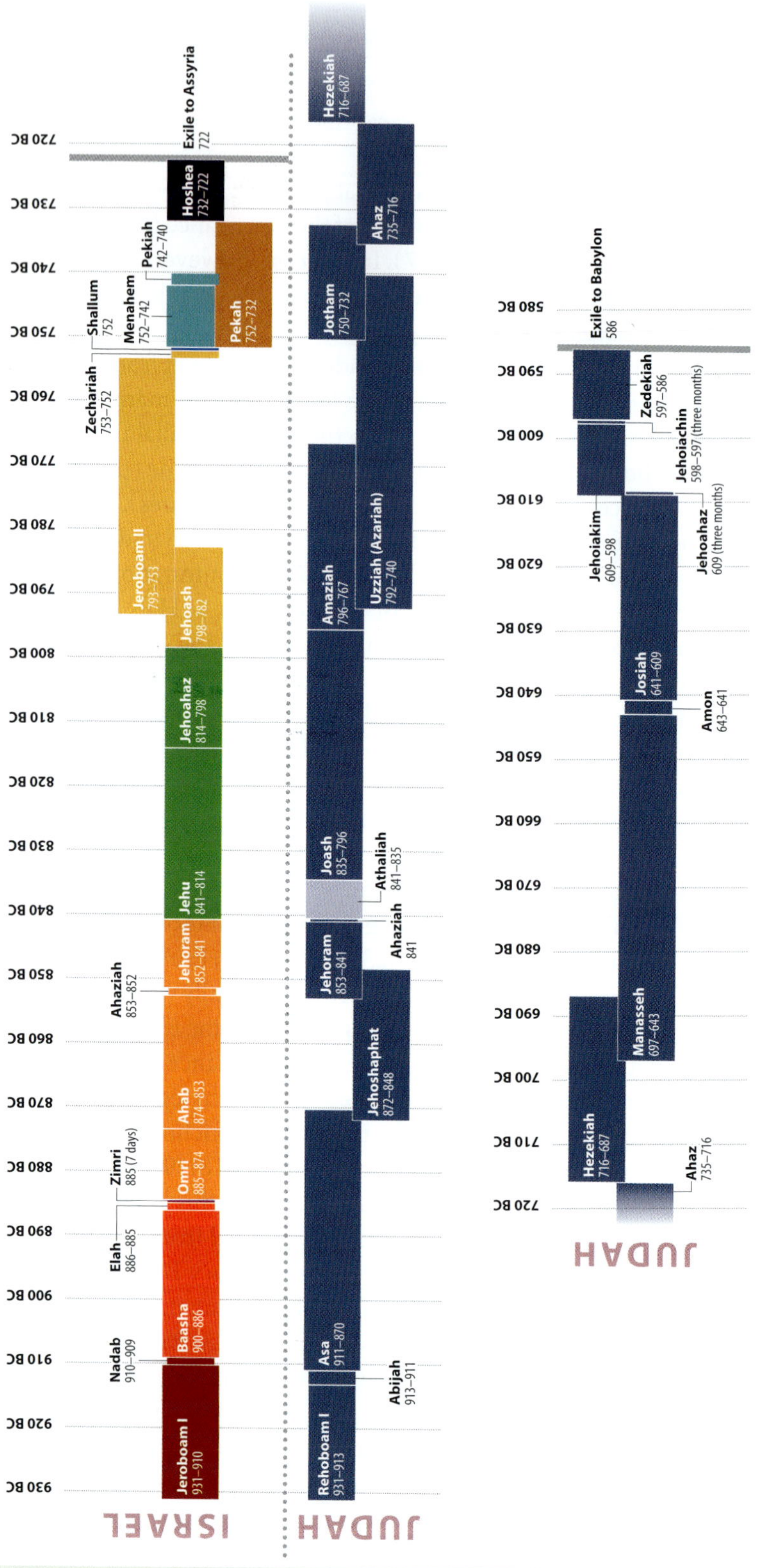

930 BC
920 BC
910 BC
900 BC
890 BC
880 BC
870 BC
860 BC
850 BC
840 BC
830 BC
820 BC
810 BC
800 BC
790 BC
780 BC
770 BC
760 BC
750 BC
740 BC
730 BC
720 BC

ISRAEL

Jeroboam I 931–910
Nadab 910–909
Baasha 900–886
Elah 886–885
Zimri 885 (7 days)
Omri 885–874
Ahab 874–853
Ahaziah 853–852
Jehoram 852–841
Jehu 841–814
Jehoahaz 814–798
Jehoash 798–782
Jeroboam II 793–753
Zechariah 753–752
Shallum 752
Menahem 752–742
Pekiah 742–740
Pekah 752–732
Hoshea 732–722
Exile to Assyria 722

JUDAH

Rehoboam I 931–913
Abijah 913–911
Asa 911–870
Jehoshaphat 872–848
Jehoram 853–841
Ahaziah 841
Athaliah 841–835
Joash 835–796
Amaziah 796–767
Uzziah (Azariah) 792–740
Jotham 750–732
Ahaz 735–716
Hezekiah 716–687

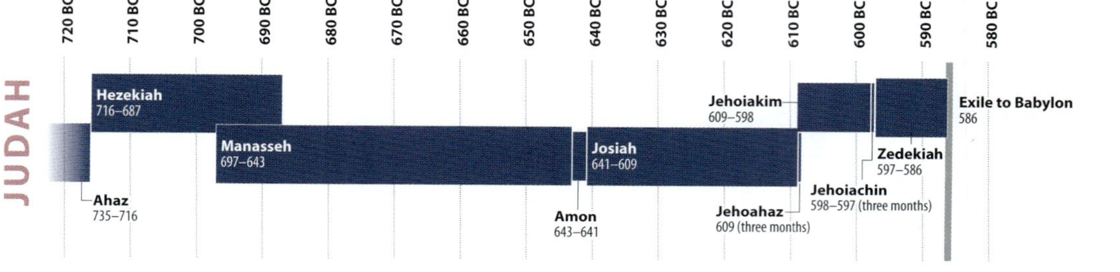

alliance between Hazael and Jehu (1 Kings 19:17) explains how both men could claim to have killed Israel's king.

Samaria (3:1). See comments on 2 Kings 1:2.

The sacred pillar of Baal (3:2). Similar stones were discovered in a Canaanite temple at Hazor dating to the fifteenth to thirteenth centuries BC, including one engraved with two arms raised in prayer or worship. Another example was found in the city gate at Geshur (Bethsaida in the NT). The stone was engraved with the image of Baal and had been placed on a platform for easy viewing. Although forbidden by the Mosaic law (Exod. 34:13; Lev. 26:1; Deut. 7:5), sacred stones were used in Israelite worship, as attested by those found in the Israelite temple at Arad.

King Mesha of Moab (3:4–5). See comments on 2 Kings 1:1.

You will cut down every good tree (3:19). Deuteronomy 20:19–20 prohibits the destruction of fruit trees in most cases, but apparently the Moabites are to be given over to desolation rather than simply subdued. Therefore their food supply is to be cut off, leaving the land desolate and uninhabitable. This action is depicted in an Assyrian relief from Sennacherib's southwest palace. After the destruction of the city of Dilbat (modern Tell ed-Duleim or Tell al-Deylam in Iraq) Assyrian soldiers work in pairs to cut down date palm trees.

Men with slings surrounded the city (3:25). See comments on 1 Sam. 17:49. Dozens of sling stones from the eighth-century-BC Assyrian invasion of Judah were discovered in the excavations at Lachish. The stones are about the size of tennis balls and weigh at least nine ounces each. The sling consisted of a shallow leather pouch with one or two cords attached at the end. The combatant placed the stone in the pouch and then swung the device over his head several times to increase speed. He then launched the stone by releasing the cord(s). Assyrian soldiers are depicted in the stone reliefs from Sennacherib's palace slinging stones at the city walls of Lachish and its citizens.

He took his firstborn son . . . and offered him as a burnt offering (3:27). Although abhorrent to us, religious rituals involving child sacrifice were not uncommon among the Canaanites and the Phoenicians, as well as the Moabites. In the Phoenician city of Carthage (near modern Tunis, the capital of Tunisia) archaeologists discovered a massive *tophet* ("place of burning") where hundreds of children had been sacrificed as burnt offerings to the god Baal Hamon and the goddess Tanit during the six-hundred-year period from the eighth to the second centuries BC. Their graves were marked by upright stone monuments, some of which were inscribed with dedications indicating that the children were sacrificed in fulfillment of religious vows made by their parents (cf. 2 Kings 23:10; Jer. 7:31; Mic. 6:7). In Israelite

Ruins of Carthage *tophet* with the upright stone markers.

tradition the firstborn belonged to God (Exod. 13:2, 12–15; 34:19–20), but those children were to be redeemed by animal sacrifice (Gen. 22:13; Exod. 34:20) rather than be sacrificed themselves. It is noteworthy that some of the burial jars in the Carthage *tophet* contained animal bones instead of human remains. This suggests that redemption by an animal substitute was known among the Phoenicians at this time, although rarely used.

The creditor is coming to take my two children as his slaves (4:1). In the ancient Near East debt slavery laws allowed for creditors to take children from their parents as a form of payment. In ancient Israel, however, it was the responsibility of the kinsman redeemer to liberate the person or dependents of a kinsman in debt (Lev. 25:35–55). Here, in the apparent absence of a true kinsman, Elisha essentially takes on this role for the widow. The proceeds from the sale of the oil will enable her to pay off her debts, free her sons, and have enough money to survive.

Mount Carmel (4:25). See comments on 1 Kings 18:19.

Gilgal (4:38). See comments on 2 Kings 2:1.

Aram (5:1). This region in southern Syria, with its capital at Damascus, reached its zenith politically during the ninth century BC.

The Lord had given victory to Aram (5:1). In the ancient Near East military victory was interpreted as a favorable act of the gods. Mesha, the king of Moab, inscribed on his victory stela, "I made this high place for Chemosh in Qarhoh [. . .] because he saved me from all the kings and caused me to triumph over all my adversaries."[17] Similarly Zakkur, the king of Hamath (ninth century BC), says of Baal, "Ba'alshamayn [raised] me and stood beside me, and Ba'alshamayn made me king over Hazrach."[18] Here, the Lord, the God of Israel, is credited with giving victory to Israel's enemy Aram (cf. Dan. 1:1–2; Jer. 20:4; 21:7; 32:3, where the Lord delivers his people into the hands of their enemies, and Jer. 44:30, where Israel's God gives the Egyptian pharaoh over to the Babylonians).

Took with him . . . silver . . . gold . . . clothing (5:5). When asking for a favor, a person customarily sent lavish gifts, which often included money and expensive textiles. In one letter a Hittite king complains to the king of Assyria, "Did [my brother?] not send you appropriate greeting-gifts? But when I assumed kingship, you did not send a messenger to me. It is the custom that when kings assume kingship, the kings who are his equals in rank, send him appropriate greeting-gifts, clothing befitting kingship, and fine oil for his anointing. But you have not yet done this."[19]

Rimmon (5:18). Rimmon, also known as Hadad-rimmon (Zech. 12:11), is another name for the Canaanite deity Baal, or Baal Hadad. "Rimmon" may be a deliberate misspelling of "Ramman," meaning "to rumble, roar, growl, howl, bellow, groan, thunder," a term used to describe Baal Hadad in several Akkadian texts. By changing the vowels, the biblical author transformed the name Hadad-ramman ("Hadad the thunderer") to the pejorative Hadad-rimmon ("Hadad the pomegranate").

Dothan (6:13). Dothan, identified with Tel Dothan, lies only ten miles north of the city of Samaria. Excavations have confirmed that there was a large settlement at Dothan during the tenth to eighth centuries BC, which included the remains of domestic and administrative buildings, the latter of which contained over one hundred large storage bins.

Samaria (6:20). See comments on 2 Kings 1:2.

King Ben-hadad of Aram (6:24). Several kings of Aram from the ninth century BC were named Ben-hadad. This one probably is Ben-hadad II (860–841 BC), also known as Hadadezer, the successor of Ben-hadad (I) named in 1 Kings 15:18–20.

A donkey's head sold for thirty-four ounces of silver . . . dove's dung sold for two ounces of silver (6:25). To avoid dying of starvation, the people of Samaria were forced to pay exorbitant prices for anything edible, including undesirable parts of an animal. The price mentioned here for bird dung was roughly the equivalent of six months' pay.

Give up your son, and we will eat him today (6:28). That famine victims resorted to cannibalism is mentioned in Lam. 2:20; 4:10; Ezek. 5:10. During the Assyrian siege of Babylon (650–648 BC) King Ashurbanipal reports, "Famine broke out among them; and to still their hunger they ate the flesh of their sons."[20] A carved stone relief from the causeway of the Pyramid of Unas (mid-twenty-fourth century BC) at Saqqara in Egypt provides a rare glimpse of ancient famine victims.

He tore his clothes (6:30). Tearing one's garments was a common sign of shock, grief, or mourning throughout the ancient Near East. In the Ugaritic mythological texts the god El rips his garments in grief upon hearing of Baal's death.

At Samaria's gate (7:1). See comments on 1 Kings 22:10. The Lord promises an end to the famine and thus the excessive price gouging.

The land of the Philistines (8:2). See the article "The Philistines." The land of the Philistines was located on the southern Canaanite coast, north of Egypt. It included the pentapolis cities of Ashkelon, Ashdod, Ekron, Gaza, and Gath. Ashkelon, Ashdod, and Ekron have been securely identified and excavated. Ancient Gaza lies beneath the modern city of the same name but is inaccessible due to the current political situation. Gath may be Tell es-Safi, about halfway between Ashkelon and Jerusalem, although this identification is uncertain.

To appeal to the king for her house and field (8:3). The kings of the ancient Near East were ultimately responsible for establishing equity, enforcing the law, maintaining peace, and administering justice. The Code of Hammurabi, king of Babylon, includes among the king's duties, "to cause justice to prevail in the land, to destroy the wicked and the evil, that the strong might not oppress the weak."[21]

Damascus (8:7). Damascus was the capital of the Aramean Empire. The king named here is Ben-hadad II, also known as Hadadezer.

Hazael (8:8). See comments on 1 Kings 19:15; 2 Kings 3:1. Hazael became king of Aram in 842 BC after the death of Ben-hadad II, and was one of Israel's bitter enemies throughout his lengthy reign (cf. 8:28; 13:22).

A mere dog (8:13). This same phrase appears in the Amarna letters (fourteenth century BC) in an address by a vassal to the pharaoh of Egypt, and several times in the Lachish letters (early sixth century BC) in which Hoshaiah, a Judean soldier, appeals to his commanding officer, Yaush/Yaosh. It is an example of the typical self-deprecating language frequently used in the ancient Near East when one was addressing a superior.

Apostasy and the Last Days of Israel (2 Kings 8:16–17:41)

Israel's King Joram son of Ahab (8:16). This king was also known as Jehoram (cf. 3:1 NRSV). Another king by the same name, distinguished by his ancestry as the son of Jehoshaphat, reigned in Judah.

Ahab (8:27). See comments on 1 Kings 16:29.

King Hazael of Aram (8:28–29). See comments on 2 Kings 8:8.

Jehu son of Jehoshaphat, son of Nimshi (9:2). Jehu is the only Israelite king whose depiction has survived antiquity. On the Black Obelisk of Shalmaneser III this king of Israel is shown bowing before his Assyrian overlord. The accompanying inscription reads, "I received the tribute of

Jehu of Bīt-Ḫumrî [the house of Omri]: silver, gold, a golden bowl, a golden goblet, golden cups, golden buckets, tin, a staff of the king's hand, (and) javelins" (see comments on 2 Kings 3:1).[22]

Ramoth-gilead (9:4). See comments on 1 Kings 22:3.

The dogs will eat Jezebel . . . no one will bury her (9:10). See comments on 1 Kings 21:23–24.

Jehu (9:14). See comments on 2 Kings 9:2.

Joram (9:14). See comments on 2 Kings 8:16.

Ramoth-gilead (9:14). See comments on 1 Kings 22:3.

King Hazael of Aram (9:14). See comments on 2 Kings 8:8.

She painted her eyes, fixed her hair, and looked down from the window (9:30). See the article "Women's Fashion in the Old Testament World." The use of eye makeup in antiquity is mentioned in a nineteenth-century-BC tomb painting found at Beni Hasan in Egypt. Asiatic merchants are shown bringing a variety of goods to sell. The painting's caption includes, "Arriving and bringing black eye-paint, which 37 Asiatics brought to him."[23]

Pile them in two heaps at the entrance of the city gate (10:8). The piling up of enemy body parts in a public place was a form of psychological warfare, intended to demoralize and terrorize the enemy. In a stone relief commemorating the fall of Babylon to Assyria in the mid-seventh century BC a pile of enemy heads appears in the center of the upper register.

Samaria (10:12). See comments on 2 Kings 1:2.

Baal (10:18–27). See comments on 1 Kings 16:32; 18:18; see the article "The Canaanites and Canaanite Religion."

The pillar of the temple of Baal (10:26). See comments on 2 Kings 3:2.

Hazael (10:32–33). See comments on 2 Kings 8:8.

The temple of Baal (11:18). See comments on 1 Kings 16:32.

The high places (12:3). See comments on 1 Kings 3:2–3.

King Hazael of Aram (13:3). See comments on 2 Kings 8:8.

His son Ben-hadad (13:3). This is Ben-hadad III (8:7), who became king of Aram in 806 BC.

The Lord gave Israel a deliverer (13:5). The deliverer mentioned here was likely Adad-Nirari III, king of Assyria, who defeated the Arameans in 802 BC. An Assyrian record of the campaign mentions "Joash the Samaritan" as an Assyrian vassal.

The Asherah pole also remained standing in Samaria (13:6). See comments on 1 Kings 15:13.

Samaria (13:10). See comments on 2 Kings 1:2.

Elisha responded, "Get a bow and arrows" (13:15). See comments on Ezek. 21:21.

King Hazael of Aram (13:22). See comments on 2 Kings 8:8.

Ben-hadad (13:24). See comments on 2 Kings 13:3. Jehoash was able to retake the Israelite cities conquered by the Syrian army during the reign of his father, Jehoahaz, because Ben-hadad III was preoccupied with the Assyrian threat on his northern border.

Jehoash (13:25). Jehoash is listed as an Assyrian vassal in an inscription of the Assyrian king Adad-Nirari III (see comments on 2 Kings 13:5).

The high places (14:4). See comments on 1 Kings 3:2–3.

Samaria (14:14). See comments on 2 Kings 1:2.

Jeroboam son of Jehoash (14:23). Jeroboam II ruled the northern kingdom of Israel for forty years. During this time Aram was weakened by the Assyrians, who were, in turn, preoccupied with defending their northern border against Urartu (modern Armenia). The resulting power vacuum enabled Israel to expand and prosper. Over one hundred ostraca (letters, receipts, and records written in ink on potsherds) dating to the reign of Jeroboam II were discovered during the excavations of Samaria. They record shipments of wine and olive oil from various administrative districts in Israel to specific individuals in Samaria. The receipts include the date, the name of the district, the recipient's name, and the identity of the item itself. One of the receipts reads, "In the ninth year from Qosah to (credit of) Gaddiyaw, a jar of old wine."[24] The goods could have been a form of tax or tribute, but they may instead be contributions for the royal household, grown on land granted by the king.

Samaria (14:23). See comments 2 Kings 1:2.

Azariah son of Amaziah (15:1). Azariah was also known as Uzziah (15:13, 30, 32, 34).

The high places (15:4). See comments on 1 Kings 3:2–3.

Tirzah (15:14). See comments on 1 Kings 16:6. Tirzah was the capital of the northern kingdom of Israel during the reigns of Baasha, Elah, Zimri, and Omri (1 Kings 15:33; 16:8, 23) before Omri relocated it to Samaria.

Menahem attacked Tiphsah (15:16–20). The city of Tiphsah was located about seventy miles south of Carchemish on the Euphrates River. "Pul" ("Pulu" in Akkadian) is another name for the Assyrian king Tiglath-pileser III, who subjugated Menahem and forced him to pay excessive tribute, as reported in one of his inscriptions: "I received tribute from . . . Rezon of Damascus, Menahem of Samaria, Hiram of Tyre" (see the article "The Assyrians").[25]

Pekah . . . became king (15:27–31). Israel remained an Assyrian vassal during Pekah's reign and even lost much of its territory to Tiglath-pileser III, who reported in his annals,

> [As for Menahem I ov]erwhelmed him [like a snowstorm] and he . . . fled like a bird, alone, [and bowed to my feet(?)]. I returned him to his place [and imposed tribute upon him, to wit:] gold, silver, linen garments with

> multicolored trimmings . . . great . . . [I re]ceived from him. Israel (lit. "House of Omri") . . . all its inhabitants (and) their possessions I led to Assyria, They overthrew their king Pekah and I placed Hoshea as king over them. I received from them 10 talents of gold, 1,000(?) talents of silver as their [tri]bute and brought them to Assyria.[26]

The high places (15:35). See comments on 1 Kings 3:2–3.

The LORD began to send Aram's King Rezin and Pekah son of Remaliah against Judah (15:37). This is the beginning of the Syro-Ephraimite war (cf. Isa. 7–9), in which Israel and Aram attacked Judah, who then appealed to Assyria for aid. Rezin, king of Aram, is named in the Assyrian annals as one of several kings defeated by Tiglath-pileser III, who claims, "I laid siege to and conquered the town Hadara, the inherited property of Rezin of Damascus, [the place where] he was born. I brought away as prisoners 800 (of its) inhabitants with their possessions . . . their large (and) small cattle."[27]

Ahaz son of Jotham became king of Judah (16:1). A seal impression found in a private collection bears Ahaz's name. It reads, "Belonging to Ahaz, (son of) Yehotam (Jotham), King of Judah."[28] He is also mentioned in the annals of Tiglath-pileser III as an Assyrian vassal. A longer form of his name, Yeho-ahaz, appears in the annals of Tiglath-pileser III as one who paid tribute to Assyria. The prefix "Yeho" refers to Yahweh ("the LORD")

Sacrificed his son in the fire (16:3). See comments on 2 Kings 3:27.

The high places (16:4). See comments on 1 Kings 3:2–3.

Rezin . . . Pekah . . . Ahaz (16:5–9). See comments on 2 Kings 15:37; 16:1.

I am your servant and your son (16:7). Ahaz submits to Assyria and requests Tiglath-pileser III's help rather than turn to the Lord. The Assyrians soundly defeat the unified forces of Pekah and Rezin, the latter of whom is put to death. By identifying himself as Tiglath-pileser's "son" Ahaz employs standard covenant terminology, derived from the realm of kinship, to denote his vassal status (see comments on 1 Kings 20:32).

He saw the altar that was in Damascus (16:10). The text provides no details as to the altar's design, but altars from this period discovered in excavations in Syria were rectangular in shape with raised, pointed corners (a good example was found at Pella). This form may have been the prototype for the four-horned altars from the tenth to early sixth centuries BC discovered at Dan, Megiddo, Shechem, Lachish, Arad, Beer-sheba, Gezer, and at the Philistine cities of Ashkelon and Ekron. Damascus was the capital and central city of Aram (Syria).

The bronze altar that was before the LORD (16:14). Ahaz will now use the bronze altar to "seek guidance." This probably means that he resorted to extispicy, the inspection of animal entrails to determine the will of the gods, which was frequently practiced among the kings of Assyria and Babylon. Priests were trained to "read" livers using clay models. One of these clay models was discovered in southern Iraq and dates to about 1900–1600 BC. Each square on its surface contains an interpretation for a corresponding blemish or mark found on the animal liver. An omen text from Mesopotamia states, "If there is a *Hal* sign at the emplacement of 'the well-being' [that is, at the groove of the liver running between the umbilical fissure and the gallbladder] the reign of Akkad is over. If the entire liver is anomalous—Omen of the king of Akkad regarding catastrophe. Omen of Ibbi-Sin when Elam reduced Ur to tell and rubble. If the 'rise of the head of the bird' is dark on the left and the right there will be *pitrusta* [an abnormality that can cause the priest to reverse his decision]."[29] Liver models have also been found at Megiddo and Hazor, although extispicy was prohibited in Israel (Deut. 18:10).

Hoshea (17:1). Hoshea, who ruled from 732 to 722 BC, was the last king of the northern kingdom of Israel before the Assyrian invasion in 722/721 BC. His name appears on an Egyptian-style seal dated to the eighth century BC with an inscription that reads, "Belonging to Abdi servant of Hoshea."[30]

King Shalmaneser of Assyria (17:3). Shalmaneser is identified here and in the Babylonian Chronicle as the conqueror of Samaria in 722 BC. However, in the Nimrud Prism the Assyrian Sargon II (722–705 BC), Shalmaneser's successor, claims the victory for himself, declaring,

> [The inhabitants of Sa]merina, who agreed [and plotted] with a king [hostile to] me, not to do service and not to bring tribute [to Assur] and who did battle, I fought against them with the power of the great gods, my lords. I counted as spoil 27,280 people, together with their chariots, and gods, in which they trusted. I formed a unit with 200 of [their] chariots for my royal force. I settled the rest of them in the midst of Assyria. I repopulated Samerina more than before. I brought into it people from countries conquered by my hands. I appointed my eunuch as governor over them. And I counted them as Assyrians.[31]

As a usurper to the throne, Sargon II perhaps takes the credit as a way to legitimize his kingship.

High places (17:9). See comments on 1 Kings 3:2–3.

They set up for themselves sacred pillars and Asherah poles (17:10). See comments on 1 Kings 15:13; 2 Kings 3:2.

An Asherah pole . . . and served Baal (17:16). See comments on 1 Kings 15:13; 16:32; 18:18; see the article "The Canaanites and Canaanite Religion."

They bowed in worship to all the stars in the sky (17:16). Astral worship was popular in Judah, as attested by the prophet Jeremiah (Jer. 7:18; 44:17, 25) and in the archaeological record. Seal impressions (bullae) from this period in Judah include symbols of the sun and moon before which human figures are worshiping.

They sacrificed their sons and their daughters in the fire (17:17). See comments on 2 Kings 3:27.

Practiced divination and interpreted omens (17:17). The art or "science" of divination—which included dream interpretation, casting lots, inspecting animal livers, consulting the dead, and astrological observations—was practiced in Israel and in the ancient Near East as a way of determining the future and/or the will of the gods (see comments on 2 Kings 16:14). Divination was prohibited in Israel (Deut. 18:10), although the priests were allowed to consult God through the Urim and Thummim (cf. Num. 27:21; 1 Sam. 14:41).

The men of Babylon made Succoth-benoth, the men of Cuth made Nergal, the men of Hamath made Ashima . . . the Sepharvites burned their children in the fire to Adrammelech and Annammelech (17:30–31). On the burning of children as sacrifices, see comments on 2 Kings 3:27. Succoth-benoth was the creator goddess Banitu, known from Neo-Assyrian and Neo-Babylonian texts and worshiped in various forms from Mesopotamia to Egypt. This deity may also be identified with Sakkut/Ninurta, a fertility god particularly associated with agriculture and animals and who is often depicted and described as a heroic hunter. Nergal was the god of the underworld in Mesopotamia and was associated with drought and death. His center of worship was in Kuthah/Cuthah (modern Tell Ibrahim), which is listed as the home of some of the exiles relocated to Samaria. Ashima is a West Semitic god mentioned in several Aramaic inscriptions, but little else is known of him. The identity of the other gods in the list is uncertain.

The Struggle with Apostasy and the Last Days of Judah (18:1–25:30)

Hezekiah son of Ahaz (18:1). Hezekiah's name appears on two clay seals (bullae) from private collections. The first example is decorated with a winged scarab (an Egyptian sacred beetle) and an ankh (an Egyptian hieroglyphic sign that means "life") with an inscription that reads, "Belonging to Hezekiah [son of] Ahaz, king of Judah."[32] The design and inscription on the second bulla are nearly identical to the first, although it is missing the name "Ahaz."

The high places (18:4). See comments on 1 Kings 3:2–3.

The sacred pillars . . . the Asherah poles (18:4). See comments on 1 Kings 15:13; 2 Kings 3:2.

The bronze snake (18:4). Archaeologists discovered an Israelite horned altar from the late eighth century BC at Beer-sheba. A serpent was incised on one of the stones of which it was built.

Philistines (18:8). See the article "The Philistines." The Philistines arrived on the southern coast of Canaan in the thirteenth century BC as one of several groups of Sea Peoples searching for a new homeland. They, along with other Sea People groups, invaded Egypt but were soundly defeated by Ramesses III. The captives were either conscripted into the Egyptian military or were given permission to settle along the southern Canaanite coast. The Philistines arrived in Canaan, displacing the local population and preventing the tribe of Dan from claiming its allotted territory. They remained in this region until they were defeated and either killed or exiled by the Babylonians at the end of the seventh century BC.

As far as Gaza (18:8). Ancient Gaza lies buried underneath the modern city of the same name. It was the southernmost of the Philistine Pentapolis cities and was located on the Mediterranean coast about nine to ten miles south of Ashkelon. Its importance derived largely from its location along the great coastal highway connecting Egypt in the south to Syria-Palestine and Mesopotamia farther north and east.

Assyria's King Shalmaneser (18:9). See comments on 2 Kings 17:3; see the article "The Assyrians."

Assyria's King Sennacherib attacked all the fortified cities of Judah and captured them (18:13). Sennacherib was king of Assyria from 704 to 681 BC. Reliefs discovered by British excavators in the throne room of Sennacherib's palace at Nineveh depict in remarkable detail the Assyrian attack on Lachish, one of the Judean cities destroyed in Sennacherib's southern campaign. The scenes, which were arranged in chronological order around the room, depict the assault by Assyrian archers, slingers, and battering rams; the vain attempt by the citizens of Lachish to defend their city with bows and arrows, flaming torches, and rocks; the death or exile of the people; the plundering of the city; prisoners of war being tortured; and the neighboring Assyrian military camp where Sennacherib received updates from his general. In the excavations of Lachish the Assyrian siege ramps have been uncovered, along with iron arrowheads, sling stones, bronze armor, and the physical remains of Judeans who lost their lives in the battle. The written accounts of the battle

The Oriental Institute Prism of Sennacherib.

are preserved here in 2 Kings 18, in Isa. 36–37, and on the Oriental Institute Prism of Sennacherib, which states,

> As for Hezekiah, the Judean, I besieged forty-six of his fortified walled cities and surrounding smaller towns, which were without number. Using packed-down ramps and applying battering rams, infantry attacks by mines, breeches, and siege machines, I conquered (them). I took out 200,150 people, young and old, male and female, horses, mules, donkeys, camels, cattle, and sheep, without number, and counted them as spoil. He himself, I locked up within Jerusalem, his royal city, like a bird in a cage. I surrounded him with earthworks, and made it unthinkable for him to exit by the city gate. His cities which I had despoiled I cut off from his land and gave them to Mitinti, king of Ashdod, Padi, king of Ekron and Ṣilli-bel, king of Gaza, and thus diminished his land. I imposed dues and gifts for my lordship upon him, in addition to the former tribute, their yearly payment. He, Hezekiah, was overwhelmed by the awesome splendor of my lordship, and he sent me after my departure to Nineveh, my royal city, his elite troops (and) his best soldiers, which he had brought in as reinforcements to strengthen Jerusalem, with 30 talents of gold, 800 talents of silver, choice antimony, large blocks of carnelian, beds (inlaid) with ivory, armchairs (inlaid) with ivory, elephant hides, ivory, ebony-wood, boxwood, multicolored garments, garments of linen, wool (dyed) red-purple and blue-purple, vessels of copper, iron, bronze and tin, chariots, siege shields, lances, armor, daggers for the belt, bows and arrows, countless trappings and implements of war, together with his daughters, his palace women, his male and female singers. He (also) dispatched his messenger to deliver the tribute and to do obeisance.[33]

It is worth noting that Sennacherib does not claim to have captured Jerusalem, but only to have imprisoned its king within the city itself.

The king of Assyria sent the field marshal . . . to King Hezekiah at Jerusalem (18:17–19:37). For the Assyrian account of this campaign, see comments on 2 Kings 18:13.

Eliakim . . . who was in charge of the palace (18:18). The royal title "over the household" (here translated as "who was in charge of the palace") was discovered on the lintel of an eighth-century-BC royal tomb in Jerusalem. The inscription identifies the person interred in the tomb as "[ ]yahu who is over the household."[34] The same title was also found on a sixth-century-BC seal impression at Lachish, which identifies the seal's owner as "Gedalyahu 'Over(seer of) the (royal) house.'"[35]

High places (18:22). See comments on 1 Kings 3:2–3.

Please speak to your servants in Aramaic (18:26). The Judean officials request that the Assyrian emissaries use Aramaic, the language used by the Assyrian Empire in international correspondence, so that the common people standing on the city wall would not understand them. The Assyrians continue to speak in Hebrew, the language of Judah, however, precisely because they are attempting to persuade the people to surrender.

He tore his clothes, covered himself with sackcloth (19:1). See comments on 2 Kings 6:30.

Eliakim, who was in charge of the palace (19:2). See comments on 2 Kings 18:18.

King Tirhakah of Cush (19:9). See the article "The Cushites." Tirhakah was the Cushite commander of the Egyptian army that invaded Judah in 701 BC. He ruled Egypt as pharaoh from 690 to 664 BC.

Esar-haddon (19:37). See the article "The Assyrians." Esar-haddon, Sennacherib's son, was the king of Assyria from 681 to 669 BC.

Merodach-baladan (20:12). "Merodach-baladan" (or in some manuscripts "Berodach-baladan") was the Hebrew name for Marduk-apla-iddina II, who became king of Babylon in 722 BC. His trip to Jerusalem occurred sometime during the first twelve years of his reign, before he was exiled by the Assyrian king Sargon II.

Hezekiah . . . made the pool and the tunnel and brought water (20:20). The Gihon Spring, located in the Kidron Valley just south of the Jerusalem temple, was the primary water source for Jerusalem. The water needed to be accessible from within the city, especially during times of war, so Hezekiah commissioned a tunnel to be constructed to carry the water from the spring to the Pool of Siloam, where residents could reach the water from within the city walls. Known as Hezekiah's Tunnel, it was a remarkable feat of engineering. Two crews worked from opposite ends to dig through the bedrock. The moment the two crews met was commemorated in antiquity by the following inscription, known as the Siloam Inscription, carved on the tunnel wall:

> [The day of] the breach. This is the record of how the tunnel was breached. While [the excavators were wielding] their pick-axes, each man towards his co-worker, and while there were yet three cubits for the brea[ch,] a voice [was hea]rd each man calling to his co-worker; because there was a cavity in the rock (extending) from the south to [the north]. So on the day of the breach, the excavators struck, each man to meet his co-worker, pick-axe against

The Cushite pharaoh Tirhakah.

> pick-[a]xe. Then the water flowed from the spring to the pool, a distance of one thousand and two hundred cubits. One hundred cubits was the height of the rock above the heads of the excavat[ors.][36]

Hezekiah's tunnel.

In addition to securing a dependable water supply prior to the Assyrian invasion, Hezekiah fortified the city by building a much thicker and stronger defensive wall, known as the Broad Wall (cf. Isa. 22:10). The partial remains of this wall were discovered in the Jewish Quarter of Jerusalem's Old City. Additional preparation may have included stocking various administrative and military centers in Judah with food and supplies. This is suggested by over one thousand *lamelek* store-jar handles from the late eighth century BC found in Judah. Each handle bears a stamp of either a four-winged scarab beetle or a two-winged sun disk or scroll with the Hebrew word *lamelek* ("belonging to the king") impressed on the clay, along with the name of one of four cities: Hebron, Ziph, Socoh, and the unidentified *mmsht*. These jars may have been used to transport supplies for the Judean army in preparation for the impending Assyrian attack.

The high places (21:3). See comments on 1 Kings 3:2–3.

Altars for Baal . . . an Asherah (21:3). See comments on 1 Kings 15:13; 16:32; 18:18; see the article "The Canaanites and Canaanite Religion."

All the stars in the sky (21:3). See comments on 2 Kings 17:16.

Sacrificed his son in the fire (21:6). See comments on 2 Kings 3:27.

Practiced witchcraft and divination, and consulted mediums and spiritists (21:6). See comments on 2 Kings 16:14. Practicing divination, seeking out omens, and consulting mediums and spiritists (or necromancers, those who consult the dead) are well attested among the Hittites, the Canaanites, in Mesopotamia, and, to a lesser extent, in ancient Egypt. In a Late Babylonian incantation from the first millennium BC, the medium prepares a special ointment made of various animal parts, wine, water, and milk. He then applies it to the eyes of a man who wants to consult the dead. The priest instructs, "You recite the incantation three times and you anoint your eyes (with it), and you will see the ghost; he will speak with you. You can look at the ghost, he will talk with you."[37] The prohibitions against and condemnations of consulting mediums and spiritists in 1 Sam. 28; Lev. 20:6, 27; Deut. 18:10–11; 2 Kings 21:6; and Isa. 8:19 indicate that these methods, although forbidden, were employed by Judeans in an attempt to determine the Lord's will or knowledge of the future.

King Manasseh of Judah (21:10). Manasseh's name appears in the campaign records of Esar-haddon, king of Assyria from 681 to 669 BC. As an Assyrian vassal, he was required to provide and ship supplies to Nineveh for the construction of Esar-haddon's royal palace. Manasseh is also mentioned in the campaign records of Esar-haddon's successor, Ashurbanipal (668–630 BC), who exacted hefty tribute and required some of the men from Judah to serve in the Assyrian military.

He tore his robes (22:11). See comments on 2 Kings 6:30.

Baal, Asherah, and all the stars in the sky (23:4). See comments on 1 Kings 15:13; 16:32; 18:18; 2 Kings 17:16; see the article "The Canaanites and Canaanite Religion."

The high places . . . they had burned incense to Baal, and to the sun, moon, constellations, and all the stars in the sky (23:5). See comments on 1 Kings 3:2–3; 16:32; 18:18; 2 Kings 17:16; see the article "The Canaanites and Canaanite Religion."

The Asherah pole (23:6). See comments on 1 Kings 15:13; 2 Kings 3:2.

Topheth . . . sacrifice his son or daughter in the fire to Molech (23:10). See comments on 1 Kings 11:5; 2 Kings 3:27.

The horses that the kings of Judah had dedicated to the sun (23:11). Over one thousand vessels and religious objects from the eighth to seventh centuries BC were found in a cave on the eastern slope of the Ophel in Jerusalem, near the Temple Mount. The objects included small, ceramic horse figurines, several of which had a disk, perhaps representing the sun, on their foreheads between the ears. If so, they may be models of the horses dedicated to the sun standing at the entrance of the temple. Alternatively, these disks could represent part of a bridle.

The altars . . . on the roof (23:12). Rooftops were a natural place to worship the starry hosts. An incense altar from the 604 BC Babylonian destruction was found atop a collapsed roof at Ashkelon.

The high places (23:13). See comments on 1 Kings 3:2–3.

Ashtoreth . . . Chemosh . . . Milcom (23:13). See comments on 1 Kings 11:5; 11:7.

Sacred pillars . . . Asherah poles (23:14). See comments on 1 Kings 15:13; 2 Kings 3:2.

The high place (23:15). See comments on 1 Kings 3:2–3.

The mediums, the spiritists, household idols, images (23:24). See comments on 2 Kings 21:6. Although forbidden by the Mosaic law, household gods were used in divination (Ezek. 21:21; Zech. 10:2), and in spiritism in particular. The worship of these family deities may have been related to the care and worship of dead ancestors. Rituals in Mesopotamia involved these types of figurines that often represented a deceased relative, who was believed to speak through the figure.

The Babylonian Chronicle.

Pharaoh Neco . . . at Megiddo when Neco saw him he killed him (23:29). Pharaoh Neco II (610–595 BC) marched north with an army from Egypt so that he, along with his Assyrian allies, could attack the united forces of the Babylonians and the Medes. The Babylonian Chronicle reports, "Seventeenth year [609 BC]: In the month of Dumuzi, Ashur-uballit, king of Assyria, and a large Egyptian army . . . cross the [Euphrates] river and marched on Harran in order to take posses[sion] of it. They massacred the garrison that the king of Akkad had set up there. Once victors, they set up camp facing Harran. Until the month of Elul, they joined battle in the city without ce[asing], but it ca[me]to nothing."[38] Josiah's attempt to prevent Egypt's reinforcements from reaching the Assyrian army cost him his life.

Jehoiakim (23:36–24:7). The Egyptian pharaoh Neco, with Judah under his tight control, removes Jehoahaz as king of Judah and replaces him with Jehoahaz's brother Jehoiakim, who will figure prominently throughout the book of Jeremiah as one of the prophet's major opponents. Politically, Jehoiakim was caught between the powerful Babylonians to his north and the powerful Egyptians to his south. In 605 BC the Babylonian king Nebuchadnezzar defeats the Assyrian-Egyptian alliance. In 604 BC Jehoiakim switches sides and pledges loyalty to the Babylonians. Three years later, however, after Nebuchadnezzar is unable to seize control of Egypt, Jehoiakim reverses his allegiance once again, rebelling against his Babylonian overlord and turning to Egypt for aid (cf. Jer. 46:14–28).

King Nebuchadnezzar of Babylon attacked. Jehoiakim . . . turned and rebelled against him (24:1). In December of 598 BC Nebuchadnezzar and the Babylonian army set out on a military campaign to the west in order to suppress Jehoiakim's revolt, a campaign mentioned in the Babylonian Chronicle (see comments on 2 Kings 24:10).

Jehoiachin (24:8). By the time Nebuchadnezzar reaches Jerusalem to dethrone his rebellious vassal, Jehoiakim has died (perhaps murdered) and eighteen-year-old Jehoiachin has replaced him as king. Jehoiachin quickly surrenders to Nebuchadnezzar, and many Judeans, especially those of the upper class, are taken into exile at this time, including the prophet Ezekiel.

The servants of King Nebuchadnezzar of Babylon marched up to Jerusalem, and the city came under siege (24:10). Babylonian records (the Babylonian Chronicle) report that Nebuchadnezzar "besieged Jerusalem and seized it on the second day of the month Adar. He then captured its king and appointed a king of his own choice, having received heavy tribute from the city, which he sent back to Babylon."[39]

King Jehoiachin of Judah (24:12–16). The exiled king Jehoiachin and his sons are mentioned specifically by name in two administrative documents found in Babylon (see comments on 2 Kings 25:29–30).

Zedekiah rebelled against the king of Babylon (24:20). The Babylonians appoint Jehoiakim's brother Zedekiah to be the new puppet king of Judah. He also foolishly rebels against the Babylonians, and this rebellion provokes a harsh military response. Nebuchadnezzar and the Babylonian army destroy much of Judah and Philistia, an event well documented in the archaeological record at Lachish, Hazor, Megiddo, Acco, Ashdod, and Ashkelon, among other cities. In Jerusalem the city walls are destroyed and buildings are burned by fire, as excavations in Jerusalem (the Citadel, the Jewish Quarter, and on the eastern slope of the city of David) attest. Much of the population was either killed or exiled (see comments on 2 Kings 25:8–10).

Nebuzaradan, the captain of the guards . . . entered Jerusalem (25:8–10). Archaeological evidence for the Babylonian invasion is well attested at many sites in Judah and Philistia. The excavations at the Philistine port city of Ashkelon revealed layers of burnt debris and smashed pottery throughout the excavated areas, along with vitrified mud-brick and clay materials. The skeletal remains of a middle-aged woman were discovered in a room full of store jars, where apparently she was hiding. A physical anthropologist determined that she died from blunt-force trauma to the head. Inland at the Judahite city of Lachish excavators found twenty-one ostraca (potsherds with letters written on them in ink) dating to the early seventh century BC that appear to have been written during the Babylonian invasion. Letter 3 was sent by a man named Hoshaiah to his commander, Yaosh, at Lachish. He writes, "Now your servant has received the following information: General Konyahu son of Elnatan has moved south in order to enter Egypt. He has sent (messengers) to fetch Hodavyahu son of Aḥiyahu and his men from here," indicating that Judah was seeking Egypt's help.[40] In letter 4 Hoshaiah reports to Yaosh, "it will be known that we are watching the (fire)-signals of Lachish according to the code which my lord gave us, for we cannot see Azeqah."[41] Hoshaiah was referring not to the city of Azekah itself but rather to smoke signals used as a means of communication. That he did not see signals from Azekah suggests that it had already fallen to the Babylonian army, which would now be marching toward Lachish.

Evil-merodach became king of Babylon (25:27). Evil-merodach (sometimes transliterated as Awel-Marduk [e.g., NIV]), known as Amel-Marduk in Akkadian, was Nebuchadnezzar's son and successor. He was king of Babylon for only two years, from 562 to 560 BC.

Jehoiachin . . . dined regularly in the presence of the king (25:29–30). Jehoiachin and his sons are mentioned by name in two administrative documents found in Babylon from the early sixth century BC. One of the documents records rations of oil given to the king and his family: "10 (sila) to Ia-ku-u-ki-nu, the son of the king of Judah, 2½ sila for the 5 sons of the king of Judah."[42]

1–2 Chronicles

SAMUEL A. MEIER

Introduction. The book of Chronicles is now formatted in Bibles as two separate books because the entire work was originally written on two scrolls. It was one of the last books of the OT to be written, penned around the fourth century BC. Chronicles uses as source material, indeed often extensively quoting, several of the earlier books of the Bible such as Genesis, Joshua, 1–2 Samuel, and 1–2 Kings.

The work focuses on the Davidic monarchy from its beginning following the death of Saul around 1000 BC (1 Chron. 10) to Zedekiah, the last "son" (descendant) of David to sit on the throne of Jerusalem before it was destroyed in 586 BC (2 Chron. 36). This central topic of the Davidic monarchy is set in the larger frame of international and pan-Israel concerns (1 Chron. 1–9) and the subsequent realities of the Persian Empire (2 Chron. 36:22–23), which replaced the Babylonians as the major power in the region.

The story of the Davidic monarchy is told with reference to its failures and successes that result from the degree of obedience that David's heirs show to the instructions that God gave to Moses and to David. These instructions have a special focus upon the Levites and the proper conduct of temple worship. Unlike 1–2 Kings, which stresses that both grace and punishment can be transferred from one generation to another, 1–2 Chronicles emphasizes that the consequences of obedience and sin have repercussions upon the individuals themselves.

1 Chronicles

Historical Records from Adam to Abraham (1 Chron. 1:1–27)

Adam, Seth, Enosh (1:1). The writer assumes that the reader has some prior knowledge, for no narrative introduces the list of names. Not even a succession of generations is indicated. In Babylonian literature, the list providing twenty-eight names in the genealogy of the Hammurapi dynasty (popularly known as Hammurabi, an ancient king of Babylon) begins similarly: "Arammadara, Tubtiyamuta, Yamquzzuhalamma, Heana. . . ."

Shem, Ham, and Japheth (1:4). Japheth's offspring are associated with Asia Minor and the Aegean and Mediterranean Seas. Ham is associated with northeast Africa and Canaan. Shem is associated with Syria, Mesopotamia, and the Arabian Peninsula. Elsewhere in the ancient Near East an interest about distant peoples is attested in the "Onomasticon of Amenemope," an extensive list compiled in Egypt of peoples, places, objects, cities, and other facts of the ancient world.

Japheth's sons (1:5). The father-son link is now made explicit in contrast to the first four verses. A similar shift appears in the Assyrian King List, where the seventeen earliest ancestors are simply listed in contrast to later names that are identified as explicitly related.

The Abydos King List records seventy-six kings (pharaohs) of ancient Egypt.

Gomer, Magog, Madai, Javan, Tubal (1:5). These names are primarily places that reflect the geography comprehensible in the middle of the first millennium BC. Here, as elsewhere in the Bible, places (cities, regions, etc.) often are personified as individuals who are related to one another. For example, the Bible speaks of cities as mothers who have satellite cities identified as daughters (2 Sam. 20:19; cf. 1 Chron. 18:1). Likewise, in Ezek. 16:3 Jerusalem is portrayed as the daughter of an Amorite and a Hittite.

Sidon as his firstborn (1:13). The firstborn had special legal privileges (Deut. 21:15–17). This practice is also found outside of Israel (e.g., Middle Assyrian Laws B.1).

Ophir, Havilah (1:23). As far as we know, outside of Cush (see the article "The Cushites") these two locations to the south of Israel were the only sources of gold in the ancient Near East (Gen. 2:11; 2 Chron. 8:18).

The Family of Abraham (1 Chron. 1:28–34)

Sons born to Keturah (1:32). Ancient writers normally did not cite their sources. Genesis is the source for this chapter. The writer assumes the reader's familiarity with it, for no reference is made to Sarah or Hagar, or to the fact that Ishmael and Isaac have different mothers.

Esau's Sons (1 Chron. 1:35–54)

Kings who reigned in the land of Edom before any king reigned over the Israelites (1:43). Reference to both kings and chiefs of Edom (1:51) reflects a transition from a tribal to a monarchic state similar to the transition that took place in Israel (1 Sam. 8–12) as well as in the Aramean kingdoms.

Israel's Sons: Judah (1 Chron. 2:1–4:23)

Er, Judah's firstborn, was evil in the Lord's sight (2:3). This first appearance of moralizing in these genealogies is simply a quotation from Gen. 38:7.

Adonijah son of Haggith was fourth (3:2). Sequential listing of sons with ordinal numbers is unusual, but it does occur, as here, in genealogies of royal families, where the order may be important for succession (1 Chron. 2:13–15; 3:15; 8:1–2, 39).

Shallum fourth (3:15). Also known as Jehoahaz, he was actually the first one of Josiah's sons to sit on the throne (Jer. 22:11).

Elioenai's sons . . . Akkub (3:24). These two names appear in an Aramaic inscription ("Akabiah son of Elioenai") found on a tombstone in Alexandria,

Egypt, dating to the third century BC, an inscription that perhaps does indeed refer to these descendants of the Davidic line.[1]

His mother named him (4:9). The naming of children apparently was done more frequently by the children's mother than by their father, although the father could on occasion override the mother's choice (Gen. 29:32–30:24; 35:18; Exod. 2:10; 1 Sam. 1:20; Luke 1:60–63).

Simeon (1 Chron. 4:24–43)

Five hundred men . . . went . . . to Mount Seir . . . and they still live there today (4:42). This account underscores the mobile and seminomadic status of the tribes, similar to the account in Judg. 18:11–29 about the six hundred men from the tribe of Dan who invaded the northern region of Galilee and settled far from their original appointed location.

Reuben (1 Chron. 5:1–10)

Tiglath-pileser (5:6). This is Tiglath-pileser III, king of Assyria (745–727 BC) (see comments on 2 Kings 15:27–31; 2 Chron. 28:20; see the article "The Assyrians," in particular the section on the Neo-Assyrian period).

Because their herds had increased (5:9). The nomadic profile of this tribe defined where they settled. Numbers 32:1 stresses the large size of the Reubenites' herds and flocks.

Hagrites (5:10). The connection between these enemies of Israel (5:19–22; Ps. 83:6) who lived on the east side of the Jordan River with the woman Hagar (Gen. 16) is possible but unclear.

Gad (1 Chron. 5:11–22)

The sons of Gad (5:11). The Moabite king Mesha in the ninth century BC indicates how he had attacked Gad in this region even though Gad had been settled there "from ancient times."[2]

The Half-Tribe of Manasseh (1 Chron. 5:23–26)

Half the tribe (5:23). This unique designation for an Israelite tribe reflects the fact that half the tribe settled on the east side of the Jordan River, lured there by its rich grazing land (Num. 32).

Tiglath-pileser . . . took them to . . . Gozan's river (5:26). On Tiglath-pileser, see the article "The Assyrians," in particular the section on the Neo-Assyrian period. Israelite personal names, probably deriving from Israelite exiles and their descendants, are preserved in texts unearthed at the city of Gozan, on the Habur River in northern Mesopotamia.

Tiglath-pileser III, with his foot on the neck of a defeated king.

Levi (1 Chron. 6:1–81)

The men David put in charge of the music (6:31). Singers and instruments were a pervasive part of temple services in the ancient Near Eastern world, in contrast to the complete absence of any divine reference to either in the detailed instructions for the tabernacle and its services in the Pentateuch. David changes the silent service of the tabernacle, preparing the way for the temple liturgies, many of which are preserved in the book of Psalms.

Their settlements in their territory (6:54). Priests in the ancient Near East often had special temple properties allotted for their sustenance. The land allotments for the tribe of Levi were similarly distinct and of a different nature than the land holdings of the other Israelite tribes.

Issachar, Benjamin, Naphtali, Manasseh, Ephraim, Asher (1 Chron. 7:1–40)

Many wives and children (7:4). Numerous offspring were universally understood in the ancient world to be a sign of divine blessing. Issachar musters more men for battle than any other tribe except Judah.

Aramean concubine (7:14). Manasseh himself had an Egyptian mother (Gen. 41:50–51). The readiness of preexilic Israelites to have offspring with spouses outside of the twelve tribes (1 Chron. 2:3, 17; 4:18) contrasts with postexilic exclusiveness (Ezra 9–10).

The Genealogy of Saul the Benjaminite (1 Chron. 8:1–9:1)

Esh-baal (8:33). Early in Israel's history those in covenant with the God of Israel could have names that contained the word *baal* (1 Chron. 5:5; 8:30, 34), since this word simply meant "lord" and only secondarily referred to a specific Canaanite god. Only later did Israelites avoid its presence in their names (Hosea 2:16–17).

An Assyrian wall relief showing Judean captives (from Lachish) going into exile.

The People in Jerusalem

(1 Chron. 9:2–34)

The first to live in their towns on their own property again (9:2). Dislocation and resettlement of populations were common realities in the ancient world. The Babylonian king Hammurabi prides himself in the prologue to his collection of laws as one "who gathers together scattered peoples." The many correspondences of this list in 9:2–21 with Neh. 11:3–19 indicate that this settlement occurs during the Persian era, after the exile to Babylon.

The Genealogy of Saul (1 Chron. 9:35–44)

Kish fathered Saul (9:39). This list, repeating 1 Chron. 8:29–38, properly begins the narrative of 1–2 Chronicles in the same way that the story of Abraham begins with his genealogy (Gen. 11:27–32), or the narrative of Jesus's life in the Gospel of Matthew begins with a genealogy specific to Jesus.

Saul Takes His Life (1 Chron. 10:1–14)

The Philistines (10:1). See the article "The Philistines."

Uncircumcised men (10:4). Circumcision was widely practiced in the ancient Near East but not in the Aegean, where the Philistines originate, making them clearly distinguishable by this physical feature.

Fell on his own sword (10:5). The suicides of Saul and his armor-bearer are among the few recorded in the Bible, for suicide was generally seen as reprehensible in the ancient Near East.

David Becomes King over Israel in Jerusalem

(1 Chron. 11:1–9)

Hebron (11:1–3). Hebron has ancient ties with the patriarchs (Gen. 23:19; 49:29–32). Confirming a new king at a traditional location is attested for other monarchs in the ancient Near East as well, such as in Egypt, where pharaohs would go to Memphis for their coronation even though the primary palace from which they ruled might be elsewhere.

Leading Israel out to battle (11:2). Since kings by definition were warriors, and Israel had asked for a king to fight their wars (1 Sam. 8:20), David's credentials as a good warrior make him a logical choice for king.

The supporting terraces (11:8). This refers to the area where terraces would later be built by Solomon (1 Kings 9:15) to transform Mount Zion's steep slopes into a level platform on which to build his palace.

David's Mighty Warriors (1 Chron. 11:10–12:40)

Killed him with his own spear (11:23). Death by one's own weapon (e.g., Goliath in 1 Sam. 17:51; Saul in 1 Sam. 31:4) illustrates proverbial wisdom (Prov. 26:27).

They . . . could use either the right or left hand (12:2). The left was regarded in the ancient Near East as sinister, but these Benjaminites (ironically, the name Benjamin means "son of the right hand") overcame that perceived liability.

Bringing Back the Ark (1 Chron. 13:1–14)

If this is from the Lord our God (13:2). Moving sacred objects in Mesopotamia required confirmation through favorable omens, just as the Israelites knew when to move the ark during the wilderness years because the cloud over the tabernacle would move (Exod. 40:36–37).

The ark of God on a new cart (13:7). See comments on 2 Sam. 6:16–19. Moving sacred objects in the ancient world required specific methods and techniques. Moving the ark by cart always resulted in catastrophe, for it was only to be carried by Levites (Num. 7:6–9; 1 Sam. 6:11–21; 1 Chron. 15:13).

Lyres, harps, tambourines, cymbals, and trumpets (13:8). See comments on 1 Chron. 15:24; see the article "Musical Instruments in Israel and the Ancient Near East."

David's House and Family (1 Chron. 14:1–7)

Cedar logs (14:1). Cedar, the most important type of timber that kings used to construct their palaces, is a high-quality and aromatic wood that was rare and difficult to acquire, for it grew only in the mountains of Lebanon, and normally could be obtained only through the nearby port city of Tyre.

David took more wives (14:3). A complex hierarchy of authority and behavior in the ancient harem is clearly depicted in the Middle Assyrian palace edicts, clarifying one reason why Deut. 17:17 specified that Israelite kings were not to have many wives.

David Defeats the Philistines (1 Chron. 14:8–17)

The Philistines . . . all went in search of David (14:8). See the article "The Philistines." The Philistines occupied the coast, for the most part exerting significant authority only in the lowlands, usually no more than twenty miles inland, making these attacks into the mountains as far as Jerusalem highly unusual.

The Ark Brought to Jerusalem (1 Chron. 15:1–29)

Pitched a tent (15:1). David does not return the ark to the tabernacle at Gibeon (16:39), but rather erects a new tent in proximity to himself in order to benefit from the ark's blessing (2 Sam. 6:11–12). The failure to return sacred objects to their designated locales for selfish reasons was a common temptation in the ancient Near East. For example, the Egyptian Bentresh Stela tells the story of how Ramesses II sent the statue of a god to the prince of Bakhtan in order to heal his daughter. The prince tries to keep the statue for himself, but the statue transforms into a falcon and flies back to Egypt.

The Lord our God burst out in anger . . . for we didn't inquire of him (15:13). See comments on 1 Chron. 13:2.

Appoint their relatives as singers (15:16). See comments on 1 Chron. 6:31.

Blow trumpets before the ark (15:24). See comments on 1 Chron. 6:31; see the article "Musical Instruments in Israel and the Ancient Near East." Specific musical instruments were designated for use in particular rituals throughout the ancient Near East. The two silver trumpets for calling to assembly and to march are the only instruments specified for Israelite ritual in the Pentateuch (Num. 10:1–10). The list of seven men here assumes seven horns, having a precedent in the seven ram's-horn trumpets accompanying the ark's movement at Jericho (Josh. 6:4). Otherwise, the instruments listed in 15:16, 28, are presented as Davidic innovations.

Ministering before the Ark (1 Chron. 16:1–43)

Burnt offerings and fellowship offerings (16:1). Because the ark is in an ordinary tent, and not in the sacred area of the tabernacle (16:39), David omits any sin (purification) offering that the tabernacle would have required for purification (contrast Hezekiah in 2 Chron. 29:21, 27, 31).

Jeiel played the harps and lyres (16:5). See the article "Musical Instruments in Israel and the Ancient Near East."

Ancient bronze trumpet.

David decreed . . . that thanks be given (16:7). Verbal rituals in temples, often sung, have a long tradition in the ancient Near East, but the Pentateuch is emphatically silent on any tabernacle liturgy. It is David who begins the hymnic tradition with the ark when it is separated from the tabernacle, here with a psalm whose words are found in their entirety in portions of Psalms 96, 105, and 106.

He is good; his faithful love endures forever (16:34). This is the refrain most often repeated in Israel's hymns (2 Chron. 5:13; 7:3; Ezra 3:11; Ps. 100:5; 106:1; 107:1; 118:1; 118:29; 136:1; Jer. 33:11).

God's Promise to David (1 Chron. 17:1–27)

A cedar house (17:1). See comments on 1 Chron. 14:1.

I have moved from one tent site to another (17:5). The principle of establishing ownership by walking over terrain (Josh. 1:3; 14:9) lies behind the mobility of the ark as God's portable throne or footstool (1 Chron. 28:2) to establish his kingdom and authority over the earth. The construction of a temple will bring this process to a halt—the only reason God gives here (17:5–6) for not wanting the temple.

I will be his father, and he will be my son (17:13; also 28:6). The unique relationship between king and god was shared by no one else, a relationship that began with the anointing of the king (Ps. 2:6–7). Some regions in the ancient Near East believed in the deification of the king (e.g., Egypt and the pharaohs), or in some participation by the king in the divine nature (e.g., Eannatum in the Vulture Stela), but Israel saw this only as metaphor.

Lord, there is no one like you, and there is no God besides you . . . you, my God, have revealed (17:20, 25). Here, in the polytheistic ancient Near East, David has deliberately chosen the Lord as his God in the midst of a variety of competing gods (cf. Josh. 24:20–23).

The Vulture Stela.

David's Victories and Administration (1 Chron. 18:1–17)

Assyrian groom with horses.

Hadadezer (18:3). This name recurs among Aramean royal names. Aram was a region in Syria, just to the north of Israel.

Zobah (18:3). This territory extended from north of Dan, the northernmost city in Israel, to south of Hamath.

Hamath (18:3). This major city on the Orontes River (in modern Syria), ninety miles from the Euphrates and 250 miles north of Jerusalem, gave its name to the Aramean kingdom of which it was the heart.

Hamstrung all the horses, and kept a hundred chariots (18:4). See comments on 2 Sam. 8:4. This text implies that David hamstrung most of the chariot horses that he captured but that he also kept some horses for the hundred chariots. This is a compromise on Deut. 17:16, which strictly forbade the king from accumulating large numbers of horses. Earlier in history Joshua, even though he was not a king, hamstrung all of the chariot horses that he captured (Josh. 11:6, 9). David's son Solomon will completely ignore the Deut. 17:16 guideline for kings and build a large army of chariots (2 Chron. 1:14).

The Arameans of Damascus (18:5). Many Aramean kingdoms, like Israel, began to come into existence at the beginning of the first millennium BC, such as the kingdoms of Zobah (18:3), Hamath (18:9), and Aram-naharaim (19:6) to the north of Damascus, and Aram-maacah (19:6) to the south of Damascus.

Administering justice and righteousness for all his people (18:14). The Babylonian king Hammurabi insisted at the beginning of his collection of laws that since he was installed as king "to make justice prevail in the land . . . , I established truth and justice as the declaration of the land, I enhanced the well-being of the people."

The Cherethites and the Pelethites (18:17). Not only was David's bodyguard composed of these Aegean warriors (in this case from the island of Crete and from Philistine backgrounds) but also Egyptian pharaohs enlisted these and other Sea Peoples in their military endeavors (see the article "The Philistines").

David Defeats the Ammonites (1 Chron. 19:1–20:3)

Ammonites (19:1). See comments on Gen. 19:37–38. Israel was not to show aggression against the kingdom of Ammon on the east side of the Jordan River (Deut. 2:19). Because it was important for kings in the ancient world to have publicly defensible reasons for going to war, this narrative demonstrates that it was Ammon who provoked Israel to war.

Aram-naharaim (19:6). "Naharaim" means "two rivers," a reference to the Balikh and Hubur Rivers, which flow into the upper Euphrates River and provide clear boundaries for this Aramean kingdom.

In the spring when kings march out to war (20:1). In many regions of the ancient Near East the rains and snows of October to March swelled the creeks and rivers and did not permit easy mustering and transport of troops.

War with the Philistines (1 Chron. 20:4–8)

The Rephaim (20:4). When referred to in narrative biblical texts like this one, the "Rephaim" or "Raphaites" are always early inhabitants of Canaan (typically of unusual size), but in biblical poetic texts (Ps. 88:10; Prov. 2:18; 9:18; Isa. 14:9; 26:14) as well as in other Canaanite languages they are nearly always (one exception is Isa. 17:5) denizens of the underworld (CSB: "departed spirits").

Shaft . . . like a weaver's beam (20:5). This Aegean-style javelin had a ring with an attached thong midway up the shaft (thus appearing like the rod and rings that lifted the heddle on a loom) that allowed the hurler to throw it with more velocity and force.

David Counts the Fighting Men (1 Chron. 21:1–22:1)

Count the people of Israel (21:1). Exodus 30:12–16 underscored that divine authorization and a very careful procedure were required when taking a census in order to prevent a plague from breaking out. As in this account, great concern and caution are reflected in many texts from the city of Mari in the early second millennium BC with respect to mustering soldiers.

Why does my lord want to do this? (21:3). A king's advisors typically are presented as less insightful than their king in ancient Near Eastern texts, but the Bible, as here, regularly and realistically presents kings as flawed humans who can ignore their wiser subjects.

Gad, David's seer (21:9). This problematic designation for a prophet is contrary to the characteristic identification of prophets as individuals who are "prophets of the LORD" (1 Kings 18:22). A prophet under the authority of a king was suspect (1 Kings 22:23; 2 Kings 3:13).

Take your choice . . . famine . . . foes . . . plague (21:11). In the Babylonian creation myth called the Atrahasis Epic (see comments on Gen. 1:1) three comparable calamities—plague, drought with famine, flood—are sent by the gods upon humanity because each one fails in sequence to achieve the desired ends anticipated by the gods.

Threshing floor (21:18). See comments on 2 Chron. 3:1.

Fire from heaven (21:26). See comments on 2 Chron. 7:1.

Preparations for the Temple (1 Chron. 22:2–19)

Immeasurable quantity of bronze and innumerable cedar logs (22:3–4; also 22:14, 16). Throughout the ancient Near East rhetorical flourish was common in describing superlative royal endeavors. The Assyrian king Sennacherib, for example, boasted, "I besieged . . . surrounding smaller towns, which were without number."[3]

Cedar logs (22:4). See comments on 1 Chron. 14:1.

Young and inexperienced (22:5). See comments on 1 Chron. 29:1.

You have shed much blood (22:8). Kings throughout the ancient Near East achieved renown for two activities: fighting wars and building temples. There is no parallel to this objection anywhere in the literature of the ancient Near East. More perplexing, this reason does not appear in God's oracle through Nathan, nor does David cite the reason God gave there (17:4–6). If this was a matter of religious impurity, there were means to purify warriors (Exod. 32:27–29; Num. 31:19). If it was a moral issue, Moses would have been prohibited from building the tabernacle (Exod. 2:12).

3,775 tons of gold, 37,750 tons of silver (22:14). This reads literally, "a hundred thousand talents of gold and a million talents of silver." The Chronicler often records large quantities of gold and silver that seem exorbitant but often are quite appropriate in light of the royal monopolies on trade in precious metals in the ancient world. For example, over a span of thirty-one years 444 tons of gold and 735 tons of silver were donated by Ramesses III just to temples (Harris Papyrus). Antiochus III had to pay 450 tons of silver to Rome (Treaty of Apamea, 188 BC). However, the amount recorded in this verse is so vague and extravagant—over 3,000 tons of gold and 30,000 tons of silver—that clearly it is intended as a hyperbolic expression.

David ordered all the leaders of Israel to help his son Solomon (22:17). Binding one's subjects to submit to the next king was a common royal strategy to confirm a stable transition to a new ruler. The seventh-century-BC

Assyrian king Esar-haddon, for example, bound his subjects by stringent oaths to support his son Ashurbanipal as the next king.

The Levites (1 Chron. 23:1–32)

He installed his son Solomon as king (23:1). This coregency, where both father and son were recognized as king, sets a precedent that was sometimes followed by Davidic heirs (e.g., 2 Kings 8:16), following the example of other kingdoms to assure a smooth transition for the successor (cf. 1 Kings 1:5–52).

Thirty years old or more (23:3). This unusually advanced age (given short lifespans in antiquity) to begin service corresponds to Pentateuchal regulations (Num. 4:35, 39, 43). It is lowered in 23:27 likely so that there would be enough men to fulfill the many new tasks associated with the novel and more complex temple administration.

Gatekeepers (23:5). See comments on 1 Chron. 26:1. The temple compound, with multiple entries, required numerous gatekeepers, unlike the smaller tabernacle, with its single entry on the east.

Their duty (23:28). The duties prescribed for the priests correspond closely to temple maintenance responsibilities for temple personnel attested from Egypt to Mesopotamia.

The Divisions of Priests (1 Chron. 24:1–19)

They were assigned by lot (24:5; also 24:31). This method of determining sequence in holding office or apportioning inheritance among brothers, both of which apply in this context, was also a regular feature of Neo-Assyrian culture, where the lot (*puru*) was cast before the god who controls its movement (cf. Prov. 16:33).

The Rest of the Levites (1 Chron. 24:20–31)

The family heads and their younger brothers alike (24:31). The use of lots in this context counters the special legal privilege granted to the firstborn in Israel (cf. Deut. 21:15–17) and in Mesopotamia (Middle Assyrian Laws B.1).

The Musicians (1 Chron. 25:1–31)

The sons of Asaph, Heman, and Jeduthun (25:1). There was a widespread tradition in the ancient Near East of guilds composed of fathers who passed on their skills and professions to their sons.

Egyptian flute player.

Lyres, harps, and cymbals (25:1, 6). See the article "Musical Instruments in Israel and the Ancient Near East." A wide variety of musical genres and instruments was an essential component of ritual in temple contexts in the ancient Near East from Egypt to Mesopotamia, with specialists developing skills that required specialization and division of labor, as here.

They cast lots for their duties, young and old alike (25:8). See comments on 1 Chron. 24:5.

The Gatekeepers (1 Chron. 26:1–19)

Gatekeepers (26:1). See comments on 1 Chron. 23:5. The regulation of traffic flow to restricted space in urban life became a common motif and plot element in numerous literary works of the ancient Near East (Enlil's gatekeepers in the Atrahasis Epic, the mayor's gatekeeper in "The Poor Man of Nippur," the gatekeeper to the underworld in "The Descent of Ishtar," the gatekeeper to the realm of the gods above in "Ea and Ereshkigal").

The east gate (26:14). In the ancient Near East one typically faced east to orient (literally "face east") oneself to the cosmos (with the exception of Egypt, where one faced south toward the source of the Nile). Thus here the east gate is listed first and the west gate last, since it is at one's back.

The Treasurers and Other Officials (1 Chron. 26:20–32)

The treasuries of God's temple (26:20). Particularly careful oversight was required in light of the huge deposits of wealth donated by worshipers, whether from mandatory tithes or from freewill offerings. Theft of temple property ranked among the most highly punishable offenses in the ancient Near East.

Army Divisions (1 Chron. 27:1–15)

The divisions . . . military duty (27:1). The names of those in charge are, appropriately, men experienced in battle (2 Sam. 23:8–9, 20, 24–30).

The first month (27:2). Because a standing army was very expensive to maintain, a king might put soldiers to work doing nonmilitary labor when there were no military crises. A monthly rotation in Israel was another solution seeking to address the expense of maintaining a standing army.

Leaders of the Tribes (1 Chron. 27:16–24)

In charge of the tribes (27:16). Many of the kingdoms in this area (e.g., Arameans, Ammonites) that, like Israel, arose in the eleventh to tenth centuries BC retained some of their old tribal traditions as they developed into monarchical states. David utilizes but dominates the old tribal structures. When Solomon succeeded David as king, he erased this tribal administration and restructured the bureaucracy to weaken the tribal loyalties that David had maintained (1 Kings 4:7–19).

The King's Overseers (1 Chron. 27:25–34)

The king's storehouses (27:25). Scores of pieces of broken pots (ostraca) from the early eighth-century-BC palace at Samaria (capital of the northern kingdom Israel) preserve the administrative records of royal scribes as they recorded transfers of oil and wine between the palace and outlying districts.

David's Plans for the Temple (1 Chron. 28:1–21)

A footstool for our God (28:2). Unlike other gods in the ancient world, who were visible and were portrayed sitting on thrones with footstools, the invisible God of Israel sat as king upon an invisible throne with only a visible footstool to identify the place of his enthronement.

You are a man of war and have shed blood (28:3). See comments on 1 Chron. 22:8.

The Lord . . . chose me . . . he has chosen my son Solomon (28:4–5). In the ancient Near East a variety of factors combined to determine who would sit on the throne of a kingdom, but it was universally recognized that it was a deity who ultimately made the succession possible for a particular individual whom the deity selected. Thus the ancient Babylonian king Hammurabi claims in the preface to his collection of laws, "The gods Anu and Enlil . . . called my name!"

The plans (28:12; also 28:19). It was important in describing the plans for the tabernacle that the design came from God (Exod. 25:9). Temple plans in the ancient world required divine

Gudea, ruler of Lagash in Mesopotamia.

approval. Gudea, ruler of Lagash in southern Mesopotamia in the late third millennium BC, had stone statues of himself carved that showed him seated with a lapboard on which was inscribed the plan of a temple that he built. He also recorded on a stone cylinder how in a dream one god told him to build a temple and another god drew the design for him.

The *daric*, a gold coin minted by the Persian Empire.

Gifts for Building the Temple
(1 Chron. 29:1–9)

Young and inexperienced (29:1; also 22:5). These liabilities in a culture that values the wisdom that should come with age (Job 32:4–7) are not insurmountable when an individual is specially gifted by God. The word translated here as "young" (*naar*, "boy, youth") is the same word that Jeremiah uses when he unsuccessfully attempts to decline God's call to become a prophet (Jer. 1:6–7).

The building will not be built for a human but for the LORD God (29:1). Temples were not structures to which most people had ready access, but were places where gods resided and revealed themselves.

Ophir (29:4). See comments on 2 Chron. 8:18.

10,000 gold coins (29:7). The gold coin referenced here is the *daric* (cf. NRSV), minted during the Persian Empire and weighing 0.3 ounces. Since the book of Chronicles was written during the time of the Persian Empire, the writer has converted the quantity of gold into a unit with which contemporaries were familiar.

David's Prayer (1 Chron. 29:10–20)

Without hope (29:15). This is a reference to the awareness of all cultures in the ancient world that there was no escaping death. For example, the Gilgamesh Epic notes, "When the gods created mankind, they allotted death to mankind."

They knelt low and paid homage to the LORD and the king (29:20). The physical act of bowing down was both a form of greeting and a means of affirming a social hierarchy, indicating submission. Bowing to a king was an act not of worship but of submission. Therefore, bowing to other gods was a problem for the Israelites, who had sworn allegiance to the Lord alone, but bowing to humans was a perfectly acceptable way of showing respect to one's social superior.

Solomon Acknowledged as King and the Death of David (1 Chron. 29:21–30)

A thousand bulls (29:21). See comments on 2 Chron. 7:5.

Pledged their allegiance to King Solomon (29:24). See comments on 1 Chron. 22:17.

Royal majesty as had not been bestowed on any king over Israel before him (29:25). This comparison might seem weak because only two earlier kings had reigned over Israel (Saul and David). However, the statement is a hyperbole whose like recurs thousands of times in royal inscriptions from Egypt to Mesopotamia whenever a king identifies something great about his reign (cf. 2 Chron. 1:12; 9:9, 11, 19, 22).

2 Chronicles

Solomon Asks for Wisdom (2 Chron. 1:1–17)

Gibeon (1:3). The Philistines destroyed Shiloh after they captured the ark (1 Sam. 4; Jer. 26:6–9). The tabernacle, however, which had been at Shiloh, had been moved before Shiloh's destruction and eventually had been erected at Gibeon.

Wisdom and knowledge are given to you (1:12). Throughout the ancient Near East monarchs repeatedly insisted that they possessed these essential features of kingship. For example, the Babylonian king Hammurabi asserts in the introduction to his collection of laws that he is the "wise one . . . , he who has mastered all wisdom."

Unlike what was given to the kings who were before you (1:12). See comments on 1 Chron. 29:25.

Solomon accumulated 1,400 chariots and 12,000 horsemen (1:14). When the horse-drawn chariot was introduced into the ancient Near East in the second millennium BC it became an essential component of a king's army and a symbol of a powerful king. In contrast to other kingdoms, however, the Lord demanded that horses and chariots not be a part of Israel's armies (Deut. 17:16; Josh. 11:6, 9). Solomon's vigorous trade in horses and chariots opened the door to his successors' continued abuse in refining this technology so that by the ninth century BC no other kingdom in the Levant could field as many chariots in battle as King Ahab (according to the inscriptions of the Assyrian King Shalmaneser III). This royal failure to obey the Lord vexed the prophets (Isa. 2:7–8; 31:1; Mic. 1:13).

Silver and gold as common in Jerusalem as stones (1:15). This description of hyperinflation results from the rapid introduction of large quantities of gold and silver, explicitly forbidden to Israelite kings (Deut. 17:17). Solomon is behaving just like the other ancient Near Eastern kings, who would write to one another, "Send me much gold!"[4]

From Egypt and Kue (1:16). This means from the south (Egypt) and the north (Kue is Cilicia in southeastern Asia Minor).

Preparations for Building the Temple (2 Chron. 2:1–18)

He assigned 70,000 men (2:2). See comments on 1 Kings 4:6. Forced labor, familiar from the Egyptian enslavement of Israelites, was an abuse about which Samuel had earlier warned when the Israelites asked for a king (1 Sam. 8:16–18). This forced labor under Solomon will be one of the primary causes of the civil war that divides Israel after Solomon's death (2 Chron. 10:14, 18–19). Even in the Mesopotamian myth of Atrahasis the institution of forced labor is criticized when the gods are forced to labor, resulting in rebellion against Enlil as the god who is in charge.

Our God is greater than any of the gods (2:5). See comments on 2 Chron. 6:14.

Send me an artisan who is skilled in engraving to work with gold (2:7). Monarchs in the ancient Near East with special needs were known to ask for assistance from other monarchs. The Hittite king Hattushili, for example, concerned about his sister's inability to give birth, wrote to Pharaoh Ramesses II in the thirteenth century BC, "Let my brother send a man to prepare medicines for her, so that she might be caused to give birth."

Cedar, cypress, and algum logs from Lebanon (2:8; also 9:10). A long-standing need for basic building materials from the forest-impoverished ends of the Fertile Crescent (Babylon and Egypt) prompts a royal tradition already in the third millennium BC to seek not simply timber from Lebanon but exotic and highest-quality wood. The three types of trees listed here are the same that the Assyrian king Sennacherib later used to build his palace in the early seventh century BC.

As rafts by sea (2:16). Mesopotamian kings portrayed on their palace walls this method of transporting logs (in their case, on the Tigris and Euphrates Rivers) as a particularly praiseworthy engineering feat.

Joppa (2:16). Joppa was the closest large port to Jerusalem, which was thirty-five miles inland from the Mediterranean Sea.

Solomon Builds the Temple (2 Chron. 3:1–17)

The threshing floor (3:1). Threshing floors were associated with harvest, fertility, and prosperity, and were places where God could be expected to reveal himself (Judg. 6:37; 2 Sam. 24:18; 1 Kings 22:10).

The length was ninety feet, and the width thirty feet (3:3). The size (90 feet by 30 feet) of the temple corresponds approximately to that of two other temples in the region from this time period that have been excavated north of Israel at Ain Dara (98 feet by 66 feet) and Tell Tainat (83 feet by 39 feet).

Palm trees (3:5). The date palm was a symbol of fertility and prosperity that commonly adorned palace and temple walls. No such decorations appeared in the tabernacle decoration proper, perhaps indicating Phoenician influence here in the temple décor.

Gold of Parvaim (3:6). This exotic source for gold, mentioned only here, may refer to the gold-producing region in the southern Arabian Peninsula, where a gold-producing locale called Farwa is attested.

Length of the wings . . . 30 feet (3:11). The gigantic size reflects an awareness that the supernatural beings associated with temples in the ancient world were much larger than humans, as evident in the huge stone guardian genii that flanked the doors of Mesopotamian palaces and temples, or the three-foot-long footprints that were carved into the stone pavers of the Ain Dara temple to represent the tracks of the deity.

Two pillars (3:15). This innovation, not found in the tabernacle, was a feature of Phoenician temples.

Jachin . . . Boaz (3:17). Architectural elements often had inscriptions. As the Hebrew name of each of the first five books of the Bible is an initial word that begins the book, so the "name" of each pillar derives from an opening word for each inscription that would have referred to the way God or Solomon established (*yakin*) some aspect of the temple with strength (*boez*).

Three-foot-long footprints at the Ain Dara temple (in Syria).

The Temple's Furnishings (2 Chron. 4:1–5:1)

15 feet high (4:1). More than twice a man's height requires a means of access that is not specified. All indications point to a ramp, not steps (cf. Exod. 20:26).

Cast metal basin (4:2). The word translated as "basin" is literally "sea" (cf. NRSV). Fresh water in this basin was for cleansing

(4:6), but its name reminded the Israelites of God's control over the most unruly element in the cosmos, transforming the sea's threatening saltwaters into a means of life (Ps. 93:3–4). Neo-Assyrian kings purified their weapons by washing them in the Mediterranean Sea. In Mesopotamian temples a water basin was called the *apsu*, the Akkadian name for the sea and deep cosmic waters.

An ivory furniture panel from Nimrud showing a winged griffin and floral motifs.

Lily blossom (4:5). Motifs of flowering plants and trees, as symbols of life, characterized temple architecture everywhere, from the intricate ivory work of Phoenician craftsmen to the huge hypostyle halls of Egypt with their columns replicating the flora of a marsh on a grand scale.

Such great abundance . . . was not determined (4:18). The claim that a king's benefaction is beyond computation is a common motif in royal inscriptions, appearing frequently in David's and Solomon's bequests on behalf of the temple (2 Chron. 5:6).

The Ark Brought to the Temple (2 Chron. 5:2–6:11)

Bring the ark of the covenant of the Lord up from the city of David (5:2). The temple was built outside the city of David on a higher level of the mountain than the king's palace (cf. 2 Kings 20:8).

In the seventh month (5:3). The Festival of Tabernacles, when Israel for seven days camped in temporary shelters (Lev. 23:42), was a propitious and appropriate time to transition the ark from its temporary shelter to the permanent structure built by Solomon.

Cherubim spread their wings over the place of the ark (5:8). Cherubim—supernatural winged creatures with composite bodies—were a regular part of the décor for temples with two primary functions in Israel, as elsewhere: protect and support the divine throne. The small cherubim on the ark (God's footstool) supported the divine throne (1 Chron. 28:2) while these large cherubim (fifteen feet high [1 Kings 6:23]) served as protectors and guards (cf. Gen. 3:24).

Carrying cymbals, harps, and lyres (5:12). See the article "Musical Instruments in Israel and the Ancient Near East."

For he is good; his faithful love endures forever (5:13). See comments on 1 Chron. 16:34.

Solomon's Prayer of Dedication (2 Chron. 6:12–42)

Spread out his hands (6:12). This gesture was used in Israel and elsewhere in the ancient Near East to address or petition a social superior, whether divine or human (cf. 6:29).

Lord God of Israel (6:14). This identification acknowledges that although Israel has chosen the Lord as their God (Josh. 24:22), the Lord is not the god whom other nations have chosen (cf. 6:33).

There is no God like you (6:14). This affirmation of God's superlative character (cf. 2:5) is a claim often made on behalf of various gods in the ancient world. For example, the Egyptian god Amun is said to be the "sole one, unique one,"[5] the Aten is the "sole god beside whom there is none,"[6] and Osiris is "the leader of all the gods."[7] Likewise, the Babylonians claim, in regard to the god Shamash, that there is "none who is supreme like you in the whole pantheon of gods."[8]

Who keeps his gracious covenant with your servants (6:14). No other god in the ancient world is known to have had a covenant relationship with any national entity.

Defeated before an enemy . . . no rain . . . famine in the land . . . blight or mildew, locust or grasshopper (6:24–28). This list not only responds to the specific curses for disobedience to the covenant made at Mount Sinai (Deut. 28:22–25, 38, 42, 52, 59) but also replicates curses found in international treaties for those who fail to keep them.

Spread out their hands toward this temple (6:29). See comments on 2 Chron. 6:12.

Then all the peoples of the earth will know your name, to fear you as your people Israel do (6:33). No other national entity in the ancient world recognized a need for its god to be recognized by all other groups, a fundamental perspective in ancient Israel (Ps. 100:1; 117:1).

Assyrian wall relief with a winged cherubim-like being.

The Dedication of the Temple (2 Chron. 7:1–10)

Fire descended from heaven (7:1). Fire sent by the Lord also confirmed his acceptance of the tabernacle (Lev. 9:23–24), Gideon (Judg. 6:21), David's altar (1 Chron. 21:26), and Elijah (1 Kings 18:38).

Twenty-two thousand cattle and one hundred twenty thousand sheep and goats (7:5). Ashurnasirpal II, king of Assyria, sponsored festivities on a similar scale in his palace and temple dedication celebrations around 879 BC. His list includes "1,000 barley-fed oxen, 1,000 young cattle and sheep from the stalls, 14,000 common sheep belonging to Ishtar my mistress, 200 oxen from the herds belonging to Ishtar my mistress, 1,000 fattened sheep, 1,000 lambs, 500 deer, 500 gazelles . . . [the list continues]."

Observed the festival at that time for seven days (7:8). At the end of the third millennium BC, Gudea of Lagash in southern Mesopotamia celebrated a seven-day festival for the dedication of a temple that he built. The duration of such observances probably was related to the sanctity of the number seven.

The Lord Appears to Solomon (2 Chron. 7:11–22)

The Lord appeared to Solomon at night (7:12). Night appears repeatedly as an appropriate time for revelations from God to kings, particularly through the medium of dreams. Likewise, in Babylon King Nabonidus records how the goddess Ishtar "revealed a dream to me in the middle of the night for the construction of the temple Eulmash."

Everyone who passes by will be appalled and will say (7:21). In the shame-oriented culture that pervaded the ancient world, what others thought of Israel was a powerful incentive to proper behavior.

Solomon's Other Activities (2 Chron. 8:1–18)

Solomon went to Hamath-zobah and seized it (8:3). Although Solomon is characterized as a king associated with peace (1 Chron. 22:9), his reign was marked by some military hostilities that he had to address (1 Kings 11:14–25).

Forced labor (8:8). See comments on 1 Kings 4:6; 2 Chron. 2:2.

My wife must not live in the house of King David (8:11). The regulation of a king's wives was a matter of highest priority (cf. 1 Chron. 14:3), but Solomon's reason here for relocating this wife has no counterpart in the ancient Near East.

Gatekeepers (8:14). See comments on 1 Chron. 23:5; 26:1.

Hiram sent ships to him (8:18). See comnments on 1 Kings 5:1; 2 Chron. 20:36.

Ophir (8:18). This location in either southern Saudi Arabia or east Africa (1 Chron. 1:23) was mentioned in an eighth-century-BC Hebrew inscription from Tell Qasile to specify a particular type of gold.

The Queen of Sheba (2 Chron. 9:1–12)

Sheba (9:1). This kingdom corresponds to modern Yemen, where thousands of inscriptions in a variety of dialects accompany a sophisticated body of artwork and architecture that extends back into the early first millennium BC. Pottery has been found in Jerusalem from the period of the Israelite monarchy that preserves examples of such writing, pointing to a trade network between Sheba and Jerusalem.

Camels bearing spices, gold in abundance (9:1). These products correspond to what Assyrian kings received from Arabs in the eighth to seventh centuries BC.[9]

It took her breath away (9:4). This unnamed queen from a land that is literally at the southern edge of the ancient Near East serves as a foil to underscore Solomon's achievements: the most exotic of kingdoms from the most distant realms acknowledges Solomon's superiority.

Lyres and harps (9:11). See the article "Musical Instruments in Israel and the Ancient Near East."

Solomon's Splendor (2 Chron. 9:13–28)

Two hundred large shields of hammered gold (9:15). Completely useless as military items, such shields are attested elsewhere in large quantities as votive offerings, even in the sacred shrine of a god, as attested in the Assyrian inscription titled "Sargon's Letter to Ashur."

The House of the Forest of Lebanon (9:16). This armory with distinctive pillars (1 Kings 7:2) seems to have had the appearance of a forest, much as the pillars in Egyptian temples were designed to look like papyrus plants in a marsh.

A large ivory throne (9:17). See comments on 1 Kings 10:18–20. Phoenicia was a center for the artistic production of carved ivories for an elite clientele, which included the northern kingdom of Israel (1 Kings 22:39; Amos 3:15; 6:4), hundreds of examples of which have been found at the ancient Assyrian capital of Calah, where they were collected by Assyrian kings. Ivory increasingly had to be imported from Africa (see the article "The Cushites") (cf. 9:21), since hippopotamuses were no longer to be found in the ancient Near East after the second millennium BC, and elephant herds diminished and then disappeared after the middle of the first millennium BC.

Two lions standing beside their armrests (9:18). See comments on 1 Kings 10:18–20. Lion imagery was a regular adjunct to thrones, whether of kings or gods.

Monarchs in the ancient Near East prided themselves in their collections of exotic animals. In this Egyptian wall relief two Cushites bring a giraffe and a monkey to the pharaoh as tribute.

Apes, and peacocks (9:21). Monarchs, such as Hatshepsut and Shalmaneser III, prided themselves when they were able to collect these exotic animals, not indigenous to the Middle East.[10]

Solomon's Death
(2 Chron. 9:29–31)

Buried in the city of his father David (9:31). Israelites consistently buried their dead away from human habitation. This deviation here, followed by most of Solomon's royal successors, provoked criticism in Israel (Ezek. 43:7–9) but had its counterpart in Mesopotamia, where royalty could be buried under the palace.

Israel Rebels against Rehoboam (2 Chron. 10:1–11:4)

Rehoboam went to Shechem (10:1). Shechem has ancient ties with Abraham, Joseph, Joshua, and kingship (Gen. 12:6; Josh. 24:25, 32; Judg. 9:1–2). Confirming a new king at a traditional location is attested for other monarchs, such as in Egypt, where pharaohs went to Memphis for their coronation even though the primary palace from which they ruled might be elsewhere.

Rehoboam consulted with the elders (10:6). When kings conducted their affairs with counselors, they typically were depicted as wiser than their counselors. The Bible takes an unusual stance in its persistent criticism of kingship in general and specific kings in particular, as here when Rehoboam follows the foolish advice of the young men.

The Israelites stoned him to death (10:18). This was not an unusual punishment in the ancient Near East. For example, in an eighth-century-BC inscription from Syria, if one betrays the royal dynasty, the king calls for both the rebel and all his male relatives to be stoned.[11]

He mobilized the house of Judah (11:1). In order to force rebels to submit, war was the standard response of new kings who often found their first years troublesome with rebellions that tested their ability to maintain their authority. The Assyrian king Sennacherib, for example, found that he had to quell rebellions throughout the Assyrian Empire when he became king in 705 BC, Judah itself being one of the kingdoms that rebelled.

Rehoboam Fortifies Judah (2 Chron. 11:5–17)

Fortified cities (11:5). These are not towns on the perimeter of the kingdom to protect the kingdom from foreign invasion. All fifteen of these locations are within thirty miles of Jerusalem, and many much closer, suggesting less a strategic defense of the kingdom than a protective perimeter primarily for Jerusalem.

The priests and Levites . . . took their stand with Rehoboam (11:13). Kings who did not have the support of the priests in a kingdom could find their policies severely compromised. The priests who were ignored by Pharaoh Akhenaten in fourteenth-century-BC Egypt completely reversed his policies and innovations after his death.

Rehoboam's Family (2 Chron. 11:18–23)

After her, he married Maacah (11:20). The next king, Abijah, is thus neither the firstborn nor a son of the first wife. Deuteronomy 21:15–17 indicates that one such as Abijah could not inherit as a firstborn. However, elsewhere in the ancient Near East the firstborn did not necessarily always follow their father as king. Two of the first three successors to David were not the eldest sons (cf. Solomon [1 Kings 2:22]), even though the firstborn could be chosen (2 Chron. 21:3).

Sought many wives for them (11:23). See comments on 1 Chron. 14:3.

Shishak Attacks Jerusalem (2 Chron. 12:1–16)

King Shishak of Egypt went to war against Jerusalem (12:2). See comments on 1 Kings 11:40. Shishak founded the Twenty-Second Dynasty, of Libyan rulers, over Egypt, uniting an Egypt that had been divided for two centuries. As part of this Egyptian renaissance, Shishak's invasion marked the first major

The canopic chest of the Egyptian king Shishak. During mummification the internal organs of the king were placed in this chest.

Egyptian presence in this area since the twelfth century BC, justifying his pride in recording, on the walls of the Amun temple at Karnak in Thebes, the names of scores of cities in Judah and Israel that he conquered.

Libyans, Sukkiim, and Cushites (12:3). The multiethnic composition of Egyptian forces reflects Shishak's own Libyan origin: the Sukkiim were a Libyan group mentioned as adjuncts to Egyptian forces in the twelfth to thirteenth centuries BC, and Cushites were from the region south of Egypt (see the article "The Cushites").

He captured the fortified cities of Judah (12:4). See comments on 1 Kings 11:40. A detailed list of these cities appears in Shishak's record of his campaign. He also recorded conquered sites in the northern kingdom of Israel, including Megiddo, where fragments of his victory stela that he erected there have been found.

Treasuries of the Lord's temple . . . he took everything (12:9). In accord with the policies of conquest and plunder in the ancient world, conquered lands would have to surrender the best and the conqueror could take what he chose.

Abijah, King of Judah (2 Chron. 13:1–14:1)

A covenant of salt (13:5). See comments on Lev. 2:13; Ezra 4:14. Since every meat offering required salt (Lev. 2:13), every covenant ratified by a sacrificial meal included the ingestion of salt (a preservative and a symbol of permanence), underscoring a covenant's inviolability (Num. 18:19).

Jeroboam . . . rebelled (13:6). Kings made a point of justifying any military action, and here Abijah is telling only half the story to account for his aggression against Israel. Jeroboam is actually in many ways like David. Both were privately anointed to be king by a prophet from Shiloh with a torn garment while there was still a reigning king on the throne (1 Sam. 15:27–28; 1 Kings 11:29–38; 2 Chron. 10:15).

The ceremonially clean table . . . the gold lampstand (13:11). These are inferior replacements (cf. 2 Chron. 12:9–10), even though nothing has been said as to how or when these items were replaced after Abijah's father lost them to Shishak (pharaoh of Egypt), or why Solomon's ten lampstands and ten tables for the sacred bread in the temple (1 Kings 7:49; 2 Chron. 4:8, 19) were reduced to the original single table and lampstand prescribed for the tabernacle.

Blew the trumpets (13:14). Up to this point in 1–2 Chronicles trumpets have been confined to use with the ark or in the temple, but now they appear on the battlefield. These trumpets used by the priests in Judah may have been similar to the two trumpets with wooden cores and silver and gold overlay discovered in Pharaoh Tutankhamun's tomb.

Asa, King of Judah (2 Chron. 14:2–15)

Shattered their sacred pillars and chopped down their Asherah poles (14:3). See comments on 1 Kings 15:13; see the article "The Canaanites and Canaanite Religion." Asherah was a mother goddess associated with fertility, physically manifested as a tree or wooden object to which upright stone pillars provided the male counterpart.

Zerah the Cushite (14:9). Cush is the kingdom located along the Nile River south of Egypt (see the article "The Cushites"). Zerah is not called "pharaoh" and thus cannot be associated with the later Cushite Twenty-Fifth Dynasty that ruled Egypt from 710 to 663 BC. Cushite troops were employed by the pharaohs of the Libyan Twenty-Second Dynasty, contemporary with King Asa (cf. 2 Chron. 12:2–3). Thus Zerah probably is a Cushite commander serving under the pharaoh Osorkon I.

As far as Mareshah (14:9). This city guards access to Judah in the southern foothills of the kingdom of Judah, thirty-five miles southwest of Jerusalem.

Do not let a mere mortal hinder you (14:11). This petition assumes that the defeat of Judah's army represents a defeat for the god whom the army follows. As David observed before his encounter with Goliath, "The battle is the LORD's" (1 Sam. 17:47). One of the most common themes in royal inscriptions of the ancient Near East is the assistance that the gods provide to protect, arm, and give victory on the battlefield to the victorious king whom they have chosen.

Pursued them as far as Gerar (14:13). This city, some thirty miles southwest of Mareshah, would lie in the direction that retreating troops from Egypt would take.

The terror of the LORD was on them (14:14). This decisive moment always results in no further opposition, a theme repeated often in royal inscriptions of the ancient Near East. For example, on an Assyrian inscription found at Nimrud, in describing his defeat of the king of Damascus, the king of Assyria proclaims, "The fearful splendor of Ashur, my lord, overwhelmed him."[12]

Asa's Reform (2 Chron. 15:1–19)

No peace for those who went about their daily activities (15:5). An inability to travel freely appeared regularly as one of the hallmarks of the breakdown of society (Judg. 5:6), as expressed in the ancient Mesopotamian story "The Curse of Agade": "Messengers no longer travel the highways, the courier's boat no longer takes to the rivers."[13]

The third month (15:10). The Festival of Weeks (Pentecost) is an appropriate occasion to enter a covenant with God because it commemorates the covenant made at Mount Sinai (no specific day in the third month is noted because the festival does not fall on a predictable day; its observance is counted seven weeks from Passover).

Sheep and goats from all the plunder (15:11). A very strict accounting of the spoil from military victories (14:14–15) included God receiving his portion (Gen. 14:14–20). Similarly, at the end of the Assyrian king Esarhaddon's letter to the gods after one of his campaigns, he closes with his description of the distribution of the spoils to various gods and temples in Assyria.

Asa's Last Years (2 Chron. 16:1–14)

Asa brought out the silver and gold from the treasuries of the Lord's temple (16:2). This impious act of temple sacrilege obliterates the careful distinction made between revenues that went to political leaders and revenues that went to God (cf. Num. 31:36–54).

Aram's King Ben-hadad (16:2). Aram was a kingdom to the north of Israel, with its capital city of Damascus (located in modern Syria). The name Ben-hadad (in Aramaic, Bar-hadad) is attested for more than one Aramean king (cf. 2 Kings 8:9; 13:3). It is possible that the Aramean king Ben-hadad who dedicated a ninth-century-BC stela to the god Melqart is this king.

Break your treaty with Israel's King Baasha (16:3). Such a request, encouraging an impious act of oath-breaking, was never defensible. All treaties to which gods were invoked as witnesses were inviolable. For this reason, Joshua cannot even break a treaty that was ratified under false pretenses (Josh. 9:3–21; 10:5–7).

A great fire in his honor (16:14). See comments on 2 Chron. 21:19.

Jehoshaphat, King of Judah (2 Chron. 17:1–19)

He did not seek the Baals (17:3). See the article "The Canaanites and Canaanite Religion." This activity is associated with this god only here in Chronicles but is assumed to be common by this negative statement in preparation for the action in the next chapter. Kings

The Melqart Stela.

had many options to attempt to discover what the future held as they made decisions: dream interpretation, prophetic oracles, consulting the dead, and interpreting omens from animal entrails, movements of stars, behaviors of animals, and the like. Many of these practices were forbidden to Israelites (Deut. 18:10–14).

They taught throughout Judah (17:9). This activity is not attested for other cultures at this time when professional scribes required years of training and had a monopoly on learning. The simple alphabet that Israel used, with its handful of characters, made literacy easily achievable for a larger portion of the population than was true for Mesopotamia (using cuneiform) or Egypt (using hieroglyphics).

The book of the Lord's instruction (17:9). This document was actually a scroll, since the book as a bound series of pages (known as a codex) will not be invented for several hundred more years.

Micaiah Prophesies against Ahab (2 Chron. 18:1–27)

Bulla (imprint from a seal) from Jerusalem that reads "Governor of the City."

Ramoth-gilead (18:2). The heights of Gilead were a strategic and hotly contested area east of the Sea of Galilee, providing access to fertile regions in the Transjordan (east side of the Jordan River) that both Israel and the Syrians claimed as their own.

My people as your people (18:3). This sentiment encapsulates the essence of treaty relationships between kingdoms, as the king of Mitanni writes about Mitanni to the pharaoh: "This country is my brother's country, and this house is my brother's house."[14]

Ask what the Lord's will is (18:4). Consulting the gods in the ancient Near East was standard procedure before going into battle (cf. 1 Sam. 23:2; Ezek. 21:21–22).

The threshing floor (18:9). See comments on Ruth 3:2; 2 Chron. 3:1.

Like sheep without a shepherd (18:16). This image anticipates King Ahab's death appropriately, since kings were metaphorically understood to be shepherds over their people. "I am Hammurabi the shepherd" is the affirmation that introduces the famous Babylonian king's collection of laws.

Governor of the city (18:25). Official seal impressions on clay (bullae) with this exact title "governor of the city" for an administrator have been discovered.[15]

Ahab Killed at Ramoth-gilead (2 Chron. 18:28–19:3)

Do not fight with anyone . . . except the king of Israel (18:30). The strategy of eliminating the leader of an army was often used to terminate a battle, notable examples including the deaths of Josiah (35:23–24) and Cyrus the Younger (as described in the Greek work *Anabasis*).

Do you . . . love those who hate the LORD? (19:2). This rhetorical question assumes with the rest of the ancient Near East that the love of one's enemies is an absurdity, and it echoes the language of treaties between kings, as seen in a Hittite treaty that states, "Whoever is my majesty's enemy shall be your enemy, and whoever is my majesty's friend shall be your friend."[16]

Jehoshaphat Appoints Judges (2 Chron. 19:4–11)

He appointed judges (19:5). There is little evidence to determine how judges and courts were constituted, beyond the role played by elders and local communities. The distribution of judicial authority seen here corresponds to the fact that the king was everywhere seen as the primary human pillar of justice in the ancient world.

Your brothers who dwell in their cities (19:10). The distinctly urban context of this judicial reform (cf. 19:5) suggests that rural justice continued to be maintained by local elders (cf. Deut. 21:1–9).

Jehoshaphat Defeats Moab and Ammon (2 Chron. 20:1–30)

Moabites and Ammonites (20:1). See comments on Gen. 19:37–38.

Together with some of the Meunites (20:1). Meunites were a nomadic people associated epigraphically with regions to the south and east of Judah (cf. 1 Chron. 4:41) and in the remainder of this passage (vv. 10, 22–23) associated with Mount Seir (i.e., Edom).

He proclaimed a fast for all Judah (20:3). This is the only fast explicitly mentioned in 1–2 Chronicles during the period of the Davidic dynasty, and it has a purpose comparable to other communal fasts, which is to gain God's attention in order to avert anticipated disaster (cf. the Ninevites' fast in Jon. 3:5–10; Esther's fast in Esther 4:16).

You did not let Israel invade (20:10). Ammon, Moab, and Edom were all relatives of Abraham—and thus of Israel—to whom God had given land, just like Israel (20:11), as a part of the blessing to Abraham (Deut. 2:5, 9, 19) (see comments on Gen. 19:37–38). In the ancient world the boundaries between national entities were recognized as inviolable unless the gods permitted or demanded their breach.

The battle is not yours, but God's (20:15). See comments on 2 Chron. 14:11.

Wilderness of Tekoa (20:20). This was located ten miles south of Jerusalem.

For his faithful love endures forever (20:21). See comments on 1 Chron. 16:34.

Nobody could carry any more (20:25). See comments on 1 Chron. 22:3–4.

Harps, lyres, and trumpets (20:28). See the article "Musical Instruments in Israel and the Ancient Near East."

The End of Jehoshaphat's Reign (2 Chron. 20:31–21:3)

Make ships to go to Tarshish (20:36). The Phoenicians became the primary maritime power in the ancient Near East. When Solomon traded by sea, he used Phoenician ships (8:18; 9:10, 21), a precedent ignored here with results that are not surprising.

He was the firstborn (21:3). See comments on 2 Chron. 11:20.

Jehoram, King of Judah (2 Chron. 21:4–20)

Killing with the sword all his brothers (21:4). Writing much later, the Greek historian Plutarch notes, "That brothers should put brothers to death was assumed like the postulate of mathematics as the common and recognized royal first principle of safety" (*Life of Demetrius*). Such a situation might have motivated the Assyrian king Esar-haddon, who before his death made his subjects swear to protect both the son chosen to succeed him and his brothers.

His people did not hold a fire in his honor (21:19). Performed for King Asa (16:14), this rite has nothing to do with cremation, which was not a normal, respectful way to treat the dead in the ancient Near East. Yet fire rituals associated with the dead are not clearly attested elsewhere in the ancient Near East.

Ahaziah, King of Judah (2 Chron. 22:1–9)

Granddaughter of Omri (22:2). Her son is thus the result of an attempt at international diplomacy in joining the two kingdoms of Israel (house of Omri) and Judah (house of David).

King Hazael of Aram (22:5). Aram was the kingdom to the north of Israel in what is now modern Syria. Hazael was a usurper (as the Assyrians would say, "a son of a nobody") who had killed his predecessor and would become one of the most powerful of all Aramean kings and a great threat to Israel at the end of the ninth century BC (2 Kings 8:7–15).

Ramoth-gilead (22:5). See comments on 2 Chron. 18:2.

Judah's king Ahaziah . . . went down to Jezreel (22:6). The descent was significant, from Jerusalem's elevation of twenty-five hundred feet above sea level to Jezreel's mere three hundred feet above sea level.

Joram was ill (22:6). Royal health was closely watched by fellow monarchs (2 Kings 20:12). Thus, for example, the king of Babylon writes to the pharaoh, "Since I was not well and my brother showed me no concern, I for my part became angry with my brother, saying, 'Has my brother not heard that I am ill?'"[17]

Jehu looked for Ahaziah (22:9). Jehu wanted to eradicate the entire dynasty of Omri and Ahab, including their descendant Ahaziah, no matter that he now ruled over Judah.

Athaliah and Joash (2 Chron. 22:10–23:21)

Annihilate all the royal heirs (22:10). This foreign princess (22:2) is vulnerable now that her ruling son has been murdered (22:9). Harem power politics appear in Nathan's words to Bathsheba when Adonijah, son of another wife in David's harem (Haggith), tried to become king: "Let me advise you how you can save your own life and the life of your son Solomon" (1 Kings 1:12). In the twelfth century BC the Egyptian queen Tiye conspired to murder her husband, Ramesses III, in order to place her son on the throne. Likewise, in the seventh century BC the Assyrian queen Zakutu placed other royal children under oath to protect her own offspring.

Athaliah reigned over the land (22:12). Usually a solitary rule by a queen was quickly remedied through remarriage or through an

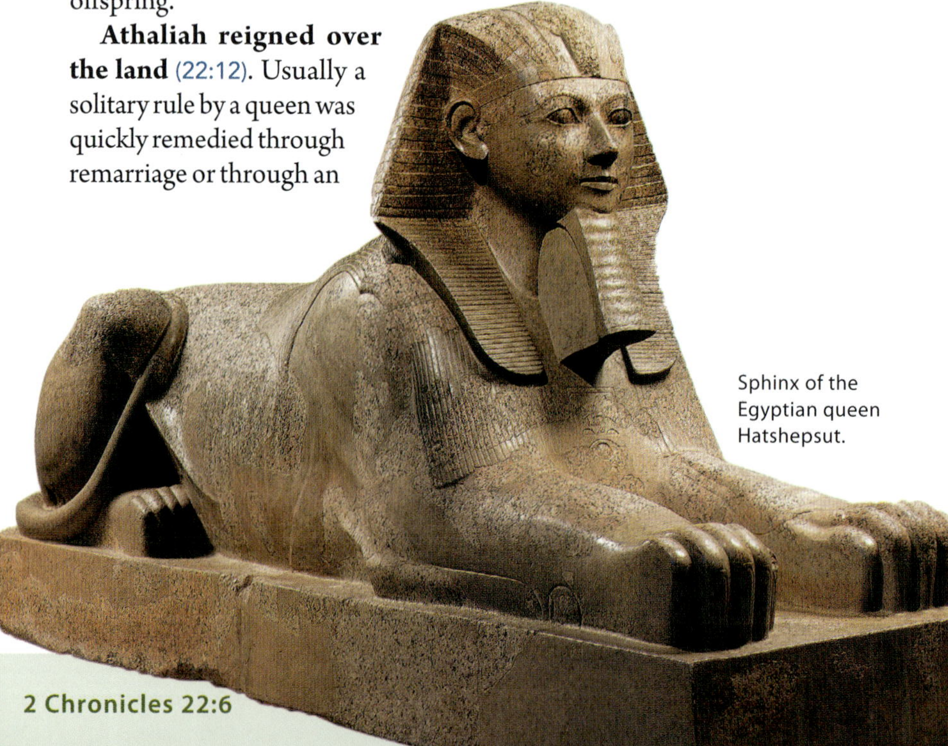

Sphinx of the Egyptian queen Hatshepsut.

alternate male family member ascending the throne. Less common were queens who continued to rule without a male consort, such as Hatshepsut in Egypt (fifteenth century BC) and Athaliah here.

Completely surround the king with weapons in hand (23:7). The sword was an important part of the history of the Levites (Gen. 34:25–26; Exod. 32:26–28) and for their role as guards for the temple precincts (cf. 23:19).

Seated the king on the throne of the kingdom (23:20). This chapter contains one of the two most detailed descriptions of the crowning of a Davidic heir (cf. 1 Kings 1:32–40).

Joash Repairs the Temple (2 Chron. 24:1–16)

Renovate the LORD's temple (24:4). Temples throughout the ancient world needed constant maintenance from normal wear and tear, their physical restoration becoming a matter of pride for kings as a means of expressing piety.

Collect silver from all Israel . . . year by year (24:5). Solomon built the temple entirely from royal revenues. Kings in the ancient Near East normally funded restorations, but the maintenance of Jerusalem's temple was to be funded by the people, with the institution of a yearly collection based upon a Mosaic precedent (Exod. 30:12–16).

He was 130 years old at his death (24:15). Unusually long lives were recorded as a mark of special blessing. The age of 104 years is recorded in the sixth century BC for Adda-Guppi, priestess of the moon god and mother of the Babylonian king Nabonidus.

The Wickedness of Joash (2 Chron. 24:17–27)

They . . . stoned him at the king's command (24:21). See comments on 2 Chron. 10:18.

In the courtyard of the LORD's temple (24:21). Such profanation of the sacred area is carefully avoided on other occasions (23:14).

Few men . . . a vast army (24:24). Such a reversal was enshrined as a consequence of violating a treaty (Deut. 28:25).

Ammonite . . . Moabite (24:26). Royal assassinations were never justified (cf. 33:24), but the blame is here deflected from Judeans to foreign conspirators.

Amaziah, King of Judah (2 Chron. 25:1–28)

They got very angry (25:10). Each soldier receives approximately four shekels for doing nothing, apparently a good deal. However, their anger stems from their lost expectations of plunder from a campaign that they take anyway in 25:13.

Salt Valley (25:11). This region in the vicinity of the Sea of Salt, or Dead Sea (Gen. 14:3), is on the way to Edom (or Seir) (on Edom, see comments on Obad. 1).

Top of a cliff (25:12). Mountains and cliffs, the distinguishing features of Edom, are stereotyped as its primary means of defense (see comments on Obad. 3). Ironically, here they become the means of destruction for its people.

They threw them off (25:12). This reprehensible military conduct is to be contrasted with 2 Kings 6:21–23. Although there were no rules in war, this kind of cruelty is what one expects more of the Assyrian army, which used cruelty in war as a calculated weapon to demoralize their foes.

Obed-edom (25:24). The ark had briefly been under his care during the reign of David (2 Sam. 6:10–12), his name an ironic allusion to Amaziah's earlier successful attack on Edom.

Lachish (25:27). See comments on 2 Chron. 32:9.

Uzziah, King of Judah (2 Chron. 26:1–23)

Rebuilt Eloth (26:2). This Red Sea port city used by Solomon (8:17) was in Edomite territory, which the Israelites were forbidden to occupy (Deut. 2:5, 8; 2 Chron. 20:10), and it will be lost by Uzziah's grandson (2 Kings 16:6).

Zechariah (26:5). Nothing more of this man is known; he is not to be confused with the Zechariah stoned during Joash's reign (24:20–21) or the postexilic literary prophet Zechariah.

Meunites (26:7). See comments on 2 Chron. 20:1.

Over the king's household (26:21). See comments on 2 Kings 18:18. This administrative position (literally "over the house") is attested on Hebrew seal impressions.[18]

Jotham, King of Judah (2 Chron. 27:1–9)

He waged war against the king of the Ammonites . . . overpowered the Ammonites (27:5). Israelites were forbidden to conquer Ammon, a people related to them as kin of Abraham (Deut. 2:19; 2 Chron. 20:10).

Ahaz, King of Judah (2 Chron. 28:1–27)

The Ben Hinnom Valley (28:3). This half-mile-long valley runs east-west immediately to the south of Jerusalem.

Burned his children in the fire (28:3). See comments on 2 Kings 3:27. The extensive cemeteries of young children found at Phoenician sites, notably Carthage, seem to be related to this same phenomenon.

The king of Aram (28:5). This king is Rezin (2 Kings 16:5), who, allied with Israel, invaded Judah (Isa. 7:1–9) but eventually was defeated by the Assyrian king Tiglath-pileser III, who destroyed his kingdom in 732 BC.

Tiglath-pileser (28:20). This Assyrian king (also identified by an abbreviated form of his name, Pul), who ruled 745–727 BC, marked the beginning of Assyria's rise to its greatest extent as an empire and reduced the northern kingdom of Israel to a vassal state (cf. 1 Chron. 5:6, 26; 2 Kings 15:19) (see the article "The Assyrians," in particular the section on the Neo-Assyrian period).

Hezekiah Purifies the Temple (2 Chron. 29:1–36)

In the first year of his reign, in the first month (29:3). Ahaz's modifications in 2 Chron. 28 require the purification of the temple. The Passover is to be celebrated on the fifteenth day of the first month, but the purification will not be completed in time.

Kidron Valley (29:16). This valley on the east side of Jerusalem with a perennial stream was conducive to purification rites.

Sin offering (29:21). This purification offering must come first to cleanse the altar that had been rendered unclean by King Ahaz. Only then can the burnt offerings be offered (29:27) in preparation for the communal sacrifices that the worshipers could eat (29:31).

Cymbals, harps, and lyres (29:25). See the article "Musical Instruments in Israel and the Ancient Near East."

They weren't able to skin all the burnt offerings (29:34). The skin was one part of the burnt offering that was not consumed on the altar and that belonged to the priest (Lev. 7:8).

Hezekiah Celebrates the Passover (2 Chron. 30:1–31:1)

Come to the LORD's temple . . . to observe the Passover (30:1). Observance of the Passover in the first month of the year, a pre-Sinai observance in Israelite homes that required no sanctuary, has not been mentioned anywhere since the entry into Canaan (Josh. 5:10–11), but now Hezekiah transforms the festival into a temple-centered observance.

Second month (30:2). Observing the Passover one month later has a precedent (Num. 9:1–14).

Israelites (30:6). The northern tribes, addressed here, had been conquered by Assyria in 722 BC.

Unclean (30:17). The first Passover in Egypt did not require ceremonial purity, for it was a life-threatening situation in no proximity to a tabernacle or temple that might require purity. This new problem arises when the observance is brought to the temple.

A thousand bulls and seven thousand sheep (30:24). See comments on 2 Chron. 7:5.

Sacred pillars . . . Asherah poles (31:1). See comments on 1 Kings 15:13; 2 Chron. 14:3.

Contributions for Worship (2 Chron. 31:2–21)

Give a contribution (31:4). It is apparent here that the tithe has not been collected for some time. Since the tithe is an institution widely attested even outside Israel, the issue in this passage is that tithes have been going elsewhere, to other deities, while the Lord's temple services have languished under Manasseh and Amon.

Freewill offerings (31:14). This refers to voluntary contributions in addition to the required tithes.

Registered by genealogy (31:16). Records of disbursements for palace and temple provisions from around the ancient Near East make it clear that a very close accounting was made of who could, or could not, benefit.

Sennacherib Threatens Jerusalem (2 Chron. 32:1–23)

Sennacherib (32:1). His reign as king of Assyria began (705 BC) with rebellions against the new king in various parts of the empire, including Judah (see comments on 2 Kings 18:13; see the article "The Assyrians," in particular the section on the Neo-Assyrian period).

Stopping up the water (32:3). See comments on 2 Chron. 32:30.

Rebuilding the entire broken-down wall (32:5). See comments on 2 Kings 20:20. This twenty-foot-thick wall, still preserved today up to ten feet high, has been uncovered for over two hundred feet in Jerusalem (cf. Isa. 22:9–11).

There are more with us than with him (32:7). Assyrian kings regularly asserted that their enemies trusted in alternate sources of power that proved inadequate and resulted in their defeat.

Besieged Lachish (32:9). See comments on 2 Kings 18:13. Lachish, one of Judah's primary fortresses, thirty miles southwest of Jerusalem, eventually fell to Sennacherib, becoming the subject of multiple stone panels in his Nineveh palace to commemorate his conquest. Sennacherib indicates that he captured forty-six fortified Judean cities and too many other unfortified towns to count, taking 200,150 Judeans into exile.[19]

He sent his servants to Jerusalem (32:9). These "servants" are further defined in 2 Kings 18:17. The Assyrian titles given there are *tartan* ("general"), *rab-saris* ("chief eunuch"), and *rab-shaqeh* ("chief cupbearer"), high-ranking Assyrian officials who accompanied the king on, and even led, military campaigns.

Jerusalem under siege (32:10). See comments on 2 Kings 18:13. Sennacherib described the event: "Hezekiah. . . . I locked up within Jerusalem, his royal city, like a bird in a cage. I surrounded him with earthworks, and made it unthinkable for him to exit by the city gate."[20]

What I and my fathers have done to all the peoples (32:13). This included mutilation, skinning alive, early forms of crucifixion, and torture, deliberately used as propaganda to terrorize Assyrian opponents.

They called out . . . to frighten and discourage them (32:18). This action is attested in other sieges in the ancient Near East where the besieger attempts to bring the siege to a close.

The king of Assyria returned in disgrace to his land (32:21). Sennacherib leaves the siege of Jerusalem in many ways unresolved when compared with other Assyrian campaigns, apart from saying, "Hezekiah was overwhelmed by the awesome splendor of my lordship, and he sent me after my departure to Nineveh . . . 30 talents of gold, 800 talents of silver."[21]

Some of his own children struck him down (32:21). The likely instigator was his eldest living son, Arad-Mulissi (referred to as Adrammelech in 2 Kings 19:37), who had been skipped over in favor of a younger son, Esarhaddon, who ultimately became king.

The Siloam Inscription, commemorating the construction of Hezekiah's water tunnel.

Hezekiah's Pride, Success, and Death (2 Chron. 32:24–33)

He made warehouses for the harvest of grain (32:28). Hundreds of storage-jar handles stamped with the mark of ownership "for the king" (*lmlk*) have been found throughout Judah, associated specifically with the reign of Hezekiah.

Blocked the outlet of the water (32:30). See comments on 2 Kings 20:20. The Hebrew term for "outlet" appears in the eighth-century-BC inscription found in the Siloam tunnel that commemorates the construction of the 583-yard-long tunnel.[22]

The Upper Gihon (32:30). See comments on 2 Kings 20:20. The small perennial stream east of Jerusalem runs south down the Kidron Valley. Hezekiah dug a tunnel through solid rock to bring this spring inside the city walls to prepare for a siege by Assyria (701 BC). "Gihon" echoes primordial waters associated with Eden (Gen. 2:13), appropriate for the temple (Ezek. 47:1).

Ambassadors of Babylon's rulers were sent (32:31). The Chaldean prince Merodach-baladan (Isa. 39:1) took control of Babylon from Assyria at the end of the eighth century BC. Hezekiah's rebellion against Assyria meant that Judah and Babylon shared similar political goals. The Assyrians finally expelled him from Babylon, and he died in exile.

Manasseh, King of Judah (2 Chron. 33:1–20)

Manesseh . . . reigned fifty-five years (33:1). King Manesseh died in 642 BC, having had the longest reign of any Israelite or Judean king, paralleled by his contemporary Pharaoh Psammetichus, who reigned 664–610 BC.

Baals . . . Asherah poles (33:3). See comments on 1 Kings 15:13; 2 Chron. 14:3; see the article "The Canaanites and Canaanite Religion."

Ben Hinnom Valley (33:5). See comments on 2 Chron. 28:3.

Bronze shackles (33:11). See comments on 2 Chron. 36:6.

They captured Manasseh with hooks (33:11). The Assyrian kings Esarhaddon and Ashurbanipal recorded Manasseh's assistance twice in providing them with tribute and building materials. Esar-haddon depicted his conquered enemies with hooks in their noses attached to ropes that he held.

Amon, King of Judah (2 Chron. 33:21–25)

Put him to death (33:24). David never saw the murder of Saul as an option in order to claim the throne to which he had been anointed (1 Sam. 26:8–11), setting a pattern that calls into question all subsequent assassinations and makes the execution of Amon's assassins (33:25) entirely appropriate.

Josiah's Reforms (2 Chron. 34:1–13)

Scattered them over the graves . . . burned the bones (34:4–5). Punishment of criminals did not stop with their death, and mistreating their dead bodies was common in the ancient Near East.

The governor of the city (34:8). See comments on 2 Chron. 18:25.

Shaphan (34:8). This official founded an influential family that later will help the prophet Jeremiah and guide Judah briefly after the destruction of Jerusalem (Jer. 26:24; 36:10–11; 40:5). One of the many clay seal imprints that remain from this era has the name of "Gedaliah, overseer of the royal house" on it, probably Shaphan's grandson (Jer. 40:5).[23]

Buildings that Judah's kings had destroyed (34:11). Temples throughout the ancient world needed constant maintenance from normal wear and tear. The reconstruction of a temple was perceived to be as pious an act as the original construction.

The Book of the Law Found (2 Chron. 34:14–33)

Found the book of the law (34:14). Pharaohs Shabaka and Amenhotep II recorded the finding of lost sacred texts that they copied afresh and revived.

Tore his clothes (34:19). Josiah is the only king who does this in the book of Chronicles, an expression of the greatest grief.

Prophetess Huldah (34:22). Female prophets appear regularly in Israel (Exod. 15:20; Judg. 4:4; Neh. 6:14; Isa. 8:3) and elsewhere in the ancient Near East.

Read in their hearing all the words of the book of the covenant (34:30). Such a public reading was often specified as mandatory for covenants made in the ancient Near East (Deut. 31:10–12).

Josiah Celebrates the Passover (2 Chron. 35:1–19)

Passover (35:1). Josiah is the second of only two kings said to observe the Passover (30:1).

You do not have to carry it on your shoulders (35:3). Sacred images and shrines of gods elsewhere in the ancient Near East were carried out on regular excursions from their temples. The ark was designed to be portable, but Hezekiah here transitions to a new and completely immobile phase for the ark.

According to the command of King Josiah (35:16). In accord with the centralization of Passover observance begun under Hezekiah (30:1), there is no mention of blood applied to the doorposts of one's home, as some Samaritans are still able to do to this day.

The Death of Josiah (2 Chron. 35:20–36:1)

King Neco of Egypt (35:20). See comments on 2 Kings 23:29. Josiah attempted in 609 BC to stop this newly crowned pharaoh from bringing his forces to help the weakening Assyrian Empire, which was under attack by Babylon.

Valley of Megiddo (35:22). The only way for the Egyptian forces to continue north was to pass through the mountains by means of the narrow pass guarded by the city of Megiddo.

Jehoahaz son of Josiah (36:1). He was not the eldest son, for the brother who succeeded him was older (36:2, 5).

Jehoahaz, King of Judah (2 Chron. 36:2–4)

Three months (36:2). This is the time required for Pharaoh Neco, after killing Josiah in battle at Megiddo, to travel north, join up with Assyria to fight (unsuccessfully) against the Babylonians, and then to return to the south, passing through Judah on his way back to Egypt.

Changed Eliakim's name (36:4). Changing a person's name signified Neco's complete sovereignty over the king of Judah.

Aerial view of the excavations at the city of Megiddo, with the Plain of Megiddo in the background.

Jehoiakim, King of Judah (2 Chron. 36:5–8)

Bronze shackles (36:6). Three kings of Judah being treated in this fashion by the Assyrians (Manasseh, 2 Chron. 33:11) and the Babylonians (Jehoiakim, 2 Chron. 36:6; Zedekiah, 2 Kings 25:7) reflects the humiliation that conquering kings often boasted of inflicting on defeated kings, binding their hands and feet with fetters of both bronze and iron.

Jehoiachin, King of Judah (2 Chron. 36:9–10)

In the spring Nebuchadnezzar sent for him (36:10). The Babylonian Chronicle records that Nebuchadnezzar "encamped against the city of Judah and on the 2nd day of the month Adar [March 16, 597 BC], he captured the city and seized its king; a king of his own choice he appointed in the city and taking the vast tribute he brought it into Babylon."[24]

Zedekiah, King of Judah (36:11–14)

Zedekiah . . . rebelled against King Nebuchadnezzar who had made him swear allegiance by God (36:13). A similar relationship is reflected in a Hittite treaty, where the Hittite king reminds his vassal, "I have made you swear an oath to the king. . . . Keep the oath of the king . . . and I, My Majesty, will protect you."[25]

The Fall of Jerusalem (2 Chron. 36:15–23)

Those who escaped from the sword (36:20). After the destruction of Jerusalem in the summer of 586 BC, in accord with Babylonian policy, only a few of the most influential among the conquered were deported to Babylon, leaving large numbers behind in a devastated land (2 Kings 25:11–12, 22).

First year of King Cyrus (36:22). Cyrus was welcomed into Babylon in the fall of 539 BC, proclaiming himself "king of Babylon, king of the four corners of the world" (see the article "The Persians," in particular the section on Cyrus).

Appointed me to build a temple at Jerusalem (36:23). According to the Cyrus Cylinder, King Cyrus decreed that the destroyed temples in many locales should be rebuilt (see the article "The Persians," in particular the section on Cyrus). The Jews were one of numerous groups whose destroyed temples fell under this decree.[26]

Ezra–Nehemiah

Gregory Goswell

Introduction. The books of Ezra and Nehemiah take place during the postexilic period, when the Persian Empire dominated the ancient Near East (see the article "The Persians"). The account of the two books covers just over one hundred years, running from the first year of King Cyrus's reign in 539 BC (Ezra 1:1) down to sometime later than the thirty-second year of King Artaxerxes I (Neh. 13:6). The last possible date for Nehemiah's return visit to Jerusalem would be the year of Artaxerxes's death in 423 BC.

There are significant chronological gaps between Ezra 6 and 7, between Ezra 10 and Neh. 1, and between Neh. 13:3 and 13:4. Likewise, these two books are not attempting to provide a complete detailed history of this one-hundred-year-plus time span, but instead focus on only a few highly significant years: the efforts to rebuild the temple in the time of Zerubbabel, the ministry of Ezra in the seventh year of King Artaxerxes I, and the efforts of Nehemiah to reestablish Jerusalem in the twentieth year of the same reign.

Early in its history, Ezra-Nehemiah probably was viewed as one book. The book incorporates what appear to be the memoirs of Ezra and Nehemiah. The division into two parts is found first at the time of Origen (AD 185–253), with a possible reason being that Neh. 1:1 could be understood to mark a new beginning ("The words of Nehemiah son of Hacaliah"). This division subsequently influenced the English Bible (via the Latin Vulgate).

Ezra

Introduction (1:1)

In the first year of King Cyrus (1:1). King Cyrus (the Great), reigning from 559 to 530 BC, was the founder of the Persian Empire and the Achaemenid dynasty of Persian kings (see the article "The Persians"). His tomb can still be seen at Pasargadae, the first capital of the Achaemenid dynasty, in the homeland of the Persians, situated on a plain northeast of Persepolis in southwestern Iran.

This was 538 BC, Cyrus's first regnal year, after his capture of Babylon in October 539 BC, which made him the lord of Mesopotamia, in effect, "king of the world." He had been king of Anshan since 559 BC and had earlier conquered Lydia and Ionia (in western Turkey) in 547–546 BC. The extent of the empire was expanded by subsequent kings. At its height the Persian Empire extended from India to Cush (Esther 1:1) and lasted until the conquests of Alexander the Great (323 BC) (see the article "The Persians").

Put it in writing (1:1). This is an indication of the importance of written documents generally in Ezra-Nehemiah and in the Persian era (cf. the book of Esther).

The Cyrus Decree (1:2–4)

This is what King Cyrus of Persia says (1:2). This text (1:2–4) and a partial parallel in 2 Chron. 36:23 are the only record of the royal decree, but its historicity is supported by the Cyrus Cylinder, found in the area of the Marduk temple in Babylon and now housed in the British Museum. This Akkadian text describes Cyrus entering Babylon and his act of returning the images of gods to the ruined temples beyond the Tigris and of repatriating people groups. Implied evidence of Cyrus's decree can also be seen in the trilingual Xanthos inscription (in Greek, Lycian, and Aramaic) on a stela from

The tomb of King Cyrus (the Great).

the city of Xanthos in southwestern Turkey. Dated to 388–358 BC, it mentions Persian aid given for the upkeep of a Lycian temple.

God of the heavens (1:2). This divine title is also found in the documents addressed to the Persians from the Jewish-inhabited Elephantine colony in southern Egypt on the Nile River.

The Cyrus Cylinder.

The Response to the Decree (1:5–11)

The family heads . . . prepared to go up and rebuild the LORD's house in Jerusalem (1:5). The route taken by this caravan would be to travel north from Babylon along the Euphrates River and then south along the Orontes Valley in Syria into Palestine.

Sheshbazzar the prince of Judah (1:8). The designation "prince" (*nasi*) need mean no more than tribal leader (as in Num. 1:16). He is later identified as "governor" (5:14), the Persian-appointed administrator. Nothing is made of any possible Davidic connection that Sheshbazzar may have had. Some have suggested that he is to be identified with Shenazzar, fourth son of Jehoiachin and the uncle of Zerubbabel (1 Chron. 3:18). The identification of the names, however, is unlikely, for Shenazzar is derived from an Akkadian name referring to the moon god (Sin), whereas Sheshbazzar comes from a name referring to the sun god (Shamash).

The First Great Caravan (2:1–70)

The number of Israelite men included (2:2–67). The listing of persons is repeated (with minor variations) in Neh. 7:6–73. The list of places resettled (2:21–35) shows the narrow geographical limits of Yehud (Judah), mostly confined to the tribal areas of Benjamin and Judah.

The temple servants and the descendants of Solomon's servants (2:58). The Hebrew word rendered as "temple servants" means "those given" to assist the Levites in the service of the sanctuary (8:20). They may have been descendants of the Gibeonites (Josh. 9:23, 27) or descendants of war captives (Num. 31:25–47). The descendants of the servants of Solomon were a closely related group, for only a joint tally is supplied. The name suggests that they were descendants of foreigners enslaved by Solomon (1 Kings 9:20–21). In both groups there are foreign-sounding names (e.g.,

Rezin, Sisera) and names with Aramaic-looking endings (e.g., Hasupha, Hakupha).

Gold coins (2:69). The word used here is a reference to the Persian daric, a gold coin named after Darius I. It is also mentioned in 8:27 and 1 Chron. 29:7.

Recommencing Worship (3:1–6)

When the seventh month arrived (3:1). This is a key liturgical period in the Jewish calendar.

The Commencement of Temple Restoration (3:7–13)

Cedar wood from Lebanon to Joppa by sea (3:7). Lebanon was famous for its cedar timbers, here floated as rafts down the coast, as had been done for the construction of Solomon's temple (1 Kings 5:9; 2 Chron. 2:15–16).

Opposition to the Project Emerges (4:1–5)

King Esar-haddon of Assyria (4:2). This Assyrian king, the successor to Sennacherib (2 Kings 19:37), reigned from 680 to 669 BC (see the article "The Assyrians").

Later Examples of Opposition (4:6–24)

The reign of Ahasuerus (4:6). This is a reference to Xerxes, the same king as in the book of Esther. The line of Persian kings is Cyrus, Cambyses, Darius, Xerxes, and Artaxerxes. Cambyses is not mentioned in the Bible. Ezra 6:14 shows that the author is aware of their order of succession. Xerxes (called Ahasuerus here and in Esther) was the son of Darius. When Darius died in 486 BC, Egypt revolted, but Xerxes repressed the revolt. He is best known for his invasion of Greece as recounted by Herodotus, but he suffered a naval defeat in the Bay of Salamis (480 BC) and lost a crucial land battle near Plataea (479 BC) (see the article "The Persians").

During the time of King Artaxerxes (4:7). This refers to King Artaxerxes I, who enjoyed a forty-year reign (464–424 BC). The missions of Ezra and Nehemiah take place during his reign.

Coin showing Xerxes, king of Persia.

The Behistun inscription, describing how King Darius came to power.

The letter was written in Aramaic and translated (4:7). Portions of Ezra-Nehemiah are written in the Aramaic language. The book of Ezra is in Aramaic from 4:8 to 6:18, and there is a smaller portion in 7:12–26. Aramaic was the lingua franca of the ancient Near East at this time period and is called Imperial Aramaic. It is in the Northwest Semitic language group and is related to Hebrew. It has a consonantal alphabet derived from Phoenician and is thus much easier to master than the Akkadian cuneiform syllabic script with its many characters (which had been used earlier in Mesopotamia as the "official" literary and diplomatic language). Aramaic documents incorporated into Ezra-Nehemiah include a letter to King Artaxerxes (4:8–16), letters from King Artaxerxes (4:17–22; 7:12–26), a letter of King Darius (5:6–17), and a letter of King Darius citing an Aramaic memorandum related to the decree of Cyrus (6:3–12).

Whom . . . Ashurbanipal deported (4:10). Ashurbanipal was the last successful Assyrian king (669–633 BC), who may be the unnamed Assyrian king who deported people groups to Samaria in 2 Kings 17:24.

The region west of the Euphrates River (4:10). The name for this region in Aramaic literally means "Across the River," referring to the area west of the Euphrates River and encompassing Syria, Phoenicia, and Palestine (1 Kings 4:24). This became the official title of the fifth satrapy (an administrative district in the Persian Empire).

Tribute, duty, or land tax (4:13). This alludes to the tribute paid annually to the Persian kings, who accumulated a vast store of gold and silver bullion by draining the empire of these precious metals.

An oath of loyalty to the king (4:14). Literally this reads, "we eat the salt of the palace," meaning that they were on the king's payroll and had the obligation of loyalty. Eating the king's food amounted to an oath of total allegiance (cf. Dan. 1:8, 16; 11:26).

Until a further decree has been pronounced by me (4:21). This was a caveat, or escape clause, a wise precaution given the irrevocable nature of Persian royal decrees (Dan. 6:8, 12, 15; Esther 8:8).

Until the second year of the reign of King Darius (4:24). The reference to his "second year" is significant because, for two years following the death of King Cambyses (his predecessor), Darius fought and defeated eight challengers to gain the throne. This is recounted in the famous Behistun inscription, written in Old Persian, Akkadian, and Elamite and carved high up on a cliff face in 518 BC. Darius organized the empire into administrative regions called satrapies, introduced coinage, built the famous road from Susa to Sardis, and established a system of mounted couriers (see the article "The Persians").

Temple Building Recommences and Finishes (5:1–6:22)

Zerubbabel son of Shealtiel (5:2). Zerubbabel was a grandson of Jehoiachin, the last legitimate king of Judah (1 Chron. 3:17). His Davidic credentials may have assisted him in gaining the governorship under the Persians (Hag. 1:1; 2:1, 21).

Tattenai the governor (5:3). The name Tattenai (5:6; 6:6, 13) appears on tablets dated 502 BC. He is called governor of Trans-Euphrates and probably was resident in Damascus (in Syria).

Ecbatana (6:2). Located in Media, this important city was one of the three main Persian capitals, along with Babylon (5:17) and Susa (Neh. 1:1). Persian monarchs would winter in Babylon and spend the summer in Susa or Ecbatana.

A scroll was found with this record written on it (6:2). A similar memorandum was found in the Aramaic papyri of Elephantine (an island in the Nile River in southern Egypt), which deals with Persian approval to rebuild a Jewish temple in that settlement.

Three layers of cut stones and one of timber (6:4). This literally reads, "rolling stones"—that is, stones so heavy that they could only be rolled, not lifted (also 5:8). The method of construction using timber beams and masonry recalls the Solomonic original (1 Kings 6:36; 7:12) and has parallels with other ancient sites.

Whatever is needed (6:9). Evidence for the interest taken by the Persian rulers in foreign religious worship/temples is seen in the ordinances of Cambyses and Darius I, in which they regulate the temples and priests in Egypt, and in a letter under the authority of Darius II (423–404 BC) concerning the holding of the Festival of Unleavened Bread at Elephantine (419 BC).

Pray for the life of the king and his sons (6:10). Likewise, the Jews of Elephantine (a colony of Jews on an island in the Nile River, originally protecting the southern border of Egypt) promise Bagoas, the Persian governor of Judah, that they will pray for him and his sons if he helps them get their temple built.

He will be impaled (6:11). Gruesome modes of execution were practiced by the Persians (7:26) and included such forms of mutilation as cutting off ears and noses, as well as impaling.

The Passover lamb (6:20). A letter from the Jewish settlement on the island of Elephantine (on the Nile in southern Egypt) to the Persian king in the fifth year of Darius II likewise deals with Passover regulations.

Ezra Comes to Jerusalem (7:1–8:36)

During the reign of King Artaxerxes of Persia . . . the seventh year (7:1, 7, 8). Artaxerxes I reigned from 465 to 424 BC, so Ezra arrived in Jerusalem in 458 BC.

Seraiah's son (7:1). Ezra's long priestly pedigree of sixteen generations (7:1–5) indicates a focus on the temple (see also Ezra's prayer in 7:27).

He was a scribe skilled in the law of Moses (7:6). Ezra was literate (see also 7:11) and a religious expert. The phrase "the law of Moses" perhaps refers to the complete Pentateuch, though we cannot be certain.

On the first day of the fifth month (7:9). From spring to summer was the best time to travel, so Ezra sets out in April. The nine-hundred-mile journey took four months.

The king and his seven counselors (7:14). This refers to an executive structure of seven aristocrats, also mentioned in Esther 1:14 and by the Greek historians Herodotus and Xenophon.

Up to 7,500 pounds of silver (7:22). Literally this reads, "one hundred talents." A talent in the Babylonian sexagesimal system was sixty minas, and a mina was sixty shekels. This comes to the enormous weight of 3.75 tons (7,500 pounds).

You do not have authority to impose tribute (7:24). In similar fashion, King Darius instructed Gadatas in a letter to exempt the sacred gardeners of the sanctuary of Apollo at Aulai in the Ionian province of Magnesia from tribute or forced labor.

The law of your God (7:26). Sweeping authority was granted to Ezra. Similar favor was granted to Udjahorresnet, an Egyptian priest and scholar, by King Cambyses and King Darius.

At the river that flows to Ahava (8:15). This was a central canal (also 8:21, 31).

Casiphia (8:17). Casiphia is literally called "the place" (omitted in most English translations), suggesting its sanctuary status, such as existed in the Jewish colony of Elephantine.

Stone wall relief depicting Persian soldiers.

The Crisis of Intermarriage (9:1–10:44)

Canaanites, Hethites, Perizzites, Jebusites (9:1). By the time of Ezra, most of these people groups no longer existed. Use of such a (purposely) archaic list of foreign people groups that no longer existed probably underscores and stresses that exogenous marriage (marriage outside the faith) was a grave sin.

All the foreign wives and their children (10:3). Women typically took their children with them when marriages were dissolved.

Excluded from the assembly (10:8). Banishment from one's group as a punishment is known elsewhere in the ancient Near East as well, mentioned, for example, in the Damascus Document at Qumran.

The heavy rain . . . it is the rainy season (10:9, 13). The ninth month, Kislev (November-December), is the wet (and cool) winter period in Palestine.

Elders and judges of each town (10:14). These were people who governed country villages and served as local magistrates (Deut. 19:12; 21:3, 19).

Nehemiah

The Crisis in Jerusalem (1:1–11)

Introduction. Ezra and Nehemiah are discussed together in the introduction to Ezra above.

Fasting and praying (1:4). Fasting in this situation is an expression of sorrow over the failings of God's people and their resultant distress (see also Ezra 10:6; Neh. 9:1).

This man (1:11). The reference "this man" is a pejorative and disrespectful reference to his royal master (in contrast to the Lord).

The king's cupbearer (1:11). This is a position of great trust and responsibility (2:1), as illustrated by Ahikar in the Jewish nonbiblical book of Tobit (1:21–22), who is said to have kept the signet ring and administered the accounts of Esar-haddon, king of Assyria.

Nehemiah Returns to Jerusalem (2:1–20)

The month of Nisan (2:1). See comments on Deut. 16:1.

To Judah and to the city where my ancestors are buried, so that I may rebuild it (2:5). Despite the later reference to "the tombs of David" within the city (3:16), this does not imply Nehemiah's royal lineage. It means only that his ancestors were buried in proximity to the city.

It pleased the king to send me (2:6). Though the biblical account is silent on the subject, it may be that part of the royal motivation was to fortify Jerusalem in response to the threat of Athenian aggression, which included the coastal city of Dor (on the northern coast of Palestine) in its Delian League.

The king's forest (2:8). The king's forest might have been in Lebanon, but there are geographically closer possibilities.

Sanballat the Horonite (2:10). Sanballat's epithet (the Horonite) probably indicates that he came from upper or lower Beth-horon, twin cities twelve miles northwest of Jerusalem (Josh. 10:10; 16:3, 5). He gave his sons good, Jewish (Yahwistic) names (Delaiah and Shelemiah), and they are mentioned in an Elephantine papyrus that also refers to him as the governor of Samaria. Papyri found in a cave in Wadi ed-Daliyeh, north of Jericho (375–335 BC), indicate that the name was used by several generations of officials in this family.

Wall panel from the palace of Darius I depicting cherubim-like winged griffins.

Tobiah the Ammonite official (2:10). Tobiah's name means "The Lord [Yahweh] is good." He may have been part of an aristocratic family with estates on the east side of the Jordan River, where Ammon was located. The word translated as "official" (*ebed*) can mean "slave," and its use may be mocking in intent. He may have been the Persian-appointed governor of the area east of the Jordan River. At the town of Araq el-Emir, located eleven miles west of the modern city of Amman, are the ruins of a large building called Qasr el-Abed ("castle of the slave"), a structure probably built by one of Tobiah's descendants.

Valley Gate (2:13). Nehemiah's night journey provides an indication of the state of the walls and gates of Jerusalem at that time (2:12–15). Nehemiah went out of the Valley Gate, so called because it led to the valley of Ben Hinnom (Jer. 19:2). This gate was on the western wall.

Serpent's Well (2:13). This probably is the same as En-rogel, located at the junction of the Ben Hinnom and Kidron Valleys (2 Sam. 17:17; 1 Kings 1:9).

Dung Gate (2:13). This was also called the Potsherd Gate (Neh. 3:13–14; 12:31; 2 Kings 23:10; Jer. 19:2). It was the southernmost exit, out of which the city garbage was carried.

Fountain Gate (2:14). At this gate the debris of the collapsed terraces of the eastern slope of the Ophel, the original ridge of "the city of David," just to the south of the Temple Mount, required Nehemiah to dismount and go on foot up "the valley"—that is, the Kidron Valley on the eastern side of the city. The failure to mention any other gates suggests that the translation "heading back" (NIV: "turned back") is correct (2:15a). Nehemiah retraced his steps (without doing a full circuit of the city) and reentered the city by the gate through which he left.

King's Pool (2:14). This probably is the Pool of Siloam.

Geshem the Arab (2:19). This is the third dangerous opponent of Nehemiah. In 6:6 he is called "Gashmu," a variant that reflects the original Arabic name inscribed on silver coins found at Tell el-Maskhuta. He was head of an Arab Qedarite confederacy that controlled southern Transjordan (having pushed the Edomites into southern Judah) and paid lip service to Persian authority. Labeling him as "the Arab" makes it obvious that he was a foreigner with no legal claim over Jerusalem.

The List of Wall Builders (3:1–32)

Sheep Gate (3:1). The list of those engaged in the rebuilding of the wall follows a counterclockwise circuit of the wall from the Sheep Gate in the north (3:1) back to the Sheep Gate (3:32). This northwestern section of the wall was close to the temple, with the Sheep Gate being the entrance through which sacrificial animals came into the city on their way to be slaughtered in the temple. Not by accident, the first construction group mentioned is "the high priest Eliashib and his fellow priests" (3:1), underlining the religious significance of the task. Eliashib (cf. Ezra 10:6; Neh. 13:4) was the grandson of Jeshua (Neh. 12:10).

Tower of the Hundred (3:1). This tower is known only from this text and 12:39. In both texts it is possible that it is equated with the better-known Tower of Hananel at the northern extremity of the city (Jer. 31:38; Zech. 14:10). The "hundred" may refer to the military unit associated with its defense (e.g., 2 Kings 11:4, 9, 19); thus it probably was a garrison post. The tower protected the vulnerable northwestern approach to the city.

Built the Fish Gate . . . with beams . . . doors, bolts, and bars (3:3). Through this gate merchants from Tyre brought fish for sale (13:16; 2 Chron. 33:14). The laying of "beams" was for a roof structure over the gate, and "bolts and bars" were the mechanism to lock the gate.

Old Gate (3:6). Literally this just reads, "old," with the term "gate" perhaps implied, but not clearly stated. It perhaps could be the old "city" or the old "wall," but most probably is the old "gate." This gate in the old western wall led into the old portion of the city (on the eastern ridge) as distinct from the new suburbs that in late preexilic times had expanded to the west and had been enclosed by a new wall. That expansion was abandoned due to the much smaller population of postexilic Jerusalem. The phrase in 3:8 that is translated as "they restored Jerusalem" could also be translated as "they left out part of Jerusalem" (cf. NLT), which probably is preferable. This would imply that the city in Persian times was confined to the old city of David and the Temple Mount, and did not include the earlier "suburban" expansion.

The men of . . . Mizpah (3:7). The official residence of the governor is specified as located in the city of Mizpah, which has also served as the administrative center of Gedaliah, whom the Babylonians appointed as governor back at the time of the exile (2 Kings 25:23) (see comments on Jer. 40:6). Nehemiah 3 mentions only a few place names, but it does suggest that the province of Judah was divided into five districts: Jerusalem (vv. 9, 12), Beth-haccherem (v. 14), Mizpah (v. 15), Beth-zur (v. 16), and Keilah (vv. 17–18). The city of Jerusalem and the (apparently large) area of Keilah consisted of two half-districts.

Broad Wall (3:8). This may refer to the late preexilic wall that was heavily reinforced and rejoined the older western wall at a point north of the Valley Gate (12:38). It had enclosed a large extension of the city required by the influx of refugees after the fall of Samaria (722 BC).

Tower of the Ovens (3:11). This tower was on the western wall, located near ovens used by bread bakers or perhaps potters.

Valley Gate (3:13). See comments on Neh. 2:13.

Fountain Gate (3:15). This gate was rebuilt and reroofed. It provided access for city dwellers to the fountain (spring) that fed the pool mentioned, which could be the same one that is called the King's Pool back in 2:14. Its waters may have been used to water the king's garden.

Pool of Shelah (3:15). This pool is given a similar but not identical name in Isa. 8:6 ("the water of Shiloah"). This was the same pool as the Pool of Siloam in the NT (John 9:7, 11).

King's garden (3:15). The king's garden is also mentioned in 2 Kings 25:4; Jer. 39:4; 52:7 as a private exit from the city (through which King Zedekiah fled from the Babylonians as Jerusalem fell).

The city of David (3:15). The area referred to as "the city of David" was the renamed Jebusite fortress that formed the inner citadel of the (by this time) expanded city.

The tombs of David (3:16). This was the royal cemetery in the city of David, where David and succeeding kings were buried (1 Kings 2:10; 11:43; 14:31; 2 Chron. 21:20; 32:33). For further architectural mentions of David, see 12:37.

House of the Warriors (3:16). This structure may have been a military headquarters, barracks, or armory, and it perhaps was named after the heroes (mighty men) who served David (2 Sam. 23:8–39).

The Angle (3:19). This refers to a pronounced bend in the wall (cf. 3:24; 2 Chron. 26:9).

The courtyard of the guard (3:25). This apparently was the prison yard.

The temple servants living on Ophel (3:26). "Ophel" refers to the heights upon which the temple had stood.

As far as the wall of Ophel (3:27). This was an internal wall that separated the city of David (3:15) from the Temple Mount to its north. The temple servants repaired this section of the wall near where they lived.

Horse Gate (3:28). The Horse Gate may be the same gate as that mentioned in 2 Kings 11:16, through which horses were brought to the royal palace. Being also near the temple, the homes of the priests were in this area.

East Gate (3:29). This gate was the eastern entrance to the temple court (cf. Ezek. 40:6, 10). In this way, the list of the builders with their sections begins and ends at a part of the wall in close proximity to the temple, making the city as a whole an extension of the temple.

Opposite his room (3:30). This refers to a chamber in the temple complex (12:44; 13:7).

The house of the temple servants (3:31). This probably refers to a structure used by the temple servants when they were on duty, as opposed to the district in which they lived when off duty (3:26).

And [the house of] the merchants (3:31). This probably refers to a place of business or lodging conveniently located near the temple. With the mention of the Sheep Gate, the circuit of the wall has been completed (3:32; cf. 3:1).

Opposition to Wall Building (4:1–23)

A fox (4:3). Tobiah used exaggeration to make his point, choosing a fox as his illustration, for this animal was a proverbial inhabitant of ruins (Ezek. 13:4 NASB) and light-footed. To call their construction a "stone wall" (literally, "the wall of your stones") implied its lack of cohesion.

Ashdodites (4:7). Ashdod was, at this stage, a leading inland city of the region of former Philistia.

The Outcry (5:1–19)

The king's tax (5:4). The Persian kings taxed their subjects heavily. This imperial Persian tax was mentioned in Ezra 4:13, 20. Poor farmers were borrowing money (weighed silver or coinage) to pay this tax. This made the Jewish officials party to foreign oppression.

We are subjecting our sons and daughters to slavery (5:5). This chapter describes an economic and social crisis and refers to the ancient institution of debt slavery, in which a person served a debt holder to work off a loan (Lev. 25:47–48).

Charging his countrymen interest (5:7). Nehemiah is accusing the nobles not so much of charging interest (despite most English translations), but rather of lending money in order to confiscate sons and daughters, fields, vineyards, and houses when the loan principal could not be repaid by the poor farmers and then heartlessly enforcing the handing over of what was pledged (Exod. 22:26–27; Deut. 24:10). The creditors agreed to return the pledges and not to require them any more (5:12; cf. 10:31b).

You sell your own countrymen (5:8). Selling fellow Hebrews to foreigners was forbidden (Exod. 21:8).

The percentage of the money (5:11). Literally this reads, "a hundred silver pieces." It could refer to interest (the one percent), but more likely the point is that it is a large number, indicating that even large pledges should be returned.

I summoned the priests (5:12). Nehemiah summoned the priests to administer the oath, as was their role under the law (Num. 5:19, 21).

Shook the folds out of my robe (5:13). This is an acted-out curse. The fold of a garment was used as a kind of pocket to carry personal items (Prov.

A Yehud (Judah) coin.

21:14). The threat was that God would shake those who broke their oath out of any possession they had.

Governor . . . from the twentieth year until his thirty-second year (5:14). That Nehemiah was appointed governor was implied in 2:9, but here his official position is made explicit (cf. 10:1, where a different Hebrew word is used; 12:26). For Nehemiah to contrast his actions with those of previous governors assumes that he was comparing like with like—that is, his own behavior with that of earlier *Jewish* governors. He was governor of Judah, whose provincial boundaries were very narrow. Nehemiah mentions "governors who preceded me" (5:15). This suggests that Judah as a district acquired administrative independence from Samaria prior to the arrival of Nehemiah. This implication is confirmed by the evidence of Yehud (Judah) coins, jar impressions, and bullae (seal impressions) discovered from this time.

Remember me favorably (5:19). The use of such expressions (cf. 13:14, 22, 31) has led to the theory that Nehemiah's memoirs were inscribed as a memorial and placed in the temple, on analogy with the autobiographical inscription recalling the meritorious deeds of the Egyptian notable Udjahorresnet written on a statue in the temple of Osiris dating from the early years of the reign of Darius I (the statue is now in the Vatican Museums).

The Wall Is Finished (6:1–19)

Ono Valley (6:2). Ono was twenty-seven miles northwest of Jerusalem, near Lod (Lydda), and it was a place of resettlement (1 Chron. 8:12; Ezra 2:33; Neh. 7:37; 11:35). It could be considered as neutral territory between the provinces of Judah (Yehud) and Samaria.

An open letter (6:5). Ancient letters usually were written on a papyrus or leather scroll, rolled up and tied with string, and sealed with a clay imprint (called a bulla). By using an open letter, Sanballat was spreading the rumor further.

The twenty-fifth day of the month Elul (6:15). This was the sixth month, the date being October 27, 445 BC.

Guarding the City (7:1–4)

Commander of the fortress (7:2). In 2:8 this is called "the temple's fortress," possibly the Tower of Hananel on the Temple Mount (3:1).

Until the sun is hot (7:3). During the middle of the day, especially when it was hot, many people would rest or sleep. The city gates were not to be left open during this time because the guards probably went off duty.

The Genealogy Repeated (7:5–73)

Genealogical record (7:5). This chapter repeats (with variations) the lists of Ezra 2. Only those who could trace their descent to the returnees included in the list would be considered bona fide Israelites.

The seventh month (7:73). This month was a highpoint of the Jewish religious calendar.

The Great Community Gathering (8:1–12)

At the square in front of the Water Gate (8:1). One perhaps would have expected this gathering to take place in the temple courtyard (cf. 3:26; 12:37). This gate stood on the eastern side of the city.

All who could listen with understanding (8:2). This refers to children with sufficient maturity to comprehend the readings. A somewhat similar expression qualifies the sons and daughters mentioned in 10:28.

A high wooden platform (8:4). The Hebrew literally says, "a wooden tower."

Ezra opened the book (8:5). This book was a scroll that was opened by unrolling it. Codices (rectangular shaped books with pages sewn together) had not been invented yet.

Translating and giving the meaning (8:8). The expression probably means "section by section." The terminology does not imply the process of translation from Hebrew to Aramaic. The need of an Aramaic translation in the early postexilic period is an unproved hypothesis. All that is meant is that the law was read section by section, with explanations interspersed.

This day is holy (8:9). The Festival of Trumpets on the first day of the seventh month is called "a sacred assembly" in Lev. 23:24 and Num. 29:1, though nothing is said in this narrative about the festival. Feast days were to be celebrated with joy (e.g., Deut. 12:12; 16:11). There is no actual mention of sacrifice, though the invitation to feast (8:10) assumes that sacrifices have been made.

Send portions to those who have nothing prepared (8:10). Thus the poor were enabled to share in the joyous occasion (cf. Deut. 14:29; 26:12).

The Festival of Shelters (8:13–18)

The Israelites should dwell in shelters during the festival (8:14). This feast (the Festival of Shelters) began on the fifteenth day of the month and continued for eight days (i.e., to the twenty-second) (8:18), so there was only a day's break before the next gathering (9:1). The thirteen-day gap was filled by the preparations described in 8:16.

Branches of olive, wild olive, myrtle, palm, and other leafy trees (8:15). The types of trees mentioned do not exactly coincide with Lev. 23:40 but were species indigenous to the Mediterranean climate.

On each of their rooftops (8:16). Typical houses in Palestine had accessible, flat roofs (Josh. 2:6; 1 Sam. 9:25–26; 2 Sam. 11.2).

Ephraim Gate (8:16). This gate was not noted in chapter 3 but is mentioned in 12:39. It probably was situated in the northern part of the western wall of the city.

The Levites' Prayer (9:1–38)

Fasting, wearing sackcloth, and had put dust on their heads (9:1). See comments on Lam. 2:10. These were outward signs of mourning over sin (cf. 1 Sam. 4:12; 2 Sam. 1:2; Ezra 9:3–5; 10:1, 6; Neh. 1:4; Job 2:12). In addition, the people were fasting (cf. Joel 2:12) and wore sackcloth as a sign of repentance (cf. Dan. 9:3; 1 Chron. 21:16).

They rule over our bodies (9:37). This refers to the Persian imposition of forced labor for things like road maintenance or military service.

We are making a binding agreement (9:38). The fact that this is written down and sealed underscores how serious they were about the promises being made. The Hebrew word translated as "binding agreement" is a strong term meaning a "fixed provision." This term is used of royal decrees, as in 11:23. Here in 9:38 it carries the nuance of

An ancient sarcophagus with mourning women wearing sackcloth, some of them with their hands on their heads.

a fixed provision for regular support for the temple.

The Community Pledge (10:1–39)

Those whose seals were on the document (10:1). This list was part of the legal document binding each of these people to the agreement.

Populating Jerusalem (11:1–36)

Excavations showing part of Nehemiah's wall.

One out of ten (11:1). The way that these people were selected to come live in Jerusalem, the holy city, was a form of tithing of the whole community, just as in the preceding verses they promised to bring a tithe of the farm produce to the storehouses (10:37–39).

The officer over them (11:9). The Benjaminite, Joel son of Zicri, was overseer of the city, an appropriate appointment, seeing that Jerusalem stood just inside Benjaminite territory.

Hinnom Valley (11:30). This valley ran along the western wall of Jerusalem, indicating that Jerusalem served as a boundary dividing line. The Hinnom Valley is also given as the northern boundary of Judah in Josh. 15:8; 18:16.

Craftsmen's Valley (11:35). The Benjaminites settled in sixteen towns, though the last seven towns on the list are located in the Ono-Lod Valley (here given another name) rather than in Benjamin proper.

Priestly and Levitical Genealogies (12:1–26)

These are the priests and Levites (12:1–26). With regard to the high priestly line (12:10–11, 22, 26), the succession of high priests (without explicitly using the title) starts with Jeshua, who was the high priest at the time of the return (Ezra 3:2; Hag. 1:1), and the list covers the entire Persian period. Eliashib (12:10) was high priest during Nehemiah's governorship (3:1, 20–21; 13:4, 7, 28). Given that this is some eighty years after the first return from Babylonia, the expression "fathered" may cover more than one generation. It is unlikely (though not impossible) that just one generation, that of Joiakim, filled that gap. The list is not necessarily complete. Joiada is mentioned in 13:28, though it is not clear that he was the high priest at that time. Nehemiah 12:22 supplies the extra name of Johanan, who was perhaps another "son of Eliashib" (cf. Jehohanan of Ezra 10:6), and so the brother of Joiada (who succeeded him) and uncle of Jonathan. The Elephantine correspondence (from the Jewish colony on the island of Elephantine on the Nile River in the southern part of Egypt), in a letter dated in the seventeenth year of Darius II (407 BC), refers to "the high priest Jehohanan and his colleagues the priests in Jerusalem."[1] According to the first-century-AD Jewish historian Josephus, Jaddua lived in the days of Alexander the Great (ca. 333 BC), but the ancient prevalence of paponymy (naming sons after fathers or grandfathers) means that this probably was a later Jaddua, so that the Jaddua found in this list may be dated to the time of Darius II (424–405 BC) (see the article "The Persians").

Darius the Persian (12:22). The priests were listed only for the first generation (12:1–7), so this probably is Darius I (the Great), the king at the time of the rebuilding of the temple in the days of Zerubbabel and Jeshua (Ezra 5–6).

The Dedication of the Wall (12:27–43)

Cymbals, harps, and lyres (12:27). See the article "Musical Instruments in Israel and the Ancient Near East."

Gate of the Guard (12:39). This gate is mentioned only here, but its association with the Sheep Gate means it was close to the temple (3:1; Jer. 32:2). It is perhaps to be identified with the Inspection Gate (3:31).

The Chambers (12:44–47)

The rooms that housed the supplies, contributions (12:44). This refers to the storage rooms that were in the exterior walls of the temple building.

The Banning of Foreigners (13:1–3)

The book of Moses was read publicly to the people (13:1). The phrase "book of Moses" typically refers to the Pentateuch (the first five books of the OT). The law in question is from Deut. 23:3–6.

Nehemiah's Second Governorship (13:4–31)

King Artaxerxes of Babylon (13:6). This title ("king of Babylon") implies that the Persian king Artaxerxes was resident in Babylon at this time. On Artaxerxes, see the article "The Persians."

Tyrians (13:16). The city of Tyre was famous in the ancient Near East for its merchants (e.g., Ezek. 27:12–36; 28:16), with a large fleet of ships that dominated the trade of the Mediterranean Sea.

Esther

Constance E. Clark Gane

Introduction. In 539 BC Cyrus united the Medes and Persians, founding one of the greatest empires of all time, the Persian Empire (see the article "The Persians"). The dynasty of kings that ruled the Persian Empire was known as the Achaemenid dynasty, so sometimes the empire is referred to as the Achaemenid Empire (synonymous with Persian Empire). The empire reached its apex during the reigns of Darius I (the Great) (522–486 BC), Xerxes I (486–465 BC), and Artaxerxes I (465–425 BC). Both Darius I and his son Xerxes I orchestrated large-scale attacks against Greece. The book of Esther is set in the historical context of these brutal Persian Wars, but never mentions them.

Queen Vashti Deposed (1:1–22)

These events took place during the days of (1:1). The book begins with a Hebrew narrative formula that indicates that the author intends the reader to understand that the account is historical.[1]

Ahasuerus (1:1). The Persian king is referred to by the Hebrew name Ahasuerus. His identity is widely accepted to be Xerxes I (486–465 BC), son of Darius I. The Greek *Xerxēs* derives from Old Persian *Khšayāršan*, which means "ruling over heroes." The author clarifies that the Xerxes of the text is he who ruled over 127 provinces, implying that there was another king by that name (i.e., Xerxes II).[2]

127 provinces (1:1). The biblical text divides the Persian Empire into 127 provinces, while the Old Persian cuneiform texts divide the empire into

A Persian king on his throne.

various "satrapies" numbering in the twenties. The quantity given here may indicate a subdivision of the Persian satrapies.[3]

India to Cush (1:1). This empire stretched from modern Pakistan to Sudan. The Daiva inscription from the time of Xerxes I corresponds to this description of the empire.[4]

Third year of his reign (1:3). The year is 483 BC; Xerxes I is thirty-five years old. The author chooses to introduce the story from the perspective of Xerxes I's days of glory and not after his defeat by the Greeks four years later.

A feast for all his officials and staff, the army . . . the nobles, and the officials (1:3). While the purpose for this gathering is not stated in the biblical text, it is clear from Persian and Greek sources that this was the period of time when Xerxes I called together critical leaders and military staff to begin planning his invasion of Greece.

A week-long banquet . . . from the greatest to the least (1:5). The feast was held in Susa and given for inhabitants of the citadel.[5] Palace intrigue and treachery reached unprecedented proportions in the Persian Empire, and the king lived in constant danger. In this seven-day feast the king may have been currying the favor of those closest to him who had recently experienced the strain of hosting the feast for the war council described in 1:3–4.

The garden courtyard (1:5). Gardens were an important feature in Assyrian, Babylonian, and Achaemenid royal cities. The palace grounds expressed an overt political statement of royal dominance over the king's empire.[6]

Gold goblets (1:7). The Persians had elaborate drinking vessels called "rhytons." These vessels generally were made of gold or silver and often were formed in the shape of an animal's head.[7] When the soldiers of Alexander the Great later conquered Persia, many of these famous vessels were taken as plunder back to Greece, where they became the inspiration for Grecian drinking vessels.

Queen Vashti (1:9). The name of Queen Vashti is found only in the biblical text of Esther. The Greek historian Herodotus identifies Amestris, the daughter of Otanes, commander of the Persian branch of Xerxes's army, as the primary queen of Xerxes and queen mother of Artaxerxes I, the heir of Xerxes I.[8] It is possible that Vashti was Amestris, and that at the time of the feast she was pregnant with the heir, Artaxerxes I. Amestris was a cruel and powerful woman, as evidenced by her mutilation of her sister-in-law after she discovered that Xerxes was having an affair with his niece. As the mother of Artaxerxes I, she would not have been executed, but she could have been banished from the king's presence.[9]

Queen Vashti also gave a feast for the women (1:9). In direct contrast to Greek culture, Persian women were involved in the social affairs of the court.[10] Royal women of Persia traveled, often controlled large units of manpower requiring organization and structure, were involved in the administration of economic affairs, and engaged the same officials as the king. Within Persian culture it was not unusual for men and women to attend feasts together.[11] During events where the men celebrated separately, drinking was heavy and the entertainment became more erotic.

Feeling good from the wine (1:10). Persians were noted for their heavy drinking.

He wanted to show off her beauty (1:11). Xerxes himself was known for being tall and handsome. It was said of him, "Of all those tens of thousands of men, for goodliness and stature there was not one worthier than Xerxes himself to hold that command."[12]

Became furious and his anger burned (1:12). Xerxes I was infamous for his hotheaded and irrational temper.[13]

Consulted the wise men (1:13). Many monarchs in the ancient Near East were illiterate and could not read the laws of their own lands. They were dependent upon advisors who had access to the written laws.[14]

The seven officials of Persia and Media (1:14). This reflects a tradition initiated by Deioces (700–647 BC), the first Median king,[15] who established the rule that his seven closest friends could have access to his presence uninvited and unannounced.[16]

Laws of Persia and Media (1:19). The concept of an irrevocable law is unknown in Persian texts and the writings of Herodotus. However, Plutarch (AD 45–120) writes that the Persian king was constrained by the law but found ways around it.[17]

Each ethnic group in its own language (1:22). According to Old Persian texts dating to the reign of Darius I, there were sixty-seven national groups in the Persian Empire.[18]

Esther Made Queen (2:1–18)

Let a search be made (2:2). This suggestion is highly unusual because a Persian king normally selected his

A gold Persian rhyton, a special cup for banquet drinking.

wife from nobility.[19] The Greek historian Plutarch, however, describes Persian kings occasionally going against the law in the selection of a consort.[20]

Young virgins (2:2). It was not uncommon for the Persian court to take by force young boys and girls for the service of the royal court. When the Persian commanders under Darius I captured Ionian settlements, they "picked the best-looking boys and castrated them, cutting off their testicles and turning them into eunuchs; they also took the most attractive girls and sent them to the king as slaves."[21]

Harem (2:3). Literally this reads, "the house of the women." In 2:3, 9, 11, the Hebrew term is *bet hannashim* ("house of the women"), which refers to the house of the virgins, while in 2:14 the text has *bet hannashim sheni* ("second house of the women"—i.e., of the concubines and wives).[22]

Hegai, the king's eunuch (2:3). Male access to women in the harem was limited to eunuchs in order to protect the progeny of the king.

A Jewish man (2:5). In this one Hebrew word, *yehudi*, translated here as "a Jewish man," the account is securely placed in the context of Jewish history. This designation is especially significant because the book of Esther never mentions the Lord, the God of Israel.

Mordecai (2:5). Two individuals in the OT are known by the name Mordecai. One returned from Babylon to Jerusalem with Zerubbabel (Ezra 2:2; Neh. 7:7). The name Mordecai is a variant of the name Marduk, the national god of Babylonia.[23]

Son of Shimei, son of Kish, a Benjaminite (2:5). Note the similarity between this family identification and that of King Saul (1 Sam. 9:1–2; 2 Sam. 16:5) from hundreds of years earlier.

He had been taken into exile (2:6). Mordecai's ancestor Kish was one of those taken to Babylon along with the king of Judah as described in Jer. 24:1, but it is not known how the family relocated to Susa.

Hadassah (2:7). This is the only biblical book that mentions the name Hadassah, which in Hebrew means "myrtle."[24] However, the name may be derived from the Akkadian name *ḫadaššatu*, which means "bride, just married, epithet of Ishtar."[25]

Esther (2:7). The origin of this name is uncertain. It may be derived from Akkadian *Ištar*, the Babylonian goddess of

The Babylonian goddess Ishtar riding on top of a lion.

sex and war, or it may also be related to the Persian word *stāreh* ("star").[26] Because the etymology of Mordecai's name is a variant form of Marduk, likewise, Esther's name is likely derived from the name of the Babylonian goddess Ishtar. The setting of the narrative is Persia, but the names are of Babylonian deities.

Esther was taken (2:8). The Hebrew uses a passive verb, indicating that, willing or not, she was taken.

Beauty treatments . . . and cosmetics (2:12). Beauty treatments and cosmetics have a long tradition in Persian history, and many of those customs continue to this day. Persian royalty, both men and women, followed beauty rituals with extreme care, applying fragrant oils to their hair and skin and using facial powders, kohl eyeliner, and rouge.[27] See the article "Women's Fashion in the OT World."

She would go in the evening, and in the morning she would return (2:14). The Hebrew terminology used here makes clear that the night with the king involved a sexual relationship and initiated the "marriage" of the young girl to the king as a concubine.

The concubines (2:14). A concubine was considered married and not a mistress, though she had fewer rights than wives.[28] Children conceived with a concubine could become high officials but were not legitimate heirs to the throne.

The month Tebeth, in the seventh year of his reign (2:16). This month corresponds to December-January and comes from the Babylonian calendar, which the Jews adopted during the exile and still use as their religious calendar.[29] The seventh year of Xerxes's reign was 479 BC, four years after Vashti was deposed. Xerxes, now thirty-nine years old, has been engaged in several historically significant battles with the Greeks over the past two years (Thermopylae, Salamis).

Mordecai Uncovers a Conspiracy (2:19–23)

The King's Gate (2:19). Only those holding high official positions in the court sat in the king's gate, where they conducted legal, civil, and commercial business transactions.

Hanged on the gallows (2:23). Hanging by the neck is not attested in the ancient Near East. Thus the phrase used here probably is describing the impalement of these men on the end of wooden poles, a practice common in both Babylonia and Assyria. It is also possible that they were nailed to a board, a fate suffered by Xerxes's governor of Sestus.[30]

Recorded in the Historical Record (2:23). These are the official records of events during the life of the Persian king. Ezra 4:15 mentions similar "record books" of the king during the reign of the Persian king Artaxerxes. As recorded by Herodotus, acts of loyalty to the Persian kings were immediately rewarded with generous gifts of land or position.[31]

Haman's Plot to Destroy the Jews (3:1–15)

The Agagite (3:1). First Samuel 15:8 identifies Agag as king of the Amalekites. The designation of Haman as "the Agagite" here connects the reader to the ancient animosity between the Israelites and the Amalekites, descendants of Esau whose brutal attack on the Israelite stragglers in the desert compelled God to order their complete annihilation (Exod. 17:18–19; Deut. 25:17–19).[32] These ironical connections are complex, because 2:5 connected Mordecai's pedigree with that of King Saul, whose final act of disobedience occurred in 1 Sam. 15, when he failed to kill King Agag of the Amalekites.

Mordecai would not bow down or pay homage (3:2). No reason is given for Mordecai's behavior. Neither act is prohibited in the biblical text, and both are attested in comparable situations.[33] Herodotus explains that the Persian protocol for exchanging greetings was done according to social standing: the inferior party is to fall to the ground and prostrate himself before the one of higher station.[34]

Since he had told them he was a Jew (3:4). This suggests a continuation of the feud between Jews and Amalekites as well as clear anti-Semitism (see comments on Esther 3:1).

He planned to destroy all of Mordecai's people, the Jews (3:6). As reflected in the law code of the ancient Babylonian king Hammurabi as well as in the OT (Lev. 24:17–22), one would expect Persian law to support the punishment of the one who had violated the law, not a total annihilation of all of his people. The design to exterminate the entire Jewish race perhaps is a reaction to the command given by God to exterminate the Amalekites (see comments on Esther 3:1).

Nisan (3:7). This corresponds to March-April, the first month of the Babylonian calendar year.

Twelfth year (3:7). The year is now 474 BC. Esther has been queen for five years.

The Pur (3:7). The word *pur* is an Akkadian word used in both Assyria and Babylonia to denote selection by lot or lottery through divination.[35]

Adar (3:7). This is February-March.

Their laws are different (3:8). Subjects of the Persian Empire usually were allowed to maintain their religious and cultural autonomy. However, Haman is stating that this ethnic group (the Jews) does not keep the king's laws. Xerxes has already recently put down revolts in Egypt (485 BC) and Babylon (484 and 482 BC); he does not need another one.

Authorizing their destruction (3:9). Total destruction of entire people groups was not a widespread phenomenon in the ancient Near East. However, gendercide, in which conquered males were destroyed while virgin girls were taken as plunder, was not uncommon throughout the second and first millennia BC. Similarly, in holy war the conquered often were dedicated to the god(s) for destruction. For example, the Ur III king Iddi(n)-Sin (ca. 2028–2004 BC) destroyed the city of Kullunum and consecrated it to the gods.[36] Mesha, king of Moab, boasted of the destruction of Nebo, in which he slew all the inhabitants because he "had dedicated it to 'Astar-Kemosh."[37] Following the takeover of the Persian throne in 522 BC by Darius the Great, the magi were all but eliminated in a purge.[38]

375 tons of silver (3:9). Literally this reads, "10,000 talents of silver." Compare this to the total annual revenue of 14,560 talents under Darius.[39] Corruption and bribery were always major issues in the Persian court.[40]

Signet ring (3:10). See comments on Hag. 2:23. Finger rings, though not common, are attested during this period along with cylinder and stamp seals.[41] All were used by a variety of individuals.[42] Sealing conferred validity on sealed items and identified the sealer.[43]

Thirteenth day of the first month (3:12). The thirteenth of Nisan is Passover Eve.

Mordecai Persuades Esther to Help (4:1–17)

Tore his clothes, put on sackcloth and ashes (4:1). This is an ancient Near Eastern sign of distress well known to the Persians, who tore their own tunics when defeated by the Greeks in the battle at Salamis.[44]

Extends the gold scepter (4:11). A relief from the treasury at Persepolis (one of the Persian Empire capital cities) depicts the seated king holding his scepter, while a guard wielding a battle-ax stands nearby.[45]

From another place (4:14). This probably is a veiled reference to God. The Septuagint (an early Greek translation of the Hebrew Scriptures) replaces this phrase with the name of God.

Esther's Request to the King (5:1–8)

The banquet (5:4). According to ancient Near Eastern etiquette, delay in making one's request signaled its importance. Food and especially wine were important precursors for making a weighty request. An invitation to a second banquet heightened the seriousness of the situation.

Haman's Rage against Mordecai (5:9–14)

A gallows seventy-five feet tall (5:14). Literally this is fifty cubits, or about the same height of a six-story building.

Mordecai Honored (6:1–14)

Honor and special recognition (6:3). According to Herodotus, those honored for helping or saving the king were called the "king's benefactors" and were rewarded with gifts such as governorship of a province.[46]

A royal garment that the king himself has worn and a horse the king himself has ridden (6:8). The king's garments were thought to possess supernatural powers,[47] and the splendor of these robes may still be seen on reliefs in the Persian capital of Persepolis.[48] Xerxes's bestowal of this privilege on Mordecai is the highest of honors.[49] Riding a royal horse also elevated one's status.[50] Horses with the royal crest can be seen on reliefs from Persepolis.[51]

Haman Impaled (7:1–10)

Haman remained (7:7). No man, except the king, was allowed to be alone in the presence of the queen. If a man approached a woman in the king's harem, he was to always maintain a distance of seven steps.[52]

The King's Edict (8:1–14)

Estate of Haman (8:1). Oroetes, the Persian governor of Sardis, rebelled against the king by murdering another governor. In turn, Oroetes was executed by order of Darius and all of his property (including slaves) reverted to the king.[53]

Removed his signet ring . . . and gave it to Mordecai (8:2). Several men named Marduka, a variant form of Mordecai, appear in Persian records from this period. One of them is an accountant who made an inspection tour of Susa during the last years of Darius I or the early years of Xerxes I. In addition, four different individuals bearing this name are mentioned in some Elamite tablets dating to 505–499 BC. However, it is not certain if any of these men named Marduka are actually the Mordecai in the book of Esther.[54]

An Egyptian signet ring.

Triumph of the Jews (8:15–9:19)

Clothed in royal purple and white, with a great gold crown (8:15). The description of the garments awarded Mordecai correlates with the known wardrobe of Persian kings.[55] Giving an individual a crown was rare, but Xerxes is known to have given a helmsman a garland of gold for saving the king's life during a storm at sea (although he then had him beheaded for the lives that were lost).[56]

These ten sons of Haman (9:7–10). Their names find parallels in Persian sources, including texts from Persepolis that linguistically date the Esther account to the time of Xerxes.[57]

Purim Established (9:20–32)

Purim (9:26). The festival of Purim was added to the five festivals commanded by Moses. Purim was celebrated on the fourteenth of Adar and, according to 2 Macc. 15:36, became known as the "Day of Mordecai" in the Hasmonean period (the intertestamental period). Because the Jews of Susa fought an extra day, they did not celebrate until the fifteenth of Adar, which became known as "Shushan Purim." Today, Purim is celebrated on the fourteenth in the "rural" areas, but on the fifteenth in Jerusalem, as it was in Susa.[58]

Queen Esther . . . wrote this second letter (9:29). The Hebrew verb for "wrote" is in the third-person feminine singular. Esther writes a letter, presumably using a scribe, giving authority to Mordecai's letter and establishing a religious festival that is still practiced today. No other woman in biblical history shares the achievement of saving an entire nation and instituting a national holiday.[59]

Scene from an Assyrian siege depicting the impalement of some of the defenders.

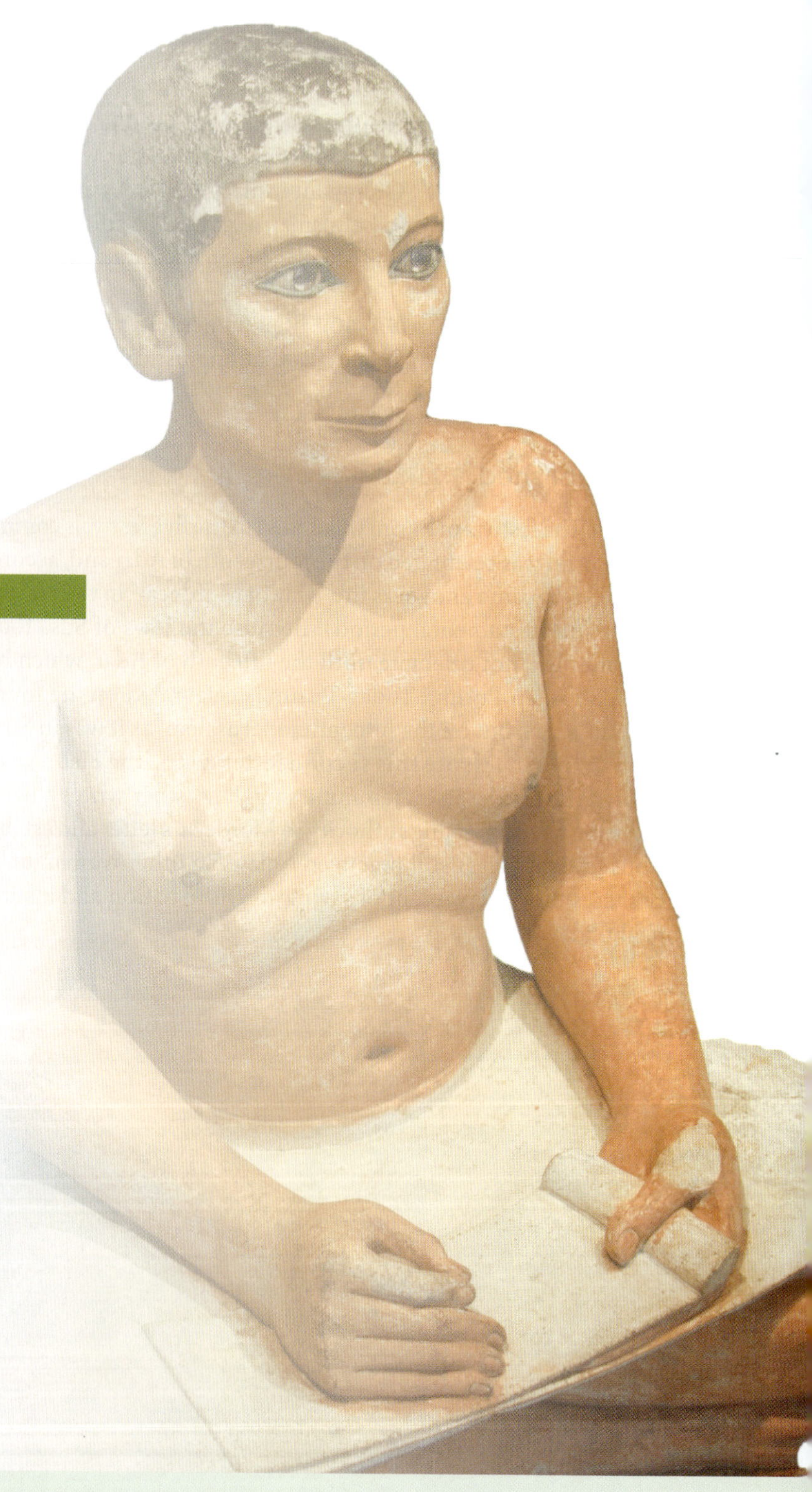

Job

John E. Hartley

Introduction. The book of Job does not mention any kings or any specific historical events that could help to date the composition of the book with any certainty. Based on some apparent interplay between texts in Job and other OT texts, especially Isaiah, one of the stronger arguments supports dating the composition of the book of Job in the seventh century BC, but this is far from certain, and there is no consensus among scholars.

The book of Job is part of the wisdom literature in the Bible. In general there are numerous parallels between Israelite wisdom literature and ancient Near Eastern wisdom literature. While we are not aware of any literature that is exactly like Job, there are several examples of wisdom literature in the ancient Near East that deal with the themes of suffering and apparent injustice. From Egypt are the texts titled "The Protests of the Eloquent Peasant"[1] and "A Dispute over Suicide."[2] Mesopotamian texts that deal with these themes include "The Poem of the Righteous Sufferer"[3] and "A Dialogue about Human Misery."[4]

In the opening of the book God has blessed Job, an upright person, richly (1:1–2:13). At a session of the heavenly council God praises Job to "the Satan" (the Hebrew text contains the definite article), whose role is to roam the world to uncover hidden opposition to God. Satan counters by asserting that Job is faithful

Tablet containing the Babylonian text of "The Poem of the Righteous Sufferer."

to God primarily because of the abundance that God provides him. Satan then puts Job to two tests: (1) a series of tragedies destroys his wealth and his children, and (2) he is afflicted with a horrible illness. This narrative sets the stage for the dialogue, lasting three rounds, between Job and his three friends, Eliphaz, Bildad, and Zophar, who have come to console him.

When Job speaks, he curses the day of his birth and longs for death (chap. 3). The three friends seek to convince him that his suffering is proof that he has sinned grievously (chaps. 4–27). Thus they urge him to repent in order to regain his health. But if Job follows their counsel, Satan's claim that Job serves God for gain would be confirmed. In his speeches Job becomes convinced that he has an advocate (redeemer) in heaven who will testify in his favor. Job brings the dialogue to an end with oaths that he will never contrive a confession as the friends have advised or say they are right (27:1–6). Then he swears a complex oath, requesting that God provide a list of his sins for which he is suffering (chaps. 29–31).

Since the three friends of Job turn silent, Elihu, a young bystander, enters and delivers four speeches in succession (chaps. 32–37). He encourages Job by pointing out that God has been speaking to him in dreams and in pain. Also, God provides an angel to announce that a ransom has been found to deliver one who is near death. Elihu also makes Job aware that when God appears, Job will have to renounce his pride and withdraw his lawsuit.

In the climax of the book God appears in a whirlwind (chaps. 38–41) and confronts Job with a series of questions about the way he has created the world and how he governs the world. In response, Job withdraws his lawsuit (42:1–7). Accepting Job's concession, God blesses him, restoring double (symbolizing completeness) all that Job had lost (42:8–17).

The region of Edom, a possible location for Job's homeland of Uz.

An Egyptian banquet scene.

Prologue (1:1–2:13)

Job . . . had seven sons and three daughters . . . seven thousand sheep and goats (1:1–3). Job, an upright, wealthy patriarch, lived in Uz, likely a village in Edom. God had blessed him with great wealth: seven thousand sheep and goats, three thousand camels, five hundred yoke of oxen, and five hundred female donkeys. He had seven sons and three daughters, the ideal family in the ancient Near East. The symbolic numbers three, seven, and ten attest that his wealth was the result of God's blessing (see chap. 29).

His sons . . . banquets . . . their three sisters (1:4). The solidarity of Job's family and their happiness is manifest in his sons' holding feasts that lasted several days to which they invited their sisters. Large and elaborate feasts and banquets like these (including both men and women) are well attested in the ancient Near East.

Offer burnt offerings for all of them (1:5). Prior to the establishment of formal worship at the tent of meeting (Exod. 25–40), the patriarchs offered their own sacrifices (see Gen. 15:8–10). Job's scrupulous devotion is attested in his offering sacrifices for his children after each celebration. He did this to atone for the possibility that one of them might have denounced God in a thought. This detail highlights the crux of Job's trial: Will loss or suffering cause Job to curse God?

The sons of God came to present themselves before the LORD (1:6). A few OT texts picture God presiding over a council of celestial agents—that is, "the sons of God" (see 1 Kings 22:19–22; Ps. 82:1).

Satan also came with them (1:6). At this session "the Satan," a roving agent who functions as a prosecuting attorney, is present. In Hebrew the term *satan*, being modified by the definite article, is a title or a function rather than a name. The Hebrew root word means "to accuse," "to oppose (legally)," or "to be an adversary." In preexilic OT texts the word *satan* is used without the definite article for human adversaries—for example, the adversaries of Solomon who lived in neighboring nations (1 Kings 11:14, 23, 25). Not until the postexilic era did this word become the name of the spiritual being who opposed God (see Zech. 3:1–2). The Satan's role in Job is to serve as God's roving eye, roaming the earth to discover any illegitimate activity. The Persian kings of the Achaemenid Empire (ca. 553–330 BC) were known to send out spies to roam throughout the empire to find out who was loyal to the king and who was not. Herodotus, a Greek historian, notes that these spies were called "the eyes and ears of the king."

At this session God brings to the Satan's attention that Job is one who truly fears God and lives blamelessly. Responding like a prosecuting attorney, the Satan counters by claiming that Job serves God only for the vast benefits that he receives. God then proposes a test to prove that Job's integrity is genuine.

The oxen were plowing (1:14). Plowing in the ancient Near East typically was done in autumn after the start of the early rains. Using scratch plows, workers cut furrows about four inches deep.[5] Seeds were planted in the trenches. Then the field was plowed again at a 90-degree angle, thereby covering the seeds with soil. This plow was made of hard wood; if the farmer could afford it, the plow had a bronze or an iron blade. The frame was constructed so that the oxen did most of the work.[6]

The Sabeans swooped down (1:15). These Sabeans probably are from the northern part of the Arabian Desert.

The Chaldeans . . . made a raid (1:17). Early in their history the Chaldeans were a seminomadic tribe, roaming the region between southern Babylonia and the northeastern portion of the Arabian Desert. Later in their history they produce the dynasty that rules over the Neo-Babylonian Empire (see comments on Jer. 38:2; see the article "The Babylonians").

God's fire fell from heaven (1:16). "God's fire" probably refers to lightning. This lightning strike was so spectacular that it was viewed as an act of God. The use of lightning and fire from heaven as divine judgment is attested both in the OT and in the literature of the ancient Near East.

Job . . . tore his robe, and shaved his head (1:20). It was customary for a person to express deep grief by tearing their outer garment. The word translated as "robe" denotes an elegant garment.[7] Shaving was uncommon, but tearing the robe and shaving the head were known as signs of grief both in the OT (2 Sam. 1:1–2; Amos 8:10) and in the ancient Near East.

He sat among the ashes (2:8). Since his illness exiled Job from community life, he sat on ashes at the gate where people disposed of ashes. The ashes represent his mourning.

Each man tore his robe and threw dust into the air and on his head (2:12). The tearing of one's garments and putting dust or ashes on one's head were typical acts of mourning in the ancient Near East (see comments on 2 Sam. 13:19).

Job's Curse-Lament (3:1–26)

May the day I was born perish (3:3). Wishing never to have been born, Job curses the day of his birth. He entreats the most highly skilled wizard

(3:8), one who could arouse Leviathan (see comments on Job 41:1–34), to pronounce a spell that would remove that day from the calendar. If that were accomplished, all that took place on that particular day would cease to exist.

Leviathan (3:8). See comments on Job 41:1–34.

Knees receive me (3:12). Family members welcomed a newborn by holding the infant on their knees (Gen. 50:23).

Then I would be at rest (3:13–19). Job poetically describes death in a way that also parallels some ancient Near Eastern texts. According to this view, death is a place where the weary rest and where slaves no longer have to obey their taskmasters.

The First Cycle of the Dialogue (4:1–14:22)

Isn't your piety your confidence? (4:6). Since Job has expressed his fear of God by helping the poor and caring for the weak (see 29:12–17), his piety (literally, "his fear of God") should now be his confidence. Then he would not long so intensely for death.

The teeth of young lions are broken (4:10–11). Even the mightiest of wild animals, here symbolic for the wicked, may experience a harsh fate. Several references to lions in the OT attest their presence throughout Palestine. In the ancient Near East lions were also used frequently as symbols of the power and aggressiveness of monarchs.

A word was brought to me in secret (4:12). In the OT it is normally only the patriarchs and especially the prophets who receive visions (e.g., Gen. 15:12–16; Amos 7:1–9). This is the only OT account of a sage (wise person who transmits wisdom) receiving a vision.

Clay houses (4:19). This refers to either small adobe dwellings or (perhaps as a metaphor) to human bodies, based on God's having formed the first human from the dust of the ground (Gen. 2:7).

Which of the holy ones will you turn to? (5:1). "Holy ones" is a reference to angels (e.g., Hosea 11:12; Zech. 14:5).

A fool . . . his children . . . with no one to rescue them (5:3–4). Inside the major gate of most cities in the ancient Near East, people gathered to converse and sell goods, and the elders settled disputes. In this example the fool's children, lacking a defender, receive a harsh penalty, enabling vagrants to consume their father's harvest. Based on retribution, they suffer the consequences of their father's folly.

As surely as sparks fly upward (5:7). When used to sharpen a metal tool, the sharpening stone often caused sparks to fly upward. With this analogy Eliphaz shows that anyone who has done wrong suffers in some way. Hardship never befalls a person by chance, he argues, for that person committed a wrong.

He will rescue you from six calamities; no harm will touch you in seven (5:19). Using a numerical saying (six . . . seven) in which the number in the second line is raised by one (cf. Amos 1:3–2:6), Eliphaz asserts that God afflicts humans in multiple ways to make them aware of having done wrong. The progression of six to seven conveys that God will rescue the devout from every trouble.

As a stack of sheaves (5:26). Stalks of ripe grain were cut and stacked on the threshing floor. A large stack from a bountiful harvest is a metaphor for a prominent grave, honoring a virtuous person who died fittingly in old age.

If only my grief could be weighed (6:2–3). Scales in the ancient Near East consisted of two pans or trays suspended by cords from the arms of a center-balanced crossbeam. In Job's analogy, if his sufferings were placed on one tray of the scale and on the other tray all the sand of the seas, his suffering would weigh heavier.

The arrows of the Almighty (6:4). Job depicts God as a warrior (see comments on Job 16:12–14), who sometimes disciplines his own by shooting them with poison-tipped arrows (Ps. 7:12–13; 38:2). The portrayal of deities in the ancient Near East as warriors was common. Likewise poison arrows were well known throughout the ancient Near East.

Does a wild donkey bray over fresh grass? (6:5). Wild donkeys had to search diligently for food, especially in the arid areas they often inhabited (24:5; 39:5–8). While feeding on grass, however, a wild donkey would not be braying loudly. Job is showing that there are solid grounds for his caustic statements.

A despairing man should receive loyalty from his friends (6:14). The term Job uses that is translated as "loyalty" indicates that he and his friends are in a covenant relationship. Thus his friends are obligated to help him face his hardship. His claim that they are failing him is a serious charge.

My brothers are as treacherous as a wadi (6:15–20). Often a creek bed (called a wadi) in southern Palestine had water flowing in it only after the mountain snow melted in the spring or right after a rain. Most of the time wadis were dry. Job's point is that the failure of his friends is as grievous as the shock experienced by a caravan crossing the desert that reaches a stream expecting to find water but discovering that it is dry.

A scene from the Egyptian Book of the Dead depicting an elaborate set of scales on which the deceased's heart is weighed.

The dry wadi (seasonal flowing stream) represents the friends' failure to provide Job relief.

Caravans of Tema . . . merchants of Sheba (6:19). These caravans are identified with two famous trading centers in the Arabian Desert. Tema (today Tayma) is in northwestern Arabia, at the intersection of three trade routes, and Sheba is in southwestern Arabia.[8]

Pay a bribe for me (6:22). Job states that if he had been kidnapped, his friends would have been obligated to rescue him by paying a large ransom or by risking their lives to free him from his captors. But presently they are failing him.

Am I the sea or a sea monster? (7:12). The Hebrew word for "sea" was the same word that the Canaanites used for the god of the sea (Yam). Common in the ancient Near East were traditions associating the sea and the sea monsters with forces of chaos that opposed the main god or gods and that had to be overcome in order to establish order in the world (see comments on Gen. 1:1; see the article "The Canaanites and Canaanite Religion"). Job feels that God is treating him as though he were God's most formidable foe, the sea or the serpentine monster that lived in the deep and opposed God.

You frighten me with dreams (7:13–14). Dreams play an important role in the book of Job (4:12–16; 33:15–20). Typically in the literature of the ancient Near East nightmares or bad dreams come from demons, but here it is God who terrifies Job with wild and frightening dreams.

What is a mere human? (7:17–18). Job expresses the depth of his despair with a parody on lines in Ps. 8 that laud the way God made humans, crowning them with honor and entrusting them with care of the earth and the animals. Job turns these accolades into an accusation against God for testing him so harshly. Job finds God's vigilance to be oppressive. In questioning the value of being human, Job reaches the lowest point of despair in his trial.

Ask the previous generation (8:8–10). Bildad bases his judgment on the teaching of the fathers, probably an allusion to a tradition of handed-down wisdom. In the ancient Near East the handed-down wisdom of the ancestors was viewed as much more authoritative than one individual's experience.

Does the papyrus grow where there is no marsh? (8:11–13). Papyrus, a luxuriant plant, grows abundantly in well-watered marshes, as found in the Nile Delta and the Hula swamps in Upper Galilee. When papyrus lacks water, it withers. This imagery indicates that Bildad concedes that the wicked may thrive for a while, but upon facing hardship, they wilt.

How can a person be justified before God? (9:2–6). Job ponders two approaches in the ancient world by which an offended person could regain honor: a legal dispute (9:3) or a wrestling match (9:4). In the legal dispute the one party that reduces the other to silence wins. Likewise, winning a

Ancient sketch of an Egyptian papyrus boat.

wrestling match proves the winner's position (similarly, the wording in 38:3, "Brace yourself like a man" [NIV], is a call to prepare for a wrestling match). Job realizes that his challenging of God, who is both wise and powerful, is not very promising, for in a legal dispute God can easily counter his arguments, and in a wrestling match God can easily defeat him.

He shakes the earth from its place (9:6). Often an earthquake attends God's appearing (Judg. 5:4–5; Ps. 18:7, 15; 46:2–3; 68:7–8).

He commands the sun not to shine (9:7). God's power is evident whenever he darkens the sun and the stars by hiding them—for example, with clouds, dust storms, or eclipses.

Treads on the waves of the sea (9:8). Treading on someone's or something's back was a demonstration of power or subjugation. In several ancient Near Eastern myths the ruling god displays his power by treading on the crests of the waves of the sea.[9]

He makes the stars: the Bear, Orion (9:9). Peoples in the ancient Near East typically viewed the constellations as gods, and study of the constellations was also a major component of divination in trying to predict the future. The Babylonians in particular interpreted the movements of the constellations as foreshadowing events on earth (Isa. 47:12–13). By contrast, the Israelites viewed the movements of the heavenly bodies as directed by God. Job mentions four constellations: (1) the Bear (perhaps the Big Dipper or the Little Dipper) or the star cluster known as Hyades; (2) Orion, based on the reference to its being bound to the heavenly dome in 38:31; (3) Pleiades (38:31; Amos 5:8); and (4) the constellations of the southern sky (see 38:32). The Israelites were likely aware of the southern stars as a result of their trading expeditions to western Arabia and the eastern coast of Africa (1 Kings 9:26–28).

Rahab's assistants cringe in fear beneath him (9:13). In the OT the term "Rahab" often is used to refer to a hostile serpentine sea creature that God subdued (slayed) prior to creation (see 26:12–13; Ps. 89:10). In the literature of the ancient Near East the pagan gods often fight against the god of the sea and associated sea monsters (like Leviathan), but the term "Rahab" is not used. In other OT texts (Ps. 87:4; Isa. 30:7) Rahab is used symbolically to represent Egypt.

My days fly by faster than a runner . . . like boats made of papyrus . . . like an eagle (9:25–26). With three metaphors Job laments the swift passing of his life: (1) a swift runner—that is, a person employed to deliver urgent messages (see 2 Sam. 18:19–23); (2) Egyptian skiffs (small boats) made out of papyrus, which, being light, appear to skim over the water (see Isa. 18:1–2); (3) an eagle, which swoops on its prey at exceedingly high speeds (see 39:27–30).

Even if I washed myself with snow (9:30). In many cultures of the ancient Near East specific ordeals sometimes were used to determine whether a person was guilty of a forbidden activity (see comments on Num. 5:24). In order to prove his innocence, Job considers performing such an ordeal. He will wash his body with soap and snow water (for its purity) and his hands with a strong cleanser, likely lye[10] (cf. Deut. 21:6–7; Ps. 26:6). The classic example is that of Pilate washing his hands at Jesus's trial in order to demonstrate to the crowd that he was innocent of Jesus's death (Matt. 27:24).

There is no mediator between us (9:33). Mediators played an important role in the complex legal system of Mesopotamia. Likewise, in some ancient Near Eastern religious beliefs people had their individual and personal (minor) gods who advocated on their behalf at the council of the great gods. Realizing that there is no way for him to challenge God, Job wishfully pleads for someone to serve as a mediator or arbiter. That person would make God remove the rod that he is using to punish Job, thereby easing his pain. Job, then, would have the composure to persuade God that he truly is innocent.

Your hands shaped me . . . you formed me like clay (10:8–9). See comments on Jer. 18:3. Job compares how God created him to how a potter forms a vessel out of clay (Gen. 2:7; Isa. 64:8).

Curdle me like cheese . . . wove me together with bones and tendons (10:10–12). Using the analogy of making cheese, Job describes the way God forms a baby in a mother's womb. It is like a shepherd pouring cream into a skin and then shaking it vigorously. Slowly the cream begins to congeal, forming a small lump—that is, an embryo. As the embryo grows, God covers it with skin and flesh, eventually adding bones and sinews. As it leaves the womb, God breathes into it the breath of life.

I cannot lift up my head (10:15–16). A bowed head indicates humiliation; an uplifted head expresses confidence, and sometimes pride.

If I am proud, you hunt me like a lion (10:16). This text is not clear. Either God is like a lion in how he hunts Job because of Job's pride,

Wall panel relief from the palace of the Assyrian king Ashurbanipal depicting his lion hunts.

or Job is like a proud lion being hunted by God. Quite a number of wall panel reliefs discovered in the palace of the Assyrian king Ashurbanipal (ca. 645 BC) depict the king's lion hunts.

Doesn't the ear test words? (12:11). For the Israelites, the ears play a vital role in gaining understanding (13:1). A person with open ears listens attentively and learns well (Deut. 4:5–8). Those with closed ears reject God's counsel (Zech. 7:11).

I will still defend my ways before him . . . I have prepared my case (13:15–18). Job continues to use typical legal language and courtroom concepts. Seeking to compel God to stop treating him so viciously, Job resolves to prove his innocence by taking God to court. Having prepared a strong defense, he is confident of winning a favorable verdict.

How many iniquities and sins have I committed? (13:23). As Job prepares to go to court against God, his initial request is for God to provide a bill of particulars.

My rebellion would be sealed up in a bag (14:17). Job envisions God's placing either a list of his sins or stones that represent his sins in a bag. He then ties the bag with a string and seals it so that the contents are never revealed.[11]

The Second Cycle of the Dialogue (15:1–21:34)

The hot east wind (15:2). In Palestine the hot east wind, the sirocco, blows in mid to late spring and in early fall, producing high temperatures. Vegetation wilts and people become irritable. Eliphaz complains that Job's words are as irritating as the east wind.

Were you the first human ever born? (15:7–10). Eliphaz is referring not to Adam (who was created, not born), but rather to a legend common in the ancient Near East associated with the wisdom tradition about the first human who existed before the creation of the world. In that legend this sage passed on the knowledge of civilization (e.g., writing) to humans who followed. Although this account is not in the OT, there is an echo of it in the description of wisdom's origin in Prov. 8:22–31 (cf. Ezek. 28:12–19). That person thus has superior wisdom because of having observed God creating the world. Because Job is not that person and the friends are older, Eliphaz rejects Job's supposed claims that he knows more than they do (cf. 12:3; 13:1–2).

His waistline bulges (15:27). Being rich, this ruthless person is well fed. He builds up his body so that he can defy God and bully people (cf. Ps. 73:4–12).

You have shriveled me up . . . a witness (16:8). In antiquity illnesses often were viewed as punishment for sin. Thus Job is greatly distressed that the sores on his body bear witness to his having sinned grievously, refuting his declarations of innocence.

He set me up as his target (16:12–14). Common in the ancient Near East was the comparison of deities to great warriors. Job compares God to a warrior repeatedly. In this text God is honing his archery skill by making Job his target (cf. 30:11–15). God's arrows have pierced Job's kidneys, vital organs that were considered the locus of deep emotions. Then like a warrior who makes repeated charges until he breaches an enemy's stronghold, God keeps rushing at Job, inflicting great pain, as evidenced by his red face and the dark shadows around his eyes (16:16).

Buried my strength in the dust (16:15). The word translated as "strength" is literally "horn." An animal's horn represents its ability (strength) to inflict deadly harm. Burying a horn is a gesture of deep humiliation as the result of being defeated.

Earth, do not cover my blood (16:18). There was a common, somewhat poetic concept that if a person has been killed and the body not buried, the uncovered blood would cry out, petitioning God to avenge that one's death (cf. Gen. 4:10; Isa. 26:21). Drawing on this norm, Job entreats the earth to prevent the burial of his body so that his blood may cry out, leading to his eventual vindication.

My witness is in heaven (16:19). Continuing with legal courtroom language, in faith Job declares that there is an advocate in heaven who will testify to his integrity. The advocate's role is counter to that of the Satan (the accuser) in the prologue. The identity of the advocate is the same as the redeemer in 19:25.

Accept my pledge (17:3). A pledge involved putting up a valuable item as a guarantee that one will perform what has been promised. Since no one will make that pledge for him, Job appears to be asking God to accept him as the pledge. Then God, being assured that Job will stand trial, may cease afflicting him.

Lamp (18:6). In the ancient Near East the most common lamp was simple, a small plate-shaped clay vessel about two to three inches in diameter that had two sides slightly folded in to form a spout-like space for the wick. Olive oil was placed in the dish, and a wick was set with one end in the oil and the other across the spout. The light of a lamp going out symbolized dying.

A net . . . mesh . . . trap . . . noose . . . rope . . . snare (18:8–10). The hazardous path of the wicked is compared to numerous traps common in the ancient Near East. (1) A net for catching birds was stretched out between two bows set in a half circle. When a bird pecked at the bait, the bows released, causing the net to encircle the bird. Another use of nets was to set them so that an animal's feet would get entangled in the netting (Ps. 9:15). (2) A mesh, comprised of a network of sticks, was placed over a pit to conceal it. When an animal walked across the mesh, it would fall into the pit. (3) A trap, used for capturing birds, had a springing mechanism that seized whatever triggered the device—a foot or another appendage (Ps. 91:3). (4) A snare with a door was configured so that when an animal nibbled at the bait, the door closed, preventing the animal's escape. (5) A rope or noose was hung from a tree or hidden on a path, and it would close on the appendage of an animal that got caught in it. (6) Another type of snare, which is hidden on a path, holds an animal that walks on it. Hunters often caught animals by driving them into a trap.

Terrors frighten him . . . he is ripped from the security of his tent (18:11–14). "Terrors" probably is a reference to a wide range of terrifying things such as bad dreams, premonitions, consuming disease, and demons. Incorporating imagery about death and the grave that was common in the literature of the ancient Near East, this description culminates with a graphic and poetic picture of death. When a wicked person dies, the body is dragged from the tent and stood before the king of terrors, the ruler of Sheol (the netherworld), to receive judgment.

Death's firstborn (18:13). This may be an epithet for the deadliest disease.[12] Being a demonic power, it consumes a person's skin and limbs.

Burning sulfur is scattered over his home (18:15). To prevent defeated villages from recovering quickly, conquering armies sometimes spread sulfur or salt over the farmland to render it infertile for years (cf. Deut. 29:23).

I cry out: "Violence!" (19:7). Under Mosaic law, a woman who was attacked in the countryside and cried out for help was innocent and had no complicity in the assault (Deut. 22:25–27). Drawing on this legal principle, Job cries, "Violence!" and tries to clear himself of any responsibility for his suffering (cf. Hab. 1:2–3).

They construct a ramp against me and camp around my tent (19:12). Job compares God's attacks against him to an army besieging a city. When confronted with a strong walled city, invading armies often constructed siege ramps and moveable siege platforms that could be pushed up to the walls so that warriors could shoot arrows and throw stones into the fortress. The fact that Job is living not in a strong walled city, but rather in a tent, turns this description into a humorous but grim oxymoron.

My words . . . inscribed in stone forever (19:23–24). A common practice in antiquity was to erect a stone, usually engraved with pictures or a text, to preserve valuable information for posterity. Such a stone is known as a stela. Several stelae have survived from the ancient Near East. One of the most famous is the large stela, over seven feet tall, of Hammurabi's law code. At the top is a depiction of the king receiving the law code from Shamash, the

sun god. The law code is inscribed below, covering all sides. Job desires that his lament be inscribed on a stone stela so that coming generations will learn of his assertions of innocence. He wants the letters to be lined with lead, likely so that they will sparkle under sunlight or perhaps to preserve the writing. The Behistun inscription recounting the Persian king Darius's victories has inscribed letters filled with lead.

My Redeemer lives . . . I will see God (19:25–26). In Israel a redeemer was a person who came to the aid of a close relative facing a hardship, such as having had to sell oneself into bondage because of a heavy debt (Lev. 25:35–54). This redeemer will serve as Job's defense attorney before the heavenly court (see Ps. 119:154; Prov. 23:10–11). Yet the redeemer appears to be God himself. This is evident given that the term "redeemer" is a beloved title for God, grounded in his delivering Israel from Egyptian slavery (see Exod. 15:13; frequent in Isa. 40–55). Since Job has suffered publicly, he declares that he will see God with his own eyes. Seeing God is necessary for him to experience fully the restoration of his honor, since during his ordeal God has remained hidden.

Terrors (20:25). See comments on Job 18:11–14.

Put your hand over your mouth (21:5). This was a gesture of silence, especially when one was amazed (cf. 29:9; 40:4).[13]

Tambourine and lyre . . . flute (21:12). See the article "Musical Instruments in Israel and the Ancient Near East."

The Third Cycle of the Dialogue (22:1–27:23)

Aren't your iniquities endless? (22:5). Disturbed by Job's resolve to pursue a lawsuit against God, Eliphaz presents a bill of particulars, listing sins commonly committed as the reason for Job's

Hammurabi's law code stela.

suffering (22:5–9). If Job accepts this list, he must repent of the sins and forsake his desire for a lawsuit. Then his health will be restored, and he can rebuild his household.

The circle of the sky (22:14). In the OT the heavens were viewed as a vault where God moves about observing affairs on earth (Gen. 1:7). But the wicked think that a heavy cloud cover keeps God from viewing activities on earth and rendering judgments.

Gold of Ophir (22:24). Ophir is likely a region in southwestern Arabia famous for its high-quality gold (28:16; 1 Kings 9:28; 2 Chron. 8:18).

A Babylonian boundary stone.

Boundary markers (24:2). In order to prevent encroachment on its property, a family set stone markers around the boundary. Moving such markers was strictly forbidden (Deut. 19:14; 27:17). Often these stones not only served as boundary markers but also contained legal descriptions of the property.

Sheol . . . Abaddon (26:6). Reflecting the common view of the afterlife, Job describes the shadowy existence of the dead in Sheol, a realm beneath the oceans, also called Abaddon, meaning "destruction" (cf. 28:22; 31:12). Although hidden from human sight, it is visible to God.

He crushed Rahab . . . the fleeing serpent (26:12–13). See comments on Job 7:12; 9:13; Gen. 1:1; see the article "The Canaanites and Canaanite Religion." Several ancient Near Eastern myths recount the primordial victory of the upright god over the malevolent god, often identified as a serpentine sea monster. For example, in the Canaanite myth Baal defeats Yam, the sea god, leading to his enthronement as king. Several OT texts refer to Yahweh proving his supremacy by decimating the primeval foe, often represented as the sea or the sea monster. That foe has various names in the OT: the Sea (Yam), Rahab (Ps. 89:10; Isa. 51:9), Leviathan (Job 41:1; Isa. 27:1), and the sea monster (7:12).

It claps its hands at him (27:23). This is a gesture of scorn.

Hymn to Wisdom (28:1–28)

The miners swing back and forth (28:4). In the ancient Near East people mined for metals (gold, silver, copper, tin, lead, iron) as well as precious stones (e.g., lapis lazuli [v. 6], quartz [v. 18], topaz [v. 19]). In 28:1–11 Job is marveling at the wisdom and skill required to mine these metals out of the depths of the earth. In order to reach these jewels buried deep in the earth, miners enter the mines by descending on ropes or possibly in baskets attached to ropes.

Where can wisdom be found? (28:12). This majestic poem (28:1–28) acclaims human technical skills that produce remarkable results. The premier example, as noted above, is the ability to penetrate deep into the earth and bring to light precious metals and stones. Human technical skills, however, fail to match the grandeur of God's wisdom.

Job's Avowal of Innocence (29:1–31:40)

Hear my case . . . let the Almighty answer me (29:1–31:40). Drawing on the legal process of the ancient Near East, and seeking to compel God to vindicate him by filing a lawsuit against God, Job supports his claims of innocence of any wrongdoing by swearing a complex oath of innocence. It has three distinct parts: (1) Job recounts his former life, emphasizing his deeds of compassion (chap. 29); (2) he describes his sufferings in detail (chap. 30); and (3) he swears an oath of clearance by naming sins that he has never committed (chap. 31).

His lamp . . . his light (29:3). See comments on Job 18:6. Before his trial Job experienced God's presence like a lamp lighting up the darkness, providing him guidance and protection (cf. 2 Sam. 22:29).

Bathed in curds . . . the rock poured out streams of oil (29:6). Being very prosperous, Job had an abundance of "curds" (dairy products) and olive oil, substances that refresh and nourish life (Deut. 32:13–14). The reference to the rock alludes to the ability of olive trees to grow in very rocky areas, even on rocky hillsides.

Young men . . . withdrew, while older men stood to their feet (29:8–10). These are cultural ways to show respect (cf. Lev. 19:32).

Bow (29:20). The bow was a symbol of strength.

Rain . . . spring showers (29:23). The heavy showers of fall enabled farmers to break up the soil for planting seeds. The light showers of March and April were necessary for the grain to ripen.

Jackals . . . ostriches (30:29). The mournful cries

An Assyrian cylinder seal that probably depicts gods fighting against the chaos sea monster.

of these inhabitants of desolate lands represent Job's agonizing pain and forlornness.

My lyre . . . my flute (30:31). See the article "Musical Instruments in Israel and the Ancient Near East."

On accurate scales (31:6). See comments on Job 6:2–3.

I threw them a kiss (31:27). Kissing the hand and extending it upward was one way of expressing devotion to a deity (cf. Hosea 13:2). Job declares that he had never shown such homage to the sun or the moon in their splendor (cf. Deut. 17:2–5; 2 Kings 23:5).

If my land cries out against me (31:38–40). Job's concern for the land is in accord with the goal of the sabbatical laws that required letting land lie fallow every seventh year (Lev. 25:2–7).

The Elihu Speeches (32:1–37:24)

Elihu son of Barachel the Buzite (32:2). Elihu ("he is my God") is introduced along with his lineage, in patriarchal style. In fact, his line may go back to Abraham, for it includes Buz, Abraham's nephew (Gen. 22:20–21).

About to burst like new wineskins (32:19). New wine is poured into new skins so that the skins can expand as the wine ferments.

I was also pinched off from a piece of clay (33:6). Elihu describes himself as a clay vessel made by God (see 4:19; 10:9). With this imagery he expresses solidarity with Job.

The Pit (33:24). A large hole dug for receiving the deceased.[14]

He scornfully claps in our presence (34:37). See comments on Job 27:23.

See how he spreads his lightning around him (36:30). To illustrate God's vast power, Elihu describes a powerful storm at sea (36:27–37:24). When it passes, there is a grand display of color in the clearing northern sky, reflecting God's glory (37:21–22).

He covers his hands with lightning (36:32). Baal, the Canaanite god of the storms (and fertility), often is

An ancient bronze mirror.

depicted with a thunderbolt in his hand (see the article "The Canaanites and Canaanite Religion").

A cast metal mirror (37:18). Ancient mirrors were primitive; the best were made of polished bronze.

The Yahweh ("the Lord") Speeches (38:1–42:6)

The Lord answered Job from the whirlwind (38:1). A grand display in nature often attends God's appearing, confirming that God is the speaker.

Answer me like a man (38:3). The Hebrew word translated as "man" implies a strong man of military fighting age. Thus the Lord addresses Job not as a disabled person, but rather as a strong man, thereby challenging him to a wrestling match, one of words (see comments on Job 9:2–6).

When I established the earth . . . fixed its dimensions (38:4–7). In wisdom God made "blueprints" for the world. Following them as he created, he provided the earth a secure foundation. There was a grand celebration at the laying of the cornerstone;[15] the morning stars (i.e., Venus and Mercury) sang and the angels shouted joyfully.

The sea . . . burst from the womb (38:8). From the heavenly womb God brought forth the turbulent sea. Given its vast power, God put in place doors and bars to keep it from inundating the land. Caring for the newborn, God wrapped it in clouds. This imagery conveys that at its origin the sea was not an evil god as recounted in various ancient Near Eastern myths (see comments on Gen. 1:1), but rather was brought into being by the Lord and thus subject to him.

The dawn . . . so it may seize the edges of the earth . . . shake the wicked (38:12–15). Figuratively, each morning the sun's rays take hold of the corners of the earth, like a tablecloth, and shake off the crumbs—that is, driving the wicked into hiding.

The sources of the sea . . . gates of deep darkness . . . home of light (38:16–24). The implication here is that whoever knows or has visited the extremities of the world—the springs deep in the earth that feed the seas, the gates of death (Sheol), the abode of light, and the sources of the wind in the east and of darkness in the west—had special power over the universe.

Snow is stored . . . storehouses of hail (38:22). The typical understanding in the ancient Near East was that behind the dome or expanse of heaven were storehouses for snow, hail, lightning, and the east wind (see comments on Gen. 1:6). These elements are available for God to use as weapons against earthly foes. Similar to the way farmers make ditches for irrigating their fields,[16] God has put in place channels for carrying water from the heavenly reservoir to fall as rain on desolate areas, enabling grass to grow as food for the wild animals (38:25–27).

Uninhabited land . . . wasteland (38:26–27). This picture and the animal portraits (38:38–39:30) show God as the creator caring for lands beyond human habitation. A common understanding in the ancient Near East was to view land as consisting of two regions: (1) sown land, where humans support themselves by farming and shepherding, and (2) the wilderness, where wild animals roam free from human control. God manages both regions for the benefit of their inhabitants.

Does the rain have a father . . . the ice . . . the frost? (38:28–30). In contrast to the views expressed in several ancient Near Eastern myths of creation, the various forms of water (i.e., rain, dew, frost, ice) are produced not by procreation of the gods, but by the cycles that God has embedded in the world.

Can you bring out the constellations? (38:32). See comments on Job 9:9.

A lioness . . . mountain goats . . . the wild donkey . . . the eagle (38:39–39:30). Animals in this list are wild except for the horse. Being untamable, they do not exist to serve humans. All of them, from the smallest to the majestic, are dependent on God, who has given to each specific traits necessary for survival.

Appetite of young lions . . . the raven's food (38:39–41). The female lion, the more skillful hunter, was the one that provided food for her cubs. Likewise, ravens, feeding on grains, fruit, small animals, insects, and eggs,[17] scavenged for food for their young.

Mountain goats (39:1–4). Palestine had several varieties of wild goats, from small goats in the Arabian Peninsula to the large Syrian mountain goat.[18] Their ability to climb steep, rocky terrain enabled them to graze in areas beyond the range of carnivorous animals.

The wild donkey (39:5–8). The reddish brown onager, a fast runner, lived primarily in more arid areas far from populated centers (cf. Jer. 2:24). Its freedom came at the price of surviving on a meager diet. Assyrian reliefs depict royal hunting parties that hunted wild donkeys.

The wild ox (39:9–12). This likely is a reference to the now extinct aurochs. Weighing about a ton and having two curved horns up to ten feet long, they were very dangerous animals. They were herbivorous and roamed in small groups (Deut. 33:17; Ps. 22:21; 92:10).[19]

The ostrich (39:13–18). The ostrich is a strange-looking bird. Though it cannot fly, it is a fast runner, faster than the horse, exceeded only by the cheetah. Several hens normally share a nest set in thick grass.[20] The dominant female lays about ten eggs, each weighing about three pounds. She places her eggs in the center. The male and the dominant female take turns sitting on the nest for about six weeks, primarily to protect them from the sun's

An Egyptian royal hunting party hunting hippopotamuses.

heat.[21] At times the hen leaves the nest, unmindful that the eggs might be stepped on (cf. Lam. 4:3).

The hawk . . . the eagle (39:26–30). The Hebrew word translated as "eagle" probably refers to the griffon vulture.[22] Hawks and griffon vultures migrated between southern Europe and the Palestine-Syria area as well as northeastern Africa.

Behemoth (40:15–24). The animal referenced here probably is the hippopotamus. The male of the species can weigh upwards of thirty-five hundred pounds. Its huge mouth, opening as much as four feet wide,[23] can close with tremendous force. Hippopotamuses consume large volumes of vegetation each day. To keep its skin from becoming dry, it spends much of the day in swamps or under trees such as the lotus and the willow (or poplar) (40:22). Lotuses are native to Syria and much of Africa. They have clusters of vivid flowers. Poplars (or willows) often grow along riverbanks.[24] Drawings from Egypt show a royal party hunting a hippopotamus; for weapons they carry hooks, harpoons, and spears. The hippopotamus was prized for its hide, fat, teeth, tusks, and meat.[25] Pharaohs hunted them to authenticate their right to rule and their ability to protect their people. Also hippopotamus bones have been found at Tell Qasile, located on the north side of Tel Aviv.[26]

Leviathan (41:1–34). The term "leviathan" in this text usually is identified as a crocodile. Crocodiles are common along the Nile. In antiquity they also lived in areas of Palestine—for example, along the seacoast from present-day Tel Aviv to Caesarea. In 41:1–12 Leviathan is described as a fierce animal, and in 41:13–34 Leviathan is described as a mythic creature. Given the fear that they inspire, crocodiles were hunted by pharaohs to prove their divine status and their ability to protect their people. Somewhat comparable are OT references that exalt the Lord as supreme over all cosmic forces by his crushing of Leviathan at the dividing of the sea so that Israel could escape from Egypt (Ps. 74:14; cf. Isa. 51:9–11). This victory demonstrated that there is no rival to the Lord's rule. Eschatological texts describe the Lord's complete victory over Leviathan, the evil force, in the final battle (e.g., Isa. 27:1). In the literature of Israel's neighbors in the ancient Near East, Leviathan is used to denote the primeval sea monster of chaos that was defeated at creation.

A lower millstone (41:24). To make flour, grain typically was ground between two millstones. The lower stone was large and stationary. A person would then rub a handheld stone over the heads of grain on the lower millstone, grinding them into flour.

Threshing sledge (41:30). This was a heavy board with several symmetrical, circular holes into which flint or basalt stones were set to protrude through the bottom. It was dragged over harvested grain to remove husks and over straw to make chaff.[27]

Epilogue (42:7–17)

Take seven bulls and seven rams (42:8). God directed Job's three friends to present the highest sacrifice, seven bulls and seven rams (cf. Num. 23:1; 1 Chron. 15:26), to make amends for wrongly advising Job to contrive repentance.

The Lord restored his fortunes and doubled his previous possessions (42:10). Doubling symbolizes that God fully restored his faithful servant (cf. Isa. 40:2).

He named his first daughter Jemimah (42:14). In the OT names of women normally occur only in a narrative along with other characters. But here the names of Job's daughters are given. Their names are of items prized by women: Jemimah, likely "turtledove"; Keziah, "cassia, cinnamon"; and Keren-happuch, "horn of antimony," a small container of pulverized dark minerals used as eye shadow (2 Kings 9:30; Jer. 4:30). Their names are connected with the senses: hearing, smell, and sight.[28] Job also breaks tradition by giving them an inheritance (see comments on Num. 27:8).

Full of days (42:17). God granted Job a full, long life; this phrase is used to honor the patriarchs—for example, Abraham and Isaac (Gen. 25:8; 35:29).

Psalms

Psalms

Christine Brown Jones

Introduction. A number of the psalms are attributed to various individuals (or groups), and the lifetimes of these individuals/groups span over eight hundred years. Thus obviously the book of Psalms was not produced overnight! The book of Psalms contains several smaller collections gathered according to title/authorship or content. Over time Israel gathered these smaller collections into larger ones and eventually gathered the full collection of 150. They divided the full book into five smaller books: Book I (Pss. 1–41), Book II (Pss. 42–72), Book III (Pss. 73–89), Book IV (Pss. 90–106), and Book V (Pss. 107–150). Some scholars suggest that this fivefold division may mirror the five books of the Torah/Pentateuch.

Headings and Titles. Of the 150 psalms, 116 contain some sort of title or heading. In the Hebrew text these headings and titles constitute verse 1 in the verse numbering system, but in our English translations they have been moved up and set apart as headings or titles and are not used at all as part of the verse numbering system. The titles serve several purposes, such as assigning authorship or assigning a collection title, identifying style, noting musical or worship instructions, and providing possible historical context for understanding the psalm (e.g., several psalms of David refer to historical events from his life). Many psalm titles mention individual or group names, and the assumption often is made that the named person(s) must have directly authored the psalm. That is, however, not necessarily the case. The Hebrew grammatical construction of these titles

A small statue of an Egyptian playing a harp.

allows for a much broader range of possibilities. The psalms assigned to a particular person (or group) may have been written by that person, commissioned by that person, written in honor of that person, or written in the same style as that person. The designation may also indicate responsibility during worship. David and the Levites appointed specific families (Heman, Asaph, Ethan, and others) as temple musicians (1 Chron. 15:16–21). Regardless of the purpose of noting names, we cannot deny the significance of those individuals/groups in the development and leadership of worship in Israel. Given the uncertainty of authorship, I will refer to the writer of the psalms simply as the psalmist, while recognizing the influence of numerous psalmists throughout the book.

Many aspects of the titles remain unclear, especially the musical and style notations. Some titles refer to instrumentation and tune (e.g., Ps. 5: "with the flutes"; Ps. 22: "To [the tune of] 'The Deer of the Dawn'"). Other terms note literary information about the form. Some of the frequent terms such as "prayer" and "psalm" are easily understood, but there are several other frequent terms, such as *miktam* and *maskil,* that are ambiguous and not clearly understood even by scholars.

Book I: Psalms 1–41

Introduction. With few exceptions (notably Pss. 1 and 2), the psalms of Book I are associated with David through the mention of David in the titles.

How happy is the one (1:1). The psalm begins with a Hebrew word translated as "happy" (other translations read "blessed"), which the ancient audience understood as general well-being or a sense that life was right or in balance. They did not understand "happy/blessed" to mean perfection or lack of negative realities.

His delight . . . the Lord's instruction (1:2). The Hebrew word translated as "instruction" is *torah.* Teaching right and orderly living greatly concerned the wisdom teachers of the day. They believed that God created an orderly world, and humans bore responsibility to live rightly within that order.[1] While early wisdom teachers found that order mainly in the natural world, later teachers added the *torah* as an equally important source. These teachers understood the *torah* to be more than simply the first five books of the OT, the Hebrew title of which is *Torah.* To them, all of God's instructions represent *torah,* and therefore *torah* could be found in other Scriptures, including the psalms.[2]

Like chaff (1:4). Chaff results from the winnowing process, which the Israelite farmers knew well (see comments on Ruth 3:2). In order to separate the usable grain from its husk, they used a forked tool to toss the grain into the air. In the breeze, the heavier grain would fall to the threshing floor and the unusable chaff would be blown away.

Why do the nations rage? (2:1). The area in and surrounding Israel/Judah represents the traditional homeland of many people groups, including the Canaanites, Edomites, Moabites, and Ammonites, among others. Biblical writers recorded some of the long-standing animosities among these groups, especially in the books of Joshua through 2 Kings. Other external threatening enemies included large empires such as Egypt, Assyria, and Babylonia. Often these nations threatened the safety and stability of Israel/Judah through battles or invasion and in doing so assumed the superiority of their own gods.

I have installed my king (2:6). In the ancient Near East several ideologies existed regarding monarchy. Some nations believed their king to be a god, while others understood their king to be a representative of their god/gods among the people, but one who was chosen and appointed by the gods. Many viewed the king's primary task as providing order, stability, and security to the nation. A secondary task included extending the rule of their god through the expansion of the kingdom. The Israelites certainly did not consider their king to be a god, but they recognized their king as God's representative with limited power and freedom (Deut. 17:14–20). In Israel God chose and anointed kings through prophets, and the kings in turn were accountable to God, not to the people. As detailed in 1–2 Samuel and 1–2 Kings, Israel and Judah had mixed experiences with the monarchy. Their kings often sinned greatly and even led their people to worship other gods at times. Sometimes,

A picture from 1940 of Middle Eastern farmers winnowing grain.

however, their kings also expanded the kingdom, protected the people during difficult situations, and occasionally brought economic prosperity.

Zion, my holy mountain (2:6). The psalms use "Mount Zion," "Jerusalem," "tent of meeting," "temple," and "holy hill" synonymously at times to represent the place where God dwelled on earth. This dwelling place was symbolized by the ark of the covenant in the tabernacle's holy of holies and later in the temple.

You are my Son; today I have become your Father (2:7). Based on the Davidic covenant, the anointed king became God's adopted son. This covenant, found in 2 Sam. 7, began when God established an enduring dynasty through David and his descendants. As God's anointed, adopted son, the king gained access to God's power on behalf of the nation. It is difficult to overestimate the importance of this covenant in the life of Israel/Judah, as it is mentioned as a motivating factor for various actions in the historical books, the Prophets, and the Psalms. In many regions of the ancient Near East the relationship between the king and his primary god was described in terms of a parent-child relationship.

When he fled from his son Absalom (Ps. 3 title). This title references a historical setting (2 Sam. 15–18) that records the account of David's conflict with Absalom, but there is nothing else mentioned in the body of the psalm that directly references this event. David, and by extension the nation, had numerous enemies, both internal and external. Absalom may poetically represent enemies in general, and the discussion of enemies need not be limited to him.

A shield around me (3:3). See the article "Warfare in the Old Testament." The psalmist mentions a shield as a metaphor for God's protection. The defensive weapon referenced was an easily maneuverable, round shield carried on the forearm to protect the chest and arms. The terminology in this psalm implies hand-to-hand battle, which was common in those days. The psalmist also mentions striking the jaw and breaking teeth, which occurred in such close battles (3:7).

Pursue a lie (4:2). While the law mandated worship of the Lord only, the people lived with the constant temptation to worship other gods and goddesses. Although we may not fully understand their temptation, given our long-standing belief in monotheism, we need to realize that most people in general across the ancient Near East probably could barely conceive of such a thing as monotheism. The Israelites often disobediently followed the Canaanite god Baal or goddess Asherah (see the article "The Canaanites and Canaanite Religion"). Numerous biblical texts place blame with leaders, especially kings, for ushering people toward apostasy. Throughout the psalms readers encounter terms and phrases that allude to this complex religious context.

An Assyrian wall carving depicting the god Assur with drawn bow, flying into battle above the Assyrian king.

Punish them, God (5:10). The people recognized God as a righteous and true judge of all people (both his covenant people and the nations). God's right character ensured perfect judgment. God's justice was not limited to punitive responses. It may be helpful to consider the image of a balance scale. In their concept of justice God kept the balance level or "right." Positive actions received rewards while negative actions received punishment of some sort.

Who can thank you in Sheol? (6:5). The people of Israel/Judah, throughout much of the OT, believed that all people—righteous and unrighteous—ended up in Sheol (the NIV often translates this as "the grave"), which was the underworld or the place of the dead (see comments on Isa. 38:10). The people feared Sheol for a number of reasons. Obviously, one's presence in Sheol meant death. Additionally, it meant losing access to God, including the ability to praise God or to call upon God's justice or mercy. Even faithful people at this stage of biblical revelation had little or no concept of resurrection. The psalmist often tried to motivate God's healing by mentioning that death affected the relationship between God and the psalmist.

The Lord judges the peoples (7:8). See comments on Ps. 5:10.

My shield (7:10). See comments on Ps. 3:3.

He has prepared his deadly weapons (7:13). Throughout the ancient Near East there are numerous depictions, both in literature and in artwork, of the pagan gods wielding various deadly weapons (swords, bows, maces, clubs, etc.).

He tips his arrows with fire (7:13). This may be an allusion to the practice of dipping arrow tips in pitch and then igniting them right before the archer shot the arrows. However, often in the OT when God uses a bow and arrow, the arrows are lightning bolts (see comments on Ps. 18:14).

When I observe your heavens . . . the moon and the stars (8:3). Here the psalmist lauds the creative power of the Lord and in doing so establishes the Lord's unique ability to rule the earth. The fact that God alone is the creator who rules from the heavens established for the people a fundamental basis for trusting God. Throughout the ancient Near East people typically believed that the moon and the stars were gods and goddesses. Here, as throughout Scripture, the moon and the stars are presented as part of the Lord's great creation (see comments on Gen. 1:14; Deut. 17:3; 2 Kings 17:16).

You made him ruler over the works of your hands (8:6). This psalm declares an important aspect of God's order on earth: humankind holds an honored place within the created order and has responsibility for earthly creatures. This honor and responsibility align with Gen. 1, especially the command of God in 1:28 for humans "to fill the earth and subdue it."

You are seated on your throne as a righteous judge (9:4). Like an earthly monarch, God rules and judges the earth. Unlike the earthly monarch, God does so with perfect justice and righteousness (see comments on Ps. 5:10). The concept that gods sat on thrones was common throughout the ancient Near East.

The Lord is a refuge for the persecuted (9:9). Throughout the OT several groups of people often are included in the category of persecuted (e.g., defenseless, vulnerable, oppressed). This includes the poor, widows, orphans, foreigners, victims of misfortune, the innocent, the weak, and the helpless. The law establishes a variety of concessions for this class, including special legal and economic protections and other assistance. The righteous are responsible to care for the people in these situations; in contrast, those who would exploit such people are out of order or unrighteous.

The gates of death (9:13). See comments on Ps. 6:5; Isa. 38:10.

Daughter Zion (9:14). See comments on Ps. 2:6.

The Lord is King forever and ever (10:16). While the people do have an earthly king, the psalmist reminds them that the Lord is the ultimate king, who rules and defends the oppressed people.

The Lord is in his holy temple . . . his throne is in heaven (11:4). God's earthly dwelling was the temple in Jerusalem, where the people housed the ark of the covenant. Yet this earthly dwelling did not limit God to earth or earthly constraints.

How long, Lord? (13:1). Psalm 13 opens with a string of questions from the psalmist. This questioning

Stela of the falcon-headed Egyptian god Ra-Horakhty, seated on a throne.

of God stands within a long tradition of OT characters who do so, such as Abraham, Moses, and Job, and is founded on the values of covenant relationship. In the case of Ps. 13, the longer God goes without acting, the more ammunition the psalmist's enemies have for believing that they will triumph.

Come from Zion (14:7). See comments on Ps. 2:6.

In your tent . . . on your holy mountain (15:1). God's first earthly dwelling was the tabernacle, a portable tent that housed the ark of the covenant and could be moved when necessary (see comments on Exod. 25:10–22). After Solomon constructed the temple (1 Kings 6–8), God's sacred tent (the tabernacle) became a synonym for the temple. Psalm 15 implies that the righteous alone gain access to the temple and therefore to God.

Those who take another god (16:4). See comments on Ps. 4:2.

You are my portion and my cup (16:5). The psalmist expresses contentment with his "portion." The terms in verses 5–6 reflect the distribution of land described in the book of Joshua. It is the Lord who portioned the land, and thus the psalmist will worship the Lord rather than the deities of the previous inhabitants.

The Egyptian goddess Isis with outstretched protective wings.

Against your right hand (17:7). The right hand (cf. 17:14) represents a place of support and protection.

Shadow of your wings (17:8). While this may refer to the safety of a mother bird, the ancient Israelites likely also considered the cherubim, the winged creatures represented on the ark and depicted in the temple (see comments on 1 Kings 6:23–28; Ezek. 10:1).

On the day the Lord rescued . . . from the power of Saul (Ps. 18 title). Psalm 18 sets the historical context of the psalm as the time when God delivered David from his enemies and from Saul. The psalm itself is included in 2 Sam. 22:1–51 toward the end of David's reign and after yet another battle with the Philistines (see comments on 2 Sam. 22:10, 13; 22:11).

The Lord is my rock . . . my God, my rock (18:2). One of the Hebrew words used in this verse portrays the image of a craggy rock face in which to shelter and hide. In light of the geography of Israel, the crags of Mount Arbel near the Sea of Galilee or the rocky hills near the Dead Sea would be good representations of such rock.

My shield (18:2). See comments on Ps. 3:3.

The earth shook and quaked (18:7). Psalm 18:7–16 also describes a theophany—an appearance of God. In the OT natural phenomena such as earthquakes, thunderstorms, and smoke often accompanied these appearances. The relationship between creator and created world is such that the world responds when God appears. In this case, God appears in order to rescue David from his enemies.

He rode on a cherub (18:10). See comments on 2 Sam. 22:11.

He shot his arrows . . . hurled lightning bolts (18:14). Throughout the ancient Near East gods frequently are portrayed as warriors, sometimes armed with bow and arrows. Likewise, lightning often is one of their fearsome weapons (see comments on 2 Sam. 22:10, 13).

The Lord repaid me (18:24). See comments on Ps. 5:10.

He is a shield (18:30). See comments on 2 Sam. 22:36.

He gives great victories to his king (18:50). The extreme intercession of Ps. 18 relates to God's covenant relationship with David (see comments on Ps. 2:7).

The heavens declare the glory of God (19:1). The first six verses of Psalm 19 address the relationship between God and creation. God's creation testifies about God's creative activity (without the need of words or sounds, 19:3).

The instruction of the Lord is perfect (19:7). The psalmist uses several synonyms for law, including statutes, precepts, commands, and decrees (vv. 7–9). Our understanding of this law should not be limited only to teachings of the Torah/Pentateuch (see comments on Ps. 1:2).

Sweeter than honey (19:10). See comments on Exod. 3:8, 17; Deut. 6:3.

May he send you help from the sanctuary (20:2). See comments on Ps. 2:6.

May he remember all your offerings . . . your burnt offering (20:3). See the numerous comments in Lev. 1:1–7:38. Psalm 20 brings momentary attention to sacrifices and offerings (this attention is renewed in Book II). Israelite worship included a number of sacrifices and offerings for known sin, unknown sin, thanksgiving, and fellowship. Israelites sacrificed animals (unblemished bulls, sheep, goats, doves, or pigeons) and grain. Their sacrificial system made up an important part of worship until the destruction of the second temple in AD 70.

The Lord gives victory to his anointed (20:6). See comments on 2 Sam. 22:21–25; Ps. 2:7.

Lord, the king finds joy in your strength (21:1). See comments on Ps. 2:6; 2:7.

Like a fiery furnace (21:9). See comments on Mal. 4:1.

My God, My God, why have you abandoned me? (22:1). For the basis of questioning God, see comments on Ps. 13:1.

You are holy, enthroned on the praises of Israel (22:3). See comments on Ps. 10:16.

Our fathers trusted in you (22:4). Here "fathers" (i.e., ancestors) included any of the covenant people from Abraham to the current time.

Out of the womb . . . my mother's womb (22:9–10). The psalmist's faith and relationship with God began at the start of life. Here the psalmist credits his mother's faithfulness for his own. Mothers provided the first source of teaching, which is likely one reason why the law forbade marrying foreign women. If these women taught their children about other gods, then it would not take long for the nation to turn away from the Lord.

Many bulls . . . strong ones of Bashan . . . lions, mauling and roaring . . . dogs . . . wild oxen (22:12–21). Animals figure prominently in Ps. 22. Bulls, oxen, and lions represented strength; in fact, the worshipers of other gods often used the bull as the image of their god (Baal being the most prominent) (see the article "The Canaanites and Canaanite Religion"). Bashan was a region east of the Sea of Galilee, famous for its cattle (see comments on Amos 4:1).

In the assembly (22:22). When the people gathered for worship and/or instruction, they were referred to as "the assembly." At different points they assembled outside the tabernacle, the temple, and, much later, in synagogues.

The Lord is my shepherd (23:1). Shepherds were a frequent sight for those living in southern Israel, and in several places the Bible mentions herding. Kings in the ancient Near East often referred to themselves as "shepherds" (see comments on Jer. 23:1; Ezek. 34:2). Likewise, the image of the shepherd frequently was applied to deities.

You prepare a table before me (23:5). This portrays God as the welcoming host, incorporating typical expectations of hospitality common at the time. Hospitality in the ancient Near East involved opening up one's home to passersby, offering food and safety.

You anoint my head with oil (23:5). Given the dirty conditions of travel, it was proper to offer anointing of the head and also the feet as a means of cleansing. This anointing also reminded the people of the anointing of kings. At installation, the king's head was anointed with oil (see comments on 1 Kings 1:39).

Collection of ancient Egyptian staffs.

He laid its foundation on the seas . . . on the rivers (24:2). Psalm 24 begins with a declaration of God as creator. God founded and established the earth on the seas. Readers should recall Gen. 1:2 and God hovering over the waters before creating.

The mountain of the Lord . . . His holy place (24:3). See comments on Ps. 2:6.

Who has not sworn deceitfully (24:4). See comments on Ps. 4:2.

Lift up your heads, you gates! Rise up, ancient doors! (24:7). Walls surrounded Jerusalem, like most other important cities in the region. At the arrival of the king, the gates were opened and the people celebrated his arrival.

This King of glory (24:8, 10). This psalm identifies the creator Lord as the true and worthy king of Israel. For the Lord as king, see comments on Ps. 10:16.

Do not let me be disgraced (25:2). The people of the ancient Near East lived in a culture of honor and shame. People prized honor and could achieve it through various means, including victory, wealth, health, and having many children (particularly sons). Shame occurred in loss, illness, barrenness, and other negative situations. Considering Israel's understanding of God's justice (see comments on Ps. 5:10), they often equated shame with unrighteousness or unfaithfulness. The righteous ones thus wanted to avoid shame and expressed offense when enemies shamed them in some way. They sought God in order to right the record and restore their honor. Additionally, they often desired that God rightfully shame the enemy.

Teach me . . . guide me (25:4–5). On God's instruction, see comments on Ps. 1:2.

He reveals his covenant to them (25:14). See comments on 2 Sam. 7:11, 16.

I have lived with integrity (26:1). It is important to understand that the Israelites did not equate being blameless (or righteous) with sinlessness. A consistent desire to remain within God's order and follow God's instructions resulted in righteousness.

I wash my hands in innocence and go around your altar (26:6). Personal righteousness allows one to enter the temple and join the congregation in order to praise the Lord.

The house where you dwell . . . where your glory resides (26:8). See comments on Ps. 2:6.

In the assemblies (26:12). See comments on Ps. 22:22.

My foes and my enemies stumbled and fell (27:2). Enemies often went unnamed, and thus they are difficult to identify precisely. The psalms often describe these enemies as unrighteous, unfaithful, wicked, and arrogant. They threatened the righteous physically and emotionally and had the potential to lead the faithful to doubt God's justice, hence the frequent calls for God's action in the psalms.

He will conceal me in his shelter (27:5). In addition to being a place of worship, the temple provides safety and security. Criminals could seek asylum at sanctuaries or temples within their nation (cf. Joab and Adonijah in 1 Kings 1–2). In the psalms the righteous seek such asylum.

I will offer sacrifices in his tent with shouts of joy (27:6). See comments on Ps. 20:3.

Show me your way (27:11). See comments on Ps. 1:2.

I lift up my hands toward your holy sanctuary (28:2). Even if one could not reach the temple, a righteous person could pray in that direction and be heard.

Repay them according to what they have done (28:4). See comments on Ps. 5:10.

Ascribe to the Lord, you heavenly beings (29:1). The Hebrew phrase translated as "heavenly beings" can literally be translated as "sons of gods," which acknowledges a time when the people believed that other deities existed (at least poetically), but that the Lord was their God and the highest God (see comments on Ps. 4:2). In this case, the other gods are acknowledging the same by ascribing splendor to the Lord.

The voice of the Lord (29:3–9). Psalm 29 describes a theophany (see comments on Ps. 18:7).

Cedars of Lebanon (29:5). Lebanon was located to the north of Israel and was famous for its timber, particularly its strong and beautiful cedar (see comments on Ezek. 27:5).

Sirion (29:6). Sirion is another name for Mount Hermon and is located in the northern region of Israel.

Wilderness of Kadesh (29:8). This desert is located in the south of Israel/Judah.

Mount Hermon (Sirion) with snow.

The Lord sits enthroned (29:10). See comments on Ps. 10:16.

Over the flood (29:10). The mention of the flood reminds readers of the flood of Gen. 6–9 (see comments on Gen. 6:7). The same Hebrew word is used in both places.

Sheol . . . the Pit (30:3). Sheol and the Pit are names that refer to the realm of the dead (see comments on Ps. 6:5; Isa. 38:10).

You removed my sackcloth (30:11). People in the ancient Near East often wore sackcloth to represent mourning, despair, and/or repentance (see comments on 1 Kings 20:31).

Let me never be disgraced (31:1). See comments on Ps. 25:2.

Worthless idols (31:6). See comments on Ps. 4:2.

I am in distress (31:9). In this case, the distress of the psalmist is a physical ailment or illness. Given the brevity of the description, it is difficult to determine the exact nature of the ailments. At times people considered illness as a just consequence of sin (as did Job's friends), and at other times as an affliction that God would heal. Illnesses tied to one's sin required repentance in order for healing to occur. Either way, illness often resulted in the shaming of the distressed person. Not only was illness difficult in terms of enduring pain, performing daily tasks, or participating in social situations, but also it possibly affected one's cleanness for worship. If the illness involved any type of discharge (i.e., from infection or leprosy), the individual was not allowed into the temple. Illness isolated individuals from the rest of society (see comments on Lev. 13:46).

I am ridiculed by all my adversaries (31:11). Perhaps the illness resulted in physical distortion, or the enemies used the illness as grounds to mock the psalmist, or both.

My bones became brittle . . . my strength was drained (32:3–4). These phrases also imply an illness of some kind (see comments on Ps. 31:9).

I will instruct you and show you (32:8). See comments on Ps. 1:2.

The lyre . . . a ten-stringed harp (33:2). See the article "Musical Instruments in Israel and the Ancient Near East"; see comments on 1 Chron. 6:31.

All the stars, by the breath of his mouth (33:6). See comments on Gen. 1:14.

He gathers the water of the sea into a heap (33:7). The creative activity of God is linked to the waters (see comments on Gen. 1:1; Ps. 24:2).

For he spoke, and it came into being (33:9). This is a reference to God's creation through speech (see comments on Gen. 1:3).

When he pretended . . . in the presence of Abimelech (Ps. 34 title). The historical notation references an event from David's premonarchy days when he fled from Saul and sought protection in Philistia (see the article "The Philistines"). The fuller biblical record of this account is found in 1 Sam. 21:10–15. In 1 Samuel, however, the Philistine king is identified as Achish, king of Gath. Genesis 26:1 refers to a king Abimelech of Philistia, but that narrative recalls Isaac's life, well before the time of David. Regardless of the name of the king, David feigned insanity because he feared the king. As with other historical references in titles, the interpretation of the psalm should not be limited to this one reference.

Musician from Ur playing a small ten-stringed harp that has a bull-shaped sound box.

The angel of the Lord (34:7). This phrase appears some fifty times in the OT, mostly in the narrative, historical books. In the psalms the phrase appears three times (34:7; 35:5, 6). Appearing often in human form, this messenger worked on God's behalf to communicate or act in the world. At times the narrative texts equate the angel with God, and at other times they seem to distinguish between them.[3]

Take your shields (35:2). See comments on 2 Sam. 22:36; Ps. 3:3.

Draw the spear and javelin (35:3). Unlike the shield, these were offensive and not defensive weapons (see the article "Warfare in the Old Testament"; see comments on 2 Sam. 22:36; 22:38–39).

Be disgraced and humiliated (35:4). See comments on Ps. 25:2.

My clothing was sackcloth (35:13). Mourning over illness (one's own or someone else's) was a common practice (see comments on 1 Kings 20:31; Ps. 30:11).

My deceitful enemies (35:19). See comments on Ps. 27:2.

Be disgraced and humiliated . . . be clothed with shame (35:26). See comments on Ps. 25:2.

Shadow of your wings (36:7). See comments on Ps. 17:8.

Because of your indignation there is no health in my bones (38:3). For a discussion of illness, see comments on Ps. 31:9. In this case, the psalmist understands his illness as a consequence of sin.

Those who run after lies (40:4). See comments on Ps. 4:2.

Be disgraced and confounded (40:14). See comments on Ps. 25:2.

Happy is the one who is considerate of the poor (41:1). See comments on Ps. 9:9.

The Lord will sustain him on his sickbed (41:3). See comments on Ps. 31:9.

Book II: Psalms 42–72

Introduction. As in Book I, many of the psalms in Book II include the phrase "of David" in their title (heading). A group of psalms titled the "Sons of Korah" (Pss. 42–49), however, comes at the beginning of Book II. The name Korah appears in a genealogy of Levi in Exod. 6:21, 24 (two different people), and also in 1 Chron. 6:22. In Num. 16 a man named Korah leads a drastically unsuccessful rebellion against Moses. It remains unclear how the Korah of Psalms relates to those mentioned in Exodus, Numbers, and 1 Chronicles. Thus it is not clear exactly who wrote the "Sons of Korah" collections. A few psalms in Book II do not include any names in their headings (Pss. 43, 66, 67, 71), and one is attributed to Asaph (Ps. 50).

How I walked with many, leading the festive procession to the house of God (42:4). The psalm does not give a reason why the psalmist no longer goes to the temple to worship. The "house of God" likely refers to the temple. Possibilities for exclusion from worship include ceremonial uncleanness, geographical distance from the temple, or potentially a time when the temple was destroyed (after 586 BC).

From the land of the Jordan and the peaks of Hermon, from Mount Mizar (42:6). The headwaters of the Jordan River come from the streams of Mount Hermon in northern Israel, through the Sea of Galilee and south into the Dead Sea. Mount Mizar is associated with Mount Hermon.

Your holy mountain . . . your dwelling place (43:3). See comments on Ps. 2:6.

You displaced the nations by your hand; in order to settle them (44:2). This psalm refers to God's actions in the conquest of Canaan (described in the book of Joshua), the land that God promised the ancestors through the covenant with Abraham. Here all success is attributed to God, not to human leaders.

You are my King, my God (44:4). See comments on Ps. 10:16.

You do not march out with our armies (44:9). In this understanding, military success depended on the strength and presence of God, not the power of the human army. If God was not present, defeat was sure.

You hand us over (44:11). There are many instances of Israel/Judah being oppressed by other nations from the time of the judges to the exile and beyond.

My disgrace is before me . . . shame (44:15). See comments on Ps. 25:2.

We have not forgotten you or betrayed our covenant (44:17). The reality of being defeated in such a way challenged their understanding of their covenant relationship with God. If they had been false, their defeat was warranted, but they do not believe that is the case.

The headwaters of the Jordan River.

Wake up, LORD! Why are you sleeping? (44:23). Many times the people feel that they must rouse God in order to prompt God's action on their behalf. This action seemed necessary when they did not believe that God was fulfilling his covenant responsibility.

Redeem us because of your faithful love (44:26). Their call for help and for God's action is based on God's covenant relationship (unfailing love).

A love song (Ps. 45 title). Unique in the psalter, this psalm depicts a princess as she regales her royal groom and calls upon God to be with the groom. The specific setting of this psalm is unknown, but a general understanding of royal matchmaking may help make sense of the psalm. Kings of large and small kingdoms regularly related to one another by making agreements for trade, protection, or other beneficial actions. Often the royal families furthered these relationships by arranging marriages between themselves or their children (see comments on Song 6:9). No doubt Solomon acquired many of his wives in this manner (see comments on 1 Kings 3:1), but he was not alone in acquiring wives this way. While politically these arrangements furthered the kingdoms, in Israel such marriages broke the covenant laws regarding marrying foreign women.

In the cause of truth, humility, and justice (45:4). All of these are traits of an ideal monarch (see comments on Ps. 2:6).

Your throne, God, is forever and ever (45:6). It is not clear who is being addressed in this passage and how the word "God" is functioning. If the bride is addressing these words to the king, it may reflect the ancient Near Eastern understanding that kings were divine, despite the fact that Israelites did not hold such a view (see comments on Ps. 2:6). If the bride is addressing

God, then it may reflect an understanding that God is the true king (see comments on Ps. 10:16).

Forget your people and your father's house (45:10). The bride is encouraged to forget her people, which may imply that she was not an Israelite, and her father's house, which likely included her father's gods.

The daughter of Tyre (45:12). Tyre was an important port city located in Phoenicia, just north of Israel (see comments on Ezek. 26:2).

The holy dwelling place of the Most High (46:4). See comments on Ps. 2:6.

A great King over the whole earth (47:2). See comments on Ps. 10:16.

He subdues peoples . . . he chooses for us our inheritance (47:3–4). See comments on Ps. 44:2.

God reigns over the nations (47:8). In the ancient Near East most people believed that deities were regional and associated with specific nations. In this verse the Israelites assert that God's power extends beyond Israel to other nations.

For the leaders of the earth belong to God (47:9). Again here, the Israelites extend God's control beyond their borders. On the ancient Near Eastern understanding of monarchy, see comments on Ps. 2:6.

The city of our God. His holy mountain (48:1). See comments on Ps. 2:6.

Mount Zion—the summit of Zaphon (48:2). Zaphon is a mountain to the north and east of Jerusalem and east of the Jordan River. "Zaphon" also means "north." Zaphon is mentioned in Josh. 13:27; Judg. 12:1.

Ships of Tarshish (48:7). See comments on Jon. 1:3. The exact location of this city remains uncertain. Tarshish, however, is mentioned several times in the OT and usually is associated with ships and storms. Many scholars believe that Tarshish was a port in the Mediterranean Sea, perhaps as far west as Spain.

Judah's villages rejoice because of your judgments (48:11). See comments on Ps. 5:10.

I turn my ear to a proverb; I explain my riddle (49:4). Both proverbs and riddles were used by teachers in the wisdom tradition. Proverbs are short statements that communicate a truth or important lesson. They were used in part because students could easily remember them. Riddles tested the students' thinking skills and knowledge as they worked to understand the concept(s) being communicated.

A psalm of Asaph (Ps. 50 title). Psalm 50 divides the Korah and David collections. The name Asaph appears for the first time in Ps. 50. See the introduction to Book III.

From Zion (50:2). See comments on Ps. 2:6.

Our God is coming; he will not be silent (50:3). The psalm describes a theophany (see comments on Ps. 18:7).

Judge his people (50:4). See comments on Ps. 5:10.

I will testify against you, Israel (50:7). The "covenant lawsuit" described here is similar to judgments in other parts of the OT, especially in the prophets. God brings charges against the people based on their unfulfilled covenant responsibilities.

For your sacrifices . . . burnt offerings (50:8). See the numerous comments in Lev. 1:1–7:38; see comments on Ps. 20:3.

I will not take a bull from your household (50:9). See comments on Lev. 3:11, 16. In other ancient Near Eastern cultures the purpose of sacrifices was to please the deity by providing the food and drink necessary for sustenance. God makes it clear that sacrifices are not necessary for his well-being.

When the prophet Nathan came to him after David had gone to Bathsheba (Ps. 51 title). The historical setting provided in the title situates the psalm after Nathan confronts David regarding David's abuse of power with Bathsheba and the death of her husband (2 Sam. 11–12). As with other historical references in titles, there is no specific mention of this event in the body of the psalm, although David's confession of sin seems to fit well.

When you pass sentence (51:4). See comments on Ps. 5:10.

When Doeg the Edomite went and reported to Saul (Ps. 52 title). This title recalls 1 Sam. 22:9–10, which recounts when Doeg informed Saul of David's past actions. When David first fled from Saul, he sought help from the priest Ahimelech. Saul responds to the priest's action by having Doeg kill Ahimelech and his family.

Come from Zion (53:6). See comments on Ps. 2:6.

When the Ziphites went and said to Saul (Ps. 54 title). This historical reference connects the psalm with Saul's pursuit of David in 1 Sam. 23:19–29.

I will sacrifice a freewill offering to you (54:6). Freewill offerings often were associated with vows and often were for the purpose of celebration.

God, the one enthroned from long ago (55:19). See comments on Ps. 10:16.

When the Philistines had seized him in Gath (Ps. 56 title). See comments on Ps. 34 title; see the article "The Philistines."

I will make my thank offerings to you (56:12). Thank

Egyptians offering various foods to their gods.

offerings, a type of fellowship offering, could be bread or meat (cf. Lev. 7:12–15).

When he fled before Saul into the cave (Ps. 57 title). This refers to 1 Sam. 24:1–3, which describes David hiding from Saul at En-gedi, an oasis near the Dead Sea.

Shadow of your wings (57:1). See comments on Ps. 17:8.

Wake up, harp and lyre! (57:8). See the article "Musical Instruments in Israel and the Ancient Near East."

God who judges on earth (58:11). See comments on Ps. 5:10.

When Saul sent agents to watch the house and kill him (Ps. 59 title). The historical information here likely references 1 Sam. 19:11, when Saul sends men to watch the house that David shares with his wife Michal, Saul's daughter.

When he fought with Aram-naharaim (Ps. 60 title). See comments on 1 Chron. 18:5. Interestingly, the historical marker in the title sets the psalms in the military victories of David and Joab (2 Sam. 8; 1 Chron. 18), which does not appear to fit the content or geography of the psalm itself.

God has spoken in his sanctuary (60:6). See comments on Ps. 2:6.

I will divide up Shechem . . . the Valley of Succoth (60:6). Shechem was a prominent city to the north of Jerusalem, lying in between Mount Ebal and Mount Gerizim. Shechem appears several times in the stories of the patriarchs (Gen. 33–37) and was the location of the covenant renewal in Josh. 24. The Valley of Succoth lies east of Shechem across the Jordan.

Gilead . . . Manasseh . . . Ephraim . . . Judah . . . Moab . . . Edom . . . Philistia (60:7–8). See comments on Gen. 19:37–38; Obad. 1; see the article "The Philistines." Gilead, Manasseh, Moab, and Edom lie east of the Jordan. Ephraim and Judah lie south of Shechem, and Philistia lies along the coast of the Mediterranean west of Judah. All of these locations recall the conquest and settlement of the land in Joshua and Judges.

Shelter of your wings (61:4). See comments on Ps. 17:8.

The king's life . . . may he sit enthroned before God forever (61:6–7). See comments on Ps. 2:6.

I gaze on you in the sanctuary (63:2). See comments on Ps. 2:6.

Shadow of your wings (63:7). See comments on Ps. 17:8.

In Zion (65:1). See comments on Ps. 2:6.

You establish the mountains . . . you silence the roar of the seas (65:6–7). These verses reference God's creative activity (see comments on Gen. 1:1).

He turned the sea into dry land (66:6). The psalmist is recalling the parting of the sea during the exodus from Egypt (Exod. 14). This event came to symbolize God's power and protection for his people (see comments on Exod. 14:9).

Cushites bringing tribute to the Egyptian pharaoh.

I will enter your house with burnt offerings . . . I will sacrifice (66:13–15). See comments on Ps. 20:3.

A great company of women brought the good news . . . she who stays at home divides the spoil (68:11–12). Women often responded to the news of victory with singing and dancing, as seen in Miriam's song and the women's dance in Exod. 15:20–21 and in the response of the women upon David's return in 1 Sam. 18:6–7. Women also participated in dividing the spoils of battle.

Zalmon (68:14). This mountain lies near the city of Shechem (see comments on Ps. 60:6).

Mount Bashan (68:15). Mount Bashan lies east of the Sea of Galilee in what is now the Golan Heights (see comments on Amos 4:1).

Why gaze with envy . . . at the mountain God desired for his abode? (68:16). In the sight of Israel, neither Mount Bashan nor Zalmon compares to Mount Zion.

The LORD is among them in the sanctuary (68:17). See comments on Ps. 2:6.

The procession of my God, my King, in the sanctuary (68:24). On God as king, see comments on Ps. 10:16.

Benjamin . . . rulers of Judah . . . rulers of Zebulun . . . rulers of Naphtali (68:27). Benjamin, Judah, Zebulun, and Naphtali are tribes of Israel. King Saul was of the tribe of Benjamin, while King David was of the tribe of Judah.

Cush will stretch out its hands to God (68:31). Cush is a region along the Nile River, south of Egypt (see the article "The Cushites").

Do not let those who seek you be humiliated (69:6). See comments on Ps. 25:2.

I wore sackcloth (69:11). See comments on 1 Kings 20:31; Ps. 30:11.

Those who sit at the city gate (69:12). See comments on Deut. 17:5.

Let them be erased from the book of life (69:28). See comments on Exod. 32:32; Mal. 3:16.

Be disgraced (70:2). See comments on Ps. 25:2.

Let me never be disgraced (71:1). See comments on Ps. 25:2.

I have leaned on you from birth . . . from my mother's womb (71:6). See comments on Ps. 22:9–10.

I will praise you with a harp . . . with a lyre (71:22). See the article "Musical Instruments in Israel and the Ancient Near East."

Of Solomon (Ps. 72 title). This is the first of two psalms attributed to King Solomon (also Ps. 127).

Give your justice to the king (72:1). See comments on Ps. 2:6; 2:7.

May the kings of Tarshish . . . Sheba and Seba . . . bow in homage to him (72:10–11). The psalmist mentions several locations to underscore the expansion of the kingdom. The psalmist hopes for renown from Tarshish in the western Mediterranean (see comments on Jon. 1:3) to Sheba and Seba (probably in the Arabian Desert, but this possibly is a reference to Cush) (see comments on 2 Chron. 9:1).

May all nations be blessed by him (72:17). The purpose of expansion and renown is that all may be blessed through the king, and by extension the Lord, a concept also found in God's covenant with Abraham (Gen. 12:3). Historically, the monarchy of Israel never achieved such renown in the world before its fall (cf. 1–2 Kings). Later audiences shifted such expectations onto the future Messiah (anointed one).

Book III: Psalms 73–89

Introduction. Book III contains a collection of psalms of Asaph (Pss. 73–83), a second "sons of Korah" collection (Pss. 84–85; 87–88), a psalm of David (Ps. 86), and a psalm of Ethan the Ezrahite (Ps. 89). Asaph (along with Heman and Jeduthun) was considered a head Levitical singer and musician (1 Chron. 25:1, 6; 2 Chron. 5:12) and the chief minister before the ark (1 Chron. 16:4–5). Asaph certainly did not write all the psalms attributed to him, for many clearly reflect events that occurred long after his lifetime. As is the case with other psalms having name attributions, subsequent people who followed in Asaph's appointed positions likely wrote many of these psalms (see comments on 1 Chron. 6:31). Ethan the Ezrahite is associated with only one psalm, Ps. 89, and is mentioned only one other time in the OT (1 Kings 4:31), where he is considered one of the wisest men around (excepting Solomon). Ethan the (Levite) musician is mentioned in 1 Chron. 6:44; 15:17, 19. First Chronicles often associates Ethan with Heman and Asaph. These probably are all references to the same Ethan of Ps. 89.

God's sanctuary (73:17). See comments on Ps. 2:6.

Why have you rejected us forever, God? (74:1). See comments on Ps. 13:1.

Remember your congregation, which you purchased . . . your own possession (74:2). See comments on Ps. 44:2.

Make your way to the perpetual ruins (74:3). The likely setting of this national disaster is the destruction of Jerusalem in 586 BC, when the Babylonians destroyed the city and the temple and removed the Davidic king (see comments on 2 Kings 24:20; 25:8–10).

Smashing all the carvings . . . they set your sanctuary on fire (74:6–7). The temple was built with a variety of materials, including cedar, pine, and olive wood in the interior, a stone exterior, and gold overlaid objects (altar, cherubim). It was a multistoried building filled with intricately carved paneling (see 1 Kings 6–7). The wielding of axes, smashing, and burning recorded in Ps. 74 fit with what is known of the temple and of its destruction (see comments on 2 Kings 24:20; 25:8–10).

They burned every place throughout the land where God met with us (74:8). While the temple was the official worship site (see Deut. 12), the people often worshiped God in other places, usually in disobedience (see comments on 1 Kings 3:2–3; 11:7; 12:29; 2 Kings 3:2).

God, how long will the enemy mock? (74:10). The destruction of Jerusalem reflected poorly not only on the inhabitants but also, from their view, on God and God's ability to protect his people. The people of Jerusalem had come to believe that Jerusalem was indestructible because God had established it and dwelled there.[4] In the minds of the Babylonians their god Marduk was surely more powerful than the God of Israel, hence Babylon's victory.

Why do you hold back your hand? (74:11). Was God not powerful enough to keep the covenants? Had God abandoned them? In addition to the basic traumas of war, the people lost their king, their temple (including the ark), and their land. Every covenant promise suddenly seemed void. On the significance of the right hand, see comments on Ps. 17:7.

God my King (74:12). See comments on Ps. 10:16.

You divided the sea (74:13). This phrase could be a reference to God's creative activity or to the parting of the sea during the exodus.

You smashed the heads of the sea monster . . . the heads of Leviathan . . . you opened up springs and streams (74:13–15). The psalmist provides a poetic account of the creation of the earth, where God brought order to the chaotic waters by force (killing the sea monster and Leviathan [see comments on Job 41:1–34]) and then established days, seasons, and the boundaries of the earth. This account is one of several descriptions of the creation in the OT (see comments on Gen. 1:1).

I will judge fairly (75:2). See comments on Ps. 5:10.

Do not lift up your horn (75:5). In the ancient Near East the horn was a symbol of power, a concept probably derived from the power of horned animals. Lifting up the horn meant claiming power or victoriously obtaining power, while cutting the horn (75:10) meant taking power away (see comments on 1 Sam. 2:1).[5]

His tent is in Salem (76:2). See comments on Ps. 2:6. "Salem" is another term for Jerusalem.

When God rose up to judge (76:9). See comments on Ps. 5:10.

The water saw you . . . you led your people like a flock (77:16–20). See comments on Ps. 66:6. The language in these verses also reflects a theophany (see comments on Ps. 18:7).

I will declare wise sayings (78:2). See comments on Ps. 49:4.

He established a testimony . . . and set up a law (78:5). The statutes and laws are a reference to the covenant, perhaps with Abraham (Gen. 12, 15, 17) and certainly with the people of Israel at Mount Sinai (Exod. 19–24).

The Ephraimite archers (78:9). Ephraim was one of the most influential of the twelve Israelite tribes and was a name often used representatively to refer to the entire northern kingdom during the time of the divided nation. In this verse, however, the reference describes an event during the time of wandering after the exodus.

They did not keep God's covenant (78:10). The psalmist does not reference the specific disobedience. The covenant referenced is the Mount Sinai covenant. It is important to remember that this covenant is the only covenant in which the people bear significant responsibility for its keeping.

He worked wonders (78:12–31). Beginning in verse 12 and continuing through verse 31, the psalmist references many events of God's provision during the exodus and wandering, which can be found in the narrative accounts of Exodus and Numbers.

When he performed his miraculous signs in Egypt . . . in the territory of Zoan (78:43–51). Zoan was a capital city in the Nile Delta of northern Egypt and is sometimes used as a synonym for Egypt, as it seems to be here in 78:43. The verses that follow describe the plagues that God sent upon Egypt. The order and number of the plagues here differs from the narrative account found in Exod. 7–11, but the psalm has the same general categories of plagues, involving water to blood, insects of various sorts, frogs, cattle, weather, and death.

Tents of Ham (78:51). The Egyptians are considered descendants of Noah's son Ham (Gen. 10:6).

He drove out nations (78:55). See comments on Ps. 44:2.

Their high places (78:58). The only specific disobedience mentioned in this psalm is the worship of idols (see comments on Ps. 4:2). Often this worship occurred on "high places" (see comments on 1 Kings 3:2–3; 11:7).

The tabernacle at Shiloh (78:60). See comments on Jer. 7:12, 14. During the time of the judges the people set up the tabernacle at Shiloh, a town in north-central Israel (Josh. 18:1), where it remained throughout much of Judges (Judg. 18:31; 1 Sam. 1:3).

He gave up his strength to captivity (78:61). For a brief time the Philistines had possession of the ark of the covenant (1 Sam. 4–6).

He chose instead the tribe of Judah, Mount Zion (78:68). See comments on Ps. 2:6. David was of the tribe of Judah, and Jerusalem was located in Judah.

The nations have invaded your inheritance, desecrated your holy temple, and turned Jerusalem into ruins (79:1). See comments on Ps. 74:3.

How long, Lord? (79:5). See comments on Ps. 13:1; 74:11.

For the glory of your name (79:9). See comments on Ps. 74:10.

You who sit enthroned between the cherubim (80:1). See comments on Ps. 10:16; 11:4. Two cherubim images sat atop the ark of the covenant representing God's earthly throne (see comments on 1 Kings 6:23–28; Ezek. 10:1).

Rally your power (80:2). See comments on Ps. 44:23.

Make your face shine (80:3, 7, 19). The shining of God's face suggests a theophany or an appearance of God. Therefore, asking God "to shine" represents their request for another personal intervention.

The tambourine . . . lyre . . . harp (81:2). See the article "Musical Instruments in Israel and the Ancient Near East."

Blow the horn on the day of our feasts (81:3). The psalmist mentions two feasts (or festivals) that have to do with the moon: one for a new moon, and one for a full moon. These feasts were not part of the major

Excavations of an Israelite idol-worship site at Dan.

prescribed feasts (Passover, Weeks, Shelters) but seem to reflect a time of celebration. Numbers 10:10 records brief instructions about the new-moon festivals indicating the sounding of ram's horns and the giving of burnt and fellowship offerings (see comments on Num. 10:2).

The Waters of Meribah (81:7). The location of Meribah is uncertain. It is mentioned twice, implying two different regions, near Rephidim in the Sinai Peninsula and Kadesh-barnea in southern Israel (cf. Exod. 17:7; Num. 20:13).

You must not bow down to a foreign god (81:9). See comments on Ps. 4:2.

God stands in the divine assembly (82:1). This psalm has a dual setting of heavenly council and judgment scene. The setting of the heavenly council is best understood in light of the religious context of ancient Israel. In their henotheistic understanding the Lord their God was the highest God, whom they worshiped, but they acknowledged the existence of other gods. In this psalm God enters the assembly of gods and holds court, proceeding to judge them. Interestingly, in this psalm God condemns all the other gods to death and thus makes them mortal. In the process God, the true and just one, claims all nations as an inheritance.

The oppressed and the destitute (82:3). See comments on Ps. 9:9.

All the nations belong to you (82:8). See comments on Ps. 47:8.

The tents of Edom . . . Ishmaelites . . . Moab . . . Hagrites, Gebal, Ammon, and Amalek, Philistia . . . Tyre . . . Assyria (83:6–8). These nations and people represent many of Israel's common enemies, especially during the time of the judges and the divided monarchy. Edom was located southeast of the Dead Sea (see comments on Jer. 49:7; Obad. 1; Mal. 1:4). The Ishmaelites were thought to be from Arabia (see comments on Gen. 37:25), while Moab, the Hagrites, and Ammon were to the east and southeast of Israel, across the Jordan River (see comments on Gen. 19:37–38). The Amalekites lived in the arid areas to the south of Judah (see comments on Exod. 17:8). Byblos and Tyre were along the Mediterranean coast in Phoenicia (see comments on Ezek. 26:2), and Philistia was on the coast south of Judah (see the article "The Philistines"). Assyria was located in Mesopotamia (see the article "The Assyrians").

Midian . . . Sisera and Jabin . . . Oreb and Zeeb . . . Zebah and Zalmunna (83:9–12). Midian was located in the eastern part of the Sinai Peninsula; Oreb and Zeeb were Midianite captains or princes defeated by Gideon (Judg. 7), and Zebah and Zalmunna were Midianite kings whom Gideon also defeated (Judg. 8). Sisera and Jabin were Canaanites defeated during the rule of the judge Deborah (Judg. 4–5).

Dwelling place . . . courts of the Lord (84:1–2). See comments on Ps. 2:6.

Set on pilgrimage (84:5). In a system of centralized worship it became necessary to take periodic journeys to the temple for the purpose of worship or sacrifice. Many did so during the three major festivals, but one could undertake a pilgrimage for a variety of reasons. Given the distance that many would travel, the journey could be long and dangerous at times, but the faithful continued to go.

Valley of Baca (84:6). Also called the Valley of Weeping, the exact location of this valley is unknown. Presumably many pilgrims passed through it on the way to Jerusalem.

For the Lord God is a sun (84:11). See comments on Mal. 4:2.

Shield (84:11). See comments on Ps. 3:3.

You restored the fortunes of Jacob (85:1). There were many times during the rule of the judges and the divided monarchy when God restored the people, such as when the Assyrians threatened Jerusalem during the reign of Hezekiah and the angel of the Lord killed thousands of them (2 Kings 18:13–19:36).

Zion's city gates (87:2). See comments on Ps. 2:6.

Rahab, Babylon, Philistia, Tyre, and Cush (87:4). All five places represent traditional enemies of Israel. Rahab refers to Egypt (see comments on Isa. 30:7; 51:9), not the Rahab of the Joshua (Jericho) story or Rahab the sea monster (see comments on Job 9:13; Ps. 89:10). Babylon, a Mesopotamian nation, was responsible for the destruction of Jerusalem (see the article "The Babylonians"). On Philistia, see the article "The Philistines"; on Tyre, see comments on Ezek. 26:2; on Cush, see the article "The Cushites."

Registers the peoples (87:6). See comments on Dan. 7:10; Mal. 3:16. While many ancient cultures believed in a book of life or destiny, this psalmist likely intends a citizens' list or temple congregation list.[6]

Going down to the Pit (88:4). "Pit" is a synonym for Sheol, the place of the dead (see comments on Ps. 6:5).

From my youth, I have been suffering (88:15). This phrase likely refers to an illness of some sort (see comments on Ps. 31:9).

I have made a covenant with . . . David my servant (89:3). See comments on Ps. 2:6; 2:7.

Assembly of the holy ones . . . council of the holy ones (89:5–7). See comments on Ps. 82:1.

You crushed Rahab (89:10). Here Rahab is a reference to the primeval chaos monster that God slays in creation (see comments on Job 9:13; 26:12–13; Ps. 74:13–15; Isa. 51:9).

Horn (89:17, 24). See comments on 1 Sam. 2:1; Ps. 75:5.

I will not violate my covenant (89:34). The Davidic covenant, which is being referred to here, was an unconditional, everlasting covenant (see comments on 2 Sam. 7:11, 16; Ps. 2:7).

But you have spurned and rejected . . . you have repudiated the covenant (89:38–39). This abrupt shift voices a feeling of rejection by God. With the abolishment of the Davidic monarchy in 586 BC, it seemed as if the Davidic covenant had been broken by God, even though it was supposed to be an everlasting covenant.

Book IV: Psalms 90–106

Introduction. Unlike most of the psalms of Books I–III, fewer than half the psalms in Book IV have titles. Of those with titles, one is attributed to Moses (Ps. 90, the only psalm title that references Moses) and two to David (Pss. 101, 103).

All our days ebb away under your wrath (90:9). After the destruction of Jerusalem in 586 BC the Babylonians deported people from the ruling class, including government officials, religious officials, and wealthy citizens. Many of the people of Judah, however, remained and had to deal with the destruction of Jerusalem and other cities in the region (see the introduction in the commentary on Lamentations). During this time some willingly left the area to settle in Egypt and other locations. From this point on Jews were scattered in many places. They were without a king, their land, and their temple and at times viewed those losses as punishment.

You will take refuge under his wings (91:4). See comments on Ps. 17:8.

His faithfulness will be a protective shield (91:4). See comments on Ps. 3:3.

A ten-stringed harp and . . . a lyre (92:3). See the article "Musical Instruments in Israel and the Ancient Near East."

You have lifted up my horn (92:10). See comments on 1 Sam. 2:1; Ps. 75:5.

Cedar tree in Lebanon (92:12). See comments on Ps. 29:5; Ezek. 27:5.

The Lord reigns (93:1). See comments on Ps. 10:16.

Shine (94:1). See comments on Ps. 80:3, 7, 19.

My God is the rock of my protection (94:22). See comments on Ps. 18:2.

Great king above all gods (95:3). On God as king, see comments on Ps. 10:16.

An Egyptian woman playing a large harp that has thirteen strings.

Meribah . . . Massah (95:8). See comments on Ps. 81:7.

For forty years I was disgusted with that generation (95:10). Here the psalmist references the years of wandering that occurred because of the people's lack of faith (Num. 14).

He is feared above all gods. For all the gods of the peoples are idols (96:4–5). See comments on Ps. 4:2.

The Lord reigns (96:10). See comments on Ps. 10:16.

He judges the peoples fairly . . . the world with righteousness (96:10–13). See comments on Ps. 5:10.

The Lord reigns (97:1). See comments on Ps. 10:16.

Clouds and total darkness . . . the mountains melt like wax (97:2–5). See comments on Ps. 18:7.

All who serve carved images . . . all the gods must worship him (97:7). See comments on Ps. 4:2.

He is coming to judge the earth . . . the peoples fairly (98:9). See comments on Ps. 5:10.

The Lord reigns (99:1). See comments on Ps. 10:16.

He is enthroned between the cherubim (99:1). See comments on 1 Kings 6:23–28; Ps. 80:1; Ezek. 10:1.

You have established fairness (99:4). See comments on Ps. 5:10.

Moses . . . Aaron . . . Samuel (99:6). The psalm recalls Moses, Aaron, and Samuel as models of people who called upon God and obeyed. Also, these men represent leaders of Israel before the institution of the monarchy.

But you, Lord, are enthroned forever (102:12). See comments on Ps. 10:16.

For the Lord will rebuild Zion (102:16). The exile ended in 538 BC by the decree of the Persian king Cyrus (see the article "The Persians"). All exiles now had permission to return to their homelands. For the Jews, this became a slow and incomplete process. Judea (as it was now called) remained largely in ruins, while life in Babylon or Persia continued for many of the Jews with stability and comfort. Those who did return did so in waves, mostly with the intention of restoring Jerusalem, the temple, and, hopefully, the Davidic monarchy. Restoration took place slowly and amid much resistance. Eventually, in 515 BC, they completed the temple, but the finished product did not match the splendor of Solomon's temple. See the introductions in the commentary on Haggai and Zechariah.

He forgives all your iniquity; he heals all your diseases (103:3). See comments on Ps. 31:9.

From the Pit (103:4). "Pit" is a synonym for Sheol, the place of the dead (see comments on Ps. 6:5).

Those who keep his covenant (103:18). Here the psalmist refers to the covenant made at Mount Sinai (Exod. 19–24).

He established the earth on its foundations (104:5). In the ancient Near Eastern understanding of the created world, the earth rested on a foundation of four pillars (see comments on Job 38:4–7).

At your rebuke the water fled (104:7). See comments on Ps. 24:2.

Leviathan, which you formed (104:26). At times Leviathan is considered a creation of God, and other times a chaotic monster that God conquered during creation (see comments on Job 41:1–34; Ps. 74:13–15).

He sent darkness . . . he struck all the firstborn (105:28–36). See comments on Exod. 10:21; Ps. 78:43–51.

In the camp they were envious . . . Dathan . . . Abiram (106:16–17). The disobedience of Dathan and Abiram is recorded in Num. 16.

At Horeb they made a calf (106:19). Horeb and Sinai are names that refer to the same mountain (see comments on Exod. 19:1–2). This disobedience is recorded in Exod. 32 (see comments on Exod. 32:4).

They aligned themselves with Baal of Peor . . . offered to lifeless gods (106:28). See comments on Num. 25:3. The Canaanites often worshiped Baal, a god of storms and agriculture (see the article "The Canaanites and Canaanite Religion").

Phinehas (106:30). Numbers 25 records the faithful actions of Phinehas, grandson of Aaron.

At the Waters of Meribah (106:32). See comments on Ps. 81:7.

They did not destroy the peoples (106:34). This is a reference back to the failure of the Israelites to completely drive out the Canaanites, as delineated in the books of Joshua and Judges.

They sacrificed their sons and daughters to demons . . . to the idols of Canaan (106:37–38). See comments on 2 Kings 3:27; see the article "The Canaanites and Canaanite Religion."

He handed them over to the nations (106:41). During the time of the judges, other nations such as Canaan, Moab, and Ammon oppressed Israel.

Book V: Psalms 107–150

Introduction. Book V contains a variety of smaller psalm collections; some are grouped by common content, others by title. Three psalms in Book V are considered thanksgiving psalms (Pss. 107; 118; 136). Each of these psalms begins with and/or repeats the phrase "Give thanks to the

A bronze bull figurine from Samaria (twelfth century BC).

LORD, for he is good; his faithful love endures forever." There are also numerous psalms of David, which mention David in their title (Pss. 108–110; 124; 131; 133; 138–145). The Psalms of Ascent (Pss. 120–134) all share that title and may represent pilgrimage songs sung as pilgrims went up to the gates of Jerusalem. The Hallelujah Psalms (Pss. 111–113, 115–117, 135, 146–150) all begin and/or end with the phrase "Praise the LORD" (Hebrew: *hallelu yah*).

He has . . . gathered them from the lands (107:3). After the destruction of Jerusalem in 586 BC the people of Judah were scattered to many places (see comments on Ps. 90:9). On the return of the exiles, see comments on Ps. 102:16; see the introductions in the commentary on Ezra-Nehemiah, Haggai, and Zechariah.

Sacrifices of thanksgiving (107:22). See comments on Ps. 56:12.

In the assembly of the people (107:32). See comments on Ps. 22:22.

Wake up, harp and lyre! (108:2). See the article "Musical Instruments in Israel and the Ancient Near East."

I will divide out Shechem . . . I shout in triumph over Philistia (108:7–9). See comments on Ps. 60:6; 60:7–8.

Put to shame (109:28). See comments on Ps. 25:2.

You are a priest forever according to the pattern of Melchizedek (110:4). The psalmist links king and priest together as dual roles of the monarch. In this linking Melchizedek, not Aaron, became the archetype of priest because he was also a king. The story of Melchizedek, found in Gen. 14:18–20, recalls him as king of Salem (another name for Jerusalem). This righteous king and priest blesses Abraham and God. The Davidic kings who later ruled Melchizedek's city maintained his dual roles.

In the assembly of the upright . . . the congregation (111:1). See comments on Ps. 22:22.

Giving them the inheritance of the nations (111:6). See comments on Ps. 44:2.

Instructions (111:7, 10). "Instructions" or "precepts" are synonyms for the laws that God gave to Israel as part of the covenant at Mount Sinai (Exod. 19–24).

His horn will be exalted (112:9). See comments on 1 Sam. 2:1; Ps. 75:5.

The one enthroned on high (113:5). See comments on Ps. 10:16.

The sea looked and fled; the Jordan turned back (114:3). The psalmist recalls the two episodes when God parts water: at the sea (Exod. 14) and at the Jordan River (Josh. 4).

Their idols are silver and gold, made by human hands . . . have mouths . . . eyes . . . ears . . . noses . . . hands . . . feet (115:4–7). This psalmist explains the absurdity of worshiping idols. Idols were created by human hands, and although they had the necessary body parts, they were still speechless, blind, and deaf. Likewise, the OT prophets regularly ridicule those who worship what their own hands have constructed from metal, wood, or stone (see comments on Isa. 40:19–20; 44:10; 44:15; Jer. 10:3).

House of Aaron (115:10, 12). In place of a Davidic leader the priests rose to prominence, particularly the priestly family of Aaron.

The silence of death (115:17). This is a synonym for Sheol (see comments on Ps. 6:5).

I will offer you a sacrifice of thanksgiving (116:17). See comments on Ps. 56:12.

The Lord's house (116:19). See comments on Ps. 2:6.

House of Aaron (118:3). See comments on Ps. 115:10, 12.

House of the Lord (118:26). See comments on Ps. 2:6.

Bind the festival sacrifice (118:27). On festivals, see comments on Lev. 23:1–44; 23:4, 37; Ps. 81:3.

Happy are those . . . the Lord's instruction (119:1). Psalm 119 is an acrostic (alphabetically structured) psalm (for more on acrostic, see the introduction in the commentary on Lamentations). It extols God's law and instruction. The form and content of this psalm seem related to the wisdom traditions of the time. Scholars do not know specifically how the wisdom "schools" of Judaism functioned, but they actively produced literature, including several psalms, Proverbs, Job, Ecclesiastes, and probably other works outside the OT. After the exile, at least in some wisdom circles, wisdom became closely related to obedience to the law. With the priestly leadership came increased attention on tradition and Torah (law/teachings). Those who observed, meditated on, and followed God's decrees were the righteous and blessed ones. The extensive acrostic of Ps. 119 celebrates such activity. In addition to law, words such as "decrees," "statutes," "(God's) ways," "commands," and "precepts" all refer to the law. Often these laws are tied to the covenant at Mount Sinai. Also, observing the law allowed Jews, particularly those who lived outside the land of Israel, to set themselves apart from other people. Their common behavior helped keep them distinct.

Be ashamed (119:6, 46, 116). See comments on Ps. 25:2.

A Song of Ascents (Pss. 120–134 title). Though a handful of these psalms also contain name attributions (David in Pss. 124, 131, 133; Solomon in Ps. 127), most contain only the title "Song of Ascents." Scholars debate the exact purpose of the collection. Some believe the priests recited these psalms as they ascended the steps of the temple, while others propose that pilgrims recited them as they walked uphill toward the gates of Jerusalem and entered the city (on pilgrimage, see comments on Ps. 84:5).

I have stayed in Meshech . . . among the tents of Kedar (120:5). Scholars associate Meshech with lands far north of Israel, perhaps as far north as the Black Sea (see comments on Ezek. 38:2). The people of that land were associated with Japheth, son of Noah (Gen. 10:2). Kedar lies in the Arabian Desert. Scholars know little about these places.

The one enthroned in heaven (123:1). See comments on Ps. 10:16.

When people attacked us (124:2). Over their history, Israel and Judah were threatened by numerous nations. The attack by the Babylonians, which ended in the destruction of Jerusalem and the temple 586 BC, had the most impact, and yet the Judahites survived and eventually returned from exile.

Mount Zion (125:1). See comments on Ps. 2:6.

The mountains surround Jerusalem (125:2). Jerusalem is located in the central hills of Israel, and its topography would serve to protect it somewhat from enemies.

Israel was not the only nation in the ancient Near East to produce acrostic prayers/songs. Shown here is an acrostic prayer of the Assyrian king Ashurbanipal (in the Akkadian language).

When the Lord restored the fortunes (126:1). The restored fortunes mentioned here likely refer to return from the Babylonian exile (see comments on Ps. 102:16).

Zion (126:1). See comments on Ps. 2:6.

Then they said among the nations (126:2). Given the ancient Near Eastern cultural assumptions that the success or failure of a nation was related to that nation's patron deity, other nations attributed the success of Judah to the Lord. The failure of a nation also reflected on the deity (see comments on Ps. 74:10).

Negev (126:4). The Negev is the dry, desert land in the south of Israel.

The watchman (127:1). See comments on Ezek. 33:2.

Sons are indeed a heritage . . . a reward (127:3). In the ancient Near East having children, particularly sons, meant the continuation of the family, and thus the people considered children a blessing from God. The people of that time experienced a high rate of infant mortality and death during childbirth so persistence from infancy into childhood could not be assumed. For that reason they desired many children, again preferring sons. On the other side, people often associated childlessness, including childless couples (such as Samson's parents in Judges, and Elizabeth and Zechariah in the Gospel of Luke) or childless women (such as Sarah, Rebekah, and Rachel in Genesis, and Hannah in 1 Samuel), with shame (see comments on Ps. 25:2). Hence the Bible contains many prayers for children.

At the city gate (127:5). See comments on Deut. 17:5.

Your wife will be like a fruitful vine (128:3). See comments on Ps. 127:3.

Zion (128:5). See comments on Ps. 2:6.

Zion (129:5). See comments on Ps. 2:6.

Be driven back in disgrace (129:5). See comments on Ps. 25:2.

More than watchmen wait for the morning (130:6). See comments on Ezek. 33:2. For those keeping watch over camps, towns, or cities, the darkness of night hindered their work. With the morning came the light needed to see approaching danger.

Remember David (132:1). See comments on Ps. 2:7.

Making a vow to the Mighty One (132:2). The psalmist refers to David's commitment to relocate the ark to Jerusalem, David's capital (2 Sam. 6), and his desire to build a permanent dwelling for the ark (2 Sam. 7).

In Ephrathah . . . in the fields of Jaar (132:6). Ephrathah is a town in Judah, perhaps near Bethlehem. Jaar is another name for Kiriath-jearim, a town northwest of Jerusalem. After the Philistines returned the ark of the covenant, it remained in Kiriath-jearim (1 Sam. 6:21) until David moved it to Jerusalem (see 1 Sam. 7).

For the sake of your servant David (132:10). See comments on Ps. 2:7.

The Lord swore an oath to David . . . forever (132:11–12). See comments on Ps. 2:7. Interestingly, in this recollection the Davidic covenant appears conditional, unlike the account in 2 Sam. 7. Psalm 132 seems to be more closely tied to God's conditional promise to Solomon in 1 Kings 9:1–9.

For the Lord has chosen Zion (132:13). See comments on Ps. 2:6.

I will make my home here (132:14). This is a reference to the Lord's enthronement (see comments on Ps. 10:16).

It is like fine oil on the head . . . running down Aaron's beard onto his robes (133:2). See comments on Exod. 30:25; 1 Kings 1:39. Exodus 30:22–33 describes the consecration of the priest Aaron and his priestly sons with oil. Often in Israel, however, as well as throughout the ancient Near East, kings too were anointed with oil. The anointing mentioned here probably would bring both types of anointing to mind for the people living after the exile.

Hermon (133:3). Mount Hermon, the highest peak in the region, is located in the north of Israel in what is now the Golan Heights.

Mountains of Zion (133:3). See comments on Ps. 2:6.

Zion (134:3). See comments on Ps. 2:6.

The Lord has chosen Jacob (135:4). The foundation for the praise of God is God's covenant relationship with the people.

Our Lord is greater than all gods (135:5). On the religious context of Israel, see comments on Ps. 4:2.

On this ancient wall relief from Egypt, the pharaoh is being anointed by the Egyptian gods Thoth and Horus.

He struck down the firstborn . . . against Pharaoh and all his officials (135:8–9). The psalmist references the plagues in Egypt (Exod. 7–11) (see comments on Ps. 78:43–51).

He struck down many nations . . . Sihon . . . Og . . . gave their land as an inheritance . . . to his people Israel (135:10–12). See comments on Deut. 1:4; 3:11. The psalmist recalls the settlement of Canaan, during which the Israelites, with God's power, drove out the nations inhabiting the land (see comments on Ps. 44:2). Specifically, the psalmist mentions two kings of the Amorites: Sihon and Og. These independent kings ruled the area west of the Jordan River from just north of the Dead Sea to near the Sea of Galilee—Sihon in Heshbon, and Og in Bashan. Sihon would not let the Israelites pass through his region on the way to the promised land, so the Israelites defeated him and took his land (Num. 21:21–26). Similarly, Og resisted the Israelites with the same result (Num. 21:33). These defeats underscored the power of God and God's ability to protect his people.

The idols of the nations . . . there is no breath in their mouths (135:15–17). See comments on Ps. 115:4–7; Isa. 40:19–20; 44:10; 44:15; Jer. 10:3.

House of Aaron (135:19). See comments on Ps. 115:10, 12.

House of Levi (135:20). The Levites were the priestly tribe of Israel.

Zion (135:21). See comments on Ps. 2:6.

He made the heavens skillfully . . . the moon and the stars to rule by night (136:5–9). See comments on Gen. 1:14; Ps. 8:3.

Sihon . . . Og (136:19–20). See comments on Deut. 1:4; 3:11; Ps. 135:10–12.

By the rivers of Babylon . . . our captors there asked us for songs (137:1–3). The exiles of 597 and 586 BC likely lived the remainder of their lives in Babylonia (see comments on Jer. 29:5–6; see the article "The Babylonians"). At first their freedom may have been restricted, but not likely in brutal ways. Some with important skills or knowledge even gained positions in Babylonian government and businesses (e.g., Daniel). Despite the option to assimilate, many of the exiles longed greatly for Zion (see comments on Ps. 2:6).

The Edomites (137:7). See comments on Ps. 83:6–8; Jer. 49:7; Obad. 1; Mal. 1:2–3; 1:4. The Edomites were Israel/Judah's neighbors to the southeast. They were a common enemy from the time of the judges forward. Although scholars are unsure of their exact role in the destruction of Jerusalem in 586 BC, several texts reference their involvement.

Happy is the one who pays you back . . . who takes your little ones (137:8–9). The exiles longed for vengeance for the atrocious acts committed against Judah. Keep in mind that Jerusalem fell to a brutal army that likely killed children as well as women and the elderly. When the people cried to God for vengeance, they exhibited trust in God's justice and recognized God's power.

I will sing your praise before the heavenly beings (138:1). See comments on Ps. 4:2; 29:1; 82:1.

The Lord upholds the just cause (140:12). See comments on Ps. 5:10.

Do not bring your servant into judgment (143:2). See comments on Ps. 5:10.

Going down to the Pit (143:7). See comments on Ps. 6:5.

Part your heavens . . . touch the mountains (144:5). See comments on Ps. 18:7.

Flash your lightning . . . shoot your arrows (144:6). See comments on 2 Sam. 22:10, 13; Ps. 18:14.

This ancient wall relief depicts captives playing their lyres for their Assyrian captors.

A ten-stringed harp (144:9). See the article "Musical Instruments in Israel and the Ancient Near East."

God the King (145:1). See comments on Ps. 10:16.

The Lord reigns forever (146:10). See comments on Ps. 10:16.

Zion (146:10). See comments on Ps. 2:6.

Israel's exiled people (147:2). See comments on Ps. 90:9.

He has raised up a horn (148:14). See comments on 1 Sam. 2:1; Ps. 75:5.

The assembly (149:1). See comments on Ps. 22:22.

Zion (149:2). See comments on Ps. 2:6.

Trumpet . . . harp and lyre . . . tambourine . . . strings and flute . . . cymbals (150:3–5). See the article "Musical Instruments in Israel and the Ancient Near East."

Proverbs

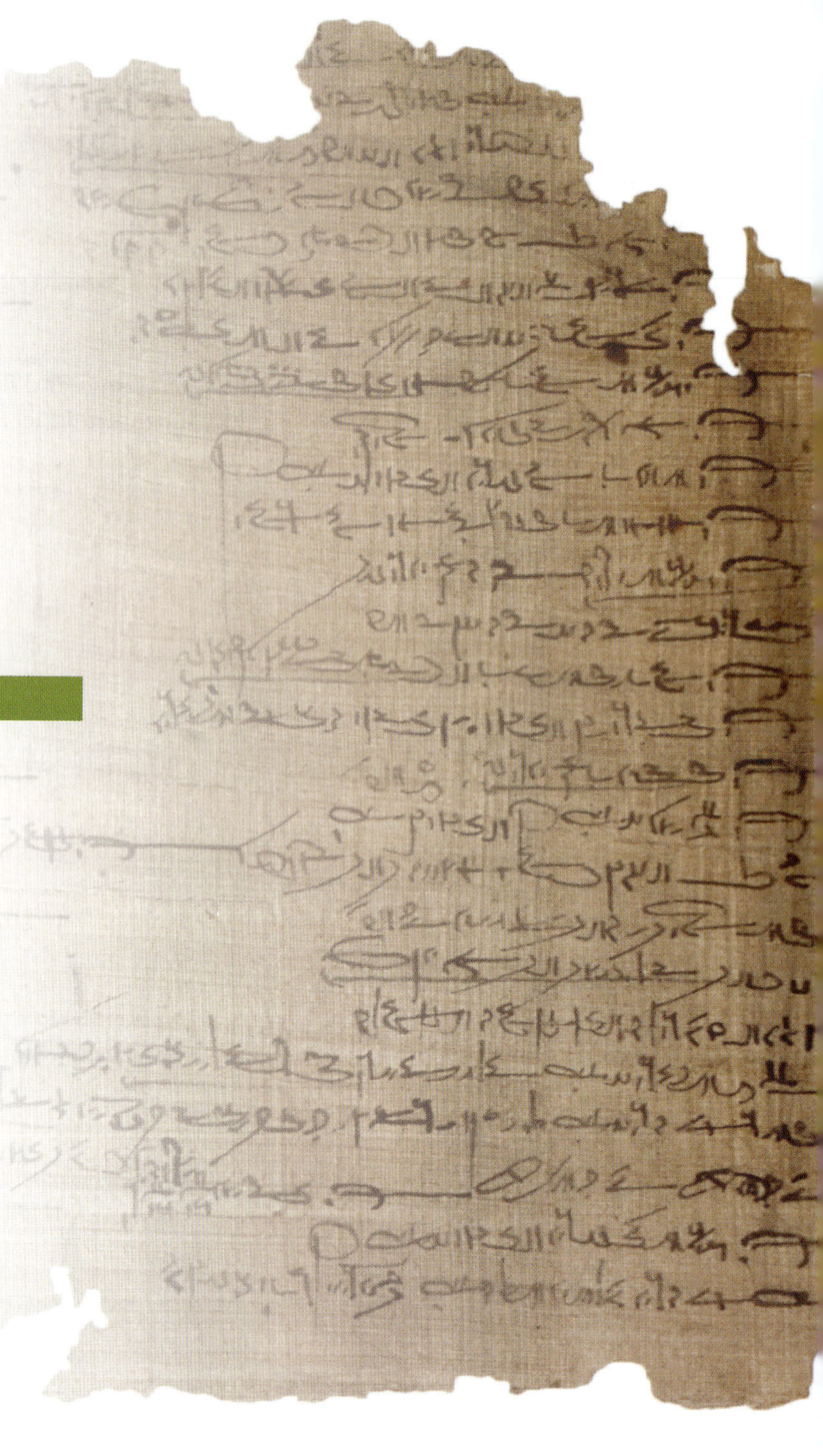

Proverbs

Richard L. Schultz

Introduction. The timeless, universal nature of the biblical proverbs can be confirmed by the existence of similar or even nearly identical sayings not only in ancient Near Eastern proverbial collections but also, for example, in modern Africa. Likewise, of all the literary forms found in the OT, no similarity is greater than that which exists between the book of Proverbs and the instructional materials of ancient Egypt. This often has led to the denigration of Proverbs as merely a compilation of commonsense reflection on everyday life (i.e., reason) or the careful observation of nature (i.e., natural revelation, as in 6:6: "Go to the ant, you slacker!"), neither of which is correct. Although one can affirm that God's providential work in the world enables individuals from other cultures to discover true things about life and ethics, this merely overlaps with the fuller revelation of "the good life" that is oriented around God. Not only does Yahweh ("the Lord"), the covenantal name of Israel's God, occur 133 times in the book but also numerous proverbs reflect the moral standards, cultural values, and religious practices of ancient Israel seen elsewhere in the OT.

Many scholars argue for a lengthy, complex compositional history for the book of Proverbs. One commentator, for example, distinguishes three types of proverbs, with each one supposedly originating in a different period of Israelite history: (1) those concerned with educating the individual, (2) those concerned with community life, and (3) those containing "God-language." More often, chapters 1–9 are viewed as the most recent (i.e., postexilic) addition to the book, due to their more cohesive "instructional" style, more frequent mention of God, overall theological orientation, and personification of "Lady Wisdom." These features often are presented as originating in a later period than the proverbial collections found in chapters 10–31. However, all of these features can be found as well in Egyptian instructional literature from the period of the Israelite monarchy or even earlier. Thus there is no compelling reason to conclude that the proverbial collections in chapters 10–31 ever circulated in ancient Israel independent of chapters 1–9 or that different types of proverbs in the book correspond to social and religious developments in the course of Israelite history.

There are more than two dozen documents of "instructions" deriving from ancient Egypt across three millennia that have been preserved and translated, as well as several proverbial collections from ancient Mesopotamia and Canaan.[1] These texts exhibit some close parallels in structure, content, style, and editorial practice to the book of Proverbs. This is not surprising, since King Solomon, the primary named author/compiler of proverbial wisdom, certainly would have been familiar with the wisdom of the ancient Near East. This familiarity is implied in 1 Kings 4:30, which characterizes Solomon's wisdom as greater than the wisdom of all the people of the East, and even greater than all the wisdom of Egypt.

A cuneiform tablet containing ancient Sumerian proverbs.

Foreword: A Foundation in the Fear of the Lord (1:1–7)

The proverbs of Solomon (1:1). King Solomon's divine endowment with, judicial demonstration of, literary production of, and widespread reputation for "wisdom" are described in detail in 1 Kings 3:5–15; 4:29–34; 5:12; 10:1–9; 11:41 (partially paralleled in 2 Chron. 1:1–12; 9:1–8, 22–33; cf. Matt. 12:42; Luke 11:31). If Solomon is the "Teacher" in the book of Ecclesiastes, we also learn about his activities as sage from Eccles. 12:9–10 (see the introduction in the commentary on Ecclesiastes).

For learning wisdom and discipline (1:2). Several Egyptian texts, most notably "The Instruction of Amenemope" (composed probably during the twelfth century BC), begin with a series of purpose statements similar in form to Prov. 1:1–7 but somewhat different in emphasis. For example:

> To set one straight on the paths of life,
> And make him prosper on earth;

To let his heart settle down in its chapel,
As one who steers him clear of evil;
To save him from the talk of others,
As one who is respected in the speech of men.[2]

"Wisdom" (Hebrew: *hokmah*) is the broadest of several related terms used in these introductory verses. In the OT "wisdom" can designate various intellectual and practical, even artistic, skills, but in Prov. 1–9 it always has a moral dimension.

The fear of the LORD is the beginning of knowledge (1:7). The non-Israelite instructional texts throughout the ancient Near East also frequently note the value of revering the gods, but only Israelite wisdom ascribes to "the fear of the LORD" a central role for acquiring wisdom and achieving God-pleasing behavior.

Prologue: Wisdom 101 (1:8–9:18)

On the basis of some Egyptian literary models, some scholars suggest that the lengthy prologue of 1:8–9:18 should be divided into ten or more originally independent "lectures." However, this compositional theory requires scholars to label some verses as "interludes" between the individual "lessons." As it now stands, the prologue to Proverbs (1:8–9:18) presents a carefully composed and unified theological introduction to proverbial wisdom.

The Appeals of Loving Parents and Lady Wisdom (1:8–33)

Listen, my son . . . don't reject your mother's teaching (1:8). Wisdom texts in the ancient Near East often feature a father addressing his son, although since scribal schools were common outside Israel, some interpreters consider this merely to be a metaphorical designation for a teacher-student relationship. The unique mention in 1:8 and 6:20 (cf. 31:1) of a mother's involvement in her son's instruction, however, points instead to a family context. As with Israel's neighbors, this may have involved training sons to follow their father's profession, but Proverbs gives less emphasis to job skills and more to moral formation than do other non-Israelite instructional texts throughout the ancient Near East.

Let's swallow them alive, like Sheol (1:12). This verse may be an allusion to Death's voracious appetite depicted in Canaanite mythology (cf. 27:20; 30:16).[3] On Sheol, see comments on Ps. 6:5.

Wisdom calls out (1:20). In this section of Proverbs "wisdom" is personified as a woman, referred to by scholars as "Lady Wisdom." Some interpreters have suggested that Lady Wisdom was modeled after an ancient Near Eastern goddess, most frequently the Egyptian goddess Ma'at. The Egyptian word *ma'at* designates the concept of truth and justice, and the goddess Ma'at personifies these traits (on Ma'at, see comments on Exod. 5:2; see the section on Egyptian religion in the article "The Egyptians"). However, Lady Wisdom in Proverbs does not clearly exhibit divine features or actions, and the Hebrew word *hokmah* ("wisdom") is not synonymous with the Egyptian word *ma'at.*

The Commendation of Wisdom's Ways (Chaps. 2–4)

It will rescue you from a forbidden woman (2:16). The meaning of the Hebrew word translated as "forbidden" is debated. This woman may be either a foreigner (i.e., a stranger), and thus likely a worshiper of a "strange" God, or merely unfaithful to (i.e., estranged from) her husband. Egyptian wisdom texts likewise warn against sexual promiscuity and marital infidelity due to the negative consequences. The Egyptian "Instruction of Any," for example, contains a strikingly similar description to that found in 2:16–19 and chapters 5–7:

> Beware of a woman who is a stranger,
> One not known in her town;
> Don't stare at her when she goes by,
> Do not know her carnally.
> A deep water whose course is unknown,
> Such is a woman away from her husband.
> "I am pretty," she tells you daily,
> When she has no witnesses;
> She is ready to ensnare you,
> A great deadly crime when it is heard.[4]

The Egyptian "Maxims of Ptahhotep" conclude even more ominously:

> One may be deceived by an exquisite body,
> But then it (suddenly) turns to misery.
> (All it takes is) a trifling moment like a dream,
> And one comes to destruction through having known them.[5]

They will bring you many days, a full life, and well-being (3:2). Literary works from throughout the ancient Near East also often invoke or promise a deity's granting of long life, prosperity, and health. For example, a Phoenician text states, "May Ba'al KRNTRYŠ and all the gods of the city give Azatiwada length of days and multitude of years and good prosperity, and mighty strength over every king."[6] Such blessing often was contingent upon ritual fidelity to the god.

Tie them around your neck (3:3). Deuteronomy 6:8 likewise mentions the use of amulets as a reminder of important instruction (cf. Prov. 6:21; 7:3).

She is a tree of life (3:18). Metaphorically, wisdom is a life-giving tree (cf. 11:30; 13:12; 15:4), alluding to the "tree of life" in the garden of Eden (Gen. 2:9; 3:22, 24; cf. Rev. 2:7; 22:2, 14, 19). An Egyptian hymn of praise to the god Amun-Re uses this same metaphor, likewise referring to the "tree of life."[7]

An Egyptian amulet, in the shape of a heart.

Listen, sons (4:1; also 4:10, 20). Wisdom texts throughout the ancient Near East frequently contain repeated calls to heed the words of an authority figure, such as the king, the sage, or even one's own "soul," often accompanied by a description of the benefits of such attentiveness. Note the similar exhortation in an ancient Egyptian text: "Listen to me! Behold, it is good for people to listen."[8]

The path of the righteous is . . . but the way of the wicked (4:18–19; also 4:11, 14–15). The "two ways" is a favorite biblical metaphor, especially within wisdom texts, for contrasting two ways of life and their respective "destinations" (cf. Deut. 11:28; Josh. 1:8; Ps. 1:1, 6; 139:24; Isa. 26:7–8).

Wisdom's Warnings against Adultery and Other Folly (Chaps. 5–7)

As sharp as a double-edged sword (5:4). Wisdom texts in the ancient Near East extol the value of a good wife while warning against the consequences of adultery, although some of them exhibit a less balanced view of women than does Proverbs, as in this Assyrian text: "Woman is a well, woman is an iron dagger—a sharp one!—which cuts a man's neck."[9]

If you have put up security for your neighbor (6:1). An Assyrian debt note from Tel Hadid (ca. 664 BC) parallels the stern warning in 6:1–5 and elsewhere in the book (11:15; 17:18; 20:16; 22:26; 27:13) against guaranteeing another's debt. According to that note, the debtor's wife and sister work for the lender at the debtor's expense for the duration of the loan, and if the principal is not repaid by the set date (in about three months), the interest rate goes to 33.33 percent.[10] Likewise, one Sumerian proverb warns, "Do not vouch for someone; that man will have a hold on you."[11] A person's warm outer garment could serve as a security deposit.

How long will you stay in bed, you slacker? (6:9). Since wisdom literature praises decisive, hard-working, and diligent behavior, laziness is

Some exquisitely dressed wealthy Egyptian women at a banquet.

viewed as foolish behavior and is regularly depicted as a serious character flaw (cf. 6:6–11; 10:26; 13:4; 15:19; 19:24; 20:4; 21:25; 22:13; 24:30–34; 26:13–16). The Egyptian "Instruction of Any" offers a similar assessment: "He who is slack amounts to nothing. Honored is the man who's active."[12]

Coverings . . . richly colored linen from Egypt . . . perfumed . . . with myrrh, aloes, and cinnamon (7:16–17). Although flax (from which linen was made) was grown in Palestine, the finest, most expensive linen came from Egypt (Ezek. 27:7), and the named spices (cf. Song 4:14) were imported from India and Arabia, suggesting that the seductive woman described here is quite wealthy.

Lady Wisdom's Final Appeals (Chaps. 8–9)

It is by me that kings reign (8:15). The most extensive personification of wisdom in Proverbs is in chapter 8, where Lady Wisdom is commonly viewed either as a goddess figure or as a divinized abstract quality. The closest ancient Near Eastern parallel to this is in the Aramaic wisdom text "Ahiqar":

> From heaven the peoples receive favor.
> Wisdom is from the gods.
> Also, she is precious to the gods.
> Rulership is hers f[or eve]r.
> She/it has been placed in heaven,
> because the lord of the holy one has exalted her.[13]

She has carved out her seven pillars (9:1). Houses (and temples) with seven pillars have been found in ancient Israel (and the ancient Near East), but the number seven used here probably is symbolic of perfection, while also indicating that it is a spacious and luxurious house.

Advanced Instructions in Wisdom (Chaps. 10–29)

There are two basic forms of ancient Near Eastern instructional texts: those in which a prologue precedes the proverbial collection and those with only a preceding title. Following the lengthy prologue in chapters 1–9, several collections of proverbs or distinct compositional units can be distinguished within the book of Proverbs: Solomonic (10:1–22:16); words of the wise (22:17–24:22); further words of the wise (24:23–34); Solomonic, edited by Hezekiah's men (25:1–29:27); words of Agur (30:1–9); numerical proverbs, perhaps also from Agur (30:10–33); words of Lemuel's mother (31:1–9); and a concluding praise of the wise woman (31:10–31). Non-Israelite ancient Near Eastern wisdom compositions, however, do not typically contain multiple collections of proverbs like this, as indicated by introductory titles. It is currently debated whether the individual proverbs within the respective collections are carefully ordered—their order therefore having interpretive importance—or largely random—each proverb therefore being properly interpreted as an independent unit. Several Egyptian texts clearly group some of their proverbs thematically; the clearest example of this is "The Instruction of ʻOnchsheshonqy."[14]

Righteousness and Wickedness as the Ultimate Contrast (Chaps. 10–15)

Whoever spreads slander is a fool. When there are many words, sin is unavoidable, but the one who controls his lips is prudent (10:18–19). God detests speech-related vices (e.g., lying, slander, false witness) because they denigrate individuals whom he has created and disrupt and destroy life within the covenantal community. Several other ancient Near Eastern wisdom texts share this perspective. Thus the Akkadian "Counsels of Wisdom" declares, "Whoever slanders (or) speaks evil, as a retribution the god Shamash will pursue after his head. Open not wide your mouth, guard your lips."[15]

Ancient temples, such as this Egyptian temple at the city of Thebes, often contained columns in rows of seven.

The fear of the LORD prolongs life (10:27). Non-Israelite wisdom texts also affirm the benefits of divine favor but are more likely to specify the cultic actions that must be carried out correctly in order to guarantee this: "Reverence (for the deity) produces well-being, sacrifice prolongs life, and prayer atones for sin. A god-fearing man is not despised by [his god]."[16]

Dishonest scales are detestable to the LORD (11:1). In ancient Israel a standardized (but easily falsifiable) weight on one plate would be balanced with a precious metal as a means of exchange (cf. 16:11; 20:10, 23). This proverb is one of many that have close parallels in the Mosaic legislation (cf. Deut. 25:13–16), even expressing divine displeasure similarly (the word translated as "detestable," traditionally translated as "an abomination," occurs in this context twenty-two times in Proverbs and seventeen times in Deuteronomy). This value is also shared by ancient Near Eastern wisdom texts, one of which similarly warns, "Do not tilt the scale nor falsify the weight."[17]

If the righteous will be repaid on earth, how much more the wicked and sinful (11:31). This proverb affirms a perspective that is prominent in the OT wisdom books: divine punishment and reward are expected in the present world. This view often is contrasted with a NT perspective that emphasizes future (postmortem) justice. This understanding need not imply, however, that the sage in Proverbs has no hope in a postmortem extension of life (see comments on Prov. 12:28).

Lying lips are detestable to the LORD (12:22). Lying qualifies as one of the most destructive speech vices throughout the ancient Near East. For example, an ancient Egyptian text states, "Do not converse falsely with a man, for it is the abomination of God."[18]

There is life in the path of righteousness, and in its path there is no death (12:28). The NIV translates the final phrase ("there is no death") as "immortality," implying that the horizon of the sage extends beyond one's present earthly existence, a perspective perhaps reflected in 15:24; 23:18; 24:14 as well. Most interpreters, however, understand 12:28 as referring simply to the avoidance of a premature death through wise living. But one should note that ancient Israel's neighbors generally shared a strong belief in the afterlife, and their burial preparations and procedures reflected that conviction (see the section on Egyptian religion in the article "The Egyptians").

The one who will not use the rod hates his son (13:24). Corporal discipline using a rigid staff (also mentioned in 19:25, 29; 20:30; 22:15; 23:13–14; 26:3; 29:15) was viewed in the ancient Near East not

An ancient set of scales.

as child abuse but as a protective demonstration of parental love. For example, an ancient Aramaic text makes a similar statement: "Do not keep your son from the rod. If you are not able to save him [from wickedness]. If I beat you, my son, you will not die" (cf. 19:18).[19] The passing on of cultural values took place primarily in the home and thus was the parents' responsibility.

In this common scene from the Egyptian Book of the Dead, the heart of the deceased is being weighed against the seated goddess Ma'at (note the feather on her head). The god Thoth writes down the results.

The one who oppresses the poor person insults his Maker, but one who is kind to the needy honors him (14:31). The protection of and provision for the needy are likewise affirmed in the Akkadian text titled "Counsels of Wisdom," which states, "The lowly, take pity on him. Do not despise the miserable. . . . Give food to eat, beer to drink. Present what is asked for, provide for and honor. One's god will be happy with him for that."[20]

The eyes of the Lord are everywhere, observing the wicked and the good (15:3). Comparatively, an Egyptian text describes the pharaoh as "Perception," whose "eyes search out everybody."[21]

The sacrifice of the wicked is detestable to the Lord (15:8). Other OT texts, such as 1 Sam. 15:22 and Isa. 1:11–17, confirm that religious ritualistic practices apart from obedience to God's law and the practice of social justice are unacceptable to God (cf. Prov. 21:3, 27).

Sheol and Abaddon (15:11; also 27:20). This is a personification of the grave and the underworld. In Canaanite mythology "Death" (*Mot*) is actually a god (see comments on Ps. 6:5; see the article "The Canaanites and Canaanite Religion").

A hot-tempered person (15:18; also 19:19; 22:24; 29:22). This description finds a close parallel in the frequent references within Egyptian wisdom literature to "the hot-headed man."[22]

Wise Counsel for Rulers and Everyday Life (16:1–22:16)

The Lord weighs motives (16:2; also 21:2; 24:12). This claim is similar to the portrayals of the Egyptian god Thoth, who weighs the heart of the deceased against the feather of truth in order to determine whether they will be permitted to enter the afterlife.

The lot is cast (16:33; also 18:18). In Israel the high priest threw the "divinely loaded" stones (i.e., the Urim and Thummim) in order to determine God's direction in a public matter (see comments on Exod. 28:2; 1 Sam. 14:41–42).

Even a fool is considered wise when he keeps silent—discerning, when he seals his lips (17:28). Self-restraint in speech is a common value in the instructional/wisdom texts of the ancient Near East. For example, "Do not reveal your heart to a stranger. . . . Choose the good one and say it, while the bad is shut in your belly."[23]

A man who finds a wife finds a good thing and obtains favor from the Lord (18:22). Proverbs emphasizes the character of a good wife (cf. 12:4; 19:14; 31:30), while ancient Near Eastern texts more often emphasize her reproductive capacity. For example, one ancient Egyptian text advises, "Be gracious to your wife . . . Rejoice her heart all the days of your life, for she is a profitable field for her lord."[24]

Wine is a mocker, beer is a brawler (20:1; also 23:20–21, 29–35; 31:4–7). Other than water, wine was the most consumed beverage in ancient Israel. Made from barley and wheat, beer was the preferred beverage in Egypt and Mesopotamia.[25] The Egyptian "Instruction of Any" also warns against drunkenness: "Don't indulge in drinking beer, lest you utter evil speech and don't know what you are saying . . . One finds you lying on the ground."[26]

Drives the threshing wheel over them (20:26). "Two or more heavy wheels were attached to a frame, which was drawn by animals over the grain to crack the husk."[27]

A king's heart is like channeled water in the Lord's hand (21:1). In the ancient Near East constructed and controlled irrigation ditches directed water from springs, rivers, or lakes into agricultural fields and gardens (cf. Ps. 1:3; 65:10).

A wise person went up against a city of warriors and brought down its secure fortress (21:22; also 24:5–6). The OT's historical accounts (e.g., 2 Sam. 20:15–22) as well as Ecclesiastes (e.g., 7:19; 9:13–18) describe the strategic advantage provided by wise advisors and military leaders.

Admonitions for Societal Relationships (22:17–24:22)

Pay attention to the words of the wise (22:17). Ever since a scholarly edition of "The Instruction of Amenemope" became available early in the twentieth century, the relationship between this Egyptian wisdom text and Prov. 22:17–24:22 has been closely examined. The usual claim is that the numerous striking verbal parallels between the two texts indicate that the author of the latter borrowed extensively from the former, based both on the proposed dates of composition for these two texts and on a careful analysis of divergent wording between individual proverbs. In turn, this claim has been used theologically to argue that divine truth can be found readily in extrabiblical texts. The two texts do, in fact, share various themes as well as specific proverbs, in addition to two notable rhetorical features: (1) a greater frequency of imperatival verb forms, found elsewhere in Proverbs only in chapters 1–9; and (2) small groups of proverbs related to a specific theme, rarely encountered elsewhere within the proverbial collections of Proverbs (but more commonly found in Egyptian instructions).

However, there are problems with the claim of literary dependence of the Israelite sage on Amenemope. These include the following: (1) Some of the parallels are created only by emending the Hebrew text to conform to the wording of their alleged Egyptian source. (2) The Egyptian parallels are confined to eight of the thirty chapters of the Amenemope text. Proverbs fails to draw on a number of Amenemope's chapters addressing themes also commonly occurring in Proverbs. (3) The parallels are found only in Prov. 22:17–23:11. (4) The parallels in Proverbs occur in a puzzling order if borrowed directly from the Egyptian text. (5) The verses commonly cited as borrowed verses are similar in content to other OT and ancient Near Eastern texts and just as easily could have been "borrowed" instead from them. Regardless of the nature of the relationship between the two texts—a few scholars even argue that Amenemope borrowed from Proverbs—the latter maintains its distinctive Israelite emphases.

That your confidence may be in the Lord (22:19). If there is direct borrowing by the author/editor of this section of Proverbs, this affirms that wise individuals everywhere can discern truth through observation and reason. The incompleteness—but not falsity—of these "truths" is highlighted by the way in which Proverbs anchors wisdom in one's relationship with the Lord.

Haven't I written for you thirty sayings? (22:20). The Hebrew text is not clear, and scholars disagree over how to translate this verse. The Hebrew appears to read "three days ago," meaning "previously." Yet this same Hebrew word is similar to the word meaning "thirty," and most English translations have concluded that the word should be emended to "thirty," based on the assumption that this section is structured like "The Instruction of Amenemope," which is subdivided into thirty "chapters/sections."

Don't move an ancient boundary marker (22:28; also 23:10). Although found in chapter 6 of "The Instruction of Amenemope," closer parallels occur in Deut. 19:14; 27:17.

Put a knife to your throat if you have a big appetite (23:2). The warning against gluttony here, especially in the presence of a ruler, is paralleled in chapter 23 of "The Instruction of Amenemope."

Beekeeping and the production of honey was practiced extensively in Egypt. This painting shows ancient Egyptians baking honey cakes.

The Indispensability of Integrity and Diligence (24:23–34)

These sayings also belong to the wise (24:23). This superscription supports the claim that there was a distinct professional group of sages in ancient Israel, perhaps serving primarily as court officials and advisors in Jerusalem (cf. Jer. 18:18).

Relating Wisely to Various Societal Groups: Rulers, Neighbors, Family, and Social Menaces (25:1–27:27)

These too are proverbs of Solomon, which the men of King Hezekiah of Judah copied (25:1). The second Solomonic collection of Proverbs, which begins here, was compiled and edited two centuries after his reign over the united nation of Israel. According to the Babylonian Talmud, *Baba Batra* 14b–15a (compiled ca. AD 500), "Hezekiah and his company wrote Isaiah, Proverbs and Song of Songs, (and) Ecclesiastes," presumably also referring to their editorial rather than authorial role (on King Hezekiah, see comments on 2 Kings 18:1).

If you find honey, eat only what you need (25:16; also 25:27). See comments on Exod. 3:8, 17. Honey was used primarily as a sweetener and could be derived from grapes, dates, figs, and bees (Judg. 14:8).[28] The reference to "finding" honey in 25:16 suggests that it is produced by bees (also 24:13; 27:7).

Like pouring vinegar on soda (25:20). The exact point of this simile is unclear. Presumably, since vinegar causes sodium carbonate to "sizzle," that sounds like enmity between the two substances.[29]

Heap burning coals on his head (25:22). It has been suggested that this passage refers to a ritual from Ptolemaic Egypt whereby a thief is exonerated, but there is no evidence that it was ever practiced in Israel.[30] More likely, this refers metaphorically to inflicting psychological pain on an enemy by treating them kindly.

Like snow in summer and rain at harvest (26:1). In Israel it does not snow in summer, and it seldom rains during the spring or summer harvest seasons.

Like glaze on an earthen vessel (26:23). Adulterated silver provides a cheap and fragile, though superficially attractive, glaze that serves to cover up flaws in a ceramic pot.[31]

Know well the condition of your flock (27:23). It is somewhat surprising that this subsection concludes with a longer instruction regarding tending one's flocks and herds (27:23–27). However, this merely reflects practical wisdom and diligence being applied to an everyday task.

Righteousness and the Health of a Nation (28:1–29:27)

Whoever increases his wealth through excessive interest (28:8). According to the Mosaic law, it was illegal to charge interest of a fellow Israelite, but it was permitted of foreigners (Exod. 22:25; Lev. 25:35–37; Deut. 23:19–20). Yet apparently this did occur sometimes (Neh. 5:9–11; Ezek. 18:13; 22:11).

A king who judges the poor with fairness (29:14; also 31:8–9). It was the expectation that rulers in the ancient Near East would establish and maintain justice in their realm, especially on behalf of those easily oppressed and exploited. It is not surprising that the prophetic promise of an ideal future Davidic ruler emphasized this responsibility as well (Isa. 9:7; 11:3–5; 32:1).

Without revelation people run wild (29:18). The crucial role of divine guidance and obedience to the revealed law is emphasized here. The same verb translated here as "run wild" occurs in Exod. 32:25 to describe the Israelites' idolatrous revelry before the golden calf.

Epilogue (30:1–31:33)

The Words of Agur Calling for Humble Reliance on God's Work and God's Word (30:1–33)

The pronouncement (30:1; also 31:1). The Hebrew word translated as "pronouncement" (*masa*) normally designates prophetic oracles (Isa. 13:1; Ezek. 12:10), but here it may instead refer to a region in the Arabian Peninsula named after a descendant of Ishmael (Gen. 25:13–14; 1 Chron. 1:29–30), which would make Agur and King Lemuel non-Israelites.

To Ithiel and Ucal (30:1). Ithiel and Ucal are unknown, apparently non-Israelite, locations. However, these Hebrew words are better translated not as names but as verbs: "I am weary, God, but I can prevail" (NIV).

Every word of God is pure . . . don't add to his words (30:5–6). Here Agur quotes from Ps. 18:30 (cf. 2 Sam. 22:31) and Deut. 4:2; 12:32, thereby asserting the flawless status of his oration.

Three things are too wondrous for me; four I can't understand (30:18). In 30:10–33 this numerical saying is the dominant form, an often riddle-like proverb in which the final item is emphasized.

An unloved woman (30:23). This expression is used of Leah in Gen. 29:31 and in marriage legislation in Deut. 21:15–17; 22:13–21; 24:1–4.

The Words of Lemuel's Mother Calling the King to Justice (31:1–9)

A pronouncement that his mother taught him (31:1). The "royal instruction" is a well-established literary genre in the ancient Near East in which an aging (or deceased) monarch prepares his successor to rule effectively. However, to ascribe such counsel to a queen mother is without parallel in the ancient Near East.

Lady Wisdom Incarnate as a God-Fearing Wife and Mother (31:10–33)

Who can find a wife of noble character? (31:10). Proverbs 31:10–31, which may also originate with King Lemuel's mother, concludes the book using an acrostic: each succeeding verse begins with the next letter of the Hebrew alphabet, a structuring technique also found in Nah. 1:2–8, Lam. 1–4, and nine psalms, as well as in several Akkadian (Mesopotamian) texts. This most likely indicates that the described woman embodies all aspects of godly wisdom (i.e., "from A to Z") that have been presented throughout the book of Proverbs. Although a few Egyptian instructions extol individual virtues of women, especially wives, this text is unique in the ancient Near East in both its length and range of described female strengths and activities. The portrait given here is somewhat idealized, since the legal rights and privileges of Israelite women were limited outside the home, making some of the commercial activities mentioned difficult to carry out.

From the ancient city of Susa, this wall relief depicts a wealthy Elamite woman working a spindle.

Fine linen and purple (31:22; also 7:16–17). These are very expensive items normally owned only by the wealthy, indicating the degree of prosperity that this woman provides for her family.

At the city gates (31:31; also 1:21; 8:3; 22:22; 24:7, 31:23). The main gateway entrance to cities is where the elders gathered to conduct legal and commercial business (see comments on Deut. 17:5; Ruth 4:1).

Ecclesiastes

Richard L. Schultz

Introduction. The book of Ecclesiastes presents the words of the "Teacher" (Hebrew: *qohelet*; see 1:1, 2, 12; 7:27; 12:8–10). Though Solomon is never mentioned by name in the book, the further description of the Teacher as the son of David and king over Israel (1:1, 12), his unsurpassed wisdom (1:16), and his royal achievements (2:4–10) indicate that Solomon is intended to be understood as the book's primary speaker. The instruction is given predominantly in the first person: "I turned . . . realized . . . knew . . . said" (2:12–15). A concluding section, however (12:9–11), contains third-person references to the Teacher and may indicate the words of an editor.

If Solomon is the primary source of the instruction in the book, then it can be dated to the mid-tenth century BC, and can be understood against the dual background of the flourishing united monarchy in Israel, when the people were "eating, drinking, and rejoicing" (1 Kings 4:20), and Solomon's reputation for unparalleled wisdom (1 Kings 4:29–34). Many interpreters, however, consider the figure of Solomon to be merely a literary persona used by a much later author in the postexilic (fifth century BC) or even the Hellenistic period (third century BC) to look at the world from Solomon's perspective. To support these later dates of composition, scholars cite specific words as indicating Persian influence, indications of a postexilic setting, and parallels to later Greek philosophy (e.g., Stoicism and Epicureanism).

The literary genre or literary style of the book is unique within the OT, and its genre as well as its ancient Near Eastern background remains disputed. The first-person discourse has prompted some interpreters to compare Ecclesiastes with the Egyptian autobiographic instructions of King Meri-Ka-Re or King Amen-Em-Het or with the fictional royal Assyrian autobiographies in Akkadian of Naram-Sin or Sennacherib. Others focus on the Teacher's complaints regarding human limitations and divine injustice and compare the book with ancient Near Eastern pessimistic/disputation literature, such as the Egyptian "Admonitions of an Egyptian Sage" and "The Man Who Was Weary of Life" (i.e., soul) or the Akkadian "Dialogue of Pessimism" and "The Babylonian Theodicy." Despite some striking parallels between such texts in style and content, Ecclesiastes remains unparalleled, given its alternating moods of celebration and resignation.

Introductory Remarks (1:1–11)

Says the Teacher (1:2). The Hebrew word translated as "Teacher" refers either to someone who assembles the people—for example, to instruct them (see 12:9)—or to a sage who assembles (i.e., edits) collected sayings into an anthology (see 12:9–11). Ecclesiastes opens (1:1–11) and closes (12:8–14) with third-person narrative text ("the Teacher") while all the interior text is in first person ("I"). Other ancient Near Eastern texts, such as "The Maxims of Ptahhotep," also use a third-person narrative framework to introduce first-person instruction.

Everything is futile (1:2). The book's theme verse occurs here and again in 12:8. The Hebrew word translated here as "futile" (*hebel*) occurs thirty-eight times in the book. It characterizes human achievements (and existence) as short-lasting and insubstantial—that is, "vapor" (cf. Ps. 144:4). It is often associated with "pursuit of the wind" (1:14, 17; 2:11, 17, 26; 4:4, 6, 16; 6:9). In the Mesopotamian Gilgamesh Epic the main character similarly states, "As for mankind, numbered are their days; whatever they achieve is but the wind!"[1]

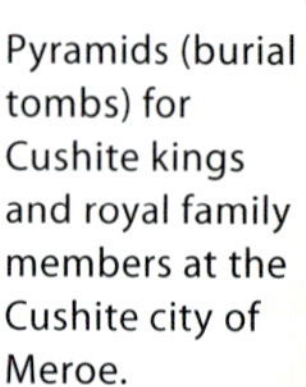

Pyramids (burial tombs) for Cushite kings and royal family members at the Cushite city of Meroe.

What does a person gain for all his efforts . . . under the sun? (1:3). This verse expresses the Teacher's quest throughout the book. The Hebrew word translated as "gain" is a commercial term, sometimes used to refer to a "surplus" of silver. The phrase "under the sun" (twenty-nine times in the book) also occurs in some ancient Near Eastern curse texts, referring to the realm of the living in contrast to the realm of the gods.

The wind returns in its cycles (1:6). The description in 1:4–7 of the constant motion within the natural world has been seen as reflecting a cyclical worldview, with "there is nothing new under the sun" (1:9) refuting the prophetic perspective that God is directing history toward a new, better future world (Isa. 65:17). However, the former (1:6) merely mirrors the lack of "gain" in the human sphere, while the latter (1:9) refers to human, not divine, limitations. In the words of the Egyptian "Complaints of Khakheperre-sonb," "From the first generation down to those who come after they imitate what is past."[2]

There is no remembrance of those who came before (1:11). Ancient Near Eastern monarchs were obsessed with preserving a record of their existence through monuments and public inscriptions, but to no avail. The ancient Egyptian song titled "The Song of the Harper" notes, ironically, that "the blessed nobles . . . are buried in their tombs. . . . Their places are no more. What has become of them?"[3]

Everything under the Sun Is Examined (1:12–5:9)

Human Achievements and Wisdom (1:12–2:26)

I applied my mind to examine (1:13). The Hebrew for "I applied my mind" translated literally is "I set my heart." Similarly, an Egyptian sage claimed to launch "the gathering of maxims, the quest of phrases with a searching heart."[4]

And explore through wisdom all that is done under heaven (1:13). The Mesopotamian Epic of Gilgamesh introduces its hero as "He who saw everything to the ends of the land, who all things experienced, considered all! . . . The hidden he saw, laid bare the undisclosed."[5]

See, I have amassed wisdom . . . I increased my achievements (1:16–2:4). Solomon's wisdom and achievements, as described in this section, are best understood against the background of the historical account of his reign in 1 Kings 3–10. It was common for ancient Near Eastern monarchs to boast of their accomplishments (cf. 2 Kings 18:28–35; Dan. 4:30). One finds in ancient Near Eastern propagandistic royal inscriptions similar claims that a specific king possesses superior, even comprehensive, knowledge and wisdom. One Phoenician king, for example, declared, "Every king made me as a father, on account of my righteousness, my wisdom, and the goodness of my heart."[6]

So I became great and surpassed all who were before me in Jerusalem (2:9). This statement is puzzling to some because only Solomon's father, David, ruled from Jerusalem prior to him, although earlier Jebusite rulers could perhaps be in view here as well (see Judg. 1:21; 2 Sam. 5:6; also Gen. 14:18). However, a similar description of Solomon is given in 1 Chron. 29:25, and this may reflect the ancient Near Eastern practice of using a phrase like "any/all who were before me" in an almost formulaic manner to emphasize the king's remarkable successes.

One fate comes to them both (2:14). Death is the great equalizer (see also 9:2), as also expressed in an ancient Akkadian document titled "The Dialogue of Pessimism," where a servant observes, "Look at the skulls of the lowly and great. Which was the doer of evil, and which was the doer of good deeds?"[7]

There is nothing better for a person than to eat, drink, and enjoy his work (2:24). This climactic, refrain-like affirmation of God's gifts to humans recurs in various formulations in 3:12–13, 22; 5:18–19; 8:15; 9:7–9. It should not be confused with the self-indulgent and God-ignoring revelry described in Isa. 22:13, which is cited in 1 Cor. 15:32 (cf. Luke 12:19). Ancient Near Eastern texts containing a similar charge to enjoy life in the face of inevitable death (e.g., "Follow the happy day and forget worry!")[8] lack the Teacher's claim in 2:24–26 that these everyday pleasures are a gift from God (also 3:13; 5:19).

Time and Eternity (3:1–22)

A time to throw stones and a time to gather stones (3:5). This is the most obscure of the fourteen contrasting activities in this so-called Catalogue of the Times (3:1–8). It is unclear which item is negative and which is positive and how verse 5a is related to 5b. Suggestions include stones for building, for destroying an enemy's field, or for executing a criminal, or as a euphemism for sexual activity (i.e., parallel to v. 5b). Some interpreters see in this poetic list a strict determinism, but the claim in 3:11 ("He has made everything appropriate in its time") suggests rather that individuals should seek to identify "appropriate" occasions for particular actions.

There is wickedness at the place of judgment (3:16). A primary responsibility of ancient Near Eastern monarchs was to maintain justice within their realm. However, too often this was not the case, as indicated by this quotation in the Egyptian document titled "The Eloquent Peasant": "Is it not wrong: a balance that tilts . . . The straight becoming crooked? Behold, justice flees from you, banished from its seat!"[9]

All come from dust, and all return to dust (3:20). The Teacher alludes here (see also 12:7) to the OT creation account (Gen. 2:7; 3:19). Similarly, the Mesopotamian creation myth Atrahasis also describes humans as being formed from clay.

Social Relationships (4:1–16)

A cord of three strands (4:12). The Mesopotamian Gilgamesh Epic also refers to the strength of a three-strand woven cord.

Better is a poor but wise youth than an old but foolish king (4:13). Interpreters have suggested some possible historical rulers that may be alluded to here (e.g., the pharaoh and Joseph, Saul and David, Nebuchadnezzar and Daniel, or, assuming a late compositional date, various Hellenistic rulers such as Ptolemy IV and Ptolemy V in the third century BC), but it is unclear whether the Teacher has any specific king in mind. None of the suggested pairs adequately fit the details of 4:13–16.

Three-stranded rope from ancient Egypt (ca. 1550–1295 BC).

Warnings against Wrong Attitudes toward God and Government (5:1–9)

When you make a vow to God (5:4). Ecclesiastes 5:4–6 takes up the specific wording of the Mosaic legislation regarding the making of vows (Deut. 23:21–23), warning against seeking to impress God by making insincere pledges. Throughout the ancient Near East proper ritual performance was essential if the gods were going to look with favor on a king or nation, but, unlike in the OT, people realized the difficulty in actually discerning the desires of the gods, as one Babylonian sage quipped: "Even if one tries to apprehend divine intention, people cannot understand it."[10]

The king is served by the field (5:9). Ecclesiastes 5:7–8 are among the most difficult verses in the book to interpret. Does the king exploit the field, as claimed in the Egyptian "Prophecies of Neferti" ("The land diminishes but its rulers are numerous"),[11] or is stable government essential if agriculture is to thrive ("After all, a king who cultivates the field is an advantage to the land"), as implied by the NASB (cf. ESV)?

Wealth (5:10–6:9)

I have seen . . . I have seen . . . I have observed (5:13, 18; 6:1). Three scenarios regarding possessions are given in this section. Proverbs shares the Teacher's perspective that poverty can have diverse causes: oppression (5:8), laziness (4:5), unwise investments (5:14), or a widespread "disaster" (11:2). "The Maxims of Ptahhotep," an ancient Egyptian document of practical wisdom, also acknowledges that wealth comes from God ("If you engage in agriculture and [your] field prospers, and God causes it to increase under your hand"), and that wealth is not always beneficial to its owner ("For wealth brings no advantage when it is a burden").[12]

As he came from his mother's womb, so he will go again, naked as he came (5:15). The statement is nearly identical to Job 1:21.

A stillborn child is better off (6:3). This negative comparison relates to the person who "has it all" but lacks the God-given ability to derive pleasure from it (v. 2). At low points in their lives, both Jeremiah (Jer. 20:18) and Job (Job 3:10) also expressed the wish that they had never been born.

Positive Attitudes in the Light of Injustice and Uncertainty (6:10–10:20)

Whatever exists (6:10). In the Hebrew text rabbinic copyists marked this verse as the middle of the book, and verses 10–12 offer a provisional summary of what the Teacher has learned (and shared) thus far.

Bad Days Can Bring About Good (7:1–14)

A good name is better than fine perfume (7:1). Though clearly affirming the superiority of character to wealth (as in Prov. 22:1; cf. Song 1:3), this statement's linkage to verses 1b–4 suggests that it is one's reputation at death that is being contrasted here with the aromatic oil used to prepare a corpse for burial.

It is better to listen to rebuke from a wise person (7:5). This accords with the perspective of Prov. 13:1; 17:10.

A bribe corrupts the mind (7:7). This is especially true of government officials: "He will be partial toward him who is generous to him and biased toward the one who pays him."[13]

Who can straighten out what he has made crooked? (7:13). Here the Teacher takes up the proverb from 1:15 and ascribes this "twisting" action—that is, "the day of adversity" (7:14)—to God. The ancient Near East was a "god-saturated" realm in which nearly every bad thing that happened was attributed to divine action, whether deserved punishment or seemingly arbitrarily. This is the basis for Job's advisor-friends' (wrongly) attributing his suffering to his alleged wicked deeds.

Righteousness and Wisdom Offer Only Limited Protection (7:15–29)

Don't be excessively righteous, and don't be overly wise (7:16). Interpreters often see here the influence of the emphasis on moderation (the "golden mean" of avoiding extremes) in Greek philosophy, especially by Theognis and Aristotle. However, it would be out of character for the Teacher to advocate any wicked or foolish action, as if an individual would avoid negative consequences merely by remaining "moderate."

Ten rulers of a city (7:19). Interpreters have seen a reference here to the "ten principal men" who governed some Hellenistic cities, including Tiberias.[14] This would require a rather late date for the book. Furthermore, the Hebrew word used here (*shallit*) is also applied to Joseph in Gen. 42:6 and does not necessarily refer to a political office; the number ten may be a hyperbolic round number.

The woman who is a trap (7:26). The servant in "The Dialogue of Pessimism" gives a similarly negative description of women: "A woman is a pitfall . . . a hole, a ditch,"[15] but it is unlikely that 7:26 is intended as a general characterization of women (cf. Prov. 7:21–23).

One Should Submit to the Government Despite Injustice (8:1–17)

Keep the king's command . . . since he will do whatever he wants (8:2–3). The criticism of the king or governing officials in this chapter and elsewhere (3:16; 4:13; 5:8; 10:5–7, 16) has been cited as a reason to deny Solomonic authorship for the book, but no specific ruler, nation, or historical period is clearly described here. Warnings against rebellion are common in ancient Near Eastern texts: "When a royal command is given you, it is a burning fire. Execute it at once, lest it flare up against you."[16]

Although a sinner does evil a hundred times and prolongs his life (8:12). The common expectation in the ancient Near East, including the OT, is that wickedness will be punished and upright behavior rewarded during one's lifetime. The Teacher focuses repeatedly on the exceptions to this principle, which is expressed in an Aramaic grave inscription: "Because of my righteousness in his presence, he [Sahar, the Aramean moon god] gave me a good name and prolonged my days."[17]

In Light of Death, One Should Redeem the Time (9:1–12)

There is one fate for the righteous and the wicked (9:2). That shared "fate" is death, the great equalizer (see comments on 2:14).

The dead don't know anything (9:5). This text should not be understood as a denial of the afterlife (see 12:7), in contrast to other OT texts that affirm it (e.g., Dan. 12:1–2; also Ps. 73:24; Isa. 26:19). The belief in some form of postmortem existence was widespread in the ancient Near East (e.g., it was the reason for mummifying deceased pharaohs). Rather, in a manner similar to Ps. 6:5; 115:17, the Teacher here is contrasting the activities that individuals "under the sun" can engage in with their cessation after death.

Let your clothes be white all the time, and never let oil be lacking on your head. Enjoy life with the wife you love (9:8–9). Because they are so easily soiled, white garments were worn only on festive occasions. Since life is short and uncertain, the Teacher, like "The Song of the Harper" ("Put myrrh on your head, dress yourself in fine linen"),[18] calls for a celebratory mood. Gilgamesh is also reminded of the inevitability of death and then told, "Make thou merry by day and by night . . . Let thy garments be sparkling fresh [i.e., white] . . . Let the spouse delight in thy bosom!"[19]

One Should Embrace Wisdom and Avoid Folly (9:13–10:20)

And built large siege works against it (9:14). The reference here is to movable assault towers, such as those used by the Assyrians to breach the walls of fortified cities (cf. Deut. 20:20; Isa. 29:3). The didactic story in 9:14–15 probably has no specific individuals in mind but is intended rather to teach a lesson (9:16), similar to Jesus's parables.

I have seen slaves on horses, but princes walking on the ground like slaves (10:7). The kind of societal chaos caused by incompetent rulers is described in "The Prophecies of Neferti" as a "land in turmoil" where there are now "lowly men in exalted positions," while the "noble woman (will toil) in order to subsist."[20] A similar thought is expressed in Prov. 19:10.

The one who digs a pit may fall into it (10:8). This popular saying occurs in variant forms in Ps. 7:15; 9:15; 35:7–8; 57:6; Prov. 26:27.

Final Encouragement to Be Bold, Joyful, and Reverent (11:1–12:7)

Send your bread on the surface of the water . . . for you don't know what disaster may happen on earth (11:1–2). It is unclear whether the proverb in 11:1 is commending acts of charity or wise investments, but a saying in "The Instructions of 'Onchsheshonqy" ("Do a good deed and throw it into the flood. When it subsides you will find it")[21] supports the first option. So does the following verse (11:2), which has a parallel in "The Maxims of Ptahhotep": "Gratify your friends with what has come into your possession. . . . No one knows what will come to pass when he considers tomorrow."[22]

Let your heart be glad . . . remove sorrow from your heart (11:9–10). The brevity of youth and of life itself is a motivation to enjoy it while one can, a sentiment found also in several Egyptian texts: "So rejoice your heart! Absence of care is good for you; follow your heart as long as you live."[23]

Before the sun and the light are darkened, and the moon and the stars, and the clouds return after the rain (12:2). A backdrop of prophetic "end times" imagery, as found in Isa. 34:4; Joel 2:10, 31; Mark 13:24–25, has been suggested for this verse. However, the "darkness" and "clouds" language here is anticipated in 11:3–4, 8.

The ones who watch through the windows see dimly (12:3). Most interpreters see in 12:3–5(6) a partly literal and partly allegorical description of the debilitating aging process, a universal problem also described by Ptahhotep: "Old age has arrived . . . the eyes are blurred, the ears are deaf, and vigor wanes."[24]

Concluding Remarks (12:8–14)

He weighed, explored, and arranged many proverbs (12:9). A similar editorial process is set forth in the opening lines of an Egyptian text: "The collection of words, the gathering of maxims, the quest of phrases."[25]

Fear God and keep his commands (12:13). The Teacher's closing admonition occurs repeatedly in Deuteronomy (see Deut. 6:2; 8:6; 13:4; 17:19).

Song of Songs

Gordon H. Johnston

Introduction. Few biblical books present modern readers with more interpretive challenges than Song of Songs (Song of Solomon). While some interpreters still follow allegorical and typological approaches, most scholars today view Song of Songs as celebrating romantic love between a man and woman as one of God's greatest gifts to humanity (cf. Gen. 2:21–25). As its title and poetic features suggest, this book reflects a unified collection of ancient Hebrew love lyrics. Indeed, many interpretive enigmas can be resolved when Song of Songs is read against the background of ancient Israelite culture and ancient Near Eastern love poetry.

Cycle #1 of Love Poems (1:1–2:7)

Your caresses are more delightful than wine (1:2). Ancient love poetry often compared the delight of romantic love to the intoxicating effect of wine. For example, in an Egyptian love song a maiden tells her beloved, "Your love is desirable . . . like dates mixed in beer," and he later replies, "I will kiss her, her lips are parted—I am happy without beer."[1] In a similar vein, the Hebrew sage advises his son to be intoxicated with the love of his wife (Prov. 5:19–20).

Tents of Kedar (1:5). The tent-dwelling nomads of Kedar were well known in the OT (Ps. 120:5) and are mentioned in other ancient Near Eastern texts as well. The maiden compares her swarthy complexion to the rustic tents of Bedouin tribes residing in the northern Arabian Desert southeast of Israel. Woven from the wool of black goats, these rugged tents were well suited for the sun-scorched desert.

Tell me . . . where do you pasture your sheep (1:7–8). In ancient Near Eastern literature the shepherd was archetypal of the ideal lover. Sumerian poems celebrating the wedding of king Amaushumgalanna metaphorically portray him as a shepherd and depict the bridal chamber as the location of a romantic rendezvous in the countryside. Since sheep grazed in a variety of unpredictable locations, finding the whereabouts of a shepherd often was a challenge. Thus the maiden in a Sumerian courtship poem muses, "Oh that I might know the way to my bridegroom's sheepfold!" The love poem in 1:7–8 reflects a similar sentiment: the maiden expresses her desire for a romantic rendezvous with her beloved, querying where she might find him.

A mare among Pharaoh's chariots (1:9). Ancient love lyrics often compared beautiful women to sleek mares and male suitors to excited stallions. Or perhaps 1:9 echoes a famous incident from about 1450 BC during the siege of Kadesh by Pharaoh Thutmose III. As Egyptian chariots rushed to battle, the prince of Kadesh released a mare in heat, creating frenzy and chaos among the pharaoh's stallions. However, since 1:10 describes her adorned cheeks and neck, it is also possible that 1:9–10 is evoking the common image of Egyptian chariot horses decorated with exquisite ceremonial harnesses and trappings, perhaps best illustrated by the renowned chariot horses of the Egyptian pharaoh Tutankhamun.

While the king is on his couch (1:12). In the social structure of the ancient world the image of a king reclining on his royal banquet couch epitomized the ideal aristocrat. There are numerous examples in ancient art that depict banquet scenes of kings eating or drinking while reclining on their banquet couches, often accompanied by a reclining woman (queen or consort). Banquet scenes highlighted the themes of royal prestige and pleasure—the epitome of the good life.

I am a wildflower of Sharon (2:1). Often translated as "rose," this refers to the meadow saffron, a wildflower indigenous to Sharon, a region encompassing the northern half of ancient Israel's coastal plain. Comparison of a maiden's beauty to flowers was a conventional theme in ancient love poetry.

Banquet hall (2:4). The maiden metaphorically depicts the bridal chamber where she and her groom consummated their love as a banquet hall (literally a "house of wine" [cf. Esther 7:8]). In the ancient Near East royalty celebrated both betrothal and marriage with lavish banquets. Ancient palaces often included banquet halls. Palace wall reliefs from Assyria feature banquet scenes depicting the king and queen drinking wine and eating fruit.

Cycle #2 of Love Poems
(2:8–3:5)

On the divided mountains (2:17). As parallel verses suggest (4:6; 8:14), this geographical reference is a metaphor for the maiden's breasts. The Hebrew may also be translated as "the Bether mountains" (CSB footnote). Bether (from the related verb *batar*, meaning "to cut in two pieces") was an ancient village located about seven miles southwest of Jerusalem on a mountain spur rising above the Sorek Valley. The plural expression refers not to twin peaks, but rather two rounded parts of the southern face of the hill. The poet compares these two round mounds to the maiden's beautiful figure—a subtle but visually appropriate metaphor. The parallel verses compare her breasts to perfumed hills (4:6; 8:14).

Egyptian servants carrying a palanquin that holds the pharaoh.

Cycle #3 of Love Poems (3:6–5:1)

Solomon's bed (3:7). This probably is not a fixed bed, but rather a portable royal throne (NIV: "carriage"). It was the central item of the royal litter, often used by kings when traveling great distances. Several examples of portable thrones have been found in ancient Egypt (about 2600–1050 BC). It is not clear whether the portable throne in 3:7 and the palanquin (i.e., a "carried litter") in 3:9 refer to two separate vehicles (one for the king, one for his bride) or if they are parts of the same mobile structure. In Egyptian texts, for example, the two terms often were interchangeable—the former for the portable throne, the latter for the whole.

Carriage (3:9). This refers to a palanquin, or royal litter, usually consisting of a throne fixed on a platform covered by a canopy that porters transported by lifting its poles on their shoulders. Used almost exclusively in Egypt, the appearance of a palanquin here may hint that it was imported from Egypt and transported the daughter of the pharaoh to Jerusalem as Solomon's royal bride (1 Kings 3:1; 9:16). Reserved almost exclusively for royalty during this period, the palanquin displayed the wealth and status of the king, who was effectively elevated and made more visible. The art and literature of

Egypt feature dozens of examples of palanquins. The frames of Egyptian palanquins often were made from cedar of Lebanon, covered with gold foil, and inlaid with costly stones (cf. 3:9–10). In Egyptian art the number of porters carrying palanquins varies from four to twenty-four. Thus the sixty warriors surrounding the palanquin in 3:7 is striking by comparison. Most likely, 3:6–11 pictures a royal entourage transporting the king and his royal bride to Jerusalem for a royal wedding.

How beautiful you are . . . eyes . . . hair . . . teeth . . . absolutely beautiful (4:1–7). Ancient love lyrics often featured poetic praise of a maiden's beauty vis-à-vis metaphoric comparison of parts of her body to objects in the natural world. Striking examples appear in ancient Sumerian, Akkadian, Assyrian, Ugaritic, and Egyptian love poetry. Similarly, the groom's lyrical anatomical praise of the maiden played a central role in traditional Syrian wedding festivities. As the wedding party watched, the bride performed a dance while the groom praised her beauty from head to foot using color metaphors—the more creative and amusing the better. This conventional form of love lyric appears in Song of Songs in contexts reminiscent of these ancient backgrounds (4:1–7; 5:10–16; 6:4–7; 7:1–7).

My sister, my bride (4:9, 10, 12; 5:1). While ancient Near Eastern kings occasionally married half-sisters, sibling marriage (consanguinity) was prohibited in Israel (Lev. 18:9). As 8:1 makes clear, the maiden in Song of Songs is not her beloved's sibling. In the ancient Near East the epithets "my sister" and "my brother" often were used as terms of endearment for wife and husband. This motif occurs frequently in ancient Near Eastern love poetry, where male and female suitors often refer to each other as "my sister" and "my brother." In Egyptian love poetry the sister/brother motif occurs in courtship contexts, but in Sumerian love poetry it occurs in courtship as well as nuptial contexts. In several Sumerian poems, for example, the groom tenderly addresses his bride as "my sister" in the context of the bridal chamber. So the expression "my sister, my bride" in Song of Songs likely echoes this ancient poetic convention of tender affection.

You are a locked garden (4:12–5:1). The bride's gift of herself to the groom is conveyed through the metaphor of the royal garden. Kings frequently built royal gardens as a source of pleasure and a display of their wealth (e.g., 1 Kings 21:1; 2 Kings 21:18, 26; 25:4; Neh. 3:15; Esther 1:5; 7:7; Eccles. 2:5). Literary and material artifacts of the ancient Near East reveal numerous examples of royal gardens in ancient Egypt, Ugarit (an ancient city in Syria), Assyria, Persia, and Israel. Enclosed in the palace to ensure its privacy and inviolability, this ideal landscape was the exclusive domain of the king. Watered by artificial means (pools, aqueducts, reservoirs), the royal pleasure garden featured exotic trees, lush plants, and imported flowers. An iconic image of splendor, the royal garden functions as a romantic metaphor in 4:12–5:1. The natural beauty of the garden expresses the physical beauty of the bride; the sensory pleasure of the garden mirrors the pleasure that the couple finds in their mutual love. The lush imagery speaks of the delight that the bride and groom find in each other; the enclosed nature of the garden reflects the privacy, intimacy, and security that they feel in their love; the walled garden also functions as a symbol of the bride's chastity.

Cycle #4 of Love Poems (5:2–6:3)

The opening (5:4). In the ancient Near East the palace women (including the king's main wife) resided in separate quarters, typically located deep within the royal complex. The women's quarters featured a series of locked doors to keep women in and men out. Castrated guards stood sentry outside the locked doors barring other males from entering the area. The right of unbridled access to the women's quarters belonged to the king alone. The image of the maiden's locked door was also a recurrent theme in ancient Near Eastern love poetry. In Egyptian love poetry, for example, the symbol conveyed the virgin's inaccessibility; the locked door of her bedroom thwarted the advances of the eager young male. Some poems personified her anatomy as a bolted door that she alone had the right to unlock. Likewise, in an Assyrian love poem that shares common themes with 5:3–6 the bride retires to the bridal chamber, locking the door and bolting the latch before bathing and climbing into bed to await her groom's arrival.

Flowing myrrh on the handles of the bolt (5:5). In the biblical world the door latches of palaces, temples, and city gates often were anointed with fragrant oils to celebrate the initial opening of the entrance. For example, filling a temple with fragrant odors apparently was meant to attract the god to it. Filling a room with fragrance was intended to enhance its ambiance, impart a contagious sanctity, and create an inviting entrance for the guest. For example, an Akkadian temple dedication text reads, "I lavish your temple with riches, I cause your door bolt to drip oil."[2] The Babylonian king Nabonidus described the dedication of the Ebabbar temple thus: "I drenched with perfumed oil the door posts, locks, bolts, and door leaves; I made the contents of the temple full of sweet fragrance for the entry of their exalted divinity."[3]

The guards who go about the city found me. They beat and wounded me (5:7). The watchmen mistakenly identify the maiden—searching in the city late at night for her beloved—as a sexually promiscuous woman, and they punish her as a harlot. Many ancient Near Eastern societies sanctioned physical violence against sexually promiscuous women. For example, Middle

Assyrian laws required that any prostitute wearing a veil in public be seized, brought to the palace, disrobed, and beaten.

Cycle #5 of Love Poems (6:4–7:11)

Sixty queens and eighty concubines (6:8–9). While ancient Israelite society tolerated polygamy, possession of a harem was a luxury few could afford; thus it normally was the privilege of kings. Ancient culture viewed a large harem as indicative of royal power and international prestige. The ancient Near Eastern ruler typically possessed (1) a primary wife of elite status or noble lineage to cement his political position, (2) secondary wives to ensure reproductive success, (3) foreign wives to secure international alliances, and (4) concubines for personal pleasure. Mirroring ancient custom, Hebrew kings often had multiple wives and concubines. While Solomon's seven hundred wives and three hundred concubines may seem extreme, historians from the Hellenistic period report that Artaxerxes II and Darius III each had 360 concubines—one for each day of the Persian calendar. Thus the sixty queens and eighty concubines (poetic approximations) in 6:8 seem modest by comparison. If this indeed pictures Solomon's entourage, it reflects his early years—after inheriting David's harem but before falling into unbridled polygamy. Moses warned against this kind of royal excess (Deut. 17:14–17), and Solomon's seven hundred wives eventually turned his heart away from God (1 Kings 11:1–7).

But my dove . . . is unique (6:9). In the world of ancient Near Eastern royalty love was rarely the initial basis for marriage. Most often, royal marriages were arranged for political advantage. Nonetheless, there were some exceptions, kings who seemed to marry for love. For example, the Hittite prince Hattusili was smitten by Puduhepa the first time he set eyes upon her. Moreover, possession of a harem did not prevent a king from being smitten with his primary wife. While the Egyptian pharaoh Ramesses II had six minor wives and two hundred concubines, his love poetry extolled Nefertari (the bride of his youth and chief royal wife) above all others, declaring, "For the one whose love shines: My love is unique—no one can rival her for she is the most beautiful woman in the world. Just by passing, she has stolen away my heart."[4] Although King Rehoboam had seventeen secondary wives and sixty concubines, he loved his main wife, Maacah, more than all others (2 Chron. 11:18–21). Solomon had numerous wives (1 Kings 11:1, 3), yet his primary wife was the celebrated daughter of the pharaoh, whom he honored more than all others (1 Kings 3:1; 7:8; 9:24). She likely was the royal bride whose procession into Jerusalem is lauded in 3:6–11, the dark-skinned foreign maiden speaking in 1:5–6, and the daughter of noble

The Egyptian queen Nefertari, the chief royal wife of Pharaoh Ramesses II and the bride of his youth.

birth praised in 7:1. Metaphoric comparison of her to a mare among the pharaoh's chariots (1:9) perhaps also suggests an Egyptian background of this image as well as an Egyptian origin of this woman.

A tower of ivory (7:4). Comparison of the maiden's neck to an ivory tower betokened its shapely form, pinkish hue, and elegant stature. Ancient artists often represented women in ivory relief due to the beauty of its color and warmth of its texture. Archaeologists have found ivory workshops and collections of ivory carvings in aristocratic and royal settings in Egypt, Phoenicia, and Assyria, as well as Israel. Ivory artifacts include artwork (statuettes, plaques), implements (decorative spoons and combs, fan and mirror handles, cosmetic boxes), royal objects (decorative daggers and knives, scarabs and seals, game boards and gaming pieces), inlaid furniture (thrones, chairs, beds), and inlaid wall panels (palaces, temples). Since ivory was harvested from elephant tusks, a real full-sized city tower could hardly have been built of ivory. Thus this reference probably is a figure of speech.

Pools in Heshbon (7:4). The ancient city Heshbon was situated on the King's Highway, located upon one of the summits of the mountains of Moab, approximately twenty miles east of the Jordan River and twelve miles

The Egyptian pharoah Tutankhamun in a royal garden with his queen, who wears a perfume cone on her head and is offering him two bouquets of special plants. The imagery depicted here is similar to that decribed in Song of Songs.

southwest of Amman. Excavations at the site (Tell Hesban) uncovered a massive open-air water reservoir on the southern slope of the acropolis, which excavators identify as the "pools of Heshbon." The reservoir was fed by runoff rainwater funneled through several channels cut into the adjoining bedrock on its eastern side. Measuring 57 feet long, 57 feet wide, and 23 feet deep with a capacity of 566,385 gallons, it was likely the largest reservoir of its day. Construction of the reservoir dates to the time of Solomon, but it continued in use for four centuries. When Heshbon was destroyed (sixth century BC), the reservoir was buried under a layer of ash; when the city was rebuilt centuries later, debris from the abandoned town was scraped into the reservoir (second century BC). The vividness of the metaphor in 7:4 suggests that the "pools of Heshbon" were still in existence when Song of Songs was composed.

Cycle #6 of Love Poems (7:12–8:4)

Mandrakes (7:13). A perennial herbaceous plant, the low-growing mandrake features fragrant rosette-shaped leaves surrounding a crown of purple flowers atop large fork-shaped taproots. The species indigenous to ancient Israel thrived in light woodlands, where it budded in early autumn and flowered in early spring. The roots contain alkaloids that, when indigested, produce pain relief, sexual excitement, and hallucinations. In the ancient Near East it was used as both an anesthetic and an aphrodisiac. Popular tradition deemed it capable of promoting conception. Nevertheless, in 7:13 the maiden highlights not the legendary effect of consuming mandrakes, but rather their alluring fragrance.

Cycle #7 of Love Poems (8:5–14)

Set me as a seal (8:6). Cylinder seals were made of semiprecious stones on which were engraved unique designs and inscriptions that could be rolled across clay surfaces to leave imprints identifying objects as the property of the seal's owner. Since it was so valuable, wise owners kept it very close.

The typical cylinder seal was one inch long with a hole running lengthwise through its center, worn on a necklace around the neck or on a bracelet around the wrist. Thus the maiden's poetic request is twofold: to be kept close to his heart in a committed relationship that would never be lost, and to be the one woman whose name, so to speak, was indelibly engraved upon his heart.

An almighty flame . . . a huge torrent (8:6–7). In the ancient world the powers of chaos often were pictured as the threatening force of pounding waves of the chaotic sea. This recurrent theme is evident in the image of "many waters" (Ps. 18:16; 144:7; Isa. 17:13; Jer. 51:55; Ezek. 31:15). While water quenches fire, true love is like a mighty flame that cannot be quenched by life's calamities and challenges.

Isaiah

GARY V. SMITH

Introduction. Isaiah prophesied in the southern nation of Judah from around 750 to 685 BC. Isaiah began proclaiming God's message during the reign of Uzziah (and Jotham) around 750–740 BC (chaps. 2–5). Second Chronicles 26:1–27:9 reports that Uzziah was a very powerful yet prideful king. Ignoring the opposition of eighty priests, he insisted on entering into the temple and burning incense himself, a function that only priests were allowed to perform. Consequently, God struck Uzziah with leprosy, so he could no longer rule as king. His son Jotham, a righteous king, replaced him and ruled for the next few years (2 Chron. 27:1–9).

Isaiah 6–12 describes events that occurred during the reign of the wicked king Ahaz (2 Kings 16; 2 Chron. 28), king of Judah, but a worshiper of Baal (on Ahaz, see comments on 2 Kings 16:1). Isaiah challenged Ahaz to trust God when Judah was attacked by a military coalition from Syria and Israel (the Syro-Ephraimite War), but instead Ahaz turned to the Assyrians to deliver him (see the section on the Neo-Assyrian period in the article "The Assyrians").

In Isaiah most of the oracles against the foreign nations (chaps. 13–23), the woe oracles (chaps. 28–33), and the surrounding chapters (plus chap. 1) come from the period when the righteous king Hezekiah (2 Kings 18–20; 2 Chron. 29–32) was under attack by the large Assyrian army led by King Sennacherib (chaps. 36–39) (on Hezekiah, see comments on 2 Kings 18:1). Isaiah challenged Hezekiah to trust in God rather than in alliances with other nations. Hezekiah listened to Isaiah and prayed for God to deliver Jerusalem from the Assyrians. In response, God destroyed the Assyrian army (37:36) (see the section on the Neo-Assyrian period in the article "The Assyrians").

There are few historical markers in chapters 40–66, so the historical setting is debatable. There are three major views. Many critical commentators think these messages come from the disciples of Isaiah during the exilic period (chaps. 40–55) and the postexilic period (chaps. 56–66). Many traditional scholars, however, believe that Isaiah himself was writing to future generations that would live in the exilic and postexilic eras. The third view maintains that the references to war and to the defeat of an enemy (41:10–14; 42:22–25) refer to Judah's conflict with the Assyrian king Sennacherib described in chapters 36–37, so they believe that in chapters 40–66 Isaiah was encouraging people in Judah to trust God during the Assyrian conflict.[1]

God Threatens to Take Judah to Court (1:1–31)

Uzziah, Jotham, Ahaz, and Hezekiah (1:1). Details about each king are provided in the introduction above. The defeat in war (1:5–9) indicates that chapter 1 is from the time of Hezekiah.

Heavens . . . earth (1:2). The creation witnessed the sinfulness of the people of Judah, as it witnessed Cain's sin (Gen. 4:10) and Israel's promise to keep the covenant with God (Deut. 4:26; 30:19).

The whole head is hurt (1:5). The metaphor of an injured soldier describes how the nation severely suffered when the Assyrian king Sennacherib conquered all of Judah except Jerusalem.

Soothed with oil (1:6). In the ancient Near East oils were poured on cleansed wounds to aid healing and to keep the wounds from drying out.

Foreigners devour your fields (1:7). The foreigners mentioned here are from the Assyrian army. When armies invaded a nation, they typically fed their soldiers and horses from the crops of the local people.

Palace wall panel depicting rows of Assyrian archers and shield bearers at the siege of the Judahite city of Lachish.

Like a shelter in a vineyard (1:8). At harvest time workers often built temporary shelters in their fields so they could protect their harvest from thieves.

Your incense is detestable to me (1:13). Incense was made of ground fragrant spices (gum resin, onycha, and galbanum) and frankincense. It was burned inside the temple on a daily basis (see comments on Exod. 30:1–10, 34–38). The word translated as "detestable" (sometimes as "abomination") often refers to pagan practices (cf. 2 Kings 21:2, 11).

An ancient incense altar.

New Moons and prescribed festivals (1:14). The beginning of every lunar month was marked by special offerings and feasting (see comments on Num. 28:17) to dedicate the activities of the month to God.

Plead the widow's cause (1:17). In the ancient Near East many men died in war, and when vulnerable widows went into debt, dishonest creditors sometimes cheated them out of their land by bribing judges.

Your silver has become dross (1:22). The smelting process required the heating of rocks to about nine hundred degrees Fahrenheit to separate the waste (dross). The purpose of smelting would be defeated if dross was added to the pure silver.

The sacred trees . . . the garden shrines (1:29). Lush gardens and sacred groves of trees often were the sacred places of the Canaanite fertility cult (57:5; 65:3; 66:17; Ezek. 6:13). Some trees were carved into the image of the goddess Asherah (2 Chron. 15:16).

Exalt God, for He Will Humble the Proud (2:1–22)

The mountain of the Lord's house (2:2). This was Mount Zion, in Jerusalem.

They will beat their swords into plows (2:4). Iron was quite rare and very expensive. Most peasants could not afford iron plow points. If a peasant soldier was fortunate enough to capture an iron sword and bring it back to the farm, he could rework it into a point (blade) for a plow, increasing the efficiency and durability of his tool.

Divination from the East . . . fortune-tellers like the Philistines (2:6). See the article "The Philistines." Sorcery or divination in the ancient Near East often was practiced by examining the organs of animals, observing the movement of stars and planets, studying the direction of rising smoke or patterns of oil on water, or speaking with the dead. Deuteronomy 18:10–11 forbids all pagan sorcery and divination.

Full of horses . . . no limit to their chariots (2:7). Uzziah had a very strong army (2 Chron. 26:11–14).

Cedars of Lebanon . . . oaks of Bashan (2:13–16). Bashan was the fertile land north and east of the Sea of Galilee. Lebanon was north of Galilee and was known for its tall cedar trees.

People will throw their silver and gold idols . . . to the moles and bats (2:20). Moles and bats were unclean animals.

Judgment on Jerusalem (3:1–4:1)

Remove from Jerusalem and Judah every kind of security (3:1). A military siege would blockade the city and prevent any supplies of water, grain, and meat from entering the city.

Heroes and warriors, judges and prophets (3:2). Through death and deportations the support of military, civil, political, religious, and economic leaders will disappear.

I will make youths their leaders (3:4). In the ancient Near East older men were honored as wise leaders, but after defeat in war, social order often degenerated into chaos. Having immature children (or childlike adults) ruling compounded the instability.

You have a cloak—you be our leader! (3:6). A cloak signified status or role (for a king or priest), but leadership involved more than just nice-looking clothing.

The Lord will shave their foreheads bare (3:17). Beautiful hair was a status symbol of wealthy women. Baldness was a sign of a slave.

Ankle bracelets, headbands, crescents . . . linen clothes, turbans, and shawls (3:18–23). Wall paintings and archaeological discoveries in graves from the ancient Near East indicate that wealthy upper-class women often owned a wide range of beautiful clothes and jewelry (see the article "Women's Fashion in the Old Testament World").

Seven women will seize one man, saying, . . . "Take away our disgrace" (4:1). Many husbands will die in this war (3:25), so the widows will forgo the normal expectation of a husband (providing food and clothing [cf. Exod. 21:10]) and will share a husband with six other women in order to survive and to restore their status of being married.

The Transformation of Zion (4:2–6)

The Branch of the Lord (4:2). A "branch, sprout" can refer to plant life (Gen. 41:6, 23; Ezek. 17:6), but here it figuratively refers to a ruler who will "sprout, go forth" from David (Ps. 132:17). A Phoenician document from

Cyprus uses this term to refer to an heir to the throne. The "Branch of the LORD" is the Messiah (cf. Jer. 23:5; 33:15; Zech. 3:8; 6:12).

A cloud of smoke by day and a glowing flame of fire by night (4:5). The cloud and fire signified the presence of God's glory with the Israelites in the wilderness (Exod. 13:21–22; 14:24).

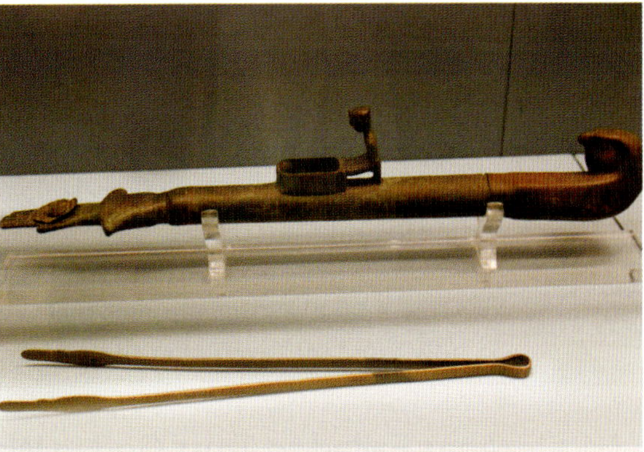

An ancient set of bronze tongs and an incense shovel ("In his hand was a glowing coal that he had taken from the altar with tongs" [Isa. 6:6]).

Judah Will Be Destroyed (5:1–30)

He broke up the soil, cleared it of stones (5:2). Israel's hills were rocky, so farmers often removed stones from their fields, using these stones to construct protective fences.

Woe to those who add house to house and join field to field (5:8). When the poor fell into debt, their wealthy creditors often cheated them and took their property (homes and fields). Apparently these landowners did not return this property in the Jubilee Year (Lev. 25).

Lyre, harp, tambourine, flute (5:12). See the article "Musical Instruments in Israel and the Ancient Near East."

Sheol enlarges its throat (5:14). The place of death (Sheol) is pictured here as a monster that swallows up many victims.

No belt is loose and no sandal strap broken (5:27). The approaching army is completely ready to fight, without even the smallest problem (a broken sandal strap) to interrupt its progress.

Their roaring is like a lion's (5:29–30). As the army charges into battle for hand-to-hand combat, the soldiers' yell resembles the roar of a lion or the crashing waves of the sea (5:30).

Light will be obscured by clouds (5:30). The burning of cities will darken the sky with clouds of smoke.

God Calls Isaiah to Serve in a New Setting (6:1–13)

In the year that King Uzziah died (6:1). On Uzziah, see the introduction above. Isaiah also prophesied during Uzziah's life (2:1–5:30), so this probably is not Isaiah's original call, but rather a new calling to prepare him for the sinful era of Ahaz.

Seraphim were standing above him; they each had six wings (6:2). Seraphim (literally, "burning ones") flew above the throne singing praise. Ezekiel describes similar beings (called cherubim) below the throne, providing locomotion (Ezek. 1; 10).

The holy seed is the stump (6:13). Life was considered to be in the stump of a tree, so the analogy implies that there would be some righteous people (a holy remnant) even after the nation was destroyed and exiled.

Ahaz Failed to Trust God in War (7:1–25)

Ahaz, son of Jotham (7:1). On Ahaz, see comments on 2 Kings 16:1.

Aram's King Rezin and Israel's King Pekah . . . went to fight against Jerusalem (7:1). On Rezin of Aram, see comments on 2 Kings 15:37; on Pekah of Israel, see comments on 2 Kings 15:27–31. Aram was the kingdom just to the north of Israel in what is now modern Syria. Some English translations render the term "Aram" as "Syria." Because Assyria threatened, Rezin, king of Aram, wanted to form a coalition with Israel (which joined) and Judah (which did not join) to stop Assyria's western advances. In 7:1 Aram and Israel tried to force Judah to join their coalition against Assyria (see the section on the Neo-Assyrian period in the article "The Assyrians").

Go . . . meet Ahaz at the end of the conduit of the upper pool (7:3). It was militarily wise to deny an enemy army easy access to water, so King Ahaz had his troops transfer water from a pool outside the north walls of Jerusalem to a pool inside the city.

Don't be afraid or cowardly because of these two smoldering sticks (7:4). Burning torches would be dangerous, but smoldering torches (representing King Rezin of Aram and King Pekah of Israel) about to go out were not a cause for concern.

A sign from the Lord your God—it can be as deep as Sheol or as high as heaven (7:10). Signs could be memorial (the rainbow in Gen. 9:12–13), symbolic (circumcision in Gen. 17), or given to produce faith (the burning bush in Exod. 3:12). Sheol referred to the underworld, the place of the dead.

Eating curds and honey (7:15). This phrase can refer to prosperity (Deut.

Throughout the ancient Near East winged composite seraphim/cherubim-like beings were common. This ivory piece from Samaria depicts a composite being with the body of a lion, the head of a man, and the wings of a bird.

32:13–14), but in the context of 7:22–23 it seems rather to refer to a time of scarcity and little agricultural production.

Before the boy knows . . . the land of the two kings you dread will be abandoned (7:16). This is the short time before the "boy" (probably Shear-jashub in 7:3, not the "child" in 7:14) is able to make moral judgments. The two kings are Rezin of Aram and Pekah of Israel (7:1).

The king of Assyria (7:17). The Assyrian king Tiglath-pileser III defeated Aram and Israel (2 Kings 16:9) and then attacked Ahaz (2 Chron. 28:20) (see the section on the Neo-Assyrian period in the article "The Assyrians").

To shave the hair on your heads (7:20). The Assyrians will treat the Israelites like prisoners, humiliating them by shaving their hair.

Fear God, Not Human Armies (8:1–22)

A large piece of parchment . . . Maher-shalal-hash-baz (8:1). This object is a large polished surface (not a scroll). The name means "swift to plunder, quick to spoil" and predicted disaster.

Rejected the slowly flowing waters of Shiloah and rejoiced with Rezin (8:6). God is symbolized as the waters of Shiloah (the Gihon Spring in the Kidron Valley). Rezin was the king of Aram who attacked Judah.

Mighty rushing water of the Euphrates . . . reaching up to the neck (8:7–8). The Assyrian army is pictured as a flood almost drowning the people in Judah with neck-deep water.

Seal up the instruction among my disciples (8:16). Written messages on scrolls in the ancient Near East often were sealed with a string and a clump of clay with a seal impression pressed into it.

Inquire of the mediums and spiritists (8:19). The consultation of pagan spiritual advisors who claimed to talk to the spirits of the dead was strictly forbidden (Deut. 18:9–11). On mediums and spiritists, see comments on 1 Sam. 28:3, 9.

The Eternal Reign of a Godly Davidic King (9:1–7)

He humbled the land of Zebulun (9:1). Zebulun and Naphtali, two of the twelve tribes of Israel, were located in northern Galilee. They were overrun (i.e., "humbled") by Assyria in 732 and 722 BC.

You have shattered their oppressive yoke . . . just as you did on the day of Midian (9:4). On Midian, see comments on Judg. 6:1; Exod. 2:15. Gideon and a small force of three hundred miraculously defeated Midian (Judg. 6–7) to remove its oppressive yoke on Judah.

This wall relief from the palace of the Assyrian king Ashurbanipal depicts the Assyrian assault on an Elamite city. Some of the Elamites have tried to escape by fleeing to the river and swimming away.

Wonderful Counselor, Mighty God, Eternal Father, Prince of Peace (9:6). Similar terms were used of kings in the ancient Near East who wanted to be known for their wisdom, power, military prowess, and ability to provide peace and stability. Egyptian pharaohs even claimed to be the son of a god (see comments on Exod. 5:2). The birth of a royal child in the ancient Near East was a highly significant event, and there are several instances of royal proclamations regarding royal births.

Proud Israel Will Be Judged (9:8–10:4)

The bricks have fallen, but we will rebuild (9:10). Falling bricks describe the destruction of the city walls of Samaria, the capital of Israel, destroyed by the Assyrians in 722 BC.

The Lord has raised up Rezin's adversaries . . . Aram . . . Philistia . . . have consumed Israel (9:11–12). The Assyrian king Tiglath-pileser III (745–727 BC) defeated and executed Rezin, king of Aram, in 734–732 BC (2 Kings 16:9) (see the section on the Neo-Assyrian period in the article "The Assyrians"). Philistia lay to the west of Israel (see the article "The Philistines").

Manasseh is with Ephraim . . . both are against Judah (9:21). Assassinations by fellow Israelites from neighboring tribes brought internal chaos in Israel, and the ten northern tribes went to war against Judah when Ahaz was king (2 Kings 15–16).

Proud Assyria Will Be Judged (10:5–34)

Assyria, the rod of my anger (10:5). A typical father might punish a disobedient son with a stick. God declares that he will discipline his sons by sending the Assyrian army (his rod) against them (10:6).

Isn't Calno like Carchemish? (10:9–11). The king of Assyria is depicted as speaking here. His human logic concluded that since he conquered the large fortified cites in the countries north of Israel, then he could also capture the capitals of Israel (Samaria) and Judah (Jerusalem).

I will punish the king of Assyria for his arrogant acts (10:12). The Assyrian king Sennacherib attacked Jerusalem and spoke with great pride (36:1–20; 37:23–29, 37), but an angel decimated his army by killing 185,000 Assyrian soldiers (37:36). On Sennacherib's siege of Jerusalem, see comments on 2 Kings 18:13; see the section on the Neo-Assyrian period in the article "The Assyrians."

Does an ax exalt itself above the one who chops with it? (10:15). An iron tool can do nothing by itself; it is the person using it who accomplishes something. This figure of speech (the iron ax) refers to Assyria.

Assyria has come to Aaith . . . Nob (10:28–32). The twelve cities referred to in these verses were fairly near and to the north of Jerusalem. This list of cities reflects the path of the invading Assyrian army coming to Jerusalem.

The Lord God of Armies will chop off the branches (10:33). The Assyrian army is compared to a great forest of tall trees, but one that God can cut down easily.

A Davidic King Will Reign and Gather the Nations (11:1–16)

A shoot will grow from the stump of Jesse (11:1). The imagery used here depicts the stump of a cut tree that appears to be dead, but out of which a new shoot grows, producing a new tree. Like Israel's stump (6:13), the stump of David's father, Jesse, will produce a branch (cf. 4:2), the Messiah of 9:6–7 (cf. Jer. 23:5–6). The imagery of a shoot in reference to descendants also occurs in literature of the ancient Near East.[2]

The wolf will dwell with the lamb (11:6). Sin's curse brought

An ancient ax.

violence among animals on the earth, so the end of sin will bring the ideal messianic period, without violence or fear. The dangerous carnivorous animals present throughout the ancient Near East also presented a constant threat to people, so similar portrayals of predators becoming harmless in future idyllic times also appear in the literature of Israel's neighbors.[3]

Assyria, Egypt . . . and islands (11:11). This list includes countries from north, south, east, and west of Israel, thus stressing people from everywhere. This includes Assyria to the north; Egypt, Pathros (a term also used for Egypt), and Cush (the region south of Egypt) to the south; Elam (the area east of Babylon) to the east; Shinar (an ancient name for Babylon) to the northeast; Hamath (in Syria) to the north; and the islands (probably Cyprus and Crete) to the west.

The Philistine flank . . . Edom and Moab, and the Ammonites (11:14). Philistia was in southwest Palestine along the Mediterranean Sea (see the article "The Philistines"), Edom was southeast of the Dead Sea, Moab was east of the Dead Sea, and Ammon was north of Moab.

The Lord will divide the Gulf of Suez . . . wave his hand over the Euphrates (11:15). The phrase translated as "Gulf of Suez" literally says "Sea of Egypt" and probably alludes back to the exodus parting of the Red Sea. The body of water that hindered travel from Egypt was the Red Sea, and from Babylon it was the Euphrates River.

A Song of Trust in God (12:1–6)

You will joyfully draw water from the springs of salvation (12:3). The joy produced by salvation will be like the joy of drawing cold water from a deep well on a hot day.

Ancient Egytians carrying banners/ standards.

God's Plan to Humble Proud Babylon and Assyria (13:1–14:27)

Lift up a banner . . . the LORD of Armies is mobilizing an army (13:2–4). The word translated as "banner" refers to the flag or standard that armies used in the ancient Near East for identification and organization. Warriors from many nations (13:4) and from heaven (13:5) will gather at the standard/banner/flag to prepare for war.

The sun will be dark when it rises, and the moon will not shine (13:10). The cosmic significance of the day of the Lord is affirmed in many eschatological prophecies (Isa. 13:13; 24:18–23; 34:1–4; Ezek. 32:6–8; Joel 2:10, 31; Matt. 24:29; Rev. 6:12–14). The imagery is that of dense smoke rising from burning cities and blocking out the light from the sun and the moon.

The Medes (13:17). The Medes lived in the region that is now northern Iran. They played an important role in the Persian Empire (see the article "The Persians"). The Persian king Cyrus will lead the Medes and Persians to defeat Babylon in 539 BC (Ezra 1; Dan. 5; the Cyrus Cylinder).[4]

Desert creatures will lie down there (13:21). War, destruction, and exile will leave the abandoned farmlands and dilapidated houses to the wild animals.

The cedars of Lebanon rejoice (14:8). Lebanon (the region north of Israel) was famous for its cedar trees. The trees will rejoice because a dead king cannot cut cedars for a new construction project.

The music of your harps (14:11). See the article "Musical Instruments in Israel and the Ancient Near East."

Shining morning star, how you have fallen from the heavens! (14:12). This text is referring to the Babylonian king's downfall. This was parallel to an ancient Near Eastern myth in which a minor god tried but failed to become the greatest god. The bright "morning star" refers to Venus, closely associated in mythology with the goddess Ishtar.

I will sit on the mount of the gods' assembly, in the remotest parts of the North (14:13). The word translated as "north" can also be understood as a mountain (Zaphon). In Canaanite mythology the god El ruled over the assembly of gods on Mount Zaphon, in the north (see the article "The Canaanites and Canaanite Religion").

But you are thrown out without a grave (14:19). Lavish royal tombs allowed the legacy of kings in the ancient Near East to last for years, but this king will be shamed by not having a royal burial tomb.

I will break Assyria in my land (14:25). This predicted what would happen in 701 BC when the Assyrian army came to Jerusalem, and an angel killed 185,000 Assyrian soldiers (37:36) (see the section on the Neo-Assyrian period in the article "The Assyrians").

God's Plans for Philistia (14:28–32)

The rod of the one who struck you is broken. For a viper will come from the root of a snake (14:29). The Philistines were struck by the rod of the Assyrian king Tiglath-pileser III (the snake), but a poisonous viper (the Assyrian king Sargon II) will bite them worse (see the section on the Neo-Assyrian period in the article "The Philistines").

A cloud of dust is coming from the north (14:31). The route and the location of an enemy army were revealed by the smoke from the cities that it burned.

God's Plans for Proud Moab (15:1–16:14)

A pronouncement concerning Moab: Ar . . . Kir in Moab is devastated (15:1). Moab was to the east of Israel, across the Dead Sea (see comments on Gen. 19:37–38). Ar and Kir were two of Moab's major cities.

Dibon went up to its temple to weep at its high places . . . every head is shaved (15:2–3). Dibon was one of the major cities of Moab. People in the ancient Near East would weep, shave their hair, and plead with their gods for help in times of war.

Whose fugitives flee as far as Zoar (15:5). Zoar probably is at the southern end of the Dead Sea. These refugees were fleeing to the southern border of Moab to escape the invading Assyrians.

The grass is withered, the foliage is gone (15:6). Survival is questionable, for those fleeing through the desert have no water to drink or food for their animals.

The Waters of Dibon are full of blood (15:9). Dibon was one of the major cities in Moab. The blood of injured soldiers has polluted its water.

Send lambs to the ruler of the land, from Sela in the desert (16:1). Sela (which means "rock") was the capital city of Edom, so these Moabites are south of Moab, probably fleeing from the invading Assyrians. The practice of sending tribute in submission to a more powerful nation to seek protection was common.

Raisin cakes (16:7). This delicacy, made of pressed dried grapes, was eaten at feasts (2 Sam. 6:19).

God's Plans for Damascus, Israel, and Cush (17:1–18:7)

The fortress disappears from Ephraim, and a kingdom from Damascus (17:3). As the largest tribe of Israel, the name of Ephraim often was used to represent Israel itself. Damascus was the capital of Aram. Both were defeated by the Assyrians in 734 BC, and Israel was finally exiled in 722 BC.

Only gleanings will be left in Israel, as if an olive tree had been beaten (17:6). To gather olives from an olive tree, harvesters struck the branches, causing the olives to fall. Usually a few unripe olives remained on the branches.

Asherahs and shrines (17:8). Canaanite places of worship frequently had wood poles carved to represent the goddess Asherah (see the article "The Canaanites and Canaanite Religion"; see comments on 1 Kings 15:13).

They roar like the roaring of the seas (17:12). When the Assyrian army charges into battle, the shouting troops sound like the roar of the sea.

Land of buzzing insect wings beyond the rivers of Cush (18:1). Cush was an African kingdom south of Egypt along the Nile in what is now the country of Sudan. They ruled over Egypt from 710 until 663 BC, when the Assyrians finally drove them out of Egypt (see the article "The Cushites"). The "rivers of Cush" refers perhaps to the Blue Nile and the White Nile, or perhaps to the cataracts on the Nile that delineated the northern boundaries of Cush. The tsetse fly or winged beetles thrived along the rivers of Africa.

A nation tall and smooth-skinned (18:2). The Cushites, an African people, were known for their unusual height. "Smooth-skinned" probably refers to the fact that they rarely had beards.

When a banner is raised . . . when a trumpet sounds (18:3). These acts signal that a war is coming.

God's Plans to Destroy and Restore Egypt (19:1–20:6)

The Lord rides on a swift cloud (19:1). This symbolized God's quick movement through the heavens to sovereignly control the earth and was a contrast to the idols, which could not move.

I will provoke Egyptians against Egyptians (19:2). Civil war broke out between Upper and Lower Egypt, lasting from around 720 to 710 BC, and ending with the Cushites ruling over Egypt (see the article "The Cushites").

I will hand over Egypt to harsh masters (19:4). In about 720 BC the Cushite king Piye invaded Egypt and established the Twenty-Fifth Dynasty of pharaohs ruling Egypt. His son Shabaka completed the consolidation of Egypt by around 710 BC. The Cushites ruled Egypt until 663 BC, when the Assyrians drove them out.

Princes of Zoan (19:11). Zoan was an Egyptian capital in the Nile Delta.

Princes of Memphis (19:13). Memphis, located south of the Nile Delta, was an ancient capital of Egypt.

Five cities in the land of Egypt will speak the language of Canaan . . . the City of the Sun (19:18). Speaking another nation's language would

King Sargon of Assyria.

indicate similar thinking and a relationship. Sun worship at the Egyptian city of Heliopolis ("city of the sun") will turn to worship of the God of Israel.

An altar to the Lord in the center of the land of Egypt and a pillar to the Lord (19:19). Altars imply worship while monuments on the border imply sovereign control of a territory.

A highway from Egypt to Assyria . . . Egypt will worship with Assyria (19:23). Egypt was to the south of Israel and Assyria was to the north. A highway symbolizes friendly relations that enable two former enemies to cooperate.

The chief commander, sent by King Sargon of Assyria, came to Ashdod and attacked and captured it (20:1). Ashdod, a Philistine city on the Mediterranean coast, was captured by the Assyrians in 711 BC (see the article "The Philistines"). This campaign is described in the annals of King Sargon.[5]

Take off your sackcloth and remove the sandals from your feet (20:2). When people lamented an approaching military disaster they wore sackcloth, but when the war was finally lost they became prisoners of war without clothes and sandals.

Those who made Cush their hope and Egypt their boast will be dismayed (20:5). Cush and Egypt were closely connected, with Cushite pharaohs ruling over Egypt at this time. Judah was allied with Cush/Egypt against Assyria, the common foe. Initially, Hezekiah trusted in help from Cush/Egypt (cf. 31:1–5a) for a defense against Assyria in 701 BC, but the Egyptians/Cushites were unable to rescue the Israelites from Assyria (37:9). See the articles "The Cushites" and "The Egyptians."

God's Plans to Defeat Babylon (21:1–10)

Desert by the sea (21:1). Assyrian sources refer to southern Babylon as the "sea land," and there are deserts on both sides of this marshy area.

Like storms that pass over the Negev (21:1). The Negev was the desert area to the south of Judah. The unstoppable power and destruction of Assyria are compared to a powerful dust storm in the desert.

I am too perplexed to hear (21:3). The news about the defeat of the powerful nation of Babylon was so bad that it astonished even the prophet Isaiah.

Rise up, you princes, and oil the shields! (21:5). Shields in the ancient Near East often were made of wood covered with leather, and apparently were oiled in preparation for going into battle (2 Sam. 1:21). In this verse a meal is suddenly interrupted by an urgent call to go fight in a battle.

Post a lookout (21:6). Reconnaissance horsemen would be stationed on high hills to observe the battle and report the outcome of the fight over Babylon.

Babylon has fallen . . . the images of her gods have been shattered (21:9). This conquest likely refers to the destruction of Babylon in 689 BC by the Assyrian king Sennacherib (cf. 46:1–47:15) (see the section on the Neo-Assyrian period in the article "The Assyrians").

God's Plans for Dumah (21:11–12)

Dumah (21:11). This was the name of a town at an oasis in the Arabian Desert in Edom. On Edom, see comments on Obad. 1.

Seir (21:11). This was another name for Edom and the mountain range south of the Dead Sea.

Watchman, what is left of the night? (21:11). Walled cities had night watchmen on the walls to warn of impending dangers. "Night" probably refers to a time of political darkness.

God's Plans for Arabia (21:13–17)

You caravans of Dedanites . . . the inhabitants of the land of Tema (21:13–14). The cities of Dedan and Tema were important towns in the northeastern part of the Arabian Desert.

Meet the refugees with food. For they have fled from swords (21:14–15). The refugees from war fled into the desert to escape the battle, but now they needed others to bring them water and food.

All the glory of Kedar will be gone (21:16). Kedar was a city north of Tema, in the Arabian Desert.

An inscripton on the lintel of an ancient tomb discovered in Jerusalem. Although the text with the name of the occupant has been damaged and cannot be read, his title, "the royal steward," is clear. This title, along with the date of the tomb, suggests that this was the tomb constructed for Hezekiah's royal steward, Shebna.

God's Plans for Jerusalem (22:1–25)

Valley of Vision (22:1). The valley was a place the prophet saw in this vision, probably a valley around Jerusalem (the Kidron or the Hinnom).

Your dead did not die by the sword (22:2). Starvation and disease often caused the death of many inhabitants within a city during a military siege.

The weapons in the House of the Forest (22:8). Since the time of Solomon weapons were stored in a building in Jerusalem called the grand House (or Palace) of the Forest (1 Kings 7:2–5).

You collected water from the lower pool (22:9). This refers to a tunneling project of Hezekiah (see comments on 2 Kings 20:20).

Shebna, that steward who is in charge of the palace (22:15). Shebna was a high administrative official in Hezekiah's court before the Assyrian attack on Jerusalem in 701 BC (see comments on 2 Kings 18:18).

The Lord is about to shake you violently . . . and sling you into a wide land (22:17–18). Shebna will be buried in another land (probably Assyria), not in the grand tomb that he was preparing.

God's Plans for Proud Tyre (23:1–18)

A pronouncement concerning Tyre: . . . be ashamed, Sidon (23:1–4). Tyre and Sidon were powerful Phoenician cities on the Mediterranean coast north of Israel. They were famous for their ships, sailors, and maritime trade. On Tyre, see comments on Ezek. 26:2.

Wail, ships of Tarshish (23:1). This refers to large cargo ships built at Tarshish, probably in Spain (see comments on Jon. 1:3).

Cyprus (23:1). This large island, approximately 140 miles long, sits in the Mediterranean Sea 60 miles west of Syria.

Inhabitants of the coastland (23:2). Tyre included a city on the shores of the Mediterranean Sea as well as a secure island city with an excellent harbor just off the mainland.

Grain from Shihor (23:3). The Phoenicians transported Egyptian grain grown near the Nile Delta channel known as Shihor.

Tyre, the bestower of crowns (23:8). Through its extensive maritime trade Tyre had the power to make a merchant rich or a ruler powerful.

Look at the land of the Chaldeans—a people who no longer exist (23:13). Chaldea is another name for Babylonia. Tyre cannot look to Babylon for help because the Assyrians leveled Babylon in 689 BC.

She will go back into business, prostituting herself . . . but her profits . . . will be dedicated to the Lord (23:17–18). Tyre's maritime trade is compared to prostitution. It is unknown what earnings came to God, unless Tyre helped Josiah repair the temple in 621 BC (2 Kings 22).

God's Final Judgment of the Heavens and the Earth (24:1–23)

Overstepped decrees, and broken the permanent covenant (24:5). These people violated the Mosaic covenant (the statutes) and the everlasting covenant with Noah (Gen. 9:8–17).

Like a harvested olive tree (24:13). At harvest time workers beat the branches of olive trees so that all the olives fell to the ground except for a few unripe olives.

The windows on high are opened, and the foundations of the earth are shaken (24:18–19). This refers to flooding and violent earthquakes.

Future Thanksgiving, Feasting, and Praise (25:1–26:6)

He will destroy the burial shroud (25:7). A burial shroud was a funeral cloth that mourners wore over their heads. These will no longer be needed, since there will be no death.

But Moab will be trampled in his place (25:10). Moab was a nation east of Israel (see comments on Gen. 19:37–38; Isa. 15:1–16:14). Here Moab seems to be used as a symbol of the destruction of all the proud people who did not trust God.

The People Lament and God Answers Their Prayer (26:7–27:1)

Lords other than you have owned us (26:13). This probably refers to Egypt's rule over Israel before the exodus, the domination of neighboring nations during the time of the judges, and Assyrian domination during Isaiah's time.

We became pregnant, we writhed in pain (26:18). In this prayer the people of the nation are in a painful situation (the pain of childbirth is associated with the Assyrian king Sennacherib's attack on Jerusalem in 37:3) and are unable to save themselves from the Assyrian attack.

Hide for a little while until the wrath has passed (26:20). God's wrath sent the Assyrian king Sennacherib against them, but the people can hide behind the walls of Jerusalem for a little while until God delivers them.

The Lord . . . will bring judgment on Leviathan (27:1). In the literature of the ancient Near East Leviathan (also known as Lotan) was a ferocious sea monster (cf. Job 41:1–3). In this context Leviathan probably is used as a figure of speech for Assyria, the monstrous nation opposing Judah that God will defeat at the siege of Jerusalem in 701 BC (cf. 37:36).

God Will Bring Salvation (27:2–13)

Did the Lord strike Israel? . . . he removed her with his severe storm (27:7–8). This probably alludes to several past judgments on Jerusalem and Judah that resulted in the exile of people: Jehoash, king of Israel, defeated Jerusalem and took captives (2 Chron. 25:21–24); Pekah, king of Israel, took 200,000 captives (2 Chron. 28:5–18); and Sennacherib, king of Assyria, took 200,150 captives.[6]

Asherah poles (27:9). See the article "The Canaanites and Canaanite Religion"; see comments on 1 Kings 15:13.

First Woeful Lament: Ephraim Was, and Judah Will Be, Judged (28:1–29)

Woe to the majestic crown of Ephraim's drunkards (28:1). This compares the grand city of Samaria, the capital of Ephraim (Israel), the crown jewel of the nation, to a drunkard wearing a celebratory wreath that was fading.

The fading flower . . . will be like a ripe fig . . . whoever sees it will swallow it (28:4). Whatever was glorious about Samaria is now like the fading flowers on a wreath, and it will quickly disappear, as fast as fresh figs disappear when eaten by hungry people.

Infants just weaned from milk (28:9). The drunken priests and prophets speak the gibberish of a two-year-old. In the ancient Near East children often nursed for two years.

Law after law . . . line after line (28:10). This could refer to stuttering or perhaps to meaningless sounds of a young child, but in any case, it is not an intelligible sentence.

With stammering speech and in a foreign language (28:11). This refers to the language of Assyria.

Law after law . . . line after line (28:13). This repeats 28:10, but now it is apparently the Assyrians who are speaking this to them. In 28:12 the Israelites refuse to listen to God, so here it seems as if God is saying that they will therefore be forced to listen to Assyrian masters, a very ominous prediction.

You said, "We have made a covenant with Death" (28:15). The proud rulers of Jerusalem had placed a false security in an agreement with the Egyptian/Cushite army that they thought would enable them to avoid death when Assyria attacked them (cf. 30:1–17; 31:1–3).

I have laid a stone in Zion . . . a precious cornerstone (28:16). "Zion" is used as another term for Jerusalem, often focusing particularly on the temple area. Not only was the foundation cornerstone critical in aligning a new building and providing support, but also in Mesopotamia there are numerous instances where the cornerstone contained (or covered) inscriptions dedicating the building (often in temples). Using this practice as an analogy, God is saying that he, and not the Egyptians, is the sure foundation needed in the coming Assyrian crisis.

Justice the measuring line and righteousness the mason's level (28:17). Continuing the building analogy from 28:16, God states that justice will be his "measuring line," a flexible cord or rope used to measure horizontal distance, and righteousness will be his "mason's level," a weight tied to a string used to determine vertical alignment, like a plumb line. The same two terms are used in the exact same order in 2 Kings 21:13.

The Lord will rise up as he did at Mount Perazim . . . at the Valley of Gibeon (28:21). God defeated the Philistines at Perazim (2 Sam. 5:20) and the Amorites at Gibeon (Josh. 10:10–12).

Cumin (28:25). Cumin is an herb from the parsley family.

A threshing board (28:27). This was a wooden platform pulled by oxen and used to thresh wheat.

Second Woeful Lament: Jerusalem (29:1–14)

Ariel, the city where David camped (29:1). The name Ariel means the "place of the altar hearth."

I will camp in a circle around you (29:3). This refers to the Assyrian siege of Jerusalem in 701 BC.

All the many nations going out to battle against Ariel . . . will then be like a dream (29:7). The defeat of the Assyrians in 701 BC was indeed dreamlike (37:36–37; 2 Kings 19:35–36). In the evening the Assyrians were encamped around Jerusalem, but in the morning most of them were either dead or running back to Nineveh.

Third Woeful Lament: The Rebellious (29:15–24)

Hide their plans from the Lord (29:15). Judah tried to hide their treaty with Egypt (30:1–2).

The deaf will hear the words of a document (29:18). God will open their ears so that they can understand God's message, reversing 29:9–12.

Fourth Woeful Lament: Trusting Egypt (30:1–33)

They make an alliance (30:1). This refers to the military agreement (the "covenant with Death" in 28:15) of Judah with Egypt/Cush for help against the Assyrians.

Take refuge in Egypt's shadow (30:2). Trusting in the Egyptians for protection from the Assyrians is compared to seeking protection from the sun by standing in the shade of a tree.

Though his princes are at Zoan . . . as far as Hanes (30:4). Judah's envoys would go to the city of Zoan (probably the city of Tanis, the Egyptian capital in the northern part of Egypt) and Hanes (probably Heracleopolis, a regional capital farther south) to meet with Egyptian officials about this military agreement.

The Negev (30:6). The name of the desert region to the south of Judah, and thus lying between Judah and Egypt.

Rahab Who Just Sits (30:7). See comments on Job 9:13. Rahab is used here figuratively to refer negatively to Egypt. Isaiah is predicting that Egypt will do nothing to defeat the Assyrians.

No fragment large enough to . . . scoop water from a cistern (30:14). Normally, broken pottery pieces were large enough to still be useful for moving hot coals in a fire or scooping up water to drink.

Meager bread and water (30:20). A major part of siege tactics was to starve out the besieged city. Assyria's siege of Jerusalem will leave it with little water or food.

Assyria will be shattered by the voice of the Lord (30:31). As described in 37:36 and in 2 Kings 19:35, God intervenes dramatically in the siege of Jerusalem by sending an angel to kill 185,000 Assyrian troops.

Tambourines and lyres (30:32). See the article "Musical Instruments in Israel and the Ancient Near East."

Topheth has been ready . . . with plenty of fire and wood (30:33). This was a place in the Ben Hinnom Valley, south of Jerusalem, where trash was burned. Later, as described in Jer. 7:30–34, the people of Jerusalem engaged in the sacrifice of children to the god Molech in this valley (probably alluded to in Isa. 57:5).

Fifth Woeful Lament: Do Not Trust Egypt (31:1–9)

Like hovering birds (31:5). Birds are well known to protect their young in the nest.

Then Assyria will fall, but not by human sword (31:8). An angel will kill the Assyrian troops besieging Jerusalem in 701 BC (37:36).

His officers will be afraid (31:9). When the Assyrian commanders realized that 185,000 of their soldiers were dead, the remaining small force fled back to Nineveh (37:37).

Whose furnace is in Jerusalem (31:9). See comments on Mal. 4:1.

Exalt God's Rule, Do Not Be Complacent (32:1–20)

You complacent women (32:9). The wealthy women believed that the Assyrian problem would be resolved in their favor, so they foolishly did not worry about it.

In little more than a year . . . the grapes will fail (32:10). This harvest will fail because the Assyrian army will eat it while they besiege Jerusalem.

Growing thorns and briers (32:13). Agricultural fields will be ruined by the invading Assyrians, so weeds and underbrush will grow in the fields.

Sixth Woeful Lament: God Will Defeat Assyria and Reign in Zion (33:1–24)

Woe, you destroyer (33:1). Assyria is the destroyer, but soon an angel will destroy it (37:36).

Your spoil will be gathered as locusts (33:4). Locusts (like the Assyrian troops) come in large swarms of thousands and ferociously eat whatever is available (see comments on Joel 1:4).

The highways are deserted . . . an agreement has been broken (33:8). Egypt/Cush failed to keep their treaty with Judah and stop Assyria, so now the Assyrians control all roads around Jerusalem.

Sharon is like a desert; Bashan and Carmel shake off their leaves (33:9). These are areas in Israel that were famous for their fertile agriculture. As the soldiers of the Assyrian army move south through each of these regions, they destroy everything, leaving only desolation behind them.

The peoples will be burned to ashes (33:12). In 701 BC an angel of God will kill 185,000 Assyrian troops ("the peoples"). Their bodies will be burned because they are too numerous for all to be buried.

A place of rivers and broad streams (33:21). Jerusalem will be as secure as the city of Nineveh, where the broad Euphrates protects it from enemy attack.

Your ropes are slack . . . then abundant spoil will be divided (33:23). After the Assyrians flee (37:36–37), the Israelites will gather the spoils of war from the abandoned tents of the Assyrians.

God's Wrath on the Nations (34:1–17)

It will then come down on Edom (34:5). See comments on Obad. 1; Mal. 1:2–3; 1:4. Edom, a nation just to the east of Judah, also served as a symbol of the nations. In Hebrew the words for "humankind" (*adam*) and "Edom" are the same except for the vowels.

Bozrah (34:6). A capital of Edom.

God Will Transform the World (35:1–10)

The glory of Lebanon will be given to it, the splendor of Carmel and Sharon (35:2). Lebanon was famous for its tall cedars (destroyed in 2:13; 10:34; 33:9). Mount Carmel and the Sharon Plain were famous for their bountiful agriculture. After being destroyed by the invading Assyrian army (2:13; 10:34; 33:9), they will once again be plush and productive.

Sennacherib Questions Hezekiah's Trust in God (36:1–22)

In the fourteenth year of King Hezekiah, King Sennacherib of Assyria attacked (36:1). See comments on 2 Kings 18:1; 18:13; see the section on the Neo-Assyrian period in the article "The Assyrians." Sennacherib attacked Judah and conquered forty-six fortified cities in 701 BC because Hezekiah refused to pay his tribute (2 Kings 18:7).[7]

Lachish (36:2). Lachish was a large fortified city in southwest Judah that Assyria captured. A large detailed wall carving depicting this siege and victory was discovered in the palace of Sennacherib during archaeological excavations of Nineveh (see comments on 2 Kings 18:13).

The Assyrian stood near the conduit of the upper pool, on the road to the Launderer's Field (36:2). This is a flat area on the north side of Jerusalem, the same place where Isaiah challenged Ahaz to trust God (cf. 7:3).

Please speak to your servants in Aramaic . . . don't speak to us in Hebrew (36:11). The international language in the ancient Near East at this time was Aramaic, which most Hebrews could not understand. If the Assyrians spoke in Hebrew, then the common people would understand the threat and might surrender.

Eat their own excrement and drink their own urine (36:12). A long siege would lead to starvation, causing people to eat and drink anything to stay alive.

Make peace with me (36:16). The Assyrians want Jerusalem to surrender (literally, "come out"), and they promise that everything will be wonderful. This is a lie, for the Assyrians usually killed, raped, and enslaved people who had rebelled against them.

Where are the gods of Hamath and Arpad? (36:19). These are cities north of Jerusalem that the Assyrians had already defeated, so the Assyrians believe that their gods must be stronger than the gods of the conquered.

God Promises to Defeat Assyria When Hezekiah Trusts in Him (37:1–38)

The king of Assyria's attendants have blasphemed me (37:6). Defying and mocking God as powerless blasphemed his reputation.

Return to his own land, where I will cause him to fall by the sword (37:7). After the death of 185,000 of his soldiers (37:36) Sennacherib returned to Nineveh, where in 681 BC he was killed by his sons (37:37–38).

Fighting against Libnah (37:8). Libnah was a fortified city a few miles north of Lachish.

King Tirhakah of Cush (37:9). See the article "The Cushites." The Cushite king Tirhakah did not become king (pharaoh) over Egypt until 690 BC. At this time he was the crown prince, a military general, and a coruler with his brother Pharaoh Shebitku.

Did the gods of the nations that my predecessors destroyed rescue them—Gozan, Haran, Rezeph, and the Edenites in Telassar? (37:12–13). Assyrian kings defeated these major fortified cities in Lebanon, Syria, and Mesopotamia. Assyrian logic deduced that since their gods were stronger than the gods of these cities, surely they were also stronger than the Hebrew God.

Daughter Jerusalem shakes her head behind your back (37:22). The people in Jerusalem will shake their heads as a sign of contempt and ridicule as the few surviving Assyrians flee.

I will put my hook in your nose and my bit in your mouth (37:29). At times the Assyrians used hooks and other instruments in the bodies of their captives to prevent them from trying to escape. Now this will happen to the Assyrians themselves.

He will go back the way he came, and he will not enter this city (37:34). After the angel of God killed 185,000 of his soldiers, Sennacherib fled home to Nineveh and never did capture Jerusalem (37:36–37). On Sennacherib's account of this siege, see comments on 2 Kings 18:13.

In the temple of his god Nisroch, his sons Adrammelech and Sharezer struck him down with the sword (37:38). Nisroch was a Mesopotamian god of agriculture. The Assyrian records confirm that Sennacherib was killed by his sons.[8]

Hezekiah Is Delivered from Certain Death (38:1–22)

In those days Hezekiah became terminally ill (38:1). In 38:6 God promises to deliver Jerusalem from Assyria. So Hezekiah's illness must have occurred before Sennacherib and the Assyrians come (chaps. 36–37) and likewise before the visitors arrive from Babylon (39:1).

The gates of Sheol (38:10). Sheol was the place of the dead. The literature of the ancient Near East frequently depicts the place of the dead, the netherworld, as having gates.

Like a weaver . . . from the loom (38:12). Hezekiah's death is compared to a weaver ending his weaving by rolling up the cloth and cutting it off the loom.

Take a lump of pressed figs and apply it to his infected skin, so that he may recover (38:21). Since a skin problem prevented one from going to the temple (Lev. 13:18–23), Hezekiah's boil is treated with a medicinal ointment from figs to help it heal quickly.

Should Hezekiah Trust in Babylon or God? (39:1–8)

Merodach-baladan . . . king of Babylon (39:1). Merodoch-baladan, king of Babylon, rebelled against Assyria in the east (704–703 BC), and he wanted Hezekiah to join him by rebelling against Assyria in the west.

Showed the envoys his treasure house . . . all his armory (39:2). Hezekiah demonstrated to the Babylonians that he had the financial and military resources to join this coalition against the Assyrians.

The days are coming when everything . . . will be carried off to Babylon (39:6). In 605, 597, and 587 BC Babylon plundered Judah and exiled thousands of Hebrews to Babylon.

Be Comforted, for God Is Coming to Shepherd His People (40:1–11)

Her time of forced labor is over (40:2). "Forced labor" often referred to warfare; thus when God comes, warfare will end (cf. 2:4).

Prepare the way of the Lord in the wilderness (40:3). In preparation for a visit by a king, often his subjects would repair the roads and make them smooth.

He protects his flock like a shepherd (40:11). A good shepherd used his power to protect his sheep and his tenderness to show his love (see comments on Jer. 23:1; Ezek. 34:2).

God's Incomparable Power Strengthens the Weak (40:12–31)

The nations . . . are considered as a speck of dust on the scales (40:15). Balance scales in the ancient Near East usually consisted of two shallow pans suspended by string on each side of a central balanced beam. A known weight was placed on one side, and the object to be weighted was placed on the other side. A small amount of dust would not affect the measurement at all.

Something that a smelter casts and a metalworker plates with gold (40:19–20). Idols in the ancient Near East could be made of stone, wood, or metal. Often they were carved out of wood and overlaid with a precious metal such as gold.[9] Whatever the material, the idols had to have a firm, flat base or else be supported laterally to prevent them from toppling over.

He brings out the stars by number (40:26). Throughout the ancient Near East the stars and planets frequently were associated with various gods (see comments on Deut. 17:3; 2 Kings 17:16). In contrast, this text stresses that they are part of God's creation, which he maintains.

They will soar on wings like eagles (40:31). The Hebrew word translated as "eagle" is used for a wide variety of large birds and not just specifically for eagles. The point is that these large birds can catch drafts of hot air and thus soar for long stretches of time without flapping their wings.

Do Not Fear, for God Is Greater Than the Nations and Their Gods (41:1–29)

Who has stirred up someone from the east? (41:2). God's sovereignty over the world will direct leaders, giving them victory to accomplish his plan. No great king is identified here, but it could refer to the Assyrian king Sennacherib (chaps. 36–37; see 41:10–12) or to the Persian king Cyrus (44:28).

Those who war against you will become absolutely nothing (41:12). Though it is not certain, this perhaps refers to the angel of God's defeat of Sennacherib's army at Jerusalem (37:36).

I will make you into a sharp threshing board, new, with many teeth (41:15). In the process of winnowing wheat sometimes a heavy wooden sled (threshing board), often with projecting stone, iron, or wooden teeth, was pulled over the stalks by oxen in order to separate the grain from the stalks and chaff. The enemy may look like an impossibly big mountain, but a threshing sled with sharp teeth underneath can pulverize almost anything.

You will winnow them (41:16). Winnowing typically took place on hilltops, where the wind was the most constant. Stalks of grain were placed on the ground, and then oxen dragged a threshing board over them to loosen the grain from the stalks and to knock off the chaff. Then the farmer tossed a load of grain up into the air to allow the lighter chaff to be blown away in the wind.

God's Servant Will Bring Justice and Light to All (42:1–12)

He will not break a bruised reed (42:3). In an Akkadian text the Assyrian king Esar-haddon brags about snapping the kings who opposed him "like a marsh-reed."[10] A bruised reed was like a weak, sick, useless person, but unlike Esar-haddon, the coming servant will help the weak, not crush them.

The settlements where Kedar dwells cry aloud (42:11). Kedar, the second son of Ishmael (Gen. 25:13), developed into one of the larger Ishmaelite tribes in northern Arabia.

Let the inhabitants of Sela sing (42:11). Sela was the capital of Edom, the kingdom to the southeast of Judah (see comments on Isa. 16:1; Obad. 1).

An Assyrian king trampling over defeated soldiers with his chariot.

Do Not Fear, for God Will Deliver His Blind Servants (42:13–43:7)

The Lord advances like a warrior (42:13). The depiction of a deity as a great warrior was a common motif in the ancient Near East (see comments on Isa. 59:17).

I will lay waste mountains (42:15). The mountains symbolized a great enemy (cf. 41:15).

But this is a people plundered and looted, all of them trapped in holes (42:22). Typically, one would hide in a pit to avoid an enemy in a time of war (Josh. 10:16; 1 Sam. 13:6). There was no war against Israel in Babylonian exile, so this must refer to a preexilic event, that of either the Assyrians (701 BC) or the Babylonians (586/596 BC).

I have given Egypt as a ransom for you, Cush and Seba in your place (43:3). Cush was the African empire located south of Egypt along the Nile River (see the article "The Cushites"). Although Seba is closely associated with Cush, its exact location is disputed (perhaps either in southern Arabia or North Africa). If these chapters reference the Assyrian crisis, this probably refers to Sennacherib's plundering of these African armies (chaps. 30–31; 37:9) instead of Jerusalem. If these chapters are referring to the time of the Babylonian/Persian exile, then this refers to the Persian invasion of Egypt by King Cambyses (see the section on Cambyses in the article "The Persians").

Do Not Fear, for the Blind Will Be Delivered (43:8–44:5)

I will send an army to Babylon . . . even the Chaldeans in the ships (43:14). The terms "Chaldean" and "Babylonian" often are used interchangeably (see the article "The Babylonians"). The city of Babylon relied upon the Euphrates River as a critical part of its defense, but here, when some unnamed nation attacks Babylon (probably Cyrus the Persian), the Babylonians will try to escape in boats on the Euphrates, but still they will be captured and become fugitives.

Who makes a way in the sea . . . they lie down, they do not rise again (43:16–17). God delivered Israel through the Red Sea, but the Egyptian army died in the sea (Exod. 14).

Look, I am about to do something new (43:18–19). A great redemption from Egypt, the exodus (43:16–17), happened in a former time, but a greater redemption will happen in the future.

So I defiled the officers of the sanctuary (43:28). The Hebrew text says that God "will disgrace" the dignitaries of the temple, a prophecy fulfilled in 586 BC, when the Jerusalem temple was destroyed by the Babylonians (Jer. 52).

My servant, Jeshurun (44:2). The name Jeshurun means "upright one," implying a future change in Israel's character (cf. Deut. 32:15).

Another will write on his hand, "The Lord's" (44:5). Throughout the ancient Near East it was common for slaveholders to write their names (by either tattoo or brand) onto the hands of their slaves to provide an uncontestable sign of ownership.

Do Not Fear Idols, Fear God (44:6–23)

There is no other Rock (44:8). A rock symbolized a solid foundation and a reliable source of security (cf. Deut. 32:4; Ps. 18:31).

Who makes a god or casts a metal image (44:10). In the ancient Near East some idols were cast from metal by blacksmiths (cf. 44:12), while others were carved from wood by carpenters (cf. 44:13–14) (see comments on Isa. 40:19–20).

A person can use it for fuel . . . he even makes it into a god and worships it (44:15). Since idols often were made out of wood, this text underscores sarcastically the illogical reality that the idol worshiper, using the same tree, could both shape a god and cook bread.

God Will Restore Jerusalem and Remove All Doubts (44:24–45:13)

Says to Cyrus . . . and says to Jerusalem, "She will be rebuilt" (44:28). Ezra 1:1–4 and the Cyrus Cylinder[11] indicate that the Persian king Cyrus allowed all exiled people to return to their land and rebuild their temples in 538 BC (see the article "The Persians").

Though you do not know me (45:4). The Persian king Cyrus probably was polytheistic, adopting the Babylonian god Marduk as his central god, but still acknowledging and worshiping numerous others. Persia later becomes a center of Zoroastrian worship, and Cyrus may have worshiped the Zoroastrian god Ahura-Mazda as well.

He will rebuild my city, and set my exiles free (45:13). The person being discussed here is the Persian king Cyrus, who in 538 BC decrees that the exiled Hebrews can return home.

All Nations Will Bow Down before God (45:14–25)

By myself I have sworn (45:23). Throughout the ancient Near East it was common for people to swear oaths in the name of their gods. Yet there are no records indicating that the pagan gods themselves ever swore an oath in their own name, as the Lord does here.[12]

God Is Superior to Babylon's Idols (46:1–13)

Bel crouches; Nebo cowers. Idols depicting them are consigned to beasts and cattle (46:1). See the section on religion in the article "The Babylonians." Bel (Marduk) rose to be the chief god of Babylon based on his defeat of the goddess Tiamat, as recorded in the Enuma Elish. His son Nebo, chief god of Borsippa, was in charge of the "tablets of destiny."

I call a bird of prey from the east, a man for my purpose from a far country (46:11). This could refer back to the Persian king Cyrus (45:1–3) or to the Assyrian king Sennacherib (41:2, 11–12, 25).

The Fall of Babylon (47:1–15)

Virgin Daughter Babylon. Sit on the ground without a throne (47:1). The capital city of Babylon was personified as a woman who will have no power or royalty.

Take millstones and grind flour (47:2). Throughout the ancient Near East grain often was ground into flour through the use of two heavy stones. The bottom stone was stationary, and the upper stone rotated around on top of the bottom one. The point here is that Babylon, former ruler of the region, will do common labor, possibly as a captive.

In spite of your many sorceries and . . . spells (47:9–11). Babylon was famous throughout the ancient Near East for its sorcery and divination. Archaeological excavations have uncovered thousands of texts with magical incantations.

Let the astrologers stand and save you (47:13). Astrology was closely connected to sorcery and divination, and Babylon was likewise well known for its astrology. Babylon's astrologers tried to predict the future by following the movement of the moon and various planets. In about 500 BC Babylonian astrologers developed the twelve signs of the zodiac.[13]

Stubborn Israel Needs to Trust God (48:1–22)

Who swear by the name of the Lord (48:1). Israel made oaths of obedience at Sinai (Deut. 5:22–27) and at Mount Gerizim (Deut. 27–28).

I have tested you in the furnace (48:10). Archaeologists have discovered several ancient Near Eastern metal-smelting furnaces. Some of these furnaces have tubes that function as bellows for injecting air into the furnace

An ancient metal-smelting furnace.

to increase the temperature sufficiently to melt metal.

The Lord loves him; he will accomplish his will against Babylon (48:14). An unnamed king (probably the one in 47:1–15, the Assyrian king Sennacherib; or perhaps Cyrus the Persian king) will defeat Babylon.

Leave Babylon, flee from the Chaldeans (48:20). The terms "Chaldean" and "Babylonian" often are used interchangeably (see the article "The Babylonians"). This could refer to fleeing either from Babylonian influence and theology (as in chaps. 46–47) or from a Babylonian location.

God's Servant Will Bring Salvation to All (49:1–13)

He made my words like a sharp sword (49:2). The term translated as "words" literally means "mouth." The comparison of the mouth (or tongue) to a sword was common throughout the ancient Near East. For example, an Egyptian text reads, "The tongue is [a king's] sword; Speaking is stronger than all fighting."[14]

God Has Not Forgotten His People (49:14–50:3)

Look, I have inscribed you on the palms of my hands (49:16). See comments on Isa. 44:5. A slave might have a permanent brand to identify the owner. In contrast, God's brand made him unable to forget his people.

Mother's divorce certificate (50:1). Deuteronomy 24:1–4 required a husband to give a written document to the wife he was divorcing.

To which of my creditors did I sell you? (50:1). In the ancient Near East parents could use their children as a pledge for securing a loan. Then if they defaulted on the loan, their children would become slaves of the creditor.

The Example of the Servant of the Lord (50:4–11)

The tongue of those who are instructed (50:4). The mouth spoke what the mind has learned, so the openness to further education was essential.

Those who beat me . . . who tore out my beard (50:6). This probably refers to a public, formal symbolic shaming.

I have set my face like flint (50:7). The word translated as "flint" is a reference to very hard rock. A related word in Akkadian is used of diamonds and other hard gems. Thus this servant's determination was unbreakable or unchangeable.

Assurance of God's Future Salvation and the End of His Wrath (51:1–23)

Look to the rock from which you were cut, and to the quarry (51:1–2). The massive building projects of kings in the ancient Near East required huge stone quarries from which large stone blocks were cut.

Wasn't it you who hacked Rahab to pieces (51:9). See comments on Isa. 30:7. Rahab apparently is similar to the chaos sea monster Leviathan (see comments on Job 26:12–13) but also is used symbolically to represent Egypt (30:7). The reference here is to the defeat of Egypt during the exodus.

The prisoner is soon to be set free; he will not die and go to the Pit (51:14). This described prisoners of war, not the condition of people living in Babylonian exile. Pits often were used as prisons in the ancient Near East. The word translated here as "Pit" can mean either a pit in the ground (i.e., a prison) or death (i.e., the grave).

Rejoice, for God's Salvation Is Here (52:1–12)

At first my people went down to Egypt . . . then Assyria oppressed them (52:4). Israel had two periods of oppression: years ago in Egypt and more recently by Assyria.

Egyptian prisoners of war.

The upper half of this ancient Egyptian wall painting depicts metalsmiths at work. The lower half shows workers making sun-dried mud bricks.

For you will not leave in a hurry . . . the God of Israel is your rear guard (52:12). In contrast to the exodus (Exod. 12:11, 33), the people here do not have to hurry, but like in the exodus (Exod. 13:21–22) God will protect them from enemies.

The Suffering and Exaltation of God's Servant (52:13–53:12)

He grew up before him like a young plant (53:2). On the comparison of people to frail plants, see comments on Isa. 11:1; 42:3.

Bore our sicknesses . . . was pierced because of our rebellion (53:4–5). The sacrificial act involving a "substitutionary atonement" was known both to Israel and to their neighbors, but usually the sacrifice was an animal or grain of some type. Human substitution was rare.[15]

Like a lamb led to the slaughter (53:7). Sheep were slaughtered throughout the ancient Near East, sometimes simply to provide food, and sometimes to provide a ritual sacrifice to the gods.

Like a sheep silent before her shearers (53:7). Because wool played such an important role in the ancient Near East (the major component in the clothes of many people), the annual shearing of sheep was a highly significant and festive event. It usually was done in the spring. Metal shears for shearing sheep were invented as early as 1000 BC.[16]

In Compassion God Will Multiply the Nation (54:1–17)

Rejoice, childless one (54:1). In the ancient Near East, for a woman to be barren was a socioeconomic disaster, and thus normally it was a cause for mourning.

Enlarge the site of your tent (54:2). This is a figure of speech alluding back to the time when the patriarchs lived in tents. Those tents typically were made of goat hair, constructed of three-foot-wide strips sewn together. A popular idiom for family growth was "enlarge your tent" (i.e., add another strip on), likewise causing the need to lengthen the ropes that held it and to increase the strength of the tent pegs.

Look, I have created the craftsman . . . no weapon formed against you will succeed (54:16–17). The word translated as "craftsman" can refer to one working in a wide variety of materials. The reference to the charcoal fire in the following lines implies that this person is a blacksmith, forging weapons from a furnace (forge) with an air bellows. Since God gave the blacksmith skill to make weapons, he can remove that skill so that no weapons will be made.

Seek God and See How He Will Fulfill His Promises (55:1–13)

Come, everyone who is thirsty, come to the water; and you without silver (55:1). Couched in the language of a generous invitation of ancient Near Eastern hospitality, this verse invites anyone to come to eat and celebrate the offer of a new covenant relationship with God (55:3).

Milk (55:1). Milk and other dairy products (cheese, yogurt, etc.) were important food products throughout the ancient Near East (see the section on provisioning life in the article "Daily Life in Ancient Israel"). Goat's milk probably was more common than cow's milk.

I will make a permanent covenant with you, on the basis of the faithful kindness of David (55:3). A covenant was a legal contractual agreement. In contrast to human covenants, which often were broken, God declares that his covenant with David (2 Sam. 7:12–16) had no ending.

God Accepts Worship from All Who Keep the Covenant (56:1–8)

No foreigner who has joined himself to the Lord should say, "The Lord will exclude me from his people" (56:3). Although certain foreigners and castrated eunuchs were excluded from the temple (Deut. 23:1–3), foreigners like Ruth the Moabite (Ruth 2:10), Rahab the Canaanite (Josh.

2:8–12), Uriah the Hittite (2 Sam. 11:11), and many other peoples (Exod. 12:38) joined the Israelites. All will be able to worship together in the future.

For the eunuchs who keep my Sabbaths . . . I will give them, in my house and within my walls, a memorial and a name (56:4–5). Eunuchs were used as court administrators and often as guardians of the king's harem. Eunuchs normally were unable to have children to carry on their name, and typically they were excluded from the temple (Deut. 23:1).

The Rejection of Godless Leaders and the Revival of the Lowly (56:9–57:21)

All you animals of the field and forest, come and eat! (56:9). Kings at war in the ancient Near East often were compared to ravaging lions and other dangerous predators. This verse probably is a figure of speech inviting enemy nations (the beasts) to attack and destroy.

Israel's watchmen are blind . . . all of them are mute dogs . . . and love to sleep (56:10–11). Cities in the ancient Near East typically had watchmen on the walls to warn of approaching armies. Dogs in the streets also tended to bark at night if someone approached one's house with hostile intent. Blind watchman and mute dogs would be of little help. Also, in Israel it was quite offensive to call someone a dog. Here it is even worse because these watchmen of Israel are compared to dogs that can't even bark when needed.

They will rest on their beds—everyone who lives uprightly (57:2). The Hebrew word translated as "beds" often is used euphemistically to refer to the bench within a tomb upon which the dead are laid (cf. 2 Chron. 16:14; Ezek. 32:25).

You witch's sons, offspring of an adulterer and a prostitute (57:3). These derogatory terms referred to the pagan practices of divination, magic, and soothsaying used to determine the will of the gods, practices strictly prohibited in Deut. 18:10. Prostitution and adultery frequently are mentioned by the OT prophets as figurative references to idolatry. These two elements are combined in 2 Kings 9:22, where Jehu refers to the "prostitution and sorcery" (i.e., idolatry and witchcraft) of Jezebel.

Who burn with lust among the oaks (57:5). In the pagan religions of Israel's neighbors large, impressive trees frequently had religious significance and also sometimes served as worship sites. Likewise, many of the gods who were worshiped (e.g., Baal) were fertility gods, and perverse sexual acts often were associated with them.

Who slaughter children in the wadis (57:5). Child sacrifice was associated with the worship of the Ammonite god Molech, a terrible practice carried out by the Israelites right outside the walls of Jerusalem in the Ben Hinnom Valley (see comments on 2 Kings 3:27; Jer. 7:31).

Your portion is among the smooth stones of the wadi (57:6). The background for "the smooth stones" is uncertain. Smooth standing stones sometimes were erected to represent gods. However, the phrase may simply refer to the smooth stones down in the creek bed. Others have suggested that the reference may be to the tombs cut into the rock of the Ben Hinnom Valley.

You have placed your bed on a high and lofty mountain (57:7). This probably refers to the sexual perversion taking place with temple prostitutes at Canaanite "high places" (worship sites).

You went to the king with oil . . . and sent them down even to Sheol (57:9). The Hebrew word translated as the "king" (Hebrew root: *mlk*) might instead be a reference to Molech (cf. NRSV; NIV), a pagan god of the region associated with child sacrifice (2 Kings 23:10) (see comments on Isa. 57:5).

God Accepts the Fasting of Those Who Please Him (58:1–14)

"Why have we fasted, but you have not seen?" (58:3). Although a common practice in Israel, fasting was not common in the religions of the ancient Near East and, when it was practiced, was associated with mourning. In Israel it often was associated with making a request. Here they apparently think that God will give them some reward for their fasting.

Is it not to share your bread with the hungry . . . to bring the poor and homeless into your house? (58:6–7). Stressed repeatedly throughout the OT, the virtue and moral "rightness" of caring for the poor and hungry (often grouped as "orphans, widows, foreigners") was also extolled throughout the ancient Near East but, as in Israel, not always practiced.

And the Lord's glory will be your rear guard (58:8). This is a reference back to the exodus story. The Egyptian army had trapped Israel in front of the Red Sea, so God's presence (a pillar of fire and the cloud) became the rear guard protecting the Israelites.

Accusations of Injustice Bring Confession of Sins and the Establishment of Justice (59:1–21)

He put on righteousness as body armor, and a helmet of salvation on his head (59:17). The practice of depicting one's deity as a great warrior was common in the ancient Near East. For example, in the Enuma Elish, the Babylonian epic of creation, the god Marduk is described as a great warrior as he goes out to fight the goddess Tiamat: "Champion of his father, Hastener to the battle, the warrior Marduk. . . . He made the bow, appointed it his weapon. . . . He took up the mace. . . . He was garbed in a ghastly armored garment."[17]

Many Will Come to Worship God in Zion (60:1–22)

Look, darkness will cover the earth (60:2). Darkness represented the hopelessness and the devastating results of God's curse on the earth, as described in Isa. 24, 34.

Caravans of camels (60:6). Camels were able to carry cargoes across the formidable deserts of the ancient Near East and thus were extremely valuable. They are included in lists of tribute given to Assyrian kings.

Midian and Ephah . . . Sheba . . . Kedar . . . Nebaioth (60:6–7). Even the smaller Bedouin tribes in the Sinai (Midian) and the Arabian Desert (Kedar and Nabaioth) will worship God in those days. The location of Sheba is uncertain, but probably it was a kingdom in southern Arabia.

The ships of Tarshish (60:8–9). Tarshish probably was a city at the far western end of the Mediterranean Sea, perhaps a trading colony founded by the Phoenicians (Canaanites). The sails of ships on the Mediterranean Sea looked like clouds or darting doves.

The glory of Lebanon will come to you—its pine, elm, and cypress together (60:13). Lebanon was famous for its forests and especially its cedar, but here other types of lumber are extolled as well.

You will nurse on the milk of nations and nurse at the breast of kings (60:16). Children in a royal family lavishly enjoyed the best that the king and the vassal nations could provide.

God's Anointed One Announces God's Favor (61:1–11)

To proclaim liberty to the captives and freedom to the prisoners (61:1). In the ancient Near East, sometimes during his first year or two, a new king would announce the release of prisoners.

Provide for those who mourn in Zion . . . festive oil instead of mourning (61:3). Anointing with oil served as a sign of consecration, but it also was used in celebration of good news or of a good event.

Strangers will stand and feed your flocks, and foreigners will be your plowmen and vinedressers (61:5). In the past foreign armies had taken Israel's animals and crops, but in the future foreigners will be the ones to care for Israel's animals and crops.

As a groom wears a turban and as a bride adorns herself with her jewels (61:10). Priests often wore elaborate and beautiful turbans/headgear.

Likewise, brides in the ancient Near East were clothed in beautiful clothes and expensive jewels (cf. Jer. 2:32).

The Transformation of Zion (62:1–12)

You [Jerusalem] will be a glorious crown in the LORD's hand, and a royal diadem (62:3). Kings (and deities) throughout the ancient Near East are depicted regularly with elaborate crowns. A royal crown was a precious, expensive, and unique treasure of the king. A Mesopotamian text even refers to a city (Borsippa) as the crown of Marduk.

God's Day of Vengeance on the Wicked (63:1–6)

Who is this coming from Edom . . . from Bozrah? (63:1). Edom was the kingdom to the southeast of Judah, but it was also used to represent all the nations that opposed God. Bozrah was one of the main cities in Edom (34:6) (see comments on Amos 1:12; Obad. 1).

Why are your clothes red, and your garments like one who treads a winepress? (63:2). When people in the ancient world trampled on grapes to make wine, their clothing would become stained with the red juice.

A Lament Remembering the Past (63:7–64:12)

In all their suffering, he suffered, and the angel of his presence saved them (63:9). When Israel was enslaved in Egypt, God felt their agony, so he revealed his glory in a pillar of fire or cloud to bring them out of Egypt (Exod. 14:19–25).

Your holy people had a possession for a little while, but our enemies have trampled down your sanctuary (63:18). Some connect this to the desecration of the holy temple during the time of Athaliah (2 Chron. 23), Ahaz (2 Chron. 28), Manasseh (2 Chron. 33), or the Babylonians (2 Kings 25).

You came down, and the mountains quaked at your presence (64:3). At Sinai the glory of God appeared at the top of the mountain (Exod. 19:16–20).

God Answers the Lament: Some Will Receive Wrath, but My Servant Salvation (65:1–25)

Sacrificing in gardens, burning incense on bricks, sitting among the graves . . . eating the meat of pigs (65:3–4). This described pagan worship at outdoor temples (probably gardens or sacred groves of trees associated with a temple [cf. 66:17]) where people were involved with many forbidden practices (Lev. 11:7; 20:27). The word translated as "brick" can also be used to refer to incense altars.

As the new wine is found in a bunch of grapes, and one says, "Don't destroy it" (65:8). Typically, when pruning his grapes, if a farmer found a cluster with only a few grapes or with grapes that were dried up, he would assume that the cluster was useless. In this case a farmer wanted to save all the grapes.

Sharon will be a pasture for flocks, and the Valley of Achor a place for herds to lie down (65:10). The Sharon Plain was a fertile area in western Judah between the coastal plain and the mountainous hill country. The Valley of Achor was a narrow valley by the Jordan River, the place where Achan was punished for stealing what belonged to God (Josh. 7).

Who prepare a table for Fortune and fill bowls of mixed wine for Destiny (65:11). The words translated as "Fortune" and "Destiny" are names of pagan gods, the god of "good fortune" and the god of "destiny." This probably references the pagan practice of seeking knowledge of the future based on the "tablets of destiny," which these gods controlled.

In her, a nursing infant will no longer live only a few days, or an old man not live out his days (65:20). In the ancient Near East the infant mortality rate was extremely high; many infants died at birth or soon thereafter. Likewise, the life expectancy for adults was low.

God Will Honor the Humble from All Nations but Judge the Wicked (66:1–24)

One person slaughters an ox, another kills a person . . . one person offers a grain offering, another offers pig's blood (66:3). This text alternates between legitimate sacrifices (ox, lamb, grain, incense) and illegitimate offerings (human being, dog, pig's blood, praise to an idol). In the ancient Near East the sacrificial use of pigs and dogs often was linked with the worship of gods associated with the netherworld.

His chariots are like the whirlwind (66:15). The depiction of a deity riding on a chariot, sometimes associated with clouds, was common in the ancient Near East.

Eating meat from pigs, vermin, and rats (66:17). This describes those who followed pagan practices (cf. 1:29; 65:3–5), doing what was strictly forbidden in Lev. 11:7, 29.

Tarshish, Put, Lud . . . Tubal, Javan, and the coasts and islands far away (66:19). Tarshish probably was located in Spain and represented the most distant known areas. Put refers to the area in northern Africa to the west of Egypt (modern Libya). Lud and Tubal refer to areas in Asia Minor (modern Turkey). Javan probably refers to the Greek settlements in the Aegean Sea and along the western coast of Turkey. "The coasts and islands far away" probably refers to the islands of the Aegean Sea, plus larger islands like Cyprus and Crete.

Jeremiah

Gary E. Yates

Introduction. Jeremiah prophesied in the final days of Judah as a nation. Jeremiah's calling occurred in 627 BC, and his ministry covered the reigns of Judah's last five kings and extended beyond the time of the fall of Jerusalem in 586 BC. Josiah was Judah's last godly king, and he reigned until his death in a battle with the Egyptians at Megiddo (609 BC). His successors included Jehoahaz (609 BC), Jehoiakim (609–598 BC), Jehoiachin (598–597 BC), and Zedekiah (597–586 BC). After the fall of Jerusalem to the Babylonians Jeremiah remained in the land of Judah until kidnapped and taken away to Egypt, where he likely died around 580 BC.

Jeremiah's ministry coincided with the rise of the Neo-Babylonian Empire under the powerful ruler Nebuchadnezzar (see the article "The Babylonians"). Jeremiah called Judah to repentance, but when repentance was not forthcoming, he announced that the Lord would use Babylon as his instrument of judgment against his disobedient people. The Babylonian king Nebuchadnezzar captured Jerusalem in 597 BC and destroyed the city in 586 BC. Nebuchadnezzar took exiles from Judah on four separate occasions and deported Judah's final two kings. Jeremiah also offered hope for Israel's future, promising that the Lord would restore the Davidic dynasty, bring his people back to their land, and bless them with peace and prosperity. The Lord would make a new covenant with Israel, forgiving the sins of the past and providing enablement for future obedience.

The book of Jeremiah is arranged more thematically than chronologically. Chapters 1–25 record Jeremiah's oracles and sermons of judgment against Judah. Chapters 26–45 contain primarily narratives from Jeremiah's life that

The Babylonian Empire and the Judean Exiles

highlight Judah's unbelieving responses to the prophetic word. The Book of Consolation in chapters 30–33 provides a detailed message concerning Israel's future restoration. Chapters 46–51 record Jeremiah's oracles against the nations, culminating with the judgment of Babylon in chapters 50–51. The appendix in chapter 52 provides an account of the fall of Jerusalem.

The Call of Jeremiah (1:1–19)

Hilkiah . . . Anathoth (1:1). Jeremiah's father was a priest in Anathoth, a village three miles northeast of Jerusalem in the territory of Benjamin. Jeremiah may have been a descendant of Abiathar, the priest whom Solomon banished to Anathoth for his support of Adonijah as David's successor (1 Kings 1:7; 2:26–27).

Thirteenth year . . . Josiah . . . Zedekiah . . . exile (1:2–3). For the chronology of Jeremiah's ministry, see the introduction to Jeremiah above.

A branch from an almond tree.

Branch of an almond tree (1:11). The vision of the almond tree (*shaqed*) reflected a wordplay signifying that God was "watching" (*shoqed*) to see that his word was fulfilled. The almond tree was also one of the first trees to blossom in the spring, and the Lord would soon bring Jeremiah's words of judgment to fulfillment.

Boiling pot . . . from the north (1:13). The boiling pot represented an enemy nation that would attack Judah from the north, the typical direction from which foreign armies invaded (1:14–15; 4:6; 6:1, 22; 10:22). Babylon is later identified as the specific nation that would carry out this invasion (cf. 20:4–6; 21:2–4; 25:9, 26).

The Lord Calls for His Unfaithful Wife to Return (2:1–4:4)

Prophesied by Baal (2:8). See the article "The Canaanites and Canaanite Religion." Baal, whose name means "lord" or "husband," was the Canaanite storm god. Worship of the fertility god, Baal, with its promises of rain, abundance, and moral license, was a common temptation in Israel, and syncretistic forms of worship that combined Baal with Israel's God were common in Israel and Judah (cf. 7:9, 11, 13, 17; 12:16; 19:15; 23:13, 27; 32:29, 35).

Cyprus . . . Kedar . . . has a nation ever exchanged its gods? (2:10–11). The use of Cyprus and the Greek islands, along with Kedar in southern Arabia, conveys the idea of "from east to west." The polytheistic cultures of the ancient Near East did not have to exchange gods but simply added other gods to their pantheons. It would have been unthinkable to reject specific nationalistic deities.

Cracked cisterns that cannot hold water (2:13). A cistern was a pit dug out of stone with a narrow opening at the top, used to store rainwater. Cisterns were needed to provide a source of water during the dry season in the late spring and summer. Cisterns often were lined with plaster to prevent leakage.[1]

Memphis and Tahpanhes have also broken your skull (2:16). Memphis and Tahpanhes are Egyptian cities, used here figuratively to represent the Egyptians, who had killed King Josiah and defeated Judah at a battle near the city of Megiddo in 609 BC (2 Kings 23:29–30; 2 Chron. 35:20–24). The Egyptians subsequently deported Jehoahaz to Egypt, installed Jehoiakim on the throne in his place, and exacted heavy tribute from Judah (2 Kings 24:33–35; 2 Chron. 36:3–4).

What will you gain by traveling along the way to Egypt . . . to Assyria? (2:18). Military alliances with other nations were not the solution for

Judah's problems. Alliances with Egypt had not helped during the Assyrian crisis (cf. Isa. 30:1–5; 31:1–3), and they would not save Judah in their struggles with Babylon either (cf. 37:5–9; Ezek. 29:6–9). Ahaz had sought help from Assyria rather than trusting the Lord during the Syro-Ephraimite War (734–732 BC) (cf. 2 Kings 16:5–18; Isa. 7–8).

Every high hill . . . green tree . . . lie down like a prostitute (2:20). Pagan rites involving sexual acts believed to bring fertility and blessing from the gods were conducted on hilltops or at sites with groves of sacred trees.[2] Israel's worship of these gods is depicted as adultery or prostitution because Israel was to be devoted exclusively to the Lord (Num. 25:1; Jer. 3:8–9; Ezek. 16; 23; Hosea 2:1; 4:13–14).

If a man divorces his wife (3:1). Jeremiah alluded to the divorce law in Deut. 24:1–4, which stipulated that the husband was required to provide a certificate of divorce and that he was not allowed to remarry his divorced wife once she married another man. Even though the Lord's marriage with Israel/Judah was more broken than what was envisioned in this law, the Lord was still willing to allow his people to return to him (3:12, 14, 22; 4:1). The requirement of a certificate for divorce is attested in the Code of Hammurabi and elsewhere in the ancient Near East.

Spring rain (3:3). The autumn or early rains (October–February) prepared the soil for planting, while the spring or later rains (March–April) provided the moisture needed to ripen the crops.

Circumcise yourselves to the Lord (4:4). Circumcision was the sign of the covenant between the Lord and the descendants of Abraham required of all males (Gen. 17:9–14), but it is used metaphorically here to refer to inner conformity and commitment to God and his commands (cf. Deut. 10:16).

Preparation for War as the Lord Sends an Invader (4:5–6:30)

Blow the ram's horn (4:5). The blowing of the ram's horn (*shofar*) was used to warn of an approaching enemy, to call the people to battle (Judg. 3:27), or to assemble the people at the sanctuary (cf. Lev. 25:9; Ps. 150:3).

Flee to the fortified cities (4:5). In times of military attack people living outside of cities would go to take refuge within the city walls. Judah had rebuilt many of its city walls and fortifications after the Assyrians had captured forty-six of its cities in the late eighth century BC.

Put on sackcloth (4:8). This coarse, black fabric made from goat hair was worn with ashes as a sign of mourning and grief (Gen. 37:34; 2 Sam. 3:31; Esther 4:1–3) or repentance (1 Kings 21:27).

Seasonal rains (5:24). See comments on Jer. 3:3. The people attributed the rains to Baal rather than to the Lord (cf. Hosea 2:8–9).

A wall panel from an Assyrian palace depicting an Assyrian battering ram.

Sound the ram's horn (6:1). See comments on Jer. 4:5.

Raise a smoke signal (6:1). Fire signals were used for communication between towns, especially in times of war or crisis. The Lachish letters make mention of fire signals being used between the cities of Jerusalem, Lachish, and Azekah (cf. 34:7).

Raise a siege ramp (6:6). As part of their siege techniques the Babylonians built siege ramps in order to use battering rams to breach the walls of the city under attack (cf. 2 Kings 25:3–4; Jer. 32:24; Ezek. 4:1–2).

I appointed watchmen (6:17). The role of watchmen stationed on the city walls was to warn of approaching armies (2 Sam. 18:24–27; 2 Kings 9:17–20; Isa. 21:6–9), and the prophets served in this role by warning the people of coming judgment (cf. Ezek. 3:17; 33:2–7).[3]

Sackcloth . . . dust (6:26). See comments on Jer. 4:8. The act of rolling in ashes seems to be a particularly intense expression of grief (cf. Mic. 1:10).

I have appointed you to be an assayer among my people (6:27). Jeremiah as a prophet would act as a refiner of metals to remove the impurities from the rebellious house of Judah. The process of smelting involved refining ore at extremely high temperature in order to remove impurities and extract the pure metal (cf. 9:7; 11:4).[4]

Jeremiah's Temple Sermon and Judah's Rebellion (7:1–10:25)

Do not trust deceitful words, chanting, "This is the temple of the LORD" (7:4). The people had come to believe that Jerusalem was inviolable and would never fall to enemy armies. This presumptuous confidence was no doubt rooted in the Zion traditions concerning the Lord's protection of the city (Ps. 46; 48: 76; 132:13–16) and the miraculous deliverance of Jerusalem from the Assyrians in 701 BC.

Den of robbers (7:11). Jeremiah compared the temple to the caves where bandits would often hide out after committing their crimes because the people believed that they could break God's commands and still enjoy his protection.

Shiloh (7:12, 14). The prophet recalled the example of Shiloh to show the seriousness of the threats concerning Jerusalem. Following the conquest in the book of Joshua, Shiloh had been the locale for the tabernacle and the ark of the covenant (Josh. 18:1, 9), but the Lord abandoned the tabernacle (Ps. 78:60) and allowed the ark to be captured by the Philistines (1 Sam. 4:4–11).

Do not pray for these people (7:16). Throughout Israel's history prophetic intercession had spared the people from divine judgment on various occasions (cf. Exod. 32:9–14; Num. 14:11–20; 1 Sam. 12:16–23; Amos 7:1–6). To forbid Jeremiah to intercede meant that the Lord had given Judah over to judgment.

Make cakes for the queen of heaven (7:18). The pagan fertility goddess in view here is most likely the Mesopotamian Ishtar or the Canaanite goddesses Astarte or Asherah, or perhaps some syncretistic combination of them all. These cakes were made in the image of a nude goddess, and women played a leading role in these worship practices.[5]

Cut off the hair (7:29). Shaving the head or face often was done as an act of mourning (Job 1:20; Mic. 1:16). The fact that these practices were prohibited in the Mosaic law (cf. Lev. 19:27–28; Deut. 14:1) may reflect that the prophet is sarcastically condemning the people here for their pagan practices.

High places of Topheth in Ben Hinnom Valley (7:31). This location southwest of Jerusalem was the site of pagan worship practices, including the sacrifice of children. Topheth ("hearth") was the name of the place where the sacrifices occurred and where the urns containing the remains of the sacrificed children were kept (see comments on 2 Kings 3:27).[6] This place would become known as the Valley of Slaughter because of all the dead bodies buried there after the Babylonian invasion (7:32).

Corpses . . . will become food . . . bones . . . will be brought out of their graves (7:33–8:1). Exposure to the elements and the consumption by wild animals of the corpses of those killed in battle was one of the covenant curses that Moses had warned of (Deut. 28:26). Exposure in some cases would come from the disinterment of the bones of the dead. Failure to receive a proper burial was considered highly shameful in this culture (2 Kings 9:7–10; Ps. 79:1–5), and the extension of this curse even to the kings, who often were buried with great ceremony in elaborate tombs, was especially significant (cf. 22:18–19).[7]

No balm in Gilead (8:22). Medicinal salve made of resin and olive oil was produced in Gilead in northern Galilee. There was no solution for Judah's crisis apart from returning to the Lord.

Wormwood (9:15). Wormwood here indicates a shrub with leaves that have an extremely bitter taste, used here as a vivid image for the bitterness of divine judgment (cf. Prov. 5:4; Amos 5:7).

Women who mourn (9:17). Mourning customs in the ancient Near East involved demonstrative expressions of grief, including tearing clothes and loud wailing. Professional mourners often joined the family to express grief (cf. Eccles. 12:5; Jer. 9:20; Ezek. 27:32; Amos 5:16).

Death has climbed through our windows (9:21). The Hebrew word for death (*mot*) and the name of the Canaanite god of death (*Mot*) are the same, so personifying death, as is done here, often carries a suggested wordplay regarding the god (see the article "The Canaanites and Canaanite Religion"). Mot, the god of death and the underworld, had a ravenous appetite for human flesh (cf. Job 18:13; Prov. 1:12; 27:20; 30:15–16; Isa. 5:14; Hab. 2:5).

Human corpses will fall like manure (9:22). See comments on Jer. 7:33–8:1.

Nations are uncircumcised (9:26). Circumcision was practiced throughout the ancient Near East, including by the nations mentioned here, but did not have the same covenantal significance as in Israel. In the Lord's eyes Judah was no different spiritually or morally from these pagan nations because they were "uncircumcised in heart."

Cuts down a tree from the forest (10:3). The prophet parodies the making and worship of idols with biting sarcasm (cf. Ps. 115:1–8; 135:15–18; Isa. 44:9–20). The prophet mocked idol worshipers for their devotion to lifeless objects that they had made with their own hands. Idol worshipers in the ancient Near East were aware that the deity and its idol were distinct from each other, and they even had a special ceremony called the "opening of the mouth," in which the presence of the deity came to indwell the image.[8]

He makes lightning for the rain (10:13). The Lord's control over the rains demonstrated his superiority to the pagan storm gods, like the Canaanite Baal and the Babylonian Marduk (see the article "The Canaanites and Canaanite Religion").

The Broken Covenant (11:1–17)

The words of this covenant (11:2). The Lord called on Jeremiah to remind the people of the terms of the Sinai covenant with its promises of blessing for obedience and warnings of cursing for disobedience (Lev. 26; Deut. 28).

They have returned to the iniquities of their fathers (11:10). King Josiah's religious reforms and covenantal renewal (cf. 2 Kings 22–23; 2 Chron. 34–35) had only a short-term effect.

Do not pray for these people (11:14). See comments on Jer. 7:16.

Jeremiah's Complaints (11:18–12:17)

I was like a docile lamb (11:19). Verses 18–20 contain the first of Jeremiah's "confessions" or prayers of lament concerning the hardships and persecution that he experienced as a prophet. Others are found in 12:1–17; 15:10–21; 17:14–18; 20:7–18. Lament was a common form of prayer in Israel and throughout the ancient Near East, and Jeremiah's prayers contain many of the elements found in the laments of the psalms (e.g., Pss. 3, 6, 13, 22, 88): vivid description of the worshiper's suffering (Jer. 15:16–17; 20:8–11, 14–18), accusatory language and questions toward God (Jer. 12:1; 15:18; 20:7), prayers for divine retribution against the wicked (Jer. 12:3; 15:15; 17:18; 18:21; 20:12), and a shift from complaint to praise and trust (Jer. 20:13).

Drag the wicked away like sheep to slaughter (12:3). The prayers of the righteous in the OT often contain imprecations or curses against the wicked (cf. Ps. 58:6–8; 69:22–28; 109:6–15; 137:8–9). These curses resemble those found in ancient Near Eastern political treaties. Despite the harsh language, Jeremiah prayed for the Lord to bring justice in accordance with the standards of *lex talionis* ("eye for eye") established in the Mosaic law (Exod. 21:24; Lev. 24:20). Jeremiah also gave over vengeance to the Lord rather than seeking it on his own.

Taught my people to swear by Baal (12:16). God originally had commanded Israel to completely destroy the Canaanites so that the Israelites would not be influenced to worship their gods (Deut. 7:1–4; 20:16–18). Rahab and others demonstrated that the sentence was not executed when the Canaanites turned to the Lord (cf. Josh. 2; 6:22–25), and here Baal worshipers who believe in the Lord are given the same promise of being "planted" in their land that was extended to Israel (24:6; 31:28; 32:41).

Judah Past the Point of No Return (13:1–17:27)

Linen undergarment (13:1). This belt was an undergarment wrapped around the body from the waist to the knees. Linen was an expensive material used for priestly garments (Lev. 16:4). The belt, as part of Jeremiah's sign-act, symbolized Judah's intimacy with the Lord and its priestly status.

Euphrates (13:4). In the OT this name normally signifies the Euphrates River, but here it most likely refers to a village with a similar-sounding name (cf. NIV, "Perath") near Jeremiah's hometown of Anathoth that is used symbolically to represent the Euphrates River. Jeremiah would have had to travel more than seven hundred miles twice to make two round trips to the actual Euphrates River. Jeremiah buried the belt on his first trip, and then he retrieved it on his second visit to find that it was "ruined and completely useless" (13:7). The people were as ruined and worthless as the belt because of their idol worship (13:10).

King . . . queen mother (13:18). This most likely refers to Jehoiachin and his mother, Nehushta, who were taken away into exile in 598 BC (cf. 2 Kings 24:8–17; Jer. 22:26; 29:2). The queen mother exercised considerable power in ancient Israel (see comments on 1 Kings 15:13).

Pull your skirts up over your face (13:26). Because of Judah's spiritual adultery, the Lord as the wronged husband would publicly shame his promiscuous wife by publicly exposing her nakedness (cf. Ezek. 16:37; Hosea 2:3). This imagery used for rhetorical effect needs to be balanced with statements in the OT concerning God's special concern for oppressed women (cf. Gen. 21:14–19; Deut. 10:18; Ps. 146:9).

Do not pray for . . . these people (14:11). See comments on Jer. 7:16.

No one to bury them (14:16). See comments on Jer. 7:33–8:1.

Worthless idols . . . bring rain (14:22). See the article "The Canaanites and Canaanite Religion." Israel had specifically turned to Baal worship because of their belief that this Canaanite god would bring them rain and abundant crops (cf. 1 Kings 18; Hosea 2:5, 8).

Even if Moses and Samuel should stand before me (15:1). Moses and Samuel were remembered as the greatest of Israel's prophetic intercessors (cf. Exod. 32:9–14; Num. 14:11–20; 1 Sam. 7:8–9; 12:16–23).

Manasseh son of Hezekiah (15:4). See comments on 2 Kings 21:10. This wicked king (697–642 BC) reversed the reforms made by his father, Hezekiah, and his sins included injustice, shedding innocent blood, idolatry, and even sacrificing his sons to the gods (2 Kings 21:1–16). The Lord had declared that he would wipe out Jerusalem for Manasseh's many sins (2 Kings 21:12–14).

Water that is not reliable (15:18). Jeremiah complains that God is unreliable and compares him to streams or wadis that filled with water after rains but that were empty streambeds at other times (cf. Job 6:15–20).

A dry streambed (wadi).

Do not marry or have sons or daughters (16:2). Jeremiah's unmarried status would have been quite unusual. Celibacy was rare because marriages were arranged by families, and men married at a young age. Jeremiah's lack of family signified the coming loss of family members through war and exile.

They will not be mourned or buried (16:4). See comments on Jer. 7:33–8:1.

Mourning feast (16:5). In light of the importance of proper mourning rites, the prohibition against visiting houses of mourning or participating in funerals would have made Jeremiah seem particularly unsympathetic to friends and loved ones.

Nor will anyone cut himself or shave his head (16:6). See comments on Jer. 7:29.

Do not enter the house where feasting is taking place (16:8). Weddings in ancient Israel were times of great celebration that might last for several days. Jeremiah was not to attend them, and this signified that marriage celebrations would cease because of the coming war and siege.

Inscribed with an iron stylus (17:1). An engraving stylus with a point made of flint or even diamond was used to carve inscriptions into metal or stone (cf. Job 19:24). The sinfulness of the people was indelibly etched into their character. The Lord promised that the new covenant would bring transformation as he would write his law on the hearts of the people (31:33).

Asherah poles (17:2). See comments on 1 Kings 15:13. These wooden poles or trees represented the Canaanite goddess Asherah and were associated with fertility rites conducted on high hills and in sacred groves (cf. 2:20, 27). Inscriptions from Kuntillet Ajrud in southern Judah attest to the syncretistic worship of "Yahweh and his asherah" (cf. Exod. 34:13; Deut. 7:5; 12:3; 1 Kings 14:15, 23). Josiah had earlier destroyed pagan worship objects as part of his reforms (2 Kings 23:4–7).

Jeremiah's Two Visits to the Potter (18:1–19:15)

Go down at once to the potter's house (18:2). Skilled potters made earthenware cups, bowls, jars, and craft items used for food production and serving, storage and transportation, as well as decoration and religious service. The availability and pliability of clay and then its durability when hardened were reasons for the widespread use of these objects.[9]

There he was, working away at the wheel (18:3). The Hebrew word for "wheel" here is "two stones." The potter's wheel consisted of a larger wheel at the bottom connected to a smaller disk at the top, on which the potter shaped the clay. The potter turned the wheel at the bottom with his foot, causing the upper wheel connected by a spindle to rotate as well.

The turning of the wheel enabled the potter to shape and mold the clay as desired.

The clay became flawed in the potter's hand (18:4). If the object that the potter was making was marred or blemished, the potter would start over by reshaping the wet clay into the desired object. The marred clay represented Judah's sinful condition, but the Lord was willing to reshape them into the people he desired, and there was still time to repent and avoid his judgment (18:5–6).

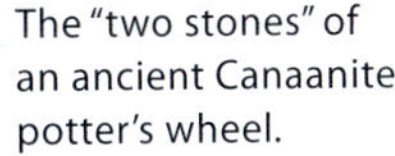
The "two stones" of an ancient Canaanite potter's wheel.

I will relent (18:8). Prophecies of judgment and salvation were implicitly conditional. Historical examples of where God relented from sending judgment in response to repentance would include Nineveh when Jonah preached there (Jon. 3) and Jerusalem in 701 BC (Jer. 26:17–19; cf. Joel 2:12–17). The Lord relented from sending judgment at other times in response to prophetic intercession (cf. Exod. 32:11–14; Num. 14:13–20; Amos 7:1–6).

Go, buy a potter's clay jar (19:1). This event may have occurred months or even years after the first visit to the potter in chapter 18 and seems to reflect a time when the opportunity to avoid judgment through repentance had passed. The jar is in its finished state, unlike the clay on the potter's wheel that could still be reshaped (18:4).

Ben Hinnom Valley (19:2). See comments on Jer. 7:31.

To burn their children in the fire (19:5). This refers to the pagan practice of child sacrifice, which here is connected to the worship of the Canaanite god Baal (cf. 7:31) (see comments on 2 Kings 3:27).

Topheth (19:6). See comments on Jer. 7:31.

Eat the flesh of their sons and their daughters (19:9). Moses had warned of this fate as one of the potential covenant curses against a disobedient Israel (Lev. 26:29; Deut. 28:53–57). The siege of cities often resulted in the conditions of extreme famine that even led to the horrific practice of parents eating their children (2 Kings 6:28–29; Lam. 2:20; 4:10).

Shatter the jar (19:10). The smashing of the jar in front of the leaders was an object lesson symbolizing the impending destruction of Judah and Jerusalem. From early times in Egypt priests inscribed the names of enemies on pottery jars and then smashed them as part of a cursing ritual.

Burned incense to all the stars in the sky (19:13). See comments on Deut. 17:3; 2 Kings 17:16.

Jeremiah Beaten and Imprisoned (20:1–18)

Pashhur the priest, the son of Immer (20:1). Pashhur's position was likely next to the high priest in authority and involved keeping order in the temple precincts (cf. 2 Kings 25:18). The authorities viewed Jeremiah as a troublemaker who needed to be disciplined because of his controversial message.

Beaten (20:2). Deuteronomy 25:2–3 stipulates that a person sentenced to a beating could not be given more than forty lashes.

Stocks (20:2). The Hebrew word (related to a verb that means to "turn" or "overturn") occurs only here, in 29:26, and in 2 Chron. 16:10. It may refer to an instrument of confinement that kept the body in a stooped position or perhaps to a small and cramped dungeon.[10] Another incident where Jeremiah is beaten and imprisoned at a makeshift dungeon in the house of a royal official is found in 37:15–16. There are recurring references to Jeremiah's more permanent confinement at the "courtyard of the guard" (32:2, 8, 12; 33:1; 37:21; 38:6, 13, 28; 39:14) during the reign of Zedekiah.

The king of Babylon (20:4). This is the first specific mention of Babylon, the previously unidentified enemy from the north; this king would be Nebuchadnezzar (see the article "The Babylonians").

The Lord Rejects Zedekiah's Request (21:1–14)

Inquire of the Lord on our behalf (21:2). King Zedekiah made this request as the Babylonians were besieging Jerusalem in the final days of his rule. The Babylonians besieged Jerusalem for eighteen months (from 588 to 586 BC) before destroying the city. Zedekiah frequently sought Jeremiah's help and counsel (cf. 37; 38:14–28) but lacked the courage to follow his advice. Zedekiah hoped that the Lord might miraculously intervene and save his people as he had done when he delivered Jerusalem from the Assyrian siege in 701 BC.

Nebuchadnezzar (21:2). This is the first mention by name in Jeremiah of the Babylonian king who reigned from 605 to 562 BC, when the Neo-Babylonian Empire was at the height of its power (see the article "The Babylonians").

With an outstretched hand and a strong arm (21:5). Jeremiah reverses Israel's holy war traditions (cf. Exod. 6:6; Deut. 4:34; 11:2) so that the Lord is now fighting against his people with the Babylonians, an idea emphasized by the Lord's repeated "I will" statements in verses 3–7.

Whoever stays in this city will die (21:9). Jeremiah advocated surrender to the Babylonians as the only way Jerusalem could be spared, because the Lord had given the city over to Babylon as punishment for Judah's apostasy (cf. 34:2–3; 37:6–10, 17; 38:1–3, 17–18, 20–23). Zedekiah did not follow Jeremiah's advice because he feared his officials who favored continued military resistance to the Babylonians and viewed Jeremiah as a traitor.

I will kindle a fire in your forest (21:14). The "forest" here refers to the palace in Jerusalem, which was called the "House of the Forest of Lebanon" because of the large amount of cedar used in its construction (1 Kings 7:2).

Judgment of Judah's Unrighteous Kings (22:1–30)

Do not weep for the dead (22:10). Josiah was killed at Megiddo in 609 BC in battle with Neco II of Egypt, and Jeremiah had composed laments after his death (2 Chron. 35:25).

For he will never return again . . . Shallum son of Josiah (22:10–12). Shallum, whose throne name was Jehoahaz, succeeded his father, Josiah, as king but was taken to Egypt three months later by Neco II (2 Kings 23:31–33; 2 Chron. 36:2–3).

Builds his palace through unrighteousness (22:13). Neco II of Egypt installed Jehoiakim as king of Judah in the place of his younger brother Jehoahaz. Despite Judah's national crisis, Jehoaikim engaged in a lavish remodeling of his palace or perhaps the construction of another royal residence (cf. 36:22), using his own people as slave labor.

Spacious upstairs rooms . . . windows . . . paneled with cedar . . . painted bright red (22:14). Roof chambers with large rooms expanded the interior space of the palace and made for cooler temperatures. Cedar paneling was the most expensive wood and a luxury reserved for palaces and temples (1 Kings 7:2, 3, 7, 12; 9:11). Red paint came from a costly dye (cf. Ezek. 23:14).[11]

They will not mourn for him . . . he will be buried like a donkey (22:18–19). Jehoiakim would die without the honors of a state funeral (cf. 36:30) (see comments on Jer. 7:33–8:1). The

Cedar trees of Lebanon.

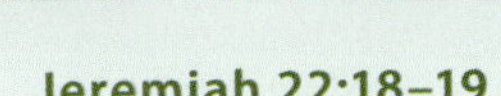

exact circumstances of Jehoiakim's death are uncertain, but it appears that he died during the Babylonian siege of Jerusalem in 598 BC.

Son of Jehoiakim . . . a signet ring (22:24). Jehoiachin (Coniah) became king after the death of his father, Jehoiakim, but was taken as a prisoner to Babylon three months later (2 Kings 24:8–16; 2 Chron. 36:9–10). A signet ring bore the owner's personal seal and was used by the king to stamp official documents. The Davidic kings reigned as the Lord's vice-regents (2 Sam. 7:13–14), but the Lord was now rejecting Jehoiachin as his representative. The reversal of this prophecy appears in Hag. 2:20–23.

Record this man as childless . . . none of his descendants will succeed in sitting on the throne (22:30). Jehoiachin (also referred to as Coniah or Jeconiah) had at least seven sons (1 Chron. 3:17–19; Matt. 1:12), but none of them would succeed him as king. The Persians appointed his grandson Zerubbabel as the governor of Judah in the postexilic period (Hag. 1:1).

Corrupt Shepherds and the Future Branch (23:1–8)

Woe to the shepherds (23:1). Shepherd was a common occupation and a metaphor for rulers throughout the ancient Near East (cf. Ps. 78:71–72). The image spoke to the care and protection that these leaders were to provide for their people, but the leaders of Israel and Judah had failed miserably to live up to this ideal (cf. Isa. 56:11; Jer. 10:21; 12:10; Ezek. 34:1–10; Zech. 10:3).

A Righteous Branch (23:5). This title refers to the future ideal Davidic ruler through whom God would fulfill his covenant promises to David (cf. 30:9; 33:15). God's judgment would cause the Davidic line to be like a tree that was cut down and reduced to nothing more than a stump. The "branch" pictures the new life that would emerge as God restored David's throne (Zech. 3:8; 6:12; cf. Isa. 11:1). The title "righteous [*tsaddiq*] branch" and name "The Lord Is Our Righteousness [*tsedeq*]" for this future king are puns on the name of Zedekiah (which means "righteousness of the Lord"), who did not embody the character reflected in his name.

Condemnation of the False Prophets (23:9–40)

Prophets of Samaria . . . prophesied by Baal (23:13). See comments on Jer. 2:8. Ahab and Jezebel had provided support for the prophets of Baal (1 Kings 18:19), but Elijah had them killed following the contest on Mount Carmel (1 Kings 18:40). Jehu had also killed Baal's prophets when purging Baal worship from the land (2 Kings 10:18–28).

Stood in the council of the Lord (23:18, 22). The council is the meeting place of the Lord and his heavenly hosts where the Lord announces his plans and commissions the members of the council to accomplish his purposes. True prophets are viewed as having access to these heavenly cabinet meetings (cf. 1 Kings 22:19–23; Isa. 6:8). The false prophets announced only their own dreams, and their failure to call the people to repentance was proof of the inauthenticity of their message.

I had a dream! I had a dream! (23:25). Dreams were a common form of divine communication in the OT and the ancient Near East at large (cf. Gen. 37; 41; Dan. 2; 7). Archaeologists have discovered numerous dream reports and manuals on how to interpret dreams in the cultures surrounding ancient Israel.

Good Figs and Bad Figs (24:1–10)

Two baskets of figs (24:1). Figs were an important part of the Israelites' diet and were eaten fresh, dried, in cakes, or preserved. They were harvested twice a year, in May-June and then again in August.

Good figs (24:2, 4). The good figs represented the exiles living in Babylon after 597 BC. They were good not in the sense of personal righteousness but in that the Lord had good intentions for the exiles to save and restore them (24:6–7).

Bad figs (24:2, 8). The bad figs represent Zedekiah and the Jews who remained in the land after 597 BC and who viewed themselves as favored by God because they had not been banished to a foreign land. The fate awaiting those who remained in the land was further judgment.

Babylon and the Cup of God's Wrath (25:1–38)

Fourth year of Jehoiakim (25:1). The year 605 BC was a critical one in Judah's history (cf. 36:1; 45:1; 46:2). Key events from this year include (1) Babylon's defeat of Egypt and Assyria at the battle of Carchemish (see comments on Jer. 46:2); (2) the deportation of the first wave of Judean exiles,

"This is what the Lord, the God of Israel said to me: 'Take this cup of the wine of wrath from my hand and make all the nations to whom I am sending you drink from it'" (Jer. 25:15). Depicted is an Assyrian king with a cup in his hand.

including Daniel; and (3) the composition of Jeremiah's scroll that was destroyed by Jehoiakim (chap. 36).

My servant Nebuchadnezzar (25:9). See the article "The Babylonians." The Lord would use the Babylonians as his instrument of judgment against Judah and the nations, just as he would use other foreign kings to accomplish his purposes (cf. Isa. 10:5; 44:28–45:1).

Seventy years (25:12). Babylon's dominion over the nations lasted from its defeat of Assyria in 609 BC to the rise of the Persians in 539 BC. "Seventy" is a round number indicating a lengthy period and is used figuratively elsewhere in the OT to indicate completeness (cf. Ps. 90:10; Isa. 23:15). An inscription of the Assyrian king Esar-haddon makes reference to Babylon being desolate for seventy years.[12]

The king of Sheshach (25:26). Sheshach is a code name for Babylon, using a technique called *atbash,* which reads the letters of the alphabet in reverse order. With this technique, in Hebrew the consonants *b-b-l* for Babylon become *sh-sh-k* for Sheshach (see also 51:1). Jeremiah may have used such coded references at times in his preaching.

Jeremiah on Trial (26:1–24)

At the beginning of the reign of Jehoiakim (26:1). Jehoiakim came to the throne in 609 BC. This message appears to be the same as Jeremiah's temple sermon in chapter 7 (or at least a similar message).

I will make this temple like Shiloh (26:6). See comments on Jer. 7:12, 14.

You must surely die! (26:8). The penalty for false prophecy was death (Deut. 18:20). Those demanding a death sentence for Jeremiah likely viewed him as a false prophet for suggesting that the Lord might destroy his own house.

Micah . . . prophesied in the days of King Hezekiah (26:18). The elders supported Jeremiah's defense by recalling Hezekiah's positive response to Micah's earlier warning that Jerusalem would be destroyed (cf. Mic. 3:9–12). Because Hezekiah sought the Lord's favor, the Lord relented from sending the threatened judgment.

Uriah . . . prophesied . . . King Jehoiakim . . . heard his words (26:20–21). See also Jehoiakim's response to Jeremiah's scroll in 36:20–26.

They brought Uriah out of Egypt (26:23). The Egyptians had installed Jehoiakim on the throne (2 Kings 23:24–25) and cooperated with him here in the extradition of Uriah. The Lachish letters also mention the sending of a Jewish commander to Egypt.

Ahikam son of Shaphan (26:24). Support from this influential official protected Jeremiah from the same fate suffered by Uriah. Ahikam's name has been discovered on a seal impression dating from the time of Jeremiah. The family of Shaphan had supported Josiah's reforms (2 Kings 22:8–14) and were also sympathetic to Jeremiah's message (cf. 29:3; 36:10–14; 40:7–10). They likely belonged to the party of Judean officials favoring submission to Babylon as the best course of action.

The Yoke of Babylon and Jeremiah's Conflict with Hananiah (27:1–28:17)

At the beginning of the reign of Zedekiah (27:1). Most Hebrew manuscripts here read "in the reign of Jehoiakim," but verses 3, 12, 20, and 28:1 clearly indicate that "Zedekiah" should be read here (as in a few Hebrew manuscripts and the Syriac). The year was 594 BC (cf. 28:1).

Make chains and yoke bars (27:2). The yoke was a wooden crossbar placed over the necks of two oxen, fastened around their necks by leather thongs, and used when plowing or threshing grain.[13] Jeremiah wore the heavy yoke as another of his sign-acts, conveying through this unusual object lesson the need for submission to Babylon.

Through messengers who are coming to King Zedekiah (27:2). Representatives from five surrounding nations had likely come to Jerusalem to discuss the possibility of revolt against Babylon. The Babylonian Chronicle indicates that Nebuchadnezzar was also dealing with internal rebellion at home at this time.

Edom . . . Moab . . . Ammonites (27:3). See comments on Ezek. 25:2; 25:9; 25:12.

Tyre . . . Sidon (27:3). See comments on Ezek. 28:21.

My servant Nebuchadnezzar (27:6). See comments on Jer. 25:9; see the article "The Babylonians."

Articles of the Lord's temple (27:16). Nebuchadnezzar had taken valued treasures and objects from the temple when he had captured Jerusalem in 597 BC (2 Kings 24:13).

Zedekiah . . . the fourth year (28:1). The events in this chapter occurred in 594 BC.

The prophet Hananiah (28:1). Representative of the prophets that Jeremiah had warned about in 27:14–17, Hananiah was offering assurances of peace and prosperity that the people wanted to hear (6:14; 8:11). Hananiah promised that the articles of the temple taken to Babylon in 597 BC, and even Jehoiachin the king, would return to Jerusalem within two years.

Prophets . . . prophesied war, disaster, and plague (28:8). The people could not tell the future to determine whether the prophets of judgment or salvation were telling the truth (cf. Deut. 18:22–23), but prophecies of judgment were the only ones that made sense in light of the people's disobedience and the severity of the Babylonian crisis. Prophets promising peace could be trusted only if there was dramatic confirmation of their message (28:9).

Jeremiah's Letter to the Exiles (29:1–32)

The letter that the prophet Jeremiah sent (29:1). This chapter focuses on three letters of Jeremiah to the exiles in Babylon written after the deportation in 597 BC (29:1–23, 24–28, 29–32). There is also mention of a letter from Shemaiah in Babylon to Jerusalem, to which Jeremiah responds (29:24–25). These letters were conveyed by officials traveling between Judah and Babylon (29:3).

Elasah son of Shaphan (29:3). See comments on Jer. 26:24.

Build houses . . . plant gardens . . . find wives for yourselves, and have sons and daughters (29:5–6). Jeremiah had to counter expectations of a short exile promoted by the false prophets among the Jews in Babylon (29:21–23, 29–32). The exiles needed to plan for a long stay in Babylon and to settle into the patterns of normal life. The best course of actions for these exiles was to accept their fate and be supportive of the empire. Ezekiel testifies to how the Jews in exile were allowed to live in their own communities and even allowed to own homes (Ezek. 3:15; 8:1; 11:17–21).[14] Likewise, the TAYN archives (a collection of nearly one hundred texts) indicate that some Jewish communities were flourishing in the later Persian Empire (see the article "The Persians").[15]

Seventy years (29:10). See comments on Jer. 25:12.

The priest Zephaniah (29:25). As high priest, Zephaniah had the role of censuring and punishing prophets who exercised their role illegitimately (cf. 36:5).

Stocks and an iron collar (29:26). See comments on Jer. 20:2.

The Promise of Israel's Restoration (30:1–31:40)

Write on a scroll (30:2). This document would have been in the form of a scroll likely made of parchment or papyrus (cf. 36:2; 51:61–63).

The wooden writing palette of an ancient scribe.

Samaria . . . Ephraim (31:5–6). The returnees from exile would include those taken away in the captivity of the northern kingdom in 722 BC, and Israel would once again be a unified nation (31:27).

Ramah . . . lament with bitter weeping (31:15). This town was located about five miles north of Jerusalem and was the staging area through which many of the Jewish exiles passed on their way to Babylon (cf. 40:1).

Rachel weeping (31:15). Back in the time of the patriarchs, Rachel grieved as she was dying while giving birth to Benjamin (Gen. 35:16–18), and her grief now represented the grieving of all women in Israel over the exile. Rachel was also the grandmother of Ephraim and Manasseh (Gen. 30:22–24; 48:1), further reflecting the focus on the northern kingdom in this passage. Rachel's burial place was located near Ramah (cf. 1 Sam. 10:2). Jeremiah perhaps had delivered these salvation oracles early in his ministry, with their being reapplied to the exile of Judah at a later time.

Fathers have eaten sour grapes . . . children's teeth are set on edge (31:29). This proverbial statement represented the claim of a present generation that they were suffering for the sins of previous generations (cf. Ezek. 18:2).

Jeremiah Purchases a Field (32:1–33:28)

Tenth year of King Zedekiah . . . eighteenth year of Nebuchadnezzar (32:1). These events occurred in 587 BC, as the Babylonians began the final siege of Jerusalem.

Imprisoned in the guard's courtyard (32:2). Jeremiah had been imprisoned at an earlier time when he attempted to leave Jerusalem during a break in the siege (cf. 37:11–16). This location was Jeremiah's primary place of confinement until he was released by the Babylonians following the capture of the city (cf. 37:21; 38:13, 28; 39:14–15).

Buy my field in Anathoth . . . you own the right of redemption to buy it (32:6). When a relative was forced to sell property because of debt, the next of kin or another close relative was to redeem the property so that the land remained in the extended family (Lev. 25:35–38). Jeremiah's purchase of his cousin Hanamel's property conveyed the certainty of the Lord's promise to bring his people back to the land (32:14). This transaction may or may not be the same as the one mentioned in 37:11–16. If the same, Jeremiah completes here the transaction that he was unable to finish when arrested in chapter 37.

Seventeen shekels of silver (32:9). Silver was commonly used as currency at this time, and this amount would be approximately seven ounces. The value or cost of this purchase is unclear, but the money needed to purchase food would have been a precious commodity in a city under siege. Land prices likely were depressed as a result of the Babylonian invasion.

Baruch son of Neriah (32:12). Baruch, Jeremiah's faithful scribe, is mentioned here for the first time in the book. Baruch is referred to as a "scribe" in 36:26, the title for a high government official. He and his brother Seraiah, a "quartermaster" for the king (51:59), belonged to a prominent family in Judah. Baruch had earlier recorded Jeremiah's messages of judgment and then read the scroll at the temple (36:1–19). Baruch would later be accused of treasonously inciting Jeremiah against his own people (43:3) and kidnapped along with Jeremiah and taken to Egypt (43:6–7). Baruch likely played a significant role in the composition of the book of Jeremiah. Two seal impressions bearing the name "Baruch son of Neriah the scribe" have been discovered, though their provenance is unknown.[16]

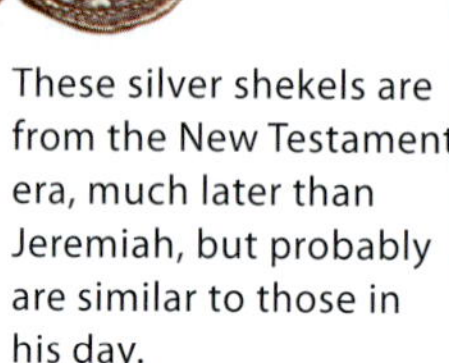

These silver shekels are from the New Testament era, much later than Jeremiah, but probably are similar to those in his day.

Siege ramps have come against the city (32:24). See comments on Jer. 6:6.

Ben Hinnom Valley to sacrifice . . . to Molech (32:35). See comments on 2 Kings 3:27; Jer. 7:31.

Houses of this city . . . torn down for defense (33:4). In besieged cities it often was necessary to demolish houses in order to provide materials for repairing breaches in the city walls as defenses against the siege ramps built by the attacking army. Excavations at the Judean city of Lachish, for example, have uncovered a counterramp inside that city that was raised during the Assyrian siege.[17]

A desolation without people, without inhabitants, and without animals (33:10). Ancient Near Eastern treaties or battle accounts often used hyperbolic language to describe the defeats inflicted on vanquished enemies (cf. Josh. 10:40; 11:8, 11, 20). The prophets employed this same type of extreme language in order to impress upon the people the seriousness of the coming judgment (cf. 44:12–14, 27–28).

A Righteous Branch to sprout up for David (33:15). See comments on Jer. 23:5.

This seal impression (bulla) bears the name of "Baruch son of Neriah the scribe," although some scholars have questioned its authenticity.

Judgment on Judah for Breaking a Promise (34:1–22)

Nebuchadnezzar . . . fighting against Jerusalem (34:1). The Babylonian king Nebuchadnezzar's invasion of Judah, which led to the fall of Jerusalem, began in 588 BC.

You will not escape (34:3). See comments on Jer. 21:9.

You will die peacefully . . . a burning ceremony for you (34:5). The positive outcome of remaining in the land and being honored in death for Zedekiah would appear to have been contingent upon the king's obedience to Jeremiah's counsel to surrender to the Babylonians. The funeral fire involved the burning of incense and spices and was part of the honors accorded to royalty in death (cf. 2 Chron. 16:14; 21:19), and it is attested archaeologically elsewhere.

Lachish and Azekah (34:7). The Lachish letters, a series of eighteen letters inscribed on clay tablets (ostraca), attest to the desperate conditions facing the Judean military during the Babylonian invasion.[18] In Letter 4 the commander at Jerusalem states that he is looking for the signal fires at Lachish and that the ones from Azekah are no longer visible, indicating a time shortly after the one described here. Lachish was located twenty-five miles southwest of Jerusalem. Azekah was a fortress city located north of Lachish and about eighteen miles southwest of Jerusalem.

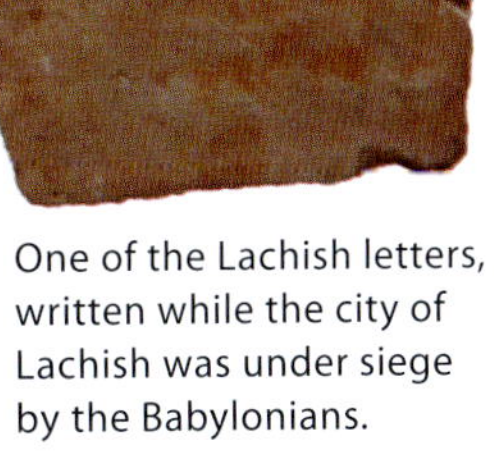
One of the Lachish letters, written while the city of Lachish was under siege by the Babylonians.

Proclaim freedom to them (34:8). As the Babylonian army threatened Jerusalem, Zedekiah and the people of the city made a covenant to release their Hebrew slaves in a desperate attempt to gain the Lord's favor. The Mosaic law stipulated that Hebrew slaves were to be released after six years of service (34:14; cf. Exod. 21:1–11; Lev. 25:39–46; Deut. 15:12–18), but the people had ignored these laws.

Taken back his male and female slaves (34:16). The king and people broke their promise to release their slaves by taking them back. The Babylonian withdrawal from Jerusalem when Egypt marched up to help Judah (37:11) is the most likely explanation for why the king and people reneged on their promise.

Calf they cut in two . . . pass between its pieces (34:18). A ritual for making a covenant involved cutting up an animal and the parties walking between the body parts as a way of symbolizing what would happen to anyone breaking the covenant (cf. Gen. 15:7–21).

The Faithfulness of the Rechabites (35:1–19)

The days of Jehoiakim (35:1). The narrative returns to the time of King Jehoiakim (609–598 BC) to provide an example of faithfulness in Judah that contrasts with the example of national infidelity in chapter 34.

The Rechabites (35:2). These were the descendants of Jehonadab, the son of Rechab, who lived during the reign of Jehu in Israel in the ninth century BC (2 Kings 10:15–17). Jehonadab had supported Jehu's bloody purge of Baal worship in Israel (2 Kings 10:18–27).

Do not drink wine . . . must not build a house or sow seed or plant a vineyard (35:6–7). For more than two centuries the clan had followed the instructions of their forefather by living in tents, not drinking wine, and not planting fields or vineyards. The Rechabites affirmed their loyalty to their family traditions by refusing to drink the wine that Jeremiah placed in front of them. They had moved into Jerusalem only as an accommodation to the Babylonian crisis (35:11). The point of Jeremiah's message was not that the Rechabites had been more faithful to the Lord than the people at large, but rather that they had been faithful to their forefather in the way that the nation should have been faithful to God's commandments (35:14–16).

Will never fail to have a man stand before me (35:19). The same promise is given to the house of David in 33:18. The Rechabite clan did continue into the postexilic period (1 Chron. 2:55).

Jehoiakim Destroys Jeremiah's Scroll (36:1–32)

Fourth year of Jehoiakim (36:1). This would be 605 BC, the same year in which Nebuchadnezzar, king of Babylonia, defeated Egypt and Assyria at the battle of Carchemish and took control of Syria-Palestine.

Take a scroll, and write on it . . . from the time I first spoke to you (36:2). Prophets most often delivered their messages orally, but there were times when God commanded them to write down their words (Isa. 8:1; 30:8; Jer. 30:2; Hab. 2:2).[19] Jeremiah began his ministry in 627 BC (1:1–3) and had been preaching for more than two decades. This scroll summarized Jeremiah's warnings of judgment.

Baruch son of Neriah (36:4). See comments on Jer. 32:12.

I am restricted (36:5). Jeremiah may have been banned from the temple because of his earlier sermon prophesying the destruction of the temple (chaps. 7, 26).

A day of fasting (36:6). The only day of fasting commanded in the Mosaic law was the Day of Atonement (Lev. 16:29, 31), but fasting and communal prayer in times of crisis were common (1 Sam. 7:5–6; Ezra 8:21–23; Neh. 9:1–3; Joel 1:13–14; 2:12–17).

In the fifth year . . . in the ninth month (36:9). Baruch read the scroll at the temple in November-December of 604 BC. The time from the command to write the scroll until its public reading was at least nine months. Nebuchadnezzar destroyed the Philistine city of Ashkelon in this same month, and the imminent threat that his campaign presented to Judah was likely the reason for this assembly.[20]

In the chamber of Gemariah son of Shaphan (36:10). Baruch read the scroll to the people from this location, which had a window looking out over the temple court. Gemariah was the royal secretary and belonged to the family of Shaphan, who supported Jeremiah (see comments on Jer. 26:24). Gemariah's son Micaiah reported the contents of Jeremiah's scroll to a select group of officials, who then asked for a private reading.

Three or four columns, Jehoiakim would cut the scroll . . . and throw the columns into the fire (36:23). Because of their size, scrolls were rolled out only three to four columns at a time when read. Jehoiakim would cut the scroll with his knife after each section was read and then toss it into the fire. Jehoiakim's reaction to this scroll stands in contrast to the repentant reaction of his father, Josiah, to the newly discovered scroll containing the book of the law in 622 BC (2 Kings 22:10–13).

Jeremiah Imprisoned during the Reign of Zedekiah (37:1–21)

Zedekiah . . . reigned as king (37:1). The narrative now moves to the time of Zedekiah (597–586 BC). Chapters 37–44 provide a chronological account of the final days of Judah as a nation and the events that occurred in the aftermath of the destruction of Jerusalem.

Please pray to the Lord our God for us (37:3). See comments on Jer. 21:2.

Pharaoh's army had left Egypt (37:5). During the Babylonian siege of Jerusalem that began in 588 BC, the armies of Pharaoh Hophra (589–570 BC) had marched north in response to Judah's request for assistance (cf. Ezek. 17:11–18). The presence of the Egyptian army caused the Babylonians to temporarily withdraw from Jerusalem (cf. 34:21) to deal with the Egyptians.

When the Chaldean army withdrew . . . Jeremiah started to leave Jerusalem (37:11–12). Jeremiah attempted to take advantage of the withdrawal of the siege by leaving Jerusalem to take possession of some family property around Anathoth. This property may or may not be the same as the field of Hanamel that Jeremiah purchases in chapter 32 (see comments on Jer. 32:6).

Beat him and placed him in jail in the house of Jonathan . . . a cell in the dungeon (37:15–16). Jeremiah was kept in a makeshift cell at the house of this royal official. The Hebrew in 37:16 describes his cell as "a house of the pit" and "the dungeon." Jeremiah likely was confined in an underground cellar that may have been used to store grain and that was cramped and uncomfortable (cf. Gen. 40:15; 41:14).

Zedekiah gave orders . . . guard's courtyard (37:21). Zedekiah moved Jeremiah to a more favorable location and provided him with food but refused to release him or follow his counsel for fear of his officials.

Jeremiah Thrown into a Cistern (38:1–28)

Heard the words Jeremiah was speaking to all the people (38:1). The chronological relationship of chapters 37 and 38 is not clear. Jeremiah appears to be preaching among the people, which means that this event occurred before his incarceration in the previous chapter. If this incident follows the events of chapter 37, then Jeremiah's message was being reported to the people by Baruch and others while he was still in prison.

Whoever surrenders to the Chaldeans will live (38:2). See comments on Jer. 21:9. The term "Chaldea" refers to a region south of Babylonia. When the Assyrians started to decline, a Chaldean dynasty consolidated power in Chaldea and Babylonia. This dynasty, which included Nebuchadnezzar, ruled in Babylon during the time of the Neo-Babylonian Empire (see the article "The Babylonians"). In several places in the Bible the term "Chaldean" is used synonymously with "Babylonian."

Weakening the morale (38:4). Literally this translates as "weakening the hands." In other words, Jeremiah's message was demoralizing the soldiers who were trying to defend Jerusalem. This same expression appears in the Lachish letters with references to how certain princes were discouraging the military officer Joash (see comments on Jer. 34:7).

Dropped him into the cistern (38:6). The officials lowered Jeremiah into a cistern (see comments on Jer. 2:13) that was empty of water but had a layer of mud on the bottom. There was no way for Jeremiah to escape, and eventually he would have died of starvation if left here. Jeremiah's enemies may have thought that by leaving him to die they could avoid the guilt of shedding the innocent blood of one recognized as a prophet (see 26:15; cf. Deut. 19:10, 13; Jon. 1:12).

Ebed-melech, a Cushite court official (38:7). This royal official was from the African kingdom of Cush, south of Egypt (see the article "The Cushites"), and his name (perhaps a title) means "king's servant." Foreigners often served in the royal court. The term *saris* likely means "eunuch" but could mean "official" (cf. Gen. 39:1). His role in this story suggests that he was a trusted advisor of the king. Legal and business proceedings often were conducted at the city gate, and the king likely was listening to cases when Ebed-melech made his appeal for Jeremiah (cf. Ruth 4:1–12; 2 Sam. 15:2–6). In 39:15–18 the Lord promises Ebed-melech that he will protect him because of how he has acted to save Jeremiah's life.

Remained in the guard's courtyard (38:13). Jeremiah was returned to prison after his rescue from the cistern and remained there until freed by the Babylonians when they took Jerusalem (38:28; 39:13–14).

I am worried about the Judeans who have defected to the Chaldeans (38:19). In addition to his fear of the officials, Zedekiah expressed his fear of the Jews who had already defected over to the Babylonian army. He feared mistreatment because he had continued the resistance that had led to the miserable conditions in Jerusalem.

All the women who remain in the palace (38:22). Typically in the ancient Near East, the conquering king would take the harem of the defeated king and his family, with the possibility of rape, torture, deportation, or execution (cf. 39:6).

The Fall of Jerusalem (39:1–10)

Ninth year of King Zedekiah . . . tenth month (39:1). Nebuchadnezzar's siege of Jerusalem began January 15, 588 BC.

In the fourth month of Zedekiah's eleventh year, on the ninth day of the month (39:2). Nebuchadnezzar's army captured the city of Jerusalem on July 18, 586 BC. The siege of Jerusalem lasted eighteen months. A second account of the fall of Jerusalem that closely parallels 2 Kings 25:1–12 is found in 52:1–16.

Zedekiah . . . and all the fighting men . . . fled (39:4). Zedekiah and his remaining troops escaped Jerusalem and fled toward the Jordan Valley, perhaps hoping to cross over into Moab. The Babylonian army captured Zedekiah in the plains of Jericho and took him to appear before Nebuchadnezzar at Riblah in Syria, where the king had his base of operations.

Passed sentence on him (39:5). Nebuchadnezzar's punishment of Zedekiah was severe, forcing him to watch the execution of his nobles and sons and then having his eyes gouged out. The blinding of conquered enemies was a common practice in the ancient Near East.[21] Zedekiah was then shackled and taken to Babylon as a prisoner. No further record is given of what happened to him in exile.

Burned down the king's palace . . . and tore down the walls (39:8). The Babylonians also burned the temple (52:13; cf. 2 Kings 25:9). Archaeological evidence attests to the destruction and burning of Jerusalem in all parts of the city from this time.

Deported the rest of the people to Babylon (39:9). Many of the survivors of the siege of Jerusalem were taken into exile. A substantial population among the poor who had no land or resources that would make them threats to the Babylonians remained in the land (cf. 2 Kings 25:22–26). The Babylonians gave them "vineyards and fields" so that they would be able to collect tribute from them (39:10).

Jeremiah's Release by the Babylonians (39:11–41:10)

Take him and look after him (39:12). Nebuchadnezzar ordered Jeremiah released from prison and likely treated the prophet favorably in light of his message that the Babylonians were the Lord's instrument of judgment.

Turned him over to Gedaliah son of Ahikam, son of Shaphan (39:14). The Babylonians appointed Gedaliah as governor to administer the province of Judah. Gedaliah was from the family of Shaphan, who had supported Jeremiah (see comments on Jer. 26:24). The Babylonians likely appointed Gedaliah as governor because his family was part of the "pro-Babylonian" faction in Judah that advocated surrender to Babylon.

Go tell Ebed-melech . . . "I will rescue you" (39:16–17). The Lord had promised to protect and deliver this official who had intervened to save Jeremiah from the cistern (38:1–13).

Nebuzaradan . . . released him at Ramah (40:1). After Jeremiah's initial release to Gedaliah at Jerusalem, Babylonian soldiers took him to Ramah (cf. 31:15), the staging area for deportation to Babylon. Nebuzaradan, the Babylonian commander, found Jeremiah at Ramah and then gave him the option of remaining in the land or going to Babylon.

Mizpah (40:6). Mizpah was a fortress town in the territory of Benjamin, approximately five to seven miles north of Jerusalem, where Gedaliah took up residence and established Judah's new capital (cf. 2 Kings 25:23) because Jerusalem was in ruins. Excavations from Mizpah have offered no signs of destruction from this time. Saul was anointed Israel's first king at Mizpah (1 Sam. 10:17–24), and during the postexilic time of Nehemiah, Mizpah once again functioned as an administrative center (Neh. 3:7, 15, 19) (see comments on Neh. 3:7).

All the commanders of the armies . . . came to Gedaliah (40:7–8). The Babylonian-appointed governor Gedaliah had initial success in gathering the leftover Judean army officers and troops who had escaped the Babylonians and were in hiding, perhaps continuing to resist the Babylonians as guerillas and insurgents. Gedaliah offered assurances that Babylon would not retaliate against them and that he would represent their interests before the Babylonians (40:9–10).

Baalis, king of the Ammonites, has sent Ishmael (40:14). Ammon was the nation just to the east of Judah (in modern Jordan) (see comments on Gen. 19:37–38; Jer. 49:1). A seal inscription found in Jordan bearing the name Baal-yisha may refer to this king. Baalis perhaps conspired to kill Gedaliah because of his hatred of the Babylonians and their supporters, as the Ammonites had participated in talks concerning an anti-Babylonian coalition in 594 BC (27:3), or he may have simply wished to destabilize Judah for his own territorial expansion. Nebuchadnezzar defeated the Ammonites in 582 BC, perhaps in response to this conspiracy.

Ishmael . . . to kill you (40:14). As a member of the family of David and one of King Zedekiah's officers (41:1), Ishmael may have sought revenge for Gedaliah's collaboration with the Babylonians, or he may have even had hopes of restoring Davidic control over Judah. Two seals reading "Ishmael son of the king" have been discovered and perhaps refer to this figure.

In the seventh month (41:1). This event occurred in Tishri (September-October), indicating that Gedaliah's murder occurred only three months after the fall of Jerusalem in 586 BC. The events that transpire in chapter 40 seem to suggest a longer period of time. Some scholars date Gedaliah's assassination to 582 BC because of the reference to another Jewish deportation by Nebuchadnezzar in that year (52:30).

Struck down Gedaliah (41:2). The assassination of Gedaliah was later commemorated by a Jewish day of fasting (cf. Zech. 7:5; 8:19). Ishmael also killed "all the Jews" at Mizpah (see comments on Jer. 40:6), likely a reference to the members of Gedaliah's administrative staff, and the contingent of Babylonian soldiers stationed there as well.

Eighty men . . . carrying grain and incense offerings (41:5). These pilgrims from the territory of northern Israel were coming to Jerusalem for the Festival of Shelters. Their shaved heads, torn clothes, and lacerations suggest that they were in mourning over the destruction of the temple. Grain and incense offerings and prayer would have continued to be offered at the temple ruins even if animal sacrifices were not. The reasons why Ishmael killed these pilgrims, beyond his own brutality, are not clear.

Ishmael took captive all the rest of the people (41:10). Ishmael also took hostages from Mizpah, which may have included Jeremiah and Baruch (see comments on Jer. 40:6). The capture of the king's daughters may have represented an attempt to make royal claims for himself or for King Baalis in Ammon (see comments on Jer. 40:14). He likely intended to sell the other captives as slaves.

Jeremiah Taken to Egypt (41:11–43:13)

Away from the Chaldeans (41:18). On the Chaldeans, see comments on Jer. 38:2. Johanan and his contingent made plans to flee to Egypt because they feared Babylonian reprisals for the brutal murders of Gedaliah and the Babylonian troops with him.

I will now pray to the Lord your God (42:4). The people of Judah were no longer under an unalterable sentence of judgment as they had been before the fall of Jerusalem, when the Lord had instructed the prophet not to pray for the people (cf. 7:16; 11:14; 14:11; 15:1).

We'll go to the land of Egypt (42:14). Johanan and his contingent believed that flight to Egypt would put them outside the reach of Babylonian reprisals for the death of Gedaliah, but Jeremiah warned them that rejecting his counsel to remain in Judah would bring upon them the covenant curses of "sword, famine, and plague" (42:17, 22).

Baruch . . . is inciting you against us (43:3). See also 32:12–13; 36:4–19, 26; 45:1–5. The accusation that Baurch is the source of the warnings not to go to Egypt is perhaps to avoid the fact that they had chosen to reject the message of a true prophet. Jeremiah is once again accused of being a traitor who has defected over to the Babylonians (cf. 37:13–14; 38:4).

They went to the land of Egypt (43:7). Johanan and his followers went to Egypt in direct disobedience to the Lord and took Jeremiah and Baruch with them. A significant Jewish population emerged in Egypt after the fall of Jerusalem. A prominent Jewish colony was established on the island of Elephantine in southern Egypt. Numerous documents and letters attest to the Jewish presence at this military outpost, and the Jews even built a small temple to Yahweh ("the Lord") at Elephantine that was destroyed around 410 BC.[22]

Pick up some large stones and set them in the mortar (43:9). Jeremiah's sign-act of burying large stones in the pavement outside the pharaoh's palace represented how Nebuchadnezzar and the Babylonians would take control of Egypt. The stones marked the place where Nebuchadnezzar would set up his throne.

Pharaoh's palace at Tahpanhes (43:9). This building likely was an administrative building that may have also served as the pharaoh's residence when he visited the city. A large rectangular building discovered at Tel Defeneh dates to this time and may be the building mentioned here.[23]

He will come and strike down the land of Egypt (43:11). Nebuchadnezzar invaded Egypt in 568–567 BC, though the Babylonians were unable to inflict the kind of total defeat and subjugation of Egypt envisioned in 43:11–14. In light of the prophet's use of stereotypical judgment language, there was an essential rather than an exact and literal fulfillment of this prophecy.

Judgment of the Jews in Egypt (44:1–30)

The Jews living in the land of Egypt (44:1). Over time, the Jews settled throughout Egypt. This message appears chronologically to be the last recorded message of Jeremiah in the book. Jeremiah announced that the Lord would judge the Jewish community for its idolatry.

From the time we ceased to burn incense to the queen of heaven (44:18). See comments on Jer. 7:18. In their paganized thinking, the Jews in Egypt believed that Josiah's purging idolatry from the land of Judah was the cause of their calamity (cf. 2 Kings 23:3–40) rather than the cause of the Lord's forestalling of the judgment threatened during the time of the wicked king Manasseh (cf. 2 Kings 21:12–15).

Hophra, Egypt's king (44:30). This ruler (named Apries outside the Bible) of the Twenty-Sixth Dynasty ruled over Egypt from 589 to 570 BC. Hophra's troops gave assistance to Judah in the siege of Jerusalem and caused the Babylonian army briefly to withdraw from the siege. Like Zedekiah, however, Hophra would be given "into the hands" of his enemies. As part of a military revolt in 570 BC, Amasis became the ruler of Egypt, and Hophra was executed.

A Promise to Baruch (45:1–5)

Baruch (45:1). See comments on Jer. 32:12.

Wrote these words on a scroll . . . fourth year of Jehoiakim (45:1). Baruch recorded the scroll of Jeremiah's prophecies in 605 BC, the same year in which Nebuchadnezzar and the Babylonians took control of Syria-Palestine with their victory over Egypt and Assyria at the battle of Carchemish in Syria.

I will grant you your life (45:5). Baruch faced grave danger by associating with a subversive prophet of judgment like Jeremiah, but the Lord provided assurance to Baruch that he would protect and preserve his life as a reward for his faithfulness (cf. 39:18).

The damaged sculptured head of Pharaoh Hophra (also know as Apries).

Jeremiah's Oracles against the Nations (46:1–51:64)

Chapters 46–51 contain Jeremiah's message concerning ten foreign nations surrounding Judah, including the powers of Egypt and Babylon at the beginning and end of this section.

Oracles against foreign nations were an important part of the prophetic message (Isa. 13–23; Ezek. 25–32; Amos 1:3–2:3; Obadiah; Nah. 1–3; Hab. 2:6–20; Zeph. 2:14–15).

Oracle against Egypt (46:1–28)

Egypt (46:2). See the article "The Egyptians." Egypt vied for control over Syria-Palestine as the Assyrian Empire declined. Judah turned to Egypt as an ally in both the Assyrian and Babylonian crises.

Pharaoh Neco (46:2). Neco ruled over Egypt as a member of the Twenty-Sixth Dynasty from 610 to 594 BC. His armies were responsible for the death of Josiah at a battle near the city of Megiddo in 609 BC, when they marched north to assist the Assyrians in their conflict with Babylon.

Defeated at Carchemish (46:2). Carchemish was a city located in northern Syria on the Euphrates River. Nebuchadnezzar, king of Babylonia, defeated the Egyptians here in 605 BC. Nebuchadnezzar then pursued Pharaoh Neco's troops toward Egypt, taking control of Syria-Palestine and deporting the first wave of exiles from Judah. Nebuchadnezzar was forced to return home upon the death of his father, Nabopolassar, in order to take control of the throne. In this oracle prior to the battle of Carchemish, Jeremiah mocked the Egyptians as they prepared for a war in which they would be soundly defeated.

Gilead . . . balm (46:11). See comments on Jer. 8:22.

Migdol . . . Memphis . . . Tahpanhes (46:14). The Babylonians eventually would invade Egypt in 568–567 BC, and the Jews who fled to these Egyptian cities (44:1) would not escape the Lord's judgment. Migdol and Tahpanhes were border towns in Egypt. Jeremiah himself was at Tahpanhes (43:7–8). Memphis was the capital of Lower Egypt.

Oracle against Philistia (47:1–7)

Philistines (47:1). See the article "The Philistines." The Philistines occupied a five-city kingdom along the coast of southwest Palestine and had been an enemy of Israel since the days of the Judges (cf. Judg. 3:31; 13:1).

Before Pharaoh defeated Gaza (47:1). Neco, pharaoh of Egypt, may have attacked Gaza in 609

The Egyptian pharaoh Neco.

or 605 BC when marching north to help the Assyrians in their fight against Babylon, or he may have captured Gaza after the battle of Carchemish (see comments on Jer. 46:2) in order to establish fortifications as a buffer against the Babylonians.[24]

Water is rising from the north (47:2). King Nebuchadnezzar and his Babylonian army inflicted a more serious defeat on the Philistines when he captured Ashkelon in 604 BC and took many of its people into captivity. The Babylonian Chronicle recounts the total destruction of the city, and excavations from Ashkelon reflect that the city was burned at this time (see the article "The Philistines").

The coastland of Caphtor (47:4). See the article "The Philistines." Caphtor was the place of origin for the Philistines and is most commonly identified with the island of Crete. The bulk of the Philistine population in Syria-Palestine had come from Crete as part of the larger Sea Peoples migration into the area around 1300 BC.

Oracle against Moab (48:1–47)

Moab (48:1). Moab was located on a high plateau on the eastern shore of the Dead Sea. The Moabites were the descendants of Lot (see comments on Gen. 19:37–38) and had a long history of conflict with Israel. Messages of judgment against Moab are found elsewhere in Jeremiah (9:26; 25:21) and in other prophetic books as well (Isa. 15–16; Ezek. 25:8–11; Amos 2:1–3; Zeph. 2:8–11).

Nebo (48:1). This Moabite town was located near the mountain from which the Lord showed Moses the promised land and where Moses died (Deut. 34:1–8). This chapter mentions twenty-five towns in Moab, reflecting the severity of the destruction to come.

Chemosh (48:7, 13, 46). This god was the national deity of the Moabites (cf. Num. 21:29; Judg. 11:24; 1 Kings 11:7, 33; 2 Kings 23:13). The depiction of Chemosh on the Moabite Stone suggests that he was a warrior god. Moab would come to "shame" over its trust in Chemosh, just like Israel for its trust in the calf gods at Bethel (48:13; cf. 1 Kings 13:26–33; Amos 7:13).

Make Moab a salt marsh (48:9). This act symbolized a curse that the defeated city was not to be rebuilt and also was done to prevent the ground from producing crops (cf. Josh. 6:26; Judg. 9:45). This action was apparently not uncommon in the ancient Near East, as Assyrian records note that Tiglath-pileser I of Assyria (ca. 1100 BC) also salted the ruins of a defeated city.

Settled like wine on its dregs. He hasn't been poured from one container to another (48:11). Moab was famous for its grape and wine production (Isa. 16:8–10; Jer. 48:32–33). In the making of wine, the grape juice was poured into a clay jar, and the dregs or sediment from the grapes assisted in the fermentation process. Wine left on its dregs too long did not have a good flavor or aroma. The imagery reflects how Moab's excessive pride and complacency would lead to its demise.

Moab's calamity is near at hand (48:16). The Babylonians invaded and destroyed Moab, though there is no actual documentation of this event from that era. Josephus, a Jewish historian in the first century AD, places the fall of Moab in 582/581 BC.

I will restore the fortunes of Moab (48:47). The same promise of future restoration given to Israel is now given to Moab and later to Ammon (49:6) and Elam (49:39). The reason why the Lord promised to restore these specific nations is not clear, but perhaps the fate of these specific nations is merely reflective of the more general promise that gentiles would share in the blessings of Israel's future salvation (cf. Isa. 2:2–4; 49:6; 60:1–3; Zeph. 3:9; Zech. 14:16).

Oracle against the Ammonites (49:1–6)

The Ammonites (49:1). These people were descendants of Lot (see comments on Gen. 19:37–38) who lived northeast of Moab. Ammon was one of the nations that sent envoys to Jerusalem to discuss an anti-Babylonian coalition (27:3). The Ammonite king Baalis participated in the conspiracy to assassinate Gedaliah of Judah (40:14; 41:15), which likely led to their subjugation to Babylon in 582 BC.

Milcom (49:1). Milcom was the chief Ammonite god (1 Kings 11:5, 33; 2 Kings 13:23). The name means "king," and apparently this is the same deity as Molech, the god commonly associated with child sacrifice in the OT (Lev. 18:21; 20:2–5; 2 Kings 23:10; Jer. 32:35) (see comments on 2 Kings 3:27).

Rabbah (49:2). This was the capital city of Ammon, the location of the present-day city of Amman, the capital of modern Jordan.

Restore the fortunes (49:6). See comments on Jer. 48:47.

Oracle against the Edomites (49:7–22)

Edom (49:7). See comments on Obad. 1; Mal. 1:2–3; 1:4. The Edomites were the descendants of Esau (Gen. 25:29–30; 36:1). Edom was a small kingdom to the southeast of Judah that lay between the Dead Sea and the Gulf of Aqaba. The name Edom means "red" and has reference to the sandstone in the area. Israel and Edom were bitter rivals, and the lack of natural boundaries between Israel/Judah and Edom was likely a key reason for their perpetual conflict.[25]

At the time I punish him (49:8). The Lord would punish the Edomites because they allied with Babylon in their assault on Jerusalem in 588–586 BC (cf. Ps. 137:7; Lam. 4:21–22). Edom used the Babylonian invasion as an opportunity to seize territory from Judah, and archaeological evidence, including military dispatches, from the fortress city of Arad in southern Judah confirms this conflict between Judah and Edom. A number of prophetic oracles against Edom are found in the OT (Isa. 63:1–6; Ezek. 25:12–14; 35:1–15; Joel 3:18; Amos 1:11–12; 9:12; Obadiah; Mal. 1:2–5). The material here in 49:9, 14–16, closely parallels what is found in Obad. 1–6 (see the commentary on Obadiah).[26]

Bozrah (49:13). This was the capital city of Edom, located twenty-five miles southeast of the Dead Sea. The fortified city had a wall around it and was built on an elevated site.

Live in the clefts of the rock (49:16). The Edomites thought that they were inviolable to enemy attack because of their rocky and mountainous terrain (see comments on Obad. 3).

Oracles against Damascus, Kedar and Hazor, and Elam (49:23–39)

About Damascus: Hamath and Arpad are put to shame (49:23). Damascus was the capital of Aram (Syria). It was captured by the Assyrians in 732 BC after Aram and Israel had formed a coalition against them, and then later came under Babylonian control as well. Hamath and Arpad were also key Syrian cities. Hamath was located 110 miles north of Damascus, and Arpad was 95 miles north of Hamath.

Kedar . . . Hazor (49:28). The name Hazor in this verse refers not to the city Hazor in Galilee but rather to an Arabian tribe. Hazor and Kedar were tribes that lived in the Arabian Desert and likely were attacked by Nebuchadnezzar in his raids on Arabia in 599 BC.

Elam (49:34). Elam was located east of Babylon, and this oracle focusing on such a distant people demonstrated the extent of the Lord's sovereignty over the nations. The Assyrians had destroyed Elam in the seventh century BC, and Nebuchadnezzar may have campaigned against them in 596 BC, shortly after this oracle was delivered.

Oracle against Babylon (50:1–51:64)

Bel . . . Marduk (50:2). The name Bel (related to the Canaanite Baal) means "lord" or "master" and was a title applied to Marduk, the chief god of Babylon. In the Babylonian creation account, Enuma Elish, Marduk creates by defeating the goddess Tiamat and the forces of chaos (see the article "The Babylonians"; see comments on Gen. 1:1).

A nation from the north (50:3). The Neo-Babylonian Empire would fall to the Medes and Persians, who came from the north (cf. 50:9, 41) (see the article "The Persians"). The Lord had used Babylon as the enemy from the north to punish Judah (1:14–15; 4:6; 6:1, 22; 10:22). The same judgment would now come upon Babylon.

No one will be living in it (50:3). The same type of hyperbolic language used to describe the destruction of Jerusalem is applied here to Babylon (cf. 50:12–13, 21, 26, 29–30, 39–40; 51:25–26, 37–39, 42, 55–57) (see comments on Jer. 33:10). The prophecy speaks of Babylon's downfall in terms of total destruction and annihilation.

As I punished the king of Assyria (50:18). The Medes and Babylonians allied to capture the Assyrian capitals of Asshur (614 BC) and Nineveh (612 BC), and then the Babylonians inflicted a final defeat of Assyria at Haran (609 BC).

Leb-qamai (51:1). This title is a code name for Babylon, using a technique called *atbash*, which reads the letters of the alphabet in reverse order (see comments on Jer. 25:26). The letters here are the Hebrew equivalent to "Chaldean" (see comments on Jer. 38:2) and also have the meaning of "the heart of those who rise against me," expressing Babylon's rebellion against the Lord.

The kings of the Medes (51:11). The kingdom of Media was located northwest of Babylon. The Medes had allied with Babylon to defeat the Assyrians, but there was an ongoing rivalry between the two kingdoms. The Medes attacked Babylon as allies of the Persian Empire after Cyrus the Persian king subjugated Media around 550 BC (cf. 51:28).

Walls of Babylon (51:12). See the article "The Babylonians." The city of Babylon was encircled by two parallel walls made of brick that were separated by a large and deep moat. The outer wall was twelve feet thick, and the inner wall was twenty-one feet thick. Nebuchadnezzar expanded the walls and fortifications of Babylon, but these walls would not protect the city against the judgment to come from the Lord (51:44, 53, 58).

Sheshach (51:41). See comments on Jer. 25:26.

Seraiah son of Neriah (51:59). Seriah was the brother of Baruch, Jeremiah's scribe, and he traveled to Babylon with Zedekiah in 594/593 BC on a diplomatic mission. The Babylonians may have summoned Zedekiah to account for the meetings in Jerusalem that had plotted revolt against Babylon (cf. 27:3).

See that you read all these words . . . tie a stone to it and throw it into the middle of the Euphrates (51:61–63). Seriah's reading of the scroll and then throwing it into the river provided an accompanying object lesson for the prophetic word (cf. 13:1–11; 18–19; 27:2; 43:8–13).

The Fall of Jerusalem (52:1–34)

Zedekiah was twenty-one (52:1). Verses 1–11 nearly replicate 2 Kings 24:18–25:7, and verses 4–11 similarly correspond to Jer. 39:1–7.

Nebuzaradan . . . entered Jerusalem (52:12). See comments on 2 Kings 25:8–10. Nebuzaradan, commander of the Babylonian army ("captain of the guards"), entered Jerusalem in August 586 BC to complete the destruction of the city. The Jews later remembered this event with a day of fasting (Zech. 7:3–5; 8:19). The destruction of the city is mentioned in 39:8; verses 12–23 here focus on the destruction of the temple.

Seraiah . . . Zephaniah . . . court official . . . sixty men (52:24–27). The Babylonians had the high priest Seriah, his chief associate, and a number of other military and civic leaders in Judah taken to Riblah and executed (cf. 2 Kings 25:18–21).

Nebuchadnezzar deported (52:28–30). The small group of exiles that were taken away when Nebuchadnezzar first came to the city in 605 BC (Dan. 1:1–3) is not mentioned here. The number of exiles taken in Nebuchadnezzar's seventh year (597 BC) was 3,023. These numbers may only represent the men taken away, because the larger number in 2 Kings 24:14–16 is 18,000 (the 10,000 in 24:14 may also represent an approximation of the 8,000 soldiers and workmen in 24:16, plus the 3,000 people mentioned here). The number taken in his eighteenth year (586 BC) was 832. The deportation in his twenty-third year (582 BC) likely was in response to the assassination of Gedaliah and totaled 745 persons (cf. 41:1–3).[27]

Thirty-seventh year of the exile . . . King Evil-merodach (52:31). Nebuchadnezzar's successor, Evil-merodach, reigned from 562 to 560 BC. The spelling "Evil" (Hebrew: *ewil*) of his name here may reflect a Hebrew word for "foolish" or "stupid" as an expression of derision (cf. 2 Kings 25:27–30).

Pardoned King Jehoiachin . . . released him from prison (52:31). The new king likely granted amnesty to Jehoiachin as an expression of goodwill. A ration list discovered in Babylon confirms that Jehoiachin did receive food supplies from the Babylonian king (see comments on 2 Kings 25:29–30).

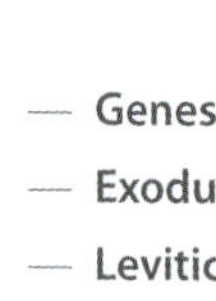

Lamentations

Lamentations

Gary E. Yates

Introduction. Lamentations consists of five distinct poems that mournfully reflect on the destruction of Jerusalem by the Babylonians in 587/586 BC. These laments vividly portray the intense suffering and grief of Jerusalem's inhabitants, while also wrestling with the theological crisis created by this national tragedy. The intensity of the poetry, along with the absence of any reference to the return to the land, suggests that the book was composed shortly after the events depicted. The book itself is anonymous, though Jewish tradition identifies Jeremiah as the author of the book (Lam. 1:1 in the Septuagint; cf. 2 Chron. 35:25; Jer. 9:1–2). The Jews observed several fasts and rites of mourning for various events surrounding the fall of Jerusalem during the exilic period (Jer. 41:5; Zech. 7:3–5; 8:19), and Lamentations has also long been used by the Jews in the observance of Tish b'Av, which commemorates the later destruction of Jerusalem in AD 70. Laments over the destruction of Jerusalem also occur several times in Psalms (Pss. 74, 79, 80, 83).

The most notable feature of the poetry in Lamentations is its use of the acrostic form, in which verses are arranged according to an alphabetic pattern. Chapters 1, 2, and 4 each have twenty-two verses corresponding to the number of letters in the Hebrew alphabet, and each verse begins with successive letters of the alphabet. Chapter 3 has sixty-six verses in which each letter of the alphabet begins three sequential verses. Chapter 5 also has twenty-two verses, but the acrostic pattern is absent. Alphabetic acrostics appear elsewhere in OT poetry (Pss. 9, 10, 25, 34, 37, 111, 112, 119, 145; Prov. 31:10–31) and are also attested in other ancient Near Eastern literature (e.g., "The Babylonian Theodicy"). The acrostic form perhaps reflects that Lamentations offers full expression of the people's grief or suggests the fullness of the suffering that they had endured.

Mourning over the Destruction of Jerusalem (1:1–22)

She . . . has become like a widow (1:1). Royal cities or temple cities often were personified as women in the ancient Near East (cf. Isa. 47). In pagan contexts these cities were closely associated with their patron goddesses. However, Jerusalem is portrayed as a widow here because she is bereft of her residents (children). The poems in Lamentations closely resemble ancient funeral dirges with their deep and elaborate expressions of grief intended to honor the dead (2 Sam. 1:17–27; 3:33–34). Women in the ancient Near East mourned the loss of their husbands and sons in times of war, and sometimes they even served as the professional mourners (Jer. 9:17; Ezek. 32:16).

The princess among the provinces (1:1). Jerusalem's exalted status was both political and religious. David had chosen Jerusalem to be his royal city, but the Lord had also chosen Zion (the hilltop in Jerusalem on which the temple was built, used here synonymously with the city of Jerusalem) as his earthly dwelling place (Ps. 132:13; cf. Deut. 12:5–7). The Lord reigned as king at the temple (2 Kings 19:15; Ps. 48:2; 80:1; 99:1), and the temple and the ark of the covenant also served as the footstool of the Lord's heavenly throne (1 Chron. 28:2; Ps. 99:5; 132:7; Lam. 2:1; cf. Isa. 66:1).

A scene from an Egyptian tomb depicting people wailing and lamenting.

From all her lovers (1:2). Israel and Judah had turned to both false gods and foreign alliances for protection and security (4:17; 5:6), viewed by the Lord (and proclaimed by the prophets) as a form of spiritual adultery, since they were expected to trust in the Lord (Ezek. 23:20–22; Hosea 2:5–7; 5:13–14; 8:9–10).

The roads to Zion mourn (1:4). Pilgrims came to Jerusalem for the three major festivals: Passover, Pentecost, and Shelters (Exod. 23:14–17; Deut. 16:16; cf. Pss. 120–134), but these times of joyous celebration had now come to an end, since the city and the temple were in ruins.

They have seen her nakedness (1:8–9). A husband might shame an unfaithful wife by exposing her nakedness (Ezek. 16:37; 23:29; Hosea 2:3). Captives often were stripped naked when taken away as prisoners (Isa. 20:2–3; Amos 2:16).

Seized all her precious belongings (1:10). It was common in the ancient Near East for victorious armies to plunder the temples of defeated peoples and to place these articles in their own temples as a way of asserting the superiority of their gods (cf. 1 Sam. 5:1–5; 2 Kings 24:13; 25:13–17; Dan. 1:2; 5:2).

In a winepress (1:15). A winepress was a stone pit where grapes were trampled by feet. The juice flowed into a smaller vat or stone jars for fermentation. The winepress here represents the crushing effect of divine judgment (cf. Isa. 63:1–6).

The remains of an ancient wine press.

The Lord's Anger Poured Out on His People (2:1–22)

Footstool (2:1). See comments on Lam. 1:1.

The Lord is like an enemy (2:5). Throughout Israel's history the Lord had fought on behalf of his people (Exod. 15:3; Josh. 10:10–11; Judg. 5:4–5; 2 Sam. 5:22–25; 2 Chron. 20:1–30; Ps. 47:3), but the poet here reverses Israel's traditions of holy war to portray God himself fighting against his people in judgment. Human warfare was viewed as an extension of the cosmic conflicts among the gods.

Stretched out a measuring line (2:8). After a city was conquered, a plumb line was used to determine which parts of the city walls were unstable and needed to be torn down (cf. 2 Kings 21:13; Isa. 34:11). Armies used siege ramps and battering rams as means to breach a city's defense walls.

Ramparts and walls (2:8). The rampart was a mound that protected the city wall from the battering ram.[1] The Broad Wall in Jerusalem, dating to the time of Hezekiah, was more than twenty feet thick. A short section of this wall is visible in Jerusalem today.

Thrown dust on their heads and put on sackcloth (2:10). The wearing of sackcloth—a coarse, black fabric made from goat hair—combined with ashes symbolized mourning (Esther 4:1, 3; Jer. 6:26) or repentance (Isa. 58:5; Jon. 3:5–6).

Where is the grain and wine? . . . Should women eat their own children? (2:12, 20). The siege of a city often would cut off food supplies completely, which usually resulted in extreme famine (cf. 2 Kings 6:24–31; 25:1–3). Starving parents might even be reduced to cannibalizing their own children. Moses had warned of the covenant curse of famine leading to cannibalism before the people had entered the land (Deut. 28:53–57).

The Suffering of Jerusalem and a Plea for Mercy (3:1–66)

The Lord is my portion (3:24). The word translated as "portion" often denotes an allotment of land (cf. Deut. 33:21; Josh. 15:13; 18:10). As a result of the exile, all the Jews had become like the Levites who had the Lord as their special "portion" instead of a designated tribal territory (Num. 18:20; Deut. 12:12; Josh. 14:4).

Crushing all the prisoners of the land beneath one's feet (3:34). Victorious kings in the ancient Near East often were portrayed as trampling their enemies underfoot or crushing their heads (cf. Num. 24:17; Ps. 44:5; 60:12; 68:21; 108:13). Egyptian art pictures the triumphant pharaoh using his defeated foes as his footstool when seated on his throne (cf. Ps. 110:1).[2]

Pay them back . . . may your curse be on them . . . destroy them (3:64–66). The prayers of the righteous in the OT often contain imprecations or curses, resembling those found in ancient Near Eastern treaties (Ps. 58:6–8; 109:6–15; 137:8–9; Jer. 11:20; 12:3; 18:20–23). These prayers seek justice so that the divine punishments against the wicked fit their crimes (cf. Lam. 1:22; 3:59–63). The Lord had promised in the Abrahamic covenant to curse those who curse Abraham and his descendants (Gen. 12:3; 27:29).

Jerusalem's Humiliation because of God's Judgment (4:1–22)

Jackals offer their breasts . . . cruel like ostriches (4:3). Food shortages had caused the people to become selfish and cruel, treating their own children worse than animals. By contrast, even scavenging jackals nursed their young. These people, however, are more like ostriches, thought to neglect their young because they buried their eggs and left the nest (cf. Job 39:13–18).

Those slain by hunger . . . have cooked their own children (4:9–10). See comments on Lam. 2:12, 20.

That an enemy or adversary could enter Jerusalem's gates (4:12). The Lord's presence brought blessing to Zion, and the Lord had promised to protect the city from its enemies (Pss. 46, 48, 76). The deliverance of Jerusalem from the Assyrians in 701 BC

An Assyrian king standing with his foot on the head of a defeated foe.

contributed to the mistaken notion that the Lord would deliver the city regardless of the people's behavior (cf. Jer. 7:4–14). The Lord, however, eventually withdrew his protective presence, departed from the temple and Jerusalem, and allowed the Babylonians to take the city (Ezek. 10:18–19; 11:23–24).

The Lord's anointed . . . was captured in their traps (4:20). The last two Davidic kings, Jehioiachin in 597 BC and Zedekiah in 586 BC, were deported to Babylon and remained there for the rest of their lives.

He will punish your iniquity, Daughter Edom (4:22). See comments on Obad. 1; Mal. 1:2–3; 1:4. Edom was located south and east of the Dead Sea. The Edomites were descendants of Esau and bitter rivals of Israel and Judah. The Lord would punish the Edomites because they allied with Babylon in their assault on Jerusalem in 588–586 BC and had used the Babylonian invasion as an opportunity to seize territory from Judah (cf. Ps. 137:7).

The People Ask God to Remember and Restore (5:1–22)

We made a treaty with Egypt and with Assyria (5:6). In times of national crisis Judah's leaders often had turned to foreign military alliances for protection rather than trusting in the Lord (Isa. 30:1–5; 31:1–3; Jer. 2:16–18, 36–37). King Ahaz, for example, had turned to Assyria for assistance during the Syro-Ephraimite War in 734–732 BC (2 Kings 16:6–18; Isa. 8:5–8). Military aid from Egypt had proved unsuccessful in delivering Jerusalem from both the Assyrians and Babylonians (Isa. 36:6–9; Jer. 37:5–7).

Princes have been hung up by their hands (5:12). In the ancient Near East the leaders of a defeated people often were either deported or executed. The Babylonians killed Zedekiah's sons after they attempted to escape (2 Kings 25:6–7; Jer. 39:5–6). The corpses of the executed sometimes were hung up in public view as a form of humiliation and shame (cf. Josh. 10:26; 2 Sam. 21:12).

Young men labor at millstones (5:13). Captive men often performed menial tasks normally assigned to slaves or women (cf. Judg. 16:21). Grain was poured on a large stone, and a smaller stone was moved over the grain to grind it into meal. Livestock sometimes was used to operate larger millstones.

Bring us back to yourself, so we may return (5:21). Lamentations is often compared to the Sumerian "city laments," initially composed following the defeat of the Ur III Empire (ca. 2000 BC).[3] These compositions attribute the destruction of the various cities and their temples to the anger of the gods, who decreed their downfall by a human army. The patron goddess of the city frequently mourns the fall of the city, similar to the role of the personified

Daughter Zion in Lamentations. These laments were part of ceremonies for the restoration of rebuilt sanctuaries and praised the gods for returning to the cities. Lamentations does not promise the rebuilding of the sanctuary or the return of the Lord to Jerusalem but does conclude with a plea for the Lord to restore his people.

Ezekiel

Mark F. Rooker

Introduction. Ezekiel was among the eight thousand citizens of Jerusalem deported to Babylonia when King Nebuchadnezzer captured Jerusalem in 598/597 BC (2 Kings 24:10–17). Five years later, in 593 BC, Ezekiel was called to be a prophet (this was also the fifth year of King Jehoiachin's exile) while he was living in Babylonia. Ezekiel ministered until the twenty-seventh year of King Jehoiachin (Ezek. 29:17), thus giving Ezekiel a ministry of twenty-two to twenty-three years.

Ezekiel lived through the greastest crisis in Israel's history: the final destruction of Jerusalem and the temple in 587/586 BC. Chapters 1–24 are saturated with oracles of judgment and punishment directed toward Judah and Jerusalem, but once the announcement comes that Jerusalem has fallen (33:21), the book moves forward to address the restoration for Israel (33:21–39:29) and the temple (chaps. 40–48). Many of the prophecies of restoration reverse the earlier images of devastation and ruin.

God Reveals Himself to Ezekiel (1:1–28)

In the thirtieth year (1:1). The reference of this opening phrase is not clear. The editorial explanation in the following verses (1:2–3) takes "the thirtieth year" as equivalent to the fifth year of Jehoiachin's exile. Some maintain that the "thirtieth year" refers to Ezekiel's age (NIV: "in my thirtieth year"). According to Num. 4:30, thirty is the age at which priests qualified for induction into their office.

The fifth year of King Jehoiachin's exile (1:2). Jehoiachin reigned only three months and ten days (see comments on 2 Kings 24:8). Ironically, Ezekiel uses the removal of Jehoiachin from the throne and his exile as the reference point for his prophecies, instead of using a king's accession to the throne as reference, as biblical prophecies typically are dated (2 Kings 25:27; Jer. 52:31). The name Jehoiachin appears in Babylonian ration lists dating from the tenth to the thirty-fifth year of the reign of Nebuchadnezzar II (595–569 BC).[1]

Land of the Chaldeans (1:3). The term "Chaldean" is interchangeable with "Babylonian" in the book of Ezekiel (12:13; 23:15, 23). See the article "The Babylonians."

I fell facedown (1:28). This is the posture that one would assume before a ruling monarch in ancient times. When a vision or manifestation of God occurs in the OT there is an inherent danger associated with such a manifestation. The Bible teaches that a human being cannot see God and live (Exod. 33:18, 20), and so what Ezekiel actually sees is a vision of God, a representation, not the true person of God. As a consequence, words such as "likeness" and "appearance" permeate the description of God throughout the chapter. Similarly, in Rev. 1:17–18 John makes the only appropriate response to the appearance of God: "I fell at his feet like a dead man."

God Calls Ezekiel to Confront the Rebellious Israelites (2:1–3:15)

The Spirit entered me (2:2). Just as the first Adam received the breath of life from God (Gen. 2:7), so Ezekiel as "son of Man/Adam" receives an infusion of the divine Spirit, which enables him to carry out his God-given task.

This is what the Lord God says (2:4). This is an adaptation of the so-called messenger formula. Numerous letters found in the ancient sites of Mari and Amarna, as well as from other sites in the ancient Near East, begin with the words "To my lord say: 'Thus says X.'"

There was a written scroll in it (2:9). Occasionally scrolls in the ancient world were quite long. One of the famous Dead Sea Scrolls, for example, measured almost twenty-four feet in length. Most often scrolls were written on only one side of the writing material. Occasionally, however, papyrus scrolls in ancient Egypt as well as in the Greco-Roman period were written on two sides.

One of over fifteen-thousand tablets discovered at the ancient city of Mari.

Words of lamentation (2:10). Following the custom of that time, the content of the scroll is summarized on the outside of the rolled document with three ominous words ("lamentation, mourning, and woe"), each of which spells disaster. One of the Dead Sea Scrolls, the *Manual of Discipline,* has precisely such a title (although only a few letters remain) written on the outside.[2]

Tel-abib (3:15). In Akkadian this phrase literally means "mound of the flood," indicating that the location was well known as a ruined site as a consequence of being on the receiving end of foreign invasions. In Hebrew the second letter of the alphabet can denote either a *b* sound or a *v* sound; thus some translations render this as "Tel Aviv" (NIV). This location, however, is in Babylonia, and thus is not the same location as the modern city of Tel Aviv in Israel.

Ezekiel's Commission to Warn the Israelites and Portray the Coming Judgment (3:16–5:17)

A watchman (3:17). See comments on Isa. 56:10–11; Ezek. 33:2. In order to provide an opportune warning of approaching danger, lookouts, serving as watchmen, were posted on the roofs of gatehouses (2 Sam. 18:24) or towers (2 Kings 9:17). These elevated positions enabled them to see approaching enemies from a distance. The comparison of the Lord's prophets to watchmen occurs also in Jer. 6:17; Hab. 2:1.

Draw the city of Jerusalem on it (4:1). Sketching city plans on clay bricks was a common practice in the ancient Near East. In the excavation of the ancient Mesopotamian city of Nippur (where Ezekiel actually resided), a clay brick was discovered on which was inscribed a plan of the city of Nippur, including gates, canals, and sanctuaries.[3]

Lay seige against it (4:2). The primary objective of siege warfare was to stop the flow of food as well as other supplies and thereby starve the enemy.

Build a ramp (4:2). Battering rams were thrust up siege ramps to attack the city walls and thereby create an entrance into a city. A wall relief in the palace of the Assyrian king Sennacherib in Nineveh depicts a very large ramp constructed in the siege of the Israelite city of Lachish. Archaeologists estimate that it took approximately twenty-five thousand tons of earth and stones to construct the ramp.[4] Battering rams frequently are pictured in Assyrian reliefs.[5] See comments on Jer. 6:6.

This will be a sign (4:3). The warning function of the sign is illustrated by a Lachish letter written in Paleo-Hebrew and dated from the time of Nebuchadnezzar's pending invasion of Jerusalem of 588/587 BC. In it the same Hebrew term for "sign" is used. The commander of a Judean fortress wrote to the army officer in Lachish, "We are watching the Lachish (fire)-signal according to the 'signs' which my lord has given."[6]

Wheat, barley, beans, lentils, millet, and spelt (4:9). Often the main strategy of a siege was to starve out the inhabitants (2 Kings 25:3; Jer. 38:2, 9). All of these food products are available in Babylonia and probably would constitute a siege diet.

The food you eat each day (**4:10**). The amount of food cited is literally "twenty shekels." This is about eight ounces of food per day, about eight to ten times less than normal daily food intake. The allotment of water too is severely reduced.[7]

You can make your bread (4:15). See comments on Mal. 4:1.

Shave your head (5:1). Shaving one's head could be associated with grief and mourning rites (see comments on Job 1:20; Jer. 7:29), but here shaving inidicates a change in the status of the Israelites from free individuals to captives submitted to their Babylonian conquerors.[8]

Fathers will eat their sons (5:10). Tragically, during the time of the siege and subsequent fall to Babylon in 588–586 BC, the Israelites were forced to resort to cannibalism in Jerusalem (see comments on Lam. 2:12, 20). Cannabilism is mentioned in the annals of the Assyrian king Ashurbanipal (668–627 BC)[9] as well as in the eighteenth-century-BC Atrahasis Epic.[10]

God's Judgment for Sin Will Be Swift and Comprehensive (6:1–7:27)

Mountains of Israel (6:2). In the ancient world mountains often were centers of idolatrous worship. Referring to Israel as "the mountains of Israel" denotes Israel's apostasy (cf. 6:13; 18:6, 11; 22:9). Shrines dedicated to Canaanite deities often were built in groves on the hills and mountains, and idolatry frequently was practiced on hilltop shrines in Canaan (1 Kings 14:23). Elijah (1 Kings 18:1–40), Hosea (Hosea 4:12–13), and Amos (Amos 7:9) acknowledged that the Israelites syncretized elements of Canaanite worship with the worship of the true God.

Your high places (6:3). See comments on 1 Kings 3:2–3; 11:7. The high places were artificially built, elevated platforms where sacrifices were carried out. These high places were supposed to have been completely destroyed when the Israelites settled in the land (Num. 33:52). However, they continue to appear consistently throughout the history of Israel, even though various kings like Josiah tried to remove them (2 Kings 23:8, 15, 19).

In front of your idols (6:4). The Hebrew word translated as "idols" occurs forty-eight times in the OT, thirty-nine of which are in Ezekiel, who seems to prefer this unusual word as his designation for idols. Through wordplay this word carries very strong and derisive connotations of excrement, implying that when Ezekiel uses this word he is comparing the idols to dung or excrement.

You will know that I am the Lord (6:7). This phrase, occuring nearly sixty times in Ezekiel, often is used as a closing statement for oracles or sections within oracles, and it expresses the intended result when the event predicted in the oracle comes to fruition. The phrase also was frequently used in the context of the exodus from Egypt (Exod. 7:5; 14:4, 18). The phrase occurs four times in this chapter alone (6:7, 10, 13, 14).

On every high hill, on all the mountaintops, and under every green tree and every leafy oak (6:13). These phrases echo Deut. 12:2 and illustrate the extent to which Canaanite worship practices had been incorporated into Judah (see comments on Jer. 2:20; see the article "The Canaanites and Canaanite Religion").

Idolatry Brings Judgment and Separation from God (8:1–11:25)

The offensive statue that provokes jealousy (8:3). The term translated as "offensive statue" (*semel*) occurs in two other OT books (Deut. 4:16; 2 Chron. 33:7, 15). It has been suggesed that the term is a foreign word and thus is associated with the worship of a foreign god. It is possible that this image may have been one of the Asherah set up in the temple by Manasseh (2 Kings 21:7; 2 Chron. 33:7, 15), or this "offensive statue" perhaps refers to the vegetation god Tammuz (Ezek. 8:14–17).

Weeping for Tammuz (8:14). Weeping for Tammuz was part of a Babylonian ritual remembering the Sumerian god Dumuzi's death and descent into the underworld. In the pagan ritual the course of death and return for Dumuzi (Tammuz) was thought to be parallel to the annual rhythm of nature (summer-fall-winter-spring).

With their backs to the Lord's temple . . . they were bowing to the east in worship of the sun (8:16). See comments on 2 Kings 23:11. Turning their backs toward the Lord in the temple implies an insulting rejection of him in favor of the sun god they were worshiping. Worship of the Mesopotamian

A cylinder seal and its clay impression depicting the god Dumuzi.

The Mesopotamian sun god Shamash.

sun god (Shamash) appears to have gained royal approval during the reign of Manasseh (suggested perhaps by 2 Kings 21:5), a practice that persisted even after Josiah removed it from the temple.

I saw six men coming . . . there was another man (9:2). Apparently there are seven men in this vision. In the Babylonian "Poem of Erra" seven executioners are available to the god of plague and war. Likewise, in an eighth-century-BC treaty there is reference to a group of seven gods ("The Divine Seven") who punish people who break covenants and treaties.[11]

Carrying writing equipment (9:2). Many commentators identify the figure holding a writing kit with the Babylonian god Nabu, the god of writing who also was in charge of writing out human destinies. The divine symbol of Nabu is the writing stick made out of a reed that carved cuneiform signs on clay tablets.[12]

Put a mark on the foreheads (9:4). The mark is a *taw* sign, which in the Paleo-Hebrew alphabet is represented by two intersecting diagonal lines, the shape of an X, and resembles a cross.

The cherubim (10:1). See comments on Gen. 3:24; 1 Kings 6:23–28. The inner curtains as well as the veil that separated the holy of holies in the tabernacle were decorated with cherubim (Exod. 26:1, 31; 36:8, 35). Two golden cherubim with outspread wings consisted of one piece with the covering of the ark within the holy of holies of the tabernacle (Exod. 25:18–22; 37:7–9). Similarly, in the Jerusalem temple cherubim covered with gold were carved into the temple walls (1 Kings 6:29; 2 Chron. 3:7; Ezek. 41:18–20), and two-winged cherubim looked down on the mercy seat of the ark (1 Kings 6:23). In the tabernacle as well as the temple the cherubim were understood to be God's throne (2 Kings 19:15 [= Isa. 37:16]; 1 Sam. 4:4; 2 Sam. 6:2; Ps. 18:10; 80:1; 99:1).[13]

The close association of God with the cherubim is also indicated by their presence to guard the garden of Eden when Adam and Eve are evicted (Gen. 3:24). Back in chapter 1 Ezekiel simply called these beings "creatures." Now, in close association with the temple, he recognizes these creatures to be cherubim.

Modern scholars have compared these creatures to the winged sphinxes and other composite quadrupeds pictured as supporting the thrones of ancient Near Eastern kings or guarding the entryways to palaces or temples. Yet numerous composite creatures with wings are also depicted with two legs, resembling humans from the shoulders down, yet having the head of an animal or a bird. These beings also are often associated with temples, thrones, and sacred trees.

An ivory carving of a winged composite quadruped.

Demonstration of the Exile (12:1–20)

An exile's bags (12:4). Numerous Assyrian reliefs depict defeated people going into captivity carrying small knapsacks. According to a talmudic source (later Jewish commentary/explanation), the exile's gear consisted of a small clay lamp, a rug on which to sleep, and a bowl for eating and drinking.

Dig through the wall and take the bags out through it (12:5). The readers would understand that breaking through a wall indicated defeat and possible exile, as the conquering armies would break through the walls at vulnerable points in order to conquer the city (Amos 4:3).

Because of the violence of all who live there (12:19). This phrase probably is an allusion to Gen. 6:11–13, where violence was the stated rationale for the judgment of the earth by the flood.

The False Leaders (12:21–14:11)

Set up idols in their hearts (14:3). This is a figurative expression conveying the notion of commitment to the service of an idol, although some think that it actually refers to amulets hung around the neck over the heart. On the word translated as "idols," see comments on Ezek. 6:4.

They will be my people and I will be their God (14:11). This formula first occurs in Exod. 6:7 with reference to the establishment of the covenant relationship between God and his people. It also recurs in the description of the covenantal blessings of Lev. 26:12. Marriage and adoption practices may have given rise to the formula.

Judgments against Jerusalem (14:12–15:8)

Noah, Daniel, and Job (14:14). In texts from the ancient city of Ugarit (in Syria) mention is made of a mythological figure by the name of Dan'el. Many scholars have argued that this is the figure that Ezekiel refers to here in connection with Job and Noah. However, the limited and scanty evidence for this figure makes it unlikely that he would be well known to Ezekiel's audience.[14] The biblical Daniel was exiled to Babylon in 605 BC (Dan. 1:1) and would have quickly developed a reputation as a wise and righteous man (see Dan. 1:17–21; 2:14, 48; 5:12). All three of these men (Noah, Daniel, and Job) were recognized for their righteous behavior, although all three lived in decadent times.

The wood of the vine (15:6). The use of the vine as an image of Israel goes back to Num. 13:23, where the vine symbolizes the richness of Canaan. The vine is used frequently throughout the OT as a symbol of the nation of Israel (Deut. 32:32; Jer. 2:21; Hosea 10:1).

The Spiritual History of Israel (16:1–63)

Your origin and your birth were in the land of the Canaanites. Your father was an Amorite and your mother a Hethite (16:3). Canaanites, Amorites, and Hethites are closely related in biblical ethnography, for they were inhabitants of Palestine before the Israelite conquest (see comments on Gen. 23:3; Deut. 1:4; Josh. 9:1). Likewise, they often symbolize the enemies of Israel. By going back to the people's origin (Hosea 2:5 may have suggested this), the prophet stresses the point that the people have always been disobedient, even from their ancestry. There is already present in the nature of the chosen people an original inclination toward paganism, which it has received as an inherited family failing and which cannot be expected to produce anything but bad results.

You were not rubbed with salt or wrapped in cloths (16:4). Exposure of unwanted babies, especially girls, was not uncommon in the ancient world. Here the abandoned infant was described as still attached to the placenta and left to die. In some Middle Eastern cultures today, after the umbilical cord is cut, midwives commonly apply a mixture of salt and oil to a newborn infant's body.

I said to you as you lay in your blood, "Live!" (16:6). It is possible that this expression refers to God's basic desire for all people to live (see 18:23, 32). Others cite an ancient Near Eastern custom in which this expression announces a formal declaration of adoption.

I spread the edge of my garment over you (16:8). This symbolic gesture constituted a proposal of marriage. In early Arabia throwing a garment over a woman symbolized acquiring her, as it is understood that henceforth the woman will be covered to all except her husband. Deuteronomy 22:30 can express the illicitness of relations of a man with his father's wife as "uncovering the edge of his father's garment." The gesture of spreading the corner of a garment as a symbol of a marriage proposal is illustrated in Ruth 3:9.

You became mine (16:8). The figure of Israel as the Lord's wife derives from the first commandment to worship God alone. To that demand of exclusive fidelity, the obligation of a wife to her husband offered a parallel. Certain usages in the Torah already reflect the figure. In the Decalogue and the Covenant Code (Exod. 21–23) the Lord is called "passionate" or "jealous" toward those who were unfaithful to him (Exod. 20:5; 34:14). In Num. 5:14, 30, related Hebrew terms describe the agitation of a husband suspicious of his wife's fidelity (cf. Prov. 6:34). In Exod. 34:14–15 and Num. 15:39 apostasy was expressed by a Hebrew word that meant "to practice prostitution" (cf. Ezek. 6:9). The prophetic development of this figure is built upon this early foundation. Sexual infidelity was used as a metaphor not only for Israel's adoption of Canaanite religion (Hosea 1:2; 2:5–13; 3:1; Jer. 2:20) but also for political alliances with foreign powers (Hosea 8:9; Jer. 2:33, 36).

I washed you with water . . . anointed you with oil (16:9). Bathing and anointing were part of wedding ceremonies described in Old Babylonian (2000–1600 BC) and Middle Assyrian (1364–934 BC) texts.[15]

Acted like a prostitute because of your fame (16:15). The accusation of prostitution referred to a spiritual turning away from the Lord often accompanied by physical involvement with the fertility rites that accompanied Canaanite paganism (Jer. 3:1–5; Hosea 4:13–14; 9:1; cf. Gen. 38:14–16) (see the article "The Canaanites and Canaanite Religion"). The unfaithfulness of Jerusalem began with Solomon's introduction of idol worship and his construction of multiple pagan shrine sites where idolaters could worship (see comments on 1 Kings 11:3; 11:5; 11:7). Jerusalem was unfaithful as it committed the sin of idolatry.

You even took your sons and daughters you bore to me and sacrificed them to these images as food (16:20). On child sacrifice in the ancient Near East, see comments on 2 Kings 3:27. Child sacrifice was practiced in Israel during the reigns of Ahaz (2 Kings 16:3) and Manasseh (2 Kings 21:6) but apparently was even more widespread during the time of Jeremiah (Jer. 7:31; 19:5; 32:35). Child sacrifice is mentioned also by Ezekiel (Ezek. 5:10; 23:37; 20:26). By sacrificing her offspring Jerusalem clearly proved that she was a moral descendant of pagan Canaanite ancestry. The Mosaic law clearly regulated against this practice (Lev. 18:21; 20:2; Deut. 12:31; 18:10).

When you paid a fee instead of one being paid to you (16:34). The figurative language here compares Jerusalem to a prostitute who pays money rather than collects money for her prostitution. Numerous Israelite and Judahite kings made alliances with foreign kings and then paid them tribute as well.

They will strip off your clothes (16:39). In the ancient Near East if a man stripped his wife in public it signified an official divorce. Contracts discovered at Nuzi (fifteenth century BC, northern Iraq) specify that if a wife were to divorce her husband, she would depart from her husband without her clothes.

Your mother was a Hethite and your father an Amorite (16:45). Ezekiel accuses Jerusalem (figuratively) of being like its mother "the Hethite" who was married to an Amorite (see comments on Gen. 23:3; Deut. 1:4), the people group that was removed from Canaan by the Israelites because their sins had reached an intolerable level before God (Gen. 15:16). The implication of this is that God's justice would now seem to require that Israelites left in their land should be removed.

The Unfaithful King (17:1–24)

A huge eagle with powerful wings (17:3). Eagles in the ancient Near East usually represented the splendor and power of monarchs, often associated with the monarch at war. The eagle mentioned here probably refers to Nebuchadnezzar, king of Babylon, the one who conquered and destroyed Jerusalem.

There was another huge eagle (17:7). While the first eagle represents the king of Babylon, the second eagle represents the Egyptian pharaoh, either Psammetichus II (595–589 BC) or Hophra (589–570 BC). King Zedekiah of Judah had sought aid from Egypt in order to break free from the Babylonian hegemony (2 Chron. 36:13; Jer. 35:5–7; 44:30; 52:11). Similarly, Hezekiah had sought aid from Egypt against the Assyrians about one hundred years earlier (cf. Isa. 28–30).

Will he not tear out its roots? (17:9). Tearing out the roots signifies the end of the national existence (Amos 2:9). Here, specifically, it would refer to the deportation and exile of the people from Judah to Babylon.

When the east wind strikes it (17:10). The east wind is the hot, dry wind of Israel known as the *chamsin*. Throughout the OT it is often depicted as an instrument of God's will (Exod. 10:13; 14:21; Ps. 78:26; Jon. 4:8; Hosea 13:15).

I will spread my net over him (17:20). Gods in the ancient Near East frequently are depicted as using nets in their acts of judgment against people.

I will pluck a tender sprig (17:22). Other prophets likewise employed a variety of horticultural expressions to designate the messianic scion from the Davidic line (Isa. 4:2; 11:1; 53:2; Jer. 23:5; 33:15; Zech. 3:8; 6:12).

Birds of every kind will nest under it (17:23). The image of birds nesting under the protection of a competent leader is a frequent motif in the Bible

(Dan. 4:20–22; Ezek. 17:23). The expression "birds of every kind" is taken from the flood story (Gen. 7:14).

I bring down the tall tree (17:24). See comments on Dan. 4:14.

Individual Responsibility (18:1–32)

He does not eat at the mountain shrines (18:6). Pagan temples and shrines often were constructed on mountaintops. In the OT the mountains frequently are cited as the location for idolatrous sacrifices (Isa. 57:7; Ezek. 20:28; 34:6; Hosea 4:13). The expression here was a way of affirming that the righteous person would avoid partipating in idolatrous practices.

Lamentation for Princes of Israel (19:1–14)

Led him away with hooks (19:4). The expression "they led him with hooks" is found in an Assyrian inscription where captives are led away during the reign of King Esar-haddon (680–669 BC). See also Hab. 1:15.

He became a young lion . . . he was caught in their pit (19:3–4). Many of the kings in the ancient Near East went on lion hunts.

The ruins of a Roman-era temple built on top of the ruins of the citadel in the ancient city of Rabbah, the capital of the Ammonites (located in the modern-day city of Amman, Jordan).

The End Is in Sight (20:1–24:27)

I swore an oath (20:5). Here the Hebrew for "I swore" is literally "I raised my hand." The method for making a commitment under oath was expressed by the physical gesture of raising one's hand to the sky/heaven. Of the eleven occurrences of this phrase in the OT, eight are in Ezekiel (Ezek. 20:5 [twice], 15, 23, 42; 36:7; 44:12; 47:14; see also Exod. 6:8; Neh. 9:15; Ps. 106:26). God had committed himself by divine solemn promise to choose his people, to rescue them from slavery in Egypt, and to settle them in the land of Canaan.

When they sacrificed every firstborn in the fire, I defiled them through their gifts (20:26). This act refers to child sacrifice, often associated with the worship of the pagan god Molech (see comments on 1 Kings 11:5; 2 Kings 3:27). According to the pagan perception, offering a sacrifice to a god would put that god in debt so as to manipulate the god to act favorably toward the one making the sacrifice.

Serve wood and stone (20:32). The derogatory designation of the heathen gods as wood and stone should have been enough to counteract the strange notion that these heathen gods really existed. See also Deut. 4:28; 28:36.

I will accept you as a pleasing aroma (20:41). Normally, the phrase "pleasing aroma" is used in regard to God's acceptance of a proper sacrifice of things such as animals, grain, flour, oil, and incense. Only here in the OT does the expression apply to people to indicate that God is pleased with them.

Strike two times, even three (21:14). The mention of three strikes of the sword may refer to the three attacks and subsequent deportations that the Babylonians carried out against Jerusalem in 605, 597, and 588–586 BC.

Rabbah of the Ammonites (21:20). Ammon was the foreign kingdom to the east of Judah and the Jordan River, now the modern-day country of Jordan. Rabbah, once the capital of Ammon, is the location of the modern capital city of Amman, Jordan. The joint conspiracy of Judah and Ammon against Babylonia in 589 BC provoked the invasion of the Babylonian army (Jer. 27:3).

He shakes the arrows, consults the idols, and observes the liver (21:21). The practice of belomancy involved shaking arrows until they fell to the ground, or simply tossing arrows or shooting them until they fell to the ground. The formation of these fallen arrows was to convey a particular interpretation with regard to future events. This was somewhat of a common practice in the ancient Near East (note the similar function of arrows in 2 Kings 13:15–19). It may have been similar to today's practice of drawing straws. If the arrows were inscribed with personal or place names, as some maintain, the practice was a form of casting lots. The "idols" (*teraphim*) appear to have been miniature household gods (Gen. 31:19; Hosea 3:4;

Zech. 10:2). Hepatoscopy, the examination of the liver taken from a sacrificial animal as a form of divination, was a widespread practice in ancient Mesopotamia, though it is mentioned only here in the OT.

Sexual intercourse with their father's wife (22:10). The "wife" referenced here probably is a stepmother, but this is nonetheless a very serious offense (Lev. 20:11).

Oholah represents Samaria and Oholibah represents Jerusalem (23:4). Samaria and Jerusalem were the capital cities of the northern and southern kingdoms, respectively.

The names Oholah and Oholibah are both related to the Hebrew word for "tent." They correspond to the two capital cities according to the number of syllables in each word. That is, "Oholah" contains the same number of syllables as the Hebrew word for "Samaria," and "Oholibah" the same number of syllables as the Hebrew word for "Jerusalem." The names recall the period when Israel lived in tents in the desert, reinforcing the notion of long-standing harlotry. The translation of "Oholibah" (Jerusalem) is "my tent is in her," indicating the fact that the temple resided in Jerusalem (2 Sam. 6:17; 1 Kings 8:4; Ps. 48:1–14). Samaria and Jerusalem were also designated as sisters in Jer. 3:6–12. The mention of the mother of the sisters would emphasize their common origin from the united nation of Israel that existed from the time of the exodus to Solomon.

She lusted after her lovers, the Assyrians (23:5). The allegiance of the northern kingdom Israel (Samaria) to Assyria during the reign of Jehu can be seen on the Black Obelisk of the Assyrian king Shalmaneser III (dated ca. 841 BC), which mentions "Jehu son of Omri" and shows the Israelite king Jehu bowing down to the Assyrian monarch, paying homage.[16] This "love affair" that Israel has with the Assyrians may be alluding to this subservience of Jehu or perhaps to the tribute paid to the Assyrians by King Menahem (see comments on 2 Kings 15:16–20) and Hoshea (see comments on 2 Kings 17:1).

All the Chaldeans; Pekod, Shoa, and Koa (23:23). The word "Chaldean," used interchangeably with the word "Babylonian," initially referred to the people occupying the region just north of the Persian Gulf. Pekod, Shoa, and Koa were Aramean tribes east of the Tigris River and were allied with Babylonia. It is possible that Ezekiel mentioned such obscure peoples in order to convey to Israel the idea that "the whole world" is or will be against the people of Israel (cf. chaps. 38–39).

The children . . . they have sacrificed (23:37). See comments on 2 Kings 3:27.

Drunkards (23:42). The word translated as "drunkards" may alternatively be translated as "men from Sheba." Sheba was located at the southwest corner of the Arabian Peninsula (modern Yemen) and was known for trading (see Job 6:19; also 1 Kings 10:1–10; Ezek. 27:22; 38:13).

Oracles against Foreign Nations (25:1–32:32)

Face the Ammonites and prophesy against them (25:2). Ammon (25:2–7), Moab (25:8–11), and Edom (25:12–14) were the three nations just to the east of Israel and Judah. The Ammonites were the descendants of Lot (the nephew of Abraham), who was both the father and grandfather of the sons of Ammon (see comments on Gen. 19:37–38). Ammon and Israel had frequent conflicts going back to the days of Jephthah in the time of the Judges (Judg. 10:6–11:33; 1 Sam. 11:1–11; 2 Kings 24:1–2; 1 Chron. 19:1–20:3; Jer. 49:1–6). Ammon played a role in a secret conspiracy to rebel against Babylon in 593 BC (cf. Jer. 27:1–7) but later allied with the Babylonians against Judah (2 Kings 24:1–2). Ammon maliciously gloated over Judah's fall (Lam. 2:15–16). The Ammonites had a reputation for their extravagant idolatry (1 Kings 11:7, 33), vicious brutality (Amos 1:13), pride (Zeph. 2:9–10), and unending hostility toward God's people (Deut. 23:3–4; Judg. 3:13; 1 Sam. 11:1–3; 2 Sam. 10:1–14; 2 Kings 24:2; Neh. 4:3, 7–8). According to the first-century-AD Jewish historian Josephus, Nebuchadnezzar, king of Babylon, campaigned against Ammon and Moab in his twenty-third year, which was 582 BC.[17] Later, Bedouins from the east plundered the Ammonites.

Seir (25:8). The term "Seir" is used as a synonym for Edom. See comments on Ezek. 35:2.

I am about to expose Moab's flank (25:9). Like the Ammonites, the Moabites were descendants of Lot and one of his daughters (see comments on Gen. 19:37–38). Shortly after the Israelites were released from Egyptian bondage the Moabites introduced the Israelites to Baal worship (Num. 21:1–25; 31:16). Later, during the time of the divided kingdom, Judah went on to dominate Moab throughout much of its remaining history. During Ezekiel's time, in the time of the destruction and exile, Moabite troops joined forces with Nebuchadnezzar and attacked King Jehoiakim (2 Kings 24:2). When Judah was defeated, the Moabites rejoiced (Jer. 48:29; Zeph. 2:8–9). According to Josephus, Nebuchadnezzar overran Moab five years after the fall of Jerusalem.[18]

Because Edom acted vengefully against the house of Judah (25:12). The struggle between Edom and Judah began on the very occasion of their birth when Jacob, the father of the Israelites, grabbed the heel of Esau, the father of the Edomites, as they emerged from Rebekah's womb (Gen. 25:21–34). In the time of Moses, as the Israelites departed from Egypt, Edom refused

Ruins from the city of Petra, built by the Nabateans, who displaced the Edomites.

to let them pass through their land en route to Canaan (Num. 20:14–21), even though Moses's appeal for special consideration was based on recognition of their "brotherhood" (Num. 20:14–17). This was the beginning of an adversarial relationship between Israel and Edom throughout much of their mutual histories. There were conflicts between Israel and Edom during the reigns of Saul (1 Sam. 14:47), Solomon (1 Kings 11:14–22), Jehoshaphat (2 Chron. 20:1–23), Jehoram (2 Kings 8:21), and Ahaz (2 Chron. 28:17). Edom even apparently played a role in the destruction of the Jerusalem temple (Ps. 137:7; Lam. 4:21–22; Obad. 1–14). Like the Moabites and Ammonites, the Edomites had an ancestral connection to the Israelites, and yet they were combatant (Gen. 27:40), idolatrous (2 Chron. 25:14, 20), and cruel (Amos 1:11–12).[19] However, unlike Moab and Ammon, Edom seems to have taken on a special role as "the archenemy of Israel."

Yet the prophets declare that Israel will one day possess Edom in the end time (Isa. 11:14; Ezek. 35:1–36:15; Dan. 11:41; Amos 9:12; Obad. 18–19) (see comments on Ezek. 35:2). During the fourth and third centuries BC the Edomites were gradually replaced by the Nabateans, who then became the dominant population in that area down into the NT era (see comments on Obad. 1; Mal. 1:2–3; 1:4).

Because the Philistines acted in vengeance and took revenge with deep contempt (25:15). See the article "The Philistines." The Philistines migrated to the coast of Canaan from Greece and the islands of the Aegean Sea (Amos 9:7; Zeph. 2:5; Jer. 47:4). As far back in Israelite history as the time of the judges they were perennial adversaries of Israel (Judg. 3:31; 10:7; 13–16; 1 Sam. 4; 13; 31; 2 Sam. 5; 2 Kings 18:8; 2 Chron. 21:16–17; 28:18). The final subjugation of the Philistines did not occur until the time of David's reign (2 Sam. 5:17–25). There is no record for the existence of the Philistines after the time of the Maccabees (second century BC). Regardless, the later name of the region of Canaan, "Palestine," was taken from the name "Philistine."

Cutting off the Cherethites (25:16). The Cherethites (possibly Cretans) are understood to be a people group of Aegean origin that settled along the southwest coast of Canaan. They lived among the Israelites to a limited degree, but later David chose several Cherethites to be part of his personal

A colorful wall painting from the palace of Knossos on the island of Crete.

guard (1 Sam. 30:14; 2 Sam. 8:18). They often are mentioned along with the Pelethite forces with which they formed a mercenary unit during the time of David (2 Sam. 8:18; 20:23; see also 2 Sam. 15:18).

Because Tyre said about Jerusalem, "Aha! The gateway of the peoples is shattered" (26:2). Tyre was a city along the Mediterranean coast, north of Israel, encompassing an island fortress along with a mainland settlement. The inhabitants of the city of Tyre (the Phoenicians) were part of the original population that lived in Canaan before the Israelites arrived under the leadership of Joshua. Tyre dominated the other coastal cities of Phoenicia, but much of the Phoenician inland was under its influence as well. Likewise, with colonies on the North African coast and a powerful fleet of ships, Tyre exercised tremendous influence throughout the entire Mediterranean region.

Tyre's Hebrew name is *tsor*, which means "rock." From a military perspective, the island fortress of Tyre, butressed by its dominating fleet, was virtually impregnable. For example, even though the powerful Assyrians were able to conquer the northern kingdom of Israel (722 BC), they were forced to abandon their unsuccessful five-year siege of Tyre. Then, as Assyrian dominance of the region began to decline in strength, Tyre exerted its complete independence. Joel 3:6 implies that Tyre and Sidon had become the Mediterranean's paramount slave-trading nation, buying masses of slaves taken in the Babylonian onslaught and reselling them far away from home in places such as Greece.

After being defeated by the Babylonians at the battle of Carchemish (605 BC), the Egyptians' influence was diminished in the region and Tyre filled that void, becoming one of the central powers opposing Babylon. Tyre, by this time the preeminent maritime power of the ancient world, aligned with Judah in rebellion against the Babylonian Empire (Jer. 27:3). After Nebuchadnezzar defeated Jerusalem and destroyed the temple, he besieged

Tyre for thirteen long years (585–572 BC). He ultimately was unsuccessful in his campaign to conquer the rock fortress located offshore, although he did destroy Tyre's mainland territories. It was Alexander the Great in 332 BC who actually conquered Tyre. Alexander built a causeway a half-mile long and two hundred feet wide from the mainland to enable his army to reach the fortress and destroy it, fulfilling much of Ezekiel's prophecy against Tyre (cf. 26:14; 27:36). This causeway is still visible today.

The sound of your lyres (26:13). See the article "Musical Instruments in Israel and the Ancient Near East."

I will turn you into a bare rock, and you will be a place to spread nets (26:14). See comments on Ezek. 26:2.

When I raise up the deep against you so that the mighty waters cover you (26:19). With these words the Lord threatens Tyre with the same language used to describe the Genesis flood (Gen. 6–8).

They constructed all your planking . . . mast . . . deck . . . sail (27:3–7). The city of Tyre was famous for its fleet of ships. Ezekiel portrays Tyre as a well-built ship to symbolize the way Tyre achieved wealth.

A cedar from Lebanon (27:5). Lebanon cedar was distinguished by its height and strength (1 Kings 4:33; 5:6; 1 Chron. 17:1–6; Ezra 3:7; Isa. 2:13), and often it was imported by Israel from Lebanon for important building projects.

Tarshish was your trading partner (27:12). The exact location of Tarshish has been debated. The location has often been linked with Tartessus of classical sources, a Phoenician colony in western Spain on the Guadalquivir River, and thus at the opposite end of the Mediterranean Sea from Tyre.

Tubal . . . Meshech (27:13). See comments on Ezek. 32:26; 38:2.

Purple and embroidered cloth (27:16). Phoenicia was famous for trade in very expensive purple dye obtained from shellfish (see the article "The Canaanites and Canaanite Religion").

Eden (27:23). In ancient Near Eastern literature Eden was south of Haran, and it is mentioned with Haran in 2 Kings 19:12. On the similar term "Beth-eden," see comments on Amos 1:5.

Assyrian wall relief depicting the transport of cedar logs by sea, probably shipped from Tyre.

Say to the ruler of Tyre (28:2). The two most likely candidates for this Tyrian king who ruled in Ezekiel's day are Ittobaal II and Ethbaal III. It is also possible that the language about this king was purposely vague in order to couch his identity so that any Tyrian king might have served as its target. Like the inhabitants of Tyre, Tyre's ruler was guilty of pride and self-aggrandizement (see 27:1–9; cf. Prov. 6:17; 8:13; 16:18).

You are wiser than Daniel (28:3). Daniel's fame had spread in the exile, even beyond the boundaries of his own nation (see Ezek. 14:14, 20; Dan. 1:20; 2:48; 4:18; 5:11–12; 6:3). The character of Daniel is antithetical to the pride and egotistical self-sufficiency of the king of Tyre.

Face Sidon and prophesy against it (28:21). Sidon, like Tyre, was a very important Phoenician port city, located twenty-five miles north of Tyre. Sidon and Tyre often are mentioned together (Jer. 27:3; 47:4; Joel 3:4; Zech. 9:2). During times when Tyre experienced weakness Sidon would increase in prominence. For example, in the Persian period Sidon was considered the chief Phoenician city. It is possible that Sidon's abrupt and brief inclusion in this collection of oracles was in order for the total number of nations addressed to equal seven. Support for this interpretation comes from the fact that chapters 29–32 contain seven oracles against Egypt. Alternatively, the present oracle may have been precipitated (as are many others) by Sidon's involvement in the revolt against Babylon during Zedekiah's reign in Jerusalem (Jer. 27:3).

Face Pharoah king of Egypt and prophesy against him (29:2). Egypt too was a perennial foe of Israel, having kept the nation in bondage for four hundred years of its early history. Somewhat unique about the present oracle to Egypt, however, is the promise of a restoration of the nation to its land after a period of forty years. If Egypt fell to the Babylonians in about 568 BC, as implied in the chronicles of the Babylonian kings, a forty-year "captivity" of Egypt would end under the Persians, who encouraged exiled peoples to return to their homelands (2 Chron. 36:22–23). However, Egypt never returned to its former position of preeminence in the international arena.

The great monster lying in the middle of his Nile (29:3). In ancient Near Eastern literature this term "monster" (*tannin*) often refers to the mythical sea monster associated with chaos, known elsewhere by the names Rahab and Leviathan. Here, because the term is closely associated with the Nile River, some argue that it refers to a crocodile. In Egyptian literature the pharaoh occasionally is compared to a crocodile. Whether or not this text refers to a crocodile, Ezekiel speaks of the king of Egypt as the great monster who, like the ruler of Tyre in chapter 28, dares to defy the Lord. In other OT texts as well Egypt is compared to a sea monster type of entity (Job 9:13; 26:12–13; Ps. 89:9–10; Isa. 30:7; 51:9–10).

The Egyptian crocodile god Sobek.

When they leaned on you, you shattered (29:7). See the article "The Egyptians." In 2 Kings 18:21 and Isa. 36:6 the Assyrians declare that placing trust in the pharaoh is like leaning on a staff that is as feeble as a reed. The reed breaks and hurts the hand that holds it. The statement here looks back specifically to the Egyptian pharaoh Hophra's later unsuccessful attempt to support Jerusalem during the military siege. His attack against the Babylonian king Nebuchadnezzar in the spring of 588 BC had failed to deliver Jerusalem (Jer. 37:5–10).

Its cities will be a desolation among ruined cities for forty years (29:12). "Forty years" is a frequent expression in the Bible for a complete and lengthy period of time (Num. 14:33; Judg. 3:11; 1 Kings 2:11). If Egypt fell to the Babylonians in 568 BC, as most ancient Near Eastern records suggest, then this forty-year "captivity" of Egypt would end under the Persians.

It will never again be an object of trust for the house of Israel (29:16). After the Babylonian defeat and the Persian rise to power, Egypt would never again be a world power as it was earlier.

Nebuchadnezzar . . . made his army labor strenuously against Tyre (29:18). See comments on Ezek. 26:2. Nebuchadnezzar's unsuccessful siege of Tyre lasted thirteen long years.[20]

Memphis . . . Zoan . . . Thebes . . . Pelusium (30:13–15). These were all important cities in Egypt.

In the eleventh year, in the first month, on the seventh day (30:20). This date formula may indicate that this oracle was announced shortly before the fall of Jerusalem to the Babylonians. It possibly alludes to Pharaoh Hophra's attempt to rescue Judah from the crisis (Jer. 37:5).

I have broken the arm of Pharaoh king of Egypt (30:21). This figurative expression refers to the Babylonian king Nebuchadnezzar's defeat of Pharaoh Hophra, who attempted to come to the aid of Jerusalem in 588 BC (2 Kings 24:7; Jer. 37:5).

A dragon on the Ishtar Gate of Babylon during the time of Ezekiel.

Think of Assyria, a cedar in Lebanon (31:3). Lebanon was known for its cedars (Judg. 9:15; 1 Kings 4:33; 5:6; 2 Kings 14:9; Ezra 3:7; Ps. 29:5; 92:12; 104:16; Ezek. 31:15–18). In the ancient Near East cedar often was a symbol of royalty and majesty, and in the Bible cedar frequently is mentioned in association with the construction of luxurious buildings such as palaces and temples. In this text the fall of Assyria is compared to a tall, magnificent cedar tree that nonetheless is cut down (31:12), and this analogy then becomes the illustration for the fall of Egypt.

You also will be brought down to the underworld (31:18). The tree would die disgracefully as an uncircumcised foreigner without a respectable burial. This reality would be particularly distressing for Egyptian royalty, as the purpose of the pyramids was to make the kings comfortable in the afterlife.

You compare yourself to a lion (32:2). Egyptian literature attests to the fact that the ancient pharaohs frequently compared themselves to fierce lions. For example, a text inscribed on the walls of a temple in the Egyptian city of Karnak describing one of the military campaigns of Pharoah Seti I (1318–1301 BC) states, "His majesty prevailed over them like a fierce lion."[21]

But you are like a monster in the seas (32:2). Many scholars see in this portrayal of the pharaoh's defeat by God an allusion to the mythological traditions of God's defeat of the sea dragon Leviathan at creation (Job 38:8–11; Ps. 74:12–17; 104:7–9; Isa. 11:15; 27:1). A good depiction of the combination of lions and dragons in a royal context can be seen on the blue ceramic panels that lined the street leading up to the Ishtar Gate of Babylon. Lions and dragons are alternately portrayed on these panels.[22]

Go down and be laid to rest with the uncircumcised (32:19). As throughout much of the ancient Near East, circumcision was practiced in Egypt, although how widely so is uncertain. Some have suggested that circumcision was practiced in Egypt only by pharoahs and priests, who viewed the uncircumsised other people disdainfully as "unclean."[23] The reference to this act thus must be seen as metaphorical to convey the notion of uncleanness and vileness. Thus it is a theological rather than a literal evaluation. The phrase "the uncircumcised" is used ten times in chapter 32 (vv. 19, 21, 24–30, 32) to emphasize the point that the death of the pharaoh is one of complete shame and defeat. Egypt joins six other nations (Assyria, Elam, Meshech, Tubal, Edom, Sidon) in the underworld, thus becoming the climactic and completing seventh nation that occupies the underworld.

Meshech and Tubal are there (32:26). Meshech and Tubal (cf. 27:13) probably were located on the northern border of modern eastern and central Turkey. In chapters 38–39 they are depicted as the allies of Gog (see comments on Ezek. 38:2).

The Watchman Recommissioned (33:1–33)

Appointing him as their watchman (33:2). In the ancient Near East major towns typically had watchmen stationed at the highest lookout post in the town, either at the city gate (2 Sam. 18:24) or on a tower built specifically for this purpose (2 Kings 9:17). The Lachish letters (a collection of short communiqués written on pottery fragments between Judean fortress commanders during the Babylonian invasion of Judah) indicate that smoke signals were used to communicate between fortress cities. Thus the watchmen probably were responsible to alert not only their own town of approaching invaders but also all other towns within range of smoke signals. Here the watchman was to blow the alarm on a trumpet (33:3–5). Watchmen (or sometimes "lookouts") and watchtowers are mentioned numerous times in the OT (2 Sam. 18:24–25; 2 Kings 9:17; Isa. 21:6–12; Jer. 4:5; 6:1,17; Hosea 8:1; Amos 3:6; Hab. 2:1). The watchman would not be responsible for the fate of the people if he warned them, but he would be fully responsible if he did not.

In the tenth month . . . a fugitive from Jerusalem came (33:21). The time it took for a messenger to reach Ezekiel was five to six months. In Ezra 7:9 this trip, going the other direction from Babylonia to Jerusalem, likewise took five months.

Abraham was only one person (33:24). This saying alludes back to the Abraham narratives in Gen. 12–22.

The Shepherds of Israel (34:1–31)

Prophesy against the shepherds of Israel (34:2). The phrase "shepherds of Israel" was a figurative expression used to refer to the political leaders of Israel, perhaps foremost the kings. This shepherd imagery is used frequently throughout the OT (2 Sam. 7:7; Ps. 78:70–72; Isa. 44:28; 63:11; Jer. 10:21; 23:1–6; 25:34–38; Mic. 5:4–5; Zech. 11:4–17). This was also a common figure of speech for kings and other leaders throughout the ancient Near East. As early as the eighteenth century BC, for example, the Babylonian king Hammurabi was called a shepherd.

I break the bars of their yoke (34:27). See comments on Jer. 27:2. The term "yoke" occurs more than fifty times in the Bible. The yoke was the wooden bar or frame used to join animals so they could pull a heavy load; the bars of the yoke consisted of wooden pegs inserted down through holes in the yoke that were tied below the animal's neck with cords, forming a collar (Lev. 26:13; Isa. 58:6; Jer. 27:2; 28:10–13; Ezek. 30:18). The yoke could be a symbol either of bondage or of joining together, but most of the time in the OT, as here in chapter 34, the imagery is one of the bondage of foreign domination (see Deut. 28:48; Jer. 27:8–12).

The Land (35:1–36:15)

Face Mount Seir (35:2). Mount Seir is the ancient name for the mountainous regions south of the Dead Sea on both sides of the Rift Valley extending south to the Gulf of Aqaba, a region inhabited during the OT era by the Edomites (Gen. 32:3; 36:8–9; Deut. 2:1–29). In Ezekiel, both here and in 25:8, the term "Seir" or "Mount Seir" is used as a synonym for Edom. Referring to Edom as "Mount Seir" here probably serves to connect it as a foil to "the mountains of Israel" in chapter 36. In light of Isa. 34:5 and 63:1–4 there is evidence pointing to the fact that Edom sometimes was used as a representative of Israel's enemies in general. Most likely Edom was mentioned here to represent the judgment that God would inflict on all nations that opposed Israel. The destruction of Edom would signal the beginning of God's judgment on all those who had opposed the nation of Israel (see comments on Ezek. 25:12).

I will treat you according to the anger and jealousy you showed in your hatred of them (35:11). This expression ("I will treat you according to"), indicating that a punishment should be commensurate with an action or crime, came to be known as the *lex talionis*. The concept can be seen in principle in Gen. 9:6 ("whoever sheds human blood, by humans his blood will be shed") and more clearly in the legal material of Exod. 21:23–25 ("life for life," "eye for eye," etc.) and Lev. 24:19–20 ("fracture for fracture," "eye for eye," etc.). These laws indicate that the execution of justice should be impartial and that the punishment should fit the crime. The principle would rule out excessive punishment for any committed offense or unlawful violation. Contrary to the common misinterpretation in our modern culture, this law does not authorize personal revenge. The point is that Edom's punishment will fit its crime.

God's Reputation (36:16–38)

I will also sprinkle clean water on you (36:25). Water was used for ritual cleansing both in Israel and throughout the ancient Near East. Although the actions and the purpose are not defined clearly, water was most likely used in ritual cleansings, as well as in practical cleanup, in association with the temple. This was accomplished to a significant degree by the huge bronze sea and the ten moveable water basins just outside the main temple building (1 Kings 7:23–39) (see comments on 1 Kings 7:23; 7:27–39).

People Revived and United (37:1–28)

The breath entered them, and they came to life (37:10). The two-stage process of forming the physical body and subsequently filling it with the breath of life is patterned after the creation of the first man, Adam, in Gen. 2:7, as indicated by the use of the same Hebrew verb (*nafah*) in both cases ("*breathe* into these slain" [Ezek. 37:9]; "*breathed* . . . into his nostrils" [Gen. 2:7]). In both cases the bodies did not come to life until they received an infusion of the Spirit.

Eschatological Judgment and Protection (38:1–39:29)

Face Gog, of the land of Magog (38:2). There has been a wide range of views regarding the identity of Gog and Magog. Regarding Gog, one theory is that this is a reference to a man named Gyges, who was king of Lysia in the seventh century BC. Yet even if this were the case, this same Gog apparently has been figuratively reenvisoned from his historical setting in the seventh century to refer to a leader who will oppose Israel in the eschatological future. Other than the brief mention of an unrelated person named Gog in the genealology of 1 Chron. 5:4, the only other occurrence of the name in the Bible is in Rev. 20:8, where Gog seems to transcend historical categories and become a symbol of the antichrist. If this is correct, then the original identity of Gog matters little because Gog becomes a transnational symbol of evil, much like Edom and Egypt (e.g., Exod. 15; Isa. 34; 63:1–6; Mal. 1:2–5).

The chief prince of Meshech and Tubal (38:2). The two names Meshech and Tubal were listed earlier (27:13) as nations with which the city of Tyre traded ("they exchanged slaves and bronze utensils for your goods") and, along with Assyria, Elam, Edom, Sidon, and Egypt, as inhabitants of Sheol, the underworld (32:26). They are mentioned in the records of the Assyrians (conquered by Sargon II) and the Persians. The ancient Greek historian Herodotus likewise mentions them. These references place their location in central and eastern Turkey. The Assyrians referred to Meshech as "Mushku," and in the eighth century BC the king of Mushku was Mita, known in Greek literature as Midas, the legendary king with the golden touch.[24]

Because the Hebrew word for "chief" (*rosh*) is similar in sound to the national name "Russia," a few writers have attempted to identify Russia with the word translated as "chief" in 38:2 ("the *chief* prince"). Although the Septuagint does transliterate the Hebrew word into Greek (*Rōs*), this is virtually the possible extent of the evidence for such a conjecture. The earliest attestation of the name Rus (Russia) dates to the ninth century AD, a name probably brought by the Vikings to the area around Kiev. The popular identification of Rosh with Russia is based on a faulty etymology, the similarities in sound between "Russia" and "Rosh" being purely accidental. Rosh never appears as a nation in any other biblical (or nonbiblical) list of place names, while all the other names mentioned in this passage are well attested (cf. Gen. 10:1–7; 1 Chron. 1:5–7; Ezek. 27:13–24; 32:26). Those who identify "Meshech" with Moscow and "Tubal" with Tobolsk likewise do so on faulty and extremely speculative etymological evidence.

I will give Gog a burial place there in Israel—the Travelers' Valley east of the Sea (39:11). This burial project will be so massive that it will block the normal passage of people. The name of the valley will be renamed as the valley of Hamon Gog ("Hordes of Gog

Valley"). The only valley that runs in an east-west direction in Israel is the Jezreel Valley. The Jezreel Valley stretched west from the town of Jezreel to the plain of Acco, south of Ibleam. The Jezreel Valley was a vital strategic link on the route from Egypt to Damascus in biblical times. Another possibility is to view "Hamon Gog" as a wordplay on "Valley of Hinnom," the valley next to Jerusalem where child sacrifice had been practiced (Jer. 2:23; 7:31–32), thus locating this valley as right next to Jerusalem.[25]

Tell every kind of bird and all the wild animals, . . . "gather . . . to my sacrificial feast" (39:17). In the ancient Near East the practice of throwing slaughtered corpses out into the open field to be eaten by birds and wild animals was viewed not only as a humiliating punishment but also as a curse. The practice is well attested in ancient Near Eastern texts, and it often occurs as a punishment (and curse) for treaty violations.[26]

New Temple (40:1–43:12)

A man . . . with a linen cord and a measuring rod (40:3). There are numerous instances from the ancient Near East, both in literary documents and in iconography (paintings, carvings, etchings, etc.), where the construction of a temple is preceded by surveying activities, often with both a measuring line and a measuring rod.[27]

The measuring rod . . . six units of twenty-one inches (40:5). Measuring rods were common tools used in surveying and in the construction

The Eastern (Golden) Gate to the Temple Mount in Jerusalem today. This gate was sealed during the time of the Crusades. Most of the wall and gate visible today was built during the Muslim occupation of Jerusalem between AD 969 and 1541. Some of the lowest stone blocks, however, and the blocks below ground may date as far back as the First Temple.

of buildings. Several Egyptian measuring rods have survived from ancient times. The common measuring unit in the Bible (as well as throughout the ancient Near East) was the cubit, approximately the distance from the elbow to the fingertips (17–18 inches). The Siloam Inscription (eighth century BC) notes that Hezekiah's tunnel was 1,200 cubits long. Actual measurement of the tunnel today, divided by 1,200, yields a cubit length of 17.6 inches. This term is used very frequently in the Bible (over two hundred times), especially when the text is dealing with the dimensions of the tabernacle (Exod. 25–38) or the temple (1 Kings 6–7; 2 Chron. 3–4). Yet both the Egyptians and the Babylonians apparently had two official cubit measurements, a "short cubit" (17–18 inches) and a "long cubit" or "royal cubit," which was longer (21–24 inches). Yet although these measurements were precise locally, one can tell from the ranges cited above that they did vary some across the ancient Near East. So it is difficult for us today to say with exact precision how long a cubit was. Second Chronicles 3:3 appears to explain that Solomon's temple had been built according to the old, shorter cubit. The Hebrew text in Ezek. 40:5 states that the measuring rod was six cubits long, each being a cubit and a span (width of a hand), probably clarifying that the surveyor in Ezekiel was using the longer, more recent cubit length in his measurement.[28]

Then he came to the gate . . . each recess was 10½ feet long and 10½ feet deep . . . three recesses on each side (40:6–16). The gate and its associated guardhouse described in this passage are similar (although larger than most) to the numerous older gates that have been excavated in Israel (e.g., the cities of Gezer, Hazor, Megiddo). Guardrooms were also a part of the Solomonic temple (1 Kings 14:28; 2 Chron. 12:11).

He led me to the gate, the one that faces east (43:1). Ezekiel mentions the eastward-facing orientation of the main gate several times (e.g., 40:6–10, 22; 42:15; 43:1–4; 44:1). Both the tabernacle and Solomon's temple were oriented in an east-west direction with the main entrance facing east (as were many temples of the ancient Near East). Just as Ezekiel witnessed the departure of the Lord from the east gate of Solomon's temple (10:18–19), so here the Lord returns through the same gate.

Regulations for Worship (43:13–46:24)

The sanctuary's outer gate that faced east . . . was closed (44:1). At this point the east gate is closed, apparently now dedicated to be used only by the Lord (44:2). The city of Babylon had a "Sacred Gate," which was closed at all times to human traffic but opened on special occasions to allow Marduk (the main god of the city) and other deities to enter.[29]

Land of Blessing (47:1–48:35)

There was water flowing from under the threshhold of the temple (47:1). Throughout the ancient Near East there is a close association between temples and flowing water. Sometimes temples were constructed on top of springs to allow the water to flow up and through the temple.[30] Similarly, there are several depictions in the ancient Near East of water in temples flowing out of vases. Some scholars propose that the Hebrew terms used here suggest the vase imagery and background.[31]

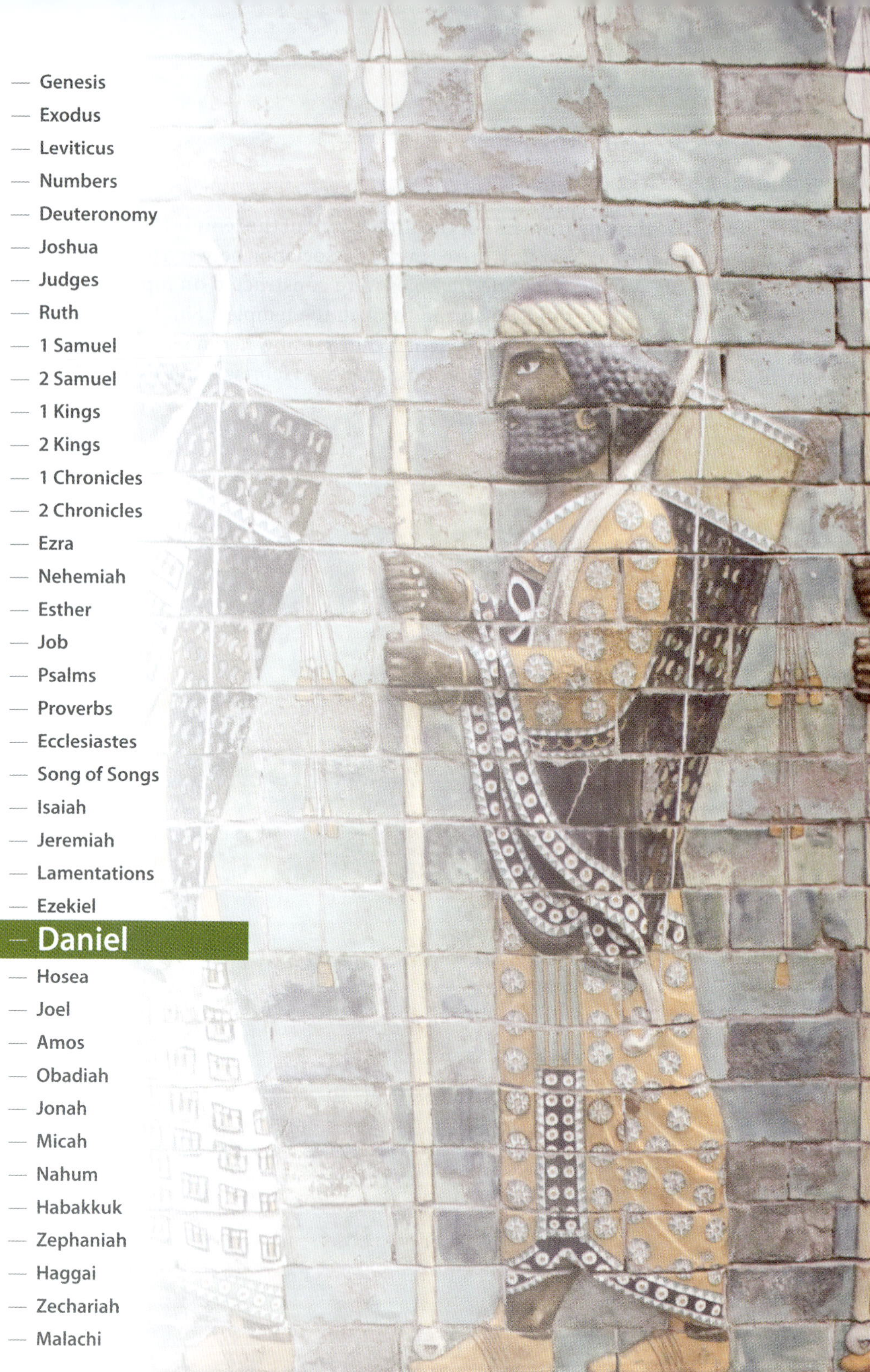

Daniel

William B. Nelson

Introduction. The genre (literary style) of Daniel is apocalyptic, which is a late form of prophecy characterized by highly symbolic cryptic visions, periodization of history, heavenly mediators, often an end-time battle, and the coming of God's eternal kingdom. The book is written in two languages: Hebrew and Aramaic. It begins in Hebrew (1:1–2:4a), shifts into Aramaic (2:4b–7:28), and then reverts to Hebrew for the last four chapters (chaps. 8–12). Furthermore, the Aramaic section is carefully organized into a chiastic pattern; that is, the six chapters form an A B C C′ B′ A′ pattern, as follows:

- A Dream of four kingdoms followed by the kingdom of God (chap. 2)
  - B Miraculous deliverance (from a furnace of blazing fire) (chap. 3)
    - C Judgment on a king (Nebuchadnezzar) (chap. 4)
    - C′ Judgment on a king (Belshazzar) (chap. 5)
  - B′ Miraculous deliverance (from a den of lions) (chap. 6)
- A′ Vision of four kingdoms followed by the kingdom of God (chap. 7)

Elamites being deported into captivity by the Assyrians.

Traditionally, this book is attributed to the prophet Daniel, who was taken to Babylon during the exile. However, many scholars believe that the book was composed by an anonymous author in the second century BC. Whether it was written early or late, however, it seems to be addressed to the context of the Jews living in the second century BC who were enduring persecution under the evil tyrant Antiochus IV Epiphanes, a Seleucid king. Its purpose is to encourage them to remain faithful even if they are martyred, because they will be raised "to eternal life" (12:2).

Daniel and His Friends Exiled to Babylon (1:1–21)

In the third year of the reign of King Jehoiakim (1:1). Jehoiakim was king of Judah, reigning in Jerusalem from 609 to 598 BC (see comments on 2 Kings 23:36–24:7). Because Jehoiakim's reign began in 609 BC, the siege and the first deportation mentioned here in 1:1 would date to 606 BC or so and would imply three different deportations. Based on 2 Kings 24 and 2 Chron. 36:5–9, however, many scholars see only two deportations and date the first deportation to 597 BC.[1]

King Nebuchadnezzar (1:1). Nebuchadnezzar II was king of Babylonia from 605 to 562 BC (see the article "The Babylonians").

Carried them to the land of Babylon, to the house of his god (1:2). The primary god of the Babylonians and head of their pantheon was Marduk (see the section on Babylonian religion in the article "The Babylonians"). Throughout the ancient Near East temples often were used to display trophies of war. The Philistines, for example, put the captured ark of the covenant in their temple of Dagon (1 Sam. 5:1–7). After killing Saul, the Philistines placed his armor in the temple of Astarte (1 Sam. 31:10).

Babylon (1:2). The Hebrew text has "Shinar" here, as the CSB footnote records. Shinar, probably originally a reference to the more general region in which the city of Babylon was located (Gen. 11:2; 14:1,9), sometimes is used to refer specifically to Babylon (Zech. 5:11), and thus many English versions translate it as "Babylon."

He was to teach them the Chaldean language and literature (1:4). "Chaldean" refers to a people group in 5:30 and 9:1. Here and in 2:2–5, 10;

The Ishtar Gate from the city of Babylon, reconstructed in a museum in Berlin.

3:8; 4:7; 5:7, 11, however, the term designates the royal advisors: astrologers, magicians, diviners, dream interpreters, and soothsayers. Their language would have been Akkadian, and their literature would have included Babylonian legends and myths, texts on dream interpretation, texts on how to read animal livers for omens (see comments on Ezek. 21:21), and texts on magical practices and religious rituals (see the section on literature and culture in the article "The Babylonians"). However, even though Daniel and his friends mastered the curriculum "ten times better than all the magicians and mediums" (1:20), when Daniel actually interpreted dreams, he did so by God's help, not by the Babylonian wisdom (1:17; 2:19, 27–28; 4:9, 18; 5:11, 14).

He would not defile himself with the king's food or with the wine (1:8). The cause of this defilement that Daniel is avoiding is not stated. Perhaps the royal food contained things prohibited by Mosaic law (e.g., blood, pork), but it is puzzling why wine is mentioned, since wine was not prohibited. Perhaps some defiling religious rituals were involved, or, since the book of Daniel was used to preach to the Jews in the later Hellenistic era, perhaps it is warning them not to participate in the cult of Dionysus, the god of wine.

King Cyrus (1:21). Cyrus was king of Persia (see the section on Cyrus in the article "The Persians").

Nebuchadnezzar's Vision of a Statue (2:1–49)

That statue, tall and dazzling, was standing in front of you (2:31). There are references to colossal images in the ancient Near East. For instance, the Greek historian Herodotus tells of a gold statue in the temple of Bel in Babylon that was twelve cubits (about 17.5 feet) high.[2] Numerous statues overlaid with metals (gold, silver, bronze) have been found by archaeologists. In addition, parallels to this dream exist: Gudea of Sumer saw a gigantic man in his dream; Pharaoh Merneptah witnessed a large apparition of the god Ptah.[3]

Pure gold . . . silver . . . bronze . . . iron . . . partly iron and partly fired clay (2:32–33). The ancient Greek writer Hesiod (eighth century BC) spoke of five historical periods characterized by metals of diminishing value: gold, silver, bronze, an age of demigods (no accompanying metal), and iron.[4] The Latin poet Ovid (late first century BC to early first century AD) divided history into similar periods: gold, silver, brass, and iron.[5]

A fourth kingdom (2:40). The motif of three successive kingdoms goes back to the Persian era and was outlined as Assyria,

Media, and Persia. The ancient Greek historian Herodotus also recounted this scheme.[6] After Alexander the Great conquered much of the known world, this motif grew to four kingdoms, Greece being the last. As time went on, Rome was appended as a fifth.[7] The author of Daniel adapted this pattern for his use. He was not concerned about Assyria so he substituted Babylon, because the Babylonians had destroyed Jerusalem and the holy temple. The fourth kingdom, both here and in chapter 7, probably is Greece, which is important because of the persecutions that the Jews endured under the wicked Seleucid king Antiochus IV, a cultural and political descendant of Alexander the Great. However, since the kingdom of God did not come in the Hellenistic era, some interpret the four kingdoms as Babylon, Medo-Persia, Greece, and Rome. This does not really help, though, because the fullness of God's kingdom, with the appearance of the one like a human being coming in the clouds (7:13), did not occur in the Roman period either.

The Fiery Furnace (3:1–30)

A gold statue (3:1). See comments on Dan. 2:31.

Ninety feet high and nine feet wide (3:1). The text reads "sixty cubits high and six cubits wide." A cubit was approximately eighteen inches, although this varied and a cubit may have been longer at this time (see comments on Ezek. 40:5). Though very tall, this statue is not unique. The colossus at Rhodes was seventy cubits high (approximately 105 feet). However, these dimensions give a very unusual height-to-width ratio for a statue (10:1); it would be extraordinarily thin. Different suggestions have been made to explain this. Maybe the author used comical dimensions to ridicule the idol. Perhaps it is meant to display the Babylonian penchant for the sexagesimal number system (based on the number sixty). Or perhaps the statue was an obelisk or pillar with a smaller, more humanly proportional image on top.

The horn, flute, zither, lyre, harp, drum, and every kind of music (3:5). The first term probably denotes a ram's horn or shofar. The second term comes from a root meaning "to whistle" or "to hiss," so usually it is rendered as "flute" or "pipe." The third is a loanword from the Greek *kitharas* or *kithara*, from which we get "guitar" and "zither." The CSB and NIV have "zither," but other versions have "harp" or "lyre." The fourth one is not as certain; it may indicate a stringed instrument shaped like a triangle, known as a "trigon" (NRSV). The CSB and NIV choose "lyre." Most agree that the fifth is a "harp." The sixth noun may designate an instrument (perhaps "drum" or "pipes"), but since it is the word from which we get "symphony," it might just suggest the beautiful harmony generated by the ensemble, hence "every kind of music" (CSB). The third, fifth, and sixth terms are of

Greek derivation, suggesting either a later date for the book of Daniel or the presence of Greeks (or Greek musicians) in the court of Nebuchadnezzar. See the article "Musical Instruments in Israel and the Ancient Near East."

A furnace of blazing fire (3:6). Certain laws in the ancient Babylonian Code of Hammurabi stipulate burning as the penalty for some offenses, and such punishment does appear in the records of the ancient Near East.[8] The Bible also appears to allow punishment by burning in certain instances (Gen. 38:24; Lev. 21:9; Josh. 7:15, 25; Jer. 29:21–22).

The fourth looks like a son of the gods (3:25). Within the Bible the sons of God typically are heavenly beings or angels who are members of the divine council or God's court (Gen. 6:2, 4; Deut. 32:8 [LXX and NIV footnote]; 1 Kings 22:19; Job 1:6; 2:1; 38:7; Ps. 29:1; 82:6). Although some writers have argued that this fourth person is the preincarnate Jesus (often based on the King James Version: "the form of the fourth is like the Son of God"), 3:28 appears to clearly identify the fourth one as an angel.

Judgment and Restoration for Nebuchadnezzar (4:1–37)

A tree in the middle of the earth (4:10). Throughout the ancient Near East the imagery of a great "cosmic tree" that ties heaven and earth together appears fairly frequently in art, iconography, and literature; here it is reminiscent of the tree of life (Gen. 2:9). It stands in the middle of the earth (not "land" as if confined to one region); it is exceedingly lofty with its branches soaring into the sky; it provides abundant food and protective shelter to all. Ancient people believed that the king could help preserve the cosmic

The Assyrian king Ashurnasirpal standing by a sacred tree flanked by winged protective genies.

order by participating in religious rites. Therefore, it is not surprising that Nebuchadnezzar is portrayed as this tree and that sometimes kings were depicted as trees in images.

A watcher, a holy one, coming down from heaven (4:13). The word "watcher" and associated concepts appear frequently in nonbiblical Jewish texts from the Greek and Roman eras. The first thirty-six chapters of *1 Enoch*, for example, are titled "The Book of the Watchers," which dates to around the third century BC. This term also occurs in the Dead Sea Scrolls. Although the term "watcher" can be used to designate fallen angels (especially in later literature), it can also denote faithful angels.[9]

Cut down the tree (4:14). On the "cosmic tree," see comments on Dan. 4:10. Imagery of a cosmic tree similar to that in 4:10–12 is found also in Ezek. 17; 31. The trees are tall with fruitful branches, offering sustenance and homes to all creatures. The tree in Ezek. 31 is even said to be greater than all the trees in Eden, the garden of God (vv. 8–9). God brings judgment on account of pride, a thread common to all three texts.

Seven periods of time (4:16). "Seven periods of time" also occurs in 4:23, 25, 32. Many scholars are convinced that there is some connection between this story in chapter 4 and a story appearing in the Dead Sea Scrolls about the Babylonian king Nabonidus, titled "The Prayer of Nabonidus." In that story Nabonidus suffers a seven-year affliction, but then he prays and confesses his sin, and subsequently is healed by a Jewish exorcist.[10]

His hair grew like eagles' feathers and his nails like birds' claws (4:33). Similar language is used of Ahiqar in the popular ancient story known as "The Words of Ahiqar" (seventh to sixth centuries BC). The story's hero, Ahiqar, was a prosperous vizier to the Assyrian king. After being falsely accused, he is condemned, but a servant rescues him and gives him refuge. During his concealment his hair grows long like an animal's and his nails become "like the claws of an eagle."[11] Eventually Ahiqar is cleared of the charges and, like Nebuchadnezzar in chapter 4, is reinstated.

The Writing on the Wall (5:1–31)

King Belshazzar (5:1). Nabonidus was the last king of Babylon. Although Belshazzar was the crown prince and regent, fulfilling some royal duties while his father, King Nabonidus, was away, Belshazzar is never actually called "king" in the ancient records;

Broken granite stela of the Babylonian king Nabonidus, covered with inscriptions.

nor was he able to celebrate the Akitu (or New Year) festival in the absence of his father, as this was something that only the king could do.

Held a great feast for a thousand of his nobles and drank wine in their presence (5:1). Both Herodotus and Xenophon, ancient Greek historians, also note that a Babylonian festival was taking place on the night the Persian king Cyrus captured Babylon. Xenophon recounts that the feast involved drinking; Herodotus mentions dancing.

Chaldeans (5:7). See comments on Dan. 1:4.

Mene, Mene, Tekel, and Parsin (5:25–29). All of these terms are words for weights, but the translation and the significance of these terms are far from clear. Complicating matters is the fact that the words used in the explanation (5:26–28) do not match exactly the words used in 5:25 for the inscription. In 5:25 the first word, repeated twice, denotes a mina, which was about sixty shekels. The third word is Aramaic for "shekel," and the fourth means "halves," probably indicating half-minas (or, less likely, half-shekels). Note that while the term "mene" is repeated twice in 5:25, in the explanation following in 5:26 only one "mene" is mentioned. Perhaps the second "mene" in 5:25 is a dittography (a scribal error by which something is accidentally repeated), or perhaps we just don't know the significance of the repetition. Also, regarding the fourth word in the inscription (5:25), the term cited is "parsin," but in the following interpretation (5:28) the word that is explained is "peres."

For interpretive purposes it appears that the explanation (5:26–28) should take priority in determining the meaning of the inscription. Scholars, however, remain divided on how to understand the weights. Some suggest that each one of the three weights symbolizes one of the three Babylonian kings (Nebuchadnezzar, Nabonidus, Belshazzar). Others propose that the weights should be added together. They note that if the final weight is a plural and means "halves," then the total is sixty shekels plus one shekel plus two halves (one shekel), which equals sixty-two shekels. Yet while the number sixty-two does occur a few verses later (5:31) as the age of Darius the Mede and does likewise figure prominently in Daniel's chronological schema (9:25–26), it is not clear at all what this connection would be, and the text itself makes no connection. In contrast, in 5:26–28 Daniel reinterprets the three nouns as verbs that pronounce judgment on Belshazzar and his kingdom.

Darius the Mede (5:31). This reference is puzzling, and, once again, there is no consensus among scholars as to how to understand this text. There is no attestation of anybody called "Darius the Mede" in historical records from this period. Both historical annals and the Scriptures affirm that it was Cyrus the Persian who conquered Babylon (in 539 BC), not Darius the Mede. Later,

A wall panel from the palace of the Assyrian king Ashurbanipal depicting the release of a lion for the royal lion hunt.

there were three Persian kings named Darius, but the first one did not come to power until 521 BC. Suggestions have been made to identify Darius the Mede with Cyrus or one of his subordinates, but there is no consensus view.

Daniel in the Lions' Den (6:1–28)

Darius decided to appoint 120 satraps (6:1). The word "satrap" refers to a provincial governor. Although Darius the Mede is unknown outside the book of Daniel (see comments on Dan. 5:31), the Persian king Darius I Hystaspes (521–486 BC) is known to have divided his empire into about twenty satrapies or provinces (see the section on Darius in the article "The Persians").

The lions' den (6:7). In ancient Mesopotamia kings apparently often participated in royal lion hunts. Discovered in the palace of Assyrian king Ashurbanipal (from around 645 BC) is an extensive series of wall panel carvings depicting these royal lion hunts. The lions initially are in mobile cages and then are released in the field to allow the king to chase them and combat them. Apparently, therefore, lions must have been housed and cared for, probably either in cages or in pits/dens somewhere near the royal court, in preparation for upcoming hunts.[12] Ezekiel 19:1–9 implies that lions were sometimes captured through the use of hand-dug pits in the ground and then forcibly placed in cages to be transported to the royal palace.

Daniel's Vision of the Five Kingdoms (7:1–28)

Four winds of heaven (7:2). In the Enuma Elish, the Babylonian creation myth, the god Marduk does battle against Tiamat, the goddess of the sea. Among his weapons are the four winds. The term "four winds" is used again in Daniel (8:8; 11:4) as well as in other biblical passages (Jer. 49:36; Ezek. 37:9; Zech. 2:6; 6:5; Matt. 24:31; Mark 13:27; Rev. 7:1).

Four huge beasts came up from the sea, each different from the other (7:3). In the ancient Near East the sea represented chaos. This nuance is suggested in 7:2, which states, "the four winds of heaven stirred up the great sea." Likewise, widespread throughout the ancient Near East was the close association of the sea with dragons and sea monsters. So readers in the ancient Near East would not be surprised at all to see violent, malevolent beasts emerge from the chaotic deep. In ancient Mesopotamian mythology the god Marduk defeats Tiamat, the sea goddess, and then splits her in two to create the cosmos. In Canaanite lore the storm god Baal vanquishes Yam, god of the sea, and also fights against Lotan (Leviathan), the dragon or twisting serpent.

These stories were commonly known in the ancient Near East and provide helpful background for understanding some of the OT texts in which Israel's God is depicted as doing some similar actions, but usually bigger and better, as a statement of how Israel's God is greater than the pagan gods (see comments on Gen. 1:1). Israel's God divides the waters below from the waters above in creation (Gen. 1:6–8). He also split the sea in the time of Moses. While there is no mythological language in the Exodus account, it comes up in other passages. The Lord, not Baal or Marduk, crushed Rahab, the sea monster (Job 26:12–13; Ps. 89:9–10). In Isa. 51:9–10 the miraculous crossing of the Red Sea is specifically tied to the defeat of Rahab, the dragon (see comments on Isa. 51:9), and the splitting of the sea is associated with crushing the heads of dragons or Leviathan (Ps. 74:12–14). One day the Lord will destroy Leviathan, the twisting serpent, the dragon of the sea (Isa. 27:1). This theme continues in the NT. A beast rises from the sea (Rev. 13:1) or from the abyss (Rev. 17:8). When Jesus returns, the sea will no longer be chaotic but will become like glass (Rev. 15:2) or will cease to be (Rev. 21:1).

The first was like a lion but had eagle's wings (7:4). Composite animals with a lion's body (or often a bull's body) and the wings of a bird are commonly depicted in the art and iconography of the ancient Near East.

These composite winged creatures are from a wall panel in the palace of Darius I in the Persian city of Susa.

Hosea mentions a lion, a leopard, and a bear, which parallels Daniel's vision, although the order is different and Hosea, unlike Daniel, portrays God coming in judgment like these animals (Hosea 13:7–8).

It had ten horns (7:7). The four beasts probably symbolize Babylon, Media, Persia, and Greece; another, less likely option is Babylon, Medo-Persia, Greece, and Rome (see comments on Dan. 2:40). The horns represent kings (7:24). In fact, it is possible to count ten kings, starting with Alexander the Great and leading up to Antiochus IV Epiphanes, who is the little horn and the eleventh king. Scholars, however, disagree as to which names to include in the list of ten.

Another horn, a little one, came up among them (7:8). Since the little horn in chapter 8 clearly depicts Antiochus IV, and since the little horns in both chapters are similar, it is best to interpret this little horn also as Antiochus IV, the tyrant who persecuted the Jews severely in the second century BC. Antiochus IV (215–164 BC) ruled over the Seleucid Empire (which controlled Palestine) from 175 to 164 BC. That he called himself "Epiphanes," which means "God manifest," is evidence that he had "a mouth that was speaking arrogantly" (7:8). However, since the kingdom of God did not come in the Hellenistic period, some say that this little horn refers to the antichrist, who comes at the end of time. Others propose a "near view" (Antiochus) and a "far view" (the antichrist) understanding.

Three of the first horns were uprooted before it (7:8). When Antiochus IV seized the throne, three other rivals were pushed aside. Antiochus, son of Seleucus IV, probably was killed by Antiochus IV; Seleucus IV was killed by Heliodorus; and Demetrius, son of Seleucus IV, was held hostage in Rome.[13]

The Ancient of Days took his seat. His clothing was white like snow, and the hair of his head like whitest wool (7:9). Just as the motif of beasts coming out of the sea frequently is found in ancient Near Eastern myths (see comments on Dan. 7:3), so too this representation of God is not unique. This depiction of God, for example, has parallels in Canaanite mythological texts from the ancient city of Ugarit. In those texts the high god El is called "father of years," which is similar to "Ancient of Days" here in Daniel. Also, El is depicted as a wise, old god with hoary head, comparable to God's white hair in this biblical vision.

And the books were opened (7:10). These books (more likely scrolls) contain the good and bad deeds of humans; they will be used for judgment when people stand before God (7:10; cf. Rev. 20:12). There are a number of other similar scrolls or books mentioned in the Bible. Malachi mentions one that contains a list of faithful Jews who speak with one another about the Lord and obey his commands (Mal. 3:16–17). Then there is the book of life (Ps. 69:28) (see comments on Dan. 12:1). In another book heaven takes account of human misery and tears (Ps. 56:8). Finally, there are books of destinies: God preordains certain events in people's lives, writing them down before they happen (Ps. 139:16).

One like a son of man was coming with the clouds of heaven (7:13). The phrase "son of man" later becomes a title: "Son of Man." Here, however, "son of man" is a term for "human being" or "mortal," similar to how it is used frequently in Ezekiel (e.g., Ezek. 3:17) and even once later in Dan. 8:17, where it refers to Daniel himself. The fact that this individual comes with the clouds shows that this being is a heavenly one, but reference to "a son of man" underscores that this one looks like a human being. To this heavenly one is given the fifth kingdom, the kingdom of God. He thus stands in dramatic contrast to the earthly, beastly kingdoms from below, from the chaos waters, because he represents a more human kingdom, from above, from heaven. Heavenly beings often are characterized as human in appearance. The angel in 8:15 "looks like a man"; Gabriel is referred to as a "man" (9:21); even God looks human in Ezekiel's vision (Ezek. 1:26).

Concerning the "coming with the clouds," similar imagery was used in Canaanite mythology in regard to Baal, the Canaanite storm god, who rode on his chariot of clouds, bringing rain to the crops. In a Canaanite myth from the city of Ugarit, Baal appears before El after defeating Yam, the god of the sea, in order to have a palace built for him so that Baal could be proclaimed king (see the article "The Canaanites and Canaanite Religion"). In Daniel this heavenly cloud rider is also given dominion over the powers of the sea. However, there is one very significant difference: the Canaanites were polytheists while the Israelites were monotheists. Therefore, when the book of Daniel was written this figure probably was understood by the Jews to be an angel, most likely Michael, because Michael plays an important role in the deliverance of the Jews a few chapters later in 12:1. However, since Christians have a trinitarian understanding of God, they understand this divine being to be the Christ or Messiah, especially because Jesus referred to himself specifically as the "Son of Man" (Matt. 8:20; 9:6; 11:19) and taught that he would fulfill this particular prophecy during his second coming (Matt. 19:28; 24:27, 30; 26:64). Elsewhere in the OT the imagery of the chariot of clouds is appropriated for God himself (Ps. 68:4; 104:3).

The holy ones of the Most High (7:18). The phrase "the holy ones" refers not to people, but to heavenly beings, as can be seen from other biblical passages. For instance, Deut. 33:2 is clearly referring to God's heavenly entourage when it states, "The LORD came from Sinai . . . with ten thousand holy ones." That God, the divine king, has a council similar to earthly kings is affirmed numerous times in the OT (e.g., Job 15:15; Ps. 89:5–7). More importantly, this concept is evident elsewhere in Daniel. Daniel 4:13 refers to "a watcher, a holy one, coming down from heaven," and 4:17 proclaims, "This word is by decree of the watchers, and the decision is by command from the holy ones" (see also 7:27). The use of "holy ones" for heavenly beings is also well attested in ancient Near Eastern texts.[14]

He will . . . oppress the holy ones . . . change religious festivals . . . for a time, times, and half a time (7:25). This refers to the persecution of the Jews by the Seleucid king Antiochus IV, which took place from 167 to 164 BC. Starting in 167 BC Antiochus slaughtered thousands of inhabitants in Jerusalem and enslaved thousands of others. He outlawed all Jewish religious festivals and practices, desecrated the Temple Mount, and rededicated the temple in Jerusalem to the Greek god Zeus (see the article "Intertestamental History"). If "a time" equals a year, "times" equals two years, and "half a time" equals half a year, the total is three and a half years, which is close to the period of Antiochus's oppression.

Daniel's Vision concerning Persia and Greece (8:1–27)

A ram . . . he had two horns (8:3). In 8:20 the angel Gabriel explains to Daniel that the two horns are Media and Persia. The second horn is longer (8:3) because Persia came after Media and was more powerful.

The goat had a conspicuous horn (8:5). This is a reference to Alexander the Great (explained clearly in 8:21), who in 334–323 BC conquered the Persians and many other nations and peoples as far as the Indus River Valley (see the article "Intertestamental History").

When he became powerful, the large horn was broken (8:8a). After vanquishing most of the known world and surviving numerous battles, Alexander died of a fever in Babylon at the age of thirty-two (323 BC).

Four conspicuous horns came up in its place (8:8b). When Alexander died he left no male heir, so his kingdom was fought over by his generals. Eventually, four kingdoms were formed by four of the generals, known as the Diadochi or "successors." These were the Ptolemaic kingdom (Egypt), the Seleucid kingdom (Mesopotamia and central Asia),

Alexander the Great.

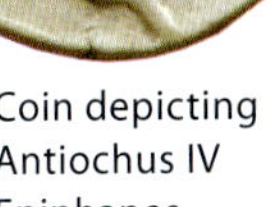
Coin depicting Antiochus IV Epiphanes.

the Attalid kingdom (Anatolia [modern Turkey]), and the Antigonid kingdom (Macedonia).

A little horn emerged (8:9). One of the generals who established a significant kingdom following the breakup of Alexander the Great's empire was Seleucus. The infamous Antiochus IV was one of his descendants and part of this dynasty. The "little horn" in 8:9 refers to Antiochus (cf. 7:8, 21).

Grew extensively . . . toward the beautiful land (8:9). This verse and the ones that follow describe how Antiochus IV outlawed Judaism, stopped the sacrifices in the Jerusalem temple, and committed the desolating sacrilege by offering an illicit offering to Zeus Olympios on the Lord's altar in the temple (see comments on Dan. 7:25; 11:31).

For 2,300 evenings and mornings (8:14). The period of oppression is often taken to mean 2,300 morning and evening sacrifices, or half that in days, which is 1,150 days, or a little more than three years.

Gabriel (8:16). This is the first time an angel is named in the Bible. Gabriel (Dan. 8:16; 9:21; Luke 1:19, 26) and Michael (Dan. 10:13, 21; 12:1; Jude 9; Rev. 12:7) are the only angels named in the Bible, although several angels are named in extrabiblical ancient Jewish books like Tobit (Raphael) and 2 Esdras (Uriel).

Daniel's Prayer and a Divine Word concerning the Seventy Weeks (9:1–27)

Until an Anointed One, the ruler, will be seven weeks (9:25). This "Anointed One" probably refers to Zerubbabel, who rebuilt the temple in 515 BC. Although he was not crowned king, he was a descendant of David who as governor gave leadership to the Jews who had returned from exile.

The Anointed One will be cut off (9:26). This was fulfilled in 171 BC when Menelaus, the high priest appointed by the wicked king Antiochus IV, had the legitimate high priest, Onias III, murdered.

And the abomination of desolation (9:27). See comments on Dan. 7:25; 8:9.

The Final Revelation: Prologue (10:1–11:2a)

Michael (10:13). See comments on Dan. 8:16.

The book of truth (10:21). The "book of truth" contains information about the predetermined future of God's people (10:14, 21; 11:1–45). This motif is found outside the Bible as well. *First Enoch*, an ancient nonbiblical Jewish text, refers to tablets on which are inscribed future destinies

(*1 Enoch* 106:19–107:1; see also 81:1–2; 93:2–3; 103:2–3). The notion of predestination is also found among the Dead Sea Scrolls at Qumran in a manuscript labeled by scholars as 4Q180 and titled "The Ages of the World." The belief that the gods fix the fates and record them ahead of time was likewise widespread in the ancient Near East. On other divine books, see comments on Dan. 7:10.

The Final Revelation: Body (11:2b–12:4)

Then a warrior king will arise (11:3). This refers to Alexander the Great (356–323 BC) (see comments on Dan. 8:5; see the article "Intertestamental History"). Almost all of the many people and events mentioned in 11:2–39 can be corroborated from ancient texts.[15]

The Greek god Zeus.

Ships of Kittim will come against him . . . then he will rage against the holy covenant (11:30). In the Dead Sea Scrolls "Kittim" is used to designate the Romans, and that appears to be the meaning here. When the Seleucid king Antiochus IV (ruled 175–164 BC) made a second attempt to take Egypt (168 BC), the Romans intervened. They sent the legate Gaius Popilius Laenas to stop the Seleucid king's advance. Humiliated on the battlefield, Antiochus IV took out his wrath on the Jews by outlawing their religion (see comments on Dan. 7:25; 8:9).

His forces . . . will abolish the regular sacrifice and set up the abomination of desolation (11:31). Antiochus IV Epiphanes stopped the sacrifices to God in the Jerusalem temple and then offered unclean animals to the Greek god Zeus Olympios, an event referred to several times in Daniel (8:13; 9:27; 12:11) as well as in the Jewish history books of 1 Maccabees (1:45–48, 59) and 2 Maccabees (6:2–5), as well as in the NT (Matt. 24:15; Mark 13:14).

He will exalt and magnify himself above every god (11:36). Antiochus IV called himself "Epiphanes," which means "(god) manifest." On coins he sometimes included the inscription "Of King Antiochus, God Manifest, Victory-Bearer." The last epithet, "Victory-Bearer," was also used of the Greek gods Zeus and Apollo.[16]

All your people who are found written in the book (12:1). See comments on Dan. 7:10; 10:21. Most likely the author is thinking of the book of life, a list of those who would survive (cf. Exod. 32:32; Ps. 69:28; Isa. 4:3). The NT continues the tradition of a book of life (Phil. 4:3; Rev. 3:5; 13:8; 17:8; 20:12, 15).

The Final Revelation: Epilogue (12:5–13)

A time, times, and half a time (12:7). See comments on Dan. 7:25.

Hosea

J. Andrew Dearman

Introduction. Hosea's ministry took place in the second half of the eighth century BC. He lived in the northern kingdom of Israel. The historical context of Hosea's ministry is summarized in 2 Kings 14:23–17:6. It was a time of international political intrigue and instability. The Assyrian king Tiglath-pileser III took over significant portions of Israel during the years 734–732 BC (see comments on 2 Kings 15:27–31; see the article "The Assyrians"). Some ten years later the Israelite capital of Samaria fell to the Assyrians, and the land of Israel was divided into several Assyrian provinces. Thousands of Israelites were taken into exile. Judah, however, managed to survive, but now as a vassal of Assyria. Hosea understood these terrible circumstances as divine judgment upon Israel for its failure to keep the covenant with the Lord, the God of Israel. At the same time, however, he indicated that there would still be a future for Israel beyond the historical failure that occurred during his day.

The book of Hosea is largely poetic in expression, making extensive use of metaphors as well as symbolism (especially regarding his marriage and children). Chapters 1–3 depict the failures of his wife, Gomer, and the symbolic names of his children as analogies of Israel's failures and future. Chapters 4–14 contain oracles directed to Israel and Judah concerning the broken covenant and the coming judgment. Egypt sought a role in influencing affairs in the region and is mentioned several times by the prophet in this section. The very last verse of the book is proverbial in expression and reminds readers that the contents of the book illustrate the way that the Lord works in the world.

The Superscription (1:1)

Reigns of Uzziah, Jotham, Ahaz, and Hezekiah, kings of Judah . . . and of Jeroboam . . . king of Israel (1:1). Four kings of the southern kingdom are listed first, and they are in chronological order, spanning almost one hundred years (783 to 687 BC). Only one king from the northern kingdom, Jeroboam II, is mentioned out of seven who reigned during this period, something rather awkward for a book addressed to the northern kingdom. If Hosea began his ministry toward the end of Jeroboam II's reign (about 750 BC) and continued until the beginning of Hezekiah's reign (about 728/727 BC), then his ministry would have overlapped with all five kings mentioned in 1:1.

Failure Personified (1:2)

Marry a woman of promiscuity . . . for the land is committing . . . promiscuity (1:2). In the ancient Near East people often were identified by the land, region, or city of their residence. Likewise, both the land and the city could be personified in representing the people. The term translated as "promiscuity" can refer to improper sexual behavior such as adultery, or, more frequently, to prostitution. Adultery in Israel referred to sexual relations between a married woman and a man who was not her husband. Both parties incurred guilt, and the recognized penalty was death (Lev. 20:10; Deut. 22:22). Adultery, promiscuity, and prostitution (Hosea 5:4), however, were also cultural metaphors for breaking sacred relationships such as a covenant.

Marriage and Children (1:3–9)

Jezreel (1:4–5). In Israelite culture names often represented a person's identity or a significant characteristic of that person. Jezreel was a fertile valley in Israel and earlier had also been the name of one of the residences of King Ahab and Jezebel (1 Kings 21:1). A bloody slaughter had taken place in this valley and city at the time of Jezebel's death (2 Kings 9–10). The name means "God sows."

Future Change of Circumstances (1:10–2:1)

The sand of the sea (1:10). This was a proverbial phrase used to express an unlimited quantity (cf. Gen. 22:17; 41:49).

They will be called: Sons of the living God (1:10). Reversing a name or changing a name was a cultural way of portraying new circumstances in a person's life.

Gomer as Israel Judged (2:2–13)

She is not my wife (2:2). This phrase functions like a legal divorce decree. As with the language of adultery, poetic references to lovers (2:5, 7, 10, 13; cf. 8:9) indicate illicit connections to others that break apart established relationships.

Baal . . . Baals (2:8, 13). *Baal* is both a Canaanite word and a Hebrew word meaning "owner," "master," or "husband," and it could be used to describe either a deity or a human. It is the name of one of the most popular gods in the Canaanite pantheon (see the article "The Canaanites and Canaanite Religion").

Future Restoration of Israel (2:14–23)

You will call me, "My husband," and no longer call me, "My Baal" (2:16). See comments on Hosea 2:8. This is a poetic wordplay in which "husband" (*ish*) is contrasted with "master/Baal" (*baal*) to emphasize the change in relationship between the Lord and Israel (cf. NIV: "you will call me 'my husband'; you will no longer call me 'my master'").

I will take you to be my wife (2:19–20). A betrothal was a contractual commitment to marry. Gifts to a bride and her family were parts of the marriage arrangement. The gifts given here represent the positive characteristics of a covenant between the Lord and his people. The cultural convention of name changes (cf. 1:10–2:1) for two of the children also indicates a positive change of status for Israel.

Bought with a Price (3:1–5)

Raisin cakes (3:1). These were offerings often made to one or more Canaanite deities (cf. Jer. 44:19).

So I bought her for fifteen shekels of silver and five bushels of barley (3:2). This quantity of silver and barley may be the price of a slave (cf. Exod. 21:32) or a debt that Gomer had incurred that bound her to a creditor. In the ancient Near East the two most common ways to become enslaved were through defaulted debts or capture in warfare.

Ephod (3:4). This was a garment or vest worn by a priest and containing special marked stones that the priest could use to discern direction from God (see comments on Exod. 28:2). It could also be used as a garment to adorn an idol (see comments on Judg. 8:27).

Household idols (3:4). The Hebrew word used here refers to small crafted images or statues kept in family homes rather than in temples.

Charging Israel with Failure (4:1–3)

The Lord has a case (4:1). In Hebrew the term translated as "case" refers to a formal charge, quite similar to a lawsuit declaration in modern society.

All of Israel Has Failed (4:4–19)

They feed on the sin of my people (4:8). This is a charge against corrupt priests. The charge assumes a common feature of the priestly privilege in the ancient Near East, that priests were entitled to eat some of the meat from animals brought as sacrifices by worshipers to a temple. Thus the priests were eating from the "sin offering" of the people, ironically eating better as the people sinned more (cf. 1 Sam. 2:12–17).

Their wooden idols . . . a spirit of promiscuity (4:12). These two references show the connection that the prophet draws between forms of forbidden worship and deception in ancient Israel. Hosea's descriptions of religious practices reflect various kinds of pagan worship activities that were popular in ancient Canaan and even in parts of Israel, even though the covenant statutes of the Torah forbade them (see the article "The Canaanites and Canaanite Religion"). This was a classic dynamic in the ancient Near East. Law codes and official priestly rituals had regulatory roles, but popular practices were very diverse and could depend on magic and superstition.

Cult prostitutes (4:14). This is a term that literally indicates women who are set apart for a sacred task. There is no consensus on how best to interpret the phrase. One possibility is that men would copulate with designated women as part of a fertility ritual in hopes for increased numbers of children, flocks, and crops. The connection between fertility and religious practices in the ancient Near East was especially strong and widespread. However, some scholars think that perhaps there were prostitutes associated with certain temples who participated in temple festivities and may also have provided part of their fees for temple support.

Problems in Israel and Judah (5:1–15)

Ephraim (5:3). The term "Ephraim," mentioned several times in chapter 5, refers to a large central tribe of the Israelite kingdom that worked closely with Manasseh, its northern tribal neighbor. Ephraim was a driving force behind the administration in the capital city of Samaria, and as such, during the eighth century BC, the term "Ephraim" was used interchangeably as a synonym for the northern kingdom of Israel.

Even Judah will stumble (5:5). Judah was the southern tribal state with Jerusalem as its capital. For much of Hosea's ministry Judah was at war with Israel, a conflict commonly referred to as the Syro-Ephraimite War (see comments on 2 Kings 15:37; see the introduction to the commentary on Isaiah).

Illegitimate children (5:7). In the ancient Near East illegitimate children were those who had no formal claim on their father's identity or a family inheritance.

Boundary markers (5:10). These boundary markers were made of stone and were used throughout the ancient Near East to delineate the boundaries of one's property, which normally was also one's inheritance received from one's ancestors. Removing or relocating these property boundary markers was considered a very serious offense, both in Israel (Deut. 19:14; Prov. 22:28) and throughout the ancient Near East.

The great king (5:13). This was a title assumed by the ruler of the Assyrian Empire, whose heartland was in northern Mesopotamia. The language of struggle and intrigue in chapter 5 may have as its background the conflict between Israel and Judah known as the Syro-Ephraimite War (2 Kings 15:29–16:20; Isa. 7:1–9), which resulted in the intervention of the Assyrian king Tiglath-pileser III, who subjugated large portions of Israel and made Ahaz, king of Judah, his vassal (see the section on the Neo-Assyrian period in the article "The Assyrians"; see the introduction to the commentary on Isaiah).

I am like a lion (5:14). God's judgment on Ephraim and Judah is compared to a lion tearing its prey to pieces. In the ancient Near East lions not only were feared but also were used as symbols of power. The Assyrian kings, in particular, depicted themselves as hunters of lions in their public art, thereby showing that they were more fierce and powerful than their opponents. Possibly Hosea's claim about the Lord acting like a lion (see also 13:7) assumes that God would use the Assyrians as an agent of judgment.

The Assyrian king Tiglath-pileser III.

Problems in Israel and Judah Continue (6:1–11)

Like the rain, like the spring showers (6:3). The seasonal rains were vital to agriculture in ancient Israel. Summers in this region are warm and dry, although there can be morning mist or dew (6:4;

cf. 13:3; 14:5). The success of the entire agricultural year, however, depends first on the winter rains that can begin in October or November, after which things like wheat and barley are planted, and then on the early spring rains, which bring the crops to maturity for harvest in April and May. In Canaanite mythology the god Baal controlled the rain, so this verse also counteracts that pagan understanding.

Gilead (6:8). This refers to the forested, hilly region east of the Jordan River. It was part of the inheritance of the tribes of Gad and Manasseh (Josh. 13:24–31; Judg. 10:6–12:2), although the region also had Aramean and Ammonite inhabitants. Ramoth-gilead (1 Chron. 6:80) and Jabesh-gilead (1 Sam. 11:1, 9) were well-known cities in the region.

Intrigue and Its Consequences (7:1–7)

Samaria (7:1). This was the capital city of Israel during most of the divided monarchy. It was built by Omri (1 Kings 16:23–24) to be the capital of the confederated northern tribes, which kept the covenant name of Israel when they separated from Jerusalem and the rule of the Davidic monarchs.

Like an oven (7:4–7). Ovens typically were made of baked clay, sometimes lined with stones to mediate heat for various cooking tasks. They usually were located in the courtyard of one's house (see the section on provisioning life in the article "Daily Life in Ancient Israel"). Fueled by wood, animal dung, or other combustible materials, well-built ovens were able to generate considerable heat.

In Danger among the Nations (7:8–16)

Unturned bread baked on a griddle (7:8). This is a reference to bread baked on hot rocks or a primitive griddle. Like a modern pancake, this bread, unless it was was turned over at the appropriate time, would be (over)cooked on one side and raw on the other.

Like a silly, senseless dove (7:11). Doves were trapped and eaten in ancient Israel. Once doves spotted appealing food such as seeds or berries, they tended to come after the food, even if danger lurked nearby. That is, in spite of a visible snare (perhaps triggered by a rope pull) in plain sight or the nearby presence of a person with a net, the birds' desire for food made them vulnerable to capture.

Like a faulty bow (7:16). Bows and arrows were used by both soldiers and hunters in ancient Israel and throughout the ancient Near East. The most powerful bows were composite bows, constructed of wood strips (sometimes from different kinds of trees), animal tendons, animal horns, and glue.[1] If not expertly made, they were subject to breaking. A faulty bow was dangerous because it could snap and injure its user. Likewise, if one's bow broke during a battle, the consequences were serious.

Trouble over God's House (8:1–6)

Like an eagle (8:1). The Hebrew word used here is the general term for any large bird of prey, including eagles or even vultures. These birds hover high overhead looking for prey or carrion.

Your calf-idol (8:5–6). Immediately after the death of Solomon a civil war split the country into two: Israel in the north and Judah in the south. In the northern kingdom of Israel, King Jeroboam had two golden calves constructed: one in the northern part of the country (Dan) and another in the south at Bethel, near the border with Judah (1 Kings 12:28–33) (see comments on 1 Kings 12:29). Note similar references in Hosea in 10:5; 13:2. Bovine symbolism (bull, heifer, calf) was used to represent several different deities in the ancient world. The text in 1 Kings 12:28–33, as here, has ironic allusions back to Israel's disastrous experience with the golden calf during the exodus (Exod. 32).

Acts and Consequences (8:7–14)

Like a wild donkey (8:9). The Hebrew word used here probably refers to an undomesticated donkey or to an onager, an equid and what is sometimes called a "wild ass." Onagers roamed over parts of western Asia, and yet they could not be domesticated (like most zebras).

No Rejoicing (9:1–4)

They will eat unclean food in Assyria . . . like the bread of mourners (9:3–4). Coming into contact with a corpse rendered one ceremonially unclean (Num. 19:11–15; Deut. 26:14). Thus the bread of mourners at a funeral would also be considered ceremonially unclean, similar to food eaten in a foreign, unclean land like Assyria.

Statue of the sacred bull Apis, which ancient Egyptians viewed as the physical manifestation of the god Ptah.

Ripe figs.

No Fruit, No Spiritual Health (9:5–17)

Watchman (9:8). See comments on Ezek. 33:2.

The first fruit of the fig tree in its first season (9:10). Figs were an important source of nourishment in ancient Israel, also highly desired because of their sweet taste. Fig trees typically produce their fruit several times per year, usually in June, August, and November.[2]

Baal-peor (9:10). This is the place in Moab where Israel had been unfaithful to the covenant with the Lord during the exodus wandering (Num. 25).

Failed Worship (10:1–8)

Altars . . . sacred pillars (10:1–2). Not all shrines in Canaan had enclosed temple buildings, but virtually all had open-air altars and sacred stones (pillars). In the book of Deuteronomy the Israelites were instructed to destroy all of these Canaanite altars and sacred stones (7:5; 12:3), but these elements remained in the land and continued to influence Israelite worship practices. Altars for animal sacrifice were built of stones or earth (cf. Exod. 20:22–26). Sacred stones often were set upright like pillars and occasionally contained carvings or etchings. They functioned to represent the presence of deities.

Beth-aven (10:5; also 4:15; 5:8). "Beth-aven" means "house of wickedness" and is an ironic play on the name of Bethel (cf. 10:15), a major sanctuary in Israel founded centuries earlier by Jacob, which means "house of God" (Gen. 28:10–22).

Great Wickedness and Great Consequences (10:9–15)

Shalman's destruction of Beth-arbel (10:14). These two names may refer to a slaughter perpetrated by the Assyrian ruler Shalmaneser III, who campaigned in the region of Israel and Gilead about a century before Hosea and whose battles were well known in the ancient Near East (see the article "The Assyrians"). Beth-arbel likely is a city on the east side of the Jordan in Gilead.

The Pain of Loving a Rebel (11:1–11)

My son (11:1). This is yet another reference to Israel as a part of God's family (cf. Exod. 4:22), and the language of God's difficulty with Israel in this chapter is cast, at least in part, as the painful experience of a father with a recalcitrant son.

Admah . . . Zeboiim (11:8). These were cities near Sodom and Gomorrah and part of the judgment on settlements in the region (Gen. 18:16–19:29; cf. Deut. 29:23). Apparently, Hosea associated this story first with these two cities.

Ephraim (Israel) Is Deceitful (11:12–12:1)

Olive oil (12:1). Olive oil was a valued commodity throughout the ancient Near East. Although olives were not grown in Egypt or Mesopotamia, they were grown in abundance in Israel, and the production of olive oil was a significant industry. Thus olive oil was a very important export commodity for Israel. Both Egypt (the main power to the south) and Assyria (the main power to the north) sought to control the land of Israel during Hosea's day. The rulers in Samaria looked for ways to preserve themselves by agreements with these two powers. It was a delicate balancing act that ultimately failed.

Jacob's Problems Continue (12:2–14)

Jacob (12:2, 12). "Jacob" is another name for Israel (cf. Gen. 32:28). Several allusions to the story of Jacob in Genesis occur in 12:3–4.

Merchant (12:7). The Hebrew word translated as "merchant" can also be translated as "Canaanite." Ephraim/Jacob is portrayed as a trader using false balances—that is, scales with improper weights—so that the customer is cheated.

This small bronze lion was an official Assyrian weight (one mina) to be used in commercial transactions.

Guilt and Death (13:1–16)

Kiss the calves (13:2). People in the ancient world showed their religious affection for various deities with kisses for the physical representation of a deity, even as they offered all manner of precious objects in sacrifice, including, on occasion, human beings.

A lion . . . a leopard . . . a bear (13:7–8). As part of the land bridge between Africa and Asia, the land of Israel had lions, leopards, and bears. A she-bear was proverbial for her ferocity in protecting her cubs (Prov. 17:12). Note the similar list of fierce animals in the vision in Dan. 7 (lion, bear, leopard) (see comments on Dan. 7:4).

The power of Sheol (13:14). The Hebrew word *Sheol* is used broadly to refer to the underworld, the place of the departed.

Israel Will Flourish Again (14:1–9)

The cedars of Lebanon (14:5). The cedars of Lebanon were recognized throughout the ancient Near East as the best trees for lumber to use in the construction of beautiful buildings. The temple in Jerusalem had such beams (1 Kings 5:1–12).

Lebanon (14:5–7). The mountains of Lebanon were near the coast of the Mediterranean Sea and thus caught a good amount of rain, producing a rich variety of plants and foods in the valleys.

A flourishing pine tree (14:8). This tree grew in the hills of northern Israel and Lebanon and was a symbol for long life.

Joel

Mark W. Chavalas

Introduction. Although the text makes it clear that Joel, son of Pethuel, penned this prophetic writing, Joel is not mentioned anywhere else in Scripture. Moreover, unlike other some of the other Minor Prophets, the book of Joel does not mention any ruling kings, nor is there explicit reference to any specific historical event. Though Joel has a number of clearly definable themes concerning the "latter days" (e.g., a call to repentance and restoration of Israel), they are not detailed enough to provide a firm historical context to this book. Because of this, there is no agreement on the date of the composition; scholars have argued for various dates, spanning from the ninth to third centuries BC, without arriving at a consensus.

The Locust Plagues: Judgment and Call to Repentance (1:1–2:17)

Hear this, you elders (1:2). Joel begins with a call to elders, and not to a king. If there was no king, then the context would place this book after the Babylonian conquest and subsequent exile (586 BC). However, it is possible to read too much into this brief introduction. The mere fact that Joel does not mention a monarch does not necessarily prove a postexilic date for the book.

Locust (1:4). The description of a locust plague dominates the first two chapters of the book. Scholars, however, are divided as to how to interpret the reference to this event. Is this locust plague a literal or figurative event?

Wall painting from an Egyptian tomb (1292 BC) depicting a locust.

If figurative, was Joel describing a particular invasion of Judah? Two are well known from this period: the Assyrian attack by Sennacherib on Judah in 701 BC, and the Babylonian invasion of the region by Nebuchadnezzar II in 598 BC. However, since locust plagues were common in the ancient Near East, many argue that the locust invasion is to be taken literally. Mesopotamian sources occasionally describe plagues of locusts. Portions survive of a remarkable hymn written in Akkadian to the goddess Nanaya during the reign of the Assyrian king Sargon II in which the monarch petitions the divinity to halt a locust plague:

> The evil locust which destroys the crop/grain,
> the wicked dwarf-locust which dries up the orchards,
> which cuts off the regular offerings of the gods and goddesses.[1]

There are at least three letters in the Assyrian royal correspondence during King Sargon's reign that mention a locust plague. Moreover, a damaged relief from Sargon II's reign presents an individual standing before an unnamed deity (perhaps Shamash or Ashur) with a locust above the worshiper's head. It is presumed that the person is pleading for the end of a locust plague. Numerous Mesopotamian incantations were employed to stop plagues by locusts or other pests.[2]

In addition, invading armies described figuratively as locusts are mentioned in Nah. 3:17 as well as in ancient Near Eastern literature from the region. For example, the Ugaritic Kirta Epic (from the Syrian coast, ca. 1400–1200 BC) depicts Kirta's army as numerous as locusts. The royal annals of Sargon II occasionally describe enemy armies as locusts as well. Interestingly, Sargon's son and successor, Sennacherib, made this comparison about the allies of Marduk-apal-iddina (biblical Merodach-baladan, the Chaldean king of Babylon): "Like the onset of locust swarms in the springtime, they kept steadily coming on against me to offer battle."[3]

Dress in sackcloth . . . announce a sacred fast (1:13–14). Perhaps in response to the locust plague, the writer of Joel anticipates that the Judahites will put on sackcloth and ironically call for a fast (ironic because the locusts have eaten all the food!). The use of sackcloth (or the ripping of clothing) was a common custom in the ancient Near East as a sign of national (or private) mourning. A Phoenician sarcophagus from Byblos (ca. 900 BC) shows mourning women with ripped clothing and unkempt hair. Worshipers put on sackcloth after the death of the god Baal in one of the Ugaritic poems of Baal and Anath.[4] Fasting and weeping were less common; after a frightening night vision, Balaam fasted and wept, according to the collection of narratives from eighth-century-BC Deir Alla.

My holy mountain (2:1). The concept of God's holy mountain was not exclusive to Israel. Mount Saphon (modern Mount Aqraa near the Orontes River in Syria) was the home of Baal in the Ugaritic Baal narratives.

The day of the Lord is coming (2:1). The concept of a "day" for a particular deity was also known in Babylon, as Marduk, its primary deity, was celebrated during the annual Akitu enthronement festival. Like the Lord, the Babylonian deity renewed his relationship with his worshipers and reaffirmed his control over the universe, although there is no evidence that the day of the Lord was celebrated on any certain day.

God's Response (2:18–3:21)

I will pour out my Spirit (2:28). In the ancient Near East the concept of God's Spirit "poured out" on individuals signified a kind of seal of approval on that person, similar to the Akkadian concept of *melammu*, a term associated with the inner essence of the deity. The Neo-Assyrian kings claimed in their annals to have this divine source.

The sun will be turned to darkness and the moon to blood (2:31). See comments on Joel 3:15. This probably is a reference to solar and lunar eclipses, which in Mesopotamian sources usually were considered to be evil omens.[5] A number of rituals were to be performed to counteract the effects.

Tyre, Sidon (3:4). See comments on Ezek. 26:2; 28:21. Tyre and Sidon were two powerful Phoenician cities on the coast north of Israel. The people of Tyre and Sidon were leading Phoenician trading peoples, with powerful maritime fleets controlling the sea trade routes in the Mediterranean Sea.

All the territories of Philistia (3:4). See the article "The Philistines."

The Greeks (3:6). These were often referred to as the Ionians (biblical "Javan," probably denoting Greek-speaking peoples from the Aegean region), who are mentioned in Assyrian sources during the reign of the Assyrian king Sargon II (ca. 721–705 BC). They are also listed as traders in Ezek. 27:13.

The Sabeans (3:8). Saba was a kingdom on the southern Arabian Peninsula (present-day Yemen).

The sun and the moon will grow dark (3:15). See comments on Joel 2:31. One of the West Semitic plaster inscriptions from a West Jordanian site presents Balaam as describing a vision of the heavens as "dense cloud, that darkness exists there, not brilliance," similar to the way that 3:15 describes the darkening of the sun and moon.[6]

Amos

M. Daniel Carroll R.

Introduction. Amos was from Tekoa, a town in the southern kingdom of Judah, but he was called to prophesy for a short time against the northern kingdom of Israel in the first half of the eighth century BC. He is described as a man of means, which may be the reason why the high priest at Bethel was fearful of this foreigner's possible impact and demanded that he return to his home country of Judah (7:10–13).

From the opening lines of this book, it is clear that the Lord is not being worshiped by the northern kingdom of Israel. He roars from Zion (the location of Judah's temple) in Jerusalem (Judah's capital). In other words, Israel's national ideology of prosperity and victory, along with the corrupt leaders and political, economic, and religious structures that sustained it, were illegitimate. God resided in the south and spoke through this southern prophet; he will judge Israel's exploitation of the poor, unacceptable religious rituals, and military complacency with an invasion and by sending many into exile (2:14–16; 3:9–4:3; 5:27; 6:7–14).

The book closes with a brief message of hope (9:11–15). After the imminent devastation Israel would be restored to the land, but under a Davidic king.

The Superscription (1:1–2)

One of the sheep breeders (1:1). Not the usual word for "shepherd" (cf. 3:12), the Hebrew term used here appears elsewhere only at 2 Kings 3:4 in relationship to the king of Moab and his huge flocks. Scholars debate its

A sycamore tree.

meaning. In 7:14 Amos calls himself a "herdsman" (NIV: "shepherd") and identifies himself as one who cares for sycamore trees. Since these did not grow in the region of Tekoa, Amos perhaps owned several properties. He was not some poor shepherd when called to prophesy in Israel.

Tekoa (1:1). Today identified with Khirbet Tequ'a, this town in Judah was located about six miles southeast of Bethlehem and ten miles south of Jerusalem. To the east the land slopes down toward the Dead Sea and an area known as the Desert of Tekoa (2 Chron. 20:20).

Uzziah . . . Jeroboam (1:1). Uzziah, also called Azariah (2 Kings 15:1–7), and Jeroboam II (2 Kings 14:23–29) were successful kings during the first half of the eighth century BC (792–740 and 793–753, respectively), although both are criticized in the biblical accounts (see comments on 2 Kings 14:23).

The earthquake (1:1). Earthquake imagery permeates the book (3:14–15; 4:11, 13; 6:11; 8:8; 9:1, 5, 9). Excavations at the ancient cities of Hazor, Gezer, and other sites indicate that this seismic event occurred in about 760 BC. A fault line extends from the Rift Valley in Africa through Israel to Asia Minor. That this earthquake is mentioned centuries later by the prophet Zechariah underscores its impact (Zech. 14:5).

The Lord roars (1:2). A lion roars when it is hungry, not when it is stalking or has just caught its prey (cf. 3:4). This jarring image portends an imminent judgment (cf. 3:12).

Zion . . . Jerusalem (1:2). The Lord speaks from the temple and capital of the southern kingdom of Judah, thereby invalidating the northern kingdom of Israel's state and popular religion, as well as its sociopolitical and economic system.

The pastures . . . mourn (1:2). Some translations render this Hebrew verb as "dry up" (e.g., NIV), but this verb can also be translated as "mourn." It reoccurs in 5:16; 8:8, 10; 9:5. It alerts the reader that death is coming.

The summit of Carmel (1:2). This is the high point of a mountain range situated close to the Mediterranean (cf. 9:3), south of the modern port of Haifa, that separates the Jezreel Valley from the Sharon Plain. It enjoys significant rainfall and mild temperatures in the summer and was a fertile area for forests and grasslands.

The Oracles against the Nations (1:3–2:16)

Damascus (1:3–5). This was the capital city of Aram (Syria), Israel's primary enemy in the ninth century BC.

They threshed . . . with iron sledges (1:3). Threshing separates the wheat from the chaff (see comments on Isa. 41:15). This could be a metaphor for a military attack (Isa. 41:15; Hab. 3:12; used of Aram in 2 Kings 13:7), or it could refer to physical torture, where a sledge runs over the backs of victims.

Gilead (1:3). This was a disputed region in the Transjordan (the region east of the Jordan River) bordering on Aram (cf. 1 Kings 22). See comments on Hos. 6:8.

Hazael's palace . . . Ben-hadad's citadels (1:4). These are two kings of Aram (Syria) (843–796 BC and 796–770 BC, respectively). Judgment on Aram would center on the capital and the royal dynasty.

I will break down the gates (1:5). The word translated as "gates" literally means "bar," referring to a horizontal shaft made of wood or bronze (1 Kings 4:13) placed behind the doors of a city gate to prohibit opening.

Valley of Aven (1:5). A wordplay meaning "valley of sin." It is to be identified with a region north of Damascus around Baalbek or the Beqaa Valley in Lebanon.

Beth-eden (1:5). This probably is a reference to an area associated in Assyrian annals with Bit-Adini, about two hundred miles northeast of Damascus along the banks of the Euphrates River.

Kir (1:5). This is the place of origin of the Arameans (9:7), whose location is uncertain. Perhaps it lay in the region of Elam, north of the Persian Gulf (Isa. 22:6).

Gaza . . . Ashdod . . . Ashkelon . . . Ekron (1:6–8). These are four of the five Philistine cities. The fifth, Gath, is mentioned in 6:2 (see the article "The Philistines"). This pentapolis (five-city kingdom) was located in the southwestern coastal region of Israel/Canaan, on a plain extending from the Brook of Egypt (Wadi el-Arish) northward to the Yarkon River. The eastern boundary was the Shephelah, the Judean foothills. Gaza, Ashdod, and Ashkelon were coastal cities on the Mediterranean Sea; Ekron and Gath were inland.

They exiled a whole community, handing them over to Edom (1:6). In the ancient Near East those defeated in war often were sold as slaves. The victims mentioned here might have been Israelites, and the repetition of

An ancient wooden threshing sledge.

this censure in 1:9 may indicate that the Philistines and the people of Tyre worked in tandem. On Edom, see comments on Amos 1:11; Obad. 1.

Tyre (1:9–10). See comments on Ezek. 26:2. This prosperous Phoenician port was located on an island, just offshore about thirty-five miles north of Mount Carmel. The coastal kingdom of Tyre had allied with David and Solomon (2 Sam. 5:11; 1 Kings 5) but later was condemned for its trading practices (Isa. 23; Ezek. 26–28).

Edom (1:11). See comments on Ezek. 25:12; Obad. 1. Edom's territory extended from west of the Wadi Arabah eastward to the Arabian Desert. It spanned from Moab in the north to the Gulf of Aqaba in the south.

Teman . . . Bozrah (1:12). Teman and Bozrah can refer to Edom in general (Isa. 34:6; 63:1; Jer. 49:20). The city of Bozrah (modern Busayra) lay in northern Edom, about twenty-one miles southeast of the Dead Sea, and was its most important city. Some identify Teman with modern Tawilan, but others believe it to be a regional designation for the southern part of Edom (see comments on Obad. 9).

The Ammonites (1:13–15). See comments on Gen. 19:37–38. Ammon was located east of Israel, on the other side of the Dead Sea. Its boundaries were the Jabbok River in the north and the Arnon River in the south, with the Arabian Desert to the east.

Ripped open the pregnant women (1:13). This is an atrocity of ancient warfare, also mentioned in 2 Kings 8:12; 15:16; Hosea 13:16.

Rabbah (1:14). Rabbah was Ammon's most important city. The citadel is located in the modern city of Amman, Jordan.

Moab (2:1–3). See comments on Gen. 19:37–38. The plateaus of Moab lay east of the Dead Sea between Ammon and Edom. The most famous document of this region is the memorial stela of King Mesha of the mid-ninth century BC, which commemorates a victory over Israel.

He burned the bones . . . to lime (2:1). It was a serious cultural offense to desecrate a tomb. To extract the bones and burn them "to lime" (cf. Isa. 33:12), perhaps for use as whitewash, was even a greater disgrace.

Kerioth (2:2). This is a town named in the Moabite Mesha Stela that was a worship center for Chemosh, the principal deity of Moab. Its location is uncertain.

A pair of sandals (2:6). This phrase could refer to a minimal debt or to a transaction involving property (Ruth 4:7; cf. Deut. 25:9–10).

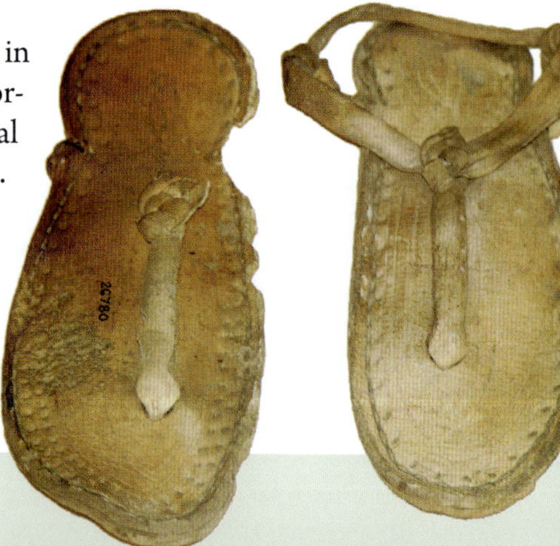

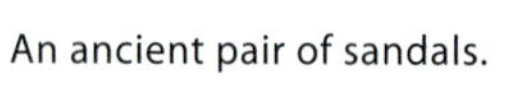

An ancient pair of sandals.

With the same girl (2:7). The language (literally, "go to the [same] girl") could suggest sexual intercourse, although this is not the usual expression for that. Some suggest that what is meant is cultic prostitution, incest (Lev. 18:6–17; 20:11–12), or the abuse of a girl living in the household as a debt slave.

Garments taken as collateral (2:8). Although this transgression may be the keeping of garments taken in pledge to secure a loan and not returning them before sunset (Exod. 22:26–27; Deut. 24:12–13), it could refer to distraint, the act of seizing something upon the default of a loan. In extreme cases this could involve children (2 Kings 4:1; Job 24:9).

The Amorite (2:9). The Amorites are first mentioned in third-millennium-BC texts from areas north and northeast of Israel. Over time they assimilated throughout Mesopotamia. In the OT the designation is used of Sihon and Og, kings in Transjordan (east of the Jordan River) at the conquest (Num. 21:21–35; Deut. 2:24–3:11), and of the inhabitants of Canaan generally (Deut. 1:7; 7:1).

Nazirites (2:11–12). Nazirites were individuals who made a vow of commitment to the Lord for a specific period (Acts 18:18; 21:23–24) or for life (Samson, Judg. 13:5–7; Samuel, 1 Sam. 1:11). Restrictions related to this pledge included prohibition of alcohol, shaving or haircutting, and contact with corpses (Num. 6:1–21).

Divine Exposure of Israel's Guilt (3:1–4:13)

Lion (3:4). See comments on Amos 1:2.

Does a bird land in a trap? (3:5). Several ancient Egyptian tombs depict scenes in which fowlers and kings hunt birds with bow and arrow, slings, and throwing sticks or catch them in nets or cages (cf. Hosea 7:12).

The mountains of Samaria (3:9). Samaria, capital of the northern kingdom of Israel, was built on a single hill (6:1; cf. 1 Kings 16:24) but was surrounded by other hills. It was strategically located at a crossroads, with Shechem to the southeast, the Jezreel Valley to the north, and the coastal plains to the west.

As a shepherd snatches (3:12). A shepherd had to produce remains as evidence of losing an animal to a predator and to dispel any suspicion of theft (Exod. 22:10–13).

Horns of the altar (3:14). The stone horns (elevated corners) of the altar were sprinkled with the blood of the sacrifice of atonement (Lev. 16:18), but they also represented a place of safety for someone seeking sanctuary (Exod. 21:12–14; 1 Kings 1:50–53; 2:28–34).

The winter house and the summer house (3:15). The wealthy, particularly royalty, might move between residences to escape uncomfortable weather,

Expensive furniture being carried away as loot by a conquering army.

whether the summer heat or the winter cold. Ahab had homes in Jezreel (probably for winter) and Samaria (a cooler region in the summer) (1 Kings 21:1, 18).

Inlaid with ivory (3:15). Excavations at Samaria uncovered ivory carvings that had been inlaid in fine furniture, an indication of an opulent lifestyle (cf. Ps. 45:8) (see comments on 1 Kings 22:39). This is mentioned also in 6:4.

Cows of Bashan (4:1). Bashan, associated today with the Golan Heights, was a fertile area east of the Jordan River, bordered by Mount Hermon in the north and the Yarmuk River in the south. It was renowned for its cattle (Deut. 32:14; Ps. 22:12; Ezek. 39:18; Mic. 7:14).

Hooks . . . fishhooks (4:2). The meaning of these terms is debated. According to this translation, the reference could be to grappling hooks used in sieges or to the Assyrian practice of piercing defeated captives through the lip, cheek, or jaw to lead them into captivity. Some commentators argue that the reference is to baskets by which fish were caught and transported.

Harmon (4:3). If this disputed term is a place name, its location is unknown. Conjectures include Mount Hermon in northern Israel or modern Hermel in northern Syria.

Bethel . . . Gilgal (4:4). Bethel has been identified with the modern Arab village of Beitin, situated about ten miles north of Jerusalem. Gilgal was on the plain west of the Jordan River near Jericho. The significance of both places went far back into Israel's history: Bethel to the patriarchal period (Gen. 12:8; 28:10–22; 35:1–15), and Gilgal to Joshua's conquest (Josh. 4–5; 10). They are mentioned again in 5:5–6.

Absolutely nothing to eat (4:6). Literally, "clean teeth," this euphemism means a lack of food, perhaps due to a famine resulting from uneven rainfall, bad crop yields, or locusts (cf. 4:7–9; 7:1–3).

This carved ivory panel with a cherubim-like creature was inlaid into a piece of furniture at a palace.

Blight and mildew . . . locust (4:9). Crop diseases and locusts appear in the curse list in Deut. 28:22, 39–42. "Blight" and "mildew" could refer to maladies that attack barley and wheat. Before the advent of pesticides a locust plague could be devastating (Exod. 10:1–20; Joel 1:2–20; 2:25). Fig trees and olive trees were important for the life and economy of Israel. A different Hebrew term for "locust" occurs in 7:1.

Lament for the Death of Israel (5:1–6:14)

Virgin Israel (5:2). This term signifies a young maiden who has not yet given birth. This scene is doubly tragic. The woman has fallen in battle with no one to pick her up or, even more shameful, no one to provide a proper burial. She also has been deprived of reaching full maturity as wife and mother.

Beer-sheba (5:5). Beer-sheba was a town in southern Judah, situated on a hill at the crossroads of important trade routes. Excavations uncovered a horned altar from the Iron II period (1000–550 BC). Beer-sheba reappears at 8:14.

Wormwood (5:7). The term refers to a bitter herb, perhaps *Artemisia absinthium* (cf. 6:12).

Pleiades and Orion (5:8). See comments on Job 9:9. These were two well-known constellations. In Mesopotamia and Phoenicia the movements of stars and constellations were studied with scientific interest (astronomy), as well as religiously to divine the will of the gods and the future (astrology). The Lord created these two prominent constellations to which other peoples looked for guidance (Job 9:9; 38:31–32) and, as heavenly king, he rules over the celestial bodies (Isa. 40:26). His unique power is underscored by the ability to control the natural rhythm of day and night and to bring disastrous floods.

The houses of cut stone (5:11). Constructed of dressed stone, these houses were a contrast to the mud-brick or rough stone homes in which most of the population lived. Such stones were used to build the temple and royal palaces (1 Kings 5:17; 6:36; 7:9, 11). This announcement of judgment echoes the curses in Deut. 28:30.

They . . . take a bribe (5:12). Fair legal proceedings were mandated in Israel (Exod. 23:6–8; Deut. 16:19; 27:25; Prov. 17:23). Those adjudicating cases were not to be swayed by social standing or gifts (Deut. 1:15–17; 1 Sam. 12:3; Isa. 1:23; Mic. 3:11).

Wailing . . . professional mourners (5:16). Mourning in the ancient Near East was very outwardly demonstrative. The bereaved would wail, tear their clothes, wear sackcloth, cover themselves with dust, and fast (e.g., Gen. 37:34–35; 2 Sam. 1:11–12; 3:31). Mourning could last for some time (Gen.

Wall relief of a Mesopotamian harpist.

50:11; Num. 20:29; 1 Sam. 31:13). Shaving the head was not uncommon (Isa. 22:12; Jer. 7:29; Mic. 1:16), but self-mutilation was prohibited (Lev. 19:28). Professional mourners could be employed at these times as well (Jer. 9:17, 20).

Songs . . . music of your harps (5:23). See the article "Musical Instruments in Israel and the Ancient Near East." The use of music was common in religious settings. The musical terms and directions of many superscriptions in the Psalter attest to the importance of music in worship (e.g., Pss. 4; 9; 55–61). The OT mentions many musical instruments (1 Sam. 10:5; 2 Sam. 6:5; Ps. 150) and describes David's organization of music for the temple (1 Chron. 25).

Sakkuth . . . Kaiwan (5:26). These probably are astral deities, although the Hebrew in this verse is not entirely clear. In the NIV's preferred translation ("shrine . . . pedestal") the verse is condemning the religious objects by which images of deities were carried. In the CSB's translation and the NIV footnote (also ESV: "Sikkuth . . . Kiyyun") the verse is censuring the astral deities themselves.

Your star god (5:26). This could refer to a standard representing a deity, which would be paraded in sacred processions on the way to a shrine.

Calneh . . . Hamath (6:2). Calneh was the capital of the Hittite state of Pattin (Unqi) in the lower Orontes River Valley (Gen. 10:10; Isa. 10:9). It has been identified as Tell Tayinat in modern-day Turkey. Hamath was a key Aramean (Syrian) city-state on the Orontes River to the south of Pattin, about 130 miles north of Damascus (see comments on Amos 6:14). The Assyrians punished these cities in 738 BC (Tiglath-pileser III) and 720 BC (Sargon II), but the event alluded to here may be to a conflict closer to Amos's time that is unknown to us.

Gath (6:2). This Philistine city, most famously connected with Goliath (1 Sam. 17:4), was located in the Elah Valley about five miles south of Ekron, another major Philistine city (see comments on Amos 1:6–8; see the article "The Philistines"). Gath is identified with the current site of Tell es-Safi. Tiglath-Pileser III attacked Gath in 734 BC, and Sargon II did so in 711 BC. This verse may allude to the destruction of Gath by Hazael of Aram in the late ninth century (2 Kings 12:17).

Beds adorned with ivory (6:4). See comments on 1 Kings 22:39; Amos 3:15.

Lambs . . . calves (6:4). The diet of the average Israelite consisted of cereals (especially wheat and barley), dairy products, olive oil, and some fruits and legumes, but little meat. Sheep were invaluable for wool and milk, and cows helped till the ground and also provided milk. The best animals were set aside for religious purposes and special occasions. That the wealthy elite in Israel were consuming stall-fattened beasts was a mark of indulgent extravagance.

Invent their own musical instruments like David (6:5). See comments on Amos 5:23; see the article "Musical Instruments in Israel and the Ancient Near East."

Wine by the bowlful (6:6). Several times in the OT the wealthy elite are condemned for drinking in excess at banquets (Isa. 5:12; 28:7–8; Hosea 7:5). The word translated with the phrase "by the bowlful," though, is not the common Hebrew term for "cup" but one that normally is used only in religious worship contexts (Exod. 27:3; 38:3; 1 Kings 7:40, 45, 50). Drinking from these special "sacred" bowls suggests that religious impropriety is in view, whether related to the Lord or another deity (cf. Dan. 5:1–4).

The finest oils (6:6). Olive oil was used to fuel lamps, to prepare food, and also as a medicine. Anointing with oil was employed to dedicate priests, prophets, and kings (Exod. 40:13, 15; Lev. 8:12; 1 Sam. 10:1; 1 Kings 19:16) and in ritual worship contexts (Exod. 29:36; 40:9, 10; Lev. 8:10, 11). These wealthy individuals in 6:6 were squandering quality olive oil on themselves, even though the country had lost many of its olive trees (4:9).

Feasting (6:7). These feast celebrations were known across the ancient Near East. Apparently this was a social institution of the well-to-do, characterized by heavy drinking. These gatherings may have been associated with funerary meals designed to commemorate the dead (cf. Jer. 16:5–8). This fact, along with other details of 6:4–6, implies an improper and irregular religious setting.

A close relative and burner will remove his corpse (6:10). See comments on Amos 2:1. Cremation was not practiced in Israel, although the burning of corpses was stipulated for some crimes (e.g., Lev. 20:14; 21:9; Josh. 7:15, 25). The burning of the corpses here, after the destruction of the attack, probably was intended to minimize the outbreak of disease and pestilence. The bodies of the dead were all around because of the enemy attack (8:3; cf. 5:3, 16–17).

Lo-debar . . . Karnaim (6:13). The first of these two fortified towns, Lodebar, was located north of the Yarmuk River in Transjordan (east of the Jordan River). It has been identified with Tell el Hamme or modern Umm el-Dabar. The variation in spelling (in Hebrew it is spelled differently at 2 Sam. 9:4–5) is designed to mock Israel's military pride: its armies had captured

"No-Thing"! Karnaim has been identified with Al Sheik Sa'ad, farther north in Bashan along a northern tributary of the Yarmuk River and northeast of Ashtaroth. Both probably were trophies of the Israelite king Jeroboam II's program of territorial expansion (2 Kings 14:23–29).

The entrance of Hamath to the Brook of the Arabah (6:14). This phrase indicates the broad geographical sweep of the coming judgment. Hamath represented Israel's far northern frontier (Num. 13:21; Josh 13:5; Judg. 3:3; 1 Kings 8:65). The Brook of the Arabah refers either to the Wadi 'el-Qelt or the Wadi Kefrein. Both are located in the upper region of the Dead Sea, which sometimes is called the "Sea of the Arabah" (Deut. 3:17; 4:49; Josh. 3:16; 12:3), located south of Israel.

Three Visions of Disaster (7:1–9)

The king's hay (7:1). The king's hay probably was a royal tax in kind on the first harvest, which was of barley and wheat. These crops were sown in the autumn and harvested in the spring. The "late crops" of various fruits and vegetables were watered by the spring rains and harvested in the summer months. That locusts had eaten what remained from the king's take spelled disaster for the general populace.

The great deep (7:4). The "great deep" was thought to be the subterranean waters from which flowed the seas and rivers. It could also represent chaotic forces, though in the OT always under the Lord's control (Gen. 1:2; 7:11–12; 8:2). God's provision of the deep (waters) was life-giving (Gen. 49:25; Deut. 33:13; Ps. 78:15), so its destruction by fire would be catastrophic.

Plumb line (7:7–8). "Plumb line" is the traditional translation of the Hebrew term used here. The idea is that Israel had been placed against the divine standard of the law (a lead plumb hanging from a string) and, like a crooked wall "out of plumb," found wanting. Recently, numerous scholars have argued instead that this word is an Akkadian loanword for "tin." From this perspective, this vision continues the critique of Israel's defenses. Their walls were not as stout as they supposed. At a distance they might look as strong as iron (Jer. 1:18; Ezek. 4:3), but in reality they were feeble as tin. The Lord had ripped out a piece of that flimsy wall and thrown it at his people's feet. Appropriately, this vision is followed by an announcement of the monarchy's demise (7:9–11).

The Confrontation at Bethel (7:10–17)

The king's sanctuary and a royal temple (7:13). In the ancient Near East the central sanctuary of the chief deity was intimately intertwined with the king, the deity's representative and patron responsible for the upkeep of the temple. Religious personnel and ceremonies were important legitimizers of the national ideology.

A Vision of Religious Failure (8:1–3)

Summer fruit (8:1–2). This vision exploits the wordplay between "summer/ripe fruit" (*qayits*) and "the time is ripe" (*qets*; literally, "end").

The Cost of Religious Perversion (8:4–14)

New Moon (8:5). The new moon was the first day of the lunar month and, evidently, the time of an important religious celebration (1 Sam. 20:5–6; 2 Kings 4:23; Isa. 1:13; 66:23).

Dishonest scales (8:5). Fraudulent balances are condemned in the law (Deut. 25:13–15), the wisdom literature (Prov. 20:10, 23), and the prophets (Hosea 12:7; Mic. 6:11).

The Nile in Egypt (8:8). In its normal inundation cycle, because of heavy rains to the south the level of the Nile River rose from August through October and then receded (cf. 9:5). The agricultural life of Egypt depended on this influx of water and its deposit of silt across the farmland. The completion of the Aswan Dam in Egypt in 1970 ended this pattern.

Mourning . . . lamentation . . . sackcloth . . . every head to be shaved (8:10). See comments on Amos 5:16.

The guilt of Samaria (8:14). This may refer to idol worship in Samaria (1 Kings 16:30–32; Hosea 8:6). The Hebrew term translated as "guilt" (*ashmah*) might be a wordplay on the god Ashima (cf. NRSV: "Ashimah of Samaria"), a god worshiped in particular by the people of Hamath, a city on the northern border of Israel (Samaria) and Syria (see comments on 2 Kings 17:30–31).

Dan (8:14). Jeroboam I set up golden calves at Dan and Bethel when the united monarchy split into the two kingdoms of Israel and Judah (see comments on 1 Kings 12:29). The goal was to institute an alternative to the temple worship system in Jerusalem.

A Vision of Divine Sovereignty in Judgment (9:1–6)

The altar . . . Strike the capitals (9:1). This probably is a reference to the sanctuary at Bethel, whose collapse sealed God's rejection of Israel (see further at 1:2; 7:13). The capitals (tops) of the pillars that support the roof will be shaken so that it will collapse upon the worshipers.

Sheol (9:2). Although English translations often properly translate this Hebrew term (Sheol) as "grave," that rendering cannot express the force of this verse. Sheol refers to the underworld, the abode of the dead (Isa. 14:9–11) over which God has control (1 Sam. 2:6; Ps. 139:8; Prov. 15:11). This is the first of several merisms in 9:2–4, a literary device stating two extremes to encompass everything in between.

The sea serpent (9:3). This is a poetic allusion to a mythical sea monster, underscoring the Lord's great power (Job 7:12; Ps. 74:13–14; Isa. 51:9).

His upper chambers in the heavens (9:6). The same Lord who decrees the destruction of Israel's fortifications and sanctuary is described as building his own cosmic palace and temple (Ps. 78:69; 104:3; Isa. 66:1; cf. Heb. 8:5) of which Eden, the tabernacle, and the Jerusalem temple were all to be a reflection.

In these excavated ruins of a temple at the city of Dan, archaeologists have used a steel frame to re-create the outline of the large altar that was used there.

The Hope beyond the Ruins (9:7–15)

Cushites (9:7). See the article "The Cushites." Cush is to be identified with the region south of Egypt, now in the modern country of Sudan (Isa. 18:1–2). For a time the Cushites controlled Egypt. Their pharaoh Tirhakah fought the Assyrians, who invaded Judah in 701 BC (2 Kings 19:9). Zephaniah may have been the son of a Cushite (Zeph. 1:1), and the Cushite Ebed-melech befriended Jeremiah (Jer. 38:7–13).

Caphtor . . . Kir (9:7). Caphtor and Kir probably were the places of origin of the Philistines and the Arameans, respectively. Caphtor is Crete. On Kir, see comments on Amos 1:5.

As one shakes a sieve (9:9). During a harvest, after the wheat was crushed and winnowed, a sieve was used to filter out the finer grain from any remaining waste, including stalks and pebbles. The desired product (here the righteous ones) falls to the ground (i.e., they are spared), while the debris (the unrighteous ones) remains in the mesh (i.e., to be judged).

The fallen shelter of David (9:11). The "fallen shelter" probably refers to the condition of the united monarchy after its division into the two kingdoms of Israel and Judah in 931 BC (1 Kings 12). The hope presented here is for a time of future reunification under a glorious Davidic king.

Obadiah

M. Daniel Carroll R.

Obadiah (1). The name Obadiah means "servant of the Lord."

Edom (1). See comments on Jer. 49:7. Edom was a kingdom on the southeastern border of Judah. The boundaries of Edom extended from the Zered River at the southern end of the Dead Sea, southward to the Gulf of Aqaba. The east was marked by the Arabian Desert, while the limits of the territory west of the Wadi Arabah varied over time. Much of Edom was mountainous, with steep ridges and deep valleys. The King's Highway, which originated in Egypt, traversed the Sinai Peninsula, turned north at the Gulf of Aqaba, and passed through the eastern part of Edom, near key Edomite cities such as Teman (v. 9) and Bozrah.

Until recently, many scholars thought that Edom did not reach mature statehood until the Assyrian period in the late eighth to seventh centuries BC. Some questioned whether Edom could have done what it is accused of in this prophetic book. A different picture, however, is emerging through recent excavations, such as at Khirbat en-Nahas, located in the western lowlands of Edom. Remains from impressive copper-smelting works, dated from the twelfth to ninth centuries BC, demonstrate that Edom was a complex society at a very early time. Other significant archaeological sites include Horvat 'Uza and Horvat Qitmit, where findings mention the Edomite deity Qaus.

Clefts of the rock (3). This description reflects the topography of the Edomite heartland. This striking landscape fueled Edom's sense of invulnerability. The Hebrew word translated here as "rock" can also be translated by the proper name "Sela," a fortress taken by Amaziah and renamed Joktheel (2 Kings 14:7; cf. 2 Chron. 25:12). Sela has been connected to an area close to Bozrah (cf. Isa. 34:6; 63:1; Jer. 49:13) or to Umm el-Biyara near the city of Petra.

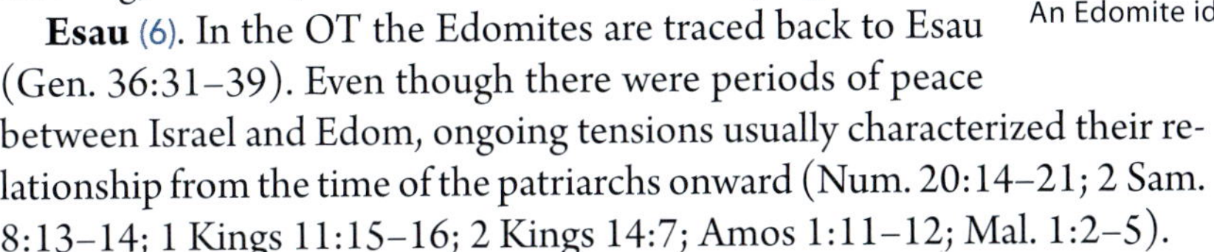
An Edomite idol.

Grapes (5). Edom was famous for its viticulture, or grape growing (cf. Isa. 63:1–6). The image here is of unconscionable seizure by future invaders. Normally the Israelites were to leave the remnants of a harvest for the needy (Lev. 19:9–10; Deut. 24:21; cf. Ruth 2; Mic. 7:1). Nothing, however, will be left to Edom in this judgment.

Esau (6). In the OT the Edomites are traced back to Esau (Gen. 36:31–39). Even though there were periods of peace between Israel and Edom, ongoing tensions usually characterized their relationship from the time of the patriarchs onward (Num. 20:14–21; 2 Sam. 8:13–14; 1 Kings 11:15–16; 2 Kings 14:7; Amos 1:11–12; Mal. 1:2–5).

Everyone who has a treaty with you (7). The terminology of this verse (literally, "men of your covenant" and "men of your peace") is the language of ancient Near Eastern covenants. Edom will be betrayed by other peoples with whom it had mutual agreements.

In that day . . . will I not eliminate . . . Edom? (8). In the middle of the sixth century BC the Babylonian king Nabonidus conquered and destroyed several sites in Edom, leaving behind an engraved celebratory stone relief near Sela.

Wise ones of Edom (8). The association of Edom with wisdom is suggested by Job's connection with Uz (sometimes linked to Edom) and his friend Eliphaz with Teman (cf. Jer. 49:7).

Teman (9). The location of Teman has been connected to Bozrah in northern Edom, though some argue for a southern location. The Kuntillet Ajrud inscription (an inscription from the ninth or eighth century BC discovered in the northeast region of the Sinai Peninsula) curiously mentions "Yahweh [the Lord] of Teman."

Because of violence . . . on the day (10–14). There is disagreement as to which event is being described. Scholars propose dates ranging from the reign of Jehoram (853–841 BC [2 Kings 8:20–22; 2 Chron. 21:16–17]) to the taking of Jerusalem by the Babylonians (586 BC). Several other passages are directed against Edom concerning the fall of Jerusalem to the Babylonians (Ps. 137; Jer. 49:7–22; Lam. 4:21–22; Ezek. 25:12–14; 35). Arad Ostracon 24 apparently alludes to the Edomite threat at that time. Edom's participation in the Babylonian capture of Jerusalem progressed from observing, to involvement in the sacking of the city, to turning over fleeing refugees to the Babylonians (see comments on Ezek. 25:12).

Your brother Jacob (10). The historic kinship connection between Jacob and Esau (Edom) made this cruelty even more unacceptable.

Foreigners . . . cast lots (11). In the ancient world lots sometimes were cast to distribute equitably the plunder of victory (cf. Ps. 22:18; Prov. 18:18). The results were believed to be in the hands of the gods.

They will drink and gulp down (16). The excessive drinking by God's enemies in their celebration of victory over Zion finds its poetic justice counterpart in fully imbibing the cup of divine wrath (cf. Isa. 51:17; Jer. 25:15–16).

From the Negev . . . the Judean foothills (19). God's people in southernmost Judah (the Negev) will move east to occupy Edom. From the Judean foothills they will regain the Philistine coastland to the west, the lands in the north conquered by Assyria (Ephraim, Samaria), as well as the region east of the Jordan River (Gilead).

Zarephath . . . Sepharad (20). Zarephath was located to the northwest in Phoenicia between the cities of Tyre and Sidon (1 Kings 17:9; cf. Luke 4:26). Sepharad probably refers to Sardis, situated in western Turkey, although some relate it to Spain. Even those who are farthest away will return.

Jonah

M. Daniel Carroll R.

Introduction. The prophet Jonah is mentioned in 2 Kings 14:25 as ministering during the reign of Jeroboam II (see comments on 2 Kings 14:23) in the first half of the eighth century BC. This time frame coincides with a time of Assyrian weakness. After the death of the Assyrian king Adad-nirari III (810–783 BC) the Assyrian Empire was beset with rebellions and suffered several natural disasters (an earthquake and an eclipse). If the book of Jonah represents a historical event, the shock of these reversals could explain why the Ninevites were receptive to Jonah's message. Ashur dan III (772–755 BC), one of the sons of Adad-nirari III, may have been the Assyrian king during the events described in this book. Assyria did not regain its former glory until Tiglath-pileser III ascended the throne in 745 BC (see the article "The Assyrians").

Jonah's Flight to Tarshish (1:1–16)

To the great city of Nineveh (1:2). Nineveh, identified with Tell Kuyunjik, is located in modern Iraq on the Tigris River some six hundred miles northwest of the Persian Gulf. A longtime center for the worship of the goddess Ishtar, Nineveh achieved its political zenith when the Assyrian king Sennacherib (704–681 BC) made Nineveh the empire's capital. He expanded its size and fortifications and built a magnificent palace there. Many of the significant archaeological remains of Nineveh are now housed in museums around the world. At the time of Jonah Nineveh would have been a major regional center. The language of Jonah's call echoes Gen. 18:20, suggesting that Jonah is commissioned to announce the destruction of the city.

Tarshish (1:3). While some scholars suggest that Tarshish was an area around Carthage in North Africa or perhaps the islands of Cyprus or Sardinia, most scholars connect Tarshish to Spain. This narrative suggests that it was far to the west. Several biblical texts associate Tarshish with trade and precious metals (1 Kings 10:22; Ezek. 27:12, 25).

Joppa (1:3). This important Mediterranean harbor was about 35 miles northwest of Jerusalem (2 Chron. 2:16; Ezra 3:7) and 550 miles from Nineveh. An Assyrian inscription from the end of the eighth century BC, decades after Jonah's possible historical setting, describes Joppa as under the control of the Philistine city-state Ashkelon, 30 miles to the south. Today Joppa is known as the modern city of Jaffa, located in the southern sector of Tel Aviv, Israel.

Ship (1:3). The Phoenicians dominated the maritime trade in the Mediterranean Sea (see comments on Ezek. 26:2), and they probably operated the ships sailing from Joppa. Phoenician ships in the first millennium BC were about seventy-five feet long and twenty feet wide and could carry a cargo of one hundred to five hundred tons. Crews numbered up to twenty sailors.

Each cried out to his god (1:5). Sailors in the ancient Near East often performed religious rituals (sacrifices, etc.) in harbor temples both before and after a voyage to ask for and celebrate safe passage. They also performed these rituals at sea when in danger. Symbols of deities often were placed in the prow or stern of ships, some of which also had a holy space to house figurines, sacred anchors, or altars. A terrible storm would have been interpreted by ancient sailors as the action of an angry deity. Sailors from different regions would have

Replica model of an ancient Phoenician merchant ship.

pleaded with their patron gods to intercede, especially before the more powerful and relevant deities, such as the storm god Hadad (also known as Baal) or Yam, the god of the sea. The sailors would seek to identify which deity had sent the storm and what was required to appease that god.[1]

Let's cast lots (1:7). In the ancient Near East lots often were cast in an attempt to discern the will of the gods and to make decisions. Lots were used for various similar purposes in the OT (e.g., Lev. 16:8–10; Josh. 7:10–26; 1 Sam. 14:41–42; 1 Chron. 24:5; cf. Prov. 16:33). Lots could be made of wood, stone, or bone, with distinguishing markings.

I worship the Lord, the God of the heavens (1:9). By describing the Lord as the "God of heaven" and the creator God, Jonah declares his god as sovereign over all other deities and natural phenomena, including the storm.

Throw me into the sea (1:12). The sailors may have understood this as a call for human sacrifice to placate Jonah's god. They fear that this deity might punish them if this were the wrong solution, hence their plea regarding shedding innocent blood (cf. Deut. 21:1–9). The text does not identify the kind of sacrifice or vow that the sailors offered, or whether these rituals were done on the ship or later on land. As polytheists, they probably accommodated the Lord within their pantheon of gods (cf. Ps. 107:21–30).

Jonah in the Fish (1:17–2:10)

A great fish (1:17). No species of fish is specified. In the ancient world sea monsters were associated with Yam, the god of the sea, but here, importantly, it is the Lord who appoints and controls this great fish.

Jonah prayed to the Lord (2:1–9). Much of this vocabulary is found in Psalms (18:4–6; 30:3; 31:22; 42:7; 69:14–15), demonstrating the prophet's familiarity with Israel's hymns. Jonah believes that he is inescapably close to perishing. He prays from "Sheol," or the grave (2:2), and "the Pit," where he is trapped by the gates of the netherworld (2:6) (cf. Job 38:17; Isa. 38:10). "The foundations of the mountains" (2:6) could refer to the cosmic mountains, which were believed to extend from the netherworld upward to hold up the sky. The temple that Jonah mentions twice (2:4, 7) could be one of the sanctuaries of the northern kingdom or the temple in Jerusalem. The promise of song, sacrifice, and vow signals not repentance, but rather appreciation for being delivered from death in the fish.

One of the gates to ancient Nineveh, partially reconstructed.

Jonah's Message to Nineveh (3:1–10)

An extremely great city (3:3). Literally, "a great city to God." This phrase could connote Nineveh's significance (1:2; 3:2) or perhaps indicate its worth to the Lord, who was willing to extend mercy to its inhabitants (3:9–10; 4:11).

A three-day walk (3:3). This time frame reflects the time needed for Jonah to proclaim his message throughout different parts of the city or within the broader province of Nineveh.

In forty days Nineveh will be demolished! (3:4). In contrast to his message to the sailors, Jonah does not describe his god or provide his name ("the Lord"). Clearly, the prophet desires that Nineveh will not repent and will be destroyed.

They proclaimed a fast and dressed in sackcloth . . . the king of Nineveh, he got up from his throne, took off his royal robe, put on sackcloth, and sat in ashes (3:5–10). This overwhelming response may have been due to other confirming omens, before or after Jonah's preaching. The "king" probably refers to the district governor, as Nineveh then was not a royal city. Fasting and sackcloth were associated with mourning. Though ignorant of the cause of the anger of Jonah's god, these funerary gestures (including symbolically even the fasting and repentance of their animals) express sincere sorrow and the hope that the god of Jonah will not bring disaster on them.

Each must turn from . . . evil ways and . . . wrongdoing (3:8). The mention of violence is apropos in light of the Assyrian reputation for cruelty.

Jonah's Reaction to Nineveh's Repentance (4:1–11)

I knew that you are a gracious and compassionate God (4:2). Jonah cites a long-standing conviction in the OT about the Lord's covenant commitment to his people (cf. Exod. 34:6; Neh. 9:17; Ps. 86:15), recognizing that God's compassion is available to all humanity, even to Israel's past and future enemy. Jonah confesses that this possibility is what drove him to run away.

Scorching east wind (4:8). The word translated as "scorching" appears only here in the OT, so its meaning is unclear. Unlike in Palestine, where an eastern wind comes from the desert and can be problematic, eastern winds in the region of Nineveh normally bring rain. Yet it is the sun's sweltering heat that exhausts Jonah.

A hundred and twenty thousand (4:11). Nineveh's population in the seventh century BC is estimated to have reached three hundred thousand, so this is a plausible number for the eighth century BC.

Micah

Stephen G. Dempster

Introduction. This book receives its name from the prophet to whom the Lord spoke. The only time his name is mentioned, however, is in the title of the book (1:1). Micah's name means "who is like the Lord?" His hometown was Moreshet-gath (cf. 1:1, 14), a town in the southwestern hill country of Judah, located about twenty miles southwest of Jerusalem and nine miles east of Gath. Often OT prophets were identified by their family name (e.g., Jonah son of Amittai, Isaiah son of Amoz), but Micah was identified by his location, which suggests that he did most of his speaking in another place, most likely the city of Jerusalem. Micah 1:1 indicates that he prophesied during the time of three kings of Judah: Jotham (742–735 BC), Ahaz (735–715 BC), and Hezekiah (715–687 BC), although much of Micah's prophesying seems to have centered on the predictions of the destruction of Samaria (722 BC) and Jerusalem (701 BC). His prophesying inspired a repentance around the time of the invasion of the Assyrian king Sennacherib (701 BC) (cf. Jer. 26:18–19).

The recipients of the prophet's messages are also mentioned in the title to the book: Samaria and Jerusalem. Each of these capitals, respectively of the northern and southern kingdoms, by extension represented its nation.

Most scholars see a tripartite structure in Micah, indicated by the three calls to hear (1:2; 3:1; 6:1). Each of these demarcated sections begins with judgment oracles issued to Micah's present audience and concludes with salvation oracles for a future audience. The whole book is united by the mention of Micah's name at the beginning (1:1) and a wordplay on the same name at the end: "Who is a God like you?" (7:18).

Part 1: Judgment, Exile, and Deliverance (1:1–2:13)

Oracle against Samaria (1:1–7)

The Lord God will be a witness against you . . . from his holy temple (1:2). The word "witness" shows the legal context, and the holy temple indicates that the Lord is also a judge and ruler of the world as he sits in his heavenly temple.

Trample the heights of the earth (1:3). To "trample" or "tread" on ground in biblical times meant that one took ownership of it. Here the Divine Owner lays claim to his land. "Heights of the earth" is a double entendre, referring both to the mountains and to the "high places," the sites of Canaanite temples and altars. These often were located on the highest point within towns and cities. Thus by treading on these high places God not only displays transcendence but also lays claim to all worship.

I will make Samaria a heap of ruins in the countryside (1:6). Samaria, the capital of the northern kingdom of Israel, was conquered by the Assyrians in 722 BC after a three-year siege. The archaeological evidence of destruction is scarce, but the city was reconstructed by the Assyrians shortly after the conquest. Thus the spirit of the prophecy came true. The Assyrian king Sargon II writes in various inscriptions, "I conquered the city of Samaria and all the land of Bit Humri." "Bit Humri" means "House of Omri" and is

The ruins of Micah's hometown, Moreshet-gath, and surrounding region.

a reference to the land of Israel as ruled by a royal dynasty initiated by Omri (886 BC) and concluded by his grandson Joram (841 BC) (see comments on 1 Kings 16:16–28). This shows the political influence of that dynasty was remembered over a century after it had perished.

All her wages will be burned in the fire (1:7). The term translated as "wages" probably refers to the price paid for services of ritual prostitutes in the service of Canaanite fertility religion. Part of the religion included sympathetic magic, in which sexual acts among humans stimulated the gods of nature to copulate and to produce their children, the plants of the earth.

Lament over Judah (1:8–16)

Because of this I will lament and wail . . . walk barefoot and naked (1:8). Mourning practices in the ancient Near East often involved radical measures such as these mentioned here. The more radical the measure, the more intense the grief. When David, for example, was running for his life with his men, they covered their heads, some of them ripped their garments, and they went barefooted (2 Sam. 15:14–33).

Gath . . . Beth-leaphrah . . . Shaphir . . . Adullam (1:10–15). The towns mentioned in this passage are from the southwestern part of Judah, where one part of the Assyrian army advanced in its invasion of Judah in 701 BC. Micah would have been familiar with these towns, as they are in proximity to his own village. Some of the names occur only in this text, and their locations have not been determined (e.g., Beth-leaphrah, Shaphir, Beth-ezel, Maroth). But the towns are chosen because of their names, which evoke an ominous note of doom. Puns or wordplays are made with the name of each town; thus these puns were chosen not for wit but for evoking a sense of impending doom in the audience. Their doom was their destiny! There are six towns containing verbal wordplays. For example, in the phrase "Don't announce it in Gath," the Hebrew words for "announce" and "Gath" sound similar. Likewise, there are six towns containing plays on meanings (usually in a semantic reversal). For example, "Shaphir" means "beauty, splendor," but the residents will "depart in shameful nakedness."

Shave yourselves bald and cut off your hair in sorrow for your precious children (1:16). These are examples of extreme rites of mourning, which generally were forbidden for the Israelites (Deut. 14:1). Here, Mother Zion, representing Judah, is being addressed as the parent of her children who are being led into captivity. The Assyrian relief drawings have many examples of children with their mothers being taken into captivity.

Judgment against the Covetous (2:1–5)

Woe to those (2:1). The Hebrew word for "woe" was used for funeral dirges in ancient Israel (1 Kings 13:30), so Micah is pronouncing a lamentation for those who engage in such practices. They are as good as dead!

They covet fields and seize them (2:2). This is a reference to the practice of foreclosure for inability to pay debts. Insolvency often was caused by dire economic circumstances, but the creditors had no mercy.

There will be no one in the assembly of the Lord to divide the land by casting lots (2:5). This is a reference back to the practice of land distribution when the Israelites took possession of the land of Canaan (Josh. 14:1–2). The current greedy land barons will be dispossessed of land in any future inheritance distribution after the exile.

False Prophets (2:6–13)

"I will preach to you about wine and beer"—he would be just the preacher for this people! (2:11). Prolific quantities of alcohol represented prosperity in Israel (Gen. 49:11–12; Amos 9:13), so these false prophets were professing an early "prosperity gospel" of sorts.

One who breaks open the way will advance before them (2:13). Ancient armies had "sappers," whose job it was to undermine the walls of besieged cities and thus to open breaches in the defenses. They also had siege engines that were used to batter breaches in the walls. Here the Lord is the one who breaks open the wall imprisoning his people.

Part 2: Judgment, Exile, and Universal Peace (3:1–5:15)

Judgment for the Courts (3:1–4)

You eat the flesh of my people after you strip their skin from them (3:3). Cannibalism was rarely practiced in the ancient Near East, usually occurring only in very desperate conditions, such as when a city was under

Captured women with a child being led into captivity by the Assyrians. Their hands on their heads represent mourning and lamenting.

siege for a long period of time (see comments on 2 Kings 6:28). Thus this image is used to shock the judicial officials to the reality of their outrageous acts of injustice. In their oppression of the poor they are just like cannibals! The flaying of the skin may be an allusion to the terror tactics of the Assyrian army, whose soldiers often would flay the skin from enemies who resisted their advances.

Judgment for the False Prophets (3:5–8)

They will all cover their mouths (3:7). The word translated as "mouth" probably refers more broadly to the lower part of the face. To cover the face was a sign of shame and degradation. It was required of lepers (Lev. 13:45), and people who felt like social lepers would voluntarily do it as a sign of unthinkable grief (2 Sam. 15:30–31).

Judgment on Jerusalem (3:9–12)

Who build Zion with bloodshed and Jerusalem with injustice (3:10). Before the Assyrian invasion and during King Hezekiah's reign major building projects were undertaken in Jerusalem, which no doubt required oppressive labor. Hezekiah built a tunnel over one hundred feet underground and approximately five-eighths of a mile in length in order to supply another part of the city with water. He also built a massive wall to protect a large part of the city that was defenseless. This particular wall was over twenty feet thick and twenty-seven feet high, spanning nearly a mile in length.

The Future of Zion (4:1–5)

The mountain of the LORD's house . . . will be raised above the hills (4:1). In Mesopotamia the ziggurats were built as large, man-made mountains on flat plains to show the unity of heaven and earth. An inscription describing how Gudea of Lagash constructed a temple for his gods reads, "They were making the temple grow (high) like a mountain range; making it float in mid-heaven like a cloud."[1]

They will beat their swords into plows, and their spears into pruning knives (4:3). This shows the transformation from militarism and aggression to peace and production (see comments on Isa. 2:4).

But each person will sit under his grapevine (4:4). This is an image of peace and plenty, particularly a result of the messianic age (Zech. 3:10). Solomon's era was the partial realization of such a hope (1 Kings 4:25).

Though all the peoples each walk in the name of their gods (4:5). To walk in the name of a god was to be identified with that god. It was to manifest the character of that god and to receive its help and strength (Zech. 10:12; cf. 1 Sam. 17:45).

Zion Judged and Restored (4:6–5:1)

Rise and thresh . . . for I will make . . . your hooves bronze, so you can crush many peoples (4:13). Cattle often were used to thresh wheat. In ancient Near Eastern artistic depictions of kings and gods, bulls sometimes are shown trampling upon enemies.

You will set apart their plunder for the Lord (4:13). The devotion to the deity of an enemy's spoil often was the last act of a holy war, as is depicted in Josh. 6:21and also on the Moabite Stone (an inscribed stone monument set up around 840 BC by King Mesha of Moab). Here Micah says that there would be no spoil for any human being; it would be devoted to the Lord in a type of sacrifice.

They are striking the judge of Israel on the cheek with a rod (5:1). To be struck on the face was a sign of humiliation (1 Kings 22:24; Job 16:10; Ps. 3:7; Isa. 50:6; Lam. 3:30). This may be a metaphorical description of what happened to Hezekiah when he was embarrassed in front of all his people by the Assyrian messenger who taunted his inability to withstand the Assyrian onslaught (2 Kings 18:18–19:4) (see comments on 2 Kings 18:13).

The Shepherd and the Sheep (5:2–9)

He will stand and shepherd them (5:4). See comments on Jer. 23:1; Ezek. 34:2. Kings in the ancient Near East often stylized themselves as shepherds who would guide their flock (their people) into safe pastures and protect them. Egyptian pharaohs often were pictured with a shepherd's staff.

Like dew from the Lord (5:7). Dew was a necessary refreshment for the pasturelands of ancient Israel particularly in the dry season, and showers were absolutely necessary in the rainy season. They literally provided life. The promise of dew was also an ancient blessing given to the people of God (Gen. 27:28).

Like a lion among animals of the forest (5:8). Lions were the most powerful and dangerous predators in the forests and fields of the ancient Near East. They often are depicted in imagery of the ancient world as animals to be feared.

Final Battle (5:10–15)

I will . . . wreck your chariots (5:10). Chariots were the rapid-deployment forces in the ancient world and were a critical component of up-to-date military power. Kings often were known by the number of their horses and chariots. The Assyrian king Shalmeneser III mentioned in an inscription (Kurkh Monolith) that Ahab, king of Israel, was reputed to have marshaled two thousand chariots in the battle at Qarqar (853 BC) (see the section on the Neo-Assyrian period in the article "The Assyrians").

Part 3: Call to Repentance, Confession, and Final Salvation (6:1–7:20)

The Lord Contends with His People (6:1–8)

Remember . . . what Balaam son of Beor answered (6:5). This story is found in Num. 22–24.

What happened from the Acacia Grove to Gilgal (6:5). The Acacia Grove (literally, "Shittim") was the last stop in the journey of the Israelites from Egypt to the promised land, while Gilgal was the first stop in the promised land (see comments on Josh. 3:1; 4:19).

Should I come before him with burnt offerings, with year-old calves? (6:6). A burnt offering was the most complete because the entire offering was burned, while one-year-old calves were the most valuable offering because the meat was the most tender.

Should I give my firstborn for my transgression, the offspring of my body for my own sin? (6:7). There is evidence that human sacrifice was practiced in some of the surrounding cultures that influenced the Israelites (see comments on 2 Kings 3:27).

The Lord Judges His People (6:9–16)

Can I excuse wicked scales or bags of deceptive weights (6:11). False weights sometimes were kept alongside true weights in order to decrease the grain being sold and to increase the money being received. Amos, Micah's colleague preaching up

The Kurkh Monolith of the Assyrian king Shalmaneser III, which mentions Ahab, king of Israel.

in the northern kingdom of Israel, had already condemned this criminal practice (see comments on Amos 8:5). In the Pentateuch and the wisdom literature there is persistent prohibition of such an unjust practice (Deut. 25:13–16; Prov. 11:1).

Zion Laments for Its People (7:1–7)

Finds no grape cluster to eat, no early fig (7:1). All the imagery in this verse derives from an agrarian culture: there is no remaining harvest at all of any crops. This represents the lack of spiritual fruit in Judah—a dire picture of spiritual desolation indeed.

Israel's Hope in Yahweh (7:8–20)

Let them graze in Bashan and Gilead (7:14). Bashan and Gilead were known for their prize cattle, precisely because of their luxurious pasturelands (see comments on Amos 4:1).

They will lick the dust like a snake (7:17). This is the posture of humiliation and defeat (Gen. 3:14; Ps. 44:25).

Who is a God like you? . . . he delights in faithful love (7:18–20). This final text is expressed in the genre of a hymn of praise. There is nothing quite like this particular hymn of praise in the literature of the ancient Near East, celebrating the divine qualities of forgiveness, compassion, and love. The Lord is truly incomparable!

Nahum

Gordon H. Johnston

Introduction. The oracle of Nahum envisioned the destruction of Nineveh, the Assyrian capital, and the subsequent demise of the Neo-Assyrian Empire. Following the death of the last mighty Assyrian king, Ashurbanipal (668–627 BC), the empire began to fracture under a series of weak and short-lived successors. In 616 BC the Assyrian homeland was invaded by a coalition of former vassals turned attackers: Babylonians, Medes, Persians, Scythians, and Cimmerians. These invaders besieged and sacked Nineveh in 612 BC. With the fall of its capital, the Assyrian remnant fled to Haran, which was subsequently captured in 609 BC. Ashur-uballit II, the last Assyrian king, fled to the city of Carchemish, which fell to the Babylonians in 605 BC, bringing Assyrian power to a complete end. See the article "The Assyrians."

The Lord takes vengeance . . . the mountains quake before him . . . he will completely destroy Nineveh (1:2–8). Conquest accounts in Assyrian royal annals typically opened with a series of boasts depicting the Assyrian king as the mighty warrior par excellence. These stereotypical epithets were repeated from one Assyrian king to another. For example, Shalmaneser III (ca. 858–824 BC) boasted, "Shalmaneser, king of the four quarters of the world, who treads the summits of mountains and hills far and near, at whose mighty battle onset all regions feel threatened . . . mighty hero who slays every foe and overwhelms them like a flood."[1] Nahum opened his oracle of God's conquest of Nineveh in strikingly similar terms, picturing the Lord as the

In this battle scene from King Ashurbanipal's palace in Nineveh, the Assyrians have chased fleeing Elamite soldiers into a river, where they either drown or get slaughtered.

Divine Warrior, who trumps all rivals, including the Assyrian king.[2]

Overwhelming flood (1:8). One of the conventional motifs in Assyrian texts was the destruction of a city by flood. Assyrian treaties in particular often threatened vassals with the curse of an overwhelming flood. For example, Esarhaddon (681–669 BC) threatened his Syro-Palestinian vassals thus: "May [Adad] submerge your land with a great flood," and "May an irresistible flood come up from the earth and devastate you."[3] Assyrian royal annals also often contained references to the devastating effects of a flood. For example, Ashurbanipal (668–627 BC) boasted, "I conquered that city and smashed it like a flood."[4] Ashurbanipal destroyed the city of Shapibel by literally flooding it: "I devastated, I destroyed, I laid waste Shapibel his stronghold by flooding it with water."[5] In similar fashion, Nahum announced that God would destroy Nineveh with an overwhelming flood.[6] Although 1:8 might simply represent conventional imagery, Nineveh was actually conquered when the attacking coalition opened the sluice gates of the water canal outside the city—already at flood stage due to unusually heavy rains—which breached the city wall, allowing the attackers to enter and conquer the city (cf. 2:8–9). Centuries later the Greek historian Diodorus Siculus provided an embellished account of the breach of Nineveh's walls as a result of the flooding of the Euphrates River.[7]

I will now break off his yoke (1:13). The imagery of the yoke was a metaphor for subjugation to a foreign power (Lev. 26:13; Jer. 27:2; 28:14; Ezek. 30:18; 34:27). Assyrian kings often boasted that they had subjugated foreign nations, causing them to pull their "yoke"—that is, submit to their rule. For example, when the Assyrian king Sennacherib forced Judah to submit to his rule, he boasted, "I put the straps of my yoke upon Hezekiah its king."[8]

The river gates are opened (2:6). Nineveh employed a system of dams and sluice gates to control the waters of the Tebiltu and Khoser Rivers that flowed through the city. However, the Tebiltu often flooded its banks inside the city, undermining palace foundations and weakening other structures. To reduce this flooding, the Assyrian king Sennacherib changed the course of the Tebiltu inside the city. Outside the city he dammed up the Khoser and created a reservoir, regulating the flow of water into the city through an elaborate system of double sluice gates. According to later Greek tradition, a succession of high rains deluged the area in the days before Nineveh fell.[9] The Khoser River swelled and the reservoir was breached. The waters rushed through the overloaded canal system, breaking an enormous hole in the city wall. When the waters receded, the Babylonians stormed into Nineveh and conquered the city.

The palace erodes away (2:6). Nahum pictures the riverbanks inside Nineveh overflowing in a torrent, crashing into the royal palace and eroding its limestone slab foundations. Earlier the Assyrian king Sennacherib had strengthened the foundations of his palace with "mighty slabs of limestone" so that "its foundation would not be weakened by the flood of high water."[10] At the time of the fall of Nineveh the royal palace was located on the edge of the sharpest bend of the Khoser River as it flowed through the city; when the Khoser overflowed its banks, the palace foundation was weakened.[11]

Where is the lions' lair? (2:11–13). The iconic image of the mighty lion as the king of the beasts frequented Assyrian royal art and literature. In their royal annals Assyrian kings often compared themselves to mighty lions raging against their enemy in battle. Wall reliefs of Assyrian palaces pictured the kings engaged in their favorite sport: hunting and killing lions. In 2:11–13 Nahum dovetailed both motifs, creating an ironic reversal of the Assyrian boast. The Assyrian king would be like a lion—but with a new twist. Rather than being like a mighty lion on the scene of battle, he would be like a lion in a royal hunt. In other words, the hunter would become the hunted. Moreover, just as the Assyrian king Ashurbanipal (668–627 BC) boasted that he had wiped out a population explosion of wild lions that had victimized Assyrian villages, Nahum proclaimed that the Lord would wipe out the Assyrian lion-kings who had been victimizing the people of the ancient world.[12]

I will make your chariots go up in smoke (2:13). Treaties in the ancient Near East featured various curses against recalcitrant vassals, including the destruction of their chariots.[13] For example, the vassal treaty of Esar-haddon threatened to destroy the chariots of rebellious vassals: "May they [Assyrian gods] turn your chariots upside down," and "Just as this chariot is spattered with blood up to its running board, so may they [Assyrian gods] spatter your chariots in the midst of your enemy with your own blood."[14] Nahum turned the table on the Assyrians: the Assyrians would not destroy the chariots of God's people; rather, God would destroy the chariots of the Assyrians.

I will lift your skirts over your face (3:5–7). In the ancient Near East prostitutes often were punished by public exposure of their nakedness. Treaty curses from the time of Nahum likewise threatened that rebellious vassals would be punished like prostitutes. For example, an Aramaic treaty warned, "Just as a prostitute is stripped naked, so may the wives of Matiilu be stripped naked, and the wives of his offspring and the wives of his nobles."[15] An Assyrian treaty likewise warned, "If Matiilu sins against this treaty with Ashurnirari king of Assyria, may Matiilu become a prostitute, his soldiers like women, may they receive [. . .] in the square of their cities like any prostitute."[16] Hence, it was fitting when Nahum announced that the Lord would punish Nineveh in similar fashion.

All your fortresses are fig trees . . . when shaken, they fall (3:12). Following Nineveh's fall in 612 BC (portrayed throughout 1:12–3:10), Ashur-uballit II, the last Assyrian king, and the remnant of his army fled west, first to the city of Haran and then to the city of Carchemish (portrayed in 3:11–19). The stronghold at Haran provided refuge for a short time (612–609 BC), but then the Assyrians were forced to flee to the fortified city of Carchemish (a former vassal of Assyria), where they held out from 609 to 605 BC. Led by the Neo-Babylonian king Nebuchadnezzar II (605–562 BC), the allied forces of the Babylonian and Median army finally destroyed the Assyrian forces (along with their Egyptian allies) at Carchemish in 605 BC. See the article "The Babylonians."

Like the young locust (3:15–17). Locust swarms often consumed crops in the ancient world, leaving entire populations desolate. Accordingly, ancient Near Eastern treaties often cursed rebellious vassals with destruction by locusts. For example, the Assyrian king Esar-haddon threatened his vassals thus: "May the locust which diminishes the land devour your harvest. . . . May they [Assyrian gods] let . . . crop-consuming devourers consume your cities, country and provinces like locusts." In their royal annals Assyrian kings likewise portrayed their armies coming upon the battlefield like a swarm of locusts that left nothing behind. For example, Sargon II boasted, "I overran these lands like a swarm of locusts," and "With the widespreading armies of Assyria I overwhelmed all of their cities like locusts."[17] Just as Assyrian kings compared their armies to a swarm of locusts, Nahum depicted the numerous Assyrian troops and their allies to a swarm of locusts. However, he reversed the imagery in an ironic manner. The numerous Assyrian troops would flee in battle just as a swarm of locusts taking flight at dawn; Assyria's numerous allies then would plunder its wealth like a swarm of locusts devouring a field.

Habakkuk

James K. Bruckner

Introduction. The prophet Habakkuk, a contemporary of Nahum, Zephaniah, and Jeremiah, was a temple prophet and musician (see 3:1, 19) who prophesied during the violent political upheaval at the end of the seventh century BC. His book is a collection of oracles written just before the invasion of Judah by the Babylonians.

The prophet began with a complaint to the Lord against local corruption, but he was drawn into a progressively more difficult understanding of faith. God took the prophet's persistent question of theodicy, "Why do you tolerate wrongdoing?" (1:3, 13), and made him wrestle with a broader international sociological reality: the unexpected rise of the Neo-Babylonians.

In preparing his faithful people for this devastating change, the Lord told Habakkuk that Judah's prosperity and autonomy would end. Yet the Lord promised that things would improve after the devastation. In the meantime, they could cling to their memory of the Lord's past faithfulness (chap. 3). They would have the benefit of forewarning and the possibility of joy in the Lord (3:17–19).

Habakkuk's Question to God about Injustice (1:1–4)

The pronouncement that the prophet Habakkuk saw (1:1). This was unique, since it was a dialogue between the prophet and the Lord. The Hebrew word translated as "pronouncement" literally means "burden." Here the "burden" of Habakkuk's message is the rise of the Neo-Babylonians, who soon would destroy Jerusalem (586 BC) (see the article "The Babylonians").

Why do you force me to look at injustice? (1:2–4). The prophet's complaint was about Jehoiakim, the corrupt king of Judah, who killed innocents and refused to pay poor laborers (2 Kings 23:35–37; Jer. 22:13–19). Under his administration prophets and priests fell into adultery and abuse of authority (Jer. 23:1–2, 9–11). Jehoiakim killed the prophet Uriah for prophesying Jerusalem's fall (Jer. 26:20–23) and burned Jeremiah's handwritten prophecy (Jer. 36).

God's Answer to Habakkuk: The Babylonians (1:5–11)

I am raising up the Chaldeans (1:6). The term "Chaldean" is often used synonymously with "Babylonian" (see the article "The Babylonians"). The Lord turned the prophet's attention to the broader international situation. Nabopolassar had destroyed Nineveh in 612 BC, and his successor, Nebuchadnezzar II, was about to defeat Egypt and Assyria at the battle of Carchemish and make Jehoiakim his vassal (605 BC). In 597 BC he would also capture Jerusalem and deport Jehoiakim's successor, King Jehoiachin, to Babylon.

Their horses . . . their horsemen (1:8). Nebuchadnezzar's cavalry was legendary for its speed, pursuing Egyptian imperial forces more than 150 miles to destroy them completely immediately after the battle at Carchemish.

Fortress . . . seige ramps (1:10). Judah had numerous heavily fortified cities. At Lachish, one of Judah's strongest fortresses, the outer wall was more than eighteen feet thick with a six-chambered main gate. Sieges against such fortifications included the building of earthen ramps to bring massive battering rams against the walls and gates or to allow troops to climb over the walls.

Habakkuk's Question and God's Answer: Wait for the Judgment (1:12–2:20)

Write down this vision; clearly inscribe it on tablets (2:2). Temple prophets such as Habakkuk often were literate. Important messages in the ancient Near East often were

An Assyrian soldier holding the reins of a cavalry horse.

inscribed on stelae (stone, wood, or clay) and taken to public squares, where the literate could read them out loud for the populace.

For the vision is yet for the appointed time (2:3). The way of faith required waiting for the Lord's vindication during seventy years of exile in Babylon.

His ego is inflated (2:4). The Hebrew word translated as "inflated" (NIV: "puffed up") is an expression that alludes to being swollen like a tumor. Here it refers to being swollen with presumptuous pride.

Won't all of these take up a taunt against him (2:6). These five "woe" taunts (2:6–20) refer to Babylon's future defeat of Jerusalem. After Jerusalem's surrender in 597 BC the Babylonian king Nebuchadnezzar took Jehoiachin, king of Judah, to Babylon along with most of the educated and skilled population of Jerusalem. The monarchy of Judah ended with Zedekiah propped up by Nebuchadnezzar as Judah's last king (597–586 BC). In Babylon the "woes" of Habakkuk would provide hope and perspective for the captive exiles.

Woe to him who (2:6–20). Five "woe" oracles are introduced as taunts in 2:6–20. The Hebrew word translated as "woe" in this context could be understood as a simple exclamation ("Hey!") introducing the taunts. However, this word is also used as a cry ("Woe!") in funeral dirges, and the captivity setting would suggest that understanding. Captives usually did not taunt their persecutors, but these exiles would have God's voice as a prophetic weapon of hope.

The earth will be filled with the knowledge of the Lord's glory (2:14). This is the centerpiece of the five woes within the oracle and the physical center of the book. It declared the international scope of God's purpose (see Exod. 9:16; Num. 14:21; Isa. 11:9).

A carved idol (2:18–19). Every culture of the ancient Near East carved wood, cast metal, or fashioned stone with tools to create idols (cf. Exod. 20:4–6; Isa. 44:9–20).

Habakkuk's Conclusion: I Will Wait and Rejoice (3:1–19)

According to *Shigionoth* (3:1). The third chapter of Habakkuk is a psalm. It reflects Habakkuk's final response to the Lord. The exact meaning of *Shigionoth* is not known, but it is clearly associated with a musical setting (cf. Ps. 7:1), further affirmed by the closing note in 3:19. This song has three musical stanzas (3:3–8; 9–13a; 13b–15), each marked by the Hebrew word *selah*.

God came from Teman, the Holy One from Mount Paran (3:3). Teman is in southern Palestine, and the Paran Mountains are on the eastern edge of the Sinai Peninsula. God's formation of Israel began there after their deliverance from the Egyptian army at the sea (Exod. 14–15).

Selah (3:3, 9, 13). *Selah* is a term used as a musical indicator, although its exact meaning is uncertain. There are three basic proposed meanings: (1) indicating a doxological interlude; (2) indicating a repetition; (3) signaling a time of bowing.[1] It occurs seventy-one times in the book of Psalms.

The tents of Cushan (3:7). The Hebrew word translated as "Cushan" occurs only here in the Bible, and apparently it refers to a group of people associated with the Midianites. They are not to be confused with the Cushites, who were located south of Egypt (see the article "The Cushites").

The tent curtains of the land of Midian tremble (3:7). The trembling of the tent curtains is idiomatic of severe fear and distress due to the fact that the Creator himself was present, fighting for Israel (cf. Num. 31:7; Judg. 3:10). In Israel's history God had used an earthquake (Josh. 6), torrential rains (Judg. 4–5), a thunderstorm (1 Sam. 7), wind (2 Sam. 5), and a plague (2 Kings 18–19) to rout Israel's enemies.

You took the sheath from your bow; the arrows are ready (3:9–13a). The second stanza begins with the Lord as a bowman (cf. Deut. 32:23; Ezek. 5:16). The collage of images that follows was based on Israel's memories of the Lord's deliverance of them in the past (cf. Josh. 10; Ps. 77:11–20).

You crush the leader of the house of the wicked (3:13b–15). This third stanza describes the memory of victory over the pharaoh of Egypt back in the book of Exodus. The "crushing " (cf. Ps. 74:12–14) recalls that the Lord established cosmic order and

Basalt rock carving of Assyrian soldiers with bows and maces.

justice (Job 26:12–13; Ps. 89:9–10; Isa. 27:1; 51:9–10). This hope would help Habakkuk's congregation face the impending devastation, for it indicated that the Lord eventually would defeat Babylon too.

I heard, and I trembled within (3:16). The psalm concludes with Habakkuk's honest fear about the impending Babylonian conquest. Although terror stricken, he accepted that the Lord would work in a new and unsettling way to accomplish his purpose.

Though the fig tree does not bud . . . yet I will celebrate in the Lord (3:17–18). The prophet named the primary agricultural commerce of the OT world: figs, grapes, olives, produce, sheep, and cattle. Even in their absence, without immediate economic evidence of favor, Habakkuk was resolved to rejoice in the Lord.

For the choir director: on stringed instruments (3:19). See comments on Hab. 3:1.

Zephaniah

Jason S. DeRouchie

Introduction. Zephaniah, a contemporary with Jeremiah in his early years (and perhaps Nahum and Habakkuk), prophesied during the days of King Josiah of Judah (640–609 BC), prior to the destruction of Jerusalem by the Babylonians (586 BC). His preaching probably aided with Josiah's reforms around 622 BC (2 Kings 23:4–20; 2 Chron. 34:8–35:19). See the introduction in the commentary on Jeremiah.

Superscription (1:1)

Zephaniah son of Cushi (1:1). Zephaniah's father is named "Cushi" ("the Cushite"), connecting him to ancient Cush, the powerful and influential black African empire along the Nile River, south of Egypt, in what is modern-day Sudan (see the article "The Cushites"). Perhaps his father was an ethnic Cushite, or perhaps he looked like a Cushite (perhaps one of his parents was a Cushite), or perhaps he was named "Cushi" in honor of the Cushites, who had been allies with Judah against the Assyrians.[1]

Son of Hezekiah (1:1). Zephaniah's great-great-grandfather probably was King Hezekiah, the faithful reformer and thirteenth king of Judah (729–686 BC) (2 Kings 18–20; Isa. 36–38). Listing four generations of ancestors was unusual, and this connection to King Hezekiah may be the reason for it.

Josiah (1:1). Josiah was Hezekiah's great-grandson, a good king who reigned in Judah from 640 to 609 BC and instituted much-needed religious reform (2 Kings 22:1–23:20; cf. 2 Chron. 34:3–35:19).

Setting: A Call to Revere God (1:2–18)

I will completely sweep away everything (1:2). This echoes the warning that God gave to Noah just prior to the flood (Gen. 6:7).

I will cut off every vestige of Baal (1:4). Baal was a prominent Canaanite god, the god of storms, rain, and thus fertility (see the article "The Canaanites and Canaanite Religion").

The pagan priests along with the priests (1:4). This suggests two corrupt groups of apostate priests: illegitimate priests of non-Levitical descent (1 Kings 12:31–32; 13:33–34) and legitimate but still apostate Levitical priests.

Who bow in worship on the rooftops to the stars in the sky (1:5). See comments on Deut. 17:3; 2 Kings 17:16. Astral deities were common in the ancient Near East. Although strictly forbidden by God (Deut. 4:19; 17:3–7), they were worshiped both in the northern kingdom of Israel (2 Kings 17:16) and in the southern kingdom of Judah (2 Kings 21:3–21; Jer. 8:2; 19:13).

Pledge loyalty to Milcom (1:5). Milcom (or Molech) is an Ammonite god, often associated with child sacrifice (Lev. 18:21; 20:2–5). Yet this term could also be translated as "their king," in which case it would be a reference to Baal, the Canaanite deity mentioned in 1:4.

He has consecrated his guests (1:7). This likely refers to the Babylonians, whom the Lord consecrated to destroy Judah (cf. Isa. 13:3).

The officials, the king's sons (1:8). These were Judah's public leaders as well as members of the royal court.

All who are dressed in foreign clothing (1:8). This may indicate foreign influence in the royal court. Some suggest that it refers to priests who worship foreign gods and thus dress in that foreign tradition.[2]

Mesopotamian king with astral deities above.

All who skip over the threshold (1:9). This probably is a reference to a pagan superstition about the entryway into a temple (1 Sam. 5:3–5).

Fish Gate . . . Second District (1:10). The Fish Gate was one of the main gates in Jerusalem, located on the vulnerable northern wall (2 Chron. 33:14; Neh. 3:3). The Second District (NIV: "New Quarter") was an expansion of Jerusalem west of the Temple Mount started during the reign of Hezekiah (2 Kings 22:14; 2 Chron. 34:22).

The Hollow (1:11). The "Hollow," or "market district" (CSB footnote; NIV), probably was located in one of the depressions in the Tyropoeon Valley, between the Temple Mount and the Second District.

Who settle down comfortably (1:12). Literally, the Hebrew phrase is "who thicken on their dregs." The idiom refers to wine that would thicken and become syrupy at the bottom of the container (the dregs). The implication is that the people were indifferent and unmoved by the prophetic preaching.

Their silver and their gold (1:18). Sometimes an invading army could be bought off by paying it tribute of silver and gold (cf. 1 Kings 20:3–4). But in this case—the invasion by the Lord—that would prove ineffective. Alternatively, often idols were constructed of silver and gold, and this may be a metaphorical reference to the ineffectiveness of the idols to deliver Jerusalem.

Seek the Lord Together to Avoid Punishment (2:1–3:7)

Gaza . . . Ashkelon . . . Ashdod . . . Ekron (2:4). These are four of the five main Philistine cities, which the Babylonian king Nebuchadnezzar destroyed in 600 BC (see the article "The Philistines"). Gath's absence from the list suggests its earlier destruction by the Assyrians (Amos 6:2).

Philistines . . . Ammonites . . . Cushites . . . Assyria (2:5–15). See the articles "The Philistines"; "The Cushites"; "The Assyrians." Zephaniah builds a "compass" of punishment around Judah: the Philistines to the west (2:5–7), the Moabites and Ammonites to the east (2:8–11), and the imperial powers of the Cushites and Assyrians to the south and north (2:12–15).

Cherethites (2:5). The Cherethites are closely affiliated with the Philistines (Ezek. 25:16), and are perhaps a subgroup whose origin is associated with the island of Crete (see the article "The Philistines").

Moab . . . Ammonites (2:8). Ammon and Moab were two neighboring countries to the east of Judah (see comments on Gen. 19:37–38).

Like Sodom . . . like Gomorrah (2:9). The destruction of Sodom and Gomorrah by God, described in Gen. 19:24–25, is used here as a graphic metaphor for upcoming terrible judgment on Moab and Ammon. The connection between this story and the Moabites and Ammonites is ironic, for

Lot, the main character in the story of Sodom and Gomorrah, who survives the judgment, was the progenitor of both the Moabites and Ammonites (Gen. 19:30–38), those who will now be judged as if in Sodom and Gomorrah.

Nineveh (2:13). Nineveh was the capital of Assyria, destroyed by the Babylonians in 612 BC (see the article "The Assyrians").

Roaring lions (3:3). Throughout the ancient Near East rulers often were depicted as lions in order to emphasize their strength and power (see comments on Nah. 2:11–13). Here, these "lions" are preying on the very people they were to protect.

Wait on the Lord to Enjoy Satisfying Salvation (3:8–20)

Beyond the rivers of Cush (3:10). This likely refers to the White Nile and the Blue Nile, the two main tributaries of the Nile River that were associated with the empire of Cush (cf. Isa 18:1–2), which lay to the south of Egypt (see the article "The Cushites").

My holy mountain (3:11). This is a reference to Mount Zion in Jerusalem (Ps. 121:1–2; 125:1–2; Isa. 2:2).

The Lord your God is among you, a warrior who saves (3:17). The image of the Lord as a powerful warrior who fights and defeats Israel's enemies is common in the OT (e.g., Ps. 24:8; Isa. 42:13; 59:17). Likewise, throughout the ancient Near East numerous deities were described and depicted as strong, valiant warriors (see comments on Isa. 59:17).

Haggai

George Athas

Introduction. Haggai addressed his oracles to the fledgling community of Judeans who had returned to Jerusalem from the exile in Babylon. Nebuchadnezzar originally had deported some Judeans to Babylon in 597 BC, and then again in 586 BC, when Jerusalem and its temple were destroyed. These Judeans were settled in Babylon, where eventually they prospered as farmers, laborers, soldiers, and businessmen. However, in 539 BC the Persian king Cyrus conquered Babylon, and in the following year he decreed that conquered peoples could return to their homelands to rebuild the temples of their gods (see the section on Cyrus in the article "The Persians"). This posed a dilemma for the Judeans. Should they remain in the land of their exile, or should they return to their distant homeland to rebuild Jerusalem and its temple?

A small group of Judeans returned, led by Zerubbabel and Joshua. Scholars often talk of their return occurring soon after Cyrus's decree in 538 BC, based on the account in Ezra 1–3. Ezra does not date these happenings with reference to external events. Haggai, however, gives precise dates for his ministry. His oracles impel the returnees to begin construction of the Lord's temple in 520 BC, which suggests that the return to Jerusalem had occurred just a year or two earlier.[1] Haggai's ministry was closely associated with that of Zechariah (Ezra 5:1; 6:14).

First Oracle (1:1–12)

In the second year of King Darius (1:1). See the article "The Persians." Darius I came to power in dubious circumstances. The previous king, Cambyses son of Cyrus, died unexpectedly in 522 BC without an heir. His brother, Bardiya, was killed at about the same time in mysterious circumstances. This plunged the Persian Empire into disarray. Numerous rebellions broke out across the empire as people groups declared their own independence. In the Behistun inscription, Darius son of Hystaspes states that he sought to rectify the situation by taking power and putting down the rebellions. Hostilities continued for the first few years of Darius's reign. It was during this period of upheaval that Haggai prophesied.

On the first day of the sixth month (1:1). This is datable to August 29, 520 BC.

Zerubbabel son of Shealtiel, the governor of Judah (1:1). Zerubbabel was the grandson of Judah's penultimate king, Jehoiachin (1 Chron. 3:16–19). Zerubbabel was born during the exile in Babylon, but he led the return to Jerusalem (Ezra 2:2; Neh. 12:1). Since he was the rightful heir to the Davidic throne, it was incumbent on him to rebuild the temple of the Lord (cf. 2 Sam. 7:11b–16). The title "governor of Judah," however, indicates that Zerubbabel was not an independent king but rather a subordinate to the Persian authorities.

The ruins at Persepolis of the palace of the Persian king Darius I.

Joshua son of Jehozadak, the high priest (1:1). Joshua was the grandson of Jerusalem's last serving high priest, Seraiah (1 Chron. 6:14–15).

A time for you yourselves to live in your paneled houses (1:4). The Hebrew word translated as "paneled" can mean either "paneled" or "roofed." Thus this verse can refer either to expensive cedar wall paneling, usually something only the very wealthy could possibly afford (1 Kings 7:7; Jer. 22:14), or to the fact that the houses were roofed and thus finished or complete (in contrast to the unfinished temple).

You have planted much but harvested little (1:6). Haggai sees the agricultural and economic failures during the early years of the return to Jerusalem as evidence that the community had failed in its obligations to the Lord as lord of the land. This dynamic stems from the integral relationship between God, the people, and the land, as established in the book of Deuteronomy (28:15–24). In this case, Haggai attributes the community's economic failure to their delay in building the Lord's temple (1:7–11; 2:15–19).

Second Oracle (1:13–15)

The house of the Lord of Armies (1:14). The "house" (i.e., the temple) was not just the place where God's presence resided and where sacrifices could be made; it was also the physical symbol of the Lord's covenant with David and his dynasty. In accordance with this covenant, it was the task of the Davidic heir to build and maintain the Lord's temple in Jerusalem (2 Sam. 7:11b–16). Furthermore, the Lord ruled his people through the Davidic dynasty. The initiation of temple construction was, therefore, the first step in restoring a Davidic kingdom.

On the twenty-fourth day of the sixth month (1:15). This is datable to September 21, 520 BC.

Third Oracle (2:1–9)

On the twenty-first day of the seventh month (2:1). This date comes a few days after the Day of Atonement and coincides with the celebration of the weeklong Festival of Shelters. It can be calculated to be October 17, 520 BC.

I am going to shake the heavens and the earth (2:6). Cosmic cataclysm is often used as a vivid way of talking about "groundbreaking" events.

I will fill this house with glory (2:7). The term "glory" has many nuances in reference to temples. First, it can refer to the crafting of luxurious articles for use in the temple. Second, it can refer to wealth stored in the temple, much like a bank. Third, it can refer to prestige and honor, pertaining both to the architecture and the reputation of the deity. Finally, it can refer to the presence of God. When Solomon dedicated his temple some 440 years earlier, the "glory of the LORD filled his temple" (1 Kings 8:11 NIV) in the form of a cloud, temporarily preventing the priests from performing their duties (cf. Ezek. 11:22–23).

Fourth Oracle (2:10–19)

On the twenty-fourth day of the ninth month (2:10). This was December 18, 520 BC, three months after construction of the temple began.

If . . . consecrated meat . . . touches bread . . . does it become holy? (2:12–14). Meat sacrificed on the altar was considered holy ("consecrated"), but this status was not transferrable to other things by contact with the meat. Consecration required specific sacrifices and was not "contagious." However, an unclean person or thing could "defile" another by mere contact, even if that other person or thing had been holy. In order to acquire holiness again, a defiled person or thing had to be cleansed and then consecrated through appropriate ritual, usually sacrifice.

Fifth Oracle (2:20–23)

I will overturn royal thrones and destroy the power of the Gentile kingdoms (2:22). Rebellions broke out across the Persian Empire after the deaths of Cambyses and Bardiya in 522 BC (see the article "The Persians"). In the Behistun inscription Darius claims to have killed an imposter king, though historians today believe that this is propaganda meant to cover up the assassination of Bardiya. In any case, Darius eventually quelled all rebellions by 517 BC.

Zerubbabel . . . like my signet ring (2:23). A signet ring bore a personal insignia that could be stamped into wax or clay to indicate the authorization of its owner, with much the same effect as a signature today. In 597 BC, God described Zerubbabel's grandfather, King Jehoiachin, as a signet ring that he was tearing off his finger (Jer. 22:24–30). This symbolized God's rejection of him and his exile to Babylon. The image here is a specific reversal of this, and it hails the reinstatement of the Davidic royal family in the purposes of God.

Zechariah

George Athas

Introduction. Zechariah prophesied to the small community of Judeans who had returned from exile in Babylon to rebuild Jerusalem. His ministry was associated with that of Haggai (see the introduction in the commentary on Haggai). Zechariah's initial prophecies addressed the community's resolve to rebuild the temple of the Lord in what was a chaotic time in the Persian Empire. Political turmoil had erupted in 522 BC after the Persian king Cambyses, son of Cyrus, died unexpectedly without an heir. Numerous nations used this uncertainty to declare independence from Persia. Darius, son of Hystaspes, eventually quelled these rebellions, but it took him some years to do so (see the article "The Persians"). It was during this time that the community in Jerusalem, under the leadership of Zerubbabel, laid the foundations for the rebuilt temple. It is possible, though not certain, that Zerubbabel also declared independence from Persia at this time, causing neighboring groups and the Persian authorities to interrupt his building efforts (Ezra 4:1–5, 24). Zechariah's lengthy vision (Zech. 1:7–6:8) addresses Jerusalem's dilemma in the face of uncertainty about the temple-building program.

The book of Zechariah also looks beyond this time, with most of the second half of the book (chaps. 9–14) coming from later periods. Some scholars date parts of this material to later in Zechariah's lifetime, while other scholars date it to sometime after Zechariah, possibly even as late as the fourth century BC. Regardless of the time frame, the book begins with an optimistic view of the possibility of restoring God's kingdom in the land of Judah. However, it moves toward a pessimistic view of history, in which

God's people are continually opposed by others, riddled by poor leadership, and ultimately disappointed in their restoration efforts. It ends, however, with an almost apocalyptic hope for God to intervene in history supernaturally and to inaugurate a totally new age.

First Oracle (1:1–6)

In the eighth month, in the second year of Darius (1:1). This is datable to November 520 BC, when the Persian king Darius (522–486 BC) was still in the process of curbing rebellions across the Persian Empire. Zerubbabel laid the temple foundations just prior to this (Ezra 3:1–8).

Zechariah's Vision (1:7–6:8)

On the twenty-fourth day of the eleventh month . . . in the second year of Darius (1:7). This is datable to February 15, 519 BC. At this time Darius sent forces to put down a rebellion in Egypt. This army must have passed through Judah, reinforcing Persian control over that region as it went. This dovetails with the report that construction of the temple in Jerusalem halted at the intervention of the Persian authorities (Ezra 4:24).

A man riding on a chestnut horse (1:8). In the ancient Near East horses generally were not associated with farming or viewed as a transportation method for regular people, but were associated almost exclusively with armies or royal messengers. The Persian army used both mounted cavalry and horse-drawn chariots, along with an extensive communication system via horseback. The Behistun inscription (western Iran) and documents from Egypt recount how Darius coordinated his forces with messengers to quash numerous rebellions all across the Persian Empire. Zechariah's vision of supernatural mounted riders and chariots (6:1–8) seems to align Darius's army with the will of the Lord.

Seventy years (1:12). According to Jeremiah, Judah's exile would last seventy years (Jer. 25:11–12; 29:10).

I am extremely jealous for Jerusalem and Zion (1:14). Zion (cf. 1:17; 2:7, 10; 8:2–3; 9:9, 13) was the fortress in Jerusalem originally captured by David (2 Sam. 5:6–10). The term is therefore specifically associated with the rule of the Davidic dynasty.

The nations that are at ease (1:15). Between 522 and 518 BC the Persian king Darius faced numerous rebellions from nations that felt confident enough to assert independence from Persia. Not one of these rebellions was successful, as Darius points out publicly in the Behistun inscription, where he lists each rebellion and how he crushed it.

I looked up and saw four horns (1:18). The horns of a bull were symbols of brute power, here standing for nations (chiefly Assyria and Babylonia) that had figuratively "gored" and "tossed" God's people.

I saw a man with a measuring line in his hand (2:1). See comments on Ezek. 40:3.

Jerusalem will be inhabited without walls (2:4). The Babylonians had broken down Jerusalem's walls when they captured the city in 586 BC. Zerubbabel naturally would have wanted to rebuild them, especially if he was planning to forge an independent kingdom of Judah.

The high priest Joshua (3:1). Joshua was the grandson of Jerusalem's last serving high priest, Seraiah (2 Kings 25:18–21). Along with Zerubbabel, he supervised construction of the temple (Ezra 3:8–9). His close association with Zerubbabel means that he may have been involved in trying to establish Zerubbabel as king of an independent Judah.

Human-headed winged lions like this one guarded the entrances to the palaces of Assyrian kings. These guardians wore caps with bull horns, symbolizing divinity and power.

On that one stone there are seven eyes (3:9). Temples in the ancient Near East usually had a dedication stone naming the royal builder or patron (cf. modern-day dedication plaques). This stone is placed not before Zerubbabel, as expected, but Joshua. This suggests that Joshua had to take over construction of the temple because Zerubbabel was absent, perhaps because the Persians arrested him for perceived rebellion. Furthermore, Darius instituted a spy system throughout his empire to discourage rebellion. These spies were known as the "eyes of the king," and they reported directly to Darius.

I see a solid gold lampstand (4:2). The lampstand was a basic part of the temple furnishings. While the tabernacle had only one golden lampstand, Solomon's temple contained ten golden lampstands (1 Kings 7:49). The temple in the NT that had been built by King Herod appears to have had one large golden lampstand. In addition to providing light, the continual flame probably symbolized the presence of God.

Two olive trees (4:3). Ancient Judah was known as a center of olive oil production. Olive oil was used in cooking, for fueling lamps, for medicinal and cosmetic purposes, and for anointing ceremonies. Since olive trees took many years to grow and to begin to produce, they were prized resources. Keeping the temple lampstand continually burning necessitated a secure supply of olive oil to the temple.

Limestone box placed in the ground, containing dedication tablets.

Zerubbabel (4:6). Zerubbabel's grandfather Jehoiachin ruled Judah for just three months in 597 BC before he surrendered to the Babylonian king Nebuchadnezzar and was exiled to Babylon (2 Kings 24:8–15). As his direct descendant, Zerubbabel would have been a focus of royal hope for the Judean exiles who returned to rebuild Jerusalem. The Davidic covenant (2 Sam. 7:8–16) informed these hopes, as the Lord had committed himself to ruling his covenant people through a Davidic king. The temple in Jerusalem was the physical symbol of this covenant. It was a permanent structure, because the Davidic covenant was to be a permanent institution. One of the central roles of any Davidic king was, therefore, to build and maintain the temple as the essential covenant symbol. The subsequent exile and destruction of the temple were a massive challenge to this understanding. By constructing the temple, then, Zerubbabel was taking the first step in the restoration of a Davidic kingdom and enacting the Lord's zeal for Zion (Zech. 1:14). If, as many scholars surmise, the Persians then removed Zerubbabel from Jerusalem, the community would have been thrown into confusion about his future, as well as God's will for them. Zerubbabel most likely returned, though, as Zechariah stakes his prophetic reputation on Zerubbabel completing the temple (4:9; cf. 9:9). The temple was dedicated three years later in 516 BC (Ezra 6:14–22).

There was a woman sitting inside the basket . . . "This is Wickedness" (5:7–8). The "basket" is specifically an "ephah," which could hold approximately six gallons of a dry substance. The woman inside the small container is named "Wickedness." The Hebrew term translated as "wickedness" is *harishah,* no doubt a wordplay on the word *asherah* ("blessed one"). "Asherah" is also the name of a pagan goddess (see comments on 1 Kings 15:13), and thus the point of this wordplay probably is to characterize the idol of the goddess Asherah as wickedness. Before the exile, people in Judah blasphemously worshiped Asherah as the Lord's consort and "queen of heaven" (Jer. 7:18; 44:17–19). The few people left behind in Judah during the exile and those in Samaria to the north most likely continued to worship Asherah. As the Lord's temple was being rebuilt, some may have expected Asherah to be worshiped there again.

The land of the north (6:8). This is a reference to Mesopotamia. Since the Arabian Desert lay directly east of Israel and Judah, armies coming from Mesopotamia had to approach from the north. Thus when the Lord describes to Jeremiah the coming Babylonian invasion of Judah, he says that he will summon "all the clans and kingdoms of the north" (Jer. 1:13–16).

Epilogue to Zechariah's Vision (6:9–15)

A man whose name is Branch (6:12). The term "branch" was synonymous with Davidic kingship. Jeremiah looks forward to the Lord raising up a new and righteous "Branch" (Jer. 23:5; 33:15). Isaiah looks to a "shoot" arising from the "stump" of Jesse (David's father), expressing hope for the renewal and reinvigoration of kingship arising from the "felled" Davidic dynasty (Isa. 11:1). Since Davidic kingship was closely associated with the Jerusalem temple (2 Sam. 7:8–16), Zerubbabel would have been viewed as the new "Branch," and therefore been the focus of royal hopes. Yet here Zechariah is told to invest Joshua, the high priest, as the new "Branch." Scholars have debated the significance of this. One possibility is the promotion of the priesthood to the same level of authority as the Davidic ruler, thus creating hope for a dyarchy. A more plausible reason is that Joshua is commissioned as "Acting Branch" while Zerubbabel is absent.

Oracle about Mourning and Fasting (7:1–8:23)

In the fourth year of King Darius . . . on the fourth day of the ninth month (7:1). This can be dated to December 7, 518 BC. By this time Darius had pacified most of his empire, and the temple in Jerusalem was nearing completion.

Bethel (7:2). Bethel lay twelve miles north of Jerusalem. It had been the site of a major worship center built by Jeroboam I in the late tenth century BC (1 Kings 12:28–33). It is unknown whether this shrine survived into the postexilic era.

Should we mourn and fast in the fifth month? (7:3). Fasts were days of communal mourning. This particular fast probably commemorated the destruction of the Jerusalem temple by the Babylonians in 586 BC (2 Kings 25:8).

Fasted and lamented in the fifth and in the seventh months (7:5). This latter fast, in the seventh month, probably commemorated the assassination of Gedaliah, son of Ahikam, whom the Babylonians appointed governor after they conquered Jerusalem in 586 BC. After Gedaliah's assassination in 582 BC the Babylonians took over direct rule of Judah, and many of the last remaining people in Judah fled the country (2 Kings 25:22–26; Jer. 40:6–43:7).

The fast of the fourth month . . . and the fast of the tenth (8:19). The fast of the fourth month probably commemorated the day in 586 BC when the Babylonians breached Jerusalem's walls and captured Jerusalem (2 Kings 25:3–6; Jer. 39:2–5). The fast of the tenth month probably remembered the beginning of the Babylonian siege of Jerusalem in 588 BC (2 Kings 25:1; Jer. 39:1).

An Oracle (9:1–11:17)

Hadrach . . . Ekron (9:1–8). All the cities mentioned in these verses were centers located on major ancient highways. It is likely that Darius's armies moved through them to assert his authority on his way to Egypt in 519 BC. Alexander the Great also asserted sovereignty over these cities when he followed a similar path after the battle of Issus in 333 BC. The list of cities therefore evokes images of foreign conquerors, showing how Jerusalem was virtually powerless to resist them. Yet it also shows how God was protecting his people and temple, keeping alive their hope for full restoration (9:8).

Tyre (9:3). See comments on Ezek. 26:2. Zechariah 9:3 uses skillful wordplay in Hebrew to allude to Tyre's downfall in 332 BC.

There will cease to be a king in Gaza (9:5). After Alexander the Great's conquest of Tyre in 332 BC, the only city in the region that resisted him was Gaza. Yet just two weeks after arriving in Gaza, Alexander captured the city and had its ruler, Batis, brutally executed by tying him behind a bolting horse.

A mongrel people will live in Ashdod (9:6). The Hebrew literally says, "A bastard will sit in Ashdod." Ashdod was a Philistine city on the Mediterranean coast. The phrase may refer to the mixing of populations, or it may be an allusion to Alexander the Great, whose mother purportedly conceived him by Zeus.

Your King is coming to you; he is righteous and victorious (9:9). The Hebrew phrase actually says "righteous and rescued." While scholars often see this as an expression of hope in a future messiah, it originally probably referred to the Persians' acquittal and release of Zerubbabel and his subsequent return to Jerusalem

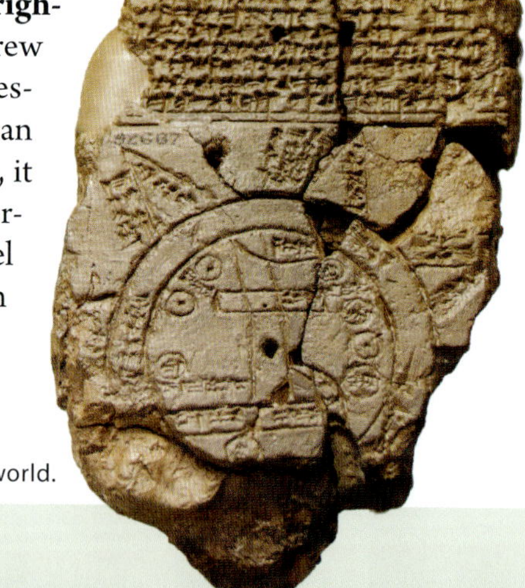

A Babylonian map of the world.

(cf. 4:9). In subsequent generations, though, this certainly took on a more eschatological significance.

Return to a stronghold, you prisoners who have hope (9:12). Some scholars understand this figuratively with reference to the return from exile. However, the connection to an acquitted and liberated royal figure (9:9) means that this probably referred in the first instance to Zerubbabel being released by the Persians. An unusual Hebrew word for "fortress" is used here (*bitsaron*), which sounds similar to the Hebrew phrase "in Zion" (*betsiyyon*). This gives the passage strong Davidic overtones (2 Sam. 5:6–10).

Judah . . . Ephraim (9:13). Judah and Ephraim were the two major tribes representing the southern kingdom of Judah and the northern kingdom of Israel. The nation had not been united since the late tenth century BC. Yet this did not quell hopes of the nation's full restoration under a Davidic king, even though this looked increasingly unlikely as history unfolded. In the later postexilic era the two halves of the nation emerged respectively as the Jewish and Samaritan communities.

Greece (9:13). Greek merchants and mercenaries had been known in Syria and Palestine for centuries. David's Cherethite and Pelethite soldiers most likely were Greek mercenaries (2 Sam. 8:18). Darius was the first Persian king to invade the Greek region, and his armies probably included Judeans. His son Xerxes (486–465 BC) continued the effort, though ultimately he was repelled. During the conquests by Alexander the Great in the late fourth century BC, Greeks took political control of Judah. This enabled the spread of Hellenism, which some perceived as a threat to the Jewish way of life. This ultimately led to the Maccabean Revolt in 167 BC. See the article "Intertestamental History."

Thirty pieces of silver (11:12). A slave was valued at thirty pieces of silver (Exod. 21:32), as was a woman who had dedicated herself by oath to the Lord (Lev. 27:4). The amount is indicative of low status and the end of a period of service.

May a sword strike his arm and his right eye (11:17). The curse pronounced on the "worthless shepherd" seems to reflect elements of Alexander the Great's career. At his first battle against the Persians at the Granicus River (334 BC), Alexander was struck above the eye and felled from his horse. As

Sarcophagus of Alexander the Great.

his assailant swung to kill him, one of Alexander's men lopped the assailant's arm off just in time to save Alexander. Had this not occurred, Alexander's entire campaign would have come to an end, and Hellenism probably never would have spread to the ancient Near East. Furthermore, Alexander was aided by Antigonus Monophthalmus ("one-eyed"), one of the generals who squabbled over his empire after Alexander's sudden death in 323 BC, and who at one point controlled Syria and Palestine.

An Oracle (12:1–14:21)

Me whom they pierced (12:10). Scholars debate the identity of this figure. Some understand it to be figurative of God himself, while others suggest that it refers to the assassination of a significant figure in the Jerusalem community, perhaps Zechariah himself.

Mourning of Hadad-rimmon (12:11). This seems to be a location in the Valley of Megiddo, which separates the hills of Samaria from Galilee. Some scholars surmise that this refers to the mourning at the unexpected death of King Josiah (2 Kings 23:29–30).

The family of David's house . . . of Nathan's . . . of Levi's . . . of Shimei (12:12–13). While the clans of David and Levi probably refer to the royal family and the priestly families, respectively, scholars are unsure of the identification of Nathan and Shimei here.

I will gather all the nations against Jerusalem for battle (14:2). In the decades after Alexander's death (323 BC), his generals fought one another for the pieces of his empire. Fighting over control of Judah were the generals Ptolemy, Antigonus, and Seleucus. Eventually, Ptolemy of Egypt conquered Jerusalem in 301 BC. He killed a significant portion of Jerusalem's population and deported half the survivors to Alexandria. Many Jews then migrated there in the following decades. This is how the large Jewish community in Alexandria began.

His feet will stand on the Mount of Olives (14:4). This mountain lies to the immediate east of the Temple Mount in Jerusalem. In the ancient world the imagery of a deity placing feet on a significant mountain is associated with both judgment and the bringing of fertility.

The earthquake in the days of King Uzziah (14:5). During the reign of Uzziah (also known as

Ptolemy I, one of Alexander the Great's generals.

Azariah), back in the eighth century BC, a devastating earthquake had struck Israel and Judah. Amos's ministry was associated with this earthquake (Amos 1:1; cf. 8:8; 9:1, 5).

Changed into a plain (14:10). The "plain" (NIV: "Arabah") in view here is the long Rift Valley, which runs the length of the Jordan River and the Dead Sea—the lowest point on the surface of the earth, some 1,300 feet below sea level. Jerusalem sits 2,460 feet above sea level. This verse pictures the land around Jerusalem falling to the level of the Arabah, leaving Jerusalem towering invincibly above the landscape.

Festival of Shelters (14:16). This festival commemorated Israel's exodus from Egypt and time of wandering in the desert on the way to the promised land, as well as the harvest of the land (Lev. 23:33–43).

The people of Egypt (14:18). Some scholars understand this phrase to refer to native Egyptians, but it may refer to Jewish people living in Egypt, such as those whom Ptolemy deported to Alexandria in 301 BC, and others who voluntarily migrated there.

Malachi

William B. Nelson

Introduction. In Protestant Bibles, Malachi is the last book in the OT and also the last of the twelve Minor Prophets. Traditionally, it has been ascribed to a prophet by the name of Malachi, but the word "Malachi" means "my messenger," as it is used in 3:1. Perhaps this is not a proper name at all but rather a title, signifying that the author was the messenger of the Lord. The book was written in the postexilic era after the temple had been rebuilt in 515 BC (1:7–14). Malachi begins with the words "A pronouncement: The word of the Lord." Interestingly, Zech. 9:1 and 12:1 begin the same way. For this reason, some scholars think that perhaps there were originally three independent collections of oracles: Zech. 9–11; Zech. 12–14; Malachi. In the editing of the prophetic corpus the first two were attached to the book of Zechariah, while the last was allowed to stand on its own as a separate book. The author uses a disputation style of writing, communicating the sins of the people or their complaints through a question-and-answer format. The book opens with a superscription, then follow six disputations, and it concludes with two appendices.

Superscription and First Disputation: The Lord Loves Israel (1:1–5)

I loved Jacob, but I hated Esau (1:2–3). Here Malachi is alluding to patriarchal history and the conflict between the twin sons of Isaac: Jacob and

Esau (Gen. 25:27–34; 27:1–45). Jacob became the father of Israel, and Esau became the father of the Edomites. (Edom was the kingdom that bordered Judah to the southeast.) Although Malachi refers to the individuals, he actually is speaking about their descendants: the peoples of Israel and Edom. Although he describes God's attitude toward them in absolute terms—love and hatred—he means that, relatively speaking, God chose Israel over Esau. This is because God made a covenant with his people, the Israelites. The intense hostility between Jacob and Esau in Genesis is exhibited in the later history between the two nations. When the Israelites sought to enter the promised land after the exodus from Egypt, the Edomites met them with well-armed soldiers, forcing the Israelites to go a long way around Edom (Num. 20:14–21). Closer to Malachi's time (the postexilic period), the Edomites had supported the Babylonians when they invaded Judah and sacked Jerusalem (586 BC), gloating over the destruction and participating in the looting (Ps. 137:7; Obad. 10–14). As a result, Edom is singled out for special condemnation by the prophets (Isa. 35:5–17; Jer. 49:7–22; Lam. 4:21–22; Ezek. 25:12–14; 35:1–15; Joel 3:19; Amos 1:11–12; Obad. 1–21). They are "a people always under the wrath of the LORD" (Mal. 1:4 NIV).

Edom (1:4). See comments on Obad. 1. Of the three Transjordan (i.e., across the Jordan River from Israel) countries during OT times, Edom was the southernmost, with Ammon and Moab to the north. Its territory was mostly south and east of the Dead Sea, extending from the Arabah, the Jordan Rift Valley, on the west to the wilderness on the east, and from the Wadi Zered, the border with Moab, on the north to the gulf of Aqabah (biblical

The mountains of Edom.

Elath and Ezion-geber) in the south. However, at times they controlled southern Judah on the western side of the Arabah to the Wilderness of Zin and the Ascent of Akrabbim (Num. 34:3–4; Josh. 15:1–3). King David subdued the Edomites (2 Sam. 8:13–14), and King Solomon built a fleet of ships at the port city of Elath on the Red Sea, from which he engaged in trade with Arabia (1 Kings 9:26; 10:19). However, Edom rebelled against Solomon later in his reign (1 Kings 11:14–22, 25). During the exilic era Edomites expanded into southern Judah; eventually they were displaced by the Nabateans, who invaded from Arabia and ruled from the city of Petra.

Second and Third Disputations: Israel's Father Deserves Honor (1:6–2:9) and the Lord Hates Divorce (2:10–16)

The LORD has been a witness between you and the wife of your youth (2:14). In the fifth century BC, very near the time of Malachi, a colony of Jews inhabited Elephantine, an island in Egypt on the Nile River. Among the many papyri documents discovered on Elephantine are several contracts relating to marriages, dowries, and inheritances.[1] The implication of the terms in these contracts is that these Jews were quite open to divorce, in contrast to 2:10–16.[2]

Fourth Disputation: God Is Just (Part 1) (2:17–3:5)

Like a refiner's fire and like launderer's bleach (3:2). In the ancient Near East launderers burned certain plants to produce a special ash residue. This alkaline residue was used to make soap, a kind of lye that cleanses because of its caustic properties. Malachi may be referring to the purifying of the Levites as one washes clothes. However, since the text also mentions metal refining in the same verse, it is possible that the prophet is describing the process where the chemicals from launderer's soap were used in the smelting process.

Refine them like gold and silver (3:3). Malachi predicts that God will purify the Levites in a "refiner's fire" (3:2) as metalsmiths purify gold and silver. When these precious metals are mined, they are found mixed with other elements, such as lead. With silver, the crude ore was heated in a furnace in order to extract the pure material. During the smelting, hot air was blown over the molten substance, causing oxidation and removal of the dross (cf. Ezek. 22:17–22). Gold was also refined with heat. Sometimes cupellation was used: a small receptacle shaped like a cup or cone was inserted into the liquid to remove the separated silver or gold.

Fifth and Sixth Disputations: God Expects His People to Give (3:6–12) and God Is Just (Part 2) (3:13–4:3)

A book of remembrance (3:16). This scroll probably contains a list of faithful Jews who speak with one another about the Lord (3:16) and obey his commands (3:16–17). They will be God's "treasured possession" (3:17). God is portrayed as a king who keeps track of those who are loyal to him in order to reward them, just as the Persian king Ahasuerus consulted his chronicles and rewarded Mordecai for saving him from assassination (Esther 6). Other scrolls or books are mentioned in the Bible, such as the book of life (Ps. 69:28 [see comments on Exod. 32:32]; Isa. 4:3; Dan. 12:1; Phil. 4:3; Rev. 3:5; 13:8; 17:8; 20:12, 15), books used for judgment (Dan. 7:10; Rev. 20:12), and the book of truth (Dan. 10:21–11:45).

Furnace (4:1). The word translated as "furnace" usually is rendered as "oven." It denotes a fired-clay structure shaped like a cylinder or a beehive and used especially for baking bread. The fire was placed inside, with dried grass and animal dung (Ezek. 4:15) used for fuel. Once the oven was hot, a thin layer of dough was placed on the wall, with the result that it cooked very quickly. Because of its great heat, its flames, and its destructive power to consume things, the oven or furnace became an apt metaphor for God's judgment, as here when Malachi predicts that the arrogant ones and evildoers will be consumed (cf. Ps. 21:9; Isa. 31:9).

The sun of righteousness will rise with healing in its wings (4:2). This image of the sun disk with wings is fairly common in ancient Near Eastern art and iconography. It signifies the benevolence of the deity. Just as the sun provides light and warmth, so God provides his presence, protection, and blessing for his people. Shamash, the Mesopotamian sun god, was understood to be the god of justice, so it is natural for Malachi to critique, correct, and borrow the image, applying it to the Lord, the God of Israel—he, not Shamash, is the sun of righteousness. Elsewhere, God is once called a sun (Ps. 84:11), but sun-like qualities often are ascribed to God: light, shining, and glory (e.g., Num. 6:24–26; Isa. 60:1).

First and Second Appendices (4:4–6)

Horeb (4:4). "Horeb" is another name for Mount Sinai, where the Lord revealed himself to Moses in the burning bush and where he then later established a covenant with Israel after delivering them from Egypt (see comments on Exod. 3:1; 19:1–2).

Intertestamental History

Larry R. Helyer

Definition. The term "intertestamental period" refers to the years intervening between the closing of the OT canon (ca. 400–165 BC) and the composition of the NT (ca. AD 48–95).[1] Many scholars prefer to designate this era as the Second Temple period, spanning the years from the destruction of the First Temple in 586 BC down to the destruction of the Second Temple in AD 70 and its aftermath in the Bar Kokhba Revolt of AD 132–35.

Importance. The importance of this era can scarcely be overemphasized for an in-depth study of the NT, because the roots of Christianity reach back into this formative period, which significantly impacted its development. Since Second Temple Judaism itself is rooted in the ancestral faith of Israel as enshrined in the Hebrew Bible, Hebraic thought is the matrix out of which the message of the NT emerges.[2]

Rather than using an expression such as "the silent years" to designate this period, one must be aware that Jews were not silent; on the contrary, they continued to reflect on God and his dealings with the world, especially his chosen people, Israel. Jewish literature produced during the intertestamental period (often referred to as the literature of Second Temple Judaism) is rich and opens a window into the important history and the thought world of this era.

Survey of the Period

Five great crises, like tsunamis, radically reshaped the cultural and historical landscape of the intertestamental period. The surviving literature reflects these epochal transitions.

The Destruction of Judah and the First Temple (586 BC). The Neo-Babylonian conquest of Judah and the destruction of its crown jewel, the First Temple (2 Kings 23–25; 2 Chron. 36), devastated the land and dispersed refugees and survivors across the region. Only the poorest remained to care for the land (2 Kings 25:12, 22). This dispersion ushered in the development of diaspora Judaism, a phenomenon that continues to this day. The OT prophets interpreted this disaster as the fulfillment of the Lord's solemn warning about continued violations of the Sinai covenant (Exod. 24; Lev. 26:14–39; Deut. 28:15–68; Jer. 1–5; Ezek. 5–24). The shattering reality of exile for the majority of Jews raised troubling questions: Was God finished with his chosen people? What could be done to regain his favor? Jewish literature of the Second Temple period reflects on this problem and offers various responses.

Collapse of the Persian Empire and the Coming of Hellenism. The Persian king Cyrus (559–530 BC) crushed the Neo-Babylonian Empire and founded the Achaemenid Persian Empire, the largest the Middle East had yet seen—one that endured for two centuries (539–331 BC) (see the section on Cyrus in the article "The Persians"). Cyrus secured for himself an honored place in Jewish history as the benevolent monarch who permitted Jews (among others) to return to their ancestral homeland and rebuild their temple, the famed Second Temple (Ezra 1:1–4; 3:1–13; 6:13–18). During this period Judah (called "Yehud" in the ancient sources from this era) was a tiny administrative district in a larger province designated as "Trans-Euphrates" (Ezra 4:11 NIV). A large majority of Jews, however, chose not to return (Ezra 2:64–65). Most of these were farmers and herdsmen (Jer. 29); some were artisans, traders, and merchants; a small number held administrative jobs in the Persian government; and a select few even rose to positions of great influence and power (Neh. 2:1; 5:14; Esther 2:5, 19–23; 3:2; Dan. 1–6; see also, in a Jewish literary work from this era, Tob. 1:12–14).

The conquest of the Persian Empire by Alexander the Great (331 BC) was nothing short of a cultural revolution.[3] More than a military conqueror, Alexander was a missionary for Hellenism (i.e., the all-encompassing aspects of Greek culture, including language, religion, philosophy, architecture, clothing, etc.). Following in his wake, Greek culture was embraced in most of the major cities across the ancient Near East. Hellenism, Alexander's greatest contribution to Western civilization, would last a thousand years.

For the Jews it constituted a serious challenge to their ancestral faith. The question of how far Jews could go in accommodating to the Hellenistic cultural imperialism while still remaining faithful to their God dominates Jewish literature of the intertestamental period. The answers given varied, contributing directly to the wide diversity of Judaism during this era. Many passages in the NT reflect a similar struggle for Christians living in a Greco-Roman environment dominated by Hellenism (e.g., 2 Cor. 6:14–7:1; Eph. 4:17–5:20; 1 Pet. 2:11–12; 2 Pet. 2; 1 John 2:15–17; Rev. 2–3).

Following the early death of Alexander the Great, his generals split his empire up into four kingdoms: the Ptolemaic kingdom (Egypt), the Seleucid kingdom (Mesopotamia and Syria), the Lysimachian and then the Attalid kingdom (Anatolia—i.e., modern Turkey), and the Antigonid kingdom (Macedonia). The Ptolemaic kingdom controlled Judea for the early part of this period (323–198 BC), but the Seleucids conquered the region in 198 BC.

Coin bearing the image of Alexander the Great.

The Maccabean Revolt (beginning in 175 BC). The challenge of Hellenism to the Jewish faith was never more acute than in the days of the Seleucid king Antiochus IV Epiphanes (215–163 BC) (see comments on Dan. 7:8). This monarch embarked on a thorough Hellenizing program whereby all citizens in his kingdom (which included Judea and Jerusalem) were required to embrace the cultural ideals and political objectives of the empire. The Jews, with their distinctive monotheism and customs, stood out as a major impediment. Antiochus mandated that Jews relinquish their religion and customs and embrace those of Hellenism.[4] This provoked one of the most remarkable resistance movements in history. Led by the Hasmonean family (better known as the Maccabees), the Jews successfully secured religious freedom and even achieved political autonomy by 140 BC. Several Jewish writings from this era reflect an epic struggle in which Jews had to decide whether their faith was worth dying for (e.g., 1–2 Maccabees, Judith, Baruch). It was also a time of bitter division and internal strife over what it meant to be a true Jew; rival sects such as the Pharisees, Sadducees, and Essenes defended quite different definitions.[5]

Roman Domination (63 BC–AD 66). Before long, however, the Hasmonean dynasty weakened and succumbed to Rome, the new superpower. Pompey the Great defeated the last Hasmonean prince and sacked Jerusalem in 63 BC. The ancestral homeland became an occupied province in the Roman Empire, ruled by either native-born client kings (Herod the Great and his successors) or directly appointed Roman governors (such as Pontius Pilate). The Gospels must be read against this backdrop (Luke 3:1).

Resentment seethed, and yearnings for independence waxed and waned in proportion to the ineptness and oppression of the Herodian dynasty or the provincial governors. Some Jewish factions, recalling the heroics of the Maccabees, clamored for violent resistance (Zealots); others counseled patience and appealed to the messianic hope of national liberation (Pharisees and Essenes); still others, with vested interests in the establishment, urged accommodation with the Romans (Sadducees).

Roman Destruction of Jerusalem and the Second Temple (AD 66–73). In AD 66 Judea and most of Galilee rose in revolt. Nero dispatched four legions of Roman soldiers under Vespasian to crush the revolt. In the summer of AD 70 Jerusalem fell, and the city and its temple were set ablaze. The loss of human life was staggering. This catastrophe again raised anguished questions: Was God finished with the Jewish people? Was there hope beyond destruction (see 2 Esdras)? The Pharisees, the only major Jewish sect to survive the disaster, set about reconstituting Judaism. Rabbinic Judaism testifies to their remarkable success, and the Mishnah (a major literary collection produced by early rabbinic Judaism) reflects that transformation.

Gold coin depicting Pompey, the Roman general who brought Judea under Roman control.

Conclusion

These tumultuous times form the backdrop for reading and understanding the NT. The rich nonbiblical Jewish literature produced during this era continues to be extremely helpful in shedding light on the background for the NT and emerging Christianity.

THE NEW TESTAMENT

Introduction to the New Testament

J. Scott Duvall

To understand the message of the NT, we need to have a sense of its context. When we read the Gospels, we don't read far before we encounter a ruler named Herod or Roman soldiers or the Sea of Galilee or a synagogue or someone taking a journey up to Jerusalem. We read about the temple, Pharisees, the Law and the Prophets, sheep, catching fish, raising crops, and sharing a meal. As the NT unfolds, the setting expands beyond the land of Israel to Asia Minor and Macedonia and even to Rome. Then we read about ships, food offered to idols, missionary journeys, synagogues, Roman emperors, and more. We quickly realize that we simply cannot make sense of the NT apart from its context, a context or setting that includes political history, geography, religious beliefs and groups and institutions and literature, as well as social and cultural values and practices. In this brief introduction we explain what to expect from this commentary in each of these areas when it comes to studying NT background.

Political History. The OT closes with the Persian period (539–331 BC), also known as the postexilic period because the Jews began to return to their homeland soon after Babylon's fall. The Second Temple period begins with this return to the land and the rebuilding of the temple in Jerusalem. The Persians rule the land of Israel for about two hundred years until the conquests of Alexander the Great, who lived 356–323 BC. As a result, Israel comes under Greek control from about 331 BC until the period of Jewish independence in 166 BC. The influence of Greek civilization over the NT world cannot be overestimated: city features (e.g., public baths, theaters, schools), a standard monetary currency, and most importantly, the Greek language, which became the common trade language of the eastern Mediterranean world (e.g., used in business, medicine, education, religion, literature, philosophy). *Hellas* means "Greece," so the term "Hellenism" refers to the spread of Greek culture and language. The NT was written in *koinē* ("common") Greek. When Alexander dies in 323 BC, two groups struggle for control of his empire: the Ptolemies based in Egypt and the Seleucids based in Mesopotamia and Syria. The Ptolemies gain control of Israel and rule until 198 BC. During this period there is a thriving Jewish community living in Alexandria, where the need arises to translate the OT into Greek since many of them no longer speak or read Hebrew. The Septuagint (LXX) was one of the most significant accomplishments from this period and serves as the primary Bible for Jews outside of Israel and early Christians.

In 198 BC the Seleucids gain control of Israel, and their ruler Antiochus IV "Epiphanes" ("manifest one"), who rules from 175 to 163 BC, becomes a key threat to Israel. He tries to suppress Judaism and superimpose Greek beliefs and customs on the Jews by controlling the high priesthood, looting the temple treasury, banning the observance of Jewish special days (e.g., the Sabbath), prohibiting circumcision, destroying copies of the Scriptures, and mandating the worship of the Greek gods. In 167 BC he sets up an altar dedicated to Zeus in the Jerusalem temple where pigs (and other unclean animals) are sacrificed. As a result of this desecration of the temple, the Jews rebel.

The Maccabean Revolt (166–135 BC) is a rebellion of pious Jews who oppose Hellenistic oppression. In the village of Modein, when Mattathias is ordered to sacrifice a pig on the altar, he initiates a rebellion. Mattathias's son Judas (nicknamed "Maccabeus" from an Aramaic word meaning "hammer") organizes the Jews into a fighting force, and they defeat the Greeks in battle and liberate the temple in 164 BC. This victory is celebrated today through the Jewish festival of Hanukkah ("dedication"). The story of the revolt is told in the apocryphal books 1–2 Maccabees. The family of Mattathias and its heirs forms the Jewish dynasty known as the Hasmonean dynasty, a group of priest-kings who rule Israel from 135 to 63 BC, when the Romans take control.

The Roman period begins in 63 BC when the Roman general Pompey captures Jerusalem from the Hasmoneans. The NT opens with Israel under the reign of Herod the Great (37–4 BC), the ruler when Jesus is born (Matt. 2:1–19; Luke 1:5). The Roman emperor at the time is Octavian, better known as Caesar Augustus. Herod was a gifted administrator and builder.

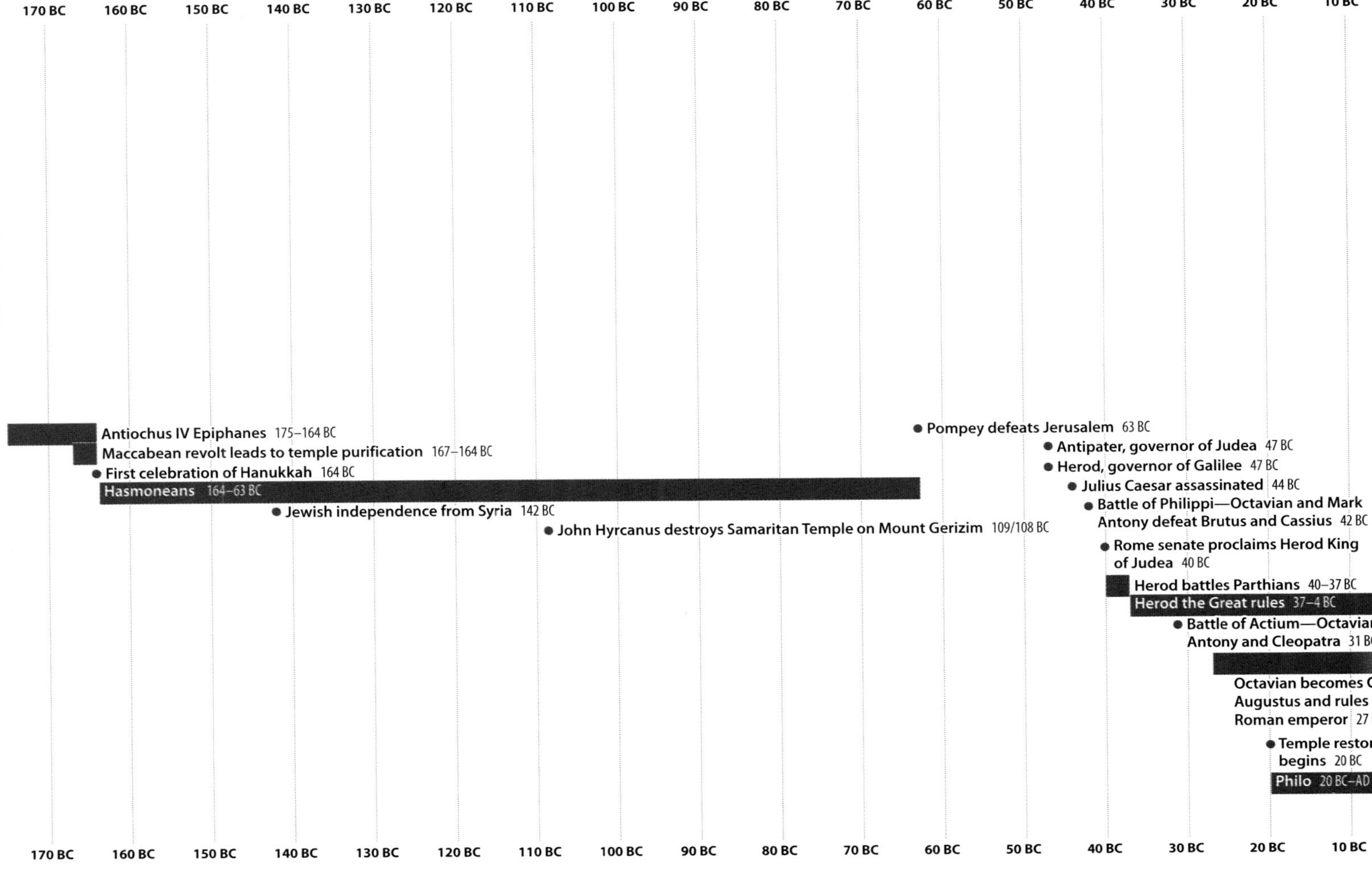

170 BC
160 BC
150 BC
140 BC
130 BC
120 BC
110 BC
100 BC
90 BC
80 BC
70 BC
60 BC
50 BC
40 BC
30 BC
20 BC
10 BC
KEY NEW TESTAMENT BIBLE EVENTS
KEY PEOPLE/EVENTS FROM THE MEDITERRANEAN WORLD
Antiochus IV Epiphanes 175–164 BC
Maccabean revolt leads to temple purification 167–164 BC
First celebration of Hanukkah 164 BC
Hasmoneans 164–63 BC
Jewish independence from Syria 142 BC
John Hyrcanus destroys Samaritan Temple on Mount Gerizim 109/108 BC
Pompey defeats Jerusalem 63 BC
Antipater, governor of Judea 47 BC
Herod, governor of Galilee 47 BC
Julius Caesar assassinated 44 BC
Battle of Philippi—Octavian and Mark Antony defeat Brutus and Cassius 42 BC
Rome senate proclaims Herod King of Judea 40 BC
Herod battles Parthians 40–37 BC
Herod the Great rules 37–4 BC
Battle of Actium—Octavian defeats Antony and Cleopatra 31 BC
Octavian becomes Caesar Augustus and rules as first Roman emperor 27 BC–AD 14
Temple restoration begins 20 BC
Philo 20 BC–AD 50

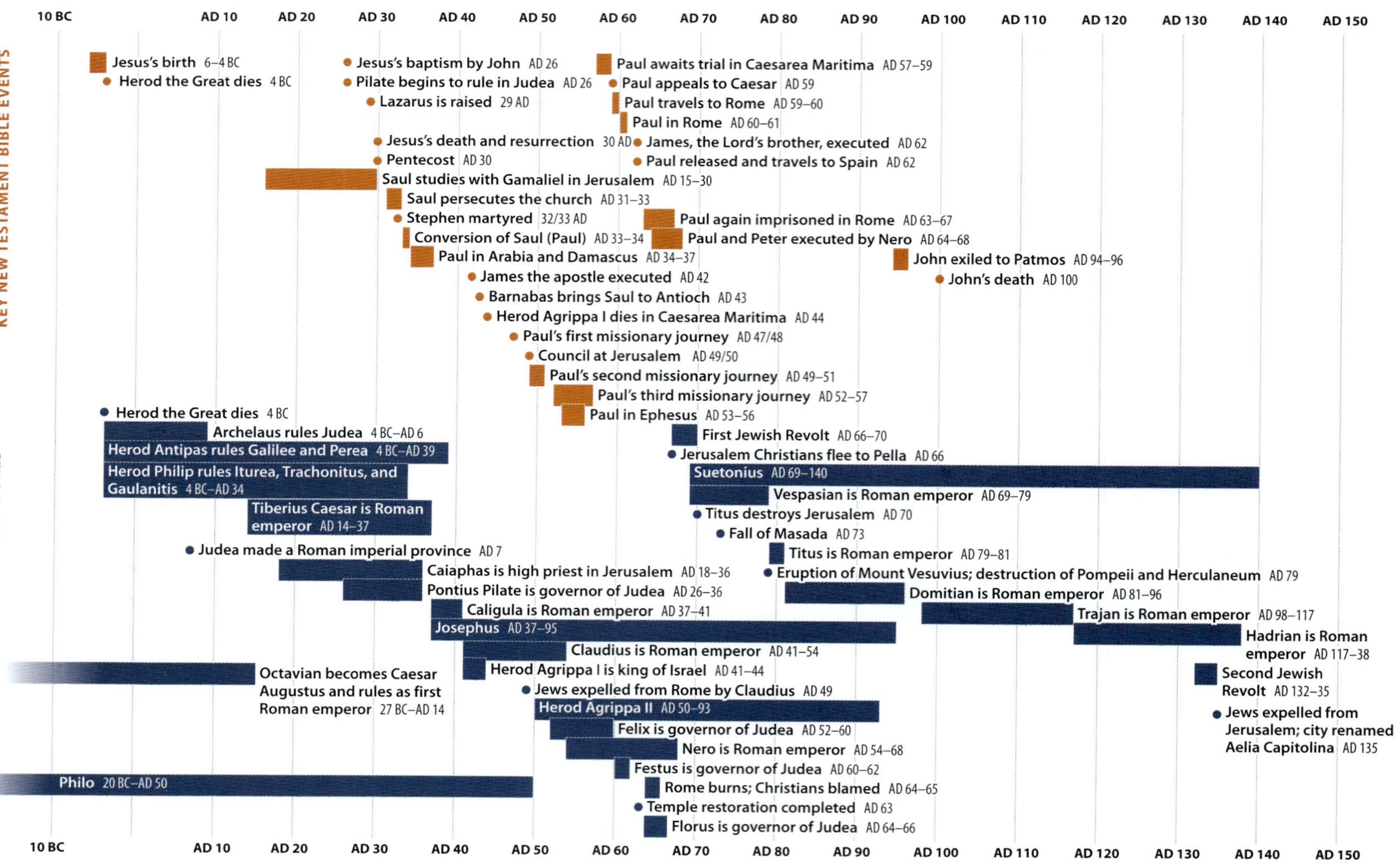
10 BC
AD 10
AD 20
AD 30
AD 40
AD 50
AD 60
AD 70
AD 80
AD 90
AD 100
AD 110
AD 120
AD 130
AD 140
AD 150
KEY NEW TESTAMENT BIBLE EVENTS
Jesus's birth 6–4 BC
Herod the Great dies 4 BC
Jesus's baptism by John AD 26
Pilate begins to rule in Judea AD 26
Lazarus is raised 29 AD
Jesus's death and resurrection 30 AD
Pentecost AD 30
Saul studies with Gamaliel in Jerusalem AD 15–30
Saul persecutes the church AD 31–33
Stephen martyred 32/33 AD
Conversion of Saul (Paul) AD 33–34
Paul in Arabia and Damascus AD 34–37
James the apostle executed AD 42
Barnabas brings Saul to Antioch AD 43
Herod Agrippa I dies in Caesarea Maritima AD 44
Paul's first missionary journey AD 47/48
Council at Jerusalem AD 49/50
Paul's second missionary journey AD 49–51
Paul's third missionary journey AD 52–57
Paul in Ephesus AD 53–56
Paul awaits trial in Caesarea Maritima AD 57–59
Paul appeals to Caesar AD 59
Paul travels to Rome AD 59–60
Paul in Rome AD 60–61
James, the Lord's brother, executed AD 62
Paul released and travels to Spain AD 62
Paul again imprisoned in Rome AD 63–67
Paul and Peter executed by Nero AD 64–68
John exiled to Patmos AD 94–96
John's death AD 100
KEY PEOPLE/EVENTS FROM THE MEDITERRANEAN WORLD
Herod the Great dies 4 BC
Archelaus rules Judea 4 BC–AD 6
Herod Antipas rules Galilee and Perea 4 BC–AD 39
Herod Philip rules Iturea, Trachonitus, and Gaulanitis 4 BC–AD 34
Tiberius Caesar is Roman emperor AD 14–37
Judea made a Roman imperial province AD 7
Caiaphas is high priest in Jerusalem AD 18–36
Pontius Pilate is governor of Judea AD 26–36
Caligula is Roman emperor AD 37–41
Josephus AD 37–95
Claudius is Roman emperor AD 41–54
Octavian becomes Caesar Augustus and rules as first Roman emperor 27 BC–AD 14
Herod Agrippa I is king of Israel AD 41–44
Jews expelled from Rome by Claudius AD 49
Herod Agrippa II AD 50–93
Felix is governor of Judea AD 52–60
Nero is Roman emperor AD 54–68
Festus is governor of Judea AD 60–62
Rome burns; Christians blamed AD 64–65
Temple restoration completed AD 63
Florus is governor of Judea AD 64–66
Philo 20 BC–AD 50
First Jewish Revolt AD 66–70
Jerusalem Christians flee to Pella AD 66
Suetonius AD 69–140
Vespasian is Roman emperor AD 69–79
Titus destroys Jerusalem AD 70
Fall of Masada AD 73
Titus is Roman emperor AD 79–81
Eruption of Mount Vesuvius; destruction of Pompeii and Herculaneum AD 79
Domitian is Roman emperor AD 81–96
Trajan is Roman emperor AD 98–117
Hadrian is Roman emperor AD 117–38
Second Jewish Revolt AD 132–35
Jews expelled from Jerusalem; city renamed Aelia Capitolina AD 135

He built the harbor at Caesarea Maritima, one of the largest harbors in the Mediterranean, which allowed ships from the west access to Israel.

Roman Emperors during the NT Period

Caesar Augustus (Octavian)	30 BC–AD 14
Tiberius	AD 14–37
Caligula	AD 37–41
Claudius	AD 41–54
Nero	AD 54–68
Vespasian	AD 69–79
Domitian	AD 81–96

His most famous project was a major remodeling of the Jerusalem temple (see the article "The Jerusalem Temple"), a project that began in 20 BC and wasn't completed until AD 63. Herod the Great placed a great tax burden on the people to finance his many projects, and he proved to be a paranoid ruler, as his attempt to kill the infant Jesus demonstrates (Matt. 2:16–18).

After Herod's death his kingdom is divided among three of his sons. Archelaus rules Judea (4 BC–AD 6). Herod Antipas rules Galilee and Perea, the region east of the Jordan (4 BC–AD 39). Jesus's ministry began under the rule of Antipas, who executes John the Baptist and confronts Jesus at his trial (Luke 23:7–12). Jesus refers to Antipas as "that fox," likely due to his deceitful ways (Luke 13:31–32). The third son is Herod Philip (4 BC–AD 34), who rules the northern regions of the kingdom. He builds Caesarea Philippi, the setting for Peter's confession of Jesus as the Messiah (Matt. 16:13–16).

Rome rules Judea not only through client kings such as Herod the Great but also through a series of governors to rule the different provinces (see the article "Roman Rule of Judea"). Perhaps the most famous such governor during the NT period is Pontius Pilate, the prefect of Judea (AD 26–36). He oversaw the trial of Jesus and called for his crucifixion (Luke 23:1). Later Jewish rulers mentioned in the NT include Herod Agrippa I (AD 41–44; Acts 12), Marcus Antonius Felix (AD 52–59; Acts 23; 27), and Porcius Festus (AD 59–62; Acts 25).

The later period of NT history politically revolves around two Jewish rebellions against Roman rule. The First Jewish Revolt (AD 66–70) occurs when Gessius Florus is procurator of Judea (AD 64–66), a man who did much to spark Jewish rebellion. The emperor Nero sends his general Vespasian to put down the revolt, and he besieges Jerusalem. Shortly thereafter Nero dies, and Vespasian returns to Rome as emperor. He then sends his son Titus to finish the job. In AD 70 Jerusalem falls, and Titus's troops destroy the temple, one of the most devastating events in all of Jewish history. A group of survivors flees to the mountaintop fortress of Masada, which falls in AD 73, when they commit suicide rather than surrender to Rome. With the destruction of the temple the high priesthood loses its influence (with no more temple for sacrifices) and fades into history, while the study of Torah and the local synagogue become central to Jewish religious life. The Second Jewish Revolt occurs in AD 132–35 when the emperor Hadrian tries to build a pagan temple on the Temple Mount and prohibits Jewish religious practices such as circumcision. Simon bar Kokhba, a gifted military leader, spearheads the fight against Rome for four years until he is killed in AD 135.

Geography. Any student of the NT needs a sense of place, a feel for the geographical layout, in order to make sense of the events reported. The "where" often helps explain the "what" and "why" and "how." We begin our overview of geography by noting that the Roman Empire at that time stretched from Spain across the Mediterranean world, down through the land of Israel and eastward into Mesopotamia and then westward across North Africa. The NT story plays out within this space.

Christianity is born in the land of Israel and, more specifically, in the city of Jerusalem (see the article "Jerusalem in the Time of Jesus"). Israel is located at the eastern end of the Mediterranean Sea and forms a land bridge between Mesopotamia and Egypt. The land itself consists of five zones that run north and south: the coastal plain next to the Mediterranean Sea; the coastal hills; the central mountains, featuring the central city of Jerusalem; the Jordan Valley, consisting of the Sea of Galilee in the north and the Dead Sea in the south connected by the Jordan River; and the plateau region to the east of the Jordan River. Three major regions make up Israel: Galilee in the north, Samaria in the central section of the country, and Judea in the south. It's worth noting also that elevation plays an important role in reading NT stories. Peter's confession of Jesus as the Messiah probably occurs on Mount Hermon, a peak north of Caesarea Philippi with an elevation of over nine thousand feet (a "high mountain" indeed [Mark 9:2]). The Sea of Galilee (a freshwater lake) is surrounded by hills rising to several thousand feet, which may explain the frequency of sudden storms. The journey from Jericho to Jerusalem would mean an elevation gain of over three thousand feet. People always "go up to Jerusalem" in the NT. The Dead Sea is about twelve hundred feet below sea level. The Judean wilderness stretches east of Jerusalem and south to the Dead Sea. This barren landscape is likely the place where Jesus was tempted for forty days and the place where John the Baptist preached.

As Christianity spreads from Jerusalem westward, we enter the wider Mediterranean world where Paul and other missionaries traveled. Paul traveled through Asia Minor (modern-day Turkey) with its three southern provinces of Cilicia, Galatia, and Asia. The Letter of 1 Peter mentions the northern regions of Asia Minor and the provinces of Pontus, Cappadocia, and

Bithynia (1 Pet. 1:1). Moving westward we see the provinces of Macedonia (including Philippi and Thessalonica) and Achaia (including Corinth and Athens). Farther west still lies Rome (see the article "The City of Ancient Rome"). Paul traveled over vast stretches of this section of the empire to take the gospel to the nations.

Society and Culture. In the NT articles we will present helpful background information and illustrations of Jewish and Roman society. Regarding

Jewish society, you will read about various groups within Judaism such as the Pharisees and Sadducees, their beliefs and practices, and how they related to the early Christians (see the article "Pharisees and Sadducees"). You will learn about the beliefs held dear within Judaism as well as the cherished organizations and institutions such as the Jerusalem temple, the local synagogue, the high priesthood, the Sanhedrin, messianic expectations, festivals and holy days, and daily life. The earliest Christians were Jews, and the church was born in Jerusalem. We cannot understand the NT apart from understanding a bit about what is commonly called Second Temple Judaism.

You will also learn about Roman society, since this culture also influences early Christianity. You will read about the Roman military, Roman citizenship, slavery in the first century, economic life, entertainment, literature, and religion. We have discussions of underlying cultural values such as honor and shame, of powerful cultural influences such as the practice of magic, of what it was like to travel by ship or on foot. You will read articles about banquets and meals, family life, hospitality practices, letter writing, and various other topics that help us grasp the message of the NT more clearly.

Literature and Sources. The authors of this commentary have drawn on many ancient sources to shed light on the background of the NT. You will see references to Jewish sources such as Josephus and Philo, the Dead Sea Scrolls, the Apocrypha and the OT Pseudepigrapha, the Septuagint, and other rabbinic writings.

You will also find references to classical and Hellenistic sources, inscriptions, philosophers, and poets, as well as to early Christian writings not found in our canon of Scripture, such as the early church fathers. There is much to study when it comes to NT background. If you want to go deeper in your study of this literature, you'll need a guide. We recommend the following for a survey of the background literature of the NT:

Evans, Craig A. *Ancient Texts for New Testament Studies: A Guide to the Background Literature.* Grand Rapids: Baker Academic, 2005.

Helyer, Larry R. *Exploring Jewish Literature of the Second Temple Period: A Guide for New Testament Students.* Downers Grove, IL: InterVarsity, 2002.

We recommend the following as trustworthy guides to the general background of the NT:

Arnold, Clinton E., ed. *Zondervan Illustrated Bible Backgrounds Commentary.* 4 vols. Grand Rapids: Zondervan, 2002.

Evans, Craig A., and Stanley E. Porter, eds. *Dictionary of New Testament Background.* Downers Grove, IL: InterVarsity, 2000.

Ferguson, Everett. *Backgrounds of Early Christianity*. 3rd ed. Grand Rapids: Eerdmans, 2003.

Green, Joel B., and Lee Martin McDonald, eds. *The World of the New Testament: Cultural, Social, and Historical Contexts*. Grand Rapids: Baker Academic, 2013.

Jeffers, James S. *The Greco-Roman World of the New Testament Era: Exploring the Background of Early Christianity*. Downers Grove, IL: InterVarsity, 1999.

Magness, Jodi. *Stone and Dung, Oil and Spit: Jewish Daily Life in the Time of Jesus*. Grand Rapids: Eerdmans, 2011.

Yamauchi, Edwin M., and Marvin R. Wilson. *Dictionary of Daily Life in Biblical & Post-Biblical Antiquity*. 4 vols. Peabody, MA: Hendrickson, 2014–16.

General Background Articles

Ancient Letter Writing

E. RANDOLPH RICHARDS

From the bogs of England, to the ravines of Judea, to the sands of Egypt, in every location where material was capable of surviving, archaeologists have uncovered lots of letters. The Roman Empire was a letter-circulating culture. Much like phone calls or text messages today, letters caught family up on news, such as the new navy recruit in a letter to his mother: "I have been assigned to Misenum."[1] Others wrote to keep a relationship warm and maybe handle a bit of business. Here is a typical letter, dated around AD 120:

> Julius Clemens, centurion, to his most esteemed Socration, greeting. I thank you for your kindness about the olive oil, as Ptolemaeus wrote to me that he had received it. And do write to me about what you may need, knowing I will gladly do everything for you. [2nd hand] I pray for your good health, my most esteemed friend.[2]

The vast majority of ancient letters averaged about 87 words, much shorter than even 3 John. The famed letter writers of that age wrote long letters, averaging 295 words (Cicero) and 995 words (Seneca). And then there was Paul, averaging 2,495 words, with Romans at a hefty 7,114. Paul's opponents ridiculed his letters as "weighty" (2 Cor. 10:10), highlighting their length as well as complexity—a pun that works in English as well as Greek.

The letter from Clemens, presented above, demonstrates another feature. Scholars noted that the handwriting changed at the end of his letter. This was common. A secretary wrote out the letter, and the sender appended a closing greeting in his or her own handwriting, a practice often used to guarantee the letter's authenticity. So Paul: "I, Paul, am writing this greeting with my

Ancient writing stylus and inkwell.

own hand, which is an authenticating mark in every letter; this is how I write" (2 Thess. 3:17).

Scholars debate ancient literacy rates, some estimates as low as 10 percent or as high (in Christian congregations) as 50 percent. Probably the vast majority of ancients were functionally illiterate. Modern literacy is commonly described as the ability to read and write, but ancient literacy was primarily the ability to read. Handwriting is a matter of practice. How well do we write with our nondominant hand?

But even the literate used secretaries. They knew the proper titles and phrases, and the appropriate rhetorical style for the occasion. Shorthand writers existed at the time but were not widely available. Generally, secretaries took notes (or slow dictation) on a wax tablet or a washable sheet of parchment. They had other skills as well. Papyrus usually was sold by the roll. Secretaries were skilled at cutting off the necessary amount, pricking and lining the sheets, mixing the ink, and writing legibly. Appearances mattered in antiquity. What would a recipient think if you sent some letter scratched messily across a sheet, especially if it was shared (cf. Col. 4:16)?

Ancient letter writing was not as easy, cheap, or convenient as today. Longer letters likely went through several rough drafts on tablets. New Testament letters show signs of thoughtful composition, likely worked and reworked before being committed to papyrus for dispatch. Since most letters were brief, the cost was not excessive. The letter of the sailor to his mother probably cost, in today's dollars, about $50 for the secretary and the materials. Paul's Letter to the Romans, though, probably cost over $2,000, including the cost of several drafts, the preparation of a nice copy for dispatch, and a copy for Paul to retain.[3]

Athletics in the New Testament World

Bernie A. Cueto

In the Greco-Roman world athletics were a demonstration of excellence and achievement, religious devotion, and entertainment. *Athleō* ("to compete for a prize") became an integral part of the social life in the Greco-Roman world and was included in the educational journey of young citizens. It was not uncommon for education to be focused on the "whole" person. The Greek word for "education" (*paideia*) means "training, discipline." It was later translated into Latin as *humanitas*, which was understood as the formation of the human person.[1] Therefore, the gymnasium included education in rhetoric, grammar, dialectic, geometry, arithmetic, astronomy, music, and philosophy, as well as physical education and competition. Physical education in classical education was not just a competition; it was the anvil for moral training, helping the pupil to become a perfect moral and physical specimen characteristic of Greek ideals.

Athletic festivals were always dedicated to Greco-Roman deities. Filled with commemorative rituals for the heroes, various games (Olympian, Pythian, Isthmian, and Nemean games) were held in honor of the prevailing deity of the time and the specific location where they were held. For example, both the Olympic and the Nemean games were dedicated to Zeus. Athletics and religion in the Greco-Roman world went hand in hand. It was not uncommon for the sports event to be seen as a form of worship. The victorious athlete would sense that he was pleasing the gods with his performance, and so would dedicate his effort and accomplishment to them.

Not only was athletics a form of worship but also, one may argue, it was the ultimate form of entertainment in the NT world. Spectators would easily number into the thousands to watch the various events (primarily running, boxing *pankration* [a no-holds-barred combination of wrestling and boxing that including kicking], and the pentathlon [running, long-jump, discus, javelin, and wrestling]) over several days of festivities and celebration. The most famous of the arenas is the Roman Colosseum, where the various tiered seats would hold an estimated fifty thousand spectators. Athletic events became so dominant that they eventually replaced Greek drama in popularity.[2]

The Roman Colosseum could seat around fifty thousand people, who watched gladiator spectacles such as mock sea battles, hand-to-hand combat, and executions.

Banquets and Meals in the Greco-Roman World

E. Randolph Richards

The standard diet in the Greco-Roman world had three elements: bread (usually wheat, but barley for the very poor), olive oil, and fruit (usually figs).[1] Vegetables were added when available; beans, peas, and chickpeas were preferred. Turnips were for the poor; hence the saying, "Woe to the house in which the turnip passes."[2] Meat was a luxury, eaten only by the wealthy or at the occasional banquet.

Banquets (*convivia*) usually concluded with wine parties (*symposia*). The ancient Mediterranean world enjoyed banquets.[3] Philo mentions the "convivial meals" of the Essenes.[4] Aulus Gellius, noting his fellow philosophers, speaks of "the entertainments [*convivia*] which it was the custom of us young men to hold at Athens at the beginning of each week."[5] Paul writes, "When you come together to eat, welcome one another" (1 Cor. 11:33). Certain religions featured banquets: Judaism (festival meals), Greco-Roman mysteries, and Christianity. Ancients also attended sacrificial meals, funerary banquets, and governmental feasts.

Regardless of the setting, banquets shared much in common. Plutarch and others wrote treatises on proper behavior at banquets. Generally, "like dined with like"—for example, slaves with slaves, Torah-obedient Jews only with their own,[6] and aristocrats together. The host was also to arrange guests according to relative social status, "according to his worth," as Plutarch notes, and not merely leave it to a "foot-race" for the best seats.[7] Jesus condemns these practices (Luke 14:1–24), as does Paul (1 Cor. 11:18–19; Gal. 2:11–13). Hosts were to honor guests appropriately (Luke 7:44–45) and to lavish wine (John 2:1–10). Hosts at Roman banquets provided male and female slave "escorts" who offered sexual favors to the guests.

Seneca, a contemporary of Paul, described a typical wealthy banquet:

> Purse-proud etiquette surrounds a householder at his dinner with a mob of standing slaves. The master eats more than he can hold, and with monstrous greed loads his belly until it is stretched. . . . All this time the poor slaves may not move their lips, even to speak. . . . When we recline at a banquet, one slave mops up the disgorged food, another crouches beneath the table and gathers up the left-overs of the tipsy guests. . . . Another, who serves the wine, must dress like a woman and wrestle with his advancing years; . . . he must remain awake throughout the night, dividing his time between his master's drunkenness and his lust; in the chamber he must be a man, at the feast a boy. Another, whose duty it is to put a valuation on the guests, must stick to his task, poor fellow, and watch to see whose flattery and whose immodesty, whether of appetite or of language, is to get them an invitation for to-morrow.[8]

Drunkenness, immorality, meats, gossiping, social stratifying—all were common fare at banquets, leading many to see banquets as a cultural challenge facing Corinthian Christians, for Paul addresses these very issues.

Jesus and his disciples would have reclined around a low table to share table fellowship on the night before he went to the cross.

Baptism in the New Testament World

Rodney Reeves

Two kinds of baptisms appear in the NT: the water ritual performed by John the Baptist, or more accurately, "John the Baptizer" (Mark 1:4–8), and the baptism offered by Jesus, his disciples, and Paul (John 3:22–26; Acts 2:38–41; 1 Cor. 1:14–17). And even though John's baptism differed from early Christian baptism, both water rituals came from Jewish rites of purification. According to the law, Jews were required to maintain their covenant relationship with God by keeping certain purity rites, which included washing themselves with the "water of cleansing" (Lev. 14:6–16; 15:5–27; Num. 19:7–22). Most of the time their impurity had nothing to do with immorality. Rather, Jews became unclean through everyday activities (contact with dead animals, mold, skin diseases)—even by keeping the law. For example, honoring parents would mean ensuring them a proper burial, which included handling a corpse—something that made the family unclean. God commanded humans to "be fruitful and multiply," which rendered couples unclean when they had sex or birthed children. Therefore, it shouldn't surprise us that baptismal pools (*mikvot*) have been discovered all over the land of Israel—going back to NT times and before—proving that the Jewish people obeyed the law and constantly baptized themselves to maintain purity.

Obviously, John's baptism wasn't a Christian baptism, immersing participants under water while reciting Paul's words "buried in the likeness

An ancient Jewish ritual bath, or *mikveh*.

of his death" (Rom. 6:5). And yet, even though it was a very Jewish ritual, John's baptism differed from customary rites of purification. For example, Jews were accustomed to baptizing themselves; John was the one who baptized the repentant. Jews baptized themselves many times to deal with impurity; John's baptism was a one-time act of repentance for the forgiveness of sin. Jews submitted to purification rites to maintain covenant with God; John's baptism prepared Israel for God's visitation at the end of the world. In other words, even though the Jews were accustomed to baptism as a religious duty, John the Baptizer offered something different: a prophetic call to Israel to confess their sins to get ready for the day of the Lord.

Even though its antecedents can be traced to the Jewish ritual of purification by water, Christian baptism is closer to John's baptism: a one-time act of repentance for the forgiveness of sin. But there is a huge difference: John didn't baptize persons in his own name, as if they were "converts"—even though some of them became his disciples (Matt. 11:2; John 1:35). Christians, however, baptize converts in the name of Jesus Christ. Baptism is more than an act of repentance; it is an entry rite into a new religion, a new identity, a new way of life. Interestingly, Jesus never said why his disciples were supposed to baptize converts, nor did he explain what the ritual meant. He simply commanded them to do it in order to "make disciples of all nations" (Matt. 28:19). The same is true for the apostles. Peter didn't explain the meaning of baptism to three thousand converts on the day of Pentecost. He simply gave an order: "Repent and be baptized, each of you, in the name of Jesus Christ for the forgiveness of your sins" (Acts 2:38), and they complied (2:41). Due to the fulfillment of the prophecy of Joel (Acts 2:16–21; cf. Joel 2:28–32), Peter knew that they would "receive the gift of the Holy Spirit" when they were baptized (Acts 2:38). And yet the fullest explanation regarding the significance of baptism comes from a man who, ironically, never followed the historical Jesus. It was Paul, apostle to the gentiles, who explained what baptism means: when we are placed in a watery grave, we are crucified with Christ, buried with Christ, and resurrected in Christ to live a new life in him, for him, through him (Rom. 6:1–14). "Therefore, if anyone is in Christ, he is a new creation; the old has passed away, and see, the new has come!" (2 Cor. 5:17).

The City of Ancient Rome

Alan S. Bandy

The city of Rome, the eternal city, was unparalleled in the ancient world, and its influence continues to this day. According to legend, it was named after Romulus, who founded the city April 21, 753 BC. It was located along the banks of the Tiber River and encompassed seven hills (Aventine, Caelian, Capitoline, Esquiline, Palatine, Quirinal, Viminal), their intervening valleys, a large defensive wall, and suburbs sprawling well beyond the seven hills.[1]

Rome became the first city in history to reach a population of over a million people.[2] The average life expectancy in Rome, however, was approximately twenty-five years, and less than 50 percent of babies lived to age twenty.[3] So the population was also fed by a steady influx of immigrants from throughout the empire, including a large Jewish community numbering forty to fifty thousand. The mixture of cultures in the city ensured that it would be home to a great variety of religions and often prone to immorality. Tacitus described Rome as "the city where all degraded and shameful practices collect from all over and become the vogue."

Emperor Augustus once boasted, "I found Rome built of bricks; I leave it clothed in marble."[4] Augustus divided Rome into fourteen administrative regions with a reorganized division of official neighborhoods.[5] At the center, located in the valley between the Palatine and Capitoline hills, was the Forum. It was the political, economic, religious, and cultural heart of the city. The Forum, as the seat of Rome's government, was the location for the

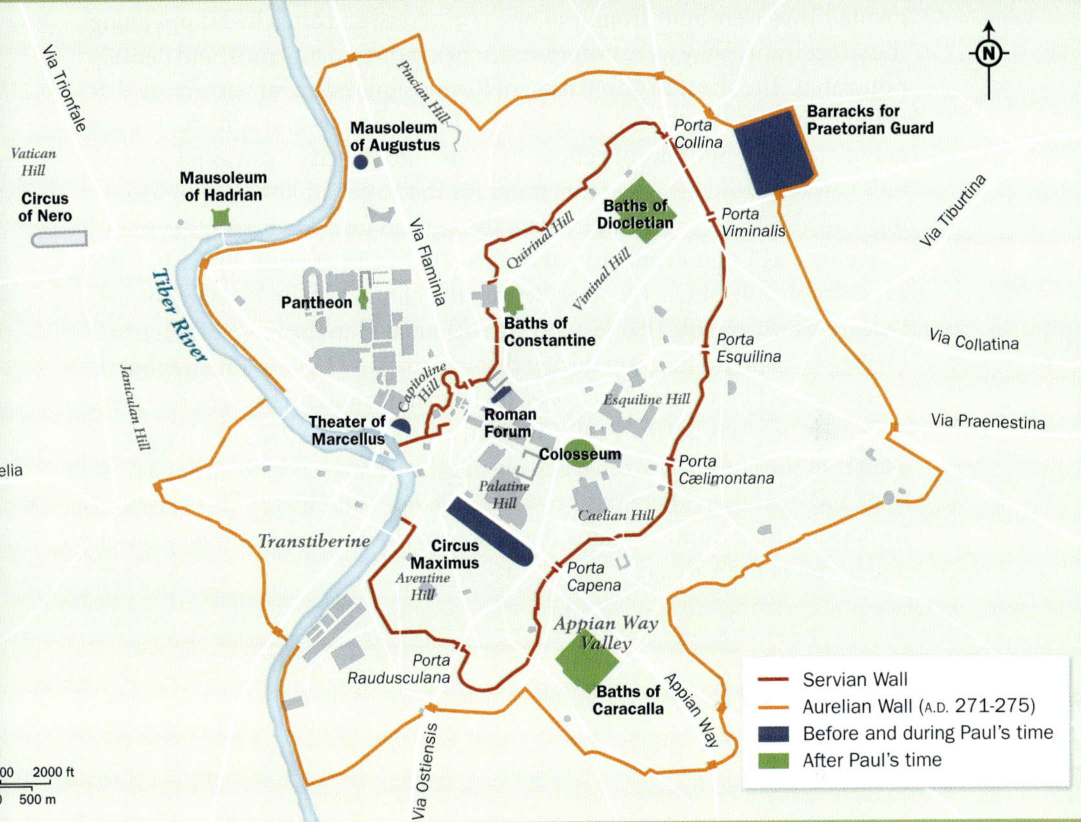

Senate, an open-air, multitier venue for public assemblies, a raised podium for announcements and speeches, an official archive, and several massive rectangular buildings, called basilicas, used for a wide range of civic activities such as public meetings, commerce, and banking. Since every aspect of Roman life, including government, was deeply religious, the Forum also housed many important temples. For example, the temple of Saturn kept the treasury, and the temple of Vesta was responsible to ensure the well-being of Rome's families with a fire that burned perpetually.

Surrounding the city's center, Rome hosted huge venues for entertainment, including several theaters. The Colosseum held seating for 50,000 spectators, and the Circus Maximus could seat upwards of 250,000.[6] The typical Roman house was constructed around an *atrium*, an open-air courtyard, with rooms for a family shrine, dining, entertaining, sleeping, cooking, and bathing surrounding it. The size and amenities in these homes depended on the wealth of the family. The majority of Romans lived in apartment blocks (*insulae*) that were owned by landlords and comprised of six to eight apartments.[7] They were built around an open courtyard and often had shops lining the street front. They were notorious for being dirty, dangerous, and densely populated. The size and population of Rome required an infrastructure that could provide all the water necessary for life, and so several aqueducts used gravity to bring millions of gallons of water into the city from as far as sixty miles away.[8] Residents used this water for the large public baths, for drinking, and also to carry out their waste through an extensive sewage system.[9]

Rome was a significant city for the growth of Christianity. In the NT the events of the life of Christ are set within the context of the Roman Empire. Luke is careful to note that Jesus's birth occurs within the reign of Augustus (Luke 2:1), and his baptism during that of Tiberius (Luke 3:1). The church in Rome was likely started by Jews who lived in Rome and became believers at Pentecost (Acts 2:10). Paul, a Roman citizen (Acts 22:25–29), penned a letter to the church at Rome, and eventually he arrived in Rome as a prisoner and died there. Peter also resided in Rome until he too was executed by Nero. Today Rome remains the center of the Roman Catholic Church and home of the Vatican.

The City of Corinth

Mariam Kamell-Kovalishyn
and Josiah McDermott

Like the churches of 1–2 Corinthians, the city of Corinth in Paul's day could be characterized by its young identity. Pausanias records that Corinth was destroyed in 146 BC and rebuilt under order of Julius Caesar in 44 BC.[1] Therefore, it is important to recognize that the city of Corinth during Paul's lifetime was thoroughly Roman.[2] The population of Corinth initially consisted of freedmen and military veterans.[3] By and large, these freedmen were former slaves with no roots in family honor or social customs on what was appropriate in their quest for an enjoyable life. Social mores and assumed cultural conventions that would have constrained a "respectable" citizen in the Roman world could not be automatically assumed by those in Corinth. Without an aristocracy, freedmen aggressively pursued power and honor, and patronage undergirded the majority of relationships.[4] Gordon Fee described it as "at once the New York, Los Angeles, and Las Vegas of the ancient world."[5]

Corinth sits on the isthmus of Greece, giving it two harbors; thus Livy calls Corinth "the meeting-place for Greece and Asia."[6] The harbors and the isthmus connecting the two brought vast resources to the city and, consequently, helped bring vast amounts of taxation income to the city. Naturally, a growing commercial industry developed, bringing a cosmopolitan expression of culture. Religion played an important social aspect in Corinthian life and was the cohesion that the Corinthian people depended on. Religious feasts provided many meals for the community and at times were the only place to eat meat.[7] Religion was intimately tied with business, and shops were in close vicinity to religious shrines.[8] The temple dedicated to the worship

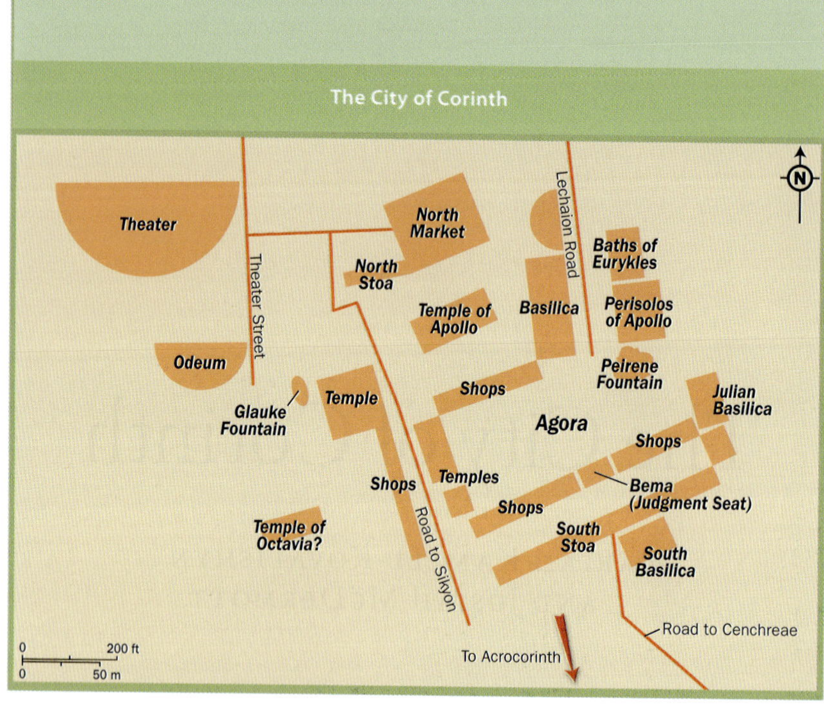

Because of its location, the city of ancient Corinth prospered as a major trading center.

of the Roman emperor had been built up to be higher than that of any of the Greek gods as a status symbol. Alongside religion, philosophy was also popular, with many major philosophers making Corinth their home for a time. This led to a popular presence of Sophists in Paul's day, teachers who flocked to wealthy cities in hopes of making money by educating on rhetoric and speechmaking.

Corinth was also the home of the Isthmian games. Traditionally, these games ranked second behind the Olympic games in importance. Under the Roman Empire the games were an important event to showcase competition, and, in true Roman fashion, these games celebrated only the winners. Though the two harbors brought an immense amount of trade, the Isthmian games brought revenue from thousands of visiting spectators.

While all of these factors played a large part in the cultural identity of Roman Corinth, none played a bigger role than the cultural impact of its founding citizens. The city was marked by its implicit culture of freedmen who were eager to accumulate wealth. They knew that there was no aristocratic restriction to flaunting their means of acquiring power and honor. In Paul's time Corinth was a young city full of upwardly mobile people showcasing their status and asserting their desire for applause and public attention.

The City of Ephesus

Mark Wilson

Roman Ephesus stood between Mounts Pion and Coressus, where Lysimachus established the Hellenistic city after 294 BC. In the first century AD it was the fourth largest city of the Roman Empire, with a population over one hundred thousand. It also served as the capital of the province of Asia. Ephesus was the guardian (*neōkoros*) of the temple of Artemis (Acts 19:35). This Artemisium was the fifth temple standing on the site and the largest temple in the ancient world, with 127 columns. It was also one of its seven wonders. Sacred processionals related to the festivals of Artemis started at the temple, wound through Ephesus around Mount Pion, and then returned to the temple, a distance of about 3.5 miles. During such a festival the riot recorded in Acts 19 took place.

Paul visited Ephesus at the end of his second journey, arriving by ship from Corinth at the Harbor Street (Acts 18:19–21). On his third journey he ministered in the city for about three years (Acts 20:31). Despite more than a century of excavations, archaeologists have failed to uncover any Jewish synagogues or the Hall of Tyrannus (Acts 19:9). The terrace houses near the city center display the affluence of the civic elite, and their atrium style suggests the type of space where early believers might have gathered. Paul, Priscilla, and Aquila passed through the Gate of Mazeus and Mithridates on their way to the commercial Tetragonos agora, where they worked as tentmakers (Acts 18:3; 20:34). (The nearby iconic Library of Celsus did not exist in the first century AD.)

In the marketplace the riot instigated by Demetrius spilled into the adjacent theater (Acts 19:23–41). Renovations in the theater began under

Curetes Street in Ephesus, one of the main thoroughfares in the ancient city.

Nero to expand its capacity to around twenty-two thousand persons. The state agora, resembling the Roman Forum, stood in the upper city and held twelve major monuments. These included a basilica dedicated to Augustus and a portico built during Nero's reign. Here Paul would have interacted with the officials of the province (Asiarchs) who were his friends (Acts 19:31). North of the state forum stood the town council building, where the city clerk had his office (Acts 19:35). Adjacent was a sacred precinct dedicated to Divus Julius and Dea Roma. This sanctuary was established by Octavian in 29 BC for the city's Roman residents. (An alternate location proposed for this sanctuary is the temple in the agora's center.) At the state agora's western end Domitian built an imperial cult temple in AD 89–90. After his assassination in AD 96 the temple was rededicated to his father, Vespasian, and his brother, Titus, as the Flavian temple of the Sebastoi ("revered ones"). Here the emperor was worshiped as a divine being, which clashed with the Christian proclamation of Jesus as Lord and God.

Tradition states that the apostle John came to Ephesus in the later first century AD. His grave is found today in the remains of a sixth-century church on Mount Ayasoluk. The area originally was a cemetery (necropolis), and after the legalization of Christianity a four-posted, canopied ciborium was built over the tomb. In the early fifth century Theodosius II built a church around the tomb, which later was destroyed by an earthquake. A century later the emperor Justinian built the cruciform-style basilica whose central dome stood above John's grave. Despite the assertion of the church historian Eusebius, two tombs of John never existed in Ephesus. The tradition of Mary the mother of Jesus coming to Ephesus developed in the 1820s. The so-called House of Mary is a Byzantine structure with no historical basis. Early church traditions state that Mary lived and died in Jerusalem.

Crucifixion

Joseph R. Dodson

Crucifixion was a widespread practice in the ancient world and arguably the most degrading form of execution in human history. Various nations employed the cross in various ways. And numerous means of torture—such as scourging, racking, and blinding—usually preceded the practice. While scholars attribute the invention of crucifixion to the Persians, the Romans are most notorious for the custom.[1] Above execution by burning and decapitation, the Roman senate considered the *maxima mala crux* (the greatest evils of the cross) the highest form of their *summa supplicia* (capital punishments).

Death by crucifixion was so grisly that the Romans usually reserved it for foreigners and those who committed treasonous crimes, such as sedition, espionage, and desertion. The cross therefore served as a political tool of intimidation. In fact, rotting corpses were set up on busy roads as a warning for any who dared to challenge the empire—such as the six thousand crucified captives involved in the revolt led by Spartacus that littered the Via Appia from Capua to Rome in 71 BC. Jews and Christians especially faced the cruelty of the Roman cross. For example, Josephus reports that Titus had five hundred Jews a day crucified until there was no longer room to station the countless crosses, nor beams upon which to fasten the bodies.[2] Similarly, Tacitus tells how Nero not only crucified innumerable Christians but also lit them on fire to provide nightlights for his parties.[3]

Remains of a heel bone with an iron nail driven through it, revealing that the victim was likely crucified.

Due to the pervasiveness of the cross as a religious symbol in many modern societies, most people have become so desensitized to the crucifix that it is difficult to recapture the unspeakable horror that the practice of crucifixion once provoked.[4] Due to paintings and pageants of Christ, the notion of the cross rightly evokes gruesome images. Nevertheless, because of their appalling nature, other obscene aspects of crucifixion often are not portrayed. For instance, most art works depict the crucified person with his genitalia covered. In reality, however, the men's private parts would have been exposed and sometimes even impaled.[5] What is more, the positioning of criminals could even emphasize their nakedness so that bloated penises and spontaneous erections would heighten the humiliation. Further, while some modern portrayals highlight the blood caked upon the criminals, few disclose men covered in their own feces, though it was common for the crucified to soil themselves. Moreover, those condemned to the cross not only faced mockery but also likely endured sexual assault when the sadism of the executioners was given full rein.[6]

Although crucifixion served as entertainment for some,[7] the nightmarish actions associated with the cross caused many to cringe. Latin authors were even reluctant to mention the cross, and civilized people frowned upon any who uttered *crux*, the shameful four-letter word.[8] Occasionally, however, writers employed the cross as a metaphor, primarily in relation to bodily suffering from which one's soul can be liberated only by death.[9]

Demonization and Exorcism in the Greco-Roman World

Bernie A. Cueto

The Greco-Roman world was saturated with the belief in supernatural forces, both positive and negative. Some of the Greek terms that refer to demons can be found in the papyri.[1] A "spirit" (*pneuma*, "wind, breath") can be understood as being an "evil," "unclean," or "foul" force. A demonic entity was called *daimōn*. Not unlike what is found in Jewish rabbinic literature, illnesses and diseases often were understood as demonic attacks. And other terms such as "encounter" (*synantēma, apantēma*) or "occurrence" (*synkyrēma*) often were associated with an attack.[2]

Greek evidence presents various rituals and amulets being used to combat demonic attack (prevention, warding off, protection), but once the person is affected, a more active wording is used, such as "exorcism" and "expulsion."[3] In that case, a deity, powerful name, or angel was seen as having the ability to bring deliverance or healing. It was not uncommon to believe that demonic forces were everywhere and were constantly impacting the lives of humans. Plutarch provides a thorough explanation of how the word for "demon" was used by many, especially philosophers, who would fault demons for various poor conditions (natural, social, etc.). This eventually led to the concept of fearing demons or superstition (*deisidaimōnia*),[4] setting the stage for

An ancient amulet that could be placed above the bed of a sick person to call on the gods for healing.

Christian apologists of the day presenting their response to the plight of humans.[5]

The Synoptic Gospels contain six accounts of Jesus performing exorcisms: (1) Mark 1:23–28 (cf. Luke 4:33–37); (2) Mark 5:1–20 (cf. Matt. 8:28–34; Luke 8:26–39); (3) Mark 7:24–30 (cf. Matt. 15:21–28); (4) Mark 9:14–29 (cf. Matt. 17:14–21; Luke 9:37–43a); (5) Matt. 9:32–34; (6) Matt. 12:22–30 (cf. Luke 11:14–15; the woman cured of a spirit of infirmity might be included as well [Luke 13:10–17]). Demonized symptoms included insanity, self-destructive behavior, seizures, deafness, dumbness, and antisocial behavior. What is clear, when compared to the Greco-Roman world and its elaborate exorcistic formulas used by Jewish and pagan magicians, is that Jesus's approach was simple. First, he expressed concern for those who were afflicted, and second, the deliverance was evidence that his kingdom was breaking into the present (e.g., Luke 10:18; John 12:31).[6] This is not surprising because Jesus often, although not exclusively, ministered to those driven to the margins of society. Also, Jesus stressed that the kingdom of God is demonstrated in power during these encounters.

Not only was Jesus successful at expelling demons and evil spirits but also his name was used to perform exorcism. Mark 9:38 records Jesus receiving a report of an unknown exorcist successfully using his name. This demonstrates that he had a reputation as an exorcist. Also, his disciples, upon returning from their mission, state, "Lord, even the demons submit to us in your name!" (Luke 10:17). The apostle Paul uses the name of Jesus to perform exorcisms as well (Acts 16:18).

The interest in exorcism is not limited to the NT canon. Plato reports a number of sorcerers who traveled through towns in order to teach their philosophies and offer people opportunity for healing.[7] Also, the Greek Magical Papyri include a popular incantation citing the god of the Hebrews for help: "I adjure you by the god of the Hebrews, Jesu, . . ."[8] That is, his reputation as a powerful healer, even for those possessed by demons, is evidenced by some of the literature of the period.

The Family of Jesus

Andreas J. Köstenberger

Jesus's mother was Mary, who conceived him by the power of the Holy Spirit while she was a virgin (Matt. 1:18–23; Luke 1:35). Joseph was therefore Jesus's adoptive father (Matt. 1:16), and Jesus can be called "the carpenter's son" (Matt. 13:55). Mary and Joseph had other children following the birth of Jesus, both brothers and sisters (Matt. 12:46; 13:55–56). Matthew identifies the brothers' names as James, Joseph, Judas, and Simon.[1]

Joseph likely died relatively early in Jesus's life, as he is not mentioned again after the visit to Jerusalem when Jesus was twelve years old (Luke 2:41–52). Mary, however, lived to see her son crucified and raised from the dead (John 19:26–27) and was part of the early church along with her other sons (Acts 1:14).

During Jesus's ministry he encountered unbelief among his family members who evidently were concerned for his welfare (Matt. 12:46–50). John records an exchange with Jesus's brothers displaying their lack of understanding of his mission (John 7:1–9). At least two of these brothers, James and Judas (Jude), later became followers and were responsible for the letters named after them in the New Testament.[2] Paul also notes that Jesus appeared to James following the resurrection (1 Cor. 15:7).

Honor and Shame in the New Testament World

Rodney Reeves

Honor is the social worth of a person affirmed by that person's group. In the NT world honor was the most important commodity, even more valuable than money, for if a wealthy man lived dishonorably, he would be shunned by the people as a threat to the community (Zacchaeus in Luke 19:1–9). That's because the honor of the group was more important than any individual member. In fact, the social worth of a person, the identity of a man or a woman, was embedded in the social group: family, village, tribe, and nation. An individual's worth was determined by the group to which he or she belonged. And it was up to the social network of families, villages, tribes, and nation to guard the honor of their corporate identity. Consequently, every person's actions reflected positively or negatively on the entire group. Compliant members were honored by their social group, raising the honorable reputation of all members. Bestowing honor to honorable members protected the honor of everyone. On the other hand, those who defied social convention (rebels) were shunned by their group, shamed into submission, or disowned by their family, village, tribe, or nation in order to protect the honor of all. Peer pressure, then, was considered a social good in an honor culture. Individualism was dismissed as a selfish way to live because it threatened social order.

Some people were born with honor; most had to achieve it by doing what was honorable. For example, kings and priests were honored at birth by virtue of their inherited positions. Since God chose certain tribes for royal (Judah) and priestly (Levi) duties, honoring them was the same as honoring God. To give credence to the king, therefore, was obedience to God; to give sacrifices to the priests was worship to God. The same was true for fathers and mothers: since God is the author of all life (he turns men and women into fathers and mothers), honoring parents was the same as honoring God. Consequently, the reverse was true: those who dishonored parents, priests, and kings automatically dishonored God. And those who dishonored God were considered dangerous fools, unwilling or unable to recognize their shameful behavior. If they persisted in their rebellion, having no sense of shame (another social good in an honor culture), these "shameless" fools were sent packing, driven from their family, village, tribe, and nation. And since no one could get by all alone—everyone needed someone to survive the hostile environment of the first-century world—persistent foolish behavior was seen as a form of suicide. Prodigal sons always perished (unless they were saved by fathers foolish enough to take them back, as in Luke 15:20–24).

Since honor was so desirable, people had to defend it all the time. One of the ways they maintained their honorable status was to boast about their importance to their group (2 Cor. 12:6). If the group affirmed an individual's worth—"Yes, he's that important to us"—then the honorable man would not have boasted in vain (2 Cor. 10:12–18). But if someone within the group decided to challenge his honor—"No, he's not that important" (2 Cor. 10:10)—then the onus was on the boaster to defend his honor: (1) he could ignore the challenge, claiming a response would be beneath his dignity (1 Cor. 4:3–4); (2) he could offer a defense, recounting all the reasons why he was so valuable to the group (1 Cor. 9:3–27; 2 Cor. 11:5–30); or (3) he could appeal directly to the group, counting on them to defend his honor (2 Cor. 12:11). Regardless of the tactic employed, the group decided the winner of the contest. Honor claimed was honor gained if the people agreed.

Hospitality in the New Testament World

Dana M. Harris

Hospitality was highly valued throughout the ancient world: Greeks and Romans considered it a moral virtue; Jews understood it to reflect God's own nature (Deut. 10:18). Hospitality usually included lodging and food with the goal of transforming strangers (potential enemies) into allies or friends, and thus differed from entertaining friends or relatives.[1] Guests (and subsequent generations) were bound to reciprocate hospitality.[2] Letters of recommendation were common (cf. Acts 18:27; Rom. 16:1–2; 2 Cor. 3:1–3; Col. 4:10).

The possibility that one might host a disguised deity (Acts 14:8–18) or angel (Heb. 13:2, perhaps alluding to Abraham's hospitality in Gen. 18:1–16) also encouraged hospitality to strangers. This background likely informs Jesus's teaching about receiving "the least of these" (Matt. 25:31–46).

Jesus frequently received hospitality from strangers, such as Zacchaeus (Luke 19:1–10), the Samaritan woman (John 4:1–26), and Mary and Martha (Luke 10:38–42). Hospitality is thus closely linked with receiving Jesus (e.g., Luke 9:11–17; 24:29–35). Moreover, Jesus is the divine host, who provides food (Mark 6:30–44) and shelter (John 14:1–4), and invites his followers to the eschatological wedding banquet (Matt. 22:1–14; Rev. 19:9; cf. Luke 22:7–23).

Missionaries in the early church depended upon hospitality. Jesus links mission and hospitality when he sends out his disciples and the seventy

The living area of a first-century home in Palestine, with stairs leading up to a storage or guest room.

missionaries (Matt. 10:5–16; Mark 6:7–13; Luke 9:1–6; 10:1–18). Hospitality is prominent in Acts (16:11–15, 25–34; 18:1–3; 21:4, 7, 17; 28:7) and in Paul's epistles (1 Cor. 9:4, 16:19; Gal. 4:14; Philem. 22), and is an essential feature in Cornelius's conversion (Acts 10:1–11:18).

Hospitality is commanded (Rom. 12:13; 3 John 5–8) and a qualification of elders (1 Tim. 3:2; Titus 1:8). Conversely, hospitality must not be extended to false teachers (2 John 10–11).

Jerusalem in the Time of Jesus

Mark L. Strauss

Jerusalem could rightly be called the most important city in human history. It was here on Mount Moriah (traditionally associated with the Temple Mount in Jerusalem) that Abraham was willing to offer his son Isaac at God's command (Gen. 22:2). It was here that David was promised that from his descendants God would one day raise up a king—the Messiah—who would reign forever in justice and righteousness (2 Sam. 7:11–16). It was here that Solomon built the one temple to the one true God (1 Kings 5–9). Jerusalem and Mount Zion became symbolic of the presence of God and an eternal resting place for God's people (Isa. 2:3; 24:23; cf. Rev. 21:2).

It was to Jerusalem that Jesus came to challenge the religious authorities of his day and to offer himself as an atoning sacrifice for the sins of the world (Mark 10:33–34, 45). Here he was arrested, tried, and crucified, and rose victorious from the dead. From the Mount of Olives, on the east side of the city, he ascended victorious to heaven, and angels announced that he would one day return in the same way (Acts 1:9–11). In the book of Acts Jerusalem becomes the birthplace of the church and the place of the outpouring of the eschatological Spirit of God. The gospel goes forth from here to Judea, to Samaria, and to the ends of the earth (Acts 1:8).

Topography. Jerusalem is located thirty-three miles east of the Mediterranean Sea and fourteen miles west of the Dead Sea. It is twenty-five hundred feet above sea level. You always go "up" to Jerusalem—not just because of its elevation, but because it is the city of God.

The Israelite city was built on three main hills. The southeast hill, comprising eight to ten acres, was the original city of the Jebusites, which King David captured and made his capital. It became the "city of David" and Mount Zion (2 Sam. 5:6–10). "Zion," of course, later became a poetic name for Jerusalem as a whole and a symbol for the eschatological city of God. On the northern hill of the city (Mount Moriah) King Solomon built his palace and the temple (2 Chron. 3:1). These two hills are part of one ridge and are flanked on the east by the Kidron Valley and the Mount of Olives. The Kidron runs north to south, where it meets the Hinnom Valley, running along the southern and western edge of the city, below the Western Hill. Running north to south through the middle of Jerusalem, just west of the Temple Mount, is the shallower Central Valley (also known as the Tyropoeon Valley).[1]

The main source of water for the city is the Gihon Spring (1 Kings 1:33), which comes from a grotto on the eastern side of the city of David. In 701 BC, when King Hezekiah was preparing for the Assyrian invasion, a tunnel 1,750 feet long was dug connecting the Gihon Spring to the southwestern side of the city (2 Kings 20:20; 2 Chron. 32:1–5, 30).

Jerusalem under Roman Authority. The Jerusalem of Jesus's day was under Roman domination. In 63 BC the Roman general Pompey arrived in Palestine. At the time Jerusalem was divided between two Hasmonean rivals, Hyrcanus II and his brother Aristobolus II. Both sought Roman support, but when Aristobolus resisted, Hyrcanus was appointed ethnarch and high priest. Increasingly, however, authority was invested in an Idumean (Edomite) administrator named Antipater, who had gained the favor and trust of the Romans. When the Parthians plundered Jerusalem and captured Hyrcanus in 40 BC, Antipater's son Herod seized his opportunity and was appointed by the Romans as king of the Jews. Herod "the Great," a skilled politician and great builder, had grand ambitions for Jerusalem. He wanted to make it his showplace and capital, a rival to Rome, Athens, and Alexandria as one of the great cultural centers of the world. On the one hand, Herod was an ardent Hellenist and supporter of Rome. He built a theater, an amphitheater, a hippodrome (racetrack), a grand palace, and several fortresses, including the great Antonia Fortress overlooking the Temple Mount. On the other hand, he sought to support and encourage Jewish identity and religion. His greatest accomplishment was the massive rebuilding and beautification of the Jerusalem temple, one of the great wonders of the ancient world (see the article "The Jerusalem Temple").

At Herod's death his son Archelaus was appointed tetrarch of Judea and Samaria. The Roman emperor assured him that if he ruled well, he would be given all the lands ruled by his father. Yet Archelaus misruled and was deposed. Judea became an imperial province, ruled by Roman governors appointed directly by the emperor. During Jesus's ministry Pontius Pilate was prefect (governor) of Judea. Though Pilate lived and governed from Caesarea Maritima, the Roman headquarters of Judea on the Mediterranean coast, he would come to Jerusalem to maintain order during the major festivals. This is why he was present in Jerusalem for Jesus's trial.

The population of Jerusalem in Jesus's day is debated but is generally viewed as around forty to fifty thousand. During major festivals, when Jewish pilgrims streamed to the city from throughout Israel and from the diaspora, this number would swell as much as tenfold. While the primary power base of the Pharisees and their scribes was the synagogue communities of the towns and villages of Judea and Galilee, in Jerusalem the high priest and the priestly aristocracy had their greatest influence. The Sanhedrin met in Jerusalem at the Hall of Hewn Stones, on the western boundary of the Temple Mount.[2]

As a faithful Jew, Jesus traveled regularly from Galilee to Jerusalem for the Jewish festivals—a requirement for all Jewish males (Deut. 16:16). Though in the Synoptic Gospels Jesus visits Jerusalem only once, at his final Passover, in John's Gospel he comes regularly for various festivals (2:13; 5:1; 6:4; 7:2; 10:22; 11:55).

Jesus clearly viewed Jerusalem with a great deal of ambivalence. It was the city of God, the place of the temple and Yahweh's glory, and yet it was also a place of priestly corruption and exploitation. After clearing the temple of dove sellers and money changers, Jesus accuses the leadership of turning God's house into "a den of thieves" (Mark 11:17). In Jesus's teaching the city becomes symbolic of Israel's rejection of God's purposes and his Messiah. Luke records Jesus's laments over the city's rejection of God's messengers and his predictions of its coming destruction: "Jerusalem, Jerusalem, who kills the prophets and stones those who are sent to her. How often I wanted to gather your children together, as a hen gathers her chicks under her wings, but you were not willing! See, your house is abandoned to you" (Luke 13:34–35).

Luke reports, "As he approached and saw the city, he wept for it, saying, 'If you knew this day what would bring peace—but now it is hidden from your eyes. For the days will come on you when your enemies will build a barricade around you, surround you, and hem you in on every side. They will crush you and your children among you to the ground, and they will not leave one stone on another in your midst, because you did not recognize the time when God visited you" (Luke 19:41–44).

The prophecy was fulfilled in the Jewish Revolt of AD 66–70. After two years of increasing tension under the corrupt and oppressive governorship of Gessius Florus, open revolt broke out in AD 66. After the Romans experienced initial setbacks, including the massacre of the Roman garrison at the Antonia Fortress, the Roman general Vespasian arrived in Palestine to suppress the revolt. Vespasian began subjugating Judea town by town, but he returned to Rome to become emperor after the death of Nero in AD 69. His son Titus completed the siege and destruction of Jerusalem in AD 70. He burned the city and the temple, massacred thousands of its inhabitants, and carried the temple treasures back to Rome.

The mosaic map of the biblical world in St. George's Church in Madaba, Jordan, features a detailed presentation of Jerusalem.

For Jews the destruction of Jerusalem and the temple meant the end of the sacrificial system and the beginning of "rabbinic" Judaism centered on the study of Torah. For Christians it meant confirmation that the OT sacrificial system was at an end, and that Jesus's sacrificial death was the once-and-for-all atoning sacrifice for sins (Heb. 7:27; 9:12). Jesus himself is the new temple (John 2:19–21), providing access to God. The church—his "body"—is the temple in which God's Spirit now dwells (1 Cor. 3:16; Eph. 1:22–23).

The Jerusalem Temple

Mark L. Strauss

The First (Solomon's) Temple. The first Jerusalem temple was built by King Solomon in the tenth century BC. Prior to that time Israel worshiped in the tabernacle, a portable temple designed and commissioned by God in the period after the exodus (Exod. 25–40). When Israel was established in the promised land, the tabernacle was set up at a variety of locations: Gilgal (Josh. 4:19), Shiloh (Josh. 18:1), Nob (1 Sam. 21:1), Gibeon (1 Chron. 16:39; 21:29), and eventually Jerusalem (2 Sam. 6:17).

The plan for a permanent temple was initiated by King David, who bemoaned the fact that he lived in a palace while God lived in a tent (2 Sam. 7:1–2). Yet God told David through the prophet Nathan that this role would go to his son (2 Sam. 7:4–17). When Solomon became king after the death of David, he initiated the task. The building of Solomon's temple and its dedication are described in 1 Kings 5–9. It was completed in seven years and dedicated in Solomon's eleventh year, around 950 BC (1 Kings 6:38). The First Temple stood for a little over 360 years, until it was destroyed in 587 BC by the Babylonians.

The Second (Zerubbabel's) Temple. The Second Temple was initiated after the Babylonian exile, when the Persian king Cyrus conquered Babylon (538 BC) and issued decrees allowing the Jews to return to the land of Israel (Ezra 1). The governor Zerubbabel and the high priest Joshua led in the task (Ezra 3), with the prophets Haggai and Zachariah encouraging the people to finish the work.

The Second Temple experienced a devastating crisis in 168 BC when Antiochus IV Epiphanes attempted to eradicate Judaism by forbidding observance of the law. He sacked the temple and desecrated the sanctuary, offering pagan sacrifices on the altar. The heroic efforts of the Maccabees, however, gained Jewish independence, and the temple was rededicated by Judas Maccabeus three years to the day after its desecration—an event celebrated in the Jewish holiday of Hanukkah.

The Rebuilding of the Temple by Herod the Great. The Second Temple was expanded on a dramatic scale in the first century BC by Herod the Great. Although Herod, an Idumean by birth, was never accepted by most Jews as their legitimate king, he was a shrewd leader and political survivor. Appointed by the Romans as king of the Jews, Herod fortified Rome's eastern frontier, strengthened Jewish nationalism, and launched many building projects. His greatest achievement was the massive rebuilding and beautification of the temple.

Herod's temple was one of the great wonders of the ancient world.[1] The massive earthen platform it stood on was almost 550 yards north to south and 330 yards east to west, a total of approximately 35 acres. Josephus describes some of the stones used in the construction as being up to 70 feet long. Their brilliant white appearance made the temple look from a distance like a snow-covered mountain. Gold shields hung on the walls and reflected sunlight with such radiance that people had to shield their eyes like they would from the sun.[2] A rabbinic proverb said, "He who has not seen the temple of Herod has never seen a beautiful building in his life."[3]

The temple complex was the center of Jewish religious life, a place for sacrifices, prayer, worship, and teaching (Mark 11:17; 12:35). The outer Court of Gentiles was lined with 162 massive fifty-foot-high pillars cut in Corinthian style. Gentiles could proceed no farther into the inner courts, and a sign warning of immediate death for any non-Jew who entered was

An artist's rendition of the Second Temple viewed from the southwest.

placed at each gate. It was here in the Court of Gentiles that Jesus turned over the tables of dove sellers and money changers (Mark 11:15–17).

The inner courts of the temple were a series of concentric and exclusionary courtyards. The Court of Women, where any Jew could go, contained the temple treasury, with thirteen trumpet-shaped chests for offerings dedicated to the temple (Mark 12:41–44; Luke 21:1–4). The Court of Israel, where only Jewish males could enter, was next, and then, around the temple building proper, was the Court of Priests. This court contained the altar of burnt offering and the bronze laver for ceremonial washing. The temple proper was 150 feet high and was comprised of the holy place and the most holy place (or holy of holies). The holy place contained the lampstand, the altar of incense, and the table for consecrated bread. The holy place was separated from the most holy place by a magnificent Babylonian curtain, embroidered with blue, scarlet, and purple, symbolically representing the universe.[4] Through this curtain the high priest entered the most holy place only once a year, on the Day of Atonement (Lev. 16:1–34). The most holy place originally contained the ark of the covenant, but presumably the ark was destroyed at the Babylonian exile and not replaced.[5] Instead, a slab of stone marked its place, where the high priest dripped the sacrificial blood.[6]

Begun by Herod in about 20 BC, work on the temple continued until AD 64, shortly before its destruction in AD 70. Jesus predicted the destruction of the temple in his Olivet Discourse (Mark 13:2; cf. Luke 13:35), and forty years later, during the Jewish Revolt of AD 66–73, the Romans besieged Jerusalem and destroyed the temple.

Modern picture of the Temple Mount in Jerusalem.

Jewish Festivals

Andreas J. Köstenberger

Of the six major festivals mentioned in the OT (Passover/Festival of Unleavened Bread; Festival of Weeks/Pentecost; Festival of Trumpets; Day of Atonement; Festival of Shelters; Sabbath), the Gospels explicitly reference three: Passover, Shelters (or Tabernacles/Booths), and Sabbath (see the article "The Sabbath"). While all three Synoptic Gospels mention a single Passover festival when Jesus celebrates the Passover with his disciples before his death (e.g., Matt. 26:1–2, 17–30), John mentions the final Passover festival (11:55), as well as two earlier celebrations (2:13, 23; 6:4). The Passover was Israel's most important feast, celebrating God's miraculous deliverance of his people from Egypt and marking the beginning of Israel's religious year. Passover was one of three pilgrimage festivals, along with Passover and Weeks, which Jewish men were supposed to celebrate in Jerusalem. In Jesus's day the Passover lambs were slaughtered at the temple in the afternoon of 14 Nisan, so that families were ready to celebrate Passover that evening on 15 Nisan.

John's Gospel also notes Jesus's celebration of the Festival of Shelters (7:2). Shelters was celebrated for seven days, as well as an additional day on which a sacred assembly was held and sacrifices were offered. This was the final festival in the Jewish calendar and the most joyous. The Israelites rejoiced in God's provision of rainfall as well as in the newly gathered harvest of grain and the pressing of grapes.[1] The festival also served to commemorate God's provision for his people during the wilderness wanderings. Following the exile, it was the first festival celebrated by those who had returned, and it became associated with the hope of new, abundant life (Neh. 8:13–18) and end-time hope.[2] According to Josephus, it was "a most holy and most eminent feast."[3]

In addition, the Gospel of John records the celebration of the Festival of Dedication. Also known as Hanukkah or Feast of Lights, the festival was not stipulated in the OT but commemorated God's deliverance and the rededication of the temple during the Maccabean era. Antiochus IV Epiphanes had desecrated the temple in 167 BC by offering a sacrifice to Zeus. When Antiochus's representatives came to the town of Modein to force the Jews to offer pagan sacrifices, Mattathias, a godly priest, refused. Upon seeing another Jew go forward to participate, he struck down both the apostate Jew and the king's official, starting a rebellion. In 164 BC the temple was rededicated and purified on 25 Chislev (December 14). The ensuing celebration lasted eight days.[4] Unlike the pilgrimage festivals celebrated in Jerusalem, the Festival of Dedication was enjoyed at home as Jews reflected on and rejoiced in God's miraculous deliverance.[5]

Jewish Marriage Customs

Alan S. Bandy

From the inception of the world in the creation narrative of Genesis, the marriage of a man and a woman was understood to be the intention of God and the ideal situation of humanity.[1] Patterned after Adam and Eve, marriage was defined as a union between a male and female (Lev. 18:22–23). Polygamy was tolerated for kings and wealthy individuals, but monogamy was clearly understood to be the original design of God.[2] Divorce typically was frowned upon, unless the woman was unfaithful, for she was supposed to be a virgin before marriage and thereafter remain faithful to her husband (Lev. 20:10; Deut. 22:21; John 8:1–4). If the husband died without a son, the widow could marry a close kin of the husband (levirate marriage) to preserve the family line of the deceased man (Gen. 38:6–11; Deut. 25:5–10; Ruth 1:11–13; 4:10).

While marriages traditionally were arranged between families by the parents (Gen. 24:1–9; Judg. 14:2), a man could also make arrangements directly with the parents of the woman (Gen. 29:16–22).[3] Sometimes in ancient Israel a father would give his daughter to a man as a reward or as part of an agreement between the two men (Exod. 2:21; 1 Sam. 17:25; 18:17–21). A woman apparently had some say in the person whom she agreed to marry or not marry.[4] Once an agreement of marriage was made, the man was expected to give a monetary gift, often called a "bride-price," to seal the betrothal of the couple (Gen. 24:53; 29:18; Exod. 22:16–17;

Roman wives wore a veil to indicate their marital status. This carved head of Livia, wife of Augustus, shows the veil covering her hair.

Hosea 3:2).[5] The betrothal was legally binding and varied in length, but usually did not exceed twelve months. The betrothal could be broken only by legal means.

During the betrothal period the man built a room onto his parents' home, where, upon the "wedding day," the woman was delivered, a marriage contract signed, consummation occurred, and their marriage was sealed. The bride was adorned in fine clothing and jewels and was covered by a veil. Both bride and groom were accompanied by groups of companions. On the evening of the marriage day the groom and groomsmen proceeded—sometimes with festive music and dancing—to the house of the bride. From there, the wedding party generally held the wedding feast at the home of the groom or his parents (John 2:11; Matt. 22:1–10). At some point in the ceremony there was likely a custom whereby the groom spread the skirt of his garment over the bride (Ruth 3:9; Ezek. 16:8) to symbolize taking her under his protection. At long last, the couple would enter the bedchamber (known as the *huppa* or *chuppa*) to consummate the marriage with a physical union.[6] Once the ceremony was over, the festivities continued on for a week or more. The couple was treated as royalty for the week.[7] The Talmud states that the husband was responsible for providing his wife with food, clothing, shelter, medical care, ransom from captivity, and honorable burial.[8]

The Jewish Rite of Circumcision

Roy E. Ciampa

Circumcision was practiced by some ancient Semitic groups and Egyptians long before the practice was adopted by the Israelites. The way circumcision is introduced in the patriarchal narratives suggests the characters are already supposed to know what it is (Gen. 17:10), but it is also introduced as an essential sign and requirement of the covenant that God was establishing with Abraham and his family.

Philo understood circumcision to have physical benefits and to symbolize the cutting off of pleasures and passions as well as human arrogance and vanity.[1] Later in the first century Josephus argued that God commanded circumcision on the eighth day in order that Abraham's "posterity should be kept from mixing with others."[2]

Circumcision was a key marker of (male) Jewish identity in Second Temple Judaism. Jewish boys were circumcised on their eighth day (Lev. 12:3; Luke 1:59; 2:21; Phil. 3:5), and male proselytes were circumcised when they became full members of the Jewish community, responsible for keeping the Mosaic law. Circumcision normally was the final and most difficult step in the conversion process, since Greek and Roman views of the body made circumcision seem unnatural to them.

Some texts (Lev. 26:41; Deut. 10:16; 30:6; Jer. 4:4; 9:25–26; Ezek. 44:7, 9) distinguish between physical circumcision and circumcision of the heart, implying that physical circumcision alone was insufficient. That distinction becomes important in the NT, especially for Paul's understanding of the status of gentile believers in Christ (see Acts 7:51; Rom. 2:25–29; Phil. 3:3; Eph. 2:11). Paul considered circumcision (or its lack) unimportant unless someone imposed it on gentiles, at which point he considered it a direct affront to the gospel (1 Cor. 7:19; Gal. 5:2–6; 6:15).

The Jewish Synagogue

Mark L. Strauss

The synagogue (Heb. *bet kenesset*; Gk. *synagōgē*) was a local Jewish gathering place for instruction in the law, worship, prayer, and administration. The term could be used for the meeting place or for the community that met there. While in Judaism there was only one temple (in Jerusalem), symbolizing the one true God, there were many synagogues scattered throughout the Roman world. Cities with large Jewish populations would have many synagogues. We know of at least eleven by name in Rome in the first century. The Jewish Talmud claims that in Jerusalem in the first century there were 480 synagogues![1] Another term for a synagogue is "house of prayer" (Heb. *bet tefillah*; Gk. *proseuchē* [cf. Acts 16:13]).

Jesus taught regularly in the synagogues of Galilee (e.g., Matt. 4:23; 9:35). Similarly, when the apostle Paul entered a city he would find a synagogue and begin his ministry there (e.g., Acts 9:20; 13:5, 14; 14:1). There he would find not only Jews but also God-fearing gentiles (Acts 13:16, 26), who were particularly open to the gospel message.

The origin of the synagogue is uncertain, but as an institution it likely arose during the Babylonian exile, after the destruction of the Jerusalem temple in 587 BC.[2] Our earliest descriptions of a synagogue service come from Christian sources: Jesus's teaching in the synagogue of Nazareth in Luke 4 and Paul's preaching in the synagogue of Pisidian Antioch in Acts 13. The similarities between these accounts and later Jewish sources suggest a basic order of service, including the following elements:

recitation of the *Shema Yisrael* ("Hear, O Israel"), comprised of Deut. 6:4–9; 11:13–21; Num. 15:37–41

various prayers, especially the *Tefillah* ("the Prayer"), also known as the *Shemoneh Esreh*, or "Eighteen Benedictions"

readings from the Hebrew Scriptures, the Law and the Prophets (Acts 13:15; cf. Luke 4:16–17)

an oral Targum, which was an Aramaic paraphrase of the Hebrew Scriptures reading, with interpretive expansions

a homily or sermon on the text or texts for the day

closing benediction

psalms may also have been sung (cf. Mark 14:26)

The synagogue did not have a pastor or minister. Any qualified male might be invited to read the Scripture and give instruction (Acts 13:15). The "synagogue leader" (Heb. *rosh hakkenesset*; Gk. *archisynagōgos*) was the chief administrator (Mark 5:22, 35; Luke 8:49; 13:14; Acts 13:15; 18:8, 17). His role was to maintain the facilities, organize services, and keep order.[3] The term sometimes is used in the plural, perhaps referring to a council of elders

Ruins of the synagogue at Arbel in Lower Galilee.

(Acts 13:15). In addition to the synagogue ruler, there was an attendant (Heb. *hazzan hakkenesset*; Gk. *hypēretēs* [Luke 4:20]). The attendant's roles likely included cleaning the facilities, removing and returning the scrolls (Luke 4:20), and educating children. He may also have carried out judicial punishment.

In addition to instruction in Torah, synagogues also functioned as administrative and judicial centers for the Jewish community. Paul says that five times he "received the forty lashes minus one from the Jews" (2 Cor. 11:24)—likely judicial punishments that took place in local synagogues. Jesus similarly warns his followers that they will be flogged in the synagogues for their faith (Matt. 23:34; Mark 13:9; cf. Acts 22:19; 26:11).

There was no single architectural model for the synagogue, and different communities built their synagogues differently. Common to most was a niche or chamber where sacred scrolls were kept. A raised platform in the center of the room served as a podium for reading Scripture and for teaching. Congregants sat on benches along the walls. Certain seats carried special honor (Mark 12:39). Synagogues generally were segregated, with men and women worshiping separately.

There is inscriptional evidence for gentile support for some synagogues,[4] and Luke 7:1–5 refers to a particular gentile centurion who loved the Jewish people and provided patronage to build their synagogue.

Magic in the New Testament World

DANA M. HARRIS

Magic involves the belief that spirits and supernatural powers can be controlled by correctly performing certain rituals or incantations. Scholars debate the distinction between magic and religion, although most view magic as deviant behavior that seeks to effect results when prevailing religious institutions fail.[1] Moreover, religious rituals tended to occur regularly (e.g., yearly) and publicly, whereas magic occurs randomly and privately.

Magic was prevalent in the ancient world. Widespread belief that spirits were everywhere and in everything fostered a highly superstitious worldview in which ordinary events (e.g., sneezing) were seen as evil portents. Greco-Roman magic was also syncretistic, blending practices and beliefs from eastern and western traditions, such as astrology from Babylon, the "secret name" idea from Egypt, and, from Persia, the belief that demons caused human misery and could be agents of magicians.[2]

Major forms of magic included protective magic (against diseases, enemies, or evil spirits); imprecatory or malevolent magic; "love" magic or control over others; and divination. Practitioners (magicians, sorcerers, witches) used incantations,

An ancient amulet claiming to offer spiritual protection for the one who wears it.

spells, and curses (often compiled into books). Talismans, amulets, and charms were common. So prevalent was the belief in magic that frauds easily took advantage of desperate, gullible individuals. Hence the Greek word for "sorcerer" (*goēs*) became nearly synonymous with "swindler."[3] Magical practices and practitioners generally were illegal throughout the Roman Empire.

Jewish law also forbade magic (Lev. 19:26; 20:6); even so, some Jews were well known as magicians. Some linked magic with Solomon's "wisdom" (1 Kings 5:12). Josephus claimed that this "wisdom" was for exorcism and healing. Jewish magicians emphasized incantations involving names of God or angels (e.g., Acts 19:13–17). Some Jewish magic books specify which angel (Michael, Gabriel, Uriel, Raphael, etc.) to invoke against specific demons associated with certain ailments (e.g., headaches, tumors, fevers).[4] Acts 19:19 records how some recent converts in Ephesus burned their extremely valuable magic scrolls.

Jesus was accused of being demon-possessed and performing miracles by Satan's power (Mark 3:22; John 7:20; 8:48, 52; 10:20) and of being a deceiver (Matt. 27:63; John 7:12, 47). Such charges were tantamount to accusations of practicing magic. The claim that Jesus was a magician is found in several nonbiblical sources (e.g., the Babylonian Talmud and Origen's apologetic work *Against Celsus*).

The book of Acts presents a distinction between miracles (often public events with soteriological and ecclesiological significance) and magic (often random, private events that opposed the gospel). Thus the impressive magic practiced by Simon was for his own reputation. He clearly recognized the superior power of the Holy Spirit, yet he tried to buy this power to increase his own, and he was sharply rebuked (Acts 8:9–25). On Cyprus Paul and his companions met Bar-Jesus, also known as Elymas. The attempt by this magician and false prophet to thwart the gospel resulted in severe punishment (Acts 13:6–12). In Philippi a slave girl fortune-teller so harassed Paul that he cast out the evil spirit within her, thereby gaining her freedom and his imprisonment (Acts 16:16–21). While in Ephesus (a well-known center for magic) Paul performed "extraordinary miracles" that brought glory to the Lord (Acts 19:11–12), whereas the exorcism attempted by Sceva and his sons exposed their deceit (Acts 19:13–17).

The accounts in Acts, together with specific prohibitions against magic and condemnation of its practitioners elsewhere in the NT (Gal. 5:20; Rev. 9:21; 18:23; 21:8; 22:15), stress that magic contradicts God's will.

Messianic Expectations in Jesus's Day

Dana M. Harris

The word "messiah" derives from the Hebrew word for "anointed one"; the word "Christ" derives from the Greek *christos,* also meaning "anointed one." Thus a messiah is one anointed by God to do his will. Additional messianic terms include the Chosen One or Elect One, the Root, the Branch, the Star, and the Son of Man.

Messianic expectations anticipate various (sometimes eschatological) events: political or military deliverance from foreign oppressors, restoration of Israel's independence and monarchy, judgment of the wicked, vindication of the righteous, inauguration of the final age and new creation, and possibly resurrection and eternal life. Such expectations were characterized by much diversity in the centuries leading to Jesus's time, and not all eschatological hopes involved a messiah.

Several key OT passages and figures, particularly Moses and Elijah, grounded later messianic expectations (e.g., Gen. 49:10; Num. 24:17; 2 Sam. 7:11–14; Ps. 2; Isa. 11:1–4; esp. Dan. 7:13–14, which presents a messianic figure "like a son of man"). Messianic expectations, however, arose more often out of desires for liberation from foreign oppression or disillusionment with political rulers than from speculation on OT texts. Indeed, some messianic expectations are not found in the OT.

Jewish writings of this period evince these diverse messianic expectations. Some Qumran manuscripts (ca. 250 BC–AD 68) speak about the Prophet,

During the Jewish Revolt against the Romans (AD 66–74), a group of Zealots captured the mountaintop fortress of Masada and held out there for several years. Shown here is an aerial view of Masada, where the Roman siege ramp is still visible.

whereas others anticipate a messiah of Aaron (the priestly line of Levi) and a messiah of Israel (the royal line of Judah). The idea of two messiahs perhaps derives from the two anointed ones in Zech. 4:14.

In the Pseudepigrapha (spurious writings ostensibly composed by ancient biblical persons or prophets but actually written sometime between ca. 250 BC and AD 100) one finds an earthly Davidic king who restores Israel (*Psalms of Solomon* 18 [first century BC]), which probably informed many messianic expectations in Jesus's day. Yet *1 Enoch* 37–71 (second century BC) describes a heavenly, non-Davidic messiah ("Son of Man," "Elect One"), eventually identified as Enoch himself. *Fourth Ezra* 7 (ca. AD 100) presents a messiah who reigns for four hundred years and then dies with humanity, after which the new age begins.

Roman occupation of Judea prompted various responses. Some claimed that resistance was futile and that Israel should wait for God to intervene or send his messiah. Others, however, believed that revolt would hasten the messiah to drive out the Romans; still others claimed to be the messiah. Both Acts and Josephus reference several messianic pretenders. Acts 5:36 mentions Theudas (ca. AD 44), and Acts 21:38 references an Egyptian who led four thousand rebels. Other false messiahs include Simon bar Giora (AD 66–73, First Jewish Revolt) and Simeon ben Kosiba, later called Bar Kokhba, "Son of the Star" (AD 132–35, Second Jewish Revolt).

All four Gospels proclaim Jesus the Christ, the true Messiah, who was the promised Son of David (Matt. 1:1; Luke 2:11) and uniquely anointed by the Spirit (Luke 4:18–19, appropriating Isa. 61:1–2). Jesus's favorite self-designation was "Son of Man," which drew upon Dan. 7:13–14 and grounded his authority (e.g., Mark 2:1–12). He himself affirmed that he was the Messiah (Mark 14:61–62), and his disciples recognized him as such (Matt. 16:16). Yet Jesus consistently rejected incorrect messianic expectations (e.g., Mark 1:40–45; John 7:25–44) and redefined these expectations according to himself and his unique mission,[1] which culminated in the redemption achieved through his crucifixion and resurrection. The expectation of a suffering messiah is unparalleled in Jewish messianic hopes, even though the OT anticipated it (e.g., Ps. 22; Isa. 53; cf. Luke 24:26–27, 45–47).

The Pauline Epistles focus especially on Jesus as the Messiah (Rom. 9:5) and affirm the early church's recognition of Jesus's messianic status, as do Acts and the General Epistles. The book of Revelation presents the eschatological victory and enthronement of Jesus, the Messiah.

Money in the New Testament World

E. Randolph Richards

Bullion were coins where the value of the metal matched the coin's value. Theoretically, a silver denarius contained a denarius's worth of silver. Initially (in 211 BC), the denarius contained 4.5 grams of silver. By the time of Jesus it was 3.9 grams. By the time of Paul, Nero further debased it to 3.4 grams and reduced the purity from 98 percent to 93.5 percent.

The Roman denarius is commonly said to be worth one day's wage. The sole basis for this claim is Jesus's parable (Matt. 20:2). Jesus's parable was stressing the generosity of the landowner at harvest. A half-denarius was more commonly a day's wage.[1] Translated into today's wages, a denarius was about $125.

Although Rome allowed many provincial cities around the empire to mint cheaper bronze coins, only a few select cities outside of Rome were allowed to mint the gold aureus and the silver denarius. Why would a Jew have a denarius with Caesar's image, especially in the temple (Matt. 22:19–21)? Coins that contained precious metal were always at risk of being shaved or "clipped." Thieves sought to discreetly remove a bit from the edges of these coins and then pass them off. (The industrial revolution brought milling or reeding—the ridges on the edges of coins—to reduce the chance of clipping.) Roman

A silver denarius of Octavian.

coins were preferred to provincial ones because Rome enforced honest coins (brutally with the sword). Jesus tells them that if they want Caesar to keep the money honest, then they have to pay his taxes (Matt. 22:21). The kingdom of God, where no one cheats a neighbor, is the other way to ensure honest money. Jesus was challenging them to pick which king and kingdom they wanted.

New Testament Household Codes

Dana M. Harris

"Household codes" (sometimes indicated by the German word *Haustafeln*) refers to several NT passages (Eph. 5:18–6:9; Col. 3:18–4:1; cf. 1 Pet. 2:13–3:7) that address individuals within a household. Thus understanding the nature of the "household" (Gk. *oikos*) in the NT world is essential for interpreting these passages. Rather than the relatively small nuclear family prevalent in much of modern society, the Greco-Roman *oikos* is best understood in terms of economic production, usually centered around a long, single-story building (*domus*), in which rooms in the front were mainly public spaces where the master of the household (the *paterfamilias*) conducted business and received clients. This area might include a shop facing the street that sold goods produced by the *oikos*, such as olive oil or grain. The back of the *domus* was the realm of the wife and especially the daughters, who usually were not permitted in the front (public) part of the *oikos*. The *oikos* was a key part of the hierarchical, tightly structured patronage system that dictated Roman society. The *paterfamilias* was a patron who assisted clients, often legally or financially, in exchange for public displays of honor, votes, or information.

Patronage similarly dictated the structure of the *oikos*. The *oikos* comprised the *paterfamilias*, his wife, children, and slaves, all of whom were considered his property (although perhaps less so in some cases for wives). The *paterfamilias* had absolute authority, such as which gods were to be worshiped and the right of life or death within the *oikos*. (The fact that the *paterfamilias* had these rights does not imply that every *paterfamilias* exercised them, however.) Members of the *oikos* benefited from the protection and provision of the *paterfamilias* and in turn owed him complete obedience. The wife's role was to produce a male heir, and female babies could be "exposed" or abandoned at the discretion of the *paterfamilias*. Failure to produce a male heir could be grounds for divorce. Thus marriage was primarily for the continuation of the *oikos*, as is implied in the oft-quoted line from Demosthenes: "Mistresses we keep for the sake of pleasure, concubines for the daily care of the body, but wives to bear us legitimate children."[1]

Philosophers (such as Aristotle)[2] and Jewish writers (such as Philo and Josephus) stressed proper "household management," focusing especially on the rights of the *paterfamilias*. Obedience to the *paterfamilias* was assumed for the proper functioning of society. There is general agreement that the NT household codes assume the context of the *oikos* and draw upon Hellenistic writings. Indeed, there are clear similarities, such as the common pairings of husband/wife, father/children, master/slaves, and the submission of wives, children, and slaves to the *paterfamilias*. Yet there are also significant differences. Whereas Hellenistic writings address only the *paterfamilias*, the NT passages address each member of each pairing, all of whom are addressed before the *paterfamilias* (e.g., wives before husbands, children before fathers, slaves before masters), arguably to indicate individual responsibility and mutual reciprocity in these relationships. Moreover, the fact that each group is independently accountable to the Lord for its behavior has no direct parallel in Hellenistic writings. Finally, the NT passages focus on the responsibilities, not the rights, of the *paterfamilias*. Thus the *paterfamilias* is repeatedly exhorted to love his *own* wife, as Christ loves the church. This countercultural emphasis undermined prevailing norms regarding mistresses and concubines. Similarly, the declaration that both masters and slaves serve the same Lord challenged key cultural assumptions. Instead, Eph. 3:14 presents God as the glorious *paterfamilias* over his *oikos*, which he is establishing in Christ.

Pharisees and Sadducees

Andreas J. Köstenberger

The Pharisees and Sadducees were two prominent religious parties in Judaism in the first century. Both groups likely originated during the Hasmonean era following the Maccabean Revolt. The Pharisees' roots went back to the Hasidim, pious Jews who lived during the second century BC. Their name means "separatists," which was reflected in their concern for ritual purity and obedience to the law (Torah) in order to see Israel live as a holy nation. The exact origins of the Sadducees are unclear, though the traditional view is that they developed from the priestly noble class that supported the Hasmonean dynasty. Their name may stem from the priestly line of Zadok.[1] During the first century AD they were connected with the priestly class, and their primary concern was with the temple and associated worship system. The Sadducees were political conservatives, which helped secure their positions of authority. According to Josephus, the two groups appealed to very different segments of society: "While the Sadducees are able to persuade none but the rich, and have not the populace obsequious to them, but the Pharisees have the multitude on their side."[2] Both parties were represented on the Sanhedrin; the Sadducees were the majority and the Pharisees an influential minority.[3]

The Gospels attest that there were some Pharisees who cautiously followed Jesus. Joseph of Arimathea, who went to Pilate and asked for Jesus's body so as to give him a proper burial, is called a secret follower of Jesus

(John 19:38–40). Nicodemus approaches Jesus privately early in his ministry, cautions the Sanhedrin against judging him rashly, and is present at his burial as well (John 3:1–15; 7:50–52; 19:39–40). Apart from these two exceptions, the Gospels present both the Pharisees and Sadducees as being largely antagonistic toward Jesus. They tested him (Mark 8:11–13), and tried to trap him with theologically and politically sensitive questions (e.g., Matt. 12:1–14; Luke 20:19–40), and eventually conspired to kill him (Matt. 26:1–5; John 11:45–53). Jesus also had harsh words for them, accusing them of being hypocrites (e.g., Matt. 15:1–9) and denouncing them (e.g., Matt. 23; Luke 11:42–52).

Josephus has an extended discussion of the two groups describing their differences. They are cast largely as opposites, and Josephus clearly favors the Pharisees.[4] The central contrasts between the Pharisees and Sadducees pertain to their views of Scripture and authority, which led to different practical concerns. The Pharisees held not only the Hebrew Scriptures as authoritative but also the oral law that had been passed down to them. They were known for emphasizing proper adherence to the law, maintaining the traditions of their ancestors, and pursuing ritual purity, especially concerning food. They believed in angels, demons, bodily resurrection, and fate. The Sadducees, however, rejected any idea of bodily resurrection (Mark 12:18; Acts 23:8),[5] as well as the existence of angels, demons, and fate. They viewed the Torah as preeminent above the rest of Scripture. Their concern for purity was focused on the temple ministry, and they were particularly strict in this regard.[6]

Pontius Pilate

Andreas J. Köstenberger

Pontius Pilate served as procurator (governor) of Judea from AD 26 to 37. Following the deposition of Herod the Great's son Archelaus by the emperor Augustus, Rome began to rule Judea directly. A series of Roman governors were put in charge, beginning with Coponius.[1] Pilate was the fifth governor, put in charge of Judea by the emperor Tiberius, likely receiving this position due to the influence of his mentor, Sejanus. Once appointed, he quickly found himself clashing with the Jews.[2]

Josephus recounts an incident in which Pilate sent troops to winter in Jerusalem. The images of the emperor on the troops' standards were forbidden by Jewish law, leading to Pilate's house in Caesarea being surrounded by angry Jews demanding that he remove the images. Upon his initial refusal, the Jews fell prostrate and stayed there, unmoved, for five days and nights. The following day he called the Jews together and ordered his soldiers to surround them. He then told them to accept the images or be cut in pieces, at which point they bared their necks, accepting death over the images. Their willingness to die caused him to relent.[3]

A later confrontation did not end as peacefully. Pilate used money from the temple treasury to construct an aqueduct, once again upsetting the Jews. When Pilate was in Jerusalem, Jews gathered at his tribunal to protest his actions, but Pilate was prepared. Having ordered some of his soldiers to dress in plain clothes, he stationed them among the protesters and then ordered them to attack the Jews with clubs. The result was that "the Jews were so sadly beaten, that many of them perished by the stripes they received, and many of them perished as trodden to death, by which means the multitude was astonished at the calamity of those that were slain, and held their peace."[4]

Josephus and Philo both characterize Pilate as a cruel, unjust leader.[5] It is likely that Pilate was able to act harshly toward the Jews because of his relationship with Sejanus, who was known as an anti-Semite.[6] Sejanus may have prevented complaints against Pilate from reaching the Roman emperor Tiberius. However, following Sejanus's death Pilate's position in Rome was not as secure, and he was forced to proceed more cautiously.[7]

Pontius Pilate was the Roman prefect over Judea and Samaria in the years AD 26–37. A building inscription with Pilate's name and title was found at Caesarea Maritima.

All four Gospels attest to Pilate's role in crucifying Jesus (Matt. 27:1–2, 11–26; Mark 15:1–15; Luke 23:1–5, 18–25; John 18:28–19:16). His role in the crucifixion is also attested outside the Gospels. The Roman historian Tacitus wrote, "Christ had been executed in Tiberius' reign by the procurator of Judea, Pontius Pilate."[8] Pilate's cruelty was not limited to the Jews, and after Pilate had killed a great number of Samaritans, Vitellius, the legate of Syria, deposed him and sent him back to Rome in AD 36/37.[9]

Roman Citizenship

Alan S. Bandy

Roman citizenship was a privilege for the freeborn inhabitants of Rome from its foundation (753 BC), and as the empire gradually expanded, other territories, colonies, and cities in Italy, Gaul, and Asia were included.[1] Roman citizens enjoyed prestige and privilege far exceeding the general population of the empire. The basic rights of Roman citizenship were the right to appeal (*provocatio*), the right to vote (*suffragium*) in the assembly, the right to choose between a local or Roman trial, and protection from degrading forms of punishment.[2] Emperor Augustus passed a law (*lex Iulia de ui publica*) that forbade any magistrate invested with the right of capital punishment (*imperium*) to kill, scourge, chain, or torture a Roman citizen if he made an appeal. A magistrate who disregarded the appeal and carried out a capital sentence was guilty of murder.[3] Most importantly, Roman citizens were exempt from death by crucifixion, so citizens were executed by beheading.[4]

The easiest path to citizenship was by birth to parents who were citizens. Parents were required to register their children within thirty days to have legal acknowledgment of the child's citizenship (*professio*).[5] Citizenship was also granted to those who served in the auxiliary militia for a certain length of time.[6] Sometimes people received citizenship because they accomplished a noble feat or simply because they were very wealthy or prominent people.[7] Slaves often gained citizenship by obtaining manumission (freedom) either by their owner or by raising sufficient money to purchase it. Only formal manumission (before a magistrate) granted both freedom and Roman citizenship.[8] Another means of obtaining citizenship came from an en bloc grant bestowed on a city or colony by an emperor. Lastly, one could purchase citizenship. To do so, however, was very expensive—possibly as much as double the average annual income of a day laborer (Acts 22:28).[9] While citizens could carry documentation to prove their citizenship, claims of citizenship generally were trusted because the penalty for impersonating a Roman citizen was death.[10]

The rights of Roman citizenship come to the forefront in the ministry of the apostle Paul. Paul was born in a Jewish family in Tarsus of Cilicia (Acts 22:3), of which he was a citizen (Acts 21:39). Moreover, Paul makes several claims that he was a Roman citizen (Acts 16:37–38; 22:25–28) and that he received his citizenship by birth (Acts 22:28). There is some debate about how Paul's family became citizens. Perhaps they purchased it, but most likely it was through an en bloc grant from Augustus. The people of the city of Tarsus sided with Octavian Augustus in opposition to Caesar's assassins, Cassius and Brutus, because many in the city were forced into slavery due to the excessive taxes mandated by Cassius. With the defeat of Cassius and Brutus at the battle of Philippi (42 BC), Tarsus was given the status of *civitas libera* and its residents were exempt from taxes. Those who were sold into slavery were freed, and many of them were granted citizenship at the same time because of their support for Augustus.[11] The fact that the apostle is named both Saul and Paul also points to his Roman citizenship because Roman citizens had to register with the government using the *tria nomina* consisting of the *praenomen* (first name), *nomen* (family name), and *cognomen* (extra name, like the modern middle name). His citizenship granted him a measure of status in the Roman world and afforded him the full rights of citizenship. This explains why he could appeal to have his case heard by the emperor (Acts 25:9–12) and why he was likely beheaded instead of crucified.

The Roman Military

Alan S. Bandy

When Polybius, the Greek historian, wrote about the rise of the Roman Empire, the question that drove him was how the Romans succeeded in bringing almost the entire known world under their rule in less than fifty-three years (from 220 BC, the start of the Second Punic War, to about 167 BC).[1] Through its military Rome became one of superpowers of the ancient world. Over the centuries the Roman military developed in a variety of ways, but during the first century AD it reached the height of its power.

While Rome had a capable navy, it is the Roman legion that is the genius and basis of its success. "Legion" (*legio*) originally meant "levy" in terms of Roman citizens capable of bearing arms (usually between the ages of seventeen and forty-six), but later it became a specific and sizable military unit.[2] There were ten cohorts in a legion, and each cohort had around five hundred soldiers. The uniformity of equipment (each solider was issued a spear [*pilum*] and a sword [*gladius*]) and training, coupled with the simplicity of the leadership structure (each cohort had an officer to relay commands) made the legion more flexible, strategic, and deadly.[3]

Emperor Octavian Augustus (27 BC–AD 14) revised, fine-tuned, and established the organization and format of the military that endured for over a century. Augustus inherited some sixty legions, but by the time of his death he reduced the total number of legions to about twenty-five.[4] A legion numbered around five to six thousand infantry and cavalry. There also were auxiliary units, which were comprised of foreign soldiers from various non-Roman peoples that fought alongside the Roman army.[5] The establishment of the Praetorian Guard and the garrison at Rome was another significant

This relief shows a well-armed Roman soldier carrying a spear, sword, and shield (second century AD).

development of this period.[6] The garrison at Rome housed nine cohorts of the Praetorian Guard as well the urban cohorts (a police force) and the *vigiles* (a fire brigade).[7] The Praetorian Guard derived their name from the word *praetorium* ("camp" or "headquarters" [cf. Mark 15:16; Matt. 27:27]), and they served as imperial bodyguards. The Praetorian Guard trained as legionaries, but their status was much higher, their dress and equipment much more elaborate, and they were better paid.[8]

The legions were numbered (e.g., X, XIII, XIV) and given titles, which gave them a unique identity and a shared sense of camaraderie.[9] In general, all legionaries were Roman citizens with the highest-ranking officers drawn from the senatorial class.[10] The emperor, as the first citizen (*princeps*), commander (*imperator*), and the highest civil authority (*consul*), technically had command of the entire army, but he delegated this command in the provinces to propraetorian legates.[11] An individual legion was commanded by the legionary legate. The administration of the legion belonged to the senior tribune—a senatorial designate who had no prior military experience—as well as five other tribunes usually from the equestrian class.[12] The largest group of officers, the centurions, could come from the common class of soldiers. Centurions commanded a "century" of about eighty soldiers, and there were ten centuries in each cohort.[13] Legions were also staffed with medical personnel, craftsmen, and scribes.

In the NT the Roman occupation in Judea created multiple tensions with the Jewish people, but some of the earliest converts to faith in Christ came from the ranks of the centurions. In the Gospels a centurion had a faith that impressed Jesus (Matt. 8:5–13), and the centurion overseeing the crucifixion declared that Jesus was the Son of God (Mark 15:39). Cornelius, a God-fearing centurion, was the one God used to teach Peter and the apostles that the gospel was to include gentiles as well as Jews (Acts 10). Several centurions in Paul's ministry were men of honor who respected Paul (Acts 22:26–30; 23:17–35; 24:23; 27).

Roman Roads and Travel

MARK WILSON

By the first century AD the Romans had built a road network that encircled the Mediterranean Sea. These roads helped Christians to disseminate the gospel from Jerusalem throughout the empire. The roads were built initially by soldiers to move the legions to their military postings. Later the local citizenry maintained the roads when their primary use became civilian.

When the Romans annexed the province of Asia in 129 BC, the governor Manius Aquillius built a road to connect Pergamum and Ephesus with the Pamphylian coastal city of Side. In 6 BC the emperor Augustus built a road from Perga to southern Galatia by paving over a section of this earlier road. It connected the newly founded colonies of Comama, Apollonia, and Pisidian Antioch, which served as the *caput viae* ("head of the road"). Later the road was extended to another colony, Lystra. Paul walked the Via Sebaste from Perga on his first journey as well as the section from Lystra to Apollonia on his second and third journeys (Acts 13:14, 51; 14:6; 16:4, 6). Although the Via Sebaste was longer, it was a much easier route inland than going northward from Perga through the mountains as depicted on most Bible maps.

The Southern, or Common, Highway ran from Antioch and Tarsus through the great Taurus pass, the Cilician Gates, into central Anatolia. Paul followed this route on his second and third journeys (Acts 15:41; 18:23). At Iconium the road forked, with the route to Pisidian Antioch going south of the modern Sultan Mountains. After leaving the Via Sebaste, it continued westward to the important road junction at Apamea. Here Paul turned northward to Bithynia on the second journey before again being redirected through Mysian

A Roman road in Tarsus, Paul's hometown.

Asia to Troas (Acts 16:6–8). On the third journey Paul probably continued westward from Apamea by connecting with the old road that passed Laodicea and then followed the Meander River valley to Magnesia ad Meandrum. The road climbed then over a low pass before descending into Ephesus (Acts 19:1).

After Paul crossed over from Troas to Neapolis on the second journey, he connected with the Via Egnatia. The construction of this road was begun by the Macedonian governor Gnaeus Egnatius in 146 BC. It linked Byzantium to Dyrrachium, a distance of 696 miles. From Neapolis the road continued through Philippi, Amphipolis, Apollonia, and Thessalonica (Acts 16:11–17:9). From the Macedonian capital the road turned westward through the modern countries of Macedonia and Albania. Paul traveled on this section of the Via Egnatia on his third journey to Illyricum (Rom. 15:19). The road had two termini on the Adriatic coast, Dyrrachium and Apollonia, and Paul probably visited both cities before continuing southward to Corinth. Paul again traveled on the Via Egnatia on his return through Macedonia before transshipping back to Troas (Acts 20:1–6).

The Via Appia ran from Brindisium to Rome. Located on the Adriatic, Brindisium was the Italian port connected by ship to Dyrrachium. From Brindisium the Via Appia ran north to Puteoli, the port where Paul disembarked on his captivity journey (Acts 28:13). He then walked through the Pontine swamps, passing the Forum of Appius and stopping at the Three Taverns (Acts 28:14–15). Paul entered Rome at the Porta Capena, the gate where the Via Appia started and ended.

Most of the roads that Paul traveled upon were paved. Bridges allowed passage across major rivers. Carts and carriages passed along them carrying trade goods and passengers. Ruts from their iron-shod wheels are still visible in places. However, Paul probably walked most of the time (Acts 20:13). The average day's travel was around nineteen miles. Milestones prominently marked the distances from major cities; some still in situ can be found along the Via Sebaste. Milestones from the Via Egnatia and Via Appia can be seen in local museums along the routes. Accommodations known as a *mansio* provided places to sleep and eat. Three Taverns was a *mansio* on the Via Appia thirty miles from Rome. Travel on Roman roads was generally safe because of the regular flow of traffic and military patrols. However, Paul did experience problems with bandits as well as natural challenges like crossing flooded rivers (2 Cor. 11:26).

Roman Rule of Judea

Mariam Kamell-Kovalishyn
and Josiah McDermott

Rome's presence in Judea, beginning with Pompey's conquering of Jerusalem in 63 BC, was a tense time full of revolts. Under the rule of Julius Caesar the Jewish nation was given semiautonomous rule. After Julius Caesar's assassination Octavian (Augustus) and Anthony vied for power, and Herod was appointed king of Judea by the Roman senate. Octavian secured his rule at the battle of Actium in 31 BC,[1] and he confirmed Herod's kingship over Judea.[2]

Herod the Great was an Idumean (Edomite), and the Jewish people did not respect his rule. Herod converted to Judaism, and skepticism met his attempts to participate in Jewish practices. Like all client kings, Herod was to ensure that tribute to Rome was consistently provided. The Romans saw Judea as the pathway to their food supply, Egypt,[3] and feared its interruption if Judea became troubled. Otherwise, Herod was given freedom to rule as he thought best. The economy of the region prospered during the stability of Herod's rule. He contributed much with his elaborate building projects, most famous of which would be the Herodian temple in Jerusalem.[4] This Second Temple became one of the most extravagant buildings in the Roman Empire, but not everyone was grateful. The people rejected Herod and his ways, leading to constant (threats of) revolts.[5] And Herod's rule came with hefty taxation that served two purposes: to pay for Herod's building projects and to supply the tribute that Rome demanded. These taxes, coupled with the Jewish religious tithes and contributions, put estimates of annual giving at about 30–40 percent from each Jewish person, rich or poor.[6]

Herodian Kings and the New Testament

King	Dates	Family Data	Area Ruled	New Testament Connection
Herod the Great	37–4 BC	Son of Antipater	King of Judea, then all of Palestine	Named king of Judea in 40 BC by the Roman senate Defeated opposition in Judea and achieved throne by 37 BC Directed the renovation of the temple in Jerusalem Ruled when John the Baptist and Jesus were born (Luke 1:5) Received the wise men and sought to execute the Christ child in Bethlehem, forcing Mary, Joseph, and Jesus to flee to Egypt (Matt. 2:1–19)
Archelaus	4 BC–AD 6	Son of Herod the Great	Ethnarch of Judea, Samaria, and Idumea	The incompetent and cruel ruler who caused Mary, Joseph, and Jesus to divert from Judea and settle in Nazareth of Galilee when they returned from Egypt (Matt. 2:22–23)
Herod Antipas	4 BC–AD 39	Son of Herod the Great	Tetrarch of Galilee and Perea	Rebuilt Sepphoris as the capital of Galilee and then built a new capital on the virgin site of Tiberias Ruled as John the Baptist preached in the wilderness (Luke 3:1) Arrested and executed John the Baptist (Matt. 14:1–12; Mark 6:14–29; Luke 3:19) Used as a threat by Pharisees seeking to manipulate Jesus's itinerary (Luke 13:31–33) Interrogated Jesus in Jerusalem prior to his execution (Luke 23:7–12)
Herod Philip	4 BC–AD 34	Son of Herod the Great	Tetrarch of Iturea, Gaulanitis, and Traconitis	Rebuilt Paneas and named it Caesarea Philippi Received only incidental mention (Luke 3:1)
Herod Agrippa I	AD 41–44	Grandson of Herod the Great	King of Judea and then added Galilee and Perea	As a friend of Emperor Claudius, he negotiated improved civil rights for the Jews. As a defender of the Pharisees, he persecuted Christians in Jerusalem (Acts 12:1). Executed the apostle James, brother of John (Acts 12:2) Arrested Peter (Acts 12:3–4) Struck down by the Lord for taking divine honor (Acts 12:19–24)
Herod Agrippa II	AD 48–100	Great-grandson of Herod the Great	Initially control of the temple in Jerusalem before adding Iturea, Gaulanitis, Trachonitis, and the Decapolis	Observed the growing social and economic tensions leading to the first Jewish revolt and destruction of the temple in Jerusalem Listened to Paul present his case in Caesarea Maritima during Paul's trial before the Roman prefect Festus (Acts 25:13–26:32)

Herod was a brutal man, constantly suspicious of threats to his throne.[7] Whether these suspicions were real or imaginary, Herod was quick to act and make sure that there were no surviving threats (cf. Matt. 2:1–18). He did not hesitate to act against his own family, and he killed his wife and two sons. Commenting on his rule and his refusal to eat pork, Caesar Augustus once remarked, "It is better to be Herod's pig [*hys*] than his son [*huios*]."[8] When Herod died in 4 BC, Rome divided the province among his three remaining sons. Philip ruled over the northern territories and the lands east of the Sea of Galilee. Herod Antipas, the "King Herod" of the Gospels, ruled over Galilee and Perea. Archelaus was to rule over Judea (including the cities of Jerusalem and Caesarea), Samaria, and Idumea.[9] Archelaus's rule was oppressive and disliked by most of the Jews, who sent a delegation to Rome petitioning Augustus's intervention.[10] By AD 6 Archelaus was banished, and his territories became provinces of the Roman Empire (with the exception of a period in AD 41–44 when Herod's grandson Agrippa I restored all the former territories).[11]

The instability of the territory due to Jewish nationalism coupled with rejection of the emperor Nero led to the general Vespasian being sent in AD 66 to quash the largest revolt yet. Vespasian returned to Rome to become emperor in AD 68, and Jerusalem and the temple were destroyed by his son Titus in AD 70, with the spoils returning to Rome.

In AD 70–135 the Roman Empire witnessed the rise of Christianity over a succession of emperors. Over this period there was still the presence of Jewish radicals with hopes for the rebuilding of Jerusalem and its temple and the establishment of God's rule through the messianic king, which came to a head in AD 135. During the emperor Hadrian's rule (AD 117–138) Rome tried to remove all religious practices that were seen to be brutal and unclean,[12] which included banning circumcision, and attempted to turn Jerusalem into a temple city to the god Jupiter.[13] In response, a revolt was led by Simeon ben Kosiba (popularly known as Bar Kokhba, "Son of the Star," from Num. 24:17), who was proclaimed as messiah by the famous rabbi Akiva.[14] Rome brutally ended the period of struggle and sold many of the surviving Jews into slavery.

The Sabbath

Andreas J. Köstenberger

The importance of the Sabbath for first-century Judaism is evident throughout Jewish literature. The Sabbath's centrality extends throughout the OT, from its establishment at creation (Gen. 2:1–3), its inclusion in the Ten Commandments (Exod. 20:9–11), and its function as a covenant marker for the Jews (Neh. 9:14; 10:28–33). Despite the importance of the Sabbath in the OT, little space is devoted to an explicit definition of "work" (but see Exod. 34:21; Num. 15:32–36; Neh. 10:31; 13:5–22). The Sabbath increasingly served as a Jewish identity marker in the later OT and Second Temple period. The book of 2 Maccabees highlights the threat to the Sabbath by Antiochus Epiphanes (5:25) and the lengths to which faithful Jews went to keep it, preferring to die rather than fight on the Sabbath (6:11; see also 6:6; 8:26–28). *Jubilees*, a retelling of Israel's history from creation through Moses, pointedly emphasizes keeping the Sabbath in framing the narrative,[1] even arguing that the Sabbath was kept in heaven prior to the commandment being given to humanity.[2] The importance of the Sabbath led to Jews strenuously seeking to define what constitutes "work." For example, the *Damascus Document* at Qumran stipulates not only that servants should not be made to work but also that animals should not be helped to give birth or helped out of a pit, nor should a person be helped who falls into a water reservoir.[3] The Mishnah, whose discussions of the Sabbath reflect first-century debates, devotes an entire tractate to the topic (*Shabbat*).

The Gospels reflect the repeated conflict that Jesus encountered over the Sabbath, specifically in his unwillingness to follow the detailed oral traditions that had developed by the first century. When Jesus's disciples pick grain (Matt. 12:1–8), the Pharisees accuse them of breaking the Sabbath, as reaping was one of the thirty-nine acts of labor prohibited on the Sabbath.[4] When Jesus heals on the Sabbath (e.g., Matt. 12:9–14; Luke 13:10–17), he violates the prevailing view that healing was allowed only when life was threatened.[5] In the healing of the man born blind (John 9:1–34), not only was the man's life not in danger but also the Pharisees may have viewed mixing mud and spittle as kneading, another prohibited act of labor.[6] Similarly, the oral law forbade carrying an object "from one domain to another,"[7] which created conflict for the formerly lame man who carried his mat after Jesus healed him (John 5:1–15). This event led to Jesus engaging in theological debate concerning working on the Sabbath and his equality with God (John 5:16–30).

The *Damascus Document* scroll, found both in Egypt and later in Qumran, spelled out rules for the community, including regulations for keeping the Sabbath.

Because God rested on the seventh day (Gen. 2:2–3), some Jewish, and later Christian, writers sought to answer the question of how the universe was maintained on the Sabbath if God was resting. The common rabbinic response was that God indeed works on the Sabbath without violating it. Thus it is impossible for God to carry an object outside his home because the entire universe is his home.[8] Later in John's Gospel Jesus touches on the question of circumcision and the Sabbath (7:22). While there is no biblical example of how to handle circumcision when the eighth day fell on the Sabbath, the Jews concluded that circumcision was permissible. Rabbi Yose ben Halafta (second century AD) said, "Great is circumcision, since it overrides the prohibitions of the Sabbath, which is subject to strict rules."[9]

Samaritans

Andreas J. Köstenberger

The background of the Samaritans is disputed. Jewish history traced their lineage to the fall of the northern kingdom in 722 BC, when Assyria deported many Israelites and settled other conquered peoples in the land. The resulting intermarriages between Jews and gentiles allegedly gave birth to the Samaritans (2 Kings 17:24–41). Some Jews believed Samaritans to be the descendants of Shechem, who raped Jacob's daughter Dinah (Gen. 34; cf. Sir. 50:25–26, which speaks of God hating "the foolish people that live in Shechem"). Josephus notes that Shechem was considered a refuge for Jewish apostates: "And if anyone were accused by those of

Mount Gerizim was sacred to the Samaritans, who believed that it, instead of Jerusalem, was the place God chose for his temple. Pictured here is a panorama of Mount Ebal and Mount Gerizim viewed from Shechem.

Jerusalem of having eaten things common, or of having broken the Sabbath, or of any other crime of the like nature, he fled away to the Shechemites, and said that he was accused unjustly."[1] The Samaritans, for their part, claimed to be descendants of Joseph through Ephraim and Manasseh, holding that they were the faithful Israelites while the Jews were apostates.[2]

The relationship between Jews and Samaritans was strained not only because of their ethnic origin but also because of religious differences. Samaritans held that God intended worship to be conducted on Mount Gerizim, a command that was disobeyed when the sanctuary was moved to Shiloh. Idiosyncratically, they recognized only the Pentateuch, the first five books of the OT, as Scripture. Consequently, the Jews viewed the Samaritans as idolaters.[3] These religious differences, in turn, led to significant conflict, including military confrontations. Antagonism erupted particularly when John Hyrcanus, an early leader of the Jewish Hasmonean dynasty, destroyed the Samaritan temple on Mount Gerizim in the late second century BC.[4] The Samaritans, in turn, were often openly hostile to the Jews. Josephus records an incident in which Samaritans tried to desecrate the temple,[5] and another in which they killed Jews traveling to Jerusalem for a festival.[6]

The Sanhedrin

Rodney Reeves

The Sanhedrin was a Jewish council that ruled on religious and civic issues in Jesus's day. Its membership, purpose, authority, and procedures changed over the years prior to and after NT times. Drawing together information about the Sanhedrin from different periods of Jewish history to create a composite picture of the council can be very misleading. For example, we should not expect the Sanhedrin that indicted Jesus to follow rules and procedures that were drawn up some time after the destruction of the temple (AD 70). According to the Mishnah (a second-century document), the Sanhedrin was not supposed to meet at night to consider a capital offense.[1] And yet, according to the Mishnah, there seem to have been three different Jewish councils: (1) a body of seventy-one legal experts (scribes, rabbis) dedicated to ruling on religious matters; (2) a group of twenty-three powerful aristocrats who were convened for a special purpose (e.g., to try capital cases); and (3) a council of three elders who settled civil disputes (e.g., property cases). Therefore, those who rely on the Mishnah to claim that the Sanhedrin violated its own rules during the trial of Jesus have to accept that there were actually three Jewish councils, even though, according to the Gospels, there was only one Sanhedrin. Consequently, we need to be careful when assessing all the information we have on the constantly evolving Jewish council(s) called "the Sanhedrin."

The origin of a ruling council consisting of seventy-one men who are "known to you as elders and officers of the people" goes back to the time of Moses (Num. 11:16).[2] During the exile there was a council made up of "priests and nobles" who appear to have functioned like a Sanhedrin, although they were never called that (Neh. 2:16–18; 5:6–13). Actually, the Hebrew word "Sanhedrin" is the transliteration of the Greek word *synedrion* ("council"), indicating that a Jewish council called a "Sanhedrin" would not have existed prior to the Hellenistic period (333–167 BC). In fact, according to Josephus, a council consisting of priests and scribes that ruled on civil and religious matters according to Jewish law was first instituted by the Seleucid king Antiochus III.[3] After the Hasmonean dynasty lost its sovereignty to the Romans (63 BC), the governor of Syria divided Israel into five districts and set up a local Sanhedrin for each district to settle civic and religious disputes.[4] After the Romans placed Israel under the rule of King Herod, the Sanhedrin in Jerusalem tried to continue to exert its authority, even over the new king, but to no avail. Herod had all of them killed because they dared to hear a case against him.[5]

When Judea came under direct Roman rule (AD 6), the Sanhedrin in Jerusalem reemerged as a powerful council that functioned much like a supreme court, adjudicating legal disputes among the Jews. Composed of priests (Sadducees) and scribes (Pharisees) and led by the high priest, the Sanhedrin was called upon to render judgment against violators of Jewish law, having to bring those guilty of capital crimes to Roman authorities because the Sanhedrin did not have the power to execute criminals—even though at times they took matters into their own hands and stoned the accused.[6] This is the picture that emerges from the NT as well. During the trials of Jesus (Luke 22:66–23:25), Peter, James, and John (Acts 5:21–41), Stephen (Acts 6:12–8:1), and Paul (Acts 22:30–23:10; 24:1–25:12) the Sanhedrin convened—probably in a hall on the west end of the temple complex—to hear charges. They were able to convince the Romans that Jesus should be crucified, but they stoned Stephen. In the trial of the apostles a divided Sanhedrin punished the apostles but continued to seek the death penalty for Paul.

Scribes and Teachers of the Law

Rodney Reeves

Since the Jews centered their lives on the Scriptures, they needed trained craftsmen to make copies of the Bible. These scribes not only learned the art of writing (even though most Jewish men knew how to read, the ability to write was an acquired skill like calligraphy) but also had to learn how to produce the materials needed to create scrolls. This included paper made from animal skin (parchment), ink (a mixture of soot, gum, and water), and pens (made from reeds or sticks). Scribes were specially trained to follow a particular regimen when transcribing the Hebrew Scriptures. First, they had to create their copy from the sacred scrolls housed in the temple. Second, once a page was completed, they counted the letters to make sure that they copied the same number of letters as the original. Finally, scribes checked one another's work to ensure the accuracy of the new scroll before sending it to the synagogue that commissioned the copy. Some of the scribes were priests; others belonged to the Pharisees. And yet, regardless of their affiliation, since scribes spent so much time reading the Hebrew Bible, they were accepted as leading authorities on

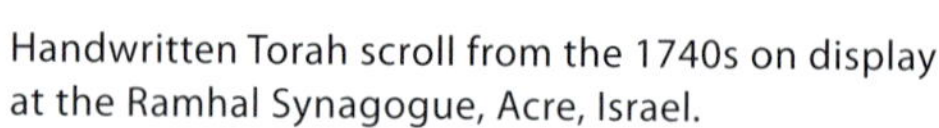
Handwritten Torah scroll from the 1740s on display at the Ramhal Synagogue, Acre, Israel.

the meaning of the Scriptures. Therefore, by NT times scribes were often referred to as "teachers of the law."

According to rabbinical tradition, Ezra was the first scribe/teacher of the law (Ezra 7:6, 10), even though scribes appear as influential interpreters of the law before the exile—much to the chagrin of Jeremiah (Jer. 8:8). But due to the venerable reputation of Ezra (and other scribes of the Levites [Neh. 8:7–9]), over the years the Jewish people looked to the scribes as reliable experts. Some scribes functioned like lawyers, having become members of the Sanhedrin, the Jewish council that ruled on religious and civic matters (see the article "The Sanhedrin"). Some scribes taught in the synagogues, earning the title "rabbi"; others, being priests, served the altar and taught worshipers in the temple.

Although most scribes were located in Jerusalem and the surrounding region of Judea, some lived in Galilee, functioning as the local expert in certain villages. During synagogue services scribes not only read from the Scriptures but also offered commentary, interpreting the requirements of the law for the people. Indeed, interpretation was necessary because many commandments are not self-explanatory. For example, the fifth commandment of the Decalogue, "Remember the Sabbath day, to keep it holy" (Exod. 20:8), is open to interpretation. Even though the law includes the prohibition "You must not do any work" (20:10), the question remains: What qualifies as work? Since scribes knew the Scriptures better than anyone, they could recall other biblical passages in which certain activities were prohibited, such as preparing meals and plowing fields (Exod. 16:5; 34:21). And, since God was emphatic about his people observing the Sabbath, commanding Israel to put to death anyone who desecrated the holy day (Exod. 31:13–15), scribal interpretation of the law became paramount to obeying God.

Of course, scribes were known to debate the finer points of the law. Different rabbis had different ideas about what constituted total obedience. But when Jesus came along and defied what teachers of the law had prohibited for centuries (e.g., reaping on the Sabbath in Matt. 12:1–2), the scribes were immediately suspicious of this rogue prophet because he ignored their interpretations (Matt. 15:1–2). As a result, the scribes were among the primary opponents of Jesus. But not all scribes were hostile to Jesus, for one wanted to follow him (Matt. 8:19), and another, according to Jesus, wasn't "far from the kingdom of God" (Mark 12:34).

The Sea of Galilee and Fishing in the First Century

Dana M. Harris

The Sea of Galilee (actually a freshwater lake) is 13 miles long, 8 miles wide, 150 feet deep, and 696 feet below sea level. It is also called the Sea of Tiberias (John 6:1; 21:1) or Lake of Gennesaret (Luke 5:1). Due to steep surrounding hills, its low elevation, and seasonally high temperatures, sudden, intense storms can occur (e.g., Luke 8:22–25). Village names along its shore reveal the importance of fishing, such as Bethsaida ("house of fishing") and Magdala, whose Greek name, Taricheae, means "place for salting or drying fish."

An important fish species is *tilapia Galilea*, the so-called St. Peter's fish. Other important species include types of carp and sardines. Fish often was broiled or roasted (Luke 24:42; John 21:9).

Casting a net, either from the shore (Matt. 4:18) or a boat (Luke 5:4), was the most common method of fishing in the first century. The dragnet, or seine net, was dragged to the shore, where the fish were sorted (Matt. 13:47–50). Fishermen often made their own nets, which required washing, drying, and mending after use (Mark 1:19). A rod or line with a hook was also used (Matt. 17:27). In 1986 a first-century fishing boat was discovered in Lake Galilee that was 26.5 feet long, 7.5 feet wide, and 4.5 feet deep and likely had a sail.

The Gospels describe small family businesses (Mark 1:19–20), although fishing in Galilee was largely controlled by local rulers. Tax collectors contracted with local fishermen on behalf of these rulers. (Matthew possibly collected taxes for fishing, as Capernaum was an important fishing center.) Local fishermen likely formed collectives (Luke 5:1–11) and hired additional labor as needed (Mark 1:19–20).

References to fishing are frequent in Jesus's teaching (Matt. 7:10; 13:47–48; Luke 11:11; cf. Mark 4:1; Luke 5:3) and miracles (Luke 9:12–17; John 6:1–14; cf. Matt. 15:32–39; Mark 8:1–10). Metaphorically, Jesus speaks of his disciples as fishers of people (Matt. 4:19; Mark 1:17; Luke 5:10).

The Sea of Galilee.

Shipping Practices in the First Century

E. Randolph Richards

Ancients stayed close to home. Travelers usually were government officials, religious pilgrims, merchants, and messengers. Travel generally was by foot, averaging about twenty miles a day. Rampant piracy made sea travel more dangerous than land travel. The Roman Empire changed that as pirate ships were attacked and torched. Taming the Mediterranean allowed an explosion of sea traffic. By NT times, ships regularly plied the seaways. Transporting cargo, along with passengers and dispatches, became profitable business. While military ships used oars for speed (4–7 mph) and dependability, commercial ships relied primarily upon sails, averaging 2–4 mph with favorable winds and half that with unfavorable winds. Common cargo ships were 70–150 feet long, carrying about 250 tons of cargo. Grain ships in Paul's day (Acts 27) routinely carried 1,300 tons, were 180 feet long, and could take twelve days to unload.[1]

A relief showing a Roman cargo ship.

The lowest level of a ship held the ballast and bilge water. The deck just above it held cargo and sometimes passengers—what we term "steerage." In general, though, passengers camped above deck, some with tents, the wealthy in cabins.[2] Josephus mentions a ship to Rome with six hundred passengers.[3] Paul's ship, which was traveling late, still managed 276 aboard (Acts 27:37).

Both land and sea travel were restricted by season. In the eastern half of the Mediterranean prevailing winds blew from northwest to southeast from June to September, marking sailing season. From November to April more fierce winds blew northeast to southwest (Acts 27:14), making sea travel too dangerous. Travelers generally restricted journeys to the middle of the season or had to stop "to winter" somewhere (Acts 28:11).

Acts notes that the prisoner Paul was placed with a centurion from the Augustan Cohort (Acts 27:1), and the second ship he boarded was an Alexandrian ship (Acts 27:6). Paul perhaps was under the control of a special type of centurion, a *frumentarius* (from *frumentum*, "grain"), those who guarded the grain shipments.[4] The Roman Empire was completely dependent upon regular shipments of grain from Egypt.[5] Massive ships traveled constantly between Alexandria (Egypt) and Rome.[6] Special centurions monitored these ships. Since these ships were constantly traveling from the provinces to Rome, they also carried imperial dispatches, passengers, and prisoners.[7]

Luke says that during the storm recorded in Acts 27 the sailors used rope cables to undergird the ship to help it stay together (v. 17)—"frapping a ship," as old English sailors called it. Modern translations often say that the ropes were passed under the ship, as in side to side under the hull. In antiquity frapping was done by wrapping the cable around the ship horizontally, just under the gunwales.[8] Like the bands holding together a barrel, these ropes were employed to help prevent the ship from sagging outward and breaking apart.

Paul was a far more experienced traveler than most. Paul was "shipwrecked" three times (2 Cor. 11:25).[9] He had the survival instincts of a seasoned traveler, able to comfort and advise others less experienced with travel (Acts 27:9–10, 30–32).

Slavery in the New Testament World

Dana M. Harris

Slavery defines a person as property (chattel), who can be bought or sold. Unlike the New World slavery of the sixteenth through the mid-nineteenth centuries (or some present-day examples of slavery), slavery in the NT world was not based on race or ethnicity; moreover, slaves could own property and often were educated or encouraged to become educated (as a means of increasing their value). Even so, violence (including sexual exploitation) and fear of punishment (including torture and even death) were inherent aspects of slavery.

Early in the Roman era slaves often were prisoners of war or had been kidnapped. Later, debt bondage became common. Impoverished day laborers could sell themselves into slavery so as to obtain secure food and shelter. Children could be sold into slavery; abandoned children often were enslaved by those who found them. A girl could be sold as a slave with the condition that she later be married to a master or his son. Children of slaves were considered slaves and became an important source of slaves. Sometimes punishment for a crime resulted in enslavement.

Slavery generally was considered necessary or inevitable by many ancient peoples, although both the Greeks and Romans depended upon slavery to such an extent as to be classified as having slave economies. The slave population of the Roman Empire is estimated at 15 to 20 percent, although slaves may have constituted up to one-third of urban populations. Greeks viewed slaves as inherently inferior, whereas Roman law viewed slavery as contrary to

One source of slaves was Roman prisoners of war, like the ones depicted on this relief from Miletus (second to third century AD).

natural law, although morally legitimate. Thus slavery was an unquestioned institution. Indeed, freed slaves often sought to own slaves themselves.

Most slaves served in urban contexts, often part of a large household (*oikos*) ruled by the head of the household (*paterfamilias*). Although slaves could be necessary for economic reasons, they also were important symbols of status and prestige. Moreover, slaves often derived their own status and honor from those of their masters. Some slaves held important positions, including doctors, teachers, accountants, ship captains, and managers. Some high-ranking slaves owned their own businesses and other slaves. Slaves even held important bureaucratic positions in the imperial court. Thus slaves were not relegated to the lowest socioeconomic level. Highly stratified Roman society, however, usually denied a freed person the same status as a never-enslaved individual. Jews enslaved by other Jews generally were treated well and often manumitted (set free) after six years.

Manumission was fairly common, but it was dependent upon the master—often for economic benefit or the desire to be seen as generous. Faithful slaves could be manumitted upon the death of the master; slaves could also amass enough funds to buy their manumission. Once free, however, slaves often were expected to show gratitude (evinced by numerous obligations) to former masters. The failure to do so could result in reenslavement. Many urban and household slaves obtained freedom and even Roman citizenship, although rural slaves rarely were manumitted. Criminals who were enslaved as punishment usually died working in mines or ship galleys or sometimes participating in gladiatorial games.

Slavery in the NT often is assumed (e.g., Matt. 18:23–34; 25:14–30; Luke 19:11–27; Eph. 6:5–9), although the institution is never endorsed. The "Freedmen's Synagogue" in Acts 6:9 likely originated with Jews who had been enslaved by Pompey in 63 BC and, having obtained their freedom, returned to Jerusalem. It is significant that Paul urges slaves to obtain their freedom if possible (1 Cor. 7:21). Moreover, by urging Philemon to receive his slave Onesimus as a brother in Christ and a partner equal to Paul himself (Philem. 15–17), Paul undermines core assumptions of slavery.

Traditional Greek and Roman Gods

Mariam Kamell-Kovalishyn
and Josiah McDermott

Ancient Greece had no sacred texts for us to study. Instead, through the transmission of epics attributed to Hesiod and Homer, we have a representation of the gods and how they were reputed to have interacted with humanity.[1] These gods ate, drank, were tempted by physical beauty and prideful desires, and could be betrayed by their tempestuous emotions.[2] They also possessed supernatural strength and intervened in human life as they saw fit. Gods were said to have defined jurisdictions. Worship of the gods involved both cult sacrifices and divination. For example, Ares, the god of war, was worshiped before battle.

The rise of Rome brought the adoption of foreign gods. Rome changed the names of the Greek gods to Latin and redefined their myths and powers.[3] The three most notable gods—Jupiter, Juno, and Minerva—were adopted from the Greek gods Zeus, Hera, and Athena. As the Roman Empire expanded south and east, other gods such as Isis or Mithras were also adopted.[4]

In addition to these gods, Caesar Augustus brought a unifying force under the guise of emperor worship.[5] With the imperial cult came a growing system of worship involving temples, sacrifices, and festivals that would honor current and former emperors as gods.[6] In varying degrees of representation and worship, the cult's presence was universal across the empire.

Commentary

— Matthew
— Mark
— Luke
— John
— Acts
— Romans
— 1 Corinthians
— 2 Corinthians
— Galatians
— Ephesians
— Philippians
— Colossians
— 1 Thessalonians
— 2 Thessalonians
— 1 Timothy
— 2 Timothy
— Titus
— Philemon
— Hebrews
— James
— 1 Peter
— 2 Peter
— 1 John
— 2 John
— 3 John
— Jude
— Revelation

Matthew

Rodney Reeves

Introduction. The first book of the NT, Matthew, is a very Jewish Gospel, presenting Jesus to Jewish readers as the Messiah of Israel for the salvation of the whole world. It probably was written after Mark (more than likely the first Gospel published), sometime shortly before or after the destruction of the Jewish temple in AD 70. Technically an anonymous work (the author having never identified himself), church tradition attributed our first canonical Gospel to Matthew from its inception—the earliest copies bear the title "According to Matthew."

It is evident that Matthew had Jewish interests in mind when he wrote his Gospel: (1) he begins his account with the genealogy of Jesus, tracing his royal lineage to Abraham through David; (2) he constantly points out how Jesus made good on promises that God gave to Israel, fulfilling prophecies pertaining to the Messiah and the messianic age; (3) he presents Jesus as the embodiment of all of Israel's heroes (Moses, David, Solomon, Elijah, and the prophets); (4) he makes it plain that Jesus came to fulfill the law, not abolish it; and, therefore, (5) Jesus's first mission was to restore Israel, then to bring salvation to the rest of the world. In fact, salvation is the key to understanding Jesus's ministry (his Hebrew name, *Yeshua*, means "Yahweh saves")—how he establishes the kingdom of heaven on earth. For if God is to reign on earth as he does in heaven, then all of God's enemies (Satan, demons, the wicked, evil, suffering, and ultimately death) must be vanquished. Indeed, according to Matthew that is the gospel story: through the words and deeds, death and resurrection of Jesus the Messiah salvation has come to Israel and all nations.

An icon of Matthew from a larger piece titled "Christ and the Twelve Apostles" (Antalya, Turkey, nineteenth century AD).

The Genealogy of Jesus (1:1–17)

An account of the genealogy (1:1). The Greek text reads *biblos geneseōs* (literally, "scroll of generation"), which may be a deliberate echo of LXX Gen. 2:4: *hautē hē biblos geneseōs* ("this is the scroll of generation"), translated as "this is the account"—a phrase that appears several times in Genesis.[1] The word translated as "genealogy" (from which we get the title of the first book of the law, Genesis) can refer to a generation, genealogy, birth, or even life history. Thus Matthew could have used this phrase to introduce the genealogy (1:1–17) or the birth of Jesus (1:1–2:23), or perhaps even as a title for his Gospel—the life and work of Jesus.

Jesus Christ, the son of David (1:1). The term "Christ" (sometimes translated as "Messiah") means "anointed one." In the OT, priests (Lev. 21:10) and kings (1 Sam. 16:1, 13) were anointed, but the title "Messiah/Christ/anointed one" came to refer to the ideal king, the descendant of David who would fulfill the royal promises God made to Israel (2 Sam. 7:11–16; Ps. 2:2–7; 89:20–37; 110:1–7).

Fathered . . . by (1:3, 5, 6). It wasn't unheard of for women to appear in genealogies, whether mothers, wives, sisters, daughters, or even concubines (1 Chron. 1:32, 39, 50; 2:3, 4, 16, 18, 19, 24, 26, 29, 35, 46, 48, 49). But why these four? Three are named (Tamar, Rahab, Ruth) and one implied ("Uriah's wife," Bathsheba). What did they have in common, other than the fact that they were included in Jesus's genealogy? Some think that their shared backstory (scandalous sexual history) explains it. Tamar acted like a prostitute to become pregnant by her father-in-law in order to honor her dead husband and preserve the family tree (Gen. 38:1–26). Rahab was a prostitute who helped the twelve tribes spy on Jericho (Josh. 2:1–24). Ruth approached Boaz to sleep with him in order to marry him (Ruth 3:1–4:12)—some take "uncover his feet" as a euphemism for sexual relations; others take it literally, meaning that she simply kept his feet warm during the night. Finally, Bathsheba and King David committed adultery and later married, and eventually she bore him Solomon, the first "son of David" to be anointed king (2 Sam. 11:1–5, 27; 12:24–25). This sets the stage for Mary, whose child was born under scandalous circumstances (Matt. 1:18–25).

Other commentators find another common denominator: all four women were gentiles. One is stated explicitly—Ruth was a Moabite (Ruth

1:22)—while the non-Israelite ethnicity of the other three must be inferred. Tamar probably was a gentile, since she wasn't identified as a member of the family. Rahab likely was a Canaanite, being a resident of Jericho. And Bathsheba probably was a Hittite, having been married to Uriah. The implication, therefore, is that Jesus's family tree included men and women with a checkered history, or that his genealogy included at least four gentiles, anticipating that Jesus would be a king for all peoples.

Used to illustrate the genealogy of Jesus, a Jesse tree is an artistic representation of a shoot from the stump of Jesse (Isa. 11:1–2).

All the generations from Abraham to David were fourteen generations (1:17). When comparing Matthew's genealogy of David's royal line (especially from Solomon to Jeconiah) to 1 Chron. 3:4–16, we see that he omitted several names in order to round out the list to fourteen generations, thereby matching the number of names from Abraham to David. Furthermore, there are only thirteen names listed from Jeconiah to Jesus (unless one of Jeconiah's brothers mentioned in 1:11 rounds out the final fourteen). Obviously, Matthew wanted the rhythm of fourteen generations to mark the three major turning points in the story of God's covenant with Israel: (1) David's monarchy, (2) the exile, and (3) the birth of Jesus, the last king of Israel, who will fulfill the covenant promises of God. When a literary device called "gematria" is applied to David's name (three letters in Hebrew: *dwd*), the numerical value equals fourteen, the implication being that Jesus arrived at the perfect time, rounding out the divine ordering of David's royal lineage.

The Birth of Jesus (1:18–25)

Mary had been engaged to Joseph (1:18). Marriages were arranged by families in order to preserve the honor of the family name and keep vital resources within the community (see the article "Jewish Marriage Customs"). The engagement was sealed when the bride-price was paid by the groom's family—often an amount negotiated between the two fathers. The betrothal period lasted about a year to ensure the purity of the bride. If she became pregnant before the wedding, the groom was expected to break the contract (and the bride's family had to return the bride-price). He could "put her away" (divorce her) publicly in order to preserve his family's honor

and shame her family, which also would signal to the community that her child was not his.

Decided to divorce her secretly (1:19). Matthew describes Joseph as "a righteous man, and not wanting to disgrace her publicly" (1:19). In other words, until an angel convinced him otherwise (vv. 20–21), Joseph was going to do the "right thing" according to the law and break the contract. By marrying Mary (v. 24) and waiting to consummate their marriage until after Jesus was born (v. 25), Joseph (and his family) would share in the shame of her "disgrace."

Name him Jesus, because he will save his people (1:21). In Hebrew this is a play on words: Jesus's name (*Yeshua*) means "Yahweh saves."

King Herod's Jealous Rage (2:1–18)

After Jesus was born in Bethlehem of Judea (2:1). This is the first mention of the location of Jesus's birth. Unlike Luke's Gospel, none of the details surrounding Jesus's birth appear here (census, no room, shepherds, manger, heavenly host). For Matthew, identifying where Mary gave birth was the only essential detail because the nativity of Jesus fulfilled prophecy, and it sets up the political fallout of the advent of the Messiah. Bethlehem (meaning "house of bread") was only a few miles from Jerusalem, where Herod ruled over all Israel (Judea, Samaria, Perea, Galilee, Transjordan) as a client king of the Roman Empire. Thus to have the long-awaited "son of David" born in David's hometown right under the nose of King Herod created political problems for the people of Judea, because Herod was an illegitimate king—not a descendant of David or even Jacob. Being an Idumean (Edomite), Herod was a descendant of Esau (Gen. 25:23, 30). As the true son of David, the Messiah was supposed to be a shepherd-king like him: "a ruler who will shepherd my people Israel" (Matt. 2:6 [cf. Mic. 5:2]).

The remains of the Herodium, the fortress that Herod built near Bethlehem.

Wise men from the east arrived in Jerusalem, saying, . . . "For we saw his star at its rising" (2:1–2). Magi (from which we get the word "magician") were sages who served as royal advisors to kings. As ancient astronomers, they believed that the heavens declared the will of the gods. Some eastern religions mapped the night sky (similar to the signs of the zodiac) and assigned certain constellations to different nations. They also read comets and other astrological phenomena as cosmic signs and omens. Evidently the appearance of a new light in the night sky (a star in the constellation of Israel?) convinced these astrologers that a powerful king had been born in Israel. Consequently, as emissaries of their kings, the magi brought gifts to Herod in Jerusalem, thinking that he must have welcomed a new son into the world. Gold, frankincense (a sacred incense used by priests), and myrrh (perfume used for interment of corpses) were luxurious gifts befitting a king (2:11).

The star . . . stopped above the place where the child was . . . the house (2:9–10). Evidently this heavenly light wasn't a literal star, since a massive planet or supernova could not hover over a house like an alien spacecraft. And, since the Jews believed that stars were heavenly powers ("angels" [Rev. 12:1–9]), it could be inferred that the "star" was an "angel" that led the magi to the *house* (not a stable!) where Jesus, Mary, and Joseph were staying in Bethlehem.

Being warned in a dream . . . an angel of the Lord appeared to Joseph in a dream (2:12–13). Dreams were accepted as means of divine communication, but sometimes they required an interpreter (Joseph in the OT was considered an expert [Gen. 40:6–41:40]). Regarding the magi, even though Matthew doesn't identify the source of the dream (God?) or describe the

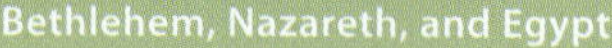

content of the dream (did it require interpretation?), it seems to have served a divine purpose: to protect Jesus from Herod's ill intent (during Herod's last days the king had his estranged wife and two sons killed due to his paranoia). Regarding Joseph, God communicated with him more directly: in three dreams (maybe four?) an angel tells Joseph what is happening—information only God would have—and, consequently, what Jesus's earthly father was supposed to do about it (1:20–21; 2:13, 19, 22).

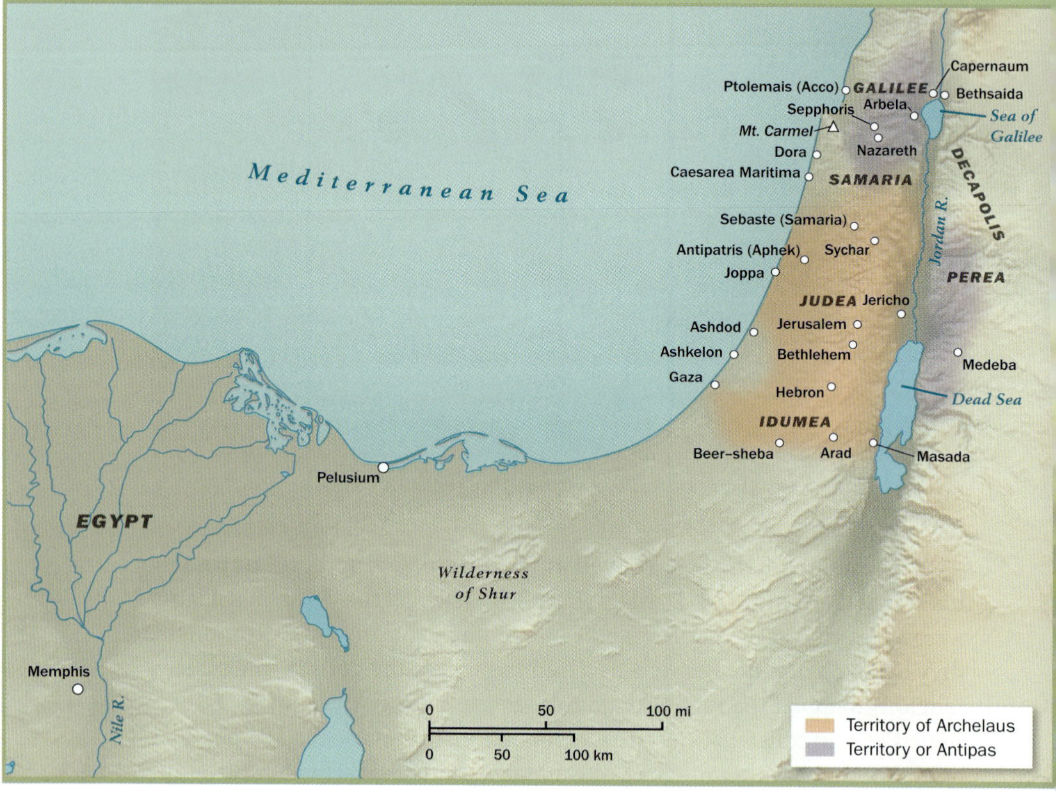

Flee to Egypt . . . *Out of Egypt I called my Son* (2:13, 15). Why Egypt? Why not find seclusion in other regions outside Herod's rule, like Phoenicia, Nabatea, or even Syria? According to Matthew, God directed Joseph to take his family to Egypt because it fulfilled prophecy (Hosea 11:1). And yet the prophecy relates to the cyclical story of the divine deliverance of Israel from exile in Egypt. The implication, therefore, is that the story of Israel (God's "son") must be played out in the story of Jesus (God's "Son").

Massacre all the boys in and around Bethlehem who were two years old and under (2:16). Herod inferred that Jesus was born at the same time the "star" appeared to the magi (2:7, 16). If Herod was right, Jesus was around two years old when Joseph took him and Mary to Egypt, which explains why the king ordered the execution of all boys "two years old and under" in and around Bethlehem. Given the small population of the village and its environs, most scholars estimate that around a dozen boys were slaughtered by order of the wicked king. And yet Herod's inference is rather flimsy—we don't know if the star appeared at the precise time Jesus was born. So the age of Jesus could have been anywhere from a few days to a few years when the magi visited him.

A voice was heard in Ramah (2:18). Matthew sees the prophecy (Jer. 31:15) fulfilled in the slaughter of the Bethlehem children because of Rachel (who was buried near Bethlehem, having died giving birth to Benjamin [Gen. 35:16–20]), or because of the location (the exiles to Babylon were gathered at Ramah [Jer. 40:1]).

Return from Egyptian Exile (2:19–23)

After Herod died . . . Archelaus was ruling over Judea (2:19, 22). After Herod the Great died (4 BC), the Romans divided his kingdom among his three sons. Herod Archelaus, the oldest, ruled Judea, Idumea, and Samaria as a "prince" (ethnarch). Herod Antipas (who executed John the Baptizer) ruled Galilee and Perea, and Herod Philip (probably not the same man whom Herodias divorced to marry Antipas) ruled the territory northeast of Galilee (often referred to as Transjordan). Both Antipas and Philip received the title "tetrarch" (ruler of a fourth). Obviously, then, Jesus was born in 4 BC or earlier. Since "BC" abbreviates "Before Christ," it is apparent that the official (Dionysius) who established the Christian calendar in the sixth century miscalculated the date of Jesus's birth by at least four years.

Settled in a town called Nazareth to fulfill what was spoken through the prophets, that he would be called a Nazarene (2:23). There is no explicit prophecy that the Messiah would live in Nazareth. Matthew probably was referring to a prophetic tradition that started with Isaiah (11:1) and continued through Jeremiah (23:5) and Zechariah (6:12–13). The prophesied "branch" that would shoot from the stump of the felled tree Israel came to be associated with the Messiah. In Hebrew the word for "branch," *netser*, sounds similar to *nazir*, "dedicated" (Nazareth and Nazarene). Thus Matthew makes the correlation: the "branch" would be known as a Nazarene because he lived in Nazareth.

John the Baptizer (3:1–12)

Preaching in the wilderness of Judea (3:1). The prophets expected God to lead Israel into the desert—just like the days of Moses—in order to teach his children to trust in him again (Isa. 40:3; Hosea 2:14). So John performed his ministry in the Judean desert in order to fulfill this prophetic expectation (Isa. 40:3; Matt. 3:3). He even wore the garments of a prophet (Zech. 13:4), appearing like Elijah in the desert (2 Kings 1:7–8; Matt. 3:4). His diet of locusts and wild honey reflects life in the desert—perhaps also intended as a sign of prophecy fulfilled (Joel 2:21–27).

They were baptized by him in the Jordan River (3:6). Obviously John's baptism wasn't a Christian ritual—he didn't place candidates under the water and declare, "Buried in the likeness of his death; raised in the likeness of his resurrection" (cf. Rom. 6:4–5). No one expected the Messiah to be crucified and raised from the dead. John's baptism was a Jewish ritual (see the article "Baptism in the New Testament World"; see comments on Mark 1:4). And yet the prophet's baptism was unique compared to other Jewish rites of purification. Jews repeatedly baptized themselves in water to remove ritual impurity. Gentile proselytes to Judaism were baptized in the temple as part of their initiation. The Jewish sectarians at Qumran (who produced the Dead Sea Scrolls) did both: they baptized initiates into their commune and practiced repeated baptisms of ritual purification. But John performed his water ritual as a one-time act of repentance for Jews who confessed their sins to escape God's imminent, end-of-the-world judgment of Israel (Matt. 3:6–11).

Many of the Pharisees and Sadducees coming to his baptism (3:7). The Pharisees were lay leaders (teachers and scribes) who emphasized the importance of obeying the law and keeping all the purification rites (see the article "Pharisees and Sadducees"; see comments on Mark 2:18). The Sadducees were priests and aristocrats who took care of the Jewish temple, where sacrifices were offered for the forgiveness of sins. They would have had a vested interest in John's baptism of repentance, perhaps even interpreting his water ritual as a threat to replace their ministry.

God is able to raise up children for Abraham from these stones (3:9). In Hebrew (and Aramaic) this is a pun: sons (*banim*) and stones (*abanim*), perhaps echoing Isa. 51:1–2.

The ax is already at the root . . . his winnowing shovel is in his hand (3:10, 12). A felled tree and winnowed chaff were common prophetic metaphors of divine judgment of Israel (Ps. 1:4; Isa. 6:13; 10:33–34; 17:13; 41:2; Jer. 11:19; Ezek. 31:10–14). Harvesters of wheat and barley beat ripened stalks of grain on a large stone floor and then used a pitchfork to throw grain up into the air, counting on the wind to blow away the chaff. In both Greek (*pneuma*) and Hebrew (*ruah*) the word "wind" also means "spirit" or "breath." Thus the Baptizer claims that the day of the Lord (the day of divine visitation) has just arrived through his ministry: he is the ax of God "already

Matthew describes Jesus as having a "winnowing shovel in his hand" (3:12). These Middle Eastern farmers are using the traditional method of winnowing grain (1940).

at the root of the trees," and Jesus, coming after him, has the winnowing shovel "in his hand" to separate the wheat from the chaff.

Thrown into the fire . . . with the Holy Spirit and fire . . . burn with fire that never goes out (3:10–12). The fiery presence of God resulted in purification, burning away impurities in order to restore divine purpose (see Mal. 3:2–4). Therefore, the Baptizer announced that the day of divine visitation would be an act of judgment against the unfruitful trees of Israel as well as a ministry of restoration performed by the Messiah, who will gather the wheat (true Israel) "into the barn," separated from the chaff via the baptism of the Holy Spirit/Wind/Breath, which is the fiery presence of God (vv. 11–12).

The Confirmation of Jesus as the Messiah, the Son of God (3:13–4:11)

The heavens suddenly opened . . . Spirit of God descending . . . a voice from heaven said (3:16–17). An invisible door in the sky, when it opened, was viewed as a portal into the presence of God (who resides above the heavens [see Rev. 4:1]). In this case the door opens and God's Spirit comes to earth and anoints Jesus, who had just been baptized by the prophet. The heavenly voice confirms that Jesus is God's "anointed one" (Messiah) by quoting Scripture, in this case a conflation of Ps. 2:7 and Isa. 42:1.

Jesus was led up by the Spirit into the wilderness to be tempted by the devil. After he had fasted forty days and forty nights (4:1–2). Why the wilderness? Since Jesus is the Messiah, shouldn't the Spirit have led him to Jerusalem to claim David's throne immediately? And yet, as the embodiment of Israel's story Jesus had to go to the desert. That's where the children of God are tested, proving that they trust him to provide (see comments on Matt. 3:1). Forty days/nights echoes forty years of Israel's life in the wilderness. Even though God provided manna in the desert for Israel, there is no miracle of bread for Jesus—even though he is God's Son. Therefore, the devil tempts Jesus to do what God did for Israel: perform a miracle to provide bread in the desert (4:3).

The Judean wilderness where Jesus faced Satan's temptations.

It is written (4:4, 7, 10). By quoting these three verses in response to the tempter (Deut. 8:3; 6:16, 13), Jesus revealed that he interpreted these three temptations as a rehearsal of Israel's experience in the wilderness. Even though Israel failed the test, Jesus succeeded: (1) Israel complained that they were hungry, but Jesus said that God's word was more important than food; (2) Israel complained about being thirsty, but Jesus said that it was wrong to test God; and (3) Israel worshiped the golden calf, but Jesus said that only God is worthy of worship.

Pinnacle of the temple (4:5). This refers either to the peak of the temple itself or to the southeast corner of the wall surrounding the temple, known as the *stoa basilica*—the most dramatic drop due to the Kidron Valley below (see the article "The Jerusalem Temple"). According to Josephus, to look down from that vantage point made one "giddy."[2]

The traditional location of the temptation to exchange the kingdom of this world for worship is a mountain near Jericho known as Jebel Quarantal.

Go away, Satan! (4:10). The greatest temptation (idolatry) occurred on a very high mountain, where devotees often built shrines to God (Deut. 12:2). Knowing that this was the greatest (and therefore last) temptation of Israel, Jesus commanded Satan to leave him. "Satan" comes from the Hebrew word *satan* (Job 1:6; Zech. 3:1; see comments on Mark 1:13), meaning "accuser, adversary." Based on Job, evidently it was Satan's divinely appointed role to test children of God to reveal the depth of their devotion. Once the devil left Jesus, angels came to his aid just as the Scriptures promised (4:11; cf. 4:6; Ps. 91:11–12).

Jesus, the Messiah, Begins His Ministry (4:12–25)

He left Nazareth and went to live in Capernaum (4:13). Jesus left his home (and family business) and moved to Capernaum, a fishing village on the northwest shore of the Sea of Galilee. Due to the rich soil in Lower Galilee and the large lake, farming and fishing were the major businesses of the region. Therefore, bread (barley and wheat) and pickled fish were the staple diet of Galileans (cf. 7:9–10). Since Jesus moved to this seaside village to begin his ministry, it comes as no surprise that his first disciples were fishermen (vv. 18–22). According to Matthew, Jesus started his messianic mission in this region to fulfill prophecy (vv. 14–16), perhaps indicating Jesus's intent to gather the ten lost tribes and draw gentiles into the kingdom according to Jewish end-time expectations.

Galilee of the Gentiles. The people who live in darkness (4:15–16). Even though Galilee was populated primarily by Jewish towns and villages, there were a few cities that had a significant gentile population, like Tiberias (south of Capernaum) and perhaps Sepphoris (north of Nazareth). Some scholars think that "living in darkness" reveals a Judean prejudice against the Galileans: they were inferior socially (rural folk) and spiritually (impious). Other scholars think that Matthew was emphasizing that the long-awaited "light" of the messianic kingdom had "dawned" on the land of the northern kingdom (Israel) before the southern kingdom (Judah).[3]

Repent, because the kingdom of heaven has come near (4:17). Repentance was the message of the prophets to prepare Israel for the day of divine visitation/judgment. "Kingdom of heaven" was an expression that signaled that God's reign "in heaven" was coming to earth, to the land of Israel, through his Messiah, Jesus (see comments on Mark 1:15).

Teaching in their synagogues (4:23). See the article "The Jewish Synagogue"; see comments on Mark 1:21. The word "synagogue" (literally, "led together," meaning "assembly" or "gathering") was used to refer to a building (sometimes called a "prayer house") and a people (a congregation gathered for Sabbath services). It was customary for visiting rabbis to be given the opportunity to teach in the synagogue.

The Sermon on the Mount (5:1–7:29)

When he saw the crowds, he went up on the mountain, and after he sat down (5:1). Matthew presents Jesus as the new Moses (see Deut. 18:18), who delivers the law on the mountain. Like the rabbis who took the seat of Moses when they taught (Matt. 23:2), Jesus sat down when he delivered his teaching to his disciples and the crowd.

Blessed are the poor in spirit (5:3). This is a contradiction in terms, because most people would have considered the poor in spirit cursed by God; spiritual poverty (disobedience) resulted in economic poverty (Deut. 28:15–68). However, with the arrival of the king and his kingdom the poor are blessed (Isa. 61:1)—all the miraculous healings by Jesus proved it (Matt. 4:23–25).

That is how they persecuted the prophets (5:12). The disciples were "Jesus prophets" who would be rejected by Israel, just like the ancient prophets (and just like Jesus).

You are the salt of the earth. But if the salt should lose its taste (5:13). Salt was used for several things (to flavor food, to preserve meat, to purify water, to purify sacrifices)—a basic mineral for life. To Jesus, the Galileans were like salt to his purpose: common and vital for life. He expected to expand his messianic mission through them. But if they refused, they would

The Church of the Beatitudes in Tabgha beside the Sea of Galilee.

be like tasteless salt—discarded and abused by others, for there is no way to make salt have flavor again. It becomes irrelevant because it no longer fulfills its purpose.

A lamp . . . on a lampstand (5:15). The most common house lamp burned oil contained in a small clay pot with a pinched-end spout that held the oil-soaked wick. Placed on a stand in the middle of a typical one-room house, it would provide enough light for all occupants.

Smallest letter . . . one stroke of a letter (5:18). The Hebrew Scriptures consist of three parts: the Law (Genesis through Deuteronomy), the Prophets (Joshua through Kings [excluding Ruth], Isaiah through Malachi [excluding Lamentations and Daniel]), and the Writings (the rest of the OT), which were preserved by scribes who followed strict production guidelines, like counting letters of every page to ensure reliability. Jesus was referring to the smallest letter of the Hebrew alphabet, *yod* (which looks like our apostrophe), and the smallest stroke (perhaps decorative) of larger letters. Obviously Jesus spoke about preserving the Scriptures with the same fervor as the scribes who copied them.

The least of these commands (5:19). There are 613 commandments in the Jewish law. And since punishment varied depending upon the commandment that was violated, rabbis debated which ones were the greatest and the least.

Righteousness surpasses that of the scribes and Pharisees (5:20). The Pharisees were the lay leaders of Israel, devoted to studying and obeying the Law and the Prophets (see the article "Pharisees and Sadducees"; see comments on Mark 2:18). Since God's blessing depended upon obedience to the Scriptures, the Pharisees were dedicated to teaching the people what was required. This meant not only interpreting vague commandments, such as "Remember the Sabbath day, to keep it holy," but also passing down their tradition—the interpretation of previous rabbis. Consequently the Pharisees were considered the most righteous people of all Israel. And yet Jesus believed that his disciples needed a better righteousness than that of the Pharisees in order to join him in the kingdom of heaven—a righteousness that fulfilled the law because he interpreted it rightly: "You have heard . . . but I tell you . . ."

Lampstands from the Roman period have been found that range from two to five feet in height, allowing light from a small oil lamp to shine throughout a room. This lampstand is from Italy (first century AD).

Whoever insults his brother or sister will be subject to the court (5:22). In an honor culture, to call your family member a "fool" was to accuse that person of being not only worthless but also dangerous to the community because fools jeopardized the social standing of the entire group. Therefore a careless accusation, "You fool!" (Aram. *raka*), could result in serious consequences, damages considered for judgment by the local court.

Subject to hellfire (5:22). Literally, Matthew wrote "Gehenna of fire." Why fire? Some scholars suggest that the valley south of Jerusalem (Gehinnom) may have been used as an ancient dump to burn trash. But since there is little evidence of Gehinnom being a trash dump, other scholars think that "Gehenna" became synonymous with hell because of the atrocity of children sacrificed by fire there during the reign of King Ahaz (2 Chron. 28:3).

Thrown into prison . . . paid the last penny (5:25–26). Debtors' prisons were the last resort for plaintiffs who had tried unsuccessfully to collect debts from borrowers. The debtor would be imprisoned until his family repaid the debt.

You have heard that it was said (5:27). The reason why Jesus didn't say, "You have read," is that people didn't own copies of the Scriptures (only the very wealthy could afford to pay a scribe to produce a personal copy [Acts 8:27–35]). In order to hear God's word, the people attended weekly synagogue services or annual temple services. Typically selections from the Torah, Isaiah, and Psalms were read/chanted in the synagogue.

Give her a written notice of divorce (5:31). According to the law, Jewish men (but not women) could divorce their spouse if they found something "indecent" about her (Deut. 24:1)—a rather vague stipulation that could mean anything from being a poor cook to being an adulteress. The certificate of divorce spelled out the indecency, giving the divorcée another chance at marriage, depending upon the severity of her shortcomings. Obviously Jesus believed that the only "indecency" that warranted divorce was adultery (5:32) (see comments on Mark 10:2).

Don't take an oath at all: either by heaven . . . or by the earth (5:34). People swore oaths to prove they were telling the truth. However, some swore oaths to cover their lies. The only way to tell the difference, besides the integrity of the person swearing the oath, was to judge the surety of the oath—that is, the sacredness of the "witness" that the swearer would call upon as proof of telling the truth. If what was sworn upon was holy, thus calling upon God as witness, then the words of the oath maker were considered golden (Lev. 19:12). But if what was sworn upon was something close to God, once or twice removed from that which was unquestionably holy, then one had to discern whether the oath maker was telling the truth. Even though the law allowed oath swearing (Num. 30:2–15), Jesus taught his disciples to dispense with the game of cloaking intent through oaths. A simple answer of yes or no should suffice.

Forces you to go one mile (5:41). According to Roman law, soldiers could impress imperial subjects to carry their load one mile.

Be perfect (5:48). The word translated as "perfect" (*teleios*) means "complete" or "mature." Children replicate the qualities of their parents.

Don't sound a trumpet before you (6:2). Alms for the poor were collected by synagogues and the temple. Since the receptacle for alms in the temple was horn-shaped, the coins tossed loudly into the metal "trumpet" called attention to the giver. If Jesus was referring to alms collected on the Sabbath in the synagogue, then he was speaking figuratively, saying that almsgivers were making some kind of ostentatious display during the offering.

As the hypocrites do (6:2). The word *hypokritēs* was the term used for actors in the Greek theater.

But when you pray, go into your private room (6:6). There were three hours of prayer: morning, afternoon, and evening (Dan. 6:10). In most homes there was a closet where valuables were stored and locked (Matt. 6:19). And so, on the heels of giving advice regarding alms for the poor, Jesus instructs his disciples to pray privately in contrast to someone playing the hypocrite in public, and perhaps also to pray in the presence of their valuables, thereby honoring God as their greatest treasure.

Don't babble like the Gentiles (6:7). Some gentiles believed that the only way to get their gods to pay attention to them was to bombard them with praise and requests, somewhat like a child trying to get the attention of their parents by nagging, "Mom, mom, mom . . ."

Give us today our daily bread (6:11). The expression "daily bread" could mean either bread for today or bread for the coming day (tomorrow). Although we may not recognize it, the request for bread relies upon community support (landowners, farmers, millers, bakers).

Forgive us our debts, as we also have forgiven our debtors (6:12). The Jews understood sin as a debt to God. "Debts/debtors" implied economic as well as spiritual and social indebtedness. To "forgive" a debt meant to cancel someone's obligation, financial as well as social. Jesus, therefore, knew that forgiveness would cost money.

Do not bring us into temptation (6:13). The word translated as "temptation" (*peirasmos*) also means "trial, testing" (James 1:2, 12), which explains why Jesus added the tagline "but deliver us from the evil one." Satan tries to turn tests into temptations (Job 1:6–11; Matt. 4:1–10).

Whenever you fast (6:16). The Jewish people fasted for two reasons: to repent of Israel's sin (Lev. 16:29–31) and to grieve over the death of a loved one (Jer. 16:7). Some fasts entailed refusing all food and drink for a brief period of time; other fasts meant abstaining from certain food/drink. Pharisees were known to fast over Israel's sin (Matt. 9:14) two days per week: Monday and Thursday (see comments on Mark 2:18).

The eye is the lamp of the body (6:22). First-century people believed that eyes not only revealed the "light" or "darkness" within a person but also were the portals through which goodness or evil could be unleashed. Therefore, to give someone "the evil eye" (literally, "eye . . . bad" [v. 23]) was to attempt to cast ill will upon an enemy.

Do not judge, so that you won't be judged (7:1). Like mercy (5:7), judgment is reciprocal: what you give is what you get (7:2).

Let me take the splinter out of your eye (7:4). Once a carpenter who worked with wood and stone, Jesus knew that sometimes a person needs help to remove foreign objects from their eyes—something first recognized by the "splinter-eyed" person, who then seeks help from the "clear-eyed" (6:22). Of course, the "beam-eyed" person (7:3), unwilling to recognize being blind, would be of no help until humbly admitting what obscured their vision: hypocrisy ("There's nothing wrong with me").

Don't give what is holy to dogs or toss your pearls before pigs (7:6). Dogs were scavengers of carcasses and trash; pigs were unclean according to the law (Lev. 11:7). No family would waste their "clean" (sacred) food on dogs; no one would dress a pig with pearls (valuables). Only clear-eyed people (humility) are wise enough not to waste sacred valuables on people who won't appreciate them.

You then, who are evil (7:11). According to Jewish ethics, what you do reveals who you are. Therefore, since all people do evil things, everyone is evil. And yet even evil people know how to do good things, especially parents for children. But since God is good, how much more will he do good things (gifts) for his children. Here Jesus uses a common rabbinical strategy, arguing from the minor ("since this is true") to the major ("how much more this will be true").

This is the Law and the Prophets (7:12). The Golden Rule appears in other Jewish writings (Tob. 4:15) and was taught by the famous rabbi Hillel (60 BC–AD 20), although both cite a negative version: "What you hate, do not do to any one."[4] And according to rabbinical tradition, Hillel declared, "This is the whole law."

Be on your guard against false prophets (7:15). Jews in Jesus's day had become convinced that most prophets were false (Zech. 13:2–6). False prophets were

Small votive images, like the pig shown here, have been found in temples to pagan gods (Temple of Demeter, Knidos, Turkey, 350–300 BC).

evident in two ways: what they prophesied didn't come true (Deut. 18:22), or they performed a miraculous sign to promote idolatry (Deut. 13:1–5). Jesus added a third: the result of their lives was evil, like a bad tree producing bad fruit (Matt. 7:16–20).

Is cut down and thrown into the fire (7:19). A tree (or vine) that produced bad fruit and was therefore felled and burned was a common prophetic image of the judgment of God (Isa. 5:1–6; Matt. 3:10).

Wise man who built his house on the rock (7:24). Unlike today, a foundation had to be located before a house could be built. Much of the ground of Lower Galilee had large, basalt rock shelves buried just below the surface (Matt. 13:5)—the perfect place for the typical one-room house to be built. Fools, however, despised conventional wisdom and built their house wherever they wanted—that is, on sand. Delivering his sermon on a "rocky" mountain, Jesus invited his listeners to build their lives upon his foundational teaching (wisdom) in order to overcome difficulties.

He was teaching them like one who had authority, and not like their scribes (7:29). If the Mishnah (the second-century collection of more than four hundred years of rabbinical teaching) gives any indication as to how rabbis taught their students, much of their instruction involved passing down what previous rabbis had taught about the Scriptures. Jesus, however, never quoted a single rabbi (he never studied the law as a rabbinical student). Instead, he told the crowd only what he thought about the Scriptures, as if his teaching was authoritative by itself.

The Cursed Are Blessed: A Leper, a Centurion's Slave, a Feverish Woman (8:1–17)

A man with leprosy (8:2). In Jesus's day the word "leprosy" was used to describe a person with any kind of skin disease, not just what we know today as Hansen's disease (see comments on Mark 1:40). The law prescribed strict guidelines to deal with all kinds of skin impurities/uncleanness, requiring those with persistent problems to live "outside the camp" (Lev. 13:1–46). If the skin disease cleared up, a protocol had to be followed in order to reinstate the "unclean" into the community (Lev. 14:1–32), which included offering a "gift that Moses commanded" (Matt. 8:4).

When he entered Capernaum, a centurion came to him (8:5). A centurion was a soldier who commanded as many as one hundred troops (see the article "The Roman Military"). There may have been a few Roman soldiers in Capernaum to help with taxation, but the largest battalion of the Roman army was based in Syria (a legion of soldiers), with two Roman auxiliaries stationed at Caesarea (on the coast) and Jerusalem. This man was either a retired soldier living in Galilee, or a Roman soldier from Syria, Caesarea, or Jerusalem who sought out Jesus's help, or a soldier who had been hired by Herod Antipas to be part of his army in Galilee.

Many will come from east and west to share the banquet with Abraham, Isaac, and Jacob in the kingdom of heaven (8:11). Jewish expectations regarding the end of the world included the idea that Jews scattered all over the world (the diaspora) would be brought back to the land of Israel by God (Isa. 56:1–8). The day of the Lord would be a day of judgment for the wicked but a day of celebration for the righteous, envisioned as a heavenly banquet on earth hosted by the patriarchs.

Sons of the kingdom will be thrown into the outer darkness (8:12). This is likely a reference to Israelites—a notion based on Isaiah's remnant theology that also shows up in Paul's letters: not all Israel are Israel (Rom. 9:6, 27; cf. Isa. 10:22–23).

When evening came, they brought to him many who were demon-possessed (8:16). Malevolent powers were said to rule the night and the sea (see the article "Demonization and Exorcism in the Greco-Roman World"). That Jesus exorcized demons "with a word" revealed his mighty power, since other exorcists had to rely upon lengthy incantations and odd rituals to cast out demons (Acts 8:9–11, 18–19; 19:13–16, 19).

A Roman centurion.

He himself took our weaknesses and carried our diseases (8:17). Isaiah prophesied that an unnamed "servant of the Lord" would reverse the curse of Israel's sin by taking upon himself the effects of their disobedience (Isa. 53:4)—a prophecy that came true in the healing ministry of Jesus according to Matthew.

The Son of Man Has No Bed (8:18–20, 23–27); Let the Dead Bury Their Dead (8:21–22, 28–34)

Lord, . . . first let me go and bury my father (8:21). Perhaps this request echoes the story of Elisha, who asked to say goodbye to his father and mother before following Elijah (1 Kings 19:19–21). One of the surest ways to keep the fifth commandment (Exod. 20:12) was to honor your father by ensuring a proper burial. More demanding than Elijah, Jesus here responds rather harshly (8:22), revealing his priorities regarding his "new family" in the kingdom—a teaching that he would emphasize later (12:46–50). This teaching would get him into trouble when he returned "home" to Nazareth (13:54–58).

What kind of man is this? (8:27). Since malevolent powers ruled the sea, only God was strong enough to make them behave (Job 41:1–34). Israel celebrated God's power over the sea and the wind (Ps. 107:23–32). Therefore, when the disciples asked, "What kind of man is this?" they already knew the answer; it's what they said after Jesus walks on the sea and calms the wind: "Truly you are the Son of God" (Matt. 14:33).

When he had come to the other side, to the region of the Gadarenes (8:28). One of the cities of the Decapolis (a constellation of ten Greek cities founded after Alexander the Great's reign), Gadara was approximately six miles southeast of the Sea of Galilee. Although some Jews lived there, it probably was populated by a majority of gentiles. Thus this may be the first time in Matthew's Gospel that Jesus traveled into gentile territory since his baptism.

Have you come here to torment us before the time? (8:29). Even the demons knew that their days were numbered, the "appointed time" when God would judge/punish malevolent powers/evil spirits on the last day—an idea that shows up in extrabiblical Jewish literature (*1 Enoch* 15–16; *Jubilees* 10.8–9) and the book of Revelation (20:1–10).

If you drive us out, . . . send us into the herd of pigs (8:30). To the Jewish mind, it would make perfect sense that "unclean" spirits would want to inhabit "unclean" animals and destroy them in the sea, where evil powers live.

God Desires Mercy, Not Sacrifice (9:1–34)

Your sins are forgiven . . . He's blaspheming! (9:2–3). For Jesus to pronounce forgiveness of sins without the necessary sacrifices required by the law was presumptuous. By divine design the temple existed to mediate the holy presence of God, and priests offering sacrifices in God's house played a significant role in maintaining holiness. Only priests had the

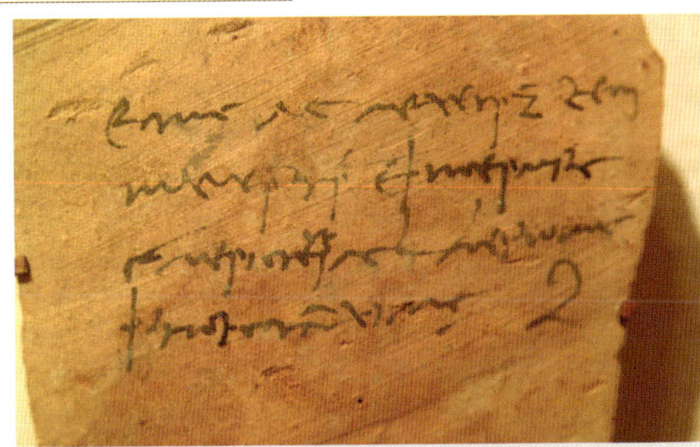

Tax receipt written in Greek from the first century AD.

right to declare whether sacrifices were acceptable to God. So for Jesus to declare the paralytic's sins forgiven outside the temple was "blasphemous" according to the scribes.

The Son of Man has authority on earth to forgive sins (9:6). The "Son of Man" is a heavenly figure who appeared in Daniel's vision and received from God an eternal kingdom (Dan. 7:13–14). Jesus claimed that through his ministry the Son of Man's heavenly kingdom had come to earth, resulting in forgiveness of sin. The fact that he reversed the curse of sin by healing the paralytic proved it.

Toll booth (9:9). Since Galilee was not under direct Roman rule—Herod Antipas was a client king of the Romans—taxes were levied by the Herodian government for its own purposes (which also included paying tribute to the Romans). Either Matthew was a tax farmer, hired by Herod to collect production taxes from farmers and fishermen, or he was a customs agent who levied tolls from merchants who traveled through Capernaum (situated on one of the major roads passing through Galilee).

Why does your teacher eat with tax collectors and sinners? (9:11). As agents of the Herodian government (proxy of the Roman Empire), tax collectors were considered traitors by the Jewish people (see comments on Mark 2:15). To associate with such people, as well as other notorious sinners, was social suicide. Since guilt by association ruled the honor game, and table company was an important public indicator of social worth, eating with shameful people revealed your place in society: you considered yourself a shameful person too. Honorable people, therefore, would share a meal only with socially acceptable people.

One of the leaders came and knelt down before him (9:18). That he knelt before Jesus while the Pharisees watched the whole affair revealed the leader's humility: a man of great influence showing deference to a rogue prophet.

A woman . . . bleeding for twelve years . . . touched the end of his robe (9:20). According to the law, a menstruating woman was unclean until her period was over and she submitted to ritual purification (Lev. 15:19–24). If her menstruation persisted, she was perpetually unclean (Lev. 15:25–27). Since Jesus wore the garments of a holy man—tassels hanging from the four corners of his robe (Num. 15:38–39)—the woman must have believed that grabbing one of these tassels would heal her, enabling her to be restored to her community. Of course, by touching Jesus she rendered him "unclean" according to the law, which may explain why Jesus singled her out. Jesus reversed the polarity of uncleanness: his clean "touch" made the unclean clean.

The flute players and a crowd lamenting loudly (9:23). Professional mourners—most often women (Jer. 9:17–20)—wailed and played laments on reed instruments and flutes to help families and the community grieve over death. They also served as experts in determining the time of death, at which time the family would be led immediately to grieve the deceased. The larger the crowd, the louder the lamentation, the more honor was shown to the family. By the time Jesus had arrived, the "funeral" for the daughter of this highly honored father had already begun.

The flute players shown here are part of a larger relief of a funeral procession from the first century AD.

Gathering the Lost Sheep of Israel (9:35–11:1)

Like sheep without a shepherd (9:36). Two of the greatest leaders of Israel, David the king and Moses the prophet, were once shepherds. Therefore, casting Israel's leaders (kings and priests) as good "shepherds" was one of the favorite analogies that prophets and psalmists used to describe Israel's need. Of course, Israel was supposed to recognize God as their supreme shepherd, and they were the "sheep of his pasture" (Ps. 100:3). Picturing Israel as scattered, shepherdless sheep was not only a commentary on the current leadership but also an expression of how much they needed God to guide them home.

Pray to the Lord of the harvest to send out workers (9:38). The day of the Lord, when God visited his people to bring justice to Israel and the land, often was pictured by the prophets as a day of harvest, most often a symbol of judgment (see comments on Matt. 3:10–12), but it could also picture a day of redemption, gathering Israel to God (Isa. 9:3).

Summoning his twelve disciples, he gave them authority (10:1). In order to expand the reach of his messianic mission, Jesus chose twelve disciples, representing the recovery of the twelve tribes of Israel—starting with the ten tribes of the old northern kingdom in Galilee (Jesus and the twelve would go to Judah, the southern kingdom, later). Matthew doesn't explain exactly how Jesus gave them authority (laying hands on them or some other ritual?), but because they were sent by Jesus, they had the power to "heal the sick, raise the dead, cleanse those with leprosy, drive out demons. Freely you received, freely give" (10:8). Since the twelve disciples were given messianic authority "freely" (they did nothing to earn it), they were to use their newfound power "freely"—healing, raising, cleansing, exorcizing without charge.

These are the names of the twelve apostles (10:2). "Apostle" means "emissary," a word used to describe messengers sent with the authority of the sender, most often political leaders or powerful businesspeople. The names of the twelve apostles listed here are the same as in Mark's Gospel (see comments on Mark 3:14; cf. Mark 3:16–19). Luke substitutes "Judas the son of James" for "Thaddaeus" (perhaps his Greek name). John never lists the twelve names. Two of the twelve had well-known nicknames or monikers, perhaps to distinguish between the "Simons": Simon also known as Peter (meaning "rock") and Simon the Zealot. Zealots were a group of Jews who became famous during the revolt that led to the first Jewish War (AD 66–73). They opposed Roman occupation of the land, using the same tactics as the Maccabeans, the insurgents who led Israel to regain their independence from the Syrians two hundred years earlier.

Don't take the road that leads to the Gentiles . . . go to the lost sheep of the house of Israel (10:5–6). Literally, Matthew wrote, "Do not travel down a road of the Gentiles." Jesus also prohibited his disciples from traveling through Samaria. In other words, the disciples were not supposed to leave Galilee during their mission of recovering the "lost sheep" of Israel. Jesus's first priority in establishing the kingdom of heaven on earth (10:7) was the reconstitution of Israel, beginning with those who lived in the land of the old northern kingdom. The "lost" sheep were the dispossessed—the sick, the dead, lepers, the demon-possessed (10:8)—those who suffered due to the absence of a "good shepherd."

The worker is worthy of his food. . . . Find out who is worthy, and stay there until you leave. . . . If anyone does not welcome you . . . more tolerable on the day of judgment for the land of Sodom and Gomorrah (10:10–15). Jesus counted on the honor code to take care of his disciples, whom he sent out as prophets to the towns and villages of Galilee. Honorable visitors could expect honorable gifts of hospitality from their hosts: a place to stay, food and drink, provisions for their journey. If the village did not esteem their visitors as "honorable," the travelers would be shunned, encouraged to move on to the next town. If the visitors were truly honorable—sent by God—the village's rejection would reflect poorly on them: they weren't honorable enough to recognize the honor of God. That's why Jesus compared his disciples to angelic visitors who were sent to warn the cities

The remains of leather sandals found in the Cave of the Letters in the Judean Desert (second century AD).

of Sodom and Gomorrah about the approaching judgment of God (Gen. 19:1–29). If any town rejected Jesus's disciples, they would be rejecting God, deserving divine judgment—pictured by the prophet shaking the dust off his feet as he departed (vv. 14–15), a sign that he left their "dirty" uncleanness behind. Consequently, the impurity of the people would remain with them; the *shalom* ("peace") of the prophet's greeting would remain with him (v. 13).

You will be given what to say at that hour, because it isn't you speaking, but the Spirit of your Father is speaking through you (10:19–20). Like Moses before the pharaoh, or the ancient prophets who declared by the Spirit of God, "This is what the Lord says," Jesus predicted that his disciples would be inspired to speak the very words of God—especially when they got in trouble with the authorities.

You will not have gone through the towns of Israel before the Son of Man comes (10:23). The appearance of the heavenly Son of Man (Dan. 7:13–14) signaled the imminent reign of God on earth. Jesus was convinced that the disciples wouldn't have a lot of time to get the message out. They wouldn't finish their mission to reclaim the lost sheep of Israel before the "Son of Man comes"—a reference either to Jesus's trip to Jerusalem to claim David's throne, to the cross, to the resurrection, or perhaps to the end of the world (see Matt. 24:27–31).

If they called the head of the house "Beelzebul" (10:25). A play on words in Aramaic, "Beelzebul" means "master of the house" (see comments on Mark 3:22). *Baal* (the Canaanite name for God, meaning "lord, master") and *zebul* ("house") was the title given to the chief adversary of God and Israel in the OT: Baal-zebul = the prince of demons = the devil.

Proclaim on the housetops (10:27). Many one-room houses had exterior steps leading to the rooftop—a workspace for certain domestic chores. To announce news from the roofs to people in the streets/footpaths below and to other residents doing chores on their roofs would be the quickest way to "get the word out."

I did not come to bring peace, but a sword (10:34). Jesus explained what he meant by this provocative claim when he appealed to the prophecy of Micah, where the prophet anticipates the time when God will visit his people—a day of battle for Israel. "Watchmen" are to warn the people that God is about to invade the land, but it will turn out to be a time of "panic" because the people will turn on one another—not only neighbor versus neighbor but also children versus parents (Mic. 7:4–6)—something that Jesus predicted would happen to his disciples too (Matt. 10:21–22). In other words, Jesus anticipated the results of his messianic mission in light of what the prophets said would happen when God visited his people.

Anyone who welcomes a prophet because he is a prophet will receive a prophet's reward (10:41). Jesus compared his disciples to the ancient prophets, who blessed those who gave them water and food (1 Kings 17:7–24). Similarly, anyone who offered the simplest act of hospitality to Jesus's itinerant disciples (Matt. 10:40–42)—a cup of *cold* water could only come straight from a well or spring—would be blessed by God, for to welcome Jesus's disciples was the same thing as welcoming him (the presumption behind the proper treatment of emissaries/apostles).

John and Jesus (11:2–30)

Go and report to John what you hear and see (11:4). Although Matthew had already indicated that the Baptizer was imprisoned (4:12), he doesn't explain the circumstances until later (14:3–5): Herod Antipas was the one who put the prophet in prison because John preached against his second marriage. Obviously John had doubts about Jesus. Prison may have intensified his concerns, which is why Jesus told John's disciples to report "what you hear and see." Then Jesus summed up for them what they had seen and heard (11:5), a veiled reference to the prophecy of Isa. 61:1–2 coming true—at least most of it. The part that Jesus omitted, about prisoners being released when the Messiah comes, may reveal the source of John's doubts, for if the Messiah was supposed to release prisoners, what about John? Thus comes the warning in the form of a beatitude: "blessed is the one who isn't offended

John the Baptist was in prison at the fortress palace of Herod Antipas at Machaerus. From there he likely sent messengers to Jesus asking him if he was "the one who is to come" (Matt. 11:3). The archaeological remains of Machaerus are located on this mountaintop to the east of the Dead Sea.

by me" (11:6)—including John. And yet, even though John had doubts about Jesus, Jesus had no doubts about the Baptizer's role in his messianic ministry: "he is the Elijah who is to come" (11:14).

Yes, I tell you, and more than a prophet (11:9). The reason why John was "more than a prophet" is that he actually fulfilled prophecy. It's one thing for a prophet to declare the message of God—to prophesy. It's quite something else to *be* the fulfillment of God's word, the embodiment of fulfilled prophecy. And, according to Jesus, John fulfilled Malachi's prophecy (Mal. 3:1; 4:5–6), being the one who would prepare Israel for the "great and terrible day of the LORD" (Mal. 4:5).

From the days of John the Baptist until now, the kingdom of heaven has been suffering violence, and the violent have been seizing it by force (11:12). Either Jesus was referring to his own ministry having been attacked by opponents ("suffering violence") and his efforts to forcibly bind the "strong man" in order to raid his house—that which Satan has stolen and Jesus recovers (12:29)—or Jesus was critiquing the Zealots, who believed that violence against Israel's enemies (the Romans) was the only way to bring the reign of God to earth.

It's like children sitting in the marketplaces who call out to other children (11:16). As children of all cultures tend to do, Jewish children in Jesus's day imitated adult rituals, playacting certain behavior associated with celebrations (festivals and weddings) and funerals. Music was an important part of both kinds of events: songs of celebration for dancing and songs of lament for grieving (11:17). Jesus compared his generation's opinion of him and John the Baptist (11:18–19) to children who were playing "grown-up," but it's difficult to determine the assigned roles: who are the children who are playing the instruments ("we played the flute for you") and the children who refused to play the game ("but you didn't dance")? If Jesus and John are the "we," then Jesus was criticizing the apathy of his generation. Jesus came "eating and drinking," but the people refused to celebrate Jesus's miracles; John "came neither eating nor drinking," but the people refused to fast—that is, to get serious about their sin. But if the children reciting the rhyme were the people of "this generation" (which seems more likely in light of vv. 18–19), then the one refusing to dance is John and the one refusing to mourn is Jesus. In other words, the people thought that John had taken repentance too far (11:18: "He has a demon"—as if to say, "He needs to loosen up and have some fun"). And Jesus needed to get serious about sin (9:14: "Why do we and the Pharisees fast often, but your disciples do not fast?"; and 11:19: "Look, a glutton and a drunkard"; cf. Deut. 21:20—what a father was supposed to say to the people to disown his rebellious son).

Wisdom is vindicated by her deeds (11:19). In the book of Proverbs "Wisdom" appears as a virtuous woman, calling out to men in the streets to listen to her words (1:20–33; 8:1–9:6), while foolishness is personified as an adulteress, soliciting young men to her house (7:7–27; 9:13–18). So when Jesus was rejected by the people as "a glutton and a drunkard," and the Galilean villages (Matt. 11:21–24) refused to repent despite the miracles of Jesus (the "deeds" of Wisdom), they revealed their own foolishness—unable to recognize Wisdom. Furthermore, even though "Wisdom" was hidden from the "wise and intelligent" (11:25), Jesus reissued his invitation, "Come to me," sounding like the voice of Wisdom calling to "all of you who are weary and burdened" needing rest (11:28). Therefore, those who listen and come to Jesus will prove that Wisdom is "vindicated by her deeds" (11:19).

Woe to you, Chorazin! Woe to you, Bethsaida . . . repented in sackcloth and ashes long ago (11:21). Ancient prophets pronounced judgments against entire cities of Israel when they didn't heed the message of God. Chorazin and Bethsaida were small villages situated on the north side of the Sea of Galilee where Jesus had performed miracles (v. 21). Jesus thought that miracles would provoke the people to repentance, evidenced by "sackcloth and ashes." Public acts of repentance looked like rituals associated with grief over death. People would shed their clothes (or tear them) and don rough garments, and would cover their faces with dirt/ashes (Job 1:20; 2:8), leaving their faces unwashed as a sign of their grief (Matt. 6:16–18).

No, you will go down to Hades (11:23). Here, Jesus echoes the words of Isaiah against the king of Babylon (Isa. 14:13–15), directing Isaiah's taunt against the fishing village of Capernaum. In Jewish parlance "Hades" referred to the place of the dead (the underworld, the grave).

I will give you rest (11:28). The Hebrew word *shabbat* ("sabbath") means "rest." Therefore, Jesus was making a significant claim when he promised that "sabbath" would be found in him.

Take up my yoke and learn from me . . . for my yoke is easy (11:29–30). The rabbis compared the law to the yoke that farmers placed on oxen to plow their fields. Similarly, the law would bridle the rebellious heart to guide them in the ways of God. But Jesus may be referring to the yoke for humans, used to carry heavy loads, like water or bags of grain. They would take a wooden pole and place it on their shoulders, having attached a load at each end, wrapping their arms around the pole to steady the weight and carry

A wooden yoke used to harness animals for plowing the fields.

their burden. In this way Jesus used the image of carrying a wooden beam on one's shoulders—reminiscent of a man carrying the crossbeam to his own crucifixion—in order to picture the cross as his "yoke" that would be "easy." The word translated as "easy" (*chrēstos*) also means "fits well." In Greek the expression "learn [*manthanō*] from me" uses the verbal form of the word "disciple" (*mathētēs*). Therefore, Jesus used a word picture, "yoke," to help his disciples see the cross that they would bear to learn what it would take to find rest in him—a yoke of discipleship that would fit them well.[5]

Could This Be the Son of David? (12:1–50)

Your disciples are doing what is not lawful on the Sabbath (12:2). Since the seventh day of the week (sundown on Friday to sundown on Saturday) was a day of rest (*shabbat* means "rest"), the law prohibited work on that day (Exod. 20:8–11) (see the article "The Sabbath"; see comments on Mark 2:23). Rabbis debated what would qualify as labor, making exceptions for dire circumstances, such as pulling sheep out of a pit (Matt. 12:11). However, to harvest grain on the Sabbath would be considered unlawful labor, no matter how hungry one might be. One had to plan for the Sabbath by preparing food in advance (Exod. 16:5). And yet the law provided for the poor to eat from unharvested fields because they had no food to prepare (Deut. 23:25; Ruth 2:2–9).

Haven't you read what David did? (12:3). Notice that Jesus referred to the Pharisees' ability to read the Scriptures—something that the average person couldn't do due to illiteracy or lack of access to copies of the law. The story comes from 1 Sam. 21:1–9, when David talked the priest into giving him and his men bread dedicated to God in his temple, bread that only priests were supposed to eat (Lev. 24:5–9). By referring to this story Jesus may have been comparing himself and his disciples to David and the ruffians who accompanied "the anointed one" while he was on the run from Saul (1 Sam. 22:2).

On Sabbath days the priests in the temple violate the Sabbath and are innocent (12:5). Priests seemed to "violate" the Sabbath because they were required to work on the Sabbath, commanded to offer sacrifices to God (Num. 28:9–10). By referring to these two examples (David eating sacred bread and priests working on the Sabbath), Jesus claimed exceptions to the rule. He used a common argument of the rabbis (argument from the minor to the major) to claim an exemption for him and his disciples: if the temple's operation is more important than Sabbath laws, and if "something greater than the temple is here" (12:6, meaning Jesus), then Jesus's disciples did not violate the Sabbath. Indeed, that his disciples harvested grain on the

Sabbath proved "the Son of Man is Lord of the Sabbath" (12:8) (see the article "The Sabbath"; see comments on Mark 2:23).

Here is my servant . . . "Could this be the Son of David?" (12:18, 23). God made several promises to Israel that he would send a special leader—someone who would be a prophet like Moses (Deut. 18:18–19), the son of David (1 Sam. 7:12–16), and the servant of the Lord (Isa. 42:1–4)—to restore the covenant and bring God's blessing. What makes Isaiah's prediction relevant regarding the "servant of the Lord" is the context of the prophecy: the servant would appear during Israel's exile (Isa. 40–55) to restore God's people back to the land of his promise. That prophecy, coupled with God's promise to raise a son of David to establish the justice of his kingdom on earth, incited the people to wonder whether Jesus was the fulfillment of every promise coming true. Through Jesus's healing ministry it appeared as though the curse of exile had been reversed. The land and the people were restored. The son of David was here to rule Israel (king) and to bless God's people and all the nations (kingdom).

This clay tablet contains part of a Greek translation of an incantation spell against evil spirits (Babylon, third to first century BC).

By whom do your sons drive them out? (12:27). Jesus wasn't the first Jewish leader to have the ability to cast out demons. Rabbis and other Jewish "holy men" before Jesus were known to cast out demons. What made Jesus unique was the relative ease with which he cast them out (he exorcized demons with a word) and the frequency of exorcisms (see the article "Demonization and Exorcism in the Greco-Roman World").

Teacher, we want to see a sign from you (12:38). Before he sent the promised leader(s) to Israel (prophet like Moses, son of David, servant of the Lord), God promised his people that he would give them a warning—a sign of the imminent "day of the Lord"—to prepare Israel for the judgment day (Mal. 3:1; 4:5–6). So when the Pharisees and the scribes asked Jesus for a sign (Matt. 12:38), they were putting him on the spot—perhaps trying to get Jesus to offer a "false sign" to prove they were right about him, that he was a "false prophet" (Deut. 13:1–5).

Parables of the Kingdom (13:1–52)

Then he told them many things in parables (13:3). Although parables were not uncommon (2 Sam. 12:1–4), that Jesus relied heavily upon them to teach Israel about the kingdom of heaven on earth surprised the disciples (see comments on Mark 1:15). As analogies, the meaning of Jesus's parables was not obvious to everyone. Those who understood them revealed that they had eyes to "see" the kingdom of heaven on earth (Matt. 13:16). Those who didn't understand revealed their ignorance about the kingdom, even fulfilling Isaiah's prophecy: when God sends his prophet to deliver his message, the people won't listen (Isa. 6:8–10). Accordingly, Jesus used parables to both reveal and conceal his teaching about the kingdom of heaven on earth.

The sower who went out to sow (13:3). The primary crop of Galilean farmers was grain (wheat or barley). Farming practices in Galilee varied: some farmers may have broadcast seed prior to tilling the ground; others sowed seed after breaking up the soil. The first sowing occurred in November, once the rainy season had begun. Then, later rains in April brought the crops to fruition (Deut. 11:14; Joel 2:23), which were harvested in May. Occasionally, grain farmers put in crops during the dry season—a second sowing that was incredibly risky—and yielded a rare harvest in October. Given his reference to the scorching sun that withered shallow plants (Matt. 13:6), perhaps Jesus compared the kingdom of heaven to this risky second sowing.

Some a hundred, some sixty, and some thirty times what was sown (13:8). If Jesus was referring to the amount of grain per stalk (wheat or barley), a hundredfold yield wouldn't be unusual. One hundred grains per head was at the top end of the average yield. But if Jesus used the common standard for figuring production taxes—the ratio of seed sown to grain harvested—then a hundredfold yield would have been a miraculous harvest, since the typical yield of Galilean farmers was tenfold.

The kingdom of heaven is like a mustard seed (13:31). Since mustard plants were so plentiful, and a little went a long way for daily use, few farmers purposely sowed mustard seeds in their vegetable garden, especially since the plants would grow so big as to attract birds—the perennial pest of farmers. That Jesus described the kingdom of heaven using negative imagery (mustard plants, leaven, thieves) may reveal the subversive reality of his ministry.

Jesus's parable of the sower pictures four soil types to represent responses to Jesus's message.

Like leaven that a woman took and mixed into fifty pounds of flour (13:33). Yeast was a Jewish symbol for impurity (Exod. 12:15–20; Lev. 2:11; Matt. 16:6). Once it is worked into a lump of dough, it eventually leavens the entire batch. A woman leavening fifty pounds of flour indicates that she was preparing bread for an entire village, enough to feed one hundred people.

The harvest is the end of the age, and the harvesters are angels . . . the angels will go out, separate the evil people from the righteous (13:39, 49). The harvest was a common prophetic image of the end of the world, the day when God would separate the righteous and the wicked for the last judgment (see comments on Matt. 3:10–12). Angels appear as God's eschatological harvesters in Jewish apocalyptic literature (*1 Enoch* 54.6) and elsewhere in the NT (Rev. 14:15–19).

Like treasure, buried in a field (13:44). In a world without banks (temples functioned like "safes" primarily for the wealthy), commoners kept their valuables in a storeroom inside their homes (Matt. 6:6; 12:29). Vulnerable to thieves (Matt. 6:19–20), treasures sometimes were buried in the ground by their owners. One of the famous Dead Sea Scrolls, known as the *Copper Scroll*, was a treasure map, locating the places where the Qumranians had buried coins, jewels, and precious metals.

Prophets without Honor (13:53–14:12)

"Isn't this the carpenter's son?" . . . And they were offended by him (13:55–57). In the first-century world people believed that God "predestined" a person's occupation. For example, in Jewish terms, kings were supposed to come from the tribe of Judah and priests were born to Levites. Such things were prearranged by the God of Israel. Similarly, if a man was born to a carpenter, the Jewish people inferred that God intended for him to be a carpenter. There was no need for trade schools, for a carpenter would teach his son their God-given trade. One can give only what has been given. To claim anything more would be pretentious—an attempt to defy God's plan, thinking that one was somehow special. When that happened, the people (family and village

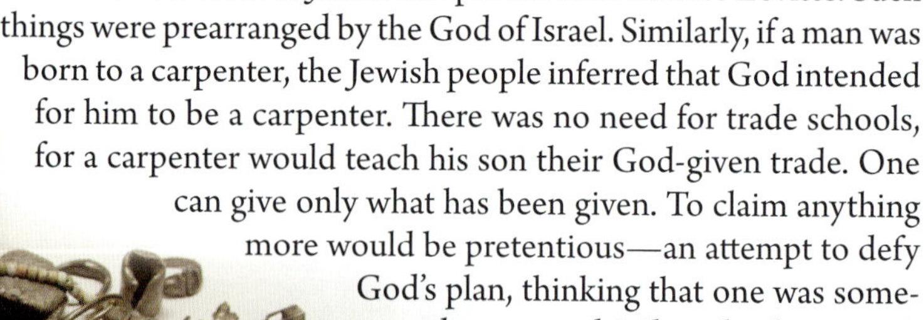

Six stashes of valuables were found during excavations at Ekron in Israel. Several were discovered hidden under floors. They often contained coins, precious stones, and fine pottery.

elders) would put the rebel in his place, reminding him of his position in society.

Herod the tetrarch heard the report about Jesus (14:1). Herod Antipas (son of Herod the Great) ruled Galilee and Perea as a "tetrarch" ("ruler of a fourth," a diminutive title two grades below "king") on behalf of the Roman Empire (4 BC–AD 39). Herod had divorced his wife (the daughter of the king of Nabatea, territory contiguous to Perea) to marry the divorced wife of his brother. When John preached against the illicit marriage while baptizing in Perea close to the border of Nabatea, it inflamed the hostilities between the two leaders. Consequently, Herod silenced the prophet by imprisoning him at Machaerus, Antipas's castle in southern Perea east of the Dead Sea.[6]

Herod's birthday (14:6). Probably seen as pretentious by commoners, birthdays were celebrated by the wealthy and the powerful. Since food and drink were in short supply, most people feasted only during holy festivals and weddings. Rulers and the wealthy, however, celebrated their birthdays with feasting (Gen. 40:20; Job 1:4–5 [NIV]).

His disciples came, removed the corpse, buried it, and went and reported to Jesus (14:12). John's disciples risked guilt by association when they came to Herod's castle to retrieve the Baptizer's headless body and bury it according to Jewish custom. In certain respects they were more faithful to John than the twelve disciples were to Jesus, since they didn't bury Jesus after he was crucified by the Romans. Rather, another disciple (not one of the Twelve), Joseph of Arimathea, approached Pilate for permission to bury Jesus (Matt. 27:57–60).

Feeding Five Thousand and Walking on Water (14:13–36)

Everyone ate and was satisfied. They picked up twelve baskets full of leftover pieces (14:20). Evidently there was an expectation that a "prophet like Moses"—the one who was to come to restore Israel (Deut. 18:18)—would perform a sign in the desert, just like Moses did in the wilderness.[7] So when Jesus miraculously fed five thousand men plus women and children in "a remote place," it was reminiscent of the times God provided manna in the wilderness for Israel. That there were enough leftovers to fill twelve baskets could symbolize God's providential care for the twelve tribes of Israel personified by the twelve disciples through this "new Moses."

It's a ghost! (14:26). First-century people believed that the waters were the ancient abode of malevolent powers (see comments on Matt. 8:27). Therefore, when Jesus appeared the disciples inferred that it had to be a ghost—an evil spirit to do them harm—since humans can't walk on water.

They came to shore at Gennesaret (14:34). This was a small village on the northwest shore of the Sea of Galilee, known in the OT as Chinnereth (Deut. 3:17; Josh. 19:35).

That they might only touch the end of his robe (14:36). Tassels hanging from the four corners of a tunic were symbols of holiness (Num. 15:38–40; Deut. 22:12). The longer the tassel, the holier the man (Matt. 23:5). Evidently people believed that the divine power of a holy man could be accessed by grabbing the "end of his robe," probably one of the tassels (see comments on Matt. 9:20).

Jewish Traditions (15:1–28)

They don't wash their hands when they eat (15:2). Since priests were required to wash their hands to serve the Lord (Exod. 30:18–21; see comments on Mark 7:1–4), some scholars think the Pharisees extended that part of the priestly purity code to all Israel. Other scholars believe hand washing became part of the holiness tradition among the diaspora—Jews living outside the land of Israel—to set them apart from pagans. Jews living in Israel eventually adopted the practice, especially the Pharisees.

Whatever benefit you might have received from me is a gift committed to the temple (15:5). The Pharisees expressed their devotion to God by consigning all of their possessions to the temple, transferable upon death. The Pharisees still used these dedicated funds for themselves. But since they had made such a vow to God, their assets couldn't be used for anything else, not even to help destitute parents. Because their possessions were *corban* ("dedicated to God" [Mark 7:11]), to use their resources for anyone but themselves would be considered "stealing from God." And yet, since the Pharisees were never commanded by God to make such a vow, Jesus accused them of breaking the fifth commandment (Exod. 20:12), nullifying the word of God for the sake of their "tradition" (Matt. 15:6).

Eating with unwashed hands does not defile a person (15:20). The word translated as "defile" (*koinoō*) means "to make common" or "to share." In a religious sense, the world was divided into two realms: common (profane/impure) and sacred (holy/pure). That which was dedicated to God was sacred, set apart from the profaned world of common life. When it came to the ritual of hand washing, Jesus did not believe that eating with "common hands" made a person any less sacred/holy/pure. Rather, one's sacredness/

Stone mugs like this one found at Masada may have been used to pour water for ritual hand washing (first century AD).

holiness/purity was revealed by one's words, "what comes out of the mouth" (Matt. 15:11).

He withdrew to the area of Tyre and Sidon (15:21). Tyre and Sidon, situated northwest of Palestine, were perennial enemies of Israel (Isa. 23:1–18; Matt. 11:21–22). And yet Elijah was sent by God to the same region to stay with a gentile widow and perform miracles, providing food and raising her son from the dead (1 Kings 17:8–24). Therefore, it isn't surprising that Jesus would meet a gentile woman in the same region and perform a miracle for the sake of her child, just like the prophets of old. What is surprising, however, is the way he treated her initially, since he had helped gentiles before (Matt. 4:24–25; 8:5–13).

Jesus traveled from Galilee to the vicinity of Tyre and Sidon and then headed back toward the Sea of Galilee. This is a map of those regions.

A Canaanite woman from that region came and kept crying out, "Have mercy on me, Lord, Son of David!" (15:22). The Canaanites were the occupiers of the promised land west of the Jordan (Canaan) before Israel took it over during the conquest led by Joshua. The Canaanites worshiped the god Baal—at times also worshiped by Israelites (Judg. 6:25–32; 1 Kings 18:16–40). But this Canaanite woman seemed to have a "Jewish" faith because she sounded like a Jew, using Jewish terms when she addressed Jesus as the "Son of David."

It isn't right to take the children's bread and throw it to the dogs (15:26). Was Jesus following his own advice (Matt. 7:6)? Even though gentiles were known to have dogs as household pets, the Jewish people despised them because they were scavengers, often found loitering around trash dumps and eating putrefied carcasses. As the "Son of David," Jesus came to restore Israel by gathering the "lost sheep" of God's pasture (15:24; 10:5–8). But when the woman admitted that she and her daughter were the "dogs" of Jesus's mini-parable (even though she had tried to sound like a Jew), she claimed that the mercy of God should be extended to her as a gentile, and that's when Jesus granted her request (15:27–28).

Feeding Four Thousand Men plus Women and Children (15:29–39)

Where could we get enough bread in this desolate place? (15:33). On a mountainside near the sea (15:29), Jesus and his entourage must have been several miles from a village where they could find food. Were they in gentile territory (see Mark 7:31–8:10)? We don't know. But some scholars see significance in the fact that the loaves and baskets of leftovers are seven in number (Matt. 15:36–37), symbolizing all humanity (seven days of the week). Thus there are two miraculous feedings: the first for Israel, the second for all people.

The region of Magadan (15:39). The location of Magadan is unknown, unless it is to be associated with Magdala (Mary Magdalene), a little village on the west shore of the Sea of Galilee that is currently being excavated by archaeologists.

The Yeast of the Pharisees and Sadducees (16:1–12)

Tested him, asking him to show them a sign from heaven (16:1). Moses performed signs to prove that he was a prophet sent by God (Exod. 4:1–9). So here the Pharisees (lay leaders of Israel) and the Sadducees (the aristocracy from Jerusalem) demand that Jesus perform a "sign from heaven" to prove that he was God's agent (see the article "Pharisees and Sadducees"). Even though these leaders of Israel could read the "sky" (literally, "heaven") to predict the weather, they were unable to see the signs that Jesus had already performed—the miracles that he called "the signs of the times" (16:3). Therefore he restated his position on the matter: since they couldn't see the signs from heaven/miracles, they would have to interpret for themselves the only sign that they would get: the "sign of Jonah" (16:4). In 12:38–41 Jesus used the story of Jonah being "in the belly of the huge fish three days and three nights" as a prophetic sign of both his own death/burial/resurrection and God's judgment against "this generation." For even Nineveh "repented at Jonah's preaching; and look—something greater than Jonah is here" (12:41).

The leaven of the Pharisees and Sadducees (16:6). The teachings of the Pharisees differed significantly from the teachings of the Sadducees (see the article "Pharisees and Sadducees"). For example, the Sadducees accepted only the law (the first five books of the OT) as Scripture; the Pharisees placed their oral tradition on the same level of authority as the law. The Sadducees denied the resurrection; the Pharisees believed in the resurrection. The Sadducees had stricter interpretation of the law; the Pharisees were known to be less literal when it came to obeying the commandments (thus the Pharisees were much more popular with the people). Furthermore, when it came to their relationship with the rulers (whether Herodian or Roman), the Sadducees and Pharisees were political enemies: when one group found favor with the rulers, the other sect was despised. That Jesus referred to the singular "yeast" (a Jewish symbol for evil) of both groups implies that they did have one thing in common: they opposed Jesus.

Jesus and Peter (16:13–28)

The region of Caesarea Philippi (16:13). Herod Philip (tetrarch of the area north and east of Galilee, sometimes called Transjordan) enlarged the Greek city known as Panea (named for the Greek god Pan, who had a shrine in a cave there), located at the base of Mount Hermon (the northernmost point of ancient Israel), and renamed it Caesarea Philippi in honor of Caesar Augustus (and himself).

Who do people say that the Son of Man is? (16:13). Jesus's favorite self-designation, "Son of Man," refers to the heavenly figure who is installed as king by the Ancient of Days in Daniel's vision (Dan. 7:9–14) (see comments on Mark 2:10). The diversity of opinion among the people regarding the identity of Jesus reveals a wide variety of bizarre end-time expectations regarding "the coming one": John the Baptist raised from the dead (Matt. 14:1–2), Elijah (Mal. 4:5–6), Jeremiah or one of the prophets (perhaps one of two "heavenly" witnesses who were supposed to warn Israel before the day of the Lord [Zech. 3:1, 8; 4:3, 11–14; Rev. 11:4–10]).

You are the Messiah, the Son of the living God (16:16). Due to passages such as 2 Sam. 7:14; Ps. 2:2, 4–7; 89:19–29, the "anointed one" (Messiah/Christ) would be considered the "Son of God" (see comments on Mark 8:29).

You are Peter, and on this rock I will build my church, and the gates of Hades will not overpower it (16:18). Here there is a pun in Greek, since "Peter" (*petros*) means "rock" (*petra*). The word for "church" (*ekklēsia*) means "assembly." The "gates of Hades" refers to the fortress of the underworld/death (Job 38:17; Ps.

An idol of the god Pan from the early second century AD.

9:13). Therefore, perhaps Jesus was claiming to be the "son of David" who would build the temple of God that would last forever (2 Sam. 7:12–13; 1 Kings 9:3) via his victory over death—a confession that Peter would make again (1 Pet. 2:4–6) and that Paul claimed for his converts (1 Cor. 3:10–17).

Ancient keys.

The keys of the kingdom of heaven (16:19). Most keys were large, made of metal, normally carried on the belt, and were used to unlock prison doors, treasure rooms, temples, and city gates. Smaller keys were used to unlock treasure chests.

Oh no, Lord! This will never happen to you! (16:22). "Oh no, Lord!" is literally, "Mercy to you, Lord!" which could be understood as a prayer to God: "May God show you mercy, Lord." It could also indicate an oath that is about to be sworn: "This shall never happen to you!"—Peter's attempt to "bind on earth" what "will have been bound in heaven" (16:19).

For the Son of Man is going to come with his angels in the glory of his Father (16:27). Jesus probably was referring to Zech. 14:1–5, where the prophet predicts that the Lord will come to Jerusalem in judgment and redemption, bringing "all the holy ones with him." Was this prophecy fulfilled in the resurrection of Jesus, when Christ "comes into his kingdom"—something that the disciples would see before they died (16:28)? Or was Jesus talking about his "second coming" (24:30–31), predicting once again that "this generation" would not "pass away until all these things take place" (24:34)? Or did Jesus's prediction regarding the Twelve—"there are some standing here who will not taste death until they see the Son of Man coming in his kingdom" (16:28)—come true in the transfiguration "after six days" (17:1–8)? Our interpretation depends upon how we answer this question: When did Jesus come into his kingdom? Was it all at once (already) or was it over time (not yet)?

The Transfiguration (17:1–13)

His face shone like the sun; his clothes became as white as the light (17:2). The face was the place where honor/glory was revealed, either bright with confidence or hidden in shame (to "save face"). Therefore, after being in the presence of God (the source of all honor) one's face would reflect divine glory (e.g., Moses's face "shown as a result of his speaking with the LORD" [Exod. 34:29]). Garments white as light indicated supreme holiness (God in Ps. 104:2; the Ancient of Days in Dan. 7:9; the saints in Rev. 3:4–5; 7:9). That Jesus radiated these traits ("transfigured") revealed his deity: God is the source of honor, glory, holiness, and light.

Moses and Elijah appeared to them, talking with him (17:3). God promised to send a new Moses and Elijah (representing the law and the prophets) to prepare Israel for the day of the Lord (Deut. 18:18; Mal. 4:5–6)—perhaps the "two heavenly witnesses" of Jewish apocalyptic eschatology (see comments on Matt. 16:13). Unlike Luke's version (Luke 9:31), Matthew doesn't give the topic of conversation—why these two prophets were talking with Jesus. And yet there was at least one common denominator: mystery surrounded the death of all three (Deut. 34:6; 2 Kings 2:11–12; Matt. 28:1–10).

I will set up three shelters (17:4). In light of the story of Abraham welcoming three divine visitors and being blessed by them (Gen. 18:1–33), Peter's request to build three shelters makes sense. He was trying to honor Jesus, Moses, and Elijah by offering acts of hospitality, perhaps in hopes of receiving a blessing. Also, the Mediterranean world was filled with shrines built to honor God/gods, either as an act of gratitude to God/gods for a benefit received (miracle or answered prayer), or as an act of obedience (having been directed in a dream to do so), or to mark the spot of a divine encounter (Gen. 28:18–19).

A bright cloud covered them (17:5). When God visited earth (theophany), strange things happened: bright lights, dark clouds, fire, lightning, and thunder (Exod. 13:21; 19:9, 16–18). What happened on the Mount of Transfiguration was similar to the times Moses and Elijah (1 Kings 19:8–12) met God on Mount Sinai/Horeb.

Elijah must come first (17:10). Due to the prophecy about a messenger who would prepare the way for the Lord's sudden visit to his temple (Mal. 3:1–4), later identified as Elijah (Mal. 4:1–6), the scribes taught that Elijah would appear as a "forerunner" before the Messiah. But the sequence of current events—Jesus the Messiah coming before the appearance of Elijah on the Mount of Transfiguration—confused the disciples. Were the scribes wrong that Elijah had to come first? No, according to Jesus, they were right. Elijah appeared before Jesus the Messiah. The prophecy of the forerunner was fulfilled in John the Baptizer (Matt. 17:12–13).

Exorcism and Temple Tax (17:14–27)

He has seizures (17:15). In Greek, the father says that his son suffers from "moon seizures"; some people believed that the moon could cause strange behavior (similar to our word "lunatic"). However, the boy's self-destructive behavior—"he often falls into the fire and often into the water"—was caused by a demon (17:18).

Those who collected the temple tax (17:24). In Jesus's day there were differences of opinion among the Jews regarding payment of the temple tax. According to the Pharisees, every Jew should pay a half-shekel annually (two drachmas, two days' wages) to support the temple (Exod. 30:12–16), regardless of where they lived. The Essenes objected to an annual tax, offering instead to make a one-time donation. The priests may have refused to pay anything because they believed that they were exempt. When Jesus referred to the children being exempt from the temple tax (17:26), his answer sounded like something a priest would say. Nevertheless, Jesus seemed to support the Pharisees' position when he instructed Peter on how to pay the tax—an odd approach that relied upon God's miraculous provision (did they have enough money in the purse to pay?)—"so we won't offend them" (17:27). After the Romans destroyed the Jewish temple in AD 70, procurators continued to collect the temple tax from the Jews in order to support Rome's pagan temples.

Little Ones, Lost Sheep, and Forgiveness (18:1–35)

Whoever humbles himself like this child (18:4). In the honor culture of the first century, children were considered as equal to slaves in status. Therefore, by placing a child before his disciples as the "greatest" in the kingdom of heaven, Jesus subverted the social standards of identity and worth. His disciples had to change the way they saw themselves and "become like little children" (18:3), choosing a life of downward mobility and embracing low social status, in order to be considered great in the kingdom.

If a heavy millstone were hung around his neck and he were drowned in the depths of the sea (18:6). Typically, large millstones were turned on a wheel to grind grain or press olives. The thought of having such a heavy stone draped around the neck like a piece of jewelry and then thrown into the sea spelled the certain doom of divine punishment. Those who died by drowning were considered cursed by God, "banished from your sight" (Jon. 2:3–4).

In heaven their angels (18:10). This is a reference either to special guardian angels of children or to the spirits of dead children who functioned like angels in God's presence.

If he listens to you (18:15). Since community was vital to living in the first-century world—no

These Tyrian shekels are from the Ussfiyeh hoard, discovered on Mount Carmel in 1960. Originally minted in the city of Tyre, Tyrian shekels were worth four drachmas each; thus one was enough to cover the temple tax for Jesus and Peter (Matt. 17:27).

one could "make it on their own"—Jesus worked with the assumption that the offender would listen to his or her brother/sister. One who refused to listen risked being shunned by the community, a dangerous situation for the rebel, then having to survive alone in a hostile world.

So that *by the testimony of two or three witnesses every fact may be established* (18:16). Sin wasn't a private matter, as if it affected no one but the sinner. Disobedience to the law resulted in injustice to the abused. Therefore sin was a community affair, a corporate reality. Thus Jesus assumed that the community must deal with the sin of one against the other according to the law—the authority for establishing justice for all (Deut. 19:15).

Tell the church (18:17). This is an unusual directive because "the church" didn't exist at the time. So either Jesus was speaking prophetically (even cryptically), since the disciples wouldn't know what the church was, or he was referring to the synagogue, since both "church" and "synagogue" could be taken as synonyms for "assembly."

Let him be like a Gentile and a tax collector to you (18:17). Literally, "let him be to *you*" (singular pronoun). In other words, Jesus was giving directions not to the assembly/church ("let him be to you all"), but rather to the one person who brought up the matter in the first place. Jesus did not teach excommunication by the church. So what did Jesus mean for one brother to treat another like a pagan (literally, "gentile") or tax collector? Was he relying upon Jewish prejudice against these two groups to encourage a disciple to reject the unrepentant sinner? Or, having just taught the Twelve that the least are the greatest in the kingdom of heaven, did Jesus expect his disciples to treat these "rebels" like he did, loving the "least of these," their enemies (e.g., healing the Roman centurion's slave [8:5–13]; eating with Matthew and his tax collector friends [9:9–13]) (see comments on Mark 2:15; 2:16)?[8]

Not as many as seven . . . but seventy times seven (18:22). In light of God's warning regarding Cain, "Whoever kills Cain will suffer vengeance seven times over" (Gen. 4:15), Peter may have reflected a common Jewish conviction that the extent of human forgiveness should equal divine vengeance. So Jesus countered the customary limitation of forgiveness by echoing Lamech's warning: "If Cain is to be avenged seven times over, then for Lamech it will be seventy-seven times!" (Gen. 4:24). In other words, since there is no limit to human vengeance (God's punishment is sevenfold, but Lamech threatened exponentially much more), forgiveness must be limitless too.

Everything he had be sold to pay the debt (18:25). No slave and his family would be worth the vast sum of his debt (ten thousand bags of gold). The master was simply cutting his losses due to the ineptitude (and perhaps crooked ways) of his slave. The slave was being disingenuous when he promised to repay the debt, for it would take a thousand lifetimes of work to earn ten thousand bags of gold.

Threw him into prison . . . handed him over to the jailers to be tortured (18:30, 34). Debtors' prisons were the last resort to exact payment for bad debts. The debtor was held for ransom until his family raised enough money to repay his debt. In light of the massive amount of the first slave's debt (it would take a thousand individuals to give all of their earnings for their entire lives to accumulate ten thousand bags of gold), to be thrown in the debtors' prison and tortured by the jailers "until he could pay everything that was owed" (18:34) was a dreadful way to picture eternal punishment.

Marriage, Divorce, and Eunuchs (19:1–12)

The region of Judea across the Jordan (19:1). This is a reference either to the west bank of the Jordan River, technically part of Judea, or to the east bank of the river ("across the Jordan"), the western edge of Perea. The location is significant, for if Jesus were passing through Perea on his way to Jerusalem, he would have continued to travel in Herod Antipas's territory (Galilee and Perea), arriving at the same location as the ministry of John the Baptizer—the prophet who was executed by Antipas for questioning the tetrarch's divorce and remarriage. Consequently, the Pharisees were being opportunistic when they questioned Jesus about divorce at this time, putting him at risk, especially since he was already "on record" regarding the matter (5:31–32).

Is it lawful for a man to divorce his wife on any grounds? (19:3). Notice two assumptions in the question: (1) only men had the ability to divorce their wives (women could not divorce their husbands), and (2) the legality of the divorce depended upon one's interpretation of the phrase "finds something indecent about her" in Deut. 24:1. What is the meaning of the word "indecent," and who has the right to determine what is indecent? What is "indecent" to one husband may be tolerable to another. Should the definition of "indecency" be left to the husband or decided by the lawyers? The rabbis in Jesus's day were divided on the issue (see comments on Mark 10:2; Matt. 5:31). Interestingly, at first Jesus didn't answer their question. Instead, he pointed to the divine purpose of marriage (Gen. 1:27; 2:24): God created male and female to become one flesh in marriage, indivisible (Matt. 19:4–6). The inference is that no man/husband should undo what God has prescribed.

Why then . . . did Moses command us to give divorce papers? (19:7). The "certificate of divorce" was prescribed by Moses in order to prevent remarriage of a divorced woman to her first husband (Deut. 24:1–4). The scenario of a man divorcing his wife, who then marries another man, who subsequently divorces her (or dies), does not make the woman available for remarriage to her first husband. In fact, according to Moses, "That would be detestable to the Lord" (Deut. 24:4). The certificate *may* have spelled out the "indecency" of the woman, the reason for divorce. But Jesus said that the provision was introduced by Moses "because of the hardness of your hearts," as if the selfish nature of husbands evident in Moses's day had never changed. Even in Jesus's day some men treated their wives like property—something that Jesus found completely "detestable" because male-initiated divorce incited adultery (19:9).

There are eunuchs who have made themselves that way because of the kingdom of heaven (19:12). Eunuchs (men without testicles) often served queens in royal courts in order to preserve the integrity of the king's wife (see Acts 8:27). Some eunuchs "were born that way"; others were "made by men" (castration or by accident and, therefore, excluded from the assembly [Deut. 23:1]). If a male disciple chose not to marry (Matt. 19:10), the only option available to him (according to Jesus) was to live like a eunuch "because of the kingdom of heaven"—that is, to father no children (and, by inference, to have no sex)—a life that must be chosen (19:12).

The Last Becoming First, and the First Becoming Last (19:13–20:34)

The disciples rebuked them (19:13). Did Jesus's teaching regarding the desirable state of becoming a eunuch (a man who has chosen not to have children) for the kingdom lead the disciples to infer that children are undesirable? Or had they so quickly forgotten the lesson Jesus recently taught them, reversing the status of the "least of these," that "whoever welcomes one child like this in my name welcomes me" (18:5)? Interestingly, the word translated as "rebuke" (*epitimaō*) is the same word used to describe Jesus's rebuke of the demons (17:18), as well as a storm (8:26) and the crowds (12:16).

Honor your father and mother (19:19). In Jesus's day the only way a young man would have "many possessions" (19:22) was through a significant inheritance received from his father. For a wealthy young man to honor his father would mean to guard his inheritance. Even though the young man claimed to have kept all the commandments that Jesus listed—including not only to "honor your father and mother" but also the command to "love your neighbor as yourself" (Lev. 19:18)—he asked Jesus, "What do I still lack?" (19:20). He needed to sell his inheritance and give it to the poor (19:21). Then he would truly love his neighbor as himself. But would he still be honoring his father? And yet Jesus required a higher allegiance to his heavenly father (6:33; 12:48–50), which is why he said, "It will be hard for a rich person to enter the kingdom of heaven" (19:23). Most wealth was inherited.

Then who can be saved? (19:25). The disciples' question was built on two assumptions: (1) God blessed the obedient with material wealth (Deut. 28:1–14) and (2) the impossibility of threading a needle with a camel (Matt. 19:24). So if those who are "blessed of God" are saved only if they give away all of their wealth—an impossible situation—and since the poor are cursed by God, "Then who can be saved?" "With man this is impossible" (19:26)—a sobering reminder that neither rich nor poor can save themselves. Only God is able to save humanity.

In the renewal of all things, when the Son of Man sits on his glorious throne (19:28). Jewish expectations of the messianic age included not only judgment of the wicked but also rewards for the righteous. And God's work of redemption at the end of time would mean not only the restoration of Israel (Jesus predicted that his twelve disciples would reign with him over Israel [v. 28]) but also the renewal of all creation—new heaven and new earth (Isa. 65:17–25; 66:10–24). Jesus saw his enthronement as the heavenly redeemer figure, the "Son of Man" (Dan. 7:9–14), as the crowning achievement of the kingdom of heaven come to earth: "the renewal of all things."

A landowner who went out early in the morning to hire workers for his vineyard (20:1). The grape harvest occurred in the fall, usually requiring many workers, for time was of the essence. The landed rich usually relied upon a foreman (20:8) to hire and supervise day laborers, who often gathered at the city gates looking for work.

I'll give you whatever is right (20:4). The fact that the landowner kept returning to hire more harvesters may reveal his inexperience in calculating how many workers he needed to bring in the harvest. "Whatever is right" implied less than a denarius (20:2), a day's wage.

Because no one hired us (20:7). That several workers were still hoping to be hired, even at the end of the day, could be interpreted to mean that (1) supply exceeded demand, (2) these were the "leftovers," the less desirable workers (old, poor health), or (3) they were desperate for work, since most agrarian people lived at subsistence level.[9]

A denarius was about a day's wage. Here are two examples of Roman denarii from the first century BC.

Are you jealous because I'm generous? (20:15). Literally, "Or is your eye evil because I am good"? To give "the evil eye" was to cast ill intent upon someone, perhaps believing one could unleash a malevolent spirit against the enemy. In other words, the daylong workers were exhibiting something more than "envy," or wanting something that didn't belong to them ("Didn't you agree with me on a denarius?" [20:13]). There was social significance to their grievance with the landowner, for in the agonistic world of agrarian life, where everyone competed for everything (not only resources but also honor), the daylong workers were angry with the landowner because he made the hour-long laborers "equal to us" (20:12) socially and economically. To their way of thinking, the landowner was implying that their daylong labor was worth the same as one hour of work. But the way Jesus tells the story, the landowner attributes equal pay to the fact that he is "good," shifting the focus from their value to his generosity. After all, it is his vineyard; they are just the workers.

While going up to Jerusalem (20:17). Since Jerusalem was situated among the highest mountains of Judea, regardless of the location of the traveler, everyone "went up" to Jerusalem. In other words, "going up" should be understood topographically, not geographically. Thus the psalms "of ascent" (Pss. 120–134) were sung as Jews traveled to Jerusalem to worship God in his temple.

The mother of Zebedee's sons (20:20). Perhaps the mother of James and John (4:21) made the request knowing that women were able to ask for things that an honorable man wouldn't request (2 Sam. 14:1–24).[10] Others think that 1 Kings 1:15–17 provides the context, where Bathsheba asked David to make Solomon the heir to his throne: (1) both women bowed before the king, (2) both David and Jesus asked the same question ("What do you want?"), and (3) both women asked for their sons to share the throne of David.[11]

Are you able to drink the cup that I am about to drink? (20:22). This probably is a reference to the cup of God's wrath/judgment (Ps. 75:7–8; Isa. 51:17–23). Therefore, Jesus knew that messianic suffering must precede messianic glory, a cross before a crown.

As they were leaving Jericho (20:29). The Jericho road to Jerusalem was steep: a fifteen-mile stretch, ascending nearly 3,200 feet to the holy city (Jericho was about 720 feet below sea level; Jerusalem was 2,450 feet above sea level)—a trip that would have taken most of the day.

Jesus, the King of Jerusalem (21:1–22)

Bethphage at the Mount of Olives (21:1). "Bethphage" means "house of unripe figs"—a detail that sets up the story of Jesus cursing the fig tree (21:18–19). The Mount of Olives was situated directly east of Jerusalem, which was built on Mount Moriah/Zion, separated by the Kidron Valley. Pilgrims traveling from Jericho to Jerusalem for Passover would travel over the Mount of Olives, down the Kidron Valley, ascend Mount Zion, and enter Jerusalem, most likely through the eastern gate.

A very large crowd spread their clothes on the road (21:8). Having taken a cue from Jesus, who orchestrated his entry into Jerusalem to fulfill prophecy (21:2–7; cf. Zech. 9:9), the Galilean pilgrims joined the procession by re-creating the scene of a newly anointed king entering Jerusalem to claim David's throne (2 Kings 9:1–13).

Hosanna to the Son of David (21:9). "Hosanna" is from a Hebrew expression that means "Save [us] now!" (from Ps. 118:25, a psalm recited during Passover).

The whole city was in an uproar . . . the crowds were saying (21:10–11). The scenario reveals the tension that existed between city dwellers and rural folk: neither group trusted the other. Urbanites consisted primarily of the retainer class, protected within the walled city. Country folk were the "working poor" who depended upon one another to survive in village life. With crowds of outsiders pouring into the big city, and with one of their own heralded as cause for the celebration ("This is the prophet Jesus from Nazareth in Galilee" [v. 11]), it's no wonder that the whole city was in an uproar and asked, "Who is this?" (v. 10). To citizens of Jerusalem, this orchestrated "triumphal entry" was a provocative, perhaps even pretentious, attempt to incite trouble.

Jesus went into the temple and threw out all those buying and selling (21:12). Why did Jesus clear the temple of commerce, especially since there was nothing in the law to prohibit leaders from selling animals for sacrifice, even in the temple courtyard? In light of Jesus's actions (overturning tables of money changers and dove sellers) and his words (21:13, a conflation of Isa. 56:7 and Jer. 7:11), scholars propose two motivations: (1) Jesus needed to "cleanse" the temple of impurity due to the corruption of the priestly leadership (because they allowed the sale of animals in the courtyard, or because they were taking advantage of the poor by selling doves [the purification sacrifice offered by the poor] and exchanging money at an exorbitant price, or because the priests were the aristocrats who abused the poor all the time, not just during Passover); or (2) Jesus performed a prophetic act predicted by Malachi, indicating that the time of divine visitation had come (Mal. 3:1–5; 4:1–6), which had nothing to do with the purity of the temple. What may lie behind both motivations, however, is the prediction that the "son of David" would build a temple that would last forever (2 Sam. 7:13). Therefore, clearing the temple was Jesus's first act in claiming David's throne (see the article "The Jerusalem Temple"; see comments on Mark 11:11).

The blind and the lame came to him in the temple, and he healed them (21:14). Was this an intentional reversal of David's curse (2 Sam. 5:6–8)?

A sycamore fig tree.

Went out of the city to Bethany (21:17). Bethany was a little village on the east side of the Mount of Olives, about two miles from Jerusalem. Evidently, Jesus stayed there during his Passover visit to Jerusalem, probably at his friends' house (26:6–13).

Found nothing on it except leaves (21:19). Since Passover was celebrated in early spring, Jesus found no figs on the tree ("for it was not the season for figs" [Mark 11:13]). Fig trees didn't bear edible fruit until June. Some fig trees were known to produce green, inedible figs as early as April. Perhaps that's why Matthew mentioned that Jesus passed through the little village of Bethphage (meaning "house of unripe figs") when he first came to Jerusalem (21:1). Jesus came to God's temple looking for fruit but found none (21:43). A fruitless fig tree judged by God was a common prophetic analogy (Jer. 8:13; Hosea 2:12; 9:10, 16–17; Mic. 7:1–8). Consequently, when Jesus "cursed" the fig tree it was a symbolic act of judgment against the "house" of Israel (either the temple leadership or the temple itself)—a dramatic performance like the prophets of old (cf. Jeremiah's broken pot [Jer. 19:1–15]).

Jesus's Authority (21:23–22:14)

When he entered the temple, the chief priests and the elders of the people came to him as he was teaching (21:23). It was customary during holidays like Passover for rabbis to gather their students in the temple and teach from the Scriptures, especially from texts typically read during the festivals. Therefore, when the chief priests and elders asked Jesus, "By what authority are you doing these things?" they were questioning not his teaching in the temple but his behavior the day before when he cleared the temple. Jesus acted like he, not the chief priests, was ultimately responsible for God's temple (see the article "The Jerusalem Temple").

There was a landowner, who planted a vineyard . . . leased it (21:33). Jesus didn't make up every parable; sometimes he found inspiration in other parables, like this one from Isa. 5:1–7. In his variation on Isaiah's parable, Jesus introduces a new character: tenant farmers who rented the vineyard, probably identified by the chief priests as the Romans, "those terrible men" whom God will "completely destroy" on the day of judgment (21:41). To their surprise, however, the chief priests realize that Jesus is pointing to them as the tenant farmers who deserved the wretched end (21:43–46).

Herod's "Second" Temple on the Temple Mount

King Herod the Great began renovations on the second temple in approximately 20–19 BC. The entire temple expansion, including the massive Temple Mount, was not completed until approximately AD 62–64, only to be destroyed by the Romans in AD 70.

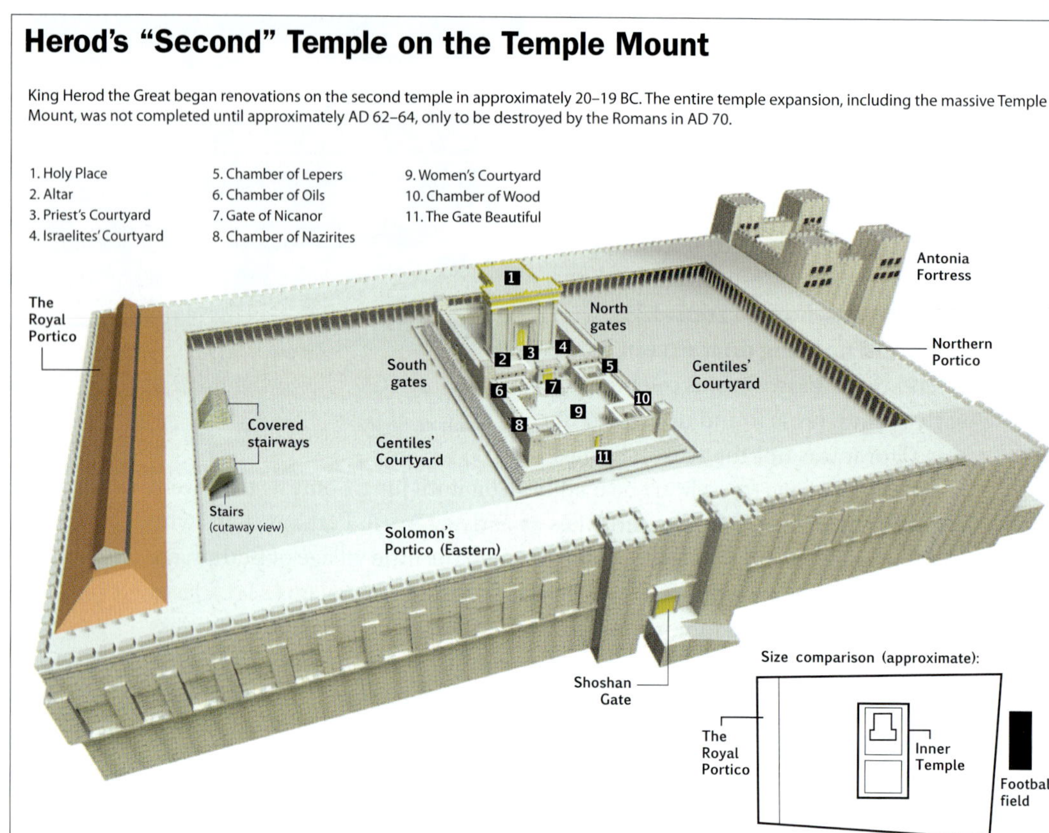

The stone that the builders rejected has become the cornerstone (21:42). Quoting Ps. 118:22–23, Jesus uses temple language as prophetic indictment (cf. vv. 26, 46) of the chief priests: (1) they rejected the cornerstone of the new temple; (2) they should have welcomed Jesus: "Blessed is he who comes in the name of the Lord" (23:39); therefore, (3) God will build the new temple using "a people producing its fruit" (21:43).

The kingdom of God will be taken away from you and given to a people producing its fruit (21:43). Here the Greek text says that the kingdom will be given to an *ethnos* ("gentile, nation, people group"), which is a reference either to the church (a people made up of gentiles and Jews) or to Jesus's disciples, replacing the priestly leadership with the Twelve.

Those invited to the banquet (22:3). Usually two wedding invitations were sent: (1) a general "save the date" invitation and then (2) the specific invitation to come to the prepared feast (see the article "Jewish Marriage Customs"). Apparently this was the second notice: the feast was ready (22:4). Dinner guests revealed the honor of the host; a king would invite only important dignitaries to the wedding of his son (the prince). And they, in return, would be honored by his invitation. But for some inexplicable reason these VIPs refused to come, dishonoring the king. By ignoring his summons, the invited guests were saying to the king (the most honorable man in the entire kingdom), "You're not worthy of our honorable presence." To make things worse, the dignitaries killed the king's servants—an act of defiance equal to anarchy—which is why the king had to "save face," protecting his honor by having his army destroy the city and kill these rebels (22:6–7).

My oxen and fattened cattle have been slaughtered (22:4). Meat, especially beef, was a delicacy enjoyed by the wealthy (oxen were indispensable to rural people for work). The expediency of the moment is heightened by a world without refrigeration. Once meat was slaughtered, it had to be eaten soon or it would turn rancid. Rather than have all this meat go to waste, the king decided to sacrifice his honor and invite the lowlifes, "both evil and good" (22:10).

He saw a man there who was not dressed for a wedding (22:11). Most people had proper attire for special occasions, especially "clean/white" garments (Rev. 6:11; 19:8). Some think that it was customary for some type of outer garment to be handed to guests as they entered the feast (Judg. 14:12). If so, the improperly dressed guest's appearance would be especially contemptuous. Wearing work clothes to a wedding would dishonor the host. The poorly dressed man was there only for the food.

Jesus and His Critics (22:15–46)

Along with the Herodians (22:16). The Herodians were a political sect that supported Herod's kingdom. It is unknown whether the Pharisees—onetime supporters of the Hasmonean dynasty (the Judean kings who ruled Israel before Rome took over in 63 BC)—would have opposed Herod's rule (even though he was a nominal Jew). It probably was a rare occurrence for these two sects to join forces politically.

Is it lawful to pay taxes to Caesar or not? (22:17). All subjects of the Roman Empire (not citizens) had to pay an annual tax to support the imperial cult (the worship of dead Caesars). They were also required to offer a sacrifice at an imperial shrine (these were located all over the empire). As conscientious objectors, Jews were exempt from burning the ashes at the shrine, but they still had to pay the tax, even though the money supported idolatry. To make matters worse, Rome minted a special coin—a denarius with the image of Caesar on one side and an inscription on the other side declaring the divinity of the emperor (22:20)—that all subjects had to use to pay the tax. Caesar would accept no other currency for the imperial tax. Consequently, not only did payment of the tax support the idolatry of the imperial cult but also Jews were forced to use "an idol" (a graven image with a sacrilegious inscription) to pay it—double jeopardy (see the article "Money in the New Testament World").

Why are you testing me, hypocrites? Show me the coin used for the tax (22:18–19). The Pharisees had placed Jesus on the horns of a dilemma: if Jesus said that his fellow Jews should pay the tax, he would be supporting idolatry; however, to refuse to pay the tax would be treason against Caesar—the only crime punishable by death according to Roman law. But Jesus saw through the ruse by revealing their hypocrisy. The reason he asked them to produce the denarius was that he didn't have one; they did, even though they were in the temple. Evidently, they had not used the money changers to exchange their Roman currency for Jewish currency before entering the temple—a service provided by the temple leadership to prevent worshipers from bringing a graven image into God's house. Therefore, by carrying a "portable idol" into the temple, they revealed that they should have no *religious* objections to paying the tax.

Whose image and inscription is this? (22:20). This is a loaded question, for they would answer "Caesar's" (22:21) but others could say "God's," since every person was made in the image of God (Gen. 1:27), even Caesar. Therefore, when Jesus said, "Give, then, to Caesar the things that are Caesar's, and to God the things that are God's," he didn't answer their question directly, but instead prompted another, implicit question: Is there anything that belongs to Caesar that doesn't belong to God?

Sadducees, who say there is no resurrection (22:23). To the Sadducees, levirate marriage not only provided the way for a dead man to live after death, "raising up" offspring for him (Gen. 38:8), but also disproved the physical "raising up" of the dead, a distinctive belief of the Pharisees (cf. Acts 23:6–8), for levirate marriage would seem to create a polygamous situation in the resurrection—something that both God and people would find reprehensible (Matt. 22:24–28).

For in the resurrection they neither marry nor are given in marriage but are like angels in heaven (22:30). Once again, Jesus never answered the Sadducees' question directly (he had his reasons [see comments on Matt. 22:33]). He said only that resurrected people neither get married nor arrange marriages for their children. He doesn't say whether husbands and wives will live as married couples in the resurrection (but his answer would imply, "It's not necessary"). Since angels were immortal, there was no need for them to procreate. However, since humans are mortal, marriage (and children) was indispensable to overcoming death. But, according to Jesus, levirate marriage didn't guarantee immortality for humans (the resurrection did), and marriage was unnecessary in the resurrection (humans become "like angels," without need to procreate).

When the crowds heard this, they were astonished at his teaching (22:33). In the honor game questions were asked in public only to shame the teacher. Students who honored their teacher would ask questions for information in private (Matt. 17:19). Therefore, in this exchange between Jesus and his opponents, the Pharisees and the Sadducees were trying to bring Jesus down in the eyes of the crowd—the group that determined who won the honor game. In this case, the crowd's approval signaled that Jesus was the winner. Eventually "no one dared to question him anymore" (22:46), because their attempts to shame him made him even more honorable in the eyes of the crowd.

Which command in the law is the greatest? (22:36). Since violating certain commandments required more severe penalties than others, rabbis commonly debated which were the greatest and the least of the 613 commandments in the law. Furthermore, they often looked for commandments that summed up the entire Law. So Jesus's answer wasn't revolutionary (see comments on Matt. 7:12). Even though an expert in the law asked the question to "test him" (22:35), Jesus's response would have been seen as conventional: quoting part of the Shema (Deut. 6:4–9, a passage recited daily by Jews) and the "love your neighbor" commandment from Leviticus (Lev. 19:18).

Jesus Excoriates the Scribes and the Pharisees (23:1–39)

Seated in the chair of Moses (23:2). This refers to the featured seat in the synagogues where teachers sat when they taught from the law on the Sabbath.

They enlarge their phylacteries and lengthen their tassels (23:5). Phylacteries were small boxes strapped to the forehead and wrist that held passages of Scripture, intended to remind the wearers and those who saw them of the Shema (Deut. 6:4–9), which instructed Israel, "Bind them [the commandments] as a sign on your hand and let them be a symbol on your forehead." Tassels on the four corners of a robe served the same

The "seat of Moses" (Matt. 23:2) was the place in the synagogue reserved for a person of authority.

purpose, to remind Israel to obey the commandments (Num. 15:38–41). Jesus questioned the width of the phylacteries and the length of the tassels worn by the scribes and Pharisees because "they do everything to be seen by others" (Matt. 23:5)—the honor game—and not to lead others to obey the commandments (23:4).

They love the place of honor at banquets, the front seats in the synagogues (23:6). Honor had to be displayed constantly in order to maintain one's sense of importance in the community. Seating arrangements at banquets and synagogues revealed social significance: the closer to the host of the banquet or to Moses's seat in the synagogue, the more honorable the person. To be seen at the most desirable place was crucial to maintaining self-image—comparable to our "selfie."

Woe to you (23:13). Like the prophets of old (Zech. 11:17), Jesus pronounced woes on the religious leadership, calling down God's curse upon them (Matt. 23:35–39).

Whoever takes an oath by the temple, it means nothing (23:16). See comments on Matt. 5:34. It's unclear as to why someone would think that swearing an oath by the temple would be nonbinding compared to swearing on oath by "the gold of the temple" (either the gold in the temple treasury, the golden utensils, or the gold inlay of the temple walls). But the Mishnah is filled with these kinds of distinctions: "[If he said, 'May it be to me] like a lamb [of the daily whole offering],' 'Like the [temple] sheds,' 'Like the wood,' 'Like the fire,' 'Like the altar,' 'Like the sanctuary,' 'Like Jerusalem'—[if] he vowed by the name of one of any of the utensils used for the altar, even though he has not used the word *qorban*, R. Judah says, 'He who says, "Jerusalem," has said nothing.'"[12]

You strain out a gnat, but gulp down a camel! (23:24). Such hyperbole makes sense (who could swallow a camel?) in light of the pun: in Aramaic, *gamla* means "camel" and *kamla* means "gnat." In order to keep from eating certain insects (Lev. 11:41–45)—the smallest of all unclean creatures—Jews had to strain their wine. And yet, because the Pharisees and scribes "neglected the more important matters of the law—justice, mercy, and faithfulness" (Matt. 23:23), Jesus accused them of swallowing the largest unclean animal, a camel (Lev. 11:4).

You are like whitewashed tombs (23:27). Since coming in contact with dead bodies rendered a person unclean (Num. 19:11–13), cemeteries were considered off-limits. Furthermore, since tombs were unclean, Jewish people, unlike the Romans and Greeks, didn't mark the significance of the deceased with large memorial stones or statues. Consequently, it was possible to traverse a cemetery without knowing it, which would have been intolerable for sojourners (especially priests [see Lev. 21:1–4]) traveling to Jerusalem to participate in holidays. Consequently, tombs were whitewashed to help visitors avoid them.

Jesus compares the Pharisees to whitewashed tombs, beautiful to look at but full of death and decay inside. Here is the inside of a tomb from the time of Jesus showing a collection of ossuaries (limestone boxes) that contained the bones of the deceased.

Brood of vipers! (23:33). Baby vipers were thought to eat their way out of their mother's womb. Thus a "brood of vipers" would be the equivalent of a nursery of "mother-killers"[13]—the ultimate epithet of inhumanity.

From the blood of righteous Abel to the blood of Zechariah (23:35). This narrative of the "bloodshed of the righteous" reveals the canon of Scripture according to Jesus: from Abel (Gen. 4:2–15) to Zechariah (2 Chron. 24:20–21)—an issue that was debated in Jesus's day (e.g., the Sadducees may have accepted only the Pentateuch as Scripture). The Hebrew canon wasn't closed until the first or second century AD. According to the Hebrew Bible (TANAK), Genesis is the first book of the Bible, but 2 Chronicles is the last book due to the canonical order of the TANAK (an acrostic derived from the first letter of each section of the Hebrew Scriptures): the Law (*Torah*), the Prophets (*Nevi'im*), and the Writings (*Ketuvim*, the last section, which begins with Psalms and ends with 2 Chronicles).

See, your house is left to you desolate (23:38). "Your house" could refer to the leaders of Jerusalem, or to Jerusalem itself, or to the temple. In light of the next few verses, when Jesus predicted the destruction of the temple (24:2), "your house" probably refers to the temple: once God's house but no more (24:15).

The Destruction of the Temple and the End of the World (24:1–51)

Not one stone will be left here on another (24:2). During the first Jewish War with Rome—incited by separate groups of Jewish resistance fighters in Galilee and in Jerusalem—the temple in Jerusalem was destroyed by the army under the command of the Roman general Titus in AD 70 (see the article "The Jerusalem Temple"). The famous Arch of Titus in Rome depicts the sacking of Jerusalem, showing soldiers carrying off the spoils of war, including the large menorah from Herod's temple.

When will these things happen? And what is the sign of your coming and of the end of the age? (24:3). The disciples now ask Jesus about two important questions: (1) when the temple would be destroyed and (2) what the sign would be that the messianic age had begun, which would also signal the end of the present age. In fact, it could be inferred that the disciples were asking just one question, wondering if the destruction of the temple would be the sign of the end of the age, signaling the beginning of the "golden age" of the Messiah's reign on earth. That the disciples were not asking about the "second coming" of Christ is evident: they didn't believe that he would ever leave them (16:22; 20:21). Therefore, when they inquired about the "sign of your coming," they were essentially asking, "How will we know that you have come into your kingdom?"

These things must take place, but the end is not yet (24:6). According to Jewish apocalyptic literature (*2 Baruch* 27.1–15; *4 Ezra* 6.18–24; 13.31–39), the beginning of the messianic age would be marked by war and turmoil, especially since the Messiah would be leading righteous forces against the wicked who had established their kingdoms on earth, unwilling to submit to the Anointed One. Sometimes these messianic "woes" were compared to birth pangs (Matt. 24:8), as if God were birthing a new creation (Isa. 13:8; 1 Thess. 5:3).

A man on the housetop must not come down (24:17). Most houses had a flat roof, accessed by outdoor steps attached to an exterior wall, that functioned as a workspace for domestic chores.

So if they tell you, "See, he's in the wilderness!" don't go out (24:26). Would-be messiahs were known to lead followers into the desert to prove their "credentials" by replicating one of the miracles performed by Moses.[14]

Then the sign of the Son of Man will appear (24:30). This points to the fulfillment of Daniel's vision when the "son of man" is given "dominion, and glory, and a kingdom" in heaven by God (Dan. 7:13–14). What is the sign? There are several possibilities: (1) cosmic collapse (Matt. 24:29), (2) the Son of Man appearing in heaven, (3) the heavenly host, (4) the trumpet blast (the ram's horn was blown to rally troops for war and to announce the forgiveness of sins on Yom Kippur, the Day of Atonement), or (5) the cross (favored by early church fathers).

This generation will certainly not pass away until all these things take place (24:34). What did Jesus mean by "this generation" and "all these things"? This generation could mean (1) "this people" (the Jews or the church), meaning that they will not perish from the earth before the end of the world; (2) "this kind" ("generation" in a qualitative sense), referring to the kind of people who reject the Messiah (i.e., people like the scribes and the Pharisees will always be around until the end); or (3) the current generation (Matt. 11:16), meaning that some would still be alive to witness "all these things" (which refers either to the destruction of the temple [vv. 4–28] or to both the destruction of the temple and the coming of the Son of Man [vv. 4–31]). If Jesus predicted that his generation would witness both the destruction of the temple (which happened in their lifetime) and the coming of the Son of Man, then scholars propose three options: (1) the coming of the Son of Man in the clouds refers to the resurrection and/or ascension; (2) the coming of the Son of Man was an apocalyptic event in heaven that was revealed only to the faithful; or (3) the coming of the Son of Man is a proleptic event, a prophecy that will be fulfilled first with the destruction of the temple (a building that was supposed to represent a microcosm of all creation)[15] and finally at the end of the world.

The flood came and swept them all away (24:39). Since Jesus compared the coming judgment of God to "the days of Noah," those who "will be taken" (24:40) are like the wicked who perished when "the flood came and swept them all away." Consequently, those "left behind" are the righteous.

Whom his master has put in charge of his household (24:45). Absentee landowners were common, having to leave a chief slave in charge of the household while they traveled to attend to business elsewhere, either other land or affairs in other cities.

While the Master Is Away, Be Faithful! (25:1–46)

Like ten virgins who took their lamps and went out to meet the groom (25:1). Even though we know very little about wedding practices in Jesus's day, the situation he described in this parable is similar to current wedding customs in the Middle East. A wedding is a weeklong celebration, culminating in the wedding banquet, hosted by the groom's family. Before the feast the groom purposely wandered through the village with his friends (sometimes taking a very long time due to a circuitous route intended to announce the upcoming event to the entire village). After retrieving the bride and her attendants from her home, the groom and his large entourage then returned to the groom's house for the feast.[16] Most often the feast occurred at night (thus the need for lamps), after which the bride and the groom retired to private quarters and consummated their marriage. See the article "Jewish Marriage Customs."

Dug a hole in the ground, and hid his master's money (25:18). On absentee landowners, see comments on Matt. 24:45. Due to the persistent threat of thieves (24:43), it was common practice among those unaccustomed to handling such wealth to bury their treasure.

You should have deposited my money with the bankers (25:27). Other than temples that functioned like depositories for the wealthy, there were no banks in the first-century world (see the article "Money in the New

Testament World"). Instead, there were money changers who operated like "loan sharks" for the wealthy—"middle men" who made loans to borrowers, exacting enough interest to make a profit and pay the guaranteed return to the wealthy. Jews collecting interest from other Jews, however, was forbidden according to the law (Exod. 22:25; Lev. 25:35–38). Furthermore, according to Jewish law, all debts were supposed to be canceled during the Sabbatical Year (Deut. 15:1–2). Therefore, Jesus's parable envisions either a pagan situation, or a Jewish master who had gentile slaves, or a Jewish master who did not keep the law (Matt. 25:24–25).

As a shepherd separates the sheep from the goats (25:32). Sheep and goats grazed in open fields together, separated for several reasons: shearing sheep, milking goats, fencing goats at night to keep them warm (woolly sheep could handle the cool evening air). To be sure, more sheep were needed for the economic and religious life of Israel. Nevertheless, even though the demand wasn't as great for goats as for sheep, goats were just as important to the cultic life of Israel: goats were sacrificed on Yom Kippur, the Day of Atonement (Lev. 16:5); sheep were used for Passover and purification (Exod. 12:3; Lev. 12:6).

I was in prison and you visited me (25:36). Of all the good works done by the righteous "sheep," visiting prisoners was the riskiest. Feeding the hungry, clothing the naked, providing hospitality to strangers, taking care of the sick—all of these were held up as virtuous deeds in the law and by the prophets. But helping prisoners was dangerous, raising the suspicions of the authorities.

Whatever you did for one of the least of these brothers and sisters of mine (25:40). The "brothers and sisters" of Jesus could be (1) his disciples (10:42; 12:50), (2) the Jewish people (5:22–24), particularly the "lost sheep of Israel" (10:6; 18:10–14), or (3) any person in need (4:24–25; 8:1–3; 15:22–27).

Sheep and goats often mix together.

Depart from me, you who are cursed, into the eternal fire prepared for the devil and his angels! (25:41). Jesus referred to hell more often than anyone else in the NT. To him, hell was never meant for humanity (perhaps because we are made in the image of God).

Rather, "the eternal fire" was intended for "the devil and his angels," even though the wicked will share their destiny. Reward for the righteous and punishment of the wicked on the last day (25:46) was a common theme in prophetic and apocalyptic literature (Isa. 66:17–24; Dan. 12:1–2; *2 Baruch* 51.6).

Plans and Preparations (26:1–16)

Why this waste? (26:8). It was customary to anoint the heads of dinner guests with oil. Either the disciples thought that such luxury was unnecessary, or they believed that the woman had used too much perfume (an amount that would have fetched a "great deal" [v. 9]), or they objected to the reason she anointed Jesus ("she has prepared me for burial" [v. 12]). Wasting myrrh (burial spices) on a man who was very much alive offended the disciples, especially since they couldn't accept the idea that Jesus was going to die.

So they weighed out thirty pieces of silver for him (26:15). This was the recompense due for the untimely death of a slave gored by a bull (Exod. 21:32). The money probably came from the temple treasury (see comments on Matt. 27:6).

The Last Supper (26:17–30)

On the first day of Unleavened Bread (26:17). The weeklong festival of eating unleavened bread began at Passover (Exod. 12:17–20).

I am celebrating the Passover at your place (26:18). Passover was one of three pilgrimage festivals (along with Pentecost and Shelters) celebrated in Jerusalem; therefore, Jesus needed accommodations in the city (see comments on Mark 14:1). That Jesus would celebrate the feast with his disciples rather than with family revealed his priorities (Matt. 12:48–50).

The one who dipped his hand with me in the bowl—he will betray me (26:23). This is either a general statement regarding the traitor (not an outsider but someone who shared table with Jesus) or a timely revelation, that Judas had dipped unleavened bread in the bowl of bitter herbs at the same moment as Jesus (a casual detail probably noticed only by the betrayer).

After singing a hymn, they went out to the Mount of Olives (26:30). Probably they sang a psalm from the Hallel (Pss. 113–118), customarily sung during Passover (imagine the irony if they sang Ps. 113:7; 115:17; 116:15; or 118:22–24!). The Mount of Olives, covered with groves of olive trees, was the first hill east of Jerusalem.

The Mount of Olives viewed from the Temple Mount.

Gethsemane (26:36–56)

A place called Gethsemane (26:36). From the Hebrew, "Gethsemane" means "oil press." The exact location of the garden is unknown. From his vantage point on the west side of the Mount of Olives, however, Jesus could have seen the mob (a trail of torches) coming for him from Jerusalem as he prayed.

If it is possible, let this cup pass from me (26:39). This is a reference to the cup of God's wrath/judgment (see comments on Matt. 20:22). Jesus recognized the possibility of not drinking from it, knowing that he could call upon God to rescue him (26:53).

Kissed him (26:49). This was a common way for good friends to greet each other in that culture.

Do what you have come for (26:50, CSB footnote). In Greek, this is an enigmatic response that could be translated several other ways: (1) "Is that [kiss or betrayal] why you are here?"; (2) "That [kiss or betrayal] is why you are here"; (3) "For that reason it happens"; or more simply, (4) "Let it be."

How, then, would the Scriptures be fulfilled? (26:54). The Scriptures (particularly Zech. 13:7, which Jesus quotes in Matt. 26:31) convinced Jesus that his upcoming death was his Father's will.

The Antonia Fortress with its four towers was connected to the temple complex. This provides the traditional location of Jesus's interrogation.

On Trial before the Sanhedrin (26:57–75)

The chief priests and the whole Sanhedrin were looking for false testimony against Jesus so that they could put him to death (26:59). The Sanhedrin was the Jewish council, composed of Sadducees and Pharisees and led by the high priest, that ruled on religious/civic matters (see the article "The Sanhedrin"; see comments on Mark 8:31). Since Judea was under Roman law, the Sanhedrin could not carry out the death penalty (there were several crimes punishable by death according to Jewish law; there was only one capital offense according to Roman law—treason). Eventually the Sanhedrin found "false testimony" against Jesus: two men testified that Jesus said that he was able to destroy the temple and rebuild it in three days (26:61)—a prophecy that hadn't come true, for Jesus's temple prediction happened on Monday, three days had passed, and the temple hadn't been destroyed (much less rebuilt). This made Jesus a "false prophet" in their eyes (Deut. 18:21–22; Matt. 27:40). And yet, according to Matthew, Jesus never predicted that *he would* destroy/rebuild the temple in three days—that's what made the two men's statement "false testimony" (but what about John 2:19?). Rather, Jesus said only that the temple would be destroyed within "this generation" (24:2–3, 34). But would Rome consider that treason punishable by death? Consequently, the Sanhedrin had to devise a plan for how to have Jesus executed (27:1).

Caiaphas was the ruling high priest before whom Jesus is brought after his arrest. Shown here is an elaborately carved ossuary (bone box) with the Aramaic inscription "Joseph son of Caiaphas." Although the bones inside may not belong to the high priest who questioned Jesus, the presence of several other ossuaries with similar inscriptions provides strong evidence that the burial place where they were found was the family tomb of the high priest referred to in Matt. 26.

Then the high priest tore his robes and said, "He has blasphemed!" (26:65). Because Jesus claimed that the Sanhedrin would see Daniel's prophecy (Dan. 7:9–14) fulfilled by him, particularly the part about "seated at the right hand of Power" (Matt. 26:64), the high priest charged him with "blasphemy"—that is, "speaking against" God. To display his contempt, the high priest tore his garments (probably not his priestly vestments, since that was prohibited [Lev. 21:10]). Ripping one's clothes was more commonly associated with acts of mourning and repentance (Job 1:20).

Your accent gives you away (26:73). Galileans were known to slur certain consonants, especially gutturals, perhaps making them sound like "country bumpkins" to the Judeans.

Then he started to curse (26:74). It's unclear whether Peter was calling God's curse upon himself, upon his accusers, or upon Jesus. Ironically, if Peter did call upon God to curse Jesus, then Jesus's prophecy in Matt. 16:19 came true: whatever Peter bound in heaven (God's curse) would be bound on earth (the crucifixion of Jesus).

On Trial before Pilate (27:1–26)

When daybreak came (27:1). Roman procurators were known to begin their workday very early in the morning, long before sunrise, so as to conclude their official business by noon.

What's that to us? (27:4). Ironically, making atonement for sin was the responsibility of the chief priests, who turn their backs on Judas as he tries to repent of his sin.

It's not permitted to put it into the temple treasury, since it is blood money (27:6). Since there is no law against accepting "blood money," perhaps the priests inferred that it was unclean due to prohibitions like the one in Deut. 23:18.

A burial place for foreigners (27:7). Corpses were interred in temporary tombs until they had decayed, then the bones were transferred to an ossuary and placed in the family tomb. Since many people visited Jerusalem, those who happened to die there would need a place to be buried until family members claimed their remains. Those who died dishonorably (like Judas or Jesus) typically were not claimed by family and thereby needed a place to be buried. The temple treasury often was used by the priests to fund community projects like this one, providing burial grounds for foreigners.

What was spoken through the prophet Jeremiah was fulfilled (27:9). The quotation in 27:9–10 is taken primarily from Zech. 11:12–13, with a few additional phrases from Jer. 18–19. When several different verses from different books were combined under a certain topic or theme, the "quotation" often was attributed to only one source (see Mark 1:2–3).

"Are you the king of the Jews?" the governor asked him (27:11). This is a dangerous question, for if Jesus had said yes, Pilate could have found him guilty of treason, since Rome ruled Judea.

At the festival the governor's custom was to release to the crowd a prisoner (27:15). Roman procurators releasing prisoners as an act of goodwill was a rare occurrence. Evidently, it was customary for procurators of Judea to offer amnesty to a Jewish prisoner during Passover, supposedly to mark the occasion of the liberation of Hebrew slaves from Egypt. Pilate, however, tried to use the custom to agitate the Jewish leadership (27:18), thinking that the citizens of Jerusalem would choose Jesus over Barabbas (27:24).

A notorious prisoner called Barabbas (27:16). The earliest Greek manuscripts omit the name "Jesus" before "Barabbas." But scholars argue that scribes most likely deleted "Jesus" from Barabbas's name in order to preserve the sacredness of Jesus's name. Ironically, in Hebrew "Barabbas" means "son of the father."

The Execution and Burial of Jesus (27:27–66)

Then the governor's soldiers took Jesus into the governor's residence (27:27). The Praetorium housed the soldiers who protected the governor. Caesarea Maritima was the headquarters for procurators who governed Judea and, therefore, where the Praetorium was located. Since the procurator needed to visit Jerusalem occasionally (certainly during Jewish festivals when disturbances were more likely), then the provisional Praetorium in Jerusalem would have been either Herod the Great's old palace (located on the west side of the city) or the Antonia Fortress (situated on the northwest corner of the temple complex).

As they were going out (27:32). Criminals were executed outside the walls of the city for Jewish and Roman reasons: (1) to protect the Jewish city from the impurity of death and the shame of crucifixion, and (2) because the Romans wanted to advertise what happened to condemned traitors, crucified on the major road leading in/out of the city.

They forced him to carry his cross (27:32). The condemned carried the crossbeam of their crucifixion to the site of execution, where it was then attached to a vertical beam permanently erected for this singular purpose. Jesus was beaten so badly that soldiers impressed a bystander to carry the crossbeam for him, probably to expedite matters. Ironically, his name was Simon (cf. Matt. 26:35).

They gave him wine mixed with gall to drink (27:34). Executioners were known to offer a drink, sometimes mixed with a numbing agent, in order to prolong the agony of crucifixion. Perhaps Matthew wanted readers to see the crucifixion of Jesus in light of Ps. 69 (especially vv. 19–21).

They divided his clothes (27:35). Victims of crucifixion usually were stripped naked before they were nailed to the cross.

Above his head they put up the charge against him in writing (27:37). The capital offense was often written on a placard in Latin and nailed to the cross above the head of the crucified. Thus the common artistic rendering of the placard, with the inscription *INRI*, is an acrostic from Latin: Jesus (*Iesus*) of Nazareth (*Nazarenus*), King (*Rex*) of the Jews (*Iudaeorum*).

Two criminals were crucified with him (27:38). Literally, two "thieves" were crucified with Jesus (see the article "Crucifixion"; see comments on Mark 8:34). Since thievery wasn't a capital offense according to Roman law, these bandits were rebels who tried to overthrow the empire via acts of economic subversion—"highwaymen" who disrupted Roman "peace" by robbing travelers on Roman roads.

For he said, "I am the Son of God" (27:43). Technically, Jesus never said, "I am the Son of God." But he did say that one day he would sit "at the right hand of the Power" (26:64), which the chief priests interpreted as a claim to deity, thus the charge of blasphemy (26:65).

My God, my God, why have you abandoned me? (27:46). This is the first verse of Ps. 22, which is a song of lament of the righteous sufferer that parallels the crucifixion of Jesus in several places (Ps. 22:2 // Matt. 27:45; Ps. 22:7 // Matt. 27:39; Ps. 22:8 // Matt. 27:43; Ps. 22:16 // Matt. 27:38–39; Ps. 22:18 // Matt. 27:35). According to Matthew, these are the only words that Jesus spoke from the cross (cf. Luke 23:34, 43, 46; John 19:26–27, 28, 30).

The curtain of the sanctuary was torn in two from top to bottom (27:51). This was either the curtain that hung in the entrance to the temple or the inner curtain that separated the holy of holies from the rest of the temple. The outer curtain was "embroidered with blue, and fine linen, and scarlet, and purple" representing the colors of the sky, sea, and earth—"a kind of image of the universe. . . . This curtain had also embroidered upon it all that was mystical in the heavens."[17] Therefore, a ripped outer curtain could symbolize the heavens opening (3:16), the destruction of the temple (24:2), or the end of the world (24:29). A torn inner curtain could symbolize access to God through the death of Christ (26:28), making the sacrificial cult obsolete. Being ripped from top to bottom signified that God was the one who tore it, perhaps picturing his departure (Ezek. 10:18; Matt. 23:38).

The tombs were also opened and many bodies of the saints who had fallen asleep were raised (27:52). This perhaps is another proleptic (symbolic, prefiguring, partial) fulfillment of messianic prophecy, particularly Isa. 26:19 and Ezek. 37:12–14.

He approached Pilate and asked for Jesus's body (27:58). Since crucifixion was such a shameful death, often the victim did not receive an honorable burial from the family. In Jesus's case, it took a wealthy man of great influence—Joseph of Arimathea—risking guilt by association, to get permission from Pilate to bury Jesus (see comments on Mark 15:46).

You have a guard (27:65). This guard was either a Jewish temple guard under the authority of the chief priests or, more likely, Roman soldiers loaned by Pilate (cf. 28:12–15).

The Resurrection of Jesus Christ (28:1–20)

Mary Magdalene and the other Mary went to view the tomb (28:1). Women were custodians of the dead—from preparing the corpse to keeping watch at the tomb.

Took hold of his feet (28:9). This is an important detail because according to Jewish belief, spirits do not have feet.[18]

Say this, "His disciples came during the night and stole him" (28:13). Ironically, the story that the Jewish leaders once tried to prevent (27:64) they now invent.

To Galilee, to the mountain where Jesus had directed them (28:16). The exact location is unknown, perhaps the Mount of Transfiguration (17:1–8) or the location of the Sermon on the Mount (5:1–8:1). The OT is filled with stories of divine encounters on mountains (e.g., with Abraham, Moses, Elijah).

But some doubted (28:17). The same Greek word translated as "doubted" appears in 14:31, and it means either "to waver" (to question something) or "to hesitate" (to be uncertain about a course of action).

Go, therefore, and make disciples of all nations (28:19). The only imperative in the so-called Great Commission is the command to "make disciples." The Greek word translated as "go" is an aorist participle, meaning more literally, "after going." Earlier, Jesus commanded his disciples to go only to the "lost sheep of the house of Israel" (10:5–6). After the resurrection—the evidence that "all authority in heaven and earth has been given to me" (28:18)—Jesus expanded the mission of his followers to make disciples of all "nations," using a Greek word that can also be translated as "gentiles."

Teaching them to observe everything I have commanded you (28:20). Rabbis made disciples by teaching them their interpretation of the Torah. Jesus instructed his followers to make disciples by teaching *his* commandments—lessons on discipleship that go all the way back to the Sermon on the Mount.

I am with you always, to the end of the age (28:20). Here is the fulfillment of the promise, made at the beginning of Matthew's Gospel, that Jesus would be Immanuel, "God with us" (1:23).

Mark

James R. Edwards

Introduction. Mark, the shortest of the four Gospels, traditionally was regarded as an inferior abridgment of the Gospel of Matthew. Since the early nineteenth century, however, careful literary analysis of the Gospels has led a majority of scholars to conclude that Mark is likely the earliest of the Gospels, and also the primary source for both Matthew and Luke. This changed perspective has resulted in renewed attention and research on the Second Gospel in modern times.

Mark nowhere identifies its author or the occasion of writing. Early and reputable witnesses, however, including Papias, Clement of Alexandria, Origen, and Eusebius, attest that the Second Gospel derives from John Mark. John Mark was the son of Mary in whose house the early church gathered in Jerusalem (Acts 12:12). He assisted on Paul's first missionary journey (Acts 12:25; 13:4, 13) and later traveled with Barnabas (Acts 15:37–41). Later NT references place him in the company of Paul (Col. 4:10; Philem. 24; 2 Tim. 4:11) and Peter (1 Pet. 5:13). According to Papias, Mark composed his Gospel while in service of Peter in Rome, whose preaching was the chief source of his Gospel. The Gospel must have been composed after AD 64 when Peter arrived in Rome, but probably before the fall of Jerusalem in AD 70, for chapter 13, which reflects some aspects of the First Jewish Revolt, does not seem to reflect the fall of Jerusalem.

Mark's primary audience was Roman gentiles, as indicated by infrequent OT quotations, explanations of Jewish customs unfamiliar to gentiles (7:3–4; 12:18; 14:12; 15:42), translations of Aramaic and Hebrew phrases by Greek

Many scholars believe that the Gospel of Mark was written for gentile readers in Rome. The center of Roman political and religious activity was the Roman Forum, shown here.

equivalents (3:17; 5:41; 7:11, 34; 10:46; 14:36; 15:22, 34), and frequent Latinisms.

The Second Gospel is action-packed, portraying who Jesus is by what he does rather than by what he teaches, or what Mark declares about him. Mark writes in an unadorned though vivid style, maintaining a vigorous tempo throughout. Mark intrudes into the narrative plot only when necessary to establish the meaning of an obscure point (e.g., 3:30; 7:19). Mark's literary techniques include the use of irony in order to challenge false preconceptions of Jesus and the kingdom of God. Mark also communicates meaning by placing stories side by side for comparison and illustration (e.g., 4:35–41 followed by 5:1–20). Especially unique among the Gospels is Mark's "sandwich technique" of inserting a seemingly unrelated story into the middle of a story in order to make a third point by implication (3:20–35; 4:1–20; 5:21–43; 6:7–30; 11:12–21; 14:1–11, 17–31, 53–72; 15:40–16:8).

Mark's two major themes are who Jesus is and what it means to be his follower. The chief characteristic that Mark wishes to convey about Jesus is his divine sonship. As the Son of God, Jesus received divine *authority* at his baptism (1:9–11) to teach, heal, minister, and even suffer. His authority is illustrated by doing what only God can do: forgiving sins (2:10), redefining the Sabbath (2:27–28), and subjugating nature to himself (4:35–41). The supreme revelation of Jesus as God's Son occurs at the crucifixion. There, he "gives his life as a ransom for many" (10:45) and is first confessed by humanity as God's Son (15:39).

Who Jesus is determines what his disciples must become. Jesus's followers must share his fate: as Jesus is with the Father, so disciples are to be with Jesus (3:13); as Jesus serves in humility and suffering, so too must his disciples deny themselves and take up their cross and follow him (8:34). In confessing and following Jesus, disciples know him and become like him.

The Preaching of John the Baptist Inaugurates Jesus's Ministry (1:1–8)

Gospel (1:1). "Gospel" can be used in three distinct senses: (1) the message of salvation that Jesus brought, (2) the summary of that message that the church teaches, and (3) a written account of the life of Jesus, such as the Gospel of Mark. Mark uses "gospel" in verse 1 with reference to the first two senses: the gospel as a story of salvation brought by Jesus and proclaimed by the church. The Greek word for "gospel" (*euangelion*) literally means "good news." In the Greek translation of the OT (1 Sam. 31:9; 1 Chron. 10:9; 2 Sam. 1:20; 4:10; 18:19–20, 26) and in Greek literature, *euangelion* (and the verb *euangelizō*) often signified victorious news from the battlefield. The birthday of Caesar Augustus (63 BC–AD 14) was likewise hailed as "the beginning of good news [*euangelion*] for the world." The Greco-Roman world typically used the word in the plural, "good tidings," but the NT uses it in the singular with reference to Jesus Christ alone. Mark uses *euangelion* in its prophetic sense (cf. Isa. 52:7; 61:1–3) of the inbreaking of God's saving intervention of peace, good news, and release from oppression for God's people.

Jesus (1:1). "Jesus" is an Anglicized form of the Hebrew name *Yeshua*, meaning "YHWH is salvation" or "YHWH saves." It was the sixth most common name among Palestinian male Jews in the first century.

Christ (1:1). See comments on Mark 8:29.

Son of God (1:1). See comments on Mark 15:39.

Wilderness (1:4). The wilderness connotes the barren badlands of Judah, which in Israel's history was a place both of testing and of repentance and grace. God brought deliverance to his people in the wilderness of Sinai (Exod. 15:22), and thereafter the wilderness became a symbol of hope in the prophetic proclamation (Jer. 2:2–3; Hosea 2:14). John appeared in the same wilderness region associated with Elijah (2 Kings 2:6–14), thereby fulfilling Mosaic prototypes in a new exodus and prophetic prototypes of the dawn of the day of the Lord.

Jesus traveled throughout Galilee performing miracles of healing and teaching in the synagogues. Other Gospels record more details about this ministry in Capernaum; its synagogue was one site for these activities. The restored interior of the synagogue in Capernaum (fourth to fifth century AD) is shown here. Remains of what many believe to be the first-century-AD synagogue lie beneath.

Baptism (1:4). The Greek word for "baptize" (*baptizō*) means "to dip fully or immerse." Rites of ritual bathing and washings were known throughout the ancient Near East, including pre-Christian Judaism, where ritual washings symbolized repentance and cleansing of God's people.[1] Ritual washings before worship (*miqvot*) were a constitutive element of Judaism, especially at

Qumran near the Dead Sea where they symbolized the eschatological cleansing of God.[2] John called people to baptism as a symbol of moral and spiritual regeneration. John's baptism was not a clear repetition of Jewish washings, however. *Miqvot* and Qumran baths were self-washings; John's baptism was administered by a second party. Proselyte baptism was an initiation into a faith community; John's baptism signified moral and spiritual renewal. Qumran washings were administered in the community; John baptized at the Jordan River. John's baptism recalled and revived God's foundational covenant with Israel at Sinai, summoning the entire people to be "a kingdom of priests and a holy nation" (Exod. 19:6; cf. 1 Pet. 2:9).

Repentance (1:4). The Greek word for "repentance" (*metanoia*) means "a change in one's thinking," connoting a rational decision and willful act as opposed an emotional feeling. Like the prophets before him, John called people to turn away from sin and show "fruit" of moral transformation (Matt. 3:8; Luke 3:8) in preparation for the imminent judgment of God.

John wore a camel-hair garment with a leather belt . . . ate locusts and wild honey (1:6). John's dress was no more typical in his day than it would be in ours. Rather, it recalled that of a prophet (Zech. 13:4), especially Elijah's "garment of hair and . . . leather belt around his waist" (2 Kings 1:8 NIV). The eating of locusts was included within Jewish dietary rules (Lev. 11:22).[3] Though foreign to modern Western tastes, locusts (or grasshoppers) are high in protein and minerals. John's diet and dress identified him with the desert region (1:4) rather than with the temple and its cult in Jerusalem. John's fearless criticism of Herod Antipas (6:18) also echoed Elijah's confrontation with King Ahab (1 Kings 18:17–18) and renewal of God's covenant with Israel on Mount Carmel (1 Kings 18:30–45).

The Baptism and Temptation of Jesus (1:9–13)

Nazareth (1:9). See comments on Mark 6:1.

Galilee (1:9). In OT times Galilee was inhabited by the tribes of Zebulun and Naphtali. It contained a mixed population of Jews and gentiles, and from the time of Isaiah onward it was called Galilee of the Gentiles. Upon the death of Herod the Great in 4 BC the Romans divided rule of Palestine into smaller regions, called tetrarchies, each assigned to one of Herod's several sons. Galilee and Perea (the region east of the Jordan River) were consolidated under the tetrarchy of Herod Antipas. Virtually all Jesus's ministry was conducted in Galilee, primarily along the northwest quadrant of the Sea of Galilee, with occasional excursions to the east of the Sea into the Decapolis. No text in the four Gospels reports a visit of Jesus to the southwest quadrant of the Sea of Galilee, or to the two major cities of Galilee, Tiberias and Sepphoris.

Baptized in the Jordan by John (1:9). The Jordan, the only major river in Israel, flows approximately seventy miles between the Sea of Galilee and the Dead Sea. It winds through the Jordan Valley, producing a narrow margin of green and fertile land along its banks but leaving barren wilderness farther away. The Gospels do not provide an exact location where John baptized in the Jordan.

Satan (1:13). The Hebrew word for "Satan" (*satan*) literally means "accuser, adversary," which in the NT designates God's personal and supernatural enemy. The other name for God's adversary, "devil," is not used by Mark, although it occurs with equal frequency in the NT. Satan and his subordinate "demons" oppose the reign of God, especially as it is manifested in God's Son, Jesus (1 John 3:8). In Mark's Gospel Jesus's first miracle (1:21–28) and first parable (3:27) are portrayed as offensives against "the strong one," Satan.

Jesus's Early Galilean Ministry (1:14–45)

Kingdom of God (1:15). The concept of the kingdom or reign of God initially began with Israel's understanding of God as king, the creator and ruler of this world (Exod. 15:18; 1 Sam. 12:12; Ps. 5:2). The exodus from Egypt and the giving of Torah were formative expressions of God's rule over Israel as a people. The promised coming of God's Messiah in the future would finally and fully restore

Jesus was baptized by John in the Jordan River. The section of the Jordan River shown here, the traditional site of Jesus's baptism, is near Bethany beyond the Jordan.

God's kingdom. Jewish conceptions of the kingdom of God usually included or excluded humanity from the kingdom on the basis of obedience to Torah. Jesus does not speak of the kingdom as a result of human effort, however, or of evolutionary development. In the Gospel of Mark Jesus does not speak of God as king, but rather of entering the kingdom as his disciples. The kingdom is a mystery (4:11) that is not explained, but rather is expressed in terms of similarities, analogies, or parables (4:26, 30). The kingdom is presently hidden, but in the future it will be manifested in power and glory (9:1; 14:25, 62). The choice to enter the kingdom cannot be deferred until its future victory, but must be made on the basis of the word and promise of Jesus. The kingdom reorders existing priorities: the rich and powerful will be admitted only with great difficulty (10:23–25), but those of humble sincerity, especially the poor, contrite, and outsiders—even children—will find ready admittance (10:14–15; 12:34). The kingdom is not only the substance of Jesus's teaching (1:15) but also is identified in the closest possible way with his own person and ministry.

Sea of Galilee (1:16). The name of the Sea of Galilee in Hebrew is *Kinneret*, meaning "harp," which describes its general shape. This body of water, which lies seven hundred feet below sea level, is thirteen miles long north to south and seven miles across at its widest east-west axis. The eastern shore rises to the mountains of the Golan Heights in the gentile Decapolis, with gentler slopes on the eastern Jewish shore. In Jesus's day this lake had as many as sixteen harbors along its shoreline, and fish from the lake were shipped to markets in Egypt to the south and Syria to the north. The confluence of hot air rising from the surface of the lake and cold air descending from the summit of Mount Hermon twenty miles to the north often caused powerful squalls on the lake. On Galilee itself, see comments on Mark 1:9.

Casting a net (1:16). The Greek verb translated as "casting a net" (*amphiballō*) means "to throw around." The verb refers to a particular circular net (*amphiblēstron* [Matt. 4:18]) that was roughly twenty feet in diameter and weighted with stones or metal on the perimeter that was used by fishermen on the Sea of Galilee. A single fisherman gathered the casting net on his upper arm and, in a discus-throwing motion, heaved it outward over the water, on which it landed like a parachute. The sinking net trapped fish within its circumference. The fisherman then dove to the bottom of the lake, gathered the weights together, and pulled the net and its catch to the shore.

Capernaum (1:21). Jesus established Capernaum, on the northwest shore of the Sea of Galilee, as the home base of his Galilean ministry. Two of his disciples (Peter and Andrew) lived in Capernaum, which lay on the Via Maris, the trade route connecting the Mediterranean coastal plain with Damascus in the north. Capernaum was outside the immediate orbits of the larger cities of Galilee—Sepphoris, Beth-shan, and especially Tiberias, where Herod Antipas located his capital—thus affording Jesus a margin of distance from Galilean political and religious leaders (1:14; 6:14–29). Capernaum was a border town between the tetrarchies of Philip and Herod, and the site of both a customs office (2:14) and a small garrison of the Roman army (Luke 7:2). Capernaum's harbor consisted of an eight-foot-wide seawall extending 2,500 feet along the shore, from which perpendicular piers reached a hundred feet into the lake. The inhabitants of Capernaum were primarily Jews who, in addition to being fishermen, were artisans, farmers, merchants, traders, and officials related to the tax office and military garrison. Capernaum's location on the Sea of Galilee and Via Maris afforded it an enviable degree of prosperity.

Synagogue and traditional house of Peter at Capernaum.

Synagogue (1:21). Unlike the temple in Jerusalem, where animals were sacrificed by priests, synagogues were "assembly halls" where Torah was read and expounded (see the article "The Jewish Synagogue"). Synagogues could be found throughout the Mediterranean world wherever ten or more Jewish males, thirteen years of age or older, were present. The white limestone synagogue visible to present-day visitors to Capernaum dates to the fourth century and is not the one visited by Jesus. The course of basalt stones visible beneath the fourth-century synagogue is, however, the foundation of the synagogue where Jesus worshiped.

A synagogue was officiated by a "ruler of the synagogue" (Heb. *rosh hakkenesset*),[4] who was not a scribe or rabbi by profession but rather a lay member entrusted with general oversight of the synagogue and orthodoxy of teaching. His responsibilities included building maintenance and security, procuring of scrolls for Scripture reading, overseeing Sabbath worship (including designating Scripture readers, prayers, and preachers), and perhaps teaching Jewish children. Mark 5:22 (also Acts 13:15) speaks of synagogue rulers in the plural, suggesting that the responsibility in some synagogues required more than one official.

Sabbath (1:21). See comments on Mark 2:23.

Scribes (1:22). Before the advent of widespread literacy, scribes were in great demand in the ancient world. They were in particular demand in Israel, where the written code of Torah formed the basis for Jewish life. Jewish scribes first appear in the reign of King David as secretaries and recorders of events related to the monarchy (2 Sam. 8:16–17; 20:24–25; 1 Kings 4:3). In postexilic Judaism scribes gained unrivaled prominence and authority in the Jewish community as experts in Torah interpretation (Ezra 7:6, 11), teachers of Torah, and legal jurists in the broad sense of the term. “Rabbi,” meaning “my great one,” was an honorary title of many scribes. The prestige of scribes on occasion surpassed that of the high priest,[5] and only scribes could enter the Sanhedrin. Scribes were highly honored in Jesus’s day: they sat in the first seats in synagogues, people rose to their feet when they entered a room, and people made way for them when they walked the streets.

Simon and Andrew’s house (1:29). No more than a hundred yards from the Capernaum synagogue is a structure (above which the Franciscans have erected a modern church that resembles a flying saucer) that is reasonably certain to have been the house of Simon (Peter). The house belongs to what archaeologists call an “insula” structure, in which dwellings face an interior court that is accessed by a gateway from the street. Stairways led to the flat roofs of the dwellings from a central courtyard, which also contained common hearths, handpresses, millstones for grinding grain, and animal holding areas. Heavy walls of black basalt were topped by horizontal support beams for the roof. These were cross-hatched by smaller poles and covered with thatch and mud (hence the reference to “digging through it” [Mark 2:4]). Flat roofs functioned much as decks do today, offering relief from dank interior quarters below, access to fresh air, and a place to dry laundry, eat, and pray (Acts 10:9). Archaeologists have discovered graffiti in Greek, Latin, Syriac, and Aramaic etched on the walls of the ostensible dwelling of Peter, indicating that it was venerated as a place of Christian assembly, and perhaps as a church, from about AD 100.

Drove out many demons . . . would not permit the demons to speak (1:34). Demons and exorcisms play an important role in the first half of Mark’s Gospel. Mark portrays Jesus’s power over demons in accord with the description of the day of the Lord in Zech. 13:2, in which the deeds and activities of Satan are vanquished. Jesus’s first miracle in Mark’s Gospel is an exorcism (1:34), and his first parable is about binding “the strong man,” Satan himself (3:27), both of which attest to his supremacy over satanic power. Demons recognize Jesus as God’s Son before his disciples do, because they, like Jesus, belong to the spiritual world.

Three reasons may be suggested why Jesus forbade the demon-possessed from making him known. First, Jesus rejected any announcement of his person and mission by those opposed to God’s kingdom, including demons. Second, it was necessary for Jesus to silence messianic utterances about himself, since “Messiah” connoted military deliverance to Jewish hearers, and Jesus was not a military deliverer (see comments on Mark 8:29). Such connotations were inappropriate to his mission, and they would invite swift retaliation from the Roman occupation. Third, and most importantly, the command to silence was rooted in the profile of the OT servant of the Lord, on whom Jesus consciously patterned his ministry (Matt. 12:15–21). The mystery of the servant's mission, influence, and power is characterized by hiddenness (Isa. 49:2). The faith of Jesus's disciples cannot be evoked through miracles and power, but only through humility and ultimately suffering.

A man with leprosy (1:40). Leprosy was a prevalent skin disease in first-century Palestine that, like all skin diseases, was hard to diagnose and difficult to heal. As a consequence, it became a subject of superstition and fear. Leviticus 13–14 reads like an ancient manual on dermatology, setting forth the OT understanding of skin diseases. In addition to the physical disease itself, leprosy carried a host of punishing social consequences as a social stigma, banishing victims from their occupations and primary communities of family, home, friends, and worship. In Israel victims needed to be cleansed of leprosy as well as healed from it (e.g., Matt. 11:5). The Hebrew term translated as "leprosy" (*tsaraat*) included, in addition to leprosy, other skin diseases such as boils (Lev. 13:18), burns (Lev. 13:24), itches, ringworm, and scalp conditions. The OT commonly speaks of leprosy in terms of divine punishment, which God alone could cure (Num. 12:10–15; 2 Kings 5:1–15). Torah required lepers to make themselves physically repugnant and keep fifty paces distant from others, and to warn others of their presence by shouting, "Unclean!" (Lev. 13:45–46).

Five Stories Depicting Jesus's Authority (2:1–3:12)

He was at home (2:1). On Palestinian houses, see comments on Mark 1:29.

Many people gathered (2:2). Crowds play an especially important role in Mark's Gospel, being referred to nearly forty times prior to chapter 10. Crowds frequently are depicted as being "amazed" at Jesus's words and deeds, and although they are the object of Jesus's compassion, they do not respond in repentance and faith, according to Mark (1:15). More often than not they prevent people from having access to Jesus. Thus Mark does not regard Jesus's popularity with crowds as a measure of his success. Following Jesus's teaching on suffering at Caesarea Philippi, crowds appear less frequently in Mark, thus fitting the category of those unwilling to "take up their cross and follow him." Since they are "outsiders," Jesus teaches the crowds in parables (e.g., 4:33–34; 7:17).

Removed the roof . . . digging through it (2:4). See comments on Mark 1:29.

Son of Man (2:10). "Son of Man" was Jesus's preferred self-designation (fourteen times in Mark), but no one other than Jesus addresses him so. It was an ambiguous title, largely free of the political and military connotations associated with "Messiah." "Son of Man" appears to have made no special claim on Jesus's hearers, for people are not amazed or offended that he calls himself the Son of Man. "Son of Man" thus offers the advantage of a title unencumbered by unwelcome associations, allowing Jesus to fill the title with his own content. In Mark's Gospel, "Son of Man" appears with reference to Jesus in three ways. First, Mark three times uses "Son of Man" in apocalyptic contexts (8:38; 13:26; 14:62), which, like its usage in Dan. 7 and *1 Enoch* 37–69, refers to the Son of Man coming in future judgment. Second, Mark twice uses the title with reference to Jesus's earthly authority to forgive sins (2:10) and to supersede the Sabbath (2:28). Third, and most predominantly, Mark uses the title nine times with reference to Jesus's suffering, often with its saving significance (8:31; 9:9, 12, 31; 10:33, 45; 14:21 [twice], 41). These uses demonstrate that "Son of Man" does not, as is often supposed, refer to Jesus's human nature rather than his divine nature (see comments on Mark 15:39). Rather, each of the three uses refers either to a divine attribute or to fulfilling a divine purpose

Tax collectors (2:15). The Roman tax system was a complex but essential element in Roman subjugation of Palestine. Fixed taxes (poll taxes) and land taxes were paid directly to the Romans, but other taxes (on transported goods, for instance) were contracted out to local agents for collection, most of whom were Jews who were willing to transact business with gentiles. People arriving in Capernaum from regions to the north and east would pay taxes to agents like Levi who were employed by Herod Antipas, tetrarch of Galilee and Perea. Such agents were middlemen for the Roman Empire whose profits were accrued by overcharging Galileans and keeping the excess money for themselves. The Roman tax system was loathed by Jews subjugated to it, not least because it attracted individuals who were not averse to graft and greed. The Mishnah and the Talmud hold tax collectors in contempt, barring them from the synagogue, disqualifying them as legal witnesses or judges, and deeming them a disgrace to families.[6] Any contact of a tax collector with a house rendered it unclean.[7] It was not acceptable for Jews to receive money or even alms from tax collectors, because such revenues were considered robbery. The disgrace to which the Mishnah relegates tax collectors is signaled by allowing Jews to lie to them with impunity.[8] Jesus is the only Jewish rabbi known to us who treated tax collectors charitably, and even on occasion used them as examples of virtue (Luke 18:9–14).

Eating with sinners and tax collectors (2:16). The contempt for tax collectors described in the comments on 2:15 obviously excluded tax collectors from table fellowship with observant Jews. Like prayer, table fellowship was regarded by Jews as a communion of trust and fellowship, and normally it was denied to those who were not Torah-observant. The Mishnah classifies various types of persons as "sinners," including thieves, shepherds, violent individuals, moneylenders, people who race animals for sport and money, and those who fail to observe Sabbath.[9] As ritually unclean persons, tax collectors and sinners were believed to defile both food and guests in dining circumstances. The willingness of Jesus to dine with tax collectors and sinners was foreign and offensive to Jewish rabbis and, along with his Sabbath healing, a primary cause for the opposition of Jewish authorities to him.

Coins from the reign of Herod Antipas.

Pharisees (2:18). See the article "Pharisees and Sadducees." The name Pharisees probably means either "separated ones" or "holy ones." The Pharisaic sect arose during the Maccabean Revolt (168 BC) when Jews launched a military offensive against the inroads of Hellenism—that is, attempts, whether outright or subtle, to transform Judaism to Greco-Roman ideals. Pharisees sought above all to be guardians of Torah, which, as the perfect expression of God's will, was the divine arbiter of human existence.[10] The primary concern of Pharisees was Torah righteousness rather than a particular political agendum; indeed, they were generally apolitical as long as they were permitted to follow Torah. One did not earn a living by being a Pharisee. Rather, Pharisaism was a lay movement, indeed, a small minority that may have numbered some six thousand persons in Jesus's day,[11] which would have comprised roughly 1 percent of Jews in Palestine. Pharisees nevertheless surpassed other Jewish parties in both number and influence—whether Sadducees, Herodians, Essenes, or Zealots. Because Pharisees were religiously fervent but politically adaptable, they alone survived the First Jewish Revolt against Rome in AD 66–70.

The religious tradition of the Pharisee was known as the "tradition of the elders" (Mark 7:5), and it was characterized by belief in the sovereignty of God, human responsibility for both good and evil, bodily resurrection of the dead, and angels and demons. Scrupulous adherence to Torah, both written in the Pentateuch and expounded orally by the rabbis, was the means of achieving righteousness. Those who neglected Torah instruction fell under stern judgment from Pharisees. Although Jesus opposed many Pharisaic practices, in his beliefs he actually stood closer to them than to other Jewish parties (e.g., Matt. 23:3). According to the Gospels, the opposition of Pharisees to Jesus occurred primarily in Galilee, for Pharisees are largely absent in the passion narratives of the Gospels (mentioned only once in Matt. 27:62 and John 18:3) and thus played little role in Jesus's death (cf. Luke 13:31).

Fasting (2:18). Along with the observance of Sabbath, circumcision, prayer, and almsgiving, fasting was a main pillar of Judaism. Only one fast was required of Jews, on Yom Kippur, the Day of Atonement (Lev. 16:29–31).[12] But three other types of fasts, as specified by Mishnah (tractate *Ta'anit*), typically were followed by Jews. One was fasting due to national tragedies, such as the destruction of the temple by Nebuchadnezzar (Zech. 7:3–7; 8:19); another was fasting due to crises, such as war, plague, drought, and famine; and a third was self-imposed fasting for various personal reasons (2 Sam. 12:16; Ps. 35:13). Yom Kippur was a twenty-four-hour fast, whereas voluntary fasts normally lasted from dawn to dusk. In Jesus's day the additional voluntary fasts were virtually expected of Jews as signs of atonement of sin, humiliation, and penitence, and as general aids to prayer. Mondays and Thursdays were normal fast days for Pharisees.[13] Rabbis considered fasting an important and sacrificial act of piety.

Wedding guests (2:19). See the article "Jewish Marriage Customs." Jesus illustrates discipleship by the metaphor of a wedding feast. Weddings were special occasions in Jewish society, normally extending to seven days for a virgin bride and three days for a remarried woman. The sole objective was for family and guests to celebrate the wedding with food, wine, song, and dance inside and outside the house. Weddings even preempted instruction in Torah, requiring both rabbis and students to join the celebration. Any thought of "the guests [Gk. *huioi*, "sons"] of the bridegroom" fasting when a wedding was at hand was out of the question.

No one puts new wine into old wineskins (2:22). In the ancient world fresh, whole animal (usually goat) hides with neck and leg holes sewn shut were used as vessels or "skins" for storing and preserving wine. New hides were sufficiently supple to expand as fermenting wine expanded, whereas the pressure of fermenting wine would burst old, brittle hides (Job 32:19).

Sabbath (2:23). Sabbath observance, which extended from sunset Friday until sunset Saturday, was the single most socially defining element in Jewish religious life. Regulations related to Sabbath observance constitute the longest of the Ten Commandments (Exod. 20:8–11; Deut. 5:12–15). The chief distinction of Sabbath observance is cessation from work. Jews were forbidden from doing any work on Sabbath that was not necessary to preserve life, nor should any work be started that could

This is a replica of a wineskin, on display at a restored third-century-AD home at Qatzrin on the Golan Heights.

not be completed before the onset of Sabbath.[14] Not only Jews but also slaves, animals, and even vegetation (which could not be cut, plucked, or uprooted),[15] were to be spared from Sabbath labors. Sabbath observance was instituted by God at creation (Gen. 2:3),[16] and thus it was the only one of the Ten Commandments delivered to Jews prior to Moses. The observance of Sabbath, according to the Talmud, makes one a partner with God in both the creation and salvation of the world.[17] The Essene community, which probably was the community of Jews that lived at Qumran, observed Sabbath more rigorously than did the Pharisees, forbidding carrying of children, assisting of birthing animals, or retrieval of animals in distress.[18] According to the Mishnah, thirty-nine classes of work are forbidden on Sabbath, including agricultural (e.g., plowing, hunting, butchering) and domestic labor (e.g., tying or loosening of knots, sewing more than one stitch, writing more than one letter).[19]

Picking some heads of grain (2:23). The Torah allowed harvesting grain from a neighbor's field if it was done by hand rather than by sickle (Deut. 23:25). Whether Jesus and his disciples were actually violating Torah is unclear in the text, unless the Pharisees considered them picking grain to excess. If they walked more than two thousand paces, however, they would have violated the Sabbath by "traveling."[20]

Herodians (3:6). The term "Herodians" occurs in only three passing references in the NT (Mark 3:6; 12:13 [8:15?]; Matt. 22:16) and thus is imperfectly understood. Josephus makes a reference to "partisans of Herod [the Great],"[21] which may allude to Herodians by a different name. Josephus's report that Herod "showed special favor to those of the city's populace who had been on his side while he was still a commoner" may be a further reference to Herodians.[22] If so, they would be sympathizers, supporters, and adherents of the Herodian dynasty rather than a distinct party defined by particular doctrines, as were Pharisees, Sadducees, and Essenes. Herodians appear in the NT only in connection with Pharisees, which is unexpected, since Pharisees opposed Hellenism as fervently as Herod promoted it. The two otherwise antagonistic parties are three times mentioned together in the NT, which may suggest that their one common denominator was their opposition to Jesus. If so, their opposition was both political and religious (Mark 6:14–29; 12:13; 15:1).

A large crowd followed from Galilee . . . from Judea, Jerusalem, Idumea, beyond the Jordan, and around Tyre and Sidon (3:7–8). The place names here indicate the distant regions to which Jesus's fame spread: not only Galilee, where he ministered, but also Judea and Jerusalem (80 miles south) and Idumea (120 miles south), Jordan (30 miles east), and Tyre and Sidon (30 miles north). Equally noteworthy is the ethnic diversity

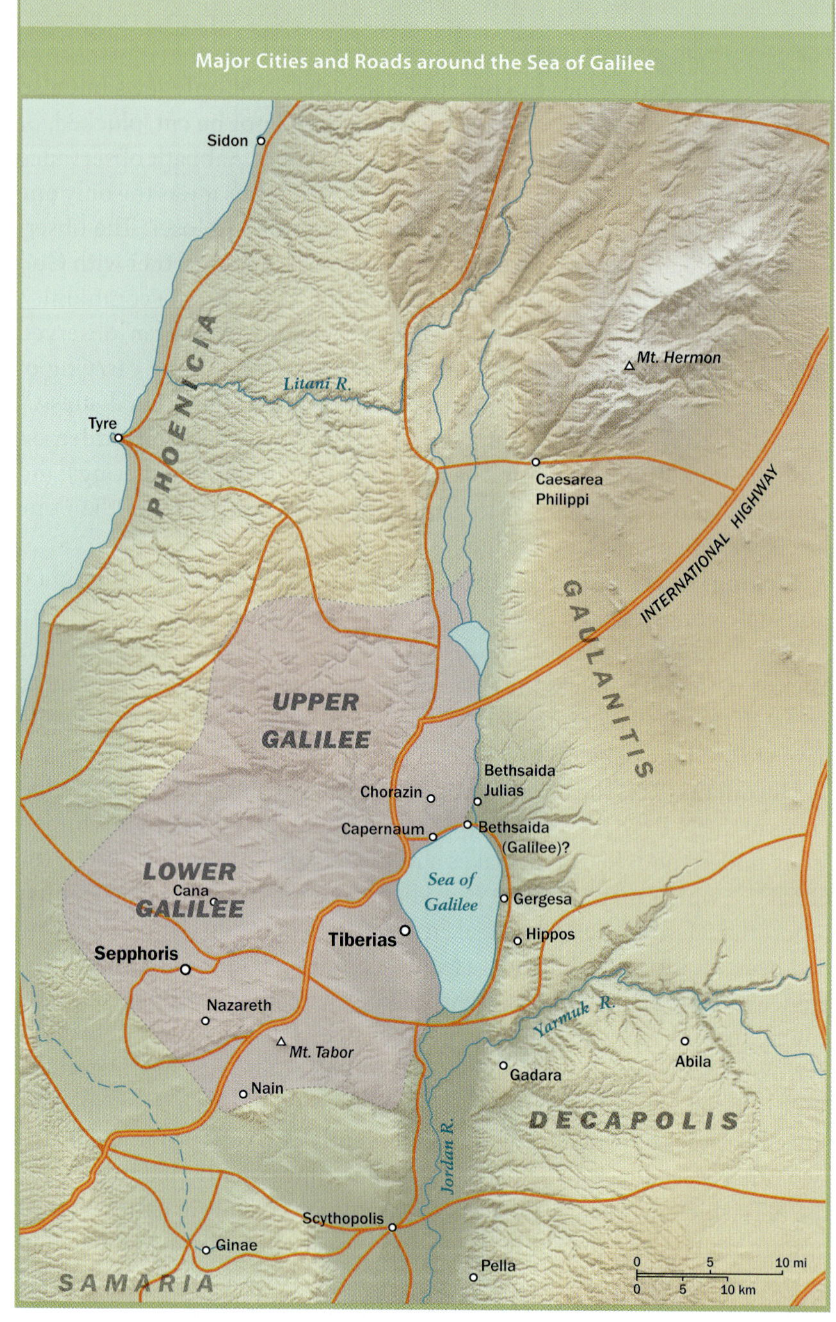

of the crowds: Judea and Jerusalem were largely Jewish; Galilee, Idumea, and Transjordan were both Jewish and gentile; and Tyre and Sidon were primarily gentile (see Matt. 11:21–22; Luke 6:17). Jesus's reputation thus transcended the ethnic diversity and divisions of the day.

Genuine Discipleship Is to Be with Jesus (3:13–4:34)

He appointed twelve . . . apostles (3:14). The Greek word *apostellō* ("send") is the root of the English word "apostle." Similarly, *shaliah* in Hebrew signified an "authorized messenger of an established community." Both terms witness to the missionary nature of the gospel. The apostle Paul first uses "apostle" to refer to one sent to proclaim the message of the gospel. There are four NT lists of the apostles (Mark 3:16–19; Matt. 10:2–4; Luke 6:14–16; Acts 1:13), each of which displays minor differences in the order of names or the names themselves, but they agree on the fixed number of twelve, which recalls Israel's twelve tribes. Jesus may have chosen twelve apostles to signify the reconstitution of Israel.

Beelzebul (3:22). The term "Beelzebul" is unique to the Gospels, but 2 Kings (1:2, 3, 6, 16) refers to a Syrian god of Ekron called "Baal-zebub." The original meaning of "Baal-zebub" seems to have been "lord of the dwelling [= temple]," which the LXX (Greek translation of the Hebrew OT) altered to a contemptuous term, *Baal muian*, meaning "lord of the flies," "lord of the dung heap." The exact Greek word in the Gospels is *Beelzeboul*. *Zebul* occurs five times in the Hebrew OT (1 Kings 8:13; 2 Chron. 6:2; Ps. 49:15; Isa. 63:15; Hab. 3:11), with reference either to an exalted temple or to heaven itself, and this meaning is carried forth in the Jewish Targums and Dead Sea Scrolls.[23] *Beelzeboul*, therefore, probably means "Baal's abode or dynasty," which is reinforced by Jesus's reference to "Beelzebul" as the "lord of the house" (Matt. 10:25). It is important to recall that in the OT the chief rival to Yahweh worship was the Baal cult. In the Bible, foreign gods frequently are called demons (LXX Ps. 95:5 [ET 96:5]; 1 Cor. 10:20); here, in fact, Beelzebul appears as the arch demon in a dynasty of evil spirits (Mark 3:26). Jewish literature rarely refers to Satan, and nowhere by the term "Beelzebul," but the rhetorical question of Jesus in 3:23 equates the two as "the prince of demons."

Your mother, your brothers, and your sisters (3:32). On Jesus's family, see comments on Mark 6:3.

He began to teach by the sea (4:1). The land between Capernaum and Tabgha slopes gently down to a bay that may have been the place of Jesus's teaching. The "Bay of Parables," as it is called, is a natural amphitheater that transmits a human voice audibly to large crowds on the shore.

He taught them many things in parables (4:2). Parables are rare in the OT (2 Sam. 12:1–14; Ezek. 17:1–10), although Greco-Roman antiquity was familiar with stories and fables similar to parables. For Jesus, however, parables were his preferred form of public teaching, and both the number and the excellence of his parables are without compare in antiquity. There are some sixty different parables in the Gospels, the majority in Matthew and Luke, fewer in Mark, and none in John. The Greek word *parabolē*, from which "parable" is derived, refers to placing a known thing alongside a lesser or unknown thing for the purposes of clarification.

The kingdom of God is the most common topic of Jesus's parables. His parables consisted of ordinary life stories that, though familiar to his hearers, contained the unexpected and even the unsettling, requiring hearers to see the ordinary in a new light. Parables are more than good advice, and often are not moral stories at all. Their purpose, rather, is to confront hearers with "good news," the transformative power of God's inbreaking presence in the world. Most parables have a single central point, although a few have allegorical qualities in which various elements of the parable represent realities in life. Jesus's parables cannot be understood by standing "outside" them, but only by allowing oneself to be drawn "into" them. Parables are like stained-glass windows in a cathedral that are colorless and dull when seen from the outside but brilliant when seen from within. The life of Jesus is itself the greatest parable, and thus it is necessary to know the Parable Teller in order to understand the parables that he tells.

The sower who went out to sow (4:3). The land and climate of Palestine—hilly terrain, rocky soil, thorns and brush, with little rain and few rivers—made farming a precarious venture (Jer. 4:3; James 1:11). The Mishnah enjoins orderly farming methods, above all, not to mix seeds.[24] Jesus's parable, by contrast, describes what appears to be a careless sowing of seed in the most unpromising conditions. The yield, however, is extraordinary for Palestine, "thirty, sixty, and a hundred times" (Mark 4:8; cf. Gen. 26:12), signifying that the harvest in the parable is more than a mere human endeavor.

In the parable recorded in Mark 4:1–20 the farmer goes out to sow seeds using the broadcasting technique by which handfuls of seed are carefully tossed in the air. This Palestinian farmer in the photograph is sowing seeds using this method. Although meant for the ground that was already cultivated or would be turned under with a plow, the seeds could settle anywhere.

The secret of the kingdom of God has been given to you (4:11). The Greek word *mysterion*, translated here as "secret," refers to knowledge of God that depends not on human abilities and resources but on God's self-revelation (LXX Dan. 2:27–28; Wis. 2:22). "It is the secret that the kingdom of God has come in the person and words and works of Jesus. That is a secret because God has chosen to reveal himself indirectly and in a veiled way. The incarnate Word is not obvious. Only faith could recognize the Son of God in the lowly figure of Jesus of Nazareth. The secret of the kingdom of God is the secret of the person of Jesus."[25]

A lamp . . . a lampstand (4:21). Oil lamps were the common and widespread source of light for interiors in the ancient world. The light of an oil lamp, like that of a candle, required open space on "a lampstand" in order to be most useful. In the OT a lamp occasionally serves as a metaphor of divine activity, for God himself (2 Sam. 22:29), the Messiah (2 Kings 8:19; Ps. 132:17), or Torah (Ps. 119:105). The Greek grammar of verse 21 makes "*the* lamp" the acting subject of the verse, a personification that makes the lamp a metaphor of Jesus, who brings God's light and revelation to those who hear him (John 1:5; 8:12).

The Power of Jesus to Save (4:35–6:6a)

He was in the boat (4:36). A drought in Galilee in 1986 exposed the hull of a fishing boat in the mud of the receded shoreline of the Sea of Galilee. The recovered boat was 26.5 feet long, 7.5 feet wide, and 4.5 feet high, a form and size similar to a first-century mosaic of a Galilean boat that has been preserved in Migdal, about a mile from the discovery site. Carbon 14 technology dates the remains of the boat between 120 BC and AD 40. The vessel, which appears to have been covered with a deck, was propelled by two rowers on each side and was capable of carrying as many as fifteen persons. The boat corresponds to the descriptions of Galilean boats in several ancient artistic renderings and is likely similar to the vessel in which Jesus and the disciples crossed the Sea of Galilee.

A great windstorm arose (4:37). On storms on the Sea of Galilee, see comments on Mark 1:16.

The region of the Gerasenes (5:1). The east side of the Sea of Galilee (referred to in the Gospels variously as the region of the Gerasenes, Gadarenes, or Gergesenes) lay in the Decapolis ("Ten Cities"), a geographical reference to a number of cities east of the Jordan River; of these cities only Beth-shan lay west of the Jordan. When Pompey invaded Palestine in 63 BC, he removed the cities of the Decapolis from Hasmonean rule and made them showcase cities of Greco-Roman culture.[26] The Decapolis was almost wholly gentile. The bulk

A first-century fishing boat discovered buried in the Sea of Galilee in the 1980s.

of the Roman army was stationed in the Decapolis, close enough to respond to disorders but distant enough so as not to antagonize without cause Jews west of the Jordan. The Decapolis was a major producer of pork, which was a staple in the diet of the Roman army but anathema to Jews. The reference to "Legion" in 5:9 recalls a Roman legion, the largest and most formidable unit of the Roman army, consisting of some five thousand well-equipped and well-trained soldiers. The association of the Decapolis with gentiles, pigs, and Roman occupation rendered it "unclean" from a Jewish perspective.

A man with an unclean spirit came out of the tombs (5:2). In Jewish and pagan societies the dead were considered both ritually and physically unclean. As a consequence, they usually were buried outside towns and cities, especially where natural or artificial caves were available.

A large herd of pigs was there, feeding on the hillside (5:11). A ridge extends down the slope of the Decapolis and meets the Sea of Galilee about two miles south of Kursi/Gergesa. At the sea the ridge breaks off in an embankment that conforms to Mark's description: "the herd of about two thousand rushed down the steep bank into the sea and drowned there" (5:13).

Synagogue leaders (5:22). See comments on Mark 1:21.

A woman suffering from bleeding for twelve years (5:25). The Torah declared that, following her monthly period, a woman was unclean for seven days. A protracted blood flow, however, such as this woman had, rendered her unclean throughout its duration. Those who came into contact with a woman with a blood flow were likewise rendered unclean and banished until evening (Lev. 15:19–27). Josephus's report that "the temple was closed to women during their menstruation" indicates this ruling was followed in Jesus's day.[27] Ironically, the *touch* of Jesus that healed the woman rendered him ritually unclean.

She came up behind him in the crowd and touched his clothing (5:27). Jewish males were required "to make tassels for the corners of their garments, and put a blue cord on the tassel at each corner," the purpose of which was to "remember all the Lord's commands and obey them" (Num. 15:38–39). The reference to the woman touching Jesus's cloak in verse 27 may refer to touching the tassels on his garment, which, in addition to signifying Jesus as an observant Jew, may indicate that the woman associates him with the God of Israel.

People weeping and wailing loudly (5:38). Funeral customs in first-century Judaism required procuring the services of a professional guild of mourners. Rabbi Judah, who lived a century after Jesus, instructed, "Even the poorest person in Israel should hire at least two flute players and one wailing woman."[28] The funeral bier was accompanied from dwelling to grave by the clapping of hands and wailing of mourners.

He . . . came to his hometown (6:1). Although Mark does not specify Jesus's hometown, the references in 1:9 and especially 6:3 imply that Jesus came from Nazareth. Nazareth was an unexceptional town in Israel, unmentioned in the OT, Josephus, rabbinic literature, Mishnah, or Talmud. In the NT it is mentioned a mere twelve times, and not until Julius Africanus, who wrote nearly two centuries after Jesus's birth, is Nazareth mentioned by a Christian writer. Until the reign of Constantine (AD 325) there is no evidence of a church in Nazareth. Beneath the Church of the Annunciation and the Church of St. Joseph in Nazareth is a series of grottoes that date to the time of Jesus. The remains that have been excavated reveal a hamlet of five hundred people at most who dwelled in caves cut into the rocky hillside, the open side of which was faced with stone. Nazareth was an agricultural village that produced wheat, millet, oil, fruit, honey, and wine. Although Nazareth itself was commonplace, the showcase city of Sepphoris lay less than three miles distant, offering Nazareth access to major traffic routes, commerce, and an impressive window into Greco-Roman culture.

Mary . . . James, Joses, Judas, and Simon . . . sisters (6:3). It was unusual in Judaism to refer to the family of an individual, as Jesus's is here, with reference to the mother and siblings but without reference to the father. Calling Jesus "the son of Mary" could have been an insult, insinuating that he was illegitimate. The OT, however, provides a few instances where a man is identified by a mother better known than his father without the insinuation of illegitimacy (e.g., Joab, Abishai, and Asahel are regularly referred to as "the sons of Zeruiah" [2 Sam. 2:18], who was David's sister [1 Chron. 2:16]). Nevertheless, Judaism was a patronymic culture, and the father's name, even when the father was no longer living, usually identified a male child, as a surname does today (e.g., Luke 4:22; John 6:42).

Leaving Jesus's sisters unnamed normally signified in Jewish custom that they had married into other households. Of the four brothers named, Joses (Joseph) and Simon disappear from record, but James later succeeded Peter as head of the church in Jerusalem, and Judas (Jude) appears as the author of the NT book bearing his name (Matt. 13:55; Luke 6:16; Acts 12:17; 15:13; 21:18; 1 Cor. 15:7; Gal. 1:19; 2:9, 12; James 1:1; Jude 1).[29] In the second century AD the reverence ascribed to Mary resulted in the above siblings of Jesus being attributed to Joseph by a former marriage, a tradition that is maintained today by Roman Catholicism and Orthodoxy. The plain sense of Mark 3:31 and 6:3 and of the NT in general, however, is that the children named or alluded to in verse 3 were born of Joseph and Mary.

Jesus Witnesses to Jews (6:6b–7:23)

Send them out in pairs and gave them authority over unclean spirits (6:7). Both Jesus and the early church continued the Jewish custom of sending disciples in pairs (e.g., Eccles. 4:9–11). Traveling in pairs was important in several respects: it provided company, the common counsel and differing gifts of the twosome strengthened the unit, and it increased their credibility, for Torah required two witnesses to establish a valid testimony (Deut. 19:15). Conferring authority over unclean spirits (cf. 3:15) on the disciples was a sign of the dawn of the messianic reign. In sending the Twelve, Jesus did not ordain them to a work separate from his own, but rather to continue and fulfill the work begun in his own ministry (1:34; 3:11–12; 5:8). In 6:8–9 the Twelve are instructed to go with cloak, belt, sandals, and staff in hand—the same items that the Israelites took when they fled Egypt (Exod. 12:11). These items symbolize the urgency of both the exodus and the mission of Jesus, and they remind the Twelve that they are to go free from encumbrances and be dependent on God in their mission for Jesus.

King Herod heard about it (6:14). This king, the second of Herod the Great's four sons, had a long reign over Galilee, extending from 4 BC until AD 39. He was named Herod Antipas and was the son of Malthace, the fourth of Herod the Great's ten wives. The father of Herodias was Aristobulus, the half-brother of Antipas, who was murdered by his father, Herod the Great. As the granddaughter of Herod the Great (through his second wife, Mariamne I), Herodias was thus a niece of Herod Antipas, whom she married. Herod Antipas furthered the magnificent building programs of his father by building the cities of Tiberias and Sepphoris in Galilee. Although he was also shrewd and a lover of luxury, he was less gifted and also less brutal than his father. Jesus's reference to Herod Antipas as "that fox" (Luke 13:32) attests to the king's cunning nature and devices. Antipas persuaded Herodias, the wife of his half-brother Herod Philip (not the tetrarch Philip of Luke 3:1), who was the son of Herod the Great's third wife, Mariamne II, to divorce Herod Philip and marry him. Before marrying Herodias, however, Antipas had to divorce his own wife, who was the daughter of Aretas, king of Nabatea east of the Dead Sea. This is the divorce that John the Baptizer denounced (Mark 6:18). In reprisal for Antipas's divorce of his daughter, Aretas inflicted a crushing defeat on Antipas in AD 36. The reign of Antipas ended in AD 39 when the emperor Caligula banished him and Herodias to Gaul.

So he went and beheaded him in prison (6:27). The Jewish historian Josephus also records the execution of John by Herod Antipas.[30] The Gospels report that John was imprisoned and killed because he condemned Herod's marriage of Herodias, his sister-in-law, whereas Josephus reports that Herod

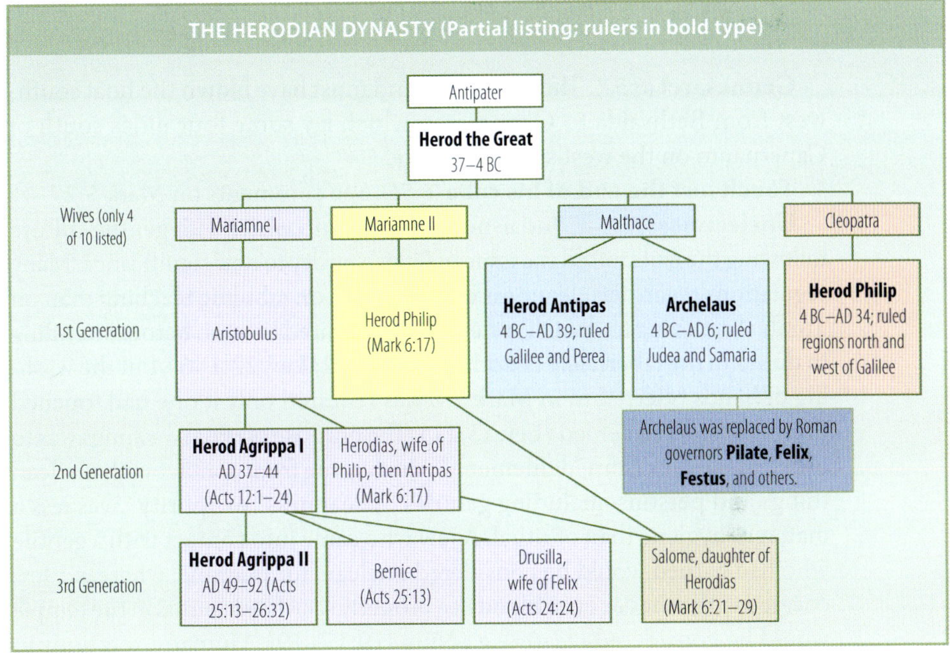

feared that John's influence over the people might lead to a revolt. Josephus reports that John was killed at Machaerus, one of the fortresses of Herod the Great east of the Jordan, a point on which the Gospels are silent. The Gospels emphasize the moral charges John brought against Antipas, whereas Josephus emphasizes the political fears he aroused in Antipas.

Twelve baskets full of pieces (6:43). On baskets, see comments on Mark 8:8.

Five thousand men (6:44). The Greek term *andres* here explicitly denotes five thousand males. The Zealot movement (Acts 5:37) took early root in Galilee in the village of Gamala,[31] which was visible from the region on the north shore of the Sea of Galilee where the feeding of the five thousand took place. According to the Gospel of John (6:15), after the feeding of the five thousand, the people "were about to come and take [Jesus] by force to make him king." This statement of the Fourth Gospel, combined with the five thousand men in the proximity of Gamala, suggests that the crowd may have intended to conscript Jesus into a messianic uprising.

He saw them straining at the oars, because the wind was against them (6:48). See comments on Mark 1:16.

Very early in the morning (6:48). "Very early in the morning" is a paraphrase of the Greek, which reads "the fourth watch of the night" (three to six o'clock in the morning). Mark follows the four Roman watches of the night rather than the three Jewish watches, presumably for the benefit of his Roman readers.

Gennesaret (6:53). The battering wind must have blown the boat southwest from Bethsaida to Gennesaret, which lay some four miles south of Capernaum on the west side of the lake.

Touch just the end of his robe (6:56). See comments on Mark 5:27.

Uncleanness (7:1–4). Judaism's increased encounter with gentile culture following the exile raised the issue of Jewish purity to new significance. Many regulations regarding cleanness depend more on rabbinic teaching than on Torah. According to the OT, priests were required to wash before attending to duties in the tabernacle (Exod. 30:19; 40:12; Lev. 22:1–6), but the washing of hands referred to in Mark 7:2 was required only if one had touched things considered defiled (Lev. 15:11). The purpose of ritual washings was to protect Israelites from "defilement," which came from contact with unclean things and persons, including gentiles. "Cleanness" or "purity" was less a matter of hygiene than of ritual. A Jew who came into contact with a gentile who had bathed would be considered unclean, for example, whereas a Jew covered with ashes or even blood of a properly sacrificial animal in the temple would be considered clean (e.g., Num. 19:17–19). Human excretions in most forms (spittle, semen, menstruation, etc.) were considered unclean, as were women following childbirth. Uncleanness also attended dead persons (corpses) or animals (carrion), most creatures that crawled, idols, and people such as lepers, Samaritans, and gentiles. The ministry of Jesus

These ruins at Machaerus are the remains of Herod's palace. The pillars in the background are part of a reconstruction and surround one of the courtyards.

brought him into contact with lepers (1:40), tax collectors (2:14), the gentile Decapolis (5:1), menstruating women (5:25), and corpses (5:35), all of which in various ways were considered ritually unclean.

The tradition of the elders (7:5). Sadducees accepted the written Torah (first five books of the OT) alone as authoritative, but Pharisees additionally accepted the oral tradition based upon it.[32] By the time of Jesus, Pharisees considered the unwritten oral tradition as authoritative as written Torah. For Pharisees, written Torah set forth "policy," whereas oral Torah declared the proper application of that policy in pertinent situations. "The tradition of the elders" in this pericope refers to the oral tradition, which, by about AD 200, was compiled and codified in the Mishnah (the "second giving of the law"). Rabbis considered the Mishnah "a fence around the Torah,"[33] "fence" being understood as proper oral interpretation of written Torah in specific cases.

Corban (7:11). Jesus critiques "the tradition of the elders" (see comment on Mark 7:5) on the issue of *corban*. *Corban* (Heb. *qorban*, "offering") was an example of the evolving rabbinic oral instruction regarding the consecration of certain goods to the Lord (Lev. 27:28; Num. 18:14). The principle behind *corban* was similar to the principle behind deferred giving today, in which capital is retained by persons during their lifetimes but surrendered for a stipulated cause at their deaths. Here in verse 11 a son declares his property to be *corban*, meaning that he bequeaths it to the temple at his death while retaining control of it during his life. In effect—and this is the reason why Jesus censures it—*corban* deprives the man's elderly parents of financial support from their son. Jesus condemns this pretense of piety as a breaking of the fifth commandment. In the words of T. W. Manson, "A man goes through the formality of vowing something to God, not that he may give it to God, but in order to prevent some other person from having it."[34]

Jesus Witnesses to Gentiles (7:24–8:9)

Tyre (7:24). Tyre (southern Lebanon today) was a city in gentile Phoenicia that lay north of Galilee. Phoenicia had a long history of antagonism toward Israel. The region had been the home of Jezebel, wife of King Ahab, whose pagan prophets had overrun the northern kingdom in Elijah's day (1 Kings 16:31–33). The wealth and fear of Tyre was of concern to the OT prophets (Ezek. 26:17; Zech. 9:3). In the second century BC Tyre, Ptolemais, and Sidon sided with the Seleucids in their effort to eradicate the religion of the Jews and co-opt Jewish Palestine as a Hellenistic kingdom (1 Macc. 5:15). In response to this attempted annihilation, Jewish patriots launched the Maccabean Revolt to preserve Israel. For Josephus, the inhabitants of Tyre were the Jews' "bitterest enemies."[35] Jesus's journey to the region might be considered an enacted prophecy, specifically, that he was the Messiah not only of Israel but also of its gentile antagonists.

Decapolis (7:31). See comments on Mark 5:1.

Seven large baskets full of leftover pieces (8:8). Here the Greek word for "basket" (*spyris*) differs from the word for "basket" (*kophinos*) in the feeding of the five thousand (6:43). *Kophinos* may have signified a smaller, perhaps stiff, wicker basket, whereas a *spyris* probably was larger and more flexible. Luke describes the apostle Paul being lowered from the city wall of Damascus in a *spyris* (Acts 9:25).

The Declaration of Jesus as the Suffering Messiah (8:10–9:29)

The region of Dalmanutha (8:10). This is the only mention in all ancient literature of Dalmanutha, a fishing village on the west shore of the Sea of Galilee about three miles north of Tiberias. The name of the village may derive from the Hebrew radicals *dylm,* meaning "wall," with reference to the cliffs or "wall" of Arbel to the west. Dalmanutha was either near or a variant name for Magadan (Matt. 15:39; some ancient manuscripts: "Magdala"). An anchorage was discovered at Magadan in 1971, and also at Magadan a 2013 excavation revealed the pavement and a beautiful stone Torah podium of the oldest synagogue yet discovered in Galilee.

Leaven (8:15). Leaven, or yeast, ferments in dough and causes it to rise. It is used here as a metaphor for something that appears more impressive or important than it is: the teaching of the Pharisees and Sadducees (Matt. 16:12), which Jesus calls "hypocrisy" (Luke 12:1).

Bethsaida (8:22). Bethsaida was a city in Gaulanitis (which belonged to the tetrarchy of Philip) that lay immediately east of the point where the headwaters of the Jordan River flow into the Sea of Galilee. The chief industry of Bethsaida was fishing, which accounts for the name of the city, which means "house of the fisher." Bethsaida Julias was built (as was Caesarea Philippi) by Philip, and named after Caesar Augustus's daughter Julia. Three of Jesus's twelve disciples—Peter, Andrew, and Philip—were from Bethsaida (John 1:44).

Laying his hands on him (8:23). Laying on of hands occurred in three contexts in the OT: in dedicating sacrifices to God (e.g., Exod. 29:10; Lev. 1:4), when Levites were installed as priests (Num. 8:10), and for general blessings (Gen. 48:14; Deut. 34:9). Jesus placed hands on people to heal them, and he did so frequently (Mark 1:41; 5:23; 7:33; 8:22, 23, 25). The hand is often a symbol of power in the OT, including the power of God. Hands were also laid on animals or persons in the OT as a means of transferring them from profane to sacred purposes. Jesus's hands, however, did not transfer power *from* the profane to the sacred, but rather transferred sacred power *to* the profane, including women (Luke 13:13); children (Luke 8:54); unclean, sinful, and suffering humanity (Luke 4:40); lepers (Luke 5:13); and gentiles (Mark 7:33).

Caesarea Philippi (8:27). Caesarea Philippi (not to be confused with Caesarea Maritima on the coast) lay in the tetrarchy of Philip, twenty-five miles north of Bethsaida. The city derived its name from Philip, who refurbished and named it in honor of Caesar Augustus.[36] The headwaters of the Jordan River gushed forth from the foot of Mount Hermon at Caesarea Philippi. This natural wonder may have accounted for the presence of cult sites of Greek gods and goddesses of nature, and especially the pastoral god Pan, at Caesarea Philippi. The Seleucids defeated the Ptolemies at Caesarea Philippi in 200 BC and proceeded to take control of all Palestine, thereby triggering the Maccabean Revolt in response from Jewish patriots in 168 BC. Caesarea Philippi demonstrated a long history of allegiance to Rome: Agrippa II attempted to dedicate the city to the emperor Nero, and following the Jewish Revolt in AD 70, Titus sacrificed Jewish prisoners in mock military battles or by throwing them to beasts. Ironically, it was in this border region between Israel and Phoenicia, with its long history of paganism and polytheism, that Jesus's disciples first declared him to be the Messiah!

Elijah (8:28). Elijah played a major role in first-century Judaism as a figure of hope and future help. Other figures such as Abraham, Moses, and David had played more important roles in the OT, but Elijah alone had been assumed bodily to heaven (2 Kings 2:11), where he was believed to strengthen

This aerial view shows the area around the shrine to the god Pan (notice the grotto), for which Caesarea Philippi was well known.

the faithful and help the needy, and from which he would return to usher in the day of the Lord (Mal. 3:1; 4:5–6).

You are the Messiah (8:29). Here "Messiah" translates the Greek word *christos*, which is a translation of the Hebrew word *mashiah*; in both Greek and Hebrew the term means "anointed." In the OT three classes of people were anointed for special tasks: prophets, priests, and kings. The Jewish concept of messiah developed from the third class, kings (e.g., 2 Sam. 7; Ps. 2). As the Israelite monarchy failed and, in the year 586 BC, succumbed to Babylonian domination, a hope arose, and from the hope a belief, that God would raise up a future king like David to fulfill God's promises to Israel (Jer. 23:5). The OT does not develop a formal doctrine of the messiah; indeed, the title "the messiah" occurs only rarely in the OT (e.g., Dan. 9:26). The pre-Christian understanding of messiah was that of an eschatological king through whom God would establish an everlasting earthly kingdom. When used in conjunction with Jesus's name ("Jesus Christ"), "Christ" is not a name but a title—that is, Jesus, the Messiah. "Messiah" is not synonymous with other titles of Jesus. Unlike "Son of God," "Messiah" signified not an eternal divine being, but rather a perfect human king chosen by God who would deliver Israel from enemies and usher in an era of peace and obedience to Torah.[37] Nor is Isaiah's "servant of the Lord" or Daniel's "son of man" associated with messianic connotations in the OT.

The elders, chief priests, and scribes (8:31). The Sanhedrin, the most authoritative ruling body in Judaism, numbered seventy-one members who were drawn from three Jewish offices: scribes, elders, and chief priests (see the article "The Sanhedrin"). The holders of these three offices could be either Sadducees or Pharisees, although the chief priest was always a Sadducee, and perhaps the majority of the Sanhedrin was as well. "Chief priests" usually occurs in the plural, which signifies a priestly dynasty that included the sitting chief priest and his predecessors and family members. Jesus was crucified when Caiaphas was chief priest (ruled AD 18–36). Caiaphas was preceded as chief priest by his father-in-law, Annas (ruled AD 6–15 [John 18:13, 24]), and was succeeded by Jonathan and his brother Theophilus (see Acts 4:6).[38] Scribes, sometimes referred to as teachers of the law, were experts in Torah and consultants to the Sanhedrin (see comments on Mark 1:22).

Take up his cross, and follow me (8:34). See the article "Crucifixion." Totalitarian regimes require terror apparatuses, and the terror apparatus of the Roman Empire was crucifixion. Death by crucifixion was both cruel, inflicting intense and prolonged pain, and shameful, for crucifixions were public spectacles. Roman citizens were exempted from death by crucifixion (although they could be executed by other means, such as beheading). Crucifixion was the most powerful and brutal symbol of Roman oppression, reserved for the lower social classes who were not Roman citizens, especially slaves and prisoners of war. In 71 BC, when the Roman general Crassus quashed the slave rebellion led by Spartacus, he crucified six thousand slaves on the Appian Way. In AD 64 the emperor Nero crucified and incinerated Christians whom he falsely accused of setting fire to Rome. Here, Jesus uses the cross as an image of discipleship to signify the total claim of the gospel on the believer's life.

Mount Hermon and Mount Tabor, the two most likely sites of Jesus's transfiguration.

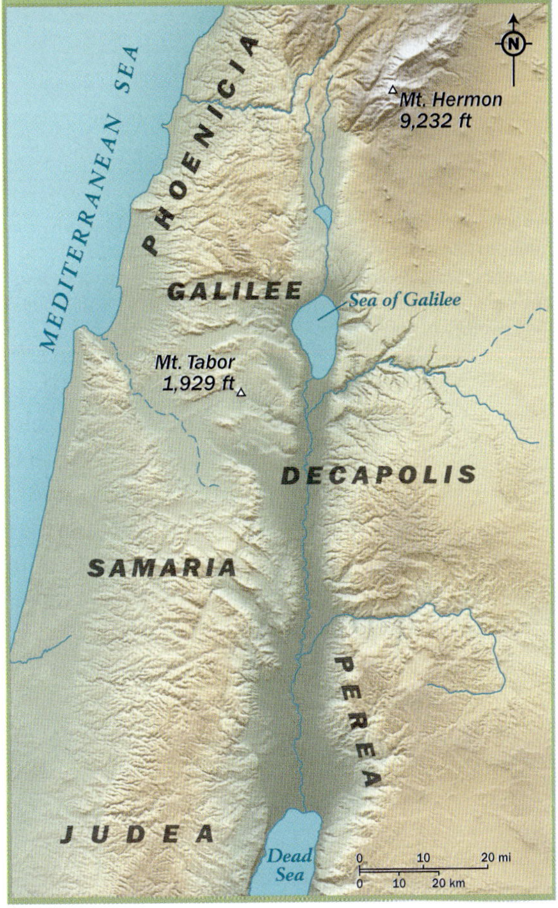

A high mountain (9:2). In Scripture mountains often are places of divine revelation. On the Mount of Transfiguration Jesus reveals his divine nature in the glorious presence of Moses and Elijah. Mark does not say where the mountain was located. Dome-shaped Mount Tabor in southern Galilee is often thought to be the site of the transfiguration. But Tabor is a great distance south of Caesarea Philippi, where Peter confessed Jesus as the Messiah. Mark 9:2 reports Jesus and the disciples being alone on a high mountain, but Tabor is not particularly high, and they would not have been alone, for in the first century the summit of Mount Tabor was surrounded by a wall in which people lived.[39] Mount Hermon is the more probable site of the transfiguration, for it is high, its summit would have been solitary, and, most importantly, it dominated the region of Caesarea Philippi, where Peter confessed Jesus as the Messiah prior to the transfiguration.

Elijah and Moses (9:4). In extrabiblical Jewish literature several OT figures are expected as precursors of the messianic era, but not Moses and Elijah.[40] The transfiguration narrative, however, likely recalls Mal. 4:4–6, where both Moses and Elijah appear as heralds of the day of the Lord.[41] In "talking with Jesus," Mark portrays them holding an audience with Jesus as their superior.

Amulets were commonly worn to ward off demonic activity, and freeborn Roman boys were given pendants (bullae) to wear to provide protection against evil spirits. The young boy standing between his parents in this funerary relief wears a Roman bulla (first century AD).

A cloud appeared, overshadowing them (9:7). In Scripture the cloud frequently symbolizes God's presence and glory. The story of Moses in Exod. 24:15–16 offers a close parallel to Jesus's transfiguration. Mark's description of the cloud overshadowing or "enveloping" (Gk. *episkiazō*) the disciples recalls the cloud that filled the tabernacle with divine glory (Exod. 40:35; cf. 1 Kings 8:10–11). The divine overshadowing of the tabernacle with God's presence and glory prefigured the ultimate overshadowing of Jesus and the disciples with God's presence and glory.

Elijah must come first (9:11). See comments on Mark 9:4.

He foams at the mouth, grinds his teeth, and becomes rigid (9:18). The boy's symptoms—convulsions, foaming at the mouth, outcries, lockjaw, rigidity, loss of consciousness—are those of tonic-clonic (grand mal) epileptic seizures (so identified in Matt. 17:15). Mark attributes the seizures to an "unclean spirit" (9:25), making his description of both the boy's suffering and father's anguish more powerful, and emphasizing that when human hopes are exhausted, hope can be expected from Jesus.

This kind can come out by nothing but prayer (9:29). Mark records only three instances of Jesus praying (1:35; 6:46; 14:32–39), each when he is alone and facing challenges in his mission and ministry. Jesus also commands the disciples to pray when facing spiritual temptations (14:38), and he enjoins prayer in adverse circumstances (13:18). He declares the temple a place of prayer (11:17), but he warns against praying in ostentation and pride (12:40). The most important text on prayer in Mark is Jesus's teaching on the relationship between prayer, faith, and forgiveness in 11:24–25. The present passage also introduces prayer in the context of faith and spiritual power. Prayer is the focusing of faith in specific requests to God. Linking prayer with faith teaches that spiritual power is *God's* power and promise to save, on which believers wait in trust.

Lessons in Discipleship (9:30–50)

Capernaum (9:33). See comments on Mark 1:21.

If anyone wants to be first, he must be . . . servant of all (9:35). The verbal form of the Greek word for "servant" (*diakonos*) in this verse often

An ancient millstone used to crush olives (Mark 9:42).

refers to waiting tables (Luke 17:8; John 12:2; Acts 6:2). The disciples, like most people, consider serving others beneath their status. In his selfless service of others, however, Jesus fills the concept of servant with new meaning: the servant is a visible manifestation of God's love (Luke 22:27). It is not the gifted and privileged who are destined for greatness in God's economy, but ordinary persons who choose to serve others in the name of Christ.

Everyone will be salted with fire (9:49). Fire and salt are cardinal metaphors of discipleship, fire because it purifies and salt because it is a preservative. Fire and salt played equally cardinal roles in temple sacrifices. A burnt offering in the temple (whether an unblemished bull, ram, or bird) needed to be wholly consumed by fire in order to be acceptable. All temple sacrifices also needed to be accompanied by salt (Lev. 2:13), which itself was a sign of the covenant (Num. 18:19). Fire and salt in the present context appear to be symbols of the costs of discipleship and total claim of the gospel on one's life (Rom. 12:1). Here, testing by fire is an offering pleasing to God, a seasoning or salting with fire.

On the Way to Jerusalem (10:1–52)

The region of Judea and across the Jordan (10:1). The shortest route from Galilee to Jerusalem followed the ridge of the Samaritan hill country connecting them both. It was more common, however, for Galilean travelers to take a longer route that proceeded south through Perea on the east side of the Jordan, then crossed the river at Jericho and climbed from there west up to Jerusalem. This latter route is implied here in 10:1. This longer route was preferred because it kept travelers within Galilee and Perea, which were ruled by Herod Antipas, and because it skirted the ethnically mixed and potential hostile region of Samaria (John 4:9).

Is it lawful for a man to divorce his wife? (10:2). See the article "Jewish Marriage Customs." The chief purpose of marriage in ancient Judaism was the establishment and continuance of the family, and its chief enemy was childlessness rather than marital discontentment of husband and wife. Jewish law clearly permitted divorce (Deut. 24:1–2), and thus the Pharisees' question here is either misleading or a trap. Divorce was not questioned in first-century Judaism, only the *grounds* for divorce. The most conservative rabbinic position allowed for divorce on the grounds of adultery alone, whereas more liberal rabbis allowed a man to divorce his wife for any number of "indecencies." The position on divorce set forth by Jesus in 10:10–13 was unique in Judaism. Jesus is the only known Jewish rabbi who unconditionally affirmed the permanence of the marriage union, and he lay responsibility for the permanence of marriage on both husbands and wives.[42]

Let the little children come to me (10:14). The ancient world rarely displayed the affection for children common in the modern West. Like that of women, children's position in society was largely determined by their relationship to adult males. Sons were of particular importance because they increased and continued the workforce of the family into which they were born, whereas daughters contributed to the economies of other families into which they married. Until children became productive family members, childhood generally was regarded as an unavoidable interim until adulthood, which a boy attained at age thirteen. The sympathy of Jesus for children is unique in both ancient Judaism and early Christian literature.

He laid his hands on them and blessed them (10:16). See comments on Mark 8:23.

He had many possessions (10:22). Wealth and possessions are regarded both positively and negatively in Scripture. They frequently are regarded as a sign of divine blessing (Job 1:10; 42:10; Ps. 128:1–2; Isa. 3:10). Poverty, by contrast, was regarded by the rabbis as an affliction that outweighed all other adversities combined. Scripture, however, also champions the poor, including the sojourner, widow, orphan, and fatherless. This latter view predominates in the NT, and especially in the teaching and ministry of Jesus, who stresses God's exaltation of the poor above wealth and power (Luke 1:46–55 [cf. 1 Sam. 2:1–10]; Mark 10:21; 12:41–44). Poverty itself does not seem to be the ideal, but rather the awareness that poverty awakens our need of God and indebtedness to God and others. Wealth, by contrast, tempts one to self-satisfaction and pride, both of which compete against faith and obedience.

A camel . . . through the eye of a needle (10:25). This statement is an example of Jesus's use of humorous hyperbole. Attempts to circumvent its trenchant point, by arguing, for example, that the Greek word for "camel" (*kamēlon*) should read "rope" (*kamilon*), are without reliable textual evidence. It is nearly as impossible, of course, for a rope to go through the eye of a needle as it is for a camel to do so. Nor is its offense resolved by supposing "the eye of the needle" to be a small gate through which camels crawled on their knees after the city gates of Jerusalem had been closed for the night. Not until the ninth century AD is there evidence for such a gate; moreover, the explanation moralizes the

Jesus says that it is easier for a camel to go through the eye of a needle than for the rich to enter God's kingdom (Mark 10:25). These bone needles from the Roman period were found at Sepphoris, just a few miles from Nazareth.

saying—as though the rich may enter God's kingdom if they humble themselves. Attempts to tame this humorous hyperbole nullify its importance.

Allow us to sit at your right and at your left in your glory (10:37). Currents of honor and shame ran strongly and deeply in ancient Near East societies. In Jewish social settings preeminent honor belonged to the person seated in the center of the company, followed by those seated to that person's right and left, respectively.

Are you able to drink the cup I drink or to be baptized with the baptism I am baptized with? (10:38). In the OT a cup is often a metaphor of God's judgment (e.g., Jer. 25:15–28), and submersion in water a metaphor of calamity (Ps. 42:7). Both metaphors are used likewise here as metaphors of trials and hardships (although not necessarily of martyrdom) that James and John will endure as disciples.

Jericho (10:46). Jericho, one of the oldest continuously inhabited cities in the world, lies 720 feet below sea level and twenty torturous miles northeast of Jerusalem, which is nearly 3,200 feet higher in elevation. Jericho is a verdant and productive oasis surrounded by extreme aridity. The description of Bartimaeus begging beside the road stigmatizes him as a social outcast.

Jesus Teaches in the Temple in Jerusalem (11:1–13:37)

Bethpage and Bethany (11:1). The order in which these two villages are named seems wrong today because the modern road runs from Bethany to Bethpage to Jerusalem. Jesus followed the ancient Roman road, however, which led southwest from Jericho along modern Wadi Umm esh Shid and then up to the summit of the Mount of Olives at or near Bethphage ("house of unripe figs"). From Bethphage a steep road ran down to Bethany, just over half a mile to the south on the east side of the Mount of Olives. The description here in 11:1 accords with the ancient itinerary.

Mount of Olives (11:1). To the east of Jerusalem a north-south ridge rising twenty-six hundred feet above sea level, and three hundred feet higher than the city itself, forms the Mount of Olives. Olivet, as it was also called, was a place of worship already in David's time (2 Sam. 15:32). A long Jewish tradition associated the Mount of Olives with the end time. Ezekiel 11:23 records a vision of the glory of the Lord departing from Jerusalem at its destruction in 586 BC and settling on the Mount of Olives. Zechariah 14:4, similarly, regards the Mount of Olives as the site of final judgment, and both rabbis and the Jewish historian Josephus associated it with the coming of the Messiah.[43] Mark rarely mentions place names, but he names Olivet perhaps to signal the messianic significance of Jesus's entry into Jerusalem.

A colt . . . on which no one has ever sat (11:2). An animal that had never been ridden or worn a yoke was deemed worthy for sacred functions in Israel (Num. 19:2; Deut. 21:3). Such an animal was thus an appropriate mount for the messianic king.

Blessed is he who comes in the name of the Lord (11:9). The crowd's acclamation was a quotation from Ps. 118:26, which Jewish pilgrims recited as they entered Jerusalem. The one blessed refers to the pilgrim entering the temple rather than to the Messiah. The waving of branches, whether palm, willow, myrtle, or citrus, and shouting of "Hosanna" (11:8–9) normally were associated with the fall Festival of Shelters rather than with Passover.[44]

He went into Jerusalem and into the temple (11:11). See the article "The Jerusalem Temple." The temple referred to here is the second Jewish temple, which was constructed by Zerubbabel (Ezra 3). The expansion of the second temple was begun by Herod the Great in 20 BC and was still in progress in Jesus's day (13:1).

The temple was divided into four areas. The largest division, the Court of Gentiles, was an open-air quadrangle some 500 yards long and 325 yards wide that was surrounded by a portico. The columns of the portico, which were 18 feet in circumference at the base, 30 feet high, and crowned with Corinthian capitals, supported an ornamental carved ceiling.[45] As the name suggests, the Court of Gentiles was open to non-Jews. Its vast thirty-five acres were a religious marketplace on which proper worship and financial revenues of the Sanhedrin depended. Sheep and doves were sold for sacrifice, and foreign currencies were exchanged into the Tyrian shekel, the currency most closely resembling the Hebrew shekel (of pure metal, and with no image) commanded in Exod. 30:13–16. According to Josephus, 256,500 Passover lambs were sacrificed when construction of Herod's temple was completed in AD 66![46] The three remaining divisions were the Court of Women, which was accessible only to Jewish women and children; the Court of Israel, which was accessible only to circumcised Jewish males; and the holy of holies, which was accessible only to the chief priest on Yom Kippur. These

Jesus's triumphal entry would have taken him down the western slopes of the Mount of Olives, across the Kidron Valley, and up through the gates into the city of Jerusalem. This is the view from the Mount of Olives into the Kidron Valley, with the walls of the Old City of Jerusalem and the modern Temple Mount in sight.

three divisions made up the temple sanctuary proper, a gleaming white free-standing edifice 150 yards long by 100 yards wide that occupied the center of the Court of Gentiles and faced east. A wall around the sanctuary, called *Soreq*, prohibited non-Jews from entering the sanctuary proper, which was open only to Jews (Eph. 2:14). The following warning was posted on the *Soreq* in Greek, Latin, and Aramaic: "No foreigner may enter within the railing and enclosure that surround the temple. Anyone apprehended shall have himself to blame for his consequent death."

If anyone says to this mountain, "Be lifted up and thrown into the sea" (11:23). Herod the Great built a fortress refuge at Herodion, about three miles south of Jerusalem, at which he surrounded a high keep with an earthen embankment of soil that he had removed from an adjacent hill. The former hill was leveled, and the embankment around the keep formed a new geological feature that resembled a volcano in shape. Herodion, which is still visible today from the east side of the Mount of Olives, may have suggested to Jesus the image of a mountain being moved.

The chief priests and scribes and elders (11:27). See comments on Mark 8:31.

A man planted a vineyard (12:1). The most common agricultural products of Galilee included olives, figs, and especially grapes. Production of grapes, known as viticulture, entailed intense labor and deferred gains, for the first grape harvest usually occurred five years after planting. The sending of the owner's son to collect the fruit of the harvest reflects a common practice in Jesus's day of absentee landowners who hired local farmers to raise their crops and supply them with the proceeds.

Taxes to Caesar (12:14). The tax referred to was an imperial poll tax first instituted in AD 6, which required of all Jewish males the annual payment of a denarius (12:15). A denarius was the average daily wage in Palestine (Matt. 20:2, 9). The obverse of the coin was stamped with a semidivine bust of Tiberius Caesar (AD 14–37) and the Latin inscription (abbreviated): *Tiberius Caesar Divi Augusti Filius Augustus* ("Tiberius Caesar Augustus, Son of the Divine Augustus"). On the reverse side was an image of Livia, the mother of Tiberius, and the inscription *Pontifex Maximus* ("High Priest").

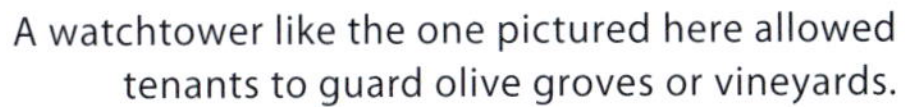
A watchtower like the one pictured here allowed tenants to guard olive groves or vineyards.

Sadducees (12:18). The two dominant Jewish religious parties in first-century-AD Palestine were the Sadducees and Pharisees (see comments on Mark 2:18; see the article "Pharisees and Sadducees"). Both parties appear to have arisen when the Maccabees revolted against Seleucid tyranny in the second century BC. Despite their common origin, their beliefs differed greatly. Pharisees believed in the sovereignty of God, whereas Sadducees believed in human free will; Pharisees accepted the existence of angels and demons, both of which Sadducees denied; Pharisees believed the written tradition (Torah, Prophets, Writings), as well as the oral tradition based upon it, to be inspired by God, whereas for Sadducees written Torah alone was inspired. As this story here indicates, Sadducees denied bodily resurrection from the dead (12:18; cf. Acts 23:8), which Pharisees affirmed. The Sadducees were fewer in number than Pharisees (perhaps twenty-five hundred compared to six thousand), but as an aristocratic dynasty that was both in charge of the temple in Jerusalem and willing to cooperate with the Roman occupation, Sadducees were wealthier and more politically influential than Pharisees.

The seven had married her (12:23). See the article "Jewish Marriage Customs." The riddle that the Sadducees propose to Jesus assumes an OT practice known as levirate marriage, in which a man was expected to marry a childless widow of his deceased brother in order to bring forth children from the widow, who would preserve the deceased man's name and retain his inheritance within the family (Gen. 38:8–10; Deut. 25:5–6). The stories of Tamar (Gen. 38), Ruth (Ruth 3–4), and Tobit (Tob. 3:7–15) reflect the practice of levirate marriage. The primary purpose of levirate marriage was social rather than sexual—that is, to preserve honor and property within a Jewish family line, and also to prevent Jews from intermarrying with gentiles.

The Messiah is the son of David (12:35). The first reference to a Davidic deliverer occurs in 2 Sam. 7:12 (further, Isa. 9; 11; Jer. 30:9; Ezek. 34:23). This deliverer was originally not identified with the Messiah/Christ, but a century before the birth of Jesus the identification of a Davidic Messiah was made and accepted.[47] Thereafter Ps. 110, which is quoted here, was customarily interpreted messianically. The point that Jesus makes in this debate is subtle: the Messiah does not follow in David's wake, but rather Davidic kingship follows in the Messiah's wake. The Messiah, in other words, sets the pattern for David, not David for the Messiah.

The crowd dropped money into the treasury (12:41). In addition to being a place of worship, the Jerusalem temple was also a repository of vast amounts of wealth that were stored and administered by the temple. The Court of Women was one place where monies and temple offerings were collected in thirteen Shofar-chests (see comments on Mark 11:11).[48] These trumpet-shaped receptacles resembled a ram's horn (Heb. *shofar*), positioned

The widow's offering was two small copper coins. These were *lepta*, like the one shown here.

with the small tapered end upward as a prevention of theft. The "two tiny coins" deposited by the widow were *lepta* (12:42), the smallest coins in circulation. For the benefit of Roman readers not familiar with Jewish coinage, Mark converts the sum into the Greek equivalent of a Roman coin, a *quadrans*.

What massive stones! What impressive buildings! (13:1). For the plan of the temple, see comments on Mark 11:11. The magnificence of the temple's stones and structures justly impressed the disciples at Passover around AD 30.

Mount of Olives (13:3). See comments on Mark 11:1.

The abomination of desolation (13:14). Three cryptic references in the book of Daniel (9:27; 11:31; 12:11) mention a scandal that would profane the temple in Jerusalem as an "abomination that causes desolation." The phrase reappears in 1 Macc. 1:54 with reference to Antiochus IV (Epiphanes), the Syrian general who outraged the Jews in 168 BC by erecting an altar to Zeus in the temple of Jerusalem and sacrificing a sow on it. The phrase in question thus originally referred to the sacrilege committed by Antiochus IV. The use of the phrase here in Mark recalls the abomination of Antiochus, but with reference to a future event that would be equally outrageous and more cataclysmic. That event appears to be the Roman destruction of the temple and Jerusalem itself in AD 70, which was unforgettably chronicled by Josephus in *Jewish War* and regarded by early Christians as a fulfillment of "the abomination of desolation."

The Son of Man coming in clouds with great power and glory (13:26). On the Son of Man, see comments on Mark 2:10. The vision of "one like a son of man . . . coming with the clouds of heaven" appears in Dan. 7:13. In the OT clouds often are symbols of God's presence and glory (see comments on Mark 9:7). The "great power and glory" with which the Son of Man will come in the future stand in ironic contrast to the humiliated Son of Man (8:31; 9:31; 10:33–34), crucified as a common criminal (Phil. 2:8).

The Disciples Abandon Jesus (14:1–72)

The Passover and the Festival of Unleavened Bread (14:1). Passover commemorated the exodus from Egypt (Exod. 12), the foundational event in Israel's history. Passover was celebrated each spring in Jerusalem by the ritual sacrifice in the temple of an unblemished male lamb or goat one year old (Exod. 12:5) on the afternoon of 14 Nisan (March/April); the lamb was then eaten after sunset on 15 Nisan in family gatherings (Exod. 12:6–20; Num. 9:2–14; Deut. 16:1–8). Following Passover, the weeklong Festival of Unleavened Bread (Exod. 12:15–20; 23:15; 34:18; Deut. 16:1–8) commemorated Israel's hasty departure from Egypt when there had been no time to allow dough to rise. Jews observed the festival by ridding their food and homes of all yeast. Mark distinguishes between Passover and the Festival of Unleavened Bread in 14:1, but their close relationship often caused them to be referred to as one event.

An alabaster jar of very expensive perfume of pure nard (14:3). Nard was an expensive aromatic oil extracted from the root of an Indian herb of the same name (see Song 1:12; 4:13–14). Matthew informs us that a normal day's wage in Palestine was a denarius (Matt. 20:2); a vial of nard worth three hundred denarii was therefore extremely valuable, the equivalent of a year's earnings. If this woman's nard was a family heirloom, which it may have been, then its dearness to her may even have exceeded its monetary value.

A man carrying a jar of water (14:13). The meeting may have occurred in the vicinity of the Pool of Siloam on Mount Zion, where Jerusalemites could draw water that had been diverted by Hezekiah's tunnel from the Gihon Spring, which was Jerusalem's only natural water source, into the city proper. In first-century Judaism water normally was carried by women or slaves. A male water carrier would have been conspicuous in the crowd, indicating perhaps that he was an Essene, for Essenes were celibate and carried their own water. The Essene Quarter was located in south Jerusalem near the Pool of Siloam.

The Mount of Olives (14:26). See comments on Mark 11:1.

Gethsemane (14:32). "Gethsemane," which comes from the Hebrew/Aramaic word *gat-shemene* ("oil press"), was the name of an olive grove east of Jerusalem in the Kidron Valley at the foot of the Mount of Olives where Jesus often gathered with his followers (Luke 22:39; John 18:1–2).

Take this cup away from me (14:36). See comments on Mark 10:38.

He went up to Jesus and said, "Rabbi!" and kissed him (14:45). The kiss of Judas is as puzzling as it is infamous, for it is the only time that Scripture records Jesus being greeted by a kiss. Kisses were practiced in Israel as gestures of honor and affection (1 Sam. 10:1; 2 Sam. 19:39; Luke 7:38; 15:20; Acts 20:37). The kiss of Judas, however, was a gesture of love used as a cloak for treachery, perhaps recalling Joab's kiss of Amasa before stabbing him (2 Sam. 20:9–10), or Jacob's kiss of his father Isaac as part of his deception in gaining Esau's blessing (Gen. 27:27).

Expensive perfumed oils, like the one made from nard that the woman used to anoint Jesus, were sealed in alabaster jars similar to the one shown here.

A certain young man, wearing nothing but a linen cloth . . . left the linen cloth behind and ran away naked (14:51–52). The identity of this unnamed and naked fugitive has been clothed in many speculations, of which perhaps the most intriguing is that verse 51 is an "anonymous signature" for the author of the Gospel, Mark himself. This relatively modern theory is possible, but it cannot be proved. Whoever he was, the naked fugitive symbolizes the flight of all Jesus's disciples.

They led Jesus away to the high priest (14:53). See comments on Mark 8:31. The church of St. Peter in Gallicantu ("cockcrow"), about half a mile to the southwest of Gethsemane on the slopes of Mount Zion, commemorates the traditional site of the house of Caiaphas, who was chief priest when Jesus was crucified. Rock-hewn cisterns and grottos dating to the Herodian period (37 BC–AD 70), which might have been used as prison cells, have been excavated beneath the church. The trial of Jesus in 14:53–65 violates the instructions in the Mishnah for such matters, however. The Sanhedrin customarily met in the temple,[49] whereas Mark reports a trial in the villa of the high priest. A quorum of twenty-three members of the Sanhedrin was required in capital cases, with a second trial the following day to confirm a verdict of guilty. Mishnah required both to be daytime trials, and neither on the eve of Sabbath or a festival.[50] In order for the charge of blasphemy to be sustained, the accused had to have cursed God's name, the punishment of which was death by stoning, followed by hanging the corpse from a tree.[51] The trial recorded here by Mark probably violates most of these prescriptions. Mark appears to describe a rump session intent on a hasty conviction of Jesus rather than a formal sitting of the Sanhedrin.

You're also a Galilean (14:70). Peter's accent or dialect, whether he was speaking in Aramaic or Hebrew, likely betrayed him as a Galilean.

Pontius Pilate Condemns Jesus to Crucifixion (Mark 15:1–41)

Pilate (15:1). See the article "Pontius Pilate." Pilate ruled as the fifth Roman "prefect" (governor) of Palestine in AD 26–37. The prefect's official residence was at Caesarea Maritima, but during festivals, and especially Passover, his presence was required in Jerusalem, where he and his Praetorian Guard most probably lodged at Herod's palace on the western wall (Jaffa Gate today). Jesus likely appeared before Pilate in Herod's palace. Pilate disdained Jewish customs and was intractable in the face of Jewish opposition, and eventually he was banished by the emperor Gaius (Caligula) for excessive brutality in dealing with Jewish grievances. Pilate's "inflexibility, stubbornness, and cruelty," in the words of Philo,[52] are filtered in the NT

Gospels in portraits that are more sympathetic of him. Particularly Mark, who most probably wrote for Christians in Rome during the reign of Nero, had to walk a narrow ridge of reporting the horrors of crucifixion without appearing to be politically subversive, the latter of which would have endangered Christians throughout the empire. The Roman Caesars were totalitarian rulers, which made "King of the Jews" (15:2) a serious charge against Jesus. Pilate did not seem to regard the charge as sufficient cause for execution, but neither did he think Jesus worthy of ultimate defense. In so doing, he abdicated his authority as prefect, consigning Jesus to crucifixion.

At the festival Pilate used to release for the people a prisoner (15:6). A Passover amnesty is unattested outside the Gospels, although Roman rulers were authorized to release prisoners at their discretion, and they occasionally did so during festivals.

The crowd came up and began to ask Pilate (15:8). The description is best understood with reference to "coming up" to Herod's palace, situated on the higher western hill of the city, where Roman prefects stayed when visiting Jerusalem.

The soldiers led him away into the palace (that is, the governor's residence) and called the whole company together (15:16–21). See the article "The Roman Military." The "company" (Gk. *speira*) refers to the Latin *cohors*, one-tenth of a Roman legion, or between five and six hundred soldiers. The "governor's residence" (Gk. *praitōrion*; Lat. *praetorium*) refers both to the elite personal guard of the Roman governor and to the place where it was housed. The Praetorium likely was located in Herod's lavish palace situated on the prominent western hill of Jerusalem (site of the Jaffa Gate today). The purple robe and crown (symbols of royalty) were placed on Jesus in cruel burlesque. "Hail, King of the Jews" was a parody of the Latin *Ave Caesar victor imperator* ("Hail Caesar, Conqueror, Ruler"). The beating of a prisoner before crucifixion, usually by flogging with a short leather whip tipped with scraps of metal or stone, was intended to weaken a prisoner and reduce the duration of his death on the cross.

A place called Golgotha (15:22). Both Jews and Romans executed victims outside their cities (Lev. 24:14; Num. 15:35–36; Heb. 13:12). Jesus evidently was crucified on a barren hill, for "Golgotha" (Aram. *gulgoltah*) means "skull" ("Calvary" comes from Lat. *calvus*, meaning "scalp" or "bald head"). A hill with a distinct skull appearance overlooking the Arab bus

The soldiers placed a crown of thorns on Jesus's head. They may have been trying to imitate the royal diadem of the emperor. The image on this coin struck during the reign of Tiberius shows Augustus wearing the radiate crown.

station in Jerusalem today has been proposed as the site of Golgotha, as has the nearby Garden Tomb, famous for its tranquility and beauty. It is far more likely, however, that the Church of the Holy Sepulchre preserves the site of Jesus's crucifixion and burial. In Jesus's day the site lay outside the walls of Jerusalem. The location was venerated from earliest Christianity as the place of Jesus's crucifixion, and the Church of the Holy Sepulchre was already there in AD 335. Excavations undertaken beneath the church from 1961 to 1980 further confirmed the site as the Golgotha referred to in the Gospels.

They tried to give him wine mixed with myrrh (15:23). Drugged wine was intended to lessen the agony of the slow and painful death of crucifixion. There is some evidence that drugged wine may have been offered by women's societies as a civic benevolence.

They crucified him (15:24). See the article "Crucifixion"; see comments on Mark 8:34.

Truly this man was the Son of God! (15:39). "Son of God" is the most preeminent title ascribed to Jesus, signifying his divine nature and equality with God. It is Mark's foremost title for Jesus, introduced already in 1:1 and further developed by divine pronouncements at the baptism (1:9–11) and transfiguration (9:7). Jesus's divine nature is recognized by demons (1:24; 3:11; 5:7) but not by his disciples. Not until the cross is Jesus declared Son of God by a human, and then by a Roman gentile responsible for his execution! For Mark, therefore, the crucifixion is the defining revelation of Jesus as God's Son. Although the title in 15:39 does not have a definite article in the Greek text, it is correctly translated as "the Son of God" rather than "a son of God," for in Koine Greek a definite predicate nominative (which this is) omits the article when it precedes the verb.

The Burial and Empty Tomb (15:42–16:8)

Joseph . . . laid him in a tomb cut out of the rock (15:46). Jews anointed corpses with spices not to embalm them but rather to lessen the odor as they decomposed in burial tombs cut in the limestone hillsides of Palestine. The Mishnah prescribes burial vaults to be six feet wide by nine feet long, and outfitted with shelves or niches on which bodies could be placed.[53] A thousand such *kokhim* (Heb. for "niche") cave tombs have been discovered in the environs of Jerusalem, some with body-shaped depressions carved on the shelf or niche. When the corpse had decomposed, its bones were deposited in ossuaries, thus freeing the niche above for another corpse. In the OT the depositing of bones in ossuaries is referred to as being "gathered to one's fathers" (e.g., 2 Kings 22:20). Large disk-shaped stones were rolled into place before the cave opening in order to seal ritual impurities in the tomb and protect the tomb and its contents from animal predators and grave robbers.

A Later Ending of the Gospel of Mark (16:9–20)

Verses 9–20 are almost certainly a later addition to the Gospel of Mark. They are wanting in the two oldest and most important manuscripts of the Second Gospel (Codices Vaticanus and Sinaiticus), as they are in its earliest translations and versions and in its most important patristic witnesses, including the Eusebian Canons. Sixteen novel words appear in the final verses of the Gospel, as do novel theological emphases, including censure of the disciples for their disbelief and appeal to charismatic signs as proof of faith. The longer ending thus represents a literary, theological, and textual miscellany that is out of character with the rest of the Second Gospel. It likely was added in the second century to compensate either for the perceived inadequacy of the ending of the Gospel at 16:8 (if that was its original ending) or for the absence of its original ending (due perhaps to the loss of the final leaf of

A tomb with a rolling stone.

the codex of the Gospel). This leaves our earliest Gospel without a resurrection appearance, but not our earliest testimony to the gospel without one, for already in 1 Cor. 15, which the apostle Paul penned no later than the mid-50s, we have the earliest and fullest witness to the resurrection of Jesus Christ from the dead.

Luke

Craig A. Evans

Introduction. The Gospel of Luke is the first volume of a two-volume work dedicated to a man named Theophilus (see Luke 1:1–4; Acts 1:1–2). The Gospel of Luke describes the ministry of Jesus, concluding with his resurrection and ascension, while the book of Acts narrates the growth of the church as it spreads from Jerusalem to Rome, from Israel's holy city to the capital city of the empire.

Early and unanimous tradition holds that the author of Luke-Acts is Luke the physician, who is mentioned in Paul's letters (Col. 4:14; 2 Tim. 4:11; Philem. 24) and traveled with the apostle, as implied by the use of the first-person-plural "we" in a number of places in Acts (16:10–17; 20:5–21; 21:1–18; 27:1–28:16).

Because the evangelist addresses Theophilus as "most honorable" (Luke 1:3), it is possible that this man was a Roman official (as in Acts 24:2; 26:25; Josephus, *Against Apion* 1.1), perhaps even the sponsor of the writing of Luke-Acts. Whatever the case, the orientation of Luke-Acts suggests that the two-volume work was intended for a general audience, including gentiles as well as Jews.

Scholars are divided on the question of the date of Luke-Acts, with some contending for a pre-70 date and others for much later dates, such as 100 or even 120. The historical accuracy and verisimilitude of Luke-Acts argue for an early date. Moreover, given the evangelist's interest in referencing significant people and events, it seems odd, if Luke-Acts is late, that we hear nothing of the martyrdom of James the brother of Jesus in 62, the removal of the Jewish high priest Annas the Younger for killing James, the great fire of Rome in 64, the martyrdoms of Paul and Peter in 65, the Jewish Revolt of 66, the suicide of Nero in 68, the accession of Vespasian in 69, and the capture of Jerusalem and the destruction of the temple in 70. If Luke-Acts had been written well after 70, one would expect reference to at least a few of these events. Acts ends in the winter/spring of 62 with Paul having arrived in Rome awaiting trial. Luke-Acts may have been written shortly after that time.

The purpose of Luke is to show that the promises and prophecies of Israel's Scriptures are fulfilled in the life, death, and resurrection of Jesus of Nazareth, and that these things are relevant for gentiles as much as they are relevant for Jews. The rapid spread of the faith fulfills the promise of the risen Jesus (Acts 1:8) and is in itself evidence that the faith is in accord with the will of God.

Luke's Preface (1:1–4)

Many have undertaken to compile a narrative (1:1). Luke knows of previous accounts of the life, teaching, death, and resurrection of Jesus. At the very least, these accounts would include the Gospel of Mark and a collection of Jesus's teachings.[1]

Just as the original eyewitnesses and servants of the word handed them down to us (1:2). Luke affirms that the material that he has used to write in an "orderly sequence" (1:3) reaches back to eyewitness testimony and "servants of the word," which probably refers to the original disciples and those they taught.

Most honorable Theophilus (1:3). Theophilus, whose name means "friend of God," may have been an official, perhaps even a magistrate. In the book of Acts the Roman governors Felix and Festus are addressed as "most excellent" (Acts 24:3; 26:25). At the beginning of his polemical work against Apion the anti-Semite, the first-century historian Josephus addresses his patron with the same title, "most excellent Epaphroditus."[2] Like Luke, Josephus appeals to historical sources.

The Births of John and Jesus Foretold (1:5–56)

Herod king of Judea (1:5). Luke could be referring to Herod the Great, who was appointed "King of the Jews" by the Roman senate in 40 BC and died in 4 BC. But Herod the Great was

Luke gathered the information for his Gospel from eyewitnesses and earlier written sources. His account was probably transcribed using the common writing implements of this period, such as the bronze pen and inkpot from Roman Britain shown here.

king of all of Israel. Luke's "king of Judea" could mean that he has in mind Herod's son Archelaus, who ruled Judea (and Samaria) from 4 BC until his removal in AD 6. Matthew believes that it is Herod the Great (Matt. 2:1–12).

A priest of Abijah's division named Zechariah. His wife was from the daughters of Aaron, and her name was Elizabeth (1:5). Being married to Elizabeth, herself of priestly lineage (a descendant of Aaron, and not simply a descendant of the great patriarch Levi), would only enhance the status of Zechariah's children, should he have any. Zechariah is said to have been "a priest of Abijah's division." Abijah was the name of one of the sons of Samuel (1 Sam. 8:2; 1 Chron. 6:28), as well as the name of one of the priests who accompanied Zerubbabel to Jerusalem in the postexilic restoration of Israel (Neh. 12:1–4). The priestly divisions are listed in 1 Chron. 24:7–20 (the division of Abijah is mentioned in v. 10). An updated list of priestly divisions was found inscribed on stone in Caesarea Maritima.

The angel Gabriel appeared to Zechariah as he was offering incense before the Lord in the holy place. Incense shovels similar to the one shown here were used to transport hot coals on which the incense would be burned. This bronze incense shovel is probably of Roman origin from the second century AD.

According to the custom of the priesthood, to enter the sanctuary of the Lord and burn incense (1:9). Incense shovels, dating to the time of the Second Temple period, have been found in Israel.

Never drink wine or beer (1:15). Abstinence from alcoholic beverages is the main requirement of the Nazirite vow (Num. 6:3; Judg. 13:7; LXX 1 Sam. 1:11).

In the spirit and power of Elijah (1:17). The language about changing hearts and minds and preparing a people for God echoes Mal. 4:6 and also reflects a growing expectation that Elijah will return to restore Israel (Sir. 48:10).

A town in Galilee called Nazareth (1:26). Archaeological excavations at Nazareth have uncovered several houses that date to the first century BC. Two of them are of special interest. One, lying beneath the ruins of a fourth-century Byzantine chapel and the modern Basilica of the Annunciation, is believed by some to have been the house in which Mary the mother of Jesus grew up. The second, a few blocks away, lying beneath the ruins of a fourth-century Byzantine chapel and the nineteenth-century Sisters of Nazareth Convent, is thought by some to have been the home of Joseph and Mary, where they raised their family, including Jesus. The stone inscription found at Caesarea Maritima (see comments on Luke 1:5) mentions Nazareth.

He will be great and will be called the Son of the Most High . . . his kingdom will have no end . . . the holy one to be born will be called

The Church of the Nativity in Bethlehem.

the Son of God (1:32–33, 35). The four things said of Jesus (he will be great, he will be called the Son of the Most High, his kingdom will have no end, and he will be called the Son of God) are said of an unnamed figure in the Aramaic scroll fragment *4QAramaic Apocalypse*, which dates to the mid-first century BC. These parallels show that the expectation of a coming Jewish deliverer, spoken of as God's Son, was part of the pre-Christian Jewish hope and not a later post-Easter embellishment inspired by the Roman cult of the divine emperor.

My soul praises the greatness of the Lord (1:46–55). Mary's "Magnificat" (so named after the first word in the Latin translation, here translated as "praises") is modeled after Hannah's praise of God in 1 Sam. 2:1–10, in gratitude for her pregnancy, for which she had prayed. (She gave birth to Samuel, the great prophet and priest who anointed David as Israel's king.) In the Aramaic paraphrase of 1 Samuel, Hannah's song becomes eschatological and messianic. Culturally, it was believed that God sometimes enabled women to conceive who otherwise seemed unable to conceive, such as Samuel's mother, Hannah, or were elderly and so well beyond child-bearing age, such as Sarah and Elizabeth.

The Birth and Circumcision of John (1:57–80)

When they came to circumcise the child on the eighth day (1:59). Circumcision on the eighth day was prescribed by the law of Moses (Lev. 12:3; cf. Acts 7:8; Phil. 3:5). Luke also records Jesus's circumcision (2:21). See the article "The Jewish Rite of Circumcision."

The Birth of Jesus (2:1–52)

A decree went out from Caesar Augustus that the whole empire should be registered. This first registration took place while Quirinius was governing Syria. So everyone went to be registered, each to his own town (2:1–3). Historians and biblical interpreters dispute what "registration" or census Luke means (and a range of proposals has been proffered). The purpose of a census usually was to ascertain the potential productivity

Statue of Caesar Augustus, the Roman emperor at the time of Christ's birth.

and income in a given region, in order then to determine levels of taxation. Registration for the census was for most people a local affair, but for some, like Joseph, it required being present at another location. Unlike Mary, who probably grew up in Nazareth (and like many in Nazareth, she was from the family of David, of the tribe of Judah), Joseph grew up in Bethlehem and so likely had property and perhaps other commercial interests in that historic village, the very village in which King David grew up. Joseph found it necessary to be present in Bethlehem and so brought his pregnant wife with him. In a decree dated to AD 104 absentee landlords are required to register in the places where they hold property.[3]

The city of David, which is called Bethlehem, because he was of the house and family line of David (2:4). Bethlehem is mentioned many times in the OT (e.g., Gen. 35:19; 48:7; Josh. 19:15; Judg. 12:8) and a few times in the OT Pseudepigrapha.[4] Bethlehem of Judea should not be confused with Bethlehem of Zebulon (Josh. 19:15), situated in the middle of Galilee. Bethlehem of Judea was the place of King David's birth and upbringing (1 Sam. 17:12, 58). Since Jesus is the son of David (Luke 3:31; 18:38–39) and was also born in Bethlehem, reference to the place of David's birth strengthens the parallel between David and Jesus.

Forty years ago an ossuary (bone box) was discovered in Jerusalem, dating to the first century. Inscribed on it were the words "belonging to the house of David" (*shel bey dawid*). The church historian Eusebius relates stories inherited from Hegesippus to the effect that the Roman emperors Vespasian (reigned AD 69–79), Domitian (reigned AD 81–96), and Trajan (reigned AD 98–117) persecuted descendants of David.[5] Rabbinic tradition also knows of surviving members of the family of David in the time of the Second Temple.[6]

Laid him in a manger (2:7). This refers to a feeding trough for animals (though no animals are actually mentioned; the presence of animals in depictions of the nativity is inspired by Isa. 1:3). The manger may be indoors or outside. The cave tradition is derived from the apocryphal work *Protevangelium of James* (18.1).

They were terrified (2:9). Terror in the presence of the divine is attested elsewhere in Scripture (e.g., 1 Chron. 21:30; Job 23:15; Isa. 30:31; 33:14).

In a typical home in Palestine, the family living space, often a single room, was either adjacent to or above an area where the animals were housed in order to secure them for the night and provide warmth in winter. This drawing illustrates a home where the animal area is adjacent to the family's living space.

I proclaim to you good news (2:10). Literally, "I evangelize you." The good news or evangelism of the NT (see comments on Mark 1:1; see also Matt. 11:5; Luke 7:22) is rooted in the proclamation of Isaiah, as seen especially in Isa. 40:9 (LXX: "Get up to a high mountain, you who evangelizes Zion!"); 52:7 (LXX: "How beautiful upon the mountains, as feet of one who evangelizes a report of peace"); and 61:1 (LXX: "The Spirit of the Lord is upon me, because he has anointed me to evangelize the poor"). The good news foretold by Isaiah has now come to pass in the birth of the son of David, the Son of God. In the Roman world there was hope that the emperor would bring good news.

A Savior (2:11). In the OT it is sometimes God himself who is Israel's Savior (e.g., Deut. 32:15; 1 Sam. 10:19; Ps. 24:5; 25:5; Mic. 7:7; Hab. 3:18). Sometimes it is a man raised up to save his people (e.g., Judg. 3:9, 15). The author of *Psalms of Solomon*, writing in the first century BC, also looked to God for salvation: "But we shall hope in God our Savior, because the power of our God is forever with mercy, and the kingdom of our God is forever over the nations in judgment" (17.3).

The Messiah, the Lord (2:11). Some manuscripts read "the Lord's Messiah," as in 2:26. "Lord" does not always imply deity, for at times it denotes nothing more than "sir." But when used in the absolute sense, the sense it appears to have here in 2:11, it refers to deity. We have an important parallel in *Psalms of Solomon*, where the author speaks of the "Lord Messiah" or perhaps "Messiah the Lord." Speaking of the awaited Davidic Messiah, the author declares, "And he himself will be a righteous king over them, taught by God. There will be no unrighteousness among them in his days, because all shall be holy and their king will be the Lord Messiah" (17.32). It is significant that the author of *Psalms of Solomon* expressed a longing for the realization of the "kingdom of our God" (17.3) and the appearance of a son of David (17.21) who will reign as the "Lord Christ" (17.32; 18.7). Luke's language is entirely consistent with Jewish Palestinian terminology and expectation. On the Messiah, see comments on Mark 8:29.

Peace on earth to people he favors! (2:14). This translation is to be preferred to the well-known translation found in the KJV, which is based on a faulty reading in some late manuscripts: "good will toward men." There are parallels to this expression found at Qumran: "Your compassion is for all the children of Your good pleasure";[7] "among men of his good pleasure."[8]

Jerusalem (2:22). The name of this historic city occurs in the Lukan writings more frequently than in any other book in the NT (see the article "Jerusalem in the Time of Jesus"). Tradition has identified the city with Salem (cf. Gen. 14:18). David conquered Jerusalem (2 Sam. 5:6–7), making it his capital city. Jerusalem later would be besieged by the Assyrians (2 Kings

18:13–19:37), and then finally be captured and destroyed by the Babylonians (2 Kings 25:1–21). After the exile the city and temple were rebuilt (Ezra-Nehemiah), and then much later, during the reign of Herod the Great, the city would undergo further expansion and beautification, including a rebuilt and expanded temple complex.[9]

Every firstborn male (2:23). The phrase reads literally, "every male opening the womb." This verse is a paraphrase of Exod. 13:2.

A pair of turtledoves or two young pigeons (2:24). Those who could not afford to offer up a lamb could offer up two pigeons (cf. Lev. 12:8).

Israel's consolation (2:25). Simeon's hope is grounded in the scriptural promises of the restoration of the kingdom to Israel (cf. Isa. 40:1; 49:6; 61:2). Sometimes in rabbinic tradition the Messiah is called a "consoler."[10]

The fall and rise of many in Israel (2:34). The reference here is to the whole story of Luke-Acts.

A prophetess, Anna (2:36). "Anna" is the Greek form of the Hebrew name "Hannah" (meaning "grace, favor"). It will be noted below that the story of Hannah's pregnancy in 1 Sam. 1–2 contributed to Luke's infancy narrative (Luke 1:46–55; 2:41–52). It is interesting to note that, according to Jewish tradition, Hannah, Samuel's mother, was a prophetess.[11]

The redemption of Jerusalem (2:38). Documents and coins produced during the Bar Kokhba Revolt (AD 132–35) refer to the "redemption of Jerusalem" and "freedom of Jerusalem."

Twelve years old (2:42). There was no requirement to participate in religious activities as an adult until the age of thirteen.[12] By showing Jesus's participation in religious activities before that age, Luke again underscores the piety and righteousness of the holy family. But there may be more to it. Luke may have been influenced by the tradition that Samuel began his prophetic activity at the age of twelve.[13] This could very well be the case in light of the deliberate and frequent allusions to the story of Samuel's birth and upbringing.

Jesus increased in wisdom and stature, and in favor with God and with people (2:52). Luke's summary of Jesus's growth and development is an unmistakable allusion to 1 Sam. 2:26 in the Septuagint: "And the boy Samuel kept going and became great and was in favor both with the Lord and with men." Luke has alluded at various points of his infancy narrative to other words and phrases and to the general framework of the Samuel story itself. Several parallels are evident: just as Samuel is presented to the Lord (1 Sam. 1:22), so is Jesus (Luke 2:22); just as Hannah (Anna in Greek) sings praises of thanksgiving because of the birth of Samuel (1 Sam. 2:1–10), so does Anna when she sees the infant Jesus (Luke 2:36–38); just as Eli blesses Samuel's parents (1 Sam. 2:20), so Simeon blesses Jesus's parents

(Luke 2:34); just as Samuel's growth is summarized (1 Sam. 2:21, 26), so is that of Jesus (Luke 2:40, 52); just as Samuel ministered in the temple and showed remarkable spiritual discernment (1 Sam. 3:1–18), so Jesus visited the temple and impressed the religious teachers (Luke 2:41–51).

The Preaching of John the Baptist (3:1–20)

In the fifteenth year of the reign of Tiberius Caesar (3:1). Tiberius succeeded Augustus, who reigned from 30 BC to AD 14, so his fifteenth year would therefore be either AD 28 or 29. Tiberius, who was not a popular emperor and was infamous for pederasty, died in 37.

Pontius Pilate was governor of Judea (3:1). Pilate's tenure in office traditionally has been dated from 26 to early 37, when he was ordered to return to Rome after the Samaritan incident (see comments on Mark 15:1). The chronology of Josephus, however, is confused; it is possible that Pilate began his term of service a few years earlier.[14]

Herod was tetrarch of Galilee (3:1). Augustus divided Herod the Great's kingdom into three uneven parts, giving the southern half (principally Samaria and Judea) to Herod Archelaus (ruled from 4 BC to his deposal in AD 6), the western portion of the northern half (principally Galilee and Perea) to Herod Antipas (ruled from 4 BC until his removal in AD 39), and the eastern portion of the northern half (principally Gaulanitis, Trachonitis, Batanaea, Auranitis, and part of Panias) to Philip (ruled from 4 BC until his death in AD 33 or 34). Herod and his brother Philip were called tetrarchs because each was a "ruler of one fourth," the literal meaning of this Greek word. (Herod Archelaus held a somewhat higher title as ethnarch, "ruler of the people.") Herod is informally called "king" (cf. Mark 6:14, 22), but technically he was never king. It was his pursuit of the title that in part resulted in his banishment to Gaul.

Lysanias tetrarch of Abilene (3:1). This man is mentioned a few times by Josephus, once as ruler of Abila[15] and again in reference to his territory being added to that of the recently deceased Philip and given to Agrippa I.[16] There are also two inscriptions that refer to "Lysanias the tetrarch."[17] We know nothing else of this man.

High priesthood of Annas and Caiaphas (3:2). Annas was appointed high priest in AD 6 by Sulpicius Quirinius, the Roman governor who replaced the deposed ethnarch Archelaus.[18] Annas was removed from office in AD 15 by Gratus. Caiaphas, son-in-law of Annas (John 18:13), was appointed high priest by Gratus in AD 18.[19] Josephus remarks on the fortune of this high priestly family: "It is said that the elder Annas was extremely fortunate. For he had five sons, all of whom, after he himself had previously enjoyed the office for a very long time, became high priests of God—a thing that had never happened to any other of our high priests."[20]

The one who has two shirts must share with someone who has none, and the one who has food must do the same (3:11). John's ethical commands in this verse are quite similar to those found in Isa. 58:7. Similar commands are found in Greco-Roman ethical writings: "Despise worldly things by sharing them."[21]

Don't take money from anyone by force or false accusation, and be satisfied with your wages (3:14). Josephus gave similar advice to his men: "I thanked them and advised them neither to attack anyone nor to sully their hands with rapine, but to . . . be content with their rations."[22]

He locked up John in prison (3:20). From Luke's point of view, the most serious sin committed by Herod Antipas was his imprisonment and eventual execution of John (9:7–9).

The Baptism and Genealogy of Jesus (3:21–38)

The Holy Spirit descended on him in a physical appearance like a dove (3:22). The addition of "in a physical appearance" (*sōmatikō*) suggests that the Spirit was substantial and real, and not merely visionary and symbolic.

Son of Joseph . . . son of Adam (3:23–38). Luke reverses the sequence of the genealogy, beginning with Joseph and working back in time to Adam (cf. Matt. 1:2–16).

Adam, son of God (3:38). Adam, like Jesus (1:35), may be called "son of God" because he was generated by God's Spirit (cf. Gen. 2:7).

The Temptation of Jesus (4:1–13)

Jesus left the Jordan, full of the Holy Spirit (4:1). Jesus's connection to the Spirit is emphasized in 1:35; 3:22; 4:14–15.

Tempted by the devil (4:2). In the temptation story Luke consistently uses the word "devil" (literally, "slanderer," from *diabolos*, from which "diabolical" is derived), although he uses "Satan" elsewhere (cf. 10:18; 11:18; 13:16; 22:3, 31; Acts 5:3; 26:18).

The Beginning of Jesus's Ministry in Galilee (4:14–5:11)

Teaching in their synagogues (4:15). As many as ten synagogues from the first century AD or earlier have been identified in Israel (see the article "The Jewish Synagogue"; see comments on Mark 1:21). The popular synagogue at Capernaum is fourth century, but the black basalt foundation beneath dates

Remains of a synagogue at Chorazin.

to the first century BC and likely is the foundation on which the synagogue of Jesus's day rested.

He entered the synagogue on the Sabbath day (4:16). The Jewish people met in their synagogues several days each week, not just on the Sabbath, which is why Luke needs to tell his readers that on this occasion it was "on the Sabbath day."

Stood up to read (4:16). Out of respect for the authority of Scripture, Jesus stands. After reading Scripture, he will sit down (as is stated in 4:20).

The scroll of the prophet Isaiah (4:17). Two large scrolls of Isaiah were recovered from cave 1 of Qumran. Both date to the second century BC.

The Spirit of the Lord is on me . . . to proclaim the year of the Lord's favor (4:18–19). Jesus reads most of Isa. 61:1–2. The passage evidently was popular in Jewish late antiquity. It is quoted and commented upon in *11QMelchizedek*, as part of an eschatological prophecy of the coming of a redeemer who will proclaim the good news, heal and forgive Israel's sins, and defeat Belial (i.e., Satan).

Doctor, heal yourself (4:23). This proverb was commonplace in both the Jewish[23] and the gentile[24] worlds.

No prophet is accepted in his hometown (4:24). Jesus's words here, and in 13:34, reflect a Jewish tradition that Israel has routinely rejected and persecuted the prophets (2 Chron. 36:15–16; Pss. 78; 105; 106; Lam. 4:13; Acts 7:51–53).

A widow at Zarephath in Sidon (4:26). Jesus refers to the story of Elijah, who provided food for a gentile widow and her son (1 Kings 17:8–16).

Naaman the Syrian (4:27). Jesus refers to the story of Elisha, who healed Naaman the leper, an enemy military commander (2 Kings 5:1–14).

Everyone in the synagogue was enraged (4:28). According to the people of Qumran, the appearance of the Messiah meant comfort for them and judgment for their enemies,[25] whereas Jesus had just told them quite the opposite. This may very well have been a widely held view.

Hurl him over the cliff (4:29). First-century-AD Nazareth was situated on a hill, alongside of which was a steep slope. What is a steep slope today could well have been a sharp drop or "cliff" in the time of Jesus.

Capernaum, a town in Galilee (4:31). Archaeological excavations in Capernaum have exposed the foundation of several small houses of first-century Capernaum. See comments on Luke 4:38.

Have you come to destroy us? I know who you are (4:34). The evil spirit rightly senses that the appearance of Jesus—no ordinary exorcist—signifies the destruction of evil (see the article "Demonization and Exorcism in the Greco-Roman World"). The declaration "I know who you are" is a threat, implying that the evil spirit can work his own spell against Jesus (by inserting the name of Jesus into an incantation that an evil spirit might use against the exorcist).

Jesus read the words of the prophet Isaiah in the synagogue at Nazareth. Here is a portion of the Isaiah Scroll, one of the Dead Sea Scrolls found at Qumran. This is the kind of scroll Jesus would have been given to read.

Came out of him without hurting him at all (4:35). Evil spirits tried to hurt humans, even when cast out. Jesus is able to cast out the spirit without injury to the sufferer.

After he left the synagogue, he entered Simon's house (4:38). The foundation of the first-century synagogue (see 7:5), the original foundation and floor of Simon Peter's house, and the Roman barracks at Capernaum have been uncovered by archaeologists.

Lake Gennesaret (5:1). This lake is also commonly referred to as the Sea of Galilee (see comments on Mark 1:16), into which and from which the Jordan River flows. Mark refers to the "shore at Gennesaret" (Mark 6:53 = Matt 14:34). Josephus refers to the "lake of Gennesar."[26] This body of water was also commonly called the Sea of Tiberias.[27]

From now on you will be catching people (5:10). The phrase may be translated literally, "You will be catching [taking] human beings alive." It has been suggested that because catching fish brings harm to the fish (in that they die), Luke has rephrased the words of Jesus to avoid such an implication. The word that Luke uses for "catching [taking] alive" (*zōgreō*) is used in the Greek OT (Septuagint) to mean "saving persons alive from danger" (e.g., Num. 31:15, 18; Deut. 20:16). Peter and his brother Andrew were from Bethsaida (overlooking the north shore of the Sea of Galilee), whose name meant "house of catching [fish]."

Followed him (5:11). This is the first time that the word "follow" (*akoloutheō*) occurs in Luke's Gospel (e.g., 5:27–28; 9:23, 49, 57, 59, 61; 18:22, 28). Josephus says that Elisha "followed" Elijah, and that as long as the latter lived, the former was his "disciple."[28] In rabbinic literature the expression "to follow after" means to be a disciple of a rabbi.[29]

The Authority of God in Jesus (5:12–6:11)

Leprosy all over him (5:12). Luke's statement that the man was covered with leprosy seems to be an attempt to provide a fuller diagnosis and thus may reflect Luke's medical interest (cf. 8:43 with Mark 5:25–26; see comments on Mark 1:40). In 2000 a tomb was discovered in Jerusalem (in Akeldama) in which one of the occupants was discovered to have died of leprosy (Hansen's disease). This discovery confirmed the reality of leprosy in Israel in the time of Jesus.

Pharisees and teachers of the law (5:17). These men were the guardians of the "oral law" (or "oral traditions"). The word "Pharisee" means "separated one" (see the article "Pharisees and Sadducees"). The Pharisees mostly were laymen (some were priests), but men very interested in the interpretation of and obedience to Scripture. The Pharisaic tradition would in large part be taken over by the "rabbis" (though they are not to be identified with the Pharisees) and be expanded, edited, and codified as Mishnah and Talmud (and other rabbinic writings). Unlike the Sadducees, who were wealthy, aristocratic, and very conservative theologically and politically, the Pharisees were more numerous and much more popular with the people. The Pharisees traced their origins back to the glorious days of the Maccabean struggle for freedom (167–146 BC). They were zealous for the Jewish faith and were champions of the messianic hope. They believed that if all Jews would dedicate themselves to a faithful observance of all of the laws of Moses (which included the observance of their oral traditions, designed as a "fence" to protect the law [see *m. Avot* 1.1]), God would raise up his Messiah and deliver Israel.

A man who was paralyzed (5:18). Paralysis was another physical condition sometimes associated with sin and divine judgment: "being paralyzed in his limbs, unable even to speak, since he was smitten by a righteous judgment" (3 Macc. 2:22 RSV); "at that time Alcimus was stricken and his work was hindered; his mouth was stopped and he was paralyzed, so that he could no longer say a word or give commands" (1 Macc. 9:55 RSV). Other examples of paralyzed persons in Luke-Acts include Acts 8:7; 9:33.

Homes during this time period had flat roofs with an outer staircase leading to the top, similar to those shown in these photos from the modern village of Der Samet near Hebron.

Friend, your sins are forgiven (5:20). In all likelihood such a connection was assumed by Jesus's audience: "The patient is not healed of his sickness until his sins are forgiven";[30] "There are no sufferings without sin";[31] "Redemption and healing come after repentance."[32] Jesus himself, however, did not necessarily make this assumption.

We have seen incredible things today (5:26). Luke's "incredible things" (*paradoxa*) connotes strangeness and unexpectedness.[33]

I have not come to call the righteous, but sinners to repentance (5:32). Luke is especially fond of this subject. In Matthew the noun "repentance" (*metanoia*) and the verb "to repent" (*metanoeō*) occur seven times, and in Mark three times. But in Luke these words occur fourteen times (and eleven more times in the book of Acts). The closely related words "conversion" (*epistrophē*) and "to convert" (*epistrephō*) also occur much more frequently in Luke's writings than in Matthew and Mark. Luke's heavy use of these words testifies to his interest in evangelism and the mission of the church.

Parable (5:36). The word "parable(s)" occurs numerous times in Luke (6:39; 8:4, 9, 10, 11; 12:16, 41; 13:6; 14:7; 15:3; 18:1, 9; 19:11; 20:9, 19; 21:29). The Greek NT word *parabolē* (as well as *mashal,* its Hebrew equivalent) has a variety of meanings and usages. It may refer to a simple illustration, a proverbial saying, or an enigmatic saying. The idea of parabolic obscurity can be seen in 8:9–11 (cf. Mark 4:10–13). The basic meaning of "parable" is "comparison." A parable usually illustrates an abstract idea (e.g., faithfulness, duty, fruitfulness, forgiveness, prayer, judgment) with common, everyday experiences and observations. Like many fables, the parable usually contains a lesson or moral. Normally, a parable is intended to make one basic point (the lesson), and it is not to be allegorized (where every detail of the parable is assigned a value). However, a few of the parables in the Gospels are allegories or at least contain some allegorical elements.

His disciples were picking heads of grain, rubbing them in their hands, and eating them (6:1). Luke adds the words "rubbing them in their hands" (cf. Matt. 12:1; Mark 2:23) probably to clarify the nature of the "work" that the disciples were doing on the Sabbath: not only were they picking grain (which, according to the oral law, approximated reaping) but also they were rubbing off the husks of each kernel (which, according to oral law, approximated threshing). Work that is forbidden includes "sowing, plowing, reaping, binding sheaves, threshing, winnowing."[34] According to rabbinic interpretation, the

A farmer of the first century AD would have used a plow and a threshing sledge (wooden sled with stones or sharp metal pieces embedded in the underside to loosen the grain), similar to the tool shown here.

mere "stripping" off the outer shell from the kernel constitutes threshing.[35] From the Pharisaic point of view, what the disciples were doing was work.

Not lawful on the Sabbath (6:2). In light of the legal interpretations cited in the comments on 6:1, the "work" being done by the disciples could be regarded as breaking Sabbath law (see comments on Mark 2:23).

What David and those who were with him did (6:3). In 6:3–4 Jesus alludes to David's actions described in 1 Sam. 21:1–6.

The Call and Instruction of the Disciples (6:12–49)

Chose twelve of them, whom he also named apostles (6:13–16). Luke provides us with twelve names, but comparison with other apostolic lists (Matt. 10:2–4; Mark 3:16–19; Acts 1:13) (see comments on Mark 3:14) suggests that there were more than twelve among the Twelve. Moreover, if the eight names given in the Gospel of John are taken into consideration (Peter, Andrew, Philip, Bartholomew, Thomas, Judas [not Iscariot], Nathanael, Judas Iscariot), there could be as many as fifteen or sixteen apostles during the time of Jesus's ministry.

We have in the Gospels and Acts the following names of men considered among the Twelve: (1) Simon Peter (Matt. 10:2; Mark 3:16; Luke 6:14; John 1:42; Acts 1:13; see also 1 Pet. 1:1; 2 Pet. 1:1), (2) Andrew, the brother of Peter (Matt. 10:2; Mark 3:18; Luke 6:14; John 1:40; Acts 1:13), (3) James, son of Zebedee (Matt. 10:2; Mark 3:17; Luke 6:14; Acts 1:13), (4) John, son of Zebedee (Matt. 10:2; Mark 3:17; Luke 6:14; Acts 1:13; see also Rev. 1:9; 22:8), (5) Philip (Matt. 10:3; Mark 3:18; Luke 6:14; John 1:43; Acts 1:13), (6) Bartholomew (Matt. 10:3; Mark 3:18; Luke 6:14; Acts 1:13), (7) Matthew (Matt. 10:3; Luke 6:15; Acts 1:13), (8) Levi (Mark 2:14; Luke 5:27), (9) Thomas (Matt. 10:3; Mark 3:18; Luke 6:15; John 11:16; Acts 1:13), (10) James, son of Alphaeus (Matt. 10:3; Mark 3:18; Luke 6:15; Acts 1:13), (11) Thaddaeus (or "Lebbaeus" in some manuscripts; Matt. 10:3; Mark 3:18), (12) Simon the Cananean (Matt. 10:4; Mark 3:18), (13) Simon the Zealot (Luke 6:15; Acts 1:13), (14) Judas, son of James (Luke 6:16; Acts 1:13; John 14:22: "Judas [not Iscariot]"), (15) Judas Iscariot, the betrayer (Matt. 10:4; Mark 3:19; Luke 6:16; John 12:4; Acts 1:16), and (16) Nathanael (John 1:45).

Since it is likely that Levi and Matthew are one and the same (cf. Matt. 9:9 with Mark 2:14, and see Mark 2:14–17; Matt. 9:9–13; Luke 5:27–32) and that Simon the Cananean and Simon the Zealot refer to the same person, our list of sixteen names is reduced to fourteen. It is also assumed that the "Judas (not Iscariot)" in John 14:22 is the same as Judas the son of James in Luke 6:16; Acts 1:13.

It is possible that other names among the remaining fourteen may in fact refer to one individual, but we have no sure way of knowing. Some efforts have been undertaken in the past to reduce the list to twelve, but ingenuity and desperation have been more in evidence than fact. For example, the suggestion put forward several centuries ago that the Bartholomew of the Synoptic tradition is the Nathanael of the Gospel of John rests on pure conjecture and not on any evidence whatsoever. Other even more improbable suggestions have been made. Consequently, it is impossible to reduce these names to no more than twelve.

The solution to the difficulty lies in recognizing that whereas the number twelve had symbolic value, and probably represented the approximate number of those men who were regarded as Jesus's closest followers, the actual number of apostles fluctuated. Evidence for this view is seen in the book of Acts. Not only is Judas Iscariot replaced by Matthias (Acts 1:26) but also Paul *and Barnabas* are numbered among the apostles (see Acts 14:14; also implied in 1 Cor. 9:6). (Paul calls himself an apostle in Rom. 1:1; 11:13; 1 Cor. 1:1; 9:1, 2; 15:9; 2 Cor. 1:1; 12:12; Gal. 1:1; see also Eph. 1:1; Col. 1:1; 1 Tim. 1:1; 2 Tim. 1:1; Titus 1:1.) In 1 Cor. 15:5–7 Paul seems to make a distinction between the "eleven" (the Twelve minus Judas Iscariot) and other apostles. From his argument in 1 Cor. 3:1–15 it would also seem that Paul regarded Apollos as an apostle. Finally, in Rom. 16:7 Paul extends his greetings to "Andronicus and Junia . . . noteworthy in the eyes of the apostles and . . . in Christ before me."

It is probably best to understand the number twelve as a general designation that is meant to have a symbolic meaning, as seen in the twelve sons of Jacob (Gen. 35:22), the twelve tribes of Israel (Gen. 49:28), the twelve stones set up as a memorial at the Jordan River (Josh. 4:8–9), and the twelve stones Elijah used to build an altar (1 Kings 18:31). Jesus's Twelve signified the restoration of Israel, but not necessarily twelve specific men without variation in membership.

Blessed (6:20–22). Beatitudes also occur in the OT (Ps. 1:1; 2:12; 34:8; 41:1; 84:4; 94:12; 119:2; Prov. 8:34; Jer. 17:7) and intertestamental writings.[36]

Woe (6:24–26). "Woe" sayings are expressed in the OT dozens of times, sometimes in series, as we find them here in Luke (e.g., Isa. 3:11; 5:8, 11, 18, 20, 21, 22; Jer. 22:13; Hab. 2:6, 9, 12, 15, 19).

Love your enemies (6:27). Loving one's enemies flew in the face of conventional morality in late antiquity.[37] However, there were voices that recommended turning enemies into friends and showing them compassion.[38]

Be merciful, just as your Father also is merciful (6:36). Jesus's command parallels quite closely a saying found in the Aramaic paraphrase (Targum): "My people, children of Israel, just as I am merciful in heaven, so shall you

This farmer's measuring bucket is full to overflowing with grain from the harvest.

be merciful on earth" (*Targum Pseudo-Jonathan* Lev. 22:28). Jesus has not quoted the Targum (this version of Aramaic Scripture postdates Jesus by centuries), nor has the Targum quoted him. Rather, Jesus in the first century and an Aramaic translator some centuries later made use of a common saying.

For with the measure you use, it will be measured back to you (6:38). There are several rabbinical parallels: "With the measure with which one measures, it will be measured to him."[39] "Moses said to Israel: 'I have measured out to you with the same measure with which you have measured out.'"[40] "All the measures have ceased, yet the rule of measure for measure has not ceased."[41] We also find a parallel in targumic literature: "In what measure a man measures, in that measure is it measured to him."[42]

Can the blind guide the blind? (6:39). Jesus's illustration is proverbial: "You can no more have a fool as a king than a blind man to lead you along the road."[43]

Everyone who is fully trained will be like his teacher (6:40). Jesus's saying closely approximates an early rabbinic saying: "It is enough for a slave that he be like his master."[44]

Figs aren't gathered from thorn bushes, or grapes picked from a bramble bush (6:44). Similar proverbs circulated among Greco-Roman writers and thinkers.[45]

More Ministry in Galilee (7:1–8:56)

Sent some Jewish elders to him (7:3). The sending (*apostellō*) of Jewish elders (*presbyteroi*) to Jesus shows the centurion's respect for Jewish customs and sensitivities. On sending Jewish elders, note the Septuagint of 2 Kings 19:2: "He sent [*apostellō*] Eliakim who was over the household with Shebna the scribe and the elders [*presbyteroi*] of the priests"; *Letter of Aristeas* 46: "I selected six elders [*presbyteroi*] from each tribe, good men and true, and I have sent [*apostellō*] them to you with a copy of our law"; and, in reverse, Acts 11:30.

Returned to the house, they found the servant in good health (7:10). There is a similar miracle story related in rabbinic literature:

> Once the son of Rabbi Gamaliel fell ill. He sent two scholars to Rabbi Hanina ben Dosa to ask him to pray for him. When he saw them he went

> up to an upper chamber and prayed for him. When he came down he said to them, "Go, the fever has left him." They said to him, "Are you a prophet?" He replied, "I am neither a prophet nor the son of a prophet, but I have learned this from experience. If my prayer is fluent in my mouth, I know that he [the sick person] is accepted; but if not, I know that he is rejected." They sat down and made a note of the exact moment. When they came to Rabbi Gamaliel he said to them, "By the temple service! You have not been a moment too soon or too late, but so it happened—at that very moment the fever left him and he asked for water to drink."[46]

Jesus gave him to his mother (7:11–17). The geographic and thematic background of this passage is found in two similar stories involving the two famous prophets. There are at least seven parallels between 7:11–17 and the stories of Elijah in 1 Kings 17:17–24 and Elisha in 2 Kings 4:8–37.

Jesus healed many people of diseases (7:21). We find significant parallels between 7:18–23 and the Qumran scroll *4QMessianic Apocalypse*, in which God's Messiah is expected to heal.

This man, if he were a prophet, would know (7:39). It was believed that a genuine prophet was clairvoyant and therefore would know things that ordinary people would not know. We have two helpful illustrations of this power at work in Elisha the prophet (2 Kings 5:25–26; 6:8–12).

A creditor had two debtors (7:41). What makes this parable work in the context of the sinful woman (7:36–50) is the ambiguity in the Aramaic word *hoba*, which means "debt" or "sin." This double meaning is at work in the parallel versions of the Lord's Prayer (cf. Matt. 6:12 with Luke 11:4).

The good news of the kingdom of God (8:1). The "good news" has its roots in the good news proclaimed by the prophet Isaiah (e.g., Isa. 40:9; 52:7; 61:1–20). The definition of the good news in terms of the rule of God or "kingdom of God" reflects the language of Scripture in Aramaic, as seen in the later Targum (see comments on Mark 1:15).

Mary, called Magdalene (8:2). She is so named because she is from the town of Magdala (possibly meaning "city of the tower"), which is on the western shore of the Sea of Galilee. Recent archaeological work at first-century Magdala has uncovered a synagogue and three ritual immersion pools.

Joanna the wife of Chuza, Herod's steward (8:3). The reference to Herod is to Herod Antipas. It has been suggested that Joanna's husband should be understood as a manager of Herod's estate.

Susanna (8:3). Outside of this reference in Luke nothing is known of this woman. This is the name of the beautiful heroine in one part of the apocryphal additions to Daniel.

The seed is the word of God (8:11). Luke qualifies it as the word of God, which is consistent with Isa. 55:10–11: "making it germinate and sprout, and providing *seed* to sow and food to eat, so *my word* [i.e., God's word]" (emphasis added).

He and his disciples got into a boat (8:22). In 1986 a first-century-AD boat was recovered from the mud along the northwest shore of the Sea of Galilee. The boat measures 26.5 feet in length, 7.5 feet in width, and 4.5 feet in depth. It once easily accommodated one dozen or more men. The boat is now housed and conserved in the Yigal Allon Museum in Kibbutz Ginosar, Galilee.

Who then is this? He commands even the winds and the waves, and they obey him! (8:25). The disciples' language may recall the boast credited to the blasphemous Antiochus IV (died 164 BC), who claimed "that he could command the waves of the sea, in his superhuman arrogance, and . . . weigh the high mountains in a balance" (2 Macc. 9:8 RSV). Jesus makes no boast; he simply does it.

The region of the Gerasenes (8:26). The Gerasenes are the people of Gerasa (or Jerash). The city itself is several miles east of the Sea of Galilee, but the "region" Gerasa extended west to the Sea of Galilee itself. The herd of pigs was near the sea, not the city.

Legion (8:30). The demonic name Legion would have brought to mind a Roman legion. Legion Fretensis X was stationed on and off in Galilee in the first and second centuries (as shown by literature and archaeological

Although the exact location where Jesus encountered the demon-possessed man is unknown, one possibility is the area near Gergesa on the eastern side of the Sea of Galilee. The steep hill-side shown here provides a logical setting for the pig stampede.

discoveries). The mascot of this legion was a boar's head, which fits well the context of the story in Luke.

Pigs . . . drowned (8:33). Casting the demons into the pigs, which then plunge into the sea and perish (and the demonic Legion perish with the pigs), foreshadows the grim fate that awaits Satan and his evil allies.[47]

When Jesus returned (8:40). Jesus and his disciples returned to the west side of the Sea of Galilee—that is, the Jewish side.

Jairus . . . a leader of the synagogue (8:41). The name Jairus in Hebrew means "he will awaken" (cf. 1 Chron. 20:5). He holds the rank of "leader of the synagogue." Inscriptions have been found in which mention is made of synagogue rulers (e.g., the well-known Theodotus Inscription found in the rubble from the destruction of Jerusalem in AD 70).

A woman suffering from bleeding for twelve years (8:43). Quite apart from the physical difficulties, the woman's condition would have kept her in a perpetual state of impurity (Lev. 15:25–28).

Touched the end of his robe (8:44). It was widely believed that touching the clothing of a holy man could confer blessing or healing. However, the woman's action of touching Jesus would have been viewed as highly presumptuous and improper. It would have been assumed that her touch would render Jesus ritually impure (Lev. 15:26–27).[48]

Daughter, . . . your faith has saved you. Go in peace (8:48). Being addressed as "daughter" signifies the woman's restoration and is a public declaration of her covenant status as a true daughter of Abraham. The command "go in peace" is a biblical idiom; for OT examples, see Exod. 4:18; Judg. 18:6; 1 Sam. 1:17; 29:7; 2 Sam. 15:9; 2 Kings 5:19; for NT examples, see Luke 7:50; Acts 16:36; James 2:16.

Not dead but asleep (8:52). Sleep often was used as a euphemism or metaphor for death, as in 1 Thess. 4:15; 5:10; 1 Cor. 7:39; 11:30; 15:6, 18, 20, 51 (where Greek verbs for "sleep" are used), and in the pagan world, as seen on epitaphs.[49]

Her spirit returned (8:55). The concept of the return of one's spirit (or breath) is paralleled in the miracle involving Elijah in 1 Kings 17:21–22: "Then he stretched himself out over the boy three times. He cried out to the LORD and said, 'LORD my God, please let this boy's life come into him again!' So the LORD listened to Elijah, and the boy's life came into him again, and he lived."

Further Instruction for the Disciples (9:1–50)

No staff, no traveling bag (9:3). A few interpreters have tried to argue that Jesus taught and behaved as a Cynic philosopher. Most scholars are rightly unconvinced. In his instructions to his disciples Jesus commands that they take no staff, no bag, no bread, no money, and so forth. Cynics always traveled with a staff and a bag (as seen throughout the *Cynic Letters*). The purpose of the latter was to collect bread and money along the way. Jesus's instructions are entirely at variance with the Cynic practice.

Shake off the dust from your feet (9:5). In Acts Luke provides us with an actual instance of shaking dust off one's feet: Paul and Barnabas shake the dust from their feet in protest against the Jews who persecuted them and drove them out of town (Acts 13:51).

Proclaiming the good news and healing everywhere (9:6). The "good news" of the kingdom of God manifests itself in healing. Healing and exorcism provide evidence that the rule of God has indeed begun.[50]

I beheaded John (9:9). According to Josephus, Herod Antipas the tetrarch of Galilee placed John in prison in Machaerus, on the east side of the Dead Sea (see comments on Mark 6:27).[51]

Everyone ate and was filled (9:17). It is likely that Luke sees the feeding of the five thousand against the background of Elisha's ministry. There are numerous points of contact between Jesus and the Elijah/Elisha stories in 1–2 Kings (cf. Luke 4:25–27; 7:11–17, 18–35, 36–50; 8:1–3; 9:51–56, 57–62). In the feeding of the five thousand Luke may have been thinking of Elisha's multiplication of the barley loaves for one hundred men (2 Kings 4:42–44). There are a number of parallels: (1) a specific number of loaves (2 Kings 4:42; Luke 9:13), (2) the command to give to the people so that they may eat (2 Kings 4:42; Luke 9:13), (3) food is "set before" the people (2 Kings 4:43; Luke 9:16), (4) after they ate there was food "left over" (2 Kings 4:44; Luke 9:17), and (5) the food was either taken from or placed into a "basket" (2 Kings 4:42 ["sack"]; Luke 9:17).

God's Messiah (9:20). The Greek *christos* ("Christ") translates the Hebrew *mashiah*, from which the word "messiah" is derived (see the article "Messianic Expectations in Jesus's Day"; see comments on Mark 8:29). The word means "anointed." But because the word is used in reference to anointed kings (1 Sam. 15:1; 16:13; Ps. 2:2), anointed prophets (1 Kings 19:15–16; 1 Chron. 16:22 = Ps. 105:15; Isa. 61:1), and anointed priests (Exod. 29:6–7; Lev. 16:32; 1 Chron. 29:22), it is not certain what Peter means by it here. Jesus's crucifixion as "King of the Jews/Israel" (Mark 15:26, 32) provides strong support for the traditional view that Peter confessed Jesus to be Israel's messianic king.

Raised the third day (9:22). The phrase "on the third day" owes its inspiration to Hosea 6:2: "He will revive us after two days, and on the third day he will raise us up so we can live in his presence." In the Aramaic paraphrase the passage is understood to refer to the "day of resurrection." Pious Jews very much believed in the resurrection.[52] Jesus was no exception.

As he was praying, the appearance of his face changed, and his clothes became dazzling white (9:28–36). Luke has made a number of subtle changes in the story of the transfiguration. Perhaps the most interesting is in verse 31, where readers are told that Jesus, Moses, and Elijah discussed Jesus's "departure" (*exodos*), which strengthens the link with Moses. When in verse 35 God commands the disciples to "listen to him" (i.e., to Jesus), we have an allusion to the words of the Septuagint of Deut. 18:15: "**God will raise up for you a prophet like me from among your brothers;** listen to him."

Discipleship and Mission (9:51–11:13)

When the days were coming to a close for him to be taken up (9:51). Luke may have been familiar with the account known as the *Ascension of Moses*, in which Moses is depicted as giving his final teaching while journeying to the place where God would take him up. If such a parallel was intended, then Luke's account would only be enriched and the interest of his first-century readers would be heightened. Just as the great lawgiver Moses, after giving the law a second time (Deuteronomy [literally, "second law"]), was taken up by God, so Jesus, after giving his "law" (cf. Luke 10:1–18:14), is taken up by God.

He determined to journey to Jerusalem (9:51). Literally, "He set his face to go to Jerusalem." The expression "to set one's face" recalls the OT idiom quite often found in the context of one being commissioned and dispatched with a message of judgment. The best example of this idea, and one that may have influenced Luke, comes from Ezek. 21:2–3: "Son of man, face Jerusalem and preach against the sanctuaries. Prophesy against the land of Israel, and say to it, 'This is what the LORD says: I am against you. I will draw my sword from its sheath.'" This is in fact very similar to the message that Jesus will deliver to Jerusalem. In 19:43 and 21:20–24, in language reminiscent of the OT prophets' description of the first destruction of Jerusalem and the temple (see Isa. 63:18; Jer. 6:6; Ezek. 4:2), Jesus woefully predicts a second destruction of the city and the temple (see the articles "Jerusalem in the Time of Jesus"; "The Jerusalem Temple").

He sent messengers ahead of himself (9:52). The language may have been intended to recall the prophecy of Mal. 3:1: "See, I am going to send my messenger, and he will clear the way before me."

The Samaritans . . . did not welcome him (9:52–53). The rivalry and hatred between Jews and Samaritans were notorious. Because of Jewish-Samaritan hostilities, Jewish pilgrims from Galilee often would cross over to the east bank of the Jordan River in order to skirt around Samaria. The first-century Jewish historian Josephus provides a graphic description of these hostilities.[53]

Do you want us to call down fire from heaven? (9:54). See 2 Kings 1:9–16, where Elijah twice calls down fire from heaven to destroy the soldiers sent by Ahaziah, the king of Samaria.

No one who puts his hand to the plow and looks back is fit for the kingdom of God (9:62). Jesus's retort to the man who wishes to say goodbye to his family before following Jesus appears to be a deliberate allusion to Elijah's summons of Elisha (see 1 Kings 19:19–21).

The Lord appointed seventy-two others, and he sent them ahead of him in pairs (10:1). Some ancient manuscripts read "seventy" (CSB footnote). In the OT the number seventy is quite significant. It can refer to the seventy who went down to Egypt (Gen. 46:27; Deut. 10:22). It is also possible that seventy alludes to the seventy gentile nations (Gen. 10:2–31).

I'm sending you out like lambs among wolves (10:3). Jesus's saying has a proverbial ring to it: "Crates said that people living with flatterers were in as bad a way as calves among wolves."[54]

Don't carry a money-bag, traveling bag, or sandals (10:4). See comments on Luke 9:3.

Whatever house you enter, first say, "Peace to this household" (10:5). Jesus's greeting of peace should be understood in the Jewish and biblical sense—for example, 1 Sam. 25:6: "Long life to you, and peace to you, peace to your family, and peace to all that is yours" (cf. 2 Chron. 18:16; Hag. 2:9). Given the judgmental element in the proclamation of the kingdom, consider Job 21:9: "Their houses are secure and free of fear [literally, "their houses have peace"]; no rod from God strikes them."

The worker is worthy of his wages (10:7). The saying is proverbial: "A good soldier is never without someone to reward his efforts, nor is a laborer or a cobbler. Do you think it is any different for a good human being? Do you think God cares so little for the servants and witnesses with whom He has had so much success?"[55]

Sodom (10:12). The notorious city was destroyed in the days of Abraham and Lot (Gen. 19:24–28).

Whoever listens to you listens to me. Whoever rejects you rejects me. And whoever rejects me rejects the one who sent me (10:16). Echoed in this statement are the conventions of the embassy or ambassador. Just as surely as the ambassador of late antiquity represented his king, so the apostles of Jesus represent their Lord. Therefore, listening to the apostles is the same as listening to Jesus himself.

I watched Satan fall from heaven like lightning (10:18). Some texts from the OT have been cited as providing the backdrop of Jesus's language (e.g., Isa. 14:12; Dan. 8:10). Qumran may also offer a relevant parallel: "When they went about in their willful heart, the Guardian Angels of Heaven fell and were ensnared by it, for they did not observe the commandments of God."[56] Another promising parallel is found in *Testament of Solomon*, the pseudepigraphal text that depicts Solomon gaining the upper hand over the demonic hosts: "But we who are demons . . . fall down like leaves from the trees and the men who are watching think that stars are falling from heaven. . . . We are dropped like flashes of lightning to the earth" (20.16–17).

I have given you the authority to trample on snakes and scorpions and over all the power of the enemy (10:19). Snakes and scorpions occur together in Deut. 8:15 and Sir. 39:30. In later traditions snakes and scorpions are understood as evil spirits. To "trample on" these powers is to exercise dominion over them. One passage from the OT Pseudepigrapha is especially relevant: "He will liberate every captive of the sons of men from Beliar, and every spirit of error will be trampled down" (*Testament of Zebulon* 9.8). This passage itself probably is inspired by Ps. 91:13: "You will tread on the lion and the cobra; you will trample the young lion and the serpent." This is especially relevant when it is noted that in the Aramaic paraphrase (Targum) Ps. 91 is understood as a psalm concerned with demons. Jesus may well have alluded to Ps. 91:13.

Rejoice that your names are written in heaven (10:20). The closest parallel to Jesus's language is found in the Jewish apocalyptic book *1 Enoch*, where the faithful are promised, "I swear unto you, that in heaven the angels remember you for good before the glory of the Great One; and your names are written before the glory of the Great One" (104.1). Being written in or blotted out of God's book is an old tradition (see Exod. 32:32–33; Ps. 69:28; 87:6; Isa. 4:3; Dan. 12:1; Mal. 3:16–17).

You have hidden these things from the wise and intelligent (10:21). Jesus's prayer of thanks for revelation echoes but reverses Daniel's similar prayer: "I offer thanks and praise to you, God of my fathers, because you have given me wisdom and power. . . . He gives wisdom to the wise and knowledge to those who have understanding" (Dan. 2:23, 21). In Daniel's prayer God is thanked for giving wisdom to the wise, but in Jesus's prayer God is thanked for hiding the truth of the kingdom of God, revealing it not to the "wise and intelligent" but to little children.

Love the Lord your God . . . your neighbor as yourself (10:27). The Double Commandment often was expressed by Jewish teachers.[57]

A man was going down from Jerusalem to Jericho (10:30–35). The well-known parable of the good Samaritan is not an allegory of the incarnation;[58] it is an illustration of what it means to love one's neighbor. The

The desolate and dangerous road linking Jerusalem and Jericho.

scriptural backdrop is the story of the good Samaritans in 2 Chron. 28:8–15. Jericho is east of Jerusalem some seventeen miles (and about thirty-three hundred feet lower), in the Jordan Valley.

Mary has made the right choice (10:38–42). Mary has acted on the teaching of Deut. 8:3: "Man does not live on bread alone but on every word that comes from the mouth of the Lord."[59]

Whenever you pray, say (11:1–4). The Lord's Prayer in Luke is much shorter than the version in Matt. 6:9–13 and parallels more closely the Jewish Aramaic prayer known as the *Qaddish*.

Suppose one of you has a friend and goes to him at midnight (11:5). Midnight is not intended as parabolic exaggeration. Such a detail is quite plausible, for people often traveled at night to avoid the heat of the day.

An egg . . . a scorpion (11:12). Some have wondered if a curled-up scorpion resembles an egg; if so, the comparison is apt.

Discipleship and Conflict (11:14–12:59)

Beelzebul (11:15). "Beelzebul" is another name for Satan or the devil. See comments on Mark 3:22.

The finger of God (11:20). Jesus's language probably refers to Exod. 8:19, where the pharaoh's magicians say of the miracles performed by Moses and Aaron, "This is the finger of God." In later Jewish tradition it was believed that the magicians were in fact in league with Satan.

A strong man, fully armed (11:21). The "fully armed" man is the soldier in full body armor and weaponry.

Anyone who does not gather with me scatters (11:23). The messianic task is to gather the elect. Satan works against this task by scattering.

As Jonah became a sign to the people of Nineveh (11:30). It's not clear in what sense Jonah was "a sign to the people of Nineveh." His sign may have been his call for the wicked city to repent. Nineveh was the capital of ancient Assyria, a kingdom that oppressed Israel and in the eighth century BC destroyed the northern kingdom of Israel.

The queen of the south (11:31). The "queen of the south" (or Sheba) came a great distance to hear Solomon's wisdom (1 Kings 10:1–13).

He was amazed that he did not first perform the ritual washing (11:38). A relevant story is found in rabbinic literature: "When I saw that you ate without washing your hands . . . I thought you were an idolater."[60]

Experts in the law (11:45). The reference is to experts in the law of Moses.

Since the foundation of the world (11:50). The turn of phrase is found in Greco-Roman writers.[61]

The blood of Abel (11:51). Abel was murdered by his brother Cain (Gen. 4:8).

The blood of Zechariah (11:51). Which Zechariah is in view is difficult to decide. Matthew says that he is the "son of Berechiah" (Matt. 23:35). The Zechariah in view probably is the son of the high priest Jehoiada, who was murdered in the temple precincts (2 Chron. 24:20–22). "Berechiah" may have come from the prophet Zechariah (Zech. 1:7: "The prophet Zechariah son of Berechiah").

This relief shows a well-armed Roman soldier carrying a spear, sword, and shield (second century AD). In Luke 11:21 Satan is portrayed as a "strong man, fully armed" who has his protective armor taken away by someone stronger (i.e., Jesus).

The leaven of the Pharisees, which is hypocrisy (12:1). Yeast, or leaven, often is a metaphor for corruption. Luke's version of this saying is based on Mark 8:15: "Beware of the leaven of the Pharisees and the leaven of Herod." It is not clear in Mark's story (Mark 8:14–21) exactly what the leaven (or yeast) of the Pharisees and the leaven of Herod is. According to Matthew, it is their teaching: "Then they understood that he had not told them to beware of the leaven in bread, but of the *teaching* of the Pharisees and Sadducees" (Matt. 16:12 [emphasis added]; note that Matthew has replaced "Herod" with "Sadducees"). Luke focuses on the hypocrisy of the Pharisees (cf. Matt. 23).

Tell my brother to divide the inheritance with me (12:13). Jesus had no legal authority to arbitrate in such a matter (a matter often settled in the synagogue or by a rabbi), as his answer in verse 14 would indicate.

Who appointed me a judge or arbitrator? (12:14). In antiquity the "arbiter" was one who divided or apportioned property or wealth, especially in disputed cases. Many papyri deal with the topic of divisions of property and inheritance. A woman named Aurelia Maria, of the village of Hermopolis, petitioned the governor, asking him to make her brother divide the family inheritance equitably.[62] Philosophers held opinions much like that expressed by Jesus. For example, to the man who says, "My brother is going to get the larger part of the farm," Epictetus advises, "Let him have all he wants."[63]

This building at Ostia Antica, where the port of Rome was located, was built as a warehouse in which foodstuffs, mostly grain and olive oil, were stored (AD 145–50).

Life is not in the abundance of his possessions (12:15). Jesus's warning about the danger of greed is commonplace in Jewish literature. The parable of the rich fool reflects the words of the psalmist: "Do not be afraid when a person gets rich, when the wealth of his house increases. For when he dies, he will take nothing at all; his wealth will not follow him down" (Ps. 49:16–17 [see also Job 31:24–28]).[64]

I'll tear down my barns and build bigger ones (12:18). The rich man's plan to pull down his barns that he might build bigger ones finds a real-life counterpart in the business correspondence of the chief steward Zenon, who served under one Apollonius, the minister of finance, during the reign of Ptolemy Philadephus, king of Egypt in the middle of the third century BC. An associate requests, in view of a good crop, "And if possible, have another granary made; the present one is not big enough to hold the year's corn."[65]

Eat, drink, and enjoy yourself (12:19). Unfortunately, the rich man is a fool, saying to himself, "Take it easy; eat, drink and enjoy yourself." Jesus has placed the words of Isa. 22:13 ("Let us eat and drink, for tomorrow we die") into the mouth of the rich man, words that Paul quotes in 1 Cor. 15:32. This sentiment, often associated with Epicureanism, was widespread in late antiquity and, interestingly enough, sometimes is found inscribed on epitaphs. For example, one inscription reads, "Play, have a good time, live; you have to die."[66] Another fool had someone inscribe this on his grave marker: "While I lived I drank freely. You who still live, drink!"[67] Even in Jerusalem a similar epitaph has been found: "Enjoy yourselves, you who are still alive, and further [. . .] eat and drink together" (uncertain date). The Jerusalem epitaph may be Sadducean, for its sentiment is consistent with what little we know of this group. In the NT we are told that Sadducees say that "there is no resurrection" (Mark 12:18; cf. Acts 23:6–8). Josephus agrees.[68] In *Testament of Moses* ruling priests, perhaps Sadducean, are severely criticized as "deceitful men, pleasing only themselves . . . loving feasts at any hour of the day—devouring, gluttonous . . . saying, 'We shall have feasts, even luxurious winings and dinings'" (7.4, 8).

Another interesting parallel is found in the writings of the Jewish philosopher-theologian Philo of Alexandria: "The farmer says, 'I will sow, I will plant, the plants will grow, seeds and plants will yield crops, not only useful as affording food that we cannot do without, but so abundant as to give us enough and to spare.' Then of a sudden a fire, or a storm, or persistent rain spoils everything. Sometimes all that he had reckoned on comes to pass, but the reckoner dies first without having had the benefits of them, and his expectation of enjoying the fruits of his toil proves a vain one."[69]

Gentile philosophers also criticized the materialistic and hedonistic lifestyle. Dio Chrysostom exclaims, "You fool! Even if everything turns out right, what assurance have you that you will live to see tomorrow, and not suddenly be torn away from all the good things you expect to enjoy?" (*Orations* 16.8).

Don't worry about your life (12:22). Jesus's admonition probably is echoed in 1 Pet. 5:7: "Cast all your cares on him, because he cares about you." Similar sentiment is found in rabbinic literature: "Will not [God], who created [the human], create for him his food?"[70]

Can any of you add one moment to his life span by worrying (12:25). Literally, the phrase is "add a cubit." According to a second-century-AD collection of sayings attributed to a sage named Sextus, "We cannot control the length of life, but we can control whether we live properly."[71]

Consider how the wildflowers grow: They don't labor or spin thread (12:27). The rabbis have pointed out, "While mortals are asleep in their beds, the Holy One causes winds to blow, clouds to rise, rains to come down, dews to glisten on plants, plants to spring up, fruits to grow plump."[72]

You of little faith (12:28). The Greek expression "little faith" (*oligopistos*) is found in *The Sentences of Sextus*: "A faithful man is an elect man. An elect man is a man of God . . . a man of little faith [*oligopistos*] is without faith."[73] Jesus's language would have resonated with most people.

Don't strive for what you should eat and what you should drink (12:29). Having little faith and being worried about food and drink come to expression in rabbinic sayings also: "Rabbi Elazar of Modi'im said, 'If a man has food for the day, but says, "What shall I eat tomorrow?" such a one lacks faith.' Rabbi Eliezer the Great said, 'He who still has bread in his basket and says, "What shall I eat tomorrow?" belongs to those of little faith.'"[74]

Don't be anxious (12:29). The Talmud advises, "Do not fret over tomorrow's troubles, for you know not what a day may bring forth. Tomorrow may come and you will be no more."[75] Jesus's language would have had wide appeal.

Where your treasure is, there your heart will be also (12:34). Jesus's saying seems proverbial, but no exact matches have been found. Greco-Roman ethicists have given expression to approximations of Jesus's teaching: "Where your mind is, there will be your good";[76] "For where one can say 'I' and 'mine,' there must the creature incline."[77] One Jewish author in the Apocrypha describes the greedy as "those who . . . hoard up silver and gold, in which men trust; and there is no end to their getting" (Bar. 3:17 RSV).

The Son of Man is coming at an hour you do not expect (12:40). This idea is consistent with Jewish messianism, which sometimes speaks of the coming of the Messiah at night, probably based on association with the night of the original Passover (see the article "Messianic Expectations in Jesus's Day").[78]

They will be divided (12:53). Here Jesus has paraphrased Mic. 7:6, a prophecy that in rabbinic interpretation signified the coming of the Messiah.[79]

A storm is coming (12:54). Predicting the weather on the basis of the color of the sky was proverbial in late antiquity: "If the wind inclined northward, then the coming rains would be abundant; if they inclined southward, there would be little rain";[80] "Is not the sun red at sunrise and at sunset?";[81] "Rabbi Yohanan said, 'Clouds are a sign of coming rain' . . . Rabbi Judah said, 'Should fine rain come down before the heavy rain then the rain will continue for some time.'"[82]

The Fate of Jerusalem (13:1–35)

Galileans whose blood Pilate had mixed with their sacrifices (13:1). Historians debate which event Jesus refers to. Josephus tells of at least one bloody clash in Jerusalem, over the use of dedicated monies for the construction of an aqueduct. Perhaps Galileans were among the protesters who were killed.[83]

The tower in Siloam fell on and killed (13:4). We have no record of this event. The tower in Siloam, if it was this structure that Jesus alluded to, was located in the southern section of Jerusalem. It may have been part of an aqueduct linked to the well-known Pool of Siloam, which archaeological excavation has uncovered.

Leave it this year also (13:8). On the fruitless fig tree, note the sage counsel offered in the Syriac version of *Ahiqar*: "My son, you have been to me like that palm tree that stood by a river, and cast all its fruit into the river, and when its lord came to cut it down, it said to him, 'Let me alone this year, and I will bring forth carobs.' And its lord said to it, 'You have not been industrious in what is your own, and how will you be industrious in what is not your own?'" (35).

There are six days when work should be done . . . not on the Sabbath (13:14). The synagogue leader refers to Exod. 20:9–10 (= Deut. 5:13–14), where work on the Sabbath is prohibited. The Mishnah tractate *Shabbat* is concerned with what is and is not lawful for the Sabbath and contains many of the oral laws and traditions that Jesus and the early church encountered (see the article "The Sabbath"; see comments on Mark 2:23).

Like a mustard seed that a man took and sowed in his garden (13:19). Matthew's "sowed in his field" (Matt. 13:31) coheres with rabbinic law that requires mustard to be sown in fields, not in gardens (as Luke has it): "They may flank a field of vegetables with mustard seed. . . . Not every kind of seed may be sown in a garden-bed . . . mustard and small beans are deemed a kind of seed."[84]

It grew and became a tree, and the birds of the sky nested in its branches (13:19). The details of "birds" and "branches" seem to allude to Ezek. 17:23: "It may bear branches . . . and become a majestic cedar. Birds of every kind will nest under it, taking shelter in the shade of its branches"; and Dan. 4:20–21: "The tree . . . in its branches the birds of the sky lived." If so, the language enriches the prophetic dimension of the parable.

Mixed into fifty pounds of flour (13:21). The phrase says literally, "hid in three measures of flour." The three measures (Gk. *sata*, an Aramaic loanword), perhaps alluding to Gen. 18:6, "Knead three measures of fine flour and make bread," probably equal one ephah (cf. Ruth 2:17), or about a dozen pints, valued at about three shekels.[85] The dough that would result should be sufficient for several loaves of bread.

Enter through the narrow door (13:24). The "two ways" theme (cf. Matt. 7:13–14) appears in OT Scripture (Deut. 11:26; 30:15; Jer. 21:8). Intertestamental expressions of the two ways include "Two ways has God given to the sons of men . . . for there are two ways, of good and evil";[86] God "showed him [Adam] the two ways, the light and the darkness, and I told him: This is good, and that bad";[87] and "Before each person are life and death, and whichever one chooses will be given."[88]

Get away from me, all you evildoers! (13:27). This language echoes several OT passages (Job 21:14; 22:17; Ps. 6:8; 139:19), but it is almost in exact agreement with Ps. 6:8 in the Septuagint: "Depart from me, all you who practice lawlessness" (LXX Ps. 6:9).

They will come from east and west, from north and south (13:29). Jesus's words allude to Ps. 107:1–3, "Give thanks to the Lord . . . he has redeemed . . . and has gathered them from the lands—from the east and the west, from the north and the south," implying that those gathered are Jews of the diaspora (or dispersion). This is expressed in Bar. 4:36–37: "Look toward the east, O Jerusalem, and see the joy that is coming to you from God. Look, your children are coming, whom you sent away; they are coming, gathered from east and west, at the word of the Holy One, rejoicing in the glory of God" (RSV).[89] According to the Aramaic paraphrase of Scripture (Targum), Israel's exiles will be gathered by the Messiah.[90]

Go tell that fox (13:32). "Fox" probably means a person of no significance,[91] or a person of cunning and treachery.[92] In Greco-Roman literature the fox serves as a figure for the sly and clever.[93] But reference to the fox is sometimes derogatory.[94] Thus the "fox" in the literature of late antiquity is not admired, whether the emphasis falls on the creature's cunning or on its insignificance.

Who kills the prophets and stones those who are sent to her (13:34). The pseudepigraphal *Lives of the Prophets* (first century AD) tells us of several prophets who were murdered, which adds color to Jesus's saying.

Your house is abandoned (13:35). This probably is an allusion to Jer. 22:5. If so, the prophetic element is enhanced.

Blessed is he who comes in the name of the Lord (13:35). This is a partial quotation of Ps. 118:26.

Lessons on Compassion and Humility (14:1–35)

A man whose body was swollen with fluid (14:2). The man suffering from abnormal swelling has dropsy. The swelling is caused by excessive fluids in various parts of the body (not just arms and legs) and usually indicates the presence of more serious problems. Dropsy was regarded by some rabbis as resulting from immorality.[95]

Which of you whose son or ox falls into a well, will not immediately pull him out on the Sabbath day? (14:5). The men of Qumran believed, "No one should help an animal give birth on the Sabbath; and if it falls into a well or a pit, he may not lift it out on the Sabbath."[96]

An ancient Near Eastern water well. Jesus posed a question to the experts of the law regarding their Sabbath regulations when he asked about the rule regarding a child or ox that falls into a well on the Sabbath.

Don't recline at the best place (14:8). The saying reflects the advice of Prov. 25:6–7: "Don't boast about yourself before the king, and don't stand in the place of the great; for it is better for him to say to you, 'Come up here!' than to demote you in plain view of a noble." A similar lesson is found in rabbinic literature: "Stay two or three seats below your place, and sit there until they say to you, 'Come up!' Do not begin by going up because they may say to you, 'Go down!' It is better that they say to you, 'Go up,' than that they say to you, 'Go down.'"[97]

Everyone who exalts himself will be humbled (14:11). Similar expressions are found in rabbinic literature: "God will exalt him who humbles himself, but God will humble him who exalts himself";[98] "Hillel used to say: 'My humiliation is my exaltation; my self-exaltation is my humiliation'";[99] "Get down to come up and up to come down: Whoever exalts himself above the words of Torah is in the end degraded; and whoever degrades himself for the sake of the words of Torah is in the end exalted."[100]

Shown here is an invitation to a birthday celebration written in about AD 97–103 and found in the remains of a Roman fort at ancient Vindolanda (modern Chesterholm), Northumberland, England.

When you host a banquet, invite those who are poor, maimed, lame, or blind (14:13). The poor and infirm often were thought to be subject to God's displeasure, perhaps because of sin. Jesus's ethic is loosely paralleled in the writings of Dio Chrysostom: "Yet the swineherd feels no surprise at the treatment and its inhumanity, as though it were the regular procedure to deal with needy strangers thus strictly and meanly and to welcome openheartedly with gifts and presents only the rich, from whom, of course, the host expected a like return" (*Orations* 7.87–88).

Blessed is the one who will eat bread in the kingdom of God! (14:15). Eating bread "in the kingdom of God" refers to the expected messianic banquet, rooted in Isa. 25:6: "On this mountain, the Lord of Armies will prepare for all peoples a feast." Qumran also anticipated a messianic feast,[101] which will set the pattern for all meals to come:[102] "The procedure for the [mee]ting of the men of reputation [when they are called] to the banquet held by the Council of the Yahad."[103]

I just got married, and therefore I'm unable to come (14:20). The three excuses in 14:18–20 are somewhat reminiscent of the three excuses in Deut. 20:5–7 (esp. v. 7, in reference to a man just engaged to be married), which exempt men from military service.

Bring in here the poor, maimed, blind, and lame (14:21). According to Lev. 21:17–23, people with such infirmities could never be qualified for priestly service (even if they were Levites). The list in Lev. 21 inspired the stipulations in at least two of the writings of Qumran, which prohibited such "defective" persons from participation in the final great holy war[104] and the messianic feast.[105]

Not one of those people who were invited will enjoy my banquet (14:24). The word translated as "invited" (*kaleō*) can also mean "chosen" or "elected." Accordingly, the men who imagined that they numbered among the chosen of Israel may in fact be excluded from the messianic banquet.

The poor and crippled—those assumed to be nonchosen—will enjoy the banquet.

If anyone comes to me and does not hate his own father and mother (14:26). This idea is expressed in Greco-Roman philosophy.[106]

My disciple (14:26). The word translated as "disciple" (*mathētēs*) comes from a root meaning "to learn." A disciple, therefore, is a learner.

Lessons on Forgiveness and Restoration (15:1–32)

Tax collectors and sinners (15:1). There are several Scriptures to which the Pharisees could have appealed in justifying their displeasure over the company that Jesus kept (e.g., Ps. 1:1–6; Prov. 1:15; 2:11–15; Isa. 52:11) (see comments on Mark 2:16).[107]

Has a hundred sheep and loses one of them (15:4). Jesus's parable of the lost sheep may have been inspired by Ezek. 34:11–16: "For this is what the Lord God says: See, I myself will search for my flock and look for them. As a shepherd looks for his sheep on the day he is among his scattered flock, so I will look for my flock. . . . I will seek the lost, bring back the strays." Note also Isa. 40:11: "He protects his flock like a shepherd; he gathers the lambs in his arms and caries them in the folds of his garment." Approximate parallels to the point of Jesus's parable are found in Greco-Roman ethics: "The true Cynic, when he is thus prepared, cannot rest contented . . . but he must know that he has been sent by Zeus to men, partly as a messenger, in order to show them that in questions of good and evil they have gone astray";[108] "If one has lost his way and is roaming across our fields, it is better to put him on the right path than to drive him out."[109]

Leave the ninety-nine in the open field (15:4). This detail may allude to 1 Sam. 17:28: "Why did you come down here? . . . Who did you leave those few sheep with in the wilderness?" The question was addressed to David the shepherd. If the allusion was intended, Jesus may have been comparing himself to Israel's great king.

There will be more joy in heaven over one sinner who repents (15:7). In the pseudepigraphal book *Joseph and Aseneth* repentance is personified and is said to be "pure and laughing" in heaven, and "all the angels stand in awe of her" (15.8). Consider also a rabbinic saying: "Fairer is one hour of repentance and good works in this world than all the life of the world to come";[110] as well as a rabbinic parable: "Moses was tested by God through sheep. Our Rabbis said that when Moses our teacher, peace be upon him, was tending the flock of Jethro in the wilderness, a little kid escaped from him. He ran after it until it reached a shady place. When it reached the shady place, there appeared to view a pool of water and the kid stopped to drink.

When Moses approached it, he said, 'I did not know that you ran away because of thirst; you must be weary.' So he placed the kid on his shoulder and walked away."[111]

The lost coin was a Greek drachma and, like a Roman denarius, was worth about one day's wages. The drachma pictured is from ancient Larissa in Thessaly, Greece (435–400 BC).

Ten silver coins (15:8). See the article "Money in the New Testament World." Commenting on Prov. 2:4, "If you seek it [wisdom] like silver, and search for it like hidden treasure," Rabbi Phineas ben Yair is remembered to have said, "If you seek after words of Torah as after hidden treasures, the Holy One, blessed be He, will not withhold your reward. If a man loses a penny or a pin in his house, he lights lamp after lamp, wick after wick, till he finds it."[112]

He distributed the assets to them (15:12). See Deut. 21:17. The younger son will receive one-third of the estate. Jewish wisdom counsels against dividing one's estate prior to death (Sir. 33:20, 24).

Traveled to a distant country (15:13). According to Quintilian (first century AD), "Children are obligated to support their impoverished parents, or they deserve to be imprisoned. There was once a man who had two sons. The one was a good manager, the other a spendthrift. Both traveled into a far country."[113]

Squandered his estate in foolish living (15:13). Such foolishness was well known in late antiquity, as seen in the comment of an ancient social critique: "The man speedily squanders the fortune he began with, or is reduced to impotent and licentious penury, and in deprivation combined with craving falls terribly short of his desires."[114]

Feed pigs (15:15). Swine were "unclean" and forbidden as food for Jews (Lev. 11:7; Deut. 14:8).

Eat his fill from the pods (15:16). The pods of the carob tree traditionally were regarded as the food of the poor. According to the rabbis, "When Israelites are reduced to eating carob-pods, they repent";[115] "The nations of the world say, 'We have no need to eat carob-pods like the Jews'";[116] "'Why are you eating carob-pods?' He says, 'I do not have honey.'"[117]

I am dying of hunger! (15:17). The rabbis were well aware of human nature: "When a son [abroad] goes barefoot [through poverty] he remembers the comfort of his father's house."[118]

This son of yours (15:30). The brothers may have been half-brothers, as in Deut. 21:15–17 (see Luke 15:12).

We had to celebrate and rejoice (15:32). The unhappy elder son no doubt would agree with Philo's remarks: "Now parents do not lose thought for their wastrel children but, in pity for their unhappy state, bestow on them care and attention. . . . Often too they lavish their kindness on the wastrels more than on the well behaved. . . . In the same way God too the Father."[119]

Lessons on Wealth and Temptations (16:1–17:10)

A rich man who received an accusation that his manager was squandering his possessions (16:1). According to Roman writers, "[Slaves] should not . . . acquire excessive power, but should all be rigorously kept under discipline, so that you shall never be brought into discredit by them. For everything they do, whether good or ill, will be set to your account";[120] "A man who entrusts his patrimony to someone whom the court has found guilty of business mismanagement will be considered a bad head of household."[121]

What will I do? (16:3). From a play from the fifth century BC: "'Is this your business? You, a sturdy youngster, live by informing on the stranger-folk?' 'What can I do? I never learned to dig.' 'O, but by Zeus, there is many an honest calling whence men like you can earn a livelihood.'"[122]

Take your invoice . . . sit down quickly, and write fifty (16:6). Perhaps the steward has reduced the bill by eliminating the interest in conformity to the OT's law against usury (Lev. 25:36–37; Deut. 15:7–8; 23:19–20).

A hundred measures of wheat (16:7). Literally, this is "one hundred *kors* of grain." It is uncertain how many bushels a single *kor* represents.

Children of light (16:8). Literally, this is "sons of light." See the similar expressions in John 12:36; Eph. 5:8; 1 Thess. 5:5. Members of the wilderness community of Qumran referred to themselves as "sons of light."[123]

Worldly wealth (16:9). The Greek word translated as "wealth" is *mamōnas* ("mammon"), and it comes from either Hebrew *mamon* or Aramaic *mamona*. Although not found in the OT, the word occurs in a few of the Dead Sea Scrolls[124] and in the Aramaic paraphrase of the OT (Targum).[125] It has been suggested that the best explanation for the meaning of the word is that it is from the root that means "firm" or "certain" (from which "amen" is derived). Therefore, mammon is "that in which one puts trust," which could be money, property, wealth (see the article "Money in the New Testament World").

Whoever is faithful in very little is also faithful in much (16:10). We have a parallel in a later collection of Greco-Roman ethical sayings: "Even in regard to the smallest matters, live scrupulously. In human life even the smallest thing is not trivial."[126]

No servant can serve two masters (16:13). Greco-Roman philosophy and ethics were largely in agreement with the position that Jesus takes: "It is impossible for the same person to be a lover of success, the body, and God. For whoever loves success, loves also the body. But whoever loves the body also loves money. But whoever loves money is also necessarily unjust. The unjust person however is an offense against the holiness of God."[127]

Everyone is urgently invited to enter it (16:16). Compare Matt. 11:12: "the violent have been seizing it by force." The idea is that violent people attempt to bring about the kingdom by force rather than by the power of God.

Jesus's parable starts, "There was a rich man who . . . lived in luxury every day" (16:19). This mosaic floor excavated in the Jewish Quarter in Jerusalem would have decorated a house occupied by a wealthy family in the first century AD.

Easier for heaven and earth to pass away (16:17). God's law is just as permanent as creation itself.[128]

A rich man (16:19). Readers in late antiquity would immediately suspect that this rich man was headed for trouble: "Luxurious living results in ruin."[129] The rich man acquires the name "Neues" in Papyrus 75 (early third century). He acquires the name "Dives" from the Vulgate (Lat. *homo quidam erat dives*), but there it is not intended to be a name; it is simply the adjective "rich."

Dress in purple and fine linen (16:19). The inference is that the rich man lived like a king.

Dip the tip of his finger in water and cool my tongue, because I am in agony in this flame! (16:24). Whereas paradise has an abundance of water, hell is dry and hot: "so the thirst and torment which are prepared await them" (2 Esd. 8:59 RSV).

Moses and the prophets (16:29). This phrase indicated that part of the OT universally recognized in the time of Jesus as authoritative Scriptures. "Moses" = Genesis, Exodus, Leviticus, Numbers, and Deuteronomy; "the prophets" = Isaiah, Jeremiah, Ezekiel, and the twelve Minor Prophets.

Millstone (17:2). Even a small millstone was quite heavy; some were used as anchors.

The size of a mustard seed (17:6). This was the smallest seed in use in ancient Israel.

Mulberry tree (17:6). The Greek word here (*sykaminos*) sometimes is translated as "sycamine tree" (KJV, ASV, RSV). It is a type of sycamore and is a very large tree, which is the point of the comparison.

We've only done our duty (17:10). This apparently is a common theme in Jewish piety. A saying attributed to Yohanan ben Zakkai sometimes is cited: "If you have accomplished much in the Law, do not claim merit for yourself; for to this end were you created."[130]

Discipleship and the Kingdom of God (17:11–18:34)

Samaria (17:11). The region of Samaria in OT times (tenth to eighth centuries BC) was inhabited by the ten northern tribes. Following the death of Solomon, the northern tribes seceded from the tribes of Judah and Benjamin in the south. The southern kingdom became known as Judah, while the northern kingdom was initially known as Israel, until eventually it came to be called Samaria after its capital city. In the eighth century Samaria was overrun by the Assyrians. The inhabitants were exiled and in their place foreign peoples were settled. In the centuries that followed a half-Jewish, half-gentile race of people emerged with whom the Jews of Judah to the south and of Galilee to the north frequently quarreled and whom the Jews loathed (cf. Luke 9:51–56).

Leprosy (17:12). The cadaver recovered from the Shroud Tomb in Jerusalem in 2000 confirmed the presence of leprosy in the time of Jesus (see comments on Mark 1:40).

Show yourselves to the priests (17:14). This command alludes to the wording of Lev. 13:49 (see also Lev. 14:2–4), where one whose leprosy or skin disease has cleared up must be inspected by a priest in order to be readmitted into society.

Gave glory to God (17:15). This possibly is an allusion to 2 Kings 5:15, where Naaman the Syrian leper praises the God of Israel for his cleansing. Allusion to Naaman is found in Luke 4:27.

This foreigner (17:18). The Samaritan is a "foreigner" (literally, "a stranger"), one who is not a pure descendant of "Father Abraham," as the rich man in 16:19–31 had been.

The kingdom of God is not coming with something observable (17:20). In the Talmud we read this exchange between a rabbi and his disciples:

> The disciples of Rabbi Yose ben Kisma asked him, "When will the Messiah come?" He answered, "I fear [giving an answer], lest you demand a sign of me [to prove that my answer is correct]." They assured him, "We will demand no sign of you." So he answered them, "When this gate [of the city of Caesarea Philippi] falls down, is rebuilt, falls again, and is again rebuilt, and then falls a third time, before it can be rebuilt the son of David will come." They said to him, "Master, give us a sign." He protested, "Did you not assure me that you would not demand a sign?"[131]

In the days of Noah (17:26). The reference is to the judgment of the flood (see Gen. 6–7).

In the days of Lot (17:28). The reference is to the judgment that befell the wicked cities of Sodom and Gomorrah (see Gen. 18–19).

Remember Lot's wife! (17:32). Lot's wife "looked back and became a pillar of salt" (Gen. 19:26).

Two will be in one bed (17:34). Some commentators have thought that homosexuality is at issue here (in view of the reference to the judgment on

Sodom in 17:28–29 and the reference to Lot's wife in v. 32). But if homosexuality is the issue, why are not *both* men judged? No, the point is quite different. The two men are not "in bed"; rather, they are reclining "at table." The Greek word *klinē* can mean either "bed" or "table"; here it means the latter. The point is the same as in the example of the two women grinding grain in verse 35 (and, in some manuscripts, the two workers in the field in v. 36): two men are at dinner; one is taken, the other is left.

A judge in a certain town who didn't fear God or respect people (18:2). One is reminded of Josephus's description of King Jehoiakim as "unjust and wicked by nature, neither reverent toward God nor kind to people."[132]

A widow (18:3). The judge's callousness toward the widow is clearly in violation of biblical injunctions (e.g., Deut. 10:18; Mal. 3:5; cf. Sir. 35:17–19).

I will give her justice, so that she doesn't wear me out (18:5). Literally, the phrase is "finally hit me under the eye." The verb *hypōpiazō* (used also in 1 Cor. 9:27) often is used in a figurative sense ("to give a black eye" [i.e., besmirch one's character] or "to wear out completely"). It is possible that Jesus intends humor (as there is in many of his sayings—e.g., Matt. 7:3–5), and so the literal rendering may be the most appropriate: "lest she come and give me a black eye."

We think of a third-century-BC papyrus written by a widow, in which she petitions a royal steward in order to have her donkey returned:

> To Zenon, greetings from Senchons. I petitioned you about my donkey which Nikias took. If you had written to me about her [i.e., the donkey], I would have sent her to you. If it pleases you, command him to return her, in order that we may carry the hives to the pastures, lest they be ruined for you and be of no use to either yourself or the king. And if you examine the matter, you will be persuaded that we are useful to you. And I will send the foal of the ass to you. Therefore, I beg and entreat you, that you not put me off. I am a widow woman. Farewell.[133]

We have another widow's petition (ca. 280 BC), this time addressed to a prefect (a governor). The woman's flock of sixty sheep and various household items had been seized by a man named Syrion shortly after her husband's death. Although we do not know the outcome, the prefect ordered the sheriff to look into the matter.[134]

Plutarch relates the story of a poor old woman who demanded justice of King Philip of Macedonia, father of Alexander the Great: "When a poor old woman insisted that her case should be heard before him, and often caused him annoyance, he said he had no time to spare, whereupon she burst out, 'Then give up being king!' Philip, amazed at her words, proceeded at once to hear not only her case but those of others."[135]

The parable Jesus told in 18:10–14 begins, "Two men went up to the temple to pray." The main staircase used to gain entrance to the various courts around the temple is shown here and is known as the monumental staircase. Much of it has been reconstructed, but the lowest steps seen in the foreground are from the first century AD.

Will not God grant justice to his elect? (18:7). The application is an instance of the form of argument *a minori ad maius* ("from minor to major"), in which it is argued that if a lesser case is valid (a dishonest, uncaring judge who finally sees that justice is carried out for an insignificant widow), then a greater case must be valid (a holy, caring God who will help his own people who ask him).

He will swiftly grant them justice (18:8). Philo remarks on Moses and prayer, "Moses retired . . . beseeching God to save the oppressed from their helpless, miserable plight. . . . God, in high approval of his spirit, which loved the good and hated evil, listened to his prayers, and *very shortly* judged the land and its doings as became His nature."[136]

A first-century inscription from Rheneia reads, "I invoke and pray to the Most High God, the Lord of Spirits and of all flesh against those who deceitfully poisoned the tragic young woman Heraclea. They unjustly spilled her innocent blood. May the same thing happen to them and to their children! Lord, you who see all, and the angels of God before whom every soul today humbly brings this supplication, avenge this innocent blood, require it, and *very quickly*!"[137]

When the Son of Man comes (18:8). On "Son of Man," see Dan. 7:13–14; see comments on Mark 2:10.

Two men went up to the temple to pray (18:10). Pharisees may have stood up to pray in a prominent location, perhaps toward the front, of the temple's Court of Israel (see the article "The Jerusalem Temple").

I fast twice a week; I give a tenth of everything I get (18:12). The Pharisee is praying the "Confession," as the rabbis came to call it (Deut. 26). The conceit of the Pharisee finds a counterpart in a rabbinic prayer:

> On leaving [the house of study] what does he [Rabbi Nehunya ben Haqaneh] say? "I give thanks to you, O God, that you have set my portion with those who sit in the House of Study and you have not set my portion with those who sit in [street] corners, for I rise early and they rise early, but I rise early for words of Torah and they rise early for frivolous talk; I labor and they labor, but I labor and receive a reward and they labor and do not receive a reward; I run and they run, but I run to life in the world to come and they run to the pit of destruction."[138]

Would not even raise his eyes to heaven (18:13). The tax collector's sense of sin is so great that he would not, as was customary, look toward heaven while he prayed.[139]

God, have mercy on me, a sinner! (18:13). One thinks of what the angel said to righteous Ezra: "But you have often compared yourself to the unrighteous. Never do so! But even in this respect you will be praiseworthy before the Most High, because you have humbled yourself, as is becoming for you, and have not deemed yourself to be among the righteous in order to receive the greatest glory. For many miseries will affect those who inhabit the world in the last times, because they have walked in great pride" (1 Esd. 8:47b–50).

The commandments (18:20). The reference is to the Ten Commandments (Exod. 20:3–17; Deut. 5:7–21).

The meaning of the saying was hidden from them (18:34). The disciples need to have their "eyes opened," as it were, in order to perceive divine truth. See 2 Kings 6:17, 20.

The Arrival of the Messiah (18:35–19:44)

Jericho (19:1). This is one of the oldest cities in the world. The Jericho "tower" excavated in the 1930s may be ten thousand years old. The city was conquered by Joshua when the people of Israel entered the land of Canaan (Josh. 6).

I'll give half of my possessions to the poor . . . I'll pay back four times as much (19:8). While it is possible that Zacchaeus has repented after conversation and supper with Jesus, and will now be honest and generous, both Greek verbs are in the present tense. Rather, the statement is "I give half of my possessions to the poor. . . . I pay back four times the amount." Zacchaeus may be responding to the grumbling crowd that complains that Jesus plans to eat supper with a wealthy tax collector, who, it is assumed, is dishonest. Contrary to the opinion of the resentful crowd, Zacchaeus gives to the poor and always repays fourfold (as in Exod. 22:1; 2 Sam. 12:6) should he overcharge.

A son of Abraham (19:9). That is, a true child of God. Although this was a common designation for a Jew (*m. Avot* 5.19), Paul uses the expression of Christians (cf. Gal. 3:29).

To seek and to save the lost (19:10). Compare Ezek. 34:16: "I will seek the lost, bring back the strays." The prophet likens Israel to sheep (cf. Ezek. 34:2, 11; Luke 15:3–7).

A nobleman traveled to a far country to receive for himself authority to be king (19:12). The parable's "nobleman" in all probability is none other than the late and unlamented Herod Archelaus, son of Herod the Great. When his father died in 4 BC, Archelaus sent an embassy to Rome, laying claim to the whole of his late father's kingdom, left household instructions to his servants, was hated by his subjects, and was pursued by an embassy that petitioned against his receiving the kingdom. Archelaus slaughtered those opposed to his rule, received half of his father's kingdom, returned as ruler, and collected tribute.[140]

Kept it safe in a cloth (19:20). The Greek word *soudarion* refers to a small piece of cloth used as a handkerchief. Hebrew sources also indicate the use of a handkerchief to secure money.[141]

Why, then, didn't you put my money in the bank? And when I returned, I would have collected it with interest (19:23). The expectation of earning interest is contrary to Jewish law (cf. Deut. 23:19–20; Exod. 22:25; Lev. 25:36–37). Jewish law allows interest to be collected from gentiles, but not from fellow Jews, and there is no reason to think that gentiles are in view (see the article "Money in the New Testament World").

Bring here these enemies of mine, who did not want me to rule over them, and slaughter them in my presence (19:27). Luke's nobleman is avaricious and vengeful; he is a gouger, possibly a thief, disregards the humane elements of the Jewish law, and shows no mercy to those who (understandably) have opposed him. Jesus's agrarian audience would have viewed the principal figure in this parable with unqualified fear and loathing. His gouging practices place a heavy financial burden on the small farmers, who pay him interest and sometimes lose their crops to this grasping, merciless man. A parallel with the hated Archelaus (see Luke 19:12) may well have been intended.

Bethphage and Bethany (19:29). These two small villages are east of Jerusalem. "Bethphage" means "house of figs"; "Bethany" may mean "house of dates."

Mount of Olives (19:29). The Mount of Olives rises twenty-four hundred feet above sea level, east of Jerusalem, separated from the city by the Kidron Valley. Atop the hill one can look down upon the Temple Mount, which stands at an elevation of about twenty-two hundred feet.

The Lord needs it (19:31). Jesus invokes the law/custom of *angareia* ("pressed transportation"), by which an animal or person can be pressed into service (but they are let go at the end of the service and usually there was compensation).

They were spreading their clothes on the road (19:36). This was a common practice in late antiquity (see 2 Kings 9:13; cf. 1 Macc. 13:51; 2 Macc. 10:7).

The stones would cry out (19:40). Jesus's curious exclamation may allude to Hab. 2:11: "For the stones will cry out from the wall, and the rafters will answer them from the woodwork."

Peace (19:42). The reference to peace may play on the popular understanding that the name "Jerusalem" meant "peace."[142]

It is hidden from your eyes (19:42). See comments on Luke 18:34.

You did not recognize the time when God visited you (19:44). The idea of the Lord "visiting" his people is found frequently in the OT (e.g., the Hebrew term is translated "pay attention" or "punish" in Exod. 3:16; Ruth 1:6; 1 Sam. 2:21; Jer. 6:15). In Luke, see 1:68; 7:16.

They will not leave one stone on another (19:44). Note 2 Sam. 17:13, where Hushai deceives Absalom into thinking that his army will enter the city to which David might retreat and "drag its stones into the valley until not even a pebble can be found there."

Teaching and Controversy in the Temple (19:45–21:4)

House of prayer (19:46). This comes from Isa. 56:7, which echoes Solomon's prayer at the dedication of the temple (see 1 Kings 8:41–43).

Den of thieves (19:46). This comes from Jer. 7:11. Josephus tells of a man who from AD 63 to 70 preached sermons of judgment on Jerusalem and the temple based on Jer. 7.[143] The ruling priests reacted violently against this man, even as they did against Jesus of Nazareth.

The leaders of the people (19:47). Literally, "leaders" is "first men" (*hoi prōtoi*). It probably refers to priestly aristocrats, for this is the same way Josephus refers to them.[144]

Proclaiming the good news (20:1). Of the fifty or so occurrences of the verb for "proclaim the good news" (*euangelizō*) in the Gospels and Acts, half appear in Luke-Acts.

All the people will stone us (20:6). Given their religious occupation, the priests' reference to stoning may imply that the people will view them as false prophets and false teachers and that therefore they will fall under the judgment prescribed by Deut. 13 (e.g., v. 10: "Stone him to death for trying to turn you away from the Lord your God").

A man planted a vineyard (20:9). These words are drawn from Isaiah's Song of the Vineyard (see Isa. 5:1–7).

Leased it to tenant farmers (20:9). Many lease agreements, some concerning planting and caring for vineyards, have been found among the thousands of papyri recovered from the dry sands of Egypt.

Everyone who falls on that stone will be broken to pieces, but on whomever it falls, it will shatter him (20:18). There is no equivalent to this saying in Mark's version (Mark 12:10–11). Luke quotes Ps. 118:22 ("The stone that the builders rejected has become the cornerstone") but omits Ps. 118:23 (cf. Mark 12:11) and adds this interesting saying about being "broken to pieces." The first half of the saying may be based on Isa. 8:14–15: "He will be a sanctuary; but for the two houses of Israel, he will be a stone to stumble over. . . . Many will stumble over these; they will fall and be broken." That the saying is based on Isa. 8:14–15 is supported by the observation that Isa. 8:14 sometimes is quoted in conjunction with Ps. 118:22 (e.g., 1 Pet. 2:4–8).

The second half of the saying ("on whomever it falls, it will shatter him") may allude to Dan. 2:34–35, 44–45, passages that describe the coming messianic stone that will shatter the image that represents the pagan kingdoms that oppress Israel. A similar rabbinic saying sometimes is cited: "If a stone falls on a pot, woe to the pot! If a pot falls on a stone, woe to the pot! In either case, woe to the pot!"[145] What is interesting here is that this saying appears in the context of a discussion of Ps. 118:22 and Dan. 2:45.

Detecting their craftiness (20:23). One thinks of the trickery of the envoys of Gibeon who deceived Joshua (Josh. 9:4). The words of the sage Yeshua ben Sira apply to those who try to trap Jesus: "There is a cleverness [*panourgia*, translated as "craftiness" in Luke 20:23] which is scrupulous but unjust, and there are people who distort kindness to gain a verdict" (Sir. 19:25 RSV).

Denarius (20:24). This was the principal coin of the Roman Empire, usually a day's wage.

Sadducees, who say there is no resurrection (20:27). For the views of the Sadducees, see Acts 23:8.[146]

The third took her. In the same way, all seven died, and left no children (20:31). The OT practice of levirate marriage is presupposed in the question put to Jesus (see comments on Mark 12:23).[147]

In the resurrection from the dead neither marry nor are given in marriage . . . they are like angels (20:35–36). In the resurrection human beings are angel-like; they no longer marry.[148] Therefore, the levirate laws that bind men and women on earth no longer apply.

Children of the resurrection (20:36). Literally, this is "sons of the resurrection," a unique expression so far as we know.

All are living to him (20:38). Compare 4 Macc. 7:19, "They believe that they, like our patriarchs Abraham and Isaac and Jacob, do not die to God, but live in God" (RSV); and 16:25, "Those who die for the sake of God live in God, as do Abraham and Isaac and Jacob and all the patriarchs" (RSV).

The Christ is the son of David (20:41). The awaited Messiah often was referred to as the "son of David" (see the article "Messianic Expectations in Jesus's Day").[149]

David calls him "Lord"; how then can the Christ be his son? (20:44). In the culture of the time the son is inferior to the father or ancestor. Therefore, calling the Messiah "Lord" implies that he is more than a mere "son of David."

Who want to go around in long robes and who love greetings in the marketplaces (20:46). The gentile world offers parallels to Jesus's invective: there are those who "preach for the sake of gain and glory and only for their own benefit"[150] and "make a great show of virtue and never practice it."[151]

They devour widows' houses and say long prayers just for show (20:47). Compare Hosea 10:4. The religious establishment was supposed to aid the widow and the orphan, not exploit them (see Exod. 22:22; Deut. 10:18; 14:29; 24:17, 19–21; 26:12–13; 27:19).

The rich dropping their offerings into the temple treasury (21:1). Money was cast into trumpet-shaped receptacles (see comments on Mark 12:41).[152]

She out of her poverty has put in all she had to live on (21:4). The poor widow cannot afford her tiny gift, which amounts to, literally, "her whole life."[153]

The Fall of Jerusalem and the Coming of the Son of Man (21:5–36)

Was adorned with beautiful stones and gifts dedicated to God (21:5). From the descriptions of Josephus and from the ruins themselves, it is not hard to imagine what it was that the disciples saw and were talking about. One such gift was one of the gates of the temple, overlaid with gold and

Now all that remains of Herod's temple are the Herodian dressed stones that were part of the Temple Mount substructure during Jesus's day. One place to view them is along the lower course of the Western Wall shown here, a place long revered by Jews.

On the ground at the southwest corner of the Temple Mount, the stones that were dismantled from the wall during the Roman destruction can still be seen as a large pile of rubble (see Luke 21:6).

adorned with a large golden grape cluster "as tall as a man."[154] The Roman historian Tacitus says, "Jerusalem is the capital of the Jews. In it was a temple possessing enormous riches."[155] See the article "The Jerusalem Temple."

Many will come in my name (21:8). Josephus speaks of many false prophets and men who desired to grasp kingship over Israel.[156] Jesus's "will come in my name" probably means that men will appear who claim to be the Messiah.

Wars and rebellions (21:9). During the Jewish Revolt the Roman Empire was convulsed with uprisings.[157]

Violent earthquakes (21:11). There were destructive earthquakes in Laodicea in AD 61 and in Pompeii in AD 62.[158]

Terrifying sights and great signs from heaven (21:11). These additional details are part of the stock vocabulary and imagery of apocalyptic.[159]

They will lay their hands on you and persecute you (21:12). As the book of Acts shows, Jesus's prediction soon came true (Acts 4:3; 5:18; 12:1; 21:27).

Not to prepare your defense ahead of time (21:14). The Greek term (*promeletaō*, "prepare") that this expression translates is a technical word that refers to memorizing a prepared text or speech.[160]

You will be hated by everyone because of my name (21:17). In Luke's time it may have been thought that this warning had been fulfilled in the aftermath of Nero's malicious suggestion that the fire that destroyed part of Rome (which Nero himself purportedly started) had been the work of the sect of Christians,[161] though most Romans suspected the depraved emperor.[162]

These are days of vengeance to fulfill all the things that are written (21:22). These words allude to Hosea 9:7: "The days of punishment have come; the days of retribution have come." The city of Jerusalem failed to recognize the day of visitation (cf. Luke 19:44); now it is the time of God's coming to the city.

There will be great distress (21:23). Compare Zeph. 1:15: "That day is a day of wrath, a day of trouble and distress, a day of destruction and desolation."

Led captive into all the nations (21:24). Compare Deut. 28:64: "Then the Lord will scatter you among all peoples from one end of the earth to the other."

Jerusalem will be trampled by the Gentiles (21:24). Compare Zech. 12:2–3: "Look, I will make Jerusalem a cup that causes staggering for the peoples who surround the city. The siege against Jerusalem will also involve Judah. On that day I will make Jerusalem a heavy stone for all the peoples; all who try to lift it will injure themselves severely when all the nations of the earth gather against her."

Until the times of the Gentiles are fulfilled (21:24). Compare Rom. 11:25–27: "A partial hardening has come upon Israel until the fullness of the gentiles has come in. And in this way all Israel will be saved." The language of Luke 20:21–24 echoes passages like Ezek. 39:23 and Zech. 12:3, passages that go on to speak of Israel's restoration (see also Ezek. 39:24–29; Zech. 12:4–9).

Signs in the sun, moon, and stars (21:25). Compare Isa. 13:10: "The stars of the sky and its constellations will not give their light. The sun will be dark when it rises, and the moon will not shine"; Isa. 34:4: "All the stars in the sky will dissolve. The sky will roll up like a scroll, and its stars will all wither as leaves wither on the vine"; Joel 2:10: "The sun and the moon grow dark, and the stars cease their shining."[163]

There will be anguish on the earth among nations (21:25). Compare Deut. 28:28: "The Lord will afflict you with madness, blindness, and mental confusion."

The roaring of the sea and the waves (21:25). Compare Isa. 17:12: "Ah! The roar of many peoples—they roar like the roaring of the seas. The raging of the nations—they rage like the rumble of rushing water"; Ps. 65:7: "You silence the roar of the seas, the roar of their waves, and the tumult of the nations."

People will faint from fear and expectation of the things that are coming on the world (21:26). Fear seized many inhabitants of the Roman Empire in the aftermath of the death of Nero, the last of the Julian Caesars. The empire became embroiled in the struggle to find a successor. Galba declared himself emperor, reigning from 9 June 68 to 15 January 69. He was succeeded by Otho, reigning from 15 January to 20 April 69. Vitellius reigned from 20 April until his defeat at the hands of Vespasian. Vespasian was declared emperor on 1 July 69, but Vitellius was not killed until 20 December 69. Thus from the end of Nero's reign until the beginning of Vespasian's reign the empire was ruled by five different emperors, from June 68 to July 69—five emperors in thirteen months!

Your redemption is near (21:28). Compare Isa. 63:4; LXX Dan. 4:34: "And in the completion of the seven years the time of my redemption has come"; *1 Enoch* 51.2: "And he shall choose the righteous and holy from among them; for the day has drawn near that they should be saved."

Minds are not dulled from carousing, drunkenness, and worries of life (21:34). Luke's language about minds being dulled (literally, "hearts weighed down") is reminiscent of the Greek text of Exod. 7:14; 8:15 (LXX 8:11); 9:7. On the warning against carousing and drunkenness, compare Rom. 13:13; Eph. 5:18; 1 Thess. 5:7.

That day will come on you unexpectedly like a trap (21:34–35). Compare 1 Thess. 5:2–3: "The day of the Lord will come just like a thief in the night. . . . Sudden destruction will come upon them."

The Last Supper and the Arrest of Jesus (21:37–22:27)

The Festival of Unleavened Bread, which is called Passover (22:1). The Passover was the great festival in which Jews remembered and celebrated their rescue from slavery in Egypt (see Exod. 12). It was celebrated on 14 or 15 Nisan (April/May) and was followed by the Festival of Unleavened Bread (Exod. 12:15), which was celebrated on 15–21 Nisan. These holidays were thought of as the "week of Passover."

Satan (22:3). "Satan" (literally, "opponent") is mentioned several times in the OT (e.g., 1 Chron. 21:1; Job 1:6–8; 2:7; Zech. 3:1–2). In the Gospels he is the tempter of Jesus (see comments on Mark 1:13). In Luke's Gospel he falls from heaven (10:18). Here he enters Judas Iscariot, the disciple who will betray Jesus.

Agreed to give him silver (22:5). Josephus reports that some ruling priests offered and received bribes.[164] In antiquity traitors were despised.[165] Betrayal for money was regarded as especially heinous.[166]

The guest room (22:11). Visitors to Jerusalem who wished to celebrate Passover had to secure a guest room. Although Jesus was residing in Bethany, the plan was to eat the Passover meal itself inside the walls of the holy city (see Deut. 16:2; *m. Pesahim* 7.9).

Make the preparations there (22:12). The preparations would include the roast lamb, the wine, the unleavened bread, and the bitter herbs, as well as the necessary furnishings.

Reclined at the table (22:14). People did not sit upright in chairs while dining. Rather, they reclined on couches or mats, with heads and hands toward the low table and legs and feet away from the eating area.

In remembrance of me (22:19). The other Gospel accounts do not contain this phrase, but it is found in 1 Cor. 11:24.

This cup is the new covenant in my blood (22:20). The words of Jesus echo key passages of Scripture, such as Exod. 24:8; Jer. 31:31; and perhaps Zech. 9:11. (In the Aramaic, reference to deliverance from Egypt is explicit.)

Those who have authority over them have themselves called "Benefactors" (22:25). A popular title for kings and potentates in the Middle East was "benefactor." The Greek word (*euergetēs*) literally means "doer of good." The title appears in inscriptions and papyri, right alongside other titles, such as "savior," "god," and "lord." It is said of Emperor Augustus that he "surpassed all previous benefactors, not even leaving to posterity any hope of surpassing what he has done, since the birthday of the god Augustus was the beginning of the good news for the world."[167] There is also an inscription in honor of Gallio, the proconsul of Greece (cf. Acts 18:12): "The city of the Plataions [honors] Lucius Junius Gallio Anianus, proconsul, her own [i.e., the city's] benefactor" (on a tablet from Pompeii).

Sit on thrones judging the twelve tribes of Israel (22:30). See comments on Matt. 19:28.

Satan has asked to sift you like wheat (22:31). See Job 1:6–12; 2:1–6, where Satan makes demands regarding Job. The point of sifting probably has nothing to do with separating wheat from chaff, but that of being shaken and blown about by the wind—that is, being thoroughly disturbed.[168]

I'm ready to go with you both to prison and to death (22:33). Here in Luke we have anticipation of Peter being cast into prison (cf. Acts 5:18; 12:3), as well as later tradition of his martyrdom.[169]

And he was counted among the lawless (22:37). Part of Isa. 53:12 is quoted. Note also *Psalms of Solomon* 16.5: "I will give thanks to you, O God, who came to my aid for my salvation, and who did not count me with the sinners for my destruction."

A kiss (22:48). A kiss is a sign of affection and loyalty, but it can be involved in treachery. See 2 Sam. 20:9–10, where Joab kisses Amasa and then kills him.

Your hour (22:53). See Luke 4:13.

The high priest's house (22:54). Archaeological excavations in Jerusalem have uncovered two or three large domestic complexes. We should assume that Caiaphas, the high priest at the time of the arrest of Jesus, lived in the same mansion as Annas, his father-in-law (see John 18:13, 24).

A fire in the middle of the courtyard (22:55). Large homes usually had a gated courtyard. Peter had access to the courtyard of the high priest's home, but not to the home itself.

Very old olive trees on the Mount of Olives.

He's also a Galilean (22:59). According to Matt. 26:73, it is Peter's accent that makes it clear that he is a Galilean. In rabbinic tradition the accent of Galilean Jews sometimes was mocked.[170]

You will deny me three times (22:61). Jesus foretold Peter's denial in 22:34.

Prophesy! Who was it that hit you? (22:64). Because Jesus is blindfolded, he cannot see who hits him. If he is a prophet, the soldiers assume, he would know even without seeing.

The Messiah (22:67). Literally, this is "the anointed." It was hoped that the Messiah, descendant of David, would come, drive the Romans out, and inaugurate a new era for Israel (see the article "Messianic Expectations in Jesus's Day"; see comments on Mark 8:29).

The Son of Man (22:69). Jesus is the figure envisioned in Dan. 7:13–14.

Seated at the right hand of the power of God (22:69). This was foretold in Ps. 110:1.

The Son of God (22:70). The confession of Jesus as "Son of God" recalls what the angel said in 1:35. This title was also applied to the Roman emperor.

The Church of Saint Peter in Gallicantu (meaning "crowing of the cock") was built to commemorate Peter's denial of Jesus in the courtyard of the high priest. It is unlikely that this is actually Caiaphas's house.

The Trial and Crucifixion of Jesus (23:1–49)

In this model of first-century Jerusalem, the traditional location of Golgotha was outside the second city wall.

Their whole assembly (23:1). Literally, this is "the whole crowd." Luke simplifies Mark's account (Mark 15:1), which speaks of a second meeting before the Sanhedrin.

Pilate (23:1). Pilate was *praefectus* of Judea and Samaria from AD 25 (or perhaps as early as 20/21) until his removal at the beginning of 37 (see comments on Mark 15:1; see the article "Pontius Pilate"). His name was found inscribed on a stone unearthed at Caesarea Maritima, on Israel's Mediterranean coast. The Jewish writers Philo[171] and Josephus[172] vilify Pilate as violent and corrupt.

Opposing payment of taxes to Caesar (23:2). This is a very serious charge, if true. There is no indication that Jesus taught his followers not to pay taxes. The accusation likely grew out of his statement about rendering to God what is God's (20:21–25).

King of the Jews (23:3). This was the official Roman title conferred upon Herod the Great.[173]

Herod's jurisdiction (23:7). The Herod here is Antipas, the tetrarch of Galilee (see comments on Mark 6:14). Antipas probably was in Jerusalem to observe the Passover.

For a long time he had wanted to see him (23:8). Earlier Luke stated that (Herod) Antipas had wanted to see Jesus (9:9; cf. 13:31).

Hoping to see some miracle (23:8). Others had demanded signs (e.g., 11:16, 29–30; 21:7).

Dressed him in bright clothing (23:11). Mockery of this nature was not uncommon in the Roman world. Philo tells the story of the mockery of Carabas, a simple-minded street person. He was dressed as a king, complete with royal scepter, and hailed as "Lord."[174]

Release Barabbas (23:18). Because Luke has omitted Mark's explanation of the Passover pardon (Mark 15:6–15), some readers will have wondered why people are shouting for the release of Barabbas. There is significant evidence that on various holidays Roman authorities released prisoners or persons accused of crimes.

They seized Simon, a Cyrenian (23:26). We probably have here another example of *angareia* (see comments on Luke 19:31). According to Mark 15:21, Simon was the father of Alexander and Rufus. We may have the ossuary (bone box) of this Alexander, for on it are inscribed these words: "Alexander [son] of Simon the Cyrene." The ossuary was found in Jerusalem.

Daughters of Jerusalem (23:28). The epithet "daughters of Jerusalem" occurs several times in Song of Songs, in romantic and joyful contexts. Here, however, the expression is filled with sorrow and pathos.

Weep for yourselves and your children (23:28). During the siege of Jerusalem (AD 69–70), according to Josephus, there was such a shortage of food that one woman actually cooked and ate her infant.[175]

Blessed are the women without children (23:29). Jesus's cynical beatitude reverses convention: "Cursed be the breast that gave suck to such a one as this."[176]

Fall on us! (23:30). The allusion is to Hosea 10:8b: "They will say to the mountains, 'Cover us!' and to the hills, 'Fall on us!'" God's wrath will be so severe that people will do anything to escape it.

If they do these things when the wood is green, what will happen when it is dry? (23:31). The saying is proverbial and probably alludes to Ezek. 17:24; 20:47.

Father, forgive them, because they do not know what they are doing (23:34). Jesus has mitigated the guilt of those who have killed him by classifying the crime as a sin of ignorance, which is far less culpable than willful sin (cf. Lev. 4:2; Num. 15:25–30; Acts 3:17; 13:27; Philo, *Against Flaccus* 7).

You will be with me in paradise (23:43). "Paradise" comes from the Septuagint translation of "garden" (*paradeisos*) in Gen. 2:8; 13:10. Eventually it came to refer to the abode of the righteous dead (cf. 2 Cor. 12:4; Rev. 2:7).

Darkness came over the whole land (23:44). Perhaps the sun refuses to shine light on what has been done to Jesus. Writing to the Jewish priest Hyrcanus (42 BC), the Roman general Mark Antony justifies his war against wicked men who are guilty of "lawless deeds against men and of unlawful acts against the gods, from which we believe the very sun turned away, as if it too were loath to look upon the foul deed against Caesar."[177]

Father, *into your hands I entrust my spirit* (23:46). Jesus has quoted Ps. 31:5.

Striking their chests (23:48). On learning of the death of his son Absalom, King David "went to the highest part of the city and bewailed his son, beating his breast, tearing his hair."[178] See also 18:13.

The Burial and Resurrection of Jesus (23:50–24:53)

Wrapped it in fine linen (23:53). Linen burial shrouds have been found in ancient Jewish tombs (see comments on Mark 15:46).

Preparation day (23:54). This refers to the day that leads up to the evening of the Passover celebration.

Spices and perfumes (23:56). It was customary to wash and anoint the corpse for burial (not embalm). The perfume masked the odor of decay, which was necessary because the funeral lasted one week and included going inside the tomb.

The first day of the week (24:1). In the Jewish calendar this is Sunday.

The stone rolled away (24:2). The phrase "rolled away" suggests that the stone was round, not a square block, as were more than 80 percent of the stones that sealed tombs (see comments on Mark 15:46).

When Joseph of Arimathea offered his tomb for the burial of Jesus, it was likely a kochim-style tomb. The main room of the tomb had a bench on its perimeter, which was used to prepare the body before placing it in one of the smaller kochim (niches). In twelve to eighteen months, the family would return to the tomb, gather the remains from the niche, and place them in a limestone box called an ossuary.

Two men stood by them in dazzling clothes (24:4). See Dan. 12:1–3, where the archangel Michael is present and the resurrected shine and are like stars. One awestruck man describes what he saw while grieving at his nephew's tomb: "I saw a figure gliding down from heaven, radiant with light like that of the stars."[179]

Why are you looking for the living among the dead? (24:5). The angels' saying is proverbial and may be compared to a rabbinic saying: "Is it the way of the dead to be sought for among the living, or are the living among the dead?"[180]

The Eleven (24:9). Judas Iscariot is no longer numbered with the Twelve.

Only the linen cloths (24:12). Had the corpse of Jesus merely been moved, the strips of linen cloth would not have been left behind.

Emmaus, which was about seven miles from Jerusalem (24:13). Luke tells us that Emmaus was about seven miles (literally, "sixty stadia" or about 6.8 miles) from Jerusalem. Some manuscripts suggest that the village was farther away. Josephus mentions a city called Emmaus.[181]

They were prevented from recognizing him (24:16). Compare 9:45; 18:34; 24:31.

Cleopas (24:18). This is a shortened form of the Greek name Cleopatros, not to be confused with Clopas (a Semitic name) found in John 19:25.

A prophet powerful in action and speech (24:19). This alludes to the promise of the great prophet who would be like Moses (Deut. 18:15–18; cf. Acts 3:22; 7:35–37).

There is much discussion about the exact location of the town of Emmaus, to which Cleopas, his companion, and Jesus walked shortly after Jesus's resurrection. Many towns were called by that name; this map shows three possibilities that have been given consideration because of their proximity to Jerusalem.

Who was about to redeem Israel (24:21). See Isa. 41:14; 43:14; 44:22–24; 1 Macc. 4:11; compare Luke 2:38; Acts 1:6.

Moses and all the Prophets . . . in all the Scriptures (24:27). See comments on Luke 24:44.

He took the bread, blessed and broke it (24:30). The breaking of bread reminded the disciples of the Last Supper (22:14–23; 24:35).

The Lord has truly been raised and has appeared to Simon! (24:34). The appearance to Simon Peter is not narrated in the Gospels, but it is mentioned by Paul in 1 Cor. 15:5.

Thought they were seeing a ghost (24:37). Given the culture of the time, the disciples were far more inclined to believe in the appearance of a ghost rather than the appearance of someone resurrected.

He took it and ate it (24:43). It was believed that angels and ghosts did not eat food.[182] Eating the fish proved that the *resurrected* Jesus stood before his disciples, not the ghost of Jesus.

The Law of Moses, the Prophets, and the Psalms (24:44). In the Greek text this reads, "the Law of Moses and the Prophets and Psalms" (i.e., there is no definite article before "Psalms"). "The Prophets and Psalms" represents one body of literature, not two. In the time of Jesus the Psalms were considered prophetic and were lumped in with the Prophets (as seen in the Dead Sea Scrolls).

The Messiah would suffer (24:46). See Isa. 53:7–8 (cf. Acts 8:26–39).

Rise from the dead the third day (24:46). See Ps. 16:8–11 (cf. Acts 2:27; 13:35).

Repentance for forgiveness of sins (24:47). See Joel 2:32 (cf. Acts 2:21). Rabbi Eliezer (ca. AD 90) said, "If Israel repent, they will be redeemed; if not, they will not be redeemed."[183]

What my Father promised (24:49). This refers to God's promise to pour out the Holy Spirit. See Acts 1:4; 2:16 (cf. Isa. 32:15; 44:3; Ezek. 39:29; Joel 2:28–29).

Lifting up his hands he blessed them (24:50). Before leaving his disciples, Jesus puts them under God's care, much as a priest might (cf. Lev. 9:22).

They were continually in the temple praising God (24:53). Luke's narrative ends where it began: in the temple (cf. 1:5, 8–9, 14, 41–44).

John

Andreas J. Köstenberger

Introduction. The "beloved disciple" is most likely the apostle John, the son of Zebedee.[1] Not only was John one of the Twelve, but also, together with Peter and John's brother James, he was one of three disciples who formed Jesus's inner circle.[2] The self-designation of "the disciple whom Jesus loved" most likely serves as an epithet of authorial modesty. It also avoids confusion with John the Baptist, who alone is called John in this Gospel.

According to early church tradition, John wrote his Gospel in the city of Ephesus.[3] His intended readership most likely was composed of both Jews and gentiles, in all probability believers who were to pass on John's eyewitness testimony regarding Jesus the Messiah and Son of God to others (20:30–31). Ultimately, like the other evangelists, John wrote for a universal audience, anyone who would want to hear the story of Jesus.

The evidence points to composition following the destruction of the Jerusalem temple by the Romans in AD 70. There is no mention of the Sadducees, who subsequently faded from view. Also, John twice refers to the Sea of Galilee as the "Sea of Tiberias" (6:1; 21:1), a name that gained prominence toward the end of the first century. The church fathers, for their part, attest to the fact that John was the last among the evangelists to write a Gospel.[4]

Most likely John wrote to present Jesus as the new spiritual temple after the Jerusalem sanctuary had been destroyed. Similar to other contemporaneous Jewish writings such as *4 Ezra* and *2 Baruch*, John's Gospel addressed the question of what God's people must do in the wake of the loss of their central place of worship. John argues that the crucified and risen Jesus is the new spiritual temple (2:19–21) and that true worship be rendered in spirit and truth (4:21–24).

Prologue (1:1–18)

In the beginning (1:1). John is drawing on Gen. 1, deliberately reflecting the opening words of the book of Genesis: "*In the beginning* God created the heavens and the earth."

Was the Word (1:1). The reference to the Word (*logos*) is based on the theology of the word of God in the OT, particularly Gen. 1 and Isa. 55:9–11. John's use of *logos* to speak of God's word would also have resonated with those familiar with Greek philosophy. The Stoics used the term to speak of "Reason," the impersonal principle that they believed governed the universe.

And the Word was God (1:1). The OT teaches that there is only one God. This is affirmed in passages such as Deut. 6:4 (the Shema): "Listen, Israel: The LORD our God, the LORD is one."

All things were created through him (1:3). Proverbs 8:22–31 affirms that God used wisdom to create all things. Yet while wisdom there is personified, the Word here is an actual person.

In him was life, and that life was the light of men (1:4). While "life" and "light" are common religious terms, John's use is grounded in Gen. 1.[5] God's first creative act involves light (Gen. 1:3) and culminates in the creation of humanity (Gen. 1:20–28).[6] Light was also a common theme in the OT, where it is given by God's word (Ps. 19:8; 119:104, 130; Prov. 6:23), and in other Jewish literature, where it emanates from the law of Moses.[7]

That light shines in the darkness, and yet the darkness did not overcome it (1:5). The imagery of light and darkness also reflects OT messianic passages (Isa. 9:2; 60:1–5). John's language of light invading darkness is markedly different from the expectations of some contemporary Jews, such as the Qumran sectarians, whose *War Scroll* pictures a battle between the "sons of light" and "sons of darkness."[8]

There was a man sent from God (1:6). "Sent from God" echoes OT language regarding the sending of prophets (e.g., Ezek. 2:3).

Whose name was John (1:6). In this Gospel "John" always refers to the Baptist; the apostle John is never mentioned by name, though he is likely "the disciple Jesus loved" and the author of the Gospel (see 13:23; 21:24–25).

The true light (1:9). The OT regularly uses the imagery of light to refer to the coming Messiah (Num. 24:17; Isa. 9:2; 42:6–7; Mal. 4:2).

Gave them the right to be children of God (1:12). In the OT God's people are said to be his children (Deut. 14:1), his son, even his firstborn (Exod. 4:22). In John's Gospel a careful distinction is made between God's children (believers) and God's one-of-a-kind Son, Jesus (e.g., 1:14, 18; 20:17).[9]

Not of natural descent, or of the will of the flesh, or of the will of man (1:13). The Jewish understanding of divine sonship was intimately tied to ethnic descent, specifically being a descendant of Abraham.

But of God (1:13). In Deut. 32:18 God is pictured as giving birth to Israel.

The Word became flesh (1:14). The idea of the divine taking on human nature would have been abhorrent to Greeks, who pitted spirit against matter. While in Greek mythology gods appeared to people, Greek thought had no place for the notion of the divine or Reason becoming an actual human being.

And dwelt among us (1:14). The word translated as "dwelt" means more literally "pitched a tent" or "tabernacled" and alludes to the way in which God and his glory dwelt with his people in OT times (Exod. 40:34–35).

His glory (1:14). The OT describes God's glory filling the tabernacle (Exod. 40:34–35) and the temple (1 Kings 8:10–11; cf. Ezek. 10:3–4, 18–19).

The one and only (1:14). The idea of a one-of-a-kind son is also used to speak of Isaac, Abraham's unique (though not only) son ("your beloved son whom you love" in LXX Gen. 22:2). Throughout the OT and Second Temple Jewish literature, Israel and the Son of David are called God's "only" or "firstborn" son (Ps. 89:27; *4 Ezra* 6.58; *Psalms of Solomon* 18.4).

Full of grace and truth (1:14). This phrase alludes to the words "love and faithfulness" found throughout the OT (Exod. 34:6; Ps. 25:10; 26:3; 40:10; Prov. 16:6).

The one coming after me ranks ahead of me, because he existed before me (1:15). John the Baptist was about six months older than Jesus. Though there are occasional exceptions, normally in Jewish culture honor and privileges were tied to one's age, so that those who were older possessed superior status (Gen. 49:3; Deut. 21:17; Prov. 16:31).[10]

The law was given through Moses; grace and truth came through Jesus Christ (1:17). In the OT the law is viewed as a gracious gift from God (Deut. 4:8; Ps. 119).

No one has ever seen God (1:18). According to Exod. 33:20, no one can see God and live. Moses, who was said to have spoken with God "face to face" (Exod. 33:11), was afforded only a glimpse of God's "back" (Exod. 33:23). The thought of seeing God typically filled people with fear (Exod. 3:6; Judg. 13:21–22; Job 13:11; Isa. 6:5).

At the Father's side (1:18). John's words could be translated "in the Father's lap" and convey intimacy.[11] Similar language is used in the OT to describe a mother's care for her children (Num. 11:12; Ruth 4:16; Lam. 2:12).

John's Witness and the Beginning of Jesus's Ministry (1:19–51)

The Jews from Jerusalem sent priests and Levites (1:19). The priests and Levites ministered in the temple and were experts in matters of purification.

I am not the Messiah (1:20). Palestine was rife with messianic fervor in Jesus's day, and many Jews were waiting for the coming son of David envisaged in the OT (2 Sam. 7:11b–16; Hosea 3:5) (see the article "Messianic Expectations in Jesus's Day").[12]

"What then?" they asked him. "Are you Elijah?" (1:21). Along with the Messiah, Jews were expecting Elijah, who would change the hearts of people (Mal. 4:5).[13]

Are you the Prophet? (1:21). A third expected figure was the prophet like Moses (Deut. 18:15, 18; cf. 1 Macc. 4:45–46). Similarly, the Jews living at Qumran were waiting "until the prophet comes, and the Messiahs of Aaron and Israel."[14]

I am *a voice of one calling out in the wilderness* (1:23). John cites Isa. 40:3 to indicate his role. The wilderness was an important place in the life of God's people. This is where God gathered his people during the exodus. The Qumran community also made use of this passage, applying it to itself.[15]

Why then do you baptize? (1:25). See the article "Baptism in the New Testament World"; see comments on Mark 1:4. In the OT water is used as a symbol for cleansing (Ps. 51:2, 7; Ezek. 36:25–26; Zech. 13:1). Baptism was not a new invention by John; it was practiced widely in first-century

John the Baptist's ministry was associated with the wilderness (cf. John 1:23). The Judean wilderness was a desolate, barren region, as this photograph illustrates.

Judaism. Apart from immersion for ritual purification,[16] the most common form was proselyte baptism of gentile converts to Judaism.[17] In cases where Jews were baptized, the practice involved self-immersion.[18]

Whose sandal strap I'm not worthy to untie (1:27). Taking off the sandals of another was considered such a menial task that Rabbi Joshua ben Levi (third century AD) said, "All manner of service that a slave must render to his master a student must render to his teacher, except that of taking off his shoe."[19]

Bethany across the Jordan (1:28). There are two sites named "Bethany" in Israel. The location mentioned here was likely the region of Batanea in the northeast, an area referred to as Bashan in the OT. The other Bethany was a village near Jerusalem.[20]

The Lamb of God (1:29). There are two places in the OT where a lamb conveys the notion of vicarious suffering for sin. The first is the exodus, where the blood of the Passover lamb spared the Israelites from receiving God's wrath (see Exod. 12). The second is Isa. 53:7, where the suffering servant is pictured as a lamb led to the slaughter.

I saw the Spirit descending from heaven like a dove, and he rested on him (1:32). While the Holy Spirit came on individuals in OT times for temporary enablement (Num. 11:25; Judg. 3:10; 6:34; 11:29; 14:19; 1 Sam. 11:6; 16:13; 2 Chron. 15:1; 20:14), the Messiah was to be full of the Spirit permanently (Isa. 11:2; 61:1).

Rabbi (which means "Teacher") (1:38). "Rabbi" is the Semitic term for "teacher." It literally means "my great one," and in Jesus's lifetime it was used by Jews to refer to any respected religious teacher.

The Messiah (which is translated "the Christ") (1:41). "Messiah" comes from the Hebrew *mashiah* (see the article "Messianic Expectations in Jesus's Day"; see comments on Mark 8:29).[21] It means "anointed one," and in the OT it could refer to the king of Israel (1 Sam. 16:6), the high priest (Lev. 4:3), or others set apart for a particular office or purpose.[22] John gives the Greek equivalent, *christos*, which likewise means "anointed one."

Simon, son of John (1:42). In biblical times a person was known not by last name but by reference to their father or location (e.g., Simon of Cyrene).

Philip was from Bethsaida, the hometown of Andrew and Peter (1:44). Bethsaida was a town located on the northeastern side of the Sea of Galilee. Andrew and Peter had likely grown up in Bethsaida and later moved to Capernaum (see Mark 1:21, 29).

Philip found Nathanael (1:45). Nathanael is not mentioned in any of the other Gospels. Because of his connection with Philip (Matt. 10:3; Mark 3:18; Luke 6:14), this is likely the personal name of Bartholomew, which means "son of Tholomaios."

You are the Son of God (1:49). "Son of God" was a messianic title (2 Sam. 7:14; Ps. 2:7) used in Jesus's day. A Qumran document says of the Messiah, "He will be called son of God, and they will call him son of the Most High."[23]

Heaven opened and the angels of God ascending and descending on the Son of Man (1:51). An "open heaven" indicates giving and receiving of revelation, as in Ezek. 1:1. The reference here is to the account of Jacob's ladder (Gen. 28:12).

Wedding at Cana (2:1–12)

A wedding (2:1). See the article "Jewish Marriage Customs." In Jewish culture weddings were important celebrations. According to the Mishnah, a man's responsibilities included "eighteen to the wedding canopy, twenty to responsibility for providing for a family."[24] It was the responsibility of the bridegroom to make preparations and pay for the wedding feast. On the night before the wedding the bride was led from her father's to her husband's house, where the marriage contract was signed and the wedding supper celebrated.[25] After the wedding celebrations would continue for up to a week.[26]

When the wine ran out, Jesus's mother told him, "They don't have any wine" (2:3). Wine was an important part of celebration in Jewish life. The Babylonian Talmud says, "There is no rejoicing save with wine."[27] An abundance of wine indicated God's blessings and was tied to messianic expectations (Amos 9:13).[28]

Various kinds of grape juice were drunk in the Greco-Roman world, both fermented and unfermented. References to wine in Scripture normally indicate a fermented drink, though wine usually was diluted with water, especially in Jewish culture. The groom and his family were responsible for providing wine, and running out would have been a social faux pas.[29]

Ancient open-mouthed stone storage jars (cf. John 2:6).

An artist's reconstruction of Herod's temple complex.

Clearing of the Temple (2:13–25)

The temple (2:14). See the article "The Jerusalem Temple"; see comments on Mark 11:11. Herod the Great significantly expanded the temple complex. The resulting edifice was magnificent to behold.[30] The temple complex consisted of more than just the temple itself. Closest to the temple, just to the east, was the Inner Court, accessible to Jewish men only. Next was the Court of Women, open to Israelite women. Last was the Court of Gentiles, the Outer Court. Jewish sources indicate that gentiles were threatened with death for passing beyond this courtyard.[31] In 1870 an ancient inscription was found that reads, "No foreigner shall enter within the balustrade of the temple, or within the precinct, and whosoever shall be caught shall be responsible for (his) death that will follow in consequence (of his trespassing)."[32]

He found people selling oxen, sheep, and doves, and he also found the money changers sitting there (2:14). The sale of animals was a necessary aspect of temple life. It allowed travelers who were coming to Jerusalem for the three pilgrimage festivals (Deut. 16:16–17) to purchase sacrificial animals on site.[33] In addition, animals were needed for regular sacrifices. Money changers helped Israelites to exchange their local currency for Tyrian coins in order to pay the temple tax, paid by Jewish men twenty years and older.[34] However, while the animals traditionally had been sold on the nearby Mount of Olives, Caiaphas set up bazaars in the Court of Gentiles around AD 30, allowing animals to be sold in the temple precincts.[35]

This temple took forty-six years to build (2:20). Herod's expansion of the temple began in 20/19 BC, in the eighteenth year of his reign. The first phase lasted a year and a half, until 18/17 BC, and ended with the completion of the temple building.[36] Renovation of the temple grounds did not finish until AD 63/64.[37] The present reference is to the forty-six years following the completion of the temple building, placing the date in AD 29.

Jesus and Nicodemus (3:1–21)

There was a man from the Pharisees (3:1). See the articles "Pharisees and Sadducees"; "The Sanhedrin." The ruling council was known as the Sanhedrin and consisted of seventy-one members from both Pharisees and Sadducees. At an earlier period there were multiple councils that had jurisdiction over individual regions. In Jesus's day the council in Jerusalem was responsible for governing matters in Israel with authority granted by Rome.[38] In the first century the Sanhedrin was controlled by the chief priests, who mostly were Sadducees; an influential minority belonged to the Pharisees. The high priest was legally responsible for calling an official meeting of the Sanhedrin and presided over it.

Rabbi (3:2). See comments on John 1:38.

No one could perform these signs you do unless God were with him (3:2). The OT mentions approximately 120 signs, most of which are clustered around two periods: the exodus and the ministry of the prophets. In both cases, the signs serve to authenticate a person as God's messenger.[39]

Unless someone is born again, he cannot see the kingdom of God (3:3). The phrase "kingdom of God" does not occur in the OT, but the concept of God's reign is found throughout, involving God as the king of all creation (e.g., Ps. 93:1–2; 103:19), the promise of a Davidic king (Isa. 9:1–7; Ezek. 34:23–24; Zech. 9:9–10), and God's future reign (Ezek. 34:11–16; Zech. 14:9). As members of the covenant, Israelites looked forward to God's coming kingdom (see comments on Mark 1:15).

Born of water and the Spirit (3:5). Jesus's language here likely draws on Ezek. 36:25–27, which speaks of God cleansing his people and giving them new hearts and a new spirit.

Just as Moses lifted up the snake in the wilderness (3:14). Jesus's reference is to the events recorded in Num. 21:4–9. After the Israelites complain about God leading them through the desert, God sends poisonous snakes in judgment. When people repent, God commands Moses to make a bronze serpent and to lift it up on a pole, promising that anyone who was bitten by a snake and looked at the serpent would live.

His one and only Son (3:16). See comments on John 1:14.

Will not perish but have eternal life (3:16). The OT calls people to choose between life and death (e.g., Deut. 28–30).

God did not send his Son into the world to condemn the world, but to save the world through him (3:17). The OT emphasizes that God's desire is to save rather than judge (Ezek. 18:23) and extends hope not only to Israel but also to the nations (e.g., Isa. 49:6). However, the typical Jewish expectation with regard to God's judgment during the Second Temple period was that Israel would be saved from its enemies while the nations would be judged. The Qumran sect was convinced that they alone were the remnant that God would deliver.

Light . . . darkness (3:19). See comments on John 1:4; 1:5.

So that his deeds may not be exposed (3:20). A parallel is found in the Qumran *Damascus Document*: "When his deeds are evident, he shall be expelled from the congregation, like one whose lot did not fall among the disciples of God."[40]

Anyone who lives by the truth (3:21). In the Greek text "lives by the truth" literally reads, "does the truth." "Doing truth" is a relatively common phrase in the Greek OT (LXX Gen. 32:11 [ET 32:10]; Neh. 9:33; Isa. 26:10) and the Apocrypha (Tob. 4:6; 13:6; Odes 5:10) and conveys the notion of acting faithfully. Doing truth was a foundational tenet at Qumran; the *Rule of the Community* exhorts sectarians "to do truth and justice and uprightness on earth."[41]

John's Witness regarding Jesus (3:22–36)

Rabbi (3:26). See comments on John 1:38.

The groom's friend, who stands by and listens for him (3:29). John compares himself to the "best man" at a wedding, a position of great honor, whose focus was nonetheless not on himself but on the groom. Both the Mishnah and later Jewish literature highlight the importance of this role.[42]

Has affirmed that God is true (3:33). "Affirmed" translates a verb meaning "to seal." The word could be used with reference to physically sealing a document, either with wax or clay, in order to authorize, protect the contents, or demonstrate ownership. By extension, the word was used to confirm that something was true or authentic.[43]

He gives the Spirit without measure (3:34). In later rabbinic thought God gave the Holy Spirit to the prophets in set amounts.[44]

Jesus and the Samaritan Woman (4:1–42)

He had to travel through Samaria (4:4). The shortest route between Galilee and Jerusalem went through Samaria (see the article "Samaritans"). Josephus writes, "I then wrote to my friends in Samaria, to take care that they might safely pass through the country: for Samaria was already under the Romans, and it was absolutely necessary for those that go quickly [to Jerusalem] to pass through that country; for in that road you may, in three days' time, go from Galilee to Jerusalem."[45]

It was about noon. A woman of Samaria came to draw water (4:6–7). Women would come to draw water from wells in groups, often in the morning

A water well from the Middle East.

or late afternoon when the heat was less intense (Gen. 24:11; Exod. 2:16; 1 Sam. 9:11). The fact that the woman came at noon may indicate she was ostracized.

For Jews do not associate with Samaritans (4:9). Jesus set aside cultural norms in speaking with the Samaritan (see the article "Samaritans"). Not only was it unusual for men to discuss theological issues with women but Jews also generally avoided contact with Samaritans, especially women, who were considered to be unclean: "Samaritan women are deemed menstruants from their cradle. And the Samaritans convey uncleanness to a couch beneath as to a cover above."[46] There were exceptions, however, and some Jews were willing to eat with Samaritans.[47]

Living water (4:10). The phrase "living water" refers to fresh, running rather than stagnant water. The well that Isaac's servants found in Gen. 26 is "living water" (Gen. 26:19; cf. Lev. 14:6, 50; Num. 19:7; Song 4:15). The OT takes this imagery and applies it to God as the source of life (see Jer. 17:13). Zechariah uses the image to speak of God's end-time provision (Zech. 14:8).

A well of water springing up in him for eternal life (4:14). The connection between water and salvation is found in Isaiah, who speaks of God's coming salvation (e.g., Isa. 12:3).[48] Similar language was used by the Samaritans. Their liturgy for the Day of the Atonement speaks of the *Taheb,* the Samaritan messiah, saying that "water will flow from his buckets" (see Num. 24:7).[49]

Our fathers worshiped on this mountain (4:20). Both Abraham and Jacob built altars in that area (Gen. 12:7; 33:20). Moses blessed the Israelites from Mount Gerizim (Deut. 11:29; 27:12), which Samaritans considered the proper location for worship rather than Shiloh or Jerusalem. This was the location of their temple prior to its destruction by John Hyrcanus (see the article "Samaritans"). Even without a temple, Samaritans continued to view the mountain as sacred.

God is spirit (4:24). The OT is clear that God, as spirit, should not be represented visually in any form (Exod. 20:4–6).

He will explain everything to us (4:25). The Samaritan expectation of a messiah was not that of a Davidic king or deliverer but that of a teacher.[50]

They were amazed that he was talking with a woman (4:27). By speaking with a woman in public Jesus here breaks social norms, as he does elsewhere

Seen here are the remains of the steps from the Samaritan temple on Mount Gerizim.

in the Gospels (Luke 7:36–50; 8:2–3; 10:38–42; John 11:21–27). Rabbinic assessments of the value of teaching a woman or talking too much with her were generally negative. Rabbi Yose ben Yohanan (second century BC) said, "Don't talk too much with women. . . . So long as a man talks too much with a woman, (1) he brings trouble on himself, (2) wastes time better spent on studying Torah, and (3) ends up an heir of Gehenna."[51]

I have food to eat (4:32). Jesus's words here may echo Deut. 8:3, a verse he cited when being tempted by Satan in the wilderness (Matt. 4:4; Luke 4:4). Jeremiah spoke about the nourishing quality of God's word as well (Jer. 15:16).

The sower and the reaper can rejoice together (4:36). Jesus's language here draws on the picture of abundance promised by God through the prophets. While reaping the harvest was a time for joy (Deut. 16:13–15; Ps. 126:5–6; Isa. 9:3), sowing was a laborious activity. Amos 9:13, however, speaks of the day when God's blessing would be so great that "the plowman will overtake the reaper and the one who treads grapes, the sower of seed."

This really is the Savior of the world (4:42). The Messiah is never referred to as "Savior" in the OT; neither did the Samaritans look to their messianic figure (the *Taheb*) as Savior (see comments on John 4:25). However, the Septuagint uses the term on a few occasions to refer to God (Isa. 45:15, 21) or to God-appointed judges or national deliverers (Judg. 3:9, 15). The term was used by Philo, a Jewish philosopher, to speak of God and also occurs in reference to the Greek gods and the Roman emperors, including Nero.[52]

Healing an Official's Son (4:43–54)

A certain royal official . . . went to him (4:46–47). Capernaum was located north of the Sea of Galilee. The travel south to Cana would have been about fourteen miles. Had he left at sunrise, the official could have reached Cana by noon, allowing him to hear Jesus's words at the seventh hour (approximately 1:00 p.m., counting from sunrise at 6:00 a.m.). By this point, however, he would not have had enough time to complete the full journey home on the same day and would have completed it the following day.[53]

Your son will live (4:50). Jesus's words may seek to call attention to Elijah's miraculous resuscitation of the son of the woman of Zarephath (see 1 Kings 17:23).

Healing a Lame Man, and Witnesses to Jesus (5:1–47)

When the water is stirred up (5:7). Some manuscripts include an additional verse between 5:3 and 5:5, which reads in part, "From time to time an angel of the Lord would come down and stir up the waters." The superstition held that the first person to reach the waters when they were stirred would be healed.

This is the Sabbath. The law prohibits you from picking up your mat (5:10). For the Sabbath controversy, see the article "The Sabbath"; see comments on Mark 2:23.

Do not sin anymore, so that something worse doesn't happen to you (5:14). It was common belief in first-century Judaism that suffering was the result of sin. The disciples' question about the man born blind reflects the same idea: "Rabbi, who sinned, this man or his parents, that he was born blind?" (John 9:2). The OT does support the idea that suffering was at times related to an individual's sin (1 Kings 13:4; 2 Kings 1:4; 2 Chron. 16:12) but also offers examples where this was not the case (Job; 2 Sam. 4:4; 1 Kings 14:4; 2 Kings 13:14).[54]

My Father is still working (5:17). For the Sabbath controversy, see the article "The Sabbath"; see comments on Mark 2:23. Jesus doesn't engage in debate about the Sabbath directly but affirms that God continues to work and that his own actions are to emulate those of his Father.[55] Jesus's practice of calling God his Father was upsetting to the Jews because they understood Jesus to be elevating himself to the same level as God by claiming a unique relationship with him. The depiction of God as Father is found in the OT but only infrequently (Ps. 89:26; Isa. 63:16; 64:8; Jer. 3:4, 19; 31:9; Mal. 2:10).

And just as the Father raises the dead and gives them life, so the Son also gives life to whom he wants (5:21). Jesus doesn't only claim he can raise the dead, an act accomplished in OT times by Elijah and Elisha, but also that he is able to grant life at his discretion. The OT teaches that raising the dead is one of the unique works of God (e.g., 1 Sam. 2:6; see also 2 Kings 5:7; cf. Deut. 32:39). Second Temple Judaism affirmed this idea as well (Wis. 16:13–14; see also Tob. 13:2), as did rabbinic texts (e.g., the *Shemoneh Esreh*, a Jewish prayer declaring, "Who is like you, O King, who makes dead and alive again?").

Anyone who does not honor the Son does not honor the Father who sent him (5:23). The connection between the honor of Son and Father reflects the Jewish background of the close connection between sender and messenger. The Mishnah says that "a man's agent is like [the man] himself."[56] To dishonor the messenger was to dishonor the sender. While true of any messenger, it was particularly true with regard to a son, because he could be trusted to accomplish his father's purposes most faithfully.[57]

If I testify about myself, my testimony is not true (5:31). The OT set guidelines for properly establishing witnesses. Two or three witnesses were necessary to establish a given fact (Deut. 17:6; 19:15). Later Jewish law, as evidenced in the Mishnah, clarified that the accused person cannot be one of the witnesses: "But a person is not believed to testify in his own behalf."[58]

John was a burning and shining lamp (5:35). Jesus may not be speaking about a lamp in general but echoing messianic references such as Ps. 132:17, which, speaking of God's promises and provision for David's descendants, says, "There I will make a horn grow for David; I have prepared a lamp for my anointed one."[59]

Ancient lamp.

You pore over the Scriptures because you think you have eternal life in them (5:39). Jewish scribes engaged in careful study of the Scriptures, noting various details such as the number of verses, letters, and words of each book. Rabbi Hillel, a famous first-century teacher, spoke of the connection between the Torah and life, saying, "Lots of Torah, lots of life . . . [If] he has gotten teachings of Torah, he has gotten himself life eternal."[60]

Your accuser is Moses, on whom you have set your hope (5:45). One of Moses's roles in the OT is intercessor, praying to God on behalf of the nation or individuals (Exod. 32:11–14, 30–32; Num. 12:13; 14:19–20; 21:7; Deut. 9:18–20, 25–29). But Moses also had a role in testifying against Israel. Both the law that God gave through Moses and the Song of Moses in Deut. 32 are said to witness against the people (Deut. 31:19, 21, 26). Second Temple Jewish literature highlights Moses's intercessory role as well.[61]

Feeding the Five Thousand (6:1–71)

Jesus crossed the Sea of Galilee (or Tiberias) (6:1). The Sea of Tiberias derives its name from the largest city on its shore (see comments on Mark 1:16). Tiberias was founded by Herod Antipas around AD 17–18. The city was named after Tiberius, the Roman emperor who reigned during the years AD 14–37. The lake did not start being referred to as the Sea of Tiberias until the latter part of the first century.

The Sea of Galilee.

Now the Passover, a Jewish festival, was near (6:4). This is the second of three Passover festivals mentioned in this Gospel (see comments on Mark 14:1). The first reference is in 2:13, the third in 11:55; both find Jesus in Jerusalem. This is the only reference to Jesus spending Passover in Galilee. The string of Passover references helps to establish the length of Jesus's ministry as spanning a minimum of two and a half years and more likely three and a half years (including a Passover mentioned or implied in the Synoptic Gospels).

Where will we buy bread so that these people can eat? (6:5). There are several close connections between John 6 and Num. 11. First, Moses asks God a similar question in Num. 11:13: "Where can I get meat to give all these people?" Second, in both narratives the people grumble (Num. 11:1; John 6:41, 43). Third, manna features prominently in both accounts (Num. 11:7–9; John 6:31, 49, 58). Finally, both passages focus on the stark difference between people's need and the available resources (Num. 11:22; John 6:7–9). Cumulatively, these parallels identify Jesus as the Messiah, who would feed people in a way similar to God's provision of manna in the wilderness (see comments on John 6:31).

Collect the leftovers so that nothing is wasted (6:12). Jesus's command reflects the common Jewish practice of collecting leftover pieces after a meal, up to the size of an olive.[62]

This truly is the Prophet who is to come into the world (6:14). On the Prophet, see comments on John 1:21. Jesus's miracle reflects both the provision of manna in the wilderness (see comments on John 6:5) and Elisha's miraculous provision of bread (2 Kings 4:42–44). In the latter event Elisha feeds a multitude (one hundred people) with a small amount of food (twenty barley loaves) and has food left over.

A high wind arose, so the sea began to churn (6:18). Strong storms were a common experience on the lake, which lies approximately six hundred feet below sea level. The interface of warm air over the lake with cool air coming from the southeast sometimes resulted in fearsome storms.[63]

The next day . . . looking for Jesus (6:22–24). The feeding of the multitude took place on the east side of the Sea of Galilee (the "far shore" [6:1], so called because most Jewish activity during the OT period took place on the western shore). During the night Jesus crossed over with his disciples to the northwest side, arriving at Capernaum (6:17, 21). In the morning

A mosaic of loaves and fishes, recalling the feeding of the five thousand, from the floor of a Byzantine church excavated on the north shore of the Sea of Galilee, near Capernaum.

boats arrived from Tiberias, which people then used to travel across the lake to Capernaum in search of Jesus.

Don't work for food that perishes but for the food that lasts for eternal life (6:27). Bread and water regularly serve as symbols for life, as they are indispensable for human existence. Later Jewish literature refers to the Torah (law) as bread.[64]

Seal of approval (6:27). See comments on John 3:33.

Our ancestors ate the manna in the wilderness (6:31). See comments on John 6:5. The provision of manna in the wilderness is celebrated in subsequent OT passages (e.g., Ps. 78:23–25).[65] Likewise, Second Temple Jewish literature reflects on God's heavenly provision of bread in contrast to God's judgment of Egypt.[66] In addition to remembering God's past provision, there was an expectation of God's future supply.[67]

No one who comes to me will ever be hungry, and no one who believes in me will ever be thirsty again (6:35). Jesus's words reflect messianic expectations found in passages such as Isa. 55:1 (see also Isa. 49:10, cited in Rev. 7:16).

The Jews started complaining about him (6:41). The grumbling of the people at Jesus's provision parallels the grumbling of the Israelites in the wilderness (Exod. 16:2, 8–9; Num. 11:4–23). See comments on John 6:5.

Unless you eat the flesh of the Son of Man and drink his blood (6:53). The Mosaic law forbids drinking blood or eating meat that still had blood in it (Lev. 17:10–14; Deut. 12:16).

The Spirit is the one who gives life. The flesh doesn't help at all. The words that I have spoken to you are spirit and are life (6:63). Passages such as Gen. 1:2 and, more prominently, Ezek. 37:1–14 indicate that the Spirit gives life. The futility of the flesh is highlighted in Isa. 40:6–8. The OT also points to God's word as the source of life (Gen. 1). Deuteronomy 8:3, cited by Jesus when tempted in the wilderness, says, "Man does not live on bread alone but on every word that comes from the mouth of the Lord."

Jesus at Shelters (7:1–8:59)

The Jewish Festival of Shelters was near (7:2). See the article "Jewish Festivals." The most recent festival mentioned was the Passover in 6:4, almost six months earlier.[68] Two relevant features of the Festival of Shelters that were in place during the first century should be mentioned here.[69] The first

The shelter was built by a Jewish family in celebration of the Festival of Shelters, the ancient religious festival that occurs at the time of the summer fruit harvest.

was a water-drawing ceremony, which commemorated God's provision of rain and involved the priests marching each day from the Pool of Siloam to the temple to pour out water at the base of the altar.[70] The Mishnah describes the celebration of drawing water as a time of such joy that "anyone who has not seen the rejoicing [at the place of the water-drawing] in his life has never seen rejoicing."[71] The second component was a candle-lighting celebration. Great bowls of oil atop large candleholders lit the women's courtyard of the temple. In addition, special wicks were made from the worn-out undergarments of the priests, which lit every courtyard in the city.[72] The lighting of the candles was accompanied by dancing and singing. A special version of both of these ceremonies took place on the seventh day.[73]

---

1 Zechariah the priest, father of John the Baptist, is burning incense when the angel of the Lord appears to him (Luke 1:8–20).

2 Joseph and Mary come to the temple to present baby Jesus and to offer doves or pigeons as a sacrifice (Luke 2:22–24). Mary would have to stay in the Court of the Women while Joseph takes the baby and the sacrifice into the Court of the Israelites.

3 Simeon and the prophetess Anna are probably in the Court of the Women when they recognize the baby Jesus as the Messiah (Luke 2:25–38).

4 Jesus's parents find him "sitting among the teachers, listening to them and asking them questions" (Luke 2:46). This could have taken place in any of the colonnaded porticos, although it is unlikely that they were in the Royal Stoa.

5 "The devil took him to the holy city and had him stand on the highest point of the temple" (Matt. 4:5). The parapet on top of the Royal Stoa in the southeast corner of the temple complex has the greatest height from top to bottom, although another possible location is the temple itself, which stood above the walls.

6 "[Jesus] spoke these words while teaching in the temple courts near the place where the offerings were put" (John 8:20).

7 "Jesus was in the temple courts walking in Solomon's Colonnade" (John 10:23).

8 "Jesus entered Jerusalem and went into the temple courts" (Mark 11:11). Jesus probably enters through the Double Gate and ascends up to the Court of the Gentiles.

9 Jesus commends the widow who gives two small copper coins (Mark 12:41–44; Luke 21:1–4).

10 When Jesus is teaching in the temple courts, he is often in one of the colonnaded porches, most likely Solomon's Colonnade (Matt. 26:55; Mark 12:35; 14:49; Luke 19:47; 20:1; 21:37–38; 28:55; John 7:28).

11 Jesus drives out the money changers and those selling animals (Matt. 21:12–16; Mark 11:15–18; Luke 19:45–47; John 2:13–22). This selling activity is in the Court of the Gentiles. It could be on either the north or south side or both.

12 "Judas threw the money into the temple and left. Then he went away and hanged himself" (Matt. 27:5). Judas probably goes into the Court of the Israelites and throws the money over the wall that separates it from the Court of the Priests.

13 "The curtain of the temple was torn in two from top to bottom" (Matt. 27:51; Mark 15:38; Luke 23:45). This could have been either the inner or outer curtain, or perhaps both.

14 After the resurrection, Jesus's disciples "stayed continually at the temple, praising God" (Luke 24:53). They are probably in Solomon's Colonnade.

Second Temple with Events from the Gospels

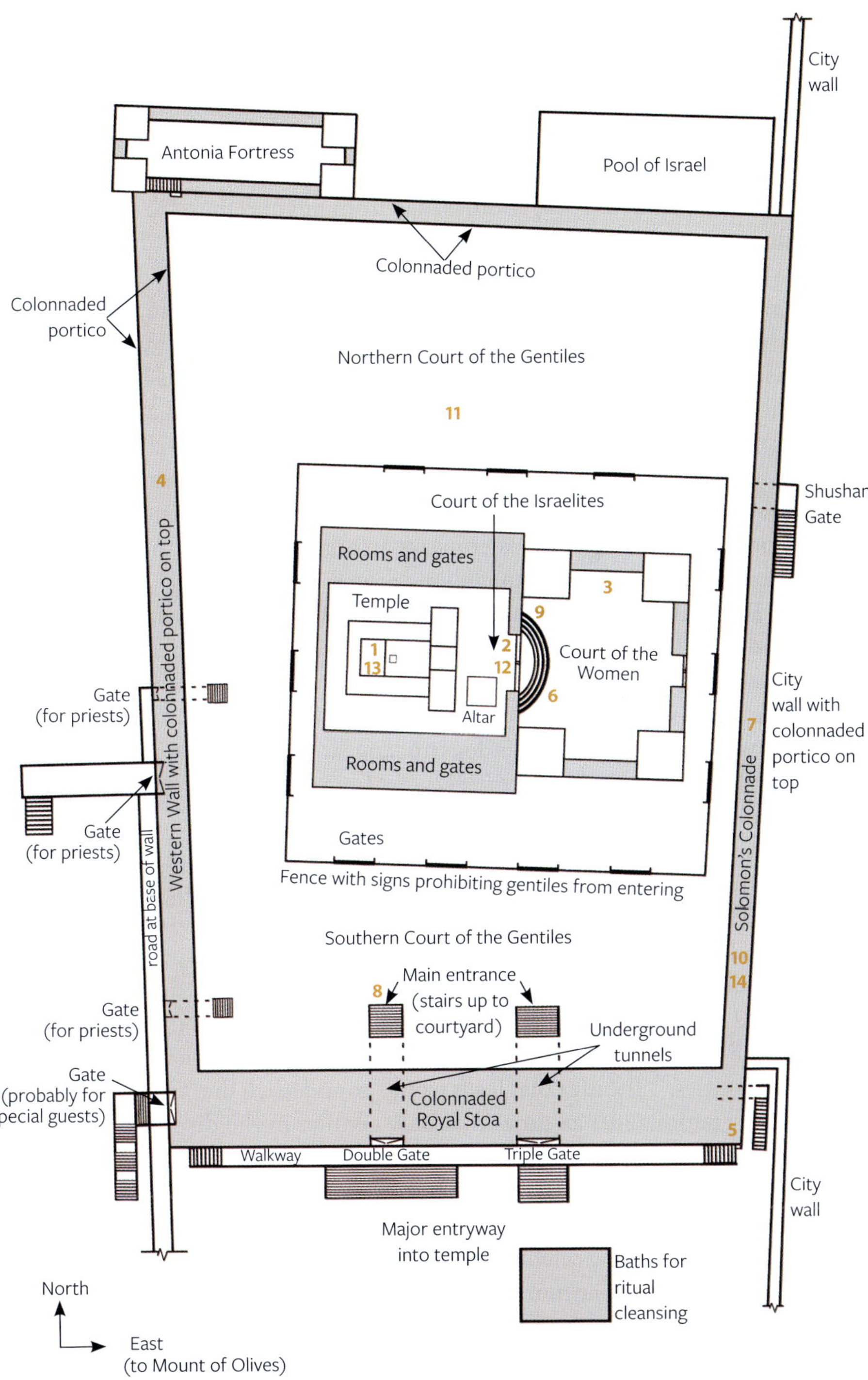

He's deceiving the people (7:12). Leading God's people astray is a serious charge. Deuteronomy 13:1–11 stipulates that a false prophet should be killed "because he has urged rebellion against the LORD your God" (13:5). Jesus was not the only person in the first century who lodged startling claims and gathered a following. According to Josephus, in AD 45 or 46 a man named Theudas, whom Josephus calls a magician, claimed that he was a prophet who would part the Red Sea; another man from Egypt claimed to be a prophet, promising to knock down Jerusalem's walls by his mere word.[74]

How is this man so learned, since he hasn't been trained? (7:15). Most Jewish males in Jesus's day were educated enough to be able to read and have a basic understanding of the Scriptures. The question posed by the Jews here relates not to Jesus's ability to read per se but rather to his lack of formal rabbinic or scribal education.[75] Jesus was able to carry on a discourse on Scripture in the same way the trained rabbis were, frequently citing Scripture.

This is why Moses has given you circumcision . . . you circumcise a man on the Sabbath (7:22). See the articles "The Jewish Rite of Circumcision"; "The Sabbath." Jesus employs an argument "from the lesser to the greater," commonly used in rabbinic discussion.

But we know where this man is from. When the Messiah comes, nobody will know where he is from (7:27). There was an expectation held by some during the Second Temple period that the Messiah had a mysterious origin and would appear unexpectedly (see the article "Messianic Expectations in Jesus's Day").[76] This does not appear to be the view of the crowd, as attested later in the passage (7:42; cf. Mic. 5:2; Matt. 2:1–6). Rather, they seem to have held that the Messiah would be an unknown figure until the time he delivered Israel.[77]

Where does he intend to go so we won't find him? He doesn't intend to go to the Jewish people dispersed among the Greeks and teach the Greeks, does he? (7:35). Jews had been living in dispersion since the Babylonian exile. While some returned following Cyrus's decree (2 Chron. 36:22–23), others continued to live away from the land of Israel. There were significant Jewish population centers in Antioch, Alexandria, Rome, and other cities.[78] The idea that Jesus would go and teach the "Greeks" (gentiles of any nationality) assumes that only gentiles in the dispersion (and not Jews) needed instruction in the Scriptures.

On the last and most important day of the festival (7:37). This was either the seventh day of the festival, which featured special water-pouring and candle-lighting celebrations (see comments on John 7:2), or the eighth day, the former being more likely. The eighth day was not properly part of the celebration of the festival but was in keeping with the scriptural command to celebrate a special solemn assembly following the Festival of Shelters (Lev.

23:34–36) (see the article "Jewish Festivals"). In Jesus's time the eighth day was formally the last day of the celebration and was marked by the singing of the Hallel (Pss. 113–118) and rejoicing as the people dismantled the temporary shelters they had constructed.

As the Scripture has said (7:38). The following phrase is not a direct scriptural quote. Rather, it constitutes a general reference to the prophetic teaching about promises of spiritual blessing, including those connected to the giving of water, that are in line with the end-time hopes of abundance celebrated at the festival.[79] Passages representative of these ideas are Isa. 12:3 and Zech. 14:8.[80]

Streams of living water flow from deep within him (7:38). For the importance of water at the Festival of Shelters, see comments on John 7:2. Later Jewish teaching also spoke of streams of water flowing from a person.[81]

They said, "This truly is the Prophet." Others said, "This is the Messiah" (7:40–41). On Jewish expectations of the Messiah and the Prophet, see comments on John 1:20; 1:21; 6:14. The Qumran community expected a prophet as well as priestly and royal messiahs; members were exhorted to continue living under the rule of the community "until the prophet comes, and the Messiahs of Aaron and Israel."[82]

The servants answered, "No man ever spoke like this!" (7:46). The temple guards were not simple soldiers, but rather were drawn from the Levites and thus religiously trained and used to hearing teaching regularly in the temple courts.

Our law doesn't judge a man before it hears from him and knows what he's doing, does it? (7:51). The OT urges that care be taken in establishing the guilt or innocence of an accused person (Deut. 1:16; 17:4; 19:18). The apocryphal book of Susanna highlights the importance of this principle, telling the story of how Daniel was able to rescue righteous Susanna from the accusations of two ungodly witnesses who falsely testified against her. The Mishnah also gives detailed instructions on the handling of litigation to ensure a fair trial.[83]

"You aren't from Galilee too, are you?" they replied. "Investigate and you will see that no prophet arises from Galilee" (7:52). This is actually an incorrect statement by the chief priests and Pharisees. Jonah son of Amittai was from the town of Gath-hepher (2 Kings 14:25), a town in the territory belonging to Zebulun (Josh. 19:10–16) located west of Mount Tabor in Galilee. In addition, Elijah (1 Kings 17:1) and Nahum (Nah. 1:1) may also have stemmed from Galilee.

A woman caught in adultery (8:3). John 7:53–8:11, the narrative unit telling the story of Jesus and a woman caught in adultery, almost certainly was added by a later scribe.[84]

I am the light of the world (8:12). This discussion takes place while Jesus is still on the temple grounds at the Festival of Shelters. The specific language of being "the light" was not unknown in Judaism. In Ps. 27:1 God is referred to as the light (see also Ps. 36:9). The OT also speaks of God's word in terms of light (Ps. 119:105; Prov. 6:23). Light is also used to characterize God's end-time presence (Isa. 60:19–22; Zech. 14:5b–8) and the coming servant of the Lord (Isa. 42:6; 49:6). In Jesus's day the language of light was applied to Israel, Jerusalem, the patriarchs (Abraham, Isaac, and Jacob), the Messiah, the temple, the Torah, Adam, and famous rabbis.[85]

Anyone who follows me will never walk in the darkness but will have the light of life (8:12). On the contrast between light and darkness, see comments on John 1:5. The connection is made between light and life in both the OT and Second Temple Jewish literature. For example, Ps. 56:13 says, "For you rescued me from death, even my feet from stumbling, to walk before God in the light of life." Similar language is used in *Psalms of Solomon* 3.12: "This is the share of sinners forever, but those who fear the Lord shall rise up to eternal life, and their life shall be in the Lord's light, and it shall never end."[86]

The seven-branched lampstand, or menorah, was a common decorative element in synagogues of the third and fourth centuries AD, such as the synagogue in Eshtemoa near Hebron, where this lintel was excavated.

You are testifying about yourself. Your testimony is not valid (8:13). On valid witnesses, see comments on John 5:31.

He won't kill himself, will he? (8:22). Earlier, Jesus's opponents wondered whether he might go to the gentiles (7:35); now they query whether he might kill himself. In Jewish thought suicide generally was considered a grievous, even unthinkable, act.[87] This stands in stark contrast to the contemporary gentile view, which often saw suicide as an "honorable death."[88]

If you do not believe that I am he (8:24). The background for Jesus's words comes from Exod. 3:13–14 as developed in Isa. 40–55, where God regularly declares, "I am he," announcing that he and he alone is God and forever the same (e.g., 43:10–13).[89] For anyone else, using this phrase would be blasphemous and render the person subject to God's wrath (Isa. 47:8–9; Zeph. 2:15).

When you lift up the Son of Man (8:28). The phrase "lift up" most likely echoes Isa. 52:13, where God says, "My servant will be successful; he will be raised and lifted up and greatly exalted."

I do nothing on my own. But just as the Father taught me, I say these things (8:28). Jesus's dependence on the Father again reflects the Jewish saying that "a man's agent is like [the man] himself."[90]

If you continue in my word (8:31). The basic idea of discipleship is that of learning from and adhering to the teachings of a master. During the first century AD the master-disciple relationship was well established in Judaism.[91] An entire tractate of the Mishnah, *Avot,* is devoted to the sayings of the fathers whose opening words extol the passing on of learning from master to student.[92] Later rabbinic teaching describes a perfect follower of a rabbi as one who has mastered his rabbi's teaching and shares it with others.[93]

You will know the truth, and the truth will set you free (8:32). Contemporary Jewish thought held that the study of the law brings freedom: "From whoever accepts upon himself the yoke of Torah do they remove the yoke of the state and the yoke of hard labor."[94] Stoic philosophers, rather than extolling the law, looked to wisdom as the source of freedom.[95]

Everyone who commits a sin is a slave of sin (8:34). Jesus's statement here should be understood against the backdrop of the common teaching of his day, according to which people possess two natures, one good and one evil: "He created man to rule the world and placed within him two spirits . . . : they are the spirits of truth and of deceit."[96] Jewish teaching held that the law helps keep the evil inclination in check and strengthen the good impulse.[97] *Testaments of the Twelve Patriarchs* (second century BC) exhorts readers, "Flee from the evil tendency, destroying the devil by your good works."[98]

We have one Father—God (8:41). There is OT precedent for the Jews to call God their father, although it was not necessarily common Jewish practice (Exod. 4:22; Deut. 32:6; Isa. 64:8).

You are of your father the devil . . . he was a murderer from the beginning (8:44). The reference here is likely to Gen. 3 and the transgression of Adam and Eve following Satan's deception of the woman. Second Temple Jewish literature identified Satan as the cause of death (see comments on Mark 1:13).[99]

You're a Samaritan (8:48). On the animosity between Jews and Samaritans, see comments on John 4:9; see the article "Samaritans."

You aren't fifty years old yet (8:57). According to the Mishnah, fifty was considered to be the age at which a man reached maturity and finished his work.[100] Judah ben Tema listed the various ages when a man would undertake activities, including "fifty to counsel."[101]

Before Abraham was, I am (8:58). Jesus's language again reflects God's name as revealed to Moses (Exod. 3:14) and highlighted in Isaiah (Isa. 43:10–13). See comments on John 8:24.

So they picked up stones to throw at him (8:59). According to the OT, stoning was the punishment for blasphemy (Lev. 24:16; cf. Deut. 13:6–11). The Mishnah likewise places blasphemers in a list of those whose actions should be punished by stoning, though both the OT and Mishnah have the punishment take place as a result of righteous judgment, not by a frenzied mob.[102]

Healing a Man Born Blind (9:1–10:21)

Rabbi (9:2). See comments on John 1:38.

Who sinned, this man or his parents, that he was born blind? (9:2). The OT is clear that while God does discipline sin, not all hardship is the result of sin (Jer. 31:29–30; Ezek. 18).[103] Second Temple Jewish literature also affirmed this principle at times. Nevertheless, the belief that suffering is always tied to sin was not uncommon and is recorded (though not affirmed) in the OT (Job 4:7) and taught by later rabbis.

Night is coming when no one can work (9:4). In the ancient world almost all work was done during the day, with some exceptions such as shepherds, watchmen, or messengers.

I am the light of the world (9:5). See comments on John 8:12.

He spit on the ground, made some mud from the saliva, and spread the mud on his eyes (9:6). The use of saliva was a relatively common practice in pagan magical practices and, as a result, was largely avoided by the rabbis.[104] In addition, the Mosaic law taught that in certain conditions saliva could bring about uncleanness (Lev. 15:8).[105] Apparently, Jesus had no such concerns; perhaps he allows the blind man to go through this process to help him realize that a powerful miracle is about to unfold. This series of actions would also make Jesus's striking messianic sign more tangible for his audience.

Stairs leading down to the Pool of Siloam (left), discovered at the south end of Jerusalem by Israeli archaeologists in 2004. This spring-fed pool, where Jesus told the blind man to go wash (John 9:7), was a source of water and ritual washing in Jesus's day.

Wash in the pool of Siloam (which means "Sent") (9:7). The Pool of Siloam connects this narrative with the previous discourse at the Festival of Shelters (8:12–59), as the water for the water-pouring ceremony was taken from the Pool of Siloam. John notes that "Siloam" means "Sent," reflecting the Hebrew *shiloah,* as in Isa. 8:6, "the slowly flowing water of Shiloah."

Isn't this the one who used to sit begging? (9:8). Beggars were a common sight in first-century Palestine, and begging may have been the only way the blind man could make a living.[106] Beggars were the truly poor in the first century, and their livelihood depended on the charity of others.[107] The OT commends almsgiving (Deut. 15:9–10; Prov. 28:27; 31:20), and Second Temple Judaism followed suit.[108]

Some of the Pharisees said, "This man is not from God, because he doesn't keep the Sabbath (9:16). On the Sabbath controversy, see the article "The Sabbath."

He's of age. He will speak for himself (9:21). At the age of thirteen a boy was considered legally able to speak for himself.[109] The Mishnah lists thirteen as the age when a boy becomes liable for taking a vow, and it was also the age, according to Rabbi Judah ben Tema, at which a boy began participating in religious duties.[110]

His parents said these things because they were afraid of the Jews, since the Jews had already agreed that if anyone confessed him as the Messiah, he would be banned from the synagogue (9:22). Expulsion from Jewish assemblies is a practice dating back at least to the return from exile, as recorded in Ezra 10:8. The practice also occurred at Qumran.[111] The decision made here likely refers to an informal decision, not to an official pronouncement against following Jesus.

Give glory to God (9:24). This phrase (or some variant) is used elsewhere in the OT and Second Temple Jewish literature as a solemn command to tell the truth, on the assumption that the person in question has done something wrong (Josh. 7:19; 1 Esd. 9:8–9).[112]

We know that God has spoken to Moses (9:29). According to the OT, God spoke to Moses "face to face" (Exod. 33:11; Num. 12:8; Deut. 34:10)—that is, with a level of intimacy not experienced by others, even prophets.[113] Rabbinic tradition held that the revelation God gave to Moses was not only the written but also the oral Torah, which had been passed down through generations.[114]

We know that God doesn't listen to sinners, but if anyone is God-fearing and does his will, he listens to him (9:31). The OT regularly connects the character of the one who prays to the response by God. Negatively, Ps. 66:18 says, "If I had been aware of malice in my heart, the Lord would not have listened"; positively, according to Ps. 34:15, "The eyes of the Lord are on the righteous, and his ears are open to their cry for help."

No one has ever heard of someone opening the eyes of a person born blind (9:32). There is only one recorded instance of blindness being cured in the OT, when Elisha prays for God to blind the army sent to capture him and then prays that God would open their eyes (2 Kings 6:18–20). Second Temple literature tells the story of the healing of Tobit's blindness, but there are no instances of people born blind being healed.[115]

In order that those who do not see will see and those who do see will become blind (9:39). The OT prophets spoke of God's judgment metaphorically as blindness (e.g., Isa. 6:10; 42:19; Jer. 5:21). The hope of the blind seeing is also a common picture associated with God's salvation.[116]

Anyone who doesn't enter the sheep pen by the gate (10:1). The image called to mind by Jesus's words may have been that of a courtyard, next to or close by a home. These courtyards could be used by a single family or shared by multiple families and could be surrounded by stone walls and topped with thorny briars. The gate would be locked and entrance be allowed by a gatekeeper (10:3).[117]

The shepherd of the sheep . . . the sheep hear his voice. He calls his own sheep by name (10:2–3). In first-century Israel shepherding generally was considered to be a lowly occupation. This stands in contrast to the OT depiction of God and his Messiah as shepherds (see comments on John 10:11).[118] The shepherd possessed unique authority over his flock. The imagery of calling sheep by name likely reflects the practice of Palestinian shepherds of giving particular names to certain sheep.[119] Correspondingly, God is said to have known both Moses and Israel "by name" (Exod. 33:12, 17; Isa. 43:1, 7). In the OT God's voice was heard through the law and the prophets.

Leads them out (10:3). The wording reflects OT passages such as Num. 27:15–17 and Ezek. 34:13. The imagery of people as sheep points to their complete dependence on God as their shepherd. The shepherd would bring out all of his sheep, and only his sheep, carefully guiding them from the crowded fold and out through the narrow gate.

He goes on ahead of them. The sheep follow him because they know his voice. They will never follow a stranger; instead they will run away from him, because they don't know the voice of strangers (10:4–5). Shepherds in the ancient Near East didn't drive their sheep from behind but rather led them in front, calling them forward as they went ahead.[120] The sheep, helpless on their own and dependent on the shepherd, were able to tell the difference between their shepherd's voice and that of strangers.

I am the gate for the sheep (10:7). The setting shifts from the sheepfold at home to the shepherd caring for his sheep out in the hills. The sheepfolds in the hills lacked doors but simply had narrow openings in the walls. The shepherd himself served as the gate at night, lying in the opening (cf. Ps. 118:20).[121]

All who came before me are thieves and robbers (10:8). Ezekiel 34 is once again in view. There, God criticizes the false shepherds of Israel who failed to care for the flock (cf. Jer. 23:1–2). There are numerous candidates who may be in view here. In the somewhat recent past the Jewish high priests Jason and Menelaus had betrayed their office (2 Macc. 4:7–14). The Pharisees and Sadducees may also be in view. The latter were known for using the temple for profit (e.g., John 2:14), while the former have just displayed their ungodly leadership in John 9.[122]

Will come in and go out (10:9). Jesus's language reflects covenant terminology for blessing, especially as found in Deuteronomy: "You will be blessed when you come in and blessed when you go out" (Deut. 28:6). It also is similar to the prayer that Moses offered up concerning the one who would be leader in his place in order to bring the people into the promised land, "who will bring them out and bring them in, so that the Lord's community won't be like sheep without a shepherd" (Num. 27:16–17). The Lord's response to the prayer was for Moses to appoint Joshua, whose name in Greek is *Iēsous*, "Jesus" (Num. 27:18).

Find pasture (10:9). "Pasture" is a common expression in the OT that speaks of God's gracious provision, both literally (1 Chron. 4:40) and metaphorically (Ps. 23:2). It is also used in contexts of looking forward to God's future restoration and salvation of his people (Isa. 49:8–12; Ezek. 34:12–16, 25–31).

As seen here, ancient sheepfolds were built of stone and had one access gate.

I am the good shepherd (10:11). Ezekiel 34 continues to be the main background for the imagery, with its comparison between the unfaithful shepherds of Israel who will be punished by God (vv. 1–10) and God as the good shepherd of his flock (vv. 11–16). The OT often refers to God as a shepherd and the people as his flock,[123] and warns that false shepherds will be judged.[124] Similarly, both Moses and the Davidic king/messiah are presented as shepherds of God's sheep.[125] The Messiah is also depicted as a shepherd in Second Temple literature.[126] The imagery was also used of gods and kings in non-Jewish literature.[127]

He is a hired hand and doesn't care about the sheep (10:13). The OT had specific regulations concerning hired hands and their responsibilities concerning animals entrusted to their care. According to Exod. 22:13, if an animal was mauled by wild beasts, the hired hand need not make restitution. The Mishnah stipulates that if a single wolf attacked the flock, the hired hand should protect it, but if two or more wolves threatened, they were no longer responsible.[128]

I have other sheep that are not from this sheep pen (10:16). The OT presents a growing expectation of gentiles becoming part of God's people. This is evidenced as early as Gen. 12 and finds full expression in passages such as Isa. 56:6–8.[129]

There will be one flock, one shepherd (10:16). See comments on John 10:11.

Jesus at Dedication (10:22–42)

The Festival of Dedication (10:22). See the article "Jewish Festivals."

No one is able to snatch them out of the Father's hand (10:29). God's sovereign care for his people is expressed in the OT in similar language: "Also, from today on I am he alone, and none can rescue from my power. I act, and who can reverse it?" (Isa. 43:13 [cf. Wis. 3:1]).

Again the Jews picked up rocks to stone him (10:31). See comments on John 8:59.

For blasphemy, because you—being a man—make yourself God (10:33). In the OT blasphemy was considered a fairly broad offense. Numbers 15:30 says that "the person who acts defiantly . . . blasphemes the Lord." Later Jewish oral law, codified in the Mishnah, narrowed the requirements for blasphemy to actually speaking the divine name.[130] However, there is no evidence that the Sanhedrin, controlled by the Sadducees, adopted such a narrow view.[131]

Isn't it written in your law, *I said, you are gods*? (10:34). Jesus quotes Ps. 82:6. The term "law" was at times extended to cover not just the first five books of the OT but the OT as a whole.[132] In its original context Ps. 82 refers to unjust judges or rulers. In typical rabbinic style, Jesus argues from the lesser to the greater: If even unjust judges can be called "gods," how much more is the designation appropriate for the Son of God?

The one the Father set apart and sent into the world (10:36). The term "set apart" is used in the OT and Second Temple literature to speak of people set apart for a particular role or task: Moses was set apart as lawgiver (Sir. 45:4–5), Jeremiah as prophet (Jer. 1:5), and Aaron and his sons as priests (Exod. 28:41; 40:13; Lev. 8:30; 2 Chron. 5:11; 26:18).

Raising Lazarus (11:1–57)

Lazarus from Bethany (11:1). The village here is different from the Bethany mentioned in 1:28 (see comments on John 1:28). This village was located east of Jerusalem and the Mount of Olives, about two miles from the city.[133]

He stayed two more days in the place where he was (11:6). Jesus is likely in Batanea, which is approximately one hundred miles to the northeast of Jerusalem. A good day of walking on Roman roads would cover approximately twenty miles.[134] At this rate, it would have taken Jesus about five days to travel from Batanea to Bethany.

Lazarus has fallen asleep (11:11). To "fall asleep" is a biblical idiom referring to death. Normally the imagery had no direct connection to the idea of "waking up" (e.g., 1 Kings 2:10; 11:21, 43; 14:20). However, Daniel uses similar language with the expectation of a future resurrection where the sleeper will awake: "Many who sleep in the dust of the earth will awake, some to eternal life, and some to disgrace and eternal contempt" (Dan. 12:2 [cf. John 5:28–29]).[135]

Lazarus had already been in the tomb for four days (11:17). Rabbinic teaching from the third century held that once three days had passed, death was final.[136] It is uncertain, however, whether this belief was common in Jesus's day. Burial normally occurred almost immediately after death, the same day if possible, as decomposition would set in quickly.[137]

The remains of the tomb of Lazarus at Bethany.

Many of the Jews had come to Martha and Mary to comfort them about their brother

(11:19). Because burial took place so soon after death, mourning normally followed the burial. Women would return to the grave alone after the burial, beginning a thirty-day period of mourning, which included wailing and pronounced demonstrations of their sorrow.[138]

"Your brother will rise again," Jesus told her. Martha said to him, "I know he will rise again in the resurrection at the last day" (11:23–24). Belief in the resurrection of the dead is affirmed in the book of Daniel (Dan. 12:2).[139] Similarly, Jews in Jesus's day generally believed in the resurrection of the dead. One of the most poignant testimonies to the expectation of resurrection comes from 2 Macc. 7:9, 11, 14, 22–23.[140] The Sadducees, however, rejected any idea of bodily resurrection. The Mishnah (compiled ca. AD 200) affirms belief in the resurrection as the generally held position.[141]

The Jews who had come along with her crying (11:33). In addition to family and friends grieving their loss, there was an expectation, even for poor families, to hire professional mourners. The Mishnah records a saying by Rabbi Judah: "Even the poorest man in Israel should not hire fewer than two flutes and one professional wailing woman."[142]

It was a cave, and a stone was lying against it (11:38). Caves, both naturally occurring and dug out, were common burial sites in first-century Palestine. The tombs normally had a hall leading from the entrance to a main room. This entryway could be either vertical or horizontal, though the main hall likely was laid out horizontally. For the first year of interment the bodies were placed in the main hall, where they decomposed. After this the bones were collected and put in small stone boxes called ossuaries, which were then put into shelves cut into the walls. Stones were regularly used to cover the entrances to these tombs.[143] The cave was located outside the village in order to avoid ritual impurity from corpses.

Bound hand and foot with linen strips and with his face wrapped in a cloth (11:44). The normal practice for wrapping a corpse was to place it on a long sheet of linen, with the feet at one end. The other end would be long enough to fold back across the entire body, reaching back down to the feet. An additional patch of cloth was used to tie up the face.[144] Other Jewish texts do not attest to the practice of wrapping the hands and feet in additional strips of linen.

A limestone ossuary (bone box) with Greek and Hebrew inscriptions.

The chief priests and the Pharisees convened the Sanhedrin (11:47). On the Sanhedrin, see comments on Mark 8:31; John 3:1; see the article "The Sanhedrin." It is unclear whether this was an official meeting of the Sanhedrin or an informal gathering, the latter being more likely.

The Romans will come and take away both our place and our nation (11:48). The destruction of the Jerusalem temple in 586 BC, followed by the exile of Jews to Babylon, was a significant event in Jewish history, as God carried out his promised judgment on his people for breaking the covenant (2 Chron. 36:15–21). The temple came under attack again when the Seleucid king Antiochus IV Epiphanes desecrated the temple (note the Festival of Dedication in John 10:22; see the article "Jewish Festivals"). Although the Jews were under Roman authority, they were granted limited self-rule. However, Rome was always ready to take away this right from provinces that caused trouble. The situation in Israel had deteriorated since the days of Herod the Great, when Judea was a client kingdom. After Herod's death his son Archelaus was appointed ethnarch of Judea, Idumea, and Samaria. When riots erupted, he was removed and Judea put under the direct control of Roman governors, though the Jews were still allowed a measure of autonomy, as is evidenced by the authority of the Sanhedrin.[145]

Caiaphas . . . was high priest that year (11:49). Caiaphas was the high priest from AD 18 to 36. Although the office of high priest didn't rotate annually (it wasn't supposed to rotate at all but was a lifetime appointment), the fact that the Romans exercised their authority in the religious sphere meant that the position of high priest was tenuous. Indeed, the three high priests prior to Caiaphas (AD 15–18), his immediate successor, and most of the high priests during AD 44 to 66 all held their position for only one year.

You're not considering that it is to your advantage that one man should die for the people rather than the whole nation perish (11:50). Caiaphas's words bring to mind passages such as Jon. 1:14–17, where the sailors cast Jonah overboard in hopes of saving themselves (cf. 2 Macc. 7:37–38).

He did not say this on his own, but being high priest that year he prophesied (11:51). In the OT the priests sometimes discerned God's will using the Urim and Thummim (lots?).[146] In addition, priests occasionally were considered prophets (Num. 27:21) or seers (2 Sam. 24:11). Josephus mentions a number of instances where the high priest acted as a prophet.[147]

Not for the nation only, but also to unite the scattered children of God (11:52). The OT repeatedly describes Israel's hope of being gathered from exile and dispersion and of returning to dwell with God.[148] It also pictures the gentiles coming to Jerusalem to be God's people and to worship him.[149]

The Jewish Passover was near, and many went up to Jerusalem (11:55). On traveling to Jerusalem for festivals, see comments on Matt. 20:17; John 2:14. This is the last Passover mentioned in John (see comments on Mark 14:1; John 6:4). If the first occurred in AD 30 (see comments on John 2:20), the year is now AD 33.[150] Josephus speaks of the crowds that traveled to Jerusalem during these festivals.[151] Although his numbers are likely inflated, historians estimate that during the pilgrimage festivals Jerusalem's population could grow from one hundred thousand to as high as one million.[152]

Purify themselves before the Passover (11:55). The law required that an individual be ceremonially clean in order to celebrate the Passover (Num. 9:6; 2 Chron. 30:17–18). This would have been particularly important for Jews living outside Israel and among gentiles. Purification rites normally lasted a week (Num. 19:11–12).

Anointing at Bethany (12:1–11)

Perfume, pure and expensive nard (12:3). Nard is a sweetly scented, fragrant oil made from the nard plant, which grows in northern India. It is sometimes known as "spikenard," as the oil is extracted from the root and "spike" (the hair stem) of the plant.[153] The perfume was expensive and so was often diluted. The reference to its purity here indicates that it was unadulterated, accounting for its high price.

Anointed Jesus's feet, and wiped his feet with her hair (12:3). Anointing with oil was a common practice in both ancient Israel and other cultures, demonstrating hospitality as the oil would soothe the skin and exude a pleasant fragrance.[154] However, anointing the feet was a somewhat unusual practice; normally, water alone would be provided for cleaning, and the head or hands were anointed (see Ps. 23:5). Nevertheless, anointing of feet was not unheard of.[155] The act would have been considered improper in Jewish eyes, especially during a meal, further aggravated by Mary using her hair to wipe Jesus's feet (it was considered a sign of loose morals for women to let their hair down in public).[156]

Three hundred denarii (12:5). A denarius was a day's wage for a laborer. Since a laborer would not work on Sabbaths or other holy days, three hundred denarii equaled approximately a year's worth of wages (see the article "Money in the New Testament World").[157]

You always have the poor with you (12:8). Jesus likely is alluding to Deut. 15:11: "There will never cease to be poor people in the land; that is why I am commanding you, 'Open your hand willingly to your poor and needy brother in your land.'"

This fourth-century-AD sarcophagus relief shows Jesus entering Jerusalem with the crowd waving palm branches and spreading their cloaks before him.

Triumphal Entry (12:12–19)

The large crowd that had come to the festival (12:12). See the article "Jewish Festivals." On the size of the crowd during the festivals, see comments on John 11:55.

They took palm branches (12:13). The palm served as an important symbol in Jewish culture. In the OT it is associated with righteousness (Ps. 92:12) as well as with the Festival of Shelters (Lev. 23:40), though not Passover. Palm branches featured in the rededication of the temple in 164 BC (2 Macc. 10:6–7) and were used to celebrate the Maccabean victory over the Syrians in 141 BC (1 Macc. 13:51). By Jesus's day they had become a national symbol and were later featured on Jewish coins minted during revolts against Rome in AD 66–70 and 132–35.[158]

Shouting: "*Hosanna! Blessed is he who comes in the name of the Lord*" (12:13). The people here are crying out Ps. 118:25–26: "LORD, save us! LORD, please grant us success! He who comes in the name of the LORD is blessed. From the house of the LORD we bless you." "Hosanna" renders "save us" in Ps. 118:25 and later became a general expression of praise. Psalm 118 was part of the Hallel (Pss. 113–118), sung on celebratory occasions. The Levites recited the Hallel as the Passover lambs were being slaughtered, repeating it as many times as necessary until sacrifices were finished. It was also sung during the eating of the Passover meal.[159] In its original context Ps. 118 was a declaration of praise to the pilgrim journeying to Jerusalem to participate in one of the festivals, perhaps when entering the temple.[160]

Jesus found a young donkey and sat on it, just as is written: *Do not be afraid, Daughter Zion. Look, your King is coming, sitting on a donkey's colt* (12:14–15). John here quotes Zech. 9:9 (with a few modifications). Zechariah's prophecy, in turn, draws on Gen. 49:10–11, itself a messianic prediction. Two ideas often were associated with donkeys: humility and peace. Although the donkey was a beast of burden, not a warhorse (Sir. 33:25), its humble and peaceful nature didn't render it unimportant. Donkeys were ridden by important figures (Judg. 10:4; 2 Sam. 17:23; 19:26) and were associated with the prophetic expectation of a king coming in peace (Zech. 9:9).

The Approaching Gentiles (12:20–36)

Some Greeks were among those who went up to worship at the festival (12:20). "Greeks" are not just people from Greece but any non-Jew (i.e., gentiles). That they are going to worship suggests they are most likely "God-fearers," non-Jewish worshipers who had not formally converted to Judaism. They were able to go to the temple court to worship, but only as far as the Court of Gentiles (see comments on John 2:14).

Unless a grain of wheat falls to the ground and dies, it remains by itself. But if it dies, it produces much fruit (12:24). Jesus uses an agricultural metaphor to make his point. The argument is a typical rabbinic one, arguing from the lesser (seeds) to the greater (human life). Later rabbinic literature also used the image of seeds dying in connection with eternal life.[161]

If anyone serves me, he must follow me. Where I am, there my servant also will be (12:26). Jesus's words about his relationship with his disciples are similar to the common expectation of teacher-student relationships in his time. Rabbinic literature frequently speaks of disciples "following behind" their teachers.[162]

Now the ruler of this world will be cast out (12:31). Second Temple Jewish literature repeatedly refers to Satan as the prince or ruler of the world.[163] In *Jubilees* Mastema is called "the chief of spirits," and the Dead Sea Scrolls speak of the "domain," "dominion," and "empire" of Belial and contrast God's rule with that of Belial.[164]

We have heard from the law that the Messiah will remain forever (12:34). The term "law" can refer to the first five books of the OT or to the OT as a whole. The common expectation in first-century Palestinian Judaism, based on OT teaching, was that the Messiah would reign forever.[165]

Walk while you have the light so that darkness doesn't overtake you (12:35). The idea of "walking" often is used with moral overtones. Psalm 1, for example, warns against walking with the wicked (v. 1).[166] The Qumran literature not only uses the imagery of walking but also speaks of walking in light and darkness.

Children of light (12:36). Being a "child of" reflects the Hebrew idiom "son of," indicating that the person displays the qualities of his or her parents.[167] The Qumran community referred to itself as "sons of light."[168]

Jewish Unbelief (12:37–50)

This was to fulfill the word of Isaiah the prophet (12:38). Jesus quotes from Isa. 53 in the following verses, drawing a connection between OT prophecies and his imminent crucifixion.[169]

Lord, who has believed our message? And to whom has the arm of the Lord been revealed? (12:38). The passage quoted is Isa. 53:1, which refers to the servant of the Lord. The message proclaimed in the associated Servant Song is both of salvation and suffering by the servant on behalf of God's people. Moreover, Isa. 53:1 speaks of people's intransigence to this message. John connects this passage with the following quotation of Isa. 6:10 (in v. 40) through the rabbinic principle of equivalent expression (*gezerah shavah,* similar to a modern cross-reference to a passage with the same or a similar topic).[170]

He has blinded their eyes . . . and I would heal them (12:40). Here Jesus quotes from Isa. 6. In its original context this passage seeks to demonstrate that, following the death of Uzziah, God's purposes toward Israel remained the same and would continue to do so until the predicted judgment occurred. God would continue to send a message of repentance to his stubborn people, many of whom would only grow more hard-hearted. Nevertheless, while their failure to repent indicated their sinfulness, it did not convey a failure of God's purposes.

So that they would not be banned from the synagogue (12:42). See comments on John 9:22.

The one who believes in me believes not in me, but in him who sent me (12:44). See comments on John 5:23.

I know that his command is eternal life (12:50). Jesus's words reflect Deuteronomy, where the people are called to build their lives on God's word and so enjoy his blessing (Deut. 8:3; 32:46–47).

Farewell and Final Prayer (13:1–17:26)

Before the Passover Festival (13:1). The opening words of the "Farewell Discourse" narrate the footwashing, which occurs before the Passover meal is eaten. For discussion of whether the meal is a Passover meal, see comments on John 18:28; 19:14.

Laid aside his outer clothing, took a towel, and tied it around himself (13:4–5). Footwashing was a common act of hospitality, attested in both the OT and Second Temple Jewish literature.[171] It was an important part of caring for one's guests, given the reality of travel in the ancient world, where walking long distances in sandals on dusty roads left travelers with dirty feet. Footwashing took place upon arrival, before the meal, with water being poured out of one basin, over the feet,

An ancient pair of sandals.

and into a second vessel. However, while a common act of hospitality, this was an act of lowly service. For Jesus, a rabbi, to take on such a role would have been shocking (see comments on John 1:27). According to rabbinic thought, "A Hebrew slave must not wash the feet of his master, nor put his shoes on him."[172] Menial service was similarly disdained in Greco-Roman culture.[173]

You have no part with me (13:8). The word translated as "part" (*meros*) is related to the word used in the Greek translation of the OT to speak of the "share" or "portion" that each of the twelve tribes of Israel (except Levi) would receive in the promised land.

One who has bathed . . . doesn't need to wash anything except his feet (13:10). There are two possible backgrounds for Jesus's statement about bathing: first, the ceremonial cleansing in which Jews took part prior to celebrating the Passover (see comments on John 11:55);[174] second, the custom observed by some to bathe before leaving home and then to wash their feet upon arriving at their destination.[175]

I have given you an example, that you also should do just as I have done for you (13:15). Both Jewish and Greco-Roman writers discuss examples of virtuous living.[176] Jewish literature also discusses setting an example in death. Second Maccabees recounts how Eleazar faced his death, saying, "Therefore, by bravely giving up my life now, I will show myself worthy of my old age and leave to the young a noble example of how to die a good death willingly and nobly for the revered and holy laws" (2 Macc. 6:27–28 NRSV).[177]

If you know these things, you are blessed if you do them (13:17). Greek literature also pronounced a blessing on those acting on their knowledge: "Blessed and fortunate is he who knowingly does all these things" (Hesiod), and "He is not happy who only knows them, but he who does them" (Seneca).[178]

I am telling you now before it happens, so that when it does happen you will believe that I am he (13:19). Jesus's language is reminiscent of words spoken by God in the prophetic books (e.g., Ezek. 24:24). The phrase "I am he" translates the Greek *egō eimi*, which was regularly used in the LXX to refer to God's identity in the book of Isaiah (43:10; cf. 41:26; 48:3, 5–6) (see comments on John 8:24).[179]

Reclining close beside Jesus (13:23). Reclining at meals was common in Jesus's day. Couches were arranged in a U shape around a table. Guests reclined with their head toward the table and their feet away from it, supporting themselves on their left arm so that they could eat with their right arm. At the bottom of the U, in between the two arms, the host reclined. The space to his left was for the guest of honor, and the space to his right was the second-most-honored position.[180] The phrase "reclining close beside him" indicates that the disciple's head was next to Jesus's chest; that is, he was lying to his right.

Some thought that Jesus was telling him, "Buy what we need for the festival" (13:29). The festival in question is not the Passover proper, as Jesus and his followers are currently eating that meal, but rather the Festival of Unleavened Bread, which followed the Passover (see Deut. 16:1–8).[181]

Give something to the poor (13:29). On almsgiving, see comments on John 9:8. It was customary to give alms to the poor on Passover night, as the gates of Jerusalem were opened after midnight and beggars gathered.[182]

Children, I am with you a little while longer (13:33). The reference to Jesus's disciples as his children is fitting for two reasons. First, he fills the role of the father at a Passover meal.[183] Second, his words in 13:31–17:26 appear to be modeled after OT farewell discourses such as Moses's parting speech to the Israelites in Deut. 31–33.[184] During the Second Temple period a specific genre of literature developed that focused on such speeches, highlighting the final words of an individual to those closest to him, such as a dying father to his children.[185] *Testament of Reuben* provides a representative example: "My children, behold I am dying, and I am going the way of my fathers" (1.3).[186]

I give you a new command: Love one another. Just as I have loved you, you are also to love one another (13:34). The command to love one's neighbor was not new. It occurs in Lev. 19:18, a passage quoted elsewhere by Jesus in the Gospels (e.g., Matt. 5:43; 19:19). Second Temple Judaism also highlighted this command. The pseudepigraphal *Testaments of the Twelve Patriarchs* contains frequent exhortations to love one another.[187] The Qumran *Rule of the Community* lists as one of its purposes "to love all the sons of light."[188] Similarly, Rabbi Hillel said, "Be disciples of Aaron, loving peace and pursuing peace, loving people and drawing them near to the Torah."[189] The newness of the command stems from its connection to Jesus's own actions as he would lay down his life for his followers at the cross.

In my Father's house are many rooms (14:2). The imagery here is drawn from the ancient Jewish practice of combining multiple homes to form an extended household.[190] When a son got married, it was common for him to build a dwelling place on his father's property, with each new building enlarging the family compound.

I am going away to prepare a place for you (14:2). In Deuteronomy God speaks with similar language, reminding the people that he went before them, preparing places for them to camp in the wilderness, and that he had promised to go before them into the promised land (Deut. 1:29–33).[191]

I am the way, the truth, and the life (14:6). Jesus's words reflect OT themes. The concept of a path of life is particularly common (e.g., Ps. 16:11).

Similarly, the OT speaks of a way of truth (often translated "faithfulness"), which often is related to God's law (Ps. 119:30). Second Temple literature contains similar language.[192] The Qumran *Rule of the Community* contrasts the paths in which the sons of truth walk with those tread by the ones who follow the spirit of deceit.[193]

Lord, . . . show us the Father (14:8). Philip appears to be asking for some form of theophany.[194] God revealed his glory in limited fashion on different occasions in the OT. When Moses asked God to see his glory (Exod. 33:18), God consented to pass before Moses but did not show him his "face." Similarly, Isaiah saw a magnificent vision of God seated on the throne in the temple (Isa. 6:1). He later spoke of God's glory being revealed at the Messiah's coming (Isa. 40:5; cf. John 12:41).

Another Counselor (14:16). The term translated as "Counselor" is *paraklētos*, a term notoriously difficult to translate. Ancient Greek literature regularly uses it to speak of a legal assistant. Later rabbinic writings picture the Holy Spirit filling the role of a legal defender.[195] The Septuagint uses related words to speak of the expected comfort in the messianic age (see LXX Isa. 40:1).

The Spirit of truth (14:17). Jewish literature in Jesus's day speaks of the "spirit of truth," but normally the phrase occurs in contexts where the "spirit of truth" is contrasted with another kind of spirit—a dualism absent from this Gospel.[196]

Will teach you all things and will remind you of everything I have told you (14:26). The OT affirms the importance of receiving correct instruction from the Scriptures as an essential aspect of living as God's people (Ps. 25:5; Neh. 9:20). At Qumran the "teacher of righteousness" interpreted the Scriptures for the community.[197] Remembering was also a central aspect of Judaism.[198] Both the OT and Second Temple literature emphasize the importance of remembering God's words and works.[199]

Peace I leave with you. My peace I give you. I do not give to you as the world gives (14:27). "Peace" was the normal Jewish greeting and farewell. The Hebrew concept of peace encompasses more than absence of strife, normally indicating the possession of blessing, especially a right relationship with God.[200] This idea is evident in the blessing God commanded Aaron to pronounce: "May the Lord bless you and protect you; may the Lord make his face shine on you and be gracious to you; may the Lord look with favor on you and give you peace" (Num. 6:24–26 [cf. Ps. 29:11; Hag. 2:9]). The future messianic age is also connected with peace. The Messiah is the "Prince of Peace" (Isa. 9:6) and is to "proclaim peace to the nations" (Zech. 9:10). Peace was an important concept in the surrounding culture as well. The first Roman emperor, Augustus (30 BC–AD 14), had secured peace for

Pressing floors used to trample the grapes and produce the juice.

the civilized world through military victory, instituting the *pax Romana*. Augustus had built his famous Peace Altar (*Ara Pacis*) to commemorate the new age of peace.[201]

I am the true vine, and my Father is the gardener (15:1). The imagery is drawn from Isa. 5:1–7, where Israel is compared to a vine and God to a gardener. Whereas God provided for the vine, tended to it, and protected it, the vine yielded bad fruit. As a result, it incurred judgment.[202] Vine imagery is not limited to Isaiah, however, but occurs extensively throughout the OT as well as in Second Temple literature.[203] While many of the references feature Israel as the vine, in later literature it also represents wisdom and the Messiah's dominion.[204] The OT also contains expectations of the Messiah being raised up as a vine (Ps. 80:14–18).[205]

He removes . . . he prunes (15:2). The vinedresser's actions here are twofold: cutting off dry and withered branches that no longer serve any purpose, and pruning small shoots so that the main branches receive more nutrients and produce more fruit.[206] The former may have occurred in the winter, pruning off branches so that only the main vine was left.[207] Similarly, Philo speaks of "superfluous shoots . . . which are a great injury to the genuine shoots, and which the husbandmen cleanse and prune."[208]

Does not produce fruit . . . produces fruit . . . produce more fruit (15:2). The concept of fruitfulness is rooted in God's work. God intends his creation to be fruitful (Gen 1:11–12, 22, 28). The prophets envision a day when "Jacob will take root. Israel will blossom and bloom and fill the whole world with fruit" (Isa. 27:6 [cf. Hosea 14:4–8]).

They gather them, throw them into the fire, and they are burned (15:6). Vine imagery in Ezekiel compares Jerusalem to a vine that is burned in the fire (Ezek. 15:1–8).[209] Fire is a common biblical picture for divine judgment (e.g., Deut. 4:24; Isa. 30:27).

No one has greater love than this: to lay down his life for his friends (15:13). The virtue of friendship is extolled in Proverbs (e.g., 17:17). Sirach has an extended discussion of friendship, warning against fickle friends and extolling faithful ones (Sir. 6:5–17). Friendship was also held in high regard in the Greco-Roman world. Aristotle observed that "a virtuous man's conduct is often guided by the interests of his friends," and "he will if necessary lay down his life in their behalf."[210]

You are my friends (15:14). To be called a "friend of God" was exceedingly rare in the OT. Abraham receives this designation (2 Chron. 20:7; Isa. 41:8), and Moses (indirectly) does as well (Exod. 33:11). Second Temple literature also notes that Abraham[211] and Moses[212] were friends of God and extended the honor to others.[213]

You did not choose me, but I chose you (15:16). Scripture records one instance each where Abraham (Neh. 9:7) and Moses (Ps. 106:23) are said to have been chosen by God. The language of God "choosing" normally is used for kings and Israel as a whole (Deut. 7:6).[214] The idea of being a chosen student was also unusual, as it was more common for students to choose a master: "Joshua b. Perahiah says, 'Set up a master for yourself.'"[215]

They hated me for no reason (15:25). Jesus here quotes from Ps. 35:19 or Ps. 69:4, the latter being more likely. Psalm 69 is a Davidic psalm depicting a righteous follower of God who suffers persecution because of his passion for the Lord.[216]

The Spirit of truth (15:26). See comments on John 14:17.

You also will testify (15:27). "Witness" language is found in the book of Isaiah, where God's end-time people are called "witnesses" (Isa. 43:10–12; 44:8).

Ban you from the synagogues (16:2). See comments on Mark 1:21; John 9:22; see the article "The Jewish Synagogue."

The Counselor (16:7). See comments on John 14:16.

I will send him to you (16:7). OT prophets regularly predicted that in the last days God would send his Spirit. At times the Messiah is the recipient (e.g., Isa. 11:1–10; 42:1–4); at other times it is God's people (e.g., Isa. 32:14–18; Jer. 31:31–34). In both cases the coming of the Spirit results in great blessings.

When he comes, he will convict the world about sin (16:8). The convicting role of the Spirit is referenced in Jewish literature: "And the spirit of truth testifies to all things and brings all accusations."[217] The idea of one who will convict the ungodly on the day of judgment was also common. In some literature the role belonged to Enoch, in other places to an unnamed scribe.[218]

The Spirit of truth (16:13). See comments on John 14:17.

Guide you into all the truth (16:13). The OT expresses the desire of God's people for his guidance (Ps. 25:4–5; 43:3; 86:11) and attests that it can be found in his word (Ps. 119:105; Prov. 6:20–24). Isaiah speaks about how God guided his people in the past (63:14) and looks forward to the day when he will once again do so (Isa. 43:19). Intertestamental literature pictures wisdom as leading God's people (e.g., Wis. 9:11). Philo speaks of "a divine spirit which guided their feet into the way of truth."[219]

He will also declare to you what is to come (16:13). The verb translated here as "declare" (*anangellō*) occurs forty-three times in the Greek text of Isaiah (e.g., Isa. 41:21–29; 42:9; 44:7), where Yahweh declares that he alone has the authority to predict the future (Isa. 48:14).[220]

Your sorrow will turn to joy (16:20). Jesus's words build on the conviction found in the OT that God is able to turn sorrow into joy (Jer. 31:13; Esther 9:22). The expectation of joy instead of sorrow is also found in Second Temple literature: "Do not be anxious, for when the day of tribulation and anguish comes, others shall weep and be sorrowful, but you shall rejoice and have abundance" (2 Esd. 2:27 NRSV).

When a woman is in labor (16:21). OT prophets used the imagery of a woman giving birth regularly, often applying it to the time when the Messiah would bring salvation (see Isa. 26:17–18; 66:7–13).[221] Similarly, the day of the Lord often is referred to as "a time of distress" (Dan. 12:1; Zeph. 1:14–15). Second Temple literature made use of the same imagery and coined the phrase "the birth pains of the Messiah" to speak about the time of suffering and trial that would precede God's salvation.[222]

You will be scattered (16:32). The words likely allude to Zech. 13:7, one of a number of OT passages that picture God's flock as scattered and without a shepherd (e.g., 1 Kings 22:17; Isa. 53:6; Jer. 23:1; 50:17; Ezek. 34:6, 12, 21).[223]

Glorify your Son so that the Son may glorify you (17:1). According to the OT, God's glory is unique, and he doesn't share it with others (Isa. 42:8; 48:11).

This is eternal life: that they may know you (17:3). Knowing God doesn't refer simply to knowledge about God but rather, in keeping with OT parlance, means enjoying personal fellowship with him.[224] The connection between knowing God and eternal life derives from OT passages in which true knowledge of God is depicted as an aspect of the new covenant (Jer. 31:34) and the future messianic age (Isa. 11:9; cf. Hab. 2:14).

I have revealed your name (17:6). God's name reveals his nature and character (Exod. 3:13–15), and in the OT his name was to be made known to his people and among the nations (Ps. 22:22; Isa. 52:6; Ezek. 39:7).[225] To "place his name" in the temple conveyed his presence in that location (Deut. 12:5; cf. 1 Kings 8:29; Isa. 18:7), and to "know [his] name" implied being committed to him (Ps. 9:10; cf. 1 Kings 8:43) and being under his care (Ps. 91:14).

I have given them the words you gave me (17:8). In passing on the Father's words, Jesus acts similarly to the prophet whom Moses predicted would come after him (Deut. 18:18).

Protect them by your name (17:11). See comments on John 17:6. This statement reflects the OT idea that God's name is powerful: "God, save me by your name, and vindicate me by your might" (Ps. 54:1).[226]

So that the Scripture may be fulfilled (17:12). The unnamed Scripture that Jesus has in mind here, in regard to the lost "son of destruction," is likely Ps. 41:9: "Even my friend in whom I trusted, one who ate my bread, has raised his heel against me" (cf. the reference to Judas Iscariot in John 13:18).

I may be in them (17:26). God dwelling with his people was a significant OT theme, with God assuring his people of his presence (Exod. 29:45–46), punishing them with the loss of his presence (Ezek. 10–11), and conveying the eschatological hope of enjoying his presence fully (Zech. 14). It was in the tabernacle and temple that God's presence resided (Exod. 40:34; 1 Kings 8:10–11). John has already drawn attention to Jesus's role in making God's presence known (see comments on John 1:14).

Crucifixion and Burial (18:1–19:42)

A company of soldiers (18:3). The soldiers in question are Roman soldiers, although the exact number is uncertain (see the article "The Roman Military"). The Greek text refers to a "company" or "cohort," which could number anywhere from a thousand to as little as two hundred.[227] The Romans were prepared to dispatch large numbers of soldiers even when dealing with individuals (as in the case of the 470 soldiers tasked with guarding Paul in Acts 23:23). The large numbers of pilgrims gathered in Jerusalem for a festival would have made a riot a distinct possibility (see comments on John 11:55).[228]

Chief priests (18:3). The "chief priests" consisted of the current high priest (Caiaphas), any former high priests who were still living (such as Annas), and members of leading families from whom the high priests were chosen.[229]

When Jesus told them, "I am he," they stepped back and fell to the ground (18:6). On the phrase "I am he," see comments on John 8:24. Falling to the ground is a common response to God's glory or divine revelation (e.g., Gen. 17:3; Lev. 9:24; Judg. 13:20; Ezek. 1:28; Dan. 2:46; 8:18).

Am I not to drink the cup? (18:11). In the OT the "cup" that God gives regularly refers to the punishment evildoers will have to bear: "Wake yourself, wake yourself up! Stand up, Jerusalem, you who have drunk the cup of his fury from the LORD's hand; you who have drunk the goblet to the dregs—the cup that causes people to stagger" (Isa. 51:17 [see also Ps. 75:8; Isa. 51:22; Jer. 25:15–17; Ezek. 23:31–34; Hab. 2:16]).[230]

Annas, since he was the father-in-law of Caiaphas, who was high priest that year (18:13). Under OT law the high priesthood was a lifelong position (Num. 35:25).[231] However, the Romans (and Seleucids before them) exercised their authority over the Jews in part by controlling the high priesthood, appointing and deposing priests. Annas had served as high priest from AD 6 to 15, until he was removed from office. A short time later one of his sons (Eleazar) was appointed high priest, and shortly thereafter his son-in-law Caiaphas. Indeed, as many as five of Annas's sons served as high priest at one time or another. Consequently, Annas was held in high esteem by the people and as former high priest still entitled to be called by that title.[232] For additional information on Caiaphas, see comments on John 2:14; 11:49.

The servants and the officials had made a charcoal fire, because it was cold (18:18). Jesus is arrested at night, and dawn has not yet arrived, as the references to the cold temperatures and the warm fire indicate. Under normal circumstances it was illegal for an actual trial to take place at night. What is more, a capital case could not take place before a festival or Sabbath: "In capital cases, they try the case by day and complete it [by] day. . . . In capital cases they come to a final decision for acquittal on the same day, but on the following day for conviction. Therefore they do not judge [capital cases] either on the eve of the Sabbath or on the eve of a festival."[233] This is one indication that the trial in question is not an official, formal one (see comments on John 18:19; 18:21).

The high priest (18:19). The high priest throughout this section is Annas (18:13, 24). Although Caiaphas was the actual high priest that year, Annas could be referred to as high priest as well, as he had served in that role and been removed from office by the Romans (see comments on John 2:14; 11:49; 18:13).

Questioned Jesus about his disciples and about his teaching (18:19). Generally it was expected that a defendant would not be questioned directly but be charged based on the testimony of witnesses. It may be that this trial is therefore informal. The questions posed to Jesus reveal a concern that his teaching was leading people astray (see John 7:12, 47; cf. Deut. 13:1–11).[234]

I have spoken openly to the world . . . I haven't spoken anything in secret (18:20). The public nature of Jesus's teaching means that eyewitnesses are readily available. His words also echo God's declaration in Isaiah: "I have not spoken in secret" (Isa. 45:19; cf. 48:16).[235]

Why do you question me? Question those who heard what I told them (18:21). It was uncommon for a defendant to be questioned, as a case was to be tried on the basis of witnesses bearing testimony (see comments on John 18:19). Jewish law considered a person's own testimony to be invalid (see comments on John 5:31). When a defendant raised an objection, the case was established through the testimony of witnesses. This is another indication that the trial is informal.

Slapped Jesus (18:22). Jewish and OT law allowed for those convicted to be punished physically (e.g., Deut. 25:2–3; *m. Hullin* 5.2). To strike a man during a trial would have been a breach of the law.[236]

Then Annas sent him bound to Caiaphas the high priest (18:24). An official trial is still needed before the Romans can get involved, which means sending Jesus to the current high priest, so that Jesus is judged by the Sanhedrin.[237]

A rooster crowed (18:27). There is debate over when roosters crowed in first-century Jerusalem. Suggestions range from as early as 12:30 a.m. to 5:00 a.m., while some suggest that the phrase here refers to a particular trumpet, the "cockcrow" blown at the end of the third watch (at around 3:00 a.m.). The crowing of the cock, whether a rooster or trumpet, signaled early morning.

It was early morning (18:28). The reference likely indicates that Jesus is being brought to Pilate before 6:00 a.m. but after sunrise. Roman officials tended to start and end the day early.[238]

They did not enter the headquarters themselves; otherwise they would be defiled and unable to eat the Passover (18:28). According to the OT, contracting uncleanness prevented people from celebrating the Passover (see Num. 9:6). Here "Passover" likely refers to the entire festival, Passover and Unleavened Bread, which extended the celebration an additional seven days (see Num. 28:16–25; 2 Chron. 30:21).[239]

Pilate (18:29). See the article "Pontius Pilate"; see comments on Mark 15:1.[240] Pontius Pilate served as procurator (i.e., governor) of Judea from AD 26 to 37. His role in the crucifixion of Jesus is attested in all four Gospels, as well as by the Roman historian Tacitus.[241]

It's not legal for us to put anyone to death (18:31). While the Sanhedrin had a degree of authority over Jewish matters, the Romans did not permit it to carry out capital punishment (see the article "The Sanhedrin"). Josephus writes of a high priest who ordered several men to be stoned as lawbreakers. Some citizens complained about this act, and Albinus, the Roman procurator who had only recently installed the high priest in office, promptly removed him.[242]

Are you the King of the Jews? (18:33). The title "King of the Jews" had definite political overtones. In the fairly recent past it had been the title of Herod the Great. Prior to that it may have been used by the Hasmonean dynasty before the Romans took control. According to Josephus, when the Roman general Pompey came to Damascus, he was met by envoys from the surrounding regions. The ambassadors from Judea brought a gift, later taken to the temple of Jupiter in Rome, bearing the inscription "The Gift of Alexander, the King of the Jews."[243]

You have a custom that I release one prisoner to you at the Passover (18:39). There is little extrabiblical support for the custom of pardoning a prisoner at Passover. However, the Mishnah does provide legal guidelines for sacrificing Passover lambs for those who may or may not be able to eat it, including "one whom they have promised to free from prison."[244] The practice may stem from the Hasmonean period and then have been carried on by the Romans.[245] It was also well within the power of a Roman governor to grant a prisoner a pardon.[246] It likely served as a goodwill gesture that was meant to relieve political tension so that pilgrims celebrating the festival in Jerusalem would know that "no one coming to Jerusalem would be caught in the midst of political strife."[247]

Barabbas was a revolutionary (18:40). The term "revolutionary" (Gk. *lēstēs*) designates Barabbas not so much as a simple robber but as an insurrectionist. Josephus uses the term and its derivatives to speak of people who participated in guerilla warfare throughout the country, and particularly of the zealots who wanted to overthrow Roman rule.[248]

Pilate (19:1). See the article "Pontius Pilate"; see comments on Mark 15:1; John 18:29.

Flogged (19:1). The Romans used three forms of beating, ranging from a less severe beating for simple criminal offenses to a horrific scourging that accompanied other forms of punishment, such as crucifixion. In the present instance, since Jesus has not yet been officially sentenced, it is likely the least severe form of beating that Pilate orders.[249]

A purple robe (19:2). Purple cloth was expensive and often associated with wealth or royalty. However, descriptions of color appear to have been somewhat fluid, and it is likely that the cloak in question was the faded red cloak of a soldier.

Hail (19:3). The guards' mockery of Jesus is highlighted by the fact that the Roman emperor normally was paid homage in similar terms.[250]

We have a law . . . and according to that law he ought to die, because he made himself the Son of God (19:7). The law may be Lev. 24:16. However, the claim to be "the Son of God" was not intrinsically blasphemous and is used in the OT and Second Temple literature to refer to the king (2 Sam. 7:14; Ps. 2:7; 89:26–27), the Messiah (*4QAramaic Apocalypse* 2.1), and Israel (Exod. 4:22; Hosea 11:1).[251] The emperor, especially Augustus, was also referred to as "son of God."[252]

You are not Caesar's friend (19:12). For a Roman government official, it was no small matter to have the emperor's favor. The term "friend of Caesar" eventually became a virtual official title, but even in Jesus's day it may have been a recognized phrase for someone in good standing with the emperor.[253] The emperor in Jesus's day, Tiberius, was known for his willingness to deal swiftly with those who were disloyal to him.[254] Pilate's mentor, Aelius Sejanus, had at one time been in good favor with the emperor, so much so that Marcus Terentius, a Roman, reportedly said that "the closer a man's intimacy with Sejanus, the stronger his claim to the emperor's friendship."[255] Some of Pilate's own harsh actions (see the article "Pontius Pilate") likely were never reported to the emperor due to Sejanus's influence and anti-Semitism. However, Sejanus himself eventually fell out of favor with the emperor and was executed in AD 31.[256] Consequently, Pilate had to tread more carefully.

The preparation day for the Passover (19:14). Here "preparation day" refers to the day of preparation for the Sabbath—that is, the day on which preparations were made so that no work would be done on the Sabbath.[257] The expression has this meaning in the Gospels as well as in contemporaneous Jewish literature.[258] In this case, the phrase "of the Passover" (*tou pascha*) refers not the Passover meal itself, which occurred the previous day, but to Passover week, the Festival of Unleavened Bread (see comments on John 18:28). The entire phrase, then, speaks of the special day preparing for the Sabbath that fell during Passover week.

They took Jesus away (19:16). It is at this point that Jesus is flogged again, this time with the horrific scourging used by the Romans accompanied by punishments such as crucifixion (see Mark 15:15). This beating was so severe as to sometimes result in death for recipients. Josephus speaks of a man being whipped by the Roman procurator Albinus "until his bones were laid bare."[259]

Carrying the cross by himself . . . they crucified him (19:17–18). Roman records attest to the practice of those sentenced to be crucified carrying their cross: "Each criminal who goes to execution must carry his own cross on his back."[260] Specifically, they carried the horizontal bar to the place of crucifixion, where the upright beam was already in place.[261] Crucifixion was a common and horrific form of execution in the ancient world (see the article "Crucifixion").[262] Cicero calls it "a most cruel and ignominious punishment" and "the most miserable and most painful punishment appropriate to slaves alone."[263] In the Roman world the practice was not to be carried out on Roman citizens without express permission from the emperor. It normally was reserved for slaves and criminals, especially for crimes that threatened the empire or social order. While there was variety in the way in which criminals were crucified, the common procedure involved nailing the criminal's hands or wrists to the horizontal beam. The person was then attached to the upright post and the feet were nailed or tied to it. A wooden footrest or seat was sometimes attached to the cross, which would prolong suffering. In addition to any beatings incurred ahead of time and the pain of being nailed to the cross, the victims often were contorted into unusual positions to increase suffering. They might be attacked by birds or other animals while hanging on their cross for hours, perhaps even days, until they died. Death normally was the result of heart failure, brain damage, suffocation, or shock.[264]

A sign made and put on the cross (19:19). A notice of a criminal's offense was at times written on a piece of board and hung from the criminal's neck. There is little evidence of such notices being hung on a cross, but given the variety with which executions were carried out, this is not improbable.[265]

Woman, here is your son . . . Here is your mother (19:26–27). Jesus's mother appears to be a widow at this point and thus depended on Jesus and his half-brothers to provide for her needs (see the article "The Family of Jesus"; cf. Exod. 20:12; Deut. 5:16). Lucian, writing in the second century AD, reflects the practice of a dying man entrusting his mother to the care of another: "The bequest of Eudamidas was, 'I leave to Aretaeus my mother to support and cherish in her old age.'"[266]

That the Scripture might be fulfilled, he said, "I'm thirsty" (19:28). This probably is an allusion to Ps. 69:21 and perhaps is also connected to Ps. 22:15.

Sour wine (19:29). Wine vinegar (sour wine) was an inexpensive drink used to quench thirst. As Plutarch discusses the character of Marcus Cato, he writes, "Water was what he drank on his campaigns, except that once in a while, in a raging thirst, he would call for vinegar."[267]

Preparation day (19:31). See comments on John 19:14.

Pierced his side with a spear, and at once blood and water came out (19:34). The presence of blood and water seems most likely to be an indication that Jesus died a truly human death. It is also possible that there are two different scriptural allusions behind the reference: the striking of the rock (Exod. 17:6) and the Passover (the hyssop [19:29], the unbroken bones [19:33], and the mingled blood [19:34]).[268]

The scripture would be fulfilled: *Not one of his bones will be broken* (19:36). It was not uncommon for Romans to break the legs of those being crucified, speeding up their death (the remains of a man crucified in the first century were discovered in Jerusalem; he had one leg fractured and the other shattered).[269] Because Jesus had already died, there was no need to break his legs. The Scriptures in question are Ps. 34:20, speaking of how God protects the righteous man, and Exod. 12:46; Num. 9:12, referring to the Passover lamb.[270]

The Church of the Holy Sepulchre marks the traditional location of Jesus's crucifixion.

Another scripture says: *They will look at the one they pierced* (19:37). The passage being quoted is Zech. 12:10, which in its original context seems to refer to the piercing of Yahweh.[271]

Asked Pilate that he might remove Jesus's body (19:38). The burial of the dead was an important rite in Second Temple Judaism (see comments on Mark 15:46). The book of Tobit records burying the dead as one of Tobit's charitable deeds (Tob. 1:16–19; 2:1–4). Josephus says that the Jews buried even those condemned to death and their enemies, extending this even to those crucified: "They took down those that were condemned and crucified, and buried them before the going down of the sun."[272] Normally, Romans let the bodies of crucified criminals hang and rot, but they allowed Jews to bury those who had been crucified on the same day in order not to incur defilement.[273] This concern to bury the body was coupled with a desire not to desecrate previously buried bodies in a family tomb, as the Mishnah attests: "And they did not bury [the felon] in the burial grounds of his ancestors."[274]

Day of preparation (19:42). See comments on John 19:14.

Resurrection (20:1–31)

Linen cloths lying there (20:5). The presence of the linen strips points to the fact that grave robbers had not taken the body, as the linen and spices used to prepare the body for burial would both have had some value.

The wrapping that had been on his head was not lying with the linen cloths but was folded up in a separate place by itself (20:7). John is either speaking to the neatness of the head wrapping or indicating that it was in the same place it had been when on Jesus's body. In either event, this again points away from grave robbers, who would neither have left the wrapping lying in its place nor rolled it up neatly but would have taken it.[275]

They still did not yet understand the Scripture that he must rise from the dead (20:9). The reference to "Scripture" may point to the whole of Scripture (see Luke 24:25–27, 32, 44–47) or to a particular passage. Suggestions regarding individual passages include Ps. 16:10, Isa. 53:10–12, and Hosea 6:2.[276]

Mary stood outside the tomb, crying (20:11). Mary is crying not because of Jesus's death but because his body has disappeared. Proper burial was important in Second Temple Judaism (see comments on John 19:38), and desecrating the dead was considered a terrible offense (1 Sam. 31:9–13). The verb used here for "crying" (*klaiō*) refers not to quiet sobbing but to the loud wailing common in mourning practices of the ancient Near East (cf. John 11:31, 33).[277]

She said to him in Aramaic, "*Rabboni!*"—which means "Teacher" (20:16). See comments on John 1:38.

Go to my brothers and tell them (20:17). The OT establishes the importance of witnesses for affirming the truthfulness of a matter (Deut. 19:15). According to the Mishnah, however, there were limitations placed on the matters concerning which women were considered competent to testify.[278]

As the Father has sent me, I also send you (20:21). The sending of the Son is an important theme throughout this Gospel. The disciples are commissioned to go with the same authority as the Son (see comments on John 5:23).[279] There is also an idea of succession present, which was important in both the OT and Second Temple Jewish literature. The most prominent OT succession narratives involve Joshua (Deut. 31:1–23; 34; Josh. 1) and Elisha (2 Kings 2:1–3:27).

He breathed on them and said, "Receive the Holy Spirit" (20:22). Jesus here draws on Gen. 2:7, where the Septuagint uses the exact same verb form to speak of God breathing on Adam and giving him life. Here, in anticipation of Pentecost, Jesus sets his apostles apart as the new messianic community.

If you forgive the sins of any, they are forgiven; if you retain the sins of any, they are retained (20:23). Jesus's words may reflect Isa. 22:22 in a way similar to Matt. 16:19. The idea of "binding and loosing" originally was used for a judge's activity of declaring persons innocent or guilty, convicting them of or setting them free from their charges. The rabbis used the language to speak of what the law allowed or forbade.[280]

A week later (20:26). The rendering "a week later" reflects the underlying "after eight days," which by inclusive reckoning refers to Sunday, a full week after Jesus's resurrection.[281]

My Lord and my God (20:28). The OT regularly refers to God by connecting "Lord" and "God" (e.g., Ps. 35:23–24; Jer. 31:18). The declaration was also in use in the Roman world, probably through Mediterranean cults, as evidenced in an inscription from 24 BC dedicating a building "to the god and lord Socnopaeus."[282] In the Roman Empire this use was later extended to at least some emperors. Domitian (AD 81–96), who likely was the reigning emperor when John wrote his Gospel, demanded that he be addressed as *dominus et deus noster* ("our lord and god").[283]

Jesus is the Messiah, the Son of God (20:31). See comments on John 1:41; 1:49.

Epilogue (21:1–25)

That night they caught nothing (21:3). Fishing was commonly done at night in the ancient world. The fish caught would then be sold in the morning.[284]

Simon Peter . . . tied his outer clothing around him (for he had taken it off) and plunged into the sea (21:7–8). The phrase "for he had taken it off" renders the more literal "for he was naked" (NRSV), though the Greek word doesn't necessarily indicate an absence of all clothing. Peter probably had taken off his fisherman's coat ("outer clothing"), so that he was wearing only his undergarments, likely the short tunic of the workman.[285] Having done so, he was now prepared to swim ashore and greet Jesus.[286]

Full of large fish—153 of them (21:11). There doesn't appear to be any symbolism behind the number 153 here. Large numbers in John are consistently used in a literal fashion (see 2:6; 12:3). The *Testament of Zebulon* (second century BC) points to an abundant catch as a sign of God's blessing: "Therefore the Lord made my catch to be an abundance of fish; for whoever shares with his neighbor receives multifold from the Lord" (6.6).

Feed my lambs . . . shepherd my sheep . . . feed my sheep (21:15–17). On the image of shepherding in the OT, see comments on John 10:2–3; 10:11. The language of "feeding" is also found in Ezek. 34:2, where the shepherds are said to feed themselves rather than the sheep. The image of leader as shepherd was also used at Qumran, where the overseer "shall have pity on them like a father on his sons, and will heal all the [afflicted among them] like a shepherd his flock."[287] The threefold repetition of the question may reflect the custom in the ancient Near East of stating a matter three times in the presence of witnesses to convey the importance of the obligation.

Stretch out your hands (21:18). In the process of crucifixion the condemned would have their arms stretched out when they were tied to the horizontal crossbeam. The word "stretch out" was used by ancient writers with reference to crucifixion: "stretched yourself out like men who have been crucified"; "stretched out both his arms and fastened them to a piece of wood."[288]

So this rumor spread to the brothers and sisters that this disciple would not die (21:23). This has been understood by some as having been written after John's death by some of his followers.[289] More likely, John himself is countering these rumors.[290]

This is the disciple who testifies to these things and who wrote them down. We know that his testimony is true (21:24). Here the author of the Gospel identifies himself as the "beloved disciple," who has been featured throughout the second half of the Gospel and is best understood as the apostle John. The solemn style was used by the authors of epistles in their closing comments to identify themselves (e.g., Gal. 6:11; Col. 4:18). The use of the third person serves to affirm the author's witness. For example, Thucydides, the noted Greek historian, introduced himself in the third person: "Thucydides, an Athenian, wrote the history of the war waged by the

Peloponnesians and the Athenians against one another. He began the task."[291] The use of the first-person "we" is an "associative collective," including both John the author and his readers.[292]

Not even the world itself could contain the books that would be written (21:25). This form of hyperbole was common in ancient literature. Rabbi Yohanan ben Zakkai (ca. AD 80) is cited as saying, "If all the heavens were sheets, all the trees quills and all the seas ink, they would not suffice for recording my wisdom which I acquired from my masters."[293] Similarly, Philo wrote, "Were he [God] to choose to display his own riches, even the entire earth with the sea turned into dry land would not contain them."[294] The OT book Ecclesiastes contains this thought near its conclusion: "There is no end to the making of many books" (Eccles. 12:12).[295]

Acts

Mark L. Strauss

Introduction. The Gospel of Luke and the book of Acts are two volumes of a single work ("Luke-Acts"), which together show how Jesus the Messiah accomplished God's promised salvation and then how the church, filled and empowered by the Holy Spirit, took that message of salvation to the ends of the earth.

Luke was a physician and missionary associate of the apostle Paul (Col. 4:14; Philem. 1:23–24; 2 Tim. 4:11). Luke likely was a gentile (Col. 4:10–14), which helps to explain his intense interest in how the message of salvation crossed the boundaries from Jews to gentiles and from Jerusalem to the ends of the earth (Acts 1:8). At various points in Paul's missionary journeys the narrative uses the first-person plural ("we"), showing that Luke was traveling with Paul at those times (Acts 16:10–17; 20:5–21; 21:1–18; 27:1–28:16).

Both Luke and Acts are addressed to Theophilus, who probably was the wealthy patron who sponsored the writing of the Gospel and Acts (Luke 1:1–4; Acts 1:1). Though the two books are dedicated to Theophilus, they are clearly directed to a larger audience, including both Jews and gentiles. Luke writes to provide Theophilus and his readers with confirmation and assurance of the truth of the gospel message and the veracity of the gospel messengers.

The date for Acts is uncertain. Some scholars date the book in the early 60s, since it ends with Paul still in prison after two years, around AD 60–62 (28:30–31). Others, however, date the book in the 70s or 80s, since Luke

The Mediterranean World

probably used Mark as one of his sources and Mark likely was written in the late 60s, shortly before the destruction of Jerusalem in 70.

Luke's overall purpose in Luke-Acts is to confirm for Theophilus and others that God's plan of salvation—promised in the Hebrew Scriptures—has come to fulfillment through the life, death, resurrection, and ascension of Jesus the Messiah and continues to advance through the proclamation of the good news to all people everywhere. More specifically, the book of Acts narrates how the followers of Jesus, filled, empowered, and directed by the Holy Spirit, take the message of salvation across geographical and ethnic bounders—from Jerusalem to Rome and from Jews to gentiles (1:8). This unstoppable advance of the gospel confirms that this is the work of God, and that Jesus's followers—made up of Jews and gentiles—are the people of God in the new age of salvation.

Jesus's Postresurrection Ministry and Ascension (1:1–11)

I wrote the first narrative (1:1). The "first narrative" is the Gospel of Luke. A scroll or codex could only be so long, and ancient authors often divided their works into two or more volumes. The Jewish historian Josephus similarly describes the second volume of his two-volume work defending Judaism against Apion, a pagan opponent: "In the former book, most honored Epaphroditus, I have demonstrated our antiquity."[1]

Theophilus (1:1). On Theophilus, see the introduction in the commentary on Luke; see comments on Luke 1:3.

The apostles he had chosen (1:2). "Apostle" (*apostolos*) means a "messenger" or someone sent with the commission (see comments on Mark 3:14; Luke 6:13–16). For the call and commissioning of the Twelve, see Luke 5:1–11; 6:12–16; 9:1–6. The apostles were chosen by Jesus to reproduce and expand his work. In Acts they will continue his work in the power of the Holy Spirit after his ascension to heaven.

Saint Peter's Church in Antioch of Syria.

The kingdom of God (1:3). The "kingdom of God" was the central theme of Jesus's preaching (Matt. 3:2; Mark 1:15; Luke 4:43; John 3:3). In its broadest sense, the kingdom means God reigns supreme over the universe (see comments on Mark 1:15). He always has and he always will: "The Lord will reign forever and ever" (Exod. 15:18). Yet since the disobedience of Adam and Eve, God's creation has been in a fallen and rebellious state. Jesus's announcement of the kingdom means that God is reclaiming his authority over creation and providing the means for a restored relationship with his people. His teaching here "about the kingdom of God" likely was explaining to his disciples the significance of his death and how his resurrection inaugurated the end-time resurrection of the dead (see Dan. 12:1–3) and launched the period of God's final salvation.

John baptized with water (1:5). John was the forerunner who prepared the way for the Messiah (Luke 1:76; 3:4–6; cf. Isa. 40:3–5). His baptism with water has parallels in Jewish ritual washings as well as Jewish proselyte (new convert) baptism, which symbolized repentance and cleansing from sin. Jesus here teaches that John's baptism was merely preparatory for the true forgiveness and empowerment that would come through the work of the Messiah and his baptism with the Holy Spirit.

Baptized with the Holy Spirit (1:5). The OT predicted God's end-time pouring out of Spirit on the people of God to fill, guide, and empower them (Isa. 32:15; Ezek. 36:26–27; Joel 2:28–29). Jesus predicts that this event is about to take place (cf. Luke 24:49).

Are you restoring the kingdom to Israel at this time? (1:6). The disciples are still expecting the kingdom to be established physically on earth through the destruction of Roman authority and the restoration of the Davidic kingdom (see 2 Sam. 7:12–16; Ps. 89:3–4, 19–37; Isa. 9:6–7; 11:1–5; Jer. 23:5–6; 33:15–16; Ezek. 37:24–25; Luke 1:32–33, 69). This hope for a warrior-king from the line of David was the most common messianic expectation of Jesus's day (see the article "Messianic Expectations in Jesus's Day").[2]

The end of the earth (1:8). In the narrative of Acts the "end of the earth" may represent Rome, since the book will end when Paul reaches Rome. More significantly, however, Isaiah predicted that God's salvation through the servant Messiah would be a light of revelation for the gentiles, reaching "to the ends of the earth" (Isa. 49:6). The whole book of Acts is about the unstoppable progress of the gospel from Jerusalem to the ends of the earth.

He was taken up (1:9). The ascension of Christ is described at both the end of Luke's Gospel (Luke 24:50–52) and the beginning of Acts. Judaism knew of various ascensions of great figures of the faith, including Enoch, Moses, Isaiah, and Elijah.[3] While these all indicated God's approval of his servants, Jesus's ascension is of much greater significance. It represents the vindication of Jesus as the Messiah, his victory over sin and death, his exaltation-enthronement as Lord and Messiah, and the pouring out of the Spirit to inaugurate the end times.

A cloud took him out of their sight (1:9). Clouds can represent the presence of God in Scripture (Exod. 40:34; Luke 9:34–36) and here signify that Jesus is returning to his Father's presence. There are also echoes here of "the son of man" of Dan. 7:13–14, who comes "with the clouds of heaven" before the Ancient of Days (God the Father) to receive all glory, dominion, and an eternal kingdom.

Two men in white clothes (1:10). Angels often are described as wearing white or linen garments, representing their purity and heavenly origin (Dan. 10:5; 12:6; 2 Macc. 11:8; *Testament of Levi* 8.2; Mark 16:5; John 20:12; Rev. 4:4; 15:6).

Judas's Replacement (1:12–26)

The Mount of Olives (1:12). It is appropriate that Jesus's ascension takes place from the Mount of Olives, since this hill east of Jerusalem has eschatological significance in the OT and Judaism. The prophet Zechariah predicts that when the Lord comes to deliver Israel and establish his kingdom, his feet will touch down on the Mount of Olives, splitting it in two: "the Lord will become King over the whole earth" (Zech. 14:3–9). Jesus also gives his famous eschatological discourse from the Mount of Olives (Matt. 24:3; Mark 13:3).

A Sabbath day's journey (1:12). This was the maximum distance Jews could walk on the Sabbath without violating the command against work (Exod. 20:10–11). The distance was based on tradition and generally considered to be about two thousand cubits (about six-tenths of a mile).[4]

The women (1:14). This probably refers to the women who supported Jesus's ministry (see Luke 8:2–3), though possibly also to the wives of the apostles (1 Cor. 9:5).

His brothers (1:14). Jesus had four brothers—James, Joseph, Jude, and Simon—and at least two sisters (Mark 6:3; see the article "The Family of Jesus"). All were presumably younger siblings (though one tradition identifies them as children of Joseph by a previous marriage). According to John's Gospel, Jesus's brothers did not believe in him during his ministry (John 7:5; cf. Mark 3:21). After his resurrection, however, they believed and became active in the early Christian movement. Paul mentions Jesus's resurrection appearance to James (1 Cor. 15:7), and James is identified by both Paul and Luke as a key leader in the Jerusalem church (Acts 15:13; 21:18; Gal. 1:19; 2:9, 12). Both James and his brother Jude wrote letters included in the NT.

He fell headfirst (1:18). Matthew reports that Judas "hanged himself" (Matt. 27:5). The two accounts may be harmonized if "hanged" meant that he was impaled on a stake or the rope or branch on which he hung himself broke and his body fell.

***Hakeldama* (that is, Field of Blood)** (1:19). *Hakeldama* means "field of blood" in Aramaic. The field may have been so named because it was purchased with "blood money" or because of Judas's gruesome death there.

Let his dwelling become desolate (1:20). This is a quotation from Ps. 69:25, which speaks of judgment against the enemies of God. Here it is applied typologically to Judas, whose death is the epitome of God's judgment. The desolation of his "dwelling" could refer to his own empty house or to his lack of heirs.

They cast lots (1:26). Casting of lots (something like throwing dice) was sometimes used in the OT for determining God's will (1 Chron. 26:13–16; Prov. 16:33; Neh. 11:1; cf. Jon. 1:7). This method is used only here in the NT. From the day of Pentecost onward the disciples will have the presence of the Holy Spirit to guide them.

Matthias . . . was added to the eleven apostles (1:26). Judas's replacement was essential to return the number of apostles to twelve, representing the restoration of the twelve tribes of Israel.

The Spirit Comes at Pentecost (2:1–13)

The day of Pentecost (2:1). Pentecost was a harvest festival, the second of three pilgrimage festivals that Jewish males were expected to attend in Jerusalem (Deut. 16:16; the other two were Passover and Shelters). It occurred seven weeks (Pentecost means "fifty days") after Passover and was also called the Festival of Weeks (Deut. 16:9–12), the Festival of Harvest (Exod. 23:16), and Firstfruits (Num. 28:26). In later Judaism Pentecost came to celebrate the giving of the law at Mount Sinai. This could be significant here, since the pouring out of the Spirit represents the inauguration of the new covenant.

Christians visit the upper-floor room of the Jerusalem Crusader Church of Saint Mary to remember the location and events of Pentecost (Acts 2:1–2).

A violent rushing wind (2:2). Wind can be a symbol for the Holy Spirit, and both the Hebrew (*ruah*) and Greek (*pneuma*) words for "spirit" can also mean "breath" or "wind" (Gen. 1:2; 2:7; John 3:8). In Ezek. 37:9 God's Spirit is portrayed as wind that breathes life into dry bones, creating the restored people of God.

Tongues like flames of fire (2:3). Fire often represents the presence of God (Exod. 3:2; 13:21; 24:17; Deut. 4:24; Heb. 12:29) and is also a symbol of judgment (Luke 3:9, 16–17; 9:54;

12:49; 16:24–25; 17:29; Acts 2:19). Both are appropriate here (2:19–21, 40).

Began to speak in different tongues (2:4). The word "tongues" (*glōssai*) can mean "languages," and it is clear human languages are intended here (2:8). For the apostle Paul's discussion of tongues as a gift of the Spirit, see comments on 1 Cor. 12:10; 13:1; 13:8b–13; 14:4; 14:10.

Aren't all these who are speaking Galileans? (2:7). Galileans would be recognized by their accents (see Matt. 26:73).

Parthians . . . Arabs (2:9–11). The people groups and geographical regions in these verses represent the primary places to which Jews had emigrated, both in the Roman Empire and beyond. The Parthian Empire extended east of Israel from the Tigris River to India. Media, Elam, and Mesopotamia were regions within the Parthian Empire (parts of modern Iran and Iraq). Cappadocia, Pontus, Asia, Phrygia, and Pamphylia were provinces within Asia Minor (modern Turkey). Libya was in North Africa, west of Egypt (modern Libya). Cretans were from Crete, the island nation south of Greece and Turkey, and Arabs were from Nabatea, to the south and east of Israel (modern Jordan and Saudi Arabia).

Converts (2:10). For a gentile to convert to Judaism (become a "proselyte") required circumcision (for males), ritual washings, and a sacrifice at the Jewish temple. They would then be required to keep the Jewish laws, including strict dietary observances.

The southern steps of the Temple Mount, a possible location of Peter's sermon (Acts 2:14–41).

Peter Addresses the Crowd (2:14–41)

The prophet Joel: . . . in the last days, says God (2:16–21). Peter quotes Joel 2:28–32 to show that the events of Pentecost represent the fulfillment of prophecy. He changes Joel's "after this" (Joel 2:28) to "in the last days" to show the end-times significance of these events. In Judaism the pouring out of the Spirit marked the dawn of the new age of salvation (Isa. 32:15; Ezek. 36:26–27; Joel 2:28–29; cf. Jer. 31:33–34).

Wonders in the heaven (2:19). Cosmic signs in the heavens and the shaking of the earth are common in the apocalyptic literature of the OT (Isa. 2:19; 13:9–13; 24:18; 29:5–6; 34:4; Ezek. 32:7–8; 38:19; Joel 2:10, 30–31),

Second Temple Judaism (2 Esd. 5:4–5; 7:39; 9:1–5; 13:31; *Testament of Moses* 10.5; *2 Baruch* 27.1–15; 70.2–8), and early Christianity (Matt. 24:29–30; Luke 21:11; Rev. 6:12; 8:12; 11:13, 19; 16:18). These images signify the upheaval and transformation of creation that come with the dawn of the new age.

Attested to you by God with miracles, wonders, and signs (2:22). Throughout the Gospel tradition Jesus's miracles confirm the validity of this message (Mark 1:27; Matt. 11:2–6; Luke 24:19; John 7:31; 9:16; 20:30–31).

His tomb is with us to this day (2:29). David's burial in the city of David on the south side of Jerusalem is described in 1 Kings 2:10, and his tomb is mentioned in Neh. 3:16. The first-century Jewish historian Josephus also repeatedly mentions David's tomb and describes attempts by the high priest John Hyrcanus (reigned 134–104 BC) and later by Herod the Great to raid the tomb for money.[5]

He was a prophet (2:30). Since David wrote psalms that are part of inspired Scripture, he can rightly be called a prophet.

God had sworn an oath . . . to seat one of his descendants on his throne (2:30). The passage echoes Ps. 132:11, which refers back to the promise that God made to David in 2 Sam. 7:12–16. This promise became the foundation for expectations related to the Davidic Messiah.

He has poured out what you both see and hear (2:33). Notice in verse 17 (= Joel 2:28) that it is God who will pour out his Spirit. Here it is Jesus who pours out the Spirit, confirming that he has the authority of God. Only God directs the Spirit of God (Isa. 40:13).

The Lord declared to my Lord, "Sit at my right hand" (2:34–35). This quotation is from Ps. 110:1, one of the OT passages most often quoted and alluded to in the NT, since it predicts the vindication and enthronement of the Messiah (see Mark 12:36; 14:62; Acts 7:56; Rom 8:34; 1 Cor. 15:25; Eph. 1:20; Col. 3:1; Heb. 1:3, 13; 8:1; 10:12–13; 1 Pet. 3:22; Rev. 3:21).

God has made this Jesus . . . both Lord and Messiah (2:36). Jesus was the Messiah-designate at his birth (Luke 1:32–33) and anointed and empowered as the Messiah at his baptism (Luke 3:21–22; 4:18; Acts 4:27; 10:38). But he became the reigning Messiah ("Lord and Messiah") at his exaltation and enthronement at God's right hand. This is similar to King David, who was anointed by Samuel as king of Israel (1 Sam. 16) long before he actually assumed the throne. There is a striking parallel between Jesus and David in that after David's anointing "the Spirit of the Lord came powerfully on David from that day forward" (1 Sam. 16:12–13).

The promise is for you and for your children, and for all who are far off (2:39). God's salvation came first to the Jews (John 4:22; Rom. 1:16), since they were to be a light to the nations (Isa. 2:3; 42:6; 49:6). But the promise was always intended also to go to the gentiles, "who are far off." This is the main theme of Acts.

The Fellowship of the Church (2:42–47)

The apostles' teaching (2:42). The content of this teaching was Jesus's words and deeds. The apostles were the official guardians of this message. This is why the replacement for Judas had to be someone who was present from the beginning of Jesus's ministry (1:21–22). It is also why the apostles could not give up "the ministry of the word of God" in order to provide service for the poor (6:2, 4).

The breaking of bread (2:42). This probably refers to participating in a common meal during which the Lord's Supper was celebrated (cf. 2:46). Meals in the ancient Near East were rituals of social status, where one would eat only with those of similar social and economic status. For church members from a wide variety of positions, eating together was a strong and countercultural sign of the unity in the church (see Gal. 3:28). In 1 Cor. 11:17–34 Paul condemns those in the Corinthian church who were breaking this unity by excluding the poor.

Held all things in common (2:44). See comments on Acts 4:32.

Meeting together in the temple . . . house to house (2:46–47). The temple was the center of Jewish community and religious life in Jerusalem, so it is not surprising that the followers of Jesus met there (see Luke 24:53; see the article "The Jerusalem Temple"). Here they could worship, teach, and share the message of Jesus with others. Their other main venue for fellowship, worship, and prayer was private homes—the beginning of the "house church."

Healing a Lame Man and Preaching the Good News (3:1–26)

The time of prayer at three in the afternoon (3:1). The Greek text reads, "the ninth (hour)" (counted from sunrise). This was one of two main times of prayer, which coincided with the morning (9:00 a.m.) and evening (3:00 p.m.) offerings.[6] Some sources mention sunset as a third prayer time.

The temple gate called Beautiful (3:2). The location of this gate is uncertain, but probably the reference is to the Nicanor Gate on the east side of the temple courts (see the article "The Jerusalem Temple"). It was one of nine gates leading from the Court of Gentiles into the temple proper. It was also called the Corinthian Gate because it was made of magnificent Corinthian bronze.[7] The lame man here is well positioned because a temple gate was a prime place to beg.

A model of the Jerusalem temple at the Israel Museum. In this view, looking toward the east, the columned porch on the far (east) side is Solomon's Colonnade. This area was a meeting place not only for Jesus but also later for his followers (Acts 3:11; 5:12).

He asked for money (3:3). Almsgiving was an important sign of piety in Judaism and was even said to atone for sins (Tob. 4:10; 12:8; Sir. 3:30; 17:22; 29:12; 40:24).

In the name of Jesus Christ of Nazareth (3:6). A name indicates authority (cf. 2:38), so to heal "in the name of Jesus" means to do so with the authority that Jesus had given to his apostles.

Solomon's Colonnade (3:11). While the entire outer court of the temple (the Court of Gentiles) was lined with porches and massive pillars, Solomon's Colonnade comprised the eastern portico, overlooking the Kidron Valley.[8]

His servant Jesus . . . Righteous One (3:13–14). Both titles have their background in the portrait of the "suffering servant" of Isa. 52:13–53:12, who will die as an atoning sacrifice for sins. Isaiah predicts that "by his knowledge my righteous servant will justify many, and he will carry their iniquities" (Isa. 53:11).

A murderer (3:14). This is a reference to Barabbas, who had been imprisoned for insurrection and murder (Luke 23:18–19, 25).

The source of life (3:15). The Greek term for "source" (*archēgos*) could be used of the founder of a city, an instigator of a movement, or one who otherwise leads the way. Elsewhere in the NT it is translated as "prince" (Acts 5:31 NIV) and "pioneer" (Heb. 2:10; 12:2 NIV). Here it likely means that Jesus is the pioneer who leads the way to resurrection life. Paul calls Jesus the "firstfruits" of the resurrection because he was the first to rise from the dead in a glorified body and because his resurrection guarantees that we too will rise (1 Cor. 15:20, 23).

You acted in ignorance (3:17). In the OT sins committed in ignorance had less severe penalties than those that were intentional (Num. 15:22–31; cf. Lev. 4:1, 13–21; 5:14–16). The same principle is found in the NT (Acts 17:30; 1 Cor. 2:8; 1 Tim. 1:13).

Predicted through all the prophets—that his Messiah would suffer (3:18). Peter doesn't specify here which prophets or OT passages predicted the suffering of the Messiah, but elsewhere in Acts there are quotations or allusions to Ps. 2:1–2 (Acts 4:25–26); Ps. 16:8–11 (Acts 2:25–28; 13:35); Ps. 118:22 (Acts 4:11); and Isa. 53:7–8 (Acts 8:32–33).

The main temple structure is to the left. In the lower right is the Court of Women. At the top is the northern Court of Gentiles, the northern portico/colonnade, and the Antonia Fortress (from the model of Jerusalem at the Israel Museum, Jerusalem).

Seasons of refreshing . . . the time of the restoration of all things (3:20–21). Israel's restoration as predicted by the prophets was closely linked to the renewal of all creation (Isa. 11:1–9; 35:1–2; 40:1–5; Hab. 2:14).

A prophet like me from among your brothers and sisters (3:22). This is a quotation from Deut. 18:15 (cf. Acts 7:37). Moses likely was predicting a line of prophets (starting with Joshua) who, like Moses, would speak God's words to the people and call them to covenant faithfulness. Jesus, however, is the ultimate fulfillment of the prophecy, since he is God's greatest and final word (Heb. 1:1–2). Expectations for a Moses-like prophet or messiah appear in various strands of Judaism, including the Dead Sea Scrolls (*1QRule of the Community* 9.9–11) and other traditions (1 Macc. 14:41; John 1:25; 6:14; 7:40). The Samaritans were expecting a Moses-like figure known as the *Taheb*, or "Restorer."[9] Josephus speaks of a certain revolutionary named Theudas, who claimed that he would part the Jordan River as Moses parted the Red Sea. Theudas was seized by the Romans and beheaded; his followers were killed, captured, or scattered.[10]

All the prophets who have spoken, from Samuel and those after him (3:24). Samuel was a transitional figure from the period of judges to the period of the monarchy and the prophets.

All the families of the earth will be blessed (3:25). This is a quotation from the Abrahamic covenant of Gen. 12:3. The universal application of the promise makes it appropriate for the book of Acts, which describes the advance of the good news from its Jewish roots to "the ends of the earth" (Isa. 49:6; Acts 1:8).

Peter and John before the Sanhedrin (4:1–36)

The priests, the captain of the temple police, and the Sadducees (4:1). The high priest and most of the influential priests were Sadducees, a political-religious party that stood in opposition to the Pharisees (see the article "Pharisees and Sadducees"). The temple was such a massive and complex institution that it had its own police force (Luke 22:4, 52; Acts 5:24, 26). Its captain was second in authority only to the high priest.

Proclaiming in Jesus the resurrection of the dead (4:2). The Sadducees did not believe in the resurrection of the dead, so the apostles' preaching about Jesus's resurrection was particularly disturbing to them.[11]

Their rulers, elders, and scribes (4:5). These three groups comprised the Sanhedrin, the Jewish high council and highest Jewish judicial and legislative body in the country (see the article "The Sanhedrin"). It was made up of seventy members plus the high priest (cf. Num. 11:16).

Annas the high priest, Caiaphas, John, Alexander, and all the members of the high-priestly family (4:6). Annas had served as high priest from AD 6 to 15, when he was deposed by the Romans. Yet he and his family continued to wield great power (Luke 3:2; John 18:13, 24), and five of his sons served as high priest after him. Caiaphas, his son-in-law, was the current high priest.

The stone rejected by you builders (4:11). This quotation from Ps. 118:22 speaks metaphorically of a stone tossed aside by masons that then becomes the most important stone of a new building. Though rejected by Israel's leaders, Jesus became the foundation of a new temple of God. Jesus quoted this same psalm at the end of the parable of the tenant farmers, which similarly allegorizes Jesus's rejection by Israel's religious leaders (Luke 20:17; cf. 1 Pet. 2:7; see also Isa. 28:16).

Uneducated and untrained men (4:13). To become a teacher of the law, one needed to be trained by a rabbi or in a rabbinic school (cf. Acts 22:3). The apostles were ordinary fishermen and other commoners, without such training (cf. John 7:15).

You said through the Holy Spirit, by the mouth of our father David your servant (4:25). Peter's introduction of the quotation of Ps. 2:1–2 reveals Jewish understanding of the nature of Scripture. It is both human ("by the mouth of our father David") and divine ("You spoke by the Holy Spirit").

Why do the Gentiles rage? (4:25–26). This quotation from Ps. 2:1–2 describes the rebellion of subject nations at the coronation of a new king of Israel. Peter appropriately applies it to the rejection of the true king of Israel, Jesus the Messiah, by both the Jewish leaders and the Roman authorities (4:27–28).

The place where they were assembled was shaken (4:31). In Scripture earthquakes are evidence of God's presence and power (Exod. 19:18; Isa. 2:19–21; 6:4–5).

They held everything in common (4:32). See also 2:44–45. The Qumran community that produced the Dead Sea Scrolls practiced a communal lifestyle, placing their resources in a common pool.[12] For the early church, such sharing was voluntary and practiced out of love for one another.

Joseph, a Levite (4:36). Levites were descendants of Levi, one of Jacob's twelve sons. The Levites did not receive an inheritance in the promised land, but were given individual towns to live in and were dedicated to God in place of Israel's firstborn children (Num. 3:41; 35:2–3; Deut. 18:1). They were a clergy class, serving as assistants to the priests in the temple.

From Cyprus (4:36). Cyprus was an island nation about seventy miles off the coast of Phoenicia. Paul, Barnabas, and John Mark go there on Paul's first missionary journey (13:4–6). It was Barnabas's home turf.

Barnabas (which is translated Son of Encouragement) (4:36). "Barnabas" is Aramaic, meaning "son of encouragement," though the exact etymology is debated.

Ananias and Sapphira, and Further Persecution (5:1–42)

Ananias, with his wife Sapphira, . . . kept back part of the proceeds (5:1–2). This is a situation similar to that of Achan (Josh. 7), who also "kept back" (*nosphizō*, the same Greek word in LXX Josh. 7:1 and Acts 5:2) and suffered divine judgment together with his family.

Why has Satan filled your heart? (5:3). Satan's mission is to attempt to defeat the work of God (Mark 1:13; 8:33; Luke 4:1–11; 22:31–32). In Luke 22:3 he similarly "entered Judas," provoking him to betray Jesus.

Ananias dropped dead (5:5). Judgment miracles appear also in the OT (Num. 16:28–35; 2 Kings 2:24; 2 Chron. 26:16–21). Elsewhere in Acts, Herod Agrippa I will be similarly judged for his arrogance before God (12:23).

Great fear came on the whole church (5:11). This is awe at God's purity, holiness, and power, similar to Isaiah's terror in the presence of God (Isa. 6:5).

Solomon's Colonnade (5:12). See comments on Acts 3:11.

At least his shadow might fall on some of them (5:15). Ancient people often considered a person's shadow to be an extension of that individual and to convey their power, whether for good or for evil.[13] Note similar beliefs regarding cloths that had touched Paul's skin (19:12).

An angel of the Lord opened the doors of the jail (5:19). An (or "the") angel of the Lord appears often in the OT to do God's bidding (e.g., Gen. 16:7; 22:11; Exod. 3:2; Num. 22:22; Judg. 2:4; 6:21; 1 Kings 19:7; 2 Kings 19:35). Sometimes this is an angelic messenger from God, while other times it appears to signify the presence of God himself.

The Sanhedrin—the full council of the Israelites (5:21). See comments on Acts 4:5; see the article "The Sanhedrin."

The God of our ancestors (5:30). "Ancestors" here refers to Abraham, Isaac, Jacob (cf. 3:13, 25), and all the faithful men and women of God from the past. The apostles do not regard themselves as founding a new religion. They are part of the fulfillment of Judaism and the establishment of God's kingdom through Jesus the Messiah.

God exalted this man to his right hand as ruler and Savior (5:31). God's "right hand" is an allusion to Ps. 110:1 and to Jesus's vindication (see comments on Acts 2:34–35); on "ruler" (*archēgos*), see comments on Acts 3:15. God often is called "Savior" in the OT (e.g., Ps. 18:46; 24:5; Isa. 17:10). Physical salvation usually is in view, but always with spiritual implications. Zechariah, the father of John the Baptist, calls Jesus "a horn of salvation . . . in the house of his servant David" (Luke 1:69), and at Jesus's birth the angel announces that Jesus is "a Savior" who is "the Messiah, the Lord" (Luke 2:11). Jesus is Savior because through him God will redeem his people (Luke 1:47, 68–69, 71; Acts 13:23). The title has political as well as religious implications. The famous Priene Calendar Inscription, celebrating the birth of Caesar Augustus, calls him a "savior" and refers to his birth as "the beginning of good news for the world."[14]

A Pharisee named Gamaliel (5:34). Gamaliel was the grandson of the famous rabbi Hillel and was one of the leading rabbis of his day. Saul of Tarsus (the apostle Paul) was one of his students (22:3). In a passage extolling the greatest of the rabbis the Jewish Mishnah says, "When Rabban Gamaliel the Elder died, the glory of the Law ceased and purity and abstinence died."[15]

Theudas rose up, claiming to be somebody (5:36). Josephus mentions a rebel named Theudas, but his revolt occurred during the governorship of Crispus Fadus (AD 44–46), which was after this time.[16] It is possible that Josephus has his dates wrong, or here Gamaliel may be referring to a different Theudas.

Judas the Galilean rose up (5:37). Josephus also refers to this man, who provoked a revolt against the Romans over taxation around AD 6. He chided his compatriots as cowards for submitting to the Romans as lords.[17] Judas became a model and inspiration for the later Zealot movement.

The Priene Calendar Inscription speaks of the birthday of Caesar Augustus as the beginning of the "gospel," or good news, announcing his kingdom.

Called in the apostles and had them flogged (5:40). Detailed guidelines related to flogging are provided in the tractate *Makkot* (meaning "stripes") of the Mishnah, the code of Jewish law.

In the temple and in various homes (5:42). See comments on Acts 2:46–47.

Choosing the Seven, and Stephen's Arrest (6:1–15)

Hellenistic Jews . . . Hebraic Jews (6:1). The former refers to Greek-speaking Jews who had returned to Israel from the diaspora, the dispersion of Jews throughout the world. The latter refers to Aramaic- or Hebrew-speaking Jews who had been born and raised in Palestine. It is not surprising that an immigrant community that had fewer ties and connections to the home culture would be inadvertently neglected.

Widows were being overlooked (6:1). There were few social welfare systems in the ancient world, so widows who had no support from family were among the most vulnerable members of society. In the OT God commands protection of widows and the fatherless and executes justice for them (Exod. 22:22; Deut. 10:17–18; 27:19).

To wait on tables (6:2). The verb used here (*diakoneō*) can mean "to serve" in a general sense. Although the Greek word for "deacon" (*diakonos*) is related to this verb, the present passage does not describe the establishment of the office of deacon. The committee here served a very specific ad hoc function in the Jerusalem church. For the office of deacon, see Rom. 16:1; Phil. 1:1; 1 Tim. 3:8.

Stephen . . . Philip, Prochorus, Nicanor, Timon, Parmenas, and Nicolaus, a convert from Antioch (6:5). All of these are Greek names, showing that the church chose leaders from within the community of need—a good precedent to set. On Nicolaus's status as a convert to Judaism, see comments on Acts 2:10.

Laid their hands on them (6:6). This action is a means of formally recognizing and affirming their call to this ministry. Later, the prophets and teachers of the church at Antioch lay hands on Barnabas and Paul in preparation for their first missionary journey (13:3).

A large group of priests became obedient to the faith (6:7). This is particularly remarkable in light of the hostility of the high priest and the leading priests of Jerusalem toward Jesus (Luke 9:22; 19:47; 20:19; 22:2; 23:10; 24:20) and more recently against the apostles themselves (Acts 4:1–3; 5:17, 33).

The Freedmen's Synagogue, composed of both Cyrenians and Alexandrians, and some from Cilicia and Asia (6:9). This synagogue evidently was made up of former slaves who had gained their freedom. Cyrene was in North Africa (2:10). Alexandria, in Egypt, had a large and thriving Jewish population and was the birthplace of Apollos (18:24). Cilicia was in the southeast coastal area of Asia Minor (modern Turkey). Saul/Paul was from Tarsus, a city of Cilicia (21:39). The province of Asia was in western Asia Minor. Stephen's opponents, like Stephen himself, are Hellenistic Jews. Expatriates can be among the most loyal citizens of a nation, and these observant Jews do not like Stephen's "radical" message about Jesus, the temple, and the law.

Blasphemous words against Moses and God (6:11). Although later Judaism defined blasphemy exclusively with reference to uttering the divine Name,[18] in Jesus's day the term was applied to a variety of offenses, including idolatry, disrespect for God, or insulting God's appointed leaders.[19] The penalty for blasphemy was death.

To the Sanhedrin (6:12). See comments on Acts 4:5; see the article "The Sanhedrin."

Speaking against this holy place and the law (6:13). Stephen is accused of blasphemy against the two great institutions of Judaism: temple and Torah.

This Jesus of Nazareth will destroy this place (6:14). This is a false charge. Jesus had predicted the destruction of Jerusalem (Luke 21:6; cf. John 2:19), but he had not said that he would destroy it himself, though this charge had been leveled against him at his trial (Mark 14:57–59). Other Jewish prophets had predicted the destruction of Jerusalem and the temple. Micah (Mic. 3:12), Jeremiah (Jer. 7:12–15; 12:7; 22:5; 26:6) and Uriah (Jer. 26:20–23) all predicted the destruction of the first temple, built by Solomon. Josephus describes predictions of the destruction of the Second Temple, including those of Joshua ben Ananus, a common herdsman, who for four years before the Jewish revolt predicted the temple's destruction.[20] Josephus himself considered the temple's destruction to be the fulfillment of prophecy.[21]

Like the face of an angel (6:15). This description recalls the glowing face of Moses when he came down from Mount Sinai (Exod. 34:29–35; cf. 2 Cor. 3:7–18) and Jesus's face at the transfiguration (Matt. 17:2; Luke 9:29).

Stephen's Speech and Martyrdom (7:1–60)

Brothers and fathers, . . . listen (7:2). In his lengthy speech, instead of directly answering the charges against him, Stephen summarizes the history of Israel from Abraham to Solomon, pointing out how God's people have consistently been stubborn, rebellious, and disobedient. The greatest focus is on Moses and the wilderness generation, since this generation epitomizes Israel's stubborn resistance against God (7:17–44).

Appeared to our father Abraham when he was still in Mesopotamia, before he settled in Haran (7:2). Although the Genesis account seems to suggest that Abraham first received his call in Haran (Gen. 11:31–12:3), there are indications here and elsewhere that God had already called Abraham while he was in Ur in Mesopotamia (Gen. 15:7; Neh. 9:7).

Left the land of the Chaldeans and settled in Haran (7:4). "The land of the Chaldeans" refers to southern Babylon. Abraham was born in Ur, a major city-state in southern Mesopotamia. Haran was about six hundred miles north of Ur.

His *descendants* would *be strangers in a foreign country, and they* would *enslave and oppress them for four hundred years* (7:6–7). This quotation from Gen. 15:13 refers to Israel's four hundred years of slavery in Egypt (Exod. 1:8–14).

The covenant of circumcision (7:8). God commanded Abraham to circumcise every male in his household as a confirmation of the covenant and a sign of Abraham's faithfulness to God (Gen. 17:10–11). Ever since, circumcision has been a key defining mark of what it means to be a Jewish male (see the article "The Jewish Rite of Circumcision").

Jacob became the father of the twelve patriarchs (7:8). Though mentioned only briefly in Stephen's speech, Jacob played a pivotal role in Israel's history (Gen. 25:19–49:33). Renamed by God "Israel" (Gen. 32:28)—meaning "he struggles with God"—his twelve sons became the twelve tribes of Israel (Gen. 29:31–30:22; 35:16–18).

Joseph (7:9–16). The story of Joseph is told in Gen. 37–50. The main theme of the Genesis account is that God took the evil plans of Joseph's brothers and turned them into good (Gen. 45:5–7; 50:20). In line with the central message of his speech, Stephen emphasizes that although Joseph was rejected by his brothers, God was with him and gave him success (Acts 7:9–10).

A different king who did not know Joseph ruled over Egypt (7:18). This likely was Ahmose I, the pharaoh who founded Egypt's Eighteenth Dynasty (reigned ca. 1539–1514 BC). Ahmose expelled the Semitic Hyksos rulers and would have been less sympathetic to the Hebrews.

Moses was educated in all the wisdom of the Egyptians (7:22). Moses's education is not mentioned in the OT, but appears in the writings of Josephus and of the Jewish philosopher Philo, who gives a detailed description of Moses's royal education and training.[22]

When he was forty years old . . . after forty years had passed (7:23, 30). Like Jewish tradition before him, Stephen breaks Moses's life up into three forty-year blocks: birth and growing up in the pharaoh's household (vv. 17–22); departure from Egypt and time in Midian (vv. 23–29); Sinai epiphany, the exodus, and wilderness wanderings (vv. 30–43).

God will raise up for you a prophet like me from among your brothers and sisters (7:37). This quotation from Deut. 18:15 was already applied to Jesus by Peter in Acts 3:22.

Our ancestors were unwilling to obey him . . . they pushed him aside (7:39). Israel's rejection of Moses is a key theme of the speech, typologically pointing forward to the rejection of Jesus by Israel's leaders.

Make us gods who will go before us (7:40–43). Beginning with the incident of the golden calf (Exod. 32:1), Israel repeatedly fell into idolatry, a violation of the first commandment (Exod. 20:3–4). The Babylonian exile served as punishment for this idolatry (vv. 42–43, citing Amos 5:25–27).

Our ancestors had the tabernacle of the testimony (7:44). The detailed plans for the tabernacle—the portable temple that Israel carried with them in the desert—are set out in Exod. 25–30 (cf. Heb. 9:1–10). It is called the tabernacle of the "covenant law" or "testimony" because it contained the ark of the covenant with the two covenant tablets from Mount Sinai.

David . . . asked that he might provide a dwelling place for the God of Jacob. It was Solomon, rather, who built him a house (7:45–47). For David's desire to build a temple for God and God's command that Solomon would build it, see 2 Sam. 7; 1 Chron. 22:7–11. Stephen's speech then jumps forward to 1 Kings 5–9, the preparation and building of the first temple.

Heaven is my throne, and the earth my footstool. . . . Did not my hand make all these things? (7:49–50). This quotation is from Isa. 66:1–2. The passage in Isaiah is not an indictment of the temple per se (which God directed to be built) but rather condemns the ritualism and even idolatry that worship can become (cf. Isa. 57:3–13; 65:1–5). God is so much bigger than the boxes (or temples) that we try to put him in. Solomon made this same point during the dedication of the first temple (1 Kings 8:27).

You stiff-necked people with uncircumcised hearts and ears! (7:51). Both expressions appear in the OT with reference to Israel as a rebellious and obstinate people, especially during the wilderness generation (stiff-necked: Exod. 32:9; 33:3, 5; 34:9; Deut. 9:6, 13; uncircumcised hearts: Lev. 26:41; Deut. 10:16; Jer. 4:4; 9:26). The two images appear together in Deut. 10:16.

Which of the prophets did your ancestors not persecute? (7:52). The persecution of the prophets, especially at the hands of Israel's wicked rulers, is a common theme in the OT (1 Kings 13:4; 18:13; 19:2; 22:26–27; 2 Kings 1:9; 6:31; 2 Chron. 24:20–21). Jeremiah was the object of repeated persecution and attempts on his life (Jer. 18:18, 23; 26:11, 20–23; 36–38). The rejection of the prophets is also a common theme in Luke's Gospel (Luke 4:24; 11:47–51; 13:34).

Righteous One (7:52). This is an allusion to Isa. 53:11 and the "suffering servant." See comments on Acts 3:13–14.

The law under the direction of angels (7:53). The mediation of the law through angels is not stated in the OT, but it appears elsewhere in the NT (Gal. 3:19; Heb. 2:2) and in Jewish tradition.[23]

Jesus standing at the right hand of God (7:55). This is an allusion to Ps. 110:1 (see comments on Acts 2:34–35). Jesus may be "standing" (instead of sitting, as in Ps. 110) to welcome Stephen into his presence or perhaps as a witness to Stephen's innocence.

Son of Man (7:56). Here we see Jesus's favorite messianic self-designation (see comments on Mark 2:10). Rarely is it used by anyone other than Jesus (cf. Rev. 1:13). Its OT background is to be found especially in Dan. 7:13–14, where it indicates the Messiah's vindication by God, his ruling authority, and his dominion over all creation. Though the Sanhedrin is judging Stephen, the Son of Man will judge them.

They yelled at the top of their voices, covered their ears, and together rushed against him (7:57). Although the Romans reserved the right to capital punishment (John 18:31), the rage of the religious leaders gets the best of them, and they proceed to execute Stephen.

Began to stone him (7:58). Stoning was the standard method of capital punishment among the Jews (Lev. 24:14). Some crimes punishable by stoning included idolatry (Deut. 17:2–7; 13:6–10), blasphemy (Lev. 24:15–16), violating the Sabbath (Num. 15:32–36), practicing magic (Lev. 20:27), adultery (Deut. 22:22–24), and rebellion against parents (Deut. 21:18–21).

The witnesses laid their garments (7:58). The primary witnesses against the condemned were required to throw the first stones (cf. John 8:7). Then the rest would join in (Deut. 17:7; cf. Lev. 24:14; Deut. 13:9–10).

Lord, do not hold this sin against them! (7:59). Stephen's request recalls Jesus's prayer for those crucifying him (Luke 23:34).

Harbona was a eunuch in the service of the king, like the eunuchs shown on this relief from Khorsabad (721–705 BC).

Philip's Outreach to Samaria, and the Ethiopian Eunuch

(8:1–40)

All except the apostles were scattered (8:1). The objects of the persecution were

primarily the Hellenistic Jewish Christians because they were identified with Stephen.

Devout men buried Stephen (8:2). In the culture of honor and shame reflected in Acts, a noble burial was an important way to show honor to the deceased. By contrast, for a body to be hung on a pole or a cross to decay or be eaten as carrion was among the most shameful and degrading things imaginable.

Philip went down to a city in Samaria (8:5). Since the Jews hated the Samaritans and vice versa, this was a surprising direction (see Luke 10:33; John 4:4, 9). Some manuscripts read "*the* city of Samaria," which would be the old capital city of Samaria, which Herod the Great had rebuilt and renamed Sebaste.[24]

A man named Simon had previously practiced sorcery (8:9). Magic or sorcery was common in the ancient world and was especially identified with magical arts from Persia. Magicians used rituals, incantations, potions, and various magical objects to manipulate good and evil spirits for healing, exorcism, and putting curses on others.[25] This was not just among pagans; there was a great deal of syncretism in Jewish and Samaritan religion (cf. Elymas in 13:6–11). In later church history Simon was called Simon Magus ("the magician") and identified as the founder of a heretical gnostic sect known as the Simonians.[26]

This man is called the Great Power of God (8:10). Since the Samaritans were monotheists, this probably means that Simon is claiming to be one manifestation of God's great power. He is the channel through which God's power is revealed.

When the apostles who were at Jerusalem heard . . . they sent Peter and John to them (8:14). In light of the bad blood between Jews and Samaritans, the news of the salvation of the Samaritans would have shocked the Jewish Christians of Jerusalem. To send such eminent apostles as Peter and John shows the gravity of the situation and the need for verification.

Simon . . . offered them money . . . Peter told him, "May your silver be destroyed with you" (8:18–20). The magical arts were considered a commodity like any other, which could be bought and sold (cf. 19:19). Peter refutes the notion that God's Spirit can be manipulated for financial gain.

"The road that goes down from Jerusalem to Gaza." (This is the desert road.) (8:26). In the OT period Gaza was one of the five chief Philistine cities, the farthest south on the road to Egypt. It was about fifty miles southwest of Jerusalem.

An Ethiopian man, a eunuch (8:27). "Ethiopia" refers not to modern Ethiopia but to the Nubian Empire in what is now southern Egypt, Sudan, and northern Ethiopia. In the OT it is known as Cush (see the article "The Cushites"). A eunuch was a castrated male (cf. Matt. 19:12). Eunuchs often served in royal courts because they did not imperil the integrity of the king's harem and could be fully devoted to the crown. Because of their defect, eunuchs could not participate fully in Jewish worship (Deut. 23:1).[27] Isaiah, however, predicts that at the time of God's final salvation eunuchs will be restored to full participation in worship (Isa. 56:3–5)—a prophecy that has great significance for this man.

High official of Candace . . . who was in charge of her entire treasury (8:27). This is a very high governmental position, equivalent to a modern finance minister or secretary of the treasury. "Candace" is a dynastic title, rather than a name, referring to the queen or perhaps the queen mother of Ethiopia.[28]

He had come to worship in Jerusalem (8:27). The Ethiopian evidently was a God-fearer, a gentile worshiper of the one true God of Israel (cf. 10:2).

Reading the prophet Isaiah aloud (8:28). The man's wealth is obvious, since such a scroll would be extremely expensive, not something that common people would own. He perhaps had purchased it in Jerusalem. Ancient peoples tended to read aloud, which explains why Philip asked about the text (8:30).

He was led like a sheep to the slaughter . . . his life is taken from the earth (8:32–33). The quotation from Isa. 53:7–8 is part of the fourth Servant Song (Isa. 52:13–53:12), one of the most important passages in the OT on the suffering role of the Messiah.

Who is the prophet saying this about—himself or someone else? (8:34). This question—the identity of the servant—has been a key point of debate among Jewish scholars, both ancient and modern. The three main possibilities are the nation Israel, or Isaiah himself, or the Messiah.[29]

Philip appeared in Azotus, and he was traveling . . . until he came to Caesarea (8:40). Azotus is known as Ashdod in the OT, another of the five main Philistine cities. It was about twenty miles north of Gaza. On Caesarea, see comments on Acts 10:1.

Saul's Conversion (9:1–31)

Went to the high priest and requested letters . . . to the synagogues in Damascus (9:1–2). The high priest in Jerusalem held the highest religious office in Judaism, so his authority would carry over into the diaspora, the Jews scattered throughout the world. Damascus had a large Jewish population, with many synagogues.

The Way (9:2). This was one of the first terms that Christians used to identify themselves (19:9, 23; 24:14, 22). It was shorthand for the way of salvation that God had provided through Jesus the Messiah (cf. 18:25–26; John 14:6).

Though his eyes were open, he could see nothing (9:8). In the OT blindness sometimes is judgment from God against sin or to prevent some evil action (Gen. 19:11; Exod. 4:11; Deut. 28:28; 2 Kings 6:18; Zech. 12:4). Here it may be both judgment and a sign, as in the case of Zechariah's muteness and deafness (Luke 1:22).

The street called Straight (9:11). This probably refers to the main east-west road of the ancient city. It had major halls with colonnades and two great city gates at each end. The street is known today as Derb el-Mustaqim.[30]

A man from Tarsus named Saul (9:11). Saul/Paul was born in Tarsus, a major commercial center in the province of Cilicia (modern southeast Turkey) (21:39), but he was educated under the rabbi Gamaliel in Jerusalem (22:3).

My chosen instrument . . . how much he must suffer for my name (9:15–16). Jesus spoke of the suffering that his disciples would experience (Mark 8:34–38; 10:39; 13:9–13). Paul later recounts his many trials when he writes to the Corinthians in what could be called his "résumé" of suffering (2 Cor. 11:23–33).

Proclaiming Jesus in the synagogues (9:20). This became Paul's pattern throughout his ministry, going first to the Jews, who would understand his message of the coming Messiah, and then turning to the gentiles.

After many days (9:23). If we compare this account to Paul's own in Gal. 1:17, we see that some of these "many days" were spent in Arabia—that is, the Nabatean kingdom south of Damascus (see Acts 9:23–25). He then returned to Damascus.

The Jews conspired to kill him, . . . but his disciples . . . lowered him in a large basket through an opening in the wall (9:23–25). Paul mentions this same event in 2 Cor. 11:32–33. There, however, he says that the governor under King Aretas was trying to catch him. Aretas IV was king of Nabatea, where Paul had ministered for some time (see Acts 9:19–22). Evidently the Jews of Damascus conspired together with Aretas's governor, labeling Paul a troublemaker who needed to be stopped.

Hellenistic Jews (9:29). See comments on Acts 6:1; 6:9.

Sent him off to Tarsus (9:30). Tarsus was Paul's hometown (see comments on Acts 9:11).

Coin of Aretas IV, king of the Nabateans (ca. 9 BC–AD 40).

Aeneas and Dorcas (9:32–43)

The saints who lived in Lydda (9:32). Lydda (called Lod in the OT) was thirty miles northwest of Jerusalem and about twelve miles from the coast.

Joppa (9:36). Joppa was a major port for Judea, second in prominence only to Caesarea Maritima. It was located about thirty-five miles northwest of Jerusalem and eleven miles northwest of Lydda. Today its location lies within the modern city of Tel Aviv.

A disciple named Tabitha (which is translated Dorcas) (9:36). Both Tabitha (Aramaic) and Dorcas (Greek) mean "gazelle."

After washing her, they placed her in a room upstairs (9:37). Bodies were washed and anointed in preparation for burial. The body's repose would give friends a place to pay their respects.

Tabitha, get up (9:40). Peter's words here recall Jesus's Aramaic expression *talitha koum* ("little girl, arise") at the raising of Jairus's daughter (Mark 5:41). Luke seems to intentionally parallel the miracles of the apostles in Acts with those of Jesus in the Gospel.

The Conversion of Cornelius's Household (10:1–48)

Caesarea (10:1). The beautiful port city of Caesarea Maritima had been built on a grand scale by Herod the Great between 25 and 13 BC. It was the residence of the procurator (governor) and the Roman administrative center and military headquarters for Judea.

A centurion of what was called the Italian Regiment (10:1). Centurions were viewed as the backbone of the Roman army, commanding a "century" of about one hundred men (see the article "The Roman Military"). Six centuries made up a regiment (or "cohort") of six hundred, and ten regiments made up a legion of about six thousand. Little is known about the Italian Regiment, though one inscription identifies it as an auxiliary force of archers.[31] It is not clear whether Cornelius is with his regiment or whether he is retired in Caesarea. Luke tells of another devout centurion in his Gospel (Luke 7:1–10).

He was a devout man and feared God (10:2). "God-fearers" were gentiles who believed in the one true God of Israel but had not gone all the way to become proselytes—full converts to Judaism (cf. 8:27; 13:16, 26; 17:4, 17).

Peter's vision at Joppa led him to travel north to the Roman city of Caesarea (Acts 10:24). This remarkable port built by Herod the Great was by this time the base of Roman military presence in the province of Judea.

Full conversion would entail circumcision (for males) as well as keeping the dietary laws of the OT. God-fearers participated in synagogue worship and often became patrons and supporters for the synagogue communities. Paul found God-fearers to be among the most receptive audience for the gospel. His message of salvation by faith in Jesus the Messiah alone, apart from the works of the law, appealed to them. So also did his preaching that the Hebrew Scriptures predicted full inclusion of the gentiles into the eschatological people of God.

Three in the afternoon (10:3). The Greek text reads, "the ninth hour" (from sunrise). This was one of two Jewish times of prayer (the other was 9:00 a.m.), coinciding with the time of offerings in the Jerusalem temple (see comments on Acts 3:1). Cornelius probably was praying when he received his vision.

Memorial offering (10:4). This language echoes OT memorial offerings, meant to commemorate God's faithfulness. Just as these offerings rise to heaven and are "a pleasing aroma to the Lord" (Lev. 2:2, 9 [cf. Phil. 4:18]), so Cornelius's prayers and gifts to the poor are well pleasing to God.

Peter went up to pray on the roof (10:9). Mediterranean roofs usually were flat and were used as living spaces—for storage, work, and sleeping on warm nights. An external staircase or ladder provided access.

All the four-footed animals and reptiles of the earth, and birds of the sky (10:12). These three groups perhaps represent the division of the animal kingdom found in passages such as Gen. 1:30; 6:20 (cf. Rom 1:23). According to the OT law, many of these animals were "unclean" and so forbidden for Jews to eat (Lev. 11).

No, Lord! . . . I have never eaten anything impure and ritually unclean (10:14). Peter thinks that he is being tested. A pious Jew would never eat such unclean animals. In times of persecution pagan rulers such as Antiochus Epiphanes had tried to force Jews to deny their religion by eating unclean foods.[32]

You know it's forbidden for a Jewish man to associate with or visit a foreigner (10:28). Although entering a pagan home was not actually forbidden in the OT law, Jewish tradition viewed pagan homes as "unclean," and pious Jews would avoid entering for fear of coming into contact with unclean food or idols.[33]

Your acts of charity (10:31). Almsgiving was viewed in Judaism as a sign of piety (see comments on Acts 3:3).

God anointed Jesus of Nazareth with the Holy Spirit and with power (10:38). The word "messiah" means "anointed one." At Jesus's baptism he was anointed and empowered by the Holy Spirit to perform miracles and fulfill the mission of the Messiah (Luke 3:21–22; 4:1, 14, 18; cf. Isa. 61:1–2).

He is the one appointed by God to be the judge of the living and the dead (10:42). This is evidence of Jesus's deity, since God alone is the final judge (Gen. 18:25; Ps. 82:8; 96:13). See Dan. 7:13–14; Matt. 25:31–46; John 5:22; Acts 17:31.

The circumcised believers who had come with Peter were amazed (10:45). It was astonishing to the Jewish believers that the gentiles could receive the end-time Spirit of God without first becoming Jews by being circumcised and keeping the law.

Peter's Report to the Jerusalem Church (11:1–18)

You went to uncircumcised men and ate with them (11:3). See comments on Acts 10:28.

John baptized with water, but you will be baptized with the Holy Spirit (11:16). See comments on Acts 1:5.

God has given repentance resulting in life even to the Gentiles (11:18). The OT (especially Isaiah) predicted that God's salvation eventually would go to the gentiles (Isa. 2:3; 49:6; 55:5; 60:3–6; 66:18; Jer. 3:17; Zech. 8:22). Yet many Jews were more focused on passages predicting the gentiles' judgment and destruction (Ps. 9:19; 110:6; Isa. 13–24; 34; Zeph. 3:8; Zech. 14:2). It took Jesus's followers some time to come to grips with God's purpose to save the gentiles.

The Church in Antioch (11:19–30)

Those who had been scattered as a result of the persecution . . . as far as Phoenicia, Cyprus, and Antioch (11:19). This is a flashback to the period after the martyrdom of Stephen (8:1). Phoenicia was the coastal region northwest of Israel (modern Lebanon). Its chief cities were Tyre and Sidon. On Cyprus, see comments on Acts 4:36. Antioch in Syria was the third largest city in the Roman Empire, behind only Rome and Alexandria. It was located on the Orontes River, fifteen miles from the Mediterranean coast, and was the Roman capital of Syria.

Men from Cyprus and Cyrene, who came to Antioch and began speaking to Greeks (11:20). Cyrene was a city in North Africa (modern Libya; see Acts 2:10). These men, like Stephen and Philip, were Hellenistic Jews, who evidently understood better than others the profound implications of the arrival of God's end-time salvation through Jesus the Messiah. Temple, Torah, and the composition of the people of God were being radically transformed through the dawn of the new age and the coming of the kingdom of God.

The modern city of Antakya, Turkey, was once known as Syrian Antioch. The church in Antioch, which launched Paul into his missionary journeys, became hugely influential in the early Christian world.

They sent out Barnabas to travel as far as Antioch (11:22). Whenever Barnabas (Joseph) appears in the book of Acts, he is building bridges of understanding and bringing people together (4:36–37; 9:27; 11:22–26, 30; 13:2; 15:37). He certainly is true to his Aramaic nickname, which means "son of encouragement."

He went to Tarsus to search for Saul (11:25). Tarsus was Paul's hometown, to which he had returned after the attempts to kill him in Jerusalem (9:29–30). See comments on Acts 9:11.

The disciples were first called Christians at Antioch (11:26). The term "Christian" evidently was coined by non-Christians in Antioch in order to distinguish the followers of Jesus from other Jews (cf. 26:28; 1 Pet. 4:16). It does not mean "little Christs," as some have claimed, but rather refers to followers or supporters of Christ.

Prophets . . . Agabus (11:27–28). The gift of prophecy, which entailed discerning God's message to his people, was common in the early church (Acts 13:1; 15:32; 19:6; 21:9; 1 Cor. 12:10, 28–29; 13:2; 14:29–32; Eph. 2:20; 3:5; 4:11; 1 Thess. 5:20; 1 Tim. 1:18; 4:14). Agabus will make another significant prediction in 21:10–11.

A severe famine throughout the Roman world . . . during the reign of Claudius (11:28). There were many food shortages and local famines during the reign of the emperor Claudius (AD 41–54), much of it due to declining grain production in Egypt. Luke may be referring to a particularly severe famine in Judea that took place in AD 44–45.[34] The Jewish Christians of Jerusalem, who already were experiencing persecution, were especially hard hit.

James's Execution and Peter's Escape (12:1–24)

King Herod (12:1). The NT uses the name "Herod" for a variety of members of the Herodian dynasty. Here the king is Herod Agrippa I, son of Aristobulus IV and grandson of Herod the Great. He had influential friends in Rome, including the emperors Caligula and Claudius, and eventually he was appointed king over Judea, Samaria, Galilee, Perea, Iturea, and Trachonitus, regions almost as vast as those ruled by his famous grandfather. He was well liked by his Jewish subjects and was viewed as a defender of the Jewish faith.

Attacked some who belonged to the church . . . executed James, John's brother, with the sword (12:1–2). As a defender of Judaism, Agrippa viewed the early Christian movement as a threat—fears perhaps stoked by the Sanhedrin and the high priest. This James is the son of Zebedee and the brother of John (Mark 1:19; 3:17; 10:35; Luke 5:10; 9:54; Acts 1:13). He was one of Jesus's "inner circle" of three disciples—Peter, James, and John (Mark 5:37; 9:2; 13:3; 14:33). Death "with the sword" usually means beheading.

The Festival of Unleavened Bread (12:3). This was one of the three great pilgrim festivals that Jewish adult males were expected to attend, along with Pentecost and Shelters (Exod. 23:14–17; 34:18–23) (see the article "Jewish Festivals"). The festival began with Passover and continued for seven days, 15–21 Nisan (March-April). Its name comes from the fact that the Israelites were commanded to remove leaven from their homes in preparation for the exodus from Egypt (Exod. 12:15–20; 23:15; 34:18; Num. 28:17; Deut. 16:1–8).

Four squads of four soldiers (12:4). The four squads probably rotated, each taking a day watch and a night watch.

An angel of the Lord (12:7). See comments on Acts 5:19.

The house of Mary, the mother of John Mark (12:12). At this time the church met in private homes. Mary perhaps was a widow whose home was large enough to house a gathering of believers. Her son John Mark will accompany Paul and Barnabas on their first missionary journey (12:25; 13:5). He is identified as Barnabas's cousin in Col. 4:10.

Tell these things to James and the brothers (12:17). This James was the half-brother of Jesus. Although he and his brothers did not believe in Jesus during Jesus's ministry, they saw the resurrected Lord and became leaders in the church (see Acts 1:14). Here we see James already assuming this role (cf. Gal. 1:19; 2:9, 12). James will render the final decision at the Jerusalem Council (Acts 15:13–21) and later will seek to make peace between Paul and some of his Jewish-Christian opponents (Acts 21:18–25). See also the introduction in the commentary on James.

Interrogated the guards and ordered their execution (12:19). Soldiers who allowed prisoners to escape often received the same punishment that their captives would have received.[35]

Very angry with the people of Tyre and Sidon (12:20). Tyre and Sidon were influential coastal cities northeast of Israel in Phoenicia. They were important trading partners with Agrippa, so he is very interested in restoring this relationship.

At once an angel of the Lord struck him because he did not give the glory to God (12:23). The Jewish historian Josephus provides a similar account of Herod's death in Caesarea, also attributing it to his arrogance at accepting the crowd's acclamation that he was a god. Josephus adds the interesting detail that, during his speech, Herod looked up and saw an owl sitting on a rope above his head, and he knew it to be an ill-fated omen. Just before collapsing, he cried out, "I, who was by you called immortal, am immediately to be hurried away by death."[36]

The First Missionary Journey: From Antioch to Cyprus (13:1–12)

Prophets and teachers: Barnabas, Simeon who was called Niger, Lucius of Cyrene, Manaen, a close friend of Herod the tetrarch, and Saul (13:1). On prophets, see comments on Acts 11:27–28. On Barnabas, see comments on Acts 4:36; 11:22. "Niger" means "black," so Simeon may have been African. The phrase "a close friend of Herod" likely means he was raised in the royal court. This demonstrates the ethnic and socioeconomic diversity of the early church. Believers were from every social class.

Worshiping the Lord and fasting . . . fasted, prayed (13:2–3). Fasting (abstaining from food for a period), worship, and prayer were ways to be sensitive to God's leading. In the OT fasting is associated with times of spiritual preparation (Esther 4:16) and repentance (2 Sam. 12:23; Joel 1:14; Jon. 3:5). The OT required fasting only on the Day of Atonement (Lev. 16:29–31), but pious Jews of Jesus's day fasted twice a week (Monday and Thursday).[37] For the reason why Jesus did not fast and his prediction that his followers would fast after his departure, see Luke 5:33–35.

Laid hands on them (13:3). This indicates a formal commissioning for service (1 Tim. 5:22; 2 Tim. 1:6; Heb. 6:2). See comments on Acts 6:6.

They went down to Seleucia, and from there they sailed to Cyprus (13:4). Seleucia was the main seaport for Antioch, which lay about fifteen miles inland (see comments on Acts 11:19; see the article "Shipping Practices in the First Century"). The port was near the mouth of the Orontes

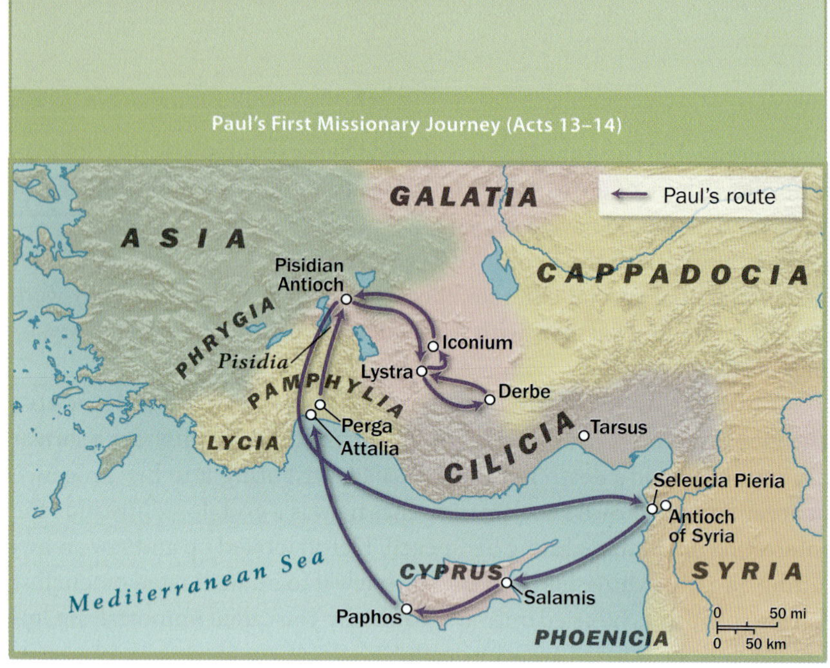

River and housed a Roman naval base. The island of Cyprus was Barnabas's homeland (4:36) and thus a good place to start.

Proclaimed the word of God in the Jewish synagogues (13:5). This would be Paul's pattern throughout his missionary journeys. In the synagogues he would find Jews, proselytes, and God-fearing gentiles. See comments on Acts 9:20; 10:2.

They also had John as their assistant (13:5). The word translated as "assistant" (*hypēretēs*) can refer to a servant, helper, aid, or official, and usually it indicates a subordinate role. John Mark likely is viewed as a missionary in training.

Salamis . . . Paphos (13:5–6). Salamis was a large port town on the eastern coast of Cyprus. Paphos was on the western coast and was the capital and Roman headquarters for the island.

A sorcerer, a Jewish false prophet named Bar-Jesus . . . Elymas the sorcerer (13:6, 8). The name "Bar-Jesus" means "son of Yeshua/Joshua." The etymology of the name Elymas is debated, and it could mean "magician," "dreamer," or "wise man." Much of Judaism was quite syncretistic (combining Jewish and pagan features) at this time, and so it is not surprising to find a Jewish sorcerer (cf. 8:9; 19:13–16).

The proconsul, Sergius Paulus (13:7). A proconsul was the governor of a Roman province, appointed for a one-year term and under the authority of the Roman senate. The proconsul had unlimited military and civil authority. Compare Gallio in 18:12.

Saul—also called Paul (13:9). As a Roman citizen, Paul would have had three Roman names: a *praenomen* (like our first name), a *nomen* (family name), and a *cognomen* (additional family name, commonly used as an ordinary personal name).[38] *Paulus* (Latin for "small" or "humble") is his *cognomen*. We do not know his *praenomen* or *nomen*. As a Jew, Paul also had a Jewish name, "Saul." Evidently Paul began using his Roman *cognomen* when he started working among the gentiles.

You son of the devil (13:10). Anyone who opposes God's work is ultimately working for Satan. In John's Gospel, Jesus refers to the religious leaders of Israel as children of "your father the devil" (John 8:44). The sectarians who produced the Dead Sea Scrolls identified themselves as the "sons of light" and their enemies as the "sons of darkness," who were working for Belial (Satan).[39]

Ministry in Antioch Pisidia (13:13–51)

Perga in Pamphylia (13:13). Pamphylia was a small Roman province in south central Asia Minor, west of Cilicia. It ran for seventy-five miles along the coast and thirty miles inland to the Taurus Mountains. Perga was its chief city.

Pisidian Antioch (13:14). Though located in Phrygia, Antioch was called *Pisidian* Antioch because it bordered on the region of Pisidia. In Paul's day the city was located in the Roman province of Galatia. The city was founded in the third century BC by the Seleucid dynasty, perhaps by Antiochus I or Antiochus II, but it gained special prominence in 31 BC when the Roman emperor Augustus annexed the central Anatolian region of Galatia and turned the city into a Roman colony.[40] Many Roman citizens, including senators, equestrians, and retired soldiers, lived there.

The reading of the Law and the Prophets (13:15). The two oldest records of synagogue services from antiquity are the one described in Luke 4:16–30 and this one (see the article "The Jewish Synagogue"). In addition to readings from the Law and the Prophets, the service likely would have consisted of prayers and a homily or sermon.

If you have any word of encouragement for the people, you can speak (13:15). Perhaps as a result of conversation prior to the service, Paul and Barnabas are recognized as qualified teachers and so are invited to give the homily. We must remember that Paul was a Pharisee (23:6) and Barnabas was a Levite (4:36).

Sergius Paulus inscription.

The God of this people Israel chose our ancestors (13:17–37). Paul begins by summarizing the history of Israel from the call of Abraham (Gen. 12) to God's choice of David to be king (1 Sam. 13; 16). He then jumps to the fulfillment of the promise that God made to David (2 Sam. 7) in the life, death, and resurrection of Jesus the Messiah.

You are my Son; today I have become your Father (13:33). This quotation from Ps. 2:7 speaks of God's vindication of his anointed king against the rebellious nations around Israel (see comments on Acts 4:25–26). Paul connects the fulfillment of the psalm to Jesus's resurrection (cf. Rom. 1:3–4; Heb. 1:5; 5:5).

I will give you the holy and sure promises of David (13:34). This quotation from Isa. 55:3 demonstrates that Jesus is the fulfillment of the promises made to David (cf. 2 Sam. 7:12–16; Ps. 89:3–4, 19–37; Isa. 9:6–7; 11:1–5; Jer. 23:5–6).

You will not let your Holy One see decay (13:35). This quotation from Ps. 16:10 shows that David himself predicted the resurrection of the Messiah (see Acts 2:25–28).

Jews and devout converts to Judaism (13:43). On proselytes, see comments on Acts 2:10.

I have made you a light for the Gentiles to bring salvation to the end of the earth (13:47). Surprisingly, Paul here applies a passage from Isaiah (Isa. 49:6) about the suffering servant to himself and his missionary companions. The point is that the missionaries represent Christ, finishing his mission by being his witnesses in bringing the light of the gospel to the gentiles (Acts 1:8).

Shook the dust off their feet (13:51). Jesus told his disciples to do this very thing if their message was rejected in a particular town (Luke 9:5; 10:11). This may recall the Jewish practice of shaking off the impurities of gentile lands when returning to the Holy Land.[41]

Ministry in Iconium, Lystra, and Derbe (14:1–28)

Iconium (14:1). Originally settled by the Phrygians, Iconium was located on several major trade routes and so was economically prosperous. The Romans made it the chief city of Lycaonia, the southern region of the Roman province of Galatia.

Entered the Jewish synagogue, as usual (14:1). See comments on Acts 9:20; 10:2; 13:5.

The Lycaonian towns of Lystra and Derbe (14:6). Lystra was about twenty-five miles southwest of Iconium. Caesar Augustus had made it a Roman colony in 25 BC because of its strategic location and settled it with many Roman army veterans. Timothy was from Lystra (16:1). Derbe was in southeastern Lycaonia, about sixty miles southeast of Lystra. It lay on the main road from Iconium and Lystra east to Tarsus in Cilicia.

They shouted, saying in the Lycaonian language (14:11). Paul and Barnabas spoke Greek, the common trade language of the eastern Mediterranean region. They did not know the local language and so were unaware of what the people were saying.

The gods have come down to us in human form! (14:11). The Roman poet Ovid recounts a local legend of how Jupiter and Mercury (the Roman names for Zeus and Hermes) visited this area in human form. They were refused hospitality by everyone except an old couple named Philemon and Baucis, who welcomed them into their humble home. The gods rewarded the old couple by turning their cottage into a gilded temple, while destroying the inhospitable neighbors with a flood.[42] The people of Lystra don't want to make the same mistake!

Barnabas they called Zeus, and Paul, Hermes (14:12). Zeus (the Roman Jupiter) was the king of the gods on Mount Olympus, the Greek pantheon. There was a temple to Zeus at Lystra. Hermes (the Roman Mercury) was the son of Zeus and messenger of the gods. Paul is called Hermes because he is the chief speaker. Perhaps Barnabas looked older and more distinguished.

Tore their robes (14:14). This act was a common way to show anguish, grief, dismay, or rage (Gen. 37:29, 34; Num. 14:6; Josh. 7:6; Isa. 37:1; Mark 14:63).

The living God, *who made the heaven, the earth, the sea, and everything in them* (14:15). Though the pagan world was thoroughly polytheistic, some Greek writers spoke of one true creator God. Paul will give a similar message at Mars Hill in Athens (17:16–34).

They stoned Paul (14:19). Stoning was a Jewish method of capital punishment (see comments on Acts 7:58). Paul will note this event when he describes his many trials for the gospel to the Corinthian church (2 Cor. 11:25).

They had appointed elders (14:23). Though no single model of church leadership is set out as normative in Acts, leadership by a council of elders (*presbyteroi*) appears to be the most common practice (11:30; 15:4; 20:17; 21:18; cf. 1 Tim. 5:17; Titus 1:5; 1 Pet. 5:1, 5). The other two church offices specifically named in the NT are deacon (*diakonos* [Rom. 16:1; Phil. 1:1; 1 Tim. 3:8, 10, 12–13]) and overseer/bishop (*episkopos* [Acts 20:28; Phil. 1:1; 1 Tim. 3:2, 7]). The latter may be the same office as elder. Elder, overseer, and deacon qualifications are set out in 1 Tim. 3:1–13; Titus 1:5–9.

The Jerusalem Council (15:1–35)

Some men came down from Judea . . . "Unless you are circumcised" (15:1). These people are sometimes called Judaizers, since they were Jewish

Christians who believed that it was necessary for gentiles first to become Jews before they could become followers of Jesus the Messiah (see the article "The Jewish Rite of Circumcision"). This issue was the greatest early challenge to the unity of the church.

They passed through both Phoenicia and Samaria (15:3). The journey from Antioch in Syria to Jerusalem was about three hundred miles. By foot it may have taken several weeks.

Some of the believers who belonged to the party of the Pharisees (15:5). It may seem surprising that some of the Jerusalem believers were Pharisees, considering Jesus's conflicts with the Pharisees in the Gospels. But the Pharisees, in contrast to the Sadducees, shared many common beliefs with Jesus and the early church, including expectations for a coming messiah, the resurrection of the dead, and the divine authority of all the Hebrew Scriptures (the Law, the Prophets, and the Writings). It is not surprising that some Pharisees became followers of Jesus.[43]

In the early days God made a choice among you (15:7). Peter is referring to the Cornelius episode in chapters 10–11.

God . . . bore witness to them by giving them the Holy Spirit (15:8). This is the key theme of the Cornelius episode (10:44–48; 11:15–17). The mission to the gentiles was initiated not by any human being but by God himself. Throughout the NT, reception of the Spirit of God is confirmation of salvation (Acts 8:15–17; Rom. 8:9–16; 1 Cor. 2:12–15; 3:16; 6:19; 12:13; 2 Cor. 1:22; Gal. 3:2, 5; Eph. 1:13; 2 Tim. 1:14; 1 John 3:24).

After they stopped speaking, James responded (15:13). James, the half-brother of Jesus, by this time had assumed a primary leadership role in the church at Jerusalem (see comments on Acts 1:14; 12:17). James's voice was well respected, since he was viewed as a pious and faithful keeper of the law of Moses, even among Jews who were not believers in Jesus.[44]

After these things I will return and rebuild David's fallen tent (15:16). See Amos 9:11–12. The "fallen tent" of David could refer to Israel generally, but probably refers more specifically to the Davidic dynasty, which collapsed at the time of the Babylonian exile. James points out that Amos predicted the time of its restoration, when gentiles would become part of the people of God.

Abstain from things polluted by idols, from sexual immorality, from eating anything that has been strangled, and from blood (15:20). The background and significance of these four stipulations are debated. Some claim that they are related to the OT requirements for resident aliens living in the land of Israel (Lev. 17–18). In this case the purpose would be to allow Jewish and gentile Christians to have table fellowship without causing offense to the Jews. Others suggest that all four are related to pagan worship and are meant to protect gentile Christians from idolatry.[45]

Food "polluted by idols" refers to food offered to pagan gods (cf. 1 Cor. 10:7, 14–22; Rev. 2:14, 20). Paul provides a more detailed and nuanced discussion of this in 1 Cor. 8–10. The OT forbade eating blood (Lev. 17:10–12), which included animals that had been strangled without draining the blood. But blood and strangulation were also associated with idolatry. Perhaps the most unusual of the four is the abstention from sexual immorality, which, one would think, would be a given for all believers. It perhaps could refer to specific types of sexual relationships that were forbidden in the OT law, such as between close relatives (Lev. 18). Or it could simply be a reminder of Christian sexual ethics, since the Greco-Roman world was so debauched in this area. It could also be related to pagan idolatry, since prostitution was a common part of pagan temple worship.

Judas, called Barsabbas, and Silas (15:22). Barsabbas means "son of the Sabbath." Nothing else is known of this Judas. "Silas" is a shortened form of "Silvanus" (cf. 2 Cor. 1:19; 1 Thess. 1:1; 2 Thess. 1:1). He will shortly join Paul on Paul's second missionary journey (see v. 40) and will work with Paul and Timothy to start churches in Philippi, Thessalonica, and Corinth (Acts 16–18). He probably was also Peter's amanuensis (scribe) for the writing of 1 Peter (1 Pet. 5:12).

Second Missionary Journey: Paul, Silas, Timothy (15:36–16:10)

They had such a sharp disagreement that they parted company (15:39). It is a common biblical theme that God takes the failings of human beings and turns them into good (see Gen. 45:5–7; 50:20). The conflict between Paul and Barnabas will result in an expanded ministry and doubling of their effectiveness.

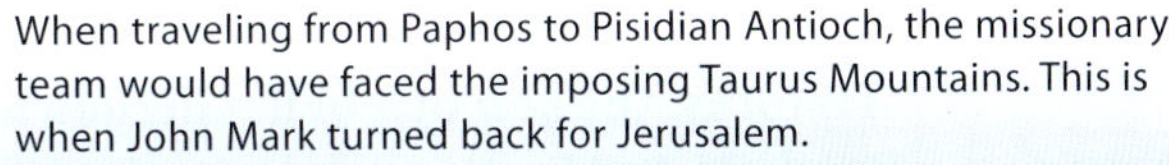

When traveling from Paphos to Pisidian Antioch, the missionary team would have faced the imposing Taurus Mountains. This is when John Mark turned back for Jerusalem.

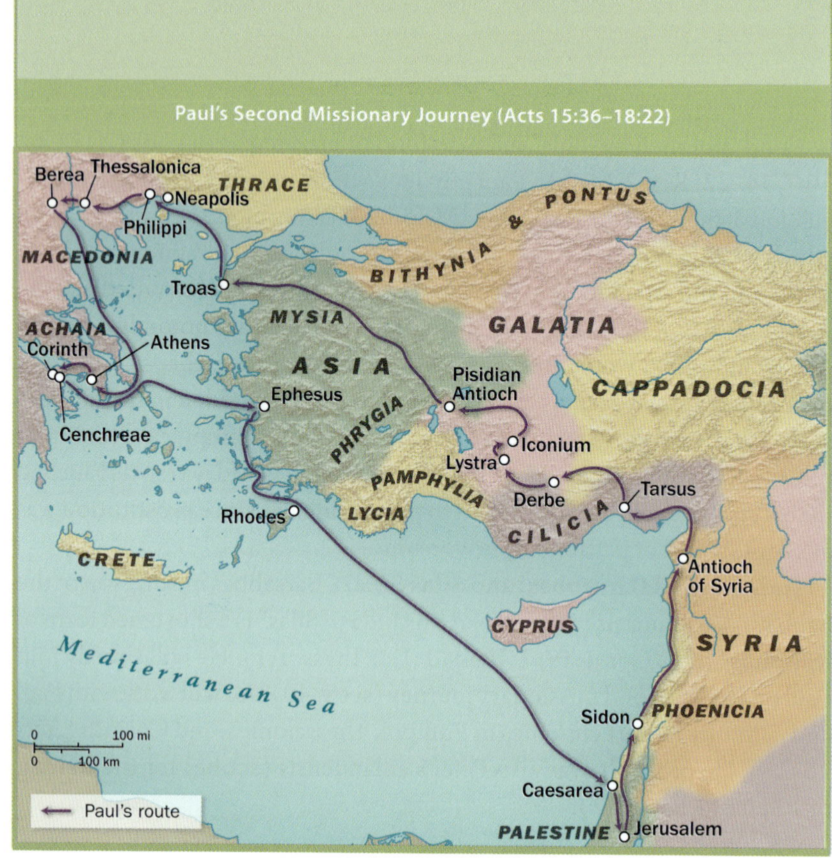

Barnabas took Mark with him and sailed off to Cyprus (15:39). Barnabas gives John Mark another chance and returns to his homeland to continue the work that Paul, he, and Mark had begun there.

He traveled through Syria and Cilicia, strengthening the churches (15:41). By taking the land route, Paul is able to visit and encourage churches in Syria and Cilicia.

Paul went on to Derbe and Lystra (16:1). See comments on Acts 14:6.

Timothy, the son of a believing Jewish woman, but his father was a Greek (16:1). Mixed marriages were quite common in the diaspora, but were frowned upon by Jews. In later rabbinic texts the mother's nationality is determinate for the child.[46] Timothy's mother (Eunice) and grandmother (Lois) are mentioned in 2 Tim. 1:5. Timothy will become one of Paul's closest and most trusted disciples (1 Cor. 4:17; Phil. 2:19–22; 1 Tim. 1:2).

Paul . . . circumcised him (16:3). Some have accused Paul here of compromising his message that salvation comes through faith alone, not by circumcision or keeping the law (Rom. 2:28–29; 1 Cor. 7:19; Gal. 2:3; 5:2, 6; 6:15) (see the article "The Jewish Rite of Circumcision"). But for Paul, Timothy's circumcision was deemed necessary because Timothy was Jewish in the eyes of his fellow Jews (because of his mother). Paul did not want to be accused of telling Jews not to circumcise their children, which would have been scandalous and detrimental to his ministry.

The region of Phrygia and Galatia (16:6). Phrygia was an inland province of southwest Asia Minor. The cities of Pisidian Antioch and Iconium were in Phrygia (see comments on Acts 13:14; 14:1).

The Holy Spirit . . . the Spirit of Jesus (16:6–7). This identification of the Holy Spirit and the Spirit of Jesus is remarkable in a Jewish context and clearly points to the deity of Christ (cf. Rom. 8:9; Gal. 4:6; Phil. 1:19; 1 Pet. 1:11).

They tried to go into Bithynia (16:7). Bithynia was the mountainous region of northern Asia Minor, bordering on the Black Sea. Though Paul was directed away at this time, Christianity must have reached Bithynia shortly after this because the Letter of 1 Peter is addressed to believers throughout Asia Minor, including Bithynia.

Troas (16:8). Troas was a large city and important seaport on the Aegean Sea in northwest Asia Minor, providing the main sea access to Macedonia. It was thirty miles south of ancient Troy. Troas became a Roman possession in 133 BC and was made a Roman colony by Caesar Augustus.

We immediately made efforts to set out for Macedonia (16:10). This is the beginning of the first "we" section of Acts. See the introduction in the commentary on Acts.

Ministry in Philippi (16:11–40)

From Troas we put out to sea and sailed straight for Samothrace, the next day to Neapolis (16:11). See the article "Shipping Practices in the First Century." Samothrace (i.e., Samos of Thrace) was an island in the northeast Aegean Sea, twenty miles south of Thrace. "Samos" means "height" or "mountain" and refers to the island's mountainous terrain. Neapolis (meaning "new city") was the seaport for Philippi, located on the northern Aegean coast, ten miles south of Philippi.

Philippi, a Roman colony (16:12). Philippi was named after Philip of Macedon, the father of Alexander the Great. It was granted status as a Roman colony after Caesar Augustus and Mark Antony defeated Cassius and Brutus in a battle nearby. The city was settled by retired soldiers and other Romans, and its citizens were very proud of their Roman heritage.

Outside the city gate by the river, where we expected to find a place of prayer (16:13). The phrase "place of prayer" may refer to the synagogue (see the article "The Jewish Synagogue"). Many commentators, however, assume that there was no synagogue in Philippi because of the small Jewish population (ten Jewish males were necessary to establish a synagogue), and that this was an informal gathering place for Jews and God-fearers to worship.

A God-fearing woman named Lydia, a dealer in purple cloth from the city of Thyatira (16:14). "Lydia" could be a nickname ("the Lydian") since Lydia was the territory in western Asia Minor where Thyatira was located. Lydia is described as a "God-fearing woman," but it is unclear whether she was a God-fearer or a Jewish proselyte. In any case, she was a merchant who sold purple cloth, a luxury item from Thyatira.

A slave girl met us who had a spirit by which she predicted the future (16:16). This "spirit by which she predicted the future" is, literally, "a python spirit." The name goes back to a Greek legend about Apollo, son of Zeus, who slayed the Python that guarded the underworld and so became lord of the underworld. At the oracle sanctuary at Delphi, priestesses of Apollo, known as Pythia, made prophecies about the future. This slave girl's owners evidently are making a significant profit from her predictions.

These men are seriously disturbing our city. They are Jews (16:20). Anti-Jewish sentiment was common in the Greco-Roman world, particularly in a Roman colony like Philippi, where citizens were proud of their Roman gods and Roman heritage.

The Temple of Apollo in Corinth. Corinth was a trading town that connected northern and southern Greece as well as sea traffic between the Aegean and Adriatic Seas. Paul visited here on his second tour and stayed for eighteen months to establish a church (Acts 18:11).

Stripped off their clothes and ordered them to be beaten with rods (16:22). Paul later says that he faced this kind of punishment on three occasions (2 Cor. 11:25).

The jailer . . . drew his sword and was going to kill himself (16:27). As in the case of the soldiers who had guarded Peter (12:19), guards who let captives escape could be subject to severe punishment and even execution.

They beat us in public without a trial, although we are Roman citizens (16:37). It was against Roman law to beat a Roman citizen without a trial.[47] In the Greco-Roman culture of honor and shame it was important that Paul and Silas be publicly vindicated so that the church would not have a shadow over it for being started by common criminals.

Ministry in Thessalonica and Berea (17:1–15)

Thessalonica (17:1). See the introduction in the commentary on 1–2 Thessalonians. This city, the chief port of Macedonia, was founded in 316 BC by Cassander, who gained control of Greece in the years after Alexander the Great's death It was named in honor of Cassander's wife, Thessalonike. The city became the capital of the Roman province of Macedonia in 147 BC. It had a large Jewish population.

A large number of God-fearing Greeks, as well as a number of the leading women (17:4). On God-fearers, see comments on Acts 10:2. Wealthy women, who had discretionary time and resources, often became patrons for cultural and religious affairs in Greco-Roman society (13:50; 16:13–14; 17:12, 34). Many were God-fearers who attended synagogue services, and Paul found them to be an audience receptive to the gospel.

The Jews . . . started a riot . . . "They are all acting contrary to Caesar's decrees, saying that there is another king—Jesus" (17:5–7). Loyalty to Caesar and to the empire was paramount for maintaining order in the Roman Empire, and any hint of revolt was violently suppressed. The claim that Jesus was the Messiah (the anointed king) seemed to many to be a direct challenge to Caesar's authority.

Taking a security bond from Jason and the others (17:9). The bond likely was money that Jason would forfeit if further unrest occurred.

Berea (17:10). This Macedonian city was about fifty miles west of Thessalonica, at the foot of Mount Bermius. Under the Romans it became a center for the imperial cult. It is now called Veria.

The people here were of more noble character (17:11). The word translated as "noble character" (*eugenēs*) means "well-born" or "of high social status." Here it obviously refers to someone who is fair-minded and willing to weigh the evidence.

A number of the prominent Greek women (17:12). See comments on Acts 17:4.

Ministry in Athens (17:16–34)

Athens (17:16). The most important city in Greece, Athens was a major center for art, science, and philosophy. The city was named after Athena, the Greek goddess of wisdom and patron of the city. At its center stood the Acropolis, a rocky hill crowned by the Parthenon (the temple of Athena) and other temples.

Epicurean and Stoic philosophers (17:18). Epicureans were followers of Epicurus, a Greek philosopher who lived 341–270 BC. He taught that nothing existed except matter and space, and that the greatest good in life was the pursuit of happiness, pleasure, and self-fulfillment. Stoicism was founded by Zeno in the third century BC. It was essentially pantheistic, believing that all is divine and that everything in the world has an essential unity. The greatest goal of life is to maintain harmony with nature and to suppress desires for excess.

Brought him to the Areopagus (17:19). The Areopagus ("Hill of Ares") was also known as Mars Hill. Mars, the god of war, was the Roman equivalent of the Greek Ares. The hill was on the western side of the Acropolis just south of the agora (marketplace). There the Council of the Areopagus met, which oversaw the civic and religious affairs of Athens.

An altar on which was inscribed: "To an Unknown God" (17:23). Other ancient authors mention similar altars in Athens.[48] Their purpose was to avoid offending gods who might otherwise be overlooked.

In him we live and move and have our being (17:28). Early church leaders attributed this quote to Epimenides, a poet of Crete (ca. 600 BC). This is debated, however, since similar statements are found elsewhere in Greek literature. Paul quotes from Epimenides again in Titus 1:12.

Some of your own poets have said, "For we are also his offspring" (17:28). This quotation from the Stoic poet Aratus (315–240 BC) shows that Paul is contextualizing his message for the philosophers in Athens, connecting the gospel to traditions that would be familiar to them.[49]

Heard about the resurrection of the dead . . . began to ridicule him (17:32). Greek philosophers were divided on the question of the immortality of the soul, but they would have rejected any thought of the resurrection of the physical body.

Ministry in Corinth (18:1–17)

Corinth (18:1). See the article "The City of Corinth"; see the introduction in the commentary on 1 Corinthians and 2 Corinthians. Corinth was strategically located on the narrow isthmus connecting mainland Greece and the Peloponnesian Peninsula. It served as the Roman capital of the province of Achaia and was a wealthy, powerful, and decadent center of trade and commerce. The city had a natural defense in the Acrocorinth, a mountain that towered fifteen hundred feet above the city. Corinth was destroyed by Rome in 146 BC and refounded by Julius Caesar in 44 BC. The city was repopulated with many colonists from Rome, especially freedmen who developed into a thriving merchant class. The city also excelled culturally with biannual Isthmian Games (second only to the Olympics), an outdoor theater that held twenty thousand people, and an indoor one that held three thousand. There was enormous religious diversity, with temples and altars scattered throughout the city.

Aquila, a native of Pontus, who had recently come from Italy with his wife Priscilla (18:2). Aquila and Priscilla (referred to by Paul as Prisca) would become key partners in Paul's ministry (18:18, 19, 26; Rom. 16:3; 1 Cor. 16:19; 2 Tim. 4:19). Priscilla normally is named first, perhaps indicating her higher social status or leadership gifts. Pontus was a region in northern Asia Minor, bordering on the Black Sea.

Claudius had ordered all the Jews to leave Rome (18:2). This event occurred in AD 49 and evidently was provoked by conflicts between Jews and Jewish Christians in Rome (see the article "The City of Ancient Rome"). The Roman historian Suetonius (ca. AD 120) writes, "Because the Jews at Rome caused continuous disturbances at the instigation of Chrestus, he [the emperor Claudius] expelled them from the city."[50] Suetonius apparently misunderstood Chrestus to be one of the leaders among the factions, when in fact it is a misspelling of *Christos* ("Christ") and refers to heated debates over whether Jesus was the Christ.

Tentmaker by trade (18:3). Most rabbis maintained a trade in addition to their study and teaching, so it is not surprising that Paul was a tentmaker (*skēnopoios*).

He shook out his clothes (18:6). This action is similar in meaning to shaking the dust off one's feet (see comments on Acts 13:51).

While Gallio was proconsul of Achaia (18:12). Gallio (his full name was Lucius Junius Gallio Annaeanus) was a well-known Roman senator and brother of the famous Stoic philosopher Seneca. Because we know from other sources that Gallio was proconsul of Achaia

Paul was brought before the proconsul Gallio at the *bēma* (judgment seat) in Corinth (Acts 18:12–17).

around AD 51–52, we can date Paul's time at Corinth to approximately AD 50–52.

I refuse to be a judge of such things (18:15). Gallio's ruling is important because essentially he declares Christianity to be a sect within Judaism and this to be an intra-Jewish debate. This would provide Christians a measure of legal protection (for a time at least), because Judaism was a legal religion (*religio licita*) and Jews were not expected to participate in emperor worship.[51]

They all seized Sosthenes, the leader of the synagogue (18:17). Anti-Semitism was common in the Greco-Roman world (16:20), so it is not surprising that Gallio's supporters vent their anger on Sosthenes for wasting the court's time. It is possible that this Sosthenes is the same individual whom Paul names as a Christian brother in 1 Cor. 1:1.

Priscilla, Aquila, and Apollos (18:18–28)

He shaved his head at Cenchreae because of a vow he had taken (18:18). Cenchreae was the southern port of Corinth, on the Aegean Sea. Paul's haircut likely signaled the end of a Nazirite vow, a period of special consecration to God (Num. 6:1–21). The vow involved abstaining from wine and grapes, not touching anything impure, and not cutting one's hair. At the end of the vow the hair was cut and brought to the Jerusalem temple, where it and other offerings were presented to the Lord.

A Jew named Apollos, a native Alexandrian (18:24). Founded by Alexander the Great in 332 BC, Alexandria was the chief port in Egypt. Since grain from Egypt fed the Roman masses, Alexandria was an enormously important center for trade and commerce. The city was also a great intellectual and university center. The library of Alexandria was the most famous in the world, reportedly housing a collection of over half a million documents and scrolls. A large and thriving Jewish population lived there. The Septuagint, the Greek translation of the Hebrew Bible, was produced there in the third century BC. As an Alexandrian Jew and a gifted speaker and scholar, Apollos represented a formidable debater and advocate for the Christian message.

Third Missionary Journey: Ministry in Ephesus (19:1–41)

While Apollos was in Corinth (19:1). On Corinth, see comments on Acts 18:1; on Apollos, see comments on Acts 18:24.

Ephesus (19:1). See the article "The City of Ephesus"; see the introduction in the commentary on Ephesians.

We haven't even heard that there is a Holy Spirit (19:2). All Jews knew about the reality of God's Spirit, so this cannot be a question of whether

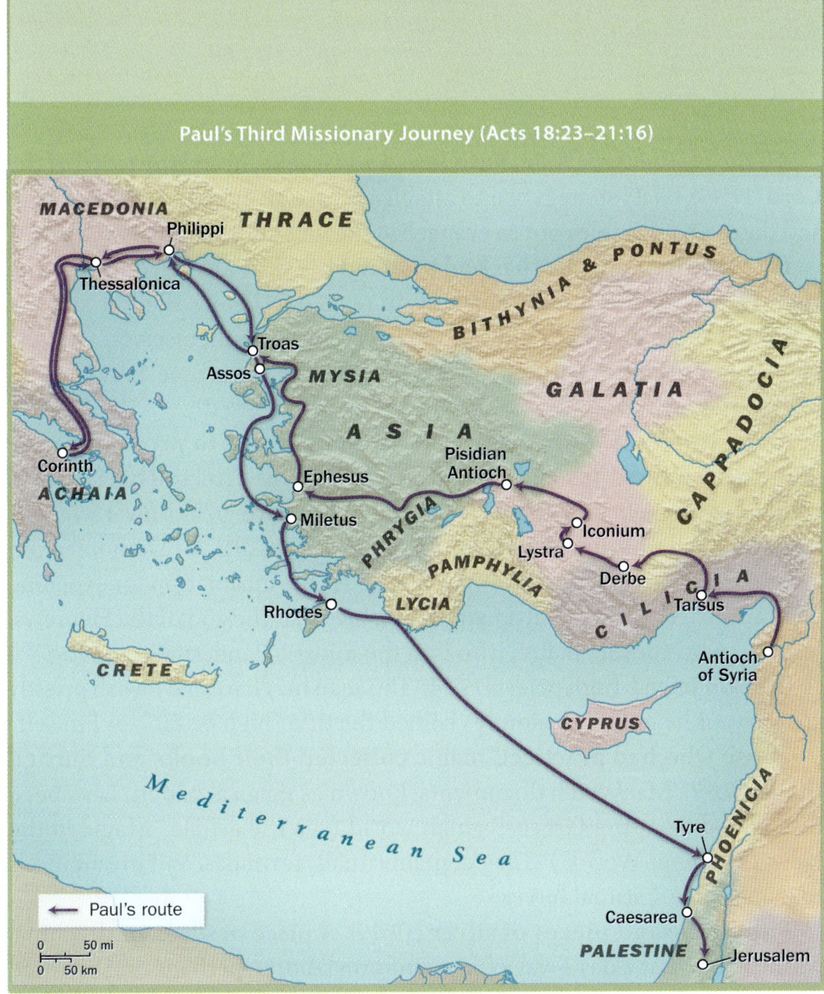

the Spirit existed. It likely means that these disciples of John did not know that the eschatological Spirit had already been poured out (see comments on Acts 1:5; 2:16–21).[52]

They began to speak in other tongues and to prophesy (19:6). Often in Acts, though not always (cf. 8:17), the reception of the Spirit is accompanied by speaking in tongues (2:4; 10:45–46).

The Way (19:9). See comments on Acts 9:2.

The lecture hall of Tyrannus (19:9). Tyrannus may have been the owner of the building, who rented it out to others, or else a philosopher or a rhetorician who ran a school there. His name means "despot" or "tyrant"—perhaps a nickname given to him by his students! Several Greek manuscripts (representing the Western text) claim that Paul taught from 11:00 a.m. to 4:00 p.m., the hottest part of the day, when people would be napping and the hall would be available.

All the residents of Asia, both Jews and Greeks, heard the word of the Lord (19:10). Paul's strategy was to establish a base of operations in a large city and then send disciples out to evangelize the neighboring towns and cities.

Facecloths or aprons that had touched his skin were brought to the sick (19:12). See the similar superstition related to Peter's shadow at 5:15. Although these items did not have magical power in themselves, God evidently honored the faith of those who touched them (see 19:11; Mark 5:27–34; 6:56).

Some itinerant Jewish exorcists also attempted to pronounce the name of the Lord Jesus (19:13). Magicians in the Greco-Roman world would invoke any name that was considered to have great power in order to accomplish a healing, exorcism, or curse (see the article "Demonization and Exorcism in the Greco-Roman World"). One incantation for expelling demons, dated to the late Roman period, invokes "the god of the Hebrews, Jesus . . . who appears in fire, who is in the midst of land, snow, and fog."[53]

Sceva, a Jewish high priest (19:14). This man may have had Jewish priestly ancestry, or he may have simply claimed the title "high priest" for himself.

Those who had practiced magic collected their books and burned them (19:19). Many such documents, known as magical papyri, have been discovered from the Greco-Roman world (see the article "Magic in the New Testament World"). They contain rituals, formulas, and incantations to manipulate spiritual forces.[54]

Fifty thousand pieces of silver (19:19). A piece of silver, or drachma, was worth about a day's wage for a common laborer, perhaps one hundred dollars by today's standards. So this amount is equivalent to five million dollars or more.

Timothy and Erastus (19:22). On Timothy, see the introduction in the commentary on 1–2 Timothy; see comments on Acts 16:1. Erastus may be the same person mentioned in Rom. 16:23 (cf. 2 Tim. 4:20), where he is called the "city treasurer," perhaps the director of public works. At Corinth archaeologists have discovered a Latin inscription reading, "Erastus in return for his aedileship laid this pavement at his own expense."[55] Aediles were responsible for maintenance of public buildings and the regulation of public festivals.

Silver shrines of Artemis (19:24). These silver shrines were small models of the temple of Artemis (see comments on Acts 19:35).

They rushed all together into the amphitheater (19:29). In addition to being a venue for plays and other performances, this was the city's official meeting place, where assemblies were held.

The city of the Ephesians is the temple guardian of the great Artemis, and of the image that fell from heaven (19:35). Artemis (the Roman Diana) was the virgin goddess of hunting, and she was widely worshiped throughout the Greco-Roman world (see the article "The City of Ephesus"). At Ephesus she was merged with an old Anatolian fertility goddess and made into the supreme goddess of love and fertility. Her massive temple was one of the great wonders of the ancient world, measuring 450 by 225 feet (over twice the size of the Parthenon) and 60 feet high, with 127 columns.[56] Her "image" was likely a meteorite that was believed to have fallen from heaven, a gift from the gods. The Ephesians had enormous pride in their goddess, and sales of religious icons and festivals in her honor brought in a huge tourist trade.

The courts are in session, and there are proconsuls. Let them bring charges (19:38). The Roman legal system was the most advanced in history, and Romans were justifiably proud of it. The town clerk appeals to the people to use the court system rather than mob rule to respond to this "blasphemy."

We run a risk of being charged with rioting (19:40). A disturbance of the *pax Romana*, the "Roman peace," was a serious offense that would result in swift reprisal by the Roman authorities.

Macedonia, Achaia, and Troas (20:1–12)

Paul . . . departed to go to Macedonia . . . he came to Greece and stayed three months (20:1–3). For more on the reasons for this journey, see the introduction in the commentary on 2 Corinthians (cf. 2 Cor. 2:12; 7:5–16). Paul is seeking reconciliation with the rebellious church at Corinth. "Greece" probably refers here to a three-month stay in Corinth. It was at this time that Paul wrote to the church in Rome in preparation for his missionary outreach to Spain (Rom. 15:23–29).

He was accompanied by Sopater son of Pyrrhus from Berea, Aristarchus and Secundus from Thessalonica, Gaius from Derbe, Timothy, and Tychicus and Trophimus from the province of Asia (20:4). Luke does not mention Paul's main reason for going to Jerusalem, but from Paul's letters we learn that he is gathering a collection for the poverty-stricken Jerusalem church (Rom. 15:25–31; 1 Cor. 16:1–4; 2 Cor. 8–9; cf. also Acts 24:17). The individuals named here are representatives from various Pauline churches, delegated to carry the collection to the Jerusalem church (cf. 1 Cor. 16:3; 2 Cor. 8:18–21). Sopater and Secundus are otherwise unknown. Gaius of Derbe is mentioned as working with Aristarchus of Thessalonica with Paul in Ephesus (Acts 19:29). Aristarchus would later join Paul on his voyage from Jerusalem to

A statue of the goddess Artemis.

Rome for trial (Acts 27:1–2). He evidently stayed in Rome with Paul and was there when Paul wrote Colossians and Philemon (Col. 4:10; Philem. 24). On Timothy, see the introduction in the commentary on 1–2 Timothy; see comments on Acts 16:1. Tychicus was another of Paul's most trusted associates (Eph. 6:21–22; Col. 4:7–9; 2 Tim. 4:12; Titus 3:12). Trophimus is mentioned again in 21:28–29, where Paul is falsely accused of taking gentiles into the Jerusalem temple (see the article "The Jerusalem Temple"; cf. 2 Tim. 4:20).

We sailed away from Philippi after the Festival of Unleavened Bread (20:6). On Philippi, see the introduction in the commentary on Philippians; see comments on Acts 16:12. Passover began on 15 Nisan (March-April) and was followed by the seven-day Festival of Unleavened Bread (see comments on Acts 12:3). This is the spring of AD 56 or 57.

On the first day of the week, we assembled to break bread (20:7). The believers evidently met for worship on the first day of the week (Sunday), the day of the resurrection, rather than the seventh day, the Sabbath (Saturday). This may be the earliest reference to Christian worship on Sunday (cf. 1 Cor. 16:2). "To break bread" refers to taking the Lord's Supper together (see comments on Acts 2:42).

Farewell Address to the Elders of Ephesus (20:13–38)

Assos . . . Mitylene . . . Chios . . . Samos . . . Miletus (20:14–15). Assos is a port on the Aegean coast, about twenty miles south of Troas. Paul travels there on foot while Luke and the others take a ship around the coast. Mitylene is the main city of the island of Lesbos (Lesvos), and Chios and Samos are islands off the coast of Asia Minor. Miletus was a port city about thirty miles south of Ephesus. See the article "Shipping Practices in the First Century."

To sail past Ephesus . . . to be in Jerusalem . . . for the day of Pentecost (20:16). Pentecost was fifty days after Passover (see the article "Jewish Festivals"). Paul knows that if he stops in Ephesus (where he had worked for three years), his meetings with close friends would delay him and prevent him from reaching Jerusalem by Pentecost. So he stops at Miletus and calls the elders of Ephesus to meet him there.

I am innocent of the blood of all of you (20:26). Paul's language echoes Ezek. 33:1–6, which describes the innocence of a watchman at the city gate who sounds the warning trumpet at the approach of an enemy but is not heeded by the people.

To shepherd the church of God (20:28). Shepherd imagery is common in the OT. It is applied to God's provision and protection of his people (Ps. 23:1–4; Isa. 40:11; Ezek. 34:11–16) but also negatively to false shepherds who lead the flock astray (Isa. 56:10–11; Jer. 23:1–4; Ezek. 34:2–10, 17–19). Jesus identifies himself as the good shepherd who gives his life for the sheep (John 10:1–18; cf. Heb. 13:20; 1 Pet. 2:25; 5:4). All Christian leaders are Christ's undershepherds, caring for God's flock (John 21:15–17; Eph. 4:11; 1 Pet. 5:2).

Savage wolves . . . men will rise up even from your own number and distort the truth (20:29–30). Ezekiel and Zephaniah describe corrupt leaders of Israel as ferocious wolves that prey on God's flock (Ezek. 22:27; Zeph. 3:3; cf. Matt. 7:15; Luke 10:3). While in Paul's early ministry external persecution from Jewish and gentile opponents was the greatest danger, soon false teachers would arise from within the church (Col. 2:8; 1 Tim. 4:1–3; 2 Tim. 2:16–18; 3:1–9; 2 Pet. 2:1–22; 1 John 2:18–19; Jude 3–16; Rev. 2:2).

I worked with my own hands to support myself (20:34). Manual labor was considered degrading by sophisticated Greeks, and philosophers and itinerant preachers expected to be compensated for their wisdom. Paul, however, continued to work as a tentmaker in order not to be a burden to others or to give the impression that his ministry was for financial gain (1 Cor. 4:12; 9:12, 15; 2 Cor. 11:7; 12:13; 1 Thess. 2:9; 2 Thess. 3:7–8).

Remember the words of the Lord Jesus, because he said, "It is more blessed to give than to receive" (20:35). This statement does not appear in the Gospels but is part of the oral tradition of Jesus's teaching passed down to Paul. Not everything that Jesus said or did appears in the Gospels (John 21:25).

Return to Jerusalem (21:1–16)

Set sail straight for Cos . . . to Rhodes . . . to Patara . . . crossing over to Phoenicia . . . arrived at Tyre (21:1–3). Cos is an island about forty miles south of Miletus, with a city of the same name (see the article "Shipping Practices in the First Century"). Rhodes is an island and city seventy miles southeast of Cos, where the famous Colossus statue, one of the seven wonders of the ancient world, once stood. Patara was the main port of the region of Lycia in southwest Asia Minor, approximately sixty miles southeast of Rhodes. After these short trips the group boards a long-distance ship that takes them approximately four hundred miles to the Phoenician coast and its chief city, Tyre.

We completed our voyage from Tyre, we reached Ptolemais (21:7). On Tyre, see comments on Acts 12:20. Ptolemais was an important seaport near Mount Carmel. Originally called Acco (Judg. 1:31), it was renamed Ptolemais during the Hellenistic period. It was strategically located at the juncture between the coastal road and the inland road that led through Galilee and Transjordan to Syria.

Came to Caesarea, where we entered the house of Philip the evangelist (21:8). On Caesarea, see comments on Acts 10:1. On Philip the evangelist, see Acts 6:1–7; 8:4–40.

Four virgin daughters who prophesied (21:9). Joel 2:28 predicted that when the eschatological Spirit was poured out, "your sons and your daughters will prophesy" (cf. Acts 2:17). Philip's daughters serve as evidence of the fulfillment of this prophecy.

Agabus . . . took Paul's belt (21:10–11). On the gift of prophecy and Agabus's previous prediction about a famine in Judea, see comments on Acts 11:27–28. The use of object lessons to illustrate God's message is common in the OT prophets (1 Kings 11:29–31; Isa. 8:1–4; 20:1–6; Jer. 19:1–13; 27:1–22; Hosea 1:2). For a similar use of a belt, see Jer. 13:1–11.

Paul's Troubles in the Temple (21:17–36)

Paul went in with us to James, and all the elders were present (21:18). As at the Jerusalem Council (15:13–21), James the half-brother of Jesus

1 "Every day they continued to meet together in the temple courts" (Acts 2:46). The apostles and new believers are meeting every day in the temple. They probably gather in Solomon's Colonnade, as indicated in Acts 5:12: "And all the believers used to meet together in Solomon's Colonnade."

2 Peter heals a man who sits begging at the temple gate called Beautiful (Acts 3:1–10). We are not certain which gate this is. It is probably the gate leading out from the Court of the Women. Another less likely option is the Shushan Gate.

3 "At daybreak they entered the temple courts, as they had been told, and began to teach the people" (Acts 5:21). This again probably takes place in Solomon's Colonnade.

4 Paul agrees to participate in purification rites along with four men who have taken vows (Acts 21:20–26). These rites probably take place in the ceremonial baths (*mikveh*) that are just to the south of the temple.

5 After the purification rites Paul goes to the temple to coordinate sacrifices/offerings (Acts 21:26). He probably makes a payment in the Court of the Women, where the treasury is.

6 After making payment for the offerings (Acts 21:26), Paul probably enters the Court of the Israelites, near the altar.

7 Thinking Paul has defiled the temple by bringing gentiles past the *soreg* (fence), a mob attacks Paul (Acts 21:27–30). He is probably in the Court of the Women or in the Court of the Israelites.

8 "Seizing Paul, they dragged him from the temple, and immediately the gates were shut" (Acts 21:30). Paul is probably dragged out of the Court of the Women and into the northern part of the Court of the Gentiles.

9 The temple gates are closed against Paul (Acts 21:30). These are probably the gates in the *soreg* (fence), but they could also be the gates leading into the Court of the Women.

10 "While they were trying to kill him [Paul], news reached the commander of the Roman troops" (Acts 21:31). This commander would be in the Antonia Fortress.

11 "He at once took some officers and soldiers and ran down to the crowd" (Acts 21:32). These Roman soldiers descend down a stairway from the Antonia Fortress into the northern colonnaded portico, and they confront the crowd.

12 As the soldiers are about to take Paul into the barracks, he asks the commander for permission to speak to the crowd from the steps (Acts 21:37–40). He is probably on the stairway leading up from the northern colonnaded porch to the Antonia Fortress.

13 "The commander ordered that Paul be taken into the barracks" (Acts 22:24)—that is, the Antonia Fortress.

Second Temple with Events from Acts

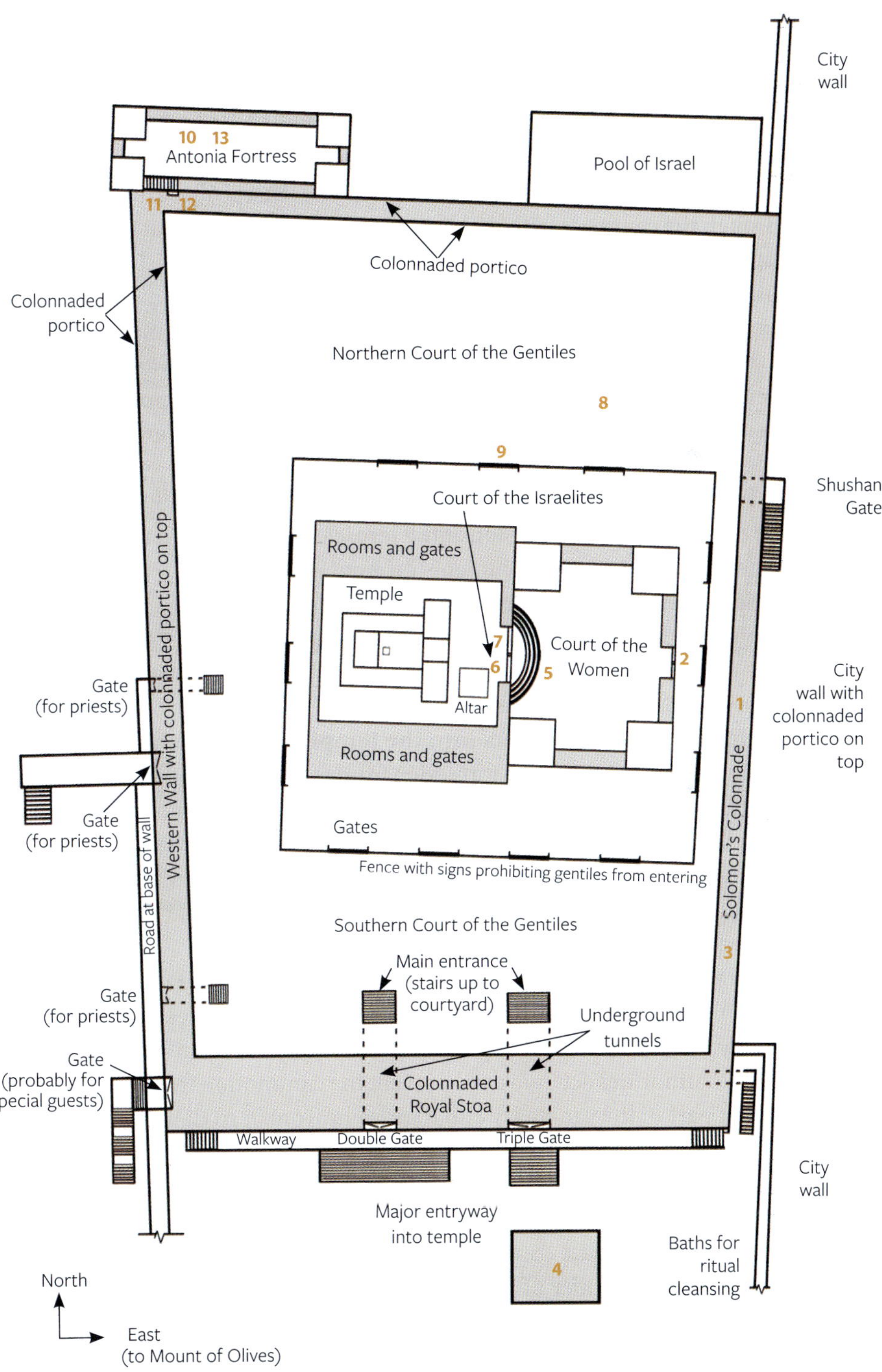

functions as the leader of the council of elders in the church at Jerusalem. See comments on Acts 1:14; 12:17; 15:13; see the article "The Family of Jesus."

Many thousands of Jews there are who have believed, and they are all zealous for the law (21:20). Faithfulness to the law of Moses remained a high priority among many Jewish Christians. This is not surprising, since through the centuries faithfulness to God's law is what separated Jews from pagans. The Mishnah says that anyone who despises the Jewish feasts voids the covenant of Abraham, or interprets the law of Moses differently from accepted rabbinic tradition "has no share in the world to come."[57]

We have four men who have made a vow (21:23). This is a Nazirite vow (see Num. 6:1–21; see comments on Acts 18:18). By supporting these men, Paul could demonstrate that he was faithful to his Jewish heritage (see v. 21).

We have written a letter containing our decision (21:25). James and the elders refer to the decision at the Jerusalem Council and the letter sent to gentile believers (see comments on Acts 15:20).

Some Jews from the province of Asia (21:27). During Paul's three-year ministry in Ephesus "all the residents of Asia, both Jews and Greeks, heard the word of the Lord" (19:10), resulting in both many converts and many enemies from among the Jewish population.

He also brought Greeks into the temple and has defiled this holy place (21:28). Gentiles were forbidden from entering the inner courts of the temple. Signs were posted warning of execution for those who would enter.[58] Fragments of two of these signs have been discovered by archaeologists. One reads, "No foreigner is to enter within the forecourt and the balustrade around the sanctuary. Whoever is caught will have himself to blame for his subsequent death."[59]

Dragged him out of the temple, and at once the gates were shut (21:30). These are the gates separating the Court of Gentiles from the inner courtyards of the temple (see the article "The Jerusalem Temple"). The temple authorities act quickly to prevent the commotion from affecting the holiest part of the sanctuary and to prevent Roman soldiers from defiling the place.

Word went up to the commander of the regiment (21:31). The Roman garrison was stationed in the Antonia Fortress, overlooking the temple compound at its northwest corner. The "commander" (*chiliarchos*) was a *tribunus militum*, a commander of a cohort of roughly one thousand troops. There were six cohorts in a Roman legion. In 23:26 the commander is identified as Claudius Lysias.

Paul Addresses the Crowd in the Temple (21:37–22:30)

Aren't you the Egyptian who started a revolt? (21:38). Josephus refers to this same Egyptian, claiming that he led thirty thousand followers to the Mount of Olives and announced that the walls of Jerusalem would fall down at his command. The Roman governor Felix sent troops against the rebels, killing and capturing many and dispersing the rest.[60] The Egyptian himself escaped, which explains why the commander suspects that Paul might be the one.

I am a Jewish man from Tarsus in Cilicia, a citizen of an important city (21:39). Tarsus was the chief city and capital of Cilicia in Asia Minor. It was a major commercial and cultural center. The Greek geographer and historian Strabo (ca. 64 BC–AD 24) claims that in the first century the city actually exceeded Athens and Alexandria in culture and learning.[61]

They heard that he was addressing them in Aramaic (22:2). The Greek word used here (*hebraïs*) could refer either to Hebrew or Aramaic but probably means the latter, since this was the common language of the Jewish people in Israel at the time (Hebrew was used mainly in the synagogue). The people evidently were expecting Greek, so they listen more carefully when Paul speaks their native tongue.

Educated at the feet of Gamaliel (22:3). Though born in Tarsus, Paul was educated in Jerusalem. Gamaliel was one of the most respected rabbis of the day. See comments on Acts 5:34.

Zealous for God (22:3). Zeal for God and for the law was highly praised among Jewish patriots. The historical exemplars were Phinehas, who satisfied God's judging zeal by killing with a single spear thrust an Israelite man and the Midianite woman with whom he was committing idolatry and sexual immorality (Num. 25:6–13), and Mattathias, who similarly speared an Israelite apostate and idolater, sparking the Maccabean Revolt (1 Macc. 2:19–28, 54).

I persecuted this Way to the death (22:4). See comments on Acts 9:1–2; 26:11; see Paul's description of his persecuting zeal in his own letters (1 Cor. 15:9; Gal. 1:13; 1 Tim. 1:13). On Christianity as "the Way," see comments on Acts 9:2.

Ananias, a devout man according to the law (22:12). Faithful adherence to the law of Moses was of utmost concern to pious Jews (6:13; 7:53; 15:21; 18:13; 21:20, 24, 28). By noting the devotion of a Jewish Christian like Ananias, Paul seeks to show the continuity between Judaism and Christianity (cf. 24:14).

The Righteous One (22:14). This is an allusion to Isa. 53:11 and the "suffering servant." See comments on Acts 3:13–14.

After I returned to Jerusalem (22:17). This visit to Jerusalem is recounted in 9:26–30 and mentioned by Paul in Gal. 1:18–19.

I will send you far away to the Gentiles . . . "Wipe this man off the face of the earth!" (22:21–22). The people listen intently until Paul points to God's desire to save the gentiles. The people of Nazareth responded to Jesus in the same violent way when he described God's favor for the gentiles (Luke 4:24–29). The Jews of Paul's day were more interested in the promises related to the judgment of the nations than those related to their salvation (see Acts 11:18).

Directing that he be interrogated with the scourge (22:24). Scourging or flogging (Lat. *flagellum*) was a standard Roman interrogation technique. A leather whip embedded with shards of metal or glass was used.

Is it legal for you to scourge a man who is a Roman citizen and is uncondemned? (22:25). Roman law did not allow a Roman citizen to be flogged without a trial (cf. Acts 16:37).[62]

The centurion . . . the commander (22:26). On centurions, see comments on Acts 10:1. On the commander, see comments on Acts 21:31. See also the article "The Roman Military."

The commander replied, "I bought this citizenship for a large amount of money." "But I was born a citizen," Paul said (22:28). Roman citizenship could be gained by birth, emancipation from slavery, or service rendered to Rome. Paul inherited it from his father or grandfather, but it is not known how they received it (making tents for the Roman army is possible but speculative). Technically, one was not allowed to purchase Roman citizenship, but gaining it through bribery was not uncommon, especially during the reign of Claudius.[63] This commander likely paid imperial agents to put his name on the list of new citizens.

Paul Addresses the Sanhedrin (23:1–11)

The Sanhedrin (23:1). Paul is addressing the seventy-member Jewish high council. See comments on Mark 8:31; Acts 4:5; see the article "The Sanhedrin."

The high priest Ananias (23:2). Ananias, son of Nedebaeus, was the Jewish high priest from AD 47 to 58. He was appointed high priest by Herod, king of Chalcis (the brother of Herod Agrippa I), after Herod deposed Joseph, son of Camydus.[64] By most accounts, Ananias was arrogant and corrupt. At the beginning of the Jewish War (AD 66) he was killed by the Zealots because of his pro-Roman sympathies.

You whitewashed wall! (23:3). This may be a metaphor for hypocrisy, meaning that Ananias appears to be one thing on the outside but is corrupt inside. Or it may echo Ezek. 13:8–15, where Israel's rulers are said to be leading God's people astray, crying out "Peace" when there is no peace and painting a flimsy wall white to hide the fact that it is about to collapse.

One part of them were Sadducees and the other part were Pharisees (23:6). The Sanhedrin was dominated by the high priest's family and the party of the Sadducees, but there was also a significant minority of influential Pharisees (see the article "Pharisees and Sadducees").

I am being judged because of the hope of the resurrection of the dead! (23:6). While the Pharisees believed in the resurrection, the Sadducees denied it (for more details on the two parties, see the article "Pharisees and Sadducees").[65] Paul sees an opportunity to divide his opponents over this crucial issue.

Neither angel nor spirit (23:8). The denial of the existence of angels by the Sadducees is not otherwise attested and seems unlikely, especially since angels appear in the Pentateuch, which the Sadducees accepted as authoritative. Luke may mean that the Sadducees did not believe in the kind of angelic hierarchies that appear in apocalyptic Jewish literature. Or it could be an expansion of the previous clause, meaning that the Sadducees did not believe in the existence of the soul after death "either as an angel or as a spirit."[66]

Plot against Paul, and Transfer to Caesarea (23:12–35)

The Jews . . . bound themselves under a curse (23:12). The oath not to eat or drink means that they were willing to forfeit their own lives rather than let Paul escape. Their failure to kill Paul does not mean that they all starved! The Mishnah allows release from an unfulfillable vow.[67]

The son of Paul's sister (23:16). Nothing else is known about Paul's relatives apart from this intriguing comment.

Felix the governor (23:24). See comments on Acts 24:1–3.

Brought him to Antipatris (23:31). Antipatris was a city and military outpost rebuilt by Herod the Great in 9 BC (formerly known as Aphek). Herod named it after his father, Antipater. The city was about thirty miles from Jerusalem and was a key way station on the road from Jerusalem to Caesarea Maritima, the Roman headquarters for Judea and Samaria.

Learned he was from Cilicia . . . "I will give you a hearing" (23:34–35). Felix perhaps is hoping to avoid the case by sending Paul back to his home province for trial. But Cilicia was at this time part of a larger Roman province of Syria-Cilicia and so was under the legate of Syria (Felix's superior).[68] Since Felix would not want to bother his boss with such a trivial case, he agrees to hear it himself.

Herod's palace at Caesarea Maritima.

Kept under guard in Herod's palace (23:35). "Herod's palace" was so called because it was built by Herod the Great and used as a royal residence. But now it was used as the Roman governor's residence and headquarters.

Paul's Trial before Felix (24:1–27)

Ananias the high priest . . . some elders and a lawyer named Tertullus (24:1). On Ananias, see comments on Acts 23:2. The elders would have been members of the Sanhedrin. Tertullus likely was a hired lawyer and orator who knew Roman law and had defended cases before Felix in the past.[69]

The governor . . . Felix (24:1–3). Marcus Antonius Felix served as procurator of Judea from AD 52 to 59. He was a freedman (a former slave) who achieved his position with the help of his brother Pallas. Both were friends and favorites of the emperor Claudius. Felix's governorship was marked by corruption and poor relations with his Jewish subjects. He instigated the murder of the high priest, allowed persecution against the Jews in Caesarea, and ruthlessly suppressed any hint of revolt. Jewish complaints eventually resulted in his recall to Rome in AD 59. The Roman historian Tacitus said of Felix that he indulged "in every kind of barbarity and lust" and "exercised the power of a king in the spirit of a slave."[70] Felix's corruption is seen in his continued incarceration of Paul despite his innocence, done in hopes of getting a bribe from him (24:26).

We enjoy great peace because of you, and reforms are taking place for the benefit of this nation because of your foresight . . . most excellent Felix (24:2–3). Gushing flattery often was used in the courtroom to

Coins minted under the procurator Antonius Felix (AD 52–58), before whom Paul went on trial (Acts 24).

gain the favor of a judge. In the forensic handbooks it is known as *captatio benevolentiae.*[71] Tertullus's words are disingenuous because Felix's rule was characterized by neither reform nor tranquility.

A plague, an agitator among all the Jews (24:5). Notice that these are political charges that would concern the governor, whose primary task was to keep the *pax Romana*—the Roman peace. It certainly was true that riots and other disturbances had broken out as a result of Paul's preaching (14:19; 16:19–21; 17:5; 19:28–41; 21:30).

A ringleader of the sect of the Nazarenes (24:5). The term "Nazarene" is used because these are followers of Jesus of Nazareth. The word "sect" could mean "a group that holds tenets distinctive to it, *sect, party, school, faction.*"[72] Though the word does not necessarily always connote heresy, it clearly is being used here in a negative sense, like the English word "cult."

To desecrate the temple (24:6). See comments on Acts 21:28.

You have been a judge of this nation for many years (24:10). Paul's introductory praise (*captatio benevolentiae*) is much more restrained and honest than Tertullus's (see comments on Acts 24:2–3).

The Way (24:14). See comments on Acts 9:2.

To bring charitable gifts and offerings to my people (24:17). This is the only hint in Acts of Paul's collection for the church in Jerusalem. See comments on Acts 20:4.

Found me ritually purified (24:18). Before entering the temple, Paul would have gone through ceremonial purification for his own vow (18:18) and for the vows of the men he was sponsoring (21:23, 26). Large numbers of *mikva'ot*, Jewish ritual baths, have been discovered around the temple in Jerusalem.

Felix came with his wife Drusilla (24:24). Drusilla was the youngest daughter of Herod Agrippa I and sister of Bernice and Agrippa II (25:13). Josephus reports that when Felix saw her beauty, he fell in love with her and sent an associate, a Cyprian Jew named Simon, to coax her to leave her husband, Azizus, king of Syrian Emesa. Simon pretended to be a magician and promised her happiness if she would come, to which she agreed (in part to escape abuse from her jealous sister).[73]

He was also hoping that Paul would offer him money (24:26). Although Greek and Roman sources portray bribes as negative and even treasonous, corruption and bribery were rampant throughout the Roman Empire.[74]

After two years had passed, Porcius Festus succeeded Felix (24:27). Felix was recalled to Rome in AD 59/60, probably because of complaints against him by the Jews.[75] By leaving Paul in prison, he hoped to gain their favor and so avoid further accusations that would hurt him in Rome. On Porcius Festus, see comments on Acts 25:1.

Paul's Hearing before Festus and His Appeal to Caesar (25:1–12)

Festus (25:1). Porcius Festus was appointed by the emperor Nero in AD 59 to succeed Felix.[76] Josephus presents a generally positive portrait of his rule, contrasting him with the corruption of his predecessor Felix and successor Albinus. Festus restored order by defeating bands of marauding bandits and treated the Jewish leaders with some respect, listening and responding to their complaints.[77] Little else is known about Festus. He died abruptly in AD 62, after only three years in office.

They were, in fact, preparing an ambush (25:3). See 23:12–22 for their previous attempt and the reason for Paul's reluctance to return to Jerusalem (25:10–11).

I appeal to Caesar! (25:11). As a Roman citizen, Paul has the right to appeal (*provocatio*) to have his case heard in Rome.[78] The emperor at this time was Nero (reigned AD 54–68). On the title "Caesar," see comments on Acts 25:21.

Paul's Hearing before Festus, Agrippa, Bernice (25:13–26:32)

King Agrippa (25:13). This is Herod Agrippa II, whose full name was Marcus Julius Agrippa II (AD 27–93). He was the son of Agrippa I, who had executed James (Acts 12:1–2), and the great-grandson of Herod the Great (Matt. 2:1; Luke 1:5). Agrippa was only seventeen when his father died, and so Judea and Samaria were given over to rule by Roman governors. Gradually, Agrippa was awarded various territories by the emperors Claudius and Nero, including portions of Galilee and Perea, but his authority was never as extensive as that of his father or great-grandfather.[79] Like his father, Agrippa was thoroughly supportive of his Roman patrons but also an advocate for Jewish culture and religion. He tried unsuccessfully to prevent the Jewish Revolt of AD 66–73. There were pervasive rumors that Agrippa had an incestuous relationship with his sister Bernice (see additional comments on Acts 25:13 below).[80]

Bernice (25:13). Bernice was a daughter of King Agrippa I, younger sister of Agrippa II (by one year) and older sister of Drusilla (Acts 24:24). After her first husband died (Marcus Julius Alexander), Bernice married her uncle, Herod of Chalcis, who also died four years later. To quell rumors of an incestuous affair with her brother, she married Polemo of Cilicia, but soon left him and returned to Agrippa.[81] Bernice, like her brother, tried unsuccessfully to stop the disastrous Jewish revolt that destroyed Jerusalem and the temple. She became the mistress of Titus, son of the emperor Vespasian and conqueror of Jerusalem, and returned to Rome after the destruction of

Jerusalem to be with him. The politics of Rome, however, prevented them from marrying.[82]

The Emperor . . . Caesar (25:21). The word translated as "emperor" is *sebastos,* meaning "revered, sovereign, august" (similar to "his/her majesty"). It is the Greek translation of the Latin *augustus,* the title conferred on Octavian by the Roman senate, "Caesar Augustus," as the first emperor of Rome. "Caesar" (Gk. *kaisar*) was originally the *cognomen* (family name [see comments on Acts 13:9]) of Julius Caesar but came to be used as a title for the emperors who followed. On the worship of emperors, see comments on Rev. 13:8.

The military commanders and prominent men of the city (25:23). Agrippa and Bernice are royalty, and so it is expected that they will be honored. The "military commanders" are likely the commanders or tribunes over the five Roman cohorts stationed at Caesarea. The "prominent men of the city" are civic leaders and elite citizens. See the article "The Roman Military."

I have brought him before . . . you, King Agrippa, so that . . . I may have something to write (25:26). Festus values Agrippa's knowledge of Judaism and hopes that Agrippa will help him prepare the case for Rome.

I consider myself fortunate, that it is before you, King Agrippa . . . you are very knowledgeable about all the Jewish customs and controversies (26:2–3). In common rhetorical fashion, Paul begins by praising the judge (*captatio benevolentiae*), though with much greater restraint than Tertullus (cf. 24:4, 10). Although it is uncertain how devoutly Agrippa lived as a Jew, like his father he was well aware of Jewish laws and traditions. He would also have stayed aware of theological controversies and new Jewish movements, such as the growing Christian community.

My way of life from my youth (26:4). See comments on Acts 22:3, where Paul refers to his training under Gamaliel in Jerusalem.

I lived as a Pharisee (26:5). Paul refers to his background as a Pharisee in Phil. 3:5 (cf. Gal. 1:14). On the beliefs of the Pharisees, see the article "Pharisees and Sadducees."

Why do any of you consider it incredible that God raises the dead? (26:8). Since the high priest and most of the ruling elite are Sadducees, who did not believe in the resurrection of the dead, Paul sees the need to make a case for the resurrection (cf. 1 Cor. 15:3–32).

Tried to make them blaspheme (26:11). Forcing a person to blaspheme their own god or perform defiling acts was a common means of religious persecution. In the days of the Maccabees, Antiochus Epiphanes sought to force Jews to perform defiling acts such as eating pork and leaving their sons uncircumcised.[83] Similarly, Pliny the Younger, the Roman governor of Bithynia in the second century, relates to the emperor Trajan that he would expose suspected Christians by requiring them to worship pagan gods and to curse Christ.[84]

I was traveling to Damascus (26:12). Paul's conversion is here narrated for a third time in Acts (cf. 9:1–30; 22:5–21).

A voice speaking to me in Aramaic (26:14). See comments on Acts 22:2. Jesus may have been speaking either Hebrew or Aramaic.

Kick against the goads (26:14). A goad is a spiked stick or prod used to drive animals. This saying was proverbial in classical Greek to express the futility of trying to escape one's destiny. In Euripides's Greek tragedy *The Bacchanals*, Dionysus says to Pentheus, "I would control my rage and sacrifice to them if I were you, rather then kick against the goad."[85]

Turn from darkness to light and from the power of Satan to God (26:18). Light and darkness were common metaphors in Judaism, early Christianity, and the Greco-Roman world for truth versus falsehood (see comments on Acts 13:10). Isaiah predicts that the Messiah would bring light to his people (Isa. 9:2–7) and to the gentiles (Isa. 42:6; 49:6; cf. Acts 13:47). Jesus calls himself the "light of the world" (John 8:12; 9:5) and calls on his followers to be the same (Matt. 5:14). Paul also frequently uses the metaphor (Rom. 13:12; 1 Cor. 4:5; 2 Cor. 4:4–6; 6:14; Eph. 5:8; 1 Thess. 5:5; cf. 1 Pet. 2:9; 1 John 2:9–10).

Saying nothing other than what the prophets and Moses said (26:22). "The prophets and Moses" is a shorthand way of referring to the Hebrew Scriptures (Luke 16:29, 31; 24:27, 44; John 1:45; Acts 28:23).

That the Messiah must suffer, and that, as the first to rise from the dead (26:23). On prophecy of the suffering of the Messiah, see comments on Acts 3:18 (cf. 17:3). Although others rose from the dead to normal mortal existence (revivifications: 1 Kings 17:17–24; Mark 5:22–43; Luke 7:11–15; John 11), Jesus was the first to rise from the dead in an imperishable, immortal body. He is the firstfruits of the final resurrection (1 Cor. 15:20; Col. 1:18).

You're out of your mind, Paul! (26:24). The ideas of the suffering Messiah and the bodily resurrection of the dead would have seemed crazy to a sophisticated Roman or Greek (cf. 1 Cor. 1:21–25).

Are you going to persuade me to become a Christian so easily? (26:28). It is unclear from the Greek text whether Agrippa's comment is an indicative ("You are so convincing that I might shortly convert") or a question ("Do you really think that you can so quickly convert me?"). The latter seems most likely. In either case, it likely is sarcastic.

From Caesarea to Malta: Storm and Shipwreck (27:1–44)

A centurion named Julius, of the Imperial Regiment (27:1). A Roman cohort or regiment (*speira*) was made up of approximately one thousand soldiers (see the article "The Roman Military"). Each had a number and a

Paul's Journey to Rome (Acts 27–28)

name. This one was called *Sebastos*, the Greek translation of the Latin *Augustus*, meaning "revered, august, imperial," and used of the emperor (see comments on Acts 25:21). Here it is an honorary title sometimes given to auxiliary cohorts. It could be translated as "Imperial" (CSB; NIV; NLT; CEB) or "Augustan" (NASB; ESV; NKJV).

A ship of Adramyttium (27:2). Adramyttium was a seaport in Mysia, on the northwest coast of Asia Minor. See the article "Shipping Practices in the First Century."

Aristarchus, a Macedonian of Thessalonica, was with us (27:2). The "us" includes Luke the author (see the introduction to the commentary on Acts). On Aristarchus, see comments on Acts 20:4.

We put in at Sidon (27:3). Sidon was in Phoenicia about seventy miles north of Caesarea Maritima.

Through the open sea off Cilicia and Pamphylia . . . Myra in Lycia (27:5). Cilicia, Pamphylia, and Lycia were provinces on the southern coast of Asia Minor (modern Turkey). Myra was the capital city of Lycia, whose port (Andriaca) was becoming increasingly important for grain shipments from Alexandria to Rome.

An Alexandrian ship (27:6). The group transfers from a smaller vessel to a large cargo ship from Alexandria, Egypt, carrying grain to Rome (27:38). Rome depended heavily on Egypt for its grain supply.[86] See the article "Shipping Practices in the First Century."

Sailing slowly for many days . . . arrived off Cnidus . . . the south side of Crete off Salmone . . . a place called Fair Havens (27:7–8). The wind from the west makes for very slow going, so at Cnidus (a city on a peninsula in southern Asia Minor between Cos and Rhodes) they turn south to catch the sheltered side of Crete. Passing by Salmone (on the eastern edge of the island), they finally reach Fair Havens, a harbor on the south coast of Crete near the town of Lasea.

Since the Day of Atonement was already over (27:9). The Greek here reads "the Fast" (*hē nēsteia* [cf. NRSV]), which refers to the Jewish Day of Atonement.[87] The holiday took place on the tenth of Tishri, equivalent to late September or early October. Romans considered sailing after mid-September dangerous, and sea travel ceased completely after mid-November (see the article "Shipping Practices in the First Century").[88]

Hoping somehow to reach Phoenix, a harbor on Crete facing the southwest and northwest, and to winter there (27:12). Phoenix was forty to fifty miles west of Fair Havens. Its exact location is unknown, though it is described by various ancient writers.[89]

A fierce wind called the "northeaster" (27:14). The "northeaster" is a dangerous high-velocity wind blowing from the northeast.[90] It likely came off of Mount Ida, an eight-thousand-foot peak on Crete. The wind blows Paul's ship south, away from Crete and the intended goal of Phoenix.

Under the shelter of a little island called Cauda . . . get control of the skiff . . . used ropes and tackle and girded the ship (27:16–17). A brief calm in the shelter of Cauda (today known as Gavdos) enables the crew to take emergency measures to try to keep the ship intact.

Fearing they would run aground on the Syrtis (27:17). These were dangerous shallows and shoals off the north coast of Africa west of Cyrene. They were a famous graveyard for ships.[91] Though the shoals are still several hundred miles away, the sailors begin to panic because the ship is out of control.

We were drifting in the Adriatic Sea (27:27). Today "Adriatic Sea" refers to the body of water between Italy and Greece (far north of where Paul's ship is). But in Roman times the term was used for a much larger area extending into the middle of the Mediterranean.[92]

They took soundings . . . dropped four anchors from the stern (27:28–29). Taking soundings involves throwing a line with a weight overboard to see how deep the water is. The anchors are to hold the ship in place until morning, when those on board can assess better how to come to shore without being dashed against the rocks. See the article "Shipping Practices in the First Century."

The soldiers' plan was to kill the prisoners (27:42). Soldiers would be held responsible and severely punished if their prisoners escaped (see comments on 12:19; 16:27).

From Malta to Rome (28:1–16)

The island was called Malta (28:1). Malta is about sixty miles south of Sicily. The island measures approximately eighteen miles at its longest point and eight miles at its widest point.

The local people (28:2). The Greek term (*barbaros*) sometimes is translated as "barbarian" (Col. 3:11), but it does not necessarily have negative connotations (translated as "barbarian" in Rom. 1:14 and as "foreigner" in 1 Cor. 14:11). It refers to someone who did not speak Greek or who was not culturally Hellenistic. The people of Malta were descendants of Phoenicians and spoke a Punic dialect, though some likely would have known Greek.

A viper . . . fastened itself on his hand (28:3). Although there are no poisonous snakes on Malta today, we do not know the conditions in the first century. Perhaps the snakes were gradually killed off by the islanders over the centuries (as in Ireland).[93]

This man, no doubt, is a murderer . . . justice has not allowed him to live (28:4). The word translated as "justice" (*dikē*) could be a general reference to divine retribution or "justice," but more likely it refers to Dikē, daughter of Zeus and Themis and the goddess of justice and moral order. She often is portrayed carrying scales. The islanders assume that Paul is being punished by the gods for some evil he has done.

The leading man of the island, named Publius (28:7). "Leading man" is an unusual title, meaning something like "first" or "preeminent" man. The title has been confirmed in first-century inscriptions from Malta.[94] It could refer to the procurator of the island or to a local officer under the authority of the procurator of Sicily.

After three months (28:11). The ship likely reached Malta at the end of October, so the three months would be November, December, and January (probably AD 59). The most dangerous winter weather had passed, but a trip in February was still risky.

An Alexandrian ship that had wintered at the island, with the Twin Gods as its figurehead (28:11). This likely was another grain ship from Alexandria heading to Rome. The Greek says that the ship had a figurehead "to the twins" (*dioskourois*), meaning the twin sons of Zeus, Castor and Pollux, who were viewed as helpers of sailors. They are also memorialized in the zodiac sign Gemini.

Syracuse (28:12). This prosperous city was located on the southeast shore of Sicily, about ninety miles north of Malta. Originally located on an island off the coast, the city spread to the mainland as it grew. It was the Roman capital of eastern Sicily. The three-day delay may have been a result of unloading or loading cargo or because of weather conditions.[95]

The Appian Way was a major road that led travelers into the city of Rome. Here remnants of it are visible. Paul certainly would have used this road in his travels to Rome.

Rhegium (28:13). This city was located on the southwest tip of the "boot" of Italy, about seventy-five miles from Syracuse. The port bordered on the Straits of Messina separating Italy from Sicily and across from the Sicilian city of Messina. Today it is known as Reggio di Calabria.

Puteoli (28:13). This major port city for grain shipments to Rome was located on the western coast of Italy about 130 miles southeast of Rome. It was known under the Greeks as Dicaearchia and today is Pozzuoli. Josephus refers to a Jewish population there,[96] which may help to explain the presence of a Christian community that welcomes Paul.

The Forum of Appius and the Three Taverns (28:15). Both of these are common stopping places on the Appian Way south of Rome. The former was a market town about forty-three miles from the city; the latter was about thirty miles away. Evidently two groups of Christians travel out from Rome, some meeting them at the first spot and some at the second.

When we entered Rome, Paul was allowed to live by himself (28:16). It is clear that Paul is not viewed as a dangerous prisoner, since he is placed under house arrest (28:30) and given a great deal of freedom. Yet he is still bound with a chain (28:20).

Paul in Rome (28:17–31)

He called together the leaders of the Jews (28:17). Despite the earlier expulsion under Claudius (see comments on Acts 18:2), there was a large Jewish population in Rome, numbering anywhere from twenty to fifty thousand (Rome had a total population of about one million). We know of at least eleven synagogues.[97] Philo says that the Jews mostly lived together on the opposite side of the Tiber River.[98]

People everywhere are speaking against this sect (28:22). Rome itself had experienced riots between Jews and Jewish Christians (see comments on Acts 18:2), and reports of other disturbances have reached the Jews in Rome.

Paul stayed two whole years in his own rented house (28:30). The dates are approximately AD 60–62. The Greek phrase translated as "in his own rented a house" (*en idiō misthōmati*) could also be interpreted as "at his own expense" (NRSV; NLT; cf. Acts 20:34). In either case, his accommodations probably were not a house per se, but rather a small apartment in a crowded, multistory tenement building known as an *insula*. Housing in Rome was extremely expensive and far from luxurious. The masses lived in general squalor.[99]

Proclaiming the kingdom of God (28:31). See comments on Acts 1:3.

Romans

C. Marvin Pate

Introduction. No modern scholar questions that Paul was the author of Romans. Moreover, many interpreters believe that the key to Paul's theology is the overlapping of the two ages: the age to come has already dawned with the first coming of Christ, but it will not be complete until the second coming of Christ. Such theology shows up in Romans. The vast majority of scholars believe that Paul wrote Romans between AD 55 and 58, from the city of Corinth on his third missionary journey.

It is clear from Romans itself that the recipients of the letter are both Jewish and gentile Christians, for both groups are addressed throughout the document (1:1–16; 2:1–3:20; 9–11; 14:1–15:13). Most likely the churches at Rome were founded by Roman Jews who were converted to Christianity in Jerusalem on the day of Pentecost (Acts 2), who then returned home to the synagogues in Rome with their newly found faith in Jesus the Messiah. It is also a very likely scenario that those Jewish Christians led to Christ the gentile God-fearers who worshiped in their synagogues. The God-fearers were gentiles who came to believe in the one true God of Israel but did not submit to circumcision or the whole of the law of Moses.[1]

Claudius, the Roman emperor during AD 41–54, expelled the Jews from Rome.

So somewhere between AD 30 and 55 Christianity became established in Rome, probably meeting in as many as five house and tenement churches, according to 16:5, 10, 11, 14, 15, and with an attendance of perhaps a few hundred (a large house church could accommodate fifty people for worship). One could see from this how the Roman believers could have become polarized into "weak" (possibly Jewish Christians) and "strong" (possibly gentile Christians) factions (see 14:1–15:13), since they met in various locations. Moreover, most scholars today think that the gentile Christian element in the house churches became dominant when Jews (Jewish Christians included) were expelled from Rome in AD 49 by the emperor Claudius. Suetonius, an early second-century Roman historian, said that the Roman emperor expelled Jews from Rome at that time because they were squabbling over a man named *Chrestus*, probably a corruption of the Greek *Christos*—Christ.[2] No doubt Suetonius was referring to the debate between Jewish Christians and non-Christian Jews over whether Jesus was the Christ. Since Rome did not distinguish between Jewish Christians and non-Christian Jews but considered all of them Jews, Claudius kicked out the whole lot of them. But after Claudius's death in AD 54 Jews were allowed to return to Rome. At that time Jewish Christians came home to house or tenement churches now dominated by gentile Christians, making for a tense relationship between the two groups.

Although there continues to be much debate as to why Paul penned his magnificent Letter to the Romans, the apostle himself leaves the reader in no doubt as to its purpose: Paul was divinely called to lead the way in bringing about the end-time conversion of the nations, a mission in which the church at Rome was to play a critical role (see 1:1–15; 15:14–33; 16:25–27). Thus Rome was to be the last major stopping point before the apostle launched the final leg of his mission to Spain, the end of the then-known world (see 15:14–33).[3] But to garner the support of the Christians in Rome, the capital city of the Roman Empire, Paul had to accomplish two tasks. First, he had to motivate the Jewish and gentile Christians in Rome to start getting along again (see chaps. 9–11; 14–15); otherwise the church would not be unified enough to support him financially and spiritually in his Spanish mission. Second, even before that, Paul had to convince the Roman Christians that he was a legitimate apostle and therefore worthy of their support.

Introduction to Romans (1:1–17)

Paul, a servant of Christ Jesus, called as an apostle and set apart for the gospel of God (1:1). Acts 13:9 says that Saul was simultaneously called Paul, thus dispelling the common misconception that the apostle's name was changed from Saul to Paul at his conversion. It was normal in antiquity for Jews to have both Semitic and Roman names. A Roman citizen such as Paul had three names: a first name (*praenomen*), a family name (*nomen*),

The Location of Rome

and a surname (*cognomen*). Concerning the apostle, we only know the last of these: Paul.

Paul describes himself in three ways. First, he is a servant of Christ Jesus. By this he means that he is a slave (*doulos*) of Jesus Christ. Besides the demeaning connotation of *doulos*, Paul may have been alluding to the very positive OT "servant of Yahweh" tradition, which was applied to Israel (Neh. 1:6; Isa. 43:10), the prophets (2 Kings 9:7; 17:23), Moses (Josh. 14:7; 2 Kings 18:12), Joshua (Josh. 24:29), and others, and especially to the suffering servant in Isaiah (Isa. 42:1–9; 49:1–13; 50:4–11; 52:13–53:12). Second, Paul is called to be an apostle, which means that he has been accorded the status of the official twelve disciples. This is so even if Paul never knew the historical Jesus. What mattered was that Paul had met the resurrected Jesus (e.g., 1 Cor. 15:8; Gal. 1:15–18). There continues to be a debate among NT scholars as to whether "apostle" referred to the Jewish rabbinic institution of *shaliah*, whereby the decisions of the Sanhedrin (the ancient governing body of Israel; cf. the Knesset today) were announced throughout Israel by official representatives of the members of the Sanhedrin. These "sent ones" were to be treated as if they too were members of the Sanhedrin.[4] Third, Paul is set apart for the gospel of God. "Set apart" probably refers to Paul's divine call from birth to be an apostle of Christ, which was actualized on the Damascus road (see Gal. 1:15–18). The term "gospel" has its taproot in the promise of the good news of the end-time restoration of Israel so prominent in the book of Isaiah, especially chapters 40 and following (see, e.g., Isa. 40:9; 42:7; 60:6; 61:1 [cf. Luke 4:18]; cf. Joel 2:32; Nah. 1:15). Such a message of good news also included the conversion of the gentiles (see Isa. 45:15; 60:15–17; Mic. 4:13; cf. Rom. 9:25–27; 15:16–33). This is the gospel of "God" in Christ because it originated in the OT as the divine promise to Israel and is fulfilled in Jesus Christ, as Rom. 1:2–6 will show.

Which he promised beforehand through his prophets in the Holy Scriptures (1:2). There is a consensus among the commentators that "prophets" here refers to the whole of the OT, not just the prophets per se. Thus Paul is saying that the OT prophetically witnesses to the gospel of God.

Concerning his Son . . . descendant of David . . . appointed to be the powerful Son of God according to the spirit of holiness by the resurrection of the dead (1:3–4). The message of this christological piece is that in Jesus Christ the promised restoration of Israel is beginning to be fulfilled. Note the following four connections between verses 3–4 and the promise in Second Temple Jewish literature of the restoration of Israel:

Jesus Christ	Restoration of Israel
the "gospel" (Rom. 1:1–7)	the good news of the restoration of Israel (e.g., Isa. 40)
the Davidic Messiah (cf. Rom. 1:3 with Matt. 1:1–16; Luke 1:27, 32, 69; 2 Tim. 2:8; Rev. 5:5; 22:16)	the Davidic Messiah will restore Israel in the age to come (2 Sam. 7:12–16; Isa. 11:1, 10; Jer. 23:5–6; 30:9; 33:14–18; Ezek. 34:23–24; 37:24–25; *Psalms of Solomon* 17.21; *4QFlorilegium*)
the Son of God, the true/restored Israel (cf. Rom. 1:3–4 with Matt. 4:1–11; Luke 4:1–13)	Israel is the son of God (Exod. 4:22–23; Jer. 31:9; Hosea 11:1; Wis. 18:13; *Jubilees* 1.24–25; *Psalms of Solomon* 18.4)
the one raised from the dead (Rom. 1:4)	the future restoration of Israel is likened to the resurrection of the dead (Isa. 26:19; Ezek. 37:1–14)[5]

To bring about the obedience of faith for the sake of his name among all the Gentiles (1:5). The "obedience of faith" of the gentiles, I suggest, refers to the OT end-time promise that gentiles will convert to the one true God upon the restoration of Israel (see again Isa. 45:15; 60:15–17; Mic. 4:13; Rom. 9:25–27; 15:16–33), except that Paul reverses that order in 11:24–27, with Israel following the gentiles. Indeed, the eschatological conversion of the gentiles is the theme of verses 5–7 as a whole.

The Obedience of Faith of the Gentiles (1:8–15)

Your faith is being reported in all the world (1:8). The obedience of the faith—the end-time conversion of the gentiles—is occurring now, in three stages, according to 1:8–15: the evangelization of gentiles to the east of Rome (v. 8), in Rome (cf. v. 8 with vv. 9–10, 13–15), and to the west of Rome in Spain, the end of the then-known world (vv. 11–12). This is nothing less than the reversal of the twofold OT promise—from restoration of Israel to conversion of gentiles—that will be the catalyst for the restoration of Israel (cf. 1:13 with 11:25–27). The Tabula Peutingeriana, a third-century-AD map of the Roman Empire, reveals the eschatological genius behind Paul's plan to visit Spain for the purpose of preaching the gospel. That map shows that the ancients believed that Illyricum was a key stopping point on the way to Rome and that Rome was halfway to Spain, the end of the then-known world. If we compare this map with 1:8–15 and 15:19–29, we arrive at the logic behind Paul's passion to go to Spain: having just evangelized Illyricum (the area of modern Albania and former Yugoslavia), Paul now needed the Roman Christians' support to conduct his mission to Spain and thereby bring about the conversion of the remaining

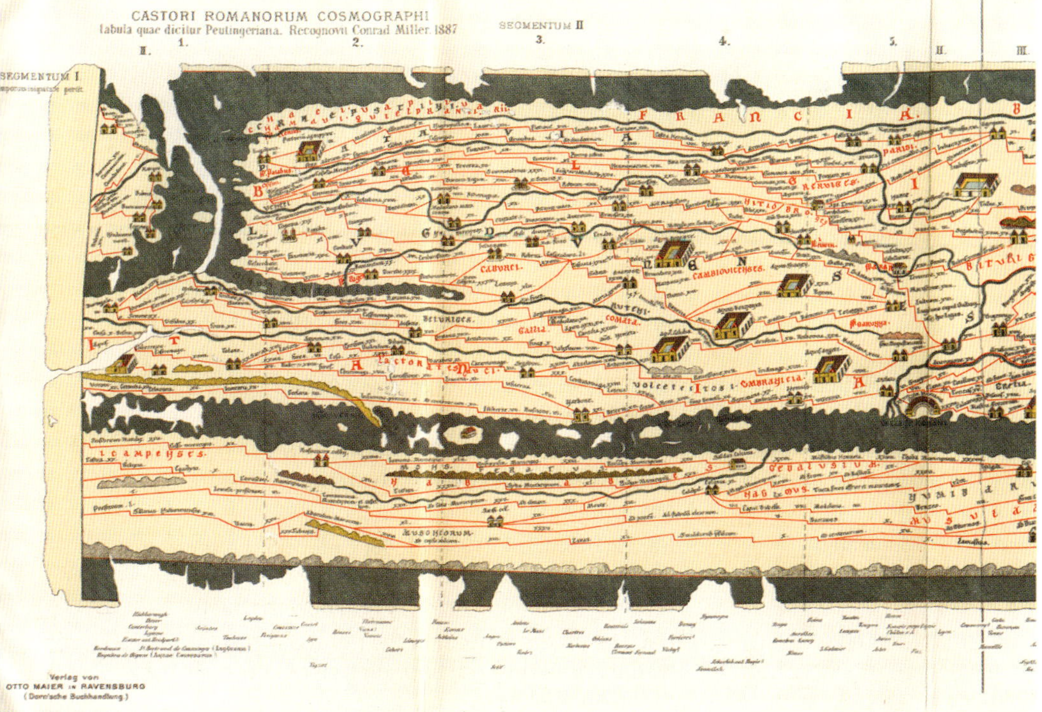

A portion of the *Tabula Peutingeriana*, an ancient road map of the Roman Empire.

gentiles. This was to bring in "the fullness of the Gentiles" right before the restoration of Israel (11:25–27). Robert Jewett puts it this way: "[Paul's] calling is to extend the gospel to the 'rest' of the Gentiles; a stunning sweeping scope whose rationale becomes clear when one realizes that Spain marked the end of the known world, the end of the 'circle' (Rom 15:19) of the known world that ran from Jerusalem through Illyricum and Rome to the Pillars of Hercules [the Strait of Gibraltar]."[6]

The Gospel of the Righteousness of God (1:16–17)

I am not ashamed of the gospel, because . . . *The righteous will live by faith* (1:16–17). A key point in the historical background of 1:16–17 is the story of Israel. That story unfolds in the OT in three stages: (1) Israel's sin of idolatry against Yahweh; (2) Israel's rejection of the prophets of Yahweh who called Israel to repentance and God's subsequent sending of Israel away into exile, first into Assyria in 721 BC and then to Babylonia in 587 BC; and (3) the promise of Israel's return/restoration to their homeland if, that is, they repent by turning back to God. It is the third point that weighs so heavily in the background of 1:16–17. The major key terms in 1:16–17 that tap into the OT promise of the restoration of Israel, especially Isaiah, are as follows:[7]

Rom. 1:16–17	Restoration of Israel (especially as recorded in Isaiah)
"not ashamed" (cf. 1:16 with 9:33; 10:11)	LXX Isa. 28:16 (in the sense that those who trust in the Lord will not be disappointed—i.e., will participate in Israel's restoration)
"gospel"	Isa. 40:9; 52:7; 61:1; LXX Isa. 60:6; Joel 2:32; Nah. 1:15 (the good news of Israel's return to their land)
"power"	Exod. 9:16; Ps. 77:14–15; 140:7 (God's saving action at the exodus, a motif applied to the return of Israel from exile in Isa. 43:2, 16–19; 52:10–12)
"salvation"	Isa. 12:2; 25:9; 46:13; 49:6; 52:7, 10 (God's deliverance of Israel from the exile)
"righteousness"	Isa. 51:5, 6, 8; Mic. 6:5; LXX Isa. 46:13; Mic. 7:9 (God's faithfulness to his covenant with Israel by restoring Israel to himself)
"revealed"	Isa. 22:14; 40:5; 43:12; 53:1; 56:1; 65:1 (in the sense that the restoration of Israel will reveal God's righteousness and his faithfulness to his covenant with Israel)
"faith"	Hab. 2:4 (in the sense that the righteous one is the one who trusts in the Lord to bring Israel out of exile back to their homeland)

The Universal Reign of Sin (1:18–3:20)

God's wrath is revealed from heaven against all godlessness (1:18). The various synonyms for truth and phrases to describe it throughout verses 18–32— "truth" (v. 18); "what can be known" (v. 19); "is evident among them" (v. 19); God's attributes of deity and power perceived in creation (v. 20); "knew God" but did not "glorify him" (v. 21); "exchanged the truth of God for a lie" (v. 25); "natural" (v. 26); "acknowledge" (v. 28); know God's "just sentence" (v. 32)—allude to the gentile Stoic concept of being in harmony with the divine being as well as to the commandments that God prescribed for the world to follow in his covenant with Noah after the flood (cf. Gen. 9:1–17; *Jubilees* 7.20; Acts 15:20–21, 29). This Noachian covenant with the world mirrors God's covenant with Israel and even overlaps with it as natural law overlaps with the Mosaic law.

Their women exchanged natural sexual relations for unnatural ones. The men in the same way also left natural relations with women and were inflamed in their lust for one another (1:26b–27). Most people in the Greco-Roman world would not have agreed with Paul's condemnation of homosexuality and lesbianism (see, e.g., Plato's *Symposium*, and note the pervasive approved practice of pederasty [adult males having sex with young boys]). Paul agreed with the OT and early Judaism that such a lifestyle was forbidden by God (see Gen. 19:1–28; Lev. 18:22; 20:13; Deut. 23:17–18; cf. Wis. 14:26; *Testament of Levi* 17.11; *Sibylline Oracles* 3.596–600).[8]

They are filled with all unrighteousness, evil, greed, and wickedness (1:29). Catalogues of vice were well known in the ancient world, particularly among the Stoics. They also were adopted in Judaism[9] and in early Christianity (e.g., Mark 7:21–22; 1 Cor. 5:10–11; 6:9–10; Gal. 5:19–21).[10]

Or do you despise the riches of his kindness, restraint, and patience, not recognizing that God's kindness is intended to lead you to repentance? (2:4). In the OT Israel labored under the assumption that their election as God's chosen people exempted them from divine judgment even if they sinned, a notion with which the prophets begged to disagree (e.g., Isa. 2:6–4:1; Jer. 2–35; Ezek. 1–24). Paul too rejects that notion in 2:1–11.

So, when Gentiles, who do not by nature have the law, do what the law demands . . . their consciences confirm this. Their competing thoughts either accuse or even excuse them on the day when God judges (2:14–16). Commentators of Romans have long noted the influence of the debating style known as the "diatribe" on 2:1–3:8, a style used by the ancient Greeks when debating. The diatribe consisted of three parts: (1) explicitly or implicitly addressing the opponent, (2) raising the opponents' criticisms, and then (3) answering those criticisms.[11] Paul employs the diatribe technique

The archaeological remains of the Forum of Caesar in Rome. Built around 46 BC, it was destroyed by fire and reconstructed several times through the third century AD. The columns typically supported a roofed portico area providing a place for public and private discourse.

precisely against the Jewish unbeliever in 2:1–3:20, specifically at three places (2:1–11; 2:17–25; 3:1–8). It is interesting by way of contrast that Paul does not use the diatribe style when dealing with the subject of the sinful status of gentiles in 1:19–32, here in 2:12–16, and in 2:26–29, presumably because his arguments therein would not precipitate any protest from gentiles.

"Conscience" (v. 15) was a Greek concept, especially the Stoic idea that the conscience is the moral mechanism within humans that convicts them of bad actions.[12] Hellenistic Judaism adopted this nuance in its usage of the term.[13] Paul refers to this negative aspect of "conscience" here (and in 1 Cor. 8:7, 10, 12; 1 Tim. 4:2; Titus 1:15), but elsewhere the conscience plays a positive role for Paul (Rom. 9:1; 2 Cor. 1:12; 1 Tim. 1:5, 19; 3:9; 2 Tim. 1:3).

Now if you call yourself a Jew, and rely on the law, and boast in God . . . having the embodiment of knowledge and truth in the law (2:17–20). Israel believed that their privileged possession of the law made them the teacher of gentiles and therefore superior to the gentiles or nations. Verses 17–20 draw upon the prevalent notion in early Judaism that the wisdom that the gentiles longed for was to be found in the Torah.[14]

You who boast in the law, do you dishonor God by breaking the law? (2:23). Paul picks up the diatribe style of argumentation again in 2:17–24, which focuses on the disingenuousness of the Jewish boast in the Torah. It is interesting that Stoic usage of the diatribe could also point out hypocritical boasts of fellow Stoics who were not actually following acceptable Stoic principles.[15]

On the contrary, a person is a Jew who is one inwardly, and circumcision is of the heart (2:29). "Circumcise your hearts" is a phrase used in the OT to express the longing that one day Israel will obey God from the heart; that is, Israel would inscribe the commandments on stone into their life (Deut. 10:16; 30:6; Jer. 4:4; 9:25–26; Ezek. 44:9).[16] Such a hope was connected with the arrival of the Holy Spirit and the new covenant (Jer. 31:31–34; Ezek. 36:26–27).

For no one will be justified in his sight by the works of the law, because the knowledge of sin comes through the law (3:20). In 3:9–20 Paul portrays the world as being on trial before God in the heavenly courtroom. The following outline unfolds the dramatic scene:

The charge: All are under sin (v. 9)

The evidence: The total depravity of humanity (vv. 10–18)

The verdict: All are guilty before God. No one will be justified in God's sight by the works of the law (implied because the law is itself under sin and therefore motivates disobedience rather than obedience) (vv. 19–20)

Justification by Faith (3:21–4:25)

God presented him as an atoning sacrifice . . . so that he would be righteous and declare righteous the one who has faith in Jesus (3:25–26). The basic background that informs Paul's language of sacrifice in 3:25–26, especially his choice of the word "atoning sacrifice" (*hilastērion* in v. 25), is the OT Day of Atonement.

If Abraham was justified by works, he has something to boast about . . . but to the one who does not work, but believes on him who declares the ungodly to be righteous, his faith is credited for righteousness (4:2–5). The following three points about Abraham help us grasp what Paul is saying in Rom. 4. First, Abraham was revered by Jews as the father of the Jewish race (Gen. 12–24; Ps. 105:6; Isa. 41:8). Second, Abraham was thought to obey the Torah in advance form and thereby was justified by his good works.[17] Third, in a number of ancient Jewish texts, Gen. 15:6 (Abraham believed God's promise that he would give him an innumerable seed and therefore God reckoned that Abraham was righteous) was interpreted through the lens of Gen. 17 (Abraham's institution of circumcision as an act of obedience

Paul uses the word "redemption" to describe the process by which slaves could be freed. This first-century-AD inscription from Thessalonica is a memorial to the freeing of a female slave by her mistress.

to God) or Gen. 22 (Abraham's offering up of Isaac) in order to show that Abraham was declared righteous because he obeyed the Torah in advance.[18] In Rom. 4 Paul begs to disagree with the second and third points above. Thus he denies that Abraham was justified by his works, and Paul severs Gen. 15:6 from either Gen. 17 or 22.

David also speaks of the blessing of the person to whom God credits righteousness apart from works: . . . *Blessed is the person the Lord will never charge with sin* (4:6–8). In verses 6–8 Paul the rabbi utilizes Rabbi Hillel's hermeneutical rule known as *gezerah shavah* (equal category) to make the controversial point that Abraham was a sinner and could therefore be justified before God only by faith. *Gezerah shavah* said that if the same key word occurs in two OT texts, then those two OT texts should be read as mutually interpretive. Thus in 4:6–8:

> Verse 3: "Abraham believed God, and it was credited [*logizomai*] to him for righteousness" (LXX Gen. 15:6)
>
> Verses 7–8: ". . . Blessed is the person the Lord will never charge [*logizomai*] with sin" (LXX Ps. 31:1–2 [ET 32:1–2])

Since the key word, *logizomai*, occurs in both Gen. 15:6 and Ps. 32:1–2, Paul, according to the principle of *gezerah shavah*, interprets Gen. 15:6 through the lens of Ps. 32:1–2 thus: what it means that Abraham was credited/counted righteous before God (Gen. 15:6) is that God did not credit/count against Abraham his sin (Ps. 32:1–2, speaking of God's forgiveness of David's sins of adultery and murder)!

For the promise to Abraham or to his descendants that he would inherit the world was not through the law, but through the

This ivory book cover (tenth to eleventh century AD) shows David dictating the psalms. Paul quotes David from Ps. 32 in Rom. 4 to make the point that God graciously forgives sins in Christ.

righteousness that comes by faith . . . because the law produces wrath (4:13–15). Paul contrasts two covenants in Rom. 4:

Abrahamic Covenant	Mosaic Covenant
4:1–5: Abraham was justified by faith.	The individual is saved by performing the works of the Torah.
4:6–8: Paul separates Gen. 15 from Gen. 17 and/or 22.	The Pentateuch and Second Temple Judaism combine Gen. 15 and Gen. 17 and/or 22.
4:9–12: Paul (like the OT prophets before him) maintains that there is discontinuity between the divine promise to Abraham that he will be the father of many nations and the divine command to Abraham to be circumcised.	The Pentateuch and Second Temple Judaism maintained that there is continuity between the divine promise to Abraham that he will be the father of many nations and the divine command to Abraham to be circumcised.
4:13–25: According to Paul, the law of Moses stirs up disobedience (vv. 13–17a), whereas the promise engenders faith and obedience (vv. 17b–25).	The law engenders obedience to God, the basis of the divine promise to Abraham.

The Assurace Provided by the Gospel: The Hope of Salvation (5:1–8:39)

Therefore, since we have been declared righteous by faith, we have peace with God through our Lord Jesus Christ (5:1). Romans 5:1–8:39 discusses the new-covenant blessings once promised to Israel that now belong to the members of the true church, those who are justified by faith. Regarding the blessing of peace, the covenant peace promised to Israel (Num. 6:22–27), especially in the new age of the new covenant (Isa. 9:6–7; 54:10; Ezek. 34:25–31; 37:26), now belongs to Christians.

And we rejoice in the hope of the glory of God . . . hope (5:2b–4). The hope of glory is the next blessing that belongs to Christians. This is the future restoration of the lost glory of Adam to Israel (1:21; 3:23), God's covenant people, but that now belongs to Christians (8:16–30) and is conditioned upon righteous suffering in this age.

God's love has been poured out in our hearts through the Holy Spirit who was given to us (5:5). God's faithful love demonstrated in his covenant with Israel now has devolved onto the church as is demonstrated by the indwelling of the Holy Spirit (cf. Isa. 32:15; 34:16; Ezek. 11:19; 36:26–27; Joel 2:28–32) and the death of Christ. This is the third new-covenant blessing that belongs to Christians, the first two being peace and glory.

Just as sin entered the world through one man, and death through sin, in this way death spread to all people, because all sinned . . . he is a type of the Coming One (5:12–14). This is the next new-covenant blessing in Christ: the new humanity in Christ is the new Adam.

How much more have the grace of God and the gift which comes through the grace of the one man Jesus Christ overflowed to the many (5:15). Paul uses the ancient rabbinic hermeneutical technique known as *qal wahomer*: if the lesser argument is true, then how much more so the greater argument is true. This technique occurs in chapter 5 in verses 9–10, 15, 17. Thus if Adam's sin affected the world, how much more Christ's obedience will affect the world.

How can we who died to sin still live in it? (6:2). The new dominion through union with Christ is the next new-covenant blessing belonging to Christians. Israel is still enslaved to sin and has, like Adam, lost its dominion over the earth (Gen. 1:26–28), but Christians have dominion over sin through their union with Christ.

Are you unaware that all of us who were baptized into Christ Jesus were baptized into his death? Therefore we were buried with him by baptism into death, in order that, just as Christ was raised from the dead by the glory of the Father, so we too may walk in newness of life (6:3–4). The major historical-cultural feature roughly contemporary with the NT that informs 6:1–14 was the practice of baptism as an entry rite into a religious community (see the article "Baptism in the New Testament World"). Some four religious groups required baptism of their new converts: rabbinic Judaism, the Dead Sea Scrolls community, John the Baptist and his disciples, and the Greco-Roman mystery religions. Most likely the origin of Paul's concept of baptism is his "in Christ" mysticism. "In Christ," or some similar wording, occurs 164 times in Paul's letters, signifying the believer's spiritual union with Christ.

Therefore do not let sin reign in your mortal body (6:12). The emphasis on obedience in verses 12–13 reminds one of a military setting (note the "weapons" in v. 13). Thus 6:12–13 (cf. vv. 4b, 6b, 11) probably draws on a familiar theme to early Jewish and Christian apocalyptic writers: the belief that at

Statue of Paul in the Basilica of St. Paul Outside the Walls in Rome.

the end of the ages the saints of God will wage war against the sons of evil.[19] What 6:12–13 thus presents is an internal, spiritual holy war between the dominion of sin and the kingdom of God, hence the injunction to Christians to align themselves with the forces of righteousness.

Don't you know that if you offer yourselves to someone as obedient slaves, you are slaves of that one you obey? (6:16). The primary background for this section is the ancient institution of slavery (see the article "Slavery in the New Testament World"). Tragically, slavery was a basic reality in Greco-Roman society, reaching its highest proportion in the first centuries BC and AD. Various estimates suggest that from one-fifth to one-third of the population was enslaved. The slave revolts in Italy and Sicily in the late republic confirm widespread social discontent at the time. Cato's account of slave labor in agriculture reveals a taskmaster mentality reminiscent of pre–Civil War slavery in the United States. Seneca relates that a proposal in the Roman senate that slaves be required to follow a distinctive dress code was defeated lest the slaves discover how numerous they were. Slavery was a despicable institution, devaluing the dignity of the human being. The legal status of a slave was that of a "thing." Aristotle defined a slave as "living property" and as a "living tool and the tool a lifeless slave."[20] In short, the slave was subject to the absolute power of his or her master.

A married woman is legally bound to her husband while he lives. But if her husband dies, she is released from the law regarding the husband (7:2). The next blessing of the new covenant is that the old dominion of sin brought about by the law over Israel is replaced by faith in Christ. Marriage and death as breaking the power of the law over Christians provide the background of 7:1–6. The main historical-cultural background for 7:1–12 is how the Jewish view of marriage differed from the Greco-Roman understanding of that institution. According to Jewish law, only the husband could divorce his wife in accordance with Deut. 24:1, and therefore the woman was bound to her husband as long as he lived, whereas in Roman law either mate could initiate divorce.[21] It is clear in 7:1–6 that the man holds all the cards in the marital relationship, for the woman is not free to remarry until her husband dies.

I would not have known what it is to covet if the law had not said, *Do not covet* (7:7b–11). Romans 7:7–11 is best understood in light of Gen. 2–3. The following chart highlights the parallels between the two passages:

Rom. 7:7–11	Gen. 2–3
7:7: "Do not covet"	3:1–6: Adam and Eve desired to be like God, thereby breaking the commandment of God not to eat of the tree of knowledge of good and evil.
7:8: Sin is personified	3:1–6: The serpent personifies sin.

Rom. 7:7–11	Gen. 2–3
7:9a: "I was alive apart from the law"	1:26–2:14: Only Adam and Eve were alive before the advent of the law, God's commandment to them not to eat from the forbidden tree (2:17).
7:9b–10: "I died"	2:17: God warns that if the couple eats from the tree of knowledge of good and evil, they will die (which happened).
7:11: "Sin . . . deceived [*exapataō*] me" (cf. 2 Cor. 11:3; 1 Tim. 2:14)	LXX Gen. 3:13: "The serpent deceived [*apataō*][22] me [Eve]."

I do not understand what I am doing, because I do not practice what I want to do, but I do what I hate (7:15). Romans 7:13–25 features the internal struggle to do good only to capitulate to evil. Thus Judaism had its duel of the two impulses.[23] So did the Greco-Roman writers. Thus Ovid writes, "I see and approve the better course, but I follow the worse."[24] And Epictetus writes, "Every sin involves a contradiction. For since he who sins does not wish to sin, but to be right, it is clear that he is not doing what he wishes."[25] Much further removed from Paul's understanding is the Platonic notion that the body is the prison of the soul, since the two are at war with each other.

The Spirit of life in Christ Jesus has set you free from the law of sin and death (8:2). The next to last new-covenant blessing that belongs to the Christian is the indwelling of the Holy Spirit, the sign above all signs that the age to come has dawned (8:1–17). Second Temple Judaism bemoaned the fact that God's presence, or Spirit, had departed from Israel. And it longed for the fulfillment of Joel's prophecy of the return of God's Spirit in the end times (Joel 2:28–29). Paul uses the term "Spirit" twenty-one times in chapter 8, signifying that Joel's prophecy had now come true. Jesus is the long-awaited Messiah, who has poured out the Holy Spirit upon the church thereby inaugurating the age to come (Acts 2:1–36). The OT also associated the coming of the Holy Spirit with the new covenant (e.g., Jer. 31:31–34; Ezek. 36:26–28). It is no surprise, then, that 8:1–17 is chock-full of the blessings of the Spirit to gentiles no less, because they have accepted Jesus as the Christ.

You received the Spirit of adoption, by whom we cry out, "*Abba*, Father!" (8:15). Above all, the Holy Spirit makes the believer a child of God. The background of "adoption" is twofold. According to Roman custom, the father could legally adopt a boy outside the father's family as a son. And then, when the boy reached the age of thirteen or fourteen, the father would bequeath to his adopted son the father's inheritance. Moreover, although adoption as a legal act was not a Jewish institution, Jews still engaged in the practice of raising others' children and treating them as their own (Gen.

15:2–4; Esther 2:7; cf. Exod. 2:10). But even more important is the fact that Israel was adopted as God's son in the OT (Exod. 4:22; Jer. 3:19; 31:9; Hosea 11:1). This background may be the nearest influence on 8:15. Furthermore, Jesus through the Holy Spirit enables believers to address God as their "Abba, Father" (Mark 14:36; Gal. 4:6).

At age forty-six Tiberius was adopted by Augustus as his son and therefore as his legitimate heir. This bronze bust of Tiberius was created to commemorate that event, which took place in AD 4. Tiberius became emperor after the death of Augustus and ruled during the time of Christ, AD 14–37.

The sufferings of this present time are not worth comparing with the glory that is going to be revealed to us (8:18). The last blessing of the new covenant is the glorious resurrection body in the new creation, but which is predicated on suffering for Christ in the present. Verses 17–18 and 28–30, preoccupied with the themes of suffering and glory as they are, form an *inclusio* or bracket around this passage. Suffering and glory combined to form a prominent notion in Jewish apocalyptic writers who believed that the suffering of the people of God in the present age would bring them glory in the age to come.[26] Yet for Paul, as for the early Christians, the relationship between suffering and glory was no longer consecutive (the one would lead to the other) but rather was dialectical (the one is intermingled with the other). Because of the death and resurrection of Christ, the glory of the age to come has broken into this age of suffering. Thus the two are intertwined in the Christian's life, as 8:17–18 makes clear. Romans 8:28–30 presents the same pattern: divine glory is the present possession of the believer, but it coexists with suffering.

Who can bring an accusation against God's elect? (8:33–34). Four juridical terms occur in verses 33–34. "Bring an accusation" is used of Paul's court trials (Acts 19:38, 40; 23:29, 38; 26:2, 7). "Justifies" is obviously a juridical term, as is "condemn." "Intercedes" is used in Heb. 7:25 of Christ's high priestly intercession for his followers. The term is also used of the Spirit's intercession for believers (Rom. 8:27).

Who can separate us from the love of Christ? (8:35–37). The main background of these verses is the affliction list in verse 35. Wolfgang Schrage has examined Paul's affliction texts from an eschatological point of view.[27] Schrage analyzes the Pauline affliction lists (esp. Rom. 8:17–18; 2 Cor. 4:7–16; 6:3–10; 11:23–29; Phil. 3:10–11) in light of Jewish apocalypticism and finds at least two major comparisons, each of which has been transformed by the Christ event. First, the paradoxical structure of Paul's affliction texts (suffering/glory; death/life; afflictions/deliverance) is the result of the modification of the two-age structure of Jewish apocalypticism[28] by the death and resurrection of Christ. That is, the age to come has broken into this present age. Second, the suffering that Paul and all Christians experience is none other than the messianic woes that Jewish apocalypticism expected would immediately precede the appearance of the Messiah,[29] though Paul believes that Jesus's resurrection has brought eschatological comfort and joy into the midst of such affliction. Thus the "already" (hope and joy) but "not yet" (messianic woes) eschatological tension initiated by the Christ event becomes the very foundation of Paul's concept of suffering.

The Problem of Israel (9:1–11:36)

Israelites (9:4). The Deuteronomic tradition is the key background to Rom. 9–11 as a whole. The application of the sixfold description of that tradition to chapters 9–11 is as follows:[30] (1) Israel has been disobedient to the law of God throughout their history (9:31; 10:21; cf. 2:1–29); (2–3) God has sent his prophets to call Israel to repentance, but Israel has repeatedly rejected them, including Paul himself (11:2–5; 10:16; cf. 15:31); (4) the Deuteronomic curses now rest on Israel in the form of foreign oppression (9:1–3; 10:3; 11:1, 5, 10, 16–25; cf. 2:6–8; 3:5); (5) it is still possible for Israel to repent (9:22; 10:16, 19; 11:11, 14; cf. 2:4–5); and (6) one day Israel will indeed repent and be restored (11:26–27).

Not all who are descended from Israel are Israel (9:6b). In 9:6–29 Paul draws on the concept of the remnant, which runs throughout Scripture. Although appearing in a wide variety of contexts, the central idea of the remnant concept or remnant theology is that in the midst of seemingly total apostasy and the consequential terrible judgment and/or destruction, God always has a small, faithful group that he has delivered and worked through to bring blessing.

I can testify about them that they have zeal for God, but not according to knowledge (10:2). Paul's mention of the word "zeal" here regarding Israel's commitment to the Torah taps into a storied tradition in the OT in Second Temple Judaism. The classic exemplars of such zeal were those who were prepared to use the sword to maintain Israel's commitment to the Torah and purity as expressed by being set apart from gentiles as God's covenant people: Simeon and Levi (Jdt. 9:4; *Jubilees* 30.5–20, referring to Gen. 34), Phinehas (Num. 25:10–13; Sir. 45:23–24; 1 Macc. 2:54; 4 Macc. 18:12), Elijah (Sir. 48:2; 1 Macc. 2:58), Mattathias (1 Macc. 2:19–26; Josephus, *Jewish Antiquities* 12.271), and, once upon a time, Saul/Paul (Acts 9:1–4; Gal. 1:13–14; Phil. 3:4b–6), not to mention the Zealot movement, which incited Israel to revolt against Rome in AD 66. "Zeal for the law" became the watch cry of the Maccabean Revolt against Antiochus Epiphanes (164–171 BC).[31] Similarly, zeal for the ordinances (of the law) became the slogan of the Essenes.[32]

But the righteousness that comes by faith speaks like this (10:6). Many commentators argue that 10:6–8 plays off of a prized equation in Second Temple Judaism: God's wisdom is embodied in the Torah.[33] The upshot of Paul's argument in 10:6–8 is that Christ is the wisdom of God who has replaced the law as the means to God's righteousness.[34]

But to Israel he says, *All day long I have held out my hands to a disobedient and defiant people* (10:21). Once again the key background to a Romans passage is the Deuteronomic tradition (see comments on Rom. 9:4). Such an OT setting heavily influences 10:14–21. Thus: (1) God sent his prophets to call Israel to repentance (10:14–15, 18); (2) but Israel persisted in the sin of unbelief (10:16, 18, 21); (3) God therefore judged Israel by sending the nation into exile—the covenant curses (compare 10:16, 18, 21 with the exilic setting of Isa. 52:7; 53:1; compare the prophecy of Deut. 32:21); (4) but if Israel repents, God will restore the nation (Isa. 52:7), yet it is the gentiles who repent that are being restored to God (the covenant blessings) (Isa. 65:1; cf. Deut. 32:21).

***I have left seven thousand for myself who have not bowed down to Baal.* In the same way, then, there is also at the present time a remnant chosen by grace** (11:4–5). The OT background idea here is from 1 Kings 18–19, when Israel forsook their God and worshiped Baal, the chief god of the Canaanites. After killing the prophets of Baal on Mount Carmel, Elijah the prophet of God fled for his life all the way to the Sinai Desert. There, God revealed to Elijah that he was not the only prophet of Yahweh left. Rather, seven thousand of God's people were still faithful to him. This is the beginning in the OT of the concept of remnant. Paul then applies the idea of the remnant to the Jewish Christians in his own day.

One way to grasp the idea of the remnant as it unfolds throughout the Bible is to use an hourglass illustration. God created the world to have fellowship with him, only to have his creation spurn that offer. To rectify this problem, God then called Abraham out from paganism in order that he might make of him a new people, Israel, to worship God and declare him to the nations. However,

This inscription from the first century AD forbids gentiles from moving beyond the Court of Gentiles into the temple area.

Israel in time disobeyed God's law just as the nations of the world had disobeyed God by worshiping other gods. Nevertheless, the purpose of God was not thereby thwarted, for God raised up for himself a remnant, a faithful few who remained true to Yahweh—for example, Elijah and the later returnees to Israel. However, by the end of the OT the hopes of Israel now rested upon one individual, the Messiah, who would turn the hearts of Jews back to God and convert the nations of the earth to the one true God. As it turns out, then, Israel's rejection of God throughout the OT actually carried along the plan of God as it narrowed its focus, culminating in the expectation of the one Messiah. But with the advent of Jesus Christ, the focus of God now widened, beginning with the apostles (the beginnings of the remnant in the NT), expanding to include the church (the replacement of Israel, however temporary that may be), and one day encompassing the world (which will bring the revelation of God full circle).

The grafting of an olive tree on the Mediterranean island of Mallorca.

If some of the branches were broken off, and you, though a wild olive branch, were grafted in among them and have come to share in the rich root (11:17). The key background material that sheds light on 11:11–24 is that of horticultural practices. Paul's argument in verses 11–24 presumes that the olive tree is the one people of God, with the patriarchs making up the root/stump of the tree. Jews are the natural branches of that tree that have been broken off because of unbelief. Gentile Christians are the wild branches grafted into the tree. Normally the opposite occurs in horticulture: a healthy, productive branch is grafted into a wild, unproductive tree to bring health to it. But Paul's reversal of that process—a wild or uncultivated branch is grafted into a healthy tree—is attested in Israel.[35] Second, Paul's condemnation of anti-Semitism in verses 11–24 was for good reason: anti-Semitism was widespread in his day (and in ours).

I don't want you to be ignorant of this mystery (11:25). The definition of "mystery" comes from Jewish apocalyptic circles: a mystery is an end-time event that God reveals to the prophetic seer.[36] This background, rather than a connection with ancient "mystery religions," informs Paul's use of the term "mystery" (Rom. 16:25–26; 1 Cor. 15:51–52). The mystery in 11:25–27 is that Israel's spiritual hard-heartedness is the occasion for the conversion of the gentiles, after which Israel will be restored to God by embracing Jesus the Messiah.

Oh, the depth of the riches both of the wisdom and of the knowledge of God! How unsearchable his judgments and untraceable his ways! (11:33). This verse is rooted in Jewish apocalypticism. Thus, for example, *2 Baruch* 14.8–9 raises similar questions as Paul does in verse 33 with regard to the destiny of God's people during their exile.[37] Moreover, the apocalyptic nuance of "mystery" (v. 25) continues to influence Paul in verse 33: the undiscoverable wisdom of God's salvation history has been revealed to Paul, the apocalyptic seer (cf. Dan. 2:20–23).

For who has known the mind of the Lord? Or who has been his counselor? And who has ever given to God, that he should be repaid? (11:34–35). Jewish wisdom traditions inform 11:33–35, particularly the notion that God's wisdom was revealed to Israel in the form of the Torah.[38] Whereas Isa. 40:13 and Job 41:3 (quoted here by Paul) were connected in rabbinic literature to say that Torah is God's preexistent wisdom,[39] Rom. 11:33–35 begs to disagree, arguing instead that the Torah is finished in God's plan of salvation (cf. Rom. 10:4) because Christ is God's preexistent wisdom (cf. Rom. 10:5–8).

For from him and through him and to him are all things. To him be the glory forever. Amen (11:36). This verse shares the language of Stoicism: "for from him and through him and to him are all things."[40] Hellenistic Judaism borrowed Stoic language in praise of the one true God.[41] Paul continues the Hellenistic Jewish pattern, except that he applies the language to God *and* Christ elsewhere (1 Cor. 8:6; Col. 1:16–17). Indeed, Paul probably applies that language to God and Christ here in 11:36.[42]

The Transforming Power of the Gospel: Christian Conduct (12:1–15:13)

Therefore, brothers and sisters, in view of the mercies of God, I urge you to present your bodies as a living sacrifice, holy and pleasing to God; this is your true worship (12:1–2). Rather than conform to this evil age begun by Adam that perverts worship of the Creator into worship of the creation and that ruins one's mind, Paul challenges Christians to worship God with a renewed mind. It is only reasonable that they worship God (cf. 12:1–2 with 1:21–25).[43] This Adam theology occurs in the context of the overlapping of the two ages:

Eschatology	this age	the age to come
Adam	the first Adam—catalyst for perverted worship	the last Adam (Jesus)—engenders true worship

As we have many parts in one body, and all the parts do not have the same function . . . one body in Christ (12:4–5). Paul's analogy of the body of Christ in 12:4–5 has been much discussed in terms of the background of that illustration (cf. 1 Cor. 12:12–28; Eph. 4:7–16; Col. 1:18). Two theories, however, dominate the discussion. First, W. D. Davies insightfully argues that the Jewish apocalyptic/rabbinic concept of the corporate body of Adam is the best antecedent to the notion of the universal body of Christ.[44] By this, Davies means that rabbis thought that Adam, as the representative of the human race, was cosmic in size. Such a cosmic or corporate body of Adam included all humanity. Second, A. J. M. Wedderburn proposes that the roots of the idea of the body of Christ stem from the ancient Hebrew mentality of corporate personality, the belief that one person represents many and many are incorporated into the one (e.g., Gen. 12:1–3; compare Gen. 14:17–20 with Josh. 7:16–26; Heb. 7:4–10).[45] This reciprocal relationship takes one a long way toward understanding the body of Christ, and it is commensurate with the Adamic theory that the first man is the representative of the fallen human race (Rom. 5:12–21). If so, we see that the church, the corporate body of Christ, is none other than the eschatological Adam (1 Cor. 15:45), the new humanity of the end time, which now has appeared in human history.

Bless those who persecute you; bless and do not curse (12:14). The main tradition informing this verse is Jesus's teachings in the Sermon on the Mount (on v. 14 see Matt. 5:44 // Luke 6:27–28; on vv. 17, 21 see Luke 6:27–36).

Let everyone submit to the governing authorities, since there is no authority except from God (13:1). The OT anticipates 13:1–7 in its recognition that no human ruler wields power except through God's appointment.[46] This applies to Israel's enemies, from Nebuchadnezzar (Dan. 4:17) to Cyrus (Isa. 45:1). Even in Paul's day Jews prayed and sacrificed to God on behalf of the Roman emperor.

For this reason you pay taxes, since the authorities are God's servants, continually attending to these tasks. Pay your obligations to everyone: taxes to those you owe taxes, tolls to those you owe tolls (13:6–7). Here Paul uses two words for taxes found in extrabiblical documents: *phoros* and *telos*.[47] The former item corresponds to the Latin term *tributum*, while the latter corresponds to *vectigalia*. *Tributum* refers to the Roman direct tax, which included property and poll taxes. *Vectigalia* refers to the

Romans coins often featured the face of a Roman emperor.

indirect tax, which covered customs, duties, toll taxes, and fees for various services. We know from the Roman historian Tacitus that the masses reached a boiling point in AD 58 over exorbitant tax rates.[48] So much so that Emperor Nero considered dropping the indirect tax but decided against doing so. So Paul here tries to keep Christians out of the debate by encouraging them to pay their taxes.

This Roman *sestertius* coin shows the image of the emperor Nero. The emperor controlled the imperial treasury, which paid all the expenses associated with administering and controlling the imperial provinces. Paul instructs his readers to pay their taxes (Rom. 13:6–7).

The one who loves another has fulfilled the law (13:8). Jesus's reduction of the law to loving God and one's neighbor informs Paul's command to love others in 13:8–10, based on Lev. 19:18 (cf. Mark 12:29–31; Matt. 22:37–39; Luke 10:27–28).

You know the time, it is already the hour for you to wake up from sleep, because now our salvation is nearer than when we first believed (13:11). Three traditions inform Paul's ethic and eschatology in verses 8–14. First, Paul's language of taking off and putting on clothing is thought by many to allude to early Christian baptism.[49] Second, verses 11–14 are thoroughly immersed in Jewish apocalypticism.[50] More specifically, verses 11–14 attest to the overlapping of the two ages in Paul's theology. Verses 11–12a emphasize that, by virtue of the Christ-event, the age to come has drawn near and, with it, the salvation of believers. However, the salvific message of verses 11–12a occurs in the context of this present age; hence Paul's emphasis in verses 12b–14 on the necessity for Christians to live holy lives. Third, Paul singles out for condemnation in verse 13 the infamous Roman banquets that turned into drunken orgies. Petronius's *Satyricon* vividly illustrates how ancient Roman banquets were characterized by overindulgence in food and drink, and how quickly they turned into sexual orgies and even violence. Petronius was Nero's advisor in matters of luxury and extravagance. As befitted his office, Petronius slept by day and partied at night, behavior that Nero took to. But Petronius fell into disfavor with Nero and was forced to commit suicide. However, before his death Petronius, in his will, lampooned Nero, whose nighttime carousing matched the characters in his *Satyricon*. Paul no doubt had heard about the Roman propensity of excess and warned the Roman Christians not to associate themselves with such debauchery.

Accept anyone who is weak in faith . . . we who are strong have an obligation to bear the weaknesses of those without strength, and not to please ourselves (14:1; 15:1). The key is the identification of the strong and the weak in faith. It seems that the "weak" were mainly Jewish Christians who refrained from certain kinds of food and observed certain days out of continuing loyalty to the Mosaic law, while the "strong" were mainly gentile Christians who felt no obligation to adhere to the diet and holy days of the week.

For whatever was written in the past was written for our instruction, so that we may have hope through endurance and through the encouragement from the Scriptures (15:4). The OT prophecies of the coming new covenant are the key background for grasping 15:1–13.[51] Such a background explains the following terms: "encouragement," "hope," "truth," "mercy," "promises" to the "fathers," along with the catena of the OT texts that Paul quotes in verses 9–12. As such, these terms emphasize the hope that Christians have in Christ not only in this life but also in the life to come.

The Letter Closing (15:14–16:27)

Serving as a priest of the gospel of God. My purpose is that the Gentiles may be an acceptable offering, sanctified by the Holy Spirit (15:16). The eschatological nature of Paul's apostleship (i.e., Paul's ministry to the gentiles is to bring about their end-time conversion) helps us understand this passage. More specifically, Paul hoped that when he brought the collection from the gentile churches to Jerusalem, then Israel would see this as the conversion of the nations that was expected to accompany the restoration of Israel. This collection was a major focus on Paul's third missionary journey (1 Cor. 16:1–2; 2 Cor. 8–9).[52] On that journey Paul took up a collection of money from the Roman provinces of Macedonia (modern northern Greece, Macedonia, and southern Albania/Macedonia) and Achaia (the bulk of modern Greece). Pauline churches included in those provinces were the congregations at Philippi, Thessalonica, Berea, and Corinth.

Whenever I travel to Spain (15:24). Paul planned to evangelize Spain. Why Spain? Three reasons. First, Spain was the westernmost edge of the then-known world, completing the arc of evangelization for Paul beginning in Jerusalem, moving to Illyricum and hopefully Rome and then to Spain. Second, Spain was populated by gentiles, not Jews.[53] Third, combining the previous two points, Paul likely understood Spain to be the Tarshish of Isa. 66:19: only when he brought Christian representatives from Spain (15:16, 24) as part of his collection enterprise (15:25–27) will the "full number" of the gentiles come in (cf. 11:25 with 15:19, 29) and the grand finale of 11:25–27 unfold.[54] Related to this is the probability that Paul's gentile collection for the Jewish Christians at Jerusalem stretching all the way to Spain, the end of the world, would fulfill the Jewish expectation that the wealth of the nations would flow into Jerusalem at the end of history in association with Israel's restoration.[55] This, for Paul, hopefully would stir Israel to jealousy to accept Jesus as their Messiah (11:13–14) and thus trigger the parousia.[56] In conclusion, although Paul's letters do not mention his visit to Spain, the late first-century document *1 Clement* (5.7) says that he did go there.

The road to the harbor in Cenchreae.

Pray that I may be rescued from the unbelievers in Judea, that my ministry to Jerusalem may be acceptable to the saints (15:31). The focus here is the nature of Paul's opposition, the "unbelievers in Judea." Quite possibly, we may identify these opponents as Palestinian Zealots pressuring Judaizers (professing Jewish Christians) to enforce the whole Torah on Jew and gentile alike, which collided with Paul's law-free gospel. This mentality ultimately fueled the Jewish Revolt against Rome of AD 66–73.

Phoebe . . . has been a benefactor of many—and of me also (16:1–2). It is widely agreed that the word "benefactor" that describes Phoebe's role here is a technical term for "patron." A patron was a wealthy person from the upper class of Roman society who gave of personal means to a cause for a city or people—civic buildings, humanitarian efforts, religious causes. In return, the recipients of such benefaction would dedicate the building to that patron in thanks for the contribution.[57] Both men and women functioned as patrons in the Roman world.[58] It is clear from this that Phoebe was a patron of Paul and, as he says, "of many" others.

Give my greetings to Prisca and Aquila, my coworkers in Christ Jesus, who risked their own necks for my life. Not only do I thank them, but so do all the Gentile churches. Greet also the church that meets in their home (16:3–5). Romans 16:3–16 provides a wealth of information about first-century Christianity in Rome, particularly how socioeconomics intersected with the house church. We can classify the thirty-six names mentioned in verses 3–16 in this way: Paul was a nonwealthy, freeborn Roman citizen, and Rufus probably was too; Phoebe and Prisca (Priscilla) were wealthy (patrons) freeborn Roman citizens; all the rest were either slaves or freedmen, including Aquila. It seems difficult to distinguish whether these names were those of slaves or freedmen, but either way they were at the lowest rungs of Roman society.[59] This evidence does seem to confirm what NT scholars have said for years: early Christianity was a movement mainly of the lower classes of Roman society, though there were important exceptions. Robert Jewett has provided a masterful analysis of the five congregations in first-century Rome to which Paul wrote, showing that only Priscilla and Aquila's worship place was located in the wealthier section of Rome; the other four were tenement churches located in the poorer sections of Rome. These were apartment complexes located above businesses.

Such people do not serve our Lord Christ but their own appetites . . . the God of peace will soon crush Satan under your feet (16:18–20). The false teachers Paul has in mind in verses 17–19 most likely were the Judaizers. There is an OT background to verse 20—"the God of peace will soon crush Satan under your feet"—which is Gen. 3:15. Genesis 3:15 is the protoevangelium—the first occurrence of the gospel. There, God promises that the seed of the woman will crush the head of the serpent. This promise of Gen. 3:15 becomes in Judaism and Christianity apocalyptic in orientation: the Messiah will come and crush Satan in the end times.[60] For Paul, Jesus is the Messiah, and he will soon crush Satan at the parousia.

I Tertius, who wrote this letter, greet you in the Lord (16:22). Romans 16:22 records that Paul used a secretary (amanuensis) to write down the Letter to the Romans (see the article "Ancient Letter Writing"). Tertius was a professional scribe (probably paid for by Phoebe). In the Roman Empire aristocrats would buy or hire amanuenses to write letters on their behalf. Like secretaries today, amanuenses had varying levels of skill, education, and political power. Some were like what we would now call "temps," offering their handwriting to whoever would pay for it. Others became very important figures in noble households, overseeing the master's correspondence and possibly acting as an editor or advisor as well. Unlike secretaries today, scribes in ancient Rome generally were men, though there were some women among them.

According to the revelation of the mystery kept silent for long ages but now revealed and made known through the prophetic Scriptures (16:25–26). Paul's language in verses 25–26 about the mystery of old being revealed to him in the

The imagery that Paul uses of crushing adversaries under one's feet (Rom. 16:20) can be seen in this statue of Hadrian, Roman emperor from AD 117 to 138. Hadrian stands in victory (note the laurel wreath on his head) over an enemy of Rome with his foot on the back of a fallen barbarian.

prophetic writings is very similar to the interpretive approach commonly used by the members of the Dead Sea Scrolls community. They claimed that God revealed the mystery of the OT Scripture to the Teacher of Righteousness, who then founded the Essene community—the new-covenant community of the end times. This is very similar to Paul's belief that Christianity is the new-covenant community.

It was common for Roman aristocrats to hire a scribe or amanuensis to write letters on their behalf.

1 Corinthians

MARK E. TAYLOR

Introduction. Paul faced significant Jewish opposition to his preaching in his initial missionary work in Corinth (Acts 18:5–6) (see the article "The City of Corinth"). Many were converted, however, including Crispus, the synagogue ruler (Acts 18:7–8). Paul remained in Corinth for eighteen months (Acts 18:11). Apollos, who followed Paul in Corinth (Acts 18:27–19:1), is mentioned at numerous places in 1 Corinthians (1 Cor. 1:12; 3:4–6, 22; 4:6; 16:12). The membership of the church was predominantly gentile (1 Cor. 6:9–10; 12:1–3). Most Corinthian Christians were of low social status, but there were some persons of rank among them (1 Cor. 1:26–31).[1]

The Corinthian correspondence reveals a contentious relationship between Paul and his converts. According to 1 Corinthians, Paul received information about the church by way of oral reports (1:11; 5:1; 11:18) and through written correspondence from the Corinthians (7:1). In 5:9 Paul mentions a prior letter that he wrote to the Corinthians, which probably occasioned the Corinthians' letter to Paul mentioned in 7:1. First Corinthians is Paul's response both to what he had heard about the church and to the content of their letter to him, which likely contained both questions and challenges to his prior instruction. The letter to Paul probably was delivered to him in Ephesus by Stephanas, Fortunatus, and Achaicus (16:8, 17), and from Ephesus Paul wrote his response,

This inscription is a copy of a letter sent by the emperor Claudius in AD 52 to Lucius Junius Gallio, the proconsul of Achaia. From this, the date of Paul's visit to Corinth can be determined, since Acts 18:12 mentions that Paul was in Corinth during the time Gallio held this administrative office.

in the spring of either AD 54 or 55. Recent scholarship has suggested that Paul wrote the letter primarily out of concerns for the purity of the church and with the conviction that the Corinthian church played a vital role in fulfilling the OT expectation of the worldwide worship of the God of Israel.[2]

The Letter Opening: Salutation and Thanksgiving (1:1–9)

The letter opening conforms to a typical first-century letter-writing pattern, which generally included a salutation, identifying the sender and recipients, along with a greeting, followed by a routine prayer or thanksgiving for good health or prosperity (see the article "Ancient Letter Writing"). The letter opening of 1 Corinthians anticipates some of its main themes, such as the purity of the church (chaps. 5–7), the Corinthians' experience of the Spirit (chaps. 12–14), and the day of the Lord (chap. 15).

Paul . . . and Sosthenes our brother (1:1). The mention of a cosender of a letter was rare in antiquity.[3] Sosthenes may be the synagogue ruler mentioned in Acts 18:17. He may have served as Paul's scribe for the writing of the letter.[4]

Called as an apostle of Christ Jesus by God's will (1:1). Paul's language concerning apostleship resembles the divine call of the OT prophets (cf. Gal. 1:15 with Jer. 1:5). Some have argued that Paul's self-identification relates to a crisis of his authority in Corinth,[5] but others have suggested that his concern is suffering associated with apostleship in contrast to the arrogance of some in Corinth (see esp. 4:6–16).[6]

Church of God (1:2). The word translated as "church" denotes a political assembly in classical Greek and carries this sense in Acts 19:32, 39–40. In the Greek translation of the OT (Septuagint) the term describes the people of Israel (Deut. 4:10; 9:10; 18:16).

Sanctified . . . called as saints (1:2). Paul's language draws from the OT background of God's people as separated from the world (see Lev. 19:2; Exod. 19:5–6). The Corinthians' status as God's holy people matters more than their human social standing.

Every place (1:2). This echoes Mal. 1:11 and evokes a tradition going back to Deuteronomy, which contains repeated references to the place where the Lord would have people call upon his name (Deut. 12:11, 21, 26; 14:23–24; 16:2, 6; 17:8; 26:2). In the OT the place was Jerusalem, but Paul now envisions believers calling upon the name of the Lord everywhere (see 2 Cor. 2:14; 1 Thess. 1:8; 1 Tim. 2:8).[7]

Call on the name of Jesus Christ our Lord (1:2). To "call on the name of the Lord" is an OT expression for the worship of Yahweh (Ps. 99:6; Joel 2:32). In the OT "name" is synonymous with character (Exod. 3:13–14).

A bema, shown here, has been excavated at Corinth. This was the place where public speakers proclaimed and where judgments may have been carried out. During Paul's first stay in Corinth some Corinthian Jews brought him to this spot in hopes that the proconsul Gallio could rule against him. Gallio refused to judge the case (Acts 18:12–17).

Grace to you and peace (1:3). The combination "grace and peace" may echo the blessing uttered by the sons of Aaron over the Israelites in Num. 6:24–26.

Enriched in him in every way, in all speech and all knowledge (1:5). The ability to speak eloquently and the acquisition of knowledge for the sake of philosophical wisdom were highly esteemed by the elite in Corinth. The Corinthian church valued, yet abused, the spiritual gifts of speech and knowledge (8:1–13; 14:1–40). Being "enriched" (*ploutizō*) may have been a Corinthian self-perception, since Paul uses a related verb (*plouteō*) sarcastically in 4:8. Here Paul reminds them of the true source of their spiritual riches (see also 2 Cor. 6:10; 9:11).

The testimony about Christ was confirmed among you (1:6). In secular contexts the Greek verb for "confirm" (translated as "strengthen" in 1:8) was used in the sense of guaranteeing legal contracts, and Paul possibly uses the term here to underscore God's approval and pledge to the Corinthians.[8]

You do not lack any spiritual gift (1:7). The meaning may be that they did not lack in the gifts they had, not that they had every gift available. The gifts listed in chapters 12–14 are not comprehensive, since other gifts are mentioned in the NT (see Rom. 12:6–8, where Paul lists serving, teaching, encouraging, giving, leading, and showing mercy as gifts, and Eph. 4:11–12, which adds the offices of evangelists and pastors in addition to the offices of prophets, apostles, and teachers mentioned also in 1 Cor. 12:28).

Blameless (1:8). In Col. 1:22 the term "blameless" (*anenklētos*) is linked to the death of Jesus as the means of believers attaining this standing before God. Paul also uses the term to refer to the moral character of church leaders (1 Tim. 3:10; Titus 1:6).

God is faithful (1:9). The phrase reflects a common OT theme (see Deut. 7:9; Ps. 145:13; Isa. 49:7).

An Appeal to a Divided Church (1:10–17)

That all of you agree in what you say (1:10). This phrase reflects political discourse used to promote unity.[9] Corinthian divisions were likely social in nature rather than theological (see 11:17–24).

It has been reported to me . . . by members of Chloe's people (1:11). The ancient household extended beyond the immediate family to include slaves and those who acted on behalf of the head of household as business agents. Since Paul writes from Ephesus, Chloe may have been a wealthy Asian with business interests that required her representatives to travel to Corinth.

I belong to Paul . . . Apollos . . . Cephas . . . Christ (1:12). Paul's description of the divisions may be a rhetorical flourish intended to describe church members' childish behavior rather than a precise description of four factions in Corinth.[10] Only Paul and Apollos figure prominently in the argument that follows (3:4–9; 4:6), and it is uncertain whether Cephas ever visited Corinth.[11] Some may have rallied around Apollos because of his rhetorical skills (see Acts 18:24).

Crispus . . . Gaius . . . Stephanas (1:14–16). Crispus probably is the synagogue ruler mentioned in Acts 18:8. In Rom. 16:23 Paul sends greetings to the Roman church from Gaius and commends him for his hospitality (see the article "Hospitality in the New Testament World"). Stephanas was among the first converts in Corinth and was part of the delegation sent to Paul in Ephesus by the Corinthians (16:17). All three men named here probably were wealthy and prominent people in the community. These three were among the few whom Paul personally baptized in Corinth (see the article "Baptism in the New Testament World").[12]

Not with eloquent wisdom (1:17). "Eloquent wisdom" translates a phrase that refers to the sophisticated and cultured speech of those with high status.[13] Some in Corinth sought to enhance their status by association with wise speakers, called Sophists,[14] thus stoking competing rivalries.

God's Wisdom and a Crucified Messiah (1:18–25)

For the word of the cross is foolishness (1:18). The contrast between wisdom and folly was common among the ancient philosophers. Judaism often personified divine Wisdom. Wisdom, in this context, is closely associated with a value system that associated sophisticated speech with social status (cf. 1:17; 2:1, 4, 13).

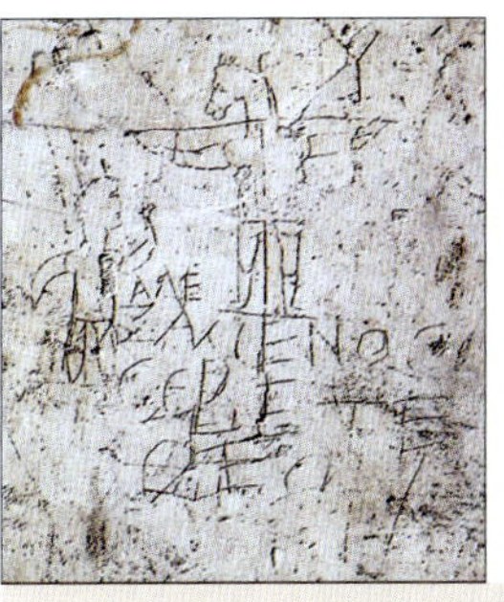

"The word of the cross is foolishness to those who are perishing" (1 Cor. 1:18). A drawing etched into some plaster was found on the Palatine Hill in Rome. It depicts a person with the head of a donkey hanging on a cross. To the left, another person stands with upraised arms. The Greek inscription reads, "Alexamenos worships [his] god." It is thought to be a caricature of a Christian worshiping a crucified god (ca. AD 225).

The Roman orator and philosopher Cicero called crucifixion a "most cruel and disgusting penalty."[15] Josephus, a first-century Jewish historian, personally witnessed crucifixion and called it "the most wretched of deaths."[16] From a Jewish perspective, the one crucified was under God's curse (see Deut. 21:22–23; cf. Gal. 3:10–14). Paul associates the message of the cross with God's power to save, countering secular notions of power as that which is miraculous or overwhelming.[17]

For it is written (1:19). Paul cites Isa. 29:14 in the Greek translation of the OT (Septuagint), possibly under the influence of Ps. 33:10 and Ps. 89:34, to show that God's sentence against human wisdom is supported by the Scriptures.

Where is the one who is wise? (1:20). The wise, the teachers of law, and the philosophers are the "experts" of the present world order. Judaism developed a belief in two successive ages: "this age" and "the age to come."[18] Paul reflects this stance in speaking of the "wisdom of the world" and the experts of "this age." The influence of Isa. 33:18 on this verse is likely.

Jews ask for signs and the Greeks seek wisdom (1:22). The Jews' demand for miraculous signs was rooted in Jewish messianic expectations (Num. 14:11, 22; John 6:30) (see the article "Messianic Expectations in Jesus's Day"). Paul may have used the term "Greeks" instead of "gentiles" as a cultural descriptor, since they were renowned for their love and pursuit of wisdom.

A stumbling block to the Jews and foolishness to the Gentiles (1:23). The proclamation of an executed criminal as "good news" would have been offensive to Jews with fervent messianic expectations and nonsense to gentiles who coveted honor, esteem, and success.

God's foolishness is wiser than human wisdom, and God's weakness is stronger than human strength (1:25). Paul preaches a crucified Messiah because this "foolishness" to the world was true wisdom and this "weakness" was God's strength. Paradox and irony play a key role in Paul's argument.

God's Wisdom and the Corinthians' Calling (1:26–31)

Not many were wise from a human perspective (1:26). Although few among the Corinthians were wise, influential, and of noble birth, some in the community enjoyed esteemed social standing. Among those in Corinth who might have been from the upper class are Crispus (1:14; cf. Acts 18:18), Gaius (1:14; cf. Rom. 16:23), Erastus the city treasurer (Rom. 16:23), Phoebe of Cenchreae (Rom. 16:1–2), and Aquila and Priscilla (16:19–20; cf. Rom. 16:3–5a).[19]

God has chosen what is foolish . . . weak . . . insignificant and despised (1:27–28). God's freedom and purpose to choose the lowly parallels his actions in the past with respect to Israel (see Deut. 7:7) and accords with the teaching of Jesus (Matt. 11:25; see also James 2:5).

Let the one who boasts, boast in the Lord (1:31). Paul's quotation from Jer. 9:23–24 sets forth the only proper grounds for boasting among the Corinthians.[20]

God's Wisdom and Paul's Ministry in Corinth (2:1–5)

I did not come with brilliance of speech or wisdom (2:1). Paul was faithful to Christ's commission to preach the gospel apart from the values embodied in the trademark competitive Greco-Roman rhetoric of the day, which emphasized audience approval (see 1:17).[21] Paul consistently employs reason and argument in his letters, including 1 Corinthians, but he rejects self-presentation and haughty speech.[22]

In weakness, in fear, and in much trembling (2:3). "Weakness" could imply a physical ailment or any number of things, such as poverty, laboring to support oneself in ministry, or persecution, all mentioned in 4:10–12. "Fear" and "trembling" may refer to Paul's demeanor in carrying out his ministry (see 2 Cor. 5:11; Phil. 2:12).

With a demonstration of the Spirit's power (2:4). Paul's claim may echo Zech. 4:6.[23]

The Wisdom of God and the Holy Spirit (2:6–3:4)

We . . . speak a wisdom among the mature (2:6). The plural "we" most likely refers to Paul and other apostles and prophets who instruct the community.[24] The term "mature" may be somewhat synonymous with the terms "spiritual" (2:13–16) and "wise" as used in Corinth. The term "mature" may have gained currency in Corinth among the self-styled elite, and Paul redefines notions of mature, wise, and spiritual in terms of behavior rather than knowledge.[25]

The rulers of this age (2:6, 8). In the NT the word for "rulers" (*archontes*) consistently refers to Jewish and Roman leaders (see Acts 3:17; 4:5, 8, 26; Rom. 13:3). The reference would then be to worldly rulers who put Jesus to death. Some scholars point out, however, that biblical and Jewish apocalyptic thought viewed hostile acts against God as inspired by evil supernatural figures.[26]

God's hidden wisdom in a mystery (2:7). "Mystery" (*mystērion*) in the NT refers to the disclosure of something previously unknown. Paul develops the concept in Eph. 3:9–13 and Col. 1:25–29 and explains the mystery as the inclusion of gentiles in God's salvation. The rulers of this age did not know that God demonstrated his secret in the crucifixion (see Luke 23:34; Acts 3:17; 4:25–28). In the OT God made known the "mystery" of Nebuchadnezzar's dream to Daniel so that he and his companions would not be destroyed along with the other wise men of Babylon, who could not interpret the king's dream (See Dan. 2:18–19, 27–30, 47).

As it is written (2:9). Some think that Paul paraphrases Isa. 64:4 in combination with Isa. 65:17. Others suggest Isa. 52:13–15 as the antecedent text. It may be that Paul brings together various formulations and concepts from a range of OT texts.[27]

By the Spirit . . . the person without the Spirit . . . the spiritual person (2:10–15). Some note the possible background of Dan. 2:19–23 with its vocabulary relating to mystery, revelation, and the deep things of God.[28] Paul distinguishes between the person with the Spirit (believer) and the person without the Spirit (unbeliever). The "person without the Spirit" denotes the worldly-wise person who belongs to this age and cannot comprehend God's wisdom (1:20; 2:6).

Who has known the Lord's mind, that he may instruct him? (2:16). Paul utilizes Isaiah's contemplation of God's incomprehensible plan to establish that those with the Spirit have the mind of Christ (Isa. 40:13).

As people of the flesh, as babies in Christ (3:1). Paul could not speak to the Corinthians as wise and mature because they were behaving like infants, as evidenced by their jealousy and quarrels. The metaphor of "milk" and "solid food" (3:2) was commonly employed in the ancient world to refer to elementary versus advanced teaching (see Heb. 5:12–14). Others think that "solid food" is a Corinthian term and thus Paul writes ironically. In other words, he wants them to see that the wisdom of the gospel (milk) is really "solid food." They had become satisfied with synthetic substitutes.[29]

The Church and Its Leaders (3:5–4:5)

Servants (3:5). The term for "servants" (*diakonos*) used here of Apollos and Paul is different from the one used for "servants" (*hypēretēs*) of Christ in 4:1.

Paul says to the Corinthians, "I gave you milk to drink, not solid food" (1 Cor. 3:2). Pictured here is a pottery piece with a nozzle through which infants were fed (Hellenistic period).

In 3:5–9 the term "servant" is associated with field workers, an image that allows Paul to emphasize the unity and equality between the one who plants and the one who waters the field. Scholars often suggest that the field image echoes the tradition of Israel and God's vineyard in Isa. 5 and related texts.[30]

The word for "servants" in 4:1 occurs frequently in the Gospels and Acts and refers to many different kinds of servants, such as attendants to a king or magistrates, officers of the Sanhedrin, or Jewish temple guards.[31] The word translated as "manager" (*oikonomos*) in 4:1 refers to the manager of an estate of an absentee landlord.

God's building (3:9b). In 3:9b–17 Paul employs the building image to emphasize the quality of materials used in construction. Some think that Paul has in mind Solomon's garden-like temple in his description of the materials used (see 1 Kings 5:17; 6:18–21, 28–30, 35; 7:18–50; cf. 1 Chron. 29:1–7) but also views the Corinthians as the fulfillment of the end-time temple prophesied in Mal. 3–4.[32] Others propose that "temple" and "building" are images of unity, which is Paul's main point.[33]

The day will disclose it (3:13). "The day" refers to the day of judgment, when the work of each one will become evident, whether that work consists of God's wisdom or human wisdom. Fire discloses the true value of something and is an image often associated with the last judgment (see Isa. 66:15; Dan. 7:9–10; Mal. 3:1–3; Matt. 3:10–12).

Only as through fire (3:15). The phrase may have become a metaphor like "a burning stick snatched from a fire" (Amos 4:11), meaning something like "saved at the last moment" or "escaping by the skin of one's teeth."[34]

If anyone destroys God's temple (3:17). Jesus associates the temple with his body (John 2:19–21), and Paul refers to the church as the "body of Christ" (1 Cor. 12:12–13, 17, 27). Thus the church is God's temple.[35] In context, destroying God's temple has to do with those causing and stoking divisions in the church.

Praise will come to each one from God (4:5). The Corinthians' craved the praise of people associated with status, but Paul reminds them that the only praise that counts is praise from God. The "human court" (4:3) is literally the "human day," and it refers to the day of judgment, when God reveals human motives. Paul's phrase "I am not justified by this" (4:4) is legal language meaning "to be acquitted." God is the final judge, and there is no further appeal.

God's Servants as Paradigms of the Cross (4:6–13)

I have applied these things to myself and Apollos (4:6). A long tradition holds that the meaning of the verb translated as "have applied"

Little remains of the amphitheater at Corinth. During the first century AD it was converted into an arena and once held up to fourteen thousand people for events such as gladiator contests and shows of wild beasts. It was even flooded for water-battle productions.

(*metaschēmatizō*) is more accurately rendered as "to transform," the same as its other NT occurrences (2 Cor. 11:13–15; Phil. 3:21), and that the so-called parties in Corinth are only veiled allusions to the real situation.[36] In other words, Paul replaces the names of the local leaders with himself and Apollos in order to avoid direct and personal rebuke.

"Nothing beyond what is written" (4:6). Paul refers to the boundaries set by Scripture concerning human wisdom, since he has quoted Scripture numerous times in the service of his argument.

You are already rich! (4:8). Paul employs irony and sarcasm, a common rhetorical and literary device, in order to confront Corinthian arrogance.

Like men condemned to die (4:9). Paul views his service in preaching a crucified Christ as analogous to the gladiator condemned to die in the arena. The phrase "men condemned to die" speaks powerfully to those who craved social standing.

Like everyone's garbage (4:13). Philosophers sometimes thought of the masses as "garbage." Paul gladly applies the image to the apostles, again, as in 4:9, speaking powerfully to those who craved social standing.

Paul's Warning and Appeal as Their Spiritual Father
(4:14–21)

I'm not writing this to shame you, but to warn you (4:14). The metaphor of father and child reminds the Corinthians that Paul is the founder of the community. Paul reminds them that his ultimate intent is not to shame, but rather to warn, his beloved children (see the article "Honor and Shame in the New Testament World").

Instructors in Christ (4:15). The "instructor" was a trustworthy slave of the upper class charged with supervising the education, life, and morals of the children of a household. There was, however, no comparison between the guardian and the father.

Therefore I urge you to imitate me (4:16). Moral teachers urged their followers to imitate their way of life, not just their teaching. Paul qualifies that he wants the Corinthians to imitate his manner of life in Christ (4:17; see also 11:1).

Should I come to you with a rod? (4:21). The "rod" depicts reproof and correction, which is Paul's prerogative as the Corinthians' spiritual father. Paul reminds them that rhetorical skills are completely irrelevant for the kingdom of God (4:20).

Directives to the Church regarding an Incestuous Man (5:1–13)

There is sexual immorality among you . . . that is not even tolerated among the Gentiles (5:1). The term translated as "sexual immorality" (*porneia*) is broad in meaning and refers to any unlawful sexual intercourse. Here Paul applies the term more specifically to incest, which was condemned in the OT [37] and by Roman law.[38]

And you are arrogant! (5:2). Recent scholarship has emphasized the social background in understanding the reasons why the Corinthians overlooked such behavior.[39] Perhaps the perpetrator was a rich patron of the church and some feared taking action against someone of such high and powerful social standing.

Shouldn't you be filled with grief and remove from your congregation the one who did this? (5:2). Mourning over the sins of others evokes an OT background, particularly Ezra, who mourned over the sins of others (Ezra 10:6).[40]

Hand that one over to Satan for the destruction of the flesh (5:5). Some think that Paul refers to physical death, but the phrase more likely describes the expulsion of the offender from the community (cf. 1 Tim. 1:19–20). Excommunication would have had the effect of ridding this individual of his sinful orientation (flesh).

A little leaven leavens the whole batch of dough (5:6). Paul explains his reasoning on the analogy of the OT feast of Passover. Fermented dough caused unleavened dough to rise but could also infect the whole if contaminated. Leaven came to symbolize the infectious power of evil (Matt. 16:6).

Do not even eat with such a person (5:11). In the ancient world refusing to eat with someone broke all social ties. Here Paul likely means exclusion from the Lord's Supper, not complete exclusion from all private meals.[41]

Remove the evil person from among you (5:13). Paul's command to expel the wicked person picks up a recurring phrase in Deuteronomy (Deut. 17:7, 12; 19:19; 21:21; 22:21–22, 24; 24:7), although without the typical formula "It is written," perhaps because of the emotionally charged tenor of the instruction.

Disputes before the Unrighteous (6:1–11)

If any of you has a dispute against another (6:1). This phrase translates a Greek idiom referring to civil litigation.

How dare you take it to court before the unrighteous? (6:1). Local civil courts often were swayed and manipulated through the social networks of powerful and influential people, leaving the poor and weak with no grounds for justice.[42] The term "unrighteous" could indicate that the secular magistrates were unjust in their judgments. Paul's exhortation to them to settle their own disputes reflects his Jewish heritage. The teaching of Jesus also underlies Paul's ethics (see Matt. 18:15–17; cf. Rom. 12:17; 1 Thess. 5:15; 1 Pet. 2:19–21).

The saints will judge the world . . . we will judge angels (6:2–3). Daniel 7:22 provides a possible background to the concept of saints judging the world. Paul does not elaborate on "judge angels" but likely has in mind fallen angels.[43]

Males who have sex with males (6:9). Of the vices that Paul lists that will exclude a person from the kingdom of God (6:9–11), the most discussed are two words translated as "males who have sex with males" (*malakos, arsenokoitēs*). Other translations list two vices, both referring to homosexual acts.[44] The second term likely derives from the language of the Greek version of the OT in Lev. 18:22; 20:13.

The Sanctity of the Body (6:12–20)

It is uncertain whether Paul opposes the sacred prostitution condoned by the pagan priesthood with ritual significance for the purpose of fertility, or the use of prostitutes for festive occasions on the temple precincts.[45]

The CSB puts quotation marks around phrases that many scholars view as Corinthian slogans or viewpoints that Paul counters (see 6:12, 13).[46]

Banquets often were a part of important social, business, religious, and political activities in the Greco-Roman world. Shown here is a banqueting scene on a funerary stela from the fourth century BC.

These slogans may have represented prevalent Greek ideas of freedom and ethics related to the body.

"Everything is permissible for me" (6:12). Paul's response to this possible slogan may have tapped into the perspective of the moral teachers of the day in order to show that even the "wise" of their own culture qualified their behavior in light of the effects such behavior had on others and on oneself.

"Food is for the stomach and the stomach for food" (6:13). Scholars commonly argue that the Corinthians correlated "the stomach and food" and the "body and sex" in a way that justified their immorality.

The two will become one flesh (6:16). Paul underscores his opposition to immorality on the basis of Gen. 2:24, which expresses God's intention for marriage. The prostitute was a symbol of darkness and defilement.

Flee sexual immorality! (6:18). This command appears in Jewish literature.[47] Paul may have in mind the story of Joseph's flight from Potiphar's wife in Gen. 39.

You were bought at a price (6:20). Some see a possible allusion to Hosea 3:1–3, which describes Hosea's redemption of his wife out of bondage back to a life of wholeness.[48]

Issues Pertaining to Marriage and Singleness (7:1–40)

The phrase "Now in response to the matters you wrote about" (7:1 [see also 7:25; 8:1; 12:1; 16:1, 12]) introduces a new stage of the letter where Paul responds directly to Corinthian questions and viewpoints.[49] The polarity of perspectives on sexual matters, from the liberated view that forms the background to chapters 6–7 to some advocating complete abstention from all sexual relations in 7:1–7, reflects the range of opinion in the gentile world of Paul's time. Some think that Paul's arguments in chapter 7 are close to arguments carried on by the philosophical schools of the Stoics and the Cynics concerning the weighty responsibilities of marriage.[50]

"It is good for a man not to use a woman for sex" (7:1). Paul may be decrying a view in Corinth that advocated celibacy in marriage, or the slogan could reflect a debate within the Roman culture on the issue of sex with one's spouse motivated by gratification and pleasure rather than for the sole purpose of procreation.[51]

But because sexual immorality is so common (7:2). Paul's view that marriage is a way to avoid the danger of sexual immorality is consistent with the OT and other Jewish literature (see Prov. 5:15–20; Tob. 4:12; *Testament of Levi* 9.9–10).[52]

A husband should fulfill his marital duty to his wife, and likewise a wife to her husband (7:3). Exodus 21:10–11 may influence Paul's instructions regarding conjugal rights within marriage. Paul's emphasis on the mutuality of the relationship between husband and wife was quite unconventional by ancient standards. Paul's allowance for the husband and wife to withdraw from each other by consent is rooted in the OT (see Exod. 19:15; Lev. 15:18; 1 Sam. 21:4–6; Eccles. 3:5; Joel 2:16; Zech. 12:12–14).

I say to the unmarried and to widows (7:8). Some think that the term "unmarried" carries the meaning of "widowers" and that Paul himself was a widower, since being married at some point in his life would have been consistent with his Jewish heritage.

To the married I give this command—not I, but the Lord—a wife is not to leave her husband (7:10). Paul reiterates the teaching of Jesus regarding divorce (Matt. 19:1–10; Mark 10:2–12; also Matt. 5:32). "Leave" does not carry a technical sense in this passage and is used interchangeably with the word "divorce."[53]

If any brother has an unbelieving wife (7:12). Paul explains that believers should remain married to unbelievers if the unbeliever consents, because the unbeliever and the children are still considered to be "holy." The principle of holiness, which extends even to the children, is established on the scriptural principle that God's blessings are not confined to the immediate recipients but extend to others (see Gen. 15:18; 17:7; 18:26; 1 Kings 15:4; Isa. 37:4).

A brother or a sister is not bound in such cases (7:15). Most scholars think that Paul means that if the unbelieving partner departs, the believing spouse is no longer bound to the marriage and therefore is free to remarry, although the term for "bound" in 7:15 is not the same as the term normally used to refer to the binding character of marriage (7:27, 39; Rom. 7:2).

He should not undo his circumcision (7:18). Paul uses two leading identity markers in the ancient world (circumcision/uncircumcision, freedman/slave) to illustrate the principle that social distinctions have nothing to do with one's standing before God. The procedure of becoming "uncircumcised" was known as "epispasm" and was a means of Jewish males masking their religious identity in order to assimilate into the Greco-Roman culture.[54] Circumcision was a covenant sign marking Jews as the people of God (Gen. 17:10–14) (see the article "The Jewish Rite of Circumcision"). The new covenant does not equate circumcision with keeping God's commands.

You were bought at a price (7:23). The phrase conjures up the imagery of slavery (see the article "Slavery in the New Testament World") in order to make a theological point (cf. 6:19–20).

Now about virgins (7:25). The identity of the "virgins" (also 7:28, 34, 36–38) is a major interpretive issue. The "virgin daughter" view (7:36–38 NASB) assumes a certain cultural background where the daughter could not marry without the permission of the father or legal guardian. More likely the term "virgins" refers to betrothed young women of marriageable age, and Paul directs his instructions primarily toward the men who took the lead in such matters.

As one who by the Lord's mercy is faithful (7:25). The term "mercy" refers to Paul's apostleship (2 Cor. 4:1; cf. Gal. 1:15–16; see also 1 Cor. 4:1–2).

Because of the present distress (7:26). Recent scholarship has suggested that Paul interprets a present crisis in Corinth, such as famine or persecution,[55] as an end-time event (cf. Luke 21:23; Mark 13:17–20).

The time is limited (7:29). The phrase could refer to both quantity and quality of time left before the second coming of Christ—that is, the character of the time remaining until the final consummation has been irrevocably altered by the event of Jesus's death and resurrection. The future has been brought into sharp focus in the present (see Rom. 13:11–14; Eph. 5:15–16).

I think that I also have the Spirit of God (7:40). The mention of being guided by the Spirit may indicate that Paul is offering a counterpoint to others in Corinth who advised otherwise under the auspices of "Spirit-inspired" advice.

This funerary monument shows several classes in the Roman social hierarchy. The large figures shown in deep relief are a family of freedmen, both male and female. The smaller figures in shallow relief are the slaves who belong to the family. The visual contrast highlights the difference in social status (Thessalonica, ca. 50 BC).

Priority of Love over Knowledge (8:1–13)

The acknowledgment of pagan gods in various settings involved eating food that had been sacrificed to an idol.[56] Remnants of the sacrifice were sold in the marketplace, making opportunities for eating such food plentiful. Some scholars have suggested that Paul prohibited eating idol food in the temple but allowed such eating in the private home (10:23–31). Others have argued that Paul's concern was the nature of the meal, whether eating religious meals with overt associations with a pagan god or eating on social occasions.[57]

Now about food sacrificed to idols (8:1). The Greek word underlying this phrase (*eidōlothytos*) does not occur in the literature prior to 1 Corinthians and probably is a Jewish/Christian polemical term. Although a variety of food products could be in view, such as grain, fruit, fish, poultry, and honey,[58] sociological approaches have preferred the idea of meat offered to idols and emphasized that the problem in Corinth had to do with social stratification between the elite and the socially disadvantaged.[59]

"We all have knowledge" (8:1). Paul agrees with a probable Corinthian slogan/viewpoint, which he sharply qualifies. The self-acclaimed "knowledgeable" may have been the wealthier members of the church.

But if anyone loves God, he is known by him (8:3). To be known by God was to be in covenant with him. The mention of one's love for God echoes Deut. 6:4–5.

We know that "An idol is nothing in the world," and that "there is no God but one" (8:4). As in 8:1, the quotations reflect the view that these words represent Corinthian slogans or viewpoints. A similar statement regarding the nothingness of gods occurs in Deut. 32:21. The whole of 8:6, regarding the uniqueness and supremacy of God the Father and the Lord Jesus Christ, likely reflects an early Christian traditional confession.

This right of yours (8:9). Paul's language indicates that the right to eat all food is a Corinthian claim. The illustration that follows in 8:10 may be purely hypothetical in order to drive home the point that Paul did not think that one had the right to eat in the temple of the idol.

One's "Rights" and the Gospel (9:1–27)

Am I not free? Am I not an apostle? (9:1). Some have suggested that Paul's discussion reflects a crisis in Corinth over his apostleship.[60] More likely, some took issue with Paul's unconventional behavior in refusing financial support.

You are the seal of my apostleship in the Lord (9:2). The word "seal" frequently meant "mark" or "stamp," referring either to the instrument used or the mark left by the signet in order to attest to the genuineness of something. The Corinthian church was proof of Paul's apostleship.

Paul tells the church at Corinth, "You are the seal of my apostleship in the Lord" (1 Cor. 9:2). Shown here is a Greek signet ring from the second or third century BC. Stamps and rings like this were used to make impressions in clay to affirm the authenticity or authority behind items such as letters, proclamations, and commercial goods.

My defense to those who examine me (9:3). The questions of 9:3–6 anticipate questions that some might raise regarding Paul's self-imposed discipline. On occasion Paul accepted material provision (Phil. 4:10–20), but normally he did not conform to this practice of the traveling rhetoricians and philosophers of the day.

Don't we have the right to be accompanied by a believing wife like the other apostles, the Lord's brothers, and Cephas? (9:5). Other apostles were married and traveled with their wives. Paul's question also reveals that the brothers of Jesus were involved in the missionary enterprise of the church.

Do not muzzle an ox while it treads out grain (9:9). Paul quotes Deut. 25:4, employing a common method of argumentation from the lesser to the greater. If God cares about oxen, then he cares even more about human beings. This supports Paul's point in 9:7 that people expect to reap benefits from their labor.

Those who perform the temple services (9:13). Paul likely refers to the temple practices described in the OT rather than the pagan temples in Corinth. Those who worked in the temple and offered sacrifices were sustained in daily provision by their service (see Lev. 7:6–10, 14, 28–36).

The Lord has commanded that those who preach the gospel should earn their living by the gospel (9:14). No saying of Jesus corresponds exactly to 9:14, but the essence is found in the gospel tradition (cf. Matt. 10:10; Luke 10:7).

I have no reason to boast, because I am compelled to preach (9:16). "Boasting" evokes a prophetic theme and shows that Paul viewed himself in the line of OT prophets who were compelled to preach.

Although I am free . . . I have made myself a slave to everyone (9:19). Paul may be referring to his financial independence that released him from any obligation to wealthy patrons.

To the Jews I became like a Jew (9:20). Paul describes his missionary life among various classes of people in order to clarify his statement of becoming a slave of all. Although Paul no longer defines his relationship to God in terms of the law, he occasionally accommodates to Jewish practice for purposes of evangelism (Acts 16:1–3; 21:23–26).

This relief shows two contestants each placing crowns on the head of their trainer and holding palm branches, which are symbols of victory (Athens, early third century AD).

I do all this because of the gospel, so that I may share in the blessings (9:23). The financial overtones of the passage may indicate that Paul refers to financial resources for the effective spread of the gospel.

Run in such a way to win the prize (9:24). The athletic metaphor was widespread among ancient philosophers[61] and would have been especially relevant to Paul's audience because Corinth hosted the biennial Isthmian Games (see the article "Athletics in the New Testament World").

God's Provision, Redemption, and Judgment of Israel (10:1–13)

Our ancestors were all under the cloud, all passed through the sea (10:1). "Ancestors" refers to the ancient Israelites. The cloud and sea were more than mere symbols of Israel's deliverance in the exodus. God himself was present in the experience (Exod. 13:21–22; 14:19–20, 24; Num. 14:14; Ps. 105:39).

All were baptized into Moses (10:2). Nothing in Jewish literature antedates Paul's use of the phrase "baptized into Moses." Paul establishes a parallel between the salvation of Israel from the Egyptians and the believer's deliverance from sin symbolized in Christian baptism.

That rock was Christ (10:4). By referring to Christ as a following "rock," some suppose that Paul draws from a Jewish interpretive tradition that sought to explain the appearance of the well at both the beginning and the end of Israel's journey (Exod. 17:6; Num. 20:11), an explanation facilitated by the ambiguity of Num. 21:16–20.[62] But Paul qualifies that the rock was "spiritual," referring to Christ as the source of Israel's provision.

They were struck down in the wilderness (10:5). "Struck down" offers the image of being slaughtered (Num. 14:22–23). The punishment for Israel's sins was physical death.

Don't become idolaters . . . *The people sat down to eat and drink, and got up to party* (10:7). Paul cites Exod. 32:6b with reference to Israel's worship of the golden calf as Moses was receiving the law on Mount Sinai.

In a single day twenty-three thousand people died (10:8). The number of deaths mentioned ties the warning against immorality to the account of Israel's harlotry with the Moabite women and their idolatrous worship recorded in Num. 25:1–9.

Let us not test Christ as some of them did (10:9). The OT passage is Num. 21:4–9, possibly used in conjunction with other texts that refer to Israel's repeated offense of putting God to the test (Exod. 17:2–7; Deut. 6:16; Ps. 78:18; 95:8–11). Testing Christ is a natural inference from the identification of Christ as the following rock in 10:4.

Killed by the destroyer (10:10). Scholars have suggested Num. 14 and Num. 16 as possible background texts, but neither refers to a destroying angel. The implication, however, is that the same instrument of death unleashed against the Egyptians (Exod. 12:23) struck the disobedient Israelites.

Flee Idolatry (10:14–22)

I am speaking as to sensible people (10:15). Paul's appeal to the Corinthians' self-perception as sensible people would reinforce the traditional opposition underlying the relationship between wisdom and idolatry. In Jewish thought those who lacked wisdom lapsed into idolatry (cf. Rom. 1:21–23).

Sharing in the blood of Christ . . . in the body of Christ (10:16). The term "sharing" translates the Greek term *koinōnia,* often rendered as "fellowship" (see 1:9). Some scholars have compared the Lord's Supper to Israel's recital of the Passover Seder. "Blood" and "body" do not have a material sense, since Paul draws upon Jesus's own interpretation of the cup as "the new covenant in my blood" (11:25).

Consider the people of Israel (10:18). The Greek reads, "Israel according to the flesh." Some scholars take the view that Paul is referring to the nation of Israel as distinct from the church, which is Israel according to the Spirit. Others think that Paul has in mind Israel's negative example in using the term "flesh," and the phrase refers to those of Israel who succumbed to idolatry and immorality in the wilderness.[63]

Do not those who eat the sacrifices participate in the altar? (10:18b). Paul refers to participation in what the altar stands for, either to sanctioned sacrifices in the OT or to participation in pagan sacrifices.

They sacrifice to demons (10:20). The Greek text leaves open the question of the subject of the verb "sacrifice," reading "what things they sacrifice, they sacrifice to demons and not to God." "They" possibly refers to Israel's participation in pagan feasts (Deut. 32). Some ancient manuscripts insert "gentiles" as a clarification.

Are we provoking the Lord to jealousy? Are we stronger than he? (10:22). The background text is the Song of Moses in Deut. 32, which recounts Israel's unfaithfulness to God through sacrificing to demons (Deut. 32:17) and arousing the Lord's anger.

Do All for the Good of Others and to the Glory of God (10:23–11:1)

Everything is permissible (10:23). See comments on 1 Cor. 6:12.

Eat everything that is sold in the meat market, without raising questions for the sake of conscience (10:25). The statement and the illustration that follows assume that the history of the food sold in the marketplace would be known by some but not by others, and that not all food sold in the marketplace would have been previously associated with idolatry. There are competing theories on the availability of meat to the poor. Some have argued that meat would have been available to those of limited financial means after the games or other civic events.[64] Others have noted that Paul's stance of asking no questions stands in sharp contrast to a typical Jewish approach.[65] Paul's rationale comes from Ps. 24:1: "The earth and everything in it, the world and its inhabitants, belong to the Lord."

If any of the unbelievers invites you over (10:27). Such invitations would have been common in the ancient world as a means of social and political networking and advancement. Paul does not specify where the meal occurs, whether in a public facility or a private home. The host of the meal may have raised the issue of sacrifice out of respect for the believer's convictions, a practice common today in Asian culture.[66]

Whether you eat or drink (10:31). Eating and drinking in the ancient world were the locus of relational interaction where dominant worldviews collided.

Husbands and Wives and the Glory of God (11:2–16)

In 11:2–16 Paul addresses proper attire for men (husbands) and women (wives) in relation to prayer and prophecy. Some think that the setting of the house church prompted wives to remove the traditional veil signifying their marital status. The Genesis account of creation is the background text that informs the interpretation of this passage (Gen. 1:26–27; 2:18–23).

The man is the head of the woman (11:3). The terms "man" and "woman" probably carry the more restricted meaning of "husband" and "wife" in this context.[67] An OT patriarchal background informs Paul's understanding of the relationship between husband and wife so that "headship" language reflects an assumed hierarchy through which glory and shame are conveyed.[68]

Dishonors his head . . . dishonors her head (11:4–5). In the honor/shame culture of first-century Roman Corinth, a married woman with an uncovered head was considered immodest with the potential to shame or embarrass her husband.[69] Since the male covered head was normal ritual behavior in the ancient Roman world for one offering ritual sacrifice, some have supposed that Christian tradition established a unique practice in contrast to pagan devotion.[70] Paul equated the uncovered head with a shaved head, which was an object of shame, perhaps referring to the social stigma of a publicly punished adulteress reduced to the status of a prostitute.[71]

Because of the angels (11:10). The most fruitful interpretation of this phrase links Paul's reference to the context of worship and to the motifs of glory and creation raised in 11:7–9. In Jewish tradition angels were perceived as participants in worship and guardians of the created order.[72]

Woman is not independent of man, and man is not independent of woman (11:11). Paul's statement mirrors rabbinic tradition that distinguished between Adam and Eve and the rest of humanity.[73] Creation validates both headship and interdependence. Gender differentiation is decreed in creation and expressed through societal convention.

If anyone wants (11:16). This type of phrase occurs for the third time in the letter (cf. 3:18b; 8:2), which may suggest that Paul is still addressing "those with knowledge" in Corinth (cf. 8:1–13) who were of high social status.

Glory and Shame in the Observance of the Lord's Supper (11:17–34)

There are divisions among you (11:18). The role of the host-patron setting may suggest that the celebration of the Lord's Supper in house groups generated a spirit focusing upon the host of the group rather than upon Christ (recall 1:10–17).[74]

It is necessary that there be factions among you, so that those who are approved may be recognized (11:19). Some think that, in keeping with the teaching of Jesus, Paul acknowledges the necessary separation between true and false believers in the last days, which have now arrived. Apocalyptic texts often warn that times of trial will bring out the true colors of those who

Paul reprimanded the Corinthian Christians for the social divisions that were occurring when the believers gathered in homes to share in the Lord's Supper. The wealthy patron would recline with friends in the triclinium, while those who were lower class or slaves would stand in the atrium and may have waited to be fed. The photo shows a triclinium scene from a mosaic from Sepphoris (third to fourth century AD).

profess faith (cf. Mark 4:14–20; 13:9–13). Or, Paul may be engaging in a bit of sarcasm toward the social dignitaries who allowed divisions between rich and poor so that they might stand out.

I received from the Lord what I also passed on to you (11:23). The language of "receiving" and "passing on" was stock language for the transmission of traditions. Paul's rendition of the received tradition of the Lord's Supper is closest to Luke's account (Luke 22:17–20).

On the night when he was betrayed (11:23). The reference to betrayal may be more wide-ranging than Judas's betrayal of Jesus, taking into account the complex of events associated with Jesus's death, including the Father's surrender of the Son and the Son's self-sacrifice.[75] Paul's word choice may echo Isa. 53:6, 12.

"Do this in remembrance of me" (11:24–25). Passover itself was a memorial (Exod. 12:14), recalling the Israelites' redemption from Egypt. The Passover celebration was explicitly tied to God's redemption of his people. Exodus 24:8 and Jer. 31:31 provide the scriptural background to Jesus's statement in verse 25, "This cup is the new covenant in my blood."

You proclaim the Lord's death until he comes (11:26). In context, proclaiming the Lord's death may have more to do with the manner of the Corinthians' observance of the meal than with verbal proclamation. Their particular behavior did not proclaim the Lord's death, even if the meal itself purported to represent his death.

Whoever eats the bread or drinks the cup of the Lord in an unworthy manner (11:27). Eating "in an unworthy manner" refers to the appalling behavior of the humiliation of the poor members of the church at the hands of the rich (11:17–22).

Let a person examine himself (11:28). If Paul refers ironically to social dignitaries in 11:19, then in 11:28 he may be engaging in wordplay by calling on the self-assured "approved" to "prove" themselves by undergoing rigorous self-examination with the intent to eat and drink in keeping with the genuine character of the meal.

Many are sick and ill among you, and many have fallen asleep (11:30). To "fall asleep" was a euphemism for death. In the OT plagues could fall indiscriminately on the community as a whole (Exod. 32:35; Num. 8:19; 11:33; Deut. 32:24; Josh. 22:17).[76]

When you come together to eat, welcome one another (11:33). In the social context of a dinner the verb underlying this phrase means "to welcome" (*ekdechomai*), and Paul may be urging the Corinthians to practice normal Christian hospitality (other translations render the phrase as "wait for each other" or "receive one another"). If taken more literally in the sense of "wait for," then Paul is literally urging the more privileged members who arrive earlier to wait for the poorer members who arrive later due to work commitments.

The Manifestation of the Spirit for the Common Good (12:1–31)

Concerning spiritual gifts (12:1). "Spiritual gifts" translates one word in the plural, which could mean "spiritual people." Paul may be picking up on Corinthian terminology and correcting the self-styled "spiritual" in Corinth (recall 2:14–3:4), who thought of themselves as spiritual, wise, and knowledgeable.

When you were pagans, you used to be enticed and led astray by mute idols (12:2). Paul contrasts the Corinthians' present experience of the Spirit with their past pagan experience of being influenced or "led astray" by mute idols. Paul's description may indicate the strong social pressure to participate in idol festivals.[77] He does not necessarily mean that their former pagan worship influenced their present Christian worship.[78]

No one speaking by the Spirit of God says, "Jesus is cursed" (12:3). Paul may be describing a hypothetical situation in order to argue that not all so-called inspired utterances come from the Spirit. A more recent view suggests the novel translation "Jesus grant a curse," based upon inscriptional evidence for the fairly widespread practice of religious curse pronouncements in the Greco-Roman world, wherein religious curses were used in various areas of life, including sports, politics, love, and business. Thus the Corinthians were acting like their pagan neighbors.[79] A simpler explanation is that the phrase alludes to an appraisal of Jesus by unbelieving Jews.[80]

To one is given . . . to another (12:8). Paul's purpose in 12:8–11 is to list, not define, the gifts in order to emphasize that all gifts have the same source. Prophecy is the only gift that occurs in all of Paul's lists (12:8–11, 28; 13:1–3; Rom. 12:6–8; Eph. 4:11–12). The lists in 1 Corinthians are representative rather than exhaustive.

Message of wisdom . . . message of knowledge (12:8). These manifestations of the Spirit held particular importance for the Corinthian congregation. The distinctions between these two gifts are not clear, but both of these speech gifts were problematic for the Corinthians.

Performing of miracles (12:10). In Greek the phrase reads, "working of powers." The working of God in power ultimately edifies the church and confirms one's faith in God rather than in human wisdom (2:4–5; cf. 12:6). "Power" (*dynamis*) was a key term in Paul's response to the self-perceived powerful speakers in Corinth (1:17–4:21).

Prophecy (12:10). Some scholars have defined prophecy rather broadly to include all forms of edifying speech. Paul describes the gift as Spirit-inspired intelligible utterances, both spontaneous and revelatory, for the benefit of the gathered church (see 14:6, 30; Acts 11:28; 13:1–3; 21:10–11). Still others have equated the gift with pastoral instruction.

Different kinds of tongues . . . interpretation of tongues (12:10). The word "tongue" means "language." Some think that Paul has in mind human languages. Others think that angelic languages are possible (13:1).[81] Tongues were capable of being understood immediately by the hearers (Acts 2:4–11) or capable of interpretation (1 Cor. 12:10; 14:5, 13). Paul insists that the interpretation of tongues is essential to edification (14:13–19, 28).

One body (12:12). Scholars have long recognized that the metaphor of the body for the society or the state, common in ancient political literature, may have influenced Paul's language.[82] Others have noted that Paul's use differs from the secular mindset, since he employs the image to advocate interdependence and the use of gifts for the common good rather than subordination of some to others for the good of the whole.[83]

The Spirit gives gifts of healing in contrast to the healing powers that were sought by the pagan community from the god Asklepios, whose statue is shown here (third to fourth century AD).

We were all baptized by one Spirit (12:13). All other occurrences of the phrase "baptized in/by the Spirit" in the NT refer to John the Baptist's prophecy that Jesus would baptize with or in the Spirit (Matt. 3:11; Mark 1:8; Luke 3:16; John 1:33; Acts 1:5; 11:16).

There are many parts, but one body (12:20). Some have suggested that a specific social context drives Paul's analogy in that 12:15–20 approaches the topic of the one body with many members from the perspective of those who perceived themselves to be inferior, and 12:21–26 approaches the topic from the perspective of those who perceived themselves to be superior.[84] The shameful treatment of the poor at the Lord's Supper by the more distinguished members of the church (11:17–34) is the background of the personification of the body that emphasizes due consideration given to the less honorable body parts (12:21–26). The head and the eye are obvious metaphors for the supposed higher-status members of the church who viewed themselves as being of greater value than others.

First apostles, second prophets, third teachers (12:28). "First . . . second . . . third" may indicate chronological priority rather than rank. Ephesians 2:20 refers to the "foundation of the apostles and prophets." Apostles were a select group who were eyewitnesses of the resurrection (1 Cor. 9:1–2; 15:5–9), including Paul, the Twelve, and others commissioned by Christ.[85]

Love: The More Excellent Way (13:1–13)

First Corinthians 13 fits the pattern of a literary discourse, called an encomium, dedicated to a person or thing (virtue).[86] Paul likely composed 13:1–13 extemporaneously for the Corinthian situation.

Human or angelic tongues (13:1). Paul refers to two different kinds of tongues hyperbolically for the sake of argument. Perhaps the Corinthians thought of their speaking in tongues as a "language from heaven."

A noisy gong or a clanging cymbal (13:1). The term translated as "gong" (*chalkos*) was used of various kinds of metals but mainly of bronze or brass. On the basis of a few references in Greco-Roman literature it has been suggested that Paul refers to the acoustic vase used in theaters in order to project and amplify sound.[87] Some think that Paul refers to the noise of pagan worship.[88]

All mysteries and all knowledge (13:2). "Mysteries and knowledge" are often conjoined in apocalyptic literature (Dan. 2:19–23;

Shown here are small cymbals from the Roman period.

1 Enoch 41.1; 52.2; 61.5; 63.3; 68.5; 71.4). The mention of "mysteries and knowledge" may evoke the portrayal of Daniel in Dan. 2; 4.[89]

Faith so that I can move mountains (13:2). This idiom for great faith resonates with the teaching of Jesus and may be derived from it (Matt. 17:19–20; 21:21; Mark 1:22–24; Luke 17:6).

Give over my body in order to boast (13:3). Some translations render the Greek text as "surrender my body to be burned" (NASB) because the terms for "burn" and "boast" are very close in Greek. One of the key arguments against "burn" is the absence of this form of martyrdom until the persecution of the church under Nero. Paul's reference, however, may be an allusion to the fiery furnace in Dan. 3.

Love does not envy, is not boastful, is not arrogant (13:4–8a). There is a consensus among scholars that Paul's description in these verses of what love *does not do* unmistakably addresses the Corinthian context and thus functions to point out their lack of love. Paul simultaneously praises love and blames the Corinthians.[90] Jealousy and quarreling, for example, underlie other portions of the letter, such as the lawsuits among believers (6:1–8) and the social divisions between the rich and the poor in the celebration of the Lord's Supper (11:17–22). Love "is not arrogant" rehearses a common theme in the letter (see 4:6, 18; 5:2; 8:1).

As for prophecies, they will come to an end; as for tongues, they will cease; as for knowledge, it will come to an end . . . but when the perfect comes, the partial will come to an end (13:8b–10). The gifts of prophecy, tongues, and knowledge are representative gifts, chosen because of their relevance to the Corinthian situation. The Greek word for "perfect" (*teleios*) also translates as "mature" in certain contexts and is used in conjunction with "infant" language (2:6; 14:20; cf. 3:1–4). Paul's language targets those in Corinth who were acting childishly.

Now we see only a reflection as in a mirror, but then face to face (13:12). The metaphor of the mirror enjoyed widespread use in the ancient world and was particularly relevant to Corinth, where bronze mirrors were manufactured. In context, the metaphor points to the indirectness of one's vision, to partial and incomplete knowledge. "Reflection" versus "face to face" refers to Num. 12:6–8, which contrasts how Moses spoke with God face to face while other prophets received revelation through visions and dreams.

Roman mirrors from Hierapolis, Turkey (first century BC to fourth century AD).

Do All for the Edification of the Church (14:1–40)

Desire spiritual gifts (14:1). Paul may have in mind gifts of speech, the focus of 14:1–40, since it is likely that the Corinthians held the speech gifts in high esteem and attached social status to them.

Not speaking to people but to God (14:2). In context, Paul means that only God comprehends an uninterpreted tongue. Only intelligible speech leads to understanding and edification.

The person who speaks in another tongue builds himself up (14:4). Paul does not commend personal edification as a function of spiritual gifts; rather, the focus of gifts is corporate edification (12:7). Paul's point is that only the speaker is edified if a tongue is not interpreted.

If I come to you speaking in other tongues (14:6). When Paul came to Corinth, it was with clear speech in a powerful demonstration of the Spirit (2:1–5). He now imagines by way of contrast that if he came to them speaking unintelligibly, there would be no benefit.

If the bugle makes an unclear sound (14:8). Paul uses a military metaphor elsewhere to describe the calling of Christians (see Rom. 6:12–14; 2 Cor. 10:3–6; Phil. 1:27–30; 1 Thess. 5:8).

There are doubtless many different kinds of languages in the world (14:10). Paul's reference to all sorts of languages in the world was especially relevant to Corinth, with its two harbors positioning the city as a major crossroads to the world and where both Greek and Latin were spoken. The citizens of Corinth would have been familiar with the alienation and frustration caused by the blend of different languages and different cultures in a major urban setting.

I will be a foreigner to the speaker (14:11). Common language is essential to unity. The Greek term for "foreigner" (*barbaros*) refers to a non-Greek-speaking person.

How will the outsider say "Amen"? (14:16). Some think that "outsider," which translates a Greek phrase of six words, is a technical term describing a prospect for membership in the community. More likely it refers to those who assume the role of the social outsider since they are alienated by unintelligible speech.

I would rather speak five words with my understanding, in order to teach others also, than ten thousand words in another tongue (14:19). The term "ten thousand" is hyperbole and means "countless."

It is written in the law (14:20–25). Social networks, marriages, and legal structures ensured that Christians interacted with non-Christians (recall 6:1–11; chaps. 8–10). Since unbelievers would have been present in the worship gatherings of the church, Paul applies Isa. 28:11–12 to the Corinthian situation in order to contrast the effect of speaking in tongues versus prophesying. In Isaiah God spoke in judgment through invaders speaking the Assyrian language (Isa. 28:11: "For he will speak to this people with stammering speech and in a foreign language"). Unlike tongues, prophecy brings about conversion.

"God is really among you" (14:25). This phrase is an echo of Isa. 45:14 (see also Isa. 49:23; 60:10–16; Zech. 8:22–23).

Everything is to be done for building up . . . decently and in order (14:26b–40). Paul sets guidelines for those who speak in tongues, for prophets, and for wives in relation to the edification of the church. Paul regulates prophetic speech similarly to tongues by instructing two to three prophets to speak and others to judge. A passage from the Dead Sea Scrolls parallels Paul's guidelines and stipulates that no one should talk during the discourse of another (*1QRule of the Community* 6.10–13).

Women should be silent in the churches . . . disgraceful for a woman to speak in the church (14:34–35). Paul has in mind a specific social situation: wives speaking in an unacceptable manner and bringing shame upon their husbands. Some have suggested that 14:34–35 forbids women from teaching (1 Tim. 2:12), a rule taken over from the synagogue and applied to the church.[91] Paul does not intend to prohibit women's speech absolutely, but rather calls for the constraint of certain kinds of speaking in order to maintain the integrity of the husband-wife relationship and the peace and order of the church gathered for worship.

If anyone thinks he is a prophet or spiritual (14:37). Paul confronts those who considered themselves a "prophet" or "spiritual" person, indicating that he is addressing a Corinthian self-perception and that the issue of what truly constitutes spirituality among the Corinthians was a major one.

The Resurrection of the Dead (15:1–58)

The problem that Paul addresses in this chapter is disclosed in 15:12b: "How can some of you say, 'There is no resurrection of the dead'?" The prevailing Greek philosophical worldview held to the immortality of the soul rather than the resurrection of a dead body. The problem for some in Corinth was not postmortem existence but rather the bodily nature of such resurrection life. It is possible that those who denied the resurrection were a minority of the socially upper class, who would have been prone to such philosophical leanings. The crux of the problem for the Greek mindset is expressed in the two questions in 15:35: "How are the dead raised? What kind of body will they have when they come?"[92]

For I passed on to you as most important what I also received (15:3). The language of receiving and handing down has long been recognized as technical vocabulary drawn from Paul's Jewish heritage related to the reception and transmission of traditions. The formulation bears the marks of a traditional confessional statement (see 11:2, 23–26).

According to the Scriptures (15:3–4). Paul probably intends the totality of Scripture rather than a passage or collection of passages. Jesus himself interpreted his death and resurrection in terms of the Scriptures (see Luke 24:25–27, 44–45). Isaiah 53 is a possible background text for the death of Jesus, and Jon. 1:17 and Hosea 6:2 are possible metaphorical references to resurrection on the third day.

He appeared (15:5–8). Paul lists appearances of the risen Christ in what seems to be chronological order. The occasion of the appearance to five hundred may have been the Great Commission (Matt. 28:16).

As to one born at the wrong time (15:8). In the Greek translation of the OT (Septuagint) the word translated as "born at the wrong time" or "abnormally born" (*ektrōma*) refers to a stillborn child (Num. 12:12; Eccles. 6:3; Job 3:16). Paul employs the metaphor in order to highlight the grace and power of God that rescued him from his deplorable condition of spiritual death.

His grace toward me was not in vain (15:10). Paul possibly reflects upon Isaiah's complaint, "I have labored in vain" (Isa. 49:4).

No resurrection of the dead (15:12–19). Paul takes the position of "no resurrection of the dead" to its logical conclusion. If resurrection is impossible, then Jesus, who was fully human, was not raised, and so all preaching and faith is vain. Further, all the witnesses listed in 15:5–8 were false witnesses, and believers are still under the power of sin and death.

Christ has been raised from the dead, the firstfruits of those who have fallen asleep (15:20). In Lev. 23:9–14 the term "firstfruits" describes a consecrated portion of the harvest offered to God in sacrifice. Here the emphasis falls more on temporal sequence. Christ is the first person to be raised from the dead, with more resurrections to come.

As in Adam all die, so also in Christ all will be made alive (15:22). Paul elaborates further upon firstfruits by comparing Adam and Christ (see 15:44–49; also Rom. 5:14). Both death and resurrection are "through a man" (v. 21).

But each in his own order (15:23). Paul uses a military metaphor denoting rank and order in reference to the resurrection of the dead. Christ will be first, followed by those who belong to him. On the resurrection of both the righteous and the wicked, see Dan. 12:2; John 5:29; Rev. 20.

Afterward, at his coming (15:23). The Greek term for "coming" (*parousia*) means "presence" and was used in some contexts in the ancient world in a technical sense to denote the coming of a political figure of high office, such as the visit of an emperor to a province. The term became a technical one denoting the second coming of Christ in certain contexts (1 Thess. 2:19; 3:13; 4:15; 5:23; 2 Thess. 2:1). The term does not always carry this meaning, however, since it is used of the arrival of Stephanas, Fortunatus, and Achaicus (1 Cor. 16:17) and of the "coming" of the lawless one (2 Thess. 2:8).

Then comes the end (15:24). Paul reads Ps. 110:1 and Ps. 8:6 christologically in order to explain that Christ must reign until all enemies are vanquished. References to Ps. 8 and Ps. 110 also occur together in Eph. 1:20–22. Psalm 8 has in mind the Genesis creation account of humankind, while Ps. 110 refers to the royal Davidic king. By combining the two psalms, Paul is able to emphasize that what was lost in Adam is regained in Christ and fulfills God's intention for humanity.

So that God may be all in all (15:28). Paul uses similar terminology in 1 Cor. 8:6a and Rom. 11:36. God's purposes take into account the whole of creation (Rom. 8:19–25; Col. 1:15–20; Eph. 1:9–10, 20–23).

What will they do who are being baptized for the dead? (15:29). The preoccupation with the dead in Corinthian culture supports the interpretation that some were being baptized on behalf of unbaptized dead people.[93] Perhaps some were being baptized for others in their household who had converted but died before their baptism. Some scholars have suggested the reference is metaphorical, and the phrase refers to the believers' soon to be dead bodies (Rom. 6:3–14; 8:10; Eph. 2:1, 5; Col. 2:13). Still others have argued that the preposition "for" is causal, and the phrase should read, "Those being baptized because of the dead." Thus "baptism for the dead" refers to the practice of those being baptized on account of what they know about the dead being raised to life.[94]

I fought wild beasts in Ephesus (15:32). "Fighting wild beasts" is a metaphor for contending with powerful adversaries. Since Paul writes from Ephesus, such conflicts are fresh on his mind (1 Cor. 16:9; see also Acts 19:23–41; Rom. 16:3–4). The metaphor occurs in Greek moralistic literature as a euphemism for self-discipline in the struggle against human passions.[95] Others have suggested a Jewish apocalyptic conceptual background where the term "beasts" denotes evil spirits, so that Paul is referring to the demon-possessed sorcerers at work in the city of Ephesus who opposed his gospel.[96] Still others have noted the symbolic use of beasts or wild animals to describe pagan rulers in Dan. 7.[97]

Let us eat and drink, for tomorrow we die (15:32). The exact words appear in the Greek version of Isa. 22:13. The saying could equally originate from secular philosophy.[98]

"Bad company corrupts good morals" (15:33). Scholars have widely recognized this phrase as a quote from the comedy *Thais* by the Greek dramatist Menander (ca. 292 BC). The proverb has a specific reference to the corrupting influence of those who denied resurrection.

I say this to your shame (15:34). Denying the resurrection was a matter of shame for the Corinthian church because the resurrection represents a fundamental truth about God's person and power (cf. Mark 12:24).

But someone will ask (15:35). Paul writes in the style of the Greek diatribe, a method of argumentation that used an imaginary opponent in order to address a real situation.[99]

There are heavenly bodies and earthly bodies (15:36–41). In these verses Paul answers the two questions posed in 15:35 in part on the analogy of the harvest already at work in creation (see Gen. 1:11–13) and on the analogy of the creation account of Gen. 1:20–27, which speaks of both earthly flesh and heavenly bodies. The link between resurrection bodies and the heavenly bodies may have as its background Dan. 12:1–3, the most explicit OT passage on resurrection.

Sown in corruption, raised in incorruption (15:42). While sowing could refer to burial or to the character of mortal life (perishable, dishonorable, weak), there are instances in Greco-Roman literature that use the metaphor to refer to human origins and generation. If this is the meaning here, then Paul is contrasting human origins with the resurrection.[100]

Sown a natural body, raised a spiritual body (15:44). The terms "natural" and "spiritual" describe the present earthly body and the future transformed resurrection body shaped in the image of Christ. Paul derives the term "natural" from Gen. 2:7 (from the Greek word translated as "being"), quoted in 15:45.

***The first man Adam became a living being*; the last Adam became a life-giving spirit** (15:45). It has been suggested that the language of "life-giving spirit" derives from Gen. 2:7 read in light of Ezek. 37, which refers to God's Spirit bringing his people to life again.[101] The phrase "living being" refers to Adam. The term "life-giving spirit" describes the risen Christ, the last Adam, in his transformed state and corresponds to the description of the resurrection body as "spiritual."

Just as we have borne the image of the man of dust, we will also bear the image of the man of heaven (15:49). The background text is still Gen. 2:7 along with Gen. 5:3, which refers to Adam bearing a son in his own image.

Flesh and blood cannot inherit the kingdom of God (15:50). Paul's affirmation of the radical incompatibility of the present human body and the future resurrection body is a theme shared with Jewish apocalyptic literature.[102]

In a moment, in the twinkling of an eye (15:52). The phrases are unique to the OT and the NT but imply an instantaneous transformation, which is consistent with the OT emphasis on God's sudden eschatological intervention (see Isa. 29:5–6; 48:3; Mal. 3:1).

The trumpet will sound (15:52). The trumpet is the sign of the day of the Lord (Isa. 27:13; Joel 2:1; Zeph. 1:14–16; Zech. 9:14).

For this corruptible body must be clothed with incorruptibility (15:53). Paul may have in mind Ps. 102:26 in using garment imagery, which is quoted in Heb. 1:11–12.

Death has been swallowed up in victory. Where, death, is your victory? Where, death, is your sting? (15:54). The conflation of Isa. 25:8 and Hosea 13:14 into a single quotation is a method of citation similar to the way the Scriptures were used in rabbinic commentaries, in the Targums, and in the Qumran literature.

In the Roman world trumpets were used to proclaim important events. In this relief a trumpet announces the triumphal return to Rome in AD 176 of the victorious emperor Marcus Aurelius.

Collection, Travel Plans, and Letter Closing (16:1–24)

The collection for the saints (16:1). The collection was an offering for believers in Jerusalem (16:3). Other NT passages provide a more complete picture of the offering and the reasons for it (Acts 24:17; Rom. 15:25–31; 2 Cor. 8–9; Gal. 2:10). The contribution was for the poor, but there were also theological motivations: to solidify and strengthen the relationship between the Jewish and gentile portions of the church, thereby contributing to the unity of the church. The collection may have originated in the Jerusalem Council (Acts 15:1–29; cf. Gal. 2:10).

I will send with letters those you recommend (16:3). The use of recommendation letters was common in the ancient world. In this case, the letters would verify the nature of the offering and introduce the contributors.[103]

I will be traveling through Macedonia (16:5). Paul often includes a travelogue toward the end of his letters (see Rom. 15:22–32; 2 Cor. 12:14–13:1, 10; 1 Thess. 2:17–20; 3:11–13; Philem. 22), which describes not only the places he intends to travel but also the people he desires to see and plans for the ministry of the gospel. Passing through Macedonia on the way to

Travelers such as Paul and Timothy would have entered the ancient city of Corinth on the Lechaion Road, the main thoroughfare that led into the city.

Corinth was a more circuitous route than traveling by sea, but Macedonia, a Roman province, was the location of other Pauline churches in Philippi and Thessalonica.

But I will stay in Ephesus until Pentecost (16:8). The reference to Pentecost provides both the location of the writing of the letter and a reference to the time of year (i.e., spring). Although it was a Jewish festival (see Lev. 23:15–21), Pentecost held great significance for the whole church in light of the events described in Acts 2.

Many oppose me (16:9). The book of Acts provides further insight into the kinds of troubles Paul faced in Asia (see Acts 19:23–41; cf. 2 Cor. 1:8–11).

If Timothy comes, see that he has nothing to fear (16:10). Paul expresses concern for the treatment of Timothy when he arrives in Corinth (cf. 4:17–21). Since Timothy is Paul's representative, how the Corinthians treat him is equated with their treatment of Paul.

Send him on his way in peace (16:11). Sending "in peace" is a traditional formula (Exod. 4:18; 1 Sam. 20:42; 2 Kings 5:19; Acts 15:33; 16:36; James 2:16).

Now about our brother Apollos (16:12). The Corinthians may have asked Paul to send Apollos for reasons unstated. Some surmise that Apollos did not return due to his disgust with the perpetuation of factions in his name.

You know the household of Stephanas: They are the firstfruits of Achaia (16:15). Paul recalls that those of the household of Stephanas were among the first converts in the Roman province of Achaia (see 1:16). Stephanas may have been the primary source of Paul's knowledge of many of the

Corinthians' problems. The mention of his household probably indicates that Stephanas was a person of considerable financial means. Not all wealthy members of the church were to be blamed for the rifts between the rich and the poor. We know nothing further about Fortunatus and Achaicus (16:17), since there is no other mention of them in the NT.

Aquila and Priscilla send you greetings warmly in the Lord (16:19). The final greetings in Paul's letters reveal his considerable support network in ministry. Aquila and Priscilla are the only persons Paul mentions by name in this concluding greeting, other than himself. This outstanding couple is mentioned elsewhere in the NT (Acts 18:1–3, 24–19:1; Rom. 16:3–4). In both Rome and Ephesus a church met in their house. Their apparent financial means enabled them to serve the church in the capacity of patrons.

Greet one another with a holy kiss (16:20). The final command "greet one another with a holy kiss" represents a common practice in Paul's world. This kiss was a gesture of respect and affection and served as an outward symbol of unity among believers.

If anyone does not love the Lord, a curse be on him (16:22). On the curse pronouncement, see comments on 1 Cor. 12:3 (cf. Gal. 1:8–9). Love was the hallmark of the Christian community, yet it was a discerning love that derived its content from a commitment to the lordship of Christ.

The grace of the Lord Jesus be with you (16:23). Paul always concludes his letters with a grace benediction. This differs markedly from other Hellenistic letters, which normally closed with a simple "Farewell."

- Matthew
- Mark
- Luke
- John
- Acts
- Romans
- 1 Corinthians

2 Corinthians

- Galatians
- Ephesians
- Philippians
- Colossians
- 1 Thessalonians
- 2 Thessalonians
- 1 Timothy
- 2 Timothy
- Titus
- Philemon
- Hebrews
- James
- 1 Peter
- 2 Peter
- 1 John
- 2 John
- 3 John
- Jude
- Revelation

2 Corinthians

George H. Guthrie

Introduction. At least three issues of background need to be considered as we approach Paul's Second Letter to the Corinthians: (1) Paul as the author; (2) the apostle's relational history with the Corinthians; (3) the city of Corinth, especially the leadership values that permeated the city's unique embodiment of Greco-Roman culture (see the article "The City of Corinth").

That the apostle Paul wrote the book we know as 2 Corinthians is not really disputed, and when he wrote the letter, he probably had been a follower of Jesus Christ for a little more than two decades. Paul was both a Roman citizen (Acts 22:27–28) and a citizen of the city of Tarsus in Cilicia (Acts 21:39; 22:3). As a Roman citizen, the apostle may have had a level of credibility with leading men in Corinth, such as Erastus (Rom. 16:23) and even the Roman official Gallio (Acts 18:12–17), since the city was a Roman colony (see the article "Roman Citizenship"). The Corinthians still prided themselves on being well connected politically and socially to the capital of the empire.

Tarsus, however, was a leading center of education, and certain rhetorical skills that we see reflected in 2 Corinthians may have had their origin in the apostle's education there. Tarsus was also known for a special type of linen woven from flax and for a local material called cilicium, woven from goats' hair. The latter was used to make materials that offered protection from bad weather.[1] Thus the apostle probably became skilled in the craft of tentmaking in his hometown (Acts 18:3), and that skill served him well by providing living expenses as he conducted his mission activities. Yet his working in

The western end of the ancient ship trackway across the Isthmus of Corinth.

"manual labor" would have been very much out of step with Corinthian leadership values.

In spite of his dual citizenship, Paul's identity centered on the fact that he was a messianic Jew—a follower of Jesus as the Messiah—and called to be the apostle to the gentiles; he had a specific ministry calling to the predominantly gentile city of Corinth (2 Cor. 10:13–15; 11:22).

Paul probably arrived in Corinth for the first time in the spring of 50, planting the church and living in the city for about a year and a half, and then leaving in the fall of 51. Having written what he refers to as a "previous letter" to the Corinthians (one lost to history) in the summer/fall of 52 (1 Cor. 5:9), the apostle penned what we know as 1 Corinthians in the summer/fall of 53 from Ephesus. Yet in the early spring of 54 Timothy arrived in Corinth to find the church in disarray, which prompted Paul to travel from Ephesus to Corinth by ship once shipping season opened later that spring. The trip turned out to be a disaster, very painful due to a public clash between Paul and an opponent, and thus Paul tags it as a "painful visit" (2 Cor. 2:1). Paul returned to Ephesus and penned a "sorrowful letter" (2 Cor. 2:3–4), in which the apostle harshly rebuked the church. Then persecution in late summer 54 drove him out of Ephesus and to the north, through Troas and into Macedonia (Acts 19:8–10; 2 Cor. 2:12–13), where he wrote 2 Corinthians in the fall of 54 or the winter of 55. Thus when the apostle wrote 2 Corinthians, the church was only about five years old, and the believers in the city still were in their spiritual adolescence, a fact that certainly relates to the problems Paul had with the church.

When Paul arrived in Corinth in the mid-first century, the city was a thriving, wealthy metropolis, situated strategically for economic growth (on the history and background of Corinth generally, see the article "The City of Corinth."). In addition to the relative immaturity of the Corinthian believers, at least three dynamics made the church an especially difficult ministry context for the apostle.

First, at some point false teachers had moved to Corinth and were offering the believers there "a Jesus other than the Jesus" Paul had preached to them, "a different spirit from the Spirit" the Corinthians had received—in short, "a different gospel" (11:4). Paul tags these opponents as "false apostles" and "servants" of Satan (11:13–15). Second, these interlopers seemed to

The remains of ancient Corinth are visible in the foreground of this northern view from the Acrocorinth (acropolis). The proximity of the ancient city to the Gulf of Corinth can be seen. The exposed excavated area reveals the center of the city that Paul knew.

fit very well Corinthian standards of leadership, placing an emphasis on the attainment of honor, advancement in social status, public-speaking ability, ministry for hire, and wealth—all values in which Paul seemed to lack interest. In short, the apostle's humility (12:21), posture as a servant, rejection of patronage and financial gain, working with his hands in manual labor, and refusal to vie for social status by flaunting his rhetorical skills all violated key leadership values and principles celebrated in Corinthian culture. Paul instead offered the Corinthians a very countercultural, biblical vision of Christian leadership. Third, the Corinthian church was diverse both socially and geographically. The church almost certainly was made up of many house churches of no more than about forty people each, and many would have included people of various social statuses. Moreover, those house churches were spread throughout the region, the letter being addressed not only to the Corinthians but also to "all the saints who are throughout Achaia" (1:1). Thus as Paul sought to pull the Corinthian church back to a firm commitment to his mission and his gospel, he almost certainly dealt with pockets of resistance spread throughout the region—not an enviable position for a leader far from the church he sought to serve.

The Letter Opening and Prologue (1:1–11)

Letters in the ancient world commonly opened with a "prescript" that included the sender's name (the *superscriptio*), the addressee(s) (the *adscriptio*), and a greeting (the *salutatio*) (see the article "Ancient Letter Writing"). In the broader culture the greeting was expressed with the Greek word *charein*, which simply meant "greetings." In Christian circles this was changed to *charis*, the Greek word for "grace." Paul's Christian greeting also adds *eirēnē* ("peace"), the Greek term taken from the common Hebrew greeting *shalom*.

Achaia (1:1). We rightly call the letter Second *Corinthians*, but notice that the letter is also addressed to "all the saints who are throughout Achaia." Achaia was a Roman province that included the whole of the peninsula south of the Gulf of Corinth, the Cyclades Islands to the east of the mainland, along with a large part of central Greece. The word comes from *Achaioi*, commonly used by Homer for the Greeks. Corinth was the capital of the province.

Blessed be the God and Father (1:3). The blessing of God here follows roughly Jewish blessings of the day, such as the Eighteen Benedictions, which repeat, "Blessed are You, Lord." However, Paul's language as he praises God comes directly from the OT (e.g., Gen. 14:20; Ps. 18:46; 66:20).

Comfort (1:3). Here the word translated as "comfort" (*paraklēsis*) should be understood as more than simply soothing a person who is suffering. Rather, the term is related to a verb often rendered as "exhort" in the NT and carries an element of emboldening someone, encouraging them as they face the future. Thus God is the "God of all comfort."

The sufferings of Christ (1:5). In broader Judaism some writings spoke of "messianic woes," birth pangs in the world that ultimately would lead to the age of the Messiah—"the Christ" (see Isa. 26:17; 66:8) (see the article "Messianic Expectations in Jesus's Day"). Paul refers to the sufferings experienced by believers as they identify with and minister on behalf of Christ in the world.

Our affliction that took place in Asia (1:8–11). Asia was a Roman senatorial province that covered most of the western part of Asia Minor, along with islands such as Rhodes and Patmos. Ephesus, where Paul spent an extended period on his third main mission journey, was the province's capital (see the article "The City of Ephesus"). In 1 Cor. 15:32 the apostle refers to fighting "wild beasts" in Ephesus, which probably is a reference to human opponents rather than literal animals, but here it seems that he refers to a life-threatening situation that happened later. "The sentence of death" of which he speaks in 1:9 most likely refers to extreme persecution, an experience that forced Paul to rely on "God who raises the dead."

Why Paul Did Not Come Directly to Corinth (1:12–2:13)

Indeed, this is our boast (1:12–14). Paul writes a good deal about "boasting" in 2 Corinthians. In the Jewish Scriptures the concept could be used positively (as here) or negatively. As with modern Western culture, the latter had to do with foolish human pride in one's abilities or accomplishments (e.g., Judg. 7:2; 1 Sam. 2:3). But the former could be used of an appropriate "pride" that celebrated the Lord's character and work in the lives of people (e.g., 1 Chron. 16:35). Paul consistently boasts in the things of the Lord.

Macedonia (1:16). Paul had communicated to the Corinthians that he planned to come visit them before traveling to Macedonia, but those plans had changed; the apostle, rather, decided to go north from Ephesus to Troas and then on to Macedonia from there. Macedonia was another Roman senatorial province, north of Achaia, that ran along the northern and western sides of the Aegean Sea.

Now when I planned this, was I of two minds? (1:17). With his change of plans, some in Corinth accused him of fickleness or of having a wishy-washy character, a flaw condemned not only in Jewish and Christian cultures but also in the broader Greco-Roman world. In ancient literature leaders were condemned for fickleness and unreliability but praised if they were true to their word. But the apostle goes on to explain why he did not come as expected.

God as a witness (1:23). This amounted to a solemn oath, taken from the law courts of the day, in effect saying, "If God, who knows the situation perfectly, took the witness stand on my behalf, I would be shown to have acted with complete integrity."

Painful visit (2:1). In the early spring of 54 Timothy traveled to Corinth and found that the church had not responded well to the letter we know as 1 Corinthians. Since the church was in a mess, Paul too traveled from Ephesus to Corinth by ship later that spring. The trip was very painful due to a public conflict between Paul and an opponent (2:5–11), and thus Paul tags it here as the "painful visit."

I wrote this very thing . . . I wrote to you with many tears (2:3–4). When he arrived back in Ephesus following the painful visit, the apostle penned a painful letter, confronting the church out of love. Letters from an authority figure carried a great deal of relational weight. The phrase "an extremely troubled and anguished heart" in 2:4 means that the letter was "gut-wrenching" to write, speaking of the internal turmoil and distress that Paul experienced in the confrontation. Evidently, the letter had the intended effect (7:7–11).

Carvings of menorahs from an ancient Jewish synagogue in Corinth.

Instead forgive and comfort him (2:7). We do not know the identity of the offender, since Paul often refers to such people without naming them. The offense seems to have been a public conflict with the apostle, which was personal rather than theological, and the punishment that the church had carried out was the withdrawal of fellowship from the offender. If the offender was a person of high social status, which seems likely, it would have made the situation even more difficult.

Troas . . . Macedonia (2:12–13). On Macedonia, see comments on 2 Cor. 1:16. The ancient writer Strabo called Troas, a Roman colony, "one of the notable cities of the world."[2] The main seaport in Mysia in northwest Asia Minor, Troas had a population of thirty to forty thousand and was on primary travel routes from east to west and north to south. This is where Paul had his "Macedonian vision" (Acts 16:8–9) to bring the gospel for the first time to what we know as modern-day Europe.

Paul Commends His Ministry of Integrity (2:14–4:6)

Triumphal procession (2:14). Paul uses a word picture of a Roman "triumphal procession" or "victory parade" to describe how God reigns victorious through the gospel of Christ and spreads that gospel through his ministers. In the Roman cultural context a general would request such a parade from the senate upon an especially significant victory over one of Rome's enemies. The general was celebrated as the elaborate parade wound its way through the streets of Rome, showcasing the general himself on a chariot pulled by four white horses, the Roman army, carts loaded with the enemy's weapons and spoils from the defeated cities, and large paintings of the battlefields or captured cities. There were also dozens of incense bearers, who filled the city with the smell of burning incense that wafted out over the crowds and rose up to the gods. In the parade were also the captive leaders from the enemy army, who sometimes were put to death at a key point in the celebration. There also were Roman citizens who had been slaves in the enemy country but had been liberated by the victorious general.

Paul picks up on aspects of the parade, depicting himself and his mission, for instance, as incense bearers and the gospel as incense wafting out over humanity, and people respond to that gospel variously (2:15–16).

A "triumphal procession" (2 Cor. 2:14) was the conclusion to a military victory when the conquerors returned home. This first-century-AD chalice displays a procession by the emperor Tiberius.

In Paul's word picture "those who are being saved" correspond to the freed slaves in the parade and refer theologically to those who have found freedom through believing the gospel. To them the "aroma" of the gospel is a sweet smell of life. "Those who are perishing," on the other hand, correspond to the enemy captives and refer theologically to those headed for destruction due to their rejection of the gospel. To them the gospel stinks, smelling of death. Thus the gospel functions as a dividing line of humanity.

Some common writing implements from the Hellenistic period, including styli for wax tablets and inkpots for pen and papyrus or parchment.

We do not market the word of God for profit (2:17). The writer Lucian spoke figuratively of false teachers who "sell their teaching like tavern keepers, and most of them mix their wine with water and misrepresent it."[3] Thus Paul uses the image of a dishonest peddler to describe his opponents, who preach their twisted messages for hire.

Commend ourselves (3:1). "Self-recommendation" was a common way to present oneself for consideration in the ancient world, whether in a business situation (think "reference letters" today) or in a social setting. There were two situations in which it was entirely appropriate to recommend yourself: (1) when you were being introduced to someone for the first time and (2) when the relationship had broken down and needed repair.

Letters of recommendation (3:1). By Paul's time recommendation letters had been used for several centuries, and there were instruction manuals on how to write one appropriately. Such letters often were used when someone traveled or moved to a new location, providing an introduction to those who might provide a job or hospitality. Paul's point is that he does not need such letters to validate his ministry to the Corinthians—they themselves are his "letter," his validation (3:2). He had brought the gospel to them and was their father in the faith.

Delivered by us, not written with ink (3:3). Paul probably presents himself in the role of an amanuensis, or secretary, a professional scribe skilled in letter writing (see the article "Ancient Letter Writing"). In the first century ink normally was black, produced by combining soot and gum. It was applied by using a reed pen.

With the Spirit . . . on tablets of human hearts (3:3). Paul probably is alluding to the new-covenant reality reflected in passages like Jer. 31:33, which speaks of the law of God being written on the hearts of believers, and Isa. 44:3, Ezek. 39:29, and Joel 2:28–29, which speak of the work of the Spirit in the lives of God's people.

Not that we are competent in ourselves (3:5). The term translated as "competent" (*hikanos*) referred to something that was sufficient or adequate, to a person measuring up to a standard or being qualified for a task. It may be that Paul has Moses's call to ministry in mind (Exod. 3:11; 4:10–12), this term being used in the Greek translation of that OT story.

The letter kills, but the Spirit gives life (3:6). The apostle refers to the OT law as "the letter," and he contrasts it with "the Spirit," who "gives life." As Paul reads the OT, he witnesses the deadly impact of the law on those who came out of Egypt, who died in the wilderness. Apart from the work of the Spirit, the impact of the law is disastrous.

The ministry that brings righteousness overflows with even more glory (3:9). In 3:7–11 Paul uses a rabbinic technique of argumentation known as *qal wahomer*, an argument "from lesser to greater." In such an argument, if something is true in a less important situation, it certainly is true in a more important situation and has greater implications. In this case, Paul reflects on the glory and veiling of Moses's face in Exod. 34:29–35. Paul's argument is that if the old-covenant ministry through Moses came with glory (the "lesser" situation), the new-covenant ministry abounds with a much greater glory (the "greater" situation). The latter is greater because the glory spreads to all God's people (3:17–18).

Glory (3:7). In the Greco-Roman culture of Corinth "glory" or "honor" was a very high social value (see 6:8). Paul, however, points to a dimension of the biblical concept of glory as a manifestation of God's presence.

Its glory, which was set aside (3:7). The Greek word translated here as "was set aside" (*katargeō*), used four times in 3:7–18, speaks of something being nullified or made inoperative. Here Paul points to the veil as "snuffing out" the glory on Moses's face. The Israelites were not able to "gaze steadily at Moses's face" because it was covered with the veil.

The veil is removed (3:16). In the ancient world veils were used to cover a person's face, either because it was sacred or shameful. As in parts of the Near East today, women at times covered their faces with a veil. In 3:12–18 Paul speaks of the veil that covered Moses's face but then transitions to a figurative veil that stands between people and God. (The same Greek word he uses for "veil" could be used for the curtain in the tabernacle, which closed off the presence of God from common people.) New-covenant ministry has a much greater glory than the old because the veil covering the hearts of people, standing between them and a relationship with God, has been "set aside" (*katargeō*, the same Greek word as above) or nullified by Christ. They have a glorious, face-to-face relationship with God that glorifies them, transforming them, by the work of the Holy Spirit, in accordance with God's character.

Commending ourselves (4:2). See comments on 2 Cor. 3:1.

The god of this age (4:4). The use of the word "god" for Satan is unique to the NT. Paul does not mean that the Enemy has divine status. Rather, he speaks of Satan's functional status as ruler of the fallen world. Similarly, John called the Evil One the "ruler of this world" (e.g., John 12:31; 14:30; 16:11). He is the one who veils the hearts of the unbelieving, blinding them to the truth of the gospel.

Image of God (4:4). An "image" truly represents the original, even as the image of a parent may be stamped on a child biologically. Biblically, glory manifests God's presence, and the emphasis on "the glory of Christ" in verse 4, coupled with "image," points to Jesus as manifesting God's presence. When you see Jesus, as borne witness to in the gospel, you are seeing God.

God who said, "Let light shine out of darkness," has shone in our hearts (4:6). In the first of these clauses Paul alludes to Gen. 1:3: "Then God said, 'Let there be light,' and there was light." Awakening people to the gospel is an act of "new creation" (2 Cor. 5:17). In the second clause the apostle alludes to another important OT passage, Isa. 9:2. The Greek translation (Septuagint) of that OT verse reads in part, "O you who live in the country and in the shadow of death, light will shine on you!"

The Suffering Involved in Paul's Authentic Ministry (4:7–5:10)

Treasure in clay jars (4:7). Clay jars were the "paper cups" of the ancient world, being mass-produced, affordable, disposable, fragile, and common. The apostle speaks of the irony of treasure being stored in such a container. Moreover, his word picture probably focuses attention on their fragility, since this section deals with the minister's vulnerability in suffering.

We are struck down (4:9). This image of persecution, if taken from the world of athletics, could allude to a person being "thrown down" in a wrestling match or being "knocked down" in a boxing match. In a military context, however, the verb (*kataballō*) could be used of someone thrown to the ground and killed. The balance here, however, is that Paul and his ministry

Paul compares messengers like himself to clay jars with precious treasure in them.

team have not been "destroyed" (*apollymi*), a word that could also be used of those killed in battle.

The death of Jesus (4:10). Here Paul uses an unusual word for "death" (*nekrōsis*), which seems to emphasize the process of dying, alluding to Jesus's suffering in his passion. This parallels the Christian minister who suffers for the gospel.

I believed, therefore I spoke (4:13). This quotation is from the Greek translation of Ps. 116:10 (LXX 115:1). The OT context of these words speaks of being delivered by the Lord but also of the preciousness of the death of those committed to the Lord. In spite of persecution and the threat of death, the apostle continues to speak the gospel because he trusts the Lord who has called him to the task.

Incomparable eternal weight of glory (4:17). Momentary troubles are "light"—that is, insignificant—compared to "eternal glory." The Hebrew word for "glory" speaks in part of weightiness or heaviness. For emphasis, Paul adds to the word "glory" the Greek word *baros*, which also could be used to speak of fullness or weightiness, but also of something being of significance or importance. He stacks up terms to show the "massiveness" of glory that makes his suffering seem paltry by comparison.

Tent . . . building . . . dwelling (5:1). As today, tents in the ancient world were both insecure and impermanent, and Paul knew them well because he was a tentmaker. In Isa. 38:12 the prophet speaks of death in terms of taking down a tent. Paul uses the twin images of a "building" and a "dwelling" or house to speak of the resurrection body as a permanent place to live. "Not made with hands" is common biblical language for something that only God can build.

Unclothed (5:4). At times writers in the ancient world described the body as clothing,[4] and death could be described with the word picture of "undressing."[5]

Spirit as a down payment (5:5). The term for "down payment" (*arrabōn*), or "deposit," was legal language. When contracts involved goods or services being transferred, the deposit was a guarantee that the transfer would take place. Thus the presence of the Holy Spirit in the life of a believer is a guarantee, an expression of God's commitment to his people, heralding things to come.

We walk by faith (5:7). The biblical concept of faith, rather than a "blind leap," has to do with trust based on what God *has revealed to be true*. In the context of this passage, trust is needed because we do not see our eternal home at present.

Judgment seat (5:10). The term translated here as "judgment seat" (*bēma*) was used in the first century of a platform that a person would ascend by steps. In the NT it primarily is used of a platform on which a Roman official, such as Pilate, Herod, or Gallio, would sit to judge cases (e.g., Matt. 27:19; John 19:13; Acts 12:21; 18:12, 16–17). Elsewhere Paul can speak also of the judgment seat of God (Rom. 14:10). Here the apostle envisions Christ as the agent of the Father in carrying out judgment at the end of the age.

"Respond to Authentic Ministry": Exhortations to the Corinthians (5:11–7:4)

Commending ourselves (5:12). See comments on 2 Cor. 3:1.

Who has reconciled us to himself (5:18). Reconciliation had to do with being brought back into right relationship with someone. In the ancient world an inferior most often would seek out reconciliation with a superior, not the other way around. But Paul emphasizes that God has taken the initiative in reconciling us to himself. Scholar Seyoon Kim believes that Paul developed his theology of God taking the initiative in reconciliation from his conversion experience on the Damascus Road.[6]

Ambassadors for Christ (5:20). An ambassador traveled and represented a person in an official capacity, and an ambassador's role was seen as highly respected and protected. In the realm of politics those to whom an ambassador was sent understood that they must treat the ambassador well, or dire consequences could take place. Normally, however, the lesser political power would send an ambassador to the more powerful to plead their case. For instance, Roman emperors often received ambassadors from lands that were subject to them. Yet in an amazing reversal of this cultural pattern, God, the all-powerful ruler of the universe, sends his ambassadors to seek out reconciliation with human beings.

He made the one who did not know sin to be sin for us, so that in him we might become the righteousness of God (5:21). Isaiah 53:4–12 almost certainly lies behind the "transformational interchange" described in 5:21. Christ "bore the sin of many" (Isa. 53:12) to "justify many" (Isa. 53:11).[7]

Ruins of the Odeon, the ancient musical theater in Corinth.

At an acceptable time . . . in the day of salvation (6:2). This quotation is from Isa. 49:8a, a passage in which the servant of the Lord serves as a representative of God's people. Thus the passage in Isaiah speaks of God's salvation, his deliverance of his people, which Paul sees as accomplished through Jesus, who through his death and resurrection accomplished reconciliation between God and people. This is a supreme expression of God's favor.

By hardships (6:4). The opponents of Paul in Corinth seemed to focus on the glory of what they perceived as great skills or accomplishments. Paul, rather, focuses on his "weaknesses" (11:22–12:10). In Greco-Roman rhetoric a speaker could focus on personal sacrifice made in service to the community. In 6:3–10 the apostle uses experiences like "by beatings, by imprisonments, by riots, by labors, by sleepless nights, by times of hunger" to validate his ministry of suffering on behalf of Christ as he preached the gospel faithfully.

I speak as to my children; as a proper response, open your heart to us (6:13). The use of *pathos*, or an emotional appeal, was a highly valued skill in Greek rhetoric. Here Paul speaks bluntly about the misplaced affections of the Corinthians and emotionally appeals to them on the basis of the social value of reciprocation, an appropriate exchange. In Greco-Roman culture it was seen as bad form to be benefited by a person and then refuse to reciprocate appropriately. This was especially the case when failing to honor a parent, and Paul was the Corinthians' spiritual father (1 Cor. 4:14–15). In that culture one of the father's responsibilities was to teach his children about what is appropriate in various life contexts, and Paul does that here.

Don't become partners with those who do not believe (6:14). The language here alludes to Lev. 19:19, a law prohibiting, among other things, the crossbreeding of livestock (literally, "breed with one of a different yoke"), and perhaps Deut. 22:10: "Do not plow with an ox and a donkey together." The ox was considered clean and the donkey unclean. The word picture here speaks of being mismatched, being in incompatible relationships with unbelievers.

What agreement does Christ have with Belial? (6:15). In early Judaism "Belial" may have been a name for Satan coined by combining the Hebrew word for "worthless" and the name of the pagan god Baal. It is absurd to think of Christ being in harmony with a pagan god!

What agreement does the temple of God have with idols? (6:16). See the article "The Jerusalem Temple." In the OT story King Manasseh at one point built altars to the heavenly host and erected an idol of Asherah in the Jerusalem temple (2 Kings 21:3–7), an egregious evil that was harshly judged by God. As the "new temple" (1 Cor. 3:16–17; 6:19–20), God's "mobile tabernacle" that moves throughout the earth with God's gospel, the people of God should have no place for idols in their lives.

Participation in pagan idolatry was an ongoing problem in the Corinthian church. The remains of the Temple of Octavia (shown here) indicate that emperor worship had a strong foothold in Corinth.

I will dwell . . . says the Lord Almighty (6:16–18). Rabbis of the first century at times bolstered an argument or exhortation by stringing together a number of OT texts having similar wording. This method was called "a string of pearls," and, playing off of the theme of God's people as his temple, Paul offers such a Scripture-saturated exhortation here.

I will dwell and walk among them (6:16b). The OT quotation is taken from a conflation of Lev. 26:11–12 and Ezek. 37:27, both passages having to do with God's promises and presence.

Come out from among them (6:17). Isaiah 52:11 is the source of this quotation, an OT passage celebrating salvation of God's people from a context of captivity and uncleanness (Isa. 52:1–2).

I will be a Father to you (6:18). The quotation in 6:18 comes primarily from 2 Sam. 7:14. The focus again is on God's presence and the promise of a family relationship with him. Rather than just "servants," we are "sons and daughters."

The Happy Result When the Corinthians Respond Well (7:5–16)

When we came into Macedonia (7:5). On Macedonia, see comments on 2 Cor. 1:16. Here the apostle picks back up his travel narrative left off at 2:13. Such a *digressio* ("digression") in a writing or speech was meant to focus the hearers' attention. When he pushes the pause button on his travel narrative at 2:13, he leaves the "tension" of his trip into Macedonia hanging in the air, resolving it here only after he has made his case for the nature of true Christian ministry. Now, in the verses that follow, Paul tells us how the situation turned out.

Titus (7:6). Titus was a gentile believer and a fellow worker of Paul who had accompanied Paul and Barnabas to Jerusalem during the controversy over the gentiles (Gal. 2:1, 3). Along with Timothy, he was one of Paul's two main liaisons with the Corinthian church during this period of ministry.

Grieved you with my letter (7:8). This is the same letter alluded to in 2:3–4. The verb *lypeō*, translated as "grieved you," could be used of stirring up negative emotions such as sadness. John Chrysostom, the great golden-tongued preacher among the church fathers, compared Paul's causing grief to the Corinthians with a father watching his son being operated on and rejoicing not because of the pain but because the pain would lead to healing.[8]

In every way you showed yourselves to be pure in this matter (7:11). The language here is from the law courts of the day.

Titus (7:13). On Titus, see comments on 2 Cor. 7:6.

If I have made any boast (7:14). As noted in the comments on 1:12–14, boasting could be perceived negatively when it focused on foolish pride in human activities, but from a biblical perspective it was seen as positive when it celebrated the Lord's character and work. Paul celebrates the work of God among the Corinthians.

The Ministry of Giving (8:1–9:15)

Brothers and sisters (8:1). The Greek term *adelphos* ("brother") is translated appropriately here as "brothers and sisters," since in the ancient world the term was used of both men and women in religious contexts.

The churches of Macedonia (8:1). The use of a positive example was a main motivational strategy in rhetorical speeches and sermons of the era, and here Paul uses the Macedonian churches (probably including the church at Philippi) as a positive example of giving.

Wealth of generosity (8:2). The Macedonians were poor but gave extravagantly. In the Greco-Roman world giving was done primarily by wealthy people giving to other elites of the culture but also, at times, for the social good. Normally, leaders were wealthy people. In the Jewish world everyone was supposed to give to the poor as an act of piety. So the members of the church in Macedonia, many of whom were from gentile backgrounds, expressed Jewish religious values in their giving. But, more importantly, they gave as devout Christ-followers (8:5). See the article "Money in the New Testament World."

The ministry to the saints (8:4). Paul alludes here to the collection for the saints in Jerusalem, the word rendered as "ministry" (*diakonia*) being a technical term referring to financial relief (Acts 11:29; 12:25; Rom. 15:31).

Just as he had begun, so he should also complete among you this act of grace (8:6). In the previous year the collection had been initiated among the Corinthians (1 Cor. 16:1–4). The Greek word *charis*, translated here as "grace," is used in at least five different ways in chapters 8–9. In the broader culture the word could refer to attractiveness, charm, winsomeness, thanks, thankfulness, grace, gift, benefit, generosity, favor, or help. Given the context, Paul here could be referring to the collection as an act of "generosity."

Though he was rich . . . he became poor (8:9). In Corinthian culture wealth and leadership were inextricably bound, so that many of the immature believers at Corinth would not have been able to imagine a poor leader. Yet Paul shows that biblical values turn that cultural assumption on its head. Christ met the need of humanity for salvation by lowering himself in the incarnation.

According to what you have (8:11). In broader Judaism teachers at times emphasized proportionate giving. The apocryphal book of Tobit exhorted, "If you have many possessions, make your gift from them in proportion; if few, do not be afraid to give according to the little you have" (Tob. 4:8).

Equality (8:13). In the ancient world the concept of "equality" (*isotēs*) had to do with being fair or balanced. The word could be used in the realms of arithmetic and geometry to refer to equal measurements or sums. In the political world the word referred to justice.

The person who had much . . . the person who had little (8:15). For the principle of equality the apostle appeals to a biblical principle, drawing on Exod. 16:18, a text concerning God's provision of food for the Israelites during the wilderness wanderings. Food wasn't to be hoarded, and people were to partake only of what they needed. Paul's point is that it is appropriate to share resources with brothers and sisters.

The brother who is praised (8:18). The word translated as "brother" (*adelphos*) may be simply a way of referring to a fellow believer, but given the context, it could refer to a "fellow worker" of Paul and his mission, chosen to serve in an official capacity (8:19). This brother is not named, and his identity is not known.

No one will criticize us about this large sum that we are administering (8:20). The terminology of administration here was used, for instance, of the annual dispatching of envoys who carried the offerings for the temple in Jerusalem from Jews scattered through the Mediterranean world.

In verse 21 Paul alludes to Prov. 3:4, which speaks of being noble before God and people.

Our brother . . . messengers of the churches (8:22–23). This is another brother who is not named. In delivering larger sums of money, officials in religious contexts of the ancient world at times used escorts to help with the delivery. The word translated as "messengers" is *apostoloi*, translated elsewhere as "apostles." Yet here the word refers to official representatives rather than those who held the apostolic office.

This ministry to the saints (9:1). See comments on 2 Cor. 8:4.

Macedonians . . . "Achaia" (9:2). See comments on 2 Cor. 1:1; 1:16.

Boasting (9:2). See comments on 2 Cor. 1:12–14.

Put to shame (9:4). The Greco-Roman world generally was a culture of honor and shame (see the article "Honor and Shame in the New Testament World"). Moving up in the culture meant doing things that accorded with gaining greater honor or status while avoiding shameful social actions. These values were attached to a strong sense of belonging to a particular family, tribe, or community. To do something shameful was to bring shame on one's whole group. For instance, in the broader culture those who defaulted on public pledges could have their names published publicly to shame them.

The person who sows sparingly will also reap sparingly (9:6). The language of sowing and reaping is taken from common proverbial language in the OT and broader Jewish literature. A familiar agricultural word picture suggested, "Little invested, little harvested." In the gentile world the word picture was used of benefiting someone and being paid back appropriately.[9]

A cheerful giver (9:7). The apostle paraphrases Prov. 22:8 in the Greek translation of the OT (Septuagint), a passage that speaks of cheerful generosity, as well as sowing and reaping.

He distributed freely . . . his righteousness endures (9:9). As Paul does here, rabbis at times reinforced a teaching by quoting a passage of Scripture. The passage that the apostle uses here is the Greek translation (LXX Ps. 111:9a) of Ps. 112:9a in the Hebrew Bible: "They have distributed freely, they have given to the poor; their righteousness endures forever" (NRSV). In this context the blessed man, living in reverent fear of God, has riches that he uses in accordance with righteousness.

The one who provides seed (9:10). The words of verse 10 almost certainly allude to the Greek translation of Isa. 55:10b, which speaks of God giving seed to the sower and bread for food. The OT context has to do with God's word being productive like the rain and snow that fall from heaven. The point of the passage, and of Paul's allusion, is to focus on God as provider, the source of what is good.

Paul's Authority and "Proper" Boasting (10:1–18)

Humble among you in person (10:1). Here Paul uses irony, which was another appropriate rhetorical technique. It is ironic that his opponents label him as "humble" (*tapeinos*) or timid. The Greek word also could be translated as "pitiful," meaning unimpressive. Leaders in Greco-Roman culture were supposed to exude confidence, and timidity in a leader was looked down upon.

According to the flesh (10:2). The false teachers in Corinth had a set of standards by which they judged leadership qualities, and their standards, rather than being biblical, were taken right out of Greco-Roman culture. These standards would have included, among other things, wealth, social connections, public-speaking ability, a high level of education, and a bold public presence.

Wage war . . . weapons (10:3–6). In these verses we have a warfare word picture used to describe the effectiveness of a Spirit-empowered ministry (over against a worldly approach to ministry). The "weapons" Paul seems to have in mind are siege engines (note "demolition of strongholds" in v. 4), which, in a world where breaking down the walls of an enemy's city could be the key to victory, would have been very familiar to the Corinthians. A "stronghold" could be demolished by various means, and once a wall was breached, an army would flood into the city and "take captive" those inside. Then the victors would prosecute or "punish" the captives. Notice that the "strongholds" Paul has in mind are false arguments raised up against a true understanding of God. He tears such arguments down by divine power, not by human means. He thus lays siege to the false ministry of his opponents in Corinth, tears down their arguments, hems in their false thinking, and is ready to punish them—all by God's power manifested in right thinking. See the article "The Roman Military."

Terrify you with my letters (10:9). Letters sent from a person in an official capacity were understood to have the same authority as if the person was present (cf. 10:11). The allusion here is to Paul's "painful letter," mentioned in 2:3–4; 7:8–12.

His public speaking amounts to nothing (10:10). Public-speaking ability—being able to wow a crowd—was one of the most important skills for leaders in Greco-Roman culture. One had to be able to move a crowd to lead them.

Classify or compare ourselves (10:12). The false teachers in Corinth seem to have been Jewish in background, to have adopted a false form of Christianity (see 11:12–15), and to have embraced an approach to leadership from Sophists—traveling, "speak for hire" philosophers who made a living by their public presentations (cf. 2:17). Drawing comparisons, moreover, was a common strategy in Greek rhetoric. In the political arena public smear campaigns sought to tear down an opponent while one was building up one's own public image. For instance, satirists at times poked fun at bogus teachers who built their own reputations by comparing themselves elaborately with others.

Area of ministry (10:13). The Greek term used here, *kanōn*, is found on an inscription from Galatia that was discovered in 1976. The inscription was an edict from Sotidius, governor of Galatia (ca. AD 13–15), and instructed the citizens to provide public transportation for officials. Our word speaks of "services" provided within certain territorial limits.[10] Paul's point is that God had given him responsibility over the church in Achaia, and the false teachers were interlopers who came there without being assigned by God to that ministry.

Regions beyond you (10:16). Paul hoped to push his mission to the west (see Rom. 15:24, 28), perhaps thinking of going as far as Spain.

Let the one who boasts, boast in the Lord (10:17). The apostle alludes to the Greek OT translation of Jer. 9:23–24. Appropriate boasting is that which boasts in the ways and work of God. On boasting, see comments on 2 Cor. 1:12–14.

Paul and the "Super-Apostles" (11:1–21a)

Foolishness (11:1). Paul is speaking ironically, adopting a posture of "foolishness" to highlight how foolish it is for the Corinthians to put up with the foolishness of the false teachers.

Godly jealousy (11:2). In the ancient world jealousy could be a negative or a positive emotion. Positively, it spoke of intense desire or dedication. In the Ten Commandments God describes himself as "jealous" (Exod. 20:5), and Exod. 34:14 even presents God's name (thus his very nature) as "Jealous." Paul shares intense, appropriate desire that the Corinthians stay true in their relationship with God.

Promised you in marriage to one husband . . . a pure virgin (11:2). The apostle uses betrothal imagery here, grounded in OT texts that present God as the groom and God's people as the beloved betrothed. It may be that Paul presents himself as the father of the bride (cf. 1 Cor. 4:15); in Jewish culture the father of the bride was responsible for protecting his daughter's purity in preparation for her wedding day (see the article "Jewish Marriage Customs").

As the serpent deceived Eve by his cunning (11:3). In Jewish theology the snake was the archetypal unclean animal and stood as a symbol of opposition to God. Here the snake is identified with Satan. The overt identification of Satan with the serpent in the garden of Eden is found in Rev. 12:9; 20:2. "Cunning" was used to describe the Sophists of Paul's day, who misled people by their public speaking.

Preaches another Jesus . . . a different spirit . . . a different gospel (11:4). The Sophists were public speakers known more for style than for substance. Their public-speaking emphasis was on the effect of their words, not the content. It seems that the false teachers in Corinth were forceful speakers, but Paul says that they did not have the true gospel.

Super-apostles (11:5). "Apostles" were sent representatives who carried the authority of the one who sent them. The prefix "super" here translates the Greek word *hyperlian*, meaning "beyond measure." These were not real apostles, such as Peter, John, and Paul, but rather were people presenting themselves as "super" on the basis of skills valued in Greco-Roman culture.

Untrained in public speaking (11:6). The term that Paul uses, translated here as "untrained" (*idiōtēs*), could carry the sense of "amateur," but it also could be used of a person who had been trained in rhetoric but chose not to use the skills in particular situations. The various rhetorical devices Paul uses in his letters seem to indicate that he had training in public speaking, but he chose not to use that ability in Corinth so that their faith would be grounded in the gospel rather than in his abilities (1 Cor. 2:1–5).[11]

I preached the gospel of God to you free of charge (11:7). Traveling professional speakers often were paid by wealthy patrons. It scandalized some in Corinth that Paul refused such support. His rejection of a patron would have been highly offensive, but Paul would have been socially obligated to that patron, so he refuses, speaking free of charge.

I robbed other churches (11:8). The term translated as "robbed" (*sylaō*) could be used of thieves ransacking a city or more mildly of someone being deprived of something.

I did not burden anyone (11:9). The word translated as "did not burden" (*katanarkaō*) was used of the social obligation in a patron-client relationship. The patron was responsible for the client, and the client was socially obligated to the patron, or to the one paying for the services.

Regions of Achaia (11:10). See comments on 2 Cor. 1:1.

Disguising themselves as apostles of Christ (11:13–15). In plays of the Greco-Roman world characters at times disguised themselves in order to deceive other characters in the play. Here the "false apostles" masquerade as "servants of righteousness."

Satan . . . angel of light (11:14). A number of Jewish works present Satan as changing himself into an angel of light to trick his targets.[12]

Fool (11:16). A worldly form of wisdom was highly valued in Greek philosophical circles, but Paul says that the approach to ministry by the false teachers amounts to them being fools. Since the Corinthians tolerate fools, Paul will gain an audience with them by taking the role of a fool. Again, he is speaking ironically, which was a rhetorical tactic.

Of boasting (11:17). On boasting, see comments on 2 Cor. 1:12–14.

To our shame (11:21a). On honor and shame, see comments on 2 Cor. 9:4; see the article "Honor and Shame in the New Testament World."

Paul Boasts Like a Fool (11:21b–12:13)

I am talking foolishly (11:21b). Paul refers to his speech as "foolish" because in 11:22–12:10 he is engaging in "boasting" about himself. But he turns the competitive boasting of the false teachers, which focused on leadership strengths, on its head, focusing rather on his weaknesses. It is a brilliant rhetorical strategy. In Greco-Roman literature philosophers could emphasize their sufferings as endured on behalf of the state or community, but they did so to emphasize their strengths.[13]

Hebrews . . . Israelites . . . descendants of Abraham (11:22). Public speakers could appeal to their ethnic identity in order to gain a hearing.

Forty lashes minus one (11:24). This was a punishment in Jewish synagogue contexts, and the punishment originated with Deut. 25:2–3, which speaks of giving a violator up to forty lashes. The collection of Jewish teachings known as the Mishnah suggested that the punishment was to be administered with a strap of three hide thongs, two-thirds on the back and one-third on the front of the offender.[14]

Beaten with rods (11:25). This was a Roman form of punishment using elm or birch rods, and Paul and Silas faced such a beating in Philippi (Acts 16:22). Normally, Roman citizens were protected from such punishment when they had not been tried and found guilty.

Stoning (11:25). This is a form of capital punishment prescribed in Deut. 17:5–7; 22:22–24. The stoning of Paul in the gentile city of Lystra (Acts 14:19–20) may have simply been a mob action.

Shipwrecked (11:25). Because of the danger, travel by sea normally was limited to the months of May through October, and people greatly feared shipwreck. Winter travel was dangerous not only due to storms but also because cloudiness made navigation impossible, and ships could be torn apart by reefs in unknown waters, which was often a death sentence for those on board the doomed ship. See the article "Shipping Practices in the First Century."

Dangers from rivers (11:26). Powerful rivers in remote areas often did not have bridges to cross, and people could easily be swept away and drowned.

Dangers from robbers (11:26). Paul could be referring to the pirates who inhabited the coast of the Mediterranean or gangs of violent outlaws who hid in the mountains. See the article "Roman Roads and Travel."

Toil and hardship (11:27). Paul's travels and his work with tentmaking were very demanding physically. Such manual labor would have been looked down upon among some in Corinth as inappropriate for a leader.

The God and Father of the Lord Jesus, who is blessed forever, knows I am not lying (11:31). On appealing to God as witness, see comments on 2 Cor. 1:23.

In Damascus, a ruler under King Aretas (11:32). This king is Aretas IV, who ruled the desert kingdom east, south, and southwest of the Dead Sea from about 9 BC to AD 40. The capital was in Petra. It seems that Aretas's power reached as far north as Damascus during the period that Paul references, and Paul probably was a fugitive (the point of the reference in v. 33 to being lowered in a basket) due to his preaching of the gospel.

Visions and revelations of the Lord (12:1). In biblical literature "visions," which involved the intersection of heaven and earth in some way, can speak of an appearance of an angel (Luke 1:22; 24:23) or of the exalted Christ, as with Paul's Damascus Road experience (Acts 26:19). Paul, for instance, also had visions of Ananias laying hands on him (Acts 9:11–12), of a request to come to Macedonia (Acts 16:9–10), and of the Lord giving him encouragement in Corinth (Acts 18:9–10). Visions were common in OT prophetic literature (e.g., Isa. 6:1; Ezek. 1:1), as well as broader Jewish apocalyptic literature. "Revelations," however, refers to a disclosure of information (e.g., Luke 2:32; Rom. 2:5; 8:19). One aspect of apocalyptic visions was a person being given insight into a present or future event.

I know a man in Christ (12:2). In Greco-Roman rhetoric a speaker could use third person, or seemingly refer to a third party, to speak of his own experience. This approach was used to deflect attention from oneself, especially when one could be heard as boasting of a great experience or accomplishment. The event that Paul mentions happened around 41–42, perhaps during a time of ministry in Syria and Cilicia.

The third heaven (12:2). It is not clear whether Jewish writings of the first century AD had complex cosmologies with multiple levels of heaven. Consequently, Paul's reference to the "third heaven" is one of the first clearly dated to the first century. "The third heaven" as used by the apostle refers to the highest heavenly realm, the location of God's throne room in the heavenly tabernacle.[15]

Paradise (12:4). The term originally was used of parks owned by Persian kings and their nobles, and the Greek translation of the OT uses the word of the garden of Eden (e.g., Gen. 2:8; 13:10). In Jewish apocalyptic literature it is

The world map by Cosmas Indicopleustes (sixth century AD) shows a rectangular landmass surrounded by the ocean, with paradise to the far right (east).

the place of ultimate blessedness in the presence of God and is identified with "the third heaven."[16]

A thorn in the flesh (12:7–9). The word rendered as "thorn" (*skolops*) could be used of something sharp or pointed, like a splinter or stake, but Paul almost certainly alludes to the Greek OT as his backdrop, to passages that speak of painful opposition as a "thorn" (Num. 33:55; Ezek. 28:24; Hosea 2:6). Given the context of the "Fool's Speech" (the apostle considered having to write this "speech" that we find in 11:22–12:10 a "foolish" enterprise), the word picture here probably refers to incessant persecution.

You ought to have commended me (12:11). On forms of commendation in the Greco-Roman world, see comments on 2 Cor. 3:1.

Signs and wonders and miracles (12:12). In the NT and broader Judaism "signs" were seen as validation of the work of God (e.g., Acts 2:22, 43; 5:12; Rom. 15:18–19), "wonders" prompted awe, and "miracles" were manifestations of God's power (e.g., Acts 6:8; Rom. 15:19; 2 Thess. 2:9; Heb. 2:4; Bar. 2:11).

Preparation for the Third Visit (12:14–13:10)

Come to you this third time (12:14). Paul often mentioned impending visits as a form of accountability. His first visit was in 50, when the church was planted. His second was in the spring of 54, called the "painful visit" in 2:1.

Children ought not save up for their parents, but parents for their children (12:14). In the Greco-Roman world parents who provided well for their children were celebrated.[17]

I took you in by deceit! (12:16). At times false teachers were described as dishonest merchants, who sought to trick their listeners into following them.[18] Paul's opponents are accusing him of using shady tactics to win the Corinthians.

God will again humiliate me in your presence (12:21). The term "humiliate" is used negatively here, referring to Paul's being shamed by the pattern of life held onto by the pockets of resistance in the Corinthian church. See the article "Honor and Shame in the New Testament World."

Third time I am coming to you (13:1). See comments on 2 Cor. 12:14.

Every matter must be established by the testimony of two or three witnesses (13:1). Rabbis often used Scripture to reinforce an exhortation or a teaching, and here Paul alludes to Deut. 19:15, which explains the "two or three witnesses" needed for dealing with an accusation that someone has sinned. The need for two witnesses, more if possible, was unique to Judaism in the ancient world.

Crucified in weakness (13:4). The apostle refers to Christ's choosing to be vulnerable, allowing himself to be crucified. Crucifixion was the most shameful form of execution in the Roman judicial system and normally was not carried out against Roman citizens (see the article "Crucifixion"). It was such a horrible, degrading form of torture that people would not speak of it in polite company.

Do you yourselves not recognize that Jesus Christ is in you?—unless you fail the test (13:5). One of the great sins of the wilderness-wandering generation was that they tested God (e.g., Exod. 17:2, 7; Num. 14:22; Ps. 78:41; Isa. 7:12), but Paul calls for the Corinthians to test themselves in terms of their commitments and patterns of life. The terminology here was used in Greek literature to speak of examining and thus validating something.

Closing Exhortations, Greetings, and Benediction (13:11–13)

Greet one another with a holy kiss (13:12). In the broader Jewish and Greco-Roman cultures greeting someone with a kiss was common, as is the case in the Near East today. It could be used as a sign of fellowship in religious contexts. The concept of a "holy" kiss seems to have originated with Paul (Rom. 16:16; 1 Cor. 16:20; 1 Thess. 5:26).

The grace of the Lord Jesus Christ, and the love of God, and the fellowship of the Holy Spirit be with you all (13:13). Greco-Roman letters often ended with a wish for good health and a farewell. Paul typically closes his letters with a benediction, and his benedictions generally have the word of blessing or wishes, God as the source, and a reference to those addressed.

Galatians

Roy E. Ciampa

Introduction. Throughout the centuries Paul's Letter to the Galatians has served as a key to understanding the grace and freedom that God has provided believers in Christ. Scholars debate whether Paul wrote this powerful letter to ethnic Galatians in the northern part of the province of Galatia or to believers living in the southern part of the province where Paul evangelized during his first two missionary journeys (Acts 13:13–14:23). Opinions similarly differ on the date of this letter, whether it was written soon after Paul's first missionary journey, and thus before the Jerusalem Council, or sometime after his second missionary journey, and thus after the Jerusalem Council. Conclusions on these issues affect one's understanding of the history of Paul's ministry more than they do key elements in the interpretation of this letter. The letter was written sometime between 48 and 57 to believers in the province of Galatia who were being pressured by false teachers to become circumcised to complete their conversion to the God of Israel.

Paul begins the letter by emphasizing his apostolic authority and his role as the divinely appointed interpreter of the gospel for gentiles (chaps. 1–2). Then he employs his interpretive authority to show that Scripture and experience support the conclusion that the Galatians were already children of God by faith in Christ and should not turn from Paul's gospel to the Mosaic covenant (chaps. 3–4). Finally, Paul warns the Galatians to hold fast to his gospel, explains that the Spirit (rather than the law, as many Jews thought) is the key to overcoming the passions of the flesh, and questions the motives of the false teachers in Galatia (chaps. 5–6).

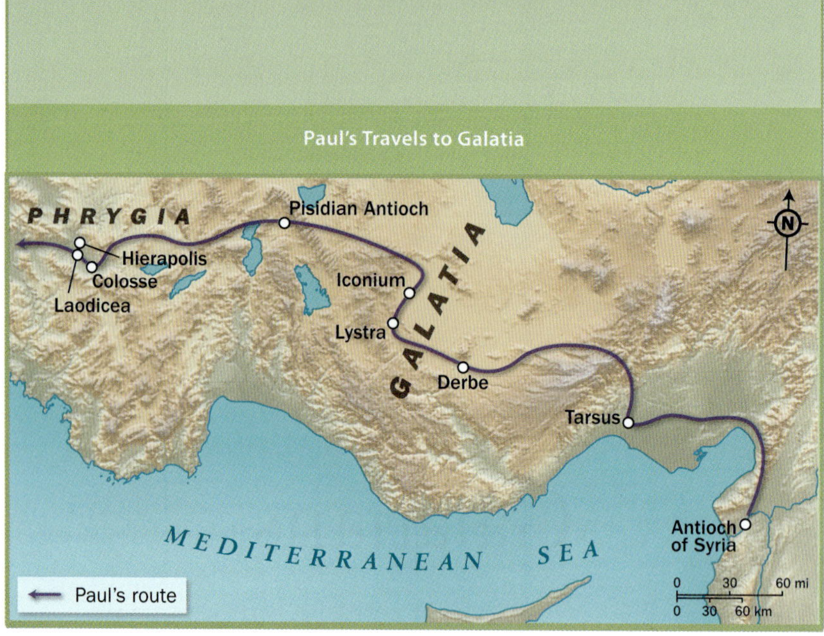

The Salutation (1:1–5)

Paul . . . to the churches of Galatia. Grace to you and peace (1:1–3). The excerpted words are all that were required in a salutation. But in verses 1–5 Paul provides much more theological material as he identifies himself and refers to God the Father and the Lord Jesus Christ, from whom they have received grace and peace. The concepts of God's fatherhood, of the Christ/Messiah, and of the resurrection from the dead (1:1) were all tied to Jewish eschatological expectations, as was the concept of this present evil age (1:4) (contrasted with "the age to come" in early Jewish thought).[1]

Gave himself for our sins (1:4). This statement may reflect an early Christian reading of Isa. 53:6 in the Septuagint: "The Lord gave him(self) over for our sins."

Paul's Opening Rebuke (1:6–10)

Amazed (1:6). At this point in his letters Paul normally included a thanksgiving section. But here he provides a rebuke instead. He is amazed: they should have rejected the message of the false teachers, not accepted it.

Quickly turning away (1:6). This expression may echo the language used for Israel's archetypal apostasy with the golden calf (Exod. 32:8; Deut. 9:12, 16) and for apostasy in general (Judg. 2:17).

Curse (1:8–9). The "curse" (*anathema*) is part of the response required by the Septuagint version of Deut. 13:16 (LXX 13:15) as punishment for people who lead God's people to apostatize.

Paul's Defense of His Apostolic Authority and Independence (1:11–2:21)

Human origin . . . human source (1:11–12). Determining divine or human origins for a message goes back to OT and early Jewish assessments of prophets, since false prophets have a message that "is not divine in its origin, but invented by themselves to please men."[2]

Persecuted . . . destroy . . . zealous (1:13–14). On violence as a manifestation of zeal in defense of God's honor, see Num. 25:1–13; Ps. 106:28–31; 1 Macc. 2:1–28, 49–58; 2 Macc. 2:19–22; Phil. 3:6.

Set me apart (1:15). Paul's description of his apostolic calling reflects the language of prophetic callings in Isa. 49:1–6 and Jer. 1:5.

Arabia (1:17). "Arabia" refers to the Nabataean kingdom (later the Roman province of Arabia, also known as Arabia Petraea or Petrea), where Paul could evangelize gentiles who had the most in common with Jews.

Jerusalem (1:18). Scholars debate whether this visit is the one referred to in Acts 9:26 or the famine visit in Acts 11:19–30; 12:25.

The regions of Syria and Cilicia (1:21). Paul's move to this region suggests that he was moving counterclockwise around the Mediterranean (as Rom. 15:19 suggests).

An Overview of the Life and Letters of Paul

30/33	Jesus's death and resurrection
32–34	Paul's conversion
46–47	Barnabas and Paul take famine relief to Jerusalem
47–49	**FIRST MISSIONARY JOURNEY** (Acts 13–14)
49?	*Galatians* (Antioch)
49	Jerusalem Council (Acts 15)
50–52	**SECOND MISSIONARY JOURNEY** (Acts 15:36–18:21)
51–52	*1–2 Thessalonians* (Corinth)
53–57	**THIRD MISSIONARY JOURNEY** (Acts 18:22–21:16)
53?	*Galatians* (Ephesus)
54	*1 Corinthians* (Ephesus)
56	*2 Corinthians* (Macedonia)
57	*Romans* (Corinth)
57–59	Arrest in Jerusalem (Acts 21:26–33)
	Two-year imprisonment at Caesarea
59	**JOURNEY TO ROME** (Acts 27:1–28:14)
60–62	Two-year house arrest in Rome (Acts 28:30)
60–62	Prison Epistles: *Philemon*, *Colossians*, *Ephesians*, *Philippians*
63	Release from prison; further work
63–67	Pastoral Epistles: *1 Timothy*, *Titus*, *2 Timothy*
64–67	Martyrdom in Rome

Fourteen years (2:1). Paul may be counting from the time of his conversion. Scholars debate whether he refers to the famine visit in Acts 11:19–30; 12:25 or to the Jerusalem Council.

Running (2:2). Paul uses an athletic metaphor for prophetic ministry (cf. Jer. 23:21; Hab. 2:2–3).

Titus . . . circumcised (2:3). Paul's opponents would have thought that Titus, being a Greek, should have been circumcised upon his conversion (based on Gen. 17).

Infiltrated our ranks to spy (2:4). Paul uses the language of military espionage in describing the false brothers.[3]

God does not show favoritism (2:6). Literally, the phrase is "does not receive a person's face"—an idiom that affirms the Jewish view of God as the model of impartiality (Deut. 10:17; cf. Acts 10:34; Rom. 2:11; Eph. 6:9).[4]

James, Cephas, and John (2:9). "Cephas" was Peter's Aramaic name. These were Christ's three most influential disciples, leaders of the church in Jerusalem.

Remember the poor (2:10). Caring for the poor was an essential moral expectation in the OT and Jewish tradition. This comment may suggest that the famine visit in Acts 11:19–30 is in view.

Opposed him to his face (2:11). In the Greek OT (Septuagint), to oppose someone to his face is a military idiom for successful resistance to an opposing power (see LXX Deut. 7:24; 9:2; 11:25; 31:21; Judg. 2:14; 2 Chron. 13:7–8; Jdt. 6:4), suggesting that Paul understood his confrontation to have been successful.

Ate with the Gentiles (2:12–13). Peter and others were sharing meals with gentile believers, but then they drew back because they suspected that visitors from Jerusalem (where purity issues where taken most seriously) would not approve (cf. Acts 11:3). Paul called it hypocrisy.

The truth of the gospel (2:14). Paul implies that the gospel, rather than the law of Moses, is the ultimate standard for Christian living.

In front of everyone (2:14). Paul's public rebuke of Peter was considered a scriptural

Relief showing comedy masks worn by actors. Paul accused Peter of hypocrisy, of wearing a spiritual mask. A "hypocrite" (*hypokritēs*) was a Greek actor.

responsibility to protect the community from an offending brother, especially a leader (Lev. 19:17; 1 Tim. 5:20; cf. Deut. 19:15).

Jews . . . "Gentile sinners" (2:15). Paul refers to the traditional Jewish ethnic dualism. "Gentile sinners" reflects the moral dualism that considered gentiles sinful and Jews righteous. As suggested by the CSB quotation marks, Paul may be using his opponents' language ("sinful Gentiles") ironically.

Works of the law (2:16). The Qumran document *4QHalakhic Letter* lists some works of the law (the community leaders' interpretations of the Mosaic law), with a promise that it would "be reckoned to [them] as righteousness" (cf. Gen. 15:6) if they followed them. Paul opposes a similar view propagated in Galatia.

Faith in Jesus Christ (2:16). This might also be translated as "the faith (or faithfulness) of Jesus Christ." "By faith" (*dia pisteōs* here and *ek pisteōs* later in the verse) reflects the influence of Hab. 2:4 in the Septuagint. Theologians agree that right standing before God is due to Christ's faithfulness (exemplified in his death on the cross) and that it is appropriated through faith in him. They debate whether the two expressions, "through faith in Jesus Christ" (*dia pisteōs Iēsou Christou*) and "by faith in Christ" (*ek pisteōs Christou*), refer to the former or the latter idea.

We . . . have believed in Christ Jesus (2:16). Paul may be echoing Gen. 15:6: Abram was justified when he believed God's promise about his seed (see Gen. 15:5–6; cf. Gal. 3:16).

By the works of the law no human being will be justified (2:16). This alludes to Ps. 143:2 ("no flesh will be justified before you" [my translation]). Paul sharpens the point by specifically ruling out justification by works of the law.

Found to be "sinners" (2:17). Some think that Paul is saying that Jews (like gentiles) are sinners because the gospel shows that all are sinners. Verses 11–14 may suggest instead that those who ate with gentile believers (in light of their understanding of justification) were found/judged to be sinners by stricter Jews from Jerusalem (cf. Acts 11:2–3).

Is Christ then a promoter of sin? (2:17). Lifestyle changes, perhaps especially the decision of Jewish believers in Christ to eat meals with gentile believers (cf. vv. 11–14), led some to wonder if Paul's teaching suggested that Christ promotes sin.

Rebuild (2:18). In Jeremiah destroying and rebuilding is a motif referring to God's judgment and then restoration of his people through his prophetic ministry (cf. LXX Jer. 1:10; 12:16–17; 18:9; 24:6; 38:4, 28 [ET 31:4, 28]; 40:7 [ET 33:7]; 49:10 [ET 42:10]; 51:34 [ET 45:4]). God called Paul to build up God's new eschatological community. He would be a lawbreaker if he were to simply rebuild the old law-based system.

The theater at Pisidian Antioch, a city in the Roman province of Galatia.

Through the law (2:19). Paul's pursuit of the law (exemplified in his persecution of Christians) led to his encounter with Christ and his experience of spiritual death to the law (cf. 2:20). Christ's own redemptive story (death followed by living) has become Paul's (and ours) as well, through union with Christ. The Messiah fulfills and establishes the destiny of God's people.

I have been crucified with Christ . . . Christ lives in me (2:20). Paul stresses again that, through union with Christ (being crucified with Christ), Christ's climactic narrative of crucifixion followed by resurrection to new life has become his own. Christ's living presence in Paul's life now ("Christ lives in me") overshadows his own life. This statement may reflect a messianic reading of Hab. 2:4, so that Christ is the "righteous one" who lives (in believers and in general) "by his faithfulness."

I live by faith in the Son of God (2:20). A reading of Hab. 2:4 in light of the Christ event suggests that it is believers, including Paul, who live by faith.

Who loved me and gave himself for me (2:20). Paul applies his understanding of Christ's sacrifice in a deeply personal way. As in 1:4, this may reflect a christocentric reading of Isa. 53:6 in the Septuagint, being read as "and the Lord gave him[self] up for our sins."[5]

Set aside the grace of God (2:21). Paul implies that Peter and others who refused to share meals with gentile believers set aside the grace of God by imposing the law. God would not have let Christ die on the cross if righteousness could be gained through the law. Such a great sacrifice points to the inability of the law to achieve God's purposes.

The Biblical-Theological Defense of Paul's Law-Free Gospel (3:1–4:31)

Galatians (3:1). It is debated whether Paul was addressing ethnic Galatians living in central Asia Minor or simply used the term "Galatians" to refer to inhabitants of the larger Roman province that extended to cities visited by Paul on his first missionary journey.

Cast a spell on you (3:1). To be bewitched was to suffer from the "evil eye"—a ubiquitous concern in the Roman world. Envious people were thought to harm others by focusing a grudging eye on people who had something they envied. People sought protection from the evil eye by posting grotesque images to distract the eye. Paul's statement that "before whose eyes Jesus Christ was publicly portrayed as crucified" (with crucifixion being an extraordinarily grotesque image) may suggest that they should have been unlikely victims of the evil eye.

The Spirit . . . the flesh (3:3). Paul reflects an eschatological dualism in which humans either live by the power of the Spirit as an end-times blessing or operate merely in the power of human flesh. In the OT the presence of the Spirit or miracles are signs of God's presence working in and on behalf of his people (besides miracles in the ministries of Moses, Elijah, and Elisha; cf. Num. 11:17–29; Isa. 42:1; 44:3; 59:21; 61:1; 63:11; Ezek. 36:27; 37:14; 39:29; Joel 2:28–31; Zech. 12:10).

Abraham . . . *believed God, and it was credited to him for righteousness* (3:6). Paul quotes from Gen. 15:6, a key text on the relationship between faith and righteousness. Abraham was considered the original gentile convert to Judaism when he was circumcised, but Gen. 15:6 indicates that he was justified while still uncircumcised (cf. Rom. 4:9–12).

All the nations will be blessed through you (3:8). Paul sees Gen. 12:3 as foreshadowing the gospel of Christ. All nations will be blessed through Abraham when they experience God's righteousness by faith. Paul reads Gen. 12:3 in light of Gen. 15:6, and vice versa.

Cursed (3:10). Paul quotes Deut. 27:26. Its reference to being cursed contrasts with the reference to being blessed in verses 8–9. Israel experienced the curses listed in Deut. 28:15–68, with repercussions extending right up to the time of Paul. The law ultimately brought curse rather than the blessing of Gen. 12:3.

Will live by faith . . . will live by them (3:11–12). Paul uses a literary device known as *gezerah shavah* (bringing together two texts that share similar wording)—here, "will live"—to contrast the promises of Hab. 2:4 and Lev. 18:5. Paul suggests that these texts pose alternative approaches to life: faith (in Christ) or doing what is written in the law of Moses. Leviticus 18:5 was cited in the OT and early Judaism in contexts that emphasized the nation's failure to cash in on its promise (cf. Neh. 9:29; Ezek. 20:11, 13, 21).

The curse of the law (3:13). Deuteronomy 21:23 helped Paul explain how Christ's death dealt with the curse of the law. In its OT context the curse applied to the public display of the corpses of those who had been executed. Later it was also applied to those who were executed for their crimes by being impaled or hung on a pole or cross. Before encountering Christ, Paul may have used Deut. 21:23 to prove that Jesus couldn't be the Messiah (as a cursed man). After encountering Christ, he realized that Christ suffered his curse to free others from the curse of the law (cf. Isa. 53:2–4).

The blessing (3:14). In verse 8 the blessing was that promised to Abram/Abraham in Gen. 12:3 that all nations ("families" in Gen. 12:3) would be blessed through him. Here Paul clarifies that the blessing of the nations is realized as Jews and gentiles experience the Spirit (and justification) in Christ.

A validated human will (3:15). Covenants could not be annulled or amended unilaterally, but only if all parties agreed on any changes. That which had been agreed upon between God and Abraham (and his seed) could not be altered by laws established centuries later.

And to your seed (3:16). The snippet of quotation comes from Gen. 13:15 (cf. Gen. 12:7; 17:8; 24:7). Paul exploits the fact that the word "seed" is grammatically singular despite being used as a collective noun to refer to one's whole progeny. In light of other Scriptures Paul has realized that the particular seed God had in mind is Christ.

430 years (3:17). The time of separation between the promise to Abraham and the giving of the law is based on Exod. 12:40, where the Masoretic text says, "The time that the Israelites lived in Egypt was 430 years."

For the sake of transgressions (3:19). Some think that this means "to incite transgressions" (and show human sinfulness), but the contents of the OT law itself suggest that the purpose was to keep Israel from sinning and to provide atonement for sins.

Through angels (3:19). That the law was given through angels is a tradition found in Josephus's *Jewish Antiquities* (15.136) as well as in Acts 7:38, 53; Heb. 2:2.

Mediator (3:20). Paul undoubtedly has Moses in mind (cf. Exod. 19:7; 20:19; 24:3; Lev. 26:46; Deut. 4:14; 5:4–5; Philo, *On the Life of Moses* 2.166). That God is one was a fundamental Jewish affirmation, based especially on Deut. 6:4. The Israelite experience of a mediator is contrasted with the direct access to God that believers have in Christ.

The ability to give life (3:21). Paul's reference to a law that could impart life probably alludes to Lev. 18:5 (quoted in v. 12), which contains a promise that went unrealized in Israel's history (cf. Neh. 9:29; Ezek. 20:11–21).

On the basis of faith (3:22). The reference to the promise being given through faith uses the unusual expression "through/by faith" (*ek pisteōs*) that comes from Hab. 2:4 and is used repeatedly in this letter (see comments on Gal. 2:16). The expression "given to those who believe" may be another way Paul rewords "through/by faith."

Guardian (3:24–25). The guardian (*paidagōgos*) was a household slave who taught the children basic virtues and morals reflecting the family's values and accompanied them outside the home until they reached adulthood.[6]

Clothed (3:27). The metaphor of being clothed with Christ through baptism reflects the practice of putting on a new clean garment upon coming out of the baptismal waters.

Jew or Greek (3:28). The three dualisms (Jew/Greek, slave/free, male/female) in this verse summarize divisions in society as seen through Jewish eyes. The wording of the third pair, "male and female" (*arsen kai thēly*), agrees exactly with the Greek text of Gen. 1:27.

Heir . . . guardians and trustees (4:1–2). In a wealthy household the *paterfamilias* appointed people to run various aspects of the household, including children. Paul compares the power that the heir would eventually have with the minor's sense of powerlessness under the authority of servants who were his social inferiors.

Elements of the world (4:3). The idea that the world was composed of four elements (earth, water, air, fire) was ubiquitous in Paul's world (see Wis. 19:18–20; Josephus, *Jewish Antiquities* 3.183–84; Philo, *On the Creation of the World* 146; *Numbers Rabbah* 14:11) and would come directly to mind. Remarkably, Paul attributes spiritual agency to the elements.

When the time came (4:4). The concept of a set time in God's unfolding plans reflects a Jewish apocalyptic motif and here refers to the time of redemption by the Messiah, God's Son.

Born of a woman (4:4). This was a Jewish expression for a human being, as reflected in the Dead Sea Scrolls.[7] To be born under the law is to be born into a Jewish family, committed to the Mosaic law.

Adoption (4:5). In Paul's world adoption was not about finding a loving home for an infant, but rather about finding a suitable heir for a wealthy adult who did not already have one. Those adopted usually were young adult males whose character would be sufficiently known to qualify them as suitable heirs.[8]

The Spirit . . . crying, *"Abba,* Father!" (4:6). In Ezek. 36:26–27 God promises to give his people a new heart and to put his own Spirit within them when he restores them to full covenant status with him in the future. *Abba* is the Aramaic term for "dad/father" that Christ uses in prayer in Mark 14:36 (cf. Rom. 8:15).

Known by God (4:9). For Paul, to be known by God "defines Christian existence" (4:8–9; 1 Cor. 8:3) and "is a measure of eschatological glory" (1 Cor. 13:12; cf. *Psalms of Solomon* 17.27).[9] On the weak and miserable forces (*stoicheia*, "elements") that Paul cautions the Galatians against in this verse, see comments on Gal. 4:3.

Days, months, seasons, years (4:10). The Galatians had begun following the Jewish calendar—one more indication of their belief that adopting the law of Moses was the key to being God's people.

Like me . . . like you (4:12). Paul became like the Galatians in assimilating as much as possible to their culture to win them for Christ. Now the Galatians are asked to become like Paul in remaining free from the Mosaic law and being faithful to the gospel.

Weakness of the flesh (4:13). We do not know what Paul's illness was, but it caused him to be laid up in Galatia long enough to establish multiple churches.

Despise (4:14). Here Paul uses a word (*ekptyō*), perhaps metaphorically, that refers to spitting to express contempt or scorn or "to ward off hostile spirits."[10]

Torn out your eyes and given them to me (4:15). Paul may have suffered some type of ailment of the eyes, but his words also may simply reflect an "idiom that speaks of going to the extreme to provide for another's needs."[11]

I am again suffering labor pains (4:19). Paul refers to the Galatians as his (spiritual-metaphorical) children and then expands on the metaphor, describing himself as a mother going through the painful process of childbirth all over again.

These things are being taken figuratively (4:21–31). Paul provides an apocalyptically influenced allegorical interpretation of Gen. 16–17; 21. Other teachers probably suggested that the Galatians were like Ishmael (almost but not quite true sons of Abraham). Paul points out that in Genesis Ishmael was harassing Isaac in some way, and in the Galatians' current context it is their other teachers who are harassing them and not vice versa. So it is their other teachers (who became Jews by the normal human processes) who are playing the role of Ishmael, and the Galatians (who have become covenant people through the fulfillment of God's special promises) who are in the role of Isaac.

Born as a result of the flesh (4:23). Paul means born either in a purely natural way or as the result of Abraham's inappropriate action when Sarah was unable to conceive. "The flesh" can have neutral or negative connotations for Paul.

Arabia (4:25). The term "Arabia" was used for the Nabataean kingdom extending east and south from Palestine (see comments on Gal. 1:17). On Jerusalem being in slavery with her children, see Ezra 9:9; Neh. 9:36.

An icon portraying the ancient rite of circumcision.

Jerusalem above (4:26). The heavenly Jerusalem is an apocalyptic motif.[12]

Rejoice, childless woman (4:27). Paul quotes Isa. 54:1, the opening of a chapter with several allusions to Abraham and Sarah, and one of the earliest texts suggesting the idea of a Jerusalem above.

Final Exhortations and Warnings (5:1–6:10)

Freedom (5:1). The theme of freedom was introduced in 2:4 and became the primary motif in the previous passage (see 4:22–23, 26, 30–31). Paul stresses that the Galatians should live in light of Christ's redemptive purpose.

Yoke of slavery (5:1). Jewish texts frequently speak of "the yoke of the law" (see *m. Avot* 3.5; cf. Sir. 51:26). A "yoke of slavery" served as an unflattering reference to the law.

Obligated to do the entire law (5:3). Jews understood that to be circumcised was to be obligated to obey the whole law. Paul assumes either that obeying the whole law is impossible or that attempting to obey the whole law would be an unnecessary burden that also nullified the grace of Christ (cf. v. 4).

Justified by the law (5:4). For a gentile, to be circumcised was to try to be justified by the law, as opposed to being justified by faith. To adopt that approach is to fall away from grace.

Neither circumcision nor uncircumcision accomplishes anything (5:6). This is a remarkable statement (cf. 1 Cor. 7:19) because (1) circumcision had been God's command, and (2) Paul gave such severe warnings not to be circumcised (vv. 3–4). Paul considers circumcision (or its lack) unimportant unless it is imposed on gentile believers, at which point it becomes a direct affront to the gospel (see the article "The Jewish Rite of Circumcision").

What matters is faith working through love (5:6). For Paul it is faith's action, actively expressing itself through love, that matters most—a clear indication that Paul does not consider "believing" and "doing" as oppositional terms.

Running well (5:7). Paul employs the athletic metaphor knowing the popularity of athletic games in the Hellenistic world (cf. 1 Cor. 9:24–27;

Paul uses breadmaking imagery in Gal. 5:8–9. The yeast refers to the leaven, bits of fermented dough that were held back before baking so they could be used to start a new batch of bread. This figurine shows bread dough being kneaded as part of the breadmaking process (ancient Medma, 490 BC).

Gal. 2:2) and describes the false teachers in Galatia as competitors who have cheated by cutting in and interfering with their progress.

Leaven (5:9). In the OT yeast (*zymē*, often translated as "leaven," as here) was prohibited during the Passover celebration (Deut. 16:1–4) and came to be used as a metaphor for contamination by unhealthy influences (Matt. 16:6–12; 1 Cor. 5:6–8).

Preach circumcision (5:11). Paul was persecuted by fellow Jews for preaching a message that did not require the circumcision of gentiles (see the article "The Jewish Rite of Circumcision"). Some may have falsely suggested that Paul did require circumcision for gentiles elsewhere.

The offense of the cross (5:11). Jews and Judaizers were offended by Paul's rejection of the circumcision requirement for gentiles, which was a basic expectation for males of God's covenant people since the time of Abraham (Gen. 17:9–14).

Let themselves be mutilated (5:12). Paul uses dark humor based on his opponents' enthusiasm for circumcision. Some suggest Paul is alluding to the Galli, pagan priests who practiced self-castration, but Jewish practices are more likely in focus.

Freedom (5:13). Freedom in Christ must not be used to satisfy one's fallen desires (the flesh), but rather to serve one another as an expression of humble love. Love (the primary fruit of the Spirit) and the flesh manifest themselves in actions that either strengthen or undermine community life.

Love your neighbor as yourself (5:14). Paul quotes Lev. 19:18. His teaching that love fulfills the entire law is reminiscent of Jesus's "golden rule" (Matt. 7:12). Romans 13:8–10 expands on this idea, reflecting Paul's indebtedness to Jesus's teaching.

Desire of the flesh (5:16–17). Stoics (and others in the Greco-Roman world) pursued mastery over the passions (similar to desires of the flesh), usually looking to reason as the key. Within Hellenistic Judaism (influenced by Stoicism) many considered the Jewish law the key to such self-mastery (e.g., 4 Macc. 1:30–2:16; Philo, *On the Virtues* 181–82). For Paul the solution is not the law but God's Spirit, given to believers. Here, "what you want" (v. 17) refers to the desires of the flesh, which the Spirit overcomes.

Works of the flesh (5:19–21). Paul offers a vice list called "works of the flesh." The main categories are sexual abuses, pagan religious practices, behaviors that undermine healthy community (the largest group of vices), and behaviors marked by a lack of self-control (a major concern in Greco-Roman moral discourse). Vice lists were common and were intended to reinforce others' commitments to rejecting such behaviors. Paul reminds his readers that these behaviors are natural manifestations of fallen human nature.

Inherit the kingdom (5:21). In the OT the language of inheritance is most often associated with God's promise that Israel would inherit the land (Exod. 32:13 and throughout the OT). In the NT those promises are understood to refer to the inheritance of the earth (Matt. 5:5), the world (Rom. 4:13), salvation (Heb. 1:14), eternal life (Matt. 19:29; Mark 10:17; Luke 10:25; 18:18), and the kingdom (Matt. 25:34; 1 Cor. 6:9–10; 15:50; Eph. 5:5).

Fruit of the Spirit (5:22–23). Paul moves from his vice list to a virtue list, which he calls "the fruit of the Spirit" and which stresses virtues that promote healthy relationships and communities. The final virtue, self-control (a central Roman virtue), reinforces Paul's point that it is the Spirit who makes such disciplined and healthy community living possible. Virtue lists served to reinforce shared community values and behaviors. Here Paul also reminds his readers that such behaviors are possible for believers thanks to God's empowering Spirit.

We live by the Spirit (5:25). Paul's words echo Ezek. 37:5–14 (which echoes Gen. 2:7) and describe a reality known by Christian experience (cf. Gal. 3:2–5). Living by or "keeping in step with" the Spirit suggests that the Spirit, rather than the Mosaic law, provides the foundation and power for Christian living (Jews commonly referred to walking according to the law).

Conceited, provoking one another, envying one another (5:26). As in the vice and virtue lists (vv. 15–23), overcoming tendencies to rivalry and other kinds of behaviors destructive to healthy community life is emphasized.

You who are spiritual (6:1). Presumably, this refers to those whose lives consistently demonstrate the fruit of the Spirit outlined in 5:22–23. Once again we see Paul's concern for maintaining a healthy community.

The law of Christ (6:2). Christ serves as the model for Christians as he carried our burdens on the cross, providing us with a new law (or an interpretation of the law different than had been known before). In 5:14 we learned that love fulfills the law (of Moses). Here that love is described as a law commanding us to serve others.

God is not mocked (6:7). Scorning or mocking God and his commands will never turn out well for anyone (cf. Prov. 1:30–31; Ezek. 8:17).

Whatever a person sows he will also reap (6:7–9). The common experience of the agricultural cycle with its sowing and reaping provided a natural metaphor for the conjunction of moral and eschatological teaching (e.g., Job 4:8; Prov. 22:8; Hosea 10:12; Matt. 13:39; 25:24–26; Luke 19:21–22;

As was customary, Paul used an amanuensis (secretary) to write his epistles. In Gal. 6:11 Paul picks up the pen and exclaims that he writes with "large letters." The parchment pages shown here, from a Coptic codex containing portions of the Gospel of John and Psalms, are an example of ancient writing (Upper Egypt, fifth century AD).

John 4:35–37; 1 Cor. 9:11; 2 Cor. 9:6). Paul has one's ultimate salvation in mind (all too often people do not reap what they sow in daily experience).

The Subscription (6:11–18)

My own handwriting (6:11). As was a common practice, Paul now takes the pen from his unnamed scribe and writes the last lines (vv. 11–18) of the letter in his own hand. Evidently his penmanship stood out in comparison with that of his scribe.

Those who want to make a good impression (6:12–13). The false teachers in Galatia want to impress people and avoid being persecuted for the cross of Christ by getting the Galatians circumcised in keeping with normal Jewish expectations.

Never boast about anything except the cross (6:14). For Paul, crucifixion was transformed from being simply a horrible Roman form of capital punishment experienced by Christ to becoming the focus of the Christian life that establishes a fundamental alienation between the believer and this world, undermining and inverting the world's values to which the other teachers were clinging.

Both circumcision and uncircumcision (6:15). In 5:6 the thing that counted was "faith working through love." Presumably, that is how the new creation should manifest itself.

The Israel of God (6:16). Those who "follow this standard" and "the Israel of God" may be two separate groups ("and/also to the Israel of God") or, since Paul has repeatedly argued that the Galatian believers are the true sons of Abraham (e.g., 3:7, 29), like Isaac (4:21–31), he may be referring to Jewish and gentile believers once again as God's Israel to reinforce that new identity.

The marks of Jesus (6:17). Like Jesus, Paul also bore marks on his body as a consequence of his faithful service to God (cf. 2 Cor. 11:23–27).

Ephesians

Osvaldo Padilla

Introduction. Ephesians was written by Paul, probably during his first imprisonment in the early 60s. With the rise of Protestant liberalism in the eighteenth and nineteenth centuries, the authenticity of the letter began to be questioned. The result is that today, outside evangelical circles, only a few still hold to Pauline authorship. However, the reasons given for the denial of Paul's authorship—Ephesians' "detached" tone and its "non-Pauline" words, sentence construction, and theology—are unconvincing. A number of reasons could be given for the differences: a different life setting from other epistles (e.g., Romans and Galatians), development in Paul's theology, and perhaps the use of an amanuensis. In any case, the argument against Pauline authorship from words peculiar to Ephesians is deficient methodologically. Since the letter claims to have been written by Paul, was accepted as such by the early church, and arguments against authenticity are wanting, it is more reasonable to accept Paul as the author.[1]

We must examine two issues before turning to the text. First, who were the recipients of this letter? The answer seems obvious, since "at Ephesus" in 1:1 is printed in our Bibles. However, there are some excellent manuscripts that omit this phrase. Ultimately, while "at Ephesus" should be preserved, it is possible that the letter circulated from Ephesus to other churches in Asia Minor (see the article "The City of Ephesus").

The second issue is the occasion of the letter. What prompted Paul to write it? From the content of Ephesians, we can suggest two reasons. First, given the religious culture of Ephesus, which is to say, its ingrained practice of

The Location of Ephesus

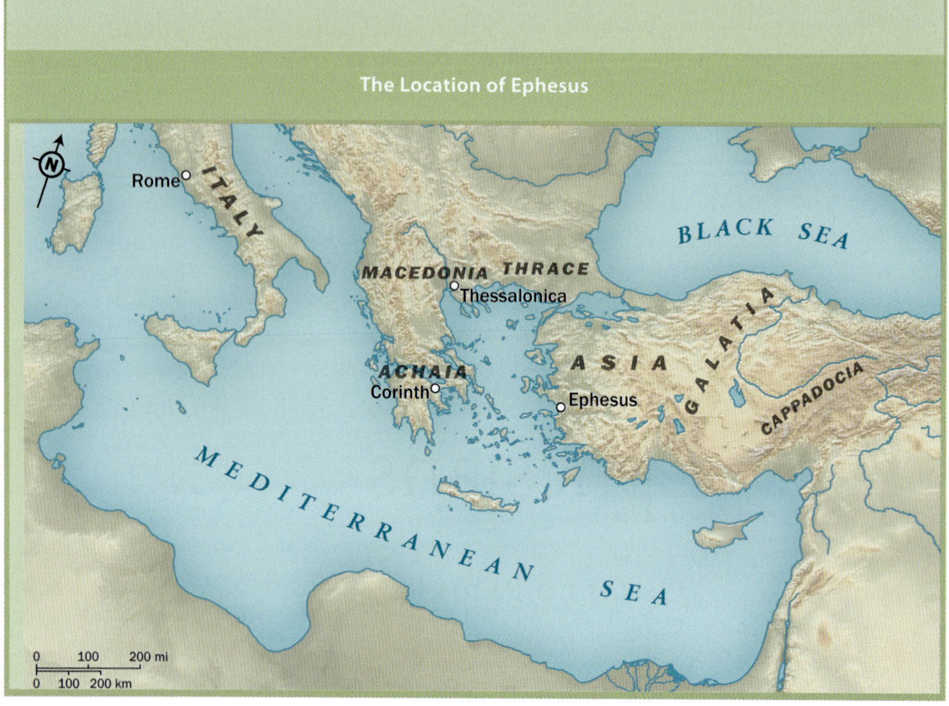

magic, it was necessary to remind the Christians that behind these practices were demonic sources. At the same time, Paul had to remind the Christians that, by virtue of their union with Christ, they did not need to be paralyzed in fear of these powers. Christ had ultimately overcome them, even though there was still a battle. The second reason why Paul penned Ephesians was to remind the believers of the unity between Jews and gentiles that Christ had won at the cross. Christian Jews and gentiles thus had to work hard at preserving that unity (4:3).

The Preface (1:1–2)

Paul, an apostle of Christ Jesus (1:1). Paul used the term "apostle" to begin his letters. Although the specific background of the term is unclear, its use by Paul highlights the following: (1) an apostle was someone commissioned by the risen Jesus to preach (Rom. 1:1; 1 Cor. 9:1; 15:9; Gal. 1:1, 15–16), and (2) an apostle, because he had been commissioned directly by Christ, had the authority to speak for God. Therefore, the apostles were the foundation for the teaching of the church (Eph. 2:20). Given this status, Paul's letters were to be treated as the word of God written (1 Cor. 14:37). Reading Ephesians was therefore reading God's revelation.

The faithful saints (1:1). The understanding of "holy" was derived from the OT. To be holy meant to have been chosen and set apart by God to be

Ephesus was one of the most spectacular cities in western Asia Minor. The theater at Ephesus went through many building and renovation phases during its long history. Reaching nearly one hundred feet in height, it could accommodate about twenty-five thousand people on its three levels.

his people and to serve him (Exod. 19:5–6; Lev. 11:44–45; 19:2). The holy ones (*hagioi*, "saints"), therefore, were called to make God the priority of life.

At Ephesus (1:1). The holy ones, who are the recipients of this letter from Paul, resided in the city of Ephesus (see the article "The City of Ephesus"). Although some very reliable manuscripts omit "in Ephesus," on the whole it is better to preserve the phrase as original. Ephesus (modern Selçuk in Turkey) was made the seat of the proconsul of Asia by Octavian in 30–29 BC. This made the city very important. In addition, because of the large size of its harbor, Ephesus prospered and grew rapidly. Seneca called it the second largest city in Asia Minor.[2]

Ephesus was best known for the massive temple of Artemis and the devotion of its citizens to the goddess (cf. Acts 19:23–28). Furthermore, it was a center for the practice of magic, the famous *Ephesia Grammata* stemming from there (see the article "Magic in the New Testament World").[3] Lastly, everyday life in Ephesus was affected by the imperial cult.[4] The cult sought to provide a pervasive worldview to the residents. The emperor Augustus, who was portrayed as Zeus, was presented as the creator or founder of a new world order. In fact, around 9 BC the calendars were changed so as to revolve around the birth of Augustus. Furthermore, the cult drove home the idea that the emperor and his dynasty would continue a rule that would be an eternal utopia. It is against this background of "power"—magical and political—that the ancient recipients of Ephesians would have read Paul's numerous statements about Christ as the one who "fills all things in every way" (Eph. 1:23).

Grace to you and peace (1:2). In the majority of his letters Paul ended the prescript with a wish/prayer for his readers. Both of the terms in this verse find their source in the OT. The combination "grace and peace" perhaps recalled the benediction that Aaron and his sons were to pray over Israel in Num. 6:23–26.

A Burst of Praise (1:3–14)

The body of the letter begins with a statement of worship. Paul was in such awe of God's character as seen in the salvation of sinners that he pushed language to the extreme. Verses 3–14 are actually one sentence in the original Greek!

Blessed is the God and Father of our Lord Jesus Christ (1:3). Paul was following a format of prayer found in the OT and other Jewish literature after the completion of the OT. This form of prayer is called a benediction or *berakah*. The Mishnah, which is the earliest written collection of rabbinic traditions, begins its first order or tractate with the subject of prayer, particularly blessings. Below is the first of the Eighteen Benedictions. Note the similarities to Paul's benediction in 1:3:

> Blessed art thou, O Lord our God and God of our fathers, God of Abraham, God of Isaac, and God of Jacob, the great, mighty, and revered God, the most high God, who bestowest loving-kindness, and possessest all things; who rememberest the pious deeds of the patriarchs and in love will bring a redeemer to their children's children for thy name's sake.[5]

So we see that the prayer is a blessing of God that is based on his greatness and covenant loving-kindness. While Paul more or less followed the format, notice that now the focus was not on Abraham, Isaac, and Jacob but on "the Lord Jesus Christ." He was the ultimate fulfillment of God's covenant with his people. Since he has come, God can be approached only through Jesus Christ.

A statement of Ephesian Artemis (first century AD), who was worshiped as a fertility goddess.

Who has blessed us with every spiritual blessing in the heavens in Christ (1:3). The phrase "in the heavens" is found several times in Ephesians: 1:20; 2:6; 3:10; 6:12. Scholars agree that it is one of the most important phrases of the entire letter. Interpreting it correctly, therefore, is important to understanding Ephesians. The phrase is found many times in Greek literature from the time of Homer forward.[6] It is also found in the OT and Jewish literature.[7] It is this latter background (which has some overlap with the Greek background, to be sure) that probably helps clarify the meaning in Ephesians. The term "heaven" (or "heavenly realms") is being used metaphorically to refer to that dimension where the spiritual powers reside. Both angels and demons operate in this realm.[8] God is also in this realm, but the heavenly throne where God and Christ are seated is even "far above" these heavenly beings (1:21).[9] Paul wants his readers to know that the one from whom and through whom they received the blessing of salvation is now seated in the heavenly realms, "far above" demonic powers. Since the believers are seated with Christ (2:6), they no longer needed to fear being under the control of demonic powers.

He predestined us to be adopted as sons through Jesus Christ (1:5). The phrase "adopted as sons" would have recalled the Roman concept of adoption. According to this custom, a male or female, when adopted, would come under the authority of the *paterfamilias*, the father of the family. The effect was that the adopted person was legally now as if he or she had been a natural-born son or daughter. Included in the adoption were the acquisition of the adopter's family name, rank, and rights.[10]

The down payment of our inheritance (1:14). Paul uses the word "down payment" to refer to the Holy Spirit. This term (*arrabōn*) was used in legal and commercial contexts to denote an earnest. The deposit served as a guarantee that once the transaction or service was completed, the remainder would be paid.[11]

Paul's Prayer (1:15–23)

The Spirit of wisdom and revelation (1:17). The terms "wisdom" and "revelation" have a rich background in the OT and subsequent Jewish literature. The first term harks back to wisdom literature, where the emphasis was on the superiority of God's ways as presented in his revelation. This wisdom was worked out in the fear of the Lord, which brought obedience to his commands (Ps. 1:2; 119; Prov. 1:7; 3:19–20; 8:22–31), and a recognition of our intellectual limits in the face of radical evil (Job) and the miseries of this life (Ecclesiastes). "Revelation" is found especially in prophetic literature to refer to God's disclosing of his eschatological mysteries. As Paul indicates, this revelation has to do with God's saving of humanity through the folly of the cross (1 Cor. 1:18–2:12) and the unity of the gentiles and Jews in one body (Eph. 3:1–13).

Every ruler and authority, power and dominion, and every title given (1:21). A number of terms were used by Paul for the supernatural forces that dwelled in the heavenlies. These were evil spirits. The first two terms, "ruler" and "authority," appear in other places in Paul's writings (Rom. 8:38; 1 Cor. 15:24; Eph. 2:2; 3:10; 6:12; Col. 1:16; 2:10, 15). They also show up in the OT and ancient Jewish texts (e.g., Dan. 7:27; *Testament of Abraham* 13.10). The third term, "power," was also used by Paul to refer to evil angels (Rom. 8:38; 1 Cor. 15:24). As the previous two, "power" was used often in Jewish literature to refer to angels. The last word, "dominion," although used in this sense only twice in the NT (here and Col. 1:16), was common in Jewish literature to refer to angels. Some scholars have suggested that the different terms reflect an angelic hierarchy. The conclusion of Clinton Arnold is more probable: "Although the terms may imply some form of order and hierarchy within the angelic realm, there is no way for us, based upon the evidence of the available texts, to determine what that was."[12]

From Death to Life (2:1–10)

You previously lived according to the ways of this world (2:2). The Greek behind this phrase is literally "the age of this world." This reflects a fundamental aspect of Paul's thought, found in the OT but developed in later Jewish writings, especially in those writings designated as apocalyptic literature. The world was understood as existing in two ages: "the present age," which was dominated by Satan and suffering and sin, and "the age to come," ushered in by God, in which he would reign and all things would be restored. Paul believed that with the coming of Jesus "the age to come" had dawned. The Holy Spirit has been given to believers, and they are already enjoying the kingdom of God. Nevertheless, "the age to come" has not come in its totality. The Christian thus lives in the tension of the "already but not yet."

Jews and Gentiles One through the Sacrifice of Christ (2:11–22)

Called "the uncircumcised" by those called "the circumcised" (2:11). Circumcision was the distinguishing physical mark of being a Jew (see the article "The Jewish Rite of Circumcision"). Jews often referred to gentiles as "uncircumcised," which was meant to label these persons as impure.

Warning inscription from the Jerusalem temple: "No intruder is allowed in the courtyard and within the wall surrounding the temple. Whoever enters will invite death for himself." Ephesians 2:14 says that Christ destroyed such dividing walls.

You are no longer foreigners and strangers, but fellow citizens with the saints (2:19). Now that they are in Christ, these gentile Christians have a different standing. Using sociopolitical terms, Paul describes their new status. In a world that was centered on the different city-states throughout the Roman Empire, those called "foreigners" and "strangers" were people who existed on the margins, with few rights. They simply did not belong. By contrast, "citizens" were at the center of the city-state and possessed every right. They were not outsiders; they belonged.[13]

Empowered to Comprehend the Incomprehensible (3:14–21)

May be able to comprehend with all the saints what is the length and width, height and depth of God's love (3:18). Paul prays that the readers would grasp the love of Christ. This love is so great that in order to "explain" it, Paul resorts to spatial dimensions. There was a similar attempt, but instead with reference to the wisdom of God, in the OT: "If only God would speak. . . . Can you fathom the depths of God or discover the limits of the Almighty? They are higher than the heavens—what can you do? They are deeper than Sheol—what can you know? Their measure is longer than the earth and wider than the sea" (Job 11:5–9).[14] Paul applies this to the love of Christ, suggesting that it is too vast to be grasped in its totality.

Preserve the Unity (4:1–16)

There is one body (4:4). Paul uses the metaphor of the "body" throughout Ephesians (e.g., 1:23; 2:16; 4:16). The most probable background is the Greco-Roman political use of the human body to denote the organic unity of the city-state.[15]

For it says: *When he ascended on high, he took the captives captive; he gave gifts to people.* But what does "he ascended" mean except that he also descended to the lower parts of the earth? The one who descended is also the one who ascended far above all the heavens, to fill all things

(4:8–10). In the context of spiritual gifts that were given to help mature and therefore preserve the unity of the church, Paul uses Ps. 68:18 to justify and further explain his argument. It is fascinating that Ps. 68:18 was used in some Jewish traditions with Moses as the subject. Thus the Targum (Aramaic translation) reads, "You ascended to the firmament, O prophet Moses, you took captives, you taught the words of the Law, you gave them as gifts to the sons of man."[16] Paul understood the psalm in a christological way. It was Christ who, having descended for his incarnation and having been exalted in his ascension, showed himself victorious over Satan and gave gifts—not the law—to build his church.

Exhortation for the Household (5:22–6:9)

Wives . . . husbands . . . children . . . parents . . . slaves . . . masters (5:22–6:9). See the article "New Testament Household Codes."

Slaves, obey your human masters with fear and trembling, in the sincerity of your heart, as you would Christ (6:5). Slavery in the Greco-Roman world was a fact of life (see the article "Slavery in the New Testament World"). Unlike modern European and American (Southern states) slavery, however, ancient slavery was not based on skin color. It was the result primarily of war. The early Christians did not view slaves as subhuman; they were viewed as full brothers and sisters in the Lord.[17]

Put On the Armor of God (6:10–20)

In the context of spiritual warfare, Paul uses as a metaphor the armor worn by a Roman soldier, probably a legionary (see the article "The Roman Military"). The attire of a Roman soldier varied throughout the centuries and also was dependent on the rank of the soldier.[18] In addition, Paul's

Bronze statuette of a second-century-AD Roman soldier wearing laminated armor.

description is general. The majority of the items are defensive: breastplate, shield, and helmet. Only the sword, which here refers to the short, dagger-style weapon, is offensive. Even though Paul gives only a general portrayal of a Roman legionary's armor, there is enough here to envision the battle as close, hand-to-hand combat. Paul envisions the spiritual warfare of the Christian as a brutal fight against an enemy who wants to maim and kill. It should also be noted that many of the items mentioned also find their background in the OT portrayal of Yahweh as a warrior (e.g., Isa. 11:4–5; 52:7; 59:17). The believer must therefore "put on the Lord Jesus Christ" (Rom. 13:14) by submitting to his will and thereby obtain victory.

Philippians

Osvaldo Padilla

Introduction. Philippians was written by Paul, and this conclusion has rarely been questioned in the history of scholarship. The letter was written probably during Paul's first Roman imprisonment, and so in the early 60s.

The city of Philippi has an intriguing history. This history, especially during the Roman period, can help shed light on the different emphases of Paul's Letter to the Philippians. The name Philippi stems from the city's having been conquered by the father of Alexander the Great, Philip of Macedon, around 356 BC.[1] The early inhabitants of Philippi were Greeks from the island of Thasos, Macedonians as well as some Thracians. From the east and southeast came people from Asia Minor, Egypt, and Israel.[2] In 168 BC the Roman general Lucius Aemilius Paullus beat the Macedonians soundly. Macedonia was then divided into four districts, to one of which, Amphipolis, the city of Philippi belonged.[3] In 42 BC the battle between Octavian and Mark Antony on the one hand and Brutus and Cassius on the other was won by the former. Mark Antony made Philippi a colony. Roman war veterans (approximately one thousand) were then sent to colonize Philippi. They were given large plots of land, and now the native inhabitants had to lease the land from the soldiers who owned it![4] After Octavian defeated Mark Antony, he renamed the city *Colonia Iula Augusta Philippensium*. It became a *Ius Italicum,* meaning that it possessed the same legal status as Italian cities.[5] Even more Roman citizens were then sent to live in Philippi. Latin was the dominant language.[6] The result of all this was that the city of Philippi had a strong Roman ethos, the effects of which we will examine below.

For what purpose did Paul write the Letter to the Philippians? In order to answer this, scholars have suggested that a grasp of Greco-Roman social conventions can aid in clarification. In particular, it may be useful to reflect on these social conventions as they were reflected in the writing of letters, specifically *reciprocal letters*. These conventions, evident in correspondence, were those of friendship, benefaction, consensual association, and patron-client relationship.[7] It appears that Paul used features found in reciprocal letters to drive home his theological message. This suggests that the Philippians viewed their relationship with Paul as loyal, "quasi-contractual commitments in this 'partnership for the gospel.'"[8] Within this framework of partnership due to their shared belief in the gospel, Paul thanks them for their financial support, recommends Epaphroditus, and warns them against false teachers. In short, Paul adapts his letter to the conventions of the period yet uses it to accomplish his apostolic work of instruction and encouragement. It is within this context that we must understand the purpose of Philippians.

Thanksgiving and Intercession (1:3–11)

In my imprisonment and in the defense and confirmation of the gospel (1:7). The theme of imprisonment figures greatly in this letter (see 1:13, 14, 16). It is important to understand the differences between modern imprisonment as done in North America and ancient Roman imprisonment. If Philippians was written between 60 and 64, Paul's custody arrangements probably were similar to those described in Acts 28:30–31, where he appears

The Via Egnatia, which passed through Philippi.

to have been under house arrest. Paul would thus not have been in a public prison in Rome. This would have been a great relief to Paul, for public prisons in Rome had a terrible reputation. The horrendous conditions were well known: darkness, overcrowding, hunger, and disease (not very different from many public prisons in Latin America today!). More than likely, Paul was under different conditions, those of house arrest. Although a better situation than a public prison, this arrangement was not a pleasant experience. Paul would have resided in an ancient apartment (*insula*) that was very restricted in size. A guard would have been with him, if not all the time, certainly during the night. Rent, food, and clothing probably were not provided by the Romans. Paul would have been totally dependent on his brothers and sisters in Christ to provide for his basic needs.[9] This is precisely the reason why Paul is so effusive in his thanksgiving for the Philippians: "I rejoiced in the Lord greatly because once again you renewed your care for me" (4:10), and, "I have an abundance. I am fully supplied, having received from Epaphroditus what you provided—a fragrant offering, an acceptable sacrifice, pleasing to God" (4:18).

Update on the Gospel (1:12–26)

It has become known throughout the whole imperial guard, and to everyone else, that my imprisonment is because I am in Christ (1:13). Paul speaks of the "imperial guard" (*praitōrion*). In all its other NT occurrences that word refers to a building, but here the reference is to a group of people.[10] That is, he is referring to the nearly nine thousand soldiers of the Praetorian Guard, the elite guards of the family of the Caesar. Despite (or because of) his imprisonment, the gospel message was finding its way into elite circles (see comments on 4:22).

Jesus Christ: The Supreme Example of Humility (2:5–11)

This magnificent passage, the center of the epistle, can be better grasped if placed in the context of Roman conventions. In particular, it must be understood that at its most basic and constitutive level the Roman ethos was one that valued honor above every other virtue. Since Philippi was a Roman colony—a miniature Rome, so to speak—the same hunger for

The remains of the bema (speaker's platform) at Philippi. This platform may be where Paul and Silas stood when they were dragged before the magistrates and subsequently beaten and thrown into prison (Acts 16:19–21).

honor that existed in Rome was also present there. At the political and therefore societal level, elite Roman males attempted to ascend in honor by means of a career path known as the *cursus honorum*. There were several steps to this climb of honor. The first office was that of *quaestor*; if that was performed well, the individual moved to the next step, *praetor*. The next step in the climb was to become a consul, which was the highest office below the emperor.

What is remarkable in our text is that the description of Christ in 2:5–8 is precisely the opposite of the *cursus honorum*. It is the ultimate descent from the highest level, "existing in the form of God," to the human level, "a man," to the lowest level of society, "a servant" (i.e., a slave). And as if this humiliation were not enough, he also went to death, "even to death on a cross," the lowest, most shameful and degrading state in which a human being could be found in the Roman world. But his humiliation was turned by God into exaltation, whereby he received the highest name, the name of God—even higher than Caesar.[11] This description of the humiliation of Christ would have been jarring to the Philippian readers. It stood in the sharpest possible contrast to the society around them.

Paul's Previous Religious Achievements (3:1–6)

In this text Paul provides in catalogue form his own religious career to demonstrate the impossibility of being justified by works of the law. Paul's religious credentials—both by birth and by merit—were impeccable. From the perspective of his former self as a Pharisee without Christ, he would have had confidence of being justified by God on the day of judgment.

Circumcised the eighth day (3:5). Thus he fulfilled the law of circumcision as commanded in Lev. 12:3.

Of the nation of Israel (3:5). The terminology here highlights Paul's race. He accomplishes this by the use of the Greek term *genos* ("nation" or "people"). The articulation of his belonging to God's chosen people is strengthened by the use of "Israel," which was the self-appellation of Israelites.

Of the tribe of Benjamin (3:5). Paul becomes more specific by pinpointing the particular tribe of the nation of Israel from which he came. The tribe of Benjamin could not only boast of being both the source of the first king of Israel and the tribe of national deliverers such as Esther and Mordecai (Esther 2:5); it also could boast of being the tribe that remained faithful to the rightful kingly house of Israel, that of David.

A Hebrew born of Hebrews (3:5). Unlike the majority of Jews outside Palestine, who spoke only Greek and read the Scriptures in Greek, Paul spoke Hebrew/Aramaic and was able to read the sacred writings in the ancestral languages.[12]

Regarding the law, a Pharisee (3:5). That is, Paul belonged to a Jewish sect that was extremely strict in matters of ceremonial purity (see the article "Pharisees and Sadducees"). This was in contrast to many in Israel who did not have the same commitment to ritual purity.

Regarding zeal, persecuting the church (3:6). Like Phinehas in the OT (Num. 25:6–13), who in ardor for the purity of Israel executed a number of Israelites, Paul's zeal was such that he persecuted the Christians. Why? Because in their worship of a crucified man, who was therefore a false teacher leading Israel astray, they were compromising the purity of Israel.[13]

Regarding the righteousness that is in the law, blameless (3:6). As a Pharisee, Paul believed that he could obtain a not-guilty verdict from God

The stadium in Aphrodisias, Turkey, was built in the first century for athletic contests. Eventually it was used for gladiatorial combat. The stadium is three hundred yards long and could seat up to thirty thousand people. Paul frames his argument in Philippians in terms of fighting alongside (*synathleō*) other Christians for the faith and work of the gospel (Phil. 1:27; 4:3).

depending to a large extent on his observance of the law. Judged purely from Pharisaic standards—that is, prior to the revelation of righteousness by faith in Christ—Paul's conduct was blameless.

The Citizenship of Christ-Followers (3:17–20)

But our citizenship is in heaven (3:20). The inhabitants of the Roman colony of Philippi were keenly aware of civic pride and status consciousness (see the article "Roman Citizenship"). This would have been particularly so of those Philippians who were Roman citizens.[14] This verse completely relativizes these social dynamics. To those Philippian Christians who were Roman citizens, the statement suggests that—should there have been unhealthy civic pride—their joy, peace, and boast should have ultimately depended on the fact that they were citizens of the kingdom of Christ. To those in the church who were not Roman citizens, the reminder was that although they may have been in a station of humiliation in the eyes of elite society, in fact they belonged to the kingdom of Christ. For both classes, the implication was that their behavior should reflect their heavenly citizenship. This heavenly citizenship was far more precious than Roman citizenship, for the king of heaven ultimately would rescue them from their shameful and perishable state. This Caesar could not do.

Paul Thanks the Philippians for Their Generosity (4:10–20)

You did well by partnering with me in my hardship. . . . I have received everything in full. . . . I am fully supplied, having received from Epaphroditus what you provided—a fragrant offering, an acceptable sacrifice, pleasing to God (4:14–18). Since Paul was a prisoner responsible for all his own expenses (rent, food, clothing, etc.), he was utterly dependent on his friends for survival. The Philippian Christians thus decided to "partner" (financially) in his troubles. They sent him aid again and again. In the phrase "I have received everything in full," the verb used for "received" (*apechō*) was a financial term for receiving a proof of receipt.[15] Paul thus had all his needs provided for, especially since Epaphroditus had brought the Philippians' gift. Although the gift was for Paul, since it was done as an act of obedience to God, Paul could use sacrificial language from the OT to describe it.

Closing Greetings (4:21–23)

All the saints send you greetings, especially those who belong to Caesar's household (4:22). This did not refer to Caesar's immediate blood relatives.

Rather, it probably referred to the hundreds who in one way or another belonged to the house of the emperor and served in some way. The majority would have been slaves. Nevertheless, the statement was surely a covert way of saying that the gospel was reaching the highest spheres of Rome. The words of Markus Bockmuehl are apt: "Concealed behind this innocuous greeting is a powerful symbol of the day when even in Rome, the seat of imperial power, 'every knee shall bow' to Christ."[16]

Colossians

Osvaldo Padilla

Introduction. Colossians was written by Paul during his first Roman imprisonment in the early 60s. There are many commentators, however, who believe that a disciple of Paul wrote it, not the apostle himself. The reasons given for the rejection of Pauline authorship are similar to those for rejecting Ephesians, but, as indicated in the introduction in the commentary on Ephesians, those reasons ultimately are unconvincing.

What prompted Paul to write Colossians? As with most of Paul's letters, there is not one reason for the composition of the letter but rather many. We can speak of areas of concentration in Paul's letter. For Colossians, there appear to be two main areas, which are related.

First, there was some false teaching afoot in the churches at Colossae, although probably it did not yet have a firm grasp on the believers. More than likely the false teaching was inspired by Jewish *merkabah* mysticism. This was a form of Jewish teaching that had assimilated Platonic thought. Among other things, this teaching emphasized the following: heavenly ascent by means of severe physical abstention (e.g., extreme forms of fasting and punishment of the body), dualism, and the role of angels in the worship of God. The belief was that the devotee could transcend the human condition in order to reach God's very presence. The way to do this was totally on the basis of the effort of the devotee, although angelic beings helped as mediators to the presence of God.[1] The false teachers in Colossae probably were arguing that this was a superior way to encounter God. This would have meant that Jesus Christ was not sufficient for a fully orbed Christian existence. As one can see, this was a significant threat to the gospel Paul preached.

The Location of Colossae

Second, and as a result of the situation noted above, Paul wrote to explain and remind the believers of the superiority (and therefore sufficiency) of Christ. He therefore articulated in majestic terms the divinity of the Son as well as the comprehensiveness of his death for us.

Prayer for the Readers (1:3–14)

In him we have redemption, the forgiveness of sins (1:14). With verse 14 Paul shifts the theme of his prayer in order to concentrate on the work of Christ. To describe the salvation that is ours through Christ, Paul uses terminology found in the manumission of slaves. Since verse 12 speaks of the "saints' inheritance," it is likely that Paul wants to link this to the paradigmatic OT event of liberation: the exodus from Egypt. Through Christ's death God liberated us from our sins and the powers of darkness so that we might serve him. This emphasis follows Jesus's own understanding of his death as presented in the Last Supper (see esp. Luke 22:19–20).

A Hymn to Christ (1:15–20)

It is probably the case that in these verses we have the fragments of an early Christian hymn that worshiped Christ as the Lord. Paul uses some of the terminology of this hymn to articulate the preexistence of Christ. He does this in the context of monotheism as well as his incarnation and ultimate death on the cross. That is to say, while affirming that there is only one God (Deut. 6:4), Paul explains that the reality and the identity of this God are such that they include the eternal Son, who is both creator and redeemer.

He is the image of the invisible God, the firstborn over all creation (1:15). The "hymn" begins by speaking of Christ as the "image" (*eikōn*) of God. The background lies in the OT emphasis on God's transcendence. That is, God created the universe, but he is totally above it and beyond it. The question became: How can such a transcendent God actually interact with human beings; how can we know him? Many Jews who wrote between the OT and the NT spoke of "wisdom" as the image of God. Since wisdom was personified in Prov. 8:22–31 as being present with God at creation, these authors spoke of wisdom as a personification of the image of God by which he interacted with the world.[2] Paul explains that it is no other than Jesus Christ who is the image of the invisible (transcendent) God. He is God in the flesh. Because he is the Word, through which God created the universe, he is "over all creation." The thought is similar to John 1:14: "The Word became flesh and dwelt among us."

Paul says, "I am struggling for you, for those at Laodicea, and for all who have not seen me in person" (Col. 2:1), as an athlete would contend in the stadium. These are the remains of the unexcavated stadium at Laodicea (built ca. AD 69–79). Paul's letter was also meant to be read to the church at Laodicea (Col. 4:16).

Paul's Ministry on Behalf of the Colossians (1:24–2:5)

I am saying this so that no one will deceive you with arguments that sound reasonable (2:4). The expression "arguments that sound reasonable" finds a useful comparison in Plato, where "attractive argument" is compared to the use of more substantial argument in order to persuade.[3] Paul's warning to the Colossians was that they should not allow clever-sounding (but not biblically substantial) eloquence to move them away from the gospel they received from Epaphras.

The Supremacy of Christ in His Person and Work (2:6–15)

The entire fullness of God's nature dwells bodily in Christ (2:9). This is one of the most stunning verses in the NT to refer to the deity of Jesus Christ. The term translated as "God's nature" (*theotēs*) was one of the most pointed ways in Greek to speak of divinity. In fact, we could perhaps think of *theotēs* as that quality which only God possesses—*what makes God God.* When Jesus took on flesh, he did not cease to share with the Father and

Holy Spirit his divine nature. Rather, the eternal Son added flesh to his being without this in any way diminishing his nature as the eternal Son. The result was that Jesus Christ was nothing less than God in the flesh.

Be careful that no one takes you captive through philosophy and empty deceit based on human tradition, based on the elements of the world (2:8). Paul continues his warning of the Colossians. The term "philosophy" itself is not negative, as it could simply refer to a body of teaching, including Jewish teaching.[4] In fact, in the ancient world philosophers were known for their dedication to a moral life. We gain clarity (but not much more) when we observe that Paul links that philosophy with "empty deceit." With this terminology, the emphasis falls on eloquent, "fluffy" popular speech, not very different from the sort of nonsense heard today on talk shows that want to pass for wisdom and that captivate the masses. Paul further qualifies the false teaching as stemming from "human tradition." Remarkably, the same phrase is used by Jesus in Mark 7:8 to refer to Jewish traditional teaching that ended up contradicting the very Scriptures it was trying to apply. Paul concludes the qualification with a devastating phrase: "based on the elements of the world." Although the meaning of the phrase is disputed, it probably refers to demonic beings. Was Paul then saying that Jewish, extrabiblical traditions had a satanic source? More likely he was saying that demonic powers co-opted this teaching in order to lead people astray away from the gospel.

He erased the certificate of debt, with its obligations, that was against us and opposed to us, and has taken it away by nailing it to the cross (2:14). In 2:11–15 Paul provides his readers with a number of metaphors to help understand salvation. In verse 14 he uses the metaphor of debt to help explain the work of Christ on the cross. Because of our failure to obey God's decrees, we incurred a debt with God. The term here for "certificate of debt" (*cheirographon*) often was used in Egyptian papyri to refer to a "record of debts."[5] This may link up with the OT and Jewish thought of there being before God a heavenly book where records of good and evil deeds were kept.[6] Paul explains that God canceled this debt on the basis of the cross. The term for "erase" (*exaleiphō*) was used in

The theater at Hierapolis, a city in Asia Minor only a short distance from Colossae.

the papyri to refer to washing out of the letters from a papyrus sheet. The standard lexicon for the NT gives the following glosses: "to remove so as to leave no trace, *remove, destroy, obliterate.*"[7] This was a powerful way of saying that God had wiped out our sins on the basis of the crucifixion.

Injunctions to the Household (3:18–4:1)

Slaves, obey your human masters in everything (3:22). Slavery was a part of life in the ancient world. Unlike modern-day slavery (European, North American, and Latin American), it was not at all based on race or education (see the article "Slavery in the New Testament World"). Rather, most slaves became such as a result of economic destitution and/or war. They often became part of households. It is clear that many early Christians belonged to these households (e.g., Acts 16:31–33). Paul commands slaves to submit in all things to their masters. There probably is some hyperbole here, since Paul would not have ordered Christian slaves (both male and female) to acquiesce to sexual intercourse with their masters, a common practice in the Roman world. Furthermore, Paul implies that slaves were not ultimately and absolutely the "property" of their masters.

Final Salutations (4:7–18)

I, Paul, am writing this greeting with my own hand (4:18). As was often the case in papyri letters,[8] Paul uses his own hand to conclude the letter (see also 1 Cor. 16:21; 2 Thess. 3:17). This probably served to authenticate that the letter was truly from him.

1–2 Thessalonians

Joseph R. Dodson

1 Thessalonians

Introduction. A Macedonian king founded Thessalonica (modern-day Salonica) in 315 BC and named it after his wife. Situated both on a natural harbor and on the Roman highway leading eastward, Thessalonica became an important commercial city in Macedonia and the capital of its province. Acts 17 provides a behind-the-scenes account that sets up Paul's letters to the Thessalonians. According to Acts, Paul arrived at the city on his second missionary journey. After he had carried out a short period of ministry, a number of Jews incited a mob in the city, because his gospel endorsed Jesus as a new king. Consequently, Paul was forced to slip away. Although he desired to return, the apostle had to settle for sending Timothy instead. Once Timothy returned with a favorable report, Paul sent him back once more with this epistle. By it, he aimed to remind the church of his love for and commitment to them and to applaud and encourage them for their enduring perseverance, as well as to reinforce and complement his former teachings on topics such as sexual purity and the second coming. Scholars consider 1 Thessalonians to have been written around 50. It therefore stands as one of Paul's first extant letters.[1]

Paul, Silvanus, and Timothy (1:1). Paul chose Silas, also known as Silvanus, to be his ministry partner on the second missionary journey (Acts

15:36–40). Silas's previous experience as an ambassador to the gentile Christians from the Jerusalem Council made him an obvious choice for Paul (Acts 15:30–33). Once they met Timothy, Paul and Silas wasted little time drafting him to be their coworker (Acts 16:1–4).

To the church of the Thessalonians (1:1). According to Acts 17:4, this church was composed of several Jews, a large number of God-fearing Greeks, and quite a few prominent women.

God the Father and the Lord Jesus Christ (1:1). This greeting may have been striking to the audience, whose coins had the image of Julius Caesar on one side and the image of Octavian on the other. Inscribed above the engraved bust of Julius Caesar on the coins was the word *THEOS* ("god") and above that of Octavian the word *THESSALONIKEŌN* ("of the Thessalonians").[2]

Grace to you and peace (1:1). The standard Greek salutation was *chairete* ("rejoice"), and the standard Jewish greeting was *shalom* ("peace"). As was his custom in his letters, Paul tweaks the former by replacing it with *charis* ("grace"), which suited his emphasis on undeserved grace.[3]

We always thank God for all of you (1:2). Many Hellenistic letters contained wishes and supplications for the well-being of the recipients.

He has chosen you (1:4). Mystery religions and philosophical competitors surrounding the church did not have a sense of divine election. In comparison then, the notion of election helped the believers have a stronger sense of community identity. Although the Jews considered themselves as God's chosen people, early believers adopted that identity for Jews and gentiles *in Christ*.

Remains from the marketplace in Thessalonica.

In power, in the Holy Spirit, and with full assurance (1:5). Philosophers sought to deliver inspired sermons that produced great conviction in their audiences. One ancient writer describes his response to a philosopher's preaching: "When he stopped speaking . . . I dripped with sweat, I stumbled . . . my voice failed, my tongue faltered, and finally I began to cry."[4]

Imitators of us and of the Lord . . . in spite of severe persecution (1:6). Many philosophical schools in the first century had disciples whose main task involved imitation—following and adhering to the example of a god or master teacher, especially in contexts of suffering.[5]

Macedonia and Achaia (1:8). Situated on the Balkan Peninsula, Thessalonica was the seat of provincial administration for the province. The example of the Thessalonian believers extended to Achaia, the province that adjoined it on the south (i.e., central and southern Greece).[6]

You turned to God from idols (1:9). Evidence from archaeology, inscriptions, and coins demonstrates that a number of idolatrous mystery cults existed in Thessalonica. The state even sponsored religions dedicated to the gods Dionysus and Cabirus, the latter of which became the chief cult of the city. Cabirus was a martyred hero whom his followers expected to return to life. Worshipers of Cabirus would confess sins and be cleansed by partaking in baptism symbolic of the god's blood.[7]

To serve the living and true God (1:9). Because of their rejection of the nations' gods, Jews and Christians were (ironically) accused of being atheists.[8]

Our visit with you was not without result (2:1). Ancient letters of friendship were replete with petitions to the audience's knowledge of certain matters meant to reinforce the relationship between the author and his audience (see also 2:5, 9–11).[9]

We had previously suffered (2:2). Before coming to Thessalonica, Paul was locked up, stripped down, and beaten with rods (see Acts 16:22–24). It would have been considered an outrage for a Roman citizen to be flogged without a trial.

Approved by God (2:4). One first-century philosopher wrote that those who have been approved by God live "above all contempt and fear, grief and terror."[10]

Not to please people (2:4). People-pleasers who used flattery to advance themselves were stock characters.[11] Paul's opponents likely accused him of being a people-pleaser, possibly because he sought to "become all things to all people" (1 Cor. 9:22).

We never used flattering speech (2:5). Ancient moralists lampooned the popular philosophers who were more interested in flattering their audiences than confronting them with truth. Such orators, it was said, were like clowns who masquerade as physicians: bringing perfume and flowers to patients instead of treatment and a cure.[12] What was needed, one moralist surmised, was the rare preacher who spoke truth in plain terms without false intentions. Such a noble soul would be willing for the sake of truth to face ridicule by and uproar from the mobs.[13]

As a nurse nurtures her own children (2:7). In a first-century essay about how to tell a flatterer from a friend (see comments on 1 Thess. 2:4), the author explains how people need gentle encouragement rather than harsh rebukes: "When children fall down, the nurses do not rush up to them to berate them, but they take them, wash them up, and straighten their clothes."[14]

Working night and day (2:9). Paul's role as a tentmaker also afforded him a locus of missionary activity outside of the synagogue. Workshops were also places for intellectual discourse. Paul's work ethic set him further apart from the host of wandering charlatans who lived at the expense of their devotees. Some rabbis claimed that the study of the Torah and a secular job made an excellent combination.[15] Paul chose a good profession, since leather products such as tents, awnings, satchels, and belts were in high demand and the tools of the trade were portable.[16]

Like a father with his own children (2:11). Good fathers were expected to rear their children in virtue so that, rather than being "spoiled pets," they would be fit for service.[17] As the head of the household, the Roman father exercised authority over his children in matters such as education, mate selection, and finances.[18]

Imitators (2:14). See comments on 1 Thess. 1:6.

You have also suffered the same things from people of your own country, just as they did from the Jews (2:14). In addition to the persecution of Stephen by the Jews in Acts 6–7 and of the believers by Herod Agrippa in Acts

This gold oak wreath (350–300 BC) was found in Turkey.

12, Paul may be referring to the pressure placed on the church by zealots pushing a campaign for circumcision around the year 48.

The Jews who killed the Lord Jesus (2:14–15). This echoes what Peter says to his fellow Israelites in Acts 3:15: "You killed the source of life." Likewise, Stephen proclaims to his fellow Jews, "As your ancestors did, you do also. . . . They even killed those who foretold the coming of the Righteous One, whose betrayers and murderers you have now become" (Acts 7:51–52). Not every Jew in Thessalonica, however, persecuted the church. Some of them were followers of Christ (Acts 17:1–9).

Wrath has overtaken them at last (2:16). This is possibly a reference to a massacre of the Jews that took place in the temple courts at the Passover in AD 49.[19] It could have also been an ominous prophecy of Jerusalem's destruction in AD 70.

We were forced to leave you for a short time (2:17). This type of sentiment was common in ancient letters. For instance, an ancient author wrote, "Even though I have been separated from you for a long time, I suffer this in body alone. For I can never forget you. . . . Knowing that I myself am genuinely concerned about your affairs, and that I have worked unhesitatingly for what is most advantageous to you."[20]

Crown of boasting (2:19). A wreath was awarded to the winners of athletic contests, which served as bragging rights for those who wore them.

In the presence of our Lord Jesus at his coming (2:19). Inhabitants celebrated the coming (*parousia*) of divine kings to their cities. One inscription states "in the year 69 of the first *parousia* of the god Hadrian."[21]

Left alone in Athens (3:1). While Paul had sent Timothy back to Thessalonica and Silas presumably back to Macedonia, Luke records the apostle as giving his famous sermon on Mars Hill (Acts 17:22–31).

Timothy (3:2). Timothy was the son of a Jewish mother and a gentile father. Although his mother and grandmother were devout, Timothy was uncircumcised until Paul saw fit to do so (Acts 16:1–3). In other letters Paul mentions more missions that he sent Timothy on (1 Cor. 4:17; Phil. 2:19) and even includes him in his salutations (e.g., 2 Corinthians, Philippians, Philemon).

We are appointed to this (3:3). A number of Jewish works that predate the first century assured readers that God's elect would have to endure sufferings before the new age dawns.[22]

This votive relief (fourth century BC), possibly associated with the founding of Thessalonica, includes images of Athena, Zeus, and Hera and is a reminder of the city's pagan heritage.

At the coming of our Lord Jesus with all his saints (3:13). Although "saints" or "holy ones" may refer to believers who had passed away, the designation often was used to refer to angels. The Qumran communities used "holy ones" for the good angels as a way to set them apart from the fallen ones.[23]

Keep away from sexual immorality (4:3). One request of the Jerusalem Council was that the non-Jewish believers abstain from sexual immorality (Acts 15:20, 29). In Thessalonica the cult of Cabirus sanctioned sexual immorality.[24] Stoics argued that setting one's mind on becoming beautiful and pure before God helped one overcome sexual attraction.[25]

Control his own body (4:4). This phrase could be a euphemism for controlling one's genitals and may be a play on words to censure the sexual activities associated with the cult of Cabirus, which used the phallus as its chief symbol.[26] Early church fathers, however, took the phrase to mean "possess one's own wife" (i.e., not somebody else's). This latter interpretation resounds with the Jewish idea of satisfying oneself sexually with one's spouse to stave off temptation (e.g., Prov. 5:15; 1 Cor. 7:2).

Not with lustful passions, like the Gentiles, who don't know God (4:5). Jewish tradition often associated the pagans' ignorance of Israel's God with sexual immorality. Roman men had mistresses to satisfy their sexual pleasures. It was common for men to have formal companions (*heterai*), sex slaves, and harlots to satisfy their lusts.[27]

One must not transgress against and take advantage of a brother or sister (4:6). In addition to satisfying their erotic desires with mistresses, men were known to commit adultery with other men's wives. Such a man was said to wrong the husband of the woman he corrupts.[28] It was also common for men to sexually exploit their slaves. Therefore, this prohibition may include a warning for Christian slave owners to abandon their old habits of taking advantage of their slaves, who are now their brothers and sisters in the faith.[29]

The Lord is an avenger of all these offenses (4:6). Romans called adultery "wife stealing," which was punishable by banishment under law. A couple caught in the act could even be in danger of being killed on the spot. If a husband learned that his wife was committing adultery, he was required by law to divorce her or face prosecution on the charge of "pimping."[30]

Seek to lead a quiet life (4:11). This notion cut against the grain of popular teaching that insisted that one could *not* achieve honor by living quietly. For the pagans, ambition necessitated pursuit for public recognition and an established reputation that resulted from conspicuous gifts and civic deeds.[31] Some philosophers, however, received criticism for promoting "quietism," that is, the practice of minding one's own business and avoiding public and political life.[32]

Mind your own business and . . . work with your own hands (4:11). While most from the social elite despised manual labor, some commended people who worked to provide themselves with what was necessary for life.[33]

Not be dependent on anyone (4:12). In this culture, rather than working hard, many people relied on patrons to take care of them. In return for the provisions that clients received, they broadcast their patron's generosity to boost the patron's reputation.[34]

So that you will not grieve like the rest, who have no hope (4:13). A large number of pagans considered death a sleep from which no one would wake. But it is an overstatement to say that pagans had no hope for an afterlife, since some did believe in an eternal soul. Some reasoned that the day of a virtuous person's death was a birthday into eternity, when the person would wake up into life and rise to the skies.[35]

The trumpet of God (4:16). In the ancient world a herald announced the coming of a king and a trumpet blast alerted the inhabitants that the king was near. The Jews used shofars to gather the people together and to give battle orders.

The dead in Christ (4:16). Some scholars argue that this phrase refers to some of the Thessalonian believers who were killed due to their association with Paul and the repercussions of the apostle's treasonous violation of Caesar's decrees (see Acts 17:1–9).[36]

Will rise first (4:16). While some people expected the soul of the virtuous to ascend to heaven (see comments on 1 Thess. 4:13), the idea of a bodily resurrection—corpses standing up in their graves—would have sounded nightmarish to most.

To meet the Lord in the air (4:17). At the coming (*parousia*) of a king, the honorable people went out to meet him, while the condemned stayed behind waiting to be judged (see comments on 1 Thess. 2:19). In the first century "the air" was thought to be the abode of demons.

We will always be with the Lord (4:17). Some pagans believed that the deceased would ascend into the heavens to dwell in peace with the gods, their loved ones, and the assembly of the saints.[37]

They say, "Peace and security" (5:3). Inscriptions decorated Rome declaring how the empire's military had produced peace and security.[38] Moreover, Roman roads allowed the military to deploy quickly and travel rapidly to eradicate any threat to the peace and safety of Rome.

We do not belong to the night (5:5). Moralists contrasted being awake and sober with being asleep and drunk.[39] "Night is the time for thieves, daylight is the time for truth."[40] Therefore, philosophers condemned people who slept during the day and spent their nights full of food and wine. It was said that those fools not only failed to know *how* to live but also they did not even know *when* to live. Moralists preached that in contrast to partying all night, "We are more industrious, and we are better men if we anticipate the day and welcome the dawn."[41]

Put on the armor of faith and love, and a helmet of the hope of salvation (5:8). While others spent their nights feasting, armed soldiers stayed awake to be on guard.[42] The notion of spiritual armor in the last days was a common Jewish idea. In canonical and apocryphal Jewish works God is the one who arms himself to fight the wicked (Isa. 59:17–18; Wis. 5:17–19).

Always pursue what is good for one another and for all (5:15). This was a common sentiment. For instance, one philosopher wrote, "Bees are of one mind, and no one has ever seen a swarm that is factious and fights against itself. Rather, they both work and live together, providing food for one another." He concluded by pointing out how shameful

Reassembled statue of Augustus from Thessalonica (first century AD). Augustus initiated the idea of *pax Romana*, the peace and security of the Roman Empire. Paul warns, however, "When they say, 'Peace and security,' then sudden destruction will come upon them" (1 Thess. 5:3).

it is when savage creatures take care of one another while human beings only look out for themselves.[43]

Don't despise prophecies, but test all things (5:20–21). Pagan cults also practiced prophecy and ecstatic inspiration. Early Christians had to test prophecies therefore, since even though a prophecy was spiritual, this did not necessarily mean that it was from God.

May your whole spirit, soul, and body be kept sound and blameless (5:23). Stoics made distinctions between the spirit and the soul. In the body the soul was the life force of the person, but when commingled with the mind (*nous*), the soul was the spirit (*pneuma*).[44]

Holy kiss (5:26). In the following centuries the holy kiss became a feature of the Eucharist. One can imagine how radical Paul's command was in light of the societal boundaries between Jews and gentiles, as well as between slaves and freepersons.

This letter be read to all (5:27). Most people in the first century were illiterate and therefore needed epistles read to them.[45]

2 Thessalonians

Introduction. Stronger in tone than 1 Thessalonians, the second letter covers some of the same topics, especially questions concerning Christ's second coming. The persecution of the believers seemed to have continued, if not increased, and adding to the crisis, they had received a false report that Jesus had already returned (cf. 2:2–3).[46] For more background information, see the introduction in the commentary on 1 Thessalonians.

Thessalonica was named after Thessaloniki, daughter of Philip II. The inscription on this base, which once held her statue, reads, "Queen Thessaloniki, [daughter] of Philip."

Paul, Silvanus, and Timothy (1:1). See comments on 1 Thess. 1:1.

To the church of the Thessalonians (1:1). See comments on 1 Thess. 1:1.

Grace to you and peace from God (1:1). See comments on 1 Thess. 1:1.

We ought to thank God always for you (1:3). See comments on 1 Thess. 1:2.

The persecutions and afflictions that you are enduring (1:4). See comments on 1 Thess. 1:6; 2:14.

It is just for God . . . to give relief to you (1:7). There was a Jewish expectation that God's faithful followers would be forced to endure an intense period of suffering before the Messiah returned and offered relief. These necessary troubles became known as "messianic woes."

The revelation of the Lord Jesus from heaven . . . when he takes vengeance with flaming fire (1:7–8). Flames often appeared at divine revelations. It was even said that the preincarnate Christ appeared to Moses in blazing fire in the burning bush at Horeb (Exod. 3:1–6).[47]

With his powerful angels (1:7). Jewish apocalyptic works prophesied that the Lord would descend from the seventh heaven with legions of angels and saints to cast Beliar (i.e., Satan) and his armies into Gehenna.[48] On saints, see comments on 1 Thess. 3:13.

Those who don't know God (1:8). Divine appearances often were associated with an agent of God such as the Son of Man, Michael, and Melchizedek. This agent would come to execute divine punishment upon the wicked.

Eternal destruction (1:9). During the persecution of the Jews in the intertestamental period, one young man proclaimed that, in contrast to the peace that welcomed his martyred brothers at their deaths, the tyrant who killed them would face "everlasting destruction" (4 Macc. 10:15). According to Plato's *Republic,* wicked people descended into the underworld after they died to be tormented for a thousand years in order to repay their sins tenfold, while the virtuous ascended into the heavens to enjoy indescribable bliss.[49]

The coming of our Lord Jesus Christ (2:1). See comments on 1 Thess. 2:19. In some Hellenistic cults there was an expectation that there would be a "coming" of certain hidden deities who would powerfully make their presence felt to the religion's initiates.[50]

Unless the apostasy comes first (2:3). Many Jews expected a revolt or falling away from God during the last days.[51]

The man of lawlessness is revealed (2:3). The first man of lawlessness was Antiochus IV Epiphanes (i.e., Epiphany). The word for "epiphany" was used of the "coming" Roman kings to imply that their visits were a manifestation of divinity.[52] In one Jewish work Pompey was called the man of lawlessness because his campaign in Judea in 63 BC resulted in widespread apostasy.[53]

The man doomed to destruction (2:3). The word translated as "destruction" (*apōleia*) was associated with Sheol, Abaddon, and Hades to signify a place for the dead.[54] Wicked people often were said to be bound for this place;[55] hence, Judas became infamously known as the "son of destruction" (John 17:12).

Proclaiming that he himself is God (2:4). Following the example of Julius Caesar, who had his statue erected throughout the empire that proclaimed him to be a god, Caligula sought to set up his statue in the Jerusalem temple (AD 39–40). Moreover, Claudius—likely the ruler during the time 1 Thessalonians was written—was declared to be the universal consolation of all humankind who governed the earth by the splendor of his divinity. It was said that Claudius was the everlasting Sun expected to heal the human race from sickness and sin and to give light to the world that had been dunked into darkness and plunged into the abyss.[56] It was not just Roman rulers who assumed the position of God, however. In AD 44 Herod allowed himself to be worshiped by the crowds.[57]

Bust of the Roman emperor Caligula, who reigned from AD 37 to 41. Paul says in 2 Thess. 2:4 that the man of lawlessness "sits in God's temple, proclaiming that he himself is God," similar to what Caligula attempted to do in the Jerusalem temple.

And you know what currently restrains him (2:6). Although neither one was the man of lawlessness, Behemoth and Leviathan were said to be held back until the time the Christ was revealed.[58] A popular early interpretation of this verse was that the Roman Empire was the restraining force holding back the man of lawlessness.[59] This would mean that some considered Claudius's death as that which would make way for Nero.

The mystery of lawlessness (2:7). The secret power of lawlessness (i.e., the "mystery of lawlessness") is similar to the "mystery of evil" that Josephus referred to in the life of Antipater.[60]

The lawless one (2:8). The Jews had a number of expectations for a lawless one who would rise when Rome fell. Some believed that this antichrist would be a fellow Jew from the tribe of Dan, while others supposed a gentile ruler. The lawless one would claim to be divine and would install a cult in the temple. Some said that Elijah would return to confront this antichrist, who in turn would kill the OT prophet and rule the world for three and half years. The lawless one would pursue those who refused to worship him into the wilderness and begin to decimate them. Finally, however, God would intervene through an agent like Michael the archangel and defeat the antichrist once for all.[61]

The breath of his mouth (2:8). One popular Jewish work, the book of Wisdom, stated that the Lord had the power to create new beasts that could slay the wicked by breathing fire and belching smoke. How much more then, that author reasoned, the impious would fall at a single burst of God's breath upon them (Wis. 11:17–20).

Based on Satan's working (2:9). Some early Christians expected Nero to return as Satan incarnate (i.e., Beliar/Belial) to persecute the church and deceive the multitudes.[62]

False miracles, signs, and wonders (2:9). The emperor Caligula claimed to work miracles and perform signs. Furthermore, there was propaganda regarding emperors' power to cure sickness, and some people invoked his spirit for healing.[63] See comments on 2 Thess. 2:4.

God sends them a strong delusion (2:11). Isaiah wrote that the Lord sent Israel a spirit to prevent people from seeing and hearing the truth (Isa. 29:10). So also God sent a spirit to deceive Ahab's prophets (1 Kings 22:22).

The word of the Lord may spread rapidly (3:1). Similar to Paul's prayer here for the word (*logos*) of the Lord to race ahead and be glorified, one Jewish work records the *logos* of the Lord springing from God's throne in heaven with the Lord's divine command in hand (Wis. 18:15).

Imitate us . . . not idle . . . working night and day (3:7–8). See comments on 1 Thess. 1:6; 2:9. Some moral philosophers celebrated hard work. In contrast to the worthless people who wasted their time amusing themselves in feasting, the virtuous people, summoned by toil, "labor, spend, and are spent."[64]

We commanded you: "If anyone isn't willing to work, he should not eat" (3:10). Rabbi Abbahu had a similar axiom: "If I do not work, I do not eat."[65] So also the Stoics urged their followers to work for their own sustenance rather than depend upon others for it.[66] An early Christian work instructs believers to feed travelers for three days, but if the guest wants to stay longer, "let him work for his bread."[67] Chrysostom later commands believers, however, not to let an idle brother or sister starve to death.[68] See comments on 1 Thess. 4:12.

Don't associate with him . . . yet don't consider him as an enemy (3:14–15). One ancient philosopher instructed his audience to avoid people who tend to get out of line in life but not to look at them askance or to conceive hatred for them.[69]

With my own hand (3:17). Ancient authors who dictated their letters would sometimes write the last couple of sentences in their own hand for authenticity and for making the epistle more personal (cf. 1 Cor. 16:21; Gal. 6:11; Col. 4:18; Philem. 19).[70]

1–2 Timothy, Titus

Ray Van Neste

Introduction. The letters 1 Timothy, 2 Timothy, and Titus have long been grouped together within Paul's other letters and since about the eighteenth century have been referred to as the Pastoral Epistles. The letters do share many similar concerns and unique vocabulary and are the only letters of Paul written to fellow workers. However, we must not forget that each of these letters has its own distinctive concerns as well. Also, while they are written to men who are serving in essentially a pastoral role, the letters do not merely address pastoral ministry issues but also speak about Christian living in general.

Each of these letters claims to have been written by Paul (1 Tim. 1:1; 2 Tim. 1:1; Titus 1:1), and this claim was affirmed by the church for the first eighteen centuries of its history. In the nineteenth century critiques of Pauline authorship began to emerge. Critics point to ways in which these three letters differ from Paul's other letters in style, vocabulary, theology, church order, and the portrait of Paul. However, the differences in theology and church order, for instance, typically are overstated based on a certain reading of Paul's earlier letters and due to reading these three letters as a unit rather than individually (as the rest of Paul's letters are read). Differences in style and vocabulary are not unusual for a creative mind, especially in light of the fact that these are the only letters written to coworkers.

These letters do not state exactly when they were written, and they do not appear to fit within the framework of the book of Acts (though some scholars argue that they do). The traditional understanding has been that Paul was released from his first Roman imprisonment (mentioned at the

This underground prison cell in the Mamertine Prison (dating back to the seventh century BC) is the traditional location where both Peter and Paul were imprisoned in Rome. Above this now stands the Church of San Giuseppe dei Falegnami, and the cell has been converted into a chapel honoring the two apostles.

close of Acts), did further mission work, and was then imprisoned a second time leading to his execution. If so, 1 Timothy and Titus would fit well during Paul's work between the two imprisonments (mid-60s). Second Timothy, which pictures Paul in prison in Rome awaiting death, would have been written during Paul's second Roman imprisonment, around 66–67. This reconstruction is supported by statements from early church writings.

1 Timothy

Salutation (1:1–2)

God our Savior (1:1). Greeks and Romans referred to human deliverers, guides, and gods as "savior." Paul makes clear that God is the Savior.

Timothy, my true son in the faith (1:2). Rabbis and philosophers referred to their disciples as their sons.

Confronting the False Teaching (1:3–20)

Macedonia . . . Ephesus (1:3). Ephesus was a major city in Asia Minor (modern-day Turkey) and a key Pauline base (see the article "The City of Ephesus"). Leaving Timothy there, Paul has crossed the Aegean Sea to Macedonia, north of Greece.

Myths and endless genealogies (1:4). "Myths" refers to traditional stories common in pagan religions. Some Jewish groups were very interested in speculations involving OT genealogies. "Myths and genealogies" had become a phrase commonly used to refer to wrongheaded teaching.

The goal of our instruction is love (1:5). This is rooted in Jesus's statement that love is the summary of the law (Matt. 22:34–40; cf. Deut. 6:6; Lev. 19:18).

Teachers of the law (1:7). Here "law" refers to OT law and suggests a Jewish background to the false teaching. The list of sins in 1:9–10 broadly corresponds to the Ten Commandments with especially horrendous violations of the commands.

Homosexuals (1:10). This term translates the word *arsenokoitēs*, which appears to have been coined by Paul (we have no examples of its use prior to Paul), and it is a combination of two words used to describe homosexual behavior in Lev. 18:22; 20:13 in the Septuagint. Although some Roman teachers opposed homosexuality, it was widespread among upper-class Romans in the first century. Jewish teaching consistently viewed homosexual behavior as unnatural and sinful.

The King eternal, immortal, invisible, the only God (1:17). In Greek thought the gods were eternal and immortal but not necessarily invisible, and certainly there was not just one god. The claim of there being only one true God was a major distinctive of Judaism and Christianity.

Hymenaeus and Alexander (1:20). The identity of these two men is not certain. They could be the same men referred to in 2 Timothy (Hymenaeus in 2:17–18, Alexander in 4:14).

Curetes Street, one of the main thoroughfares in ancient Ephesus, near the ruins of the Memmius Monument.

Corporate Prayer and Issues Arising from It (2:1–15)

One God (2:5). This is a basic OT affirmation (see Deut. 6:4), and it stood in contrast to the understanding in the rest of the ancient world, which assumed the existence of many gods.

In every place (2:8). This phrase seems to allude to Mal. 1:11, a text that looks to a day when people from all over the world will call upon the Lord. This connects to the prayer for mission, which is a key theme here and suggests that this is not merely instruction for one isolated church.

Lifting up holy hands (2:8). Raising hands in prayer was a common Jewish practice (see Exod. 9:29; Ps. 28:2), which came readily into the early church.

Dress themselves in modest clothing (2:9). Jewish and Greco-Roman writers rebuked women who dressed so as to attract the attention of men other than their husbands. Gaudy and showy dress seems to have been common in the Greco-Roman world, though many writers condemned it.

I do not allow a woman to teach or to have authority over a man (2:12). Male leadership was typical in the first-century world, although various sources record women in leadership positions politically, militarily, and religiously.

Qualifications for Overseers and Deacons (3:1–13)

Overseer (3:1). This word (*episkopē*) had a broad range of uses in the Greco-Roman world for people who watch over others—students, a city, and so on—and could even refer to a guardian deity. The idea of guarding or protecting is prominent, then, as Paul uses this term to refer to the pastoral office.

Above reproach (3:2). Priesthoods in the Roman world typically were awarded to people based on their political connections or even given to the highest bidder. Stringent moral requirements were not typical. Thus Paul's list of necessary qualities that follows here stands in marked contrast with the broader culture but in keeping with the purity required of the leaders of God's people

The head from a statue of Julia Titi (AD 61–91), daughter of the emperor Titus and mistress to her uncle Domitian. Notice the elaborate hairstyle. The diadem may have contained precious gems, and the complete statue would have been adorned with earrings and a necklace. Paul instructs women believers not to follow this trend in fashion but rather to dress themselves "in modest clothing, with decency and good sense" (1 Tim. 2:9).

in the OT (e.g., Lev. 21). The list is similar to a list composed by a Greek philosopher (Onasander, first century AD) discussing qualities that one should look for in a military leader.

He must manage his own household (3:4). See the article "New Testament Household Codes." Household management was very significant in the ancient world, and several treatises on the topic have survived. Politicians often were judged by how well their children obeyed them. The idea was well established that the family was a microcosm of society, so leadership in the home was the necessary prerequisite to leadership in broader society. The Greek historian Herodotus (fifth century BC) tells of people in Miletus (very near Ephesus) choosing political leaders based entirely on who was managing his own lands well.

Deacons (3:8). The Greek word translated as "deacon" (*diakonos*) means "servant." Many understand the choosing of seven men to distribute food in Acts 6:1–6 as the origin of this office.

Purpose of Writing: Behavior in the Church (3:14–16)

God's household (3:15). The portrayal of the church as God's household resonates in different ways with Greco-Roman and Jewish backgrounds. Like a typical Greco-Roman household, the church has established "house rules" and a leadership structure that have just been described. The church is a household in which God is the ruling Father. However, the phrase "house of God" is commonly used in the OT to refer to the temple (Exod. 23:19; 34:26; Deut. 23:18; 1 Chron. 9:13; Ezra 5:2, 13; 6:5; Ps. 55:14; Eccles. 5:1; see also Matt. 12:4), so it seems that the church is being referred to as the new temple (cf. 1 Cor. 3:16–17).

Church of the living God (3:15). The word translated as "church" (*ekklēsia*) could refer to any assembly in the Roman world. "Living God" is a common phrase in the OT pointing to the Lord as the true God (1 Sam. 17:26; Isa. 37:4; Jer. 10:10). It is also used to point to God's real presence among his people (Josh. 3:10; Ps. 42:2). Thus the church is the assembly where the presence of God is truly manifested. This is another way in which the church is the new temple.

The pillar and foundation of the truth (3:15). These architectural terms would be particularly significant in Ephesus, which was experiencing a significant building program, including the Temple of Artemis, one of the seven wonders of the ancient world.[1] Since "truth" is a synonym for "gospel" in these letters, this picture demonstrates the responsibility of the church to protect and promote the gospel.

Identifying the False Teachers (4:1–5)

Teachings of demons (4:1). The word "demon" would not have necessarily sounded bad to people in the first century. People used the word to refer to various spiritual beings to whom they sacrificed and who might provide direction. Paul states that such teaching or direction is categorically bad, pointing people instead to the work of the Spirit.

Consciences are seared (4:2). Branding with a hot iron was a well-known punishment in Paul's day, so this image of a person's conscience becoming dead and unfeeling would have been all the more striking.

They forbid marriage and demand abstinence from foods (4:3). Abstaining from certain foods was a common part of Judaism, but prohibiting marriage was uncommon in both Greco-Roman and Jewish cultures. The background of this asceticism is unclear, though it bears some similarity with concerns raised in 1 Corinthians and Colossians.

Everything created by God is good (4:4). This truth is rooted in God's assessment of creation recorded in Genesis (Gen. 1:4, 9, 10, 12, 18, 21, 25, 31). Giving thanks to God for meals was a common Jewish practice.

Instruction to Timothy (4:6–16)

Train yourself in godliness . . . the training of the body has limited benefit (4:7–8). The words used for "train" and "training" here are the source of our word "gymnasium." The physical training of the *gymnasia* was a key part of Greek culture. Greek and Roman moral teachers often used such physical exercise as an illustration for moral and intellectual development in a way similar to what Paul does here (see the article "Athletics in the New Testament World").

The living God, who is the Savior of all people (4:10). See comments on 1 Tim. 3:15. In the Greco-Roman world various people were referred to as "saviors" when they gave help or rescue. In Ephesus, where this letter was received, there was an inscription honoring Julius Caesar as "universal savior of human life." The inscription was on the base of a statue erected in Caesar's honor in 48 BC, after he had rescued the province from financial ruin.[2] Thus both of these phrases are polemical, noting God as the true Savior.

Don't let anyone despise your youth (4:12). Greco-Roman and Jewish society held age in high esteem (see Lev. 19:32), as is seen later in 5:1–2. This statement, then, challenges prevailing cultural norms, placing authority in one who is younger and basing that authority on exemplary behavior rather than age alone.

Public reading (4:13). This refers to the public reading of Scripture, which was central in Jewish worship in synagogues at this time. In general, public reading was common because books were expensive and difficult to obtain.

Laying on of hands by the council of elders (4:14). The "laying on of hands" was a recognized way of authorizing someone for leadership in Judaism (Num. 27:18–23). "Elder" was a common term for leaders in the Jewish community and synagogue and was thus taken up by the early Christian communities (throughout the OT, including Exod. 3:16; 4:29; Lev. 9:1; judging cases in Deut. 21–22; Ruth 4:4; 1 Kings 8:1; Ps. 107:32; Prov. 31:23).

Behavior of Specific Groups in the Church (5:1–6:2a)

Don't rebuke an older man (5:1). Respect for those who are older was a common value among ancient cultures. Thus Timothy is to exercise authority even as a younger man (4:12), but to do so in a respectful way.

Widows who are genuinely in need (5:3). Widows were especially vulnerable in the ancient world. Women usually were not heirs, and there was nothing like insurance or governmental help. Thus they were in particular need of help in what was often a brutal setting. Care of such widows was a long-standing concern among the Jews (Deut. 14:29), with God describing himself as "champion of widows" (Ps. 68:5). Stern judgment was pronounced on those who exploited widows (Isa. 10:2; Mal. 3:5). This concern was picked up quickly by the early church (Acts 6:1; James 1:27).

Worse than an unbeliever (5:8). Even pagans thought that one should care for widows in their own families. Roman law required children to support their aging parents.

At least sixty years old (5:9). In the regulations of Lev. 27:7, old age began at sixty years of age. This is picked up in some other Jewish writings, though Jewish and Greco-Roman writings presented a range of ages for the beginning of old age.

Well known for good works (5:10). The actions that follow in this verse are standard activities highly esteemed for women in the ancient world.

Busybodies (5:13). There was significant concern in the ancient world about people getting into other people's business and upsetting the culture by leaving their proper sphere of responsibility and trying to get into the spheres of others. This appears to be what is in view here, so Paul encourages younger widows to engage in appropriate behavior (5:14).

I want younger women to marry (5:14). Quick remarriage for widows was the social ideal in Roman and Jewish cultures.

Elders (5:17). See comments on 1 Tim. 4:14.

For the Scripture says (5:18). For a Jew, "Scripture" would refer to the OT. Paul uses the term in connection with Deut. 25:4 and a saying of Jesus found in Luke 10:7, demonstrating that the early church saw Jesus's teaching as Scripture early on.

Two or three witnesses (5:19). This was a central requirement of Jewish law (Deut. 17:6; 19:15).

I solemnly charge you before God and Christ Jesus and the elect angels (5:21). To call witnesses for a charge was a way of increasing the solemnity and gravity of the charge. Calling three witnesses here may echo the requirement referred to in 5:19. Jewish writings referred to "elect angels" in contrast to the fallen ones.[3]

Use a little wine (5:23). The moderate use of wine was commended by various ancient authors. All wine used in antiquity was alcoholic, since without refrigeration or chemical preservatives grape juice quickly turns to vinegar. Fermentation was a means of preservation. Wine typically was weak by modern standards, being cut with water. Sometimes wine was used to disinfect drinking water. It is particularly interesting that Pliny the Elder, in the mid-first century AD, discussed the wine of Ephesus in his *Natural History*. He singled out Ephesian wine as particularly bad because seawater was used in making it.[4] Perhaps this is why Timothy had abstained from drinking it previously!

The beautiful mosaic floors and frescoed walls in these ancient terraced houses in Ephesus (occupied from the first century BC through the seventh century AD) attest to the wealth that some individuals possessed. Paul addressed the dangers of wealth: "Those who want to be rich fall into temptation" (1 Tim. 6:9).

Under the yoke as slaves (6:1). Most households in the Greco-Roman world had slaves, and the situation of slaves varied widely (see the article "Slavery in the New Testament World").

Confronting False Teaching Again (6:2b–21)

We brought nothing into the world, and we can take nothing out (6:7). This is a truth also stated by various Greco-Roman philosophers as well as in the OT (Job 1:21; Ps. 49.17; Eccles. 5:15).

The King of kings and the Lord of lords (6:15). Eastern kingdoms, such as Babylon, used this title for their supreme ruler, and some Greek writers used this title for Zeus. Its use here distinguishes the Christian God as superior to all other powers, human or divine.

2 Timothy

Salutation (1:1–2)

My dearly loved son (1:2). See comments on 1 Tim. 1:2.

Call to Endurance for the Gospel (1:3–2:13)

Your tears (1:4). Tears were a common and appropriate expression in Eastern cultures when people were parting and expecting not to see one another for a long time.[5]

Your grandmother Lois . . . your mother Eunice (1:5). In Jewish families the father was considered responsible for the religious instruction of children, though this does not mean that mothers weren't involved. Timothy's father was a gentile and unbeliever (Acts 16:1–3), so his mother would have been the key person to instruct him. In the book of Tobit we have a Jewish account of a grandmother playing a key role in raising a son in the faith after the death of the son's father (Tob. 1:8).

Laying on of my hands (1:6). This was a common way in the OT to indicate someone being dedicated to God's service (Num. 8:10).

Fear (1:7). The Greek word here (*deilia*) is stronger and more specific than simply "timid" (NIV). It is used in other writings to refer to soldiers running away and abandoning their post. The writer Theophrastus (fourth century BC) described this as "a sort of fearful yielding of the soul."[6] Philo (first century AD), using this same word, said that cowardice "is a disease graver than any that affects the body since it destroys the faculties of the soul . . . cowardice is an inbred evil" that can be healed only by God.[7] Paul here shows how God delivers us from this disease of the soul.

Don't be ashamed . . . of me his prisoner (1:8). Imprisonment was not used by itself as a punishment by the Romans, so Paul must be awaiting either trial or the death penalty. This also highlights why imprisonment was particularly shameful in the ancient world. Timothy would lose face by being associated with someone on the wrong side of imperial power.

Herald (1:11). In the Greco-Roman world heralds announced good news ("gospel") on occasions such as military victories, births in the imperial family, and the ascension of a new emperor. Heralds also appeared in religious literature serving as prophets or teachers.

The good deposit (1:14). A "deposit" referred to anything entrusted to another for safekeeping, from a harvest to money or treasure. This trust was crucial for economy and society. Philo wrote, "The most sacred of all the dealings between human beings is the deposit on trust."[8]

The province of Asia (1:15). This refers to the western portion of Asia Minor (modern-day Turkey), of which the major city was Ephesus.

Onesiphorus (1:16). This man, who supported Paul, is mentioned in the NT only here and in 4:19.

Suffering as a good soldier (2:3). The suffering of soldiers in the imperial army was legendary, enduring boiling oil and other terrible fates without giving up their cause. Those who cowered in battle and deserted their position were subject to beating and execution.

No one serving as a soldier gets entangled in the concerns of civilian life (2:4). At this time Roman soldiers were not allowed to marry or carry on private business while enlisted.

Please the commanding officer (2:4). Military discipline depended on complete obedience to one's commander, seeking to please the commander, not one's self or some rival. Near the time of the writing of

A bronze statue of a boxer (third or second century BC).

this letter (68–69), over an eighteen-month period there were four changes of emperor due to the loyalty (or lack thereof) of each man's soldiers.

Competes as an athlete (2:5). Athletic games were a major aspect of Greco-Roman culture and included the Olympian Games and the Isthmian Games, near Corinth (see the article "Athletics in the New Testament World"). The emperor Nero even participated in some of these events. These events included judges whose duty it was to catch cheaters, and some of these judges were equipped with rods to strike violators. One rule in some of the events was a mandatory training period of ten months.

Crowned (2:5). This refers to a wreath made of different plants, depending on the event that the athlete was competing in.

Hardworking farmer (2:6). Scholars estimate that 85–90 percent of people in the ancient world were directly involved with farming, most of them being peasant farmers (which seems to be suggested by the word used here) who knew that their survival depended on diligent, determined labor.

Descended from David (2:8). For Jews or Christians, this phrase automatically connects to the Messiah.

Bound like a criminal (2:9). Not all prisoners were chained, so this shows that Paul was considered particularly dangerous. This phrase also points to the shame of being imprisoned (see comments on 2 Tim. 1:8).

Dealing with False Teachers (2:14–3:9)

Fight about words (2:14). Many popular teachers in the Greco-Roman world specialized and delighted in wrangling over minute details with little practical value. Athenagoras, a church leader from about a century later, contrasted such teaching focused on logical subtleties and etymology to the life-changing power of Christian teaching.[9]

Gangrene (2:17). Without antiseptics gangrene was a common and fearful problem in the ancient world. Starting in one affected area, it could spread throughout the body and eventually cause death. This made gangrene a powerful illustration of the dangerous effects of false teaching.

Hymenaeus and Philetus (2:17). Paul called for the excommunication of Hymenaeus in 1 Timothy (1:20). Philetus is not mentioned elsewhere in Scripture.

Solid foundation . . . inscription (2:19). Paul uses common architectural images here. The ancients were well aware that the stability of a building (here, the church) depended on a firm foundation. The image may allude to Isa. 28:16. Buildings often had inscriptions in this setting, denoting ownership and authenticity—God knows who are his, and they act a certain way.

The two statements of the inscription are drawn from the OT (Num. 16:5 and Isa. 26:13).

A large house (2:20). This is the dwelling of a wealthy person. Only these houses would have contained the wide range of vessels mentioned here.

Vessels . . . for honorable use and some for dishonorable (2:20). Some vessels were special, prized by the owner, and displayed prominently. Vessels for "dishonorable" use would include containers for garbage or chamber pots. These are not displayed, and in Jewish settings these containers were destroyed when they became unclean.

Last days (3:1). Ancient Jewish writings commonly anticipated particularly difficult days marked by evil and apostasy at the end of time.

Gullible women (3:6). Stories abounded in the ancient world (historical and fictional) of women being duped by false teachers. Paul applies this to the situation at hand without generalizing to all women.

Jannes and Jambres resisted Moses (3:8). According to Jewish tradition (picked up in some Greco-Roman writings), Jannes and Jambres were brothers and were the pharaoh's magicians who opposed Moses in Exod. 7.

Exhortation in Contrast to the False Teachers (3:10–4:8)

Antioch, Iconium, and Lystra (3:11). These three cities of Asia Minor were destinations in Paul's early mission journeys (Acts 13:14–14:23). Timothy was from this area (Acts 16:1).

From infancy you have known the sacred Scriptures (3:15). "Sacred Scriptures" refers to what we call the OT. It was common for Jewish boys to begin instruction in the Scriptures at age five. Most families did not have a copy of the Scriptures, so learning occurred in the synagogue and in the home with the portions that were memorized.

All Scripture is inspired by God (3:16). Other religions at this time believed that the gods inspired messages through humans, but these messages were not always reliable. Judaism and Christianity were unique in the importance and reverence given to their inspired writings.

An itch to hear what they want to hear (4:3). Phrases similar to this were used by other writers of the time to describe public speakers who told people only what they wanted to hear.

Drink offering (4:6). Pouring out a drink as an offering to a god was a common practice among Greeks, Romans, and Jews. Paul probably has in mind the OT sacrifices (Lev. 23:13; Num. 15:5; 28:7), and he pictures his life as being poured out as an act of worship in service to God.

Fought the good fight . . . finished the race (4:7). The "fight" here refers to athletic events (wrestling or running) rather than to military combat.

The crown of righteousness (4:8). The "crown," a wreath made of branches, was a well-known award for athletic contests in the Greek world.

Conclusion (4:9–22)

Demas . . . to Thessalonica (4:10). Only a few years earlier Demas, who now has deserted Paul, was a "coworker" with him (Philem. 24; see also Col. 4:14). One likely route for Timothy to take in traveling to Paul in Rome would take him through Thessalonica, so Paul might be letting Timothy know that he could encounter Demas.

Crescens . . . to Galatia (4:10). We do not know more about Crescens. Galatia is the region Paul visited on his first mission journey.

Titus to Dalmatia (4:10). Titus was a longtime companion of Paul (e.g., 2 Cor. 7:6, 13; Gal. 2:1; Titus). Dalmatia was a province farther north from Greece along the Adriatic coast.

Luke (4:11). Luke was another well-known coworker with Paul (Col. 4:14) and was the author of the Gospel of Luke and the book of Acts.

Mark (4:11). John Mark, the author of the Gospel of Mark, had abandoned Paul on an earlier mission journey (Acts 13:5, 13; 15:36–40). They have now obviously reconciled.

Tychicus (4:12). Tychicus was another well-known coworker with Paul (Acts 20:4; Eph. 6:21; Col. 4:7; Titus 3:12).

Cloak (4:13). This refers to a heavy overcoat worn in cold weather, typically a round piece of material with an opening in the middle for one's head. Anticipating winter in a Roman prison, Paul needs this garment.

In Troas with Carpus (4:13). We have no other information on Carpus. Troas is a town in northwest Asia Minor (Acts 20:5–12) on the common route through Asia westward.

The scrolls, especially the parchments (4:13). These are standard forms of written material and could refer to Paul's own notes or to copies of the Scriptures.

Alexander the coppersmith (4:14). Perhaps this is the same man referred to in 1 Tim. 1:20, but we cannot be sure. There was a guild of metalworkers at Troas, the city just mentioned, so this may be a warning for Timothy when he passes through Troas en route to Rome.

Photo of an amphora from Italy used to transport and store wine (first century BC). Wine probably was the most common drink in the Mediterranean region. It was also used by pagan cultures as a libation offering to the gods. Paul can speak of his own life as a "drink offering" (2 Tim. 4:6).

First defense (4:16). In common Roman practice there was a preliminary hearing before a magistrate preceding the full trial, perhaps before the emperor.

The lion's mouth (4:17). This is a common OT image (see Ps. 22:21) representing deliverance from death in general.

Prisca and Aquila (4:19). Greetings were common at the close of ancient letters. These two coworkers are mentioned also in Acts 18:24–26.

Erastus (4:20). A man named Erastus is mentioned in Rom. 16:23 as a Christian who is "the city treasurer" in Corinth and also in Acts 19:22 as one who "assisted" Paul alongside Timothy. It seems likely that all three instances refer to the same person.

Trophimus sick at Miletus (4:20). Trophimus is another known companion of Paul (Acts 20:4; 21:29). Miletus is a town on the west coast of Asia (Acts 20:15) located on the route west.

Before winter (4:21). Sea travel stopped for the winter due to dangerous conditions (see the article "Shipping Practices in the First Century"), and at least one part of Timothy's travel would have to be by sea. Thus if he delayed he would have to wait until spring.

Eubulus . . . Pudens, Linus, Claudia (4:21). These were all common names of the time, though they are not mentioned elsewhere in Scripture. According to some early Christian tradition, Linus was the first bishop of Rome.

Titus

Salutation (1:1–4)

Servant of God (1:1). This was a common designation in the OT for individuals who served as God's representatives: Moses (Ps. 105:26), David (2 Sam. 7:8), and the prophets (Jer. 7:25; Amos 3:7; Zech. 1:6). As God's servants, they belonged to him and thus bore his authority.

God, who cannot lie (1:2). In the Greeks' stories their gods commonly lied and deceived. Their chief god, Zeus, was particularly given to deceit in his pursuit of sexual escapades with mortal women. Thus the utter truthfulness of the God of the Bible stands in stark contrast to the religious ideas of the day.

Titus, my true son (1:4). See comments on 1 Tim. 1:2.

Occasion: The Need for Proper Leadership (1:5–9)

Crete (1:5). An island south of Greece in the Mediterranean Sea, in a strategic location for trade, Crete was also a place proverbial in the ancient world for its moral decadence. Polybius, the ancient historian, wrote that it was almost "impossible to find . . . personal conduct more treacherous or public policy more unjust than in Crete."[10] Cicero also comments, "Moral principles are so divergent that the Cretans . . . consider highway robbery honorable."[11] Although these quotations come from a time prior to Paul's ministry, they aptly describe the general view of Crete in the ancient world.

Elders (1:5). See comments on 1 Tim. 4:14.

In every town (1:5). Crete was famous for its "hundred cities,"[12] which were notorious for their fierce rivalries.

Blameless (1:6). This term and the list that follows stand in stark contrast to the general reputation of Crete noted above.

Children . . . not accused of wildness or rebellion (1:6). Greco-Roman and Jewish society both considered the obedience of children to their parents to be a prerequisite for respectability. See comments on 1 Tim. 3:4.

Not greedy for money (1:7). This would contrast with general Cretan behavior. One ancient historian stated, "So much in fact do sordid love of gain and lust for wealth prevail among them that the Cretans are the only people in the world in whose eyes no gain is disgraceful."[13]

Problem Stated: False Teachers (1:10–16)

The circumcision party (1:10). "Circumcision" had become a way to refer to Jews, since this was the mark of the covenant with Abraham (Gen. 17:9–14) (see the article "The Jewish Rite of Circumcision").

Get money dishonestly (1:11). As noted at 1:7, Cretans were proverbial for seeking dishonest gain.

One of their very own prophets (1:12). Most scholars agree that the person being quoted here is Epimenides, a religious teacher and worker of wonders from the seventh or sixth century BC. He was regarded as a prophet by various writers in antiquity, including Plato, Aristotle, and Cicero.

Cretans are always liars (1:12). This view of Cretans was proverbial and widespread in the ancient world. In fact, "to Cretize" meant "to lie."

Evil beasts, lazy gluttons (1:12). Cretans were well known for brutal, coarse behavior, with many stories of double-dealing, piracy, and even pederasty.

Jewish myths (1:14). This sounds like a reference to speculative readings of the OT that were common in certain groups within Judaism at the time.

Proper Christian Living Grounded in the Gospel, Part 1 (2:1–15)

Crete is the fifth-largest island in the Mediterranean Sea. Paul explains to Titus why "I left you in Crete" (Titus 1:5) and advises him on the continuing ministry there. This shows a portion of the harbor at Fair Havens on the island of Crete.

Self-controlled, worthy of respect, sensible (2:2). These three characteristics were prized in antiquity, especially for older men.

Not slanderers, not slaves to excessive drinking (2:3). Carelessness with words and wine was commonly discussed by ancient writers in relation to older women.

Slaves . . . may adorn the teaching of God our Savior (2:9–10). It is striking for the behavior of the people in the lowest social class to be given this much importance.

A people for his own possession (2:14). This echoes a phrase used of Israel in various places in the OT (e.g., Exod. 19:5; Ps. 135:4; Mal. 3:17).

Proper Christian Living Grounded in the Gospel, Part 2 (3:1–8)

Enslaved by various passions (3:3). The idea of being enslaved to sin was commonplace in Greco-Roman and Jewish thought. One school of Greek thought, the Stoics, regarded being enslaved to "passions" and "pleasures" as the lowest condition.

Not by works of righteousness that we had done (3:5). Some Jews thought that obedience to the Mosaic law could be the basis of receiving God's favor. Several schools of moral thought in the Greco-Roman world relied on human effort to achieve righteousness. Paul counters all of these thoughts, which have been common throughout human history, rooting salvation in God's grace alone.

Problem Restated: False Teachers (3:9–11)

Genealogies, quarrels, and disputes about the law (3:9). "Law" here refers to OT law. Speculation about various ways to spiritualize the law and OT genealogies was popular in certain branches of Judaism.

Closing Exhortation (3:12–15)

Artemas or Tychicus (3:12). Artemas is not mentioned elsewhere in the NT. Tychicus was sent with letters to the Colossians and Ephesians (Col. 4:7; Eph. 6:21) and accompanied Paul on his last journey to Jerusalem (Acts 20:4).

Nicopolis (3:12). The major city of its region, Nicopolis was located on the western side of Greece. This fits Paul's pattern of spending longer amounts of time ("winter") in major cities.

To spend the winter there (3:12). In antiquity people did not travel during the winter, especially by sea, when rough weather made sea travel treacherous (see the article "Shipping Practices in the First Century").

Zenas the lawyer and Apollos (3:13). Zenas is not mentioned elsewhere in the NT; Apollos is known as a powerful Christian preacher (Acts 18:24; 1 Cor. 1:12). A "lawyer" among Jews would be a scribe, one trained in OT law. Among Romans it would refer to a jurist. We do not know which is in view here.

Philemon

Osvaldo Padilla

Introduction. Like the other Prison Epistles—Ephesians, Philippians, and Colossians—this letter was written during Paul's first Roman imprisonment in the early 60s. That it was written by Paul the apostle has never been seriously questioned in the history of scholarship.

In attempting to put forth the occasion for the composing of this letter, we must read its actual statements and also read "between the lines." Although some gaps remain, the following reconstruction can be given with a healthy amount of confidence.

Onesimus was a slave who belonged to the household of Philemon, a Christian who was very close to the apostle Paul—indeed, converted under his ministry (v. 19). It is probably the case that Onesimus had landed on the wrong side of his owner. Had he stolen something (vv. 18–19)? Did he feel that he was being mistreated and so he left? Or did he simply flee to Rome to "start a new life"? We cannot be certain. What is clear, given the dynamics expressed in the letter, is that Onesimus went to Rome to find Paul. It is probably not the case that Onesimus was a runaway slave, a fugitive, who while fleeing his master happened to run into Paul, who happened to be his master's spiritual father. It is much more likely that Onesimus consciously went to Paul to ask him to intervene on his behalf before Philemon, since he knew that Paul held considerable influence with his master. While Onesimus was with Paul, he became a follower of Christ (v. 10).[1]

It appears that both Paul and Onesimus wanted a reconciliation between Onesimus and Philemon. Thus Paul wrote a letter of recommendation, a letter of appeal (v. 9) on behalf of Onesimus—but with a significant twist: Philemon was to receive Onesimus back, "no longer as a slave, but more than a slave—as a dearly loved brother" (v. 16).

A number of commentators have noted a similar situation in a letter that Pliny the Younger (ca. AD 61–112) wrote to his friend Sabinianus. Although the man on whose behalf Pliny wrote was no longer a slave but a freedman of Sabinianus, the letter sufficiently illustrates the dynamics of the letter to Philemon. Pliny intervened on behalf of the freedman, asking Sabinianus to receive him back. Consider the following statements from this letter:

- "Your freedman with whom you said you were angry has been with me; he threw himself at my feet."
- "He earnestly requested me with many tears . . . to intercede for him."
- "I know you are angry with him, and I know too, it is not without reason; but mercy is never more worthy of praise than when there is the justest cause for anger. You once loved this man . . . in the meanwhile, let me only prevail with you to pardon him."[2]

As Pliny did for the freedman, Paul intercedes on behalf of Onesimus. But there is a fundamental difference: Paul bases his intercession and accompanying requests on the love of Christ. It is no accident that the term *agapē* ("love") and its cognate *agapētos* ("beloved") appear five times in this short letter (vv. 1, 5, 7, 9, 16). There is also the use of a term "heart" (*splanchna*), which denotes heartfelt emotion (vv. 7, 12, 20).

One commentator speaks of the significance of Philemon in the following way:

> Historically and theologically [Philemon] is of considerable interest because it reveals and allows us to comprehend a delicate problem: how the apostle takes responsibility for his gospel of justification and his conception of the Christian community . . . in the practical, day-to day life of a Christian community. . . . In 2 Cor. 5:17 Paul highlights the following: the baptized Christian is a new creation, and in Gal. 3:26–28 he provocatively explains that

The scene on this gravestone (ca. 50 BC) depicts a slave holding a scroll and standing before Caius Popillius (the deceased).

in the Christian community the distinctions between Jew and Greek, man and woman, slave and free, already are surpassed through the unity of all in Christ. Is this, in view of the letter to Philemon, only enthusiastic theory?[3]

Salutation (1–3)

To Philemon our dear friend and coworker (1). Paul designates Philemon as a "coworker," a term that Paul often uses to refer those who help him in the preaching and teaching of the gospel (e.g., Rom. 16:3, 9, 21; Phil. 2:25; 4:3). Philemon was no passive Christian; he labored with Paul in the gospel.

To Apphia our sister, to Archippus our fellow soldier, and to the church that meets in your home (2). Apphia, whose name was a common one in the region of Colossae, probably was the wife of Philemon. In the early period of the church the believers met for worship in the homes of Christians. Although there were other places for meetings,[4] in the case of Philemon clearly the believers in the surrounding area met at his "home." This, along with the fact that Philemon owned slaves, suggests that he was well-to-do. The mention of Apphia, Archippus, and their house church suggests that the letter was meant to be read openly, not only by Philemon. This would make sense given that Onesimus as a household slave would have been well known by the members of the family and friends.[5]

Thanksgiving (4–7)

I have great joy and encouragement from your love, because the hearts of the saints have been refreshed through you, brother (7). Paul uses a unique phrase in describing the results of Philemon's love: "the hearts of the saints have been refreshed." Andrew Clarke has argued convincingly that the phrase was peculiar to Paul and that the apostle uses it in contexts where the action of refreshing could cut across various social barriers. This

The freeing of slaves (manumission) by their owners was a frequent event in the Roman world. The Greek inscription on this relief commemorates the freeing of a female slave by her mistress (first century AD).

certainly is the case here. Philemon, a wealthy man, could now refresh the prisoner Paul's own heart by receiving Onesimus back.[6]

Request (8–20)

Perhaps this is why he was separated from you for a brief time, so that you might get him back permanently, no longer as a slave, but more than a slave—as a dearly loved brother. He is especially so to me, but how much more to you, both in the flesh and in the Lord (15–16). This is the heart of the letter. Paul's plea on behalf of Onesimus is made explicit: he wants Philemon to receive Onesimus back "no longer as a slave, but more than a slave—as a dearly loved brother." It is doubtful that Paul is requesting for Philemon to free Onesimus.[7] Nevertheless, although Paul is not laboring to undo the institution of slavery directly,[8] he is in effect relativizing it (see the article "Slavery in the New Testament World"). After all, how long could slavery endure when the owner was to treat his fellow Christian slave "as a dear brother" or fellow believer? Paul lit a spark that eventually would explode into the fire of freedom.

Hebrews

Hebrews

Dana M. Harris

Introduction. Who wrote Hebrews remains unknown. Early on, the epistle was circulated with the Pauline Epistles, but some doubted Pauline authorship. The author likely was part of Paul's circle (e.g., "our brother Timothy" [13:23]), but there are compelling reasons to reject Pauline authorship. Paul generally uses legal imagery to discuss Christ's substitutionary death, whereas Hebrews uniquely presents Jesus as the high priest and stresses Christ's fully efficacious sacrifice that cleanses the conscience. The Pauline Epistles focus on Christ's resurrection, whereas Hebrews stresses his exaltation. For Paul, Scripture (the OT) is a written testimony that supports christological points, whereas Hebrews views Scripture as God's word that still speaks. Finally, the author appears to consider himself a "second-generation" believer (Heb. 2:3–4), something that Paul explicitly denies (Gal. 1:12).

There are also notable differences in style between the Pauline Epistles and Hebrews. For example, Hebrews does not begin with the designations of sender and recipient used in other NT epistles. Also, the expression "Christ Jesus" occurs over ninety times in Paul's letters but not once in Hebrews.

The epistle's tone indicates that the author was well known by the recipients. Thus, although the author is unknown to us today, Hebrews is not pseudonymous (falsely ascribed authorship). Although it is possible that Apollos is the author, it is best to conclude with the early church leader Origen: "Who the author of the epistle is, God only knows."

The epistle's recipients are unknown. They were likely second-generation believers (2:3) who had suffered for the gospel (10:32–35). Extensive knowledge of the OT is assumed. The traditional view of the recipients as persecuted Jewish believers tempted to apostatize and return to Judaism is likely.

The probable destination is Rome, which had a significant Jewish population (forty to sixty-thousand) in the first century. The gospel presumably came to Rome by converts from Pentecost (Acts 2:5–11). The recipients likely were part of a local house church, which was tempted to withdraw from a larger association of house churches (Heb. 10:25, 32–34). A Roman destination may be supported by distinctive terminology (*hēgoumenoi* in Heb. 13:7) and Clement of Rome's appropriation of Hebrews around AD 95.

The date for Hebrews is also unknown. It was likely written before the temple was destroyed (AD 70), as there is no allusion to this event, which is somewhat remarkable given the author's overall argument. A likely date is some time in the 60s. Clement's citation of Hebrews indicates that it could not have been written later than 95.

The author of Hebrews describes the work as a "message of exhortation" (13:22), which is a term indicating a sermon, although Hebrews is meticulously written, unlike an actual transcription. "Exhortation" also fits the five "warning passages" in Hebrews (2:1–4; 3:7–4:11; 6:4–8; 10:26–31; 12:25–29). Hebrews urges perseverance and faithfulness. Moreover, Hebrews stresses the incomplete and temporary nature of the Levitical priesthood and Mosaic covenant by showing how these institutions ultimately pointed to Christ—return to the old order was not possible.

The author cites exclusively from the Septuagint (LXX), the Greek translation of the Hebrew Scriptures, which differs sometimes from the Hebrew text (the basis of English Bibles) in chapter and verse numbers as well as wording. Reference numbers here follow English Bibles, but "LXX" is added when citations differ in exact wording.

The God Who Speaks and the Son (1:1–4)

These last days (1:2). This Jewish apocalyptic expression separates history into two successive ages, the latter of which Hebrews interprets eschatologically as the time between Jesus's exaltation and his return.

Heir of all things (1:2). "Heir" alludes to Ps. 2:8, linking sonship and inheritance. This psalm was understood as both messianic and eschatological prior to Christ (see the article "Messianic Expectations in Jesus's Day"). Inheritance language is prominent in Hebrews (e.g., 1:4, 14; 6:12; 9:15; 11:7, 8; 12:17) and draws upon God's promises to

A Roman coin with the emperor Nero's portrait.

Abraham. Parallels to the Greco-Roman legal realm are possible but problematic (e.g., the heir, the Son, would receive the inheritance at the eventual death of the testator, God the Father).

Made the universe (1:2). See comments on Heb. 11:3.

Radiance of God's glory (1:3). Glory is an essential aspect of God's nature (e.g., Exod. 24:15–17; 40:34–35; Lev. 9:23; Num. 14:21–22; 1 Kings 8:11; Isa. 40:5) and indicates his presence and honor (e.g., Isa. 60:19; Tob. 13:14–17). The Son's glory was seen in his transfiguration (Matt. 17:1–9; Mark 9:2–10; Luke 9:28–36). See comments on Heb. 2:10.

Exact expression of his nature (1:3). "Exact expression" (*charaktēr*) refers to an imprint for coins. "Nature" (*hypostasis*) indicates a fundamental, essential reality or substance. See comments on Heb. 11:1.

Purification for sins (1:3). This recalls the Day of Atonement; the wording reflects LXX Job 7:21. See comments on Heb. 9:7.

Sat down . . . the Majesty on high (1:3). Sitting contrasts with Levitical priests, who stood during their cultic service (Deut. 10:8; 1 Kings 13:1; 2 Chron. 29:11). "Majesty" is a reverential but roundabout way of referring to God (so also Heb. 8:1; cf. Deut. 32:3; 1 Chron. 29:11; Mark 14:62).

Right hand (1:3). See comments on Heb. 1:13.

Angels (1:4). Angels were believed to have mediated revelation (Deut. 33:2; Ps. 68:17; *Jubilees* 1.27–29) and interceded for humanity (Tob. 12:1; *1 Enoch* 9.10). They could be called "sons of God" collectively (Gen. 6:2, 4; Job 1:6; 2:1; 38:7; *Psalms of Solomon* 17.26), but never a "son of God" individually. See comments on Heb. 2:5.

The name he inherited (1:4). A new name often reflects a changed status (e.g., Gen. 17:5, 15; 35:10; Matt. 16:18). "The Name" in the OT is a title for God (Deut. 12:5, 11; 1 Kings 8:17–19; cf. 2 Sam. 7:9).

Seven Old Testament Citations Revealing the Son (1:5–14)

My Son . . . your Father (1:5). A catena, or "chain," of OT quotations was a common Jewish technique. The messianic Ps. 2:7 is also cited at Jesus's baptism (Matt. 3:17; Mark 1:11; Luke 3:22) and his transfiguration (Matt. 17:5; Mark 9:7; Luke 9:35).

His Father . . . my Son (1:5). This citation (2 Sam. 7:14) is part of Nathan's prophecy regarding the everlasting Davidic dynasty.

His firstborn (1:6). "Firstborn" indicates status and privilege and is applied to Israel (Exod. 4:22; Jer. 31:9), the Davidic king (Ps. 89:27), and Christ (Rom. 8:29; Col. 1:15, 18; Heb. 12:23; Rev. 1:5).

Into the world (1:6). See comments on Heb. 2:5.

Angels worship him (1:6). This citation may derive from Deut. 32:43 and Ps. 97:7 or from a rabbinic tradition that associated angelic worship with the first Adam, here applied to the Son.[1]

His angels winds . . . his servants a fiery flame (1:7). LXX Ps. 104:4 stresses the transient nature of angels and their subservient role as God's servants and created beings. See comments on Heb. 1:4.

Your throne . . . is forever (1:8). Psalm 45:6–7 is part of a royal wedding ode extolling the righteous rule of God, who bestows his authority on the Davidic king.

Scepter of your kingdom (1:8). A scepter indicated the Davidic king's authority and power as God's earthly representative.

Anointed you with the oil of joy (1:9). Israelite kings were anointed at their enthronement (1 Sam. 10:1; 15:17; 2 Sam. 12:7; 2 Kings 9:3; Ps. 89:20).

Established the earth . . . the heavens . . . roll them up like a cloak (1:10–12). This cites Ps. 102:25–26 (echoing Isa. 34:4; 50:9; 51:6). The universe's ultimate decay was part of Jewish eschatology, which contrasted with the Platonic idea that the world is changeless.

Angels (1:13). See comments on Heb. 1:4.

Sit at my right hand (1:13). Cited from Ps. 110:1, the right hand indicates authority and power (Exod. 15:6; Ps. 20:6; 44:3; 89:13; Isa. 41:10; 48:13) and honor (Gen. 48:18; 1 Kings 2:19; Ps. 48:10; cf. Rev. 3:21).

Pay Attention (2:1–4)

What we have heard (2:1). This likely refers to the initial gospel message preached to the audience.

Drift away (2:1). This image may reflect an anchor that does not hold, a boat that drifts off course, or a ring that slips off a finger.

Spoken through angels (2:2). See comments on Heb. 1:4.

Signs and wonders . . . gifts from the Holy Spirit (2:4). Signs and wonders accompanied the giving of the law at Sinai and the exodus; miracles attest Jesus's divinity. Here the allusion is to Pentecost and the accompanying signs and wonders (Acts 2).

Jesus, the Perfect Human Being (2:5–9)

Subjected to angels (2:5). Jewish tradition maintained that angels participated in the governance of the world (based on Deut. 32:8). In Dan. 10:20–21 angels battle the princes of Persia and Greece.

World to come (2:5). "World" (*oikoumenē*) could indicate "the inhabited world," while the "world to come" includes all of creation, including the heavenly realm. Hebrews uses *kosmos* for the present world (4:3; 9:26; 10:5; 11:7, 38). The "world to come" is key in Jewish apocalyptic thought.

Son of man (2:6). Most likely "son of man" simply refers to a human being in this context (e.g., Ps. 144:3; Ezek. 2:1, 3, 6).

Crowned (2:9). Both kings and victorious athletes received crowns (1 Cor. 9:25; 2 Tim. 2:5).

Taste death (2:9). To "taste" something is a Semitic expression for experiencing it fully.

Suffered death (2:9). See comments on Heb. 12:2.

The Son Leading the Sons and Daughters to Glory (2:10–18)

Bringing many sons and daughters (2:10). This language recalls the exodus.

Glory (2:10). Psalm 8:5 indicates that God created humankind for glory (cf. Rom. 8:17; 1 Cor. 15:43; Phil. 3:21; Col. 3:4). See comments on Heb. 1:3.

Appropriate that God (2:10). Philo claimed that it was fitting for God to swear by himself,[2] and Greek philosophers considered it fitting for the gods to direct the universe.[3]

Source of their salvation (2:10). "Source" (*archēgos*) could refer to a pioneer, the founder of a city or a school, the leader or scout of an army (e.g., LXX Num. 10:4; 13:2–3; Judg. 5:15 [B]; 9:44 [B]; 11:6, 11 [B]). It could also indicate a champion, like Hercules.

Perfect (2:10). "Perfect" (*teleioō*) is used in the Septuagint for the consecration of priests. Perfection in Hebrews is closely associated with access to God and completely fulfilling that which God intended.

Sanctified (2:11). God alone makes his people holy (e.g., Exod. 31:13; Lev. 20:8; 21:15; 22:9, 16, 32; Ezek. 20:12; 37:28). Consecration and cleansing from defilement were essential functions of the Levitical priesthood (Exod. 29:44; Lev. 21:8).

Jesus is not ashamed (2:11). In Greco-Roman culture honor was diligently sought and shame strenuously avoided. This verse likely alludes to Mark 8:38; Luke 9:26.

The children God gave me (2:13). In Isa. 8:18 Isaiah's children were signs to Israel of God's faithfulness. This is the only place in the NT where believers are called Jesus's children.

The devil (2:14). "Devil" (*diabolos*) means "slanderer" or "accuser"; see Jesus's teaching (e.g., Mark 3:20–29; Luke 11:17–23). Hebrews draws upon the OT theme of the divine warrior (Exod. 15:1–18; Isa. 42:13; 49:24–26).

Held in slavery all their lives by their fear of death (2:15). In Greco-Roman thought fear of death was considered a form of slavery.[4]

Faithful (2:17). In 1 Sam. 2:35 God promises to raise up a faithful priest unlike the faithless priest Eli and (especially) his sons.

High priest (2:17). The high priest had to descend from Aaron's son Eleazar (Num. 20:25–28). Priests had to be ceremonially pure (Lev. 21:1–4, 7–8) and free from defect (Lev. 21:16–23; cf. Lev. 10:6; 21:5–6). Only in Hebrews is Jesus called high priest.

Make atonement (2:17). See comments on Heb. 9:7.

Suffered when he was tempted (2:18). Most likely Jesus's struggle in Gethsemane (Matt. 26:36–46; Mark 14:32–42; Luke 22:39–46) is in view here, although an allusion to Jesus's temptation by Satan in the wilderness also is possible.

Jesus Compared to Moses (3:1–6)

Apostle (3:1). An apostle is a person sent, usually as an official representative. Moses was sent by God to free God's people; Jesus's apostles were sent to proclaim the gospel. This is the only place in the NT where Jesus is called apostle.

High priest (3:1). See comments on Heb. 2:17.

Moses (3:2). Moses is a key OT figure, to whom God spoke "directly" (Num. 12:8; cf. Exod. 33:11; Deut. 34:10; Sir. 45:5). Philo claimed that Moses ascended into heaven.[5] Rabbinic tradition claimed that Moses was superior to angels.

God's household (3:2). This referred to the tent of meeting (Num. 12:4–5; cf. Gen. 28:17), the tabernacle (Exod. 25:8–9; 34:26), the temple (1 Kings 8:10–11), the people of God (Exod. 40:38; Ps. 114:1), or a specific dynasty (2 Sam. 7:11–16; cf. 1 Sam. 2:30–34). God's house indicated the heavenly realm in rabbinic thought and the created world in that of Philo.

Mishkan (tabernacle) at Sinai.

Servant (3:5). The title "servant" indicated Moses's honored status before God (Num. 12:7; cf. Exod. 4:10; 14:31; Num. 11:11; Deut. 3:24; Josh. 1:2). A faithful servant or slave was highly valued.

The Wilderness Generation (3:7–19)

Today, if you hear his voice (3:7–11). Psalm 95:7–11 warns against disobeying God, using the example of the wilderness generation, recalling Num. 14; 20 (cf. 1 Cor. 10:6; Jude 5).

Harden your hearts (3:8). A hardened heart indicates refusal to do God's will (e.g., the pharaoh in Exod. 8:15, 32; 9:34).

Rebellion . . . day of testing (3:8). The Septuagint translated the names of the locations Meribah and Massah according to their symbolic significance: "rebellion" and "testing" (see Exod. 17:7; cf. Exod. 15:22–25).

My works (3:9). This includes the exodus, the crossing of the Red Sea, and the provision of manna, quail, and water (see Exod. 12–17).

My anger (3:11). God's anger was provoked against Israel's enemies (Exod. 15:7; Jer. 10:25; Ezek. 25:12–14) and against Israel when they rebelled (Exod. 22:21–24; Isa. 1:23–24).

My rest (3:11). God promised his people rest in land (e.g., Deut. 3:20); rest is linked with God's "dwelling place" (e.g., Num. 10:33–36; Ps. 132:13–14).

Living God (3:12). The "living God" contrasts with dead idols (Jer. 10:5) and is associated with God's judgment (2 Kings 19:4, 16; Isa. 37:4, 17; Jer. 10:10). But the "living God" also helps (Dan. 6:20).

The reality (3:14). See comments on Heb. 11:1.

Who heard and rebelled? (3:16). The rhetorical questions in this verse draw upon the citation from Ps. 95:7–8 (in 3:15) and allude to Num. 14:13, 19, 22.

With whom was God angry? (3:17). The rhetorical questions in this verse draw upon the citation from Ps. 95:10 (in 3:10) and allude to Num. 14:16, 29, 32.

To whom did he swear? (3:18). This rhetorical question draws upon the citation from Ps. 95:11 (in 3:11) and alludes to Num. 14:30, 33, 43.

The Promised Rest (4:1–13)

On the seventh day God rested . . . my rest (4:4–5). "My rest" in Ps. 95:11 suggests God's rest in Gen. 2:2, where God ceased his work of creation, although his sustaining works were seen by the wilderness generation (Ps. 95:9). Genesis 2 does not record the end of the seventh day, which led to speculation that God's rest continues. See comments on Heb. 3:11.

Speaking through David (4:7). The Septuagint attributes Ps. 95, quoted three times in this chapter, to David, although "speaking through David" could indicate the Psalter as a whole. If David wrote about rest long after the conquest, then the promised rest must remain.

Sabbath rest (4:9). "Sabbath rest" (*sabbatismos*) likely was coined by the author of Hebrews (cf. LXX Exod. 16:30; Lev. 23:32). God's rest formed the basis of the Sabbath commandment (Exod. 20:8–11; Deut. 5:12–15; cf. Exod. 23:12; 35:2).

Word of God (4:12). God's word is an active agent (e.g., Ps. 33:6; Isa. 55:11; cf. Jer. 23:29).

Double-edged sword (4:12). This likely refers to the short sword used by Roman soldiers that was especially effective in combat (see the article "The Roman Military"), or possibly Ehud's sword (cf. Judg. 3:16). This may also allude to those of the wilderness generation who fell by the swords of the Amalekites and Canaanites (Num. 14:43–45).

No creature is hidden (4:13). Both Jewish writers[6] and Greek philosophers[7] claimed that nothing was hidden from God (cf. Ps. 139:11–12).

Jesus, the Great High Priest (4:14–16)

Great high priest (4:14). This exact expression occurs only in extrabiblical Jewish writings (e.g., 1 Macc. 13:42). The "high priest" is mentioned in Num. 35:25; Josh. 20:6; Zech. 6:11. See comments on Heb. 2:17.

Through the heavens (4:14). "Heavens" (plural) reflects Hebrew usage and possibly levels of heavens. The image here is of the high priest moving though the partitions of the tabernacle to the holy of holies. See comments on Heb. 9:2–3.

Tempted in every way (4:15). See comments on Heb. 2:18.

Throne of grace (4:16). This refers to the "mercy seat," the cover on top of the ark of the covenant, the place of God's presence where sins were forgiven. See comments on Heb. 9:5.

Qualifications for High Priests (5:1–10)

Taken from among men (5:1). High priests were set apart as Levites (Num. 3:5–13, 44–45), and as Aaron's descendants (Num. 3:10).

Deal gently (5:2). The high priest was to show restraint (Lev. 21:10–12; cf. Aaron's forbearance in Num. 14:5;

Roman double-edged swords.

16:22, 47–48). Later Jewish writings did not speak of gentleness regarding the office.

Ignorant (5:2). Numbers 15:28 (cf. Lev. 4:2; 5:15; 22:4) contrasts sins of ignorance with willful apostasy, for which there is no forgiveness (Num. 15:30–31).

His own sins . . . the people (5:3). See comments on Heb. 9:7.

No one takes this honor on himself (5:4). The OT condemns individuals illegitimately acting as priests (Num. 16:40; 1 Kings 12:31). During the Hasmonean (152–37 BC) and Herodian eras (37 BC–AD 66) the high priest often was politically appointed.

My son . . . your Father (5:5). This citation of Ps. 2:7 supports Christ's divine priestly appointment; in 1:5 it supports his enthronement (see comments on Heb. 1:5).

Order of Melchizedek (5:6). "Order" (*taxis*) denotes type or kind, not succession (i.e., a priesthood distinct from the Aaronic one). On Melchizedek, see comments on Heb. 7:1; 7:2; 7:3.

Offered prayers and appeals (5:7). This may refer to Jesus's prayers in Gethsemane (Matt. 26:36–46; Mark 14:32–42; Luke 22:40–46) or allude to Ps. 22 and Ps. 116. Loud cries and tears are not mentioned in the NT texts but were common in prayers for deliverance (e.g., 2 Macc. 11:6; 3 Macc. 1:16; 5:7, 25).

Learned obedience from what he suffered (5:8). Learning from suffering was a common Greco-Roman idea underscored by the similarity between the Greek words for "learn" (*mathein*) and "suffer" (*pathein*). See comments on Heb. 12:5–6.

Perfected (5:9). See comments on Heb. 2:10.

Eternal salvation (5:9). See comments on Heb. 13:20.

Exhortation to Maturity (5:11–6:3)

Basic principles (5:12). The word translated as "basic principles" (*stoicheia*) could indicate basic principles, elementary truths, rudimentary elements (such as letters in an alphabet), the material elements of the world, or even elemental spirits believed to govern the world.

Milk . . . solid food (5:12, 14). The use of food imagery as an analogy for levels of education was common in Greco-Roman writings. Here milk parallels immaturity, whereas solid food indicates maturity.

Trained (5:14). "Trained" (*hexis*) indicates a habit that produces a state or condition. The word was used by philosophers to urge a state of maturity.

Ritual washings (6:2). "Washings" (plural) suggests ceremonial purification or cleansing rites (which were important to many Jewish groups) rather than Christian baptism.

Laying on of hands (6:2). This practice was associated with commissioning for service (Num. 27:18, 23; Deut. 34:9) or sacrificial offerings (e.g., Lev. 1:4; 3:2; 4:4). In the book of Acts it is associated with the impartation of the Spirit (8:17; 9:17; 19:6), commissioning for service (6:6), and healing (9:12).

Resurrection of the dead (6:2). Jewish literature discusses a general resurrection of the righteous, which may be inferred from Isa. 26:19 and Dan. 12:3.

A Stern Warning (6:4–8)

Enlightened (6:4). Enlightenment is a common metaphor for conversion. Light frequently is associated with God (Ps. 27:1) and his word (Ps. 19:8; 119:105, 130).

Tasted the heavenly gift (6:4). This may be a reference to the Eucharist. See comments on Heb. 2:9.

Tasted God's good word (6:5). Psalm 34:8 urges, "Taste and see that the LORD is good" (cf. 1 Pet. 2:3). See comments on Heb. 2:9.

Coming age (6:5). See comments on Heb. 2:5.

Receives a blessing . . . about to be cursed (6:7–8). Covenant blessings were set in the context of the land (Deut. 11:11–12; 28:1–14). Cursed land recalls Isa. 5:1–7 (cf. Gen. 3:17–18; Ezek. 19:10–14).

Assurances and Promises (6:9–20)

The love you demonstrated (6:10). See comments on Heb. 10:32–34.

Promise to Abraham (6:13). God's promise focused on descendants, land, and covenantal relationship (Gen. 12:1–3; 13:14–18; 15:1–21; 17:1–27; 22:15–19).

He swore by himself (6:13). God's oath underscores the reliability of his promise (Gen. 22:17; cf. Exod. 32:13). See comments on Heb. 2:10.

Abraham obtained the promise (6:15). Genesis 21:1–7 records the birth of the promised descendant, Isaac.

People swear by someone greater than themselves (6:16). Swearing by someone (e.g., God, the emperor) or something (e.g., the temple, heaven) greater was commonplace in the ancient world.

Two unchangeable things (6:18). This likely refers to God's promise to Abraham and his oath (in Gen. 22:17 and Ps. 110:4).

Impossible for God to lie (6:18). The OT (Num. 23:19–20; 1 Sam. 15:29; Ps. 89:35; Isa. 31:2), Greco-Roman (e.g., Plato), and Jewish writers (e.g., Philo) all affirmed this truth.

Fled for refuge (6:18). This imagery recalls the Levitical cities of refuge (Num. 35:25–26; Deut. 4:42) and/or the sanctity of the altar (1 Kings 1:50;

2:28). Temples in Greco-Roman times were also considered to be places of refuge.

Ancient anchors on display at Caesarea, Israel.

Anchor (6:19). Anchors were made of stone or sometimes iron. Some philosophers referred to virtues as anchors (e.g., Pythagoras, Plutarch).

Behind the curtain (6:19). See comments on Heb. 9:2–3.

Jesus has entered there on our behalf as a forerunner (6:20). The image here is of a forerunner or trailblazer (*prodromos*). See also Heb. 2:10.

Order of Melchizedek (6:20). See comments on Heb. 5:6.

The Priest, King Melchizedek (7:1–10)

King of Salem, priest of God Most High (7:1). The background is Gen. 14:17–20 (esp. v. 18). Melchizedek, the first OT priest mentioned (cf. Exod. 2:16), uniquely combined the offices of king and priest in the OT.

Met Abraham and blessed him (7:1). Genesis 14:1–24 recounts Abraham's defeat of foreign kings, after which he was met by Melchizedek, the king of Salem. See comments on Heb. 7:6.

King of righteousness (7:2). The name Melchizedek derives from the Hebrew words for "king" (*melek*) and "righteousness" (*tsedeq*).

King of Salem . . . king of peace (7:2). Salem would later become Jerusalem (under David). The word "Salem" derives from the Hebrew *shalom*, meaning "peace."

Without father, mother, or genealogy (7:3). Genesis does not include Melchizedek's genealogy, in contrast with the genealogies required for priests (Lev. 21:13–14; Ezra 2:62; Neh. 7:64). Hebrews follows a well-known rabbinic technique of inferring from what is unsaid in the text to argue that there exists another priesthood—one not dependent upon Levite genealogy.

Neither beginning of days nor end of life (7:3). Melchizedek's birth and death are not recorded in Genesis. Qumran writers claimed that Melchizedek was an angelic, messianic figure.[8] Hebrews, however, applies

Ivory altar fragment showing Christ blessing the sacrifices of Melchizedek and Abraham (eleventh century AD).

this observation to the priesthood associated with Melchizedek, not to the person.

A priest forever (7:3). Genesis does not mention an end to Melchizedek's priesthood, suggesting that it is ongoing. Hebrews alludes here to Ps. 110:4 to support what was implied in Gen. 14.

The patriarch (7:4). The reference to "the patriarch" underscores Abraham's greatness as the founder of Israel.

Collected a tenth (7:5). Israelites were required to pay tithes to the Levites (Num. 18:21–24).

Blessed the one (7:6). By blessing Abraham, Melchizedek performs the role of a priest (e.g., Num. 6:22–27). By paying a tenth of the spoils to Melchizedek, Abraham recognizes his priestly status.

The inferior is blessed by the superior (7:7). In an honor/shame culture, often someone of lesser status blessed someone of greater status. The readers of Hebrews would have assumed that Abraham was greater than Melchizedek. In Gen. 14, however, Melchizedek's priestly status and blessing of Abraham shows his superiority to Abraham, which was likely unexpected for the epistle's original recipients, hence the author's comment.

Scripture testifies that he lives (7:8). The fact that Genesis does not record Melchizedek's death allows the author to draw a parallel to Christ, who was resurrected from the dead.

Jesus and the Levitical Priesthood (7:11–28)

Perfection (7:11). See comments on Heb. 2:10.

Order of Melchizedek (7:11). See comments on Heb. 5:6.

Order of Aaron (7:11). See comments on Heb. 2:17.

Change of the priesthood . . . change of law (7:12). The law prescribed ordinances for the Levitical priesthood (e.g., Lev. 18).

Tribe . . . Judah (7:13–14). Only Levites were allowed to serve at the altar (Lev. 16:7–9, 18), whereas Jesus descended from the tribe of Judah (Matt. 1:2–3; Luke 3:33; Rev. 5:5).

Order of Melchizedek (7:17). See comments on Heb. 5:6.

Became a priest with an oath (7:21). A divine oath was not associated with the Levitical priesthood (cf. Exod. 29; Lev. 8). The oath in Ps. 110:4, quoted in this verse, regarding the order of Melchizedek indicates its unique (and superior) status, just as the oath associated with the Abrahamic promise confirmed its permanence. See comments on Heb. 6:13.

Guarantee (7:22). *Engyos* ("guarantee") indicates a guarantor or surety, who was liable to the same punishments as those for whom they stood, including lawsuits, imprisonment, or even death. The term occurs only here in the NT, although it was a common Hellenistic legal term. It could also indicate a promissory note.

Oath (7:21). See comments on Heb. 8:6–12.

Prevented by death (7:23). Josephus claimed that there were eighty-three high priests from the inception of the Aaronic priesthood to AD 70.[9]

Holy, innocent, undefiled (7:26). The Greek word *hosios* indicates both "holy" and "devout," especially regarding covenantal faithfulness (e.g., LXX Ps. 31:6 [ET 32:6]); "pure" or "undefiled" indicates cultic purity (e.g., Lev. 21:11).

Heavens (7:26). See comments on Heb. 4:14.

Offer sacrifices every day . . . first for their own sins, then for those of the people (7:27). The high priest offered sacrifices for himself and others only on the Day of Atonement. Hebrews likely conflates this day with the daily ministry of the high priest in order to stress the totality of Jesus's priesthood. See comments on Heb. 9:7.

Offered himself (7:27). This likely alludes to Isa. 53:10 and Mark 10:45.

The New Covenant (8:1–13)

High priest (8:1). See comments on Heb. 2:17.

Right hand (8:1). See comments on Heb. 1:13.

True tabernacle . . . set up by the Lord and not man (8:2). A tabernacle not made by humans is mentioned also in Mark 14:58; John 2:19–22; Acts 7:48; 17:24 (cf. Num. 24:6).

Copy and shadow (8:5). The Greek term *hypodeigma* ("copy") could signify a pattern, model, or copy. This language resembles that of Philo and some Platonists, who aligned the shadow with the material world and the true with the spiritual world. Hebrews, however, contrasts the shadow with the world to come, indicating that the copy and shadow correspond to the old Mosaic order. The true corresponds with the new covenant, its mediator, and the world to come.

Be careful to make everything according to the pattern (8:5). This warning occurs in Exod. 25:40 (also Exod. 25:9, 40; 26:30; 27:8; cf. Acts 7:44). It is unclear what Moses saw (e.g., blueprint, model, or the heavenly sanctuary itself). The idea that a god's earthly dwelling would reflect the heavenly one was common in the ancient world.

Mediator (8:6). A mediator was an arbitrator or intermediary between two parties (e.g., Exod. 24:1–8).

First covenant (8:7). The Mosaic covenant was a bilateral agreement between God and the people (Exod. 19:3–8; cf. Deut. 29–30).

A second one (8:7). The former covenant was limited by repetition (e.g., daily sacrifices, yearly Day of Atonement), restricted access (only the high priest could enter the holy of holies once a year), the eventual death of the high priest, the use of animal blood (Heb. 10:4), and so forth. See comments on Heb. 9:2–3; 9:7.

The days are coming . . . when I will make a new covenant (8:8–12). The new covenant, referred to in these verses in the quotation of Jer. 31:31–34, was promised when the southern kingdom, Judah, was facing exile for failing to keep the Mosaic covenant (Jer. 7:24–26; cf. Jer. 11:6).

The Tabernacle (9:1–10)

First covenant (9:1). See Heb. 8:6–12.

Tabernacle was set up (9:2). Exodus 25–31 outlines instructions for the tabernacle; Exod. 35–40 outlines its actual construction.

Holy place . . . most holy place (9:2–3). Priests passed through the outer curtain (Exod. 26:36–37) of the tabernacle (the holy place), but only the high priest could pass through the second curtain (Exod. 26:31–35) to enter the holy of holies, and only on the Day of Atonement. See comments on Heb. 2:17; 9:7.

Lampstand (9:2). The gold lampstand had a central shaft with three flowering branches extending from either side, supporting seven lamps (Exod. 25:31–40; 37:17–24).

Table (9:2). The table was made of acacia wood covered with gold (Exod. 25:23–30; 37:10–16).

Loaves (9:2). Twelve loaves of bread were placed on the table and replaced weekly (Lev. 24:5–9).

Gold altar of incense (9:4). Incense was offered on this altar daily; on the Day of Atonement the high priest put blood on it (Exod. 30:1–10).

Ark of the covenant, covered with gold . . . tablets of the covenant (9:4). The ark was made of acacia wood covered with gold and contained the tablets of the covenant (Exod. 25:10–22).

Jar containing the manna (9:4). A jar of manna, food that God provided to Israel in the wilderness, was kept with the tablets of the covenant (Exod. 16:32–34).

Aaron's staff (9:4). Aaron's staff budded as a confirmation of his priestly role (Num. 17:1–11).

Cherubim of glory (9:5). These two golden winged figures faced each other with their wings overshadowing the ark (Exod. 25:18–22; cf. 1 Kings 6:23–28). God promised to meet Moses "between the two cherubim" (Exod. 25:22; Num. 7:89), where God was enthroned (1 Sam. 4:4; 2 Sam. 6:2; Ps. 80:1).

Mercy seat (9:5). The lid of the ark was called the mercy seat, above which God was enthroned. God's throne was the source of mercy (Isa. 16:5). Only the high priest could approach the mercy seat (Lev. 16).

Their ministry (9:6). The priests' ministry included trimming lamps (Exod. 27:20–21; Lev. 24:1–4), offering daily sacrifices (Exod. 29:38–42), and replacing the bread (Lev. 24:5–9).

High priest . . . once a year . . . never without blood (9:7). On the Day of Atonement the high priest sacrificed a bull for his own sins and a goat for the people's sins; he sprinkled the blood from both on the mercy seat (Lev. 16:11–16). Only the high priest could enter the holy of holies and only on the Day of Atonement (Exod. 30:10; Lev. 16:16–17).

Still standing . . . present time (9:8–9). The author aligns the first section of the tabernacle with the physical tabernacle and Levitical priesthood, and the second with the true tabernacle and Christ's priesthood. See comments on Heb. 8:5.

Food, drink, and various washings (9:10). This likely refers to regulations for food offerings (e.g., Num. 15:5–10; 28:7–10), clean and unclean food (Lev. 11; cf. Dan. 1:8), and cleansings for priests (Exod. 29:4; Lev. 8:6; 16:4, 24) or defilement (e.g., Lev. 15).

Christ's Blood (9:11–28)

High priest (9:11). See comments on Heb. 2:17.

Perfect tabernacle (9:11). See comments on Heb. 8:2; 8:5.

He entered the Most Holy Place (9:12). See comments on Heb. 9:2–3.

Blood of goats and calves (9:12). See comments on Heb. 9:7.

Redemption (9:12). Property (Lev. 25:25–29) or persons (Lev. 25:35–55) could be bought back and thus redeemed (e.g., Israel from Egypt [Deut. 7:8; 15:15]). Jesus's own life was so understood (Matt 20:28; Mark 10:45).

Blood of goats and bulls (9:13). See comments on Heb. 9:7.

Ashes of a young cow (9:13). Ashes of a red heifer were part of a purification ritual (Num. 19:1–21).

Without blemish (9:14). This refers to sacrificial animals that were without defect (e.g., Num. 6:14).

Eternal Spirit (9:14). This may allude to the Spirit who rested upon the Lord's servant (Isa. 42:1; 61:1) and thus the Holy Spirit.

Living God (9:14). See comments on Heb. 3:12.

Mediator (9:15). See comments on Heb. 8:6.

Inheritance (9:15). See comments on Heb. 1:2.

Redemption (9:15). See comments on Heb. 9:12.

Will (9:16–17). The Greek word *diathēkē* can be translated as "will" or "testament," but here most likely it means "covenant," indicating a parallel between the inauguration of the Mosaic covenant and the new covenant. Similarly, the death associated with a covenant (Gen. 15:9–21; Jer. 34:17–20) is linked to Jesus's death.

Water, scarlet wool, and hyssop (9:19). Water, scarlet material, and hyssop are associated with purification rites (Lev. 14:4–6, 49–52; Num. 19:1–10, 17–18).

Blood of the covenant **. . . sprinkled the tabernacle** (9:20–21). The first covenant was ratified by the sprinkling of sacrificial blood (Exod. 24:3–8).

Without the shedding of blood there is no forgiveness (9:22). This summarizes the Day of Atonement (Lev. 16:14–19) and sin offerings (e.g., Lev. 4:5–7, 16–18). See especially Lev. 17:11.

Copies of the things in the heavens . . . a model (9:23–24). See comments on Heb. 8:5.

High priest . . . yearly (9:25). See comments on Heb. 9:7.

Will appear a second time . . . those who are waiting (9:28). The Israelites waited expectantly for the reappearance of the high priest from within the holy of holies on the Day of Atonement (Sir. 50:5).

Christ's Sacrifice (10:1–18)

Law (10:1). See comments on Heb. 7:12.

Shadow (10:1). See comments on Heb. 8:5.

Same sacrifices they continually offer year after year (10:1). This alludes to the Day of Atonement. See comments on Heb. 9:7.

Perfect (10:1). See comments on Heb. 2:10.

Hebrews 10:11 describes the religious duties performed by the priests at the Jerusalem temple: "Every priest stands day after day ministering and offering the same sacrifices time after time." The gentile readers of Hebrews could identify through their own experience of the repeated offerings given to Greco-Roman deities. This Roman relief shows a man offering incense to his gods (first century AD).

Reminder of sins year after year (10:3). This alludes to the Day of Atonement and possibly Num. 5:15. See comments on Heb. 9:7.

Blood of bulls and goats (10:4). See comments on Heb. 9:7.

The world (10:5). Here "world" (*kosmos*) indicates Jesus's incarnation. See comments on Heb. 2:5.

You did not desire sacrifice and offering (10:5). This citation is from Ps. 40:6 (LXX 39:7). See comments on Heb. 10:8.

You prepared a body for me (10:5). The Hebrew text of Ps. 40:6 reads "my ears you have pierced/opened," indicating complete obedience to God. The Septuagint translators apparently understood the part ("ear") in terms of the whole ("body"). Hebrews applies Ps. 40:6 to Christ's incarnation and its significance for Christ's priesthood and sacrifice.

You did not desire or delight in sacrifices and offerings (10:8). Psalm 40:6–8 indicates that sincere obedience is better than perfunctory sacrifices, a common OT refrain (e.g., 1 Sam. 15:22; Isa. 1:10–13; Jer. 7:21–24; Amos 5:21–27; cf. Ps. 50:8–10; Hosea 6:6). The terms—"sacrifice," "offering," "burnt offerings," and "sin offerings"—reflect the main types of Levitical offerings.

Takes away the first to establish the second (10:9). The reference is to the Mosaic covenant and its ordinances.

Sanctified (10:10). See comments on Heb. 2:11.

Every priest stands day after day (10:11). See comments on Heb. 1:3.

Sat down at the right hand of God (10:12). See comments on Heb. 1:13.

Perfected (10:14). See comments on Heb. 2:10.

Sanctified (10:14). See comments on Heb. 2:11.

This is the covenant I will make with them . . . I will never again remember their sins (10:16–17). This citation is from Jer. 31:33–34. See Heb. 8:6–12.

An Exhortation to Persevere (10:19–39)

The sanctuary (10:19). See comments on Heb. 9:2–3.

Curtain . . . his flesh (10:20). This may allude to the tearing of the temple veil during Jesus's crucifixion (Matt. 27:51; Mark 15:38; Luke 23:45). See comments on Heb. 9:2–3.

Great high priest (10:21). See comments on Heb. 2:17; 4:14.

House of God (10:21). See comments on Heb. 3:2.

Sprinkled (10:22). See comments on Heb. 9:7; 9:20–21.

Washed in pure water (10:22). "Pure water" alludes to ritual purification (Num. 5:17; Ezek. 36:25) or the cleansing by Jesus's blood anticipated by the sprinkling of the covenant blood (Exod. 24:3–8; cf. Ezek. 36:25–26). The reference here could also be to baptism. See comments on Heb. 9:10.

He who promised is faithful (10:23). God's faithfulness is a consistent OT affirmation (Deut. 7:9; 32:4; Ps. 145:13; cf. 1 Cor. 1:9; 2 Cor. 1:18; 1 Thess. 5:24).

Gather together (10:25). It is likely that the audience was part of a local house church that was loosely connected with other house churches. Due to persecution, this group may have been tempted to withdraw from this larger association. See comments on Heb. 10:32–34.

The day approaching (10:25). The day of the Lord was associated with divine vindication and judgment (e.g., Joel 1:15; Amos 5:20; Zeph. 1:14–18).

Deliberately go on sinning (10:26). See comments on Heb. 5:2.

Fire about to consume the adversaries (10:27). This alludes to Isa. 26:11 and possibly Num. 16:35; 26:10 (cf. Zeph. 1:18).

Died without mercy (10:28). This alludes to Deut. 13:8; 19:13.

Testimony of two or three witnesses (10:28). This alludes to Deut. 17:2–7 (cf. Deut. 19:15–21), which prescribes death as the penalty for idolatry, based on the testimony of two or three witnesses.

Trampled on the Son of God (10:29). Trampling someone or something under foot was an indication of contempt (e.g., Mic. 7:10).

Blood of the covenant (10:29). See comments on Heb. 9:20–21.

Spirit of grace (10:29). This may allude to Zech. 12:10.

Vengeance belongs to me; I will repay (10:30). This quotation from the Song of Moses (Deut. 32:35) concerns God's judgment against his enemies.

The Lord will judge his people (10:30). This quotation, also from the Song of Moses (Deut. 32:36; cf. Ps. 135:14), indicates God's impartial judgment.

Fall into the hands of the living God (10:31). This may allude to 2 Sam. 24:14. See comments on Heb. 3:12.

Earlier days . . . sufferings (10:32–34). This likely refers to the expulsion of Jews from Rome by Claudius in AD 49 (cf. Acts 18:1–2). Romans initially viewed Christianity as a Jewish sect. If the audience was Jewish believers, they likely faced public shaming (both from Romans and other Jews), confiscation of their possessions, and imprisonment. Tacitus noted that Christians were accused of various crimes.[10] The sufferings and afflictions mentioned in these verses likely do not refer to the martyrdom of Christians by Nero in 64.

Enlightened (10:32). See comments on Heb. 6:4.

Struggle (10:32). See comments on Heb. 12:1.

Prisoners (10:34). Prisoners relied on family and friends to bring them food and other provisions, although supplying such aid may have put these individuals in danger of imprisonment themselves.

Promised (10:36). See comments on Heb. 6:13.

Very little while, the Coming One (10:37). The first part of this citation is from Isa. 26:20, which mentions hiding until God's wrath has passed—an action discouraged here. "He who is coming" (or "the coming one") is from LXX Hab. 2:3, which was understood as a messianic title (cf. Matt. 11:3; Luke 7:19).

My righteous one will live by faith (10:38). This cites Hab. 2:4. The prophet Habakkuk (seventh century BC) cried out for God's vindication in the face of foreign oppression. He was exhorted to persevere in faith.

The Nature of Faith (11:1–3)

Reality of what is hoped for (11:1). The Greek word *hypostasis* can have an objective sense ("reality, substance") or a subjective one ("confidence, assurance, conviction, steadfastness"). Both fit the context here. See comments on Heb. 1:3.

Our ancestors (11:2). The author draws upon a well-known rhetorical device, the exemplar list, which was common in Jewish[11] and early Christian writings[12] and sought to motivate an audience to emulate virtuous behavior.

The universe was created by the word of God (11:3). This refers to Gen. 1:1–2:4 (cf. Ps. 33:6, 9). Unlike Greek philosophers, the author of Hebrews is consistent with other Jewish writings (e.g., 2 Macc. 7:28; *2 Baruch* 21.4; cf. John 1:1–4; Col. 1:16–17) that claim that God created the world out of nothing (*creatio ex nihilo*).

Early Faith (11:4–7)

Abel offered to God a better sacrifice than Cain did (11:4). This refers to Gen. 4:2–5.

Even though he is dead, he still speaks (11:4). See comments on Heb. 12:24.

Enoch was taken away (11:5). Genesis 5:18, 21–24 records that Enoch lived 365 years before the Lord took him. Based on his unique experience, Enoch was the subject of much speculation in Jewish writings[13] and the purported author of numerous pseudepigraphal writings.[14]

God . . . exists (11:6). Monotheism was a core tenet of Jewish belief, which included affirmations of God's existence (e.g., 4 Macc. 5:24; Wis. 13:1).

He condemned the world (11:7). Tradition held that Noah preached repentance before the flood.[15]

Faith of the Patriarchs (11:8–22)

City that has foundations, whose architect and builder is God (11:10). The understanding of the land promised to Abraham as a (heavenly) city is common in Jewish writings,[16] likely based on Isa. 54:11–12 (cf. Isa. 28:16).

Offspring as numerous as the stars . . . innumerable as the grains of sand (11:12). This reflects God's promise to Abraham (Gen. 15:5; 22:17). See comments on Heb. 6:13.

Had not received the things that were promised (11:13). Hebrews distinguishes between the Abrahamic promise of descendants, which was obtained (see Heb. 6:15), and the promise of land, which was not.

Foreigners and temporary residents on the earth (11:13). The status of "foreigners and temporary residents" (a fixed expression [cf. Gen. 23:4]) was precarious in the ancient world, often resulting from famine or war.

Where they came from (11:15). Abraham and his family first left the Mesopotamian city of Ur (Gen. 11:28), in modern-day Iraq, and then the city of Haran (Gen. 11:31), in modern-day Turkey.

Offered up Isaac (11:17). This account became paradigmatic for faithfulness in trials (Gen. 22:1–19; cf. *Jubilees* 17.15–16; 18.16; 4 Macc. 16:20).

Your offspring will be traced through Isaac (11:18). This quotation is from Gen. 21:12.

God to be able even to raise someone from the dead (11:19). This could be inferred from Gen. 22:5.

Isaac blessed Jacob and Esau (11:20). See Gen. 27:27–40.

Jacob . . . blessed each of the sons of Joseph (11:21). See Gen. 48:11–20.

Joseph . . . gave instructions (11:22). See Gen. 50:24–25 (cf. Exod. 13:19; Josh. 24:32).

Faith during Moses's Time (11:23–31)

His parents (11:23). Moses's parents and his exceptional childhood are noted in Exod. 2:2 (cf. Acts 7:20). Jewish tradition ascribed remarkable qualities to Moses.[17]

Son of Pharaoh's daughter (11:24). This refers to Exod. 2:5–10 and alludes to Exod. 2:11–15. Both the author of Hebrews and Stephen share a similar understanding of Moses (see Acts 7:20–29).

Reproach for the sake of Christ (11:26). Hebrews understands Moses's rejection of his Egyptian status and the ensuing shame as parallel to the reproach that Christ faced (cf. 12:1–3).

He left Egypt (11:27). Moses's first departure from Egypt likely is in view. Jewish tradition did not associate his departure with fear.[18]

The Passover (11:28). See Exod. 12:1–49.

The Red Sea (11:29). See Exod. 13:17–14:31 (cf. Exod. 15:1–21; Ps. 106:9–12).

Walls of Jericho (11:30). See Josh. 5:13–6:27.

Rahab (11:31). See Josh. 2:1–21 (cf. Matt. 1:5; James 2:25).

Further Examples of Faith (11:32–40)

What more can I say? (11:32). Beginning in verse 30, the narration reverses chronological order (Jericho fell after Rahab helped the spies, Gideon after Barak, etc.) and compresses the narration to stress the great number of exemplars in anticipation of 12:1.

Gideon (11:32). Judges 6:34 says that the Spirit of God was on Gideon, who defeated the Midianites (see Judg. 6–8).

Barak (11:32). See Judg. 4–5. Barak defeated the Canaanite Sisera, but only with Deborah and Jael's assistance.

Samson (11:32). See Judg. 13–16. Although Samson was driven by his passions, the Spirit of God was on him (Judg. 13:25) as he fought the Philistines.

Jephthah (11:32). See Judg. 10:5–12:7. The Spirit of God was also on Jephthah (Judg. 11:29) as he fought the Ammonites (see esp. Judg. 11:14–27).

David (11:32). The life of David spans 1 Sam. 16:1 through 1 Kings 2:12 (cf. 1 Chron. 10:14–29:30). Despite his many faults, he was faithful (e.g., 1 Sam. 13:14).

Samuel (11:32). Samuel's faithfulness (1 Sam. 1:1–25:1) was commended in Jewish literature (e.g., Sir. 46:13–15).

Shut the mouths of lions (11:33). See Dan. 6:1–23 (esp. v. 22).

Quenched . . . fire (11:34). This likely refers to Shadrach, Meshach, and Abednego (Dan. 3).

Escaped . . . sword (11:34). Elijah escaped from Jezebel (1 Kings 19:1–9), and Elisha from Jehoram (2 Kings 6:24–7:2).

Women received their dead (11:35). This likely refers to the widow of Zarephath (1 Kings 17:7–24) and the Shunammite woman (2 Kings 4:8–37).

Tortured . . . better resurrection (11:35). This may refer to the Jewish martyr Eleazar, who was tortured to death for his faith in God (2 Macc. 6:18–19, 28; cf. 4 Macc. 5:32), or to a mother and her sons who suffered the same fate (2 Macc. 7:1–41; 4 Macc. 8:1–17:24).

Mocking and scourgings, as well as bonds and imprisonment (11:36). This could refer to Jeremiah (e.g., Jer. 20:1–10; 37:15; 38:6–13), or even to the audience's own experience. See comments on Heb. 10:32–34.

Stoned (11:37). Jewish tradition claims that Jeremiah was stoned to death in Egypt. Zechariah was stoned to death by King Joash (2 Chron. 24:21; cf. Luke 11:51).

Sawed in two (11:37). The apocryphal writing *Martyrdom and Ascension of Isaiah* records that the prophet was sawed in two (5.1–16).

Died by the sword (11:37). This could refer to prophets (e.g., 1 Kings 19:10; Jer. 26:23), or to James the brother of John (Acts 12:2).

In sheepskins, in goatskins . . . in caves and holes in the ground (11:37–38). This could refer to prophets, such as Elijah (2 Kings 1:8), or to persecuted Jews (1 Macc. 2:28–38; 2 Macc. 5:27; 6:11; 10:6).

Made perfect (11:40). See comments on Heb. 2:10.

Persevering in the Race (12:1–13)

Cloud of witnesses (12:1). This Greco-Roman metaphor for a crowd emphasized vastness and unity. The contest imagery in 12:1–3 suggests a stadium or amphitheater.

Every hindrance (12:1). Athletes were encouraged to shed excess body weight before competitions. Philosophers also discussed being weighed down with excessive pride, concern for reputation, or other vices.

Sin that so easily ensnares us (12:1). The image probably is of a robe that would hinder an athlete, who normally would compete naked or minimally clad.

The race that lies before us (12:1). Athletic contests were popular and prestigious in the Roman Empire. These included running (a predetermined

The stadiums in Greek cities hosted footraces and other athletic events. The stadium shown here at Nemea, about eleven miles from Corinth, was the site of the Nemean Games, part of the Panhellenic game cycle.

course of several miles), jumping, discus and javelin throwing, wrestling, and boxing. Athletic imagery for moral struggles was common in Hellenistic Jewish literature (e.g., 4 Macc. 16:16–23; 17:11–16; cf. Acts 20:24; 1 Cor. 9:24–27; Gal. 2:2; Phil. 2:16; 3:12–14; 2 Tim. 4:7–8).

Eyes on Jesus (12:2). Athletes often looked down the track to the one seated in the place of honor (cf. 4 Macc. 17:10).

Source and perfecter of our faith (12:2). *Teleiōtes* ("perfector") likely was coined by the author. See comments on Heb. 2:10.

Endured the cross (12:2). Crucifixion was designed to prolong torture, maximize pain, and strip away all dignity. It was considered the most shameful death; Roman citizens were exempt from it and were discouraged from even discussing it.[19] See the article "Crucifixion."

Sat down at the right hand (12:2). See comments on Heb. 1:13.

Throne of God (12:2). See comments on Heb. 9:5.

Shedding your blood (12:4). Blood was commonplace in athletic contests, although this could allude to martyrdom (cf. 11:35–38).

My son . . . the Lord disciplines (12:5–6). Proverbs 3:11–12 is cited here, where discipline and sonship are linked (cf. Prov. 29:17).

Endure suffering as discipline (12:7). "Discipline" (*paideia*), or instruction, was considered necessary and could involve nonpunitive suffering (cf. Rom. 5:3–4; James 1:2–3).[20]

Father of spirits (12:9). This may allude to Num. 16:22; 27:16, and it contrasts earthly fathers.

Peaceful fruit of righteousness (12:11). This may allude to Isa. 32:17 (cf. Ps. 119:67, 71).

Trained (12:11). See comments on Heb. 12:1.

Strengthen your tired hands and weakened knees (12:12). This adapts Isa. 35:3, which originally offered encouragement for returning exiles.

The Example of Esau (12:14–17)

No root of bitterness (12:15). This alludes to Deut. 29:18, where Moses exhorted the Israelites against Canaanite idolatry (cf. Heb. 3:12).

Immoral . . . person like Esau (12:16). The word translated as "immoral person" is *pornos* ("fornicator"), which also could mean "apostate." The OT does not record sexual immorality with Esau (although it could be inferred from his two Hittite wives [Gen. 26:34–35; cf. Gen. 28:6–9]), but Jewish tradition ascribed immorality to Esau.[21]

Sold his birthright . . . for a single meal (12:16). This refers to Gen. 25:29–34. As firstborn, Esau would have inherited the blessing.

Pictured here is Jebel Katerina, a peak in the mountains of Sinai.

From Sinai to Zion (12:18–24)

Come to (12:18). In the Septuagint *proselēlythate* ("proselyte" derives from this Greek word) indicates a ceremonial approach to God; in Hebrews it is associated with Jesus's entry into the heavenly sanctuary (4:16; 7:25; 10:19–22).

What could be touched, to a blazing fire (12:18). The terrifying description of Sinai in verses 18–19 is based on Exod. 19:16–19; 20:18–21 (cf. Deut. 4:11–12).

If even an animal touches the mountain (12:20). See Exod. 19:12–13.

I am trembling with fear (12:21). These words occur with the incident of the golden calf rather than the Sinai encounter (Deut. 9:19). Jewish tradition, however, describes Moses's fear, perhaps also reflected in Acts 7:32.

Mount Zion (12:22). Zion was the site where David built Jerusalem and brought the ark (2 Sam. 5–6; cf. 1 Kings 8:1); "Zion" and "Jerusalem" often occur interchangeably (e.g., Ps. 51:18; 102:21).

The city of the living God (the heavenly Jerusalem) (12:22). Rabbinic and Jewish apocalyptic writings include much speculation on the heavenly Jerusalem,[22] likely based on Pss. 48; 87; Isa. 28:16; 54:11–12, although the term "heavenly Jerusalem" is unique to Hebrews (cf. 1 Esd. 4:58; Gal. 4:26; Rev. 21:2; Heb. 13:14).

Myriads of angels (12:22). This may allude to Deut. 33:2 (cf. Ps. 68:17–18). Myriads of angels are associated with the heavenly court (Dan. 7:10; cf. Rev. 5:11; 7:11).

Assembly of the firstborn (12:23). In the Septuagint "assembly" (*ekklēsia*) describes the wilderness gathering (e.g., Deut. 31:30), and in the NT the early church (e.g., Acts 9:31; 1 Cor. 1:2). On "firstborn," see comments on Heb. 1:6.

Names have been written in heaven (12:23). Citizens' names were legally registered at birth. Names being written in the book of life is a common biblical theme (e.g., Exod. 32:33; Ps. 69:28; Dan. 12:1; Luke 10:20; Phil. 4:3; Rev. 21:27).

Spirits of righteous people made perfect (12:23). This expression is common in apocalyptic literature.[23] Here these are likely OT believers who lived by faith (e.g., Heb. 11). See comments on Heb. 2:10.

Jesus, the mediator of a new covenant (12:24). See comments on Heb. 8:6.

Sprinkled blood . . . Abel (12:24). Sprinkled blood alludes to the Day of Atonement (see 9:7). Whereas Abel's blood cried out for vindication (Gen. 4:10–12), Jesus's blood inaugurated the new covenant. Abel's speaking in Heb. 11:4 refers to his faithful witness.

Final Warning (12:25–29)

Warned them on earth (12:25). See comments on Heb. 3:7–11.

His voice shook the earth (12:26). This alludes to the description of Sinai from Ps. 68:8.

Once more I will shake . . . the earth . . . the heavens (12:26). This quotes Hag. 2:6. Shaking (earthquakes) is linked to the day of the Lord. See comments on Heb. 10:25.

Removal of what can be shaken (12:27). The Greek word *metathesis* can indicate either "transformation" or "removal." See comments on Heb. 1:10–12.

Remain (12:27). In Hebrews what "remains" includes the Son (1:11), Christ's priesthood (7:3, 24), and the better possession of the faithful (10:34).

A kingdom that cannot be shaken (12:28). The kingdom here may allude to Dan. 7:18. The unshakable nature of God's dwelling is common in the OT (e.g., Ps. 93:1; 96:10; 125:1; Isa. 33:20).

God is a consuming fire (12:29). This likely alludes to Deut. 4:24. See comments on Heb. 10:27.

Final Exhortations and Prayers (13:1–24)

Let brotherly love continue (13:1). Familial love was esteemed in both Jewish (e.g., Ps. 133:1) and Greco-Roman sources, but loving nonrelatives as brothers and sisters was unique to Christianity (e.g., 1 Thess. 4:9; 1 John 3:16).

Show hospitality . . . welcomed angels (13:2). This alludes to Gen. 18:1–15. Both Jews and Romans considered hospitality to strangers an important virtue. See the article "Hospitality in the New Testament World."

Those in prison (13:3). See comments on Heb. 10:32–34.

Keep your life free from the love of money (13:5). This saying was proverbial (e.g., 1 Tim. 6:10; cf. 3:3). Jesus warned about excessive love of money (e.g., Matt. 6:24; Luke 12:13–21; 16:19–31). The connection between sexual immorality and greed was common in both Jewish and Greco-Roman thought.[24]

Be satisfied (13:5). Contentment was a common teaching of philosophers[25] and Jewish writings.[26]

I will never leave you or abandon you (13:5). The citation is based on God's assurance to Joshua regarding entering the land (Deut. 31:6, 8; Josh. 1:5; cf. Gen. 28:15).

Your leaders (13:7). *Hēgoumenoi* ("leaders") was a general term for leadership, but its use for church leaders appears to be limited to Rome,[27] which supports the view that Hebrews has a Roman audience in mind. These leaders may have initially preached the gospel to the audience.

Jesus Christ is the same yesterday, today, and forever (13:8). This wording may reflect an early Christian creed.

Strange teachings . . . food regulations (13:9). It is not clear whether these strange teachings were Jewish, although it is likely. See comments on Heb. 9:10.

Altar (13:10). The altar is here associated with Jesus's crucifixion.

Tabernacle (13:10). See comments on Heb. 8:2.

Most holy place by the high priest (13:11). See comments on Heb. 9:7.

Burned outside the camp (13:11). The carcasses of the bull and goat sacrificed on the Day of Atonement were burned outside the camp (Lev. 16:27; cf. Num. 19:3).

Jesus also suffered outside the gate (13:12). Jesus was crucified at Golgotha, which was outside Jerusalem's city wall (John 19:20). According to Roman practice, crucifixions normally were done outside city gates.

An enduring city . . . the one to come (13:14). See comments on Heb. 11:10; 12:22.

A sacrifice of praise, that is, the fruit of lips that confess his name (13:15). The sacrifice is anticipated in Ps. 50:14–15; 141:2. The "fruit of lips" alludes to Hosea 14:2.

God is pleased with such sacrifices (13:16). See comments on Heb. 10:8.

Blood of the everlasting covenant (13:20). An eternal covenant is anticipated in Isa. 55:3; 61:8; Jer. 32:40; Ezek. 16:60; 37:26. The eternal work of Christ is summarized here ("eternal salvation" [5:9], "eternal redemption" [9:12], "eternal Spirit" [9:14], "eternal inheritance" [9:15]).

Great Shepherd of the sheep (13:20). Shepherd imagery is prevalent in the OT. The wording here may allude to Isa. 63:11–14. Jesus as a shepherd is common in the NT (e.g., John 10:1–18, 26–29; 21:15–17; cf. 1 Pet. 2:25; 5:4).

Our brother Timothy (13:23). This is most likely the Timothy associated with Paul (e.g., Acts 16:1–5), since no further information is supplied. There is no NT account of his imprisonment, but it is likely.

Those who are from Italy (13:24). It is possible that this expression refers to individuals originally from Italy who were with the author somewhere outside Italy at the time of writing; this would also support the view that Hebrews has in mind an audience in Rome (see comments on Heb. 13:7).

James

James

Mariam Kamell-Kovalishyn
and Josiah McDermott

Introduction. The Letter of James, potentially from the head of the Jerusalem church and one of the earliest epistles written, is a key example of early Jewish Christianity.[1] It is our NT example of wisdom literature (like Proverbs), but it also shows influence from genres such as prophecy (Jeremiah) and law (Deuteronomy). In this epistle the motivation for relating to others as members of God's covenant people is not merely the earthly covenantal curses (cf. Deut. 28:15–57) but also cautions of future judgment (cf. *1 Enoch* 42.1–2; 98.6–16). The author echoes concerns, so abundant in the prophets of the OT, that God desires mercy above sacrifice, and James structures the epistle around character and justice and mercy rather than ethnic identifying marks such as circumcision or sacrifice. Jesus's Sermon on the Mount as recorded in Matt. 5–7 is also heavily influential.[2] It is generally agreed that the "James" of verse 1 at least refers to "James, the Lord's brother" (Gal. 1:19), leader of the Jerusalem church (Acts 15; 21). This James appears to have been well known to the Jews of the time, for Josephus describes the politically motivated murder of James as a significant event leading to the downfall of Jerusalem (*Jewish Antiquities* 20.9.1).

Salutation and Greeting (1:1)

James . . . greetings (1:1). This verse displays the standard way that ancient letters began: author, audience, and greetings. The title "slave" or "servant" likely echoes OT language of Abraham, Moses, and David as "servants" of

God, a title of calling rather than of subservience (e.g., Gen. 18:5–6; Num. 12:8; 2 Sam. 7:5, 8). The language of "diaspora" ("dispersed," used elsewhere only in 1 Pet. 1:1), combined with the identifier of the "twelve tribes," signals a Jewish Christian audience (i.e., an Israel formed from Israelites who identify Jesus as the Messiah).

Trials, Maturity, and God's Good Gifts (1:2–18)

Mature and complete (1:4). Perfection and wholeness are key themes throughout the epistle, reflecting the maturity to which God called his covenant people in the OT (e.g., Lev. 19:1–2).

Wisdom (1:5). As seen in OT texts such as Proverbs, wisdom is a gift from God that teaches us how to live lives pleasing to him. The language of "asking" echoes that of Jesus in Matt. 7:7.

Double-minded (1:8). The double-minded are those, such as Israel in the time of Elijah, who wanted to worship both God and Baal (cf. 5:13–20). They doubt God's sufficiency and goodness and thus seek to "cover their bases" with other things.

Exaltation . . . humiliation (1:9–10). The description of a change of fortune, while biblical, also was familiar in the ancient world. All tragedy involves a change of fortune. In a "simple" story this is gradual; in a "complex" story it is catastrophic, a sudden revolution of fortune's wheel.[3]

He will pass away like a flower of the field (1:10–11). This echoes Isa. 40:7. In the desert parts of Palestine this imagery would have been familiar.

Endures trials . . . is tempted (1:12–15). Returning to the theme of 1:2–4, James in these verses gives readers an eschatological perspective on temptation: endurance leads to life and defeat leads to death. The reference to not testing God alludes to the behavior of Israel in the wilderness. The Greek word is the same but shifts in meaning from "trial" to "temptation" in this section, following tradition (such as Sir. 15:11–17) in which it is possible for God to test people to discern their faithfulness (e.g., in the Exodus narrative), but temptation to sin comes from within the individual.

Father of lights . . . shifting shadows (1:17). The shifting likely alludes to planets that wander irregularly through the sky in contrast to the steadiness of the stars, a common contrast through Greek philosophy.

He gave us birth by the word of truth (1:18). Instead of sin, which "gives birth" to death (v. 15), God has "given birth" to his people; thus they are already in the new creation. This imagery echoes OT prophetic as well as covenantal language (cf. Jer. 31:33). It is also strikingly feminine imagery applied to God, as the verb *apokyeō* generally refers to the female capacity for birth.[4] Throughout the epistle the "word" and the "law" are closely tied together (see comments on James 1:22–25), and so the "word" here for rebirth seems to be the OT law *as communicated through Jesus*, thus closely tied to, or an alternate way of speaking of, the gospel inclusive of Jesus's teaching.

New-Creation Doers of God's Word (1:19–27)

Quick to listen, slow to speak, and slow to anger (1:19). The general content of verse 19 is fairly standard in both wisdom and philosophy of the time. The description, particularly that of "slow to anger," echoes God's self-revelation in Exod. 34:6, "The LORD—the LORD is a compassionate and gracious God, slow to anger and abounding in faithful love and truth," fitting with James's concern that people begin to imitate God's character.

The implanted word (1:21). The imagery of the "implanted word" in verse 21 could well be drawing on the parable of the four soils (Matt. 13:3–9), with the need for the seed to be planted in prepared ground rather than in untended soil choked with sins. Here it seems to be the fulfillment of Jer. 31:33, when God promised to put his law in his people's hearts and they would know him.

Be doers of the word and not hearers only (1:22–25). Of note in these verses is the smooth transition linking the "word" with the "perfect law of freedom," a phrase distinctly echoing Pss. 19 and 119, particularly the liberating aspect of the law. James clearly views the law in an OT covenantal way, even if now it is viewed through Jesus's life and teaching.[5] The "mirror" is a common image from ancient philosophical and wisdom teaching, meant to reveal the truth about a person.[6] The significance here is not the quality of the mirror, often made from polished silver, but rather the response to what is seen in the mirror.

Pure and undefiled religion (1:26–27). Following the OT prophets, true religion in James is defined not by religious rites that mark out who is included or excluded (e.g., circumcision or table fellowship), and not even by sacrifice (cf. Ps. 40:6–8; Isa. 1:11–18), but rather by a controlled tongue, moral purity, and justice and mercy in one's society (cf. Matt. 15:8–11 with Isa. 29:13). "Orphans and widows" is a stock characterization for those who have no voice in a patriarchal society.

Ancient mirrors.

Partiality and God's Mercy (2:1–13)

Glorious Lord Jesus Christ (2:1). The reference to Jesus can be either "our glorious Lord" or "the Lord of glory," with overtones of the *shekinah* glory of God, which rested on the tabernacle and temple.[7] This marks a high view of Jesus in an epistle that otherwise does not name him widely. The language of "favoritism" (*prosōpolēmpsia*, literally, "receiving a face") comes from the Hebrew "showing the face"—that is, looking only at the external.

If you look with favor on (2:2–4). Like a standard wisdom text, James then illustrates the problem raised in verse 1. The rich person in "shining" clothes and "gold fingered" (wearing a gold ring) is flaunting wealth, but the condemnation is on the one judging between the rich and poor.

Didn't God choose the poor? (2:5). Verse 5 reflects a growing tradition regarding the righteous poor who remain faithful to God despite their difficult situation (cf. Isa. 61:1).

The rich oppress you and drag you into court (2:6). A common way wealthy people gained further wealth and honor was through lawsuits against "inferior" members of society (cf. Amos 5:11–12). This raises the question of whether these wealthy are members of the church or external visitors.

The royal law . . . *Love your neighbor as yourself* (2:8). Leviticus 19:18 is the first and only OT appearance of this love command, but it becomes central to Jesus's summary of the law (Matt. 22:37–39; Mark 12:30–31; cf. Rom. 13:9; Gal. 5:14).

You show favoritism (2:9–11). A further problem with partiality is that it breaks half of the double love command (Lev. 19:18; Matt. 22:37–39; Mark 12:30–31). One cannot claim obedience to God's law while favoring the wealthy. It is as illogical as holding one command but breaking another command of the Decalogue and claiming innocence.

Mercy triumphs over judgment (2:12–13). Other Jewish literature of the time, such as *1 Enoch*, also explored the implications of the Deuteronomic covenant, wherein God's final judgment is in accordance with a person's actions of mercy or lack thereof (cf. Prov. 21:13).

Faith and Works (2:14–26)

Faith, if it doesn't have works (2:14–17). James again begins with a practical example—a person who lacks basic clothing and food—paralleling the structure of 2:1–4. The blessing "Go in peace" likely echoes the Jewish blessing *shalom* ("peace").[8]

Even the demons believe (2:18–19). Demons, not a common feature in OT thought, have become a common stock feature of those who oppose

God, and throughout the Gospels we see them recognizing Jesus's identity (cf. Mark 1:34; Luke 4:34).

Abraham believed God (2:20–24). As the great hero of the Jewish faith, Abraham's whole life was lived-out faith, from leaving Ur without a clear destination to his greatest deed, being willing to sacrifice his son Isaac. As a result, in common with Jewish tradition, James applies the statement from Gen. 15:6 (quoted in 1:23) to his own situation.[9]

Rahab the prostitute (2:25–26). Rahab is an unlikely exemplar of faith, the exact opposite of Abraham. Whereas he was a patriarch, wealthy, and a man, she was a prostitute, a refugee into Israel, and a traitor to her city (see Josh. 2). In contrast to the people of her town, who, like the demons (see comments on James 2:18–19), recognized that Yahweh was God and were terrified but opposed him, her faith leads her to act in accordance with her recognition of God's character.

Control of the Tongue (3:1–12)

Not many should become teachers (3:1–2). In a culture where honor was sought by all, becoming a teacher was one way to accrue honor in this new Christian society.[10] James warns against this way of thinking. In verse 2, "not stumble in what he says" may be reflective of Jesus (cf. 1 Pet. 2:22), but Job is also praised in the OT for refusing to blame God (Job 1:22; 2:10; cf. James 1:13; 5:11; Sir. 14:1).

The tongue (3:3–8). Like a standard wisdom teacher or philosopher, James consistently points to the world around for illustrations. The tongue can be positive, like a bridle or a rudder, or negative, like an out-of-control fire or a poison.

Fire (3:6). This may be an "eye for an eye" construction (*lex talionis*): here the tongue sets fires, and thus it is justly punished by fire.[11] "Hell" translates *gehenna*, referring to the valley outside Jerusalem that was the pit for burning garbage and had even been a place of child sacrifice (Jer. 32:35). This saying likely reflects Jesus's teaching (Matt. 5:22), the only other place where this term appears in the NT and also in context of sins of speech.

God's likeness (3:9). This is a rare NT allusion directly to Gen. 1:26–27, grounding the ethics of

An ancient decorated horse bit.

the command "love your neighbor as yourself" (see comments on James 2:8) in creation theology.

These things should not be this way (3:10–12). In these verses we have a different take on the nature imagery, this time pointing out the singleness to be seen in nature. Nothing acts like humans do in their speech, with complete opposites, "blessing and cursing," coming from the same source.

Wisdom from Above (3:13–18)

His works are done in the gentleness that comes from wisdom (3:13). This passage ties wisdom and righteousness together, as in Prov. 2 or Sir. 24. Wisdom is just as demonstrable by its works as is faith (James 2).

The wisdom from above (3:17). The list of the characteristics of wisdom is closely related both to Matt. 5:1–12 and Gal. 5:22–23.

The fruit of righteousness . . . peace (3:18). This likely draws on Jesus's beatitudes, particularly Matt. 5:9.

Idolatry of the Double-Minded (4:1–10)

Your passions that wage war within you (4:1–3). Selfishness, driven by the false "wisdom" described in 3:14–15, leads to fractured communities when everyone fights for their own honor (see comments on James 3:1–2). The language that speaks of waging war "in your members" (v. 1, CSB footnote) may be related to Paul's "body of Christ" imagery (cf. Rom. 12; 1 Cor. 12).

You adulterous people . . . friendship with the world (4:4). James echoes OT prophetic language (particularly Hosea) with the covenantal cry "Adulteresses!" Friendship in the ancient world was more than just a "liking"; rather, it meant a commitment to the same ideals and goals.[12] Abraham was God's friend (James 2:23), not the world's.

God resists . . . but gives grace (4:6). This is one of James's few direct quotations, from Prov. 3:34. It also occurs in 1 Pet. 5:5, one of many overlaps between James and 1 Peter.

Cleanse your hands . . . purify your hearts (4:8–10). The language in these verses is drawn from all the OT prophets. As in 1:27, ritual cleanliness stands for moral purity (e.g., Ps. 51:2; Isa. 1:16; Jer. 4:14).

God Alone Is Judge (4:11–12)

Lawgiver and judge (4:12). This looks back to the Exodus narrative, wherein God is the lawgiver (Exod. 20). Compare Isa. 33:22, which emphasizes God's role as judge who is able to save.

Warning to the Merchants (4:13–17)

Traditional Middle Eastern balance scale a merchant would use when conducting business.

You who say, "Today or tomorrow we will travel" (4:13). In view are the businesspeople (merchants) who traveled around the ancient world, where travel was notoriously dangerous. This is yet another example of a sin of speech (see comments on James 3:1–2).

Vapor (4:14). Echoing Ecclesiastes, this verse warns that making money for its own sake is vanity, as is overconfidence of our control of the future.

If the Lord wills (4:15). This prayer is enshrined in the modern Arabic phrase *Inshallah*, used by Christians and Muslims alike to indicate dependence on the will of God for the future.

Warning to the Rich (5:1–6)

Your wealth has rotted (5:1–3). In these verses warning the wealthy, James uses language that echoes that of Jesus in Matt. 6:19.

Has reached the ears of the Lord of Hosts (5:4). The hoarded wealth "cries out" to God much as the Israelites "cried out" to God from Egypt. "Lord of Hosts" invokes the tradition of the Warrior God of Israel (cf. 1 Sam. 17:45; Isa. 5:16). The Greek phrase for "Lord of Hosts" (*kyrios sabaōth*) is a transliteration of the Hebrew (*YHWH tsebaot*), and in the same way God heard the Israelites, the implicit threat here toward the rich is that he still hears and acts on behalf of the oppressed (e.g., 1 Sam. 15:2; Ps. 46:7, 11).

Call for Patient Endurance (5:7–12)

See how the farmer waits (5:7–9). Due to the weather and seasonal conditions, crops in Palestine were grown in the winter months, and they required the seasonal rains brought off the Mediterranean to flourish.[13]

The judge stands at the door (5:9). This likely refers to Jesus and the imminence of his return as judge (cf. Matt. 25:31–46).

The prophets (5:10). Prophets such as Moses, Nathan, and Isaiah spoke challenging words to the powers that be and advocated for justice. Generally, they were not well received, and they needed endurance to continue in their calling.

Job's endurance (5:11). Likewise, Job was noted in the biblical account both for his wrestling with God and for his refusal to blame God (see comments on James 3:1–2). The intertestamental book *Testament of Job* (included in the Pseudepigrapha, likely written in the first century BC or AD) highlights Job's passive endurance, but likely the biblical story is James's point here, as James otherwise does not teach endurance as a passive virtue.

Do not swear (5:12). Compare Matt. 5:34–37. Again a sin of speech here, possibly by the impoverished people of verses 7–11 "swearing" to repay debts they knew they could not afford.

Effective Prayer and a Call to Remain Faithful to the Truth (5:13–20)

Pray . . . sing . . . call . . . confess (5:13–16). James concludes in a standard way for ancient epistles with a series of commands regarding daily life.

Anointing him with oil (5:14). This could be a reference to spiritual purpose (dedication [e.g., Exod. 28:41; 1 Sam. 10:1]) or medical purposes, as oil was commonly used for treatment in the ancient world. The line between the two probably was not sharply demarked.[14]

According to James 5:14, those who are sick are to call the elders of the church to pray over them and anoint them with oil. The ointment bottles seen here were found in graves near Akko, Israel (first century AD).

Elijah (5:17–18). James marks 1 Kings 17–18 as his reference to this last named exemplar. There, the announcement of no rain in the start of chapter 17 and then the coming of rain at the end of chapter 18 clearly reveal a prophet "who spoke in the Lord's name" (see comments on James 5:10) and his confidence in prayer. Those chapters also include the raising of a dead boy (the ultimate healing [cf. James 1:14–15]) and a calling of Israel back from their double-minded worship of Baal and Yahweh.

Whoever turns a sinner . . . cover a multitude of sins (5:19–20). The epistle ends with the challenge developed from Elijah's example of restoring Israel to their proper worship of God. The imagery in these verses can be traced to Proverbs (10:12; 17:9), but it is unclear whose sins are being covered, and may also include the faithful person's own sins (cf. Ps. 32:1–2; 85:2).[15]

1–2 Peter

Kelly D. Liebengood

1 Peter

Introduction. Generally, scholars have argued either that 1 Peter was written by the apostle Peter (or by means of Peter's secretary or amanuensis, Silvanus [5:12]), or that 1 Peter is a pseudonymous document, perhaps written by someone within a "Petrine circle" of disciples in Rome. Those who doubt that Peter authored the letter do so in part because the Greek of the letter seems too polished for an uneducated fisherman from Galilee (Acts 4:13) (although this could be explained with an amanuensis). In the end, the letter does not offer enough historical information to enable us to situate it within a precise historical setting. If Peter stands behind the letter in some way (whether independently or with the help of Silvanus), then the letter most likely was completed prior to or just after his martyrdom (ca. 64–65). If one judges that the letter is pseudonymous, it most likely was composed no later than 92.

Even though the letter opening seems to be addressing Jews who are scattered throughout Asia Minor (see 1:1), and in spite of the proliferation of OT citations and allusions, the identification of gentiles as the out-group (2:12), and the usage of Israel as the principal metaphor for the addresses, most scholars argue that 1 Peter was written either to an exclusively gentile audience or to a mixed group that was predominately gentile in makeup. In

An icon of Peter from a larger piece titled *Christ and Twelve Apostles* (Antalya, Turkey, nineteenth century AD).

their view, several references in the letter can accurately describe only a gentile convert (1:14, 18, 21; 2:10; 4:2–5).

The Opening Address (1:1–2)

Peter (1:1). At this time period "Peter" was not a proper name. In Matt. 16:18 and John 1:42 we learn that Simon, the fisherman from Galilee, was given the nickname *Cephas* (Aramaic for "rock" or "stone") by Jesus. In Greek, *Cephas* is translated to *Petros,* which is where we get the English version, "Peter" (on Peter's names, see also 2 Pet. 1:1).

Apostle (1:1). See comments on Acts 1:2; 2:42.

Chosen (1:1). In the OT the term "chosen" (sometimes translated as "elect") was used to express a privileged relationship with God that required an obedience and faithfulness intended to bring forth God's redemption to the world (e.g., Gen. 12:1–3; Exod. 19:5–6; Isa. 41:8–9; 42:1; 44:1; 49:7; 65:9).

Living as exiles dispersed abroad (1:1). The term translated here as "exiles" (*parepidēmos*) can also indicate strangers (foreigners), resident aliens, or sojourners. It was used to describe people who were away from their homeland. The translation "dispersed abroad" comes from the Greek word *diaspora,* from which we get the English term "diaspora." Most scholars think that the description "living as exiles dispersed abroad" should not be understood as a concrete reality of the audience. Rather, Peter describes them in this manner to point out that at their conversion, followers of Jesus become foreigners (with a new way of life) in the cultures they were born into (2:12; 4:4).

Pontus, Galatia, Cappadocia, Asia, and Bithynia (1:1). These five names designate Roman provinces in the western and central part of Anatolia (modern-day Turkey). This letter is addressed to a larger territory than any other NT letter, approximately 129,000 square miles. The province of Asia was strongly influenced by Roman imperial ideology (cf. Rev. 2–3) (see comments on 1 Pet. 2:17).

Sprinkled with the blood of Jesus Christ (1:2). This phrase seems to allude to the establishment of the Mosaic covenant in Exod. 24:3–8, where the people pledge obedience to God, and the blood of the covenant is applied to them. In this sense, Peter would be suggesting that Jesus initiates a

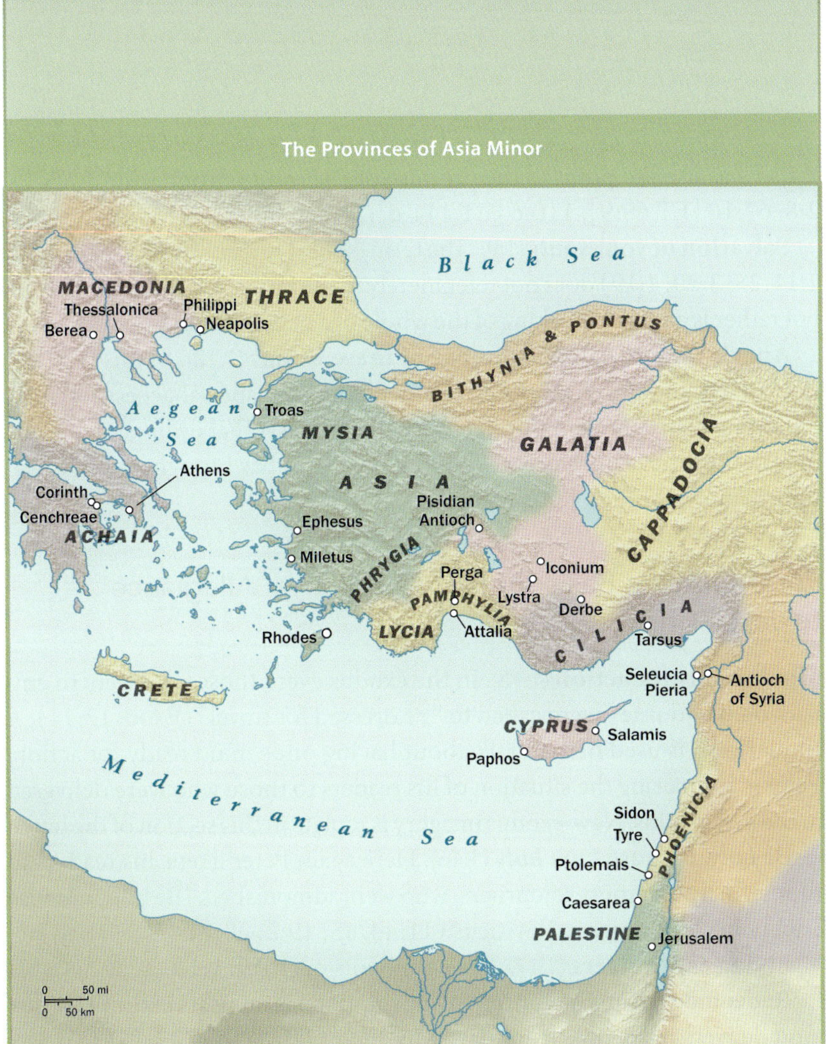

new covenant and a new exodus (a theme prominent in this letter) through his sacrificial death.

The Letter Introduction (1:3–12)

New birth (1:3). The concept of new birth was not common in this time period. It could be that Peter has been influenced by Jesus's teaching about new birth as witnessed to in John 3:3–7. It may also be the case that Peter draws the concept from the new exodus promises of Isa. 43:1, 7; 44:2, 21, 24; 45:11; 49:5. Thus as Israel was "formed from the womb," these people have been born anew through Jesus Christ.

Inheritance (1:4). In the OT this term (*klēronomia*) was shorthand for arriving in and possessing the promised land (LXX Num. 34:2; 36:2; Deut. 12:9; Josh. 1:15; 13:1; Judg. 2:6; 18:1; Ps. 134:12 [ET 135:12]; Jer. 2:7), and it also was used to point to the promise of restoration from exile (LXX Ps. 2:8; 67:10 [ET 68:9]; 110:6 [ET 111:6]; Isa. 49:8; Jer. 12:15; Ezek. 45:1).

Salvation of your souls (1:9). The term "soul" (*psychē*) (used also in 1:22; 2:11, 25; 3:20; 4:19) does not refer merely to the immaterial part of a person, but rather is a way of speaking of the whole of a person's being—"your lives."

Angels long to catch a glimpse of these things (1:12). In this time period angels and prophets were considered to have special access to God's unfolding plans of redemption. Here Peter suggests that ordinary believers in Jesus now have unique revelation of how God has brought about salvation, namely, through Jesus Christ.

Peter Offers a Basis for Hope and Loyal Allegiance to Jesus Christ (1:13–2:10)

Minds ready for action (1:13). In the exodus event those who were to embark on the journey were called to "be dressed for travel" (Exod. 12:11). A similar verb is used here to talk about having one's mind ready for action. Peter is comparing the situation of his readers to those who were delivered in the first exodus. New-exodus imagery is replete in this section of the letter.

Be holy, because I am holy (1:16). Here again Peter likens his readers to the original wilderness sojourners, who were admonished, "Be holy, because I am holy," four times in Leviticus (11:44, 45; 19:2; 20:7).

Living as strangers (1:17). See comments on 1 Pet. 1:1.

Redeemed (1:18). The concept of redemption first appears in the OT when God delivers his people from slavery in Egypt (Exod. 6:6; 13:15; 15:13).

Your empty way of life inherited from your fathers (1:18). Depending upon one's view of the makeup of the original recipients, this could either be an intra-Jewish critique of the unfaithfulness of their ancestors (e.g., Ps. 78:8; Zech. 1:4) or a critique against the Greco-Roman lifestyle that the readers inherited.

Precious blood of Christ . . . unblemished and spotless lamb (1:19). Jesus, and in particular his sacrificial death, is likened to the unblemished lamb that is killed in the Passover to preserve God's people from judgment (see Exod. 12:5–13).

All flesh is like grass . . . but the word of the Lord endures forever (1:24–25). This is a citation from the Greek translation of Isa. 40:6–8. Peter declares that the word announcing Jesus as the Christ and the means of salvation is what Isa. 40 was announcing. Isaiah 40 was the programmatic text for the book of Isaiah, announcing God's new-exodus deliverance of God's people who were in exile (see comments on 1 Pet. 1:1).

Spiritual house (2:5). The term "house" (*oikos*) can refer to a household, a dynasty, or a place where a deity dwells (temple). That it is a "spiritual" house is not to suggest that it is immaterial, but rather that it is made so by the generative power of the Spirit (see 1:2).

Holy priesthood (2:5). Just after God delivered his people from Egypt in the exodus, he declared them to be a kingdom of priests and a holy nation (Exod. 19:6). See comments on 1 Pet. 2:9.

Spiritual sacrifices (2:5). The word "sacrifices" is modified by the word "spiritual," which indicates that sacrifices are made acceptable through the power of the Spirit.

I lay a stone in Zion . . . the stone that the builders rejected . . . a stone to stumble over (2:6–8). In this time period some interpreted "stone" passages as pointing to a messianic king who would restore Israel. In this passage Peter links three "stone" texts (Isa. 28:16; Ps. 118:22; Isa. 8:14) together to explain why Jesus was rejected by his own people. Jesus identifies himself as the rejected stone in Mark 12:10–11; Matt. 21:42–44; Luke 20:17–18.

A chosen race, a royal priesthood, a holy nation, a people for his possession, so that you may proclaim the praises (2:9). These descriptors are taken from Exod. 19:5–6 and Isa. 43:20–21. Peter is claiming that the new-exodus promises of Isa. 43 are being actualized in and through Jesus Christ.

Once you were not a people, but now you are God's people (2:10). This is a reference to Hosea 2:23, in which God promises to redeem his people from their covenant infidelity. Peter claims that what his readers are experiencing in Jesus Christ is a fulfillment of Hosea 2:23.

Peter Exhorts His Readers to Pattern Their Lives after Jesus (2:11–3:12)

Strangers and exiles (2:11). Their status as strangers and exiles was a result of their faith in Jesus Christ; it was their new way of life (1:17–19; 2:12) in Jesus that made them outsiders in their own culture.

Slander you as evildoers (2:12). Slander was a common way in which a culture steered a straying member back on to the right path. Early Christians were called evildoers by their peers in order to make them feel ashamed of their negative association with other Christians.

On the day he visits (2:12). There is no clear reference to the OT or the teachings of Jesus here. It may allude to the final day of judgment (see also 1:5, 7, 13; 4:7, 13, 17; 5:1; cf. Isa. 10:3; Jer. 6:15; Luke 1:68), or it may refer to God's visitation to test nonbelievers who have witnessed faithful Christian living and are invited to join in fellowship.

God's slaves (2:16). In the exodus tradition God delivered the slaves (Israel) from Egypt so they could serve God and humanity (Exod. 7:16; 8:1, 20).

Honor the emperor (2:17). In this time period Roman imperial ideology demanded that the emperor receive supreme honor (see comments on Rev. 13:8). In this passage, however, the honor due the emperor is no more unique than what is owed to everyone. What is more, the meaning of "honor" has been subtly nuanced such that it cannot refer to "worship," as it often did in the eastern part of the empire (Asia Minor). Instead, worship (fear) is to be offered to God alone.

Household slaves (2:18). This address to slaves begins what many scholars have argued is a modified "household code" (see the article "New Testament Household Codes"). In this time period in Greco-Roman culture moral philosophers believed that the most fundamental unit in society was the household (which also consisted of adult children and slaves). As a result, we have a number of household codes in the ancient world that discuss household management and roles within the family. What is unique about Peter's household code is that slaves are addressed as free moral agents (most thought of slaves as incapable of such instruction), and that both slaves and wives are not exhorted to worship the god of the master/husband.

No deceit was found in his mouth . . . by his wounds you have been healed . . . were like sheep going astray (2:22–25). Peter links the pattern of Jesus's trial, suffering, and death with the prophetic text of Isa. 53, which speaks of a coming agent of God who will bring redemption for God's people through suffering. Peter does not cite the verses from Isa. 53 in proper order, instead lining up key verses with the events of Jesus's arrest and death (Isa. 53:9, 7, 5, 6).

Shepherd (2:25). While God at times is referred to as a shepherd (e.g., Ps. 23), the title here refers to Jesus, who is seen as fulfilling the role described in Ezek. 34:23–24 and Zech. 13:7.

Beauty . . . elaborate hairstyles . . . gold jewelry . . . fine clothes (3:3). In this time period there emerged a cultural phenomenon that scholars call the "new Roman woman": elaborate, provocative dress that was intended to communicate independence, power, and at times promiscuity.

A Roman woman with braided hair (early second century AD).

In the past, the holy women . . . Sarah (3:5–6). Rather than take their cues from the inherited culture, Peter urges his female audience to learn from Sarah (Gen. 18:12).

Weaker partner (3:7). It is not clear what Peter means with this statement, but he may be referring to the fact that under Roman law women did not have inheritance rights, nor could they become a member of their husband's kin group.

The one who wants to love life . . . those who do what is evil (3:10–12). This passage is a quotation from the Greek version of Ps. 34:12–16, which describes how God rescues those who suffer righteously.

Peter Reminds His Readers That God Delivers Those Who Suffer for Righteousness (3:13–4:11)

Ready at any time to give a defense (3:15). The term "defense" (*apologia*) may suggest that some Christians are being accused in a legal context, but it may simply point to the fact that their neighbors and peers are claiming that in following Jesus they are abandoning Roman culture and therefore are evildoers.

He also went and made proclamation to the spirits in prison (3:19). Most scholars think that Peter is drawing from *1 Enoch*, a popular extracanonical Jewish book (see comments on 2 Pet. 2:4; Jude 14) that explains where Enoch went when God took him away (Gen. 5:24) and that Enoch was involved in proclaiming eternal doom to the "spirits" whom God had locked in the abyss. In the cosmology of the day these spirits would be located not down or below, but rather in between earth and the highest heaven (*1 Enoch* 6–16; 21; cf. Eph. 2:2; 6:12). The verb "went" offers no directional cues, and given 1 Pet. 3:22, it seems best to consider that the proclamation was made to the spirits as Christ ascended into heaven.

Disobedient . . . in the days of Noah (3:20). The tradition of Noah and the flood received much attention in Asia Minor in this time period. Additionally, *1 Enoch* offers a popular interpretation of the increase of evil in the days of Noah (Gen. 6:1–4), which Peter likely has just drawn upon in 3:19.

Who has gone into heaven (3:22). This is a reference to the ascension of Jesus to the right hand of God (Acts 1:6–11; Heb. 1:1–14; 4:14–16; 8:1–7; 10:19–25; 12:25–29).

The end of all things is near (4:7). The word "end" (*telos*) points more to purpose or goal than to time running out. Thus Peter is claiming that God's purposes are coming to their intended goal.

Be hospitable (4:9). Hospitality was an essential element of early Christian development (see the article "Hospitality in the New Testament World").

Since Christians did not have official meeting places, their fellowship depended upon those with resources generously sharing with others.

Peter Exhorts His Readers to Not Be Surprised If They Suffer for the Sake of Christ (4:12–5:11)

If anyone suffers as a Christian (4:16). Disciples of Jesus were first called "Christians" in Antioch of Syria (Acts 11:26). It is likely that the term was developed by outsiders meaning to mock the followers of Christ. The term was not, however, the name by which Roman officials designated followers of Jesus as criminals.

Judgment to begin with God's household (4:17). It is likely that Peter has Zech. 13:9 and Mal. 3:2–13 in mind, which project a pattern of judgment that begins with the house of God and then moves outward to the nations.

Chief Shepherd appears (5:4). In John 10:11 Jesus refers to himself as the good shepherd who lays down his life for the sheep. See comments on 1 Pet. 2:25.

Unfading crown of glory (5:4). In the Greco-Roman world crowns were given to citizens who were distinguished in public service or who won important battles.

Mighty hand of God (5:6). This phrase is used repeatedly in the Septuagint translation of the exodus tradition to depict God's display of power as he redeemed his people out of Egypt (Exod. 13:9; Deut. 3:24; 4:34; 5:15; 7:19; 9:26; 11:2).

Adversary the devil (5:8). The word translated as "adversary" (*antidikos*) is used to describe an opponent in court, or someone opposed to God's chosen people. The term "devil" (*diabolos*) means "slanderer" or "accuser."

Parting Words (5:12–14)

Through Silvanus (5:12). This may indicate that Silvanus was Peter's amanuensis, or secretary, which may also explain how Peter, a fisherman from Galilee, was able to write this letter. Silvanus was among those chosen to deliver to Antioch the apostolic letter written at the Jerusalem Council (Acts 15:22–23), which may suggest that Silvanus did not write 1 Peter but instead delivered the letter—though possibly he did both (see the article "Ancient Letter Writing").

Babylon (5:13). This likely is a reference to Rome (see Rev. 17:5; 18:2), which at this time was playing the role that Babylon played in Israel's history by oppressing God's people and opposing God's ways. The term was not meant to conceal anyone's location but rather to reveal the true nature of Rome as an oppressive empire whose judgment was pending.

Mark, my son (5:13). This may be a reference to the Mark who traveled with Paul and Barnabas (Acts 12:25; 15:37; Col. 4:10; 2 Tim. 4:11), who also seems to have known Peter (Acts 12:12)

Kiss of love (5:14). In Roman culture one greeted family members and close friends with a kiss to express belonging and solidarity.

2 Peter

Introduction. Even though the author identifies himself in this letter as Simeon Peter (1:1)—a clear reference to the fisherman and apostle we see in the Gospels, Acts, and Galatians—many scholars think that the historical Peter did not write this letter. The main argument for this is that 2 Peter is an example of an ancient testament, a popular genre in Jewish literature in which an anonymous writer speaks on behalf of a hero to offer moral exhortation in light of his pending death and the coming of God's judgment. If 2 Peter falls into this genre category, then it is an assumed literary feature of the letter that Peter did not write it. Unfortunately, we do not have enough historical material from Peter himself to be able to determine whether these claims are sufficiently warranted. If the apostle Peter wrote the letter, then it was likely before 68, probably in Rome.

Information on the setting of the letter is lacking. We perhaps can assume that it is written to the same audience as 1 Peter (2 Pet. 3:1; cf. 1 Pet. 1:1). Although some scholars have argued that the author of the letter is responding to threats of gnosticism (a second-century heresy), this stretches the evidence. The following is what we do know about the false teachers referenced in the letter: (1) they reject apostolic authority (1:16–19; 3:2–4); (2) they do not believe that Christ will return in judgment of wrongdoing (3:4–5); (3) they deny Jesus's lordship and redemption from sin (2:1); (4) they promise freedom from moral and ethical obligations for the sake

Extrabiblical stories referred to in 2 Peter were known to first-century Jews from texts like the book of *Jubilees*. The Hebrew version of *Jubilees* exists today only in fragments, such as the ones shown here (Qumran, second century BC).

of pursuing lust and greed (2:19); and (5) they are leading astray new and immature followers of Jesus Christ (2:11–19).

The Letter Introduction (1:1–2)

Simeon Peter (1:1). Peter's Aramaic name is "Simeon," which was the most popular male name in Palestine during this period. His name means "hearing" or "obedient." The Greek equivalent is "Simon," which is how his name appears seventy-five times in the NT. Jesus gave Simeon the nickname *kēphas* (transliterated as "Cephas" in English), which means "rock, stone" (Matt. 16:18). The Greek equivalent of *kēphas* is *petros*, which is where we get the English nickname for Simeon, "Peter." The introduction of the author with his Hebrew name and Greek nickname (Simeon Peter) is perhaps suggestive of the bridge-building role that Peter played between the Jewish and gentile followers of Jesus. There are 181 NT references to Peter (either as Simon, Simeon, Peter, Cephas, or some combination), which is more than to the apostle Paul (Saul).

Servant (1:1). See comments on Mark 9:35.

Apostle (1:1). See comments on Acts 1:2; 2:42.

To those who have received a faith (1:1). The word translated as "received" is *lanchanō*, which often is used in the context of benefactors giving an inheritance or an allotted portion to a beneficiary. Some hearers may have understood Peter to be referring to God as a benefactor who apportioned to them the gift of faith.

The righteousness of our God and Savior Jesus Christ (1:1). The syntax of this phrase in Greek makes it clear that Jesus Christ is referred to both as Savior and as God (for similar grammatical constructions where the two titles both refer to Jesus, see 1:11; 2:20; 3:2, 18).

God Provides Us with All We Need for Life and Godliness (1:3–11)

Share in the divine nature (1:4). In some Greek religious and philosophical thought the goal of life was to be reunited with the divine and participate in immortality. Peter is likely aware of this, but he was more dependent upon Hellenistic Jewish developments that never considered the goal to be absorption into God and did not blur the lines between God and creation. Thus Peter is not suggesting that humans have the potential of becoming divine beings, but rather that the goal of humankind is to share in God's incorruptibility and immortality and in his virtue of love (see comments on 1:5–7).

Make every effort to supplement your faith with goodness . . . with love (1:5–7). Peter uses a well-known rhetorical device common in Hellenistic moral philosophy and adapted within both Jewish and early Christian modes of instruction known as *sorites* (cf. Rom. 5:3–5), in which character traits or virtues are catalogued in a chain-link fashion. The elements included in the *sorites* are the necessary characteristics or practices that one needs to acquire in order to reach the goal that this particular way of life is pressing toward. Thus embedded within the catalogue of virtues is an implicit vision of the good life. In the case of 2 Peter, the foundational characteristic is faith (1:1), and all the other characteristics work together to climax in becoming a person characterized by love. It is not the case that one virtue must be completed before the next is added; rather, each characteristic is necessary in order to reach the goal—love.

Christ Will Return as Promised (1:12–21)

Bodily tent (1:13). In Hellenistic thought of this time the word *skēnōma* (translated here as "bodily tent" and simply as "tent" in 1:14) often was employed as a metaphor to distinguish the body from the soul or spirit of a person, and to convey the temporary, mortal nature of the body over and against the immortal soul. Here (also in 2 Cor. 5:1, 4) it does not appear that the author wishes to affirm that the body is the temporary dwelling of the immortal soul, but rather to underscore his impending death (see comments on 2 Pet. 1:14).

As our Lord Jesus Christ has indeed made clear to me (1:14). Most likely this is a reference to Jesus's conversation with Peter recorded in John 21:18–19. In this exchange Jesus tells Peter, "When you grow old, you will stretch out your hands and someone else will tie you and carry you where you don't want to go." To this conversation the Fourth Evangelist adds this editorial comment: "[Jesus] said this to indicate by what kind of death Peter would glorify God."

Cleverly contrived myths (1:16). While Greco-Roman culture often used myths to communicate moral and philosophical truths, in this period the term "myth" often could be used in a pejorative sense to connote a farcical story that lacked credibility and was morally deceptive (see also 2 Pet. 2:3; 1 Tim. 4:7; 2 Tim. 4:4; Titus 1:14).

Coming of our Lord Jesus Christ (1:16). Jesus taught his disciples that judgment (separation) and redemption would be complete when he came again with power and glory (Matt. 25:31; Luke 21:27–28). In so doing, he drew on imagery from Dan. 7:13. This theme of the second coming of Jesus is picked up in Acts 1:11 and is central to the book of

Revelation (1:7; 22:20), which also draws on imagery from Dan. 7 as well as Zech. 12:10.

Eyewitnesses of his majesty (1:16–18). This phrase likely introduces Peter's claim that while on a mountain, he, James, and John were eyewitnesses of Jesus being radiantly transfigured in front of Moses and Elijah (see Matt. 17:1–6; Mark 9:2–7). The account in 2 Peter most closely resembles the transfiguration account in Matt. 17, where a voice from heaven said, "This is my beloved Son, with whom I am well-pleased."

Morning star rises (1:19). In Judaism of the time, Num. 24:17 was recognized as a text that pointed to a coming messiah who would deliver and restore God's people: "a star will come from Jacob." Revelation 22:16 uses similar language to speak of God's approaching rule and the advent of his Messiah.

God Will Judge False Teachers Who Promise Freedom but Promote Slavery and Destruction (2:1–22)

They will exploit you in their greed (2:3). The term "greed" (*pleonexia* [also in 2:14]) could be a reference to the lust for power, food, sex, or financial gain (see comments on 2 Pet. 2:13).

Condemnation, pronounced long ago (2:3). This probably is a response to the false teachers who were mocking the notion of a coming divine judgment. Peter does not indicate when or where the pronouncement of condemnation was made. Perhaps he considers the general OT pronouncement of judgment on all false prophets and teachers to be in play with these particular opponents.

God didn't spare the angels who sinned but cast them into hell and delivered them in chains of utter darkness to be kept for judgment (2:4). There is no clear reference to a biblical passage in view. Both Jewish and early Christian literature shared a popular assumption about an angelic fall (see comments on Jude 6) and a pending judgment that is illustrated in the extrabiblical text *1 Enoch,* a book that explains that evil has entered the world through fallen angels (Watchers) who fornicated with human women (Gen. 6:1–4) and who produced giants who incited Noah's generation to unprecedented evil. In *1 Enoch* 10 we see an example of these angels being bound and cast into the darkness for judgment. The verb *tartaroō,* used here in the phrase "cast them into hell," refers to Tartarus, which in Greek mythology was the underworld where disobedient gods and rebellious humans were sent for punishment.

He didn't spare the ancient world (2:5). Peter points to the flood and the preservation of Noah and his family, as narrated in Gen. 6–8.

Sodom.

Noah, a preacher of righteousness (2:5). The OT accounts of the flood do not mention Noah as a preacher, but some Jewish writings from this time period do refer to Noah's proclamation to sinners of his day.

Sodom and Gomorrah (2:6). Peter references the account of the destruction of Sodom and Gomorrah from Gen. 19.

He rescued righteous Lot, distressed by the depraved behavior of the immoral (2:7). This point is not clearly made in the narrative of Gen. 19, but Peter either interpolates this from Abraham's conversation with certain messengers (Gen. 18:22–33) or borrows this notion from Jewish literature in this time period.

Not afraid to slander the glorious ones (2:10). See comments on Jude 8.

Angels . . . do not bring a slanderous charge (2:11). See comments on Jude 9.

Delighting in their deceptions while they feast with you (2:13). In the early church the Lord's Supper was regularly celebrated as a meal (see 1 Cor. 11:17–34). Here the word for "deceptions" (*apatē*) can also be translated as "dissipation" or "deceitful pleasure," and Peter likely points to the fact that the false teachers join the fellowship but treat the meal like a Greek symposium, which usually involved intoxication and often was followed with sexually immoral acts.

Hearts trained in greed (2:14). See comments on 2 Pet. 2:3.

The path of Balaam (2:15). As a result of the OT narrative (Num. 22–24) and consequent Jewish literature, in this time period Balaam became a paradigmatic negative example of one who was motivated by greed and who enticed God's people to sin. See comments on Jude 11.

A dog returns to its own vomit (2:22). This maxim is taken from Prov. 26:11. Dogs in this period usually were not domesticated and were considered to be savage and destructive (cf. Phil. 3:2).

The Balaam Inscription (800 BC), found at Deir Alla in what is now Jordan, is so named because it mentions Balaam son of Beor (see Num. 22–24). In 2 Pet. 2:15–16 the false teachers are accused of following the way of Balaam, who had to be rebuked by his donkey.

"A washed sow returns to wallowing in the mud" (2:22). This saying does not come from Proverbs. Pigs were considered unclean animals in Jewish culture.

Remain Faithful because the Day of the Lord Is Coming (3:1–13)

Second letter (3:1). The reference to another letter is vague, but probably it points to what we now call 1 Peter.

Scoffers will come in the last days (3:3). See comments on Jude 17.

His "coming" (3:4). See comments on 2 Pet. 1:16.

By the word of God the heavens came into being (3:5). Peter reminds his readers of the account in Gen. 1, which emphasizes that God only needs a word to speak creation into existence.

Present heavens and earth are stored up for fire (3:7). That the world will be judged by fire is a consistent theme in the OT (Deut. 32:22; Isa. 29:6; 30:27, 30, 33; 33:14; 66:15–16, 24; Joel 2:30; Nah. 1:6; Zeph. 1:18; Mal. 4:1).

Day of the Lord (3:10). This is a common phrase used by the OT prophets to speak of God's decisive and final intervention in history to judge his enemies and to vindicate those who have been faithful to him (e.g., Isa. 2:12; 13:6, 9; Ezek. 13:5; 30:3; Joel 1:15; 2:1, 11; 3:14; Amos 5:18, 20; Zech. 14:1; Mal. 4:5).

Come like a thief (3:10). Jesus used this imagery in Matt. 24:43–44 (cf. Luke 12:39–40) to talk about the last days before his coming.

Elements (3:10). The Greek word for "elements" (*stoicheia*) is difficult to translate. It can mean "elements" (fire, air, water), "heavenly bodies," or "malevolent angelic powers," which often are regarded as presiding over the heavenly bodies. It seems that Peter has the latter two possibilities in mind, and is perhaps alluding to Isa. 34:4.

The heavens will be dissolved with fire (3:12). Fire imagery, found not only in the OT prophets but also in the Jewish literature of the time and in the NT, is regularly used metaphorically to refer to both the purging of the righteous and the destruction of all evil (e.g., Isa. 30:30; 66:15–16; Nah. 1:6; Zeph. 1:18; 3:8; Zech. 13:7–9; Mal. 3:2–3; 4:1–2; Sir. 2; Wis. 3; 1 Cor. 3:10–15; 1 Pet. 1:5–7; 4:12–13). The word translated as "dissolved" (*lyō*) in 2 Pet. 3:10, 11, 12, does not indicate annihilation, but rather radical transformation, or being undone.

New heavens and a new earth (3:13). The promise of a renewed (not annihilated) creation comes from Isa. 65:17; 66:22 and is also picked up in Rom. 8:19–21; Rev. 21:1.

Grow in the Grace and Knowledge of Jesus Christ As You Wait for His Coming (3:14–18)

Our dear brother Paul (3:15). Paul wrote several letters to the same region that 1 Peter addressed (Ephesians, Colossians, Galatians). Despite their confrontation in Gal. 2:11–14, Peter here affirms Paul as a wise, reliable, and "dear" (*agapētos*, "beloved") brother and teacher.

The rest of the Scriptures (3:16). Paul's letters were copied and circulated soon after they were written, and Peter here suggests that they were already considered to be as authoritative as the OT writings.

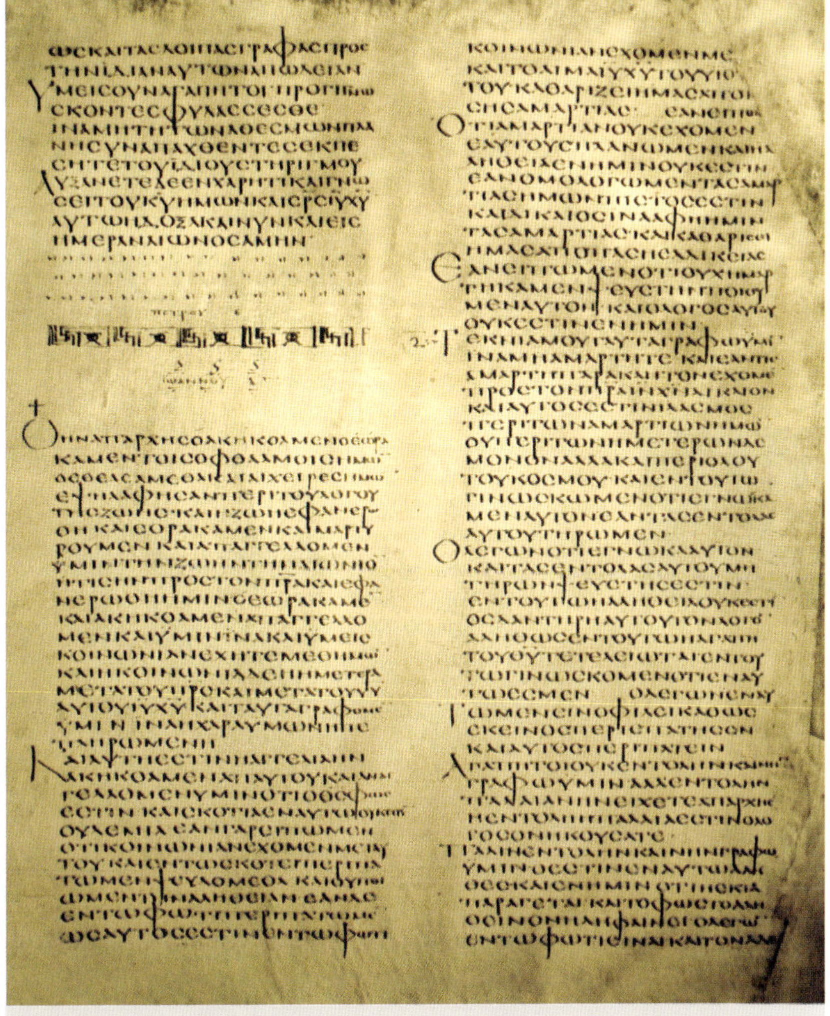

The end of 2 Peter and the beginning of 1 John in Codex Alexandrinus, an important early manuscript of the New Testament.

1–3 John, Jude

DAVID L. TURNER

Introduction. Collectively, 1–3 John are known as the Johannine Epistles (Letters), but 1 John is a homily or word of exhortation (cf. Acts 13:15; Heb. 13:22). It begins with its anonymous author's desire that the readers share in the author's own intimate familiarity with the "word of life" (1 John 1:1–4). This first involves correct thinking about the incarnate Jesus, thinking tied to the teaching of his chosen successors, the apostles (1 John 1:3; 3:23; 4:2–3, 9–10, 14–16; 5:1, 6–12, 20). Those who believe in this Jesus share in his victory over the devil, the world, and the false teachers (1 John 2:13–14; 4:4; 5:4–5, 18–19). This victory leads to an obedient lifestyle (1 John 1:5–10; 2:1, 3–6, 29; 3:3, 7 10; 5:2–3, 18; 2 John 6; 3 John 11), focused on Jesus's command to love one another (1 John 2:7–11; 3:11–18, 23; 4:7, 11–12, 19–21; 5:1–2; 2 John 1, 5–6; 3 John 1, 6; cf. John 13:34; 14:15, 21, 23–24, 28; 15:9, 12, 17; Rev. 2:4). Some have already abandoned this apostolic teaching and the church that affirms it, yet these secessionists (those who left the church) still attempt to lead the community astray (1 John 2:18–27; 3:7; 4:1–6; 2 John 7–11; cf. Rev. 2:2, 14–15, 20). The community's spiritual anointing enables it to distinguish between teaching that is faithful to Christ and that which is not (1 John 2:20, 27; 3:24; 4:2, 6, 13; 5:6–7). The homily weaves these main themes together in cycles rather than discussing them consecutively as distinct topics.[1]

Second John and 3 John clearly fit the conventions of the ancient Hellenistic (Greek) letter form. Many examples of such letters have been discovered, typically written on a single sheet of papyrus, containing personal correspondence about family or business matters (see the article "Ancient

Ancient Byzantine baptismal font at the Church of St. John near Ephesus.

Letter Writing").[2] Letters began with a prescript naming the author and audience, followed by good wishes for the audience, a central section or body containing the author's reason for writing, and a concluding postscript. The central sections of both 2 John and 3 John contain the author's concern that his readers maintain a loving lifestyle (2 John 1, 3, 5, 6; 3 John 1, 6) consistent with the truth of the apostolic tradition (2 John 1–4; 3 John 3, 4, 8, 12). Second John warns of false teachers, while 3 John recommends reliable teachers.

The details of the historical origin of 1–3 John are not clear. Christian tradition from the second century on places John the beloved disciple (John 13:23; 19:26; 20:2; 21:20; cf. Rev. 1:1, 4, 9; 22:8) in Ephesus, so it is plausible that these books reflect his ministry in the Roman province of Asia, today's western Asia Minor. According to the ancient church historian Eusebius, Papias (second century) spoke of an "elder John" in Ephesus in distinction from the beloved disciple.[3] Christ's directives for the seven churches of Asia (Rev. 2–3) likely reflect historical situations similar to those addressed in 1–3 John. Paul and Timothy also ministered in this region (Acts 19; 20:17–38; Ephesians; Colossians; 1–2 Timothy).

The historical interrelationship of John's Gospel, Epistles, and Revelation is unclear. The Johannine Epistles likely reflect varied responses to the Fourth Gospel. First John could be a homily based on the Gospel, reaffirming its central teachings and warning against misunderstandings. Second John could have been read (cf. Rev. 1:3; 22:18) to the church as an introduction to 1 John. Third John introduced Demetrius, the messenger who likely brought 1 John to the church.[4]

1 John

Sharing in the Word of Life (1:1–4)

What was from the beginning (1:1). Ancient people tended to respect continuity with the past more than many current cultures that value novelty. In 1 John the term "the beginning" may refer to the original creation of

In Ephesus today the traditional grave site for John is located in the Basilica of St. John, a church built by the emperor Justinian (527–65) over an earlier site thought to be John's grave.

the world (Gen. 1:1; Ps. 102:25; Prov. 8:22–23; Isa. 41:4; Matt. 19:4, 8; 24:21; John 1:1–2; 8:44; 2 Pet 3:4; 1 John 2:13, 14; 3:8) or to when the community first heard about Jesus (1 John 2:7, 24; 3:11; 2 John 5–6). The former is in view here.

What we have heard (1:1). The author repeatedly uses first-person plural pronouns ("we," "our," "us") in 1:1–4 and many other times throughout the book. Many times in 1 John these pronouns include the readers with the author (e.g., 1:6–10). But when the author is speaking about his personal experience of Jesus, as in 1:1–5, "we" implies that his message is what he and the other original apostles exclusively and directly received from Jesus (cf. John 21:24). This is a significant counterpoint to the recent teaching of the secessionists (1 John 2:18–27; 3:7; 4:3–5, 20), who had no claim to tradition personally received from Jesus. The readers must not abandon this original apostolic tradition (1 John 2:24; 3:11). Faithfully handing down revealed tradition to the next generation orally and in writing is important in the Bible and early Judaism (Deut. 31:14; 34:9; Josh. 1:1–2; 2 Kings 2:9–15; 1 Cor. 11:2; 2 Tim. 2:1–2; *m. Avot* 1.1–12).

The word of life (1:1). This "word" is not a mere message. It likely alludes to John 1:1, 14, and from there to Gen. 1:1. The "word" (*logos*) in this Johannine sense portrays Jesus as God's ultimate messenger who reveals God's glorious truth by embodying it as much as by speaking it (John 1:14–18; 14:6–11, 23; 17:6–8, 17; 20:27–28; 1 John 4:2; 2 John 7; Rev. 5:6, 12; 19:13; cf. Heb. 1:1–4). This "word of life" is not only heard but also seen and touched. Jesus does not merely speak the message—he *is* the message.

In the OT God creates and reveals by his word (Gen. 1:3, 6, 9, 11, 14, 20, 22, 24, 26, 28, 29; Ps. 33:6, 9; Isa. 55:10–11). His word is associated with personified wisdom in the OT and in Hellenistic Jewish texts (Prov. 8:22–29; Bar. 4:1; Sir. 24; Wis. 7; 9:1; 18:15; *m. Avot* 5.1). Aramaic Targums (interpretive translations of the OT) maintained God's absolute transcendence by speaking of his powerful revelatory relations with humans and angels as performed by his *memra* ("word").[5] In Greek philosophy the *logos* was the impersonal, rational, orderly structure of the world. John's "word of life" could have been understood against any of these conceptual backgrounds, depending on the culture of the individuals who heard it being read. Yet John's *logos* as both the original creator of the world and ultimate incarnate revealer of God transcends all of this.

Living in the Light (1:5–2:2)

God is light, and there is absolutely no darkness in him (1:5). The ethical dualism of light and darkness ultimately comes from the creation narrative (Gen. 1:1–5, 14–18). Satan's original rebellion against God brought cosmic conflict. Obeying Jesus means living in the light of God's will as opposed to the darkness of the devil's rebellion. Obedient lifestyles show that God's creative light is progressively renewing his original creation, which had been darkened by sin (1 John 1:5–7; 2:8–10; cf. John 1:4–9; 3:19–21; 8:12; 12:46; Acts 26:18; Rom. 13:12; 2 Cor. 4:4–6; Eph. 5:8; 1 Pet. 2:9). This way of thinking has affinity with that of the Qumran community.[6] In contrast to the God of the Bible, the mythological Greco-Roman deities commonly behaved shamefully, manifesting darkness as well as light. Their egregious behavior was no different from that of sinful humans.

We have an advocate with the Father (2:1). In NT times an "advocate" came to the aid of another by helping, advising, and interceding (sometimes as an attorney). We are told in John's Gospel that the Holy Spirit will come to minister to the disciples as "another advocate" in the place of Jesus (John 14:16, 26; 15:26; 16:7). Paul speaks of both the Spirit and Jesus as intercessors (Rom. 8:26–27, 34).

He himself is the atoning sacrifice for our sins (2:2). The "atoning sacrifice" concerns the appeasement of a deity's anger against sin. In ancient times pagans were preoccupied with maintaining the favor of their capricious deities by repeatedly offering sacrifices. In stark contrast, the NT portrays God as graciously taking the initiative in Christ to remove the barrier of sin once for all. This leads followers of Jesus away from fear of God's anger to assurance of God's love (1 John 4:18). Assurance of God's love in Christ motivates Christians to love one another (1 John 4:11). The OT "mercy seat" may be in the background of "atoning sacrifice" and related words in the NT (Heb. 9:5–8; cf. Exod. 25:17–22; Ezek. 43:20).

Loving One Another (2:3–11)

If we keep his commands (2:3). Obeying the stipulations of a contract or covenant was required to maintain its validity. So it was with God's covenant with Israel (Deut. 4:1–8; 6:1–9; Jer. 31:31–34), and so it is with the followers of Jesus (Matt. 7:21; John 13:17; 14:15; 15:9–14).

I am not writing you a new command (2:7). Strictly speaking, Jesus's new commandment (John 13:34) was not new—it had been taught in the OT (Lev. 19:18; cf. Matt. 22:37–40). What was new was the energizing example Jesus provided ("as I have loved you") and the dawn of God's rule in Jesus's ministry (1 John 2:8).

The true light is already shining (2:8). See comments on 1 John 1:5.

Hates his brother or sister (2:9). Compare Lev. 19:17–18, 33–34; see comments on 1 John 3:12.

Victory over the World of the Evil One (2:12–17)

Little children (2:12). This term (cf. 2:1, 28; 3:7, 18; 5:21) is figurative, speaking of the loving relationship (cf. 2:7; 4:1, 7; 3 John 1, 5, 11) between the author and his readers. "Children" in 2:14 (cf. 2:18; 3:1–2, 10; 5:2; 2 John 1, 4, 13) and "brothers" (3:12–17; 5:16) are also terms of endearment for the whole congregation. The terms "fathers" and "young men" (2:13–14) focus on men in the congregation, as would be typical in ancient cultures, without necessarily disregarding the women. Fathers presumably would exhibit wisdom from experience, and young men would be known for vigor.

You have conquered the evil one (2:13–14). In NT times the language of overcoming was used for military, athletic, and legal victories. Roman coins of the emperors featured images of the goddess Victoria, since victory was viewed as an attribute of the emperor. The King of kings (Rev.

A relief of the goddess Nike, uncovered during the excavations at Ephesus.

17:14; 19:16) spoke of his own overcoming the world through the cross in John 16:33 (cf. Rev. 5:5). Followers of Jesus share his victory (1 John 4:4; 5:4–5; Rev. 2:7, 11, 17, 26; 3:5, 12, 21; 12:11; 15:2; 17:14; 21:7).

The Anointing That Abides and Antichrists Who Deceive (2:18–27)

Many antichrists have come (2:18). In the NT the word "antichrist" occurs only in 1–2 John (1 John 2:18, 22; 4:3; 2 John 7), but the idea of an end-time archenemy of God who brings unprecedented trouble to God's people is widespread (e.g., Matt. 24:4–5, 21–28; 2 Thess. 2:1–12; Rev. 13; *Didache* 16.3–5). First John speaks of antichrist not as an end-time persecutor but in generic theological terms: anyone who presently does not acknowledge Jesus's having come in the flesh is a harbinger of the ultimate antichrist. Certain OT texts provide background for the NT texts about antichrist (Ezek. 38–39; Dan. 7:19–27; 8:11, 13, 23–25; 9:25–27; 12:11). Second Temple Jewish literature also speaks of an end-time oppressor of God's people.[7] The historical figure foreseen by Daniel was the Seleucid king Antiochus IV Epiphanes (reigned 175–164 BC) (cf. 1 Macc. 1:54; 2 Macc. 9), but in NT times Jews and Christians tended to think of Rome and its emperors as antichrist.

They went out from us (2:19). The secessionists are likely people who took the Gospel of John in the wrong direction toward what would later be systematized as the heresy of gnosticism. This way of thinking denied the goodness of the world as God's creation and affirmed salvation by illumination of the mind, not redemption of the whole person, body and soul. Various versions of this teaching include docetism and Cerinthianism. Docetism (from the Greek verb *dokeō*, "seem, appear, think") taught that Jesus appeared to be human but in reality was only divine.[8] Cerinthianism (based on the teachings of Cerinthus, who flourished around AD 100) taught that Jesus was the human son of Joseph and Mary. The Christ-spirit descended upon him at his baptism and departed before his crucifixion. According to the second-century bishop Polycarp, John rushed from the public baths at Ephesus when Cerinthus entered for fear that the roof would cave in.[9] Later gnostic systems advocated by Basilides and Valentinus, among others, carried on the doctrinal and ethical aberrations whose roots are confronted in 1 John. Ancient gnostic Christian writings known today include *Gospel of Thomas* and *Gospel of Judas*.

The secessionists left because they rejected the apostolic teaching about the incarnate Jesus (John 1:1–18; 6:53–58; 14:9; 20:24–29; 1 John 1:1; 4:2; 5:6–9; 2 John 7–9), who taught obedience to his commands. These secessionists are in view in the passages in 1 John that distinguish Christ's true followers from (1) those who deny Jesus having come in the flesh (2:22–23;

4:1–6, 14–15; 5:10–12), (2) those who do not obey God's commands (1:6, 8, 10; 2:4; 3:3–10), and specifically, (3) those who do not love brothers and sisters (2:9, 11, 15; 3:10, 14–15, 17; 4:8, 20). Even after they departed they still attempted to persuade members of the community to embrace their counterfeit version of Jesus (1 John 2:26–27; 2 John 7–11; 3 John 9–11).

You have an anointing (2:20). OT priests and kings were anointed with oil to consecrate them for their offices (Exod. 29:29; 40:15; 1 Sam. 10:1; 2 Kings 9:6). Jesus understood his own ministry in terms of the Spirit's anointing (Luke 4:16–21; cf. Isa. 61:1–2; Acts 4:26; 10:38). Later he promised to send the Holy Spirit to guide his followers in discernment (1 John 4:13; cf. John 7:37–39; 14:16–18, 25–26; 15:26–27; 16:7–15; 20:21–23).

Distinguishing between the Children of God and the Children of the Devil (2:28–3:10)

When he appears . . . at his coming (2:28). The "appearance" of Jesus may refer to either his first (1 John 3:5) or second coming to the earth (1 John 2:28; 3:2). His "coming" (Matt. 24:3; 1 Cor. 15:23; 1 Thess. 3:13; James 5:7; 2 Pet. 3:4) speaks of his glorious personal presence at his return. The coming of God in judgment was prophesied in the OT (Amos 5:18–20; Mal. 3:2). The term translated as "coming" (*parousia*) was used for the presence of gods such as Dionysus and for the visits of emperors and kings to areas they ruled.

The devil has sinned from the beginning (3:8). The deceptive work of the devil began in Gen. 3 and will end in Rev. 20:10 (cf. John 8:44; Rev. 12). The devil has enlisted demons and sinful humans to aid him in this rebellion. Willful disobedience to God's commands signals the devil's work in humans (1 John 3:10).

Believing in Jesus and Loving One Another (3:11–24)

Unlike Cain (3:12). Cain is notorious for killing his brother Abel and becoming the first murderer in human history (Gen. 4; cf. Heb. 11:4; Jude 11). Killing one's own sibling is an especially egregious sin. As Jesus taught that anger and lust were tantamount to murder and adultery (Matt. 5:21–30), so 1 John teaches that lack of love for fellow believers is tantamount to murder. This provides an emphatically affirmative answer to Cain's question "Am I my brother's guardian?" (Gen. 4:9). The book of *Jubilees* (a retelling of Genesis based on forty-nine-year divisions of time, dating from around 100 BC) finds poetic justice in Cain's death: Cain killed Abel with a stone, and so Cain was killed by a stone when his house collapsed upon him (*Jubilees* 4.31).

If anyone has this world's goods (3:17). If love for fellow believers could lead to giving up one's very life (1 John 3:16; cf. Rev. 2:13), it certainly would include giving up one's possessions. The OT provided instructions for helping the poor (Exod. 23:11; Lev. 19:10; 23:22, 35; Deut. 15:1–11; 24:14; Ruth 2; cf. Sir. 12:1–7). Early Christians also took this obligation seriously (John 13:29; Acts 4:32–37; 11:27–30; Gal. 2:10; Eph. 4:28; James 2:1–7, 14–17; 5:1–6; *Didache* 4.6–8).

Testing the Spirits of Truth and Falsehood (4:1–6)

Do not believe every spirit (4:1). This text assumes that unseen spiritual powers influenced human teachers. False prophets were viewed as mouthpieces of the evil spiritual powers anticipating the coming antichrist (4:3; cf. 2:18, 22; see also Acts 13:6–11; 16:16–18; *Testament of Judah* 20). The document of community rule from Qumran spoke of all humans being led by one of two "spirits," either a spirit of truth that motivated the children of light to righteous behavior or a spirit of falsehood that motivated the children of darkness to unrighteous behavior.[10]

Jesus Christ has come in the flesh (4:2). The secessionists (see comments on 1 John 2:19; 5:6) did not believe that Jesus was truly human. They may have thought of Jesus as a human form of a deity, as Paul and Barnabas were viewed in Lystra and Derbe (Acts 14:11–13). Perhaps they emphasized the Gospel of John's teaching on Jesus's heavenly origins (John 1:1–5; 3:13; 8:58; 17:4–5) to the detriment of its teachings on Jesus's humanity (John 1:14–18; 6:51–58; 11:35; 19:38–20:2; 20:20, 24–29; 2 John 7; Rev. 5:6).

The Gift of the Spirit Confirms God's Love to Us (4:7–21)

The atoning sacrifice for our sins (4:10). See comments on 1 John 2:2.

There is no fear in love (4:18). As with Adam and Eve, fear is the result of sin and a guilty conscience (Gen. 3:8). Ancient pagan deities acted arbitrarily, leaving their followers to repeatedly offer sacrifices to placate gods they may have unknowingly offended. Followers of Jesus are assured of God's love through Christ's gracious life, death, resurrection, intercession, and promised coming (1 John 3:16; 5:20).

Believing in Jesus and Accepting the Spirit's Witness (5:1–12)

The one who came by water and blood (5:6). The phrase "water and blood" probably refers to the incarnate Jesus's baptism and crucifixion, which bracketed his ministry on earth (John 1:29–34; 19:34). The secessionists' denial of Jesus as God-in-flesh would compromise the apostolic teaching on both of these areas. For instance, Cerinthus evidently taught that the divine Christ-spirit came on the man Jesus at his baptism and departed before his crucifixion. See comments on 1 John 2:19.

Knowing the True God and Eternal Life (5:13–21)

Sin that leads to death (5:16). This is one of the more difficult passages in 1 John. Most likely the sin that leads to death is secession from the community due to disbelief in a truly human Jesus and disobedience to his commands.

Guard yourselves from idols (5:21). Idols could be understood metaphorically as anything that one values over God, such as greed (Col. 3:5). More likely literal objects are intended here. The OT resoundingly condemns the worship of any idol (Exod. 20:4–6; Deut. 5:8–10; Isa. 40:18–22; 41:22–24; 44:6–20; cf. Acts 7:39–50). Second Temple Jewish literature likewise condemned and lampooned idol worship.[11] The gospel of Christ conflicted with the worship of various Greco-Roman gods as well as emperor worship (Acts 14:8–18; 15:29; 17:16–29; 19:23–41; Gal. 5:20; 1 Cor. 10:14; 12:2; 1 Thess. 1:9; Rev. 9:20; 13:3–8, 11–15; 16:2; 22:15). Around 112 Pliny the Younger, governor of Pontus and Bithynia, corresponded with the emperor Trajan about trying and executing Christians who refused to burn incense to statues of the emperor and the gods.[12] Whether Christians should even eat meat that had been offered to idols was a serious pastoral problem (Acts 15:20, 29; 21:25; 1 Cor. 8; Rev. 2:14, 20).

2 John

The elder (1). Mature leaders were respected early in the history of Israel and later in the synagogues. In keeping with this, pastoral leaders of the early Christian congregations were also called elders. In 2 John "the elder" appears to have apostolic authority over the affairs of multiple congregations, somewhat like that of bishops in later church hierarchies (cf. 3 John 1; 1 Pet. 5:1).

To the elect lady and her children (1). Although women were prominent in early churches (e.g., Luke 8:2–3; Acts 12:12; 16:14–15; 18:26; Rom. 16:1, 3–5), the words "lady" and "children" more likely are metaphorical references here to a congregation and its members (cf. 1 Pet. 5:13 and note the female imagery for God's covenant people in texts such as Isa. 61:10;

62:5; Jer. 2:2, 32; Hosea 2:2–6; 2 Cor. 11:2–3; Eph. 5:27, 32; Rev. 19:7; 21:2, 9; 22:17). The "children of your elect sister" in 2 John 13 probably are members of another congregation.

Many deceivers have gone out into the world; they do not confess the coming of Jesus Christ in the flesh (7). This likely refers to false teachers of the same stripe as the secessionists in 1 John. Their view of Jesus and their ethics were both deficient. See comments on 1 John 2:19; 4:1; 4:2.

Do not receive him into your home, and don't greet him (10). Early Christian congregations met in the houses of more prominent members

Many of the historic churches of Rome were built on the sites of house churches, homes where believing Jews and gentiles gathered for teaching, fellowship, worship, and prayer, and where they could celebrate the unity that they had in Christ. The remains of Roman houses from the second and third centuries have been found beneath the Basilica of Sts. John and Paul on the Caelian Hill in Rome, pictured here.

(Acts 12:12; Rom. 16:5; 1 Cor. 16:19; Col. 4:15; Philem. 2). This warning forbids supporting false teachers, not merely conversing with them. Showing hospitality to strangers was a key virtue in ancient times (Gen. 18:1–15; Job 31:32), one all the more incumbent upon followers of Jesus (Matt. 10:11–15, 40–42; Acts 16:15, 34; 21:8, 16; Rom. 12:13; 1 Tim. 5:10; Titus 3:13; Heb. 13:1–2; 1 Pet. 4:9). Early Christian writings confirm that false teachers and lazy charlatans commonly attempted to take advantage of the hospitality of early Christians.[13] A dispute over hospitality is the occasion for the writing of 3 John.

I don't want to use paper and ink (12). "Paper" (*chartēs*) was made from the inner pith of the papyrus reed that grows in marshy areas. The inner pith was flattened into strips and dried. Another layer of strips was laid at a ninety-degree angle to the first layer. Writing typically began on the layer with fibers running horizontally (the *recto*), and only if necessary on the back (the *verso*), where the vertical fibers made writing more difficult. Ink was made by mixing carbon from charcoal or soot with various liquids. See the article "Ancient Letter Writing"; see comments on 3 John 13.

The children of your elect sister (13). See comments on 2 John 1.

3 John

The elder (1). See comments on 2 John 1.

To my dear friend Gaius (1). Gaius evidently was the leader of a congregation under the elder's supervision. His was a common name. A man by this name had been baptized by Paul in Corinth (1 Cor. 1:14); likely he is also the Gaius mentioned in Rom. 16:23. Another man named Gaius, a resident of Derbe in Asia Minor, was a companion of Paul on his third mission trip (Acts 19:29; 20:4).

I pray that you are prospering in every way and are in good health (2). Such wishes were common after the greeting in ancient letters (cf. Philem. 4–7; 2 Tim 1:3–5).

Fellow believers came (3). These "believers" (literally, "brothers") are those mentioned in 3 John 5–8, 10.

You are acting faithfully in whatever you do for the brothers and sisters (5). Gaius was faithfully ministering to the traveling teachers sent out by the elder. The *Didache*, likely written only a few decades after 1–3 John, gave detailed instructions on how to discern which traveling teachers were worthy of hospitality and which were simply lazy or, worse yet, false teachers (*Didache* 11–13). See comments on 2 John 10.

Accepting nothing from pagans (7). The fact that the elder's traveling teachers were not aided by "pagans" (*ethnikoi*, "gentiles" [cf. Matt. 5:47; 6:7; 18:17]) may indicate that the elder and his teachers are ethnic Jews involved in mission to gentiles.

I wrote something to the church (9). This could be a reference to 1 John and/or 2 John, or to an unknown letter that has not been preserved.

Diotrephes . . . does not receive our authority (9). Diotrephes was a rival to Gaius, perhaps the leader of a sister congregation (cf. 2 John 13). Why Diotrephes strenuously opposed the elder is not clear. Perhaps there was merely a personality conflict or difference of opinion over procedures. More likely, given the theological unity of 1–3 John and their canonical grouping, Diotrephes agreed with the secessionists, who did not accept the apostolic tradition of an incarnate Jesus and the ethic of obedience to his commandments. This may be confirmed by 3 John 11, which starkly contrasts Diotrephes and Demetrius (cf. 1 John 3:6; 4:20; 2 John 7–11).

Demetrius (12). Evidently Demetrius was the bearer of the letter or was someone who would soon arrive. He was one of the genuine teachers sent out by the elder. Third John not only commends showing hospitality to genuine teachers but also serves as a commendation of Demetrius. Such letters were common in ancient times (2 Kings 5:6; Neh. 2:7; Acts 18:27; Rom. 16:1–2; 1 Cor. 16:3–4; 2 Cor. 3:1–3; Phil. 2:25–30; Col. 4:7–9).

I don't want to write to you with pen and ink (13). The word translated as "pen" (*kalamos*) may refer to a reed (Matt 11:7; 12:20) or to a pen made from a reed. See the article "Ancient Letter Writing"; see comments on 2 John 12.

Peace to you (15). The wish for peace may indicate the Jewish background of Gaius and his congregation (see John 20:19, 21, 26; 2 John 3; cf. Dan. 10:19; Matt. 10:11–13; Luke 10:5; 24:36; James 2:16; Rev. 1:4). "Peace" (Heb. *shalom*) in the OT was not simply the absence of conflict but the full, flourishing life of those blessed by God (Isa. 48:18; 55:12; 66:12).

A reed pen with a split nib, from Egypt during the Roman period.

Jude

Introduction. Jude (Gk. *Ioudas*) was a common name in this time period. The author of this letter identifies himself as the brother of James (1), which has been understood to mean he was either the half-brother of Jesus (since Jesus did not have a human father) or a relative of Jesus. Unfortunately, there is not enough content in the letter to enable us to date the composition with any certainty. If Jude the brother of Jesus wrote the letter, then it was composed probably no later than 80.

Jude addresses a situation in which people claiming to be followers of Jesus are living falsely within the community and persuading others to do the same: they reject apostolic authority (18), rely upon their own revelation (8, 10), and practice sexual immorality (6–8, 10). We have very little information that helps us know where the original audience was living, but we do know that Jude often alludes to the Hebrew version of the OT rather than the Greek version, and that Jude and James had influence and oversight in Palestine. Since the letter was written in Greek, it is thought that perhaps the letter was written to Jewish followers of Jesus Christ living outside Palestine who did not speak Hebrew/Aramaic but thought of Jerusalem as the center of authority.

The Letter Introduction (1–2)

Brother of James (1). This likely refers to James the brother of Jesus (Matt. 13:55; Mark 6:3) and the leader of the church in Jerusalem (Acts 15:13–21; 21:18; Gal. 2:9, 12). In this time period the honor (or shame) of one family member was ascribed to the others. Jude's reference to his brother James underscores his authority to give the following directives.

Jude's Purpose for Writing (3–4)

Contend for the faith (3). Here the word "faith" does not seem to mean the act of believing but rather refers to a body of belief (contents of belief). Jude draws on athletic imagery to exhort his readers to actively fight ("contend") for maintaining the proper boundaries of the content of their belief, which is under threat by the false teachers in their midst.

Delivered to the saints once for all (3). Jude describes the faith (content of belief) as that which has been handed over or "delivered" (*paradidōmi*), a term that often refers to the tradition of teachings and patterns of life that

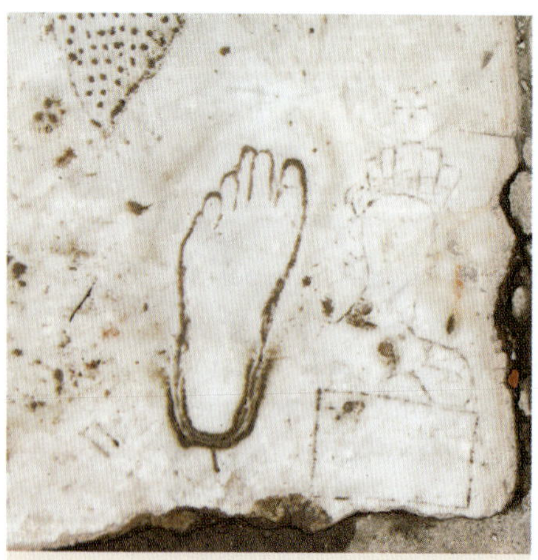
This footprint points the way to a brothel in Ephesus (first century AD).

have been affirmed by authoritative figures and then transmitted to a new generation of adherents who are called to faithfully maintain those traditions.

Designated for this judgment long ago (4). Jude likely has no particular OT passage in view, but rather, in keeping with Jewish interpretive strategies of the day, reads OT accounts of God's judgment of false teachers (see 5–8) typographically; that is, they prefigure God's judgment of the false teachers who have infiltrated the community.

The Basis for God's Judgment on False Teachers (5–19)

In this section Jude draws on OT events and people in order to demonstrate that God will indeed judge the false teachers who have infiltrated the community. It is important to note, however, that he often characterizes the events and people through the lens of traditions within Judaism that were developed beyond the OT Scriptures. Thus the examples that Jude uses (e.g., Israelites in the wilderness, disobedient angels, Sodom and Gomorrah, Cain, and Balaam) are not randomly selected, but rather function as archetypes of sin and judgment that appear frequently together in Jewish literature of this time period.

Jesus saved a people out of Egypt (5). There is some variation among the earliest texts of Jude. Some texts read "Jesus," while others read "Lord" or "God." There is no doubt that this is a reference to God's deliverance of Israel from the pharaoh's rule in Egypt (Exod. 12–14). If "Jesus" is the original reading, this identification is not unique in the NT: Paul identifies the rock that followed Israel in the wilderness as Christ (1 Cor. 10:4).

Angels who did not keep their own position (6). This is likely drawn from the extracanonical book *1 Enoch* (since Jude quotes from *1 Enoch* in 14–15), which reflects a common Jewish interpretation of Gen. 6:1–4 as a reference to sinful angels ("sons of God") who transgressed their established boundaries by fornicating with women ("daughters of mankind"). This transgression led to the intensification of evil on earth and consequent judgment (the flood).

Kept in eternal chains in deep darkness for the judgment (6). There is no OT reference for this. See comments on 2 Pet. 2:4.

Sodom and Gomorrah (7). Jude references God's destruction of Sodom and Gomorrah (Gen. 19), characterizing it as punishment because of their acts of sexual immorality.

Sexual immorality and perversions (7). What Jews (and the earliest Christians) condemned as sexual immorality was not seen as such in the Greco-Roman world of this time period. Jewish and Christian polemics against sexual immorality, and in particular homosexual practice, were seen to be intolerant and overly restrictive. A variety of homosexual relations (including same-sex monogamy) were practiced and accepted in this time period. It appears that Jude is an early response to those within the church who were teaching that freedom in Christ allowed for sexual immorality.

Relying on their dreams (8). These false teachers were rejecting apostolic teaching (v. 3) and instead relying upon special, nonapostolic revelation to determine what God wanted for their lives.

Slander glorious ones (8). This most likely is a reference to angelic beings (especially given the context of v. 9). In both Judaism and early Christianity (Acts 7:38; Gal. 3:19–20), angels are the agents that mediate God's revelation (whether it is the law or the announcement of the coming Messiah) to his people. By relying on their own revelation (dreams) and denying the authority of apostolic teaching, these false teachers are speaking falsely about what angels have revealed.

Michael the archangel was disputing with the devil (9). This account is not found in the Bible or in any available literature of the time period. Clement of Alexandria (second century), however, mentions that the story comes from a text called *Assumption of Moses* (although none of the incomplete copies of *Assumption of Moses* that we have discovered contain the account we read about in Jude).

The way of Cain (11). Here Jude relies on the interpretive tradition regarding Cain rather than the actual account from Gen. 4. By the time Jude writes this letter, Cain had become an archetypal sinner who taught others that it was acceptable to sin, since God was not going to judge their wrongdoing.

Balaam's error (11). In Num. 31:16 Balaam is blamed for enticing Israelite men to commit sexual immorality and idolatry with Moabite women (Num. 25:1–5). See comments on 2 Pet. 2:15.

Korah's rebellion (11). Numbers 16 (also Num. 26:9–11; Ps. 106:16–18) recounts the judgment that fell upon Korah (and 250 others) for opposing Moses's authority and the revelation given him by God.

Enoch . . . prophesied (14). This is not a reference to something that Enoch (Gen. 5:18, 21–24) said in the OT, but rather a direct quotation from *1 Enoch* 1.9. In the time period before Jesus, known as the intertestamental period, a significant interpretive tradition developed regarding

Icon of the archangel Michael (tenth century AD). Jude 9 holds up Michael as an example, possibly referring to an account from *Assumption of Moses*.

the Gen. 5 story of Enoch, who "walked with God; then he was not there because God took him" (Gen. 5:24). One of those interpretive traditions is found in the book *1 Enoch*, which is more properly seen as a collection of distinct literary units. It seems that *1 Enoch* was a well-known text during the NT era, as it is referenced in 1 Pet. 3:19–20; 2 Pet. 2:4; and Jude. It likely was not considered canonical in the early church but was considered illustrative for teaching.

Predicted by the apostles (17). We have no reference in the NT to any apostle saying the precise words cited in verse 18 about end-time scoffers, but we do have examples of apostles warning the church about false teaching, deception, and apostasy (e.g., Acts 20:29–30; 1 Tim. 4:1–3; 2 Tim. 3:1–5).

Encouragement to Remain Faithful (20–24)

Hating even the garment defiled by the flesh (23). The word Jude uses here for "garment" (*chitōn*) refers to the inner garment worn closest to the body (flesh). Jude uses this imagery metaphorically to talk about sexual immorality as a result of inordinate fleshly desires (similar to the angels in v. 7).

Stand in the presence of his glory (24). The imagery used here is of one who stands before a judge.

Revelation

Revelation

Mark Wilson

Introduction. As the final book of the NT and of the Bible, Revelation holds an important place in the canon of Scripture. Its backgrounds are rich and diverse, which makes reading the book both interesting and challenging. The OT is an important source for its language and imagery. It is estimated that Revelation contains almost three hundred OT allusions, mostly drawn from Psalms, Isaiah, Ezekiel, Jeremiah, and Daniel in their Hebrew and Greek versions. The exodus motif is prominent as well. Whether there are any exact quotations is debated; however, Rev. 2:27 quoting Ps. 2:9 is a strong candidate. John uses OT names (Balaam, Jezebel), activities (eating a scroll), and events (judgments of plagues and frogs) without explanation, presuming that his audience is familiar with these OT stories. Similarities to Jesus's teaching are featured in the seven beatitudes as well as the repeated "call to hear" what the Spirit is saying (chaps. 2–3). The vision of the woman, male child, and dragon in chapter 12 seemingly follows the plot of an ancient pagan myth about Apollo and Leto. The Greco-Roman world was a visual one, in part because of the high rate of functional illiteracy. Ideas, even imperial propaganda, were communicated visually through coins, statues, and friezes. This setting, foreign to us now, is encountered in visions such as the two beasts, the woman on seven hills, and the mystery of Babylon. The audience in the seven churches, familiar with this world, was able to calculate the number of the beast and to identify the seven emperors. However, to understand such references now is challenging unless the reader becomes familiar with the Greco-Roman background of the first century. Otherwise, they fall prey to distortions and bizarre interpretations of the text, practices for which Revelation has suffered throughout church history. The discussion here aims to immerse readers in the social, cultural, and religious environment of the Asian churches so that the eternal message that Jesus and John wanted to communicate can be received and applied today.

Prologue: Greetings and Doxology (1:1–8)

Revelation of Jesus Christ (1:1). The Greek word *apokalypsis* ("uncovering, disclosure, revelation") serves as the title of the book. Revelation is from Jesus and about him as well as his soon coming return. Both Paul (1 Cor. 1:7) and Peter (1 Pet. 1:7, 13) wrote about the "revelation of Jesus Christ" in speaking of Christ's second coming (*parousia*).

His angel (1:1). Angels appear repeatedly in Revelation to mediate heavenly visions to John. They frequently interpreted visions to prophets such as Daniel (Dan. 9:21–23) and Zechariah (Zech. 1:9). Angels appear in mediatorial roles in Jewish apocalyptic and apocryphal works: Raphael, Sariel, Raguel, and Uriel.[1] Angels were regarded as God's supernatural ministering spirits (Heb. 1:14).

John (1:1). The human author calls himself John four times (cf. 1:4, 9; 22:8). Church tradition has identified this John as the son of Zebedee, brother of James, and one of the Twelve (Mark 1:19–20; 3:17). The church father Irenaeus (second century) also claimed that the author of Revelation was none other than the beloved disciple who also wrote the Fourth Gospel in

The apostle John received the visions he recorded in the book of Revelation while exiled on the island of Patmos.

Ephesus.[2] The church historian Eusebius, quoting Papias (second century), claimed that there were two tombs of John in Ephesus, thus suggesting there was an elder named John too.[3] However, Ephesus has had only one tomb of John. Shortly after the legalization of Christianity in the fourth century a simple four-posted monument with a canopy was built over the grave. Visitors today see John's grave set amid the Basilica of St. John built by the emperor Justinian (527–65).

Blessed is (1:3). Seven unnumbered beatitudes appear in Revelation (1:3; 14:13; 16:15; 19:9; 20:6; 22:7, 14). Jesus spoke similar beatitudes to his disciples (Matt. 5:3–11). Like the beatitude that closes Daniel (Dan. 12:12), those in Revelation relate to the end times, especially Jesus's second coming and the promised blessings in new Jerusalem.

One who reads aloud the words . . . those who hear the words (1:3). The public reading of Scripture was a part of worship in the early church (1 Tim. 4:13). This followed the practice in synagogues, where Scripture was read each Sabbath (Luke 4:16–17; Acts 13:15). A lector was necessary in the churches because as much as 80 percent of the audience was functionally illiterate. A higher percentage of Jews usually could read because of Judaism's emphasis on the written word. Lois and Eunice, Timothy's grandmother and mother, taught him the Scriptures from infancy (2 Tim. 3:15).

This prophecy (1:3). Revelation is called a "prophecy" six times (1:3; 19:10; 22:7, 10, 18, 19). Like prophets in the OT, John has visionary experiences, is commissioned by angels, and does prophetic acts. His frequent allusions to Ezekiel, Daniel, and Zechariah reveal his self-identification with them as a prophet. The Greek phrase *tade legei* ("thus says" or "these are the words") begins each prophetic message in chapters 2–3. In the Greek OT (Septuagint) the phrase introduces prophetic declarations over three hundred times (e.g., Amos 1:6). Its only other NT use occurs when the prophet Agabus addresses Paul (Acts 21:11).

Asia (1:4). Asia was the first province established by the Romans in Asia Minor. It was formed by the senate in 129 BC after the king of Pergamum, Attalus III, willed his kingdom to the Romans in 133 BC. In the first century AD Asia consisted of what is today the western third of Turkey. Since it was one of the wealthiest provinces in the empire, officials vied to be appointed as its governor.

From the one who is, who was, and who is to come (1:4). God revealed himself to Moses as the God "who is" (LXX Exod. 3:14). In Revelation God is referred to several times with his eternal name as past, present, and future (1:8; 4:8; 11:16).

From the seven spirits (1:4). The placement of this phrase between Father and Son suggests that the image represents the Holy Spirit. The CSB footnote assumes this understanding: "the sevenfold Spirit." Jesus later holds the seven spirits (3:1), which are blazing as lamps before the heavenly throne (4:5) and become the Lamb's seven eyes dispatched into all the earth (5:6). Zechariah had a similar vision in which he saw seven lamps on a golden lampstand, which are interpreted as the Lord's seven eyes ranging throughout the earth (Zech. 4:2, 10).

From Jesus Christ, the faithful witness, the firstborn from the dead and the ruler of the kings of the earth (1:5). The messianic Davidic king is prophetically called "my firstborn" and "faithful witness" (Ps. 89:27, 37). Paul also called Jesus "the firstborn over all creation" as well as "the firstborn from the dead" (Col. 1:15, 18). In Revelation Jesus similarly calls himself "the originator of God's creation" (3:14). Jesus will triumph over the kings of the earth in the last battle (19:19–21). However, some redeemed kings will inhabit the new Jerusalem (21:24).

Look, he is coming with the clouds . . . mourn over him (1:7). The imagery of this four-line poem with its synonymous parallelism is drawn from Dan. 7:13 and Zech. 12:10. Jesus predicted that the Son of Man would come on the clouds with glory and power (Mark 13:26; 14:62).

I am the Alpha and the Omega (1:8). The first and last letters of the Greek alphabet are *alpha* (Α) and *ōmega* (Ω). Although here and in 21:6 the title refers to the Lord God, Jesus assumes it in 22:13. The titles Alpha and Omega, First and Last, and Beginning and End (see 22:13) are examples of *merism*—a figure of speech that combines two contrasting words to refer to an entirety, in this case the eternal nature of the God of all time.

John's Vision of the Son of Man (1:9–20)

Island called Patmos (1:9). A small, volcanic island now a part of the Greek Dodecanese chain, Patmos is located about forty miles west of the Turkish coast. In the first century it was under the jurisdiction of Miletus. John probably arrived in Ephesus sometime after the Jewish revolt against Rome that began in AD 66, heeding the warning of Jesus to flee Judea (Matt. 24:15–20; Mark 13:14–18; Luke 21:20–23). He was doubly suspect as a Jew from the war zone and as a Christian leader. Both Caligula and Nero are known to have exiled individuals to islands in the Aegean Sea. In a similar fashion the governor of Asia apparently banished John to Patmos. The Church of the Apocalypse now stands over the mouth of the cave where, according to tradition, John received his vision.

Because of the word of God and the testimony of Jesus (1:9). This is the reason for John's exile. That a closely similar phrase is used five times

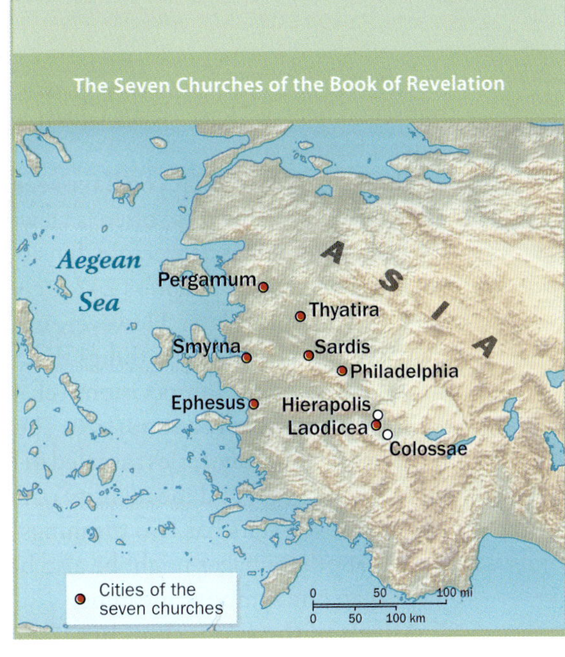

in Revelation (cf. 1:2; 6:9; 12:11; 20:4) suggests it is the main activity of God's people on earth.

I was in the Spirit on the Lord's day (1:10). The Lord's Day was Sunday, the first day of the week when Christians gathered (Acts 20:7; 1 Cor. 16:2). Like Ezekiel (Ezek. 11:24; 37:1), John was caught up "in the Spirit." During the four times he is in the Spirit in Revelation, an angel shows him visions of the Son of Man (1:10), the heavenly throne (4:2), the great prostitute Babylon (17:3), and the new Jerusalem (21:10).

Seven churches (1:11). Revelation is addressed to Christians in seven cities in Asia. Ephesus, Smyrna, and Pergamum were the "First" cities of the province and situated on the Aegean coast; the other four were inland cities. They were linked by an efficient road system along which a messenger could deliver the document (see the article "Roman Roads and Travel"). Since the gospel had spread to more than seven cities with congregations (cf. Acts 19:10), these seven churches seem to represent all the churches in the province. The church in Laodicea presumably shared John's vision with its neighbors in Colossae and Hierapolis (cf. Col. 4:13, 16). This is the first of four series of sevens—churches, seals, trumpets, bowls—used to structure the book's visions.

One like the Son of Man (1:13). John's description uses imagery from Daniel's visions of a son of man. The figure's white hair resembling wool and snow connects him to the "Ancient of Days" (Dan. 7:9–10). The imagery and titles for Jesus found in this opening vision are reused by Jesus to introduce himself at the beginning of each prophetic message in chapters 2–3.

Sharp, double-edged sword (1:16). The image of the sharp sword coming from Jesus's mouth is used four times (see also 2:16; 19:15, 21). Using the metaphorical sword of his tongue (cf. Heb. 4:12), Jesus speaks judgment against his enemies.

I am the First and the Last (1:17). Isaiah used this title for the Lord Almighty (Isa. 44:6; 48:12); now Jesus assumes it. The word "eschatology," referring to the study of last things, comes from the word *eschatos*, translated here as "Last." Jesus Christ as the *Eschatos* is the focus of Christian eschatology.

Therefore write what you have seen, what is, and what will take place after this (1:19). This verse often is viewed as a key to Revelation's structure. If we interpret this as a threefold division of its contents, chapter 1 contains what has been seen, chapters 2–3 are what is now, and chapters 4–22 are what will take place later. However, an alternative translation—"the things that are now as well as the things that will happen after this"—suggests a twofold division for John's visions (cf. 4:1).

Mystery of the seven stars (1:20). The interpretation of John's initial vision is the first of three mysteries revealed in Revelation. The other two are God's divine plan (10:7) and the identity of the prostitute (17:5, 7). Because the image of seven stars has two meanings—angels and menorahs—this suggests that other images might be also be polyvalent; that is, they may have more than one symbolic meaning.

Angels of the seven churches (1:20). These angels are addressed at the beginning of each message. Because angels are a common feature of apocalyptic literature, these messengers should be understood as actual angels rather than human leaders.

Seven lampstands are the seven churches (1:20). The menorah with its seven branches and seven lamps was a development of postexilic Judaism (Zech. 4:2). Antiochus Epiphanes took the menorah from the temple in 167 BC (1 Macc. 1:21). After the temple was purified by Judas Maccabees in 165 BC, a new menorah was among the sacred objects made for it (1 Macc. 4:49). Mattathias Antigonos issued a lepton coin in 39 BC with a menorah on it. Josephus mentioned that a seven-branched golden menorah stood in

A relief featuring a menorah (lampstand) on the Arch of Titus in Rome.

Herod's rebuilt temple. This menorah was among the objects taken to Rome after the temple's destruction in AD 70, and it can still be seen today on the Arch of Titus. The menorah became the most common identity symbol for Jews in Asia Minor in the postbiblical period and is found on lamps, plaques, and columns.

The Christians in Ephesus had endured hardships and persevered as they lived in their cosmopolitan, pagan city. But they were receiving a warning and a call to repentance because their love had diminished. Shown here is one of the main thoroughfares in ancient Ephesus known as Curetes Street.

The Messages to the Seven Churches (2:1–3:22)

Ephesus (2:1). See the article "The City of Ephesus."

Holds the seven stars in his right hand (2:1). The depiction of the seven stars of Ursa Major on Roman coins began in the period of the Roman Republic. To celebrate the deification of Domitian's infant son after his death, coins were issued in AD 83 that show the child seated on a globe and reaching out to seven stars surrounding him.

Abandoned the love you had at first (2:4). Inscriptions erected by the elites appeared in Ephesus in the first century AD using the terms *philokaisar* ("friend of Caesar") and *philosebastos* ("friend of Augustus"). Through these they expressed particular friendship and devotion to the living emperor. Christians, especially those of higher civic status, would feel social pressure to declare who was the object of their worship, Christ or Caesar. Some apparently had left their first love, Jesus.

Remove your lampstand (2:5). Jesus's warning might better be understood as "move" their lampstand from its place. Ephesus was the apostolic church in Asia from which the other churches were birthed (Acts 19:10). Paul, Priscilla, Aquila, Apollos, and John all ministered in Ephesus. The threat was that Ephesus would lose its preeminent position among its daughter churches unless it repented.

Practices of the Nicolaitans (2:6). "Nicolaitan" ("victor over the people") is a play on a key word in Revelation, *nikaō* ("to be victorious"). This heretical sect also plagued the church in Pergamum (2:15) and apparently taught that eating food sacrificed to idols and worshiping the emperor were acceptable activities for Christians. Such accommodation was not acceptable to Jesus.

Roman coin depicting the seven stars of Ursa Major.

Eat from the tree of life, which is in the paradise of God (2:7). "Paradise" is the word used for Eden in the Septuagint version of Gen. 2–3. Adam and Eve were prohibited from eating of the tree of life after their disobedience. Near Ephesus at Ortygia stood a sacred grove called Paradise (*paradeisos*), thought to be the traditional birthplace of the Greek goddess Artemis.

Smyrna (2:8). Smyrna was founded at the head of the Gulf of Smyrna in the eleventh century BC. Tradition has it that Homer was from Smyrna, and its coinage depicts the poet. Around 600 BC the city was destroyed by the Lydians and again by the Persians in 545 BC. Alexander the Great founded a new city at the base of Mount Pagos in 334 BC. This acropolis, 460 feet tall with walls dating to the Late Roman, Byzantine, and Ottoman periods, looms over Izmir (the modern name for ancient Smyrna) today. The remains of a theater rest on its northern side. In the stadium that formerly stood on Pagos, the bishop Polycarp was martyred in AD 156. Smyrna's relationship with Rome began in 195 BC, and Cicero called the city one of Rome's most faithful and most ancient allies.[4] Smyrna was a judicial center for the province, and the Roman governor conducted court sessions here. Archaeologists have excavated the Roman civic agora in downtown Izmir. An earthquake in AD 178 destroyed earlier structures on the site. Excavations in the agora basilica's basement have revealed over a thousand graffiti whose subjects include sex, love, politics, and religion. Perhaps the earliest Christian graffito has been found here: *ho dedokōs pneuma* ("the one who has given the Spirit"), referring to Jesus.

Synagogue of Satan (2:9). Certain Jews in Smyrna and Philadelphia (3:9) constituted a synagogue of Satan. Rulers of synagogues persecuted Paul during his ministry travels (e.g., Acts 13:50; 14:2, 19). The marginalization of Jewish believers in Asia at this time reflects the parting of the ways wherein followers of Jesus were no longer welcome in the synagogues.

Experience affliction for ten days (2:10). Ten days symbolizes a brief period of time. Daniel and his three friends were tested for ten days regarding their diet of vegetables (Dan. 1:12–15).

The crown of life (2:10). The wreath was made of perishable foliage like oak or laurel leaves (cf. 1 Cor. 9:25) and awarded to the victors in the Greek games (see the article "Athletics in the New Testament World"). The goddess Nike usually is depicted holding a wreath. Paul and Peter also mentioned that Christians will receive a wreath of eternal life at the Lord's coming (2 Tim. 4:8; 1 Pet. 5:4).

Pergamum (2:12). This city was founded on a hill thirteen hundred feet high, and on this acropolis Alexander's general Lysimachus stored a large treasure. His steward Philetaerus gained control after Lysimachus was defeated by Seleucus in 282 BC. Philetaerus adopted his nephews, and the oldest,

Eumenes I, succeeded him in 263 BC. During the years 263–133 BC Pergamum served as the capital of the Attalid Empire, named after Attalus I, Eumenes's son. In 133 BC Attalus III bestowed his kingdom on the Romans. Pliny the Elder called the city "the most famous place of Asia."[5] The Attalid city was constructed on three levels with the royal palaces, theater, and primary sanctuaries standing in the upper city. The most important temple was that to Athena Nikephoros ("victory-bearer"). The Roman city developed at the foot of the acropolis where a theater, stadium, and amphitheater stood. In 29 BC Asia's first imperial cult temple—the temple of Rome and Augustus—was dedicated here.

This inscription at Pergamum uses divine titles for the Roman emperor.

Although Ephesus later surpassed Pergamum in importance, Pergamum remained influential. The fourth imperial cult temple to Trajan, the remains of which still stand on the acropolis, was built in the early second century AD. Pergamum was famous as a healing center of Asclepius, the Greek god of medicine. Galen, antiquity's most famous physician, was born in Pergamum, and he gained his knowledge of the human body by treating injured gladiators. Within the temple of Serapis a church was built in the fifth century. A small Jewish community also existed in Pergamum.

Sharp, double-edged sword (2:12). The long *rhomphaia* was a sword used for piercing and cutting. Asia's governor held the right of the sword (*ius gladii*) in his province in representing the emperor and Roman senate. He had the sole responsibility for capital

Pergamum was a challenging city in which to be a Christian. It is described as the place "where Satan's throne is" (Rev. 2:13). One of the interpretations of Satan's throne is that it was the altar to Zeus at Pergamum. Shown here is the western side of the altar that has been reconstructed and restored (second century BC).

punishment and thus held the power of life and death over those in his jurisdiction. Pilate had a similar role in the death of Jesus (John 18:31; Acts 13:28).

Where Satan's throne is (2:13). Various interpretations have been suggested for this image: the altar of Zeus, the temple of Asclepius, even the acropolis's shape. Rome was the greatest enemy of the churches at this time, and the presence of the imperial cult temple in Pergamum made it a throne of satanic power.

Antipas, my faithful witness (2:13). The only Christian leader (other than John himself) named in Revelation, Antipas probably was an elder in the church. "Witness" is the Greek word *martys*, from which "martyr" was derived. Jesus was the first faithful witness to shed his blood (1:5; 3:14). Martyrdom is a major theme in Revelation (6:9; 11:7; 12:11; 17:6).

Teaching of Balaam (2:14). Balaam was the quintessential false prophet in the OT (cf. 2 Pet. 2:15; Jude 11). His greediness caused him to disobey God and assist the Moabite king Balak in his seduction of the Israelites to sexual immorality and idolatry (Num. 24:25–25:3). The teaching of the "Balaamites" was similar to that of the Nicolaitans.

Meat sacrificed to idols (2:14). Before meat was sold in the public marketplace (*macellum*), choice portions were sacrificed by priests to the gods and goddesses in the pagan temples. Philo decried Jewish participation in pagan feasts where such meat was eaten, and it became an issue for early Christians whether to eat such meat.[6] The Jerusalem Council instructed that idol meat not be eaten (Acts 15:29; 21:25). It was a major issue addressed by Paul in his letter written from Ephesus (see 1 Cor. 8:1–13; 10:19–33).

Hidden manna (2:17). God sustained the Israelites in the wilderness for forty years through the supernatural provision of manna (Exod. 16:14–31; Josh 5:12). An omer of manna was placed by Aaron in the ark as a memorial to be seen by future generations (Exod. 16:32–34). Hidden manna suggests a heavenly provision to be eaten at the future messianic banquet.

White stone, and on the stone a new name is inscribed (2:17). White stones had various uses, including as a token of admission and a means of voting. Whether this new name relates to the believer or to Jesus is unclear. Jesus is identified with several names at his return: Word of God, King of kings and Lord of lords (Rev. 19:13, 16).

Thyatira (2:18). This city was situated on a fertile plain in Lydia at a strategic crossroads linking Sardis, Pergamum, Smyrna, and the province of Bithynia. Seleucus I founded a military colony here in the early third century BC. Control of the city switched among the Galatians, Seleucids, and Attalids until the Romans arrived in 129 BC. Helius Pythius Tyrimnaeus Apollo was the city's primary deity. A shrine of Sibyl Sambathe, an oriental deity, was located outside the city at a sacred precinct of the Chaldeans. Numerous trade guilds flourished in this important commercial center, and a Thyatiran woman named Lydia was representing the purple-dyers in Philippi when Paul met her (Acts 16:14). A Jewish inscription mentions the presence of a *sabbateion* ("Sabbath building") in the city. Archaeologists, however, have never located it. A local cult for Rome and Augustus was organized before 2 BC. By AD 200 Thyatira had many Christians who were associated with Montanus and his teachings.

Son of God (2:18). This expression is used only here in Revelation. The Anointed One is twice called "Son" in Ps. 2:7, 12. Augustus adopted for himself the title "son of God," as did other emperors, and this title often was used on imperial inscriptions in Asia.

Feet are like fine bronze (2:18). Only here and in 1:15 is *chalkolibanos* used in Greek literature. Although the KJV translates this word as "brass" (an alloy of copper with zinc), "bronze" (an alloy of copper with tin) is a better translation. After being refined in a smelting furnace, bronze becomes hard and durable.

Jezebel, who calls herself a prophetess (2:20). "Jezebel" is the code name for a false teacher who advocated compromise, suggesting that Christians could eat food sacrificed to idols and commit sexual immorality without spiritual consequences. Jezebel was the quintessential false prophetess/queen who introduced Baal worship to the Israelites (1 Kings 16:31–32) and threatened Elijah (1 Kings 19:2).

Sickbed (2:22). This Hebrew idiom suggests punishing an individual with illness (cf. 1 Macc. 1:5; Jdt. 8:3). The Greek word *klinē* can also be translated as "couch." Diners reclined at their banquets on such dining couches, and upon these couches acts of sexual immorality sometimes occurred as part of the after-dinner entertainment (see the article "Banquets and Meals in the Greco-Roman World").

Will rule them with an iron scepter; he will shatter them like pottery (2:27). This is the only clear OT quotation in Revelation, from Ps. 2:9. The authority granted to the Christians will be exercised at Jesus's return when he strikes the nations with his iron scepter (Rev. 19:15).

Morning star (2:28). This image is drawn from Balaam's third oracle (Num. 24:17), which also prophesied that a scepter would rise out of Israel, both of which are fulfilled in Jesus (Rev. 12:5).

Sardis (3:1). This important city was located in the fertile Hermus River valley east of Smyrna. It became famous as the capital of Lydia. The Lydian king Croesus (reigned 560–546 BC) became rich from gold panned from the Pactolus River that flowed through the city. Cyrus the Great captured Sardis in 546 BC and made it the capital of Persia's westernmost satrapy and terminus

In spite of their reputation of being a vibrant church in the wealthy, powerful, pagan city of Sardis, the Sardis believers were warned of unexpected judgment if they did not change their ways. Shown here are the impressive restored remains of the entrance to the Roman gymnasium complex at Sardis. Activities related to the imperial cult may have been held here (second century AD).

of the Royal Road. Alexander the Great captured Sardis in 334 BC, whereupon it became the western capital of the Seleucid Empire from 281 to 190 BC. The Attalids of Pergamum ruled until the Roman annexation of Asia in 129 BC. Sardis attempted to build Asia's second imperial cult temple in AD 26, but the Roman senate decided that the city lacked sufficient financial resources to maintain it. The largest Jewish synagogue ever found outside Israel was discovered in Sardis. It dates from the fourth to fifth centuries AD, although a Jewish community is known from the second century BC. Melito was the well-known bishop of the city in the second century AD.

Like a thief (3:3). This simile was also used by Jesus (Matt. 24:42–44), Paul (1 Thess. 5:2), and Peter (2 Pet. 3:10) and suggests the element of surprise and lack of readiness that unbelievers will experience at the time of Jesus's return.

Walk with me in white . . . dressed in white clothes (3:4–5). White is a metaphor used to portray moral and ritual purity (cf. 3:18). The diners at the messianic feast were to be sealed and dressed in white.[7] The victors in heaven seen by John were wearing white robes (6:11; 7:9, 13).

Erase his name from the book of life (3:5). This book was the register of God's people (Exod. 32:32–33; Dan. 12:1). To have one's name erased meant to lose the privileges of his covenant. David pleaded that the names of his enemies be erased from the book of life (Ps. 69:28). Male citizens of Greek cities were enrolled in a public register, and those who committed capital crimes lost their citizenship and faced subsequent erasure from the public roll.

Philadelphia (3:7). Located thirty miles southeast of Sardis, Philadelphia was founded as a military colony with Macedonian soldiers either by Eumenes II (reigned 197–159 BC) or his brother Attalus II (reigned 159–138 BC). When the Romans tried to turn Attalus against Eumenes, he stayed loyal and earned the nickname Philadelphus ("brother-loving"). The city's name thus describes the love between these brothers. According to an inscription dating from around 100 BC, cultic altars for at least ten gods and goddesses existed. A priesthood for the imperial cult began to function as early as 27/26 BC; however, the first imperial cult temple was not constructed until AD 214 when Caracalla visited the city. A temple, theater, and stadium were built on the city's acropolis, but there are few archaeological remains of these monuments today.

Key of David (3:7). This symbol of authority was taken from the account of the prideful steward Shebna, who lost the right to the key of David to a more faithful servant, Eliakim (Isa. 22:15–22). The keys of the kingdom were promised by Jesus to his followers (Matt. 16:19).

Pillar in the temple of my God (3:12). Greco-Roman temples were supported by pillars capped with capitals of the Doric, Ionic, or Corinthian orders. Columns were of two types: monoliths or drums. Monoliths consisted of one piece of marble or granite, while drum columns were built of multiple round drums connected by a metal peg or wooden dowel. Because of earthquakes, the foundations of temples rested on charcoal beds covered with fleeces to provide flexibility during seismic activity. The coins of the seven cities featured illustrations of many of their multicolumned temples. The temple of Artemis was famous for its forest of 127 columns.

I will write on him the name of my God (3:12). The Doric pillars of Ephesus's Prytaneion are inscribed with the names of members of the town council and league of Curetes who served at the Artemis festivals. These forty-six lists, dating from the first century AD, name hundreds of Ephesus's elite citizens.

Laodicea (3:14). Situated in the Lycus River valley about one hundred miles east of Ephesus, Laodicea was ten miles west of Colossae and six miles south of Hierapolis. Located in southwestern Phrygia and founded around 260 BC, Laodicea was named by Antiochus II after his wife, Laodice. Zeus was the city's main deity, and originally it was called Diospolis ("city of Zeus"). In 188 BC its control passed from the Seleucids to the Attalids. After 129 BC it became a judicial center of the Romans. Jews were brought to Phrygia as colonists in the second century BC, and the Roman governor Flaccus confiscated gold here in 62 BC that was bound for Jerusalem to pay the temple tax. Laodicea was devastated by earthquakes in AD 17 and 60 and subsequently rebuilt. The site finally was abandoned after another earthquake in the seventh century AD. Two theaters stand on the site's northern side; a stadium, bath, and bouleterion (council house) remain on its southern side. Excavations beginning in 2003 have rapidly uncovered the ancient city with restorations following. The remains of twelve churches have been discovered, with the primary basilica located east of Temple A.

Lukewarm, and neither hot nor cold (3:16). This reference often is taken to be a reference to the city's water system. The white travertines of Hierapolis were visible to the north, the product of the calcareous thermal springs

The unpalatable lukewarm water received by the residents of Laodicea was used to illustrate the Lord's response to the church's lukewarm deeds. Shown here are the remains of water pipes excavated at ancient Laodicea.

around that city. However, this hot water was never channeled to Laodicea. Above Colossae rose Mount Cadmus, often covered with snow and whose snowmelt provided cold water to the local Lycus River. Laodicea's water system, still visible today, channeled its supply from underground springs to the south through pipes, an aqueduct, and two water towers to users in the city.

I'm rich; I have become wealthy (3:17). The boast of the Laodiceans is the same as Ephraim's (Hosea 12:8). After the earthquake in AD 60 Laodicea was the only city in Asia to refuse Roman aid to rebuild, determining that it was sufficiently wealthy to recover with its own financial resources.

Shameful nakedness (3:18). This observation is ironic because the local textile factories manufactured a sleeved tunic and a hooded cloak that were exported even to Rome. Such a thriving industry was another reason for the city's prosperity.

Ointment to spread on your eyes (3:18). Laodicea was the home of a medical school, and one of its graduates, Demosthenes Philalethes, was a renowned ophthalmologist. He wrote a textbook on the healing of eyes. Eye salves made of zinc and alum, common around Laodicea, were marketed by local doctors.

The Throne in Heaven (4:1–11)

Throne in heaven and someone was seated on it (4:2). During his second "in the Spirit" experience John sees a heavenly throne occupied by a divine figure, similar to one seen by Isaiah (Isa. 6:1).[8]

Appearance of jasper and carnelian stone. A rainbow that had the appearance of an emerald (4:3). Jasper is an opaque red, brown, or yellow color, while carnelian (or sard) is translucent, ruby red, and highly valued for making jewelry. Jasper and emerald were stones on the high priest's breastplate (Exod. 28:18, 20). Ezekiel also compared the heavenly throne to a sapphire (Ezek. 1:26).

Twenty-four elders (4:4). Twenty-four divisions of priests rotated through their temple ministry (1 Chron. 24:3–19), and twenty-four groups of singers prophesied with their instruments (1 Chron. 25:1–31). The sum of the twelve tribes and the twelve apostles is twenty-four (Rev. 21:12, 14).

Sea of glass, similar to crystal (4:6). The Greeks believed that crystals formed like clear ice, a fact underlying the Greek OT translation of Ezek. 1:22. Crystal drinking bowls and cups were luxury items for the Romans.

Four living creatures (4:6–8). Their description is drawn from imagery in Ezekiel (Ezek. 1:10; 10:14) and Isaiah (Isa. 6:2). Winged creatures appear often in ancient Near Eastern mythology, and statues of such figures dating back to 1200–800 BC have been discovered at Carchemish, Aleppo, and Nimrud.

Holy, holy, holy, Lord God, the Almighty (4:8). The seraphim gave a similar acclamation to one another (Isa. 6:3). "Lord God Almighty" is the creator of the world (Amos 4:13). This liturgical formula was used by Clement in his letter to the Corinthians.[9]

Fall down before the one seated on the throne and worship (4:10). Ancient worship involved bowing and kneeling. Both the psalmist (Ps. 95:6) and Paul (Eph. 3:14) bowed and knelt before their God and Father. The Jewish delegation to Rome led by Philo refused to bow before Caligula in Rome in AD 39/40, thus offending the emperor.

They cast their crowns before the throne (4:10). A vassal would present a crown to a superior ruler to indicate submission. After the Parthian king Tiridates was defeated in AD 63, he laid his crown before Nero's effigy. Titus received a golden crown from the Parthian king Vlogeses I after his victory in Judea in AD 70.

The Scroll and the Lamb (5:1–14)

Scroll with writing on both sides, sealed with seven seals (5:1). A scroll with writing on both sides is called an opisthograph (cf. Ezek. 2:9–10). There were two types of written documents in antiquity: parchments and

John was instructed, "Write on a scroll what you see and send it to the seven churches" (Rev. 1:11). Scrolls were made from parchment, vellum, or papyrus. Ink was made from charcoal and soot. In order to secure the scroll, a string was tied around it and a lump of clay was placed across the string and pressed with a seal that left an impression. To open the scroll required breaking the clay lump, known as a bulla. Pictured here is a Roman bronze pen and inkpot (first century AD) and a modern scroll tied with string and sealed with a lead bulla (Byzantine period).

scrolls (2 Tim. 4:13) (see the article "Ancient Letter Writing"). Parchment (from the Latin word *pergamena,* referring to its source, Pergamum) was made from the skins of sheep and goats. Scrolls were made of papyrus from the Nile Delta. Parchment was more expensive than papyrus, but its greater durability and erasability caused it to become the predominant book material by the fourth century AD. A scroll with seven seals was discovered among a number of papyri in caves north of Jericho in 1962. It contained a legal document dating to 335 BC.

The Lion from the tribe of Judah, the Root of David, has conquered (5:5). The Lamb has two messianic titles: lion of Judah (Gen. 49:9; cf. *4 Ezra* 12.31–32) and root of Jesse (LXX Isa. 11:1; cf. Rom. 15:12). His victory authorizes him to open the seven seals on the scroll.

Slaughtered lamb (5:6). Unblemished lambs were ritually sacrificed at Passover with their throats cut. John identified this Lamb's purpose from the paschal stigma on its neck. "Lamb" is Jesus's most common name in Revelation, used twenty-eight times.

Harp and golden bowls filled with incense, which are the prayers of the saints (5:8). David played the harp (1 Sam. 16:23) and sang his psalms accompanied by it (superscriptions to Pss. 4; 61). The Levites played harps while prophesying and praising God (1 Chron. 25:3). Incense censers fit in the palm of the hand. The leaders of Israel's twelve tribes used golden censers as part of the dedication of the altar (e.g., Num. 7:14, 20), and similar bowls were used in the temple (2 Chron. 4:22). Incense as a simile for prayer is seen also in Ps. 141:2.

You purchased people for God by your blood (5:9). "Purchased" (*agorazō*) is a term of the agora, or public marketplace, where slaves were bought and sold. John used the metaphor of the slave auction to describe Christ's redemption of his people (cf. 14:4). Paul and Peter likewise used this redemptive metaphor (1 Cor. 7:23; 1 Pet. 1:18–19).

From every tribe and language and people and nation (5:9). Despite the OT's focus on Israel as God's covenant people, hints of salvation's universal nature were already given in texts such as Dan. 7:14, where all peoples worshiped God. Four more times Revelation reiterates the universal scope of salvation regardless of a person's ethnic identity (7:9; 11:9; 13:7; 14:6).

Priests (5:10). All religions in the Roman Empire, including Judaism, had a priesthood to conduct ritual ceremonies. But because the early church had no temple for priests to offer regular sacrifices (cf. Heb. 9:11–12), society regarded its members as atheists. At Polycarp's trial the Roman governor asked the bishop to forsake his fellow believers by saying, "Away with the atheists!"[10] Revelation emphasizes that all believers are priests (cf. 1:6; 20:6), as does Peter (1 Pet. 2:9).

The First Six Seals (6:1–17)

Seven seals (6:1). A close literary connection exists between the first six seals and Jesus's prediction of events to be fulfilled in Jerusalem within a generation (Matt. 24:3–10, 29; Mark 13:3–13, 24–25; Luke 21:7–12, 25–26). These included false Christs, wars, famines, earthquakes, persecutions, and heavenly signs. This correlation suggests a specific historical period: from the ascension of Jesus to the fall of Jerusalem (30–70). The Jewish historian Josephus recorded similar signs accompanying the fall of Jerusalem.[11]

White horse (6:2). The four horsemen of the apocalypse is a trope familiar from films and works of art that feature dystopian themes. The imagery of riders on colored horses is likewise found in Zech. 1:8–11. The colors of the horses are symbolic: white for victory, red for blood, black for famine, and pale (gray) for death.

Its rider held a bow (6:2). The Parthians were noted for their cavalry and thus feared by the Romans. However, their threat was minimized after a peace was secured in AD 63. In Greek mythology Apollo is often depicted with a bow as the god who inspires prophecy.

Large sword (6:4). In the OT the sword is often depicted as an instrument of slaughter (Ezek. 21:3, 15) and with famine and pestilence as a threefold means of divine judgment (2 Chron. 20:9; Jer. 14:12).

Set of scales (6:5). The balance depicted was the steelyard type that used only one pan and a counterpoise. Merchants used balance scales to weigh coins, metal, and spices (Isa. 46:6). Scales also were a metaphor for measuring human lives (Ps. 62:9).

A quart of wheat . . . and three quarts of barley for a denarius (6:6). Famine is depicted as producing inflated prices for grain products, with the cost of wheat eleven to sixteen times higher than normal. Egypt produced much of the grain used in Rome. In AD 51 a famine produced a grain shortage, and a hostile crowd tried to fix the blame on the emperor Claudius.

Do not harm the oil and the wine (6:6). Because olive trees and vineyards took such a long time to grow, they often were spared destruction during times of war. An overproduction of wine and lack of grain prompted Domitian in AD 92 to order that one-half of all

Parthian horseman warrior (first to third century AD).

vineyards be cut down. However, the outrage from the provinces caused the emperor never to implement his edict.

Its rider's name was Death, and Hades followed (6:8). The release of the pale horse triggers a fourfold judgment—sword, famine, wild beasts, and plague—similar to that prophesied earlier against idolatrous Jerusalem (Ezek. 14:21). Thanatos was the personification of death in Greek mythology. As the god of the underworld, Hades also gave his name to the realm of the dead.

Killed just as they had been (6:11). Martyrdom was a reality for the early Christians, with Stephen and James being the first victims (Acts 7:58–60; 12:2). Until Nero's reign Christianity was viewed as a sect of Judaism. But this changed in 64 when Nero made Christians a scapegoat for the fire in Rome. In the persecution that followed, Peter and Paul were both martyred in Rome. After passing through many of the seven churches and writing letters to them, Ignatius, bishop of Antioch, was thrown to the beasts in the Roman Colosseum in 110.

Sun turned black like sackcloth made of hair (6:12). Such heavenly signs were also a feature of OT prophecy (Isa. 13:10; Joel 2:10–11) as well as Jesus's prophecy of his return (Matt. 24:29). The ancients were very superstitious, and the Romans viewed such wonders as omens of divine wrath. Ancient historians such as Tacitus, Suetonius, and Josephus frequently mentioned prodigies that accompanied significant historical events.

Moon became like blood (6:12). An ensanguinal moon was prophesied to announce the day of the Lord (Joel 2:31). This lunar spectacle occurs during a total eclipse when the moon becomes a deep copper color.

144,000 and the Great Multitude (7:1–17)

Seal the servants of our God on their foreheads (7:3). Revelation mentions two marks: the seal of the living God for believers and the mark of the beast for the unrepentant. The observance of Passover was to be a sign on the foreheads of the Israelites for perpetuity (Exod. 13:9, 16). Paul taught that believers were marked with the seal of the Holy Spirit (Eph. 1:13; 4:30).

144,000 sealed from every tribe of the Israelites (7:4). The number of those sealed was twelve thousand from each tribe of Israel (12 × 12,000 = 144,000). Various lists of the twelve tribes are found in the OT (Gen. 49:2–28; Num. 1:5–15; Deut. 33:6–25). While Reuben as the firstborn typically begins these lists, John lists Judah first because Jesus was the promised son of David (5:5). Another difference is the inclusion of Manasseh while his younger brother Ephraim and Dan are omitted. The reason for their omission is unclear but perhaps related to their sin (Hosea 8:11) and idolatry (Judg. 18:30).

Vast multitude (7:9). Tacitus and Clement both wrote about great multitudes of Christians who lost their lives during Nero's persecution.[12]

With palm branches in their hands (7:9). The victors hold palm branches as a symbol of their triumph and immortality (cf. 2 Esd. 2:45–46). The palm branch also symbolized victory for the Jews (1 Macc. 13:51). Nike, the Greek goddess of victory, usually was depicted with a palm branch in her hand.

Great tribulation (7:14). Both Daniel (Dan. 12:1) and Jesus (Matt. 24:21) predicted that the saints would endure great tribulation in the end times.

Washed their robes (7:14). Fullers washed clothing using ammonia from degraded urine collected in pots in front of their shops. The washing here is a spiritual consecration similar to what the Israelites did at Mount Sinai before the law was given (Exod. 19:14).

They will no longer hunger; they will no longer thirst (7:16). Isaiah prophesied that one of the restorative benefits of the salvation brought by the servant of the Lord was that Jews and gentiles would never hunger or thirst again (Isa. 49:10).

Seventh Seal and First Six Trumpets (8:1–9:21)

Seven trumpets (8:2). Trumpets made of metal or ram's horn (shofar) were used for various purposes in ancient Israel: warning (Ezek. 33:6), call to battle (2 Sam. 2:28), and announcing feasts (Lev. 23:23–25). Sabbaths were announced with a trumpet from the southwestern corner of the Temple Mount, called the "Place of Trumpeting." The blowing of the trumpet will signal the day of the Lord (Joel 2:1; Zeph. 1:16) and announce the return of Jesus (Matt. 24:31; 1 Thess. 4:16).

Golden incense burner (8:3). Altars functioned as stone platforms upon which incense and animal offerings were made to gods and goddesses. The wilderness tabernacle and the Jerusalem temple had both an altar of burnt offering and an altar of incense (Exod. 30:27–28; 1 Chron. 22:1; 28:18). Zechariah burned incense on the temple's incense altar (Luke 1:9–11).

Incense to offer (8:3). Incense was presented to Jesus by the magi (Matt. 2:11). Like frankincense and myrrh, incense was a product of southern Arabia and among the luxury trade items brought by merchants to Rome (Rev. 18:13). The Romans periodically tried to make Christians such as Polycarp take a loyalty oath by burning incense to the gods and to the health of the emperor.[13]

Great star, blazing like a torch, fell from heaven (8:10). Falling stars are apocalyptic cosmic signs (6:13; 9:1; 12:4). At Edom's judgment the starry host would fall (Isa. 34:4). According to Jesus, a sign of the last days is that stars will fall from the sky (Matt. 24:29; Mark 13:25).

Wormwood (8:11). Also called bitterwood, *Artemesia absinthium* is a perennial herb with small yellow flowers that grows in the eastern Mediterranean. Wormwood contains thujone, a nonlethal toxin that causes intoxication, hallucinations, and convulsions.

Abyss (9:1). This subterranean prison of evil spirits became the destination for the disobedient angels of Noah's day (Gen. 6:1–4). This well-known Jewish tradition is repeated in the NT (2 Pet. 2:4; Jude 6).[14] After his death Jesus descended into the realm of the dead—the Abyss (Rom. 10:7, quoting LXX Deut. 30:13). The Plutonium in Hierapolis claimed to provide entrance to the underworld ruled by Pluto, also called Hades.

Smoke from a great furnace (9:2). The smoke that arose from Sodom and Gomorrah's destruction resembled that from a furnace (Gen. 19:28). Jesus spoke of the "fiery furnace" when speaking about hell (Matt. 13:42, 50).

Locusts (9:3). The winged *Acrididae* was God's eighth plague of judgment against the Egyptians (Exod. 10:15). If Israel did not repent, God would command a locust plague to devour the land (2 Chron. 7:13). Swarms of locusts would leave devastated land in their wake (cf. Nah. 3:16).

A scorpion when it stings someone (9:5). Scorpions were a divine means of punishing the wicked (Sir. 39:30). While the venom of the eastern Mediterranean species was painful and toxic enough to torture its victims for five months, it was not lethal.

Appearance of the locusts was like horses prepared for battle (9:7). Locusts had the proverbial appearance of horses galloping like cavalry, and they made a noise like chariots (Joel 2:4–5).

Angel of the abyss; his name in Hebrew is Abaddon, and in Greek has the name Apollyon (9:11). In the OT Abaddon, meaning "destruction," is connected with Sheol, meaning "death" (Job 26:6; 28:22; Prov. 27:20). "Abaddon" usually is translated in the Greek OT by *apōleia*, with Apollyon representing its personal form.

Great river Euphrates (9:14). After the Jordan, the Euphrates is the most mentioned river in the Bible. Its source is in eastern Turkey, and the river courses 1,780 miles into the Persian Gulf. It is also called "the great river" (Gen. 15:18; Josh. 1:4). The Euphrates was the eastern boundary of the Roman Empire in the first century AD.

Mounted troops (9:16). Rome's enemy Parthia was known for its armored horses and riders. Parthian soldiers used a flexible but strong scale armor to protect themselves and their horses. The Parthian cavalry handily defeated the Romans at Carrhae (Haran) in 53 BC. The Romans used their mounted cavalry in Judea to quell the Jewish Revolt (AD 66–70).

Did not repent of the works of their hands (9:20). John offers three lists of vices (9:20; 21:8; 22:15). These resemble those found in other Jewish literature (e.g., Wis. 14:22–29) and in Paul's letters (cf. Rom. 1:29–31; Gal. 5:19–21). Violation of the first two commandments, which prohibited the worship of other gods and the making of idolatrous images (Exod. 20:3–4), was humanity's greatest sin. Greek and Roman religions were polytheistic (Acts 17:16), and the Ephesians worshiped some thirty other gods and goddesses besides Artemis.

Sorceries (9:21). The word "pharmacy" is derived from the Greek word *pharmakon* used here. The *pharm-* word group is used exclusively in Revelation (cf. 18:23; 21:8; 22:15) except for Gal. 5:20. See the article "Magic in the New Testament World."

The Angel and the Little Scroll (10:1–11)

His legs were like pillars of fire (10:1). The angel's appearance resembles that of the legendary Colossus of Rhodes. This 110-foot-tall statue depicted the sun god Helios. Although it was destroyed by an earthquake in 227 BC, this wonder of the ancient world was known by its depiction on Rhodian coins of this period.

Little scroll opened in his hand (10:2). While the form of the Greek word used here is a diminutive, there need not be a distinction among the scrolls seen by John. The scroll's small size is mentioned only in relation to the angel's large hand, and "scroll" and "little scroll" are used interchangeably in the chapter (10:8, 9, 10).

Seal up what the seven thunders said (10:4). Daniel sealed up his visions to be revealed later (Dan. 8:26; 9:24; 12:4). This is the only vision in Revelation that John is told to seal up.

Take and eat it; it will be bitter in your stomach, but it will be sweet as honey in your mouth (10:9). At his prophetic commissioning Ezekiel was also commanded to eat a scroll (Ezek. 2:8; 3:1). His scroll, like John's, was sweet like honey in his mouth but became sour after being swallowed (Ezek. 3:3).

As John's vision continues, a mighty angel appears, holding a scroll. Scrolls are significant in Revelation because they reveal God's redemptive plan. Scrolls were made from parchment, vellum, or papyrus like the one shown here from the second century AD.

Two Witnesses and the Seventh Trumpet (11:1–19)

A measuring reed like a rod . . . measure the temple of God (11:1). See the article "The Jerusalem Temple."

Ezekiel also received a vision of worshipers in the temple (Ezek. 8:1–11:25). Reeds served as ancient measuring rods, and their length was either three or six cubits (five or ten feet). To measure the new temple seen in his vision, Ezekiel used a rod six cubits long (Ezek. 40:3, 5).

Trample the holy city for forty-two months (11:2). Trampling the holy place was a common theme in OT apocalyptic texts (LXX Isa. 63:18; Dan. 8:13; Zech. 12:3). Jesus also prophesied that Jerusalem would be trampled (Luke 21:24). When Titus and his Roman armies entered the city in AD 70, these prophecies were fulfilled. The forty-two months is equal to the 1,260 days that the two witnesses prophesied as well as to the period of three years and six months of judgment prophesied by Elijah against Ahab and Israel (Luke 4:25; James 5:17). Because the Jewish calendar is lunar, each month has thirty days.

Two witnesses . . . dressed in sackcloth (11:3). While the witnesses are never specifically identified, their activities are done in the spirit of Moses and Elijah. They call down fire (cf. 2 Kings 1:10–14), prevent the heavens from raining (1 Kings 17:1), turn the waters into blood (Exod. 7:17–21), and send plagues (Exod. 5:3; 9:14). Sackcloth typically was black and made from goat's hair (cf. Rev. 6:12). It was worn by mourners as a sign of repentance by those seeking to lessen God's judgment (2 Kings 19:2; 1 Chron. 21:16; Neh. 9:1).

Two olive trees (11:4). Zechariah also saw a vision of olive trees and was told that they were the Lord's two anointed servants (Zech. 4:3, 14). Olive trees produced the oil used as fuel in ancient lamps, especially the menorah in the temple (see Rev. 1:20). The Levites also used it for preparing the anointing oil (Exod. 35:28).

Figuratively is called Sodom and Egypt (11:8). Sodom was the proverbial city of wickedness destroyed by God with burning sulfur (Gen. 19:24). Until being delivered by God, Israel was oppressed in Egypt, thus making it a symbol of bondage (Exod. 3:7–9). Ezekiel identified both Sodom and Egypt as godless places where Israel had turned away from God (Ezek. 16:26, 46–56).

Not permit their bodies to be put into a tomb (11:9). The failure to bury a corpse was a great insult in antiquity (cf. 1 Sam. 31:10–13; Jer. 16:4). During the revolt against Rome by Mithridates in 88 BC this Pontic king ordered that the bodies of the tens of thousands massacred in Asia be left unburied. Any Greeks who attempted to bury the Roman dead would be punished. During the siege of Jerusalem in AD 70 the Zealots did not allow the burial of the Jewish dead and killed those who tried to bury their relatives.

Ark of his covenant (11:19). The ark of the covenant was the main fixture in the wilderness tabernacle and the temple of Solomon (cf. Heb. 9:4). When the temple was destroyed by the Babylonians in 586 BC, the ark and its contents were lost. When the Second Temple was rebuilt after the exile, the ark was no longer in the holy of holies.

John sees the ark of the covenant in God's heavenly temple. Shown here is a Bar Kokhba coin, AD 133, depicting the Jerusalem temple with a view inside to the ark of the covenant.

The Woman, Male Child, and Dragon (12:1–17)

Woman clothed with the sun (12:1). Israel was prophesied as pregnant and giving birth to a son (Isa. 66:7). Mary was the virgin Israelite chosen to give birth to the promised Messiah (Luke 1:27). Roman Catholic scholarship often interprets this woman who gives birth in Rev. 12 as Mary. Above Ephesus today there is a shrine called the House of Mary. A late tradition claims that Jesus's mother accompanied John to Ephesus (cf. John 19:25–27). However, early church traditions suggest that Mary lived and died in Jerusalem, with her burial place being the Church of the Sepulchre of Mary in the Kidron Valley.

Great fiery red dragon having seven heads and ten horns (12:3). The dragon, the beast out of the sea (13:1), and the great prostitute (17:3, 7) all had ten horns, a symbol of complete power.

Dragon . . . might devour her child (12:4). The account parodies the Hellenistic combat myth of Leto, Apollo, and Python. Python the dragon pursued the goddess Leto, who was pregnant with Apollo. Leto fled to an island to give birth to Apollo, who killed Python. Artemis, the daughter of Leto and twin sister of Apollo, traditionally was born just outside Ephesus. One of her attributes was that of a virgin who protected women in childbirth.

She gave birth to a Son, a male who is going to rule all nations with an iron rod (12:5). Isaiah prophesied that a virgin would give birth to a son named Immanuel (Isa. 7:14). David likewise spoke of an anointed Son who would rule the nations with an iron scepter (Ps. 2:7–9). The male child clearly is Jesus the Messiah, but his earthly life is passed over in Revelation with only his ascension being mentioned (cf. Acts 1:9).

A seven-headed dragon appears in John's vision (Rev. 12:3) and is later identified as Satan. Shown here is a shell carving (ca. 1450 BC) that depicts a seven-headed monster with flames shooting from its back. An ancient Mesopotamian god kneels before the fearsome creature, ready to do battle.

Michael . . . fought against the dragon (12:7). Michael is the archangel and great prince of the Jews who helped Daniel (Dan. 10:21; 12:1–2). He disputed with the devil over the body of Moses (Jude 9) and is numbered among the seven archangels.[15]

Great dragon . . . ancient serpent, who is called the devil and Satan (12:9). The devil is formally introduced here, although previously he was mentioned as Satan (2:9, 13, 24; 3:9). The dragon's demise is portrayed using a similar series of names (20:2). In the Greek OT the word *diabolos* ("devil") translates the Hebrew *satan*, which means "adversary." The Greek god of healing, Asclepius, usually was depicted holding a staff around which a serpent was coiled.

Accuser of our brothers and sisters . . . has been thrown down (12:10). Satan is portrayed as the one who accused Job and the high priest Joshua before God (Job 1:9–11; Zech. 3:1). During his ministry Jesus saw Satan fall (Luke 10:17–19).

Two wings of a great eagle, so that she could fly from the serpent's presence to her place in the wilderness (12:14). Israel's exodus through the wilderness also was on eagles' wings (Exod. 19:4). Jesus warned his followers to flee Jerusalem before the Romans surrounded it (Matt. 24:16; Mark 13:14). An early tradition holds that the Jewish believers fled to Pella before Jerusalem's fall.

Time, times, and half a time (12:14). This is the same time period for the fulfillment of Daniel's vision that he asked the angelic interpreter about (Dan. 12:7). It is also identical to the forty-two months/1,260 days mentioned previously during which the two witnesses would prophesy and the woman would be protected (Rev. 11:2–3; 12:6).

River that the dragon had spewed from his mouth (12:16). An Israelite traditional myth concerned God's triumph over a sea monster named Leviathan, often translated as "dragon" in the Greek OT. Job 41:1–34 provides the fullest description of this primeval beast. Asaph also exalted that God had crushed the heads of Leviathan (Ps. 74:14; LXX: "dragon").

War against the rest of her offspring (12:17). After the fall of Adam and Eve, God told the serpent that the woman's offspring would crush his head, while the serpent would only strike the offspring's heel (Gen. 3:15). The Greek word *sperma* ("offspring, seed") in the NT can refer in the singular to Jesus (John 7:42) or can be plural in meaning, as here, referring to the collective people of God.

The Beasts out of the Sea and the Earth (13:1–18)

Beast coming up out of the sea (13:1). Daniel's vision of four beasts likewise portrays them arising from the sea, and his fourth beast with ten horns devoured the other three (Dan. 7:3–7). Rome traditionally is viewed as the fourth beast.[16] The beast's seven heads symbolize rulers, while the ten horns symbolize their client kings. Both Ephesus and Smyrna were ports on the Aegean Sea. Ephesus was the first port of landing when a new governor arrived from Rome.

One of its heads appeared to be fatally wounded, but its fatal wound was healed (13:3). The death and healing of one of the beast's heads mimics the death and resurrection of the Lamb (5:6) and the two witnesses (11:7–11). After Nero's suicide in AD 68, an urban legend arose that the emperor would return to life—the Nero *redivivus* myth. Within years of Nero's death three impostors arose who claimed that they were the emperor returned to life.

All those who live on the earth will worship it (13:8). Emperor worship was a political and spiritual reality of life in the seven cities of Asia. Greek residents viewed the living emperor as the empire's savior and lord. In the first century, imperial cult temples stood in Pergamum, Smyrna, and Ephesus; cult sanctuaries stood in most other cities. A city privileged to host an imperial cult temple was called a *neōkoros* ("guardian of the temple" [Acts 19:35]). Cities with this honor boasted about it in inscriptions and depicted these temples on their coins.

Many Roman emperors were deified upon their deaths and temples erected for their worship. The archaeological remains shown here are from the temple of Augustus at Pisidian Antioch in Turkey, built in the early first century AD.

If anyone has ears to hear, let him listen (13:9). This exhortation resembles the call to hear at the end of each of the seven messages. Its language warning of captivity and killing in 13:10 is drawn from Jer. 15:2.

This calls (13:10). This is the first of four exhortations (*hōde* sayings) to the Christian audience: the first exhorts them to endurance and faithfulness, the second to calculate the beast's name (13:18), the third also calls for endurance (14:12), and the fourth calls for understanding John's vision of the seven heads and ten horns (17:9).

Another beast coming up out of the earth (13:11). The second beast represents the priesthood of the imperial cult in Asia. The leader of its league (*koinon*) of 150 delegates, the leading citizens of the province, was the Asiarch (cf. Acts 19:31), who also served as the cult's chief priest. Augustus formed a choir of thirty-six of Asia's elite to sing praises to him in Pergamum's imperial cult temple.

It also performs great signs (13:13). The second beast promoted worship of the first beast through deceptive wonders. Trickery was commonly practiced by sorcerers in antiquity, and special-effects machines producing thunder and lightning were used in theatrical productions.

Image of the beast (13:14). Nebuchadnezzar likewise commanded that his image be erected for worship (Dan. 3:1–17). Statues (*eikōn*) of the emperor were ubiquitous around the Roman Empire. He was depicted in three main ways: (1) in his military armor as leader of the Roman legions, (2) naked as a Greek god, or (3) in a Roman toga as the ideal Roman citizen.

Permitted to give breath to the image of the beast, so that the image of the beast could . . . speak (13:15). Statues speaking oracular utterances were known. Alexander of Abonuteichos erected an image of the serpent Glaucon-Asclepius that had a movable mouth and concealed speaking tubes. The "Talking Statues" show in Las Vegas attempts to replicate this phenomenon.

No one can buy or sell unless he has the mark (13:17). The mark of the beast on the right hand and forehead parodies the seal of the 144,000 (7:3). The mark's position parallels that of the phylacteries worn by Jews, a practice reflecting God's command that his word be bound on the hand and forehead (Exod. 13:9; Deut. 6:8).

Calculate the number of the beast . . . 666 (13:18). Isopsephy (Heb. *gematria*) reflects the ancient practice in the Greek and Hebrew languages of calculating names using numbers. This was possible because the letters of these languages also represented numbers. Examples of isopsephy have been found in graffiti at Pompeii and Smyrna; for example, a man loves the girl whose number is 731 (Anthousa) or 1,308 (Tyche). Nero's name in Hebrew, NERON KAISAR, equals six hundred sixty-six (not 6-6-6). The alternate reading "616" in some ancient manuscripts is derived from dropping the letter *nun* (transliterated as "N") at the end of NERON.

The Lamb, 144,000, and Two Harvests (14:1–20)

Mount Zion (14:1). The city of David was founded on Mount Zion (2 Sam. 5:7), and upon its mount Solomon built the temple as the dwelling place of God (Ps. 50:2; 65:1). Zion also became a metonym for Jerusalem (Ps. 147:12; Isa. 33:20). Zion later was understood as the heavenly Jerusalem inhabited by God, the angels, and the saints (Heb. 12:22–23).

His Father's name written on their foreheads (14:1). When God determined to destroy the ungodly residents of Jerusalem, he sent an angel to mark the foreheads of those who lamented its sins. These were spared from divine wrath, while those who did not receive the mark were slaughtered (Ezek. 9:3–7).

Firstfruits for God and the Lamb (14:4). "Firstfruits" originally was an agricultural term (Exod. 23:16) that later connoted Israel as the spiritual harvest (Jer. 2:3). Firstfruits also describes a variety of spiritual blessings in the NT (Rom. 8:23; 1 Cor. 15:20). Paul called Israel a holy firstfruits (Rom. 11:16) from which all believers now make up the firstfruits of God's spiritual creation (James 1:18).

Eternal gospel (14:6). The "good news" is about Jesus Christ (Mark 1:1). Nevertheless, an alternative gospel circulated in Asia. In 9 BC the governor Paullus Fabius Maximus recommended that the province's calendar be changed to begin on Augustus's birthday, September 23. Its "gospel" message was political propaganda that celebrated Augustus's victories and the peace, prosperity, and honor that he had brought to the empire. The edict's closing declares that Augustus's birth "was the beginning for the world of the good tidings [*euangelion*, often translated as "gospel" in the NT] that came by reason of him."

Babylon the Great (14:8). This is the first of six usages of the cipher Babylon (also 16:19; 17:5; 18:2, 10, 21), a name found in intertestamental literature.[17] Babylon was the capital of the empire that captured Jerusalem in 586 BC, thus becoming synonymous with cruelty and oppression (Jer. 51:7). Peter similarly used Babylon as a cipher for Rome (1 Pet. 5:13).

Full strength into the cup (14:10). In the ancient world wine usually was mixed with water before it was drunk. The typical ratio was one part wine to three parts water, depending on the type. To drink wine full strength was considered a sign of debauchery and revelry. A cup of unmixed wine became a metaphor for God's unmitigated judgment (LXX Ps. 74:9 [ET 75:8]; Jer. 32:15 [ET 25:15]).

Fire and sulfur (14:10). Sulfur is a yellowish element that burns with a blue flame and emits a noxious sulfur dioxide gas. God destroyed Sodom and Gomorrah with burning sulfur (Gen. 19:24). When the Son of Man is revealed, sulfur will again rain down from heaven as in the days of Lot (Luke 17:29–30). In Revelation John always associates burning sulfur with divine punishment (cf. 19:20; 20:10; 21:8).

John sees "one like the Son of Man" (Rev. 14:14) holding a sharp sickle. Shown here is an ancient agricultural sickle from Egypt.

Use your sickle and reap . . . the harvest of the earth is ripe . . . use your sharp sickle and gather the clusters of grapes from the vineyard of the earth (14:15–18). "Sickle" can refer to either of two types of curved knives used for harvesting. A short-handled hand scythe was used to harvest grain, while vintagers used a small knife to cut grape clusters from the vine. Wheat was harvested in June, while grapes for wine production were harvested in September. The prophets compared the judgment of the nations to a spiritual harvest (Jer. 51:33; Joel 3:13). Two groups—the righteous and the wicked—are to be harvested at the end of the age, a harvest that Jesus spoke about in his parables (Matt. 13:30–40).

Winepress (14:19). Winepresses were square or circular pits, hewn out of rock or dug into the ground and then lined with rocks and sealed with plaster. Grapes were placed in a press and then trampled underfoot. The juice then flowed through a channel to a wine vat where the grape juice was collected and allowed to ferment. The winepress became a spiritual trope for the judgment of the nations (Isa. 63:2–3; Joel 3:13).

The Song of Moses and Seven Last Plagues (15:1–8)

Song of God's servant Moses (15:3). Moses sang two songs after the exodus: one about the Israelites' triumph over the Egyptians (Exod. 15:1–18) and one about the judgment of Israel's enemies and the reward of the faithful (Deut. 32:1–43).

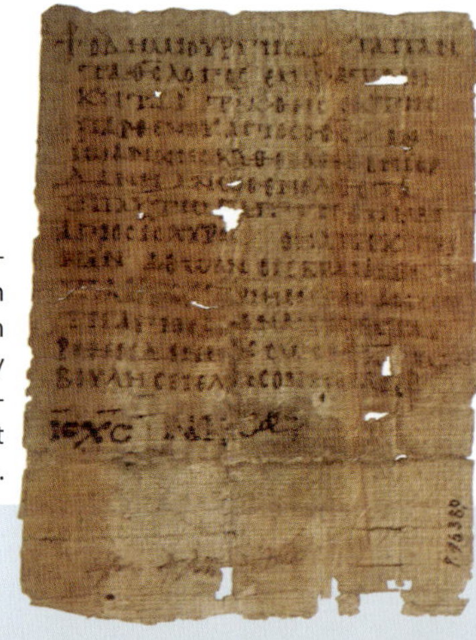

The song of heavenly saints includes praise for God's holiness. Modern church liturgies may include the words of an ancient hymn of the church known as the Trisagion, which proclaims the holiness of the Godhead: "Holy God, Holy Strong, Holy Immortal, have mercy on us." The seventh-century-AD papyrus shown here is a hymn to Christ that includes the words of the Trisagion.

Tabernacle of testimony (15:5). The tabernacle of testimony was the portable tabernacle that accompanied Israel in the wilderness (Exod. 40:36; Acts 7:44). The "testimony" refers to the twin stone tablets containing the Decalogue (Exod. 31:18), later housed in the ark of the covenant (Heb. 9:4).

Seven golden bowls filled with the wrath of God (15:7). The golden bowls seen earlier (5:8; 8:3–5) were censers full of incense. The pouring function of these other bowls suggests that they are libation bowls. Moses made similar sprinkling bowls to use at the altar of burnt offering (Exod. 27:3). Solomon had a hundred gold sprinkling bowls made for pouring out wine at the temple sacrifices (2 Chron. 4:8; Hosea 9:4). The libation bowls here contain the judgments to be poured out in chapter 16.

Temple was filled with smoke from the glory of God (15:8). The glory of God so filled the tabernacle after it was erected that Moses could not enter it (Exod. 40:35). Similarly, the cloud of God's glory so filled the temple when the ark was brought into it that the priests could not minister (1 Kings 8:6–11).

The Seven Bowls of God's Wrath (16:1–21)

Severely painful sores (16:2). Six of the ten plagues against Egypt are replicated in the trumpet and bowl judgments. As in Exodus, the judgments in Revelation are arranged with increasing intensity: the seals affect one-fourth of the earth, the trumpets one-third, and the bowls the entire world. The

The "mountain of Megiddo" in Israel becomes a symbol for the final battle between God and the forces of evil— Armageddon in Rev. 16:12–16.

first bowl parallels the sixth Egyptian plague, which produced festering boils both on people and animals (Exod. 9:8–11).

Poured out his bowl into the sea. It turned to blood . . . into the rivers and springs of water, and they became blood (16:3–4). The content of the second through fourth bowls resembles the first three trumpets. Saltwater turns to blood in the third bowl, while freshwater becomes bloody in the fourth bowl. In the first Egyptian plague the sea was not turned to blood, but only the Nile River and freshwater sources (Exod. 7:17–21).

You are just, the Holy One (16:5). John's language is borrowed from Moses's second song: "just [*dikaios*] and holy [*hosios*] is the Lord" (LXX Deut. 32:4). In Phrygia and Lydia around Laodicea, Philadelphia, and Sardis, a syncretistic religion developed featuring gods named *Hosion kai Dikaion*, "Holy and Just."

Blood to drink; they deserve it! (16:6). This statement expresses the judicial principle of reciprocity known as *lex talionis* (an eye for eye, a tooth for a tooth, etc.), which was a basis of biblical law in the OT (Exod. 21:23–25; cf. Matt. 5:38).

They did not repent (16:9–11). Just as the inhabitants of the earth had earlier refused to repent of their sins (9:20–21), they again refuse to repent and glorify God. Similarly, the pharaoh, despite the judgments brought against the Egyptians, repeatedly hardened his heart (Exod. 7–14).

Three unclean spirits like frogs (16:13). In the second Egyptian plague God released frogs to cover the land; however, the pharaoh's magicians duplicated this miracle (Exod. 8:1–14). Similar demonic deception now proceeds from the mouths of the unholy trinity. The second beast is now called "the false prophet" (cf. 19:20; 20:10).

Kings of the whole world (16:14). The civilized world of the first century AD was "the whole [Roman] empire" (Luke 2:1). Josephus called Caesar "the lord of the universe" (*oikoumenē*).[18] The goddess Oikoumene was the idealized form of this concept, and her statues sometimes were used as lighthouses to announce Rome's global dominion.

Naked and people see his shame (16:15). Greek athletes competed in the nude at the gymnasium (*gymnos*, "naked") and in the games. Romans, however, were more conservative about nudity, so their statues usually depicted clothed individuals. Jews shunned public nudity, so they objected when a gymnasium was built in Jerusalem. Jewish youth began to practice the Greek custom, and this was one of the offenses underlying the Maccabean rebellion (see 2 Macc. 4:9–15).

Place called in Hebrew, Armageddon (16:16). John transliterated the Hebrew phrase *har Megiddo* ("mountain of Megiddo)" as *Harmagedōn* (NRSV: "Harmagedon"). Megiddo was located in the Jezreel Valley in the lower Galilee

(1 Kings 4:12) and became the scene of battles between the Israelites and Canaanites (Judg. 5:19) and Judah and Egypt (2 Kings 23:29–30). Gog's defeat on the mountains of Israel is the final eschatological battle (Ezek. 39:4).

Babylon, the Prostitute on the Beast (17:1–18)

Notorious prostitute who is seated on many waters (17:1). Several cities—Jerusalem (Isa. 1:21), Tyre (Isa. 23:15–17), and Nineveh (Nah. 3:4)—were called prostitutes because of their faithlessness. Babylon was called a city of many waters because the Euphrates River flowed through it (Jer. 51:13). The Tiber River flowed through the city of Rome. However, the waters are not literal, because they are interpreted in 17:15 as "peoples, multitudes, nations, and languages."

Woman sitting on a scarlet beast (17:3). John is "in the Spirit" for a third time. The woman he sees in the desert is the antithesis of the pregnant woman in 12:14; nevertheless, she sits on the same beast seen in 13:1. The goddess Roma personified Rome, and Smyrna in 195 BC became the first city anywhere to build a temple for her worship. A sanctuary for the Romans to worship Dea Roma and Divus Julius was built in Ephesus in 29 BC.

Dressed in purple and scarlet (17:4). Purple was the color of the Roman elite and displayed their social status. The imperial family was entitled to wear purple garments. Senators wore togas with a wide purple stripe; equestrians wore togas with a narrow purple stripe. Thyatira was a production center for purple-dyed cloth (cf. Acts 16:14).

Everything detestable (17:4). Daniel prophesied that an "abomination of desolation" (*bdelygma,* translated here as "everything detestable") would desecrate the temple (Dan. 9:27; 11:31; 12:11). Antiochus IV Epiphanes erected such an abomination in the temple in 167 BC (1 Macc. 1:54), which provoked the Maccabean rebellion. The abomination was removed in 164 BC when Jerusalem was recaptured (1 Macc. 6:7). The temple's cleansing and rededication initiated the Feast of Hanukkah (cf. John 10:22). In AD 40 Caligula ordered that his image be erected in the temple, but he died before it was set up. According to Jesus, Daniel's prophecy about an abomination causing desolation would be fulfilled before Jerusalem's destruction (Matt. 24:15; Mark 13:14). It is significant to note that John never uses the word "antichrist" in Revelation.

On her forehead was written a name, a mystery (17:5). The woman's title, like the mark of the beast, is placed on her

An angel explains John's vision, saying, "The seven heads are seven mountains on which the woman is seated" (Rev. 17:9). Rome was described as a city on seven hills, and the Roman emperor Vespasian (reigned AD 69–79) issued a coin, shown here, that depicted the goddess Roma seated on the seven hills of Rome.

forehead (cf. 13:16). The "mystery" related to the woman is explained by the angelic interpreter in verses 8–18, the longest explanation in Revelation.

Seven heads are seven mountains (17:9). The city of Rome sat on seven hills: Capitoline, Aventine, Caelian, Esquiline, Quirinal, Viminal, and Palatine (see the article "The City of Ancient Rome"). A coin issued during Vespasian's reign shows Dea Roma seated on seven hills. "Seven hills" became a metonym for Rome.

Seven kings (17:9). In the Greek East the Roman emperor was called a king. However, "emperor" is the preferred translation for the ruler of the Roman Empire. Which emperor should be the first? Suetonius began his *Twelve Caesars* with Julius Caesar; Tacitus's *Annals* started with Augustus. Jesus's birth occurred during Augustus's reign (Luke 2:1). Since Augustus reconciled himself with Asia after defeating Antony and began the principate, he is the emperor who most likely begins the list.

Ten kings (17:12). These ten represent the client kings who were raised in Rome with the imperial family and then sent out to rule kingdoms throughout the empire. Herod the Great was such a king who was appointed king of Judea in 40 BC. His descendants—Archelaus, Antipas, Philip, Agrippa I, and Agrippa II—likewise ruled client kingdoms in Palestine in the first century AD.

The Fall of Babylon (18:1–24)

Fallen, Babylon the Great has fallen! (18:2). The language and imagery of Jeremiah's prediction of Babylon's fall (Jer. 50–51) are referenced twelve times in chapter 18. Six different voices lament or celebrate Babylon's demise.

Merchants of the earth have grown wealthy (18:3). Many merchants brought their commodities to Rome because of the potential for great profits. One merchant, T. Flavius Zeuxis, mentioned on his tomb in Hierapolis that he had made seventy-two passages during his lifetime around Cape Malea, the southern tip of Greece, while traveling to Italy.

Excess . . . excessive ways (18:3–9). The *strēn-* word group, suggesting luxury and sensuality, is used only here in the NT. The luxurious living of several Caesars is well known from various Roman historians who documented their profligacy. Nero never wore the same clothes twice, fished with a golden net strung with purple and scarlet threat, and traveled with at least one thousand carriages drawn by mules shod with silver.[19] Like John, Roman writers such as Lucan and Petronius decried such a lifestyle of dissipation.

Come out of her, my people (18:4). Jeremiah uttered this same exhortation to the Jews in Babylon to flee before its destruction (Jer. 51:6, 45).

Smoke from her burning (18:9). Rome experienced a great fire in AD 64 that burned ten of its fourteen districts. To deflect charges that he was the arsonist, Nero blamed the Christians and began the first great persecution of the church.

No one buys their cargo any longer (18:11). Verse 12 lists the cargoes of the merchants: twenty-eight items that they brought to Rome from around the world. Seventeen were among the trade goods that merchants brought to Tyre (Ezek. 27:12–24). Asia supplied wine, marble, olive oil, textiles, and parchment to Rome. See the article "Shipping Practices in the First Century."

Slaves—human lives (18:13). The final commodity—human bodies and souls (*somatōn kai psychas*)—is an idiom indicating slaves. See the article "Slavery in the New Testament World."

Every shipmaster, seafarer, the sailors, and all who do business by sea (18:17). A flourishing maritime network helped to maintain the Roman economy. Massive ships brought grain from Egypt to satisfy the demand for bread in Rome (cf. Acts 27:5–6). See the article "Shipping Practices in the First Century."

Threw dust on their heads (18:19). This act was a sign of mourning in antiquity (Josh. 7:6). The mariners and sea captains who witnessed Tyre's destruction also sprinkled dust on their heads (Ezek. 27:29–30).

Threefold Hallelujah and the Wedding Supper of the Lamb (19:1–10)

Hallelujah! (19:1). The four uses of "hallelujah" in chapter 19 (vv. 1, 3, 4, 6) are its only appearance in the NT. In its frequent OT usage, particularly in Psalms, the Hebrew word is translated as "Praise the LORD" (e.g., Ps. 106:1).

Marriage of the Lamb has come, and his bride has prepared herself (19:7). The wedding is a familiar metaphor describing God's relationship with his people, both in the OT (Isa. 49:18; Jer. 2:2) and in the NT (John 3:29; Luke 5:35; 2 Cor. 11:2). In Revelation the church is referred to four times as the bride of Christ (see also 21:2, 9; 22:17). See the article "Jewish Marriage Customs."

Marriage feast of the Lamb (19:9). Isaiah prophesied an end-time feast composed of guests from all nations (Isa. 25:6). At Jesus's last supper he announced that he would next drink wine with his disciples in his Father's kingdom (Matt. 26:29). The celebration of the Eucharist anticipates the wedding supper to occur at Jesus's return (1 Cor. 11:26).

I fell at his feet to worship him, but he said to me, "Don't do that!" (19:10). Other apocalyptic texts similarly show angels forbidding worship.[20]

God's heavenly celebration with his people is called "the marriage feast of the Lamb" (Rev. 19:9). Banquet scenes were frequent motifs in funerary art in the Greco-Roman period. They may have communicated a hope for an enjoyable afterlife. Frescoes of banquet scenes, like the one shown here, have been found in Christian burial areas in the catacombs outside Rome. There are many different interpretations of their purpose, and they may have developed layers of meaning over time. One interpretive suggestion, beyond that of the traditional funerary meal, is participation in the future heavenly banquet.

Paul condemned the worship of angels in Colossae (Col. 2:18). John is rebuked in 22:8–9 for again attempting to worship the angel.

The Heavenly Rider Defeats the Beasts (19:11–21)

White horse. Its rider is called Faithful and True (19:11). Roman generals celebrating a military triumph rode into Rome on a white horse. After his victory in North Africa, Julius Caesar drove a chariot drawn by white horses through the city.

Many crowns (19:12). "Crowns" (*diadēmata*) is more accurately translated "diadems." Greeks and Romans adopted the diadem as a regal badge and distinguished it from the wreath (cf. 2:10: *stephanos*, "wreath" [CSB footnote]). The dragon wore a diadem on each head (12:3), and the beast had a diadem on each horn (13:1; cf. 17:12). Ptolemy VI Philometer wore two diadems on his head after conquering Antioch in 169 BC (1 Macc. 11:13).

He will rule them with an iron rod (19:15). The male child's destiny was to rule with an iron scepter (12:5). The fulfillment of the messianic Ps. 2:9 has now arrived. Jesus will rule the nations with the victors, as promised to the Thyatirans (2:26–27).

He has a name written on his robe and on his thigh (19:16). Inscriptions sometimes were placed on the thighs of statues. Examples include a statue of Apollo mentioned by Cicero,[21] and a statue of Zeus at Olympia, both with their names written on their thighs.

All the birds ate their fill of their flesh (19:21). This gruesome description involving unclean birds of prey resembles the carnage following Gog's destruction (Ezek. 39:17–20).

The Thousand Years and Judgments of Satan and the Dead (20:1–15)

Great chain (20:1). Chains were used to bind fallen angels awaiting the day of judgment (Jude 6). This trope of chains binding Satan and his fallen angels is found in other apocalyptic works.[22]

Thousand years (20:2). A thousand years had been compared to a day (Ps. 90:4; 2 Pet. 3:8). Jewish rabbis estimated that the messianic age was a thousand years long, which was also the life span of individuals in the messianic age.[23] The seven days of creation were allegorized to represent the seven millennia of human history; the Son would come in the final thousand years and judge the ungodly.[24]

Thrones . . . authority to judge (20:4). The promise of thrones from which to judge is now fulfilled (2:26; 3:21). Jesus similarly promised that the apostles would judge on thrones (Luke 22:30); Paul likewise wrote that the saints would judge the world and the angels (1 Cor. 6:2–3).

John sees a rider called "Faithful and True" on a white horse leading the armies of heaven. Depictions of military leaders on horseback communicated their power and military success. This bronze statue of Marcus Aurelius on horseback, erected in the second century AD, is the only equestrian statue remaining from the imperial Roman period.

Beheaded (20:4). Under Roman law there were two types of capital punishment: (1) crucifixion, exposure to wild animals, or burning at the stake for slaves and the lower classes; (2) beheading for Roman citizens. According to tradition, Paul was beheaded in Rome.

First resurrection (20:5). Those victorious over the beast now receive their promised reward: they come to life to rule during the thousand years. The dead who worshiped the beast and took his mark later participate in an unnamed "second resurrection," whose destiny is the second death.

Priests of God and of Christ (20:6). That saints would reign as priests was announced earlier (1:6; 5:10). Peter similarly wrote that the people of God constituted a royal priesthood (1 Pet. 2:5, 9).

Gog and Magog (20:8). The battle of Armageddon, announced in 16:14–16, now occurs as the last battle against Gog and Magog. The language and the sequence of events parallel the eschatological restoration and battle described in Ezek. 37–39. The Lydian king Gyges, known from Assyrian inscriptions as Gugu, is the historical figure behind the

The angel holds a chain with which Satan is bound before being imprisoned in the Abyss. Two prisoners with chains fastened to their necks and ankles are depicted in this relief (first or second century AD).

Jewish tradition of Gog as the personification of evil that would come against Israel in the last days.

Encampment of the saints (20:9). This fortified military facility (*parembolē*) could also refer to a Roman barracks (Acts 21:34). Jesus warned that army camps would surround Jerusalem before its destruction (Luke 19:43; 21:20). During their siege of Jerusalem the Romans established several camps to quarter their legions. "Army" is another possible translation (Heb. 11:34), and the people of God were described as an army in 19:14.

Lake of fire and sulfur (20:10). The fate of the wicked is to burn in an unquenchable fire (Isa. 66:24; Mark 9:48). The unrighteous are destined to burn and die eternally as punishment on the day of judgment.[25] The lake of fire is also the fate of the beast and the false prophet (19:20) as well as death and Hades and the unrighteous dead (20:14–15).

Great white throne and one seated on it (20:11). This scene of judgment, announced in 11:18, draws its imagery from Dan. 7:9–10. There the enthroned Ancient of Days opens the heavenly books and executes judgment. The Jewish apocalyptic book *2 Baruch* also mentions books to be opened in which the sins of the wicked are recorded (24.1).

Book of life (20:12). The saints in the second resurrection who had their names recorded in the book are now awarded eternal life (cf. Dan. 12:1–2).

The second death, the lake of fire (20:14). This death is eternal and a punishment about which Jesus warned (Matt. 10:28). Death is the last enemy to be destroyed (cf. 1 Cor. 15:26).

New Heaven, New Earth, New Jerusalem (21:1–22:5)

A new heaven and a new earth (21:1). Isaiah prophesied the coming of new heavens and a new earth (Isa. 65:17; 66:22). The day of God will bring a new heaven and a new earth (2 Pet. 3:13).

Holy city, the new Jerusalem (21:2). The descent of the new Jerusalem is first compared to a bride (21:2–4) and then a city (21:10–22:5). The bridal imagery resumes from the announcement of the wedding supper (19:7–9).

God's dwelling is with humanity, and he will live with them (21:3). The OT is replete with statements of God's desire to live with his people in covenant relationship (e.g., Lev. 26:11–12; Ezek. 37:27; Zech. 2:11). This often went unrealized because of Israel's disobedience; now that relationship is realized forever.

I will freely give to the thirsty from the spring of the water of life (21:6). Water and thirst are common metaphors for spiritual life in Scripture. The righteous drink from God's river because the fountain of life is with them (Ps. 36:8–9). In the Jewish apocalyptic book *1 Enoch* the thirsty drink from the fountain of righteousness that never runs dry and thus are filled with wisdom (48.1).

John sees the holy city coming down out of heaven and hears God say, "I am making everything new" (Rev. 21:5). Woven in the fourteenth century AD, the Apocalypse Tapestry of Angers shows scenes from the book of Revelation. The tapestry shown here illustrates the new Jerusalem coming down out of heaven.

The one who conquers will inherit these things (21:7). In the OT sons usually became the heirs of property, with the firstborn son receiving twice as much (Deut. 21:15–17). Greek custom provided that an estate be divided by lot equally among the surviving sons. Under Roman law the father retained full legal authority until death and could disinherit his children if he wished. Paul likewise expressed the certainty that all of God's sons and daughters were his spiritual heirs (Rom. 8:17; Gal. 4:7).

I will be his God, and he will be my son (21:7). God made a similar promise to Israel that they would be his people (Jer. 32:38), something Paul reiterates in his exhortation to the Corinthians (2 Cor. 6:18). This adoption language is reminiscent of God's covenants with Abraham (Gen. 17:7–8) and Solomon (2 Chron. 7:18). Greek men could adopt any male citizen as a son. Roman men could easily adopt fatherless males. A notable example is the adoption of Octavian by his great-uncle Julius Caesar. An adoptive father could never disinherit his new son or reduce him to slavery.

Cowards, faithless, detestable, murderers, sexually immoral, sorcerers, idolaters, and all liars (21:8). This is the more complete of the two vice lists found in chapters 21–22 (cf. 22:15). Two additional sins are named in 21:27: shameful or deceitful acts.

Holy city, Jerusalem (21:10). OT prophecies describe Zion as the Lord's city (Isa. 60:14) situated on a holy mountain as the Faithful City (Zech. 8:3). The images of new Jerusalem are drawn from Ezekiel's vision of renewed temple, land, and city (Ezek. 40–48). This same conjunction of city, bride, and wife is found in the Jewish work *Joseph and Aseneth* (15.7, 9; 18.11; 21.4–9).

Massive high wall, with twelve gates . . . names of the twelve tribes of Israel's sons (21:12). Cities founded during the Hellenistic period were built with defensive walls. Lysimachus's wall around Ephesus ran over five miles. Pergamum, Smyrna, and Sardis had walls surrounding their acropolises. Roman rule brought the *pax Romana*; hence cities no longer needed walls for protection. Gates were the means of entrance to an ancient city, and Ephesus had four: Magnesian, Harbor, Koressos, and Agora. Ezekiel's visionary city also had twelve gates (Ezek. 48:31–34). But his list of the tribes differs from that in Rev. 7:4–8, where Manasseh is included and Dan omitted.

Twelve foundations . . . names of the twelve apostles of the Lamb (21:14). The twelve apostles are named in the Synoptic Gospels (Matt. 10:2–4; Mark 3:16–19; Luke 6:13–16); however, Judas was replaced by Matthias (Acts 1:16–26).

City is laid out in a square (21:16). Earlier John measured the temple of God (11:1); here an angel measures the city. The high priest's breastplate was square (Exod. 28:16); the holy of holies in Solomon's temple was also square (2 Chron. 3:8). The commercial marketplace in Ephesus was called the "Square [*tetragona*] Agora." The length, width, and height of the new Jerusalem each measures 12,000 stadia (12 × 1,000 [= 1,400 miles]), while the walls are 144 cubits thick (12 × 12 [= 200 feet]). The city, like the holy of holies (1 Kings 6:20), is shaped like a cube. The city's immense dimensions suggest that these numbers should be understood figuratively.

Wall was jasper, and the city was pure gold clear as glass (21:18). Jasper is a precious stone previously associated with God (4:3). The purity of the city and its streets is compared to gold and glass. Since gold usually was alloyed with silver, pure gold was especially valuable in antiquity. Glassblowing techniques were discovered by the Phoenicians near Sidon around 50 BC, and soon glass tableware and vessels came into common use. Since impurities often were introduced during production, pure glass was highly valued. Sardis was a production center for both gold and glass.

Foundations of the city walls were adorned with every kind of jewel (21:19). The future Zion seen by Isaiah had foundations, walls, and gates of precious stones (Isa. 54:11–12; cf. Tob. 13:16–18). The high priest's breastplate held twelve precious stones upon which the names of the twelve tribes were engraved (Exod. 28:17–20; 39:10–13). A similar list of these precious stones adorned the king of Tyre (LXX Ezek. 28:13).

Nations will walk by its light (21:24). Isaiah prophesied that people from all nations would worship on Jerusalem's holy mountain (Isa. 66:20), a theme echoed in Zechariah (Zech. 14:16–19; cf. Tob. 14:6–7).

River of the water of life (22:1). A river watered the garden of Eden (Gen. 2:10), and living waters were prophesied to flow from the future new Jerusalem (Ezek. 47:1–10; Zech. 14:8). The river's source at the throne of God and the Lamb suggests that these waters may be a metaphor for the Holy Spirit (cf. John 7:38–39).

Tree of life was on each side of the river (22:2). After the fall, access to the tree of life was denied to Adam and Eve (Gen. 2:9; 3:17–24). The victorious, redeemed nations are now given access to the tree (cf. Rev. 2:7).

Ezekiel also saw trees on each bank of the river, which produced fruit for food and leaves for healing (Ezek. 47:12).[26]

There will no longer be any curse (22:3). The pain, toil, and mourning that resulted from the curse (Gen. 3:16–19) are reversed with the passing away of the order of things on the old earth (cf. Rev. 21:4).

Three times Jesus reminds John and his readers that he is coming soon. John may have recalled the words of the angels at his ascension: "This same Jesus, who has been taken from you into heaven, will come in the same way that you have seen him going into heaven" (Acts 1:11). This ivory relief depicting the ascension of Jesus is from the late tenth century AD.

Epilogue: Jesus Is Coming Soon (22:6–21)

Look, I am coming soon! (22:7). This is the first of three announcements by Jesus of his imminent return (also 22:12, 20). Three times the Spirit and the bride respond antiphonally to these declarations of Christ's return by saying, "Come" (22:17, 20).

Blessed is the one who keeps the words of the prophecy of this book (22:7). The sixth beatitude largely repeats the first beatitude (1:3); both promise a blessing for those who keep and obey Revelation's prophetic words.

Don't seal up the words of the prophecy of this book (22:10). Although the angel previously had ordered John to seal up the words of the seven thunders (10:4), he now orders John to reveal the larger vision. In the Jewish apocalypse *4 Ezra*, Ezra was told to hide his vision but to teach its contents to the wise, who could keep its secrets (12.37–38; cf. 14.5–6, 45–46).

Let the filthy still be filthy . . . let the holy still be holy (22:11). Both the unrepentant and the victors continue to be addressed in these four exhortations. A similar contrast between the pure and the wicked is found at the end of Daniel's prophecy (Dan. 12:10).[27]

Blessed are those who wash their robes (22:14). In this seventh and final beatitude imagery related to clothing, whether clean or defiled, is again used (cf. 3:4; 7:14). The earlier promise of entry through new Jerusalem's gates to eat from the tree of life is now fulfilled for those dressed in clean robes.

Outside are the dogs (22:15). Jews had a negative attitude toward dogs (cf. 1 Sam. 17:43); thus "dog" became a derogatory term. It was also a euphemism for a male temple prostitute (Deut. 23:18) as well as for gentiles (Matt. 15:26–27). Paul called the Judaizers "dogs" (Phil. 3:2), while Ignatius, in his *Letter to the Ephesians,* called false teachers "mad dogs" (7.1).

Sexually immoral (22:15). Both heterosexual and homosexual practices were included in the general Greek term *porneia*. Sexual immorality is a practice repeatedly condemned in Revelation (e.g., 2:21; 9:21; 14:8; 21:8). Jewish wisdom literature connected the idolatry of gentiles with their immorality (cf. Wis. 14:12). Demosthenes expressed the Greek perspective on sexuality, stating that mistresses were for enjoyment, concubines for service, and wives for bearing and raising legitimate children.[28] Paul decried the view that sexual relations were a bodily function like eating and drinking (1 Cor. 6:12–13). For the Romans, adultery was illegal because it violated the husband's property rights, not because it transgressed divine law. Slaves commonly were used to gratify the sexual needs of their owners.

I testify to everyone who hears the words of the prophecy of this book (22:18). Warning formulas were used to validate the reliability of a document. Moses commanded the Israelites not to add or subtract from the commandments that he gave (Deut. 4:2; 12:32). After completing their translation of the Pentateuch into Greek, the translators commanded that a curse be laid on anyone who added or deleted any of its written text.[29] In *Epistle of Barnabas* readers are similarly warned not to add or subtract from what they received.[30]

Amen! Come, Lord Jesus! (22:20). Revelation closes with an invitation similar to the Aramaic phrase *marana tha*. Writing from Ephesus, Paul also used *marana tha* in his closing to 1 Corinthians (16:22). In the *Didache* the thanksgiving offered over the Lord's Supper also ends, "Maranatha! Amen" (10.6).

Abbreviations

Bible Versions

ASV	American Standard Version
CEB	Common English Bible
CSB	Christian Standard Bible
ESV	English Standard Version
KJV	King James Version
NASB	New American Standard Bible
NIV	New International Version
NKJV	New King James Version
NLT	New Living Translation
NRSV	New Revised Standard Version
RSV	Revised Standard Version

Rabbinic Literature

b.	Babylonian Talmud
m.	Mishnah
t.	Tosefta
y.	Jerusalem Talmud

Secondary Sources

AB	Anchor Bible
ABD	*Anchor Bible Dictionary*. Edited by David Noel Freedman. 6 vols. New York: Doubleday, 1992
ABRL	Anchor Bible Reference Library
AEL	*Ancient Egyptian Literature: A Book of Readings*. Edited by Miriam Lichtheim. 3 vols. Berkeley: University of California Press, 2006

AfO	*Archiv für Orientforschung*
AfOB	Archiv für Orientforschung: Beiheft
AGJU	Arbeiten zur Geschichte des antiken Judentums und des Urchristentums
AIO	*Archaeologia Iranica et Orientalis*
AnBib	Analecta Biblica
ANEP	*The Ancient Near East in Pictures Relating to the Old Testament.* Edited by James B. Pritchard. 2nd ed. Princeton: Princeton University Press, 1994
ANET	*Ancient Near Eastern Texts Relating to the Old Testament.* Edited by James B. Pritchard. 3rd ed. Princeton: Princeton University Press, 1969
AOTC	Apollos Old Testament Commentary
APR	Ancient Philosophy and Religion
ARAB	*Ancient Records of Assyria and Babylonia.* Daniel David Luckenbill. 2 vols. Chicago: University of Chicago Press, 1926–27. Reprint, New York: Greenwood, 1968
ArBib	The Aramaic Bible
ARM	Archives royales de Mari
ARWAW	Abhandlungen der Rheinisch-Westfalischen Akademie der Wissenschaften
ASP	American Studies in Papyrology
AUSS	*Andrews University Seminary Studies*
AYB	Anchor Yale Bible
BA	*Biblical Archaeologist*
BAFCS	The Book of Acts in Its First Century Setting
BAI	*Bulletin of the Asia Institute*
BAR	*Biblical Archaeological Review*
BASOR	*Bulletin of the American Schools of Oriental Research*
BBR	*Bulletin for Biblical Research*
BDAG	Danker, Frederick W., Walter Bauer, William F. Arndt, and F. Wilbur Gingrich. *Greek-English Lexicon of the New Testament and Other Early Christian Literature.* 3rd ed. Chicago: University of Chicago Press, 2000
BEB	*Baker Encyclopedia of the Bible.* Edited by Walter A. Elwell. 2 vols. Grand Rapids: Baker, 1988
BECNT	Baker Exegetical Commentary on the New Testament

BES	*Bulletin of the Egyptological Seminar*
BETL	Bibliotheca Ephemeridum Theologicarum Lovaniensium
Bib	*Biblica*
BibOr	Biblica et Orientalia
BJRL	*Bulletin of the John Rylands University Library of Manchester*
BJS	Brown Judaic Studies
BNTC	Black's New Testament Commentaries
BRev	*Bible Review*
BSac	*Bibliotheca Sacra*
BSL	Biblical Studies Library
BTNT	Biblical Theology of the New Testament
BZ	*Biblische Zeitschrift*
CAD	*The Assyrian Dictionary of the Oriental Institute of the University of Chicago*. 21 vols. Chicago: Oriental Institute of the University of Chicago. 1956–2010
CBC	Cornerstone Biblical Commentary
CBET	Contributions to Biblical Exegesis and Theology
CBQ	*Catholic Biblical Quarterly*
CC	Continental Commentaries
CEP	Contemporary Evangelical Perspectives
CGTC	Cambridge Greek Testament Commentary
CHANE	Culture and History of the Ancient Near East
CIG	*Corpus Inscriptionum Graecarum*. Edited by August Boeckh. 4 vols. Berlin: Reimer, 1828–77
CIJ	*Corpus Inscriptionum Judaicarum*. Edited by Jean-Baptiste Frey. 2 vols. Rome: Pontifical Biblical Institute, 1936–52
CIL	*Corpus Inscriptionum Latinarum*. Berlin, 1862–
CNTUOT	*Commentary on the New Testament Use of the Old Testament*. Edited by G. K. Beale and D. A. Carson. Grand Rapids: Baker Academic; Nottingham: Apollos, 2007
COS	*The Context of Scripture*. Edited by William W. Hallo. 4 vols. Leiden: Brill, 1997–2017
CP	*Classical Philology*
CRINT	Compendia Rerum Iudaicarum ad Novum Testamentum
CTH	*Catalogue des textes hittites*. Emmanuel Laroche. Paris: Klincksieck, 1971

CTN	Cuneiform Texts from Nimrud
CTR	*Criswell Theological Review*
CUSAS	Cornell University Studies in Assyriology and Sumerology
DDAH	Debates and Documents in Ancient History
DDD	*Dictionary of Deities and Demons in the Bible.* Edited by Karel van der Toorn, Bob Becking, and Pieter W. van der Horst. Leiden: Brill; Grand Rapids: Eerdmans, 1999
DDL	*Dictionary of Daily Life in Biblical and Post-Biblical Antiquity.* Edited by Edwin M. Yamauchi and Marvin R. Wilson. 4 vols. Peabody, MA: Hendrickson, 2014–16
DJG[1]	*Dictionary of Jesus and the Gospels.* Edited by Joel B. Green, Scot McKnight, and I. Howard Marshall. 1st ed. Downers Grove, IL: InterVarsity, 1992
DJG[2]	*Dictionary of Jesus and the Gospels.* Edited by Joel B. Green, Jeannine K. Brown, and Nicholas Perrin. 2nd ed. Downers Grove, IL: InterVarsity, 2013
DMOA	Documenta et Monumenta Orientis Antiqui
DNTB	*Dictionary of New Testament Background.* Edited by Craig A. Evans and Stanley E. Porter. Downers Grove, IL: InterVarsity, 2000
EA	El-Armana tablets. According to the edition of Jørgen A. Knudtzon, *Die el-Amarna-Tafeln.* Leipzig: Hinrichs, 1908–15. Reprint, Aalen: Zeller, 1964. Continued in Anson F. Rainey, *El-Amarna Tablets,* 359–79. 2nd rev. ed. Kevelaer: Butzon & Bercker, 1978
EBC	*The Expositor's Bible Commentary.* Edited by Tremper Longman III and David E. Garland. Rev. ed. 13 vols. Grand Rapids: Zondervan, 2006–12
EBT	Explorations in Biblical Theology
EC	*Early Christianity*
ECC	Eerdman's Critical Commentary
EDEJ	*The Eerdmans Dictionary of Early Judaism.* Edited by John J. Collins and Daniel C. Harlow. Grand Rapids: Eerdmans, 2010
EG	*Epigrammata graeca.* Edited by G. Keibel. Berlin: G. Reimer, 1878.
EGGNT	Exegetical Guide to the Greek New Testament
EKKNT	Evangelisch-katholischer Kommentar zum Neuen Testament

EncJud	*Encyclopedia Judaica*. Edited by Fred Skolnik and Michael Berenbaum. 2nd ed. 22 vols. Detroit: Macmillan Reference USA, 2007
EPSC	Evangelical Press Study Commentary
ErIsr	*Eretz-Israel*
ESVEC	ESV Expository Commentary
EvQ	*Evangelical Quarterly*
EvT	*Evangelische Theologie*
ExpTim	*Expository Times*
FAT	Forschungen zum Alten Testament
FCGRW	First-Century Christians in the Greco-Roman World
FRLANT	Forschungen zur Religion und Literatur des Alten und Neuen Testaments
GD	Gorgias Dissertations
GNS	Good News Studies
HALOT	*The Hebrew and Aramaic Lexicon of the Old Testament*. Ludwig Koehler, Walter Baumgartner, and Johann J. Stamm. Translated and edited under the supervision of Mervyn E. J. Richardson. 4 vols. Leiden: Brill, 1994–99
HCNT	*Hellenistic Commentary to the New Testament*. Edited by M. Eugene Boring, Klaus Berger, and Carsten Colpe. Nashville: Abingdon, 1995
HIBD	*Holman Illustrated Bible Dictionary*. Edited by Chad Brand, Charles Draper, and Archie England. Nashville: Holman, 2003.
HMSCS	Hearing the Message of Scripture Commentary Series
HNCT	Harper's New Testament Commentaries
HOTC	Holman Old Testament Commentary
HOTE	Handbooks for Old Testament Exegesis
HSM	Harvard Semitic Monographs
HUCA	*Hebrew Union College Annual*
ICC	International Critical Commentary
IEJ	*Israel Exploration Journal*
ISBE	*International Standard Bible Encyclopedia*. Edited by Geoffrey W. Bromiley. 4 vols. Grand Rapids: Eerdmans, 1979–88
IVPBBCNT[1]	*IVP Bible Background Commentary: New Testament*. Craig S. Keener. Downers Grove, IL: InterVarsity, 1993

IVPBBCNT[2]	*IVP Bible Background Commentary: New Testament*. Craig S. Keener. 2nd ed. Downers Grove, IL: InterVarsity, 1993
IVPBBCOT	*IVP Bible Background Commentary: Old Testament*. John H. Walton, Victor H. Matthews, and Mark W. Chavalas. Downers Grove, IL: IVP Academic, 2000
JANES	*Journal of the Ancient Near Eastern Society*
JAOS	*Journal of the American Oriental Society*
JARCE	*Journal of the American Research Center in Egypt*
JBL	*Journal of Biblical Literature*
JCS	*Journal of Cuneiform Studies*
JEBS	*Journal of European Baptist Studies*
JETS	*Journal of the Evangelical Theological Society*
JGRChJ	*Journal of Greco-Roman Christianity and Judaism*
JHebS	*Journal of Hebrew Scriptures*
JJS	*Journal of Jewish Studies*
JNES	*Journal of Near Eastern Studies*
JPSTC	Jewish Publication Society Torah Commentary
JQR	*Jewish Quarterly Review*
JSNT	*Journal for the Study of the New Testament*
JSNTSup	Journal for the Study of the New Testament: Supplement Series
JSOTSup	Journal for the Study of the Old Testament: Supplement Series
JSPSup	Journal for the Study of the Pseudepigrapha: Supplement Series
JTS	*Journal of Theological Studies*
KBo	*Keilschrifttetxte aus Boghazköi*. Leipzig: Hinrichs, 1916–23; Berlin: Gebr. Mann, 1954–
KEL	Kregel Exegetical Library
KHNTE	Kregel Handbooks for New Testament Exegesis
KTU	*Die keilalphabetischen Texte aus Ugarit*. Edited by Manfred Dietrich, Oswald Loretz, and Joaquín Sanmartín. Münster: Ugarit-Verlag, 2013. 3rd enlarged ed. of *KTU: The Cuneiform Alphabetic Texts from Ugarit, Ras Ibn Hani, and Other Places*. Edited by Manfred Dietrich, Oswald Loretz, and Joaquín Sanmartín. Münster: Ugarit-Verlag, 1995
LAE	*The Literature of Ancient Egypt: An Anthology of Stories, Instructions, Stelae, Autobiographies, and Poetry*. Edited by William Kelly Simpson. 3rd ed. New Haven: Yale University Press, 2003
LAPO	Littératures anciennes du Proche-Orient

LASBF	*Liber Annuus Studii Biblici Franciscani*
LEC	Library of Early Christianity
LNTS	Library of New Testament Studies
LSJ	Liddell, H. G., R. Scott, and H. S. Jones. *A Greek-English Lexicon*. 9th ed., with revised supplement. Oxford: Clarendon, 1996
LUA	Lunds universitets årrskrift
MC	Mesopotamian Civilizations
NAC	New American Commentary
NBBC	New Beacon Bible Commentary
NCamBC	New Cambridge Bible Commentary
Neot	*Neotestamentica*
NICNT	New International Commentary on the New Testament
NICOT	New International Commentary on the Old Testament
NIDB	*New Interpreter's Dictionary of the Bible*. Edited by Katharine Doob Sakenfeld. Nashville: Abingdon, 2006–9
NIDNTT	*New International Dictionary of New Testament Theology*. Edited by Colin Brown. 4 vols. Grand Rapids: Zondervan, 1975–85.
NIDNTTE	*New International Dictionary of New Testament Theology and Exegesis*. Edited by Moisés Silva. 2nd ed. 5 vols. Grand Rapids: Zondervan, 2014
NIGTC	New International Greek Testament Commentary
NIVAC	NIV Application Commentary
NovT	*Novum Testamentum*
NovTSup	Novum Testamentum Supplements
NSBT	New Studies in Biblical Theology
NTM	New Testament Monographs
NTS	*New Testament Studies*
OCM	Oxford Classical Monographs
OEANE	*The Oxford Encyclopedia of Archaeology in the Near East*. Edited by Eric M. Meyers. 5 vols. New York: Oxford University Press, 1997
OGIS	*Orientis Graeci Inscriptiones Selectae*. Edited by Wilhelm Dittenberger. 2 vols. Leipzig: Hirzel, 1903–5
OIP	Oriental Institute Publications
OLA	Orientalia Lovaniensia Analecta

PGM	*Papyri Graecae Magicae: Die griechischen Zauberpapyri*. Edited by Karl Preisendanz. 2nd ed. Stuttgart: Teubner, 1973–74
PMIRC	Penn Museum International Research Conferences
PNTC	Pillar New Testament Commentary
PS	Pauline Studies
QMHSS	Quantitative Methods in the Humanities and Social Sciences
RA	*Revue d'assyriologie et d'archéologie orientale*
RAr	*Revue archéologique*
RB	*Revue biblique*
ResQ	*Restoration Quarterly*
RS	Ras Shamra
RSAW	Routledge Sourcebooks for the Ancient World
RTR	*Reformed Theological Review*
SAA	State Archives of Assyria
SAAB	*State Archives of Assyria Bulletin*
SAHL	Studies in the Archaeology and History of the Levant
SBJT	*Southern Baptist Journal of Theology*
SBL	Studies in Biblical Literature
SBLAB	Society of Biblical Literature Academia Biblica
SBLABS	Society of Biblical Literature Archaeology and Biblical Studies
SBLDS	Society of Biblical Literature Dissertation Series
SBLMS	Society of Biblical Literature Monograph Series
SBLWAW	Society of Biblical Literature Writings from the Ancient World
SBT	Studies in Biblical Theology
SDAIBC	Seventh-Day Adventist International Bible Commentary
SGBC	Story of God Bible Commentary
SGLG	Studia Graeca et Latina Gothoburgensia
SHBC	Smith & Helwys Bible Commentary
SHCANE	Studies in the History and Culture of the Ancient Near East
SJ	Studia Judaica
SJLA	Studies in Judaism in Late Antiquity
SJT	*Scottish Journal of Theology*
SNTSMS	Society for New Testament Studies Monograph Series
SP	Sacra Pagina
Str-B	Strack, H. L., and P. Billerbeck. *Kommentar zum Neuen Testament aus Talmud und Midrasch*. 6 vols. Munich: Beck, 1922–61

TDNT	*Theological Dictionary of the New Testament*. Edited by Gerhard Kittel and Gerhard Friedrich. Translated by Geoffrey W. Bromiley. 10 vols. Grand Rapids: Eerdmans, 1964–76
TDOT	*Theological Dictionary of the Old Testament*. Edited by G. Johannes Botterweck and Helmer Ringgren. Translated by John T. Willis et al. 8 vols. Grand Rapids: Eerdmans, 1974–2006
THOTC	Two Horizons Old Testament Commentary
TLZ	*Theologische Literaturzeitung*
TNTC	Tyndale New Testament Commentaries
TOTC	Tyndale Old Testament Commentaries
TTCS	Teach the Text Commentary Series
TynBul	*Tyndale Bulletin*
UBCS	Understanding the Bible Commentary Series
UCOIP	University of Chicago Oriental Institute Publications
UNHAIİ	Uitgaven van het Nederlands Historisch-Archaeologisch Instituut te İstanbul
VAB	Vorderasiatische Bibliothek
VT	*Vetus Testamentum*
WBC	Word Biblical Commentary
WMANT	Wissenschaftliche Monographien zum Alten und Neuen Testament
WTJ	*Westminster Theological Journal*
WUNT	Wissenschaftliche Untersuchungen zum Neuen Testament
ZAW	*Zeitschrift für die alttestamentliche Wissenschaft*
ZEB	*Zondervan Encyclopedia of the Bible*. Edited by Merrill C. Tenney and Moisés Silva. 5 vols. Grand Rapids: Zondervan, 2009.
ZECNT	Zondervan Exegetical Commentary on the New Testament
ZECOT	Zondervan Exegetical Commentary on the Old Testament
ZIBBCNT	*Zondervan Illustrated Bible Backgrounds Commentary: New Testament*. Edited by Clinton E. Arnold. 4 vols. Grand Rapids: Zondervan, 2002
ZIBBCOT	*Zondervan Illustrated Bible Backgrounds Commentary: Old Testament*. Edited by John H. Walton. 5 vols. Grand Rapids: Zondervan, 2009
ZNW	*Zeitschrift für die neutestamentliche Wissenschaft und die Kunde der älteren Kirche*

Notes

The Assyrians

1. "Texts from Hammurabi to the Downfall of the Assyrian Empire," trans. A. L. Oppenheim (*ANET* 274).

2. "Texts from Hammurabi," 274–75.

3. "Texts from Hammurabi," 279–81.

4. "Texts from Hammurabi," 281.

5. "Texts from Hammurabi," 284.

6. "Texts from Hammurabi," 287–88.

7. "Texts from Hammurabi," 291.

The Canaanites and Canaanite Religion

1. Philip Schmitz, "Canaan," *ABD* 1:828–31.

2. Jack Sasson, "The Earliest Mention of the Name 'Canaan,'" *BA* 47 (1984): 90.

3. "The Story of Idrimi, King of Alalakh," trans. A. L. Oppenheim (*ANET* 557–58).

4. Anson Rainey, "Who Is a Canaanite? A Review of the Textual Evidence," *BASOR* 304 (1996): 1–15.

5. Anson Rainey, "A Canaanite at Ugarit," *IEJ* 13 (1963): 43–45.

6. Ann E. Killebrew, *Biblical Peoples and Ethnicity: An Archaeological Study of Egyptians, Canaanites, Philistines, and Early Israel, 1300–1100 B.C.E.*, SBLABS 9 (Atlanta: Society of Biblical Literature, 2005), 94.

7. Anson Rainey, "Amenhotep III's Campaign to Takhsi," *JARCE* 10 (1973): 71–75.

8. William L. Moran, ed. and trans., *The Amarna Letters* (Baltimore: Johns Hopkins University Press, 1992).

9. Jo Ann Hackett, "Canaanites," *OEANE* 1:409–14.

10. Claude F. A. Schaeffer, *Ugaritica* (Paris: Paul Guethner, 1939–); *Ugaritica II: Nouvelles études relatives aux découvertes de Ras Shamra* (Paris: Paul Geuthner, 1949). See also Claude F. A. Schaeffer, "Les Fouilles de Minet-el-beida et de Ras Shamra: Deuxième Campagne (printemps 1930) Rapport Sommaire," *Syria* 12, no. 1 (1931): 1–14; "Les Fouilles de Minet-el-beida et de Ras-shamra: Troisième Campagne (printemps 1931) Rapport Sommaire," *Syria* 13, no. 1 (1932): 1–27; "Les Fouilles de Minet-el-beida et de Ras-shamra: Quatrième Campagne (printemps 1932) Rapport Sommaire," *Syria* 14, no. 22 (1933): 93–127.

11. For a brief summary of Canaanite temples, see Killebrew, *Biblical Peoples and Ethnicity*, 105–7.

12. Ze'ev Meshel, "Did Yahweh Have a Consort? The New Religious Inscriptions from the Sinai," *BAR* 5 (1979): 24–34.

13. W. G. Dever, "Iron Age Epigraphic Material from the Area of Khirbet el-Kôm," *HUCA* 40–41 (1970): 139–204.

The Cushites

1. J. Daniel Hays, "The Cushites: A Black Nation in Ancient History," *BSac* 153 (1996): 275–78.

2. For a good discussion on Piye, see Robert G. Morkot, *The Black Pharaohs: Egypt's Nubian Rulers* (London: Rubicon, 2000), 179–96.

3. For a history of the Twenty-Fifth Dynasty, see K. A. Kitchen, *The Third Intermediate Period in Egypt (1100–650 B.C.)* (Warminster: Aris & Phillips, 1973).

4. Donald B. Redford, *Egypt, Canaan, and Israel in Ancient Times* (Princeton: Princeton University Press, 1992), 356.

5. "Sennacherib's Siege of Jerusalem," trans. M. Cogan (*COS* 2.119B:303).

6. Morkot, *The Black Pharaohs*, 154.

7. Stephanie Dalley, "Foreign Chariotry and Cavalry in the Armies of Tiglath-Pileser III and Sargon II," *Iraq* 47 (1985): 44. The texts themselves are published in Stephanie Dalley and J. N. Postgate, *The Tablets from Fort Shalmaneser*, CTN 3 (London: British School of Archaeology in Iraq, 1984), nos. 99–118.

8. Dalley, "Foreign Chariotry," 46.

9. Nadav Na'aman argues that the Cushite king Piye is "So, king of Egypt" mentioned in 2 Kings 17:4 as conspiring with Hoshea of Israel. Na'aman likewise concludes that the Cushite troops depicted in the Assyrian reliefs as fighting against the Assyrians in the 720 BC campaign of Sargon II suggest that the Cushite king had dispatched this army and not the weak remains of the earlier Egyptian dynasty. Na'aman also provides an extensive bibliography on the portrayal of Cushites in the Assyrian reliefs. See Na'aman, "The Historical Background to the Conquest of Samaria (720 BCE)," *Bib* 71 (1990): 206–25.

10. Kitchen, *The Third Intermediate Period in Egypt*, 384–85.

11. The best solution appears to be that by Kitchen, *The Third Intermediate Period in Egypt*, 161–72, 385–88. Kitchen argues convincingly that Tirhakah, the younger brother of the pharaoh, was appointed commander of the expedition to Palestine and was the titular king of this expedition.

12. Sennacherib's account of this battle, recorded on a Neo-Assyrian inscription, reads as follows: "The kings of Egypt, and the bowmen, chariot corps and cavalry of the kings of Ethiopia [Cush] assembled a countless force and came to their [i.e., the Ekronites'] aid. In the plain of Eltekeh, they drew up their ranks against me and sharpened their weapons. Trusting in the god Ashur, my lord, I fought with them and inflicted a defeat upon them. The Egyptian charioteers and princes, together with the charioteers of the Ethiopians [Cushites], I personally took alive in the midst of the battle." "Sennacherib's Siege of Jerusalem," trans. M. Cogan (*COS* 2.119B:303).

13. Kitchen, *The Third Intermediate Period in Egypt*, 384–85.

14. Pauline Albenda, "Observations on Egyptians in Assyrian Art," *BES* 4 (1982): 10.

15. Kitchen, *The Third Intermediate Period in Egypt*, 384–85.

16. Redford, *Egypt, Canaan, and Israel in Ancient Times*, 357–58.

17. For a discussion of this time period, see Kitchen, *The Third Intermediate Period in Egypt*, 393–97.

Daily Life in Ancient Israel

1. J. David Schloen, *The House of the Father as Fact and Symbol: Patrimonialism in Ugarit and the Ancient Near East*, SAHL 2 (Winona Lake, IN: Eisenbrauns, 2001).

2. Sandra L. Richter, *The Epic of Eden: A Christian Entry into the Old Testament* (Downers Grove, IL: IVP Academic, 2008), 69–91.

3. Daniel Fleming, "From Joseph to David: Mari and Israelite Pastoral Traditions," in *Israel: Ancient Kingdom or Late Invention?*, ed. Daniel I. Block (Nashville: B&H Academic, 2008), 78–96.

4. Philip J. King and Lawrence E. Stager, *Life in Biblical Israel* (Louisville: Westminster John Knox, 2001), 112–22.

5. F. Nigel Hepper, *Baker Encyclopedia of Bible Plants: Flowers and Trees, Fruits and Vegetables, Ecology* (Grand Rapids: Baker, 1992).

6. Leann Pace, "Feasting and Everyday Meals in the World of the Hebrew Bible," in *Feasting in the Archaeology and Texts of the Bible and the Ancient Near East*, ed. Peter Altmann and Janling Fu (Winona Lake, IN: Eisenbrauns, 2014), 179–98.

7. Oded Borowski, *Daily Life in Biblical Times*, SBLABS 5 (Atlanta: Society of Biblical Literature, 2003), 16–21.

8. Victor H. Matthews, *Manners and Customs in the Bible: An Illustrated Guide to Daily Life in Biblical Times*, 3rd ed. (Peabody, MA: Hendrickson, 2006), 99–104.

The Egyptians

1. Kasia Szpakowska, "Religion in Society: Pharaonic," in *A Companion to Ancient Egypt*, ed. Alan B. Lloyd (Oxford: Wiley Blackwell, 2014), 507.

2. John H. Taylor, *Death and the Afterlife in Ancient Egypt* (Chicago: University of Chicago Press, 2001), 198.

3. Jan Assmann, *The Search for God in Ancient Egypt*, trans. David Lorton (Ithaca, NY: Cornell University Press, 2001), 5.

4. Assmann, *The Search for God in Ancient Egypt*, 3.

5. Szpakowska, "Religion in Society," 512–14.

6. Garrett Galvin, *Egypt as a Place of Refuge*, FAT 2/51 (Tübingen: Mohr Siebeck, 2011), 131, 135.

7. Safwat Marzouk, *Egypt as a Monster in the Book of Ezekiel*, FAT 2/76 (Tübingen: Mohr Siebeck, 2015), 29–44.

8. Ellen F. Morris, "The Pharaoh and Pharaonic Office," in *A Companion to Ancient Egypt*, ed. Alan B. Lloyd (Oxford: Wiley Blackwell, 2014), 216.

9. Michael V. Fox, "From Amenemope to Proverbs: Editorial Art in Proverbs 22,17–23,11," *ZAW* 126 (2014): 76–91.

Musical Instruments in Israel and the Ancient Near East

1. Philip J. King and Lawrence E. Stager, *Life in Biblical Israel* (Louisville: Westminster John Knox, 2001), 285.

2. See the list provided by Ivor H. Jones, "Musical Instruments," *ABD* 4:934–35.

3. Bo Lawergren, "Distinctions among Canaanite, Philistine, and Israelite Lyres, and Their Global Lyrical Contexts," *BASOR* 309 (1998): 43–55.

4. See the sketches in Lawergren, "Lyres," 50.

5. King and Stager, *Life in Biblical Israel*, 294.

6. King and Stager, *Life in Biblical Israel*, 296–97; Adam L. Bean, "Music," *DDL* 3:419.

7. Jones, "Musical Instruments," 936.
8. John W. Hilber, "Psalms," *ZIBBCOT* 5:444.
9. Bean, "Music," 420.

The Persians

1. "Cyrus Cylinder," trans. M. Cogan (*COS* 2.124:314–16).
2. Laurie E. Pearce and Cornelia Wunsch, *Documents of Judean Exiles and West Semites in Babylonia in the Collection of David Sofer*, CUSAS 28 (Bethesda, MD: CDL Press, 2014).
3. L. W. King and R. Campbell Thompson, *The Sculptures and Inscription of Darius the Great on the Rock of Behistûn in Persia: A New Collation of the Persian, Susian, and Babylonian Texts, with English Translations, Etc.* (London: British Museum, 1907).
4. Pearce and Wunsch, *Documents of Judean Exiles.*
5. Eric M. Meyers, "The Shelomith Seal and Aspects of the Judean Restoration: Some Additional Reconsiderations," *ErIsr* 18 (1985): 33*–38*.
6. See T. Fish, "The Murashu Tablets," in *Documents from Old Testament Times*, ed. D. Winton Thomas (New York: Harper & Row, 1958); Matthew W. Stolper, *Entrepreneurs and Empire: The Murašû Archive, the Murašû Firm, and Persian Rule in Babylonia*, UNHAIİ 54 (Istanbul: Nederlands Historisch-Archaeologisch Instituut, 1985).
7. Bezalel Porten, *The Elephantine Papyri in English: Three Millennia of Cross-Cultural Continuity and Change*, DMOA 22 (Leiden: Brill, 1996).

The Philistines

1. Trude Dothan, *The Philistines and Their Material Culture* (New Haven: Yale University Press, 1982), 3–12.
2. *ANET* 262–63.
3. Lawrence E. Stager, "The Fury of Babylon," *BAR* 22 (1996): 56–69, 76–77.
4. Stager, "The Fury of Babylon"; Seymour Gitin, "Excavating Ekron: Major Philistine City Survived by Absorbing Other Cultures," *BAR* 31 (2005): 40–56.
5. *ANET* 308.
6. D. J. Wiseman, *Nebuchadrezzar and Babylon* (Oxford: Oxford University Press, 1985), 25.
7. R. Zadok, "Phoenicians, Philistines, and Moabites in Mesopotamia," *BASOR* 230 (1978): 61.

Women in the Old Testament World

1. For ancient Near Eastern laws, see Martha Roth, *Law Collections from Mesopotamia and Asia Minor*, 2nd ed. SBLWAW 6 (Atlanta: Scholars Press, 1997). For laws concerning women, see Martha Roth, "Women and Law," in *Women in the Ancient Near East: A Sourcebook*, ed. Mark W. Chavalas, RSAW (London: Routledge, 2014), 144–74.
2. Harold Torger Vedeler, "Naditum and Daughter: An Analysis of the Letters of Erishti-Aya of Mari (ARM X:36–43)" (MA thesis, University of Minnesota, 2000), 32–59.
3. Martha Roth, "Gender and Law: A Case Study from Ancient Mesopotamia," in *Gender and Law in the Hebrew Bible and the Ancient Near East*, ed. Victor H. Matthews, Bernard M. Levinson, and Tikva Frymer-Kensky, JSOTSup 262 (Sheffield: Sheffield Academic Press, 1998), 173–84.
4. See Cécile Michel, "Women in Letters: Old Assyrian Kaniš," in *Women in the Ancient Near East: A Sourcebook*, ed. Mark W. Chavalas, RSAW (London: Routledge, 2014), 205–12.

5. For an overview, see Stephanie Dalley, *Mari and Karana: Two Old Babylonian Cities* (London: Longman, 1984).

6. Stephanie Dalley, C. B. F. Walker, and J. D. Hawkins, *The Old Babylonian Tablets from Tell al Rimah* (London: British School of Archaeology in Iraq, 1976), 130.

7. Mark Chavalas, "Nuzi," *NIDB* 4:301–4.

Women's Fashion in the Old Testament World

1. Elizabeth Wayland Barber, *Women's Work: The First 20,000 Years; Women, Cloth, and Society in Early Times* (New York: Norton, 1994), 158.

2. Jennie R. Ebeling, *Women's Lives in Biblical Times* (London: T&T Clark, 2010), 91.

3. William G. Dever, *The Lives of Ordinary People in Ancient Israel: Where Archaeology and the Bible Intersect* (Grand Rapids: Eerdmans, 2012), 178.

4. Barber, *Women's Work*, 202–3.

5. J. A. Thompson, *Handbook of Life in Bible Times* (Downers Grove, IL: InterVarsity, 1986), 97.

6. Dever, *The Lives of Ordinary People in Ancient Israel*, 178.

7. Ebeling, *Women's Lives in Biblical Times*, 91.

8. Philip J. King and Lawrence E. Stager, *Life in Biblical Israel* (Louisville: Westminster John Knox, 2001), 265.

9. Victor H. Matthews, "Cloth, Clothes," *NIDB* 1:692.

10. Dorothy Irvin, "Clothing," *OEANE* 2:39.

11. Barber, *Women's Work*, 133–34.

12. Barber, *Women's Work*, 201.

13. Irvin, "Clothing," 39.

14. Barber, *Women's Work*, 202.

15. Irvin, "Clothing," 39.

16. W. H. Mare, "Dress," *ZEB* 2:186.

17. Dennis R. Cole and S. Cameron Coyle, "Cloth, Clothing," *HIBD* 311.

18. Douglas R. Edwards, "Dress and Ornamentation," *ABD* 3:235.

19. Irvin, "Clothing," 39.

20. King and Stager, *Life in Biblical Israel*, 283.

21. Darlene R. Gautsch, "Cosmetics," *HIBD* 351.

22. Barber, *Women's Work*, 204.

23. Barber, *Women's Work*, 172.

24. Barber, *Women's Work*, 181–82.

25. Barber, *Women's Work*, 181–82.

26. Mare, "Dress," 186.

27. Mare, "Dress," 186.

28. King and Stager, *Life in Biblical Israel*, 273.

29. Michael Dayagi-Mendels, "Cosmetics," *OEANE* 2:68.

30. Dayagi-Mendels, "Cosmetics," 67.

31. Gautsch, "Cosmetics," 350.

32. Gautsch, "Cosmetics," 350.

33. Dayagi-Mendels, "Cosmetics," 68.

34. Gautsch, "Cosmetics," 351.

35. Dayagi-Mendels, "Cosmetics," 67.

36. Barber, *Women's Work*, 201.

37. Gautsch, "Cosmetics," 351.

38. Gautsch, "Cosmetics," 351.
39. King and Stager, *Life in Biblical Israel*, 280.
40. Gautsch, "Cosmetics," 351.
41. King and Stager, *Life in Biblical Israel*, 276.
42. Elizabeth E. Platt, "Jewelry," *NIDB* 3:299.
43. Mare, "Dress," 2:187.
44. Platt, "Jewelry," 302.
45. Platt, "Jewelry," 299.
46. Platt, "Jewelry," 303.
47. Robin Ngo, "Givati Parking Lot Dig Unearths Rare Seal of Woman," *Bible History Daily*, http://www.biblicalarchaeology.org/daily/biblical-artifacts/inscriptions/givati-parking-lot-seals/.
48. Platt, "Jewelry," 299.

Genesis

1. "Epic of Creation," trans. B. R. Foster (*COS* 1.111:390–402).
2. "Atra-hasis," trans. B. R. Foster (*COS* 1.130:450–52).
3. "The Ba'lu Myth," trans. D. Pardee (*COS* 1.86:241–74).
4. W. Randall Garr, "'Image' and 'Likeness' in the Inscription from Tell Fakhariyeh," *IEJ* 50 (2000): 228.
5. "The Adapa Story," trans. B. R. Foster (*COS* 1.129:449).
6. Jeremy Black et al., *The Literature of Ancient Sumer* (Oxford: Oxford University Press, 2004), 86–88.
7. Thorkild Jacobsen, *The Sumerian King List* (Chicago: University of Chicago Press, 1939).
8. Irving Finkel, *The Ark before Noah: Decoding the Story of the Flood* (London: Hodder & Stoughton, 2014).
9. "The Aqhatu Legend," trans. D. Pardee (*COS* 1.103:343–56).
10. "The Amarna Letters," trans. W. F. Albright (*ANET* 486; EA 254).
11. Juris Zairns, "Camel," *ABD* 1:825.
12. Iain Provan, *Seriously Dangerous Religion: What the Old Testament Really Says and Why It Matters* (Waco: Baylor University Press, 2014), 258.
13. Kenneth A. Kitchen, "Genesis 12–50 in the Near Eastern World," in *He Swore an Oath: Biblical Themes from Genesis 12–50*, ed. Richard S. Hess, Gordon J. Wenham, and Philip E. Satterthwaite (Cambridge: Tyndale House, 1993), 79–80.
14. John H. Walton, "Genesis," *ZIBBCOT* 1:125–26.
15. James K. Hoffmeier, *Israel in Egypt: The Evidence for the Authenticity of the Exodus Tradition* (Oxford: Oxford University Press, 1997), 89–91.
16. Hoffmeier, *Israel in Egypt*, 88–89.
17. Hoffmeier, *Israel in Egypt*, 92.
18. Hoffmeier, *Israel in Egypt*, 93–95.
19. Hoffmeier, *Israel in Egypt*, 84–88.
20. "The Instruction for King Meri-ka-re," trans. J. A. Wilson (*ANET* 416).

Exodus

1. For a late date, this pharaoh/date could be the *terminus ante quem* for the oppression to begin, if Moses's age (eighty at the exodus event, and the oppression would need to begin at least by his birth [Exod. 7:7]) were read literally. One might argue that the age of Moses

could be read as two generations in age (literarily stylized as two "forty-year" time frames and added together, but perhaps literally two actual generations adding up to forty to fifty years of age). If so, the author would also be considering Aaron's age as two generations plus three years, since his age is mentioned in the same verse (7:7). See Bryant G. Wood, "The Rise and Fall of the 13th-Century Exodus-Conquest Theory," *JETS* 48 (2005): 478. Many thanks to Mark D. Janzen, PhD, Egyptologist and assistant professor of history and archaeology at Southwestern Baptist Theological Seminary, for his thoughts on refining several concepts here and elsewhere.

2. James K. Hoffmeier, *Ancient Israel in Sinai: The Evidence for the Authenticity of the Wilderness Tradition* (Oxford: Oxford University Press, 2011), 64.

3. Hoffmeier, *Ancient Israel in Sinai*, 57.

4. K. A. Kitchen, *On the Reliability of the Old Testament* (Grand Rapids: Eerdmans, 2006), 310.

5. Kitchen, *On the Reliability of the Old Testament*, 255.

6. James K. Hoffmeier, "A Response to Bryant Wood," *JETS* 50 (2007): 233.

7. See also Nahum M. Sarna, *Exploring Exodus: The Heritage of Biblical Israel* (New York: Schocken, 1986), 29–31.

8. "The Birth Legend of Sargon of Akkad," trans. B. R. Foster (*COS* 1.133:461).

9. Kitchen, *On the Reliability of the Old Testament*, 251.

10. James K. Hoffmeier, *Israel in Egypt: The Evidence for the Authenticity of the Exodus Tradition* (Oxford: Oxford University Press, 1997), 150.

11. *AEL* 2:199.

12. Herodotus, *Histories* 1.321–22.

13. "Locusts," *National Geographic*, http://animals.nationalgeographic.com/animals/bugs/locust; s.v. "Locust," *Encyclopedia Britannica*, http://www.britannica.com/animal/locust-insect.

14. Jonathan Grossman, "The Structural Paradigm of the Ten Plagues Narrative and the Hardening of Pharaoh's Heart," *VT* 64 (2014): 607.

15. Hoffmeier, *Israel in Egypt*, 187–88.

16. Hoffmeier, *Ancient Israel in Sinai*, 86, 107–8. See also Kitchen, *On the Reliability of the Old Testament*, 261–63.

17. Hoffmeier, *Ancient Israel in Sinai*, 105.

18. Hoffmeier, *Israel in Egypt*, 169–70.

19. Hoffmeier, *Israel in Egypt*, 190.

20. Hoffmeier, *Ancient Israel in Sinai*, 106.

21. Hoffmeier, *Israel in Egypt*, 170–71.

22. John R. Tower, "The Red Sea," *JNES* 18 (1959): 150–53; see also Hoffmeier, *Israel in Egypt*, 213–14.

23. Sarna, *Exploring Exodus*, 14; Hoffmeier, *Ancient Israel in Sinai*, 115, 286.

24. Hoffmeier, *Ancient Israel in Sinai*, 44.

25. Hoffmeier, *Ancient Israel in Sinai*, 120.

26. Kitchen, *On the Reliability of the Old Testament*, 287–90.

27. Meredith G. Kline, *Treaty of the Great King: The Covenant Structure of Deuteronomy; Studies and Commentary* (Grand Rapids: Eerdmans, 1963).

28. John H. Walton, *Ancient Near Eastern Thought and the Old Testament: Introducing the Conceptual World of the Hebrew Bible* (Grand Rapids: Baker Academic, 2006), 69.

29. *AEL* 1:169.

30. John H. Walton, *Israelite Literature in Its Cultural Context: A Survey of Parallels between Biblical and Ancient Near Eastern Texts* (Grand Rapids: Zondervan, 1994).

31. Scott B. Noegel, "The Egyptian Origin of the Ark of the Covenant," in *Israel's Exodus in Transdisciplinary Perspective: Text, Archaeology, Culture, and Geoscience*, ed. Thomas E. Levy, Thomas Schneider, and William H. C. Propp, QMHSS 2 (New York: Springer, 2015), 223–42.

32. Hoffmeier, *Ancient Israel in Sinai*, 110.

33. Kline, *Treaty of the Great King*; Elmar Edel, *Die ägyptisch-hethitische Korrespondenz aus Boghazköi in babylonischer und hethitischer Sprache*, 2 vols., ARWAW 77 (Opladen: Westdeutscher Verlag, 1994).

34. "Instructions regarding Tunic," trans. B. Porten (*COS* 3.87J:216).

35. *AEL* 1:159.

36. "The Victory Stela of King Piye," trans. M. Lichtheim (*COS* 2.7:48).

37. "The 'Sun Disk' Tablet of Nabû-apla-iddina," trans. V. Hurowitz (*COS* 2.135:367).

38. Douglas K. Stuart, *Exodus*, NAC (Nashville: Broadman & Holman, 2006), 685.

39. Michael M. Homan, "The Divine Warrior in His Tent: A Military Model for Yahweh's Tabernacle," *BRev* 16, no. 6 (2000): 22–33, 55.

Leviticus

1. Gary M. Beckman, "Blood in Hittite Ritual," *JCS* 63 (2011): 98.

2. "Instructions to Priests and Temple Officials," trans. G. McMahon (*COS* 1.83:218–20). Sections 4, 6, 12 cite warnings against priests performing rituals when drunk or quarrelsome.

3. Jacob Milgrom, *Leviticus 1–16: A New Translation with Introduction and Commentary*, AB 3 (New York: Doubleday, 1991), 188–89.

4. "Prayer to Re-Harakhti," trans. M. V. Fox (*COS* 1.29:47).

5. "The Poem of the Righteous Sufferer," trans. B. R. Foster (*COS* 1.153:488).

6. "The Mythological Origin of Certain Unclean Animals," trans. J. A. Wilson (*ANET* 10); "Cultic Abomination of the Pig," trans. R. K. Ritner (*COS* 1.19:30–31). See also Lidar Sapir-Hen, "Pigs as an Ethnic Marker? You Are What You Eat," *BAR* 42 (2016): 41–43, 70.

Numbers

1. Dennis Olson, *The Death of the Old and the Birth of the New: The Framework of the Book of Numbers and the Pentateuch*, BJS 71 (Chico, CA: Scholars Press, 1985), 83–125. For more on the message of the book, see Roy E. Gane, *Leviticus, Numbers*, NIVAC (Grand Rapids: Zondervan, 2004); *In the Shadow of the Shekinah: God's Journey with Us* (Hagerstown, MD: Review & Herald, 2009); "Numbers," in *The Baker Illustrated Bible Commentary*, ed. Gary M. Burge and Andrew E. Hill (Grand Rapids: Baker Books, 2012), 116–45.

2. Jacob Milgrom, *Numbers: The Traditional Hebrew Text with the New JPS Translation*, JPSTC (Philadelphia: Jewish Publication Society, 1990), xiii.

3. "The Kirta Epic," trans. D. Pardee (*COS* 1.102:334).

4. José M. Galán, "The Ancient Egyptian *SED*-Festival and the Exemption from Corvée," *JNES* 59 (2000): 255–64.

5. "Instructions to Priests and Temple Officials," trans. G. McMahon (*COS* 1.83:219), §10; see also §11.

6. Michael M. Homan, "The Divine Warrior in His Tent: A Military Model for Yahweh's Tabernacle," *BRev* 16, no. 6 (2000): 22–33, 55; *To Your Tents, O Israel! The Terminology, Function, Form, and Symbolism of Tents in the Hebrew Bible and the Ancient Near East*, CHANE 12 (Leiden: Brill, 2002), 111–16; Bruce Wells, "Exodus," *ZIBBCOT* 1:250–51; K. A. Kitchen, *On the Reliability of the Old Testament* (Grand Rapids: Eerdmans, 2006), 278, 470.

7. Kitchen, *On the Reliability of the Old Testament*, 280.

8. Kitchen, *On the Reliability of the Old Testament*, 276–77. Daniel E. Fleming, "Mari's Large Public Tent and the Priestly Tent Sanctuary," *VT* 50 (2000): 486–98.

9. David P. Wright, *The Disposal of Impurity: Elimination Rites in the Bible and in Hittite and Mesopotamian Literature*," SBLDS 101 (Atlanta: Scholars Press, 1987), 272.

10. Wright, *The Disposal of Impurity*, 248–71.

11. Wright, *The Disposal of Impurity*, 272–74.

12. On the nature of physical ritual impurity, see Gane, *Leviticus, Numbers*, 224–77; Hyam Maccoby, *Ritual and Morality: The Ritual Purity System and Its Place in Judaism* (Cambridge: Cambridge University Press, 1999), 31–32, 48–50, 207–8; Jacob Milgrom, *Leviticus 1–16: A New Translation with Introduction and Commentary*, AB 3 (New York: Doubleday, 1991), 766–68, 1000–1004.

13. "Shuruppak," trans. B. Alster (*COS* 1.176:569, 33–34).

14. "The Laws of Hammurabi," trans. M. Roth (*COS* 2.131:344).

15. Herbert C. Brichto, "The Case of the *ŚŌṬĀ* and a Reconsideration of Biblical 'Law,'" *HUCA* 46 (1975): 64–66. See also Tikva Frymer-Kensky, "The Strange Case of the Suspected Sotah (Numbers V 11–31)," *VT* 34 (1984): 25, esp. n19 on the drinking of potions outside the Bible.

16. Anthony Spalinger, "The Limitations of Formal Ancient Egyptian Religion," *JNES* 57 (1998): 241–60.

17. P. Kyle McCarter, *Ancient Inscriptions: Voices from the Biblical World* (Washington, DC: Biblical Archaeology Society, 1996), 121–22; Emile Puech, "Palestinian Funerary Inscriptions," *ABD* 5:127.

18. Milgrom, *Numbers*, 360–61.

19. "The Cylinders of Gudea," trans. R. E. Averbeck (*COS* 2.155:431–32).

20. "The Installation of the Storm God's High Priestess," trans. D. Fleming (*COS* 1.122:427–28).

21. Kitchen, *On the Reliability of the Old Testament*, 280.

22. Timothy R. Ashley, *The Book of Numbers*, NICOT (Grand Rapids: Eerdmans, 1993), 217; John Wilkinson, "The Quail Epidemic of Numbers 11.31–34," *EvQ* 71 (1999): 196–97; Gordon J. Wenham, *Numbers: An Introduction and Commentary*, TOTC 4 (Leicester, UK: Inter-Varsity, 1981), 109.

23. Josephus, *Jewish Antiquities* 10.1–2. For more discussion on Moses's marriage to a Cushite, see J. Daniel Hays, *From Every People and Nation: A Biblical Theology of Race*, NSBT 14 (Downers Grove, IL: InterVarsity, 2003), 70–76.

24. "Plague Prayers of Muršili II," trans. G. Beckman (*COS* 1.60:157).

25. "Regular Afternoon Meal for Bel," in Roy E. Gane, *Ritual Dynamic Structure*, GD 23/6 (Piscataway, NJ: Gorgias, 2004), 204, lines 385–94; also in "Temple Program for the New Year's Festivals at Babylon," trans. A. Sachs (*ANET* 334).

26. See also Roy E. Gane, "Leviticus," *ZIBBCOT* 1:294.

27. "Prayer to Marduk," trans. B. R. Foster (*COS* 1.114:416).

28. "The Ba'lu Myth," trans. D. Pardee (*COS* 1.86:264–66, 270).

29. "Instructions to Priests and Temple Officials," trans. G. McMahon (*COS* 1.83:218), §6.

30. "The Installation of the Storm God's High Priestess," trans. D. Fleming (*COS* 1.122:431).

31. Wright, *The Disposal of Impurity*, 120–22; and see references there.

32. *IVPBBCOT* 157.

33. Anson F. Rainey and R. Steven Notley, *The Sacred Bridge: Carta's Atlas of the Biblical World*, rev. ed. (Jerusalem: Carta, 2014), 41.

34. See R. Dennis Cole, "Numbers," *ZIBBCOT* 1:375; and other examples cited there. See Milgrom, *Numbers*, 459–60; Baruch A. Levine, *Numbers 21–36: A New Translation with Introduction and Commentary*, AB 4A (New York: Doubleday, 2000), 88–89.

35. "Kurkh Monolith," trans. K. L. Younger Jr. (*COS* 2.113A:263).

36. For example, "The Autobiography of Idrimi," trans. T. Longman III (*COS* 1.148:480), lines 92–97a; "Hadad-yith'i," trans. A. Millard (*COS* 2.34:154).

37. "The Exaltation of Inanna," trans. W. W. Hallo (*COS* 1.160:520), lines 93–96.

38. "The Deir 'Alla Plaster Inscriptions," trans. B. A. Levine (*COS* 2.27:140–45). For detailed discussion of these fascinating texts, see Levine, *Numbers 21–36*, 241–75; Milgrom, *Numbers*, 473–76.

39. "The Story of Two Brothers," trans. J. A. Wilson (*ANET* 24).

40. Klaas Spronk, "Baal of Peor," *DDD* 147–48; cf. "The Ba'lu Myth," trans. D. Pardee (*COS* 1.86:241–74).

41. Raymond Westbrook, *Property and the Family in Biblical Law*, JSOTSup 113 (Sheffield: JSOT Press, 1991), 161–63.

42. "The Cylinders of Gudea," trans. R. E. Averbeck (*COS* 2.155:432).

43. "The Laws of Lipit-Ishtar," trans. M. Roth (*COS* 2.154:411).

44. See Roy E. Gane, "'Bread of the Presence' and Creator-in-Residence," *VT* 42 (1992): 199–203.

45. "Daily Ritual of the Temple of Amun-Re at Karnak," trans. R. K. Ritner (*COS* 1.34:55).

46. Atraḫasis III v 30–36. See Wilfred G. Lambert and Alan R. Millard, *Atra-Ḫasīs: The Babylonian Story of the Flood* (repr., Winona Lake, IN: Eisenbrauns, 1999), 98–99.

47. Mark E. Cohen, *The Cultic Calendars of the Ancient Near East* (Bethesda, MD: CDL Press, 1993).

48. Cohen, *The Cultic Calendars of the Ancient Near East*, 437–51.

49. Hans Güterbock, "An Outline of the Hittite AN.TAḪ.ŠUM Festival," *JNES* 19 (1960): 80–89; Gary Beckman, "The Religion of the Hittites," *BA* 52 (1989): 103.

50. "Votive Records," trans. H. A. Hoffner Jr. (*COS* 3.36:66).

51. "The Autobiography of Idrimi," trans. T. Longman III (*COS* 1.148:479).

52. "The Asiatic Campaigns of Thut-mose III," trans. J. A. Wilson (*ANET* 235–38).

53. "The Asiatic Campaigns of Thut-mose III," trans. J. A. Wilson (*ANET* 234–55).

54. "Hittite Laws," trans. H. A. Hoffner Jr. (*COS* 2.19:107).

55. "Plague Prayers of Muršili II," trans. G. Beckman (*COS* 1.60:156–57).

56. Westbrook, *Property and the Family in Biblical Law*, 164.

Deuteronomy

1. Consequently, the Nephilim of Deut. 1 have no *genetic* relationship to the Nephilim of Gen. 6. The descriptive title makes an impressive association between the two historical settings.

2. Michael A. Grisanti, "Deuteronomy," *EBC* 2:502.

3. Examples can be found in the Code of Hammurabi ("The Code of Hammurabi," trans. T. Meek [*ANET* 178]), and the Vassal-Treaties of Esar-haddon ("The Vassal-Treaties of Esarhaddon," trans. D. Wiseman [*ANET* 538, lines 410–13]); Meredith G. Kline, *Treaty of the Great King: The Covenant Structure of Deuteronomy; Studies and Commentary* (Grand Rapids: Eerdmans, 1963), 43.

4. "God List, Blessings and Curses of the Treaty between Suppiluliumas and Kurtiwaza," trans. A. Goetze (*ANET* 205); Meredith G. Kline, "The Two Tables of the Covenant," *WTJ* 22 (1960): 133–46.

5. Moshe Weinfeld, *Deuteronomy 1–11: A New Translation with Introduction and Commentary*, AYB 5 (New Haven: Yale University Press, 2008), 410.

6. Jack M. Sasson, "Circumcision in the Ancient Near East," *JBL* 85 (1966): 474.

7. Eugene E. Carpenter, "Deuteronomy," *ZIBBCOT* 1:469.

8. "The Disputation between Ewe and Wheat," trans. H. Vanstiphout (*COS* 1.180:575–76).

9. *IVPBBCOT* 182.

10. Daniel I. Block, *Deuteronomy*, NIVAC (Grand Rapids: Zondervan, 2012), 326; Carpenter, "Deuteronomy," 471–74.

11. "A Divine Oracle through a Dream," trans. J. A. Wilson (*ANET* 449); "Oracles concerning Esarhaddon," trans. R. H. Pfeiffer (*ANET* 250–51); "The Interpretation of Dreams," trans. J. A. Wilson (*ANET* 495); "Ugaritic Dream Omens," trans. D. Pardee (*COS* 1.93:293–94); "The Sippar Cylinder of Nabonidus," trans. P. Beaulieu (*COS* 2.123A:311); "The Cylinders of Gudea," trans. R. Averbeck (*COS* 2.155:419–21).

12. Numerous treaties (*ANET* 533–41); "Proclamation of Anitta of Kussar," trans. H. Hoffner (*COS* 1.72:183); "Lamentation over the Destruction of Sumer and Ur," trans. J. Klein (*COS* 1.166:537).

13. Carpenter, "Deuteronomy," 478.

14. *IVPBBCOT* 184.

15. *IVPBBCOT* 184.

16. Jacob Milgrom, "An Archaeological Myth Destroyed," *BRev* 1, no. 3 (1985): 52–55.

17. Carpenter, "Deuteronomy," 479.

18. "The Code of Hammurabi," trans. T. Meek (*ANET* 170–71).

19. Carpenter, "Deuteronomy," 480–81.

20. "The Code of Hammurabi," trans. T. Meek (*ANET* 166).

21. "The Aqhatu Legend," trans. D. Pardee (*COS* 1.103:346); "The Zukru Festival," trans. D. Fleming (*COS* 1.123:432–46).

22. Carpenter, "Deuteronomy," 481–82.

23. *IVPBBCOT* 188.

24. Carpenter, "Deuteronomy," 486.

25. *IVPBBCOT* 188.

26. *IVPBBCOT* 191.

27. Carpenter, "Deuteronomy," 486–87.

28. Carpenter, "Deuteronomy," 490.

29. Carpenter, "Deuteronomy," 490. See "The Gebel Barkal Stela of Thutmose III," trans. J. Hoffmeier (*COS* 2.2B:15); one example of many similar statements in the annals of Shalmeneser III, "Annals: Calah Bulls," trans. K. L. Younger Jr. (*COS* 2.113C:267).

30. Carpenter, "Deuteronomy," 492.

31. Jeffrey H. Tigay, *Deuteronomy: The Traditional Hebrew Text with the New JPS Translations*, JPSTC (Philadelphia: Jewish Publication Society, 1996), 196.

32. *IVPBBCOT* 251.

33. Carpenter, "Deuteronomy," 493.

34. "The Code of Hammurabi," trans. T. Meek (*ANET* 178); "The Middle Assyrian Laws (Tablet A)," trans. M. Roth (*COS* 2.132:354, 359), laws 12, 55.

35. Carpenter, "Deuteronomy," 495–96.

36. "Lipit-Ishtar Lawcode," trans. S. N. Kramer (*ANET* 160), law 27; "The Code of Hammurabi," trans. T. Meek (*ANET* 170–71), law 117; "The Middle Assyrian Laws," trans. T. Meek (*ANET* 183–85), laws 40, 49, 52.

37. Carpenter, "Deuteronomy," 500.

38. "Hittite Laws," trans. H. A. Hoffner Jr. (*COS* 2.19:107), laws 1–4.

39. "The Code of Hammurabi," trans. T. Meek (*ANET* 171), laws 130–31.

40. Carpenter, "Deuteronomy," 503.

41. Carpenter, "Deuteronomy," 505.

42. *IVPBBCOT* 261.

43. K. A. Kitchen, *On the Reliability of the Old Testament* (Grand Rapids: Eerdmans, 2006), 292–93; *IVPBBCOT* 263.

44. "The Aramaic Text in Demotic Script," trans. R. C. Steiner (*COS* 1.99:323); "The Vassal-Treaties of Esarhaddon," trans. D. Wiseman (*ANET* 539), §69.

45. "The Epic of Gilgamesh," trans. E. A. Speiser (*ANET* 91–92).

46. "The Poem of the Righteous Sufferer," trans. B. Foster (*COS* 1.153:488); "The Babylonian Theodicy," trans. B. Foster (*COS* 1.154:493).

47. Eugene H. Merrill, *Deuteronomy*, NAC (Nashville: Broadman & Holman, 1994), 415.

48. Carl G. Rasmussen, *Zondervan Atlas of the Bible*, rev. ed. (Grand Rapids: Zondervan, 2010), 273.

Joshua

1. "The Code of Hammurabi," trans. T. Meek (*ANET* 170).

2. *ARAB* 2:195.

3. "Sinuhe," trans. M. Lichtheim (*COS* 1.38:79).

4. "The Laws of Hammurabi," trans. M. Roth (*COS* 2.131:345).

5. K. Lawson Younger Jr., *Ancient Conquest Accounts: A Study in Ancient Near Eastern and Biblical History Writing*, JSOTSup 98 (Sheffield: JSOT Press, 1990), 202–3.

6. Dominique Charpin, "I Am the Sun of Babylon," in *Experiencing Power, Generating Authority: Cosmos, Politics, and the Ideology of Kingship in Ancient Egypt and Mesopotamia*, ed. Jane A. Hill, Philip Jones, and Antonio J. Morales (Philadelphia: University of Pennsylvania Museum of Archaeology and Anthropology, 2013), 79.

7. RS 20:33.

8. Younger, *Ancient Conquest Accounts*, 210.

9. Younger, *Ancient Conquest Accounts*, 213.

10. Younger, *Ancient Conquest Accounts*, 215–16.

11. Younger, *Ancient Conquest Accounts*, 215–16.

12. "The (Israel) Stela of Merneptah," trans. J. K. Hoffmeier (*COS* 2.6:41).

13. "The Inscription of King Mesha," trans. K. A. D. Smelik (*COS* 2.23:137).

14. James K. Hoffmeier, *The Archaeology of the Bible* (Oxford: Lion, 2008), 48.

Judges

1. "Cyrus Cylinder," trans. M. Cogan (*COS* 2.124:315).

2. "The Inscription of King Mesha," trans. K. A. D. Smelik (*COS* 2.23:138).

3. K. A. Kitchen, *On the Reliability of the Old Testament* (Grand Rapids: Eerdmans, 2006), 217.

4. "The Inscription of King Mesha," trans. K. A. D. Smelik (*COS* 2.23:137).

5. Nahum M. Waldman, "The Imagery of Clothing, Covering, and Overpowering," *JANES* 19 (1989): 165.

6. "The Panamuwa Inscription," trans. K. L. Younger Jr. (*COS* 2.37:158).

1–2 Samuel

1. Roland de Vaux, *Ancient Israel*, 2 vols. in 1 (New York: McGraw-Hill, 1965), 1:25.
2. "Ugaritic Prayer for a City Under Siege," trans. D. Pardee (*COS* 1.88:284–85).
3. See Ps. 22:25; 50:14; 56:12; 61:5, 8; 65:1; 66:13; 76:11; 116:14, 18; 132:2.
4. William F. Edgerton and John A. Wilson, *Historical Records of Ramses III: The Texts in Medinet Habu* (Chicago: University of Chicago Press, 1936), 57.
5. G. R. Driver and John C. Miles, ed. and trans., *The Babylonian Laws*, 2 vols. (Oxford: Clarendon, 1955), 2:8–9.
6. "The Ba'lu Myth," trans. D. Pardee (*COS* 1.86:254–55).
7. "The Kirta Epic," trans. D. Pardee (*COS* 1.102:341).
8. David G. Firth, *1 & 2 Samuel*, AOTC 8 (Downers Grove, IL: IVP Academic, 2009), 68.
9. "Gilgamesh," trans. B. R. Foster (*COS* 1.132:459).
10. *AEL* 2:62–71.
11. John H. Walton, *Ancient Near Eastern Thought and the Old Testament: Introducing the Conceptual World of the Hebrew Bible* (Grand Rapids: Baker Academic, 2006), 114–18.
12. Robert B. Chisholm Jr., *1 & 2 Samuel*, TTCS (Grand Rapids: Baker Books, 2013), 33.
13. "The Ba'lu Myth," trans. D. Pardee (*COS* 1.86:250).
14. Walton, *Ancient Near Eastern Thought*, 240.
15. Walton, *Ancient Near Eastern Thought*, 249.
16. See Walton, *Ancient Near Eastern Thought*, 249–63, on which this summary of deductive divination is based.
17. Walton, *Ancient Near Eastern Thought*, 265.
18. Walton, *Ancient Near Eastern Thought*, 259.
19. P. Kyle McCarter Jr., *I Samuel: A New Translation with Introduction, Notes, and Commentary*, AB 8 (Garden City, NY: Doubleday, 1980), 133.
20. John Day, *Yahweh and the Gods and Goddesses of Canaan*, JSOTSup 265 (Sheffield: Sheffield Academic Press, 2000), 68–69, 131.
21. Day, *Yahweh and the Gods and Goddesses of Canaan*, 128.
22. Robert B. Chisholm Jr., "Yahweh versus the Canaanite Gods: Polemic in Judges and 1 Samuel 1–7," *BSac* 164 (2007): 180.
23. *AEL* 2:36.
24. Simon B. Parker, ed., *Ugaritic Narrative Poetry*, trans. Mark S. Smith, SBLWAW 9 (Atlanta: Society of Biblical Literature, 1997), 137.
25. K. A. Kitchen, *On the Reliability of the Old Testament* (Grand Rapids: Eerdmans, 2006), 95–96.
26. V. Philips Long, "1 Samuel," *ZIBBCOT* 2:311.
27. *AEL* 2:41.
28. *AEL* 2:41–42.
29. *AEL* 2:39.
30. Robert R. Wilson, *Prophecy and Society in Ancient Israel* (Philadelphia: Fortress, 1980), 103–6.
31. "The Report of Wenamun," trans. M. Lichtheim (*COS* 1.41:90).
32. Chisholm, *1 & 2 Samuel*, 69.
33. See Long, "1 Samuel," 322–23.
34. See Oded Borowski, *Agriculture in Iron Age Israel* (Winona Lake, IN: Eisenbrauns, 1987), 31–38, 88; Philip J. King and Lawrence E. Stager, *Life in Biblical Israel* (Louisville: Westminster John Knox, 2001), 86.

35. "The Annals of Thutmose II," trans. J. K. Hoffmeier (*COS* 2.2A:12); "Kurkh Monolith," trans. K. L. Younger Jr. (*COS* 2.113A:263).

36. McCarter, *I Samuel*, 229.

37. Chisholm, *1 & 2 Samuel*, 83.

38. Long, "1 Samuel," 329.

39. See the helpful discussions in Long, "1 Samuel," 330–31; King and Stager, *Life in Biblical Israel*, 167–69.

40. King and Stager, *Life in Biblical Israel*, 197.

41. McCarter, *I Samuel*, 250.

42. Chisholm, *1 & 2 Samuel*, 98.

43. "The Inscription of King Mesha," trans. K. A. D. Smelik (*COS* 2.23:137–38).

44. Chisholm, *1 & 2 Samuel*, 111.

45. Long, "1 Samuel," 342.

46. See Othmar Keel, *The Symbolism of the Biblical World* (Winona Lake, IN: Eisenbrauns, 1997), 59 (figs. 60, 61), 229 (fig. 313).

47. For a debate over Goliath's height, see J. Daniel Hays, "Reconsidering the Height of Goliath," *JETS* 48 (2005): 701–14; Clyde E. Billington, "Goliath and the Exodus Giants: How Tall Were They?" *JETS* 50 (2007): 489–508; J. Daniel Hays, "The Height of Goliath: A Response to Clyde Billington," *JETS* 50 (2007): 509–16.

48. See Yigael Yadin, *The Art of Warfare in Biblical Lands in the Light of Archaeological Discovery*, trans. M. Pearlman (London: Weidenfeld & Nicolson, 1963), 265.

49. "Sinuhe," trans. M. Lichtheim (*COS* 1.38:79).

50. "Apology of Hattusili III," trans. T. P. J. van den Hout (*COS* 1.77:201). See Harry A. Hoffner, "A Hittite Analogue to the David and Goliath Contest of Champions?," *CBQ* 30 (1968): 220–25.

51. King and Stager, *Life in Biblical Israel*, 228–29.

52. McCarter, *I Samuel*, 313.

53. Wilson, *Prophecy and Society in Ancient Israel*, 103.

54. "Epic of Creation," trans. B. R. Foster (*COS* 1.111:398).

55. King and Stager, *Life in Biblical Israel*, 54.

56. See Long, "1 Samuel," 354; David Toshio Tsumura, *The First Book of Samuel*, NICOT (Grand Rapids: Eerdmans, 2007), 486.

57. Chisholm, *1 & 2 Samuel*, 128.

58. Patrick D. Miller, *The Religion of Ancient Israel* (Louisville: Westminster John Knox, 2000), 56.

59. See Moshe Greenberg, *The Ḫab/piru* (New Haven: American Oriental Society 1955), 75–76. For a sociological analysis of these groups as depicted in Judges-Samuel, see Gregory Mobley, *The Empty Men: The Heroic Tradition of Ancient Israel*, ABRL (New York: Doubleday, 2005), 36–38.

60. See "The Autobiography of Idrimi," trans. T. Longman III (*COS* 1.148:479); Long, "1 Samuel," 357–58.

61. See Ada Taggar-Cohen, "Political Loyalty in the Biblical Account of 1 Samuel XX–XXII in the Light of Hittite Texts," *VT* 55 (2005): 263–65.

62. Long, "1 Samuel," 361.

63. McCarter, *I Samuel*, 250.

64. "The Kulamuwa Inscription," trans. K. L. Younger Jr. (*COS* 2.30:148).

65. "The Azatiwada Inscription," trans. K. L. Younger Jr. (*COS* 2.31:149).

66. King and Stager, *Life in Biblical Israel*, 118–19.

67. See McCarter, *I Samuel*, 384–85; Tony W. Cartledge, *1 & 2 Samuel*, SHBC (Macon, GA: Smyth & Helwys, 2001), 483.

68. King and Stager, *Life in Biblical Israel*, 113–14, 147–48.

69. See King and Stager, *Life in Biblical Israel*, 104.

70. Tsumura, *The First Book of Samuel*, 605.

71. See *TDOT* 1:130–34; Walton, *Ancient Near Eastern Thought*, 325. However, Ann Jeffers rejects this interpretation. She is content to say that an *ob* simply "appears at times to be a tool, an instrument used to get in touch with the spirits of the dead." See Jeffers, *Magic and Divination in Ancient Palestine and Syria*, SHCANE 8 (Leiden: Brill, 1996), 171.

72. McCarter, *I Samuel*, 250.

73. For a translation of the text, see "A Psephomancy Ritual from Assur," trans. V. Hurowitz (*COS* 1.127:444). For bibliography and discussion, see Kenton L. Sparks, *Ancient Texts for the Study of Scripture: A Guide to the Background Literature* (Peabody, MA: Hendrickson, 2005), 222.

74. "The Sarcophagus Inscription of Tabnit, King of Sidon," trans. P. K. McCarter (*COS* 2.56:181–82).

75. See King and Stager, *Life in Biblical Israel*, 117–18; Long, "1 Samuel," 385–86.

76. "The Ba'lu Myth," trans. D. Pardee (*COS* 1.86:250).

77. James B. Pritchard, ed., *The Ancient Near East in Pictures*, 2nd ed. (Princeton: Princeton University Press, 1969), 451.

78. Ronald F. Youngblood, "1, 2 Samuel," *EBC* 3:291.

79. Cartledge, *1 & 2 Samuel*, 343.

80. "The Aqhatu Legend," trans. D. Pardee (*COS* 1.103:351); see also V. Philips Long, "2 Samuel," *ZIBBCOT* 2:417.

81. See King and Stager, *Life in Biblical Israel*, 230; Long, "2 Samuel," 417.

82. J. A. Thompson, "The Significance of the Verb *Love* in the David-Jonathan Narratives in 1 Samuel," *VT* 24 (1974): 334–38.

83. See Robert B. Chisholm Jr., *From Exegesis to Exposition: A Practical Guide to Using Biblical Hebrew* (Grand Rapids: Baker, 1998), 40; Long, "2 Samuel," 417–18.

84. See de Vaux, *Ancient Israel*, 1:218; Long, "2 Samuel," 422–23.

85. See de Vaux, *Ancient Israel*, 1:242; Long, "2 Samuel," 423.

86. De Vaux, *Ancient Israel*, 1:115–16.

87. Long, "2 Samuel," 425.

88. "The Laws of Eshnunna," trans. A. Goetze (*ANET* 162).

89. "The Code of Hammurabi," trans. T. Meek (*ANET* 171, paragraphs 135–36).

90. On the legal background of this passage, see P. Kyle McCarter Jr., *II Samuel: A New Translation with Introduction, Notes, and Commentary*, AB 9 (Garden City, NY: Doubleday, 1984), 115; Cartledge, *1 & 2 Samuel*, 390.

91. *HALOT* 933.

92. See Long, "2 Samuel," 426; Cartledge, *1 & 2 Samuel*, 394.

93. Long, "2 Samuel," 426. For the text, see "The First Soldiers' Oath," trans. B. J. Collins (*COS* 1.66:166).

94. Cartledge, *1 & 2 Samuel*, 405.

95. For numerous examples from Egypt and Mesopotamia, see Jeffrey J. Niehaus, *Ancient Near Eastern Themes in Biblical Theology* (Grand Rapids: Kregel, 2008), 34–50.

96. "The Birth of Shulgi in the Temple of Nippur," trans. J. Klein (*COS* 1.172:553).

97. Niehaus, *Ancient Near Eastern Themes*, 46.

98. "Akkadian Oracles and Prophecies," trans. R. D. Biggs (*ANET* 605).

99. "The Inscription of Zakkur, King of Hamath," trans. A. Millard (*COS* 2.35:155).

100. Edgerton and Wilson, *Historical Records of Ramses III*, 45.

101. "The Tell Dan Stele," trans. A. Millard (*COS* 2.39:161). For Assyrian parallels to this motif, see "The Tell Dan Stele," trans. A. Millard (*COS* 2.39:161), n5.

102. For a discussion of these Assyrian examples, see McCarter, *II Samuel*, 180–81.

103. On the question of the relationship between royal grants and OT covenants, see Moshe Weinfeld, "The Covenant of Grant in the Old Testament and in the Ancient Near East," *JAOS* 90 (1970): 189–93.

104. Gary N. Knoppers, "Ancient Near Eastern Royal Grants and the Davidic Covenant: A Parallel?," *JAOS* 116 (1996): 670–97.

105. Knoppers, "Ancient Near Eastern Royal Grants," 682–83.

106. "The Treaty of Tudhaliya IV with Kurunta of Tarhuntassa of the Bronze Tablet Found in Hattusa," trans. H. A. Hoffner Jr. (*COS* 2.18:103–4).

107. "The Treaty of Tudhaliya IV with Kurunta of Tarhuntassa of the Bronze Tablet Found in Hattusa," trans. H. A. Hoffner Jr. (*COS* 2.18:105).

108. "The Azatiwada Inscription," trans. K. L. Younger (*COS* 2.31:149).

109. "The Ba'lu Myth," trans. D. Pardee (*COS* 1.86:246).

110. King and Stager, *Life in Biblical Israel*, 35. McCarter (*II Samuel*, 285) suggests that David's bed was on the roof.

111. King and Stager, *Life in Biblical Israel*, 70.

112. McCarter, *II Samuel*, 288.

113. Long, "2 Samuel," 460.

114. See "The Descent of Ishtar to the Underworld," trans. S. Dalley (*COS* 1.108:381–84). See also Ps. 9:13; 107:18; Jon. 2:6.

115. See McCarter, *II Samuel*, 312; de Vaux, *Ancient Israel*, 1:234–35.

116. McCarter, *II Samuel*, 312.

117. "The Two Brothers," trans. M. Lichtheim (*COS* 1.85:87); see McCarter, *II Samuel*, 326.

118. "The Epic of Gilgamesh," trans. E. A. Speiser (*ANET* 75).

119. Long, "2 Samuel," 464.

120. "The Kirta Epic," trans. D. Pardee (*COS* 1.102:342).

121. See de Vaux, *Ancient Israel*, 1:122–23; McCarter, *2 Samuel*, 372.

122. "Sennacherib's First Campaign: Against Merodach-Baladan," trans. M. Cogan (*COS* 2.119A:301); "Sennacherib's Siege of Jerusalem," trans. M. Cogan (*COS* 2.119B:303).

123. Long, "2 Samuel," 467.

124. De Vaux, *Ancient Israel*, 1:255.

125. McCarter, *II Samuel*, 406.

126. McCarter, *II Samuel*, 407.

127. McCarter, *II Samuel*, 409. For the text, see "Letter of Abdi-Heba of Jerusalem," trans. W. Moran (*COS* 3.92:237) (*EA* 286).

128. De Vaux, *Ancient Israel*, 1:141–42; McCarter, *II Samuel*, 434.

129. See, for example, "Treaty between Ashurnirari V of Assyria and Mati'ilu of Arpad," trans. E. Reiner (*ANET* 532–33), paragraph 4; "The Vassal-Treates of Esarhaddon," trans. E. Reiner (*ANET* 534–41), paragraph 56; "The Treaty between *KTK* and Arpad," trans. F. Rosenthal (*ANET* 659–61).

130. For discussion of the Hittite parallel, see McCarter, *II Samuel*, 444; see also Cartledge, *1 & 2 Samuel*, 639.

131. Simeon Chavel, "Compositry and Creativity in 2 Samuel 21:1–4," *JBL* 122 (2003): 41.

132. Jacob Milgrom, *Leviticus: A Book of Ritual and Ethics*, CC (Minneapolis: Fortress, 2004), 52–53.

133. Milgrom, *Leviticus*, 53.

134. For a detailed study of ancient Near Eastern, especially Hittite, parallels, see Jacob Milgrom, *Cult and Conscience: The Asham and the Priestly Doctrine of Repentance*, SJLA 18 (Leiden: Brill, 1976), 16–35.

135. For numerous parallels, see Robert Bruce Chisholm Jr., "An Exegetical and Theological Study of Psalm 18/2 Samuel 22" (ThD diss., Dallas Theological Seminary, 1983), 160–62, 166–67, 170, 172–78, 181–83, 190–92, 196.

136. See "The Ba'lu Myth," trans. D. Pardee (*COS* 1.86:262–63); Parker, *Ugaritic Narrative Poetry*, 111–12, 129, 136–37.

137. "Ishkur and the Destruction of the Rebellious Land," trans. S. N. Kramer (*ANET* 578).

138. W. G. Lambert and A. R. Millard, *Atra-Ḫasīs: The Babylonian Story of the Flood* (Oxford: Clarendon, 1969), 121–22.

139. Chisholm, "Psalm 18/2 Samuel 22," 211–12.

140. Chisholm, "Psalm 18/2 Samuel 22," 41–44.

141. See Chisholm, "Psalm 18/2 Samuel 22," 229–30.

142. Keel, *The Symbolism of the Biblical World*, 265.

143. Chisholm, "Psalm 18/2 Samuel 22," 260–61.

144. Edgerton and Wilson, *Historical Records of Ramses III*, 4.

145. Edgerton and Wilson, *Historical Records of Ramses III*, 207.

146. Chisholm, "Psalm 18/2 Samuel 22," 260–61.

147. Chisholm, "Psalm 18/2 Samuel 22," 268.

148. Chisholm, "Psalm 18/2 Samuel 22," 280–81.

149. For numerous examples, see Chisholm, "Psalm 18/2 Samuel 22," 131n2. See also McCarter, *II Samuel*, 484.

150. See de Vaux, *Ancient Israel*, 1:119–20; McCarter, *II Samuel*, 256.

151. See Long, "2 Samuel," 479–80.

152. See Long, "2 Samuel," 480; King and Stager, *Life in Biblical Israel*, 240.

153. See McCarter, *II Samuel*, 513–14.

1–2 Kings

1. ARM 6.76:20–25.

2. William L. Moran, ed. and trans., *Les Lettres d'El-Amarna: Correspondance diplomatique du pharaon*, LAPO 13 (Paris: Cerf, 1987), 221; ET in William L. Moran, ed. and trans., *The Amarna Letters* (Baltimore: Johns Hopkins University Press, 1992), 122.

3. Nahman Avigad, "The Chief of the Corvée," *IEJ* 30 (1980): 170–73.

4. Kenneth A. Kitchen, "Shishak's Military Campaign in Israel Confirmed," *BAR* 15 (1989): 32–33.

5. Othmar Keil and Christoph Uehlinger, *Gods, Goddesses, and Images of God in Ancient Israel*, trans. Thomas H. Trapp (Minneapolis: Fortress, 1998), 225–27.

6. "The Tale of Aqhat," trans. H. L. Ginsberg (*ANET* 153).

7. RS 25.460, line 11.

8. "A Hymn to Baal Enthroned" (*KTU* 1.101).

9. "Texts from Hammurabi to the Downfall of the Assyrian Empire," trans. A. L. Oppenheim (*ANET* 280).

10. "Texts from Hammurabi to the Downfall of the Assyrian Empire," trans. A. L. Oppenheim (*ANET* 297).

11. Daniel David Luckenbill, *The Annals of Sennacherib* (Chicago: University of Chicago Press, 1924), 111.

12. *ARAB* 2:795, 304.

13. Letter 26 385 in Wolfgang Heimpel, *Letters to the King of Mari: A New Translation with Historical Introduction, Notes, and Commentary*, MC 12 (Winona Lake, IN: Eisenbrauns, 2003), 333.

14. "The Moabite Stone," trans. W. F. Albright (*ANET* 320).

15. Georges Boyer, *Archives royales de Mari VIII: Textes juridiques et administratifs* (Paris: P. Geuthner, 1957), no. 1, lines 19–26.

16. Avraham Biran and Joseph Naveh, "The Tel Dan Inscription: A New Fragment," *IEJ* 45 (1995): 13.

17. "The Moabite Stone," trans. W. F. Albright (*ANET* 320).

18. "The Inscription of Zakkur, King of Hamath," trans. A. Millard (*COS* 2.35:155).

19. *KBo* 1.14 (*CTH* 173), rev. 4–10 9.

20. Pamela Gerardi, "The Arab Campaigns of Assurbanipal: Scribal Reconstruction of the Past," *SAAB* 6, no. 2 (1992): 73.

21. "The Code of Hammurabi," trans. T. Meek (*ANET* 164).

22. "Black Obelisk," trans. K. L. Younger Jr. (*COS* 2.133F:270).

23. Janice Kamrin, *The Cosmos of Khnumhotep II at Beni Hasan* (New York: Routledge, 2011), 93.

24. Ivan T. Kaufman, "Samaria Ostraca," *ABD* 5:921.

25. "Texts from Hammurabi to the Downfall of the Assyrian Empire," trans. A. L. Oppenheim (*ANET* 283).

26. "Texts from Hammurabi to the Downfall of the Assyrian Empire," trans. A. L. Oppenheim (*ANET* 283–84).

27. "Texts from Hammurabi to the Downfall of the Assyrian Empire," trans. A. L. Oppenheim (*ANET* 283).

28. Robert Deutsch, "First Impression: What We Learn from King Ahaz's Seal," *BAR* 24 (1998): 55.

29. "Mesopotamian Omens," trans. A. Guinan (*COS* 1.120:423).

30. André Lemaire, "Royal Signature: Name of Israel's Last King Surfaces in a Private Collection," *BAR* 2 (1995): 49.

31. "Nimrud Prisms D & E," trans. K. L. Younger Jr. (*COS* 2.118D:295–96).

32. Frank Moore Cross, "King Hezekiah's Seal Bears Phoenician Imagery," *BAR* 25 (1999): 42.

33. "Sennacherib's Seige of Jerusalem," trans. M. Cogan (*COS* 2.119B:303).

34. Nahman Avigad, "The Epitaph of a Royal Steward from Siloam Village," *IEJ* 3 (1953): 143.

35. "Seal and Seal Impressions: Hebrew," trans. J. H. Tigay and A. R. Millard (*COS* 2.70D:198).

36. "The Siloam Tunnel Inscription," trans. K. L. Younger Jr. (*COS* 2.28:145–46).

37. BM 36703 and K 2779 in Irving L. Finkel, "Necromancy in Ancient Mesopotamia," *AfO* 29/30 (1983): 10.

38. Jean-Jacques Glassner, *Mesopotamian Chronicles*, ed. Benjamin R. Foster, SBLWAW 19 (Atlanta: Society of Biblical Literature, 2004), 223–34.

39. D. J. Wiseman, *Chronicles of Chaldaean Kings (626–556 B.C.) in the British Museum* (London: Trustees of the British Musuem, 1956), 33.

40. "Lachish Ostraca," trans. D. Pardee (*COS* 3.42B:79).

41. "Lachish Ostraca," trans. D. Pardee (*COS* 3.42C:80).

42. "The Neo-Babylonian Empire and Its Successors," trans. A. L. Oppenheim (*ANET* 308).

1–2 Chronicles

1. "Tombstone Inscription," trans. B. Porten (*COS* 2.66:190–91).

2. "The Inscription of King Mesha," trans. K. A. D. Smelik (*COS* 2.23:137).

3. "Sennacherib's Siege of Jerusalem," trans. M. Cogan (*COS* 2.119B:303).

4. EA 16.33.

5. "Two Hymns to the Sun God," trans. M. Lichtheim (*COS* 1.27:43).

6. "The Great Hymn to the Aten," trans. M. Lichtheim (*COS* 1.28:46).

7. "The Great Hymn to Osiris," trans. M. Lichtheim (*COS* 1.26:42).

8. "The Shamash Hymn," trans. B. R. Foster (*COS* 1.117:418–19).

9. "The Calah Annals," trans. K. L. Younger Jr. (*COS* 2.117A:284–86); "Summary Inscription 4," trans. K. L. Younger Jr. (*COS* 2.117C:287–88).

10. "Black Obelisk," trans. K. L. Younger Jr. (*COS* 2.113F:269–70).

11. "The Hadad Inscription," trans. K. L. Younger Jr. (*COS* 2.36:158).

12. "Calah Orthostat Slab," trans. K. L. Younger Jr. (*COS* 2.114G:276).

13. "The Curse of Agade," 1.162–63.

14. EA 19.

15. "Seal and Seal Impressions: Hebrew," trans. J. H. Tigay and A. R. Millard (*COS* 2.70U:201).

16. "Treaty between Mursili and Duppi-Tesub," trans. I. Singer (*COS* 2.17B:97).

17. EA 7.14–16.

18. "Seals and Seal Impressions: Hebrew," trans. J. H. Tigay and A. R. Millard (*COS* 2.70T:200).

19. "Sennacherib's Siege of Jerusalem," trans. M. Cogan (*COS* 2.119B:303).

20. "Sennacherib's Siege of Jerusalem," trans. M. Cogan (*COS* 2.119B:303).

21. "Sennacherib's Siege of Jerusalem," trans. M. Cogan (*COS* 2.119B:303).

22. "The Siloam Tunnel Inscription," trans. K. L. Younger Jr. (*COS* 2.28:145).

23. "Seals and Seal Impressions: Hebrew," trans. J. H. Tigay and A. R. Millard (*COS* 2.70D:198).

24. D. J. Wiseman, *Chronicles of Chaldaean Kings (626–556 B.C.) in the British Museum* (London: Trustees of the British Musuem, 1956), 33.

25. "Treaty between Mursili and Duppi-Tesub," trans. I. Singer (*COS* 2.17B:96).

26. "Cyrus Cylinder," trans. M. Cogan (*COS* 2.124:315–16).

Ezra–Nehemiah

1. "Request for Letter of Recommendation (First Draft)," trans. B. Porten (*COS* 3.51:128).

Esther

1. This introductory formula appears in other historical books such as Joshua, Judges, Ruth, and Samuel. The author provides precise descriptions of Persian society and the Persian court, revealing intimate and extensive knowledge of the times and setting.

2. A later Xerxes II ruled for a very short period of time (forty-five days in 424 BC). See Pierre Briant, *From Cyrus to Alexander: A History of the Persian Empire*, trans. Peter T.

Daniels (Winona Lake, IN: Eisenbrauns, 2002), 772; Edwin M. Yamauchi, *Persia and the Bible* (Grand Rapids: Baker, 1997), 392n98.

3. Yamauchi, *Persia and the Bible*, 178–79.

4. Briant, *From Cyrus to Alexander*, 173.

5. These would have included princes, nobles and eunuchs, counselors, the cupbearer, court physicians, maids, and servants.

6. On the political statement of gardens, see David Stronach, "The Royal Garden at Pasargadae: Evolution and Legacy," *AIO* 1 (1989): 475–502; David Stronach, "The Garden as a Political Statement: Case Studies from the Near East in the First Millennium BC," *BAI* 4 (1991): 171–80.

7. John Curtis and Nigel Tallis, eds., *Forgotten Empire: The World of Ancient Persia* (Berkeley: University of California Press, 2005), 121–22, illus. 118–21.

8. Herodotus, *Histories* 7.61. While it is known that the king had other wives, Herodotus mentions only queen mothers.

9. William H. Shea, "Esther and History," *AUSS* 14 (1976): 235, 240. Amestris does reemerge in Herodotus's *Histories* in her old age. Following a known practice in Persia, Amestris buried alive seven pairs of youths as a thank offering to the netherworld god (Herodotus, *Histories* 7.114).

10. Maria Brosius, *Women in Ancient Persia, 559–331 BC*, OCM (Oxford: Oxford University Press, 1996), 94–97.

11. There were many different feasts that women attended, including New Year's feasts, the king's birthday, religious feasts, weddings, funerary banquets, and feasts held for the army.

12. Herodotus, *Histories* 7.187.

13. Herodotus, *Histories* 7.34–35. In the most shocking account of Xerxes's temper, the king ordered the beheading of his engineers after the new bridge they built at the Hellespont was destroyed in a violent storm.

14. Michael V. Fox, *Character and Ideology in the Book of Esther* (Grand Rapids: Eerdmans, 2001), 20.

15. Herodotus, *Histories* 1.99.

16. Herodotus, *Histories* 3.77. Because of their unrestricted access to the king, they were potentially also his most dangerous enemies.

17. See Plutarch, *Artaxerxes*. There Plutarch speaks of Persian royalty who went against the law in their selection of wives: Artexerxes II took Atossa, his own daughter, as wife (23.3), and Darius, Artexerxes II's son, requested Aspasia, an Ionian freewoman, concubine of Cyrus the Younger (27.2). In the biblical text irrevocable laws are mentioned in Esther 1:19; 8:8; Dan. 6:8, 12, 15.

18. Most royal inscriptions during this period were written in Old Persian, Elamite, and Babylonian or Aramaic. The Hebrew text says "and speak according to the tongue of his people," implying that there were mixed marriages among the various people groups with parents speaking different languages. This is a social dilemma echoed in the family dynamics of the returned exiles (Neh. 13:23–24). For a further discussion on matrimonial influence through language, see Karen Jobes, *Esther*, NIVAC (Grand Rapids: Zondervan, 1999), 82.

19. Herodotus, *Histories* 3.84.

20. Plutarch, *Artaxerxes* 23.3.

21. Herodotus, *Histories* 6.32.

22. A beautiful blue chalcedony gem discovered in Eretria, Greece, depicts a Persian woman dressed in a flowing robe and holding flowers. It dates to around 400 BC and is now

in the British Museum (BM 1895,0511.7). See John L. Papanek, ed., *Persians: Masters of Empire* (Alexandria, VA: Time-Life Books, 1995), 106.

23. *HALOT* 632.

24. The myrtle tree or branch is also referred to in Neh. 8:15; Isa. 41:19; 55:13; Zech. 1:8, 10.

25. *CAD* 6:22.

26. *HALOT* 76.

27. Lloyd Llewellyn-Jones, *King and Court in Ancient Persia 559 to 331 BCE*, DDAH (Edinburgh: Edinburgh University Press, 2013), 57.

28. "Concubine," in *Kohlenberger/Mounce Concise Hebrew-Aramaic Dictionary of the Old Testament*, ed. John R. Kohlenberger III and William D. Mounce, digital ed. (2012), H7109.

29. Anthony Tomasino, "Esther," *ZIBBCOT* 3:485.

30. Herodotus, *Histories* 7.33.

31. Herodotus (*Histories* 8.85) refers to list of "benefactors" who were given large rewards for their deeds.

32. Chaim Miller, ed., *The Gutnick Edition Chumash: The Book of Deuteronomy; With Rashi's Commentary, Targum Onkelos, Haftoras and Commentary Anthologized from Classic Rabbinic Texts and the Works of the Lubavitcher Rebbe* (Brooklyn: Kol Menachem, 2005), 185.

33. Kings of nations bowed before Solomon (Ps. 72:9); Jacob and his family bowed before Esau (Gen. 33:7).

34. Herodotus, *Histories* 1.134.

35. *CAD* 12:528–29.

36. "Simmurum—Iddi(n)-Sin," trans. D. Frayne (*COS* 2.106:225).

37. Shmuel Ahituv, *Echoes from the Past: Hebrew and Cognate Inscriptions from the Biblical Period* (Jerusalem: Carta, 2008), 394–95.

38. According to Herodotus, "If night had not intervened they would not have left a single one alive" (*Histories* 3.79).

39. Herodotus, *Histories* 3.95.

40. Xenophon, *Cyropaedia* 8.8.13.

41. For examples, see Curtis and Tallis, *Forgotten Empire*, 146, illus. 180–82.

42. All three types of seals have been found at Persepolis. See Erich F. Schmidt, *Persepolis*, vol. 2, *Contents of the Treasury and Other Discoveries*, OIP 69 (Chicago: Oriental Institute, 2010), plate 2, PT4 619. See also Nils C. Ritter, "On the Development of Sasanian Seals and Sealing Practice: A Mesopotamian Approach," in *Seals and Sealing Practices in the Near East: Developments in Administration and Magic from Prehistory to the Islamic Period; Proceedings of an International Workshop at the Netherlands-Flemish Institute in Cairo on December 2–3, 2009*, ed. Ilona Regulski, Kim Duistermaat, and Peter Verkinderen, OLA 219 (Leuven: Peeters, 2012), 108. A royal cylinder seal belonging to Xerxes's father, Darius I, depicts the king in his royal chariot drawn by the royal horse. See Curtis and Tallis, *Forgotten Empire*, 221, illus. 398 (British Museum 89132).

43. Dominique Collon, *First Impressions: Cylinder Seals in the Ancient Near East* (London: British Museum Publications, 2005), 113.

44. Herodotus, *Histories* 8.99. For a Babylonian example of self-affliction before the gods, see "The Adad-Guppi Autobiography," trans. T. Longman III (*COS* 1.147:477–78).

45. John Boardman, *Persia and the West: An Archaeological Investigation of the Genesis of Achaemenid Art* (London: Thames & Hudson, 2000), 142, fig. 4.13. This relief is now in the National Archaeological Museum in Tehran. Josephus describes the setting: "Men, with axes in their hands, stood around his throne, in order to punish such as approached to him without being called" (*Jewish Antiquities* 11.205).

46. Herodotus, *Histories* 8.85; 9.107.

47. For a detailed discussion, see Llewellyn-Jones, *King and Court in Ancient Persia*, 66.

48. Amélie Kuhrt, *The Persian Empire: A Corpus of Sources from the Achaemenid Period* (London: Routledge, 2010), 473. See also David Stronach's discussion on the Persian royal robe in David Stronach and Hilary Gopnik, "Pasargadae," in *Encyclopaedia Iranica*, http://www.iranicaonline.org/articles/Pasargadae.

49. In a contrasting scenario, Plutarch describes Artaxerxes II giving Tiribazus his torn robe but not allowing him to wear it (*Artaxerxes* 5.2).

50. Xenophon, *Cyropaedia* 8.3.23.

51. Royal horses with crests can be seen on reliefs of the Eastern Stairway of the Apadana at Persepolis. See "The Apadana," *The Oriental Institute of the University of Chicago*, https://oi.uchicago.edu/gallery/apadana#1F10_72dpi.png. A royal cylinder seal belonging to Xerxes's father, Darius I, depicts the king in his royal chariot drawn by the royal horse. See Curtis and Tallis, *Forgotten Empire*, 221, illus. 398 (British Museum ANE 89132).

52. Yamauchi, *Persia and the Bible*, 262.

53. Herodotus, *Histories* 3.127–29.

54. Yamauchi, *Persia and the Bible*, 238.

55. Llewellyn-Jones, *King and Court in Ancient Persia*, 63–66; Xenophon, *Cyropaedia* 8.3.13.

56. Unfortunately, at the request of Xerxes, many on board the ship jumped overboard so as to lighten the load. (Herodotus, *Histories* 8.118).

57. Yamauchi, *Persia and the Bible*, 235.

58. Chone Shmeruk, "Purim," *EncJud* 13:1390–403. According to *Megillah* 1:1 in the Mishnah, "The Scroll [of Esther] is read on the eleventh, twelfth, thirteenth, fourteenth, [or] fifteenth [of Adar], no earlier, no later. Cities surrounded by a wall from the time of Joshua bin Nun read [the Scroll of Esther] on the fifteenth. Villages and large towns read it on the fourteenth. But villages push it up [a day early] to a day of assembly [a Monday or a Thursday]." Jacob Neusner, trans., *The Mishnah: A New Translation* (New Haven: Yale University Press, 1988).

59. Jobes, *Esther*, 224.

Job

1. "The Protests of the Eloquent Peasant," trans. John A. Wilson (*ANET* 407–10).

2. "A Dispute over Suicide," trans. John A. Wilson (*ANET* 405–7).

3. "The Poem of the Righteous Sufferer," trans. B. R. Foster (*COS* 1.153:486–92).

4. "A Dialogue about Human Misery," trans. R. H. Pfeiffer (*ANET* 438–40).

5. John A. Beck, *The Baker Illustrated Guide to Everyday Life in Bible Times* (Grand Rapids: Baker Books, 2013), 195–97.

6. Philip J. King and Lawrence E. Stager, *Life in Biblical Israel* (Louisville: Westminster John Knox, 2001), 195.

7. King and Stager, *Life in Biblical Israel*, 269.

8. C. L. Seow locates the Sabeans in the vicinity of Tema rather than in Sheba, given that location is too far south. *Job 1–21: Illumination and Commentary*, Illuminations (Grand Rapids: Eerdmans, 2013), 277–78.

9. Seow, *Job 1–21*, 558.

10. An alkaline solution. See David J. A. Clines, *Job 1–20*, WBC 17 (Dallas: Word, 1989), 220n30.c.

11. Seow, *Job 1–21*, 678.

12. Seow, *Job 1–21*, 786.

13. David J. A. Clines, *Job 21–37*, WBC 18A (Nashville: Thomas Nelson, 2006), 524.

14. Othmar Keel, *Jahwes Entgegnung an Ijob: Eine Deutung von Ijob 38–41 vor dem Hintergrund der zeitgenössischen Bildkunst*, FRLANT 121 (Göttingen: Vandenhoeck & Ruprecht, 1978), 72.

15. Or it may have been at the setting of the capstone. See David J. A. Clines, *Job 38–42*, WBC 18B (Nashville: Thomas Nelson, 2011), 1160.

16. Clines, *Job 38–42*, 1110.

17. Clines, *Job 38–42*, 1119.

18. Clines, *Job 38–42*, 1120.

19. Clines, *Job 38–42*, 1123.

20. Clines, *Job 38–42*, 1125–26.

21. Clines, *Job 38–42*, 1126.

22. Keel, *Jahwes Entgegnung an Ijob*, 69n234.

23. Clines, *Job 38–42*, 1189.

24. Keel, *Jahwes Entgegnung an Ijob*, 132–39.

25. Clines, *Job 38–42*, 1189.

26. Simon Davis, "The Large Mammal Bones," in *Excavations at Tell Qasile*, vol. 2, *The Philistine Sanctuary: Various Finds, the Pottery, the Conclusions*, ed. Amihai Mazar, Qedem 20 (Jerusalem: Institute of Archaeology, Hebrew University, 1985), 148–50.

27. King and Stager, *Life in Biblical Israel*, 89; Clines, *Job 38–42*, 1199.

28. Clines, *Job 38–42*, 1238.

Psalms

1. Jerome F. D. Creach, *The Destiny of the Righteous in the Psalms* (St. Louis: Chalice, 2008), 3.

2. Creach, *The Destiny of the Righteous in the Psalms*, 136.

3. Gerald Wilson, *Psalms*, vol. 1, *Psalms 1–72*, NIVAC (Grand Rapids: Zondervan, 2002), 569.

4. Frank-Lothar Hossfeld and Erich Zenger, *Psalms 2: A Commentary on Psalms 51–100*, ed. Klaus Baltzer, trans. Linda M. Maloney, Hermeneia (Minneapolis: Fortress, 2005), 256.

5. Hossfeld and Zenger, *Psalms 2*, 387.

6. Hossfeld and Zenger, *Psalms 2*, 383.

Proverbs

1. Kenneth A. Kitchen counts forty works of instructional "wisdom." *On the Reliability of the Old Testament* (Grand Rapids: Eerdmans, 2006), 135.

2. "The Instruction of Amenemope," trans. W. K. Simpson (*LAE* 224).

3. "The Ba'alu Myth," trans. D. Pardee (*COS* 1.86:264–66).

4. "Instruction of Any," trans. M. Lichtheim (*COS* 1.46:111).

5. "The Maxims of Ptahhotep," trans. V. A. Tobin (*LAE* 138).

6. "Azatiwada Inscription," trans. K. L. Younger Jr. (*COS* 2.31:150).

7. "The Great Cairo Hymn of Praise to Amun-Re," trans. R. K. Ritner (*COS* 1.25:38).

8. "The Dispute between a Man and His Ba," trans. N. Shupak (*COS* 3.146:323).

9. "A Pessimistic Dialogue between Master and Servant," trans. R. H. Pfeiffer (*ANET* 438). Note, however, that the complaints in this text perhaps are intentionally and humorously contrarian.

10. "A Debt Note," trans. K. L. Younger Jr. (*COS* 3.116:263).

11. "Shuruppak," trans. B. Alster (*COS* 1.176:569).

12. "Instruction of Any," trans. M. Lichtheim (*COS* 1.46:112).

13. This translation of lines 94b–95, which involves some textual reconstruction, is cited by Michael V. Fox, *Proverbs 1–9: A New Translation with Introduction and Commentary*, AB 18A (New York: Doubleday, 2000), 332.

14. "The Instruction of 'Onchsheshonqy," trans. R. K. Ritner (*LAE* 497–529).

15. "Counsels of Wisdom," trans. R. H. Pfeiffer (*ANET* 427).

16. "Counsels of Wisdom," trans. R. H. Pfeiffer (*ANET* 427).

17. "The Instruction of Amenemope," trans. W. K. Simpson (*LAE* 237).

18. "The Instruction of Amenemope," trans. W. K. Simpson (*LAE* 232).

19. From "Ahiqar," as cited in Michael V. Fox, *Proverbs 10–31*, AYB 18B (New Haven: Yale University Press, 2009), 734.

20. Benjamin R. Foster, *Before the Muses: An Anthology of Akkadian Literature*, 3rd ed. (Bethesda, MD: CDL Press, 2005), 413.

21. "The Divine Attributes of Pharaoh," trans. J. A. Wilson (*ANET* 431).

22. See, for example, "The Instruction of Amenemope," trans. W. K. Simpson (*LAE* 227).

23. "Instruction of Any," trans. M. Lichtheim (*COS* 1.46:112–13).

24. "The Maxims of Ptahhotep," trans. V. A. Tobin (*LAE* 139).

25. Philip J. King and Lawrence E. Stager, *Life in Biblical Israel* (Louisville: Westminster John Knox, 2001), 101–2.

26. "Instruction of Any," trans. M. Lichtheim (*COS* 1.46:111).

27. Fox, *Proverbs 10–31*, 676.

28. King and Stager, *Life in Biblical Israel*, 106.

29. Fox, *Proverbs 10–31*, 786.

30. Cited in Fox, *Proverbs 10–31*, 787.

31. Fox, *Proverbs 10–31*, 800.

Ecclesiastes

1. "The Epic of Gilgamesh," trans. E. A. Speiser (*ANET* 79).

2. "The Complaints of Khakneperre-sonb," trans. N. Shupak (*COS* 1.44:105).

3. "The Song of the Harper," trans. V. A. Tobin (*LAE* 332).

4. "The Complaints of Khakneperre-sonb," trans. N. Shupak (*COS* 1.44:104).

5. "The Epic of Gilgamesh," trans. E. A. Speiser (*ANET* 73).

6. "The Azatiwada Inscription," trans. K. L. Younger Jr. (*COS* 2.31:149).

7. Benjamin R. Foster, *Before the Muses: An Anthology of Akkadian Literature*, 3rd ed. (Bethesda, MD: CDL Press, 2005), 925.

8. "The Dispute between a Man and His Ba," trans. N. Shupak (*COS* 3.146:323).

9. "The Eloquent Peasant," trans. N. Shupak (*COS* 1.43:101).

10. "The Babylonian Theodicy," trans. B. R. Foster (*COS* 1.154:494).

11. "The Prophecies of Neferti," trans. N. Shupak (*COS* 1.45:109).

12. "The Maxims of Ptahhotep," trans. V. A. Tobin (*LAE* 134–35).

13. "The Teaching for King Merikare," trans. V. A. Tobin (*LAE* 156).

14. Josephus, *The Life* 69; 296.

15. Foster, *Before the Muses*, 924.

16. "Ahiqar," trans. J. M. Lindenberger, in *The Old Testament Pseudepigrapha*, ed. James H. Charlesworth, 2 vols. (Peabody, MA: Hendrickson, 1983), 2:500.

17. "The Tomb Inscription of Si'gabbar, Priest of Sahar," trans. P. K. McCarter (*COS* 2.59:185).

18. "The Song of the Harper," trans. V. A. Tobin (*LAE* 333).
19. "The Epic of Gilgamesh," trans. E. A. Speiser (*ANET* 90).
20. "The Prophecies of Neferti," trans. V. A. Tobin (*LAE* 219).
21. "The Instructions of 'Onchsheshonqy," trans. R. K. Ritner (*LAE* 519).
22. "The Maxims of Ptahhotep," trans. V. A. Tobin (*LAE* 139).
23. "The Song of the Harper," trans. V. A. Tobin (*LAE* 332–33).
24. "The Maxims of Ptahhotep," trans. V. A. Tobin (*LAE* 130).
25. "The Complaints of Khakneperre-sonb," trans. N. Shupak (*COS* 1.44:104).

Song of Songs

1. Michael V. Fox, *The Song of Songs and the Ancient Egyptian Love Songs* (Madison: University of Wisconsin Press, 1985), 33–34.

2. W. G. Lambert, "Three Literary Prayers of the Babylonians," *AfO* 19 (1959–60): 59, lines 163–64 [47–66]. The translation above follows Kyle Greenwood, "A Shuilla: Anu 1," in *Reading Akkadian Prayers and Hymns: An Introduction*, ed. Alan Lenzi (Atlanta: Society of Biblical Literature, 2011), 225, lines 13–14 [217–26].

3. VAB 4 258 ii 13–14.

4. Kenneth A. Kitchen, *Ramesside Inscriptions: Translated & Annotated, Translations*, Volume II (Oxford: Blackwell, 1996), 2:499.

Isaiah

1. For the critical approach, see John L. McKenzie, *Second Isaiah: Introduction, Translation, and Notes*, AB 20 (Garden City, NY: Doubleday, 1968), xv–xxx. For the traditional approach, see John N. Oswalt, *Isaiah 1–39*, NICOT (Grand Rapids: Eerdmans, 1986), 17–28; Gary V. Smith, *Isaiah 40–66*, NAC (Nashville: B&H, 2009), 26–48.

2. David W. Baker, "Isaiah," *ZIBBCOT* 4:61–62.

3. Baker, "Isaiah," 63.

4. "Cyrus Cylinder," trans. M. Cogan (*COS* 2.124:315–16).

5. "Texts from Hammurabi to the Downfall of the Assyrian Empire," trans. A. L. Oppenheim (*ANET* 286).

6. "Texts from Hammurabi," 288.

7. "Texts from Hammurabi," 287–88.

8. "Texts from Hammurabi," 288–89.

9. "Temple Program for the New Year's Festivals at Babylon," trans. A. Sachs (*ANET* 331).

10. Baker, "Isaiah," 139.

11. "Cyrus Cylinder," trans. M. Cogan (*COS* 2.124:315–16).

12. Baker, "Isaiah," 155.

13. *IVPBBCOT* 632.

14. "Merikare," trans. M. Lichtheim (*COS* 1.35:62).

15. Baker, "Isaiah," 168.

16. *IVPBBCOT* 634.

17. "Epic of Creation," trans. B. R. Foster (*COS* 1.111:394, 397).

Jeremiah

1. See Philip J. King, *Jeremiah: An Archaeological Companion* (Louisville: Westminster John Knox, 1993), 154–57.

2. On fertility rites, see Richard S. Hess, *Israelite Religions: An Archaeological and Biblical Survey* (Grand Rapids: Baker Academic; Nottingham: Apollos, 2007), 258–60.

3. Aaron Chalmers, *Interpreting the Prophets: Reading, Understanding and Preaching from the Worlds of the Prophets* (Downers Grove, IL: IVP Academic, 2015), 19–20.

4. For more on this process, see King, *Jeremiah*, 179–84.

5. King, *Jeremiah*, 102–7.

6. King, *Jeremiah*, 136–39.

7. See Steven Voth, "Jeremiah," *ZIBBCOT* 4:257–58, 271–72.

8. For more on these practices, see Michael B. Dick, ed., *Born in Heaven, Made on Earth: The Making of the Cult Image in the Ancient Near East* (Winona Lake, IN: Eisenbrauns, 1999).

9. On the craft of pottery and Jeremiah, see King, *Jeremiah*, 164–74.

10. Voth, "Jeremiah," 280.

11. Voth, "Jeremiah," 284.

12. Voth, "Jeremiah," 290.

13. King, *Jeremiah*, 159–62.

14. See Peter Van Der Veen, "Sixth-Century Issues: The Fall of Jerusalem, the Exile, and the Return," in *Ancient Israel's History: An Introduction to Issues and Sources*, ed. Bill T. Arnold and Richard S. Hess (Grand Rapids: Baker Academic, 2014), 401–2.

15. Laurie E. Pearce and Cornelia Wunsch, *Documents of Judean Exiles and West Semites in Babylonia in the Collection of David Sofer*, CUSAS 28 (Bethesda, MD: CDL Press, 2014).

16. King, *Jeremiah*, 7–8.

17. Voth, "Jeremiah," 308.

18. For translations of these letters, see "The Lachish Ostraca," trans. W. F. Albright (*ANET* 321–22); "Lachish Ostraca," trans. D. Pardee (*COS* 3:42:78–81).

19. Chalmers, *Interpreting the Prophets*, 23–26.

20. Voth, "Jeremiah," 317.

21. Voth, "Jeremiah," 324.

22. Voth, "Jeremiah," 331.

23. Voth, "Jeremiah," 330.

24. Voth, "Jeremiah," 340.

25. See Van Der Veen, "Sixth-Century Issues," 396–98.

26. See also Daniel I. Block, *Obadiah: The Kingship Belongs to YHWH*, HMSCS (Grand Rapids: Zondervan, 2013), 39.

27. Van Der Veen, "Sixth-Century Issues," 383–84.

Lamentations

1. Paul W. Ferris Jr., "Lamentations," *ZIBBCOT* 4:386.

2. For representative examples, see Othmar Keel, *The Symbolism of the Biblical World* (Winona Lake, IN: Eisenbrauns, 1997), 254–55.

3. For the laments over the destruction of Sumer and Ur, see "Lamentation over the Destruction of Sumer and Ur," trans. S. N. Kramer (*ANET* 611–19).

Ezekiel

1. "The Neo-Babylonian Empire and Its Successors," trans. A. L. Oppenheim (*ANET* 308n11).

2. Daniel Bodi, "Ezekiel," *ZIBBCOT* 4:409.

3. *ANEP* no. 260.

4. Bodi, "Ezekiel," 413.

5. For example, see *ANEP* no. 369.

6. John C. L. Gibson, *Textbook of Syrian Semitic Inscriptions*, 4 vols. (Oxford: Clarendon, 1971–2009), 1:41.

7. *IVPBBCOT* 693.

8. See Saul M. Olyan, "What Do Shaving Rites Accomplish and What Do They Signal in Biblical Ritual Contexts?," *JBL* 117 (1998): 611–22.

9. "Texts from Hammurabi to the Downfall of the Assyrian Empire," trans. A. L. Oppenheim (*ANET* 298).

10. "Atrahasis," trans. E. A. Speiser (*ANET* 105–6).

11. Bodi, "Ezekiel," 423–24.

12. *IVPBBCOT* 697.

13. Carol Meyers, "Cherubim," *ABD* 1:900.

14. For a fair discussion of the views, see Daniel I. Block, *The Book of Ezekiel: Chapters 1–24*, NICOT (Grand Rapids: Eerdmans, 1997), 447–49.

15. Bodi, "Ezekiel," 438.

16. "Shalmaneser III," trans. A. L. Oppenheim (*ANET* 280, 281).

17. Josephus, *Jewish Antiquities* 10.181.

18. Josephus, *Jewish Antiquities* 10.181–82.

19. Lamar Eugene Cooper Sr., *Ezekiel*, NAC (Nashville: Broadman & Holman, 1994), 248.

20. Josephus, *Against Apion* 1.156.

21. "Campaigns of Seti I in Asia," trans. J. A. Wilson (*ANET* 254); Bodi, "Ezekiel," 473.

22. *IVPBBCOT* 719.

23. Bodi, "Ezekiel," 474; "Circumcision," in Ian Shaw and Paul Nicholson, *The Dictionary of Ancient Egypt* (New York: Harry Abrams, 2003), 65.

24. *IVPBBCOT* 723; Daniel I. Block, *The Book of Ezekiel: Chapters 25–48*, NICOT (Grand Rapids: Eerdmans, 1998), 433–34.

25. Bodi, "Ezekiel," 487; Block, *The Book of Ezekiel: Chapters 25–48*, 469–70.

26. Bodi, "Ezekiel," 487–88.

27. Victor Hurowitz, *I Have Built You an Exalted House: Temple Building in the Bible in Light of Mesopotamian and North-West Semitic Writings*, JSOTSup 115 (Sheffield: JSOT Press, 1992), 326–27.

28. Bodi, "Ezekiel," 491; Marvin A. Powell, "Weights and Measures," *ABD* 6:899–901.

29. *IVPBBCOT* 726.

30. *IVPBBCOT* 728.

31. Bodi, "Ezekiel," 494–96.

Daniel

1. For further discussion, see William B. Nelson, *Daniel*, UBCS (Grand Rapids: Baker Books, 2012), 54–59.

2. Herodotus, *Histories* 1.183.

3. A. Leo Oppenheim, *The Interpretation of Dreams in the Ancient Near East* (Philadelphia: American Philosophical Society, 1956), 189.

4. Hesiod, *Opera et dies* 1.109–201.

5. Ovid, *Metamorphoses* 1.89–150.

6. Herodotus, *Histories* 1.95, 130.

7. For a much more detailed discussion, see John J. Collins, *Daniel: A Commentary on the Book of Daniel*, ed. Frank Moore Cross, Hermeneia (Minneapolis: Fortress, 1993), 166–70.

8. John B. Alexander, "New Light on the Fiery Furnace," *JBL* 69 (1950): 375–76; P.-A. Beaulieu, "The Babylonian Background of the Motif of the Fiery Furnace in Daniel 3," *JBL* 128 (2009): 273–90.

9. Angela Kim Harkins, Kelley Coblentz Bautch, and John C. Endres, eds., *The Watchers in Jewish and Christian Traditions* (Minneapolis: Fortress, 2014).

10. For further discussion, see Nelson, *Daniel*, 142–43; Collins, *Daniel*, 217–18.

11. R. H. Charles, ed., *The Apocrypha and Pseudepigrapha of the Old Testament*, 2 vols. (Oxford: Clarendon, 1913), 2:754.

12. A. Leo Oppenheim, *Ancient Mesopotamia: Portrait of a Dead Civilization* (Chicago: University of Chicago Press, 1977), 46.

13. For more details on the ten kings and the three uprooted ones, see Collins, *Daniel*, 320–21.

14. For the occurrences in Ugaritic, Phoenician, Aramaic, and the Dead Sea Scrolls, see Collins, *Daniel*, 314.

15. See Nelson, *Daniel*, 270–88; Collins, *Daniel*, 377–88.

16. Collins, *Daniel*, 387.

Hosea

1. Yigael Yadin, *The Art of Warfare in Biblical Lands in the Light of Archaeological Discovery*, trans. M. Pearlman (London: Weidenfeld & Nicolson, 1963), 1:7.

2. *DDL* 2:333.

Joel

1. Victor Avigdor Horowitz, "Joel's Locust Plague in Light of Sargon II's Hymn to Nanaya," *JBL* 112 (1993): 597–603.

2. For example, the series *Zu-buru-dabbeda* (Sumerian: "to seize the 'locust tooth'"), which was a collection of incantations against field pests. See A. R. George, Junko Taniguchi, and M. J. Geller, "The Dogs of Ninkilim, Part Two: Babylonian Rituals to Counter Field Pests," *Iraq* 73 (2010): 79–148.

3. Daniel David Luckenbill, *The Annals of Sennacherib*, UCOIP 2 (Chicago: University of Chicago Press, 1924), 43.

4. "Poems about Baal and Anath," trans. H. L. Ginsberg (*ANET* 141).

5. *Enuma Anu Enlil*, an omen series of about sixty to seventy tablets with nearly seven thousand celestial observations, was used by Neo-Assyrian scribes to report to the monarchs. The lunar eclipses have been published by Francesca Rochberg-Halton, *Aspects of Babylonian Celestial Divination: The Lunar Eclipse Tablets of Enūma Anu Enlil*, AfOB 22 (Horn, Austria: Berger, 1988).

6. "The Deir Alla Plaster Inscriptions," trans. B. A. Levine (*COS* 2.27:140–45).

Jonah

1. Aaron Jed Brody, *"Each Man Cried Out to His God": The Specialized Religion of Canaanite and Phoenician Seafarers*, HSM 58 (Atlanta: Scholars Press, 1998).

Micah

1. "The Cylinders of Gudea," trans. Richard A. Averbeck (*COS* 2.155:428).

Nahum

1. *ARAB* 1:596.

2. Gordon Johnston, "Nahum's Rhetorical Allusions to Assyrian Conquest Metaphors: The Rhetorical Use of Allusions in Nahum, Part 3," *BSac* 160 (2002): 42–43.

3. D. J. Wiseman, ed., *The Vassal-Treaties of Esarhaddon* (London: British School of Archaeology in Iraq, 1958), 62 (line 442), 66 (lines 448–49); Simo Parpola and Kazuko Watanabe, eds., *Neo-Assyrian Treaties and Loyalty Oaths*, SAA 2 (Helsinki: Helsinki University Press, 1988), 46 (line 442), 49 (lines 448–49).

4. *ARAB* 2:906.

5. *ARAB* 2:788.

6. Gordon Johnston, "Nahum's Rhetorical Allusions to Neo-Assyrian Treaty Curses: The Rhetorical Use of Allusions in Nahum, Part 2," *BSac* 158 (2001): 415–36.

7. Diodorus Siculus, *Bibliotheca historica* 2.26–27.

8. "Sennacherib: The Siege of Jerusalem," trans. A. L. Oppenheim (*ANET* 288).

9. Diodorus Siculus, *Bibliotheca historica* 2.26–27; 27.1–3; Xenophon, *Anabasis* 3.4.12; Paul Haupt, "Xenophon's Account of the Fall of Nineveh," *JAOS* 28 (1907): 65–83; Aron Pinker, "Nahum and the Greek Tradition on Nineveh's Fall," *JHebS* 6 (2006): Article 8 (http://www.jhsonline.org/Articles/article_58.pdf).

10. *ARAB* 2:99–100.

11. Julian Reade, "Studies in Assyrian Geography, Part I: Sennacherib and the Waters of Nineveh," *RA* 72 (1978): 51.

12. Gordon Johnston, "Rhetorical Allusions to Assyrian Lion Motifs in the Book of Nahum: The Rhetorical Use of Allusions in Nahum, Part 1," *BSac* 158 (2001): 287–308.

13. Delbert R. Hillers, *Treaty-Curses and the Old Testament Prophets* (Rome: Pontifical Biblical Institute, 1964), 60; K. J. Cathcart, "Treaty-Curses and the Book of Nahum," *CBQ* 35 (1978): 182.

14. Wiseman, *The Vassal-Treaties of Esarhaddon*, 72 (lines 573–75), 76 (lines 612–16); Parpola and Watanabe, *Neo-Assyrian Treaties and Loyalty Oaths*, 63 (lines 573–75), 65 (lines 612–16).

15. Sefire I, A, lines 40–41. Joseph A. Fitzmyer, *The Aramaic Inscriptions of Sefire*, BibOr 19A (Rome: Pontifical Biblical Institute, 1967), 15.

16. "Treaty between Ashurnirari V of Assyria and Mati'ilu of Arpad," trans. E. Reiner (*ANET* 533), §5, lines 8–10.

17. *ARAB* 2:10, 59, 163, 164.

Habakkuk

1. Hans-Joachim Kraus, *Psalms 1–59: A Commentary*, trans. Hilton C. Oswald (Minneapolis: Augsburg, 1988), 27–28.

Zephaniah

1. J. Daniel Hays, *The Message of the Prophets: A Survey of the Prophetic and Apocalyptic Books of the Old Testament* (Grand Rapids: Zondervan, 2010), 335.

2. O. Palmer Robertson, *The Books of Nahum, Habakkuk, and Zephaniah*, NICOT (Grand Rapids: Eerdmans, 1990), 276.

Haggai

1. Such a delay between Cyrus's decree (538 BC) and the return would explain why the temple rebuilding seemed to be a surprise to neighboring peoples (Ezra 4:1–5), and why the Persians themselves needed to confirm its legality (Ezra 4:24–6:22).

Malachi

1. Bezalel Porten, "Elephantine Papyri," *ABD* 2:450–53.

2. Andrew E. Hill, "Malachi," *ZIBBCOT* 5:237–38.

Intertestamental History

1. James L. Johns, "The History of Palestine between the Old and New Testaments," in *The Baker Illustrated Bible Handbook*, ed. J. Daniel Hays and J. Scott Duvall (Grand Rapids: Baker Books, 2011), 465–68; Chris Seeman and Adam Kolman Marshak, "Jewish History from Alexander to Hadrian," in *The Eerdmans Dictionary of Early Judaism*, ed. John J. Collins and Daniel C. Harlow (Grand Rapids: Eerdmans, 2010), 25–55.

2. Larry R. Helyer, *Exploring Jewish Literature of the Second Temple Period: A Guide for New Testament Students* (Downers Grove, IL: InterVarsity, 2002).

3. 1 Macc. 1:1–9; Josephus, *Jewish Antiquities* 11.304–12.10.

4. 1 Macc. 1:41–62.

5. Michelle Lee Barnewall, "Pharisees, Sadducees, and Essenes," in *The World of the New Testament: Cultural, Social, and Historical Contexts*, ed. Joel B. Green and Lee Martin McDonald (Grand Rapids: Baker Academic, 2013), 217–27.

Ancient Letter Writing

1. *Michigan Papyri* 8.490.

2. *Michigan Papyri* 8.483.

3. See E. Randolph Richards, *Paul and First-Century Letter Writing: Secretaries, Composition and Collection* (Downers Grove, IL: InterVarsity, 2004), 165–69.

Athletics in the New Testament World

1. Everett Ferguson, *Backgrounds of Early Christianity* (Grand Rapids: Eerdmans, 2003), 109.

2. Alan Cameron, *Bread and Circuses: The Roman Emperor and His People* (London: King's College, 1974); Magnus Wistrand, *Entertainment and Violence in Ancient Rome: The Attitudes of Roman Writers of the First Century A.D.*, SGLG 56 (Göteborg: Acta Universitatis Gothoburgensis, 1992).

Banquets and Meals in the Greco-Roman World

1. See Ze'ev Safrai, *The Economy of Roman Palestine* (New York: Routledge, 1994), 106–7.

2. *b. Berakhot* 44b. For information on a Palestinian diet in the Roman period, see Magen Broshi, *Bread, Wine, Walls and Scrolls*, JSPSup 36 (Sheffield: Sheffield Academic Press, 2001), 121–43.

3. For a fuller discussion of ancient banquets, see Dennis E. Smith, *From Symposium to Eucharist: The Banquet in the Early Christian World* (Minneapolis: Fortress, 2003).

4. Philo, *On the Contemplative Life* 40.

5. Aulus Gellius, *Attic Nights* 15.2.3.

6. Sir. 9:15–16.

7. Plutarch, *Table Talk* 1.2.4.

8. Seneca, *Moral Epistles* 47.

The City of Ancient Rome

1. Rome was built on seven hills (Virgil, *Georgics* 2.535; *Aeneid* 6.738; Horace, *Odes* 7; Cicero, *Letters to Atticus* 6.5; Suetonius, *Domitian* 4; *Sibylline Oracles* 2.18; 13.45; 14.108). See also Lesley Adkins and Roy A. Adkins, *Handbook to Life in Ancient Rome* (New York:

Facts on File, 1994), 105; Raymond Van Dam, *Rome and Constantinople: Rewriting Roman History during Late Antiquity* (Waco: Baylor University Press, 2010), 6.

2. While there is some debate about this figure, the population count is based largely on a calculation from the daily grain dole mentioned by Emperor Augustus in the *Res Gestae.* He gave grain to 320,000 adult male citizens. When one estimates the number of women, children, and slaves, the total sum reaches well over a million. See Van Dam, *Rome and Constantinople,* 6; Whitney J. Oates, "The Population of Rome," *CP* 29, no. 2 (1934): 101–16; Jérôme Carcopino, *Daily Life in Ancient Rome: The People and the City at the Height of the Empire,* ed. Henry T. Rowell, trans. E. O. Lorimer (London: Routledge, 1946), 18.

3. Van Dam, *Rome and Constantinople,* 14.

4. Suetonius, *Augustus* 28.

5. J. Bert Lott, *The Neighborhoods of Augustan Rome* (Cambridge: Cambridge University Press, 2004), 1–12.

6. Van Dam, *Rome and Constantinople,* 6.

7. Adkins and Adkins, *Handbook to Life in Ancient Rome,* 143.

8. Van Dam, *Rome and Constantinople,* 10–13.

9. Carcopino, *Daily Life in Ancient Rome,* 257.

The City of Corinth

1. Jerome Murphy-O'Connor, *St. Paul's Corinth: Texts and Archaeology,* GNS 6 (Wilmington, DE: Michael Glazier, 1983), 5.

2. Timothy B. Savage, *Power through Weakness: Paul's Understanding of the Christian Ministry in 2 Corinthians,* SNTSMS 66 (New York: Cambridge University Press, 1996), 35.

3. Murphy-O'Connor, *St. Paul's Corinth,* 5.

4. David E. Garland, *1 Corinthians,* BECNT (Grand Rapids: Baker Academic, 2003), 2.

5. Gordon D. Fee, *The First Epistle to the Corinthians,* 2nd ed., NICNT (Grand Rapids: Eerdmans, 2014), 3.

6. Livy, *History of Rome* 33.32.2.

7. Savage, *Power through Weakness,* 32.

8. Strabo, *Geography* 5.3.10.

Crucifixion

1. Martin Hengel, *Crucifixion in the Ancient World and the Folly of the Message of the Cross* (Philadelphia: Fortress, 1977), 22–23.

2. Josephus, *Jewish War* 5.449–51.

3. Tacitus, *Annals* 15.44.4.

4. F. F. Bruce, *The Epistle to the Galatians: A Commentary on the Greek Text,* NIGTC (Grand Rapids: Eerdmans, 1982), 271. See also Sean A. Adams, "Crucifixion in the Ancient World: A Response to L. L. Welborn," in *Paul's World,* ed. Stanley E. Porter, PS 4 (Leiden: Brill, 2008), 111.

5. Seneca, *On Consolation to Marcia* 20.3.

6. Adams, "Crucifixion."

7. Philo, *Against Flaccus* 72, 84.

8. Cicero, *On Behalf of Gaius Rabirius on a Charge of Treason* 5.16. See Bruce, *Galatians,* 271.

9. Hengel, *Crucifixion,* 88. See James D. G. Dunn, *The Epistle to the Galatians,* BNTC (Peabody, MA: Hendrickson, 1993), 314. In contrast to the generally absent mention of the cross in high literature, some Greek writers used crucifixion for crass comedic relief.

Aside from Paul, only one other first-century philosopher that we know of depicted himself as having been crucified to his sinful passions. See Joseph R. Dodson, "Paul and Seneca on the Cross: The Metaphor of Crucifixion in Galatians," in *Paul and Seneca in Dialogue*, ed. Joseph R. Dodson and David E. Briones, APR 2 (Leiden: Brill, 2017), 247–66.

Demonization and Exorcism in the Greco-Roman World

1. Hans Dieter Betz, ed., *The Greek Magical Papyri in Translation, Including the Demotic Spells*, 2nd ed. (Chicago: University of Chicago Press, 1992).

2. D. R. Jordan and R. D. Kotansky, "Two Phylacteries from Xanthos," *RAr* 1 (1996): 161–74.

3. Roy Kotansky, "Incantations and Prayers for Salvation on Inscribed Magical Amulets," in *Magika Hiera: Ancient Greek Magic and Religion*, ed. Christopher A. Faraone and Dirk Obbink (Oxford: Oxford University Press, 1991), 107–37. *Testament of Solomon* presents Solomon using a magic ring to control demons that were disturbing and provoking a young boy. This document (first to third century AD) highlights the growing intersection of the time between Jewish tradition, pagan magic, and demonology.

4. See Plutarch, *Moralia* 164E–171F.

5. Plutarch, *Moralia* 361B-C; Paul, 1 Cor. 10:20; Justin, *First Apology* 5; *Second Apology* 5; Tertullian, *The Shows* 13.

6. L. R. Fischer, "Can This Be the Son of David?," in *Jesus and the Historian*, ed. F. Thomas Trotter (Philadelphia: Westminster, 1968), 82–97. See also Klaus Berger, "Die königlichen Messiastraditionen des Neuen Testaments," *NTS* 20 (1973): 1–44, esp. 3–9.

7. Plato, *Republic* 364B–365A. See also Origen, *Against Celsus* 1.68; Diogenes Laertius, *Lives of the Eminent Philosophers* 6.101; Lucian, *The Passing of Peregrinus* 10–11.

8. *PGM* 4.3019–20.

The Family of Jesus

1. The traditional Roman Catholic view has been that these were Jesus's cousins. See *Catechism of the Catholic Church*, 2nd ed. (Vatican City: Libreria Editrice Vaticana, 1997), 126–28, §§499–507. For a discussion of the issue, see C. Marvin Pate, *40 Questions about the Historical Jesus* (Grand Rapids: Kregel, 2015), 163–71.

2. Andreas J. Köstenberger, L. Scott Kellum, and Charles L. Quarles, *The Cradle, the Cross, and the Crown: An Introduction to the New Testament* (Nashville: B&H Academic, 2013), 703–11, 765–66; Peter H. Davids, *A Theology of James, Peter, and Jude*, BTNT (Grand Rapids: Zondervan, 2014), 253–57; Craig L. Blomberg and Mariam J. Kamell, *James*, ZECNT (Grand Rapids: Zondervan, 2008), 27–28.

Hospitality in the New Testament World

1. Joshua W. Jipp, *Divine Visitations and Hospitality to Strangers in Luke-Acts: An Interpretation of the Malta Episode in Acts 28:1–10*, NovTSup 153 (Leiden: Brill, 2013), 19.

2. J. T. Fitzgerald, "Hospitality," *DNTB* 522.

Jerusalem in the Time of Jesus

1. Josephus, *Jewish War* 5.136–41. The name means "Valley of the Cheesemakers."

2. *m. Middot* 5.4; *m. Sanhedrin* 11.2; Josephus, *Jewish War* 5.144; 6.354.

The Jerusalem Temple

1. Detailed descriptions of the temple are provided by Josephus (*Jewish War* 5.184–246; *Jewish Antiquities* 15.380–425) and in the Mishnah (tractate *Middot*).
2. Josephus, *Jewish War* 5.222–24.
3. *b. Bava Batra* 4a; *b. Sukkah* 41b.
4. Josephus, *Jewish War* 5.212; Exod. 26:33–37; 27:16.
5. C. L. Seow, "Ark of the Covenant," *ABD* 1:390–91.
6. *m. Yoma* 5.2.

Jewish Festivals

1. G. H. Twelftree, "Feasts," *DJG*[2] 274.
2. See especially Zech. 14:16–17, which was read on the first day of the festival (*b. Megillah* 31a). See also Twelftree, "Feasts," 274; C. E. Armerding, "Festivals and Feasts," in *Dictionary of the Old Testament: Pentateuch*, ed. T. Desmond Alexander and David W. Baker (Downers Grove, IL: InterVarsity, 2003), 312. For the end-time dimension, see D. A. Carson, *The Gospel according to John*, PNTC (Grand Rapids: Eerdmans, 1991), 326–28; Andreas J. Köstenberger, "John," *CNTUOT* 454.
3. Josephus, *Jewish Antiquities* 8.100.
4. The entire story is recounted in 1 Macc. 1:1–4:60; 2 Macc. 5:1–9. For later rabbinic traditions that the eight-day celebration took place because of God's miraculous provision of eight days of light from a single day's worth of purified oil, see *b. Shabbat* 21b.
5. Josephus, *Jewish Antiquities* 12.325. See C. K. Barrett, *The New Testament Background: Selected Documents*, rev. ed. (London: SPCK, 1987), 139–41; Daniel K. Falk, "Festivals and Holy Days," *EDEJ* 644.

Jewish Marriage Customs

1. "Marriage, Marriage Customs," *BEB* 2:1405.
2. "Monogamy and Polygamy," in *The New Encyclopedia of Judaism*, ed. Geoffrey Wigoder, Fred Skolnik, and Shmuel Himelstein (New York: New York University Press, 2002), 546–47.
3. See also *m. Qiddushin* 2.1.
4. *m. Qiddushin* 3.1. Also, according to the Mishnah there was a tradition that allowed young women to borrow a white garment and dance in the vineyards to seek a potential husband (*m. Ta'anit* 4.8).
5. The "bride-price" (*mohar*) was the amount paid by the groom or the groom's family to the bride's family, and the "dowry" (*nedunyah*) consisted of household goods, personal items, and money brought into the marriage by the bride. See Michael L. Satlow, *Jewish Marriage in Antiquity* (Princeton: Princeton University Press, 2001), 199; see also Tracy M. Lemos, *Marriage Gifts and Social Change in Ancient Palestine: 1200 BCE to 200 CE* (Cambridge: Cambridge University Press, 2010); David Instone-Brewer, *Divorce and Remarriage in the Bible: The Social and Literary Context* (Grand Rapids: Eerdmans, 2002), 4–8. Compare *m. Qiddushin* 1.1, which states that a woman is acquired as a wife in one of three ways: through money, a written agreement, or sexual intercourse. Rabbis debated the amount required.
6. Kaufmann Kohler, "Huppah," *JewishEncyclopedia.com*, http://www.jewishencyclopedia.com/articles/7941-huppah.
7. "Marriage," in *Dictionary of the Bible*, ed. James Hastings, Frederick C. Grant, and H. H. Rowley (New York: Macmillan, 1963), 626. The article suggests that the groom was dubbed "Solomon" for the week.

8. “Matrimony,” in *The Oxford Dictionary of the Jewish Religion*, ed. R. J. Zwi Werblowsky and Geoffrey Wigoder (New York: Oxford University Press, 1997), 446.

The Jewish Rite of Circumcision

1. Philo, *On the Special Laws* 1.4–10; *On the Migration of Abraham* 92; *Questions and Answers on Genesis* 3.47.
2. Josephus, *Jewish Antiquities* 1.192; cf. Acts 11:3.

The Jewish Synagogue

1. E. M. Meyers, “Synagogue,” *ABD* 6:251–60.
2. On the history of the synagogue, see Donald D. Binder, *Into the Temple Courts: The Place of Synagogues in the Second Temple Period*, SBLDS 169 (Atlanta: Scholars Press, 1999); Lee I. Levine, “The Nature and Origin of the Palestinian Synagogue Reconsidered,” *JBL* 115 (1996): 425–48.
3. W. Schrage, “συναγωγή,” *TDNT* 7:847; BDAG 139.
4. Schrage, “συναγωγή,” 813.

Magic in the New Testament World

1. David E. Aune, “Magic in Early Christianity,” in *Apocalypticism, Prophecy, and Magic in Early Christianity: Collected Essays*, WUNT 199 (Tübingen: Mohr Siebeck, 2006), 376–77.
2. D. E. Aune, “Magic; Magician,” *ISBE* 3:218.
3. Moyer V. Hubbard, “Greek Religion,” in *The World of the New Testament: Cultural, Social, and Historical Contexts*, ed. Joel B. Green and Lee Martin McDonald (Grand Rapids: Baker Academic, 2013), 119.
4. Clinton E. Arnold, “Sceva, Solomon, and Shamanism: The Jewish Roots of the Problem at Colossae,” *JETS* 55 (2012): 9–14.

Messianic Expectations in Jesus’s Day

1. L. W. Hurtado, “Christ,” *DJG*[1] 110.

Money in the New Testament World

1. See E. Randolph Richards, *Paul and First-Century Letter Writing: Secretaries, Composition and Collection* (Downers Grove, IL: InterVarsity, 2004), 51–52, 165–69.

New Testament Household Codes

1. Demosthenes, *Orations* 59.122.
2. Especially Aristotle, *Politics* 1.1253B.

Pharisees and Sadducees

1. Roland Deines, “Pharisees,” *EDEJ* 1061–63; M. L. Strauss, “Sadducees,” *DJG*[2] 824.
2. Josephus, *Jewish Antiquities* 13.298.
3. G. H. Twelftree, “Sanhedrin,” *DJG*[2] 836–40.
4. Josephus, *Jewish War* 2.162–65.
5. Josephus, *Jewish War* 2.165.
6. L. Cohick, “Pharisees,” *DJG*[2] 673; Günter Stemberger, “Sadducees,” *EDEJ* 1180–81; Strauss, “Sadducees,” 825.

Pontius Pilate

1. Josephus, *Jewish War* 2.117.

2. H. Bond, "Herodian Dynasty," *DJG*² 381; "Pontius Pilate," *DJG*² 679–80; B. M. Rapske, "Roman Governors of Palestine," *DJG*¹ 978–84; H. W. Hoehner, "Pontius Pilate," *DJG*¹ 615.

3. Josephus, *Jewish War* 2.169–74.

4. Josephus, *Jewish War* 2.175–77.

5. Philo, *On the Embassy to Gaius* 301–2; Josephus, *Jewish Antiquities* 18.55–62; *Jewish War* 2.169–77. See Hoehner, "Pontius Pilate," 615.

6. See Philo, *On the Embassy to Gaius* 159–60.

7. H. W. Hoehner and J. K. Brown, "Chronology," *DJG*² 137.

8. Tacitus, *Annals* 15.44.

9. Josephus, *Jewish Antiquities* 18.85–89. See E. Mary Smallwood, "The Date of the Dismissal of Pontius Pilate from Judea," *JJS* 5 (1954): 12–21; Helen K. Bond, *Pontius Pilate in History and Interpretation*, SNTSMS 100 (Cambridge: Cambridge University Press, 1998), 680.

Roman Citizenship

1. Michael Grant, *The World of Rome: The History of the Roman Empire from 133BC to AD217* (London: Phoenix, 2000), 77.

2. Grant, *The World of Rome*, 79–80.

3. Grant, *The World of Rome*, 80.

4. Cicero once said, "The very word 'cross' should be far removed, not only from the Roman citizen, but from his thoughts, his eyes and his ears. . . . The mere mention of such a thing is shameful to a Roman citizen and a free man" (*On Behalf of Gaius Rabirius on a Charge of Treason* 5.16). See also Martin Hengel, *Crucifixion in the Ancient World and the Folly of the Message of the Cross* (Philadelphia: Fortress, 1977); Sean A. Adams, "Crucifixion in the Ancient World: A Response to L. L. Welborn," in *Paul's World*, ed. Stanley E. Porter, PS 4 (Leiden: Brill, 2008), 111–30.

5. F. F. Bruce, *Paul: Apostle of the Heart Set Free* (Grand Rapids: Eerdmans, 1977), 39–40.

6. Lesley Adkins and Roy A. Adkins, *Handbook to Life in Ancient Rome* (New York: Facts on File, 1994), 78.

7. A. N. Sherwin-White, *The Roman Citizenship* (Oxford: Clarendon, 1973), 226–36.

8. Adkins and Adkins, *Handbook to Life in Ancient Rome*, 141–42.

9. Adkins and Adkins, *Handbook to Life in Ancient Rome*, 5. See also Cassius Dio, *Roman History* 34.21–23; 60.17.6.

10. Suetonius, *Claudius* 25.3.

11. Martin Hengel, *The Pre-Christian Paul*, trans. John Bowden (London: SCM, 1991), 5.

The Roman Military

1. Polybius, *The Rise of the Roman Empire*, trans. Ian Scott-Kilvert (London: Penguin, 1979), 41.

2. Adrian Goldsworthy, *The Complete Roman Army* (London: Thames & Hudson, 2003), 27; Pat Southern, *The Roman Army: A Social and Institutional History* (Oxford: Oxford University Press, 2007), 92.

3. Goldsworthy, *The Complete Roman Army*, 47–48.

4. Michael Grant, *The World of Rome: The History of the Roman Empire from 133BC to AD217* (London: Phoenix, 2000), 91; Goldsworthy, *The Complete Roman Army*, 27.

5. Goldsworthy, *The Complete Roman Army*, 55–58; Lesley Adkins and Roy A. Adkins, *Handbook to Life in Ancient Rome* (New York: Facts on File, 1994), 67.

6. Adkins and Adkins, *Handbook to Life in Ancient Rome*, 53.

7. Adkins and Adkins, *Handbook to Life in Ancient Rome*, 66.

8. Southern, *The Roman Army*, 115.

9. Southern, *The Roman Army*, 98.

10. Goldsworthy, *The Complete Roman Army*, 60.

11. Adkins and Adkins, *Handbook to Life in Ancient Rome*, 64.

12. Adkins and Adkins, *Handbook to Life in Ancient Rome*, 64.

13. Adkins and Adkins, *Handbook to Life in Ancient Rome*, 64.

Roman Rule of Judea

1. James S. Jeffers, *The Greco-Roman World of the New Testament Era: Exploring the Background of Early Christianity* (Downers Grove, IL: InterVarsity, 1999), 314.

2. E. P. Sanders, *Judaism: Practice and Belief, 63 BCE–66 CE* (London: SCM, 1992), 32.

3. Ben Witherington III, *New Testament History: A Narrative Account* (Grand Rapids: Baker Academic, 2001), 114.

4. Howard Clark Kee, *The Beginnings of Christianity: An Introduction to the New Testament* (New York: T&T Clark, 2005), 21.

5. N. T. Wright, *The New Testament and the People of God* (Minneapolis: Fortress, 1992), 160.

6. Sanders, *Judaism*, 157–69.

7. Witherington, *New Testament History*, 59–60.

8. Witherington, *New Testament History*, 61, citing Macrobius, *Saturnalia* 2.4.11.

9. Sanders, *Judaism*, 34.

10. Sanders, *Judaism*, 38, citing Josephus, *Jewish War* 2.80, 91.

11. Witherington, *New Testament History*, 80–84.

12. Cassius Dio, *Roman History* 69.13.1–14.4.

13. Kee, *The Beginnings of Christianity*, 24.

14. Wright, *The New Testament and the People of God*, 166.

The Sabbath

1. *Jubilees* 2.17–33; 50.1–13.

2. *Jubilees* 2.30.

3. *Damascus Document*[a] 11.12–14, 16–17.

4. *m. Shabbat* 7.2.

5. *m. Shabbat* 14.3–4; 22.6; *m. Yoma* 8.6–7. See J. Nolland, "Sabbath," *DJG*[2] 822.

6. *m. Shabbat* 7.2.

7. *m. Shabbat* 7.2.

8. *Genesis Rabbah* 11.10; *Exodus Rabbah* 30.9.

9. *m. Nedarim* 3.11. See also *m. Shabbat* 18.3; 19:1–3.

Samaritans

1. Josephus, *Jewish Antiquities* 11.346–47.

2. Josephus, *Jewish Antiquities* 9.291; 11.341, 344.

3. *m. Hullin* 2.8; Josephus, *Jewish Antiquities* 11.346–47.

4. Josephus, *Jewish Antiquities* 13.254–56.

5. Josephus, *Jewish Antiquities* 18.29–30.

6. Josephus, *Jewish Antiquities* 20.118–36. See Alan D. Crown, ed., *The Samaritans* (Tübingen: Mohr-Siebeck, 1989); Joachim Jeremias, "The Samaritans," in *Jerusalem in the Time of Jesus: An Investigation into Economic and Social Conditions during the New Testament Period*, trans. F. H. Cave and C. H. Cave (London: SCM, 1969), 352–58; James A. Montgomery, *The Samaritans: The Earliest Jewish Sect; Their History, Theology, and Literature* (1907; repr., New York: Ktav, 1968); H. G. M. Williamson and M. Kartveit, "Samaritans," *DJG*[2] 832–36. See also Helen K. Bond, *Pontius Pilate in History and Interpretation*, SNTSMS 100 (Cambridge: Cambridge University Press, 1998), 71–73, 89–93 (esp. 71n69).

The Sanhedrin

1. *m. Sanhedrin* 4.1.

2. See *m. Sanhedrin* 1.6.

3. Josephus, *Jewish Antiquities* 12.129–44.

4. Josephus, *Jewish Antiquities* 14.89–91.

5. Josephus, *Jewish Antiquities* 14.168–76.

6. Josephus, *Jewish Antiquities* 20.197–203.

Shipping Practices in the First Century

1. For evidence, see Lionel Casson, *Ships and Seamanship in the Ancient World* (Baltimore: Johns Hopkins University Press, 1995), 184–89.

2. *Zenon Papyri* 10.

3. Josephus, *The Life* 15.

4. See F. F. Bruce, *The Acts of the Apostles: The Greek Text with Introduction and Commentary* (Grand Rapids: Eerdmans, 1951), 452, following Mommsen and Ramsay. Recent excavations in Caesarea of extensions to Herod's palace mention four kinds of military personnel active in the governor's office. One group are *frumentarii.* See J. Patrich, "The Martyrs of Caesarea: The Urban Context," *LASBF* 52 (2002): 321–46, esp. 331.

5. When Mark Anthony consorted with Cleopatra in Egypt, it was for the control of the grain. Augustus attacked to keep from being starved out.

6. A ship made three one-way trips per season. Thus a ship would start one year in Egypt, travel to Rome, back to Egypt, and back to Rome by winter. The next spring it would travel to Egypt, back to Rome, and back to Egypt for winter.

7. A generation after Paul (at the time the book of Revelation was written), these *frumentarii* (centurions) were the "secret police" of Caesar, like an ancient Gestapo, doing the "dirty work" of the empire. In Paul's day they had not reached this level.

8. See Casson, *Ships and Seamanship*, 91. This is contrary to older opinions, but a recently discovered relief and several old coins illustrate it. See Casson, *Ships and Seamanship*, figs. 108, 119–21.

9. Since 2 Corinthians came before the voyage recorded in Acts 27, we must conclude *at least* four times.

Traditional Greek and Roman Gods

1. Mary R. Lefkowitz, *Greek Gods, Human Lives: What We Can Learn from Myths* (New Haven: Yale University Press, 2003), 13.

2. Lefkowitz, *Greek Gods, Human Lives*, 30.

3. Mary Beard, John North, and Simon Price, *Religions of Rome*, 2 vols. (Cambridge: Cambridge University Press, 1998), 1:30.

4. Paul R. Swarney, *The Ptolemaic and Roman Idios Logos*, ASP 8 (Toronto: A. M. Hakkert, 1970), 57–59, 83–96.

5. Seneca writes that "Caesar owned all things" (*On Benefits* 7.5.3); Ovid writes that "whatever exists beneath Jupiter on high, Caesar possesses" (*The Festivals* 2.138).

6. Beard, North, and Price, *Religions of Rome*, 1:348.

Matthew

1. See Gen. 2:4; 5:1; 6:9; 10:1, 32; 11:10, 27; 25:12, 19; 36:1; 37:2.

2. Josephus, *Jewish Antiquities* 15.412.

3. R. T. France, *The Gospel of Matthew*, NICNT (Grand Rapids: Eerdmans, 2007), 136–41.

4. *b. Shabbat* 31a.

5. See the section on Matt. 11:29–30 in Rodney Reeves, *Matthew*, ed. Scot McKnight, SGBC (Grand Rapids: Zondervan, 2017), 233.

6. Josephus, *Jewish Antiquities* 18.109–19.

7. Josephus, *Jewish Antiquities* 20.97–99.

8. Reeves, *Matthew*, 365–67.

9. Bruce W. Longenecker, *Remember the Poor: Paul, Poverty, and the Greco-Roman World* (Grand Rapids: Eerdmans, 2010), 53–57.

10. Craig S. Keener, *A Commentary on the Gospel of Matthew* (Grand Rapids: Eerdmans, 1999), 485.

11. W. D. Davies and Dale C. Allison, *A Critical and Exegetical Commentary on the Gospel according to Saint Matthew*, 3 vols., ICC (Edinburgh: T&T Clark, 1988–97), 3:87.

12. *m. Nedarim* 1.3, trans. Jacob Neusner, *The Mishnah: A New Translation* (New Haven: Yale University Press, 1988).

13. Keener, *Matthew*, 122–23.

14. Josephus, *Jewish Antiquities* 20.167–72.

15. John H. Walton, *The Lost World of Genesis One: Ancient Cosmology and the Origins Debate* (Downers Grove, IL: IVP Academic, 2009), 81–85.

16. See Kenneth Bailey, *Jesus through Middle Eastern Eyes: Cultural Studies in the Gospels* (Downers Grove, IL: IVP Academic, 2008), 271–73.

17. Josephus, *Jewish War* 5.212–14.

18. Davies and Allison, *Saint Matthew*, 3:669.

Mark

1. *Jubilees* 1.22–25.

2. In the Mishnah, see the tractate *Mikwa'ot*; for Qumran, see *1QRule of the Community* 4.21–22.

3. See also *m. Hullin* 3.7.

4. *m. Yoma* 7.1; *m. Sotah* 7.7–8.

5. *b. Yoma* 71b.

6. *b. Sanhedrin* 25b.

7. *m. Tohorot* 7.6; *m. Hagigah* 3.6.

8. *m. Nedarim* 3.4.

9. *m. Sanhedrin* 3.3.

10. *Pirqe Avot* 3.19.

11. Josephus, *Jewish Antiquities* 17.42.

12. See also *m. Yoma* 8.1–6.

13. *Didache* 8.1; *b. Ta'anit* 12a.

14. *m. Yoma* 8.6.
15. Philo, *On the Life of Moses* 2.22.
16. See also *Mekilta Exodus* 20.17.
17. *b. Shabbat* 118–99b.
18. *Damascus Document*[a] 10–11.
19. *m. Shabbat* 7.2.
20. *Damascus Document*[a] 11.5–6.
21. Josephus, *Jewish Antiquities* 14.450.
22. Josephus, *Jewish Antiquities* 15.2.
23. *1QWar Scroll* 12.1–2; *1QRule of the Community* 10.3.
24. *m. Kil'ayim* 2.3.
25. C. E. B. Cranfield, *The Gospel according to St Mark: An Introduction and Commentary*, CGTC (Cambridge: Cambridge University Press, 1959), 153.
26. Josephus, *Jewish War* 1.155; *Jewish Antiquities* 14.74–75.
27. Josephus, *Jewish War* 5.227.
28. *m. Ketubbot* 4.4.
29. See also Josephus, *Jewish Antiquities* 20.200.
30. Josephus, *Jewish Antiquities* 18.116–19.
31. Josephus, *Jewish War* 2.118; *Jewish Antiquities* 18.4.
32. Josephus, *Jewish Antiquities* 13.297.
33. *m. Avot* 3.14.
34. T. W. Manson, *The Teaching of Jesus: Studies of Its Form and Content* (Cambridge: Cambridge University Press, 1951), 317.
35. Josephus, *Against Apion* 1.70.
36. Josephus, *Jewish Antiquities* 18.28; *Jewish War* 2.168.
37. *Psalms of Solomon* 17; *Sibylline Oracles* 3.286–94.
38. See also Josephus *Jewish Antiquities* 18.26, 34, 95, 123.
39. Josephus, *Jewish Antiquities* 13.396.
40. Ezra (*4 Ezra* 14.9), Baruch (*2 Baruch* 76.2), Enoch, Seth, Abraham, Isaac, and Jacob (*Testament of Benjamin* 10.5–6).
41. For Moses alone, see also Deut. 18:15, 18, and in the Dead Sea Scrolls, *4QTestimonia* 5–8.
42. It is possible, though not certain, that the exception of adultery is implied in 10:11–12; cf. Matt. 5:32; 19:9.
43. Josephus, *Jewish Antiquities* 20.169.
44. *m. Sukkah* 3.3–9.
45. Josephus, *Jewish Antiquities* 15.391–425.
46. Josephus, *Jewish War* 6.422–27.
47. *Psalms of Solomon* 17.21.
48. Josephus, *Jewish Antiquities* 19.294; *m. Sheqalim* 6.5.
49. *m. Sanhedrin* 11.2.
50. *m. Sanhedrin* 4.1.
51. *m. Sanhedrin* 7.5.
52. Philo, *On the Embassy to Gaius* 301–2.
53. *m. Bava Batra* 6.8.

Luke

1. Probably the source known as "Q."
2. Josephus, *Against Apion* 1.1; cf. 2.1.

3. See *Greek Papyri in the British Museum* 904, lines 20–21.

4. For example, *Jubilees* 32.34; *Testament of Reuben* 3.13.

5. Eusebius, *Ecclesiastical History* 3.12; 3.19–20; 3.32.3–4.

6. "The wood offering . . . was brought . . . by the family of David, of the tribe of Judah" (*m. Ta'anit* 4.5).

7. *1QHodayot*[a] 19.9.

8. *4QVisions of Amram*[c] *ar* frag. 3, line 5.

9. Josephus, *Jewish Antiquities* 15.380–425.

10. See *b. Sanhedrin* 98b; *Lamentations Rabbah* 1.16 §51.

11. *b. Megillah* 14a.

12. *m. Niddah* 5.6.

13. "Samuel had now completed his twelfth year when he began to act as a prophet" (Josephus, *Jewish Antiquities* 5.348).

14. Josephus, *Jewish Antiquities* 18.33–38.

15. Josephus, *Jewish Antiquities* 19.275.

16. Josephus, *Jewish Antiquities* 18.237; "he granted to Agrippa the tetrarchy of Philip together with Batanaea, adding to it Trachonitis and Lysanias' former tetrarchy of Abila" (20.138).

17. *CIG* 4521; 4523.

18. Josephus, *Jewish Antiquities* 18.26.

19. Josephus, *Jewish Antiquities* 18.35.

20. Josephus, *Jewish Antiquities* 20.198.

21. *The Sentences of Sextus* 82b.

22. Josephus, *The Life* 244.

23. For example, "Physician, heal your own lameness" (*Genesis Rabbah* 23.4 [on Gen. 4:23–25]).

24. For example, "A physician for others, but himself teeming with sores" (Euripides, *Fragments* 1086).

25. See *1QM* 15.13–15; 18.14–15.

26. Josephus, *Jewish War* 3.506; cf. 1 Macc. 11:67.

27. See John 6:1; 21:1; Josephus, *Jewish War* 4.456; in rabbinic literature, *b. Bava Qamma* 81b.

28. Josephus, *Jewish Antiquities* 8.354; cf. LXX 1 Kings 19:21.

29. For example, "disciples who follow you" (*m. Avot* 1.11). Note also: "If you recognize that it is God who has put the thoughts into the hearts of the lawgivers that the lives of men might be preserved, you will follow them" (*Letter of Aristeas* 240).

30. *b. Nedarim* 41a.

31. *b. Shabbat* 55a.

32. *b. Megillah* 17b.

33. For example, "They all ran together, both small and great, for it was unbelievable [*paradoxos*] that she had returned" (Jdt. 13:13 RSV); "If anything unexpected [*paradoxos*] happened or any unwelcome news came, the people throughout the realm would not be troubled" (2 Macc. 9:24 RSV).

34. *m. Shabbat* 7.2; cf. *b. Shabbat* 73ab.

35. *b. Shabbat* 73b.

36. Sir. 14:1, 2; 25:8, 9; 28:19; *Psalms of Solomon* 5.16, 18; 6.1; *2 Enoch* 62.1; esp. *4QBeatitudes*.

37. As expressed in Hesiod, *Works and Days* 342; Pindar, *Pythian Odes* 2.83–84. Lysias wrote, "I consider it established that one should do harm to one's enemies and be of service to one's friends" (*For the Soldier* 20).

38. As in Thucydides, *History of the Peloponnesian War* 4.19.1–4; Diogenes Laertius, *Lives of the Eminent Philosophers* 8.1.23; Epictetus, *Discourses* 4.5.2; Seneca, *On Leisure* 1.4.

39. *m. Sotah* 1.7; *t. Sotah* 3.1, 2; *Sifre Numbers* §106 (on Num. 12:1–16); *b. Sotah* 8b; *b. Sanhedrin* 100b; cf. Wis. 11:15–16.

40. *Sifre Deuteronomy* §308 (on Deut. 32:5).

41. *Genesis Rabbah* 9.11 (on Gen. 1:31).

42. *Fragmentary Targum* and *Cairo Targum* D Gen. 38:26.

43. Cassius Dio, *Roman History* 62.7.

44. *Sifra Leviticus* §251 (on Lev. 25:18–24).

45. Epictetus wrote, "How can a vine be made to stop behaving like a vine and start behaving like an olive tree; or, for that matter, an olive tree like a vine?" (*Discourses* 2.20.18); and Seneca, "Evil no more gives birth to good than an olive tree produces figs" (*Moral Epistles* 87.25).

46. *b. Berakhot* 34b.

47. Note *Testament of Solomon* 5.11, where a demon pleads, "Do not condemn me to water."

48. Compare *m. Teharot* 5.8.

49. For example, "Sleep holds you fast . . . You sleep as if yet living" (*EG* 433).

50. See the linkage in the Dead Sea Scrolls manuscript *4QMessianic Apocalypse*.

51. Josephus, *Jewish Antiquities* 18.116–19.

52. Dan. 12:1–3; *1 Enoch* 22–27; 92–105; *Jubilees* 23.11–31; 4 Macc. 7:3; Josephus, *Jewish Antiquities* 18.14, 18.

53. Josephus, *Jewish War* 2.232–33.

54. Diogenes Laertius, *Lives of Eminent Philosophers* 6.92; cf. Epictetus, *Discourses* 3.22.35.

55. Epictetus, *Discourses* 3.26.27–28.

56. *Damascus Document*[a] 2.17–18.

57. For example, "Love the Lord and your neighbor" (*Testament of Issachar* 5.2); "Love the Lord with all your life and one another with a true heart" (*Testament of Dan* 5.3); "But among the vast number of particular truths and principles [are] two main heads: one of duty to God . . . one of duty to humans" (Philo, *On the Special Laws* 2.63); Philo, *On the Decalogue* 109–10.

58. As in Origen, *Commentary on Luke* §34; Augustine, *Questions on the Gospels* 2.19.

59. For a rabbinic parallel, note *m. Avot* 1.4: "Let your house be a meeting place for the sages, and sit amid the dust of their feet and drink in their words with thirst."

60. *Numbers Rabbah* 20.21 (on Num. 24:3).

61. For example, Polybius, *Histories* 1.36.8; Diodorus Siculus, *Library of History* 12.32.1.

62. *Papyri greci e latine* 452.

63. Arrian, *The Discourses of Epictetus* 3.3.9.

64. Note also the wisdom of Sirach: "There is a man who is rich through his diligence and self-denial, and this is the reward allotted to him: when he says, 'I have found rest, and now I shall enjoy my goods!' he does not know how much time will pass until he leaves them to others and dies" (Sir. 11:18–19 RSV).

65. Zenon Papyri in the Cairo Museum 59.509.

66. *EG* 362; Cotiaeum (second to third century AD).

67. *CIL* II 293.

68. Josephus, *Jewish War* 2.165; *Jewish Antiquities* 18.16.

69. Philo, *Allegorical Interpretation* 3.227.

70. *Pesiqta of Rab Kahana* 8.1.

71. *The Sentences of Sextus* 255.

72. *Pesiqta of Rab Kahana* 8.1.

73. *The Sentences of Sextus* 1–2, 6.

74. *Midrash Tanhuma, Beshallah* 117b; cf. *b. Sotah* 48b.

75. *b. Sanhedrin* 100b; cf. *b. Berakhot* 9b.

76. *The Sentences of Sextus* 316.

77. Epictetus, *Discourses* 2.22.19.

78. Compare *Targum Neofiti* Exod. 12:42: "It is a night reserved and set aside for redemption . . . when the world reaches its appointed time to be redeemed . . . and the King Messiah will go up . . . and lead at the head of the flock . . . it is a night reserved and set aside for the redemption of all Israel."

79. *m. Sotah* 9.15.

80. *b. Yoma* 21b.

81. *b. Bava Batra* 84a.

82. *b. Ta'anit* 9b.

83. Josephus, *Jewish Antiquities* 18.60–62.

84. *m. Kil'ayim* 2.8; 3.2.

85. Compare Josephus, *Jewish Antiquities* 9.85.

86. *Testament of Asher* 1.3–5.

87. *2 Enoch* [J] 30.15.

88. Sir. 15:17 NRSV.

89. See also 2 Macc. 1:27–29.

90. For example, *Targum Isaiah* 28:1–6; the Messiah "will bring our exiles near" (*Targum Isaiah* 53:8); "They shall be gathered from among their exile, they shall dwell in the shade of their Messiah" (*Targum Hosea* 14:8); "From you shall come forth before Me the Messiah . . . and they shall be gathered in from among their exiles" (*Targum Micah* 5:1–3).

91. As in *m. Avot* 4.15: "Be a tail to lions and not a head to foxes."

92. As in Rabbi Akiva's fable of the fox and the fish, in *b. Berakhot* 61b, where the fish reply to the fox's dubious proposal, "Are you the one they call the cleverest of animals? You are not clever but foolish!"

93. As in Pindar, *Pythian Odes* 2.77–78; Plutarch, *Solon* 30.2.

94. Compare the warning offered by Epictetus: "Most of us become foxes, that is to say, rascals of the animal kingdom. For what else is a slanderous and malicious man but a fox, or something even more rascally and degraded? Take heed, therefore, and beware that you become not one of these rascally creatures" (*Discourses* 1.3.8–9).

95. For example, *b. Eruvin* 41b; *b. Shabbat* 33a.

96. *Damascus Document*[a] 11.13–14.

97. *Leviticus Rabbah* 1.5 (on Lev. 1:1).

98. *b. Eruvin* 13b; cf. *b. Sanhedrin* 17a.

99. *Leviticus Rabbah* 1.5 (on Lev. 1:1).

100. *Avot of Rabbi Nathan* A 11.2.

101. *1QRule of the Congregation* 2.11–17.

102. *1QRule of the Congregation* 2.17–22.

103. *1QRule of the Congregation* 2.11.

104. *1QWar Scroll* 7.4–6.

105. *1QRule of the Congregation* 2.5–22.

106. "Isocrates the rhetor used to advise his students to honor their teachers above their parents, because the latter are the cause only of living, while teachers are the cause of living nobly" (Isocrates, *Chreia* 41, according to Theon).

107. For rabbinic literature, note *Mekilta* on Exod. 18:1: "Let a man never associate with a wicked person, not even for the purpose of bringing him near to the Torah" (*Amalek* §3).

108. Epictetus, *Discourses* 3.22.23.

109. Seneca, *On Anger* 1.14.3; cf. Seneca, *Moral Epistles* 34.1.

110. *m. Avot* 4.17.

111. *Exodus Rabbah* 2.2 (on Exod. 3:1).

112. *Song Rabbah* 1.1 §9.

113. Quintilian, *Declamations* 5.

114. Dio Chrysostom, *Orations* 4.104.

115. *Leviticus Rabbah* 13.4 (on Lev. 11:2); 35.6 (on Lev. 26:3); *Song Rabbah* 1.4 §3.

116. *Lamentations Rabbah* proem §17; 3:14 §5.

117. *Sifre Numbers* §89 (on Num. 11:7–9).

118. *Lamentations Rabbah* 1.7 §34.

119. Philo, *On Providence* 2.4–6.

120. Cassius Dio, *Roman History* 52.37.5–6.

121. Seneca, *On Benefits* 4.27.5.

122. Aristophanes, *Birds* 1430–33.

123. *1QRule of the Community* 1.9; 2.16; 3.13; *1QWar Scroll* 1.3, 9, 11, 13.

124. For example, *Damascus Document*[a] 14.20; *1QRule of the Community* 6.2.

125. For example, *Targum Neofiti* Gen. 37:26; Num. 35:32.

126. *The Sentences of Sextus* 9–10.

127. *Pythagorean Sentences* 110.

128. For example, "The law, however, does not perish but remains in its glory" (2 Esd. 9:37 RSV); "the law that endures for ever" (Bar. 4:1 RSV); "the eternal Law" (*1 Enoch* 99.2); "though we depart, yet the Law abides" (*2 Baruch* 77.15).

129. *The Sentences of Sextus* 73.

130. *m. Avot* 2.8.

131. *b. Sanhedrin* 98a.

132. Josephus, *Jewish Antiquities* 10.83.

133. *Michigan Papyri* 29.

134. Greek and Latin Papyri in the John Rylands Library 2 = The Archive of Aurelius Sakaon 36; cf. The Archive of Aurelius Sakaon 31.

135. Plutarch, *Sayings of Kings and Commanders: Philip the Father of Alexander* 31. The story is repeated in Plutarch's *Life of Demetrius* 42; it also appears in Stobaeus, *Anthology* 13.28, but the remark of the peasant is directed to Antipater.

136. Philo, *On the Life of Moses* 1.47 (emphasis added).

137. *CIJ* 2 (emphasis added).

138. *b. Berakhot* 28b.

139. Compare *1 Enoch* 13.5, which in reference to the fallen angels states that "they did not raise their eyes to heaven out of shame for their sins."

140. For various connections between the parable and Josephus, see Josephus, *Jewish Antiquities* 17.219–20, 223, 227, 237, 239, 300, 302, 320, 339; *Jewish War* 2.14, 19, 22, 93.

141. For example, "Rabbi Abba used to wrap money in his handkerchief" (*b. Ketubbot* 67b); "if someone gives money to another for safe keeping, and he wraps it up in a handkerchief" (*m. Bava Metzi'a* 3.10).

142. From an association between Salem (Gen. 14:18) and *shalom*, the Hebrew word for "peace"; according to *Genesis Rabbah* 56.10 (on Gen. 22:14), "Jerusalem" means "he will see peace."

143. Josephus, *Jewish War* 6.300–309.

144. See Josephus, *Jewish Antiquities* 18.63–64, in reference to the "first men" who condemned Jesus; see also 11.140–41; 18.121; 20.251.

145. *Esther Rabbah* 7.10 (on Esther 3:6).

146. See also Josephus, *Jewish War* 2.154–66.

147. Gen. 38:8; Deut. 25:5–6; Ruth 4; Josephus, *Jewish Antiquities* 4.254–56. For an example of seven men who married a woman and produced no children, see Tob. 3:7–15.

148. In *2 Baruch* 51.10 it is said that the righteous "will be like the angels"; cf. *2 Enoch* 22.10. According to *b. Berakhot* 17a, "in the world to come there is no . . . propagation."

149. See *Psalms of Solomon* 17.21 (first century BC).

150. Dio Cocceianus, *Orations* 13.32.30.

151. Aelius Aristides, *Platonic Discourses* 307.6.

152. *m. Sheqalim* 6.5.

153. For parallels to this idea, see Julianus of Egypt, *Greek Anthology* 6.25; note *Leviticus Rabbah* 3.5 (on Lev. 1:17): "It is regarded as if she [a poor widow] had sacrificed her own life."

154. Josephus, *Jewish Antiquities* 15.395.

155. Tacitus, *Histories* 5.8.1. See the lengthy description of the temple in Josephus, *Jewish War* 5.184–247.

156. Examples from *Jewish Antiquities* include the unnamed Samaritan (18.85–87), a man named Theudas (20.97–98), and the unnamed Jew from Egypt (20.169–70).

157. Josephus, *Jewish War* 7.79, 89–95.

158. See also *2 Baruch* 27.2, 7; *Testament of Moses* 10.4.

159. See 2 Macc. 5:2–3; *Sibylline Oracles* 3.796–808; 8.175; *Testament of Judah* 23.3.

160. For example, Aristophanes, *Women of the Assembly* 117.

161. See Tacitus, *Annals* 15.38–44; Suetonius wrote, "Punishment was inflicted on the Christians, a class of men given to a new and mischievous superstition" (*Nero* 16.2).

162. Pliny, *Natural History* 17.1.5; Suetonius, *Nero* 38.1–3; Cassius Dio, *Roman History* 62.6.

163. See also *1 Enoch* 80.4–7; *Testament of Moses* 10.5.

164. "The high priest Ananias . . . was a great hoarder of money; he cultivated the friendship of [Roman governor] Albinus, and high priest Joshua, by giving them bribes" (Josephus, *Jewish Antiquities* 20.205).

165. Babrius, *Fables* 138.7–8; Livy, *History of Rome* 1.11.6–7; 5.27.6–10.

166. Demosthenes, *On the Liberty of the Rhodians* 23; *On the Crown* 46–49.

167. Priene Calendar Inscription = *OGIS* 458 (9 BC).

168. As in *Testament of Benjamin* 3.3: "Even if the spirits of Beliar seek to derange you with all sorts of wicked oppression, they will not dominate you."

169. See John 21:18–19; Eusebius, *Ecclesiastical History* 2.25.5, where we are told that under Nero "Peter was crucified."

170. See *b. Eruvin* 53b.

171. Philo, *On the Embassy to Gaius* 301–2.

172. Josephus, *Jewish War* 2.171–74; *Jewish Antiquities* 18.55–59.

173. Josephus, *Jewish Antiquities* 15.373, 409.

174. Philo, *Against Flaccus* 36–39.

175. Josephus, *Jewish War* 6.205–12.

176. *Genesis Rabbah* 5.9 (on Gen. 1:13).

177. Josephus, *Jewish Antiquities* 14.309.

178. Josephus, *Jewish Antiquities* 7.252. See also Arrian, *Anabasis of Alexander* 7.24.3.

179. *CIL* XXI.521.

180. *Exodus Rabbah* 5.14 (on Exod. 5:2); see also *Leviticus Rabbah* 6.6 (on Lev. 5:1).

181. Josephus, *Jewish War* 7.217; see also 1 Macc. 9:50.

182. See Judg. 13:16; Tob. 12:19; Philo, *On the Life of Abraham* 118.

183. *b. Sanhedrin* 97b. See also *Testament of Judah* 23.5; *Pirqe Rabbi Eliezer* 43.

John

1. See John 13:23; 19:26; 20:2; 21:7, 20; cf. 21:24. See also 1:35–40; 18:15–16; cf. 20:2.

2. Matt. 17:1–3; Mark 5:37–43; 9:2–3; 14:33–34; Luke 9:28–29.

3. Irenaeus, *Against Heresies* 3.1.1–2.

4. Clement of Alexandria, cited by Eusebius, *Ecclesiastical History* 6.14.7.

5. See D. H. Johnson, "Life," *DJG*[1] 469–71; C. Hartsock, "Light and Darkness," *DJG*[2] 522–23.

6. Leon Morris, *The Gospel according to John*, NICNT, rev. ed. (Grand Rapids: Eerdmans, 1995), 74–75.

7. *2 Baruch* 59.2. All quotations from the Pseudepigrapha are taken from James H. Charlesworth, *The Old Testament Pseudepigrapha*, 2 vols. (New York: Doubleday, 1983).

8. All quotations from the Dead Sea Scrolls are from Florentino García Martínez and Eibert J. C. Tigchelaar, *The Dead Sea Scrolls Study Edition*, 2 vols. (Leiden: Brill, 1997–98).

9. T. E. Pollard, "The Father-Son and God-Believer Relationships according to St. John: A Brief Study of John's Use of Prepositions," in *L'Évangile de Jean: Sources, rédaction, théologie*, ed. M. de Jonge, BETL 44 (Gembloux: Duculot, 1977), 363–69, esp. 367.

10. See R. K. Harrison, "Firstborn," *BEB* 1:791.

11. Daniel B. Wallace, *Greek Grammar beyond the Basics* (Grand Rapids: Zondervan, 1996), 360.

12. See R. A. Horsley, "Messianic Movements in Judaism," *ABD* 4:791–97; Stuart D. Sacks, "Messiah," *BEB* 2:1446–49.

13. Cf. *4 Ezra* 6.26–27. All quotations from the Apocrypha are from the NRSV unless otherwise stated.

14. *1QRule of the Community* 9.11.

15. *1QRule of the Community* 8.12–14.

16. See *m. Parah* 11.6.

17. See *y. Qiddushin* 3.15 64d.

18. Morris, *John*, 123. On Jewish baptism practices, see Craig Keener, *The Gospel of John: A Commentary*, 2 vols. (Peabody, MA: Hendrickson, 2003), 1:440–48.

19. *b. Ketubbot* 96a. See David Daube, *The New Testament and Rabbinic Judaism* (London: Athlone, 1956), 266–67.

20. See R. Riesner, "Archaeology and Geography," *DJG*[2] 47, 52–53.

21. On how "Christ" is used as a title, see L. W. Hurtado, "Christ," *DJG*[1] 106–17.

22. See William Horbury, *Jewish Messianism and the Cult of Christ* (London: SCM, 1998), chap. 1.

23. *4QAramaic Apocalypse* 2.1.

24. *m. Avot* 5.21. All Mishnah quotations are from *The Mishnah: A New Translation*, trans. Jacob Neusner (New Haven: Yale University Press, 1988).

25. See D. J. Williams, "Bride, Bridegroom," *DJG*[1] 86–88; S. Safrai, "Home and Family," in *The Jewish People in the First Century: Historical Geography, Political History, Social, Cultural, and Religious Life and Institutions*, ed. S. Safari and M. Stern, 2 vols., CRINT 1/1 (Philadelphia: Fortress, 1974–76), 2:728–92; J. D. M. Derrett, *Law in the New Testament*

(London: Darton, Longman & Todd, 1970), 227–38; Everett Ferguson, *Backgrounds of Early Christianity*, 2nd ed. (Grand Rapids: Eerdmans, 1993), 68–69; Keener, *John*, 1:498–99.

26. See Gen. 29:27; Judg. 14:12; Tob. 8:20; *y. Ketubbot* 1.1 25a.

27. *b. Pesahim* 109a. All Talmud quotations are from *The Babylonian Talmud*, 18 vols. (London: Soncino, 1935–52).

28. See also Jer. 31:12; Hosea 14:7; *2 Baruch* 29.5; *1 Enoch* 10.19.

29. See A. J. Köstenberger, "Wine," *DJG*² 993–95; Keener, *John*, 1:500, 503.

30. Josephus, *Jewish War* 5.222–23.

31. Josephus, *Jewish Antiquities* 15.417.

32. Ephraim Stern, ed., *The New Encyclopedia of Archaeological Excavations in the Holy Land*, 5 vols. (New York: Simon & Schuster, 1992), 2:744; Alan Millard, *Discoveries from Bible Times* (Oxford: Lion, 1997), 243.

33. This practice is explicitly permitted for the giving of annual tithes (see Deut. 14:22–26).

34. See *m. Bekhorot* 8.7; Josephus, *Jewish Antiquities* 3.193–96.

35. *y. Ta'anit* 4.5; *b. Rosh HaShanah* 31a–b. See Grant R. Osborne, *Matthew*, ZECNT (Grand Rapids: Zondervan, 2010), 762.

36. Josephus, *Jewish Antiquities* 15.380, 421.

37. Josephus, *Jewish Antiquities* 20.219.

38. See G. H. Twelftree, "Sanhedrin," *DJG*² 836–40.

39. Andreas J. Köstenberger, "The Seventh Johannine Sign: A Study in John's Christology," *BBR* 5 (1995): 90–91.

40. *Damascus Document*[b] 20.3–4.

41. *1QRule of the Community* 1.5–6; cf. 5.3–4.

42. *m. Sanhedrin* 3.5; see Keener, *John*, 1:579–80; *m. Bava Batra* 9.4; *Exodus Rabbah* 20.8.

43. "σφράγις," *NIDNTTE* 4:410–16.

44. *Leviticus Rabbah* 15.2. See D. A. Carson, *The Gospel according to John*, PNTC (Grand Rapids: Eerdmans, 1991), 213.

45. Josephus, *The Life* 269; cf. Josephus, *Jewish Antiquities* 20.118.

46. *m. Niddah* 4.1–2.

47. *m. Berakhot* 7.1; 8.8. See David Daube, "Jesus and the Samaritan Woman: The Meaning of συγχράομαι," *JBL* 69 (1950): 137–47; Daube, *The New Testament and Rabbinic Judaism*, 373–82; J. D. M. Derrett, "The Samaritan Woman's Purity (John 4.4–52 [*sic*])," *EvQ* 60 (1988): 291–98.

48. See Carson, *John*, 220.

49. Cited in A. Cowley, "The Samaritan Doctrine of the Messiah," *Expositor* 5, no. 1 (1895): 163.

50. See John Bowman, "Samaritan Studies," *BJRL* 40 (1958): 298–308.

51. *m. Avot* 1.5.

52. For Philo, see *On the Special Laws* 2.198. See Craig R. Koester, "'The Savior of the World' (John 4:42)," *JBL* 109 (1990): 665–80, esp. 666–67; *HCNT* 268.

53. See Gustaf Dalman, *Sacred Sites and Ways: Studies in the Topography of the Gospel*, trans. Paul P. Levertoff (London: SPCK, 1935), 105.

54. See J. H. Walton, "Retribution," in *Dictionary of the Old Testament: Wisdom, Poetry & Writings*, ed. Tremper Longman III and Peter Enns (Downers Grove, IL: InterVarsity, 2008), 653–54.

55. See Carson, *John*, 247.

56. *m. Berakhot* 5.5.

57. Andreas J. Köstenberger, *The Missions of Jesus and the Disciples according to the Fourth Gospel: With Implications for the Fourth Gospel's Purpose and the Mission of the Contemporary Church* (Grand Rapids: Eerdmans, 1998), 115–21; see also "ἀποστέλλω," *NIDNTTE* 1:365–67.

58. *m. Ketubbot* 2.9.

59. See Morris, *John*, 289n100; Carson, *John*, 261; C. K. Barrett, *The Gospel according to St. John: An Introduction with Commentary and Notes on the Greek Text*, 2nd ed. (Philadelphia: Westminster, 1978), 265. Second Temple Jewish literature compared the prophet Elijah to a burning lamp (Sir. 48:1).

60. *m. Avot* 2.7.

61. *Assumption of Moses* 11.17.

62. See *b. Berakhot* 50b; 52b.

63. Carson, *John*, 275.

64. For example, *Genesis Rabbah* 54.1 understands the bread and water mentioned in Prov. 25:21 as referring to the Torah. See also *Genesis Rabbah* 70.5; *Song of Songs Rabbah* 1.2 §3.

65. Maarten J. J. Menken, *Old Testament Quotations in the Fourth Gospel: Studies in Textual Form*, CBET 15 (Kampen, Netherlands: Kok Pharos, 1996), 47–54. See Ps. 105:40; Neh. 9:15.

66. Wis. 16:20; also 2 Esd. 1:19.

67. *2 Baruch* 29.8. See *Sibylline Oracles* frag. 3.49, which speaks of feasting on manna as an eternal reward for those who honor God.

68. The Festival of Shelters is mentioned in Lev. 23:33–44; Num. 29:12–39; Deut. 16:13–15; Neh. 8:13–18; Hosea 12:9; Zech. 14:16–19.

69. For further rabbinic sources, see *Pesiqta Rabbati* 52.3–6; *b. Sukkah* 30a–41b. See B. H. Grigsby, "'If Any Man Thirsts . . .': Observations on the Rabbinic Background of John 7,37–39," *Bib* 67 (1986): 101–8.

70. *m. Sukkah* 4.1, 9–10. For more details on the water celebration, see Keener, *John*, 1:722–24.

71. *m. Sukkah* 5.1.

72. *m. Sukkah* 5.2–3.

73. For more details, see *m. Sukkah*, especially 4.1, 9–10; 5.1–5. See also G. H. Twelftree, "Feasts," *DJG*[2] 274.

74. For Theudas, see Josephus, *Jewish Antiquities* 20.97–98; cf. Acts 5:36; for the Egyptian, see Josephus, *Jewish Antiquities* 20.169–72; cf. Acts 21:38. See also Josephus's mention of an "impostor" (*Jewish Antiquities* 20.188) and Jonathan, who claimed that he would show "signs and apparitions" (*Jewish War* 7.437–42).

75. Chris Keith, "The Claim of John 7:15 and the Memory of Jesus's Literacy," *NTS* 56 (2010): 50–54.

76. See *1 Enoch* 48.2–7; 62.7; *4 Ezra* 12.32; 13.25–26, 51–52.

77. Carson, *John*, 317–18.

78. See Morris, *John*, 370–71.

79. See Carson, *John*, 326–28.

80. Both Isa. 12 and Zech. 14 were associated with the festival. For further details, see Andreas Köstenberger, "John," *CNTUOT* 453–54.

81. See *m. Avot* 2.8; 6.1; *y. Sukkah* 5.8 55a. See also Joel Marcus, "Rivers of Living Water from Jesus' Belly (John 7:38)," *JBL* 117 (1998): 328–30.

82. *1QRule of the Community* 9.11.

83. *m. Sanhedrin* 3–5. See Severino Pancaro, "The Metamorphosis of a Legal Principle in the Fourth Gospel: A Closer Look at Jn 7,51," *Bib* 23 (1972): 340–51.

84. For a discussion of the textual evidence, see Bruce M. Metzger, *A Textual Commentary on the Greek New Testament*, rev. ed. (New York: United Bible Societies, 1994), 187–89.

85. For example, Rabbi Yohanan ben Zakkai (*b. Ber.* 28b).

86. See also Job 33:30; Ps. 36:9; *4 Baruch* 9.3; *1 Enoch* 58.3–6; 92.4; *1QRule of the Community* 3.7.

87. Josephus, *Jewish War* 3.375–77. Though see passages such as Judg. 16:30 and 2 Macc. 14:37–46, exceptional cases in which taking one's own life was viewed as an act of bravery.

88. See Arthur J. Droge and James D. Tabor, *A Noble Death: Suicide and Martyrdom among Christians and Jews in Antiquity* (San Francisco: HarperSanFrancisco, 1992).

89. See Isa. 41:4; 43:25; 46:4; 48:12; also Deut. 32:39.

90. *m. Berakhot* 5.5.

91. M. J. Wilkins, "Disciples and Discipleship," *DJG*[2] 203.

92. *m. Avot* 1.1.

93. *b. Yoma* 28b.

94. *m. Avot* 3:5. See Carson, *John*, 349.

95. See Epictetus, *Discourses* 4.1.114; see also 1.19.9; 4.7.16–17. See *HCNT* 282.

96. *1QRule of the Community* 3.17–19; cf. *Damascus Document*[a] 2.14–16.

97. See Herman Ridderbos, *Paul: An Outline of His Theology*, trans. John Richard de Witt (Grand Rapids: Eerdmans, 1975), 130–35, esp. 131n98.

98. *Testament of Asher* 3.2.

99. Wis. 2:23–24. See also Sir. 25:24, where sin and death are linked to Eve's transgression. For further discussion, see Köstenberger, "John," 458.

100. See Num. 4:3, 39; 8:24–25. See Colin G. Kruse, *The Gospel according to John: An Introduction and Commentary*, TNTC (Nottingham, UK: Inter-Varsity, 2003), 217.

101. *m. Avot* 5.21. See George R. Beasley-Murray, *John*, 2nd ed., WBC 36 (Waco: Word, 1987), 139.

102. *m. Sanhedrin* 7.4. See Carson, *John*, 358.

103. See Walton, "Retribution," 653–54.

104. See *t. Sanhedrin* 12.10.

105. See Carson, *John*, 363–64.

106. See Joachim Jeremias, "The Samaritans," in *Jerusalem in the Time of Jesus: An Investigation into Economic and Social Conditions during the New Testament Period*, trans. F. H. Cave and C. H. Cave (London: SCM, 1969), 116–19.

107. P. H. Davids, "Rich and Poor," *DJG*[1] 704; C. M. Hays, "Rich and Poor," *DJG*[2] 800–802.

108. See Tob. 4:6–11, 16; 14:2, 8–11; Sir. 3:30–31; 35:1–4; *m. Avot* 1.2.

109. See Carson, *John*, 368; Keener, *John*, 1:788.

110. *m. Niddah* 5.6; *m. Avot* 5.21.

111. *1QRule of the Community* 6.24–7.25. See Keener, *John*, 1:787.

112. See also LXX Jer. 13:16; 2 Chron. 30:8; *m. Sanhedrin* 6.2. See Colleen M. Conway, *Men and Women in the Fourth Gospel: Gender and Johannine Characterization*, SBLDS 167 (Atlanta: Scholars Press, 1999), 131.

113. Carson, *John*, 373; Jacob Milgrom, *Numbers: The Traditional Hebrew Text with the New JPS Translation*, JPSTC (Philadelphia: Jewish Publication Society, 1990), 95–96.

114. *m. Avot* 1.1–18. See Jacob Neusner, *The Oral Torah: The Sacred Books of Judaism; An Introduction* (San Francisco: Harper & Row, 1986), vii–viii, 47–55.

115. Tob. 2:10; 11:10–14. See Carson, *John*, 292.

116. Ps. 146:8; Isa. 29:18; 35:5; 42:6–7, 18.

117. Gustaf Dalman, *Arbeit und Sitte in Palästina*, 7 vols. (Gütersloh, Germany: Bertelsmann; Hildesheim, Germany: Olms, 1928–39), 6:284–85.

118. K. Lewis, "Shepherd, Sheep," *DJG*[2] 859–61. Shepherding imagery pervades the OT (e.g., Gen. 49:24; Ps. 23:1–4; 77:20; 78:52; Isa. 63:11, 14; Mic. 2:12). See Urban C. von Wahlde, *The Gospel and Letters of John*, 3 vols., ECC (Grand Rapids: Eerdmans, 2010), 2:453.

119. C. T. Wilson, *Peasant Life in the Holy Land* (London: John Murray, 1906), 165; Dalman, *Arbeit und Sitte in Palästina* 6:250–51; Keener, *John*, 1:805.

120. Carson, *John*, 383.

121. William Barclay, *The Gospel of John*, rev. ed., 2 vols. (Philadelphia: Westminster, 1975), 2:58; see E. F. Bishop, "The Door of the Sheep—John x.7–9," *ExpTim* 71 (1959–60): 307–9.

122. For further examples of "thieves and robbers," see Andreas J. Köstenberger, *John*, BECNT (Grand Rapids: Baker Academic, 2004), 303.

123. Gen. 48:15; 49:24; Ps. 23:1; 28:9; 74:1; 77:20; 78:52; 79:13; 80:1; 95:7; 100:3; Isa. 40:11; Jer. 3:15; 23:1–6; Ezek. 34:11–31. See J. G. S. S. Thomson, "The Shepherd-Ruler Concept in the Old Testament and Its Application in the New Testament," *SJT* 8 (1955): 406–18.

124. Jer. 23:1–4; Zech. 11:4–17.

125. 2 Sam. 5:2; Ps. 78:70–72; Isa. 63:11; Ezek. 37:24; Mic. 5:3–5.

126. See *Psalms of Solomon* 17.21–44, especially v. 40; also *2 Baruch* 77.13–17; *Damascus Document*[a] 13.7–9. For a discussion of messianic shepherd imagery in Second Temple literature, see Andreas J. Köstenberger, "Jesus the Good Shepherd Who Will Also Bring Other Sheep (John 10:16): The Old Testament Background of a Familiar Metaphor," *BBR* 12 (2002): 75–86.

127. Barrett, *John*, 374.

128. *m. Bava Metzi'a* 7.8–9. See Dalman, *Arbeit und Sitte in Palästina* 6:233–35; Morris, *John*, 454.

129. Ps. 22:27–28; 102: 13, 15–16, 21–22; Isa. 19:24–25; Ezek. 37:15–28; Amos 9:11–12; Mic. 2:12; Zech. 2:10–11; 8:18–23. See Andreas J. Köstenberger and Peter T. O'Brien, *Salvation to the Ends of the Earth: A Biblical Theology of Mission*, NSBT (Downers Grove, IL: InterVarsity, 2001), 25–71; Christopher J. H. Wright, *The Mission of God: Unlocking the Bible's Grand Narrative* (Downers Grove, IL: InterVarsity, 2006), 474–500.

130. *m. Sanhedrin* 7.5.

131. Carson, *John*, 396. For the charge of blasphemy, see Larry W. Hurtado, "Pre–70 CE Jewish Opposition to Christ-Devotion," *JTS* 50 (1999): 35–58, esp. 36–37.

132. Severino Pancaro, *The Law in the Fourth Gospel: The Torah and the Gospel, Moses and Jesus, Judaism and Christianity according to John*, NovTSup 42 (Leiden: Brill, 1975), 175–92.

133. See Riesner, "Archaeology and Geography," 47; W. H. Brownlee, "Whence the Gospel according to John?," in *John and Qumran*, ed. James H. Charlesworth (London: Chapman, 1972), 167–74.

134. L. J. Kreitzer, "Travel in the Roman World," *DJG*[1] 945.

135. Carson, *John*, 409; see H. Balz, "ὕπνος," *TDNT* 8:552.

136. *Leviticus Rabbah* 18.1; see *Ecclesiastes Rabbah* 12.6.

137. *m. Yevamot* 16.3; *Leviticus Rabbah* 18.1. See J. B. Green, "Burial of Jesus," *DJG*[1] 89.

138. Raymond E. Brown, *The Gospel according to John: Introduction, Translation, and Notes*, 2 vols., AB 29, 29A (Garden City, NY: Doubleday, 1966–70), 1:424.

139. For discussion of how the hope of resurrection develops through the rest of the OT, see Mitchell L. Chase, "'From Dust You Shall Arise': Resurrection Hope in the Old Testament," *SBJT* 18, no. 4 (2014): 9–29; Byron Wheaton, "As It Is Written: Old Testament

Foundations for Jesus' Expectation of Resurrection," *WTJ* 70 (2008): 245–53; Robin L. Routledge, "Death and Afterlife in the Old Testament," *JEBS* 9 (2008): 22–39.

140. See Richard Bauckham, "Life, Death, and the Afterlife in Second Temple Judaism," in *Life in the Face of Death: The Resurrection Message of the New Testament*, ed. Richard N. Longenecker (Grand Rapids: Eerdmans, 1998), 80–95.

141. *m. Ketubbot* 10.1; cf. *m. Berakhot* 9.5.

142. *m. Ketubbot* 4.4. See Carson, *John*, 415.

143. Michael Avi-Yonah, *The World of the Bible: The New Testament* (Yonkers, NY: Educational Heritage, 1964), 147; Keener, *John*, 2:848; *m. Bava Batra* 6.8; *m. Ohalot* 2.4.

144. Carson, *John*, 418–19.

145. R. B. Edwards, "Rome," *DJG*[1] 171–73. The fate of the temple and of the nation is connected in 2 Macc. 5:19–20.

146. See R. K. Duke, "Priests, Priesthood," in *Dictionary of the Old Testament: Pentateuch*, ed. T. Desmond Alexander and David W. Baker (Downers Grove, IL: InterVarsity, 2003), 653; C. Van Dam, "Priestly Clothing," in Alexander and Baker, *Dictionary of the Old Testament: Pentateuch*, 644.

147. Josephus, *Jewish Antiquities* 11.327–39; 13.299–300. See C. H. Dodd, "The Prophecy of Caiaphas: John 11:47–53," in *More New Testament Studies* (Manchester, UK: Manchester University Press, 1968), 58–68. See also Josephus, *Jewish War* 1.68–69; *Jewish Antiquities* 6.115–16; 13.282–83.

148. Ps. 106:47; 107:3; Isa. 11:12; 43:5–7; 49:5; Jer. 23:3; 31:8–14; Ezek. 34:11–16; 36:24–28; 37:21–28; Mic. 2:12.

149. Isa. 2:2–3; 56:6–8; 60:6; Zech. 14:16.

150. Andreas J. Köstenberger, "The Date of Jesus's Crucifixion," *ESV Study Bible* (Wheaton: Crossway, 2008), 1809–10; Colin J. Humphreys and W. G. Waddington, "The Jewish Calendar, A Lunar Eclipse and the Fate of Christ's Crucifixion," *TynBul* 43 (1992): 331–51; Harold W. Hoehner, *Chronological Aspects of the Life of Christ*, CEP (Grand Rapids: Zondervan, 1977), esp. 44, 63, 143.

151. Josephus, *Jewish War* 6.423–25.

152. Wolfgang Reinhardt, "The Population Size of Jerusalem and the Numerical Growth of the Jerusalem Church," in *The Book of Acts in Its Palestinian Setting*, ed. Richard Bauckham, BAFCS 4 (Grand Rapids: Eerdmans, 1995), 262–63.

153. R. K. Harrison, *Healing Herbs of the Bible* (Leiden: Brill, 1966), 48–49; Winifred Walker, *All the Plants of the Bible* (London: Lutterworth, 1958), 196.

154. D. H. Engelhard, "Anoint; Anointing," *ISBE* 1:129.

155. Homer, *Odyssey* 19.503–7; Athenaeus, *The Deipnosophists* 12.553. For a more detailed listing of ancient references to anointing of feet, see J. F. Coakley, "The Anointing at Bethany and the Priority of John," *JBL* (1988): 247–48.

156. See Num. 5:18; Morris, *John*, 512. See also Coakley, "The Anointing at Bethany," 246–52.

157. Carson, *John*, 429.

158. J. F. Coakley, "Jesus's Messianic Entry into Jerusalem (John 12:12–19 par.)," *JTS* 46 (1995): 472; W. R. Farmer, "The Palm Branches in John 12:13," *JTS* 3 (1952): 62–66; Carson, *John*, 432; see Gary M. Burge, *John*, NIVAC (Grand Rapids: Zondervan, 2000), 341.

159. *m. Pesahim* 5.7; 9.3; 10.7. See Coakley, "Jesus's Messianic Entry into Jerusalem," 473–74; Solomon Zeitlin, "The Hallel," *JQR* 53 (1962): 22–29.

160. Brown, *John*, 1:457; Köstenberger, "John," 470–71; Nancy DeClaissé-Walford, Rolf A. Jacobson, and Beth LaNeel Tanner, *The Book of Psalms*, NICOT (Grand Rapids: Eerdmans, 2014), 864.

161. *b. Sanhedrin* 90b. The saying is attributed to Rabbi Meir (ca. AD 150).

162. See references in Andreas J. Köstenberger, "Jesus as Rabbi in the Fourth Gospel," *BBR* 8 (1998): 119, esp. n90.

163. See A. F. Segal, "Ruler of This World: Attitudes about Mediator Figures and the Importance of Sociology for Self-Definition," in *Jewish and Christian Self-Definition*, ed. E. P. Sanders, 3 vols. (Philadelphia: Fortress, 1981), 2:245–68, 403–13.

164. *Jubilees* 10.8; 11.5, 11; *1QRule of the Community* 1.18; 2.5, 19; *1QWar Scroll* 1.5; 4.2; 13.2, 4–5, 11–12; 14.9, 10; 15.2–3; *Damascus Document*[a] 12.2.

165. For example, *1 Enoch* 62.14; *Psalms of Solomon* 17.4.

166. This usage of *halak* ("walk") is very common (e.g., Exod. 18:20; Lev. 18:3–4; Deut. 5:33; Judg. 2:17; Prov. 2:20).

167. See Carson, *John*, 446.

168. For example, *1QRule of the Community* 1.9; 2.16–17; 3.13, 24, 25; *1QWar Scroll* 1.1, 3, 9, 11, 13.

169. See Craig A. Evans, "On the Quotation Formulas in the Fourth Gospel," *BZ* 26 (1982): 79–83; Evans, "Obduracy and the Lord's Servant: Some Observations on the Use of the Old Testament in the Fourth Gospel," in *Early Jewish and Christian Exegesis: Studies in Memory of William Hugh Brownlee*, ed. Craig A. Evans and William F. Stinespring (Atlanta: Scholars Press, 1987), esp. 225–26. See also Köstenberger, "John," 476–83.

170. Craig A. Evans, *To See and Not Perceive: Isaiah 6.9–10 in Early Jewish and Christian Interpretation*, JSOTSup (Sheffield: JSOT Press, 1989), 132–34.

171. See, for example, Gen. 18:4; 19:2; 24:32; 43:24; Judg. 19:21; 1 Sam. 25:41; *Testament of Abraham* 3.7–9; *Joseph and Aseneth* 7.1. See John Christopher Thomas, *Footwashing in John 13 and the Johannine Community*, JSNTSup 61 (Sheffield: JSOT Press, 1991), 35–40, 46–50, which also lists Greco-Roman examples.

172. *Mekilta Exodus* 21.2. The *Mekilta* records commentary on the book of Exodus, possibly based on discussions taking place in the mid-second century AD. See Günter Stemberger, *Introduction to the Talmud and Midrash*, trans. and ed. Markus Bockmuehl, 2nd ed. (Edinburgh: T&T Clark, 1996), 255.

173. Suetonius, *Caligula* 26.2. See Carson, *John*, 463.

174. See Keener, *John*, 2:909.

175. Barrett, *John*, 441. See Plutarch, *Cato the Younger* 67.1; *Pompeius* 55.6; Lucian, *The Dream* 7.9; *Timon* 54; *The Passing of Peregrinus* 6.

176. For examples from Greek literature, see Diodorus Siculus, *Library of History* 30.8; Plutarch, *Marcellus* 20.1.

177. See 2 Macc. 6:31; 4 Macc. 17:22–23; Josephus, *Jewish War* 6.103, 106.

178. Hesiod, *Works and Days* 826–27; Seneca, *Moral Epistles* 75.7.

179. See Herman Ridderbos, *The Gospel according to John: A Theological Commentary*, trans. John Vriend (Grand Rapids: Eerdmans, 1997), 467.

180. Morris, *John*, 555–56; see Joachim Jeremias, *The Eucharistic Words of Jesus*, trans. Norman Perrin (London: SCM, 1966), 48–49.

181. See Carson, *John*, 475.

182. Jeremias, *The Eucharistic Words of Jesus*, 54. For a discussion of begging and charity, see Jeremias, *Jerusalem in the Time of Jesus*, 116–19, 126–34.

183. Carson, *John*, 483.

184. See also Gen. 49; Josh. 23–24; 1 Sam. 12; 1 Kings 2:1–12; 1 Chron. 28–29.

185. *Testaments of the Twelve Patriarchs*; *Assumption of Moses*; see also *Jubilees* 22.10–30; 1 Macc. 2:49–70; Josephus, *Jewish Antiquities* 12.279–84. On ancient farewell discourses, see L. S. Kellum, "Farewell Discourse," *DJG*[2] 266–69.

186. See Brown, *John*, 2:611.

187. See *Testament of Gad* 4.1–2; 6.1; *Testament of Zebulun* 5.1; 8.5; *Testament of Joseph* 17.1–2; *Testament of Issachar* 7.6–7; *Testament of Simeon* 4.7; *Testament of Reuben* 4.5.

188. *1QRule of the Community* 1.9. Josephus notes this as a distinctive of the Essenes (*Jewish War* 2.119).

189. *m. Avot* 1.12.

190. For the idea of "father's house" representing a family in the Septuagint and Second Temple literature, see James McCaffrey, *The House with Many Rooms: The Temple Theme of Jn. 14,2–3*, AnBib 114 (Rome: Editrice Pontificio Istituto Biblico, 1998), 50–51.

191. Peter W. L. Walker, *Jesus and the Holy City: New Testament Perspectives on Jerusalem* (Grand Rapids: Eerdmans, 1996), 186–90, esp. 188.

192. Tob. 1:3; see also Wis. 5:6.

193. See *1QRule of the Community* 4.2–8 and 4.9–17, respectively.

194. Morris, *John*, 571.

195. *Leviticus Rabbah* 6.1.

196. For example, *Testament of Judah* 20.1–5, which speaks of "the spirit of truth and the spirit of error." See Carson, *John*, 500. See *1QRule of the Community* 3.17–19; 4.20–26; *1QWar Scroll* 13.1–13; also *Jubilees* 25.14; *Joseph and Aseneth* 19.11, where no contrasting spirit is mentioned.

197. *1QPesher to Habakkuk* 2.1–2. See Shani Berrin Tzoref, "Pesharim," *EDEJ* 1052–53.

198. Ernst Bammel, "The Farewell Discourse of the Evangelist John and Its Jewish Heritage," *TynBul* 44 (1993): 108.

199. Isa. 44:21; *Jubilees* 32.25.

200. See Leon Morris, *The Apostolic Preaching of the Cross*, 3rd ed. (London: Tyndale, 1965), 237–44.

201. Beasley-Murray, *John*, 262.

202. Carson, *John*, 513.

203. See also Ps. 80:8–17; Isa. 27:2–6; Jer. 2:21; 6:9; 12:10–13; Ezek. 15:1–8; 17:5–10; 19:10–14; Hosea 10:1–2; 14:7; Sir. 24:17–23; 2 Esd. 5:23; *Leviticus Rabbah* 36.2.

204. Sir. 24:17–23 and *2 Baruch* 39.7, respectively.

205. Carson, *John*, 513–14; E. M. Sidebottom, "The Son of Man as Man in the Fourth Gospel," *ExpTim* 68 (1956–57): 234; Bruce Vawter, "Ezekiel and John," *CBQ* 26 (1964): 450–58; Barrett, *John*, 472; R. A. Whitacre, "Vine, Fruit of the Vine," *DJG*[1] 867–68.

206. Dalman, *Arbeit und Sitte in Palästina* 4:312–13; Brown, *John*, 2:675; Rudolf Schnackenburg, *The Gospel according to St. John*, trans. Cecily Hastings et al., 3 vols. (New York: Crossroad, 1990), 3:97.

207. F. G. Engel, "The Ways of Vines," *ExpTim* 60 (1948–49): 111.

208. Philo, *On Dreams* 2.64.

209. Carson, *John*, 517.

210. Aristotle, *Nicomachean Ethics* 9.8.9; see also Plato, *Symposium* 179B. See G. Stählin, "φίλος," *TDNT* 9:151–54; Bruce J. Malina and Richard L. Rohrbaugh, *Social-Science Commentary on the Gospel of John* (Minneapolis: Fortress, 1998), 236.

211. *Jubilees* 19.9; *Damascus Document*[a] 3.2; *Apocalypse of Abraham* 9.6; 10.5.

212. Philo, *Who Is the Heir?* 21; *On the Sacrifices of Cain and Abel* 130; *On the Cherubim* 49; *On the Life of Moses* 1.156.

213. *Damascus Document*[a] 3.3–4; cf. *Jubilees* 30.20–21; Wis. 7:27.

214. See G. Schrenk, "ἐκλέγομαι," *TDNT* 4:155–68.

215. *m. Avot* 1.6. See Morris, *John*, 600n36.

216. Marvin E. Tate, *Psalms 51–100*, WBC 20 (Waco: Word, 1990), 196.

217. *Testament of Judah* 20.5.

218. Enoch: *Jubilees* 4.23; 10.3–4, 17; *1 Enoch* 14.1; the scribe: *1 Enoch* 89.62–63, 70; 90.17.

219. Philo, *On the Life of Moses* 2.265; cf. *On Giants* 54–55. See also *1QRule of the Community* 4.2.

220. Brown, *John*, 2:708. See Franklin W. Young, "A Study of the Relation of Isaiah to the Fourth Gospel," *ZNW* 46 (1955): 224–26.

221. Carson, *John*, 544. See Isa. 13:8; 21:3; 42:14; Jer. 4:31; 6:24; 13:21; 22:23; 30:6; 49:22–24; 50:43; Mic. 4:9–10.

222. See *1QHodayot*[a] 11.8–12; *1 Enoch* 62.4; *b. Sanhedrin* 98b; *b. Ketubbot* 111a. See William H. Brownlee, "Messianic Motifs of Qumran and the New Testament," *NTS* 3 (1956–57): 12–30, esp. 29.

223. See Schnackenburg, *John*, 3:165.

224. Carson, *John*, 556; Barrett, *John*, 504.

225. Brown, *John*, 755; Carson, *John*, 558; Morris, *John*, 640; Schnackenburg, *John*, 3:175.

226. See Brown, *John*, 759; contra Carson, *John*, 562.

227. See Polybius, *Histories* 11.23.

228. Craig Blomberg, *The Historical Reliability of John's Gospel: Issues & Commentary* (Downers Grove, IL: InterVarsity, 2001), 228–30; Carson, *John*, 577; Mark W. G. Stibbe, *John as Storyteller: Narrative Criticism and the Fourth Gospel*, SNTSMS 73 (Cambridge: Cambridge University Press, 1992), 170.

229. See Emil Schürer, *The History of the Jewish People in the Age of Jesus Christ*, ed. Geza Vermes et al., rev. ed., 3 vols. in 4 (Edinburgh: T&T Clark, 1973–86), 2:203–6.

230. See Gerhard Delling, "*Baptisma Baptisthēnai*," *NovT* 2 (1957): 92–115, esp. 110–15; L. Goppelt, "πίνω, ποτήριον," *TDNT* 6:149–53.

231. See also the mishnaic legislation in *m. Horayot* 3.4; *m. Megillah* 1.9; *m. Makkot* 2.6.

232. Josephus, *Jewish War* 4.151, 160. See C. Fletcher-Louis, "Priests and Priesthood," *DJG*[2] 700–701; L. D. Hurst and J. B. Green, "Priest, Priesthood," *DJG*[1] 635; Morris, *John*, 663–64; Ridderbos, *John*, 579.

233. *m. Sanhedrin* 4.1. See Keener, *John*, 2:1087; Carson, *John*, 583.

234. Carson, *John*, 583–84.

235. See Brown, *John*, 2:826.

236. Keener, *John*, 2:1095; Morris, *John*, 670.

237. Carson, *John*, 585. See P. S. Alexander, "Jewish Law in the Time of Jesus: Towards a Clarification of the Problem," in *Law and Religion: Essays on the Place of the Law in Israel and Early Christianity*, ed. Barnabas Lindars (Cambridge: James Clarke, 1988), 44–58, esp. 46–49; Schürer, *History of the Jewish People*, 2:199–226; Twelftree, "Sanhedrin," 837–39.

238. A. N. Sherwin-White, *Roman Society and Roman Law in the New Testament* (Oxford: Oxford University Press, 1963), 45; Carson, *John*, 588.

239. See C. C. Torrey, "The Date of the Crucifixion according to the Fourth Gospel," *JBL* 50 (1931): 239–40; Carson, *John*, 590.

240. See also H. W. Hoehner, "Pontius Pilate," *DJG*[1] 615.

241. Tacitus, *Annals* 15.44.

242. Josephus, *Jewish Antiquities* 20.197–203. See the discussion in Morris, *John*, 695–97.

243. Josephus, *Jewish Antiquities* 14.34–36.

244. *m. Pesahim* 8.6. The existence of legislation for such an event indicates that it was not uncommon. See Carson, *John*, 596.

245. See Josephus, *Jewish Antiquities* 20.208–9; Livy, *History of Rome* 5.13; Josef Blinzler, *The Trial of Jesus: The Jewish and Roman Proceedings against Jesus Described and Assessed from the Oldest Accounts* (Westminster, MD: Newman, 1959), 218–21.

246. Keener, *John*, 2:1116.

247. Charles B. Chavel, "The Releasing of a Prisoner on the Eve of Passover in Ancient Jerusalem," *JBL* 60 (1941): 277.

248. Josephus, *Jewish Antiquities* 17.285. See G. Bornkamm, "λῃστής," *TDNT* 4:257–62.

249. Malina and Rohrbaugh, *Social-Science Commentary on the Gospel of John*, 263; Sherwin-White, *Roman Society and Roman Law*, 27–28; Carson, *John*, 597.

250. See Paul Winter, *On the Trial of Jesus*, ed. T. A. Burkill and Geza Vermes, 2nd ed., SJ 1 (New York: de Gruyter, 1974), 148–49.

251. "υἱός," *NIDNTTE* 4:522–26; O. Michel, "Son," *NIDNTT* 3:637.

252. Adolf Deissmann, *Bible Studies: Contributions, Chiefly from Papyri and Inscriptions, to the History of the Language, the Literature, and the Religion of Hellenistic Judaism and Primitive Christianity*, trans. Alexander Grieve (Edinburgh: T&T Clark, 1901), 167.

253. Ernst Bammel, "*Philos tou Kaisaros*," *TLZ* 77 (1952): 205–10.

254. See Suetonius, *Tiberius* 58; Tacitus, *Annals* 3.38.

255. Tacitus, *Annals* 6.8.

256. H. W. Hoehner and J. K. Brown, "Chronology," *DJG*[2] 137.

257. See Torrey, "The Date of the Crucifixion," 233–36.

258. See Matt. 27:62; Mark 15:42; Luke 23:54; Josephus, *Jewish Antiquities* 16.163.

259. Josephus, *Jewish War* 6.303–4. See Carson, *John*, 597.

260. Plutarch, *On the Delays of Divine Vengeance* 554A/B. See also Artemidorus, *The Interpretation of Dreams* 2.56; Chariton, *Chaereas and Callirhoe* 4.2.7.

261. John Granger Cook, "John 19:17 and the Man on the Patibulum in the Arieti Tomb," *EC* 4 (2013): 427–53.

262. See David W. Chapman, *Ancient Jewish and Christian Perceptions of Crucifixion* (Grand Rapids: Baker Academic, 2010); Martin Hengel, *Crucifixion in the Ancient World and the Folly of the Message of the Cross* (Philadelphia: Fortress, 1977). For a comprehensive collection of primary source materials, see David W. Chapman and Eckhard J. Schnabel, *The Trial and Crucifixion of Jesus: Texts and Commentary*, WUNT 344 (Tübingen: Mohr-Siebeck, 2015).

263. Cicero, *Against Verres* 2.5.165; 2.5.169.

264. J. Dennis, "Death of Jesus," *DJG*[2] 173–74; Morris, *John*, 712n46; Keener, *John*, 2:1134–36; Frederick T. Zugibe, "Two Questions about Crucifixion," *BRev* 5, no. 2 (1989): 41–43.

265. Keener, *John*, 2:1137n608.

266. Lucian, *Toxaris* 22. See Brown, *John*, 2:907.

267. Plutarch, *Cato the Elder* 336.

268. Barrett, *John*, 557; J. Massingberd Ford, "'Mingled Blood' from the Side of Christ (John XIX.34)," *NTS* 15 (1969): 337–38.

269. See N. Haas, "Anthropological Observations on the Skeletal Remains from Giv'at ha-Mivtar," *IEJ* 20 (1970): 38–59; J. Zias and E. Sekels, "The Crucified Man from Giv'at

ha-Mivtar," *IEJ* 35 (1985): 22–27; Hershel Shanks, "New Analysis of the Crucified Man," *BAR* 11 (November/December 1985): 20–21.

270. Brown, *John*, 2:952–53.

271. For an extended discussion, see Köstenberger, "John," 504–6.

272. Josephus, *Jewish War* 4.317. See D. W. Chapman, "Burial of Jesus," *DJG*[2] 98.

273. Deut. 21:22–23; Philo, *Against Flaccus* 83–86; Quintilian, *Declamations* 6.9. See Dennis, "Death of Jesus," 175; J. B. Green, "Death of Jesus," *DJG*[1] 147.

274. *m. Sanhedrin* 6.5; see also Josephus, *Jewish Antiquities* 5.1.14 §44. See Carson, *John*, 629.

275. See B. F. Westcott, *The Gospel according to St. John: The Greek Text with Introduction and Notes*, 2 vols. (London: Murray, 1908), 2:340.

276. Carson, *John*, 639.

277. Morris, *John*, 739n30.

278. *m. Rosh HaShanah* 1.8. A. J. Köstenberger, "Witness," *DJG*[2] 999–1000; see Robert G. Maccini, *Her Testimony Is True: Women as Witnesses according to John*, JSNTSup 125 (Sheffield: Sheffield Academic Press, 1996), 207–33.

279. See Köstenberger, *The Missions of Jesus and the Disciples*, 180–94, esp. 190–94.

280. J. A. Emerton, "Binding and Loosing—Forgiving and Retaining," *JTS* 13 (1962): 325–31; Beasley-Murray, *John*, 383.

281. Carson, *John*, 657.

282. Adolf Deissmann, *Light from the Ancient East: The New Testament Illustrated by Recently Discovered Texts of the Graeco-Roman World*, trans. Lionel R. M. Strachan (London: Hodder & Stoughton, 1927), 361–62.

283. Suetonius, *Domitian* 13.2.

284. Brown, *John*, 2:1069.

285. Morris, *John*, 763; Avi-Yonah, *The World of the Bible*, 155.

286. Barrett, *John*, 580–81; Brown, *John*, 2:1072; Morris, *John*, 762n19.

287. *Damascus Document*[a] 13.9.

288. Epictetus, *Discourses* 3.26.22, and Dionysius of Halicarnassus, *Roman Antiquities* 7.69, respectively. See Beasley-Murray, *John*, 408–9; Hengel, *Crucifixion*, esp. chap. 4. For further uses of the phrase, see Seneca, *On Consolation to Marcia* 20.3; Tertullian, *Modesty* 22.

289. Barrett, *John*, 587; Schnackenburg, *John*, 3:371; Brown, *John*, 2:1117–19.

290. Carson, *John*, 682; Howard M. Jackson, "Ancient Self-Referential Conventions and Their Implications for the Authorship and Integrity of the Gospel of John," *JTS* 50 (1999): 1–34.

291. Thucydides, *History of the Peloponnesian War* 1.1.1; see also 4.104–7; 5.26.1. See Jackson, "Ancient Self-Referential Conventions," 27–30.

292. Jackson, "Ancient Self-Referential Conventions," 23–24.

293. *Soferim* 16.8.

294. Philo, *On the Posterity of Cain* 43.144; see Philo, *On Drunkenness* 9.32; *On the Life of Moses* 1.38.213.

295. See Brown, *John*, 2:1130; *HCNT* 308.

Acts

1. Josephus, *Against Apion* 2.1.

2. *Psalms of Solomon* 17–18.

3. Enoch: Gen. 5:24; Sir. 49:14; Heb. 11:5; Moses: *Sifre Deuteronomy* 357.10.5; Isaiah: *Ascension of Isaiah* 6–11; Elijah: 2 Kings 2:1–18; 1 Macc. 2:58. See Craig S. Keener, *Acts: An Exegetical Commentary*, 4 vols. (Grand Rapids: Baker Academic, 2012–15), 1:718–19.

4. *m. Eruvin* 4.3; 5.7–9.

5. Josephus, *Jewish Antiquities* 7.392–94; 13.249; 16.179–83; *Jewish War* 1.61.

6. Jdt. 9:1; Josephus, *Jewish Antiquities* 14.65.

7. Josephus, *Jewish War* 5.201.

8. Josephus, *Jewish Antiquities* 20.221; *Jewish War* 5.185.

9. *Memar Marqah* 4.3; cf. John 4:19, 25.

10. Josephus, *Jewish Antiquities* 20.97–99; cf. Acts 5:36–37.

11. Josephus, *Jewish Antiquities* 18.16; cf. Acts 23:8.

12. *1QRule of the Community* 1.11–12; 5.2; 6.13–25; Josephus, *Jewish War* 2.122.

13. For references, see P. W. van der Horst, "Peter's Shadow: The Religio-Historical Background of Acts v.15," *NTS* 23 (1977): 204–12.

14. See Craig A. Evans, "Mark's Incipit and the Priene Calendar Inscription: From Jewish Gospel to Greco-Roman Gospel," *JGRChJ* 1 (2000): 67–81.

15. *m. Sotah* 9.15.

16. Josephus, *Jewish Antiquities* 20.97–99; cf. Acts 3:22.

17. Josephus, *Jewish Antiquities* 17.271–72; *Jewish War* 2.118.

18. *m. Sanhedrin* 7.5; cf. Lev. 24:10–23.

19. See Darrell L. Bock, *Blasphemy and Exaltation in Judaism: The Charge against Jesus in Mark 14:53–65*, BSL (Grand Rapids: Baker Books, 2000), 30–112.

20. Josephus, *Jewish War* 6.300–309.

21. Josephus, *Jewish War* 6.109, 311.

22. Josephus, *Jewish Antiquities* 2.229–30, 236; Philo, *On the Life of Moses* 1.20–24.

23. *Jubilees* 1.27–29; *Mekilta of Rabbi Ishmael, Bahodesh* 9; cf. Acts 7:35, 38.

24. Josephus, *Jewish Antiquities* 15.296.

25. For examples of incantations, see Hans Dieter Betz, ed., *The Greek Magical Papyri in Translation, Including the Demotic Spells*, 2nd ed. (Chicago: University of Chicago Press, 1992).

26. Irenaeus, *Against Heresies* 3.12.

27. See *1QRule of the Congregation* 2.5–6.

28. Pliny the Elder, *Natural History* 6.186. For other references, see C. K. Barrett, *A Critical and Exegetical Commentary on the Acts of the Apostles*, 2 vols., ICC (London: T&T Clark, 2004), 1:425.

29. On the debate of whether first-century Jews interpreted the servant as Messiah, see J. Jeremias, "παῖς θεοῦ," *TDNT* 5:684–89; Barrett, *Acts*, 1:430–31.

30. Darrell L. Bock, *Acts*, BECNT (Grand Rapids: Baker Academic, 2007), 360.

31. Hermann Dessau, ed., *Inscriptiones latinae selectae*, 3 vols. in 5 (Berlin: Weidmann, 1892–1916), 9168.

32. 1 Macc. 1:62; 2 Macc. 6:18, 21; 7:7; 4 Macc. 4:26; 5:2, 6; 8:2.

33. *m. Ohalot* 18.7.

34. Clinton Arnold, "Acts," *ZIBBCNT* 2:321.

35. The later Code of Justinian (9.4.4) formalized this law, though no doubt it was practiced earlier (Arnold, "Acts," 329).

36. Josephus, *Jewish Antiquities* 19.343–52.

37. Luke 18:12; *b. Ta'anit* 12a; *Didache* 8.1.

38. See the helpful chart in Arnold, "Acts," 338.

39. *1QRule of the Community* 1.9–10; *1QWar Scroll* 1.1.

40. S. Mitchell, "Antioch of Pisidia," *ABD* 1:264.

41. Str-B 1:571; H. J. Cadbury, "Note XXIV: Dust and Garments," in *The Acts of the Apostles*, ed. F. J. Foakes-Jackson and Kirsopp Lake, 5 vols. (London: Macmillan, 1920–33), 5:266–77.

42. Ovid, *Metamorphoses* 8.611–724.

43. For example, Paul (Acts 23:6), Nicodemus (John 3:1–2), and Joseph of Arimathea (Mark 15:43; Luke 23:50–51; John 19:38).

44. Josephus, *Jewish Antiquities* 20.200–201; Eusebius, *Ecclesiastical History* 2.23.

45. See A. J. M. Wedderburn, "The 'Apostolic Decree': Tradition and Redaction," *NovT* 35 (1993): 362–89; Arnold, "Acts," 361–62.

46. *b. Yevamot* 45b; *y. Yevamot* 2.6. Note also *m. Qiddushin* 3.12, which says that the nationality goes with the parent of lower social status, which in this case would be the mother.

47. Brian Rapske, *Paul in Roman Custody*, BAFCS 3 (Grand Rapids: Eerdmans 1994), 49; A. N. Sherwin-White, *Roman Society and Roman Law in the New Testament* (Grand Rapids: Baker, 1978), 144–62.

48. Pausanias, *Description of Greece* 1.1.14; Philostratus, *Life of Apollonius of Tyana* 6.3.5; Diogenes Laertius, *Lives of the Eminent Philosophers* 1.110.

49. Aratus, *Phenomena* 5.

50. Suetonius, *Claudius* 25.4.

51. See Bruce W. Winter, "Gallio's Ruling on the Legal Status of Early Christianity (Acts 18:14–15)," *TynBul* 50 (1999): 213–24; Keener, *Acts*, 3:2773.

52. Bock, *Acts*, 599; Eckhard J. Schnabel, *Acts*, ZECNT (Grand Rapids: Zondervan, 2013), 788.

53. Cited in Betz, *The Greek Magical Papyri*, 96; cf. *PGM* 4.3007–25.

54. See Betz, *The Greek Magical Papyri*.

55. David W. J. Gill, "Erastus the Aedile," *TynBul* 40 (1989): 293–301.

56. On ancient sources related to the temple of Artemis, see Jerome Murphy-O'Connor, *St. Paul's Ephesus: Texts and Archaeology* (Collegeville, MN: Liturgical Press, 2008), esp. 20–24.

57. *m. Avot* 3.12.

58. Josephus, *Jewish War* 5.194; 6.125; cf. *m. Middot* 2.1–3.

59. Barrett, *Acts*, 2:1020; Arnold, "Acts," 435.

60. Josephus, *Jewish Antiquities* 20.169–72; *Jewish War* 2.261–63.

61. Strabo, *Geography* 14.5.131.

62. Sherwin-White, *Roman Society and Roman Law*, 57–59; Colin Hemer, *The Book of Acts in the Setting of Hellenistic History*, ed. Conrad H. Gempf (1909; repr., Winona Lake, IN: Eisenbrauns, 1990), 180, referring to *lex Iulia de vi publica*.

63. Keener, *Acts*, 3:3253; Sherwin-White, *Roman Society and Roman Law*, 154–55.

64. Josephus, *Jewish Antiquities* 20.103.

65. See Acts 23:8; cf. Luke 20:27; Josephus, *Jewish Antiquities* 18.16; *Jewish War* 2.165.

66. Schnabel, *Acts*, 929–30.

67. *m. Nedarim* 3.1–3.

68. Sherwin-White, *Roman Society and Roman Law*, 31; Keener, *Acts*, 3:3345–46.

69. Rapske, *Paul in Roman Custody*, 159.

70. Tacitus, *Histories* 5.9.

71. Bruce W. Winter, "The Importance of the *captatio benevolentiae* in the Speeches of Tertullus and Paul in Acts 24:1–21," *JTS* 42 (1991): 505–31.

72. BDAG 27.

73. Josephus, *Jewish Antiquities* 20.139–44.

74. For references, see Keener, *Acts*, 4:3437–38.

75. Josephus, *Jewish Antiquities* 20.182; *Jewish War* 2.270–71.

76. The date is disputed by some who suggest a date as early as AD 55. See the discussion in J. B. Green, "Festus, Porcius," *ABD* 2:795.

77. Josephus, *Jewish Antiquities* 20.182–96; *Jewish War* 2.271–72.

78. On the complexities of Roman law and various precedents, see Sherwin-White, *Roman Society and Roman Law*, 57–70; Rapske, *Paul in Roman Custody*, 186–89.

79. Josephus, *Jewish Antiquities* 20.159; *Jewish War* 2.252.

80. Josephus, *Jewish Antiquities* 20.145; Juvenal, *Satires* 6.158.

81. Josephus, *Jewish Antiquities* 20.145.

82. Suetonius, *Titus* 7.

83. 1 Macc. 1:44–50, 60–63; 2:17–22.

84. Pliny the Younger, *Epistles to Trajan* 10.96.

85. Euripides, *Bacchanals* 795, cited in Arnold, "Acts," 465.

86. Josephus, *Jewish War* 2.385–86. See Barrett, *Acts*, 2:1185.

87. *m. Yoma* 8.1; Josephus, *Jewish Antiquities* 17.165; 18.94.

88. Barrett, *Acts*, 2:1188, citing Vegetius, *On Military Matters* 4.39.

89. Strabo, *Geography* 10.4; Ptolemy, *Geography* 3.17; see Bock, *Acts*, 734.

90. On the etymology, see Keener, *Acts*, 4:3609–10.

91. For ancient references, see Hemer, *The Book of Acts*, 144.

92. Ptolemy, *Geography* 3.4.1; 3.15.1; 3.17.1; Josephus, *The Life* 15.

93. F. F. Bruce, *The Book of Acts*, NICNT (Grand Rapids: Eerdmans, 1988), 499.

94. Barrett, *Acts*, 2:1224–25.

95. A. Betz, "Syracuse," *ABD* 6:270–71.

96. Josephus, *Jewish Antiquities* 17.328.

97. Barrett, *Acts*, 2:1238.

98. Philo, *On the Embassy to Gaius* 155–58. See John B. Polhill, *Acts*, NAC (Nashville: Broadman, 1992), 710.

99. See Rapske, *Paul in Roman Custody*, 228.

Romans

1. See Acts 10:2, 22; 13:16, 26; 16:14; 17:17; 18:7. For further discussion, see C. Marvin Pate, *The Reverse of the Curse: Paul, Wisdom, and the Law*, WUNT 114/2 (Tübingen: Mohr Siebeck, 2000), 326–30.

2. Suetonius, *Claudius* 25.4.

3. Robert Jewett has shown convincingly that Paul's mission to Spain was uppermost in Paul's mind when he wrote Romans (Robert Jewett, *Romans: A Commentary*, assisted by Roy D. Kotansky, ed. Eldon Jay Epp, Hermeneia [Minneapolis: Fortress, 2007]). I agree with Jewett for the most part, but I think that he did not give sufficient focus to the eschatological status of Paul's mission to Spain via Rome.

4. See the discussion by K. H. Rengstorf in *TDNT* 1:414–22, agreeing with the identification. Not all recent scholars agree with this conclusion.

5. See N. T. Wright's convincing discussion on this point in *The New Testament and the People of God* (Minneapolis: Fortress, 1992), 320–34.

6. Jewett, *Romans*, 130.

7. See Douglas J. Moo, *Romans*, NIVAC (Grand Rapids: Zondervan, 2000), 63–89; N. T. Wright, *What Saint Paul Really Said: Was Paul of Tarsus the Real Founder of Christianity?*

(Grand Rapids: Eerdmans, 1997), 95–107. I seem to be the first author to root "not ashamed" and "revealed" in Isaiah's promise of the restoration of Israel.

8. One of the first NT scholars to question this traditional reading of Paul in Rom. 1:18–32 concerning this matter was Robin Scroggs, *The New Testament and Homosexuality: Contextual Background for Contemporary Debate* (Philadelphia: Fortress, 1983). Scroggs's argument that Paul was not all that upset by that practice because it was an acceptable norm in the apostle's day has not met with general approval among NT scholars.

9. For example, Wis. 14:25–26; 4 Macc. 1:26–27; 2:15; *1QRule of the Community* 4.9–11.

10. For further documentation, see James D. G. Dunn, *Romans 1–8*, WBC 38A (Waco: Word, 1988), 67.

11. See Stanley K. Stowers, *The Diatribe and Paul's Letter to the Romans*, SBLDS 57 (Chico, CA: Scholars Press, 1981).

12. For example, Seneca, *On Anger* 3.36.1; *Moral Epistles* 28.10.

13. For example, Wis. 17:11; Philo, *On the Special Laws* 2.49; *On the Virtues* 134; Josephus, *Jewish Antiquities* 16.103.

14. See Sirach; Baruch; the Dead Sea Scrolls; *4 Ezra*; *2 Baruch*; 4 Maccabees.

15. Epictetus, *Discourses* 2.19–20; 3.7, 17. See Stowers, *Diatribe*, 112.

16. See also *1QPesher to Habakkuk* 11.13; *1QRule of the Community* 5.5; *Jubilees* 1.23.

17. For example, Sir. 44:19–20; 1 Macc. 2:52; *Jubilees* 19.8–9; 23.9–10; *Damascus Document*[a] 3.2–4.

18. For Gen. 15:6/Gen. 17, see Sir. 44:19–20; *m. Nedarim* 3.11; for Gen. 15:6/Gen. 22, see 1 Macc. 2:52; cf. *Jubilees* 23.10 with *Jubilees* 17.15–18, 19; 19.8; see *m. Avot* 5.3; Philo, *On the Life of Abraham* 191–99; Josephus, *Jewish Antiquities* 1.223–25, 233–36; Pseudo-Philo, *Biblical Antiquities* 40.2; 4 Maccabees; *Damascus Document*[a] 3.2–4; James 2:21–24. There is much debate as to whether Paul and James 2:21–24 are actually divided on this issue.

19. See Dan. 7:21; *1QWar Scroll* 15; Rev. 19.

20. Aristotle, *Politics* 1.2.4–5; *Nicomachean Ethics* 8.2.

21. For further discussion and documentation, see Dunn, *Romans 1–8*, 360.

22. *Exapataō* is the intensive form of *apataō*.

23. For example, *4 Ezra*.

24. Ovid, *Metamorphoses* 7.21.

25. Epictetus, *Discourses* 2.26.1–2; cf. 2.26.4–5.

26. For example, *1 Enoch* 1.2–8; 96.3; *2 Baruch* 48.49–50; 51.3–11; *4 Ezra* 7.14–16, 95–98.

27. Wolfgang Schrage, "Leid, Kreuz und Eschaton: Die Peristasenkatologe als Merkmale paulinsicher *theologia crucis* und Eschatologie," *EvT* 34 (1974): 141–75.

28. For example, *4 Ezra* 4.27, 7.12, 89; *2 Baruch* 15.8; 48.50.

29. See *4 Ezra* 7.1–9.14; *1QRule of the Community* 3.23.

30. See also Odil Hannes Steck, *Israel und das gewaltsame Geschick der Propheten: Untersuchungen zur Überlieferung des deuteronomistischen Geschichtsbildes im Alten Testament, Spätjudentum und Urchristentum*, WMANT 23 (Neukirchen-Vluyn: Neukirchener Verlag, 1967).

31. 1 Macc. 2:26, 27, 50, 58; 2 Macc. 4:2.

32. For example, *1QRule of the Community* 4.4; 9.23; *1QHodayot*[a] 14.14. For further discussion, see James D. G. Dunn, *Romans 9–16*, WBC 38B (Waco: Word, 1988), 586–87.

33. For example, Deut. 30:12–14; Bar. 3:29–30; cf. Philo, *On the Posterity of Cain* 84–85; *Targum Neofiti* on Deut. 30; cf. also the Dead Sea Scrolls.

34. For discussion and documentation, see Pate, *Reverse of the Curse*.

35. See W. M. Ramsay, "The Olive-Tree and the Wild Olive," in *Paul and Other Studies in Early Christian History* (London: Hodder & Stoughton, 1908), 219–50. The ancient texts cited are Columella, *On Rural Affairs* 5.9.16; Palladius, *On Grafting* 53–54.

36. For example, Dan. 2:18–19, 27–30; *1 Enoch* 41.1; 46.2; 103.2; 2 *Enoch* 24.3; *4 Ezra* 10.38; 12.36–38; *1QRule of the Community* 3.23; 4.18; 9.18; *1QHodayot*[a] 9.21; 10.13.

37. See also *1 Enoch* 63.3; 93.11–14; *4 Ezra* 4.21; 5.36–40; 8.21.

38. For example, Sir. 24:23; Bar. 4:1. See Pate, *Reverse of the Curse*, 252–60.

39. A. T. Hanson, *The New Testament Interpretation of Scripture* (London: SPCK, 1980), 85.

40. Pseudo-Aristotle, *On the Universe* 6; Seneca, *Moral Epistles* 65.8; Marcus Aurelius, *Meditations* 4.23.

41. Philo, *On the Special Laws* 1.208; *On the Cherubim* 125–56.

42. Although many commentators think that Paul's doxology in 11:36 is only to God, others have argued elsewhere that Paul also includes Christ in the doxology in that verse (see Pate, *Reverse of the Curse*, 253–55), for at least two reasons. First, the language of 11:36 is applied to Christ in other texts by Paul: "riches" (Phil. 4:19; Col. 1:27), "wisdom" (1 Cor. 1:21–24, 30), "knowledge" (1 Cor. 8:3; Gal. 4:9), "from him, through him, for him, by him" (1 Cor. 8:6; Col. 1:16–17). Second, the context of 11:36 refers to Christ. All of this is to say that the doxology to God in 11:36 involves Christ as the means to culminating the divine plan of salvation history.

43. Commentators regularly note the connection between 12:1–2 and 1:21–25 but without specifying the Adam theology that undergirds 12:1–2.

44. W. D. Davies, *Paul and Rabbinic Judaism: Some Rabbinic Elements in Pauline Theology* (New York: Harper & Row, 1948), 57; cf. 53–57.

45. A. J. M. Wedderburn, *Baptism and Resurrection: Studies in Pauline Theology against Its Graeco-Roman Background*, WUNT 44 (Tübingen: Mohr Siebeck, 1987), 350–56. Wedderburn also convincingly responds to criticisms of the Hebrew corporate personality theory. For more discussion, see C. Marvin Pate, *The End of the Age Has Come: The Theology of Paul* (Grand Rapids: Zondervan, 1995), 170–72.

46. For example, 1 Sam. 12:8; Prov. 8:15–16; Isa. 41:2–4; 45:1–7; Jer. 27:5–6; Dan. 2:21, 37–38; 4:17, 25, 32; 5:21; cf. Wis. 6:1–3; Sir. 4:27; Josephus, *Jewish War* 2.140.

47. See K. Weiss, "φόρος," *TDNT* 9:80–81; Josephus, *Jewish Antiquities* 5.181; 12.182.

48. Tacitus, *Annals* 13.

49. See the bibliography in Dunn, *Romans 9–16*, 790–91.

50. Evald Lövestam points to Jewish eschatological texts such as Isa. 60:19–20; Amos 5:18, 20; *1 Enoch* 10.5; 92.4–5; 108.11; *2 Baruch* 18.2; 48.50; *1QRule of the Community* 1.9; 2.16; 3.13; *1QWar Scroll* 1.1 that undergird Rom. 13:11–14. See Evald Lövestam, *Spiritual Wakefulness in the New Testament*, trans. W. F. Salisbury, LUA 55/3 (Lund: Gleerup, 1963), 10–27, 34–35.

51. See, for example, Dunn, *Romans 9–16*, 840, 845, 847, 850.

52. Keith F. Nickle's study on the subject is excellent: *The Collection: A Study in Paul's Strategy*, SBT 48 (London: SCM, 1966).

53. Jewett, *Romans*, 74–77.

54. Roger D. Aus, "Paul's Travel Plans to Spain and the 'Full Number of the Gentiles' of Rom. XI.25," *NovT* 21 (1979): 232–62. Aus ties together 11:25–27; 15:16, 24, 25–27 to advance his thesis.

55. For example, Isa. 45:14; 60:5–17; 61:6; Mic. 4:13; Tob. 13:11; *1QWar Scroll* 12.13–15. See Dunn, *Romans 9–16*, 874.

56. Aus, "Paul's Travel Plans." It is splitting hairs to object to Aus's eschatological reading of Paul's gentile collection by saying that the offering of the gentiles is not the gentiles themselves, for the one (the collection) was the extension of the other (the gentiles). Furthermore, though Paul doesn't make it explicit, it seems that the apostle implies that the Roman Christians and soon the newly evangelized gentiles in Spain should also contribute to the gentile collection to the saints in Jerusalem.

57. See Bruce Winter's extensive documentation of the Roman patronage system: *Seek the Welfare of the City: Christians as Benefactors and Citizens*, FCGRW (Grand Rapids: Eerdmans, 1994).

58. See bibliography supporting this from the archaeological evidence in Jewett, *Romans*, 947.

59. Jewett, *Romans*, 954–74.

60. See, for example, *Testament of Levi* 18.12 for Judaism, and Rev. 12:17 for Christianity.

1 Corinthians

1. Erastus, the city treasurer in Corinth, is mentioned in Rom. 16:23, and Sosthenes (1 Cor. 1:1) and Crispus (1 Cor. 1:14), both synagogue rulers, may be the same men mentioned in Acts 18 (see Acts 18:8, 17). In 1 Corinthians Paul mentions the household of Stephanas (1:16; 16:15) and the household of Chloe (1:11), who may have been a Corinthian. The mention of the household suggests that these were individuals of financial means. Aquila and Priscilla, who were among the original members of the Corinthian church, traveled extensively (see comments on Acts 18:2; Rom. 16:3–5; 1 Cor. 16:19). On social stratification in Corinth, see comments on 1 Cor. 1:26.

2. Roy E. Ciampa and Brian S. Rosner, "The Structure and Argument of 1 Corinthians," *NTS* 52 (2006): 205–18. More recently, see Roy E. Ciampa and Brian S. Rosner, *The First Letter to the Corinthians*, PNTC (Grand Rapids: Eerdmans, 2010), 21–35. Ciampa and Rosner argue that 1 Corinthians is fundamentally of Jewish character, that purity concerns outweigh concerns for unity, and that the central portion of the letter is structured around the parallel commands to flee from the two chief gentile vices, sexual immorality and idolatry, and to glorify God (6:18–20; 10:14, 31).

3. See Gordon J. Bahr, "Paul and Letter Writing in the First Century," *CBQ* 28 (1966): 476–77.

4. See Jerome Murphy-O'Connor, "Co-authorship in the Corinthian Correspondence," *RB* 100 (1993): 562–79.

5. So Gordon D. Fee, *The First Epistle to the Corinthians*, NICNT (Grand Rapids: Eerdmans, 1987), 28.

6. See Anthony C. Thiselton, *The First Epistle to the Corinthians: A Commentary on the Greek Text*, NIGTC (Grand Rapids: Eerdmans: 2000), 66. Thiselton notes that this view extends from the patristic era (Chrysostom, AD 390) to the present time, calls attention to God's grace (15:9–10), and is associated with lowliness (4:9).

7. See especially Ciampa and Rosner, *First Letter to the Corinthians*, 57.

8. See Peter T. O'Brien, *Introductory Thanksgivings in the Letters of Paul*, NovTSup 49 (Leiden: Brill, 1977), 121–22.

9. See Margaret M. Mitchell, *Paul and the Rhetoric of Reconciliation: An Exegetical Investigation of the Language and Composition of 1 Corinthians* (Louisville: Westminster John Knox, 1991), 68.

10. The view of John Chrysostom (*Homilies on the First Epistle to the Corinthians* 3.1), based upon his interpretation of 4:6, that Paul tactfully used the four names as substitutes

for the real offenders still lingers in modern scholarship. Some think that Paul employs rhetorical exaggeration that would have been unmistakable to the original hearers.

11. Cephas is the Aramaic name for Peter.

12. For inscriptional evidence that "ruler of the synagogue" was an honorific title bestowed on wealthy patrons, see Jerome Murphy-O'Connor, *Paul: A Critical Life* (Oxford: Oxford University Press, 1996), 267. The home and those who served as patrons of the church performed an important role in the early church. In 1 Corinthians references to the "home" occur in 11:22, 34; 14:35; 16:19. For scholarship regarding the ancient household, see Thiselton, *First Epistle to the Corinthians*, 141.

13. See the extensive study by Stephen M. Pogoloff, *Logos and Sophia: The Rhetorical Situation of 1 Corinthians* SBLDS 134 (Atlanta: Scholars Press, 1992).

14. See Bruce W. Winter, *Philo and Paul among the Sophists*, SNTSMS 96 (Cambridge: Cambridge University Press, 1997).

15. Cicero, *Against Verres* 2.5.165.

16. Josephus, *Jewish War* 7.203. For a thorough study of the cross in its historical context see Martin Hengel, *Crucifixion in the Ancient World and the Folly of the Message of the Cross*, trans. John Bowden (Philadelphia: Fortress, 1977).

17. Thiselton, *First Epistle to the Corinthians*, 155. On the association of "power" with rhetoric and eloquence in Hellenistic literature, see Peter Marshall, *Enmity in Corinth: Social Conventions in Paul's Relations with the Corinthians*, WUNT 2/23 (Tübingen: Mohr, 1987), 387.

18. As reflected in the Jewish writing *4 Ezra* 7.113: "The day of judgment will be the end of this age and beginning of the immortal age to come."

19. For a complete analysis, see Gerd Theissen, *The Social Setting of Pauline Christianity: Essays on Corinth*, trans. John H. Schütz (Philadelphia: Fortress, 1982), 69–120.

20. The Septuagint version of Jer. 9:22–23 and 1 Sam. 2:10 are equally likely sources of the quotation, and both may have influenced the vocabulary, structure, and theme of 1 Cor. 1:26–31 (see also 2 Cor. 10:17).

21. See Winter, *Philo and Paul among the Sophists*, 147–49, 155–59.

22. See Stanley K. Stowers, "Paul on the Use and Abuse of Reason," in *Greeks, Romans, and Christians: Essays in Honor of Abraham J. Malherbe*, ed. David L. Balch, Everett Ferguson, and Wayne A. Meeks (Minneapolis: Fortress, 1990), 253–86.

23. H. H. Drake Williams III, *The Wisdom of the Wise: The Presence and Function of Scripture within 1 Cor. 1:18–3:23*, AGJU 49 (Leiden: Brill, 2001), 156.

24. So Ciampa and Rosner, *First Letter to the Corinthians*, 121. They clarify, however, that this is not the case with every "we" or "us" in the passage, since 2:10, 12 refer to all believers.

25. See Joseph A. Fitzmyer, *First Corinthians: A New Translation with Introduction and Commentary*, AYB 32 (New Haven: Yale University Press, 2008), 174–75. Fitzmyer thinks that Paul could be speaking in "no little irony."

26. See Oscar Cullmann, *Christ and Time: The Primitive Christian Conception of Time and History*, trans. Floyd V. Filson (London: SCM, 1951), 191–201; more recently, Ciampa and Rosner, *First Letter to the Corinthians*, 125.

27. See the discussion in John Paul Heil, *The Rhetorical Role of Scripture in 1 Corinthians*, SBLMS 15 (Atlanta: Society of Biblical Literature, 2005), 53–57.

28. See Williams, *Wisdom of the Wise*, 168; Fee, *First Epistle to the Corinthians*, 111.

29. See Morna D. Hooker, "Hard Sayings: 1 Corinthians 3:2," *Theology* 69 (1966): 21.

30. See the discussion in Thiselton, *First Epistle to the Corinthians*, 302. See also Jer. 18:9; 24:6; Ezek. 36:9–10.

31. Johannes P. Louw and Eugene A. Nida, *Greek-English Lexicon of the New Testament: Based on Semantic Domains* (New York: United Bible Societies, 1988), §35.20. BDAG defines it as "one who functions as a helper or assistant."

32. See G. K. Beale, *The Temple and the Church's Mission: A Biblical Theology of the Dwelling Place of God*, NSBT (Downers Grove, IL: InterVarsity, 2004), 246; Ciampa and Rosner, *First Letter to the Corinthians*, 150.

33. So Mitchell, *Paul and the Rhetoric of Reconciliation*, 99–105.

34. Ben Witherington III, *Conflict and Community in Corinth: A Socio-Rhetorical Commentary on 1 and 2 Corinthians* (Grand Rapids: Eerdmans, 1994), 134.

35. On "temple" language, see John R. Lanci, *A New Temple for Corinth: Rhetorical and Archaeological Approaches to Pauline Imagery*, SBL 1 (New York: Peter Lang, 1997).

36. David R. Hall, "A Disguise for the Wise: ΜΕΤΑΣΧΗΜΑΤΙΣΜΟΣ in 1 Corinthians 4.6," *NTS* 40 (1994): 143–49.

37. On the OT underpinnings of Paul's ethics in 1 Cor. 5–7, see especially Brian S. Rosner, *Paul, Scripture, and Ethics: A Study of 1 Corinthians 5–7*, AGJU 22 (Leiden: Brill, 1994).

38. For the Greco-Roman sources indicating the universal rejection of incest as socially unacceptable, see Thiselton, *First Epistle to the Corinthians*, 385.

39. See Andrew D. Clarke, *Secular and Christian Leadership in Corinth: A Socio-Historical and Exegetical Study of 1 Corinthians 1–6*, AGJU 18 (Leiden: Brill, 1993), 76–87; John K. Chow, *Patronage and Power: A Study of Social Networks in Corinth*, JSNTSup 75 (Sheffield: JSOT Press, 1992), 130–41.

40. See also Neh. 1:4, 8:9; 1 Esd. 8:72, 9:2; Dan. 10:2. See Ciampa and Rosner, *First Letter to the Corinthians*, 201.

41. But see Ciampa and Rosner, *First Letter to the Corinthians*, 218, proposing that the case of the incestuous man is so serious that the words "not even" suggest exclusion from private meals in this case.

42. Thiselton, *First Epistle to the Corinthians*, 419–22. See Also Alan C. Mitchell, "Rich and Poor in the Courts of Corinth: Litigiousness and Status in 1 Corinthians 6:1–11," *NTS* 39 (1993): 562–86; Bruce W. Winter, "Civil Litigation in Secular Corinth and the Church: The Forensic Background to 1 Corinthians 6:1–8," *NTS* 37 (1991): 559–72.

43. Paul M. Hoskins, "The Use of Biblical and Extrabiblical Parallels in the Interpretation of First Corinthians 6:2–3," *CBQ* 63 (2001): 287–97.

44. For a book-length discussion on this issue, see Robert A. J. Gagnon, *The Bible and Homosexual Practice: Texts and Hermeneutics* (Nashville: Abingdon, 2001).

45. See the discussion in Ciampa and Rosner, *First Letter to the Corinthians*, 246–49.

46. See J. E. Smith, "Slogans in 1 Corinthians," *BSac* 167 (2010): 68–88.

47. *Testament of Reuben* 5.5.

48. George L. Klein, "Hos 3:1–3: Background to 1 Cor 6:19b–20?" *CTR* 3 (1988): 374.

49. Not everything from 7:1 forward is a response to a question from the Corinthians. Paul refers to what he has heard in 11:18, and there is no introductory "now about" introducing the topic of head coverings (11:2–16) or the lengthy discussion of the resurrection (15:1–58). Margaret Mitchell has set forth arguments showing that the phrase "now about" may only indicate movement from one topic to another. See Margaret M. Mitchell, "Concerning περὶ δὲ in 1 Corinthians," *NovT* 31 (1989): 229–56.

50. See Will Deming, *Paul on Marriage and Celibacy: The Hellenistic Background of 1 Corinthians 7*, 2nd ed. (Grand Rapids: Eerdmans, 2004).

51. See Roy Ciampa, "Revisiting the Euphemism in 1 Corinthians 7:1," *JSNT* 31 (2009): 325–38. See also Ciampa and Rosner, *First Letter to the Corinthians*, 268–69. In this view,

Paul rejects any notion that married couples should avoid sexual relations for pleasure or passion, something idealized in the Scriptures in Song of Solomon. This background to the slogan is based upon a detailed linguistic study of the euphemism "to touch" in ancient literature, translated "have sexual relations with" in 7:2, and the discussion within Roman culture on the issue of sexual relations.

52. So Ciampa and Rosner, *First Letter to the Corinthians*, 277.

53. The verb "to leave" (*chōrizō*) appears in the papyri referring to divorce.

54. See Robert G. Hall, "Epispasm: Circumcision in Reverse," *BRev* 8 (1992): 52–57.

55. See Bruce W. Winter, "Secular and Christian Responses to Corinthian Famines," *TynBul* 40 (1989): 86–106.

56. The religious significance of food was an important issue in the ancient world and is still a persistent problem in some contemporary societies. See Alex T. Cheung, *Idol Food in Corinth: Jewish Background and Pauline Legacy*, JSNTSup 176 (Sheffield: Sheffield Academic Press, 1999).

57. For a helpful summary of recent scholarship on 1 Cor. 8–10, see Wendell Willis, "1 Corinthians 8–10: A Retrospective after Twenty-Five Years," *ResQ* 49 (2007): 103–12.

58. See John Fotopoulos, *Food Offered to Idols in Roman Corinth: A Social-Rhetorical Reconsideration of 1 Corinthians 8:1–11:1*, WUNT 2/151 (Tübingen: Mohr Siebeck, 2003), 49–157, 208.

59. See Theissen, *Social Setting of Pauline Christianity*, 126–27.

60. Fee, *First Epistle to the Corinthians*, 392–94.

61. On the image of the athletic games in pagan moral philosophy, see Victor C. Pfitzner, *Paul and the Agon Motif: Traditional Athletic Imagery in the Pauline Literature*, NovTSup 16 (Leiden: Brill, 1967), 23–37.

62. Peter E. Enns, "The 'Moveable Well' in 1 Cor 10:4: An Extrabiblical Tradition in an Apostolic Text," *BBR* 6 (1996): 23–38.

63. See David E. Garland, *1 Corinthians*, BECNT (Grand Rapids: Baker Academic, 2003), 479.

64. So Raymond F. Collins, *First Corinthians*, SP 7 (Collegeville, MN: Liturgical Press, 1999), 383; Jerome Murphy-O'Connor, *St. Paul's Corinth: Texts and Archaeology*, GNS 6 (Wilmington, DE: Michael Glazier, 1983), 32.

65. Leon Morris, *1 Corinthians*, TNTC (Grand Rapids: Eerdmans, 1985), 146.

66. Cheung, *Idol Food in Corinth*, 158n240.

67. Note the NRSV translation: "the husband is the head of his wife." So also Bruce W. Winter, *After Paul Left Corinth: The Influence of Secular Ethics and Social Change* (Grand Rapids: Eerdmans, 2001), 127, noting that the very mention of the covered head would indicate that the females under discussion were married.

68. Ciampa and Rosner, *First Letter to the Corinthians*, 509.

69. See Preston T. Massey, "The Meaning of κατακαλύπτω and κατὰ κεφαλῆς ἔχων in 1 Corinthians 11.2–16," *NTS* 53 (2007): 502–23. Some have argued on the basis of 11:14–16 that hairstyle is the issue. If hairstyle was the issue, then the central concern might be either blurred gender distinctions or disorderly worship with possible pagan associations.

70. See David W. J. Gill, "The Importance of Roman Portraiture for Head-Coverings in 1 Corinthians 11:2–16," *TynBul* 41 (1990): 245–60; Winter, *After Paul Left Corinth*, 121–23. Winter thinks that Paul is equally concerned about veiled men.

71. So Winter, *After Paul Left Corinth*, 128.

72. For a possible connection with Ps. 8, see Heil, *Rhetorical Role of Scripture*, 183–84. Evidence from Qumran that speaks of angels present at gatherings of the Essene community

bolsters the interpretation linking angels with worship (see *1QRule of the Congregation* 2.3–9; *1QWar Scroll* 7.4–6). See Fitzmyer, *First Corinthians*, 418–19.

73. Such as *Genesis Rabbah* 8.9: "In the past Adam was created from dust and Eve was created from Adam; but henceforth it shall be 'in our image, after our likeness' [Gen. 1:26]; neither man without woman nor woman without man, and neither of them without Shekinah." See also 1 Esd. 4:14–17. Noted in Ciampa and Rosner, *First Letter to the Corinthians*, 534.

74. So Thiselton, *First Epistle to the Corinthians*, 850. See also Bruce W. Winter, "The Lord's Supper at Corinth: An Alternative Reconstruction," *RTR* 37 (1978): 73–82.

75. Archibald Robertson and Alfred Plummer, *A Critical and Exegetical Commentary on the First Epistle of St. Paul to the Corinthians*, 2nd ed., ICC (Edinburgh: T&T Clark, 1914), 243.

76. Ciampa and Rosner, *First Letter to the Corinthians*, 556.

77. Wayne A. Grudem, *The Gift of Prophecy in 1 Corinthians* (Lanham, MD: University Press of America, 1982), 164; Garland, *1 Corinthians*, 565.

78. For a discussion of idol festivals, see Terence Paige, "1 Corinthians 12:2: A Pagan Pompe?," *JSNT* 44 (1991): 57–65.

79. Winter, *After Paul Left Corinth*, 167. Winter notes that twenty-seven curse tablets have been unearthed in Corinth in recent years and provide a possible background understanding for 1 Cor. 12:3a. Winter further notes that over one thousand examples have come to light of the widespread pagan practice of cursing others.

80. Garland, *1 Corinthians*, 568–71.

81. See M. Christopher Forbes, *Prophecy and Inspired Speech in Early Christianity and Its Hellenistic Environment*, WUNT 2/75 (Tübingen: Mohr, 1995), 57–72; also Thiselton, *First Epistle to the Corinthians*, 970–88.

82. See M. Mitchell, *Paul and the Rhetoric of Reconciliation*, 157. Commentators routinely cite the speech of Menenius Agrippa as one of the best-known examples of the use of the body image to exhort the Roman populace to stop their revolt against the state and to submit to the aristocracy (see Livy, *History of Rome* 2.32.7–33.1).

83. See Collins, *First Corinthians*, 460.

84. So Ciampa and Rosner, *First Letter to the Corinthians*, 589.

85. For example, the term "apostle" (*apostolos*) is used of Titus (2 Cor. 8:23), Epaphroditus (Phil. 2:25), James (Gal. 1:19), and Andronicus and Junia (Rom. 16:7).

86. See James G. Sigountos, "The Genre of 1 Corinthians 13," *NTS* 40 (1994): 246–60.

87. William V. Harris, "'Sounding Brass' and Hellenistic Technology: Ancient Acoustical Device Clarifies Paul's Well-Known Metaphor," *BAR* 8 (1982): 38–41; William W. Klein, "Noisy Gong or Acoustic Vase? A Note on 1 Corinthians 13:1," *NTS* 32 (1986): 286–89.

88. See C. K. Barrett, *A Commentary on the First Epistle to the Corinthians*, HNTC (New York: Harper & Row, 1968), 300; Fee, *First Epistle to the Corinthians*, 632.

89. So Ciampa and Rosner, *First Letter to the Corinthians*, 632.

90. Sigountos, "The Genre of 1 Corinthians 13," 256–57.

91. Robertson and Plummer, *The First Epistle of St. Paul to the Corinthians*, 325.

92. Scholars have proposed different groups of people who denied the resurrection as a possible background: (1) Jewish opponents who held the same view as the Sadducees, (2) gnostics who emphasized spirit over matter, (3) those who claimed that a resurrection had already occurred in a "spiritual" sense (see 2 Tim. 2:17–18), and (4) some among the Corinthians who emphasized the spirit to the exclusion of the body and thus held to a spiritualized eschatology.

93. See Richard E. DeMaris, "Corinthian Religion and Baptism for the Dead (1 Corinthians 15:29): Insights from Archaeology and Anthropology," *JBL* 114 (1995): 661–82.

94. For this view and a recent full-length treatment of 1 Cor. 15:29, see Michael F. Hull, *Baptism on Account of the Dead (1 Cor. 15:29): An Act of Faith in the Resurrection*, SBLAB 22 (Atlanta: Society of Biblical Literature, 2005). There are further nuances to the "causal" view. See Joel R. White, "'Baptized on Account of the Dead': The Meaning of 1 Corinthians 15:29 in Its Context," *JBL* 116 (1997): 494; James E. Patrick, "Living Rewards for Dead Apostles: 'Baptised for the Dead' in 1 Corinthians 15.29," *NTS* 52 (2006): 71–85.

95. Abraham J. Malherbe, "The Beasts at Ephesus," *JBL* 87 (1968): 71–80.

96. Guy Williams, "An Apocalyptic and Magical Interpretation of Paul's 'Beast Fight' in Ephesus (1 Corinthians 15:32)," *JTS* 57 (2006): 45.

97. Ciampa and Rosner, *First Letter to the Corinthians*, 789.

98. Scholars point out that Paul may have been referring to a sentiment found in Epicurean philosophy of his day. Gordon Fee notes that Plutarch, speaking against the Epicureans, referred to "eating and drinking" as an empty way of life. See Fee, *First Epistle to the Corinthians*, 772, citing Plutarch, *Moralia* 1098C; 1100D; 1125D.

99. Stanley Porter ("Diatribe," *DNTB* 296) notes the basis of this form of argumentation in noted philosophers such as Socrates and Plato. Some of the best-known authors of the Greco-Roman period who used this method of argumentation include Epictetus, Dio Chrysostom, Teles, and Musonius Rufus.

100. Jeffrey R. Asher, "ΣΠΕΙΡΕΤΑΙ: Paul's Anthropogenic Metaphor in 1 Corinthians 15:42–44," *JBL* 120 (2001): 102.

101. Ciampa and Rosner, *First Letter to the Corinthians*, 820.

102. Collins, *First Corinthians*, 575–76.

103. For ancient sources, see Collins, *First Corinthians*, 589. See also Acts 9:2; 13:2–3; 15:23–29; 22:5; Rom. 16:1–2; 2 Cor. 3:1; 8:16–24.

2 Corinthians

1. F. F. Bruce, *Paul, Apostle of the Heart Set Free* (Grand Rapids: Eerdmans, 1977), 35.

2. Strabo, *Geography* 13.1.26.

3. Lucian, *Hermotimus* 59.

4. For example, Seneca, *To Lucilius* 66.3; Epictetus, *Discourses* 1.25.21; Marcus Aurelius, *Meditations* 10.1.

5. For example, Philo, *Allegorical Interpretation* 2.56; Porphyry, *To Marcella* 33.501–5. See Craig S. Keener, *1–2 Corinthians*, NCamBC (Cambridge: Cambridge University Press, 2005), 180.

6. Seyoon Kim, "2 Cor 5:11–21 and the Origin of Paul's Concept of 'Reconciliation,'" *NovT* 39 (1997): 360–84.

7. See Murray J. Harris, *The Second Epistle to the Corinthians: A Commentary on the Greek Text*, NIGTC (Grand Rapids: Eerdmans, 2005), 456.

8. John Chrysostom, *Homilies on the Second Epistle to the Corinthians* 15.1.

9. Keener, *1–2 Corinthians*, 213.

10. James F. Strange, "2 Corinthians 10:13–16 Illuminated by a Recently Published Inscription," *BA* 46 (1983): 168.

11. Bruce W. Winter, *Philo and Paul among the Sophists: Alexandrian and Corinthian Responses to a Julio-Claudian Movement*, 2nd ed. (Grand Rapids: Eerdmans, 2002), 224–25.

12. For example, *Life of Adam and Eve* 9.1.

13. See the discussion in Craig Keener, *The IVP Bible Background Commentary: New Testament*, 2nd ed. (Downers Grove, IL: IVP Academic, 2014), 518.

14. *m. Makkot* 3.10–15.

15. Jonathan T. Pennington, *Heaven and Earth in the Gospel of Matthew*, NovTSup 126 (Leiden: Brill, 2007), 129.

16. *Apocalypse of Moses* 37.5; *2 Enoch* 8.1.

17. Seneca, *On Benefits* 2.11.4–5. See Keener, *1–2 Corinthians*, 242–43.

18. Lucian, *Hermotimus* 59.

Galatians

1. See Roy E. Ciampa, *The Presence and Function of Scripture in Galatians 1 and 2*, WUNT 2/102 (Tübingen: Mohr Siebeck, 1998), 60–61.

2. Karl Olav Sandnes, *Paul—One of the Prophets? A Contribution to the Apostle's Self-Understanding*, WUNT 2/43 (Tübingen: Mohr Siebeck, 1991), 56.

3. See Hans Dieter Betz, *Galatians: A Commentary on Paul's Letter to the Churches in Galatia*, Hermeneia (Philadelphia: Fortress, 1979), 90–91.

4. See Jouette M. Bassler, *Divine Impartiality: Paul and a Theological Axiom*, SBLDS 59 (Chico, CA: Scholars Press, 1982).

5. See Ciampa, *Scripture in Galatians 1 and 2*, 212.

6. See Plutarch, *Can Virtue Be Taught?* 439D–440A; Plato, *Greater Alcibiades* 121E–122B.

7. See *1QRule of the Community* 11.20–22; *4QRule of the Community*[j] 8–10; *4QApocryphal Lamentations B* 5; *1QHodayot*[a] 5.20; 23.12–13.

8. On adoption and inheritance, see the helpful discussion in James C. Walters, "Paul, Adoption, and Inheritance," in *Paul in the Greco-Roman World: A Handbook*, ed. J. Paul Sampley (Harrisburg, PA: Trinity Press International, 2003), 42–76.

9. Brian S. Rosner, "'Known by God': The Meaning and Value of a Neglected Biblical Concept," *TynBul* 59 (2008): 208.

10. The word was used "orig[inally] of spitting motion 'spit, spit out', then metaph[orically] to eject saliva as an expression of contempt . . . or to ward off hostile spirits" (BDAG 309).

11. Richard N. Longenecker, *Galatians*, WBC 41 (Dallas: Word, 1998), 193.

12. See Ezek. 40–48; *1 Enoch* 53.6; 90.28–29; *2 Enoch* 55.2; *Psalms of Solomon* 17.33; *4 Ezra* 7.26; 8.52; 10.25–28; *2 Baruch* 4.2–6; 32.2; 59.4; Rev. 21:10–27.

Ephesians

1. See the vigorous defense of Pauline authorship in Harold Hoehner, *Ephesians: An Exegetical Commentary* (Grand Rapids: Baker Academic, 2002), 1–114.

2. See Hubert Cancick and Helmuth Schneider, eds., *Brill's New Pauly: Encyclopaedia of the Ancient World* (Leiden: Brill, 2004), s.v. "Ephesus."

3. These were "letters" used as magic spells to keep away demons, to gain luck, to use in performing an exorcism, etc. See Clinton E. Arnold, *Ephesians, Power and Magic: The Concept of Power in Ephesians in Light of Its Historical Setting*, SNTSMS 63 (Cambridge: Cambridge University Press, 1989), and the literature there cited.

4. See Steven J. Friesen, *Imperial Cults and the Apocalypse of John: Reading Revelation in the Ruins* (Oxford: Oxford University Press, 2001).

5. *The Authorized Daily Prayer Book of the United Hebrew Congregations of the British Commonwealth of Nations*, trans. Simeon Singer (London: Eyre & Spottiswoode, 1962), 46.

6. For example, Homer, *Iliad* 6.129, 131; *Odyssey* 17.484; Theocritus, *Idylls* 25.5; Lucian, *Alexander* 9.18; 35.14; *Dialogue of the Gods* 10.3.

7. For example, Ps. 89:2; 2 Macc. 3:39; 3 Macc. 6:28; 7:6; Philo, *Allegorical Interpretation* 3.168; *On Giants* 62; *Testament of Abraham* 2.3; 4.9; 6.4; 17.11.

8. *Testament of Abraham* 4.9; Eph. 6:12.

9. See fig. 1 in Arnold, *Ephesians, Power and Magic*, 154.

10. Simon Hornblower and Antony Spawforth, eds., *The Oxford Classical Dictionary*, 4th ed. (Oxford: Oxford University Press, 2012), s.v. "adoption."

11. See Frank Thielman, *Ephesians*, BECNT (Grand Rapids: Baker Academic, 2010), 81.

12. Clinton E. Arnold, *Ephesians*, ZECNT (Grand Rapids: Zondervan, 2010), 114.

13. See Tet-Lim N. Yee, *Jews, Gentiles, and Ethnic Reconciliation: Paul's Jewish Identity and Ephesians*, SNTSMS 130 (Cambridge: Cambridge University Press, 2005), 191–95.

14. See also *1 Enoch* 93.11–14; *2 Baruch* 54.1–4.

15. See Dionysius of Halicarnassus, *Roman Antiquities* 6.86; Livy, *History of Rome* 2.32; Seneca, *On Mercy* 1.3.

16. David M. Stec, trans. and ed., *Targum of Psalms: Translated, with a Critical Introduction, Apparatus, and Notes*, ArBib 16 (Collegeville, MN: Liturgical Press, 2004), 131.

17. Helpful here is Murray J. Harris, *Slave of Christ: A New Testament Metaphor for Total Devotion to Christ*, NSBT 8 (Downers Grove, IL: InterVarsity; Nottingham: Apollos, 1999).

18. Hornblower and Spawforth, *The Oxford Classical Dictionary*, s.v. "armor."

Philippians

1. On what follows, I depend on the helpful work of Eduard Verhoef, *Philippi: How Christianity Began in Europe; The Epistle to the Philippians and the Excavations at Philippi* (London: Bloomsbury T&T Clark, 2013). Crucial also is Peter Oakes, *Philippians: From People to Letter*, SNTSMS 110 (Cambridge: Cambridge University Press, 2001), building on the work of Peter Pilhofer.

2. Verhoef, *Philippi*, 2.

3. Verhoef, *Philippi*, 4.

4. Verhoef, *Philippi*, 5.

5. Verhoef, *Philippi*, 7–8.

6. Verhoef, *Philippi*, 8–9.

7. See Markus Bockmuehl, *The Epistle to the Philippians*, BNTC (Peabody, MA: Hendrickson, 1998), 35–37.

8. Bockmuehl, *Philippians*, 37.

9. See Brian Rapske, *Paul in Roman Custody*, BAFCS 3 (Grand Rapids: Eerdmans, 1994), 9–35, 195–225, 227–81.

10. Bockmuehl, *Philippians*, 75, building on the classic essay by J. B. Lightfoot.

11. On the *cursus honorum* and the context of Philippi, see Joseph H. Hellerman, *Reconstructing Honor: Carmen Christi as* Cursus Pudorum, SNTSMS 132 (Cambridge: Cambridge University Press, 2005).

12. See Bockmuehl, *Philippians*, 196.

13. *b. Sanhedrin* 43a.

14. See Hellerman, *Reconstructing Honor*, 113–16.

15. Bockmuehl, *Philippians*, 265.

16. Bockmuehl, *Philippians*, 270.

Colossians

1. See Ian K. Smith, *Heavenly Perspective: A Study of the Apostle Paul's Response to a Jewish Mystical Movement at Colossae*, LNTS 326 (London: T&T Clark, 2006).

2. See the discussion in James D. G. Dunn, *The Epistles to the Colossians and to Philemon: A Commentary on the Greek Text*, NIGTC (Grand Rapids: Eerdmans, 1996), 87–90.

3. LSJ, s.v. πιθαναλογία.

4. See Josephus, *The Life* 7–12.

5. BDAG, s.v. χειρόγραφον.

6. Dunn, *Epistles to the Colossians and to Philemon*, 164–65.

7. BDAG, s.v. ἐξαλείφω.

8. See Adolf Deissmann, *Light from the Ancient East: The New Testament Illustrated by Recently Discovered Texts of the Graeco-Roman World* (New York: Doran, 1927), 170–72.

1–2 Thessalonians

1. For more on the purposes of this letter, see David A. deSilva, *An Introduction to the New Testament: Contexts, Methods & Ministry Formation* (Downers Grove, IL: IVP Academic, 2004), 535–39; Leon Morris, *The First and Second Epistles to the Thessalonians*, NICNT (Grand Rapids: Eerdmans, 1991), 1–10; Michael W. Holmes, *1 and 2 Thessalonians*, NIVAC (Grand Rapids: Zondervan, 1998), 17–28.

2. Karl Paul Donfried, *Paul, Thessalonica, and Early Christianity* (Grand Rapids: Eerdmans, 2002), 139–62.

3. See John M. G. Barclay, *Paul and the Gift* (Grand Rapids: Eerdmans, 2015).

4. Lucian, *Nigrinus* 35. See Moyer V. Hubbard, *Christianity in the Greco-Roman World: A Narrative Introduction* (Grand Rapids: Baker Academic, 2010), 92.

5. For example, Epictetus, *Enchiridion* 51.3; Seneca, *Moral Epistles* 6.5–6; Philo, *On the Life of Moses* 1.158–59; Josephus, *Jewish Antiquities* 1.19.

6. F. F. Bruce, *1 & 2 Thessalonians*, WBC 45 (Waco: Word, 1982), 16.

7. For more on this, see Charles A. Wanamaker, *The Epistles to the Thessalonians: A Commentary on the Greek Text*, NIGTC (Grand Rapids: Eerdmans, 1990), 4–5, 12.

8. For example, Cassius Dio, *Roman History* 67.14.2.

9. For more on this, see Holmes, *1 and 2 Thessalonians*, 60.

10. Epictetus, *Discourses* 1.9.

11. Bruce, *1 & 2 Thessalonians*, 29.

12. Seneca, *Moral Epistles* 75.7.

13. Dio Chrysostom, *Orations* 32.11. For more on this, see Bruce W. Winter, *Philo and Paul among the Sophists*, SNTSMS 96 (Cambridge: Cambridge University Press, 1997), 40–58.

14. Plutarch, *How to Tell a Flatterer from a Friend* 69.

15. *Pirqe Avot* 2.2. See Bruce, *1 & 2 Thessalonians*, 27, 34.

16. Hubbard, *Christianity in the Greco-Roman World*, 159.

17. See Seneca, *On Providence* 1.5–6.

18. Hubbard, *Christianity in the Greco-Roman World*, 180.

19. Josephus, *Jewish Antiquities* 20.105–12.

20. Pseudo-Demetrius, *Epistolary Types* 1.

21. Ben Witherington III, *1 and 2 Thessalonians: A Socio-Rhetorical Commentary* (Grand Rapids: Eerdmans, 2006), 91.

22. For example, Dan. 12:1; *2 Baruch* 70.2–10; 2 Esd. 5:1–12. See Witherington, *1 and 2 Thessalonians*, 94.

23. For more on this, see Morris, *First and Second Epistles to the Thessalonians*, 111.

24. See Bruce, *1 & 2 Thessalonians*, 113.

25. For example, Epictetus, *Discourses* 2.18.19–23; Seneca, *Moral Epistles* 37. See Hubbard, *Christianity in the Greco-Roman World*, 103.

26. See C. Marvin Pate, *Apostle of the Last Days: The Life, Letters and Theology of Paul* (Grand Rapids: Kregel, 2013), 90–91; Wanamaker, *Epistles to the Thessalonians*, 153.

27. Bruce, *1 & 2 Thessalonians*, 82, 87.

28. See Wanamaker, *Epistles to the Thessalonians*, 155.

29. For a fuller discussion, see E. Randolph Richards and Brandon J. O'Brien, *Paul Behaving Badly: Was the Apostle a Racist, Chauvinist Jerk?* (Downers Grove, IL: InterVarsity, 2016).

30. *IVPBBCNT*[1] 591.

31. For example, Plutarch, *On Tranquility of Mind* 465F–66A; Thucydides, *History of the Peloponnesian War* 2.44.

32. *IVPBBCNT*[1] 591.

33. For example, Dio Chrysostom, *Orations* 7.103–13, 124. See Witherington, *1 and 2 Thessalonians*, 123.

34. See Bruce Winter, *Seek the Welfare of the City: Christians as Benefactors and Citizens*, FCGRW (Grand Rapids: Eerdmans, 1994), 42–60.

35. Seneca, *Moral Epistles* 102.2, 26.

36. See Witherington, *1 and 2 Thessalonians*, 138.

37. For example, Seneca, *On Consolation to Marcia* 11–26. See Joseph R. Dodson, "Elements of Apocalyptic Eschatology in Seneca's Writings and Paul's Letters," in *Paul and the Greco-Roman Philosophical Tradition*, ed. Joseph R. Dodson and Andrew W. Pitts, LNTS 527 (London: Bloomsbury T&T Clark, 2017), 33–54.

38. See Pate, *Apostle of the Last Days*, 86.

39. For example, Plutarch, *To an Uneducated Ruler* 781D. See Witherington, *1 and 2 Thessalonians*, 149.

40. Euripides, *Iphigeneia at Tauris* 1025–26.

41. Seneca, *Moral Epistles* 122.1–10.

42. *IVPBBCNT*[1] 594.

43. Dio Chrysostom, *Orations* 48.

44. Troels Engberg-Pedersen, *Cosmology and Self in the Apostle Paul: The Material Spirit* (Oxford: Oxford University Press, 2010), 20.

45. *IVPBBCNT*[1] 595.

46. See deSilva, *Introduction to the New Testament*, 539–49.

47. For example, Justin, *First Apology* 62–63.

48. *Martyrdom and Ascension of Isaiah* 4.14. See Bruce, *1 & 2 Thessalonians*, 172.

49. Plato, *Republic* 10.615A–616A. See Joseph R. Dodson, "The Transcendence of Death and Heavenly Ascent in the Apocalyptic Paul and the Stoics," in *Paul and the Apocalyptic Imagination*, ed. Ben C. Blackwell, John K. Goodrich, and Jason Maston (Minneapolis: Fortress, 2016), 163.

50. Wanamaker, *Epistles to the Thessalonians*, 238.

51. For example, *Jubilees* 23.14–21; 2 Esd. 5:1–12; *1 Enoch* 91.7; 93.9. See Witherington, *1 and 2 Thessalonians*, 216.

52. See Bruce, *1 & 2 Thessalonians*, 173.

53. *Psalms of Solomon* 17.11–22. See Witherington, *1 and 2 Thessalonians*, 217.

54. For example, Prov. 15:11; 27:20; Job 26:6; Rev. 9:11.

55. For example, LXX Isa. 34:5; 57:4; *Psalms of Solomon* 2.31; 3.11; Rom. 9:22; 2 Pet. 2:3.

56. Seneca, *On Consolation to Polybius* 12–14. See Dodson, "Elements of Apocalyptic Eschatology."

57. See Acts 12:21–23; Josephus, *Jewish Antiquities* 19.343–47.

58. *2 Baruch* 29.4. See Witherington, *1 and 2 Thessalonians*, 222.

59. For example, Tertullian, *The Resurrection of the Flesh* 24; John Chrysostom, *Homilies on the Second Epistle to the Thessalonians*.

60. Josephus, *Jewish War* 1.470. See Witherington, *1 and 2 Thessalonians*, 222.
61. See Bruce, *1 & 2 Thessalonians*, 179.
62. *Martyrdom and Ascension of Isaiah* 4. See Bruce, *1 & 2 Thessalonians*, 182.
63. Tacitus, *Annals* 4.81. See *IVPBBCNT*[1] 602.
64. Seneca, *On Providence* 5.4.
65. *Genesis Rabbah* 2.2 on Gen. 1:2. See Bruce, *1 & 2 Thessalonians*, 206.
66. For example, Musonius Rufus, *Lectures* 11.16.
67. *Didache* 12.2–5.
68. John Chrysostom, *Homilies on the Second Epistle to the Thessalonians* 5.13.
69. Marcus Aurelius, *Meditations* 6.20. See Bruce, *1 & 2 Thessalonians*, 210.
70. See E. Randolph Richards, *Paul and First-Century Letter Writing: Secretaries, Composition and Collection* (Downers Grove, IL: InterVarsity, 2004), 171–75.

1–2 Timothy, Titus

1. S. M. Baugh, "1 Timothy," *ZIBBCNT* 3:462.
2. Baugh, "1 Timothy," 465.
3. *1 Enoch* 39.1; *Odes of Solomon* 4.8.
4. Baugh, "1 Timothy," 469.
5. *IVPBBCNT*[2] 617.
6. Theophrastus, *Characters* 25.1.
7. Philo, *On the Virtues* 26.
8. Philo, *On the Special Laws* 4.30.
9. Athenagoras, *A Plea for the Christians* 11.
10. Polybius, *Histories* 6.47.
11. Cicero, *On the Republic* 3.9.15.
12. Homer, *Iliad* 2.649; *Odyssey* 19.172–79; Horace, *Odes* 3.27.33.
13. Polybius, *Histories* 6.46.

Philemon

1. Here I follow the convincing reconstruction by James D. G. Dunn, *The Epistles to Colossians and to Philemon: A Commentary on the Greek Text*, NIGTC (Grand Rapids: Eerdmans, 1996), 301–7.

2. Translation from Stanley Stowers, *Letter Writing in Greco-Roman Antiquity*, LEC 5 (Philadelphia: Westminster, 1986), 160.

3. Peter Stuhlmacher, *Der Brief an Philemon*, 3rd ed., EKKNT18 (Neukirchen-Vluyn: Neukirchener Verlag, 1989), 17 (my translation).

4. Such as workshops, barns, and inns. See Edward Adams, *The Earliest Christian Meeting Places: Almost Exclusively Houses?*, LNTS 450 (London: T&T Clark, 2013).

5. Thus Stuhlmacher, *Philemon*, 31. Peter O'Brien's suggestion that the letter is exclusively for Philemon because "the matter Paul is dealing with is a personal affair which concerns Philemon alone and the decision to be arrived at is not a concern of the entire community" not only is doubtful for grammatical reasons but also underestimates the public ethos of ancient culture (Peter O'Brien, *Colossians, Philemon*, WBC 44 [Waco: Word, 1982], 273).

6. Andrew D. Clarke, "'Refresh the Hearts of the Saints': A Unique Pauline Context?," *TynBul* 47 (1996): 277–300.

7. However, there is enough ambiguity in v. 16 to allow Philemon perhaps to read the request as one of manumission. Whatever the case, Paul would have expected Philemon not to punish Onesimus when he returned.

8. How could he? He was living not in a modern Western European or North American democracy, but under an imperial dictatorship.

Hebrews

1. *Life of Adam and Eve.*
2. Philo, *Allegorical Interpretation* 3.203.
3. For example, Plato, *Laws* 10.
4. For example, Euripides, *Orestes*; Plutarch, *Moralia.*
5. Philo, *On the Life of Moses* 1.158.
6. For example, Philo, *On Providence* 2.35; Sir. 16:17.
7. For example, Seneca, *Moral Epistles* 83.1–2.
8. *11QMelchizedek.*
9. Josephus, *Jewish Antiquities* 20.227.
10. Tacitus, *Annals* 15.44.
11. For example, Philo, *On the Virtues* 199–255; Sir. 44:1–50:1; 1 Macc. 2:51–60.
12. For example, *1 Clement* 17.1–19.3.
13. For example, *Jubilees* 4.16–26; Sir. 44:16; Wis. 4:10–15; cf. Jude 14–15.
14. Note esp. *1 Enoch*; *2 Enoch*; *3 Enoch.*
15. Josephus, *Jewish Antiquities* 1.74; *Sibylline Oracles* 1.147–198; cf. 2 Pet. 2:5; *1 Clement* 7.6.
16. For example, Philo, *Allegorical Interpretation* 3.83; *2 Baruch* 4.1–4; *4 Ezra* 7.26; 8.52; cf. Rev. 21:1–9.
17. For example, Philo, *On the Life of Moses.*
18. Philo, *On the Life of Moses* 1.49–50; Josephus, *Jewish Antiquities* 2.254–56.
19. Cicero, *On Behalf of Gaius Rabirius on a Charge of Treason* 5.16.
20. Also Philo, *On the Preliminary Studies* 175.
21. *Jubilees* 25–26; 35; Philo, *Questions and Answers on Genesis* 4.201; *Allegorical Interpretation* 3.2.
22. For example, *2 Baruch* 4.2–6; *4 Ezra* 13.35–36.
23. For example, *1 Enoch* 22.3–7.
24. For example, Exod. 20:14–15; Deut. 5:18–19; Philo, *On the Posterity of Cain* 34; Epictetus, *Enchiridion* 3.7.21 (cf. Col. 3:5).
25. For example, Epictetus, *Discourses* 1.
26. For example, *Psalms of Solomon* 16.12.
27. For example, *1 Clement.*

James

1. David A. deSilva, *The Jewish Teachers of Jesus, James, and Jude: What Earliest Christianity Learned from the Apocrypha and Pseudepigrapha* (Oxford: Oxford University Press, 2012).
2. See Christopher W. Morgan, *A Theology of James: Wisdom for God's People*, EBT (Phillipsburg, NJ: P&R, 2010).
3. Aristotle, *Poetics* (ca. 335 BC).
4. William Baker, "Who's Your Daddy? Gendered Birth Images in the Soteriology of the Epistle of James (1:14–15, 18, 21)," *EvQ* 79 (2007): 195–207.
5. Mariam J. Kamell, "Incarnating Jeremiah's Promised New Covenant in the 'Law' of James: A Short Study," *EvQ* 83 (2011): 19–28.
6. Luke Timothy Johnson, "The Mirror of Remembrance: James 1:22–25," in *Brother of Jesus, Friend of God: Studies in the Letter of James* (Grand Rapids: Eerdmans, 2004), 168–81.

7. Jack Freeborn, "Lord of Glory: A Study of James 2 and 1 Corinthians 2," *ExpTim* 111 (2000): 185–89.

8. Dale C. Allison Jr., *A Critical and Exegetical Commentary on the Epistle of James*, ICC (London: Bloomsbury T&T Clark, 2013), 465–66.

9. For all the four named exemplars in James, see Robert J. Foster, *The Significance of Exemplars for the Interpretation of the Letter of James*, WUNT 2/376 (Tübingen: Mohr Siebeck, 2014).

10. J. L. P. Wolmarans, "The Tongue Guiding the Body: The Anthropological Presuppositions of James 3:1–12," *Neot* 26 (1992): 524.

11. See Richard Bauckham, "The Tongue Set on Fire by Hell (James 3.6)," in *The Fate of the Dead: Studies on the Jewish and Christian Apocalypses*, NovTSup 93 (Leiden: Brill, 1998), 119–31.

12. Darian R. Lockett, *Purity and Worldview in the Epistle of James*, LNTS 366 (London: T&T Clark, 2008).

13. Luke Timothy Johnson calls this description of the early and late rains "a touch of genuine local color" (*The Letter of James: A New Translation with Introduction and Commentary*, AB 37A [New York: Doubleday, 1995], 315).

14. John Wilkinson, "Healing in the Epistle of James," *SJT* 24 (1971): 326–45.

15. Ben Witherington III, *Letters and Homilies for Jewish Christians: A Socio-Rhetorical Commentary on Hebrews, James and Jude* (Downers Grove, IL: IVP Academic, 2007), 549.

1–3 John, Jude

1. Robert Law, *The Tests of Life: A Study of the First Epistle of St. John* (Edinburgh: T&T Clark, 1909). This book has been reprinted several times and is now available online (https://openlibrary.org/books/OL7208295M/The_tests_of_life).

2. The Hellenistic letter form is clear in Philemon and Jude, as well as Acts 15:23–29; 23:25–30. Other NT "letters" adapt this form into longer treatises addressing practical and theological concerns. See further Stanley K. Stowers, *Letter Writing in Greco-Roman Antiquity* (Philadelphia: Westminster, 1986).

3. Eusebius, *Ecclesiastical History* 3.39.14; cf. 3.39.6.

4. For a more detailed yet accessible introduction to 1–3 John, see C. Marvin Pate, *The Writings of John: A Survey of the Gospels, Epistles, and Apocalypse* (Grand Rapids: Zondervan, 2011), 226–46. A very thorough discussion is found in Robert Yarbrough, *1–3 John*, BECNT (Grand Rapids: Baker Academic, 2008), 3–28.

5. John Ronning, *The Jewish Targums and John's Logos Theology* (Grand Rapids: Baker Academic, 2010).

6. For example, *1Rule of the Community* 3; *1QWar Scroll* 1; 13.

7. For example, *Testament of Dan* 5.10–11; *Testament of Levi* 18.12; *Testament of Judah* 25.3; *1QWar Scroll* 1.4; 11.1–17; 13.1–12; 14.7–10; 15.1–3; 17.5; 18.1; *11QMelchizedek* 2.12–13; *4 Ezra* 11–12; *2 Baruch* 40; *Sibylline Oracles* 3.75–90.

8. See Ignatius, *To the Trallians* 9.1–2; Ignatius, *To the Smyrnaeans* 6.1–7:1.

9. Irenaeus, *Against Heresies* 3.3.4; cf. 1.24.3–4; 1.26.1; 3.16.1.

10. *1QRule of the Community* 3.15–4.26.

11. Tob. 14:6; Wis. 14:11–12, 22, 27–30; 15:15–17; Letter of Jeremiah; Bel and the Dragon.

12. See Pliny the Younger, *Letters* 10.96. Working from the martyrdom of Antipas in Rev. 2:13, Bruce Longenecker's historical novel *The Lost Letters of Pergamum: A Story from the New Testament World*, 2nd ed. (Grand Rapids: Baker Academic, 2016), shows how

emperor worship was problematic for followers of Jesus. Many scholars read Rev. 13 against the background of emperor worship.

13. *Didache* 11.1–2; Ignatius, *To the Ephesians* 7.1; 8.1; 9.1; Ignatius, *To the Smyrnaeans* 4.1; 5.1; 7.2; cf. Sir. 11:29–34.

Revelation

1. See Tob. 12:15; *1 Enoch* 20.1–3; *4 Ezra* 5.20.
2. Irenaeus, *Against Heresies* 3.1.1.
3. Eusebius, *Ecclesiastical History* 3.39.6; cf. 3.39.14.
4. Cicero, *The Philippics* 11.
5. Pliny the Elder, *Natural History* 5.121.
6. Philo, *On Drunkenness* 20–29, 95.
7. *4 Ezra* 2.38–40.
8. Compare *1 Enoch* 14.18–25.
9. *1 Clement* 34.6.
10. *Martyrdom of Polycarp* 9.2.
11. Josephus, *Jewish War* 5.424–38; 6.193–309.
12. Tacitus, *Annals* 15.44.30; *1 Clement* 6.1.
13. *Martyrdom of Polycarp* 8.2.
14. *1 Enoch* 12.1–16.4.
15. *1 Enoch* 20.1–7.
16. Compare *4 Ezra* 12.10.
17. For example, *4 Ezra* 15.46; *2 Baruch* 11.1; *Sibylline Oracles* 5.143.
18. Josephus, *Jewish War* 1.633.
19. Suetonius, *Nero* 30.3.
20. Tob. 12:16–22; *Martyrdom and Ascension of Isaiah* 7.21.
21. Cicero, *Against Verres* 4.43.
22. *1 Enoch* 54.3–6; *2 Baruch* 56.13.
23. *Jubilees* 23.15, 27.
24. *Epistle of Barnabas* 15.4–5.
25. *1 Enoch* 10.12–13; cf. 103.7–8.
26. Compare *4 Ezra* 2.18.
27. Compare *Didache* 10.6.
28. Demosthenes, *Against Neaera* 59.122.
29. *Letter of Aristeas* 311.
30. *Epistle of Barnabas* 19.11.

Image Credits

Photo on page 9 © isawnyu / Wikimedia Commons, CC by 2.0.

Photos on pages 29 (lower), 64, 147, 197, 330, 394, 401, 429, 563, 578, 607, 615, 642 (upper), 644, 677, 1199, 1235 (lower) © Baker Publishing Group and Dr. James C. Martin. Courtesy of Musée du Louvre; Autorisation de photographer et de filmer: Louvre, Paris, France.

Photo on page 34 © Bridgeman Images. Courtesy of the Egyptian National Museum, Cairo, Egypt.

Photo on page 41 © Balage Balogh (www.archaeologyillustrated.com).

Photos on pages 42, 118, 134, 231, 504 © Baker Publishing Group and Dr. James C. Martin. Courtesy of the Egyptian Ministry of Antiquities and the Cairo Museum.

Photos on pages 50, 277, 403, 487, 502, 668 © Werner Forman Archive / Bridgeman Images.

Photo on page 52 © Túrelio / Wikimedia Commons, CC by-sa 3.0.

Photos on pages 70, 620, 789, 1081, 1102 © Baker Publishing Group and Dr. James C. Martin. Courtesy of the Istanbul Museum, Turkey.

Photo on page 76 © Look and Learn / Elgar Collection / Bridgeman Images.

Photo on page 87 (lower) © Gts-tg / Wikimedia Commons, CC by-sa 4.0.

Photo on page 89 © Bouarf / Wikimedia Commons, CC by-sa 3.0.

Photo on page 91 is public domain. Courtesy of the Metropolitan Museum of Art, Rogers Fund, 1915.

Photo on page 92 © Michael Lubinski / Wikimedia Commons, CC by 2.0.

Photo on page 116 © Morburre / Wikimedia Commons, CC by-sa 3.0.

Photos on pages 122 (lower), 455, 597 © Rémih / Wikimedia Commons, CC by-sa 3.0.

Photo on page 127 (lower) © Guillaume Blanchard / Wikimedia Commons, CC by-sa 1.0.

Photo on page 129 © New York Public Library Digital Collections. Accessed July 17, 2018. http://digitalcollections.nypl.org/items/510d47d9-4808-a3d9-e040-e00a180 64a99.

Photo on page 135 © Roland Unger / Wikimedia Commons, CC by-sa 3.0.

Photos on pages 150, 177, 189, 190, 199, 213, 288, 336, 339, 373, 409, 415, 427, 435, 453, 456, 458, 467, 510, 520, 539, 549, 552, 585, 611, 665, 672, 687, 688, 690, 694, 808, 820, 834, 898, 927, 978, 1079, 1084, 1085, 1114, 1160, 1193, 1290, 1313, 1324 (upper), 1331 (lower) © Baker Publishing Group and Dr. James C. Martin. Courtesy of the British Museum, London, England.

Photo on page 158 (lower) © Joe Goldberg / Wikimedia Commons, CC by 2.0.

Photo on page 162 is public domain. Courtesy of University Museum of Pennsylvania, object number 31-43-421.

Photo on page 165 © Marc Ryckaert / Wikimedia Commons, CC by-sa 3.0.

Photos on pages 174, 450, 555, 729, 766, 814, 822, 849, 899, 907, 970, 1055 © Baker Publishing Group and Dr. James C. Martin. Courtesy of the Israel Museum. Collection of the Israel Museum, Jerusalem, and courtesy of the Israel Antiquities Authority, exhibited at the Israel Museum, Jerusalem.

Photo on page 182 © Harris Brisbane Dick Fund, 1959.

Photo on page 194 © Naunakhte / Wikimedia Commons, CC by-sa 3.0. Courtesy of the Aegyptisches Museum, Berlin.

Photo on page 215 © locanus / Wikimedia Commons, CC by-sa 3.0.

Photo on page 221 © Markh / Wikimedia Commons.

Photo on page 223 © Tarker / Bridgeman Images.

Photo on page 237 © David Stanley / Wikimedia Commons, CC by 2.0.

Photo on page 247 © Hanay / Wikimedia Commons, CC by-sa 3.0.

Photos on pages 253, 441, 464, 470, 491 are public domain. Courtesy of the Metropolitan Museum of Art, Rogers Fund, 1930.

Photos on pages 262, 423, 460, 508, 633, 680, 1019 © Baker Publishing Group and Dr. James C. Martin. Courtesy of the Oriental Institute Museum, University of Chicago.

Photo on page 264 © Collection of the Israel Antiquities Authority / Photo © The Israel Museum, Jerusalem, by Yoram Lehmann / Bridgeman Images.

Photo on page 266 © Khruner / Wikimedia Commons.

Photos on pages 269, 271, 496 © Mike Peel (www.mikepeel.net) / Wikimedia Commons, CC by-sa 4.0.

Photo on page 273 is public domain. Courtesy of the Metropolitan Museum of Art, Rogers Fund, 1924.

Photo on page 278 © beivushtang / Wikimedia Commons, CC by-sa 3.0.

Photos on pages 279, 338, 343, 349, 692 © Marie-Lan Nguyen / Wikimedia Commons.

Photos on pages 281, 656 © Fredarch / Wikimedia Commons, CC by-sa 3.0.

Photos on pages 282, 301, 333, 334, 575, 612, 674 © Osama Shukir Muhammed Amin / Wikimedia Commons, CC by-sa 4.0.

Photo on page 294 © Golf Bravo / Wikimedia Commons, CC by-sa 3.0.

Photo on page 295 © Archivio J. Lange / De Agostini Picture Library / Bridgeman Images.

Photos on pages 296, 375 © Hara1603 / Wikimedia Commons.

Photo on page 297 © Bertramz / Wikimedia Commons, CC by-sa 3.0.

Photo on page 298 © O.Mustafin / Wikimedia Commons.

Photo on page 305 © Francesco Gasparetti / Wikimedia Commons, CC by 2.0.

Photo on page 312 © GIRAUD Patrick / Wikimedia Commons, CC by-sa 2.5.

Photo on page 322 © M0tty / Wikimedia Commons, CC by-sa 3.0.

Photo on page 325 © Zev Radovan / Bridgeman Images. Courtesy of the British Museum, London, UK.

Photo on page 337 © Eric Gaba / Wikimedia Commons, CC by-sa 3.0.

Photos on pages 344, 484, 892, 1162 © Baker Publishing Group and Dr. James C. Martin. Courtesy of the Bode Museum, Berlin, Germany.

Photo on page 347 © Odilia / Wikimedia Commons, CC by-sa 3.0.

Photos on pages 352, 360 are public domain. Courtesy of the Metropolitan Museum of Art, Rogers Fund, 1931.

Photo on page 353 © Brooklyn Museum, Creative Commons 33.586.

Photo on page 356 © AlexanderVanLoon / Wikimedia Commons, CC by-sa 4.0.

Photo on page 357 © Extended loan from J. Chaim Kaufman, Antwerp / Bridgeman Images. Courtesy of The Israel Museum, Jerusalem, Israel.

Photo on page 372 © Alireza Javaheri / Wikimedia Commons, CC by-sa 3.0.

Photos on pages 374, 500, 554 (upper), 1095, 1319 (lower) © Zev Radovan / Bridgeman Images.

Photo on page 386 © Library of Congress Prints and Photographs Division [LC-DIG-matpc-03493].

Photo on page 392 © A.Davey / Wikimedia Commons, CC by 2.0.

Photo on page 393 © Bridgeman Images. Courtesy of the National Museum of Iran, Tehran, Iran.

Photo on page 399 © Zunkir/Wikimedia Commons, CC by-sa 4.0.

Photo on page 406 © Manfred Werner / Wikimedia Commons, CC by-sa 3.0.

Photo on page 408 © Djehouty / Wikimedia Commons, CC by-sa 4.0.

Photo on page 413 © Mbzt / Wikimedia Commons, CC by-sa 3.0.

Photo on pages 425, 801 © Library of Congress Prints and Photographs Division [LC-DIG-matpc-20316].

Photo on page 428 © Guillaume Blanchard / Wikimedia Commons, CC by-sa 3.0.

Photo on page 437 © Lalupa / Wikimedia Commons, CC by 2.0.

Photos on pages 439, 929 © Baker Publishing Group and Dr. James C. Martin. Courtesy of the Art Institute of Chicago.

Photo on page 448 © Manfred Niermann / Wikimedia Commons, CC by-sa 4.0.

Photo on page 463 is public domain. Courtesy of the Metropolitan Museum of Art, Purchase, Edward S. Harkness Gift, 1926.

Photos on pages 472, 795, 1074, 1130 © Marie-Lan Nguyen / Wikimedia Commons. Courtesy of the Louvre.

Photo on pages 476–77 © Hans Birger Nilsen / Wikimedia Commons, CC by 2.0.

Photo on page 479 is public domain. Courtesy of the Metropolitan Museum of Art, Rogers Fund, 1912.

Photo on page 491 © Apasova / Wikimedia Commons, CC by-sa 3.0.

Photos on pages 492, 1294 © The Yorck Project / Wikimedia Commons.

Photo on page 497 is public domain. Courtesy of the Metropolitan Museum of Art, Gift of Dr. Sidney A. Charlat, in memory of his parents, Newman and Adele Charlat, 1949.

Photo on page 503 is public domain. Courtesy of the Metropolitan Museum of Art, Rogers Fund, 1916.

Photos on pages 524, 545, 619, 759, 830, 1260, 1319 (upper) © Baker Publishing Group and Dr. James C. Martin. Courtesy of the Eretz Israel Museum, Tel Aviv, Israel.

Photo on page 525 © Mmelouk / Wikimedia Commons, CC by-sa 4.0.

Photo on page 537 © Daniel Case / Wikimedia Commons, CC by-sa 3.0.

Photo on page 543 © AinAnepaio / Wikimedia Commons, CC by-sa 3.0.

Photo on page 554 (lower) © Bridgeman Images. Courtesy of the Israel Museum, Jerusalem, Israel.

Photo on page 564 © Charles Edwin Wilbour Fund / Bridgeman Images. Courtesy of the Brooklyn Museum of Art, New York, USA.

Photo on page 572 © Bridgeman Images. Courtesy of the Louvre, Paris, France.

Photo on page 583 © Applejuicc / Wikimedia Commons, CC by-sa 4.0.

Photo on page 594 © Jebulon / Wikimedia Commons, CC0 1.0.

Photo on page 595 is public domain. Excavations of Paul-Émile Botta, 1843–1844, courtesy of Wikimedia Commons.

Photo on page 603 © Thomasccnawiki / Wikimedia Commons, CC by-sa 4.0.

Photo on page 608 © Radomir Vrbovsky / Wikimedia Commons, CC by-sa 4.0.

Photo on page 627 © Jastrow / Wikimedia Commons, CC by 2.5.

Photo on page 630 © Stefan Thiesen / Wikimedia Commons, CC by-sa 3.0.

Photo on page 642 (lower) is public domain. Courtesy of the Metropolitan Museum of Art, Rogers Fund, 1962.

Photo on page 651 © Baker Publishing Group and Dr. James C. Martin. Courtesy of the Israel Museum. Collection of the Israel Museum, Jerusalem, and courtesy of the Israel Antiquities Authority, exhibited at the Israel Museum, Jerusalem.

Photo on page 654 © Bukvoed / Wikimedia Commons, CC by-sa 4.0.

Photo on page 732 © Rama / Wikimedia Commons, CC by 2.0. Courtesy of the Louvre.

Photos on pages 741, 1014, 1089 are public domain. Courtesy of Wikimedia Commons.

Photo on page 748 © Baker Publishing Group and Dr. James C. Martin. Courtesy of the Greek Ministry of Antiquities and the National Archaeological Museum, Athens, Greece.

Photos on pages 770, 921, 1215 © Baker Publishing Group and Dr. James C. Martin. Courtesy of the Antikensammlung, Berlin.

Photo on page 777 © Library of Congress, courtesy of the Israel Antiquities Authority.

Photo on page 782 © Ijon / Wikimedia Commons, CC by-sa 3.0.

Photos on pages 794, 1097, 1264 © Baker Publishing Group and Dr. James C. Martin. Courtesy of the Antalya Archaeological Museum, Turkey.

Photo on page 824 © Baker Publishing Group and Dr. James C. Martin. Courtesy of the Masada Museum.

Photos on pages 827, 1073, 1091, 1093, 1099, 1104, 1107, 1131, 1194, 1197, 1221 © Baker Publishing Group and Dr. James C. Martin. Courtesy of the Greek Ministry of Antiquities (Athens, Corinth, Delphi, Thessalonica).

Photo on page 838 © 2008 Karbel Multimedia, Logos Bible Software.

Photo on page 856 © Carla Tavares / Wikimedia Commons, CC by-sa 3.0.

Photo on page 870 © Library of Congress Prints and Photographs Division [LC-DIG-matpc-02971].

Photos on pages 882, 981 © Baker Publishing Group and Dr. James C. Martin. Courtesy of the Vatican Museum.

Photos on pages 883, 1076, 1186, 1280, 1305 (upper) © J. Scott Duvall.

Photos on pages 884, 1311 © Baker Publishing Group and Dr. James C. Martin. Courtesy of the museum at Sepphoris.

Photo on page 890 © Baker Publishing Group and Dr. James C. Martin. Courtesy of The Field Museum, Chicago.

Photo on page 908 © Bridgeman Images.

Photo on page 912 © Library of Congress Prints and Photographs Division [LC-DIG-ppmsca-18419-00055].

Photo on page 922 © Patrick Denker / Wikimedia Commons, CC by 2.0.

Photo on page 931 © Baker Publishing Group and Dr. James C. Martin. Courtesy of the Wohl Museum, Jerusalem.

Photo on page 939 © Diego Delso / Wikimedia Commons, CC by-sa 3.0.

Photo on page 1000 © someone10x / Wikimedia Commons.

Photos on pages 1010, 1011, 1148 © Baker Publishing Group and Dr. James C. Martin. Courtesy of the Holyland Hotel, Jerusalem, 2001. Present location: The Israel Museum, Jerusalem.

Photo on page 1069 © Konrad Miller / Wikimedia Commons.

Photo on page 1082 © Chixoy / Wikimedia Commons, CC by-sa 3.0.

Photo on page 1088 © G.dallorto / Wikimedia Commons, courtesy of the Istanbul Archaeology Museum.

Photo on page 1106 © Marie-Lan Nguyen / Wikimedia Commons, CC by-sa 3.0.

Photo on page 1111 © Carole Raddato / Wikimedia Commons, CC by 2.0.

Photo on page 1113 © Michael F. Mehnert / Wikimedia Commons, CC by-sa 3.0.

Photo on page 1115 © Baker Publishing Group and Dr. James C. Martin. Courtesy of the Hierapolis Museum, Turkey.

Photo on page 1121 © José Luiz Bernardes Ribeiro / Wikimedia Commons, CC by-sa 3.0.

Photo on page 1122 © Jeanhousen / Wikimedia Commons, CC by-sa 3.0.

Photo on page 1126 © Dan Diffendale / Wikimedia Commons.

Photo on page 1133 © Hintau Aliaksei / Shutterstock.

Photo on page 1146 © Baker Publishing Group and Dr. James C. Martin. Courtesy of St. Catherine's Museum, Sinai.

Photo on page 1168 © Baker Publishing Group and Dr. James C. Martin. Courtesy of the Ephesus Museum, Turkey.

Photo on page 1212 © Marie-Lan Nguyen / Wikimedia Commons. Courtesy of the National Museum of Rome, Palazzo Massimo alle Terme.

Photo on page 1240 © Bibi Saint-Pol / Wikimedia Commons. Courtesy of the Glyptothek in Munich.

Photo on page 1246 © Itzhak Baum / Wikimedia Commons, CC by-sa 3.0.

Photo on page 1257 © Ealdgyth / Wikimedia Commons.

Photo on page 1268 © Giovanni Dall'Orto / Wikimedia Commons. Courtesy of the National Archaeological Museum, Athens.

Photos on pages 1271, 1275 (lower) © Baker Publishing Group and Dr. James C. Martin. Courtesy of the Amman Museum, Jordan.

Photo on page 1302 © Anthony M. from Rome, Italy (Flickr) / Wikimedia Commons, CC by 2.0.

Photo on page 1303 (lower) © Steerpike / Wikimedia Commons, CC by-sa 3.0.

Photo on page 1305 (lower) © Jan Mehlich / Wikimedia Commons, CC by-sa 3.0. Courtesy of the Pergamon Museum.

Photos on pages 1317, 1324 (lower) © Baker Publishing Group and Dr. James C. Martin. Courtesy of the Aegyptisches Museum and Papyrussammlung, Berlin, Germany.

Photo on page 1327 © A. De Gregorio / De Agostini Picture Library / Bridgeman Images. Courtesy of the Palazzo Massimo alle Terme & Museum, Rome, Lazio, Italy.

Photo on page 1330 © De Agostini Picture Library / Bridgeman Images. Courtesy of the Cimitero dei SS. Marcellino e Pietro, Rome, Italy.

Photo on page 1331 (upper) © G. Dagli Orti / De Agostini Picture Library / Bridgeman Images.

Photo on page 1333 © Bridgeman Images. Courtesy of the Musee des Tapisseries, Angers, France.